BRITISH KINGS & QUEENS

BRITISH KINGS & QUEENS

The Complete Biographical Encyclopedia of the Kings & Queens of Great Britain

MIKE ASHLEY

BARNES
& NOBLE
BOOKS
NEW YORK

CONTENTS

The Kings and Queens of Britain

The Genealogical Tables (Charts)

The Maps

INTRODUCTION

This book is the most complete record of the kings and queens of Britain ever compiled. It contains details on almost one thousand rulers from the earliest times to the present day.

It may come as a surprise to realize that there have been a thousand kings and queens in Britain. After all, there have only been forty-three rulers of England since 1066 when William the Conqueror defeated king Harold at Hastings. Where have the other nine hundred or so come from?

The United Kingdom has only existed for about three hundred years, since the Act of Union of 1707. Before that England and Scotland were separate kingdoms and, prior to 1603, with the accession of James VI of Scotland as James I of England the two kingdoms were ruled by different kings. In fact there have been more kings of Scotland than of England. Some of them are familiar to those of us who do not live in Scotland, especially Robert the Bruce and Macbeth. The kingdom dates back to around AD 500, when Fergus established himself as lord of the Irish settlers in Kintyre and Argyll. This territory became known as Dál Riata. The settlers were known as the Scots but the real masters of northern Britain were the Picts who had their own kings. The raids of the Vikings brought them closer together and allowed the Scots the upper hand. Even then, although Scotland gradually emerged as one kingdom, the descendants of the Picts remained vehemently independent as the Highlanders who looked to their own rulers, first amongst the men of Moray and then the Kings of the Isles.

Wales also had its own kings and princes before Edward I brought an end to their independence in 1284. Wales was in fact a conglomeration of kingdoms with no political unity but some of these kingdoms, particularly Gwent, have a line of kings that go back before the Roman conquest to the earliest known British kings and queens. The earliest king covered in this book is Beli the Great who ruled at the start of the first century BC. Others from that period that we are likely to know include Boudica or Boadicea, Cymbeline or Cunobelin and Caratacus.

Prior to the Norman conquest England had striven for unity under the Saxons. There had originally been seven main Saxon kingdoms, called the heptarchy, of which Wessex, Mercia and Northumbria were the strongest. All had their major kings who had an influence upon the whole of Britain. It was thanks to Oswy of Northumbria that we adopted the practices of the Church of Rome rather than the Celtic church. Under Offa of Mercia, England became a European force for the first time and almost a united kingdom. Under Alfred of Wessex, Alfred the Great as we know him, the Saxons managed to drive back the Danes. We tend to forget that the Danes won in the end. Canute of Denmark ruled England almost a thousand years ago, and William of Normandy was himself descended from the Vikings. The Norse had a hold over parts of Britain until the fifteenth century, where there were separate earldoms and kingdoms of the Orkneys, the Hebrides and the Isle of Man.

Before the Saxons invaded Britain during the fifth century, and after Roman administration collapsed, Britain reverted to some of its native kings. This was the mysterious time of King Arthur and of Old King Cole – or Coel to give him his proper name. He really did exist.

Perhaps that gives some idea of where these thousand rulers come from. Some may be no more than names to us, lost in legend, but in many cases they existed and this book sets them in their historical context and shows what contribution they made to the development of Britain.

This book is divided into four main sections.

1. **The Royal Book of Records.** Here you will find the answers to such questions as who had the shortest reign, or who lived the longest? This section will introduce you to many familiar names but also a surprising number of less familiar ones.

2. **The Kingdoms of Britain.** This provides a historical introduction which traces the history of all of the different kingdoms of Britain. The time chart allows you to follow the development of each kingdom and show how they gradually merged to form the United Kingdom as we know it today.

3. **The Kings and Queens of Britain.** This is the largest part of the book and has biographical entries on every known ruler. To make it easy to use the section is divided into each separate kingdom. For each kingdom there is a

map, to show you where that kingdom existed; a succession list, which shows you the sequence of rulers at a glance; and a family tree, which shows you the relationships between the rulers. The biographical entries follow in chronological order so that you can trace the history of each kingdom. Every ruler has a unique reference number shown in brackets before their name (e.g. [G5]) and that number is used throughout in cross-reference elsewhere (in the tables, family trees and index) to keep track of each name. A few people who were not rulers in their own right, but who claimed regal status, are accorded entries and are inserted in boxed form in their right sequence. This applies to certain pretenders or claimants to the throne such as Perkin Warbeck or Bonnie Prince Charlie.

This section is also split into four main parts which help follow through the chronological sequence. The first part is called "The Dark Ages" and covers all of the rulers from the earliest mists of time to the point when more established kingdoms in England, Wales and Scotland began to emerge in the tenth century.

The second part is "The Fight for Britain". This takes us from the tenth century through to the emergence of England as the dominant power at the time of Edward I. It traces the fight for supremacy from the time of the Danish and Norman conquests through to the English domination of the Welsh princes, and the almost total subjugation of Scotland until its revival under Robert the Bruce.

The third part is "The United Kingdom". This follows the lives of the kings from Edward I of England and Robert the Bruce of Scotland down through the amalgamation of England and Scotland at the time of James VI/I, the Civil War and the restoration of the monarchy under Charles II to the modern day, when the institution of the monarchy is again under threat.

The fourth part is "The World About Them". This covers two elements which help us understand the bigger picture within which the rulers of Britain have operated. Firstly there are the legendary kings, many of whom have become part of our language and culture, like King Lear, and who have stood as icons for historical kings. Secondly there are all of the European kingdoms or territories which, at different periods of history, have had domination over parts of Britain or have been ruled by

British monarchs. For instance, for over four hundred years the kings of England also called themselves kings of France, and one ruler – Henry VI – was crowned as king of both kingdoms. Britain has also had a strong relationship with Ireland. Henry VIII declared himself king of Ireland and, a thousand years earlier, the Irish kings themselves laid claim to parts of Wales and northern Britain. This part therefore contains a series of succession lists which help explain the relationship between the rulers of Britain and the island's European neighbours.

4. **The Royal Gazetteer.** This identifies the key places in Britain with royal associations. Wherever you live, be it York, Chester, London, Exeter, or anywhere else, this will help you not only to see the royal connections but also see where your town or city was in relation to each king and kingdom.

There are several ways to use this book. The key to it is the index. This lists the names of every ruler covered, as well as many other individuals. For every ruler it notes their unique reference number and the pages where they are cited, with their main entries in bold. If you ever get lost for a king or queen, check the index.

You can of course just start at the beginning of the book and read through to the end. This will allow you to trace the development of the British monarchy and the time chart will help you follow through each contributory kingdom. You can use the book to find the royal associations near where you live. Just check the maps for the kingdom or kingdoms in your area, and also check out the gazetteer for local connections. You may want to check relationships across Britain at different periods of time. Just use the time chart to identify the kingdoms prevalent at any one time and then check out the succession lists to find the contemporary rulers.

Whichever way you choose I hope you gain as much pleasure from this book and exploring the past as I did researching and writing it. You'll discover hundreds of kings, some with unpronounceable names, but most with lives that we can relate to, and from understanding them we can understand how Britain became what it is today.

Mike Ashley,
July 1998.

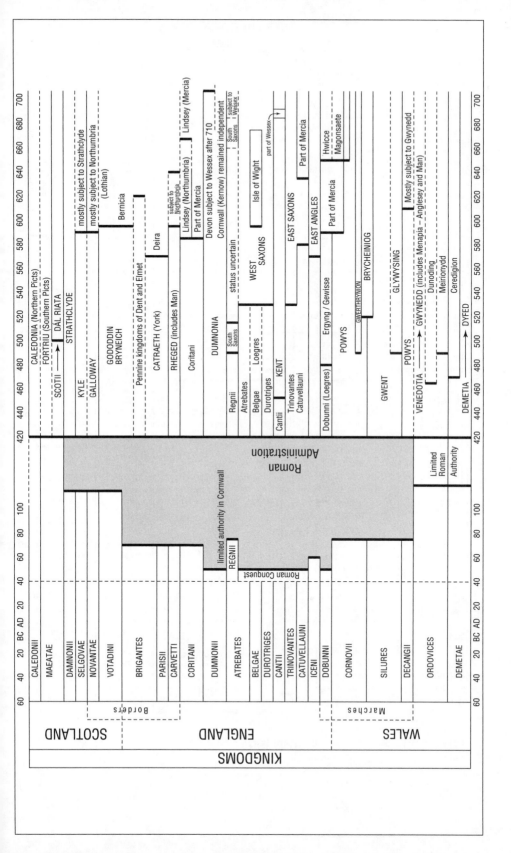

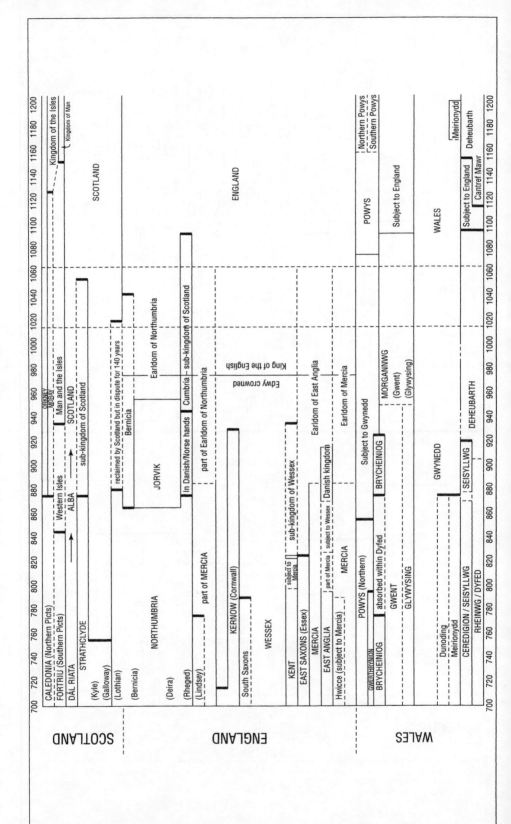

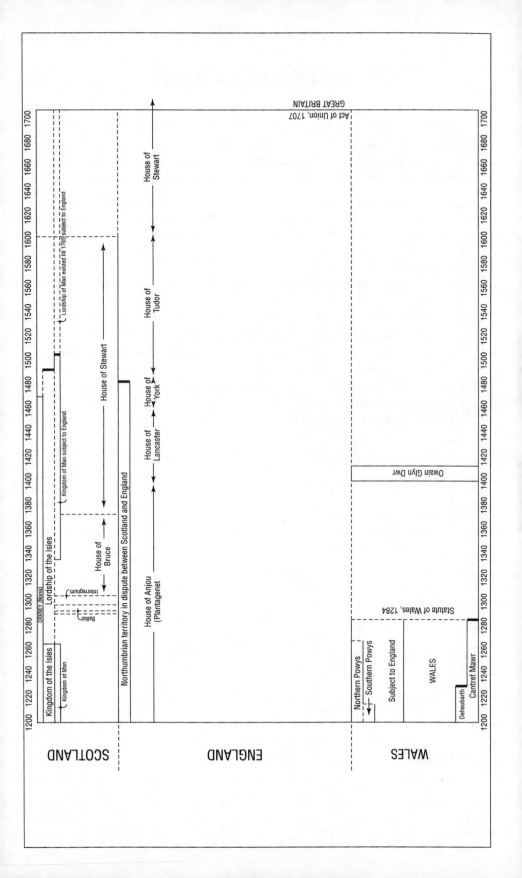

ABBREVIATIONS

I have kept the use of abbreviations to a minimum in this book. However there are occasions where abbreviations are more practical, but they mostly relate to the tables, charts and gazetteer than to the main biographical entries. The following abbreviations have been used on occasions at various places in this book.

ASC   Anglo-Saxon Chronicle

c   circa, used in relation to a date where only an approximation is known.

C   century or centuries as in 13thC – thirteenth century.

d.   died

dau.   daughter of

fl.   flourished - the approximate dates when someone lived.

illeg.   illegitimate

k.   killed. This is also represented by † in the family trees which means the individual died a violent death, either in battle or was murdered.

NS   New Style, representing the change in calendar in 1752 when September 2nd was followed by September 14th.

OS   Old Style, which are the dates under the old system of reckoning before the calendar changed in 1752.

†   died violently. See under k.

THE
ROYAL BOOK
OF
RECORDS

THE ROYAL BOOK
OF RECORDS

1. THE YOUNGEST CHILDREN TO BE DECLARED MONARCH

The earliest known child to become a king before the age of maturity, which was 14 to the Saxons, was Edward the Martyr who acceded to the throne in 975 aged 12 or 13. He was murdered three years later and succeeded by his half-brother, Athelred, who was 9 or 10. Since then eleven other monarchs have come to the throne even younger. Scotland had more infant rulers than anywhere else: eight of the ten listed below were all proclaimed monarchs before their tenth birthday.

1. Mary, Queen of Scots, 7 days, 1542
   Mary was only one week old when her father died. Scotland was governed for a period by James, earl of Arran, but Mary was still crowned, the youngest infant to so be, on 9 September 1543 aged 9 months 2 days.

2. Henry VI of England, 8 months 25 days, 1422
   Henry not only became king of England before his first birthday, but also king of France a month later. England was governed by John, duke of Bedford, as Protector of the Realm until Henry assumed control three weeks before his 16th birthday.

3. James VI of Scotland, 1 year 36 days, 1567
   James succeeded his mother Mary after she was deposed. He was the third infant in succession to the Scottish throne, and the second youngest to be crowned, which happened five days later.

4. James V of Scotland, 1 year 5 months, 1513
   James's father, James IV, was the only Scottish James who did not succeed to the throne as an infant – he was a princely fifteen. James V was succeeded in turn by Mary, Queen of Scots.

5. Margaret of Scotland, 2 years 11 months 11 days, 1286
   The last of the line of Dunkeld, Margaret was proclaimed queen on the death of her grandfather Alexander III. She was never crowned, indeed never lived in Scotland, as she died at sea coming over from Norway when only 7.

6. David II of Scotland, 5 years 3 months 2 days, 1329
   When he came to the throne David had already been married for eleven months! He was the first Scottish king to be formally anointed and crowned.

7. James II of Scotland, 6 years 4 months 5 days, 1437
   James was one of twins, the elder of which died within a few weeks of birth. James was crowned five weeks after his accession.

8. Alexander III of Scotland, 7 years 10 months 5 days, 1249
   The last of the male line of Scotland's native dynasty.

9. James III of Scotland, 8 years 3 months, 1460
   He was crowned a week later.

10. Osred (I) of Northumbria, 8 years, 705
    Osred was the son of one of the greatest Saxon kings, Aldfrith of Northumbria. Alas, he turned out to be a hopeless king.

The only other monarchs to reign before their tenth birthdays were the appropriately nicknamed Athelred the Unready in 978, Henry III in 1216 and Edward VI in 1547. In addition Harald II became earl of Orkney in 1133, when he was seven.

2. THE OLDEST SUCCESSORS TO BE DECLARED MONARCH

If you total all the known ages for when rulers came to the throne you discover that the average age of accession is just over 29 years old. There are, however, ten monarchs who did not succeed to the throne until they were over fifty.

1. William IV, 64 years 10 months 6 days, 1830
   As the third son of George III, William did not expect to become king, but he accepted the role with considerable glee.

2. Donald III of Scotland, 60 years, 1093
   Donald's precise birthdate is not recorded but has been assessed as 1033, so that he was 60 years old when he usurped his brother's throne. He was soon deposed but came back again, making him the oldest king to regain the throne.

3. Edward VII, 59 years 2 months 14 days, 1901
   Queen Victoria's son had to live a long time to outlive his formidable mother.

4. George IV, 57 years 5 months 18 days, 1820
   Effectively George IV had inherited the throne nine years earlier when he was made Prince Regent on the incapacity of his father George III.

5. Robert II of Scotland, 54 years 11 months 21 days, 1371
   The first of the Stewart kings.

6. George I, 54 years 2 months 5 days, 1714
   The first of the Hanoverian kings of England.

7. Swein of Denmark, 53 years, 1013
   Swein's birthdate is uncertain; it is possible he was a year or two younger. He had been King of Denmark since AD 986 and seized the English throne.

8. Robert III of Scotland, 52 years, 1390
   Robert's birthdate is also uncertain and he may have been a year or two younger.

9. James II of England (VII of Scotland), 51 years 3 months 24 days, 1685
   James was the first king to succeed jointly to the kingdoms of England and Scotland and to be crowned king of both on the same day, eleven weeks later.

10. Malcolm II of Alba, 51 years, 1005
    Malcolm had been king of Strathclyde since the year 990. Around the year 1016 he also inherited the kingdom of Lothian thus effectively becoming the first king of all Scotland when he was 62.

Interestingly most of the oldest new kings either conquered or usurped the throne.

3. THE LONGEST REIGNING MONARCHS

The average length of reign of all the known rulers of the British Isles is a little over fifteen years – in fact the reign of George VI was the exact average. There are only ten monarchs known to have ruled for fifty or more years. One ruler who governed even longer than Victoria was Harald II, earl of Orkney, who ruled for 66 years from

1140 to 1206, though he was only six when he was granted the earldom. At that time the Isles of Orkney were subject to the Kings of Norway, so Harald was not a monarch in his own right. He formally administered the islands from 1151.

1. Victoria, 63 years 7 months 3 days, 1837–1901
   Victoria had just passed her eighteenth birthday when she became queen, and thus is not only the longest reigning monarch, but was an adult for her entire reign.

2. Aescwine of the East Saxons, 60 years, 527–87
   Aescwine's dates are far from certain and it is not clear that he ruled as a king. He may have been a governor installed by the kings of Kent in c560 or so.

3. George III, 59 years 3 months 5 days, 1760–1820
   Effectively George III ceased to rule in 1811, when he was declared insane and his son became Prince Regent. The true length of his reign is therefore 50 years 3 months 10 days, and would place him seventh on this list.

4. James VI of Scotland, 57 years 8 months 4 days, 1567–1625
   As one of the youngest rulers, James was king virtually all of his life. He was the first king of a combined Scotland and England, though he ruled England for less than 22 years. James did not technically take authority into his own hands until his twelfth year, which reduces his official length of reign to 47 years.

5. Henry III of England, 56 years 1 month, 1216–72
   Another king who started young and managed to hold the throne during a period of upheaval. Henry did not declare his majority until his nineteenth birthday, so the length of his reign as an adult was 46 years and 5 weeks.

6. Gruffydd ap Cynan of Gwynedd, 56 years, 1081–1137
   A remarkably strong and powerful king who re-established the kingdom of Gwynedd and held back the onslaught of the Normans. Had Gruffydd inherited the throne in 1075, when he was defeated by his rival Trahern ap Caradog, he would have reigned for 62 years, making him second only to Victoria, but arguably the most resilient of all monarchs considering the turbulence of Wales at that time.

7. Hywel ab Owain, 53 years, c990–c1043
   The exact length of Hywel's reign is uncertain but there is no doubt that he ruled Glywysing for over fifty years, though he left surprisingly little mark.

8. Edward III, 50 years 5 months, 1327–77
   One of England's most powerful monarchs. He was fourteen when his father abdicated. Edward assumed personal control on 20 October 1330, so the effective length of his reign was 46 years 8 months.

9. Ealdwulf of the East Angles, 50 years, 663–713
   The longest reigning of the Anglo-Saxon kings, all the more amazing because of the considerable turbulence in neighbouring kingdoms during his reign.

10. Olaf of Man, 50 years, 1103–53
    The peace-loving king of Man and the Isles who co-operated so well with all of his contemporaries that he was allowed to govern without threat or hinderance; that is until his nephews murdered him. Technically Olaf should have come to the throne in 1096, but he was considered too young to rule. Had he done so he could have ruled for 57 years. Some records suggest that Olaf did not succeed to Man until around 1113, which reduces his rule to forty years.

4. THE SHORTEST REIGNING MONARCHS

It should come as no surprise that many of Britain's kings fought hard to cling on to their kingdoms for only a handful of years. Over sixty of them barely remained kings for a full year. You will not know many of the following names – who remembers monarchs who only ruled for a few weeks – but there are some fascinating stories behind these names. The earliest recorded reign of under a year was that of the Emperor Marcus in 406 who survived for four months.

1. Ragnald of Man, 4 days, 1164
   Usurper who seized power on Somerled's death but was killed four days later.

2. Jane, 9 days, 1553
   Lady Jane Grey, the nine-day queen. She was only fifteen at the time.

3. Elfweard, 16 days, 924
   Elfweard was elected king of Wessex for just sixteen days, and may well have been murdered by his elder brother Athelstan.

4. Ragnald II of Man, 24 days, 1249
   Another who seized power and was murdered soon after.

5. Osbald of Northumbria, 27 days, 796
   Raised to the kingship by the local nobles, they turned on him within the month and deposed him.

6. Brude mac Ferat, 1 month, 842
   One of a short-lived dynasty of Pictish nobles who sought to retain the kingdom after the slaughter of the Pictish royal household in 839 by the Vikings and the usurpation of Pictish rule by Kenneth macAlpin. Pictish king lists accord Brude a rule of just one month, but it is not known just how many days that was. He was almost certainly murdered.

7. Swein of Denmark, 40 days, 1013–1014
   Although king of Denmark for 27 years, Swein only held dominion over England for 40 days before he died.

8. Edgar the Atheling, 2 months 12 days, 1066
   Edgar was proclaimed king by the Saxon nobles after Harold's death, but he soon submitted to the overlordship of William the Conqueror.

9. Edward V, 2 months 17 days, 1483
   The young king who became one of the Princes in the Tower.

10. Connad Cerr of Dál Riata, 3 months, 629
    Connad is an example of the consequences of not minding your own business. Within a few months of becoming king he involved himself in a squabble amongst his kinsfolk in Ireland which turned into a major battle in which he was slain.

Others who ruled less than six months include Eochaid of Dál Riata in 697, Beornred of Mercia in 757, Oswulf of Northumbria in 758, Egfrith of Mercia in 796, Redwulf of Northumbria in 844, Canute of Jorvik about 900, and Duncan II of Scotland in 1094.

5. THE YOUNGEST MONARCHS TO DIE

When a young monarch accedes to the throne it is normally in the interest of the Regent to keep him or her alive, because he can exercise his own power in the name of the king. Thus it is unusual if young monarchs fail to survive into adulthood. Insofar as we know monarch's ages, I know of only five ruling monarchs who failed to make their eighteenth birthday.

1. Margaret of Scotland, 7 years 5 months 18 days
   A weak child, Margaret was proclaimed queen on the death of her grandfather, Alexander III, in 1286, when she was two years old. She was the daughter of Eric II of Norway and was considered too frail to make the journey to Scotland until she was seven. Unfortunately she was taken ill on the voyage and died on the Orkneys on 26 September 1290.

2. Edward V of England, 12 years 10 months
   One of the Princes in the Tower who was deposed by Richard III in June 1483 and murdered by his orders some ten weeks later. The exact cause of death has never been certain but it is likely he was smothered.

3. Edward VI of England, 15 years 8 months 25 days
   The only son of Henry VIII, in whom he stored such hopes. Although apparently a healthy child, Edward inherited congenital syphilis from his father. This weakened his system and by his teens he was suffering from many ailments, but died of pulmonary tuberculosis.

4. Edward the Martyr of Wessex, about 16 years
   Edward's year of birth is not certain but was probably 962, so when he died in March 978 he was probably still in his sixteenth year. He was murdered with the connivance of his stepmother, being stabbed in the back and then dragged along by his bolting horse.

5. Lady Jane Grey, about 16 years 4 months
   The innocent victim of the politico-religious machinations after the death of Edward VI. Jane was put forward as the Protestant candidate in place of the Catholic Mary. Jane was soon deposed and imprisoned, found guilty of treason, and beheaded.

6. THE OLDEST REIGNING MONARCHS

Only five monarchs were still reigning into their 80s and just one survived to over 90.

1. Meurig of Gwent, 90 years, *c*570
   Meurig's dates are uncertain. He was born around AD 467 or 487 and certainly was alive in AD 562. He had abdicated as king in favour of his son Athrwys but returned to the throne in his final years.

2. Gruffydd ap Cynan of Gwynedd, 82 years, 1137
   The powerful king who founded the kingdom of Gwynedd and ruled for 56 years.

3. George III, 81 years 8 months 5 days, 1820
   George III remained king in name until 1820, although his son had taken over as Prince Regent from 1811.

4. Victoria, 81 years 7 months 29 days, 1901
   Victoria shared her birthday with George III and died just one week younger than he had.

5. Malcolm II of Alba, 80 years, 1034
   Malcolm's birthdate is not certain but is usually cited as 954, so he was around 80 when he died.

7. THE YOUNGEST MARRIED MONARCHS OR CONSORTS

The average age at marriage for all the monarchs in Britain (where the relevant dates are known) is between twenty-eight and twenty-nine, which I found surprisingly old considering the number of child marriages in the Middle Ages. If we exclude Henry, "the Young King" (the son of Henry II who was crowned but who never lived to succeed his father), who was married at the age of 5 yrs 8 months (to an infant aged only 2), there were ten future monarchs who married before they were sixteen. The average age for the queen consorts to marry is eight years younger, at about twenty. There were over twenty-four consorts married before their sixteenth birthday. The following covers the twelve youngest partners.

1. David II of Scotland, 4 years 4 months 13 days
   and Joan, 7 years 12 days, 1328
   A political marriage between the son and heir of Robert I of Scotland and the daughter of Edward II of England with the result that Joan was known as Joan Makepeace. Although they were married for over thirty-four years they had no children.

2. Isabella of France, 6 years 11 months 25 days
   and Richard II of England, 29 years 10 months, 1396
   Another political marriage arranged to seal the peace between England and France. Hardly surprisingly the marriage was never consummated though Richard, something of a child at heart, became close friends with Isabella. After his death she married again, to Charles of Angoulême, but died giving birth to her first child when she was not quite twenty.

3. Alexander III of Scotland, 10 years 3 months 22 days
   and Margaret, 11 yrs 2 months 28 days, 1251
   A political marriage between the young Scottish king and the eldest daughter of his overlord, Henry III. Margaret was eleven months older. Her first child was born ten years later and, though she had two more, none survived their father. Margaret also predeceased her husband, dying in 1275.

4. Joan, 10 years 10 months 28 days
   and Alexander II of Scotland, 22 years 9 months 26 days, 1221
   This had been an earlier attempt at sealing a treaty between Henry III and a Scottish king, this time with the marriage of his sister, Joan. The couple were married for nearly seventeen years but had no children.

5. Mary de Bohun, about 11 years
   and Henry Bolingbroke (future Henry IV), probably about 13 years 10 months, 1381
   Henry married Mary for power and land as she was the heiress of Humphrey de Bohun, the earl of Hereford, Essex and Northampton. Her first child was born the

following year, when she was still under thirteen, but it died after four days. She bore Henry another six children, dying in childbirth with the last, when she was twenty-four.

6. Matilda, Lady of the English, 11 years 4 or 5 months
   and Henry V of Germany, 32 years, 1114
   One of a chain of marriages designed by the ambitious Henry I with the royalty of Europe. Matilda, his eldest surviving daughter (whose date of birth is in dispute but was probably in August 1102) was married to the German emperor Henry or Heinrich V. It was not a love match and she bore him no children during eleven years of marriage.

7. Eleanor of Castile, 13 years
   and Edward I, 15 years 4 months, 1254
   One of the great love matches in history, the two remaining devoted to each other for thirty-six years until Eleanor's death in 1290. Their first child was born prematurely in May 1255 and did not live. The couple waited five years before trying again. During her marriage Eleanor gave birth to sixteen children.

8. Margaret of Denmark, 13 years 17 days
   and James III of Scotland, 17 years 2 months, 1469
   A most profitable marriage for Scotland as Margaret brought with her as part of her dowry the islands of Orkney and Shetland. She bore James three children, the first three years later when she was still only sixteen.

9. Judith, 13 years
   and Athelwolf of Wessex, 61 years,　856
   Child brides were not solely the province of the Late Middle Ages. Athelwolf had abdicated as king and was returning from his pilgrimage to Rome when Charles the Bald, king of the Franks, presented him with his young daughter, who may even have been a few months under thirteen. This was the greatest age range between bride and groom (others are listed below). Not surprisingly the couple had no children, but Judith, who had already caused a scandal by being crowned queen, went on to cause further apoplexy among the witan by marrying her stepson. Through a third marriage she become a forebear of Matilda, the wife of William the Conqueror.

10. Eleanor of Provence, 13 years
    and Henry III, 28 years 3 months 14 days, 1236
    Another devoted marriage which lasted for thirty-six years. Eleanor's date of birth is uncertain and she may have been a year or two older. Their first child, the future Edward I, was born in June 1239 when she was about sixteen.

11. Isabella of Angoulême, 13 years
    and John of England, 32 years 8 months, 1200
    Isabella was John's second wife. His first had also been called Isabella, and had not been much older, probably just about fourteen. John and Isabella waited six years before conceiving their first child. They seemed ideally suited to each other, though both were highly sexed and had a succession of lovers – Isabella led an adventurous life after John's death.

12. Margaret Tudor, 13 years 8 months 11 days
    and James IV of Scotland, 30 years 4 months 22 days, 1503
    Margaret was the daughter of Henry VII of England and it was because of this marriage that James VI of Scotland came to inherit the throne of England exactly one hundred years later.

In addition Sigurd the Crusader, earl of Orkney and later King of Norway, married Blathmina in 1102 when he was about 13 and she was only 5.

8. THE OLDEST MONARCHS TO BE MARRIED

Most royal marriages happen when the king is under forty and the wife is in her early twenties. Later marriages are usually the king's second or third. Seven kings married when they were over fifty.

1. Athelwolf of Wessex, 61 years
   and Judith, 13 years, 856
   This was Athelwolf's second marriage. The age difference between the partners, 48 years, is the greatest of any royal couple.

2. Edward I, 60 years 2 months 23 days
   and Margaret of France, 19 years, 1299
   Edward had so long mourned the death of his treasured first wife Eleanor of Castile that it was surprising that he married again. Despite their age difference Margaret was a devoted wife, a good stepmother, and bore Edward two more children.

3. Gruffydd ap Llywelyn, about 57 years
   and Edith, about 15 years, c1057
   Gruffydd's year of birth is uncertain and it is possible that he was five or so years younger. There is no record that he married in his youth, though he may have had some illegitimate offspring. His marriage to Edith arose from his alliance with Alfgar, earl of Mercia. After Gruffydd's death, Edith married Harold II of England.

4. Aldfrith of Northumbria, about 55 years
   and Cuthburh, (age not known), c695
   Aldfrith had not expected to become king and had led more of a monastic life. Once king, at the age of forty-five, he must have eventually decided he needed an heir, though it took him about ten years to select a bride, the sister of Ine of Wessex. It was not a love match, but served its purpose.

5. William IV of Great Britain, 52 years 10 months 24 days
   and Adelaide, 25 years 11 months, 1818
   Like Aldfrith, William did not expect to be king, and rather enjoyed himself being a sailor. But when the heir to the throne died, William and his brothers hastened to marry to provide a future monarch in the next generation. The marriage seemed to work remarkably well, considering.

6. Henry I of England, 52 years 4 months
   and Adeliza, about 16 years, 1121
   Another quick marriage to produce an heir when Henry's son by his first marriage predeceased him. Henry was not to be blessed, however. Adeliza, nevertheless, was a loyal wife and stepmother.

7. Henry VIII, 52 years 14 days
   and Katherine Parr, about 31 years, 1543
   Henry was old before his time and riddled with gout when he married for the sixth and final time to a remarkably patient wife, who served him well as nursemaid and stepmother.

The oldest wife of a monarch, or in this case ex-monarch, was Wallis Simpson who married the former Edward VIII when she was sixteen days away from her forty-first birthday. The oldest consort to marry a reigning monarch was Matilda, who married David I of Scotland when she was about forty. Her exact date of birth is not known and she might have been a little older.

9. THE GREATEST AGE DIFFERENCES BETWEEN MONARCH AND CONSORT

The fascination for child brides meant that kings were often twice the age of their bride, and sometimes much older than that. At least six monarchs, listed below, were more than thirty years older than their brides.

1. Athelwolf of Wessex and Judith, 48 years
   Athelwolf's date of birth is uncertain, but he is unlikely to have been much younger. Judith was his second wife and seems to have been given to him more as a present than as a wife.

2. Gruffydd ap Llywelyn and Edith, 42 years
   Both dates of birth for these partners are uncertain, but the age difference is unlikely to have been less than 37 years. The marriage was part of a treaty between Gruffydd and his Mercian ally, Aelfgar.

3. Edward I of England and Margaret of France, 41 years
   Margaret's date of birth is not known for sure; Edward was certainly over forty years her senior, yet she still bore him two more children.

4. Henry I of England and Adeliza, about 36 years 4 months
   Adeliza's date of birth is uncertain, but this was another second marriage, late in life, in the hope of providing a new heir to the throne.

5. Edward the Elder of Wessex and Edgiva, 34 years
   Further uncertain dates. Edgiva was Edward's third wife.

6. Henry VIII and Katherine Howard, just over 30 years
   After the disastrous match with Anne of Cleves Henry became besotted by the teenage Katherine Howard. The age difference here was going to prove disastrous for Katherine, and her desire for young men resulted in Henry having her executed.

10. THE YOUNGEST PARENTS

The average age at which kings (or future kings) became parents, where the dates are known, is twenty-eight, whereas the average age for their wives is about twenty-one. Only two kings became parents (of legitimate children) before they were eighteen, but at least ten wives were mothers before that age. The following lists the eight youngest wives and the two youngest husbands.

1. Mary de Bohun became mother to Edward, aged 13 years, 1382
2. Henry IV became father to Edward, aged about 15 years
   Mary was the child bride of the future Henry IV. Her exact date of birth is uncertain, but she was probably under thirteen when their first child, Edward, was born in April 1382. He only survived four days.

3. Margaret Beaufort became mother to Henry (VII), aged 13 yrs 7 months 28 days, 1457
Margaret was not herself a queen or consort, but she lived long enough to see her only child, Henry, become the first Tudor king of England. Her husband, Edmund Tudor, was about 26 years old.

4. Mary (II) became mother of a stillborn child, aged 16 years, 1678
All of Mary's children were stillborn. Her husband, the future William III, was 27.

5. Eleanor of Provence became mother to Edward (I), aged 16 years, 1239
Eleanor's date of birth is uncertain. It is usually cited as 1223, but she may have been slightly older. Her husband, Henry III, was nearly thirty-two.

6. Edgiva became mother to Edmund (I), aged 16 years, c921
Edgiva was the third wife of Edward the Elder. Her date of birth is uncertain to within a year, so she may have been several months younger. Edward was about fifty.

7. Edith (or Eadgyth) became mother to Mareddud, aged 16 years, 1058
The young wife of Gruffydd ap Llywelyn had three children in the five years of their marriage.

8. Mary of Modena became mother to Katherine, aged 16 years 3 months 6 days, 1675
Mary was James's second wife, and he was aged forty-one. There had been a stillborn child in March or May 1674, though this was more likely a miscarriage.

9. Margaret of Denmark became mother to James (IV), aged 16 years 8 months 23 days, 1473
A youthful bride who bore two further children.

10. Edward III became father to Edward (the Black Prince), aged 17 years 7 months 3 days, 1330
In this instance the groom was younger than the bride. Philippa of Hainault was a mature nineteen year old (all but nine days).

11. THE OLDEST PARENTS

Several kings continued to father children well into their fifties, but perhaps more surprisingly are those queen consorts who continued to bear children into their forties. The following lists the oldest king to sire a son and the five oldest mothers.

1. Edward I, 66 years 10 months 18 days
Edward's last child, Eleanor, was born on 4 May 1306 and died in 1311. Edward's wife, Margaret, was 26.

2. Eleanor of Aquitaine, 44 years
Eleanor was the formidable wife of Henry II and at least eleven years his senior. Her date of birth is usually given as 1122, though some sources cite 1120. Her last son, the future king John, was born on Christmas Eve 1166.

3. Philippa of Hainault, 43 years 6 months 14 days
Philippa, the wife of Edward III, bore him thirteen children in twenty-seven years. The lastborn was Thomas, born in January 1355.

4. Elizabeth Wydville, 43 years
Elizabeth bore Edward IV ten children in fifteen years. The last, Bridget, was born in November 1480 and became a nun. Elizabeth's own date of birth is uncertain but was probably 1437.

5. Eleanor of Castile, 42 years 6 months
The first wife of Edward I, Eleanor had sixteen children, though there is some confusion over their sequence and dates of birth. It seems likely that her last child was the future Edward II, born in April 1284, but the possibility remains that she had at least one later child sometime before 1287, when she was about forty-five.

6. Caroline of Ansbach, 41 years 8 months 27 days
Caroline was the wife of George II and bore him ten children in nineteen years. The last born was Louisa, in December 1724, who went on to have five children of her own.

12. THE MONARCHS WITH THE MOST CHILDREN

Early records are often incomplete and inaccurate about the children of monarchs, especially their daughters. Records are also sparse about illegitimate children. It is probable that the early Saxon and Viking rulers fathered many illegitimate children, but none of these are recorded. The tradition that Brychan fathered thirty-six children may well be true, but probably not by the same wife. I am indebted to *Britain's Royal Families* by Alison Weir which enabled me to compile the following.

1. Henry I of England, 29 (25 illegitimate)
Henry only had four legitimate children, all from his first marriage, and the legitimacy of one of those is questioned. The first born died an infant and two others were drowned. Henry's favourite mistress (of whom he had at least eight) seems to have been Sybilla Corbet who gave him six children. There is apparently some dispute about the paternity of four of the illegitimate children by unknown mothers. (See Chart 37 on page XX)

2. James II of England, 27 (7 illegitimate)
James fathered the most legitimate children, eight from his first marriage and twelve from his second, although five of the latter were stillborn. James's favourite mistress was Arabella Churchill, sister of the first earl of Marlborough, who bore him four children.

3. Robert II of Scotland, 22 (8 illegitimate)
Robert had fourteen children from his two marriages.

4. Edward I of England, 20 (1 illegitimate)
Edward had 16 children by his first marriage to Eleanor of Castile, the most from any single union. Edward's reputed illegitimate child is still in doubt as he was a devoted husband and family man.

5. Henry II of England, 20 (12 illegitimate)
Henry had eight children by his wife Eleanor of Aquitaine, including Richard the Lionheart and the notorious John. Eleanor had previously borne two children to her first husband Louis VII of France.

6. Edward the Elder of Wessex, 19 (1 illegitimate)
Edward, the son of Alfred the Great, married three times, resulting in three, ten and five children respectively. Surprisingly for that period, all of the children bar one survived into adulthood.

7. Charles II of England and Scotland, 19 (16 illegitimate)
Charles' marriage to Caterina Henrietta resulted in three stillborn children and a miscarriage. Charles had at least eight mistresses of whom the best known was Nell

Gwynne, who bore him two children. Barbara Villers, who later became duchess of Cleveland, bore Charles five, possibly six children. The paternity of two of his putative children remains uncertain. (See Chart 51 on page XX)

8. Anne, 18
Anne's story is the most tragic of them all. Thirteen of her children were stillborn, including twins, and she had at least one miscarriage. Two, who were born alive, died within hours. Two more never made their second birthday, and only one, William, lived to any age at all, dying just after his eleventh birthday.

9. William IV, 17 (11 illegitimate)
Of William's six legitimate children four were stillborn, one died the same day and Elizabeth lived for nearly three months. Yet his children by his mistress Dorothea Bland all lived well into adulthood.

10. John of England, 17 (12 illegitimate)
John had no children by his first wife, but five by his second, Isabella of Angoulême. She married again after John's death, producing a further eleven children.

Despite Henry VIII marrying six times he sired only ten legitimate children, four of which were stillborn, plus four illegitimate children. Of the 43 monarchs who have ruled England since the Norman Conquest, eight sired no children at all, although four of them were married (Richard II twice). The other 34 (counting William and Mary as one) had overall 243 legitimate children out of 46 marriages (5.3 children per marriage) plus a further 116 known illegitimate children – 359 children in all (10.6 children per marriage). Just nine English monarchs account for over half of those births (183), the ninth being Edward III, who sired 16.

---

13. THE LONGEST ROYAL MARRIAGES

In a period when royal marriages seem to be evaporating like a desert mirage, it is worth reminding ourselves that the marriage of Elizabeth II and Prince Philip is the second longest in history amongst ruling monarchs. Only one other has exceeded fifty years, and four others exceeded forty years. Those top six are listed below.

1. George III and Queen Charlotte (1761–1818), 57 years 2 months 10 days
Too often we think of George III as the Mad King. He was devoted to his wife and their last years were very sad, with George confined at Windsor without his wife and gradually forgetting who she was. George survived his wife by fourteen-and-a-half months.

2. Elizabeth II and Prince Philip (1947–), 50 years and counting
The couple celebrated their fiftieth wedding anniversary on 20 November 1997. Their marriage has lasted longer than the total years for the marriages of their children.

3. Edward VII and Queen Alexandra (1863–1910), 47 years 1 month 27 days
Despite the playboy life of Edward when he was Prince of Wales, or maybe because of it, this remained a long and happy marriage. Alexandra survived her husband by fifteen-and-a-half years.

4. George V and Queen Mary of Teck (1893–1936), 42 years 6 months 15 days
Victoria's successors followed the rules of the day, and enjoyed long marriages. Mary survived her husband by 17 years and 2 months.

5. Gruffydd ap Cynan and Angharad (c1095–1137), about 42 years
   In days when life expectancy was little more than forty, such a sustained marriage was rare. Both partners lived to a great age, though Angharad was at least 25 years younger than Gruffydd. She survived him by some 25 years.

6. Edward III and Queen Philippa (1328–69), 41 years 6 months 23 days
   Despite the extra-marital passion of the Plantagenet kings, many of them enjoyed long marriages. The longest was that of Edward and Philippa and he was distraught when she died, even though by then he already had a mistress. He survived her by 7 years and 10 months.

Other monarchs with marriages of a respectable duration were Henry II and Eleanor of Aquitaine (37 years 1 month 19 days); Henry III and Eleanor of Provence (36 years 10 months) and Edward I and Eleanor of Castile (36 years 1 month). The longest duration for a Scottish marriage was between Robert III and Annabella which survived for 35 years 7 months.

14. THE SHORTEST ROYAL MARRIAGES

The average duration of a marriage between a king and queen (where dates are known) is 17 yrs 11 months. Ten marriages lasted less than two years and five less than a year. Those top five are listed here.

1. Alexander III and Yolande (1285–6), 4 months 19 days
   One of the great royal tragedies. Alexander's children from his first marriage all died and Alexander married again. Soon after he was killed in a fall from his horse while returning to his wife from state business.

2. Edmund I and Athelfleda (946), 5 months
   Dates are not certain. Edmund's first wife died in 944, and Edmund may have married soon after, but most records suggest he remarried early in 946. He was killed in a brawl five months later.

3. Henry VIII and Anne of Cleves (1540), 6 months 4 days
   This marriage was doomed from the start. The moment Henry saw Anne he disliked her and wanted a divorce. Anne had similar feelings. The divorce went through on the grounds that it was not consummated. Interestingly the two became good friends afterwards and for a while there was even rumours that they might remarry.

4. James V of Scotland and Madeleine of France (1537), 6 months 7 days
   Another sad story. Madeleine was a frail child, and only sixteen when she married. When she returned to Scotland with her husband in the spring her constitution could not cope with the Scottish climate and she died of consumption.

5. Jane Grey and Guilford Dudley (1553–1554), 8 months 23 days
   Yet more tragedy. A political marriage and ambition brought together two teenagers. Jane ruled for just nine days before she was deposed and imprisoned. Both Jane and Guilford were executed a few months later.

It is also likely that the marriage of Harald I of Man and his wife Christina lasted less than a year as they were married either at the end of 1247 or early 1248 and were drowned when returning to Man from Norway in October or November 1248.

15. MONARCHS WHO WERE OR MAY HAVE BEEN HOMOSEXUAL

Except for a few obvious examples one must draw conclusions from inferences rather than real data about the sexual proclivities of monarchs. The following list, however, is almost certainly incomplete.

1. Maelgwyn of Gwynedd
   Gildas listed Maelgwyn amongst his five tyrants, calling him "first in evil" and stating that he was "drunk on wine pressed from the vine of the Sodomites". Geoffrey of Monmouth was more specific, stating that he "made himself hateful to God, for he was given to the vice of homosexuality." Maelgwyn was a tall handsome man who also had his way with the ladies, for Gildas also reprimanded him for being an adulterer.

2. Offa of Essex
   Offa may have been a repressed homosexual. Bede tells us how much everyone adored him – he was "so lovable and handsome". But Offa had no desire to be a king. He abdicated and went to Rome with Cenred of Mercia where both became monks.

3. William II
   William seemed to love dressing up, often like a Roman emperor, and he encouraged men to his court who were effeminate and wore women's clothing and extravagant dress.

4. Richard I
   Our greatest national hero was almost certainly homosexual. Although he purportedly had an illegitimate son, and although he married (but had no children), he enjoyed more the company of men, especially soldiers on the Crusade. He had a love-hate relationship with Philippe of France and apparently had an affair with his wife's brother, Sancho.

5. Malcolm IV
   Malcolm was nicknamed "the Maiden" because of his girlish looks. His father had died when he was only ten and he had been raised amongst the company of women. He may have been a repressed homosexual. He never married and was an ineffectual ruler, losing most of the territorial gains made by his grandfather.

6. Edward II
   Edward had little paternal affection during his childhood and instead grew close to the knight Piers Gaveston. Their relationship became the scandal of the court and many of the barons were incensed at the open show of affection between them at Edward's marriage to Isabella. Edward banished many women from court, but was also forced to banish Gaveston, although he kept forgiving him until the barons took matters into their own hands and murdered Gaveston. When Edward II was himself brutally killed at Berkeley Castle there may have been good reason why his murderers thrust a red-hot poker up into his bowels.

7. Richard II
   Richard II was Edward II's great-grandson. He is frequently charged with being homosexual, but this may have been no more than a desire for affection. He was devoted to his first wife Anne and went mad with grief at her death. He had his court favourites with whom he was overly affectionate, and he became something of a dilettante, delighting in extravagant and foppish dress. He is supposed to have invented the handkerchief.

8. James VI and I

James, like Edward and Richard, was raised a lonely child starved of affection and in his youth became enamoured of his French cousin, Esmé Stuart. James was an unattractive child and notorious for dribbling, which rather disgusted the noblemen of his court when upon kissing them he "sladdered" in their mouth. Nevertheless James seemed to have no shortage of male lovers at court until at last he received the female love he so badly needed from his new wife, Anne of Denmark. After a few years, however, he distanced himself from his wife. When he moved south to London in 1603 he brought some of his male lovers with him, most notably Robert Carr, who became gentleman of the bedchamber, and the profligate George Villiers, who also became gentleman of the bedchamber and who was twenty-six years younger than James.

9. Mary II

Our only joint monarchs were not that well matched. In the end they distanced themselves from each other, William taking a mistress (Elizabeth Villiers) whilst Mary was devoted to Frances Apsley, whom she called Aurelia. Ironically after Mary's death William left his mistress and became attached to a young page, Arnold Van Keppel, which gave rise to rumours of a homosexual affair. Jonathan Swift would later reveal that he believed William had always been homosexual and had covered this from his wife by his affair with Elizabeth Villiers.

10. Anne

Like her sister Mary, Anne preferred the company of women, in particular Sarah Jennings, the mistress of the robes. They referred to each other as Mrs Morley and Mrs Freeman. Anne's romantic entanglements would later cause considerable friction at court. Sarah married the heroic John Churchill and made herself the power behind the throne. She became furious when she discovered that Anne had transferred her affections to a chamber maid, Abigail Hill, and when Anne dismissed Sarah, Sarah threatened to publish her memoirs of life at Anne's court. However, Sarah's financial mismanagement of the privy purse was discovered and this was used to blackmail her into silence. Her memoirs were not published until 1742.

---

16. THE LONGEST RULING REGAL NAMES

For over 63 years Great Britain was ruled by just one queen, Victoria. Her reign was longer than the reign of all four Williams who ruled England for a total of 53.65 years. However, there was also a William, king of Scotland, who ruled for nearly 49 years, making the total time when a William was king, 102.64 years. The following lists the longest duration for which rulers bore the same name.

1. Henry, 249.40 years
   The 8 Henrys of England were enough to amass this total, an average of 31 years each.

2. Edward, 229.43 years
   There were 11 Edwards of England (including three Saxon Edwards), although the last two Edwards were known as Albert and David when they were Princes of Wales and could have ruled as such.

3. Owen or Owain, 215.00 years
   This comes as a surprise. It covers the primary Welsh princes called Owain; the Scottish kings called Eogan or Eoganan which later evolved into Owen, and the Celtic ruler Owain of Rheged.

4. James, 210.95 years
   These are the six Jameses of Scotland plus James II/VII of Scotland and England.

5. Donald, 190.42 years
   Probably another surprise. This covers the many Celtic and Scottish rulers called either Donald or the Celtic equivalent of that name, Dumnagual or Dumnall or Dyfnwal.

6. Gruffydd, 186.00 years
   The longest running Welsh name, held by the rulers of Gwynedd, Deheubarth and Powys, some of whom ruled consecutively.

7. Hywel, 158.00 years
   The Welsh rulers of Gwent and Deheubarth. It would increase even more if it was easy to ascertain the reigns of early Celtic rulers of Dumnonia called Hoel.

8. George, 156.76 years
   The six Georges of Great Britain, helped considerably by the long reign of George III.

9. Rhodri, 124.00 years
   Six different Welsh rulers.

10. Malcolm, 112.88 years
    The period covered varies depending on how much you include tenure as sub-king of Strathclyde, often ruling in their own right. The figure quoted here is the minimum span.

17. THE LONGEST PERIODS OF IMPRISONMENT

When thinking of kings or queens in prison the likeliest to spring to mind is Mary, Queen of Scots. She was confined for over nineteen years, though her often comfortable if occasionally damp surroundings were not like other medieval castle dungeons. Compare this to the fate of Donald the Black, self-declared king of the Isles, who, apart from a few years of freedom between 1501 and 1505 was held in prison for almost all of his life, a total of forty-nine years. As Donald was not of the blood royal he is not included in the following list which covers the longest periods of confinement for more than ten years of either rulers or heirs to the throne.

1. Eleanor of Brittany, 39 years
   Eleanor was the niece of Richard I and John. After Richard's death in 1199 she and her brother Arthur had arguably greater claims to the throne than John. After Arthur's death in 1203 Eleanor might have been seen as the rightful queen. John had captured her on or soon after 1 August 1202 and she remained in captivity until her death on 10 August 1241 at Bristol Castle, having lived well into the reign of Henry III. Although her confinement was comfortable, she was never allowed to marry. There were allegations that she had been starved to death but there is no proof of this and she probably died of natural causes at the age of 57.

2. Isabella of France, 28 years 4 months
   Isabella was the queen of Edward II and daughter of Philippe IV of France. Isabella had become the lover of Roger Mortimer and between them, they plotted the downfall and death of Edward II. Her son, Edward III subsequently had her and Mortimer arrested. Mortimer was executed whilst Isabella was forced to

remain at Castle Rising in Norfolk where she was held in almost perpetual detention from April 1330 until her death on 22 August 1358.

3. Robert of Normandy, 27 years 4 months 14 days
   Robert was the eldest son of William I on whose death he succeeded as Robert III, duke of Normandy. As the eldest son he had great claim to England on the death of his brother, William II, but his younger brother Henry claimed the throne while Robert was away on Crusade. He was an ineffectual ruler and Henry invaded Normandy in 1106, taking Robert captive at Tinchebrai on 28 September. He was kept prisoner, mostly at Cardiff Castle, for the rest of his life, dying at the age of eighty-two on 10 February 1134.

4. Mary Queen of Scots, 19 years 7 months 10 days
   Mary was forced to surrender herself to the Scottish lords at Carberry on 15 June 1567 and was confined at Lochleven Castle. She officially abdicated on 24 July 1567 so was only strictly the Queen Regnant in prison for five weeks. She escaped from Lochleven on 2 May 1568 but after her defeat at Langside on 13 May she was forced to flee into England. She was taken into custody at Carlisle Castle on 16 May and remained in various castles for the rest of her life until her execution at Fotheringhay on 8 February 1587.

5. Ieuaf ap Idwal of Gwynedd, 19 years
   Ieuaf was co-ruler of Gwynedd with his brother Iago until he was defeated and imprisoned in 969. It is uncertain whether Ieuaf was released when Iago was defeated by Ieuaf's son Hywel in 980, but as he played no further part in affairs it is as likely that Hywel kept his father imprisoned until his death in 988, when he must have been into his late sixties.

6. James I of Scotland, 17 years 10 months
   This is the longest period for a ruling monarch to be held prisoner. He was only eleven years old when he was captured at sea in April 1406 on his way to safekeeping in France. His father died on the same day. James came into the custody of Henry IV of England who kept him confined first at the Tower of London and later at Nottingham Castle, though he frequently toured with Henry's court around England and spent much time at Windsor. His confinement was not onerous and James became well educated in the English court system. He also spent his time writing poetry and it was while he was held captive that he first set eyes on Lady Joan Beaufort, whom he promptly married upon his release in February 1424.

7. Edward Plantagenet, 15 years 6 months
   Edward, who was styled the earl of Warwick, was the nephew of Edward IV and Richard III. He was apparently declared the heir apparent after the believed death of the young king, Edward V, but being only eight years old Richard III allowed him a degree of freedom for a while. However by the summer of 1484 Edward was being held in custody at Sheriff Hutton castle. With the succession of Henry VII, who was well aware of Edward's prior claim, the young prince was escorted to the Tower of London where he remained confined for the rest of his life. He was often believed dead, which allowed pretenders to claim the throne, most notably Lambert Simnel and Perkin Warbeck. Having been held in prison since his childhood, Edward remained uneducated and was later accused of being simple-minded. He was eventually executed on a trumped-up charge of treason in November 1499.

8. Duncan II of Scotland, 15 years
   Duncan was the eldest son of Malcolm III. He was taken hostage by William I following a raid by Malcolm into English territory in 1072 when Duncan was only

twelve. *It did not stop Malcolm making further raids, suggesting that he cared little for Duncan's safety and may already have disinherited him. Duncan remained a prisoner in Normandy and England until 1087 by which time he was more favoured amongst the Normans than the Scots. He gained Norman support for usurping the Scottish throne in 1094 but was killed six months later.*

9. Gruffydd ap Cynan of Gwynedd, 12 years
   Gruffydd had spent much of his youth in exile in Ireland and had sought once to regain the throne of Gwynedd in 1075 before his eventual success in 1081. However within the year Gruffydd was captured by the Normans at Corwen and held in prison at Chester for twelve years until his conditional release in 1094. This was the longest period for an adult king who had not been deposed to be held prisoner.

10. David II of Scotland, 10 years 11 months 17 days
    David was taken prisoner after he was wounded at the Battle of Neville's Cross in October 1346 and was held captive in England until released under the terms of the Treaty of Berwick in October 1357.

18. THE WORST AILMENTS OR ILLNESSES

The English royal family seems to suffer from a hereditary illness known as porphyria, a metabolic disorder which causes both abdominal pains and mental confusion. It is this ailment that is now generally associated with the apparent madness of George III and probably entered the royal blood from Catherine daughter of Charles VI of France. However similar symptoms have been ascribed to earlier monarchs and thus may have been in the blood of kings since Saxon or even Celtic times. The following lists some of the more severe or unusual afflictions in chronological order of monarch.

1. Pebiau of Ergyng
   Pebiau (early 6th C) was known as Claforawg or Spumosus, both of which refer to his affliction of constantly frothing at the mouth and dribbling.

2. Eadbald of Kent
   According to Bede, Eadbald, who succeeded his father in 616, turned his back on the Christian faith and as a consequence was "afflicted by frequent fits of madness and possessed by an unclean spirit." Is this an early exaple of porphyria or, as it is more often interpreted, does it mean that Eadbald was an epileptic?

3. Alfred the Great
   According the Asser, the alleged biographer of Alfred, the king had suffered from piles from his youth. He prayed that he be relieved of this affliction and granted another less obvious malady. Although apparently cured of piles he was struck down by this new ailment on his wedding night in 868. According to Asser he was "struck without warning" by "a sudden severe pain that was quite unknown to all physicians," and which afflicted him for the rest of his life. These ailments have an uncertain basis in fact, though Alfred's own writings suggest that he did suffer physically. It is possible that Alfred had a form of porphyria, which may have given him severe stomach cramps without the associated mental decline, and that in later years he might have again developed piles.

4. Eadred of Wessex
   Eadred was a surprisingly strong king despite a weak constitution which meant he found it difficult to hold down his food. He was the grandson of Alfred the Great and may therefore have inherited something of his malady, though whether this was porphyria cannot be said with any certainty. It contributed to Eadred's early death in 955, aged 32.

5. Robert the Bruce
   The king who saved Scotland died in June 1329 of a wasting disease normally described as leprosy, though whether it was remains uncertain.

6. Henry IV
   Henry was also alleged to have contracted leprosy which the clergy maintained was divine retribution for Henry's execution of Archbishop Scrope of York. It may merely have been an extreme form of eczema and Henry's second wife, Joan of Navarre, was later accused of inflicting the ailment through witchcraft.

7. Henry VI
   Starting from 1453 Henry suffered recurrent bouts of melancholia and depression which, at their most severe would find him lost in his own world, oblivious to his surroundings and apparently imbecilic. The malady was almost certainly inherited from his maternal grandfather Charles VI of France who suffered similar bouts, and although the symptoms were not recognized at the time, they are so similar to those suffered by George III that it is likely that Henry also had porphyria.

8. Edward VI
   Although Edward was the only healthy son to be born to Henry VIII, it later emerged that he was suffering from congenital syphilis. In his last year he also contracted consumption – thus his last months not only saw him constantly wracked with coughing, bringing up foul-smelling black sputum, but also his body broke out in boils and eruptions. Amongst the potions administered to him was arsenic which, though prolonging his life, almost certainly increased the pain. His skin discoloured, his hair and nails fell out and he developed gangrene. He died after tremendous suffering in the midst of a thunderstorm on 6 July 1553, aged 15.

9. James VI of Scotland and I of England
   Although he lived to be nearly sixty, James had a poor constitution. He not only looked ungainly – he was short, had bow-legs, a large head and rheumy eyes – but, like Pebiau, he drooled frequently, had rickets and was a martyr to diarrhoea. Some of this may have been indicative of porphyria, which he is alleged to have inherited. Yet this man was also the first king to rule both England and Scotland after 1603.

10. George III
    George III's frequent bouts of porphyria have done much to sully the image of a king who was otherwise caring, thoughtful and intelligent. At times he became violent, especially towards his son, who became the Prince Regent. His final years were sad, incarcerated almost entirely alone at Windsor Castle, seldom recognizing anyone and having virtually forgotten who he was.

19. THE MOST GRUESOME OR UNUSUAL DEATHS

"Uneasy lies the head that wears the crown" is true of so many monarchs. Many were killed in battle, and many were murdered. The following lists ten of the more unusual deaths in chronological order.

1. Mul of Kent
   Mul was established as sub-king of Kent by his brother Caedwalla in 686, but a few months later the Kentish people rebelled, surrounded Mul and his men in a house near Canterbury and burned them alive.

2. Ceolred of Mercia
   Ceolred had upset the church by his wicked practices and so it was deemed he received due retribution. According to Boniface, Ceolred, who was "feasting in splendour amid his companions", was "suddenly in his sin sent mad by a malign spirit" so that "without repentance and confession, raging and distracted, conversing with devils and cursing the priests of God, he departed from this light without a doubt to the torments of hell." It may be that Ceolred was epileptic or that he suffered a seizure.

3. Edmund of East Anglia
   Edmund, who was later canonized and is now the king remembered in Bury St Edmunds, was cruelly murdered by the Danes in 869. He was flayed, an eagle was carved into the flesh of his back, he was tied to a tree, shot to death with arrows and then beheaded. Tradition recounts that the severed head was subsequently found protected by a wolf.

4. Sigurd I of Orkney
   Sigurd the Mighty conquered much of northern Scotland which brought him into conflict with Maelbrigte of Moray. Sigurd defeated Maelbrigte in 892 and strapped his decapitated head to his saddle as a sign of triumph. As he rode, however, Maelbrigte's tooth rubbed against Sigurd's leg causing a wound which turned septic and Sigurd died of the poison. He is the only ruler known to have been bitten to death by the dead.

5. Edmund II of England
   The death of Edmund Ironside so soon after his peace treaty with Canute has always been suspicious. Although the official story was that he died of natural causes, at least one chronicler claimed that he was murdered. The assassin apparently hid under the king's privy and, when the king came to relieve himself, he was stabbed twice up through the bowels. He is the only king believed to have been murdered on the toilet, though George II also died (of a heart attack) while going to the lavatory.

6. Harthacanute
   Like Ceolred, the highly unpopular Harthacanute died while drinking, this time at a wedding feast in 1042. The Anglo-Saxon Chronicle records that he "suddenly fell to the earth with an awful convulsion." Although those nearby rushed to his side, he never spoke again and died soon after. It seems he must have died of a fit, or perhaps a heart attack, but one cannot rule our the possibility of poison.

7. Harald I of Orkney
   Harald was co-earl with his half-brother Paul. His mother Helga and his aunt Frakok plotted to kill Paul and made him a poisoned shirt. Harald was unaware of this but became jealous when he saw such a fine shirt for his brother while he was wearing such old clothes. Without heeding their warning he quickly donned the

shirt. The Orkneyinga Saga *tells us that no sooner had he done so than "his flesh started to quiver and he began to suffer terrible pain. He had to go to bed and it was not long before he was dead." He died in 1131.*

8. Henry I
Henry loved lampreys even though they always disagreed with him. In 1135, after hunting in the forests near Gisors in Normandy, Henry had a feast of lampreys and died of ptomaine poisoning.

9. John
John was another who loved his food. In 1216, although already suffering from a fever, he overindulged in peaches and cider which led to dysentery and he died two days later. The suspicion has always lingered that he was poisoned by a monk or on the orders of his wife Isabella.

10. Edward II
Having deposed her husband, Queen Isabella was determined to see Edward dead but with all the appearance of a natural death. The story of his death, as recorded by the notoriously unreliable Raphael Holinshed, is that he was disembowelled by a horn being inserted into his anus through which a red-hot spit was inserted and wriggled about until he was dead.

20. MONARCHS WHO ALSO WROTE OR COMPOSED

Early monarchs were famed for their battle prowess and had little time for reading and even less for writing. Nevertheless at least six monarchs have produced books or poetry of some note. Here they are in chronological order.

1. Aldfrith of Northumbria
Aldfrith was a scholar before he became king and produced his own book on riddles called Enigmata *during the 670s or early 680s. He also wrote a study of poetry called* Epistola ad Adcircium *and some have stated he could have been the author of* Beowulf, *or certainly encouraged its production. It was during Aldfrith's reign that the Lindisfarne* Gospels *were produced by Bishop Eadfrith.*

2. Alfred the Great
Alfred was an extremely religious man and towards the close of his reign he produced several translations of his own, including Gregory's Regula Pastralis *and Boethius's* Consolation of Philosophy *to which Alfred added much of his own thinking. Alfred also produced a very free translation of Augustine's* Soliloquies. *He also encouraged the production of the Anglo-Saxon* Chronicle *and the translation of Bede's* Historia Ecclesiastica *and of Orosius'* Historia Adversus Paganos, *with additional travellers' tales.*

3. James I of Scotland
James is credited with The Kingis Quair, *a poem written when he was a prisoner in England in the early 1420s to record his love for Joan Beaufort, his future wife. He is suspected of having written other poems but their identity remains uncertain.*

4. Henry VIII
Henry loved music and delighted in composing songs and hymns. Greensleeves *has been attributed to him, but other more definite productions include the hymn* O Lord, the Maker of All Things *and the songs* Green Groweth the Holly (*written for Katherine of Aragon) and* Adieu Madame et ma Maistresse (*written for Anne Boleyn). Henry was also a noted theologian and co-wrote with Thomas More* The

Defence of the Seven Sacraments *(1520) a rebuttal of the teachings of Martin Luther. It was the Pope's appreciation of this book that caused him to bestow the title of Defender of the Faith upon Henry.*

5. James VI of Scotland and I of England
   A very learned man, he was the most prolific of the royal authors. His works include The Essays of a Prentice in the Divine Art of Poesy *(1584), a collection of poems, translations and criticism,* His Majesty's Poetical Exercises at Vacant Hours *(1591),* Daemonologie *(1598), an attack upon witchcraft,* The Trew Law of Free Monarchies *(1598), which, with* Basilikon Doron *(1599), established his principles and philosophy of kingship and government, and the anonymous* Counterblast to Tobacco *(1604). So productive was he with his pen that some have even claimed he helped write some of the plays attributed to Shakespeare.*

6. Victoria
   Victoria was so delighted with her and Albert's home at Balmoral that after his death she found solace in producing two books of memorabilia about it: A Journal of Our Life in the Highlands *and* More Leaves from Our Life in the Highlands.

21. THE SAINTLY KINGS

In the early days of the Christian church, when miracles happened at the drop of a hat, many rulers were subsequently credited with saintly attributes. It happened as much to queen consorts as kings, but the following list covers kings only, in chronological order of their life, together with their feast day.

1. Gwynllyw of Gwent, 29 March
   The husband of St Gladys and the father of St Cadoc, Gwynllyw was himself something of a seasoned warrior before his son turned him against violent ways. Gwynllyw then went to the other extreme, becoming a hermit and living a life of extreme asceticism.

2. Athelbert of Kent, 25/26 February
   Athelbert was the first Christian Anglo-Saxon king and appears to have become canonized purely because he welcomed Augustine to Kent in 597 and allowed him to establish a church. No miracles are attributed to Athelbert. Although there was clearly a local cult in Kent soon after his death his feast day was not celebrated until the 13th C.

3. Edwin of Northumbria, 12 October
   Edwin was one of those rulers, like the Emperor Constantine, who converted to Christianity because it served his purpose and who subsequently believed it helped his conquest and subordination of England. It did not entirely work as he was killed in battle by the pagan Penda in 633 or 634. Edwin became a hero to the Northumbrians and was regarded as a Christian warrior by the church who established a shrine to him at York and another at Whitby, a location apparently determined by divine revelation.

4. Sigebert of East Anglia, 16 January
   A pious and learned king, Sigebert encouraged the spread of Christianity throughout East Anglia along with the construction of monasteries and seats of learning. He abdicated to become a monk but in 635 he was forced to come out of retirement to lead an army into battle against Penda. It was believed Sigebert's

presence would raise the morale of the troops. Sigebert refused to arm himself and marched into battle with only a staff. He and his army were annihilated. He was soon venerated as a martyr.

5. Oswald of Northumbria, 5 August
   A devout Christian, raised in the faith while in exile on Iona, he established the monastery on Lindisfarne. He was known for his generosity and piety as well as his bravery and military skill. He was captured in battle in 642 against the pagan Penda of Mercia and was ritually sacrificed, dying a martyr's death. His relics became distributed across Britain and even parts of Europe and many miracles were attributed to these shrines, and to the spot where he died.

6. Oswine of Deira, 20 August
   Portrayed as a peaceful king, Oswine sought to avoid battles but was betrayed and murdered in 651. His murderer, Oswy, built a shrine to Oswine at Gilling, and a cult grew around Oswine's memory.

7. Cadwaladr of Gwynedd, 12 November
   A pious king who hated war, he nevertheless led the Welsh against the Saxons in 658 and was utterly defeated. Yet he was venerated as a hero, although he lived on for another six uneventful years.

8. Caedwalla of Wessex, 20 April
   Caedwalla was a bloodthirsty warrior and the least saintly of all of the West Saxon kings. He used the church to further his own ends and, when he was mortally wounded in battle in 688, he thought it best to be baptized in Rome so as to be purged of his sins. Bede speaks unduly kindly of him and it was probably for that reason that he became sanctified.

9. Sebbi of Essex, 29 August
   Sebbi's name became sanctified primarily because of his continued support for the church during a time of considerable pagan opposition. He was pious and generous and is believed to have built the first church at Westminster.

10. Offa of Essex, 15 December
    In his day Offa was regarded as having all the saintly virtues. Such was his calling to God that he abdicated his kingship in 709, travelled to Rome and became a monk.

11. Ceolwulf of Northumbria, 15 January
    Ceolwulf seems to have become sanctified because he was kind to the monks of Lindisfarne. In 737 he joined them as their abbot and brought with him so much of his wealth that he was able to convert their water into wine. After his burial near the tomb of St Cuthbert on Lindisfarne miracles were attributed to his tomb.

12. Elfwald of Northumbria, 23 September
    A young king who tried to retain Christian virtues against an ever more oppressive nobility. The pope sent a delegation to Northumbria where they believed that the holy authority of the kingship was being undermined. None of this did Elfwald much good for he was murdered in 788. Thereafter witnesses maintained that a light shone over the spot where he was killed.

13. Athelbert of East Anglia, 20 May
    Like his Kentish namesake, Athelbert performed no miracles but became worshipped as a saint because of his violent murder by the Mercians in 794. His body, which had been buried near Marden, was removed to Hereford Cathedral which was later consecrated in his honour.

14. Edmund of East Anglia, 20 November
Edmund, after whom Bury St Edmunds became known, was worshipped as a martyr after his ritual murder by the Danes in 869. His body was originally buried in a small chapel at Hellesdon but about fifty years later it was found to be incorrupt and it was removed to Bedricsworth.

15. Edgar of England, 8 July
Edgar was the first to be crowned as king of all England in 973. Prior to this he had led far from an exemplary life and was often admonished by Dunstan. Nevertheless he served his country well, establishing a period of firm and peaceful government and founding many monasteries not simply as religious foundations but as centres of learning and culture. It is unlikely he was regarded as a saint either during his life or soon after his death but he became closely associated with the monastic revival and when his tomb was opened in 1052 his body was found to be incorrupt and even bled when cut. Thereafter he was revered at Glastonbury where he was buried.

16. Edward the Martyr, 18 March
Edward was the son of Edgar who was murdered by his stepmother in 978. He was first buried at Wareham and miracles were soon attributed to the site. His relics were removed to Shaftesbury in 980 and he was soon being venerated as a saint. His remains were rediscovered this century but an argument over his final resting place means that they have not been reburied. Edward must thus be the only saint whose relics remain in a bank vault.

17. Edward the Confessor, 13 October
Edward was noted for his piety and holiness, though it might be argued he took this to extremes. He determined to remain celibate, which is why he had no heir, and at times treated both his wife and mother with severity. He was almost certainly a weak individual who had no great desire to be king. He clearly did not live up to his own expectations and spent the latter part of his life devoted to the foundation of Westminster Abbey where he lies buried. It was consecrated within days of his death in 1066. In 1102 Edward's body was found to be incorrupt and in 1161 Henry II succeeded in obtaining Edward's canonization. For a while Edward along with Edmund were regarded as England's patron saints.

18. Magnus of Orkney, 16 April
Magnus was a Viking earl of Orkney who was as much a pirate as his forebears in his early life but who later converted to Christianity. Forced by his king to undertake raids along the Welsh coast Magnus refused and fled to the king of Scotland where he lived as a penitent. He later returned to Orkney where he was murdered. Magnus became revered as a martyr. Kirkwall Cathedral, where he is buried, was raised in his honour.

19. David I of Scotland, 24 May
David rivals Robert the Bruce as Scotland's most important king and certainly one who was more pious and had less stain upon his character. Apart from his wars with England, which he endeavoured to curtail, David spent his time improving both the secular and ecclesiastical administration of his realm founding many churches and monasteries and reorganizing the church in Scotland. He sought to lead by example in his devout religious practices. He died in 1153.

David was the last king to be canonized, although attempts have been made over the years to recognize Henry VI as a martyr because of his extreme piety and his murder. David Stewart, the son of Robert III, and who was starved to death in 1402, was also regarded as a martyr by some, although no formal cult was established. In life David was a dissolute youth with no saintly virtues.

22. THE KINGS AND QUEENS WHO NEVER WERE

It was not until the time of William the Conqueror in England or Malcolm III in Scotland that patrilinear succession (that is the eldest son succeeding the father) became largely accepted practice; even then it was challenged for many generations. Previously the Celtic rule of tanistry, whereby a king was elected from amongst nominated successors (usually related to the royal line), prevailed, and even then territory was subdivided amongst brothers. Prior to the eleventh century, therefore, almost anyone related to the royal line had a claim on the throne, hence the many rival kings. From the eleventh century on the heir to the throne was generally accepted as the eldest son (or occasionally daughter) of the monarch. Not all of these heirs survived to inherit the throne. In some alternate world we can imagine that some of these heirs did become kings. Here are those alternate monarchs. Only those heirs who survived infancy are listed.

England

1. Robert I, could have reigned after 1100
   The eldest son of William I. He was made duke of Normandy on William's death and his brother, William II, became king of England. On William II's death, Robert could rightly have claimed the English throne, but he was duped and later imprisoned by Henry I.

2. William (III), could have reigned after 1135
   William was the eldest son of Henry I, but drowned when the White Ship sank off Normandy in 1120, when he was seventeen. His brother Richard drowned with him.

3. Eustace, could have reigned after 1154
   The son of Stephen, he was crowned as king of England in 1152 but died a year later, a year before his father, aged about twenty-two.

4. Henry (III), could have reigned after 1189
   Henry was the son of Henry II and was crowned as heir in 1170. He was known thereafter as "the Young King". However he died in 1183, aged twenty-eight.

5. Alfonso, could have reigned after 1307
   The eldest surviving son of Edward I, he died at the age of ten in 1284. He was named after his mother's half-brother, Alfonso X of Castile, who was also the child's godfather.

6. Edward (IV) – "The Black Prince", could have reigned after 1377
   One of the best known of the kings who never were, the Black Prince was the eldest son of Edward III. He was created prince of Wales in 1343. He died in June 1376, a year before his father. His son succeeded to the throne as Richard II.

7. Edmund, could have reigned after 1399
   Edmund was the great-great grandson of Edward III, but had a stronger claim to the throne than Henry IV who usurped the throne with the deposition of Richard II. He never pressed for his claim to the throne and had a good relationship with

both Henry IV and Henry V. He was made Lieutenant of Ireland and died there of the plague in 1425.

8. Arthur, could have reigned after 1509
   The eldest son of Henry VII and the first husband of Katherine of Aragon. He was named Arthur to demonstrate the link from his father through the ancient Welsh line back to the early British kings. He was always of a weak constitution and died in 1502, aged fifteen, probably of tuberculosis.

Scotland

9. Henry, could have reigned after 1153
   The eldest surviving son of David I, he became earl of Huntingdon in 1136 and earl of Northumberland in 1139. He died in 1152, aged about thirty-five, a year before his father. His sons Malcolm IV and William both succeeded him.

10. David (III), could have reigned after 1406
    The eldest son of Robert III he was made duke of Rothesay, the title borne by the heir, in 1398, as well as Lieutenant of Scotland. However he was a fairly hopeless man and was cast into prison where he died, probably of dysentery, in 1402, aged twenty-three.

England and Scotland

11. Henry (IX), could have reigned after 1625
    The eldest son of James I (James VI of Scotland) who was duke of Rothesay, lord of the Isles, duke of Cornwall and prince of Wales. But he died of typhoid in 1612, aged eighteen.

12. James (II), duke of Monmouth, could have reigned after 1685
    James was the illegitimate son of Charles II and Lucy Walter, but he claimed his parents were married and that he was the legitimate heir to the throne. He had many supporters and raised the Monmouth rebellion in 1685, but he was defeated and executed, aged thirty-six.

13. James (III), "The Old Pretender", could have reigned after 1701
    James was the Catholic heir to the throne, though the Act of Settlement barred him from inheriting. He had many supporters in Scotland who raised a rebellion in 1715, but this soon petered out. James survived until 1766. His son was Bonnie Prince Charlie, regarded by many as Charles III of England and Scotland.

14. William (IV), could have reigned after 1714
    William was the only child of Anne to survive infancy, but he had a weak constitution and died of hydrocephalus in 1700 aged eleven.

15. Frederick, could have reigned after 1760
    The wayward son of George II who was created prince of Wales in 1729. Despite his ways he would probably have made a good king, though he may have been a forerunner of his grandson George IV. He died of a ruptured aneurysm in 1751, aged forty-four. His son became king as George III.

16. Charlotte, could have reigned after 1830
    The daughter and only child of George IV, she died in childbirth in 1817 aged twenty-one. Her husband, Leopold, who might otherwise have become Prince Consort of Great Britain, subsequently became Leopold I of the Belgians.

17. Edward (VIII), could have reigned after 1910
    The eldest son of Edward VII, he was christened Albert Victor Christian Edward, but was always known as Prince Eddy. He was made duke of Clarence in 1890. He

was a rather lazy and wayward youth and caused a scandal because of his habit of frequenting male brothels in London. His name became associated with the Jack the Ripper murders, though with little basis in fact. He died of pneumonia in 1892, aged twenty-eight, even before his father had become king.

23. NOTABLE CORONATIONS

The following lists all coronations for completeness and notes where applicable interesting or unusual events that happened. There were doubtless ceremonies to ordain kings far back into prehistory, but records of such events are rare until the ninth century. It is recorded that the high kings of Tara in Ireland were ordained on a ceremonial stone which was brought to Scotland by Fergus of Dál Riata. It was later removed to Scone by Kenneth macAlpin and has ever since been called the Stone of Scone. Nevertheless it was not until the union of a secular event with religious ordination that the coronation took on a greater significance, with the king recognized as a servant of God and his secular representative on Earth. The first such recorded anointment was that of Aedán mac Gabhrain of Dál Riata by Columba in 574. The Scottish ritual remained an ordination without a formal crowning until the reign of Robert I. The first recorded Saxon coronation was that of Egfrith of Mercia who was consecrated king in 787 by Hygeberht of Lichfield. Saxon rulers were inaugurated with the placement of helmets instead of crowns until 900. There were doubtless many other coronations and ceremonies but the following lists all of those for which there are records. Coronations of queen consorts are included for completeness.

Note: The name of the monarch is followed by the date of the coronation, the officiant and the location. The officiant for all English coronations from 839 was the archbishop of Canterbury and for Scottish coronations the bishop of St Andrews unless otherwise stated.

1. Egfrith of Mercia, 787, Hygeberht, Lichfield

2. Eardwulf of Northumbria, 14 May 796, Eanbald of York, York

3. Athelwolf of Wessex, 839, Ceolnoth (?), Kingston
   Although details of this coronation are not recorded it was almost certainly the first formal coronation of the kings of Wessex by the archbishop. In 838 Egbert had bestowed many gifts upon the see at Canterbury and recognized its authority over the Kentish minsters. With this act Canterbury shifted its allegiance from the kings of Mercia to those of Wessex and thus Athelwolf's coronation ushered in a new era.

4. Kenneth I macAlpin, (?) 843, Scone
   Although there is no record of this event it is nevertheless significant. Kenneth brought the sacred inauguration Stone of Destiny from Dunstaffnage to Scone and there held a ceremony which ordained him as the king of the Scots and the Picts. The ceremony was probably already old by then and would remain much the same for a further four hundred years until the reign of Alexander III. After a service in the Abbey the king was led out to the adjoining moot hill to which the Stone of Destiny had been moved. The king was set upon the Stone and his

peers paid homage to him. The king took an oath and then a bard would recite the king's pedigree back to the time of Fergus mac Ferchard. There was no crowning.

5. Judith, wife of Athelwolf, 1 October 856, Hincmar, Verberie-sur-Oise
Judith was Athelwolf's second wife and the daughter of Charles the Bald, king of the Franks. The marriage was political, confirming an important alliance, and Charles insisted that at the ceremony Judith be crowned Queen, which was traditional amongst the Franks but had been abandoned by the Saxons. The officiant was Hincmar, archbishop of Rheims.

6. Athelbald of Wessex, 858, Ceolnoth (?), Kingston

7. Athelbert of Wessex, 861, Ceolnoth (?), Kingston

8. Athelred I of Wessex, 866, Ceolnoth (?), Kingston

9. Alfred the Great, 871, ?, ?
There is no record of Alfred's coronation and it is quite possible that there was no formal ceremony because Wessex was in the midst of the Danish threat. It would nevertheless be surprising for there to be no ordination ceremony and this probably happened soon after Athelred's funeral at Wimborne in late April or early May 871, but it is not known who officiated. The archbishop of Canterbury at that date was Athelred.

10. Edward the Elder, 8 June 900, Plegmund, Kingston
This is believed to be the first ceremony where a formal crown was used instead of a ceremonial helmet.

11. Constantine, 900, ?, Scone Abbey

12. Athelstan, 4 September 925, Wulfhelm (?), Kingston

13. Edmund I, 29 November 939, Wulfhelm (?), Kingston

14. Malcolm I, 943, ?, Scone Abbey

15. Eadred, 16 August 946, Oda, Kingston

16. Indulf, 954, ?, Scone Abbey

17. Edwy, 26 January 956, Oda, Kingston

18. Duff, 962, ?, Scone Abbey

19. Cuilean, 967, ?, Scone Abbey

20. Kenneth II, 971, ?, Scone Abbey

21. Edgar and Elfrida, 11 May 973, Dunstan, Bath Abbey
Edgar may have had a prior coronation at Kingston upon his accession in October 959 – it would be strange not to have had at least a formal initiation ceremony – but the record suggests that Dunstan refrained from crowning Edgar because of his immorality and then subsequently devised a more extravagant coronation ceremony to recognize Edgar's elevation as king of all the English. Following the ceremony Edgar went on a royal progress to Chester where he was rowed along the river Dee with his subordinate kings.

22. Edward the Martyr, *after* 8 July 975, Dunstan, Kingston

23. Athelred II, 4 April 978, Dunstan, Kingston

24. Constantine III, 995, ?, Scone Abbey

25. Kenneth III, 997, ?, Scone Abbey

26. Malcolm II, March *or* April 1005, ?, Scone Abbey

27. Edmund II, April 1016, Lyfing, St Paul's Cathedral

28. Canute, 6 January 1017, Lyfing (?), St Paul's Cathedral

29. Duncan I, November 1034, ?, Scone Abbey

30. Harold I, 1037, ?, Oxford

31. Harthacanute, 18 June 1040, Eadsige, Canterbury Cathedral

32. Macbeth, August 1040, Maelduin, Scone Abbey

33. Edward the Confessor, 3 April 1043, Eadsige of Canterbury and Ethelric of York, Winchester Cathedral
Because of the deep religious nature of Edward this ceremony, which to a great extent followed the precedent established by Dunstan for Edgar, must have held great significance and Edward may well have regarded the anointing as a special link with God. Hitherto kings had been buried in their crown but hereafter Edward's crown and other regalia (with the exception of the ring) became the crown jewels of England and were used in all future ceremonies until the reign of Charles I, after which they were broken up by the Commonwealth.

34. Edith, wife of Edward, 23 January 1045, Eadsige, Winchester Cathedral

35. Lulach, November (?) 1057, Tuthald (?), Scone Abbey

36. Malcolm III, 25 April 1058, Tuthald (?), Scone Abbey

37. Harold II, 6 January 1066, Ealdred of York, Westminster Abbey
This was the first coronation to take place at Westminster Abbey and it followed on from the funeral of Edward the Confessor. The ceremony followed a new ceremonial adapted by Ealdred from that performed on the continent. Ealdred officiated because Stigand's appointment as archbishop of Canterbury had become regarded as uncanonical. The later Norman historians recorded that Stigand was the officiant in order to undermine Harold's legality as king.

38. William I, 25 December 1066, Ealdred of York, Westminster Abbey
William was fearful at his coronation that there might be an uprising and he was so nervous that he shook visibly. His soldiers were equally on edge and those on guard outside the Abbey mistook the cries of acclaim for a call to arms and set about attacking the local populace.

39. Matilda, wife of William I, 11 May 1068, Ealdred of York, Winchester Cathedral

40. William II, 26 September 1087, Lanfranc, Westminster Abbey

41. Donald III, (?) November 1093, ?, Scone Abbey
It is not certain whether Donald was formally ordained upon his first accession to the throne or following his restoration in November 1094.

42. Duncan II, May *or* June 1094, ?, Scone Abbey

43. Edgar, (?) October 1097, ?, Scone Abbey

44. Henry I, 6 August 1100, Maurice, bishop of London, Westminster Abbey
Henry's coronation happened with such unseemly haste after the sudden death of William II – three days – that it had all the hallmarks of being planned. It

was a quick and simple ceremony after which Henry issued his proclamation that he would revoke the practices of his brother and reinstate those of his father.

45. Matilda, 1st wife of Henry I, 11 November 1100, Anselm, Westminster Abbey
     Henry's wedding to Matilda was followed quickly by the coronation ceremony. Matilda was descended from Edmund II, and Henry saw this dual ceremony as uniting the Norman and Saxon dynasties.

46. Alexander I, (?) January 1107, ?, Scone Abbey

47. Adeliza, 2nd wife of Henry I, 3 February 1122, Ralph d'Escures, Westminster Abbey
     The death of Henry's first wife and of his heirs prompted Henry to remarry quickly. The coronation of his second wife came five days after the wedding. It was noted for the aging and confused Archbishop d'Escures mistakenly believing he was crowning the king and becoming enraged when discovering Henry was already crowned. In a fit of temper he knocked the king's crown off and would only replace it with due ceremony before proceeding to Adeliza's coronation.

48. David I, (?) May 1124, (Robert ?), Scone Abbey

49. Stephen, 26 December 1135, William de Corbeil, Westminster Abbey
     Stephen acted quickly after the death of Henry I. His coronation was arranged within less than four weeks, in which time not only had news had to reach Stephen in France but he had to travel to England, secure the Treasury and convince William de Corbeil that he was the only successor and that Corbeil should conduct the ceremony. Just how many agreed with this is uncertain for the historian William of Malmesbury records that there were hardly any nobles or prelates present.

50. Matilda, wife of Stephen, 22 March 1136, William de Corbeil, Westminster Abbey

51. Stephen (second coronation), 25 December 1141, Theobald, Canterbury Cathedral
     Stephen believed it necessary for his barons to re-establish their fealty to him and so insisted upon a second coronation following his release from prison and restoration to the throne.

52. Stephen (third coronation), 25 December 1146, Lincoln Cathedral
     This was not so much a formal coronation as a display of authority.

53. Malcolm IV, (?) June 1153, Robert, Scone Abbey

54. Henry II, 19 December 1154, Theobald, Westminster Abbey

55. Eleanor, wife of Henry II, 25 December 1158, Theobald, Worcester Cathedral

56. William the Lyon, 24 December 1165, Richard, Scone Abbey

57. Henry, the Young King, 14 June 1170, Roger of York, Westminster Abbey

58. Henry, the Young King and Margaret, 27 August 1172, Rotrou, archbishop of Rouen, Winchester Cathedral
     Henry II had secured the coronation of his son, Henry, so as to cement the succession. However Louis VII, the father of the Young King's wife, Margaret, objected to the fact that she had not also been crowned, so Henry had a second

coronation at Winchester, and brought over the archbishop of Rouen for the ceremony. The Young King was a spoilt brat and was not satisfied with either ceremony, starting to regard himself as superior to his father. The first coronation had contributed to the rift between Henry II and Thomas Becket.

59.   Richard I, 3 September 1189, Baldwin, Westminster Abbey
      Many thought it was an ill omen at Richard's coronation when a bat continually circled his head as he was crowned. The circumstances were made even more contentious by Richard taking the crown himself from the altar and handing it to the archbishop. England was in the grip of crusade fever at this time and Richard's coronation was marred by an outbreak of hostility against the Jews.

60.   Berengaria, wife of Richard I, 12 May 1191, John FitzLuke, Bishop of Evreux, St George's Chapel, Limasol, Cyprus
      A combined marriage and coronation ceremony, Berengaria was only the second queen to be crowned outside Britain (see number 5, Athelwolf's wife Judith).

61.   Richard I (second coronation), 17 April 1194, Hubert Walter, Winchester Cathedral
      Richard insisted on a second coronation upon his release from captivity and return to England from the Crusades in order to re-establish his authority following John's attempt to usurp the throne. It was a simple ceremony and within a month Richard had returned to France, never to set foot again in England.

62.   John, 27 May 1199, Hubert Walter, Westminster Abbey
      If John had any redeeming feature it was his sense of humour and, to the exasperation of his lords, he had little regard for ceremony. He dropped the regalia spear at his investiture in the duchy of Normandy on 25 April, and spent much of the English coronation smiling and laughing.

63.   Isabella, 2nd wife of John, 8 October 1200, Hubert Walter, Westminster Abbey

64.   Alexander II, 6 December 1214, William Malvoisine, Scone Abbey

65.   Henry III, 28 October 1216, Peter des Roches, Gloucester Cathedral, bishop of Winchester
      The sudden death of John during his war with the barons meant that his son, Henry, who was in safekeeping at Gloucester, had to be crowned quickly. John had lost the state crown in the Wash and the royal regalia was at Westminster, so the nine-year old king was crowned with his mother's gold torque.

66.   Henry III's full coronation, 17 May 1220, Stephen Langton, Westminster Abbey

67.   Eleanor, wife of Henry III, 20 January 1236, Edmund Rich, Westminster Abbey
      Eleanor's coronation was a major occasion. Henry had spent a vast sum on having the Palace of Westminster refurbished to a standard previously unknown in England in readiness for the Queen. This was the first time the coronation procession left from the Tower of London to Westminster and Henry took this opportunity for a great display of pageant and grandeur.

68. Alexander III, 13 July 1249, David de Bernham, Scone Abbey
   This was the last occasion of the ancient ceremony described under Kenneth macAlpin above and doubtless held for all Scottish monarchs back to the time of Fergus mac Erc, and probably before him amongst the high kings of Tara.

69. Edward I and Eleanor, 19 August 1274, Robert Kilwardby, Westminster Abbey
   Edward's coronation ceremony may be viewed as an interruption between festivities. Building upon the coronation procession of his father, Edward had the streets hung with tapestries and the conduits flowing with wine while he flung coins to the crowd. After the coronation there was feasting and celebration for two weeks. This was the first double coronation in England since the Conquest and was used as a show of wealth and authority.

70. John Balliol, 30 November 1292, William Fraser (?), Scone Abbey

71. Robert Bruce, 27 March 1306, Isabella, countess of Buchan, Scone Abbey
   This was the first recorded crowning of a Scottish king. Although the ceremony happened in something of a hurry, special robes for the occasion were made at Glasgow Cathedral. The bishop of Glasgow also brought the Banner of Scotland which had been hidden from the English. Edward I had removed the Stone of Destiny from Scone so there was no historic inauguration as in past rites. Instead, in addition to the oath and homage, the king was crowned with a circlet of gold. In past ceremonies the king had been led to the Stone of Destiny by the earl of Fife who, for centuries, had been regarded as the senior peer. On this occasion Duncan, the earl of Fife, was held prisoner in England so the crowning was performed by his sister, Isabella. The choice of Isabella was bound to incense Scottish loyalties since she was the wife of John Comyn, earl of Buchan, the cousin of Red Comyn whom Bruce had murdered just prior to claiming the Scottish throne.

72. Edward II and Isabella, 25 February 1308, Henry Merewell, bishop of Winchester, Westminster Abbey
   This ostentatious coronation was organized by Edward's favourite Piers Gaveston who accorded himself the honour of carrying the Crown of England and made himself the centre of attraction, as a result of which many of the other peers of the realm nearly ended up having a brawl with him. Their fury was made all the worse at the ensuing banquet which Gaveston had organized and which was served both late and cold. Historically more significant was that this ceremony saw the first use of the coronation chair which incorporated the Stone of Scone which Edward I had stolen from Scotland and has been used at every English coronation ever since.

73. Edward III, 1 February 1327, Walter Reynolds, Westminster Abbey

74. Philippa, wife of Edward III, 20 February 1328, Simon de Meopham, Westminster Abbey

75. David II and Joan, 24 November 1331, James Ben, Scone Abbey
   David was only seven at the time of his coronation and did not realize its full significance. He was the first Scottish king to be both anointed and crowned, the pope having recognized Scotland as a separate sovereign state and granted the king the right to a formal anointment. A new crown was made for the occasion,

plus a small sceptre which the young David could hold. It was a double occasion as David's infant bride, Joan, the sister of Edward III, was the first consort to be crowned formally as queen consort.

76. Edward Balliol, 24 September 1332, ?, Scone Abbey

77. Robert II, 26 March 1371, William de Laundels, Scone Abbey

78. Euphemia, wife of Robert II, 1372, Alexander de Kyninmund, bishop of Aberdeen, Scone Abbey

79. Richard II, 16 July 1377, Simon Sudbury, Westminster Abbey
Richard was only ten at the time of his coronation. His procession from the Tower was another elaborate affair and clad in his white robes Richard was described as being like an angel. The whole ceremony lasted so long that the young king was exhausted and had to be carried from the Abbey to Westminster Hall. En route he lost one of his shoes and one of his spurs and the crown fell from his head, three omens that onlookers believed meant that he would in time lose the support of his people and of his army and at length his throne. Perhaps it was ironic, therefore, that it was at this coronation that Sir John Dymoke claimed his right, as lord of the manor of Scrivelsby, to serve as the King's Champion, an honour that has remained in the Dymoke family ever since (though since the coronation of Edward VII this has taken the form of Standard Bearer). At the coronation banquet the Champion rides into the Hall in full armour and challenges anyone to mortal combat who disputes the sovereign's right to the throne.

80. Anne, 1st wife of Richard II, 22 January 1382, William Courtenay, Westminster Abbey

81. Robert III and Annabella, 14 August 1390, Walter Trayl, Scone Abbey

82. Isabella, 2nd wife of Richard II, 8 January 1397, Thomas Arundel, Westminster Abbey

83. Henry IV, 13 October 1399, Thomas Arundel, Westminster Abbey
Henry was anxious that his coronation be special because he was a usurper. He was to be anointed with oil which was supposed to have been given to Thomas Becket by the Virgin Mary herself to be used only when a monarch regained the kingdom lost by his forebears. Unfortunately when Arundel came to administer the oil he discovered the king's head was alive with lice. There was a further ill omen when Henry came to place his gold coin in the offertory. He dropped it and it could not be found. It was at his coronation that Henry inaugurated the Order of the Bath.

84. Joan, 2nd wife of Henry IV, 26 February 1403, Thomas Arundel, Westminster Abbey

85. Henry V, 9 April 1413, Thomas Arundel, Westminster Abbey

86. Katherine, wife of Henry V, 24 February 1421, Henry Chichele, Westminster Abbey

87. James I and Joan, 21 May 1424, Henry de Wardlaw, Scone Abbey
James had been held captive in England since his infancy and thus it was a full eighteen years from the time he was declared king until he was crowned, the longest such period.

88. Henry VI, 6 November 1429, Henry Chichele, Westminster Abbey
It was seven years before Henry was crowned. Even then he was only eight and found the ceremony tiring, though he bore it with due authority despite the discomfort of the heavy crown. Henry was also crowned king of France at the Cathedral of Notre Dame in Paris on 16 December 1431.

89. James II, 25 March 1437, Michael Ochiltree, bishop of Dunblane, Holyrood Abbey
This was the first Scottish crowning to be held away from Scone, where it was considered too dangerous because of the recent murder of James I.

90. Margaret, wife of Henry VI, 30 May 1445, John Stafford, Westminster Abbey

91. Mary, wife of James II, 3 July 1449, James Kennedy, Holyrood Abbey

92. James III, 10 August 1460, James Kennedy, Kelso Abbey
The nine-year-old James was crowned almost in a war zone. His father had been killed during the siege of Roxburgh Castle. His widow and heir rushed to the scene and James was hastily crowned at nearby Kelso Abbey, only five miles from the English border, in the presence of all the lords spiritual and temporal. After the ceremony the siege continued with renewed vigour and the Castle was captured for the Scots.

93. Edward IV, 28 June 1461, Thomas Bourchier, Westminster Abbey

94. Elizabeth, wife of Edward IV, 26 May 1465, Thomas Bourchier, Westminster Abbey

95. Margaret, wife of James III, 13 July 1469, James Kennedy, Holyrood Abbey

96. Henry VI (readeption coronation), 6 October 1470, St Paul's Cathedral

97. Richard III and Anne, 6 July 1483, Thomas Bourchier, Westminster Abbey
This was one of the most sumptuous coronations of the Middle Ages and certainly the best attended as almost all the peers of the realm were present amongst some of the tightest security seen in London. Despite the mood of the festivities it was apparent amongst the crowds that shouted at the coronation procession that Richard was not a welcome monarch. Nevertheless the ceremony went without a hitch and was done by the book, even though Archbishop Bourchier was reluctant and refused to attend the coronation banquet.

98. Henry VII, 30 October 1485, Thomas Bourchier, Westminster Abbey
Henry's unease over his safety and position caused him to form his own personal bodyguard, the Yeomen of the Guard, who were first seen at Henry's coronation.

99. Elizabeth, wife of Henry VII, 24 November 1487, John Morton, Westminster Abbey

100. James IV, 26 June 1488, William Scheves, Scone Abbey
James IV had been involved in the death of his father, and at the coronation the king did penance by wearing an iron belt by which he became known as James of the Iron Belt.

101. Margaret, wife of James IV, 8 August 1503, ?, Holyrood Abbey

102. Henry VIII and Katherine of Aragon, 24 June 1509, William Warham, Westminster Abbey

    As one might expect, the coronation of Henry VIII was a most sumptious occasion, although the very religious king took the ceremony itself with due solemnity. The greatest splendour was in the coronation procession. The streets from the Tower of London were lined with tapestries, pageants were performed along the route and the goldsmiths' houses along Cheapside were hung with cloth of gold. After the coronation there was a lavish banquet followed by weeks of feasting, tournaments and other celebrations.

103. James V, 21 September 1513, ?, Stirling Castle

    James was less than eighteen months old when he was crowned. A special crown and sceptre were made with which he could be ceremonially ordained.

104. Anne Boleyn, 2nd wife of Henry VIII, 1 June 1533, Thomas Cranmer, Westminster Abbey

    Cranmer performed the full ceremony of anointing and coronation thus making Anne a queen regnant, something not granted a queen consort before or since. The ceremony went without a hitch but despite the overall grandeur the public viewed it coldly, few of them welcoming Anne as they had Katherine twenty-four years earlier.

105. Mary, 2nd wife of James V, 22 February 1540, David Beaton, Holyrood Abbey

106. Mary, Queen of Scots, 9 September 1543, David Beaton, Stirling Castle

    Mary had been less than a week old when her father died and was only nine months old at her coronation. She was crowned at the Chapel Royal in Stirling Castle where she was being held for safekeeping. The crown was too heavy to place on her head so it was held over her head by the Cardinal.

107. Edward VI, 20 February 1547, Thomas Cranmer, Westminster Abbey

    Edward was only nine when he was crowned but undertook the ceremony with all due seriousness. Part of the ceremony involved the presentation of three swords, representing Edward's three kingdoms (England, Ireland, France), but Edward demanded a fourth, to represent his defence of the Holy Spirit.

108. Mary I, 1 October 1553, Stephen Gardiner, bishop of Winchester, Westminster Abbey

    Mary entered upon her coronation procession with some trepidation because news had reached her of a possible death threat against the officiating bishop, Stephen Gardiner. Despite the festivities of the coronation procession Mary remained reserved and often withdrawn, and she looked uncomfortable throughout the ceremony, though this was partly because of the heaviness of her pearl caul. The chronicles record that 7112 dishes were prepared for the banquet of which only a third were eaten, the rest being distributed to the poor of London.

109. Elizabeth I, 15 January 1559, Owen Oglethorpe, bishop of Carlisle, Westminster Abbey

    Compared to Mary's coronation procession, Elizabeth's was joyous. The journey to Westminster from the Tower took much longer than planned because Elizabeth wished to witness the many pageants en route and to talk to the

players. There was a wonderful atmosphere. The coronation service was, for the first time, performed in English as well as Latin, a convention which has remained ever since with the exception of George I's coronation.

110. James VI, 29 July 1567, Adam Bothwell, bishop of Orkney, Stirling Castle
The realm was in such turmoil following the imprisonment of Mary that there were few peers prepared to be seen supporting her forced abdication. James's coronation was thus a simple and very solemn affair witnessed by only five earls and eight lords. He was only thirteen months old and the special sceptre and crown for the past infant kings were used again. The coronation sermon was given by John Knox.

111. Anne, wife of James VI, 17 May 1590, David Lindsay, chaplain to James VI, Holyrood Abbey

112. James I (VI) and Anne, 25 July 1603, John Whitgift, Westminster Abbey
The first coronation of a king of the Scots and the English. At the ceremony James was officially proclaimed "King of England, Scotland, France and Ireland, Defender of the Faith."

113. Charles I, 2 February 1626, George Abbot, Westminster Abbey
Much has been made of the fact that as Charles I arrived at the Abbey he stumbled, another ill omen for the coronation soothsayers. Because his queen, Henrietta Maria, was Catholic she was denied a joint coronation.

114. Charles I, 18 June 1633, John Spottiswoode, Holyrood Abbey
It was seven years before Charles visited the land of his birth and underwent an official inauguration as the king of Scotland. By this stage, nearly sixty-six years after his father's coronation, the country was staunchly Protestant. Thus the form of English ceremony used, which included not only anointing, but ceremonial robes, an altar and crucifix, and songs sung in an English so alien to Scotland that it sounded like Latin, meant that many regarded the ceremony as a Papist service and found it very distasteful.

115. Charles II, 1 January 1651, Archibald Campbell, marquess of Argyll, Scone Abbey
By contrast with his father's coronation, that of Charles II in Scotland, was a simple and open affair. There was no anointing and Charles was obliged to subscribe to the Covenants. Charles was received with overwhelming support. He was the last king to be crowned in Scotland with the ancient Scottish regalia and the recitation of the long line of royal forebears.

116. Charles II, 23 April 1661, William Juxon, Westminster Abbey
This was the first coronation in England since the Commonwealth. Because the original crown jewels had been broken up a new set had to be created and this has formed the core of the coronation regalia ever since. It was a sumptuous and almost theatrical affair, but was the last occasion when the monarch made the eve-of-ceremony procession from the Tower of London to Whitehall.

117a. James II and Mary (Catholic ceremony), 22 April 1685, Whitehall Palace

117b. James II and Mary (Anglican ceremony), 23 April 1685, William Sancroft, Westminster Abbey
James had already converted to the Catholic faith and had a special Catholic chapel built at Whitehall where he and his wife went through the Catholic

mass before the full pomp and regalia of the official service the next day. It was noticeable that James omitted to take the formal coronation oath whereby the Scottish kings defended the Protestant religion. James had played his hand and it was poorly received north of the border. Both services had their moments. The king nearly lost his crown during the procession to Whitehall, while at the coronation banquet the King's Champion fell in full armour as he dismounted.

118. William III and Mary II, 11 April 1689, Henry Compton, bishop of London, Westminster Abbey
This is the only occasion that joint king and queen regnants have been crowned and a duplicate set of regalia had to be created specially for the ceremony.

119. Anne, 23 April 1702, Thomas Tenison, Westminster Abbey
By the time of her coronation Anne was overweight and suffered from gout. As a consequence she had to be carried in a chair to the ceremony. Anne was also the first queen regnant to be married on her accession and so, for the first time at a coronation, the Queen's husband paid homage to her.

120. George I, 20 October 1714, Thomas Tenison, Westminster Abbey
Although George had some understanding of English, it was limited; to avoid the language problems almost the entire coronation ceremony was conducted in Latin.

121. George II and Caroline, 11 October 1727, William Wake, Westminster Abbey
For this coronation, George Frederic Handel composed four anthems, of which Zadok the Priest, prior to the anointing, has been performed at every subsequent coronation.

122. George III and Charlotte, 22 September 1761, Thomas Secker, Westminster Abbey
The omen-mongers were ready again at George's coronation when a jewel fell from the crown, which was subsequently interpreted as signifying the loss of the American colonies. It might just as easily have meant the loss of France for this was the last coronation at which the king was crowned as king of France.

123. George IV, 19 July 1821, Charles Manners-Sutton, Westminster Abbey
This coronation was amongst the most opulent of all, costing £243,000. It was an exceptionally hot day and the king nearly wilted in his heavy robes until revived by sal volatile. Queen Caroline was barred from the ceremony and all the doors were locked, turning the Abbey into an oven. It was the last coronation at which the sovereign walked from Westminster Hall to the Abbey and back again. It was also the last at which the King's Champion rode into the banquet to take on any challengers.

124. William IV and Adelaide, 8 September 1831, William Howley, Westminster Abbey
William, disliking all the flummery, opted for a more basic and frugal ceremony. In fact the coronation was done so much on the cheap, with the Queen providing her own jewels, that it became mocked as only half a coronation. At nearly 65, William was the oldest monarch to be crowned and was rather doddery as he walked from the throne.

125. Victoria, 28 June 1838, William Howley, Westminster Abbey
Despite the grandeur of Victoria's coronation it was rather chaotic. She was half-an-hour late, Baron Rolle fell down the stairs to the throne, and the bishop of Bath turned over two pages at once in his reading of the service and became rather confused.

126. Edward VII and Alexandra, 9 August 1902, Frederick Temple, Westminster Abbey
The coronation was originally fixed for 26 June but had to be postponed because the king was struck with acute appendicitis. It was a difficult service for Archbishop Temple who was eighty and in failing health – he died only four months later. He nearly collapsed with the crown, and was only just in time stopped from placing it on the king's head the wrong way round. Elgar composed his Coronation Ode *for this ceremony which included his famous* Pomp and Circumstance *march with the words of* Land of Hope and Glory.

127. George V and Mary, 22 June 1911, Randall Davidson, Westminster Abbey
Of more significance than this coronation was that held at New Delhi on 11 December 1911 at which George and Mary were crowned as emperor and empress of India in one of the most colourful ceremonies ever held.

128. George VI and Elizabeth, 12 May 1937, Cosmo Lang, Westminster Abbey
This was the first coronation to be filmed. It went fairly smoothly though there was a slight panic when the orb was lost, but they found the young Princess Margaret playing with it.

129. Elizabeth II, 2 June 1953, Geoffrey Fisher, Westminster Abbey
This was the first coronation to be televised and, apart from the rain, was probably the best organized of them all.

THE
KINGDOMS
OF
BRITAIN

The time chart on pages vii, viii and 1 shows how the many kingdoms that existed in Britain before the Roman conquest evolved, mutated, coalesced and eventually came together, willingly or by force, to create what became known as the United Kingdom after 1707. To help an understanding of the nature and history of these kingdoms this chapter traces that evolution.

1. Prehistory

There have been kings and chieftains in Britain for at least three thousand years, and probably much longer than that. It is unfortunate that we do not know any of their names until the time of the Roman invasion. Because of that it is easy to believe that there have only been kings since Julius Caesar. A few of their names, especially Cymbeline and Boudica or Boadicea, live on. But there were kings long before this.

Britain has been occupied by man since the end of the last Ice Age, but it was not until the New Stone Age, in about 3000BC, that a social structure began to emerge that brought with it the need for more powerful and organized leaders. These leaders were little more than tribal chieftains, but they were imbued by their subjects with something close to godhead. The connection between kings and religion emerged very early in the development of kingships, and it was well before the existence of any written records that an orderly kingship appeared across Britain. This would have consisted of a duality: a secular king, who defended the tribes in times of conflict, and a religious ruler who looked after the spiritual concerns of the tribe and would have been responsible for ensuring prosperity, in particular the right conditions for raising crops and animals. The latter was the more important individual, and it is of no surprise that the monuments that survive from ancient Britain signify the strength and power of the religious ruler or priest rather than of the secular ruler. It required someone of tremendous authority to organize the construction of Stonehenge, which was built around 1800BC, and the stone circle at Avebury, yet we have no idea who these individuals were.

Britain was subject to various waves of invasions by tribes from across Europe. The most organized was that of the Celts which began about 800BC. Within a few centuries the Celts had total control of the British Isles, including Ireland. The tribes who settled in Britain were related to the Gallic and Belgic tribes of the continent. Again, historically we have no idea of their names, although Celtic legend fills in the gaps that history misses.

According to the twelfth-century *Leabhar Gabhála Eireann*, known colloquially as the *Book of Invasions*, the sixth and last invasion of Ireland (and technically the British Isles) was that of the Milesians or sons of Milesius, who came from Spain. They encountered the Tuatha dé Danann, the existing occupants of Britain, who have since been regarded as the fairy folk. The Tuatha used various magical measures to drive the Milesians out of Britain but to no avail. Eventually the Milesians prevailed and established themselves in Ireland. They had two leaders. It was judged that Eremon should rule first but another of the leaders, Eber Finn, contested this and consequently the island was divided into two, with Eremon ruling the north. Soon after, however, the two kingdoms fought each other and Finn was killed, so that Eremon became the first king of all Ireland. These events are traditionally dated to about 800–1000BC.

The twelfth-century writer Geoffrey of Monmouth, whose book *The History of the Kings of Britain* was a medieval best-seller, has a slightly different chain of events, though with some similarities. He suggested that the first king was Brutus, was the great-grandson of the Trojan prince Aeneas. After the siege of Troy Aeneas and his son Ascanius wandered through the Greek world, eventually settling in Italy, where they founded the city of Alba Longa, the forerunner of Rome. Ascanius's son Silvius was the father of Brutus. Brutus inadvertently killed his father and fled to Greece and from there to Britain which he found uninhabited, "except for a few giants". The traditional dating of the siege of Troy is about 1180BC although recent reassessments of Egyptian and Greek chronology have shifted the date forward by at least two hundred and fifty years, placing it around 900BC and much closer to the traditional founding of Rome, which the Romans date to 753BC. We may regard Geoffrey's largely mythical first king as settling in Britain some time around 700–800BC.

Both these dates have much in common with the arrival of the Celts, and though we can make only limited sense of the Celtic myths in terms of a sequential history, there is little doubt that they are a folk memory of the arrival of heroic leaders in Britain at the time of the Celtic settlement. These eventually established dominance after a struggle with the native inhabitants who, because of their magical practices and amazing stone circles, appeared as giants or fairy-folk.

Celtic tradition has kept alive many of the names of the Irish kings and there are also many stories about the Irish settlement of parts of Britain. One story tells us that around the year 330BC Fergus, the son of Feradach, a descendant of Conn of a Hundred Battles, high king of Ireland, settled in the western highlands of Argyll. There is also the legend, variously dated, that Cruithne, the ancestor of the Picts, settled in northern Britain from Ireland and from his sons sprang the seven provinces of Pictland. Setting aside the likelihood of such legends there is little doubt that there was much relationship between the Celts of Britain and of Ireland throughout the pre-Roman era, and that this continued beyond the Roman conquest.

2. The Roman Era

The Celts in Britain established a significant tribal structure. When the Greek navigator Pytheas visited Britain in the fourth century BC and sailed around the island, he noted that it was a country of many kings. Pytheas visited the tin mines of

Cornwall where there was a thriving trade with the Greek and Roman world. Britain was known to the Greeks as the Cassiterides or Tin Isles, although Pytheas called them specifically the Pretanic Isles. The use of the word Pretani for the British evolved into Prydain as the name for Britain and later the word Britain itself.

Just how many kings Pytheas observed we do not know, and he named none. It is not until the arrival of Julius Caesar in 55BC, and the writings of Pliny the Elder and Ptolemy over the next century and a half, that the tribal make-up of Britain is recorded. Ptolemy mentioned over thirty tribes in Britain plus fifteen to twenty more in Ireland. Although he does not name their rulers, each of these tribes would have had a war-leader and a chief priest and, depending on the size of their territory, may have had sub-kings, or co-rulers who governed as a council of kings. It would not be difficult to imagine Britain in the centuries before the Romans with up to a hundred kings ruling at once. From time to time they would almost certainly have nominated a high king for major occasions. The first of these we know by name was Cassivelaunos, the leader of the Catuvellauni. From what Caesar tells us the Catuvellauni were the dominant tribe in the south, but this may not always have been so, and certainly there were other strong tribes, including the Brigantes in Yorkshire and the Silures in Wales. Although the Romans eventually conquered the tribes in the territory we now call England, they had little impact on the Celts of Wales or Scotland. It is quite likely that the rulers of the Silures, Demetae and Ordovices in Wales, and the Caledonii of Scotland (known generally as the Picts) continued to rule throughout the period of Roman occupation but we know almost nothing about them.

The Romans established their own communities or *civitates*, based largely upon the former British tribes. Although they brought in their own Roman administrators for these towns, they also married into the local nobility, and it is probable that descendants of the former tribal chiefs served as senior government officials within a Roman *civitas*. Early in their domination the Romans established a few client kings, of whom the best known are Cogidubnus of the Regnii, Prasutagus of the Iceni and queen Cartimandua of the Brigantes, but this practice ceased after their deaths. By the time of the governor Julius Agricola in AD 78 the hierarchy of military, judicial and civic administration was established. Although none of these posts held the authority of king, and were not hereditary (although that did not stop a son being named to his father's post in due course) they did have considerable power. The senior post was that of governor, appointed directly by the emperor, and of senatorial rank. Details of the origins of these governors are patchy. Initially most came from Italy but in later years they may have originated elsewhere in the Empire. The only governor likely to have been of British origin was Marcus Statius Priscus, who governed between 160 and 161 and is believed to have been born in Colchester. Whether any of his forebears were native to Britain, which might make him a relative of the Trinovantian royal family, is not known. It is more likely that the magistrates of the *civitates* were Romanized Britons (Attus of Glevum or Gloucester may be such an example), but all too few of these are known.

Roman emperors seldom came to Britain. Those who did are covered in the biographies. The best known must be Hadrian, because of his Wall, though Claudius is arguably more significant, because he formally conquered Britain and incorporated it into the Roman Empire. In the latter days of the Roman Empire it became increasingly common for soldiers or provinces to put forward their own candidates for emperor, sometimes declaring them in opposition to the existing ruler. Britain became notorious for this. The first was the governor Clodius Albinus who was elected emperor in 193; more notable were Carausius and Allectus who declared themselves emperors of Britain in 286 and 293. By their day Britain was already regaining some form of quasi-independence and though the Emperor Septimius Severus came to Britain to reorganize its administration, the fourth century saw an increasing number of emperors declared in Britain. The most famous was Constantine who was responsible for making Christianity the official religion of the Empire. By the close of the fourth century there was a cluster of British-made emperors, and Magnus Maximus passed into Welsh tradition as being descended from the kings of the Silures in Gwent.

Within a generation of Maximus's death in 388 Britain was no longer part of the Roman Empire. Britain, like the rest of the Roman frontier, was coming under increasing threat from the Germanic tribes who, in 410, crossed the Rhine and invaded the Empire. The British wrote to the emperor Honorius for help, but Honorius had his hands full protecting Rome itself. He wrote back telling the British to look after themselves. This was not a formal expulsion from the Empire. It just meant Rome could not help. No doubt Honorius expected at some future date that he or his successors would regain control and Britain would continue to be treated as part of the Empire. But it did not happen. After 410 Roman rule and Roman law no longer applied in Britain.

3. The Dark Ages

The release of Roman authority had the same effect fifteen hundred years ago as the end of Communism in the Soviet Union and in Yugoslavia. The tribalism and the local cultures which had for so long been repressed and restrained by Roman rule erupted. Warfare spread right across Britain. For the most part it was a clash between those who sought to defend and maintain the Roman *status quo*, fighting invasions from the Picts to the north, the Irish to the west, and the Germanic tribes from the east. But there was internal fighting between tribes who sought to gain power over the old tribal territories and, where possible, conquer neighbouring lands which might be richer. The period between 410 and 450 saw an almost complete breakdown of the social order, particularly in the north. Famine and pestilence swept across Britain. By 450 Britain was in a sorry state and what remained of administration in the south appealed to the Roman consul in Gaul, Agitius Aetius, for help, but none came.

During this first forty years certain chieftains had become warleaders to defend their lands and conquer enemies. These were regarded as kings by their country-men, though they did not have quite the mystical status of the kings in the pre-Roman era, or the power and authority of those who would emerge under the Saxons, but they were still kings. The best known was Coel, the Old King Cole of the nursery rhyme. Today, many believe him to be a figure of fable, but he was a real king who sought to maintain order against the Picts in the territories bordering Hadrian's Wall. It is possible that his territory stretched from Yorkshire through to Strathclyde and Lothian, though he probably focused on Galloway and Kyle: the very name Kyle may come from Coel. Others from this period in the north were Ceretic, who ruled from Dumbarton, and Cunedda, who seems to have been a war leader in the area of the Votadini, in Lothian, before he migrated to north Wales. Although these kings had certain territories within which they operated they did not have kingdoms in the sense we understand them today. They were leaders of their people, not rulers of land. Thus Cunedda was king of the Votadini, meaning that tribe, not of the land associated with them.

The kingship in southern Britain is more confusing, surprisingly so, since it is likely that it was here that some semblance of Roman administration continued, almost certainly based around one of their key provincial centres at Glevum (Gloucester), and possibly also at St Albans (Verulamium). The best known of the southern kings was Vortigern, a name which is really a title (it means High King) and not a personal name. Vortigern is known because of his associations not only with Merlin and indirectly with King Arthur, but also as the king who invited the Saxons Hengest and Horsa into Britain and thus opened the door to the Saxon invasion.

The period from 450 to 550 is aptly called the age of Arthur. Whoever this king was, he symbolizes the oppressive nature of the period when Britain was riven with warfare and strife until one master war-chief struck back so decisively that peace and prosperity returned for the first time in nearly a century. No wonder that chieftain, and we may as well call him Arthur as any other name, became such a hero of legend. There were many other heroes and villains from this period: ranging from Urien and Peredur to Maelgwyn the Tall and the treacherous Morcant.

By the late fifth century and early sixth a pattern was emerging as the kingdoms gradually settled down. The Celtic chiefs had ruled a tribe rather than land but by the start of the sixth century the surviving Celtic rulers did establish territories for themselves based on the surviving Roman strongholds, themselves built upon former Celtic centres. It would be another century before the Saxon kingdoms became established but for a generation or two during and after the lifetime of Arthur, Britain's Celtic kingdoms reappeared, many with new names. These were sufficiently well established that, when the Saxons overran England during the sixth and seventh centuries, their kingdoms absorbed, to a large degree, the old British boundaries. There is a remarkable consistency between these pre-Roman tribes, the Roman *civitates* and the emerging Saxon kingdoms. When these are compared to the existing counties of Britain, it can be seen how continuous this thread has been and how important historical roots are in Britain which, after two thousand years and more, is still essentially a tribal or at least a regionalistic nation.

These kingdoms are covered in detail from page 65 onwards, but it is worth considering here the nature of each kingdom and its survival through the Dark Ages.

4. The Emerging Kingdoms

The transition from squabbling tribe to kingdom is far from clear cut, but it is evident that through the chaos a few strong British kingdoms emerged. These were mostly in the north and west, because the Saxon raids and settlements came from the east. For instance, there is strong circumstantial evidence that a Trinovantian and Catuvellaunian kingdom established itself around London and Essex in the fifth century but no records remain of their kings because this territory was decisively overrun by the Saxons and Angles during the sixth century. The same applies to the territory of the Regnii in southern Britain which was destroyed by the Saxons under Aelle who drove the Britons north and west. Thus, although we know British kingdoms existed in the south, records of their rulers have vanished.

The kingdoms we know are those that survived the initial Saxon invasion and were documented in the battles that followed as the Saxons and Angles drove westward. In the north there was a British kingdom based on the tribe of the Votadini, which later became known as the Gododdin. These are remembered amongst the Welsh triads and poems. One of their rulers, Leudonus, later gave his name to the northern part of the territory, known to this day as Lothian. Another of their rulers, Morcant, betrayed Urien and allowed the Angles to gain their foothold on Deira (the southernmost of these northern kingdoms) and later Bryneich, or Bernicia. This territory remained a battlefield between the Angles and the Picts. No doubt many British remained in the area, but many more moved west toward the kingdom of Alclud (or Strathclyde) based on its fortress at Dumbarton. This was one of the longest surviving British kingdoms and included amongst its early kings the great Rhydderch Hen.

The Picts are a complicated people to assess. They were Celtic, like the other tribes, but seem to owe their origins to an earlier Irish migration around the third century BC. The Picts had established an inheritance based on matrilinear succession, the only one of the races to do so. It means that the king was selected on the basis of his mother, not his father, and the Pictish princesses were much honoured, since only they could confer kingship. The Picts were really an amalgam of tribes, and although Pictish king lists survive, they do not necessarily distinguish between the kings of the southern Picts (later called the Maeatae), who were based around Stirling and Fortrenn (Forteviot) and the northern Picts, or Caledonians, (based at Inverness). The greatest of the early Pictish kings, Bruide mac Maelcheon, was a northern Pict. Interestingly he was believed to be the son of Maelgwyn of Gwynedd who had evidently married a Pictish princess at some stage. There were many Pictish chieftains across the Scottish glens and highlands and the Isles. There is evidence to suggest each individual island or group of smaller islands was ruled by its own chief, but insufficient names survive to make any coherent sense. Certainly the Orkney and the larger Hebridean islands (Skye and Lewis) had their own chiefs who were originally Picts but later were displaced by the Irish and, by the ninth century, the Norse.

One Irish settlement changed the name of Pictland. This was Dál Riata, a kingdom settled by the Irish of Dál Riata in Northern Ireland who came across to Argyll and Kintyre and established their stronghold at Dunadd. There is evidence that this migration had been happening from at least the third century – tradition states that the name came from Cairbre *Riata*, son of the Irish high king, whose followers moved here around the year AD 220. These settlers were called "Scotii" by the Picts, a word which means "skirmisher". They eventually became known as Scots and their name gradually became applied to the whole of Pictland.

Another major northern British kingdom was Rheged. Its borders evidently changed considerably depending upon the strength of its ruler. At its greatest expansion under Urien, it covered all of Lancashire south to the Ribble, and north through Cumbria and into Galloway. Its rulers were also believed to exercise authority over the Isle of Man, though this island has often been in dispute and has a very checkered history. The territory between Rheged and Strathclyde sometimes had rulers strong enough to establish kingdoms of their own – Galloway and Kyle – but it was more often subject to a larger domain, and regularly disputed between all the northern kingdoms.

One other kingdom survived in northern Britain well beyond its expected shelf life and this was Elmet. Records about this kingdom are confusing, as it is possible the name also applied to a small territory along the Clyde between Lothian and Strathclyde, sometimes called Elfed or Elfet. There may therefore be two kingdoms called Elmet. But there is no doubt that a small British enclave in southern Yorkshire, around Leeds, survived into the early seventh century until crushed by Northumbria. There may have been other anomalous British kingdoms around at that time, though records of their survival are contradictory and confusing. A candidate is Lindsey, in what is now Lincolnshire, which seems to have had some British rulers before the Angles dominated it towards the end of the sixth century.

The major surviving British kingdoms were in Wales. Although the Romans had infiltrated southern Wales they never conquered north Wales and it is certain that kings of the Ordovices continued to rule there. Unfortunately we know none of their names (unless they are amongst those preserved by Geoffrey of Monmouth). By the end of Roman domination in Britain Irish settlers were invading Wales. One tradition states that the British under Cunedda came south from Gododdin to fight the Irish, and they settled in North Wales. Although this event is recorded by Nennius and other historians, its veracity has been cast into doubt by certain modern scholars but others are re-evaluating its authenticity. Archeological evidence strongly suggests some form of migration as there is little of the native Ordovician culture surviving into medieval Wales. Cunedda established the kingdom of Gwynedd, which became the strongest of all the Welsh kingdoms. Traditionally each of Cunedda's sons received a share of his lands and it was from them that many of the smaller Welsh kingdoms owed their origins. This may be an exercise in backward etymology, identifying people on the basis of place names, but regardless of Cunedda's progeny, the kingdoms of Ceredigion, Meirionydd, Rhos and others emerged in the shadow of Gwynedd but seldom had much independence. Only Ceredigion grew sufficiently strong to take on the might of Demetae, or Dyfed, a colony of Irish settlers in south-west Wales, eventually to form one kingdom, called Seisyllwg after its conqueror and subsequently Deheubarth, when it expanded to take in other territories of south-west Wales.

Deheubarth did not emerge until the tenth century. Two other Welsh kingdoms existed in the fifth century: Powys and Gwent. Powys was in eastern Wales and formed the border between Wales and England, once the Angles migrated that far west. It was essentially the old British territory of the Cornovii, and no doubt their rulers had survived through Roman occupation to re-establish themselves. The earliest known ruler of Powys, Cadell, was probably a Romano-Briton Catellus.

Gwent is another matter entirely. This was the old kingdom of the Silures, and there are many ancient records which suggest that the Silurian ruling family continued to survive throughout Roman occupation, no doubt in senior administrative posts, and it was from them that the kings of Gwent and Glamorgan, and probably Brycheiniog, emerged. It was also from them that many British migrated south to Cornwall and Devon and from there to Brittany (then called Armorica) in northern France. This territory also included the Gewisse, whom we shall return to shortly.

There were certainly other British tribes around the Severn Valley at Cirencester and Gloucester and south towards Bath. The *Anglo-Saxon Chronicle* refers to the defeat of three kings of these territories by the Saxons in 577, whilst Gildas refers to the notorious Aurelius Caninus who seems to have ruled somewhere in this region a generation or two earlier. He might possibly have been descended from Ambrosius Aurelianus, one of the great defenders of Britain. It is certain that one or two rich and important British kingdoms existed in the area of Shropshire, Herefordshire, and Gloucestershire, which formed the core of the British resistance against the Saxons in the south.

The only other British kingdom of significance was Dumnonia, which originally covered Cornwall, Devon, Dorset and Somerset, but which under pressure from the Saxons was driven back into the peninsula until only Cornwall or Kernow survived as a kingdom into the ninth century.

These kingdoms held out against the Saxons and Angles who began to settle Britain from the middle of the fifth century. Traditionally the first settlers were the Jutes in Kent under Hengest invited to Britain by Vortigern to help in the battle against the Picts. It seems somewhat strange that someone should settle in Kent when their employment was in northern Britain and we need to separate the fact from the fiction. The Saxons and Angles were raiding and settling all along the eastern coast of Britain. At the same time that Hengest was establishing the core of his future kingdom on the Isle of Thanet in Kent, there were settlers in Bernicia and Deira, led by Soemil and others, seeking territory in Lindsey and East Anglia. It was only in Kent that land was given as a payment in return for services and it is likely that, having fought in the north, Hengest and Oisc were granted land in the south in the hope that they would also help protect southern Britain from Germanic invaders from Gaul.

The remaining Saxons and Angles had to fight to gain their territory. Aelle, who landed in what is now Sussex, virtually wiped out the resident British to establish his kingdom, though he in turn seems to have been killed by resurgent British forces at the start of the sixth century. Cerdic led the next wave. He may well have been of British stock. He is identified as the leader of the Gewisse, a name which really refers to a confederate army of several tribes, and which originated in the area of Herefordshire and Shropshire in the Welsh marches. It is possible that Cerdic had been expelled from Britain and had marshalled forces in Brittany and Gaul to lead his own invasion back into southern Britain. It was he who led the offensive into Wiltshire, Somerset and Gloucestershire and drove back the British into Wales and Dumnonia, and from his battles the kingdom of Wessex began to emerge. Wessex was not really a single kingdom. It was a conglomerate of southern tribes who were probably as much British as Saxon. The British of the south – particularly the Belgae and Atrebates – may have learned by the early sixth century that the only way to survive was to join with the Saxons.

As the Saxons endeavoured to control the south, the Angles were moving into eastern and middle England. There is little doubt that there were settlements in the late fifth century, and we may deduce from the genealogies of the first kings the names of some of these settlers. The Mercians, for instance, called themselves the Iclingas, descendents of Icel, who was the great-grandfather of Creoda who is usually identified as the first king of Mercia. Since Creoda is dated to around the year 585, Icel probably settled in Britain in about AD 500, probably in the area around Lindsey in Lincolnshire. The forebears of Ida of Bernicia had settled along the Northumbrian coast a generation or two earlier, the progenitor of this royal line bearing the name Soemil. Further south, Wehha the father of Uffa or Wuffa settled in East Anglia around the year 540. Although Kent had apparently been settled since 455, there is some uncertainty about Hengest's immediate successors, and it is not until Eormenric around the year 550 that we are on firmer territory.

We thus have a period of a hundred years from 450–550 when the Celtic kingdoms remained dominant in Britain but fought against each other as much as against the Saxon and Angle settlers. Around 500 the Celts under Arthur (or a series of such war-leaders) established a bridgehead in central Britain which for a generation or two held the Saxons at bay, but by 550 the latter were on the move again under stronger leaders with firmly established settlements down the east coast. Between 550 and 600 the balance began to shift in southern and central Britain away from the Celtic kingdoms to the Saxon.

4. The Saxon Kingdoms

The significance of Kent was that it was not only the first discrete Saxon (or more properly Jutish) kingdom in Britain, but it was also the first Saxon kingdom to convert to Christianity. By the reign of Athelbert at the close of the sixth century Kent was a rich and prosperous kingdom with strong links with the Merovingian kings of France. In fact the Jutish origins of the kingdom had given way to a major Frankish element which moulded Kent's culture. There is no doubt that, regardless of claims amongst the South and West Saxons, Kent was the first important kingdom in England, and because of its position of power and authority it was able to influence the other kingdoms. Bede recognized certain Saxon rulers as *bretwalda*, the equivalent of a high king. His first was Aelle of the South Saxons, but this was almost certainly because Aelle was the main war leader of the few Saxon armies in Britain at that time (*c*500) engaged in fighting the Britons. His death (possibly at Badon) may have made him something of a martyr to the Saxon cause. The second *bretwalda* was Ceawlin of the West Saxons but he, like Aelle, was another war leader who succeeded in uniting a range of confederate Saxon tribes against the British. Athelbert, the third *bretwalda*, was different. He was an established king of a settled kingdom who exerted his influence over his countrymen in matters of culture, religion, education and trade – the first Saxon coins in England were minted by Athelbert.

Athelbert's kingdom was larger than the current county of Kent. It is likely his authority extended into Surrey and parts of Sussex, though we must remember that Sussex was separated from Kent by the vast expanse of the Anderidan Forest (the Weald), of which the Ashdown Forest is all that remains. Athelbert also held authority over Essex. The earliest known ruler of the East Saxons was Aescwine whose son Sledda married Athelbert's daughter. Aescwine's name is Kentish and he was probably established in Essex as a sub-king by Athelbert's father Eormenric, perhaps around the year 560 (not 530 as some records maintain). This probably means that Eormenric was responsible for driving the British out of the Trinovantian kingdom believed to exist in Essex and London at that time. It is interesting that all the subsequent East Saxon rulers have names beginning with S, which may have had some association with the Trinovantes. Aescwine may have married into the Trinovantian nobility and British blood flowed in the veins of the East Saxon kings. However, there is also a strong possibility that many of the East Saxons were also the Angles of East Anglia. For all that these two races fought each other during the early years of their kingdoms, there was almost certainly trade between them and some intermarriage. The East Anglian kingdom emerged at about the same time, in the 580s, and soon established itself. Redwald, who ruled around the year 600, was the next *bretwalda* after Athelbert and professed Christianity (though he was somewhat duplicitous in this respect). The East Anglian kingdom kept close to the former kingdom of the Iceni and remained ferociously independent for over three hundred years.

The distant relatives of the East Anglian kings migrated westward. Although there was a grouping called the Middle Angles, nothing is known of their rulers, and they were soon subjugated by the West Angles who established the kingdom of Mercia. The word Mercia means borderland and is the same word we use for the Welsh Marches. The early Mercian kings fought alongside the Welsh rather than against them, since they both had a common enemy in the form of the Northern Angles or Northumbrians. The Northumbrians had tenaciously clung to the east coast of northern Britain for over a century before the Bernician king Athelfrith united them under one kingdom and set out to subjugate the north. The enmity between him, his rival Edwin, and Edwin's rival Cadwallon of Gwynedd, would make an excellent film, for it was their battles that established the English in the north and decided the fate of the Welsh. Athelfrith was intent on murdering Edwin, the son of the rival king Aelle of Deira, whom Athelfrith had killed. Edwin escaped and sought refuge in Gwynedd and Powys. Athelfrith invaded Wales, slaughtering a whole abbey of monks at Bangor-on-Dee who got in his way, and killing the king of Powys. Edwin fled to Mercia, marrying the king's daughter to gain support, but was later driven out and fled to Redwald of East Anglia. It was Redwald who had the power to bring together an army that killed Athelfrith in 616AD and placed Edwin on the Northumbrian throne.

Edwin was no better than his predecessor. He was intent on total conquest. He soon conquered Elmet, the last remaining British kingdom within central England. He ravaged north Wales, despite the fact that these kingdoms had once been his protectors, and drove Cadwallon out of Gwynedd and into Ireland. Edwin was probably overlord of Rheged, assuming that kingdom survived in more than name by then, and extended his authority to the Isle of Man. By 625 Edwin dominated the north of England. But Cadwallon returned, combined forces with Penda of Mercia and killed Edwin at the battle of Hatfield Chase in 633. Cadwallon went on to devastate Northumbria. Had he not been so overcome with his war lust, but thought a little more strategically, it is possible that Cadwallon might have re-established British rule over parts of Northumbria – remember that much of the population of Northumbria was probably still native British. Cadwallon had an opportunity to turn the tables on the Angles, but he became too sure of himself and was surprised by Athelfrith's son Oswald who killed him in battle in 634. That was the Welsh's last major opportunity to reclaim land from the Angles and Saxons.

Penda was probably the greatest warrior of his age, the epitome of the war-lord. Because Mercia was the enemy of Northumbria, and because Bede was a Northumbrian, he identified Oswald of Northumbria as the next high king after Edwin, but in truth Penda dominated Britain from 633 to 655. His successors Wulfhere and Athelred were also powerful kings. Between them they created a major Mercian kingdom that ruled all of central England and stretched as far south as Sussex, Surrey and Kent, and even the Isle of Wight. They almost dominated Wessex until the rise of Caedwalla and Ine in the 680s. It was during this Mercian domination that Wulfhere established several sub-kingdoms, mostly for administrative reasons, but they served as a buffer against Wales, Northumbria, Wessex and Kent, which these subkingdoms bordered. These were the kingdoms of the Hwicce, Magonsaete, Lindsey, Surrey and Chilterns.

Because Bede refused to honour any Mercian with the title of *bretwalda*, his seventh to hold that title was Oswy of Northumbria, who was a contemporary of Wulfhere. Oswy's rule was of major importance because he called the Council of Whitby in 664 to consider whether the English Christians should follow the rules of the Roman church or the Celtic church. He found in favour of the Roman church (although he himself had been raised amongst the Celtic monks of Iona). This brought England in line with Europe and further alienated the Celts who continued to follow their own teachings.

During the seventh century, therefore, the English kingdoms of Mercia and Northumbria dominated central and northern England, whilst Wessex and Kent struggled to hold on to their power in the south. Northumbrian power was broken following the death in battle of Egfrith in 685. He had believed himself invincible, having already once subjugated the southern Picts and Strathclyde, and he marched into the heart of Pictland again to teach them another lesson only to have his army slaughtered. Thereafter Northumbria was ruled by weaker kings who, like the Celts, reduced their power by continual in fighting. The only remaining Northumbrian king worth noting here is Aldfrith, who became king unexpectedly. He was a scholar and lover of art, and it was under him that many of the beautiful illuminated books of the Northumbrian monasteries (such as the Lindisfarne *Gospels*) were produced. Some have even attributed the poem *Beowulf*, the first great work of English literature, to Aldfrith or one of his fellows at court.

Mercian power continued under a few more kings, notably Offa, who was without any shadow of a doubt the most powerful king in Britain of his day, and should certainly have been honoured as a *bretwalda*. Offa's authority was acknowledged by all the other rulers of England, and to a large extent in Wales, though less so in Scotland. It is a shame that Offa was such a proud and cruel king, as he might be remembered more than he is. He held authority over more of England than some later kings, including Alfred the Great, who are usually regarded as kings of England.

A young man at Offa's court was Egbert, in exile from his father's kingdom in

Kent. Egbert was soon banished from Mercia, as he was seen as a problem to the West Saxon kingdom then ruled by Offa's son-in-law Beorhtric, but after Beorhtric's death, Egbert returned and became king of Wessex in 802. He lay relatively low for some years, though it was during the first part of his reign that he subjugated the British of Dumnonia and absorbed Devon (though not Cornwall) into Wessex. Then from 823 on Egbert began to look to the other kingdoms. With the help of his son Athelwolf he regained Sussex, Surrey, Kent and Essex, and helped the East Anglians defeat and kill the Mercian kings Beornwulf and Ludeca. Egbert expelled Wiglaf from Mercia, and marched on Northumbria where king Eanred recognized Egbert as overlord without a fight. Although the kingdoms of Mercia and Northumbria remained in existence for another sixty years or more, Wessex was now the dominant kingdom.

5. The Viking Threat

Egbert is usually regarded as the last *bretwalda* and the first king of England. The first title is certainly correct; the second is debatable. He held a degree of authority over England, but he ruled Northumbria and East Anglia in name only. The same might be said of his successors, Athelwolf, Athelred and Alfred the Great. Alfred was the last great defender of England. Starting in Egbert's day the Vikings began to raid and plunder the British coast. By the 850s they were settled along the eastern Irish coast at Dublin and Waterford under Olaf the White and the Dane Ivarr the Boneless. From here, in the short space of twenty years, they conquered the Hebrides and the Isle of Man by the year 855, Deira in 866 (establishing their kingdom of Jorvik), East Anglia in 869, the Orkneys by 874 (and soon after Caithness and Sutherland) and throughout the 870s encroached further into England. By 878 only Alfred stood between the Danes and total domination of England, but Alfred's defeat of the Danes at Edington saved Wessex. The Danes, under Guthrum, were given the kingdom of East Anglia.

Alfred's son Edward and grandson Athelstan were equally great warriors and administrators. Edward drove the Danes out of York and East Anglia, though the Norse moved into the vacuum that was left. Athelstan briefly drove the Norse out of York, though it was not until the reign of Eadred that the Norse were finally defeated and Northumbria formally became part of England (though the earls of Bernicia retained considerable autonomy). Eadred was the first king of all the English in 954, though it was his son Edgar who was the first to be formally crowned king of the English in a special ceremony in 973 at Bath. Part of this ceremony also involved a row along the river Dee at Chester where Edgar was accompanied by at least eight other kings who recognized him as his overlord. This included some of the kings of Wales and Scotland and even Man and the Isles, but did not include other Welsh kings or the earl of Orkney. Nevertheless, as a symbolic act it was very significant, because it was the last show of power the Saxon kings were able to make. Edgar's son Edward was murdered soon after his accession, and his successor, Athelred, known notoriously as "the Unready", was an amazingly inept king who was unable to control the concentrated power of the Danes. By 1013 Sweyn held power over England and his son Canute succeeded to the English throne in 1016. Despite the valiant battles of Alfred, Edward and Athelstan a century earlier, Athelred and his weak ealdormen gave way to the Scandinavian threat and the Danes controlled England.

Even though Canute's sons were weaklings and the Saxons, under Edward the Confessor, regained the throne in 1042, it was not for long. The Vikings had not only conquered England but, as early as 911, had settled in northern France where their duchy became known as Normandy, after the Northmen. These Normans became more civilized than their Norse or Danish counterparts, heavily influenced by the French courts, but they were still of Norse stock, and retained that vicious fighting streak that never admitted defeat.

During the reign of Edward the Confessor, the young Norman duke William believed he had been acknowledged as the successor to the throne and when it went to Harold Godwinson instead, William regarded that as an act of treachery and prepared to invade. This was in the fateful year 1066. Harold had more than enough to contend with as his brother Tostig had been expelled the previous year from Northumbria and had convinced the Norwegian king, Harald Haadraada, that England was his for the taking. Harald was already king of Orkney and the Western Isles and, as the fiercest Viking warrior of his age, no doubt believed he could conquer England. Within one month in the autumn of 1066 Harold Godwinson had to face two powerful invasions. He defeated the first and almost defeated the second, but William's tactics were just too clever for Harold. Harold was killed at the Battle of Hastings and William became king of England. The rule of the Saxons was over.

Although most books about the kings of England begin with William I, it was the Saxons who united England in a long, long series of battles and alliances that started with Athelfrith of Northumbria four hundred years earlier.

6. The Union of Scotland

The same process that had unified England was working in Scotland, though rather more haphazardly. The Celtic rule of partible succession meant that kings divided their land amongst their sons so that the work of any king to establish a stronger and larger kingdom was immediately undone when it was subdivided amongst his successors, few of whom were of the same ability as their father. This rule weakened the Welsh kingdoms more than the Scottish, but it had its effect in the British kingdom of Strathclyde, which had few strong kings (see Owen map Bili and Teudebur) and many weak ones. By the late eighth century Strathclyde had been overrun by Northumbria and although it existed in name it was no longer a power. Nevertheless its fortress at Dumbarton was a key site to control, and the fight for Strathclyde continued through many generations.

The Scots of Dál Riata had been growing in power, but then fell foul of an interdynastic struggle between the main ruling family, the Cenél Gabhrán, and their distant cousins the Cenél Loarn, both descended from the father of the founding ruler Fergus. For a period at the start of the eighth century this in-fighting weakened the Scots and allowed the king of the Picts, Angus, who was the victor of their own interdynastic struggle, to take control. For the first time in 736 the Picts and the Scots were ruled by one king. This did not last because of the rules of succession, but it was the start of the inevitable. The Picts remained the dominant force for the next few generations, and then the Dál Riatan dynasty began to get the upper hand. By marrying with Pictish princesses, the Scots succeeded in gaining the throne of the Picts, starting with Constantine mac Fergus in 811. This paved the way for the major takeover by Kenneth macAlpin, whose ancestry and origins are somewhat dubious but who, with the help of the Danes, united the Picts and the Scots in 848. They were still known as separate kingdoms and the overall control of his immediate successors was somewhat tenuous. Even Eochaid, the sub-king of Strathclyde succeeded in gaining the throne of the Scots. This brought Strathclyde firmly into the Scottish domain and Eochaid's successor, Donald II was the first king to be recognized as king of Scotland (or Alba as it was then known).

Scotland at this stage did not include the territories of Caithness and Sutherland which were nominally under the control of the earls of Orkney who were subject to the kings of Norway. This authority also stretched to the Hebrides and the Isle of Man. On the other hand Scottish control now included Strathclyde which stretched down into Cumbria, a territory which was a mixture of Norse and British peoples in the tenth century. The King of the Scots had a rather tenuous hold over the territory of Moray, which was ruled by the Cenél Loarn who continued to feud with the main ruling family. This rule came to a head during the reign of Malcolm II who endeavoured to eradicate the Moray dynasty but instead paved the way for the head of the Moray clan, Macbeth, to assume the Scottish throne. Macbeth was another strong king succeeded by a weak one, Lulach, after whose death the Moray dynasty fell into decline. Scotland was then ruled by Malcolm III, known as Bighead. He was a powerful king and the one ruling at the time of the Norman conquest. He shielded the last Saxon heir to the throne, Edgar Atheling, and married Edgar's sister Margaret, which infuriated William the Conqueror. Although William made a show of force against Malcolm, he clearly did not intimidate the Scottish king. Malcolm, however, knew when to be wise and when to be rash, and he humoured William. William may have regarded himself as the superior monarch but in reality he had no control over Malcolm. Nevertheless, the cards were played. The successors of William were determined to conquer and rule the whole island. It would be another two centuries before that came close.

7. The Demise of Wales

The Welsh kingdoms also suffered from the rule of partible succession and from there being too many children of Welsh kings. The whole history of Wales from 500 to 1200 is one of constant fighting between brothers, cousins, uncles, nephews and any other relative who got in the way. And when they were not fighting each other within their kingdom, they fought their neighbours. In these conditions it was rare for a strong king to unite more than one kingdom and even rarer for that to remain united under his successors.

Wales was not really a country of discrete kingdoms. It was a country where the internal boundaries changed with every passing king, making up a cauldron of smaller kingdoms. Occasionally one of these would bubble to the surface and remain dominant before simmering down and awaiting the next eruption.

The major struggles for power were between Gwynedd in the north and Deheubarth in the south, with Powys and Gwent occasionally getting in the way.

After the defeat of Cadwallon of Gwynedd in 634, it took the rise of Rhodri the Great in 844 for Wales again to see a ruler of kingly power. He was what Wales needed at the time, for the land was under threat from the Vikings. He succeeded in uniting Gwynedd with Powys and Seisyllwg to become ruler of all North Wales and was acknowledged as overlord by the southern Welsh. After his death his son Anarawd ruled with equal power, as did his successor Idwal. After Idwal, Gwynedd was inherited by Hywel the Good of Deheubarth in 942, who united both kingdoms. Hywel was a good warrior and a good administrator. He learned from the English and applied what he believed was appropriate to Wales, especially in developing his law code and introducing coinage. Hywel ruled all of Wales except Gwent where the formidable old warrior Morgan Hen held sway.

After Hywel, Gwynedd and Deheubarth kept switching between the controlling royal houses and it was not until the rise to power of Gruffydd ap Llywelyn that Wales saw another king of superior quality. In fact Gruffydd, from 1055 until his betrayal and murder in 1063, was the only king to be recognized as ruler of all of Wales. Gruffydd had fallen foul of the vindictive strength of Harold Godwinson of England and these two mighty soldiers clashed on several occasions.

Because of Gruffydd's death, power in Wales was weakened at the crucial moment of the Norman invasion. William the Conqueror established Marcher Lords along the Welsh border and these Norman barons soon infiltrated and conquered southern Wales. Gwent and Glamorgan fell to William II in 1091, and Deheubarth was overrun in 1093 with the death of their king Rhys ap Tewdwr. Although Rhys's grandson Maredudd managed to rebuild Deheubarth, his authority was short lived. Maredudd's brother, Rhys, submitted to Henry II of England in 1158 and was therefater known as the Lord Rhys. Powys put on a show of remaining an independent kingdom, but it existed only at the whim of the English and effectively lost its power after the death of Madog ap Maredudd in 1160.

Gwynedd alone held out as it had against the Romans and to some extent against the Saxons. It was now that the greatest of the Welsh rulers emerged, Llywelyn the Great, who was acknowledged as ruler of Wales from 1216. Llywelyn endeavoured to secure the succession for his descendants but everything crumbled after his death. Llywelyn ap Gruffydd sought to hold the kingdom together but met his death in 1282. With the Statute of Wales, issued on 19 March 1284, Wales passed under the government of England, and the direct rule of Edward I who appointed his son as the new Prince of Wales.

8. The Amalgamation of Scotland

Although Scotland may have appeared to be one kingdom with the arrival of Malcolm III, it was still divided. The authority of the Scottish kings effectively covered the lowlands and the Borders plus much of the eastern seaboard. Orkney, Shetland and the Western Isles, as far south as the Isle of Man, were still answerable to the king of Norway whilst the Highlands on the mainland, where the people were Gaelic speaking, regarded themselves as independent even if recognizing the authority of the crown. The Isle of Man had always had a degree of independence especially since it became the base of the formidable Godred Crovan in 1079. A few generations later Somerled established his own Kingdom of the Isles in 1156. Both of these rulers and their successors acknowledged the sovereignty of Norway, not Scotland. Their lands remained separate kingdoms until they were officially ceded to Scotland under the Treaty of Perth of 2 July 1266. This followed the defeat of the Norse at the Battle of Largs three years earlier and the subsequent subjugation of the islands and mainland territories by Alexander III. Alexander later invested the title of Lord of the Isles in the head of the Macdonald family and over the next two centuries these lords would operate as if they were kings in their own right, frequently opposing the Scottish monarch. Orkney remained under Norse sovereignty until 20 May 1469.

In the meantime the kingdom of Scotland itself came under threat with the death, on 26 September 1290, of Margaret, known as the Maid of Norway, the infant queen of Scotland. There was no immediate successor to the throne though there were no shortage of claimants. The Scottish lords agreed that Edward I of England would arbitrate upon the final shortlist of thirteen claimants. There followed an interregnum of over two years whilst the English king and his judges decided. In the meantime Edward took advantage of the situation by claiming the Isle of Man for England in 1290 and apart from efforts by Scotland to reclaim it in 1293 and again in 1313, it remained an English territory thereafter.

On 17 November 1292 Edward I nominated John Balliol as Scottish king, a justifiable decision but one also convenient to Edward as Balliol had strong English sympathies. Balliol subsequently cast off the English yoke but following his defeat at Dunbar was forced to abdicate in July 1296. Edward set about bringing Scotland under English control and his first act was to remove the Stone of Destiny from Scone and bring it to Westminster. In effect he had taken the heart out of Scotland. Distracted by problems with France, Edward was unable to hammer home his advantage straightaway with the consequence that there was time for rebellion to ferment in Scotland, first under William Wallace and then under Robert Bruce. Edward I died without seeing Scotland absorbed into England even though he had proceeded as far as preparing a new constitution. His son, Edward II, was a much weaker ruler and after his defeat at Bannockburn in June 1314, Scotland was lost to the English. It was not, however, till the Treaty of Northampton on 4 May 1328 that the English formally recognized the sovereign independence of Scotland.

Robert Bruce had applied to the Pope for recognition of Scotland as a sovereign state with the authority to anoint its monarchs. The Scottish kings had no such right previously and this had always made them secondary to the English kings in the eyes of the Church. Pope John XXII granted this right to Robert on 13 June 1329, though unfortunately for Robert he had died six days earlier and did not know of his success. Nevertheless the combination of the Treaty of Northampton and the papal bull meant that Robert's successor, David II, was the first Scottish king to be crowned and anointed as monarch of an independent sovereign state.

Scotland was still a land divided, however. It was not until 1469 that Orkney and Shetland were ceded to Scotland by Norway. Soon after, in 1493, John MacDonald forfeited the lordship of the Isles to the Crown and though the title was reinstated to his descendants it did not carry the same authority. It was thus only by 1493 that Scotland, then under James IV, became the whole kingdom we would recognize today.

9. France and Ireland

Although the Normans had dominated Wales and Scotland by the late thirteenth century, they still regarded their heartland as Normandy and France rather than England. England was a rich country, the revenues from which allowed the kings to finance their campaigns in France and, in the case of Richard I, the Crusades. Henry II established a large Angevin Empire where he held territories in fief to the French king across most of northern and western France. The centre of this Empire was Anjou; it also included the territories of Brittany, Aquitaine and Normandy. Henry even made moves into Ireland. Following the Treaty of Windsor, signed on 6 October 1175, Rory O'Connor, the last hereditary High King, recognized Henry as his overlord in most of eastern Ireland (primarily Meath, Leinster, Munster, Waterford and Ulster). O'Connor remained king of Connaught on payment of a tribute to Henry, and other tributory kings remained. Henry made his son John "Lord of Ireland" in 1177.

John, the suitably nicknamed Lackland, who started with nothing, nearly ended with nothing since he died in the middle of a civil war in England in 1216, with the heir to the French throne having been brought over as king. John had already lost much of France and it remained a passion of all successive kings down to Henry VIII the recovery of the French lands. One of the most successful, in terms of territorial gain, was Edward I, though the more memorable, because of such battles as Crecy and Agincourt, were Edward III and Henry V. This struggle with France became known as the Hundred Years War since it dragged on from 1337 to 1453. Edward III laid claim to the French throne in 1340, and Henry V had the triumph of being recognized as heir to the French throne but died before he could inherit the title. It was his son, Henry VI, who had the rare distinction of being crowned both king of England (1429) and of France (1431). The English kings retained the title "King of France" until 1801, although it had become anachronistic soon after the death of Henry VI.

10. Great Britain

Henry VI had enough on his hands holding on to the crown of England. The Wars of the Roses between the descendants of Edward III representing the dynasties of York and Lancaster divided England between 1455 and 1487 and led to the succession of Henry Tudor, as Henry VII. Tudor was of Welsh descent and one might argue that the Welsh at last claimed the English throne, defeating the last of the Plantagenets (the direct descendants of the Normans), Richard III, at Bosworth in 1485. Certainly with the accession of Henry, the struggle between the English and the Welsh virtually ceased and Henry showed some preference for the Welsh lords, though he operated like an English king. His successor, Henry VIII, had more imperialistic intentions – he bid to be elected Holy Roman Emperor in 1519 but was not successful and he was never able to gain the ground in Europe that he wished. Indeed, breaking with the Pope and creating his own Church of England in 1534 limited his scope for further European expansion. Instead he consolidated matters at home. The Act of Union of 1536 formally absorbed Wales into the English administrative and legal systems. Henry was unable to do quite the same for

Ireland, though he imposed the administrative system where he could and formally proclaimed himself "King of Ireland" in 1542.

Another far-reaching event had already happened in 1503 when Henry's sister, Margaret, married James IV of Scotland. This union of the two royal families did not stop the discord between the kingdoms and indeed James IV was killed by the English at the battle of Flodden Field in 1513, but it meant that Margaret's children were not only direct heirs to the Scottish throne but were remote heirs to the English throne. This remoteness grew steadily more tangible. Henry VII had already ensured most of his rivals for the throne had disappeared and Henry VIII had limited success at fathering an heir. Edward VI died a teenager with no children; Mary I married but had no children, and Elizabeth, despite many suitors, never married. By the time of her death in 1603 there was only one plausible successor to the throne and that was James VI of Scotland, Margaret Tudor's great-grandson.

James was the first king who could claim the title "King of England and Scotland". James preferred the title "King of Great Britain" and used it himself, but it was never official. In fact, although James was also proclaimed "King of Ireland and France", there was little doubt that he operated parochially as a king of England. One significant event happened in 1607 when the Irish earls of Tyrone and Tyrconnell, who were staunch Catholics, found they could no longer operate under the conditions imposed upon them from England. Along with about a hundred other local chieftains from northern Ireland they fled to Catholic Europe in an episode known as the "flight of the earls". This left a vacuum into which Britain flooded English and Scottish Protestants and thus established a strong Protestant base in northern Ireland.

James VI revisited Scotland only once in the twenty-two years of his reign in England. Whereas a hundred and eighteen years earlier a Welsh prince had inherited the English throne, now it was a Scottish king. It was easy to argue that the native dynasties had at last ousted the line of William the Conqueror, and it is certainly true that the blood of the ancient lines was strong in the veins of James VI, now better known as James I of England. But it is also true that James rapidly adopted the lifestyle of the English kings as developed by the Plantagenets and Tudors, and apart from his mother tongue, which the English found difficult to understand, brought little of his Scottish heritage with him. Except, that is, in one vital matter, and that was James's belief in the divine right of kings. This wasn't exclusive to the Stewart kings – all kings regarded themselves as God-given in some form or another. But James believed that he was God's anointed ruler, that he operated by divine right and was thus above human authority. This belief came to its most extreme under James's son Charles I who flagrantly ignored the wishes of Parliament; in fact he ceased to summon it, and operated by absolute rule. This led inevitably to a clash with Parliament and the outbreak of the English Civil War in 1642. The Royalists lost and Charles I was beheaded in 1649.

A Commonwealth was established in England, run by the House of Commons. In 1653 Oliver Cromwell was created Lord Protector, effectively king in all but name. The Protectorate extended into Scotland where it was grudgingly acknowledged. The Scots had accepted Charles II as their king in 1650, and he had been crowned at Scone, but was driven out of Britain by Cromwell's forces. The Protectorate was short-lived. Cromwell's son, Richard, had no interest in governing. He was eased out of power in 1659 by which time the mood of the nation had changed. The royalist General Monck succeeded in maintaining military peace and engineered the restoration of the monarchy with the return of Charles II in 1660.

Charles had nothing of the absolute pretensions of his father or grandfather, nor anything of the religious intolerance of the Tudors and early Stewarts. Charles's *joie-de-vivre* did much to help the restoration and acceptance of the monarchy, but this was nearly undone by Charles's brother, James, the duke of York, who succeeded as James II in 1685. He was a proclaimed Catholic and efforts had been made by Parliament to exclude him from the succession. The prospect of the country returning to Catholicism led to a break with James and an invitation by the Lords to William of Orange to protect the Church of England. This led to the almost bloodless revolution of 1688 when James II fled to France, and William subsequently succeeded as William III of England. James was still accepted as king of Ireland until his defeat at the Battle of the Boyne in 1690.

William III ruled jointly with his wife, Mary II. Otherwise it was unlikely that this rather obnoxious king would have been accepted by the English and even less by the Scots. With no surviving children the crown passed to Mary's sister Anne in 1702. It was during her reign that the Act of Union was passed (1707) which formally merged Scotland with England and brought an end to the Scottish parliament. Anne was the first monarch to be recognized as queen of Great Britain.

With Anne's death in 1714 the Stewart ruling dynasty came to an end and the crown passed to George, elector of Hanover, a great-grandson of James I. He was not used to governing with a Parliament from which he needed to seek permission to raise money, and his Germanic temper and demeanour were not appreciated in England. He was even less liked in Scotland where the Highlanders believed that James Stewart, the young son of James II, was their rightful ruler and referred to him as the "king over the water", because he lived in exile in France and Rome. Their support led to the Jacobite rebellion of 1715 when James was declared James VIII of Scotland but this fizzled out when they first met James and discovered what a weak and facile man he was. He remained a figurehead of rebellion for some years, however, increasingly known as the Old Pretender. His son, Charles Stewart (or more properly Stuart, having adopted the French spelling), known as the Young Pretender or Bonnie Prince Charlie, was altogether more acceptable and he was able to ferment rebellion in 1745 with some success until his defeat at Culloden. Thereafter although his descendants have been regarded as the Stewart claimants to the throne there was no further serious attempts to oust the Hanoverians.

The other significant change during this period was the movement away from direct rule to a constitutional monarchy. This began under William III with the Bill of Rights (1689), which established the relationship between monarch and parliament and repudiated the belief in absolute power of the monarch as exercised by Charles I and attempted by James II. Kings had always had leading advisers and ministers, in particular the Privy Council, which was the executive through which the sovereign ruled, but there had never been any official post of Prime Minister. This began to emerge with the creation of the Cabinet, a smaller executive body which consulted with the monarch. This was given additional impetus with the accession of George I whose limited knowledge of English made it difficult to discuss policy and caused him to rely increasingly on his ministers. The first to take full advantage of the situation and establish himself in the position recognized now as Prime Minister was Robert Walpole in 1721. His premiership lasted until 1742 during which time Walpole had done enough to establish a working constitutional monarchy and thus deflected the direct authority of the monarch. From the reign of George II the king had become a figurehead and no longer a direct administrator.

11. The Rise and Fall of Empire

The seeds of the British Empire were sewn in the sixteenth century with the exploration of and trading with North America and the West Indies. A colony was established at Roanoke Island (off North Carolina) in 1587 and Queen Elizabeth I could claim her first territory on another continent. This settlement had vanished by 1590 but Jamestown, established in 1607 and named after James I, became Britain's first permanent colony in the New World.* The Bermudas followed in 1609 and the New England colonies under the Pilgrim Fathers in the 1620s. Many of the small islands in the Caribbean were also colonized in the 1620s followed by Jamaica in 1655. Much of the North American continent remained in French and Spanish hands until the 1750s. The war between the French and English led to the defeat of the French and the capture of Quebec (1759) and Montreal (1760). This success cemented the British control of Canada but also fuelled the bid for freedom amongst the American colonies who rebelled against the taxes placed upon them. The colonies declared independence in 1776 and, after defeating the British, were recognized as the United States of America in 1782. Britain, under George III, had thus lost a large part of its empire early in its evolution. Other changes rapidly followed, however. At home were two significant changes. On 1 January 1801 the Act of Union between Great Britain and Ireland came into force whereby the United Kingdom of Great Britain and Ireland was formally created. On the same day George III relinquished his title to the crown of France. In the meantime the Empire recovered from the loss of America and began to grow, with colonies emerging on all continents but most significantly in India, Australia (New South Wales), Cape Colony and the Gold Coast. The expansion of empire reached its greatest extent under Queen Victoria who was declared empress of India in 1876. George V and Queen Mary were crowned as emperor and empress of India at New Delhi in 1911.

In 1867 Canada had become a Dominion as distinct from a colony, and though this gave it a degree of independence it still recognized Victoria as its monarch and this was the start of what would emerge in 1931 as the British Commonwealth. At its greatest extent, in the period 1870 to 1914, the British Empire and Dominions covered over 11 million square miles or just under 20% of the land surface of the globe. By comparison the Soviet Union at its greatest extent occupied 8.7 million square miles or a little over 15% of the land surface area.

Since 1914 the British Empire has decreased and the British Commonwealth has grown. The majority of countries which once formed part of the Empire are now separate sovereign states. The most significant loss from the perspective of the

* One might treat the colonies established by Henry St Clair, earl of Orkney, in Labrador in 1398 as the first "British" settlements in the New World, although at that time St Clair was a vassal of the Norwegian king.

monarch's role was that of India in 1947, which meant that George VI had to relinquish the title of emperor of India. All that remain as Crown Dependencies are the Isle of Man, as part of the British Isles, and the Channel Isles, Gibraltar and scattered islands around the globe. Elizabeth II is now styled "Queen of the United Kingdom of Great Britain and Northern Ireland and of Her other Realms and Territories, and Head of the Commonwealth".

* * * * *

This history has followed the remarkable ascent of an island, once divided among hundreds of petty chieftains, to a united kingdom whose monarch had authority over a fifth of the globe. Whether one is a staunch royalist or a devout republican one cannot but be fascinated by the process that caused this evolution and by the one thousand or so known monarchs who have ruled all or part of Britain. This book covers them all and explores the contribution made by each and every one to the fortunes of Britain.

THE
KINGS
AND
QUEENS
OF
BRITAIN

To make this book easier to use and to place the rulers in their historical context, the coverage of kings and queens is divided into their individual kingdoms and those kingdoms are grouped according to their period in history. There are three main sections:

1. The Dark Ages, from earliest times to about AD 900
2. The Fight for Britain, from around 900 to 1300
3. Uniting the Kingdom, from 1300 to the present day.

In addition a fourth section covers the legendary kings and those European rulers closely related to the English throne.

This first part covers all of the kingdoms of Britain from before the Roman conquest to the Danish and Viking invasions in the reign of Alfred the Great. Strictly the Dark Ages, as we traditionally call them, did not start until after the end of the Roman Empire, but the phrase seems ideally suited to the earlier history of Britain as well, since so much of it remains dim and distant. This section therefore spans the thousand years from about 100BC to about AD 900.

1. THE DARK AGES

The kingdoms are divided as follows. For legendary rulers both before and after 100BC turn to page 711.

A. Pre-Roman Conquest
Known historical and quasi-historical rulers of the British tribes from about 100BC to AD 200.

B. Roman Emperors
C. Roman Governors
Lists the Emperors during the time of Roman occupation (from AD 43 to 410) with special coverage of those with a more direct involvement in Britain, plus the Governors appointed over Britain.

D. The British Kingdoms
   DA. Northern Britain
   DB. Southern Britain
   DC. The South-East (Cantii) and South-West (Dobunni and Dumnonia)
Covers the British kingdoms that emerged in the immediate post Roman period from about 410 to around 600 when the Saxon kingdoms were becoming established in England and the Celtic tribes retained their independence only in Wales, northern Britain and Cornwall.

E. The Welsh Kingdoms
   EA. Gwent and Glywysing
   EB. Ceredigion and Seisyllwg
   EC. Demetia and Dyfed
   ED. Venedotia and Gwynedd
   EE. Powys
   EF. Gwerthrynion
   EG. Brycheiniog
   EH. Meirionydd
   EI. Dunoding
   EJ. Ergyng
Covers the many Welsh kingdoms that became established after the Roman occupation from about 420 to approximately 850/900 when medieval Wales began to take shape under Rhodri the Great and Hywel the Good.

F. The Scottish Kingdoms
   FA. The Picts
   FB. Strathclyde
   FC. Dál Riata
Covers the Celtic, British and Irish settlements in northern Britain from the end of the Roman period in about 410 to the start of Scottish unification under Kenneth mac Alpin in the 840s.

G-M. The Saxon Kingdoms
   G. Kent
   GA. Isle of Wight
   H. South Saxons
   I. East Saxons
   J. East Angles
   K. Mercia, with sub-kingdoms Hwicce, Magonsaete, Lindsey, Chilterns and Surrey
   L. Northumbria, including Bernicia and Deira
   M. West Saxons
Covers the Germanic settlement of England from around 450 till the time of the Danish invasions in the reign of Alfred the Great, ending in 900 with the unification of the Saxon kingdoms and the starts of the Danish settlement.

A. PRE-ROMAN CONQUEST

No names of British kings will be found in the historical record prior to the Roman invasion of 55BC. We know that many kings and chieftains existed but the only names to survive are in Celtic legend. Some were also preserved in the *History of the Kings of Britain* by Geoffrey of Monmouth, though most of this is also more legend

Map 1 **The Celtic Tribes of Britain at the time of the Roman Conquest**

1. Celts (1) – **Early Britain**

This chart is a blending of historical sources with traditional genealogies. The two are not always compatible and therefore some of the links, represented by dotted lines, are conjectural.

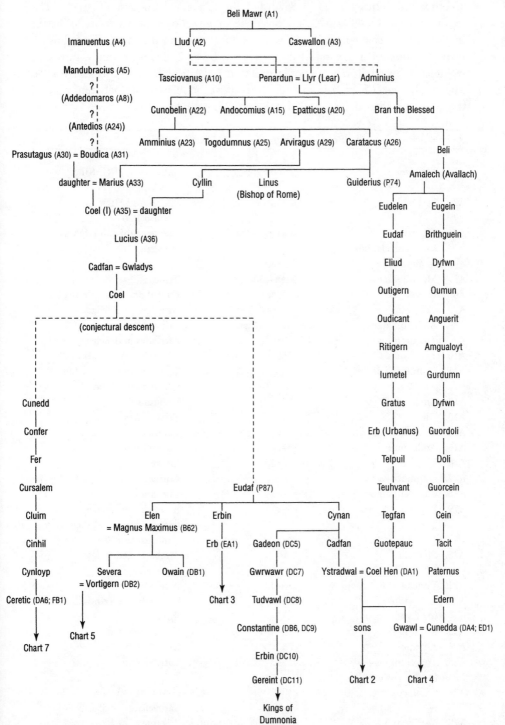

than fact (*see page 711*). There is sufficient credibility amongst Welsh legend to accept the authenticity of Beli Mawr who is the starting point in this chronology. The rulers of the British tribes were first identified by the Roman chroniclers who accompanied Julius Caesar in 55BC and the Claudian conquest of AD 43. The leading tribe was the Catuvellauni, but there were well over twenty tribes in Britain including the Trinovantes, the Silures, the Brigantes and the Picts. The following does not attempt a separate listing by tribe because there are many gaps and overlaps. Their territories are noted and Map 1 clarifies the main tribal territories. The family tree (*Chart 1*) is an attempt to show the relationship between some of the kings and their descendants in the post-Roman period.

Ref.	Ruler	Born	Reign	Died	Notes
A1.	Beli *Mawr*		*fl* 100BC		Silures and High King; see also P69
A2.	Lud or Llud		*fl* 70BC–*c*60BC		Silures and High King; see also P70
A3.	Caswallon (or Cassivelaunos)		*fl* 60BC–*c*48BC		Catuvellauni and High King; see also P71
A4.	Imanuentius		*fl* 55BC		Trinovantes
A5.	Mandubracius		54BC–*c*30BC		Trinovantes
A6.	Cingetorix		*fl* 55BC		Cantii; one of four co-rulers
A7.	Commius	*c*80BC	*c*50BC–*c*20BC		Atrebates and Belgae
A8.	Addedomaros		*c*30BC–*c*20BC		Trinovantes
A9.	Tincommius		*c*20BC–*c*AD 5		Atrebates and Belgae
A10.	Tasciovanus		*c*20BC–*c*AD 10		Catuvellauni; see also P72
A11.	Dumnovellaunos		*c*20BC–*c*AD 5		Trinovantes and Coritani; Cantii from *c*15BC
A12.	Antedrigos		*c*10BC		Dobunni
A13.	Diras		*fl* AD 1		Trinovantes
A14.	Vosenos		*fl* AD 5		Cantii
A15.	Andocomius		*c*5–*c*15		Catuvellauni
A16.	Volisios		*c*5–*c*20		Coritani
A17.	Dumnocoveros		*c*5–*c*20		Coritani
A18.	Cartivel(launos)		*c*5–*c*20		Coritani
A19.	Eppillus		*c*5–*c*10		Atrebates and Belgae; deposed but ruled the Cantii from *c*10–*c*25
A20.	Epatticus		*fl* 10		Atrebates and Belgae; deposed.
A21.	Verica (or Bericos)		*c*10–40		Atrebates and Belgae
A22.	Cunobelin (or Cymbeline)		*c*10–41		Catuvellauni; Trinovantes from *c*1; see also P73
A23.	Amminius		*c*25–*c*40		Cantii; deposed
A24.	Antedios		*c*25		Iceni
A25.	Togodumnus (or Teneuvan)		41–43		Catuvellauni
A26.	Caratacus		*c*40–51	*c*54	Cantii *c*40–43 then Catuvellauni; exiled in Rome
A27.	Cartimandua		43–69		Brigantes

A28.	Venutius	69–72		Brigantes
A29.	Arviragus	*fl* 44–74	*c*74	Silures; see also P75
	(or Gweirydd)			
A30.	Prasutagus	47-59		Iceni
A31.	Boudica	59–61		Iceni
	(or Boadicea)			
A32.	Cogidubnus	43–75		Regnii
A33.	Marius	*c*74–*c*125		Silures; see also P76
A34.	Calgacus	*fl* 80		Caledonii
A35.	Coel (I)	*fl c*125–*c*150		Silures; see also P77
A36.	Lleirwg *Mawr*	*fl c*150–*c*180		Silures; see also P78
	or Lucius			
A37.	Argentocoxos	*fl* 208		Caledonii. May be father of Ciniod of the Picts (see FA*e*).

[A1] **BELI *MAWR* (*the GREAT*)** A semi-legendary British king who was probably an historical ruler, though any facts have become so covered by the dust of myth that it is impossible to be certain about his true basis. Bel was the name of one of the principal Celtic deities, the god of the sun and of light, and it is not surprising that the name would be adopted by later warrior kings, though how much the episodes about Bel in myth are derived from those of a real king of that name (or vice versa) cannot be determined. To have acquired the cognomen *Mawr* must mean that Beli was a great king and it is likely that he was one of the first to impose his authority over many of the tribes of Britain, most likely over southern Britain and Wales. The Welsh legends make him the father of LUD and Llefelys and possibly of CASWALLON. Since Caswallon was High King at the time of Caesar's invasion, this would place Beli's existence at the start of the first century BC. It is possible to trace most of the British and Welsh rulers back to Beli.

[A2;P70] **LUD or LLUD** Legendary king of the British mentioned in Geoffrey of Monmouth's *History*. Lud is listed as the eldest son of Heli (or Beli), and the brother of the historically real CASWALLON, which would place Lud's existence at about 60BC. Lud was that rare combination of warrior king and town planner. He rebuilt New Troy, or Trinovantum as it was then known, and renamed it KaerLud after him. This became Lud's Town or London. When he died he was buried by the city wall where Ludgate is named after him. There is a story of Lud in the Welsh tale "Lludd and Llefelys" collected in the *Mabinogion*, wherein Lud consults his brother Llefelys on how to combat three supernatural plagues that are smiting Britain. He succeeds in defeating the source of the plagues and rules peacefully thereafter. This tale, like that of Merlin's, to which it is closely related, may be about a real British prince who ruled later than Geoffrey's Lud, possibly in the first or second century AD. He has become remembered in Welsh legend as the Celtic god Llud, also known as Nudd, the Celtic form of Nodens. A temple to Nodens was built at Lydney in Gloucestershire, where there are other places starting with Lyd-, and which may have some relation to a local prince who assumed the name Lud.

[A3;P71] **CASWALLON or CASSIVELAUNOS** Catuvellauni, *fl* 60–*c*48BC.
The earliest known historical British king, Caswallon (known to the Romans as Cassivelaunos) was ruler of the Catuvellauni tribe who dominated the lands to the

north of the Thames, and most of what is now Bedfordshire, Hertfordshire, Berkshire, Oxfordshire and into Wiltshire. His stronghold was at what is now Wheathamstead. We know nothing of Caswallon's background, other than that he was allegedly the son of BELI and brother of LUD. He was evidently a powerful warrior king able to establish himself as the high-king of the British tribes as, before Caesar's invasion of Britain in 55BC, Caswallon had already attacked the tribe of the Trinovantes in Essex and killed their king (see IMANUENTIUS). Other, smaller tribes looked to Caswallon as their overlord and, more importantly, protector, as Caesar prepared for his invasion. It is recorded that Caswallon had an army of over 4,000 charioteers let alone infantry. Even these, though, were no match for the Romans. After a series of battles and sorties, the British were forced into an encampment guarded by stakes along the north side of the Thames. Realising the strength of the Roman army, Caswallon negotiated with Caesar via COMMIUS. Caesar succeeded in exacting tribute and hostages, and returned to Gaul, fearing an uprising of the Gallic tribes. The fact that Caesar was unable to conquer Britain outright says something for the power and determination of the British tribes and of Caswallon as leader. We do not know how much longer Caswallon remained in power. Evidence suggests that he continued to expand his influence during the next ten or twenty years. At some stage around 50 or 45BC he was succeeded by his son Andoco with whom he perhaps showed part of his territory, and subsequently by TASCIOVANUS, who may have been his son or nephew.

[A4] **IMANUENTIUS** Trinovantes, *d* 55BC.
The ruler of the Trinovantes in Essex who was murdered by CASWALLON of the Catuvellauni, probably as part of a power struggle.

[A5] **MANDUBRACIUS** Trinovantes, 54–*c*30BC.
The son of IMANUENTIUS, who was murdered by CASWALLON in 55BC. Denied his kingdom, Mandubracius fled to Gaul where Julius Caesar had established his base. Caesar used this as an opportunity to strengthen his power for his second expedition into Britain. Caesar succeeded in subduing the native tribes of the Cantii and Catuvellauni forcing them to pay tribute. As part of the arrangement, Mandubracius was restored as king of the Trinovantes. He almost certainly remained so until the assassination of Caesar in 44BC and the subsequent power struggles would have left him in a less certain position. How long he remained in power is uncertain, but by 30BC he had been succeeded by ADDEDOMAROS. Some genealogies suggest he may have been the grandfather or great-grandfather of BOUDICA.

[A6] **CINGETORIX** Cantii, *fl* 55BC.
One of the four tribal leaders of the Cantii in Kent (the others named are Carvilius, Taximagulus and Segovax) who responded to the demands of CASWALLON and led an attack on Caesar's ships which were harboured off the Kentish coast near Thanet. Cingetorix was probably already one of the leaders who had faced Caesar's first landing and the battle near the river Stour which led to the Britons entrenching themselves at the fortress of Bigbury, near Canterbury. Their attack on the Romans was unsuccessful, and another of the chieftains, Lugotorix, was captured. Whether Cingetorix and his fellows survived is not recorded. The similarity of his name to

that the Gallic chieftain and rebel Vercingetorix does not imply an immediate family connection, though they were almost certainly of the same Gallic tribe.

[A7] **COMMIUS** Atrebates, c50BC–c20BC.

When Caesar planned his invasion of Britain in 55BC he chose an agent from amongst the Belgic tribe of the Atrebates to act on his behalf. This man was known as Commius. The Atrebates had already settled in Britain as part of the Belgic incursion that had happened the previous century. Nevertheless the native population of Britain were not yet fully integrated with the continental invaders and Commius was not welcomed. In fact the British, under CASWALLON, pounced on him, imprisoned him in chains and sent him back to Caesar. Commius returned with Caesar as translator and negotiator, and remained with Caesar upon his return to Gaul, where he was placed in charge of a Gallic army. Commius now saw the error of his ways and, in 52BC, he joined in the rebellion against the Romans in Gaul. Caesar's army was victorious and resistance collapsed. Despite assassination attempts on Commius, he survived and returned to Britain, where he was now welcomed. He established a kingdom amongst his own tribe, which covered parts of what is now Hampshire, Wiltshire and Berkshire, with his capital at Calleva, later known as Silchester. He also struck his own coins, the first to appear in Britain identifying a king. Commius ruled for about thirty years, dying sometime around 25–20BC. He was probably aged about 60. He was succeeded by his son TINCOMMIUS.

[A8] **ADDEDOMAROS** Trinovantes, c30–c20BC.

Coins identifying Addedomaros as king are difficult to date but are amongst the earliest in Britain. It is possible that at this time the Trinovantes were again subjugated by the Catuvellaunii under CASWALLON or his successor TASCIOVANUS and that Addedomaros ruled as a sub-king until he in turn was overthrown by DUMNOVELLAUNOS, who re-established a pro-Roman base in Essex.

[A9] **TINCOMMIUS** Atrebates, c20BC–cAD 5.

Probably the son of COMMIUS, he succeeded him as king of the Atrebates. Whereas Commius had become an enemy of Rome, his son seems to have been won over by Augustus Caesar in the early years of his reign, as his coins shifted to reflect a more Roman appearance. It is possible that Tincommius visited Rome and became assured of Roman support against the Catuvellauni whose territory was expanding under TASCIOVANUS. For a couple of decades Tincommius ruled a strong kingdom, probably allied with DUMNOVELLAUNOS of the Cantii, and with the tribe of the Regnii. However, toward the end of his reign there are signs of weakness. It is possible that the increasing power of the Catuvellauni caused struggles within the Atrebates as to how to deal with the problem and sometime around AD 5, Tincommius was deposed by his son or brother EPPILLUS. Tincommius fled to Rome with Dumnovellaunos and probably died there.

[A10] **TASCIOVANUS** Catuvellauni, c20BC–cAD 10.

The first chief of the Catuvellauni to mint coins. These are found extensively along the route of the Thames and even into the territory of the Trinovantes in Essex. Whether or not Tasciovanus is a son or nephew of CASWALLON is not certain, but he was clearly operating from a similar power base to his predecessor. Tasciovanus made incursions into the territories of the Atrebates and the Cantii and established the Catuvellauni as the primary tribe of south-east Britain. Exactly when Tasciovanus died is unclear as the end of his reign blurs into the rise in power of CUNOBELIN. Tasciovanus is the same as Geoffrey of Monmouth's Tenvantius. He makes him a nephew of Caswallon and son of LUD who ruled Cornwall before he became High King of Britain. He was, according to Geoffrey, a very warlike king who nevertheless pursued rigorously the rule of law.

[A11] **DUMNOVELLAUNOS** Trinovantes and Coritani *c*20BC–*c*AD 5; plus Cantii *c*15BC–*c*AD 5.
Although his name is far less well known than other British leaders of the period it is possible that Dumnovellaunos was a respected and powerful leader. Coins bearing his name (sometimes as Dubnovellaunos) have been found throughout eastern and south-eastern Britain. The evidence suggests that he was a chieftain who took control of the Trinovantes in Essex, possibly by usurpation from ADDEDOMAROS. Coins bearing the prefix DUMNO have also been found amongst the Coritani, around Leicester, but whether this is the same name or another is not certain. It is quite possible that early in his reign Dumnovellaunos became pro-Roman and may even have reached agreement with Augustus Caesar over trading and access routes. With this increased power Dumnovellaunos invaded the territory of the Cantii establishing a base in East Kent, around Canterbury. Together with the Atrebate chief TINCOMMIUS, whose territory ran into west Kent, Dumnovellaunos held a strong pro-Roman frontier against the strong anti-Roman Catuvellaunians. However the latter, under TASCIOVANUS, ultimately proved too powerful and Dumnovellaunos and Tincommius were defeated and fled to Rome some time around AD 5. Dumnovellaunos probably spent the rest of his days there.

[A12] **ANTEDRIGOS** Dobunni, dates uncertain but possibly *c*10BC.
A name found, in part, on coins in the Midlands. It has been confused with that of Antedios and the dating of the reigns of these two chieftains is still uncertain. They may have been contemporary, or it may be that Antedrigos reigned around 10BC. Nothing else is known about him.

[A13] **DIRAS** Trinovantes, *c*AD 1.
A name of uncertain origin inscribed on a few coins found in the territory of the Trinovantes in Essex. If it refers to a name of a chieftain at all it may well have been a usurper who attempted to rule over the land of DUMNOVELLAUNOS when the latter shifted his power base to Kent. If this is so then his period of authority was brief.

[A14] **VOSENOS** Cantii, *fl* AD 5.
A name found on a few coins of the Cantii around the first decade AD. Nothing, is known of the king, but it is possible he was a Catuvellaunian who, along with EPPILLUS, succeeded in expelling DUMNOVELLAUNOS and TINCOMMIUS from their kingdoms and ruled briefly in their place. Eppillus later fled to Kent after he was overthrown and may have ruled jointly with or in turn overthrown Vosenos.

[A15] **ANDOCO[MIUS]** Catuvellauni, *c*5–*c*15.
A little-known and rather shadowy figure, the evidence for whom is known only from his coins, dated to the first decade AD. It is possible that he was a son of

TASCIOVANUS who ruled jointly with his father in his last years and then briefly succeeded him, or he may have been a usurper who took over the Catuvellaunian lordship during the rise to power of CUNOBELIN.

[A16] **VOLISIOS** Coritani, *dates uncertain*, possibly c5–c20.

[A17] **DUMNOCOVEROS** Coritani, *dates uncertain*, possibly c5–c20.

[A18] **CARTIVEL(LAUNOS)** Coritani, *dates uncertain*, possibly c5–c20.

Volisios is known only by the appearance of his name on coins. These are quite plentiful and date probably to the period 5–20. The name Volisios is usually accompanied by a suffix – Dumnocoveros, DUMNOVELLAUNOS or Cartivel(launos) – but it is not clear whether this represents the name of an overlord, or of joint rulers, or of a family relationship. It is possible that Volisios was a kinsman of Dumnovellaunos who succeeded in establishing himself briefly in opposition to the Catuvellauni after the other's overthrow, but this is not certain.

[A19] **EPPILLUS** Atrebates, c5–c10; Cantii c10–c25.

Styled the son of COMMIUS, Eppillus may have been his grandson. He succeeded TINCOMMIUS around AD 5, at the time of the Catuvellaunian expansion under TASCIOVANUS, and it is possible that he was a Catuvellaunian sympathiser. If so this did not last long for he was soon deposed by Tasciovanus's son EPATTICUS and fled into Kent where he became king of the western Cantii. He managed to hold Kent against the Catuvellauni, probably in alliance with his kinsman VERICA who had regained the Atrebatian kingship, for fifteen years until he was defeated and (probably) killed by CUNOBELIN or his son AMMINIUS.

[A20] **EPATTICUS** Atrebates, *fl* 10.

A son of TASCIOVANUS who briefly conquered the Atrebates, deposing their king EPPILLUS, but who was in turn deposed by VERICA. It is possible Epatticus made later incursions into Atrebatian territory as coins bearing his name have been dated to the years 25–35, though he may have been acting as a sub-king for his kinsman CUNOBELIN.

[A21] **VERICA** Atrebates 10–40.

Verica (also called Bericos) regained the kingdom of the Atrebates after his kinsman (probably his father or elder brother) EPPILLUS was driven out by EPATTICUS. Verica was loyal to Rome and held a treaty with the emperor Augustus and his successors. This kept Verica's position strong despite the constant opposition of the anti-Roman Catuvellaunian tribe to the north ruled by CUNOBELIN. However anti-Roman factions within the Atrebates finally led to Verica's deposition in 40, when he fled to Rome. Verica arrived in Rome just at the time that CLAUDIUS had become emperor and was one of the key factors in enabling Claudius to develop his plans for the invasion and conquest of Britain in 43. As Verica is not mentioned again it is presumed that he must have died in Rome, for he was probably well into his 60s.

[A22;P73] **CUNOBELIN** Trinovantes from AD 1 and Catuvellauni from c10–41.

Immortalised by Shakespeare as Cymbeline, Cunobelin was one of the most powerful kings of the ancient British. He was probably a son of TASCIOVANUS, although that is not known for certain. His rise to fame was rapid and it is possible that he was an exile of the royal court who sought revenge. He first overran the Trinovantes and established his base at Camulodunum (Colchester) around AD 1, and then laid claim to the Catuvellaunian lordship. He may at this time have been embattled with ANDOCO, but by the second decade AD, Cunobelin was fully in power along the northern bank of the Thames and making encroachments south of the Thames. By about 20 he ruled all of the south-east, finally deposing VERICA around 40, by which time he must have been into his sixties. He died soon after, probably in 41, leading to family squabbles (*see* AMMINIUS, TOGODUMNUS and CARATACUS). The power of Cunobelin concerned the Roman emperors Augustus, Tiberius and Caligula, all of whom considered campaigns against him, but they became more pre-occupied with the German hostilities. Cunobelin may thus be seen as the last great pre-Roman British king.

[A23] **AMMINIUS** Cantii c25–c40.

A son of CUNOBELIN who received overlordship of the Cantii around 25 when EPPILLUS was deposed. In the last years of Cunobelin, family rivalry resulted in the expulsion of Amminius who, with a few faithful followers, fled to the Continent. These events may have been prompted by the threatened invasion of Britain by the emperor Caligula whose troops were stationed in northern Gaul. Amminius went to Caligula, presumably in the hope that Caligula would send soldiers to help him regain his kingdom. Caligula, however, accepted the surrender of Amminius as sufficient sign of conquest and went home in triumph! Nothing more was heard of Amminius, though it is possible he returned to Britain with the Romans as what may have been his tomb was discovered at St Albans.

[A24] **ANTEDIOS** Iceni, dates uncertain but possibly c25.

The name of this king is easily confused with that of ANTEDRIGOS, a ruler of the Dobunni, whose territory was far to the west of the Iceni, and who probably reigned in the last decade BC. Whether or not the names suggest a family relationship is uncertain. The names and coins may indicate a migration of tribal factions from the Midlands toward the east coast during a period of Catuvellaunian expansion when tribes wrestled with their stance toward Rome. Antedios probably ruled later than Antedrigos, around 25. Other coins inscribed with the name Eisu found in the Dobunni territory may also be the same as Aesubelinus in Iceni territory. The latter name, which implies a warrior, may suggest a gathering of arms under a war-like leader in the east Midlands and the Fens during this thirty year period which subsequently became the base for the Iceni.

[A25;P72] **TOGODUMNUS** Catuvellauni, 41–43.

One of the sons of CUNOBELIN who succeeded to the territory of the Catuvellauni along the north of the Thames and into Wiltshire. Together with his brother CARATACUS he led the native armies against the Roman invasion of 43 under Aulus Plautius. The British initially remained in hiding hoping to confuse and weaken the Romans, but the army remained solid. Caratacus was defeated in Kent, and Togodumnus then led a second army against the Romans somewhere in Hampshire. He was defeated and killed. It has been suggested that the name may simply be a title, Tog y Dymnaint or Chief of the Dumnonii, which would have made him originally a ruler of the tribe in south-west Britain. *See also* GUIDERIUS.

[A26] **CARATACUS** Cantii from *c*40, and Catuvellauni and Silures from 43–51.
Younger son of CUNOBELIN who succeeded to the southern half of the Catuvellaunian territories particularly in Kent (Cantii), after his brother AMMINIUS was
deposed, and Surrey (Atrebates). Along with his brother TOGODUMNUS, Caratacus
(the Latin equivalent of Caradog) led the main armies in defence of Britain against
the Roman invasion of 43. Caratacus was defeated in Kent at the Battle of the
Medway and fled west. Initially he built defences in the lands of the Dobunni,
around Gloucestershire, but the advancing Roman army forced him further
westward. Caratacus gained the support of the Silures and Ordovices in south
and central Wales, and from 47 on he maintained a guerilla warfare against the
Romans. Eventually there was a decisive battle in northern Wales near the source of
the Severn in the Cambrian mountains. Caratacus amassed forces of over 15,000
but was defeated. His brother and children were taken as hostages but Caratacus
fled to the land of the Brigantes hoping to raise more troops. However the
Brigantian queen, CARTIMANDUA, had already made a deal with the Romans, and
she promptly handed Caratacus over. He and his family were taken to Rome in
chains. His reputation was well known which gave even more power to CLAUDIUS
who displayed them as evidence of his power and authority. Caratacus may have
expected to be executed but he gave such a stirring speech that Claudius pardoned
him and he lived in comfort in Rome for the remainder of his days. It is not exactly
sure when he died, but it was probably around 54. His children probably remained
in Rome but it has been suggested that they returned to Britain around 60 as
converted Christians.

[A27] **CARTIMANDUA** Brigantes, 43–69.

Queen of the Brigantes, the dominant tribe of mid-northern Britain whose territory
covered most of what is now Yorkshire and Lancashire. No earlier rulers of the
Brigantes are named, even though the size of the tribe would suggest they would
have had many powerful rulers. They were native to Britain and not allied to the
Gallic invaders who came across in the first century. Cartimandua thus readily
allied herself to Rome at the time of the Claudian invasion in 43, presumably with
an eye to keeping her territory whilst the Gallic tribes to the south were subdued.
The Romans supported her throughout, and there can be little doubt that through
her actions and inactions the Romans were able to keep control over Britain. In 51,
when CARATACUS sought refuge with her, hoping to raise an army in revolt, she
betrayed him to the Romans. This certainly caused much dissent amongst the
Brigantes, some of whom had sided with the Silures, and she did not carry the
support of her husband VENUTIUS, but with continued Roman support she
sustained her position. Similarly when she chose not to become involved in the
British revolt under BOUDICA nine years later, she helped sow the seeds of Roman
victory, for had she brought the weight of her troops in to support the Iceni and
Trinovantes the British might well have succeeded. Cartimandua remained in a
strong position until 69. In that year she cast aside her husband, Venutius, in favour
of his armour-bearer Vellocatus. Venutius raised an army against Cartimandua
who, although she was rescued by the Romans, was overthrown. She and Vellocatus
are not heard of again. She is identified by the Welsh with the traitor queen
Aregwedd Foeddawg. Although Cartimandua was a more powerful and certainly

more tactical queen that Boudica – indeed she was a queen in her own right, not just a consort – she has come to be regarded by history as a traitor and is not as revered as her valiant contemporary.

[A28] **VENUTIUS** Brigantes, 69–72.

Husband and consort of CARTIMANDUA. After she cast him aside in 69 in favour of his armour-bearer Vellocatus, Venutius raised an army against Cartimandua and drove her out of the territory. Venutius proclaimed himself king of the Brigantes and remained at war with Rome. He maintained a bloody resistance for three years until he was defeated by Petillius Cerialis, probably at Stanwick. It is not recorded that Venutius was killed in that battle, and there is a suggestion that he fled into the Vale of Eden in Lancashire and maybe over to Ireland. With his defeat the lands of the Brigantes came under Roman domination.

[A29;P75] **ARVIRAGUS** Silures, fl 44–74.

Only one classical reference exists to Arviragus and that is in a poem by Juvenal which calls Arviragus a "black bull", probably meaning his strength and his dark flowing hair, as he rode his chariot recklessly through the Roman streets terrifying Nero. There is a strong Welsh belief that Arviragus, or Gweirydd, was the king of the Silures who joined forces with CARATACUS (possibly his brother) against the Romans. He was captured alongside the Catuvellaunian chief and taken to Rome where he was also pardoned. Tradition states that Arviragus returned to Wales and established the royal line from which King ARTHUR was descended. Arviragus is treated as the king who welcomed Joseph of Arimathea to Britain in about 63 and granted him land at Glastonbury for his church. The date 67 has been assigned to his death on the basis of the Welsh genealogies. Geoffrey of Monmouth extends the independence of Arviragus, making him a tribute-paying king who marries the daughter of the Emperor CLAUDIUS. Through the friendship of Claudius, Arviragus is installed as ruler of Britain and the city of Gloucester is built. Arviragus later defends Britain from an invasion by Vespasian and dies in old age, much loved and honoured. According to Geoffrey he was succeeded by his son MARIUS.

[A30] **PRASUTAGUS** Iceni, 47–59.

A client-king of the Romans who was assured rule of the Iceni thanks to services rendered to Claudius during the invasion of 43. These services probably included local intelligence as well as support in men and supplies. It is not clear whether Prasutagus was already a king of the Iceni before the invasion, but it is likely he was not. Some of the Iceni joined in the revolt of CARATACUS in 47, but as Prasutagus remained king he was evidently not associated with this uprising. If anything the uprising may as much have been against his imposed rule as any other factor. Tacitus refers to the "long lasting prosperity" of Prasutagus which suggests he may well have been an Icenian merchant of high noble rank who had benefitted from trade with the Romans. It probably also means that Prasutagus was reaching old age when he was made client-king, since he already had two teenage daughters by his wife, the considerably more famous BOUDICA. The client-king arrangement was not hereditary and Prasutagus had already bequeathed the kingdom to be shared between his daughters and Claudius. This meant that upon the death of Prasutagus the Romans promptly claimed the territory as their own. The subsequent pillaging led to the British revolt of 60.

[A31] **BOUDICA** Iceni, 59–61.
Queen of the Iceni, and wife of the client king PRASUTAGUS. Under the arrangements of his office, Prasutagus's territories passed to Rome after his death. The Romans, stationed at Colchester, took this rather too literally and began pillaging the land. When Boudica objected she was flogged and her two teenage daughters raped. This was the final outrage to the British who rose up in revolt. The rebellion

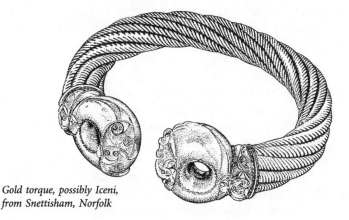

Gold torque, possibly Iceni,
from Snettisham, Norfolk

was not well organized and may not initially have been led by Boudica, though its main forces were the Iceni and the Trinovantes. The first strike was at the Roman city of Camulodunum (Colchester) where a new temple to Claudius was being completed. The town and its occupants were totally destroyed. The British then turned on London, which was not yet the main centre it became. Although the London merchants had time to flee, many others were massacred. There are sites traditionally associated with Boudica at Stanmore in Middlesex and Ambersbury Banks in Epping Forest. The Iceni and Trinovantes then turned on their old enemy the Catuvellauni, who had found favour under the Romans, in their town of Verulamium (St Albans). The British rebels, now led by Boudica, advanced on the main Roman army which had been forced to return from Wales. The site of the battle is uncertain but was probably at Mancetter, midway between Birmingham and Leicester. Even though the British must have outnumbered the Romans by ten to one the lack of organization amongst the British was no match for the hardened Roman discipline and, after a day of intense fighting, the British were defeated. By one account Boudica poisoned herself, whilst others say she fell ill and died. Boudica, under the more popular rendition of her name as Boadicea, became symbolic in Victorian times as the defender of the British Empire, a kind of Britannia, the embodiment of power – the name Boudica means Victoria. The truth was not quite the same but Boudica's was the last open rebellion against the Roman occupation of eastern Britain.

[A32] **COGIDUBNUS** or **COGIDUMNUS** Regnii, 43–75.
The last significant British king at the time of the Roman occupation. He was a client of the Romans, who, because of his help and support, was given the

kingdom of the Regnii in Sussex, spreading to Hampshire and Kent. Because of his help to the Romans, not only in the invasion of 43AD but in the later revolutions of CARATACUS and BOUDICA, Cogidubnus became increasingly wealthy and powerful ultimately becoming a Roman legate. He established a magnificent palace at Fishbourne, near Chichester, and took on the Roman name, Tiberius Claudius Cogidumnus. He became an example to others of how compliance with the Romans was beneficial. He was the first of the Romano-British elite and it is almost certain that many of the British nobility subsequently followed his example. They were not offered kingdoms but became magistrates of the cities, and few of their names are recorded. The name Cogidubnus may be a Latinised version of Tog y Dobunni, or King of the Dobunni – in return for his support Cogidubnus was perhaps granted land in southern Britain away from his Gloucester heartland.

[A33;P76] **MARIUS** A legendary king of the British mentioned in the *History* of Geoffrey of Monmouth. Since he is described as the son of ARVIRAGUS, he might just be a real ruler of the Silures, and would have ruled toward the end of the first century AD. Geoffrey suggests that he lived in Rome for some time, which is quite likely if he were a son of one of the British chieftains who were taken captive to Rome by Claudius, who included both Arviragus and CARATACUS. Once established as king of the British, he is supposed to have paid his taxes willingly to the Romans and was of upstanding character. This makes him sound like one of the client kings that Claudius established, of whom the best known were PRASUTAGUS and COGIDUBNUS, but there is no reason to doubt that there could have been others. Geoffrey describes how Marius fought and made peace with the Picts who invaded northern Britain at this time. Marius set up a stone marking his victory in Westmoreland which is supposed to be named after him. To be present that far north Marius, if he existed at all, may have been a British chief of the Brigantes, though his ability to grant the Picts land as far north as Caithness is total fabrication. Marius's historical nature must be in severe doubt, though there may be a grain of truth in how the royal line of the British continued. One tradition states that Marius married a daughter of Bran the Blessed, who was a granddaughter of Joseph of Arimathea and that through this union the British kings became cousins of the Fisher Kings or guardians of the Holy Grail. The name Marius is a Romanization of Meurig, which is itself a corruption of the Celtic Y-Veurig, which is the same as Arviragus. Geoffrey may therefore have confused two names of the same king. He was succeeded by his son COEL.

[A34] **CALGACUS** Caledonii, *fl* 80.
The last independent chieftain to be identified amongst the British tribes. Calgacus was a chieftain of the Caledonii who led the last resistance in the Scottish hills and was at last defeated at the battle of Mons Graupius in 84, though what became of him thereafter is not recorded. He may not have been a king in his own right but a resistance leader – his name is derived from *calgach* meaning swordsman. Although he is the earliest known named Pictish Celt, he was almost certainly but one of many local chieftains whose names we shall never know. His name does not appear amongst the traditional Pictish king lists.

[A35;P77] **COEL** Legendary ruler identified by Geoffrey of Monmouth. He was the son of MARIUS and was raised, and probably educated, in Rome. This means he would have been taken there at the time the British chieftains ARVIRAGUS and CARATACUS were captured by Claudius in 51, when he was probably a young boy, and would have returned with his father (and grandfather) around 60 or soon after. On these assumptions Coel, who respected and honoured the Romans, paying his taxes when due, may have lived to the turn of the first century. He was succeeded by his son LUCIUS. It is interesting to speculate whether this Coel is Geoffrey's version of COGIDUBNUS who was highly rewarded by the Romans. He is not the same as "Old King Cole" who was a post-Roman ruler, see page 97.

[A36;P78] **LUCIUS** or **LLEIRWG** *MAWR* A semi-legendary king of the British. If our only record of Lucius was from the writings of Geoffrey of Monmouth we might discount him like many of his fabrications, but Lucius is recorded elsewhere, not only by the Venerable Bede but also in the early sixth century *Liber Pontificalis*. All these sources state that Lucius was a king of the Britons in the mid second century who sent his emissaries to the Bishop of Rome, Eleutherius, seeking help in the Christian ministry in Britain. Eleutherius did not become Pope until about the year 174, so if we are to accept Lucius as the great-grandson of ARVIRAGUS, who died about a hundred years earlier (as the Welsh genealogies suggest), then Lucius must have been quite old by this time, probably in his seventies. Eleutherius responded and sent two missionaries, Faganus and Duvanus, who helped re-establish the Christian church in Britain, building the first of the churches at Glastonbury, and the church of St Peter at Cornhill in London in the year 179. Some efforts have been made to discredit the existence of this king, stating that Lucius was also the name applied to Agbar IX of Edessa, although this Agbar lived forty years later. A British Lucius is certainly possible, particularly in south-west Britain which the Romans only sparsely colonized. At this same time there was considerable persecution of the Christians in Gaul and many fled to Britain for safety. Lucius (or someone) must have protected them there and become sufficiently established to be remembered centuries later. Interestingly there was a Roman general, Lucius Artorius Castus, who was prominent in Britain at this time as he led the army that helped quell the civil unrest in Brittany. It is possible that Geoffrey latched on to his name, but it is unlikely that this same Roman would have become regarded as a protector of Christians. Geoffrey states that Lucius died with no heirs which left Britain in a state of turmoil, prone to usurpers. Welsh tradition however lists many descendants of Lucius including the future rulers of Gwent, Powys, Strathclyde, Cornwall and Brittany.

[A37] **ARGENTOCOXOS** Caledonii, *fl* 208.
A high official of the Caledonii who is mentioned in an anecdote recorded by Dio Cassius in his *History of Rome* where Argentocoxos sealed a treaty between the Caledonii and the Romans. Whether or not he was a king is not noted though his wife is recognized as having a high rank since she was able to talk freely with Julia Augusta, the wife of SEPTIMUS SEVERUS. The anecdote tells us little about Argentocoxos but tells us much about the nature of Celtic women, who were proud of their ability to have sex with other high born Celtic noblemen – unlike the Roman wives, who did it in secret. This refers to the matrilinear succession of the

Pictish kings whose authority descended through the female line and thus emphasised the importance of women in Pictish society. It is just possible that Argentocoxos is the same as Artcois the father of CINIOD MAC ARTCOIS a semi-legendary Pictish ruler (see page 169).

Map 2 **Roman Britain at the start of the Fourth Century**

ROMAN OCCUPATION (43AD–410AD)

This section is divided into two parts. All Roman emperors whose authority extended to Britain are listed. Very few visited Britain, and even fewer had any interest in the island. Those of special relevance to Britain are marked [b] and have biographies in this section. The second part covers all the governors who were appointed directly by Rome and vested with imperial authority. These were not hereditary monarchs, and are not included in the biographical section. The full list is provided for completeness, though details are uncertain towards the end of the period. All existing Celtic kingdoms became forfeit upon Roman occupation, though Claudius and his successors allowed some client kings to remain, as listed in Part A. These were soon abandoned and descendants of the tribal nobility were treated as senior administrators within the states or civitas established in Britain. Only in the northernmost parts of Britain did the Celtic tribes remain independent. Details of their rulers are uncertain but some quasi-historical kings of the Picts are listed on page 165.

B. ROMAN EMPERORS

Ref.	Ruler	Born	Reign	Died	Notes
B1.	Claudius[b]	10BC	41–54	54	probably poisoned
B2.	Nero	37	54–68	68	committed suicide
B3.	Galba	3BC	68–69	69	murdered after 7 months
B4.	Otho	32	Jan–Apr 69	69	committed suicide after 3 months
B5.	Vitellius	15?	Apr–Dec 69	69	murdered after 8 months
B6.	Vespasian	9	69–79	79	
B7.	Titus	39	79–81	81	
B8.	Domitian	51	81–96	96	murdered
B9.	Nerva	30	96–98	98	
B10.	Trajan	53	98–117	117	
B11.	Hadrian[b]	76	117–138	138	
B12.	Antoninus Pius[b]	86	138–161	161	
B13.	Marcus Aurelius	121	161–180	180	ruled jointly with Lucius Verus
B14.	Lucius Verus	130	161–169	169	ruled jointly with above
B15.	Commodus	161	180–192	192	murdered
B16.	Pertinax	126	Jan–Mar 193	193	murdered after 3 months; see C31
B17.	Didius Julianus	133	Mar–Jun 193	193	murdered after 66 days
B18.	Decimus Clodius Albinus[b]		193–197	197	committed suicide; see C32
B19.	Pescennius Niger		193–194	194	murdered after a battle
B20.	Septimius Severus[b]	145	193–211	211	
B21.	Caracalla[b]	188	211–217	217	ruled with his brother; murdered; see P80
B22.	Geta	189	Feb–Dec 211	211	ruled with Caracalla; murdered

Ref.	Ruler	Born	Reign	Died	Notes
B23.	Macrinus	164	217–218	218	murdered
B24.	Elagabalus	203	218–222	222	murdered
B25.	Severus Alexander	208	222–235	235	murdered
B26.	Maximinus	172	235–238	238	murdered
B27.	Gordianus (I)	158	Jan 238	238	committed suicide after 20 days
B28.	Gordianus (II)	c192	Jan 238	238	ruled jointly with father; murdered
B29.	Pupienus	c164	Feb–May 238	238	ruled jointly with Balbinus; murdered
B30.	Balbinus		Feb–May 238	238	ruled jointly with Pupienus; murdered
B31.	Gordianus III	224	238–244	244	murdered
B32.	Philippus	c204	244–249	249	killed in battle
B33.	Decius	c190	249–251	251	killed in battle
B34.	Trebonianus Gallus	c206	251–253	253	murdered
B35.	Aemilius Aemilianus	c207	Aug–Oct 253	253	murdered after 88 days
B36.	Valerianus	c195	253–260	after 260	died in captivity
B37.	Gallienus	c213	253–268	268	emperor in the west; murdered

Valerianus and his son Gallienus split the empire between them with Gallienus ruling the West. Gallienus subsequently faced an uprising from Marcus Cassianus Postumus, governor of Lower Germany, who declared a separate Gallic Empire in 260. This covered all of the Roman empire west of the Rhine, including Britain. It shrank to cover only Gaul and Britain by 269 and was eventually reabsorbed into the Roman Empire in 274 under Aurelianus.

Gallic Empire

B38.	Postumus		260–269	269	murdered
B39.	Laelianus		Feb–Apr 269	269	usurper; killed in battle (?)
B40.	Aurelius Marius		Apr–Jul 269	269	murdered
B41.	Victorinus		269–271	271	murdered
B42.	Tetricus		271–274		abdicated authority back to Rome

Roman Empire *restored*

B43.	Aurelianus	214	270–275	275	murdered
B44.	Tacitus	c200	275–276	276	murdered after eight months
B45.	Florianus		Jul–Sep 276	276	murdered after 88 days
B46.	Probus	232	276–282	282	murdered
B47.	Carus	c224	282–283	283	purportedly killed by lightning!
B48.	Carinus	c250	283–285	285	emperor in the west; murdered
B49.	Diocletian	245	284–305	311	retired

Although Diocletian remained the senior emperor he divided the Empire into two in 286 (East and West) delegating authority in the west to Maximian

B50.	Maximian	c250	286–305	310	retired; tried to regain the imperial throne and was killed

During Maximian's reign Britain declared independence under Carausius and Allectus (see B51 and B52 below).

B51	Carausius[b]		286–293	293	murdered; see P81
B52	Allectus[b]		293–295	296	deposed; see P82
B53.	Constantius (I) Chlorus (the Pale)[b]	c250	305–306	306	emperor in the west; see P85
B54.	Severus (II)		306–307	307	emperor in the west; forced to abdicate then killed
B55.	Constantine (I)[b]	272	306–337	337	declared emperor in Britain; see P86

Constantine was declared emperor in Britain before he was acknowledged as Augustus in the west in 307; he shared this with Licinius from 308 to 311, but thereafter Licinius gradually overpowered others to become emperor in the east. Constantine subsequently defeated and killed Licinius and from 324 was sole emperor.

B56.	Constantine II[b]		337–340	340	emperor of Britain, Gaul and Spain; killed in battle; see P92
B57.	Constans[b]		340–350	350	ruled Italy and eastern Europe until 340, then ruled all Europe; murdered; see P93
B58.	Magnentius		350–353	353	killed in battle
B59.	Constantius II		353–361	361	had been emperor in the east since 337
B60.	Julian *the Apostate*		360–363	363	died of battle wounds

Julian was appointed Caesar in the West from 355.

B61.	Jovian		363–364	364	accidentally gassed to death
B62.	Valentinian (I)		364–375	375	emperor in the west
B63.	Gratian	359	375–383	383	killed in battle; see P91

Britain declared its own emperor in 383 with Magnus Maximus.

B64.	Magnus Maximus[b]	c300	383–388	388	Britain and Gaul; killed in battle; see P88
B65.	Valentinian II	370	388–392	392	killed nominal co-emperor with Gratian from 375
B66.	Eugenius[b]		392–394	394	killed in battle; see DB1 and P87

After Eugenius's death Rome was briefly united under the eastern emperor Theodosius who died a few months later.

B67.	Honorius	384	395–423	423	

Stilicho was effectively ruler of Rome during Honorius' minority until his death in 408. The Western empire began to crumble and Britain declared several claimants to the throne:

B68.	Marcus[b]		406	406	murdered
B69.	Gratian[b]		407	407	deposed and murdered
B70.	Constantine (III)[b]		407–411	411	legitimized emperor in 408

In 410 AD, Honorius withdrew his support from Britain leaving the island to defend itself. Thereafter Britain was no longer part of the Roman Empire.

C. ROMAN GOVERNORS OF BRITAIN

Ref.	Ruler	Born	Reign	Died	Notes
C1.	Aulus Plautius		43–47		
C2.	Publius Ostorius Scapula		47–52		
C3.	Aulus Didius Gallus		52–57		
C4.	Quintus Veranius Nepos		57–59		
C5.	Gaius Suetonius Paulinus		59–61		
C6.	Publius Petronius Turpilianus		61–63		
C7.	Marcus Trebellius Maximus		63–69		
C8.	Marcus Vettius Bolanus		69–71		
C9.	Quintus Petillius Cerialis		71–74		
C10.	Sextus Julius Frontinus	c40	74–78	103	
C11.	Gnaeus Julius Agricola	37	78–85	93	
C12.	Sallustius Lucullus		85– ?		
C13.	Publius Metilius Nepos		c95–c98		
C14.	Titus Avidius Quietus		c98–c101		
C15.	Lucius Neratius Marcellus		101–103		
C16.	Publius Pomponius Mammiliaus		103–109		
C17.	Marcus Appius Bradua		?115–118		first term?
C18.	Quintus Pompeius Falco	118–122			
C19.	Aulus Platorius Nepos		122–126		
(C17)	Marcus Appius Bradua		126–129		second term?
C20.	Sextus Julius Severus		129–133		
C21.	Publius Mummius Sisenna	133–138			
C22.	Quintus Lollius Urbicus		138–144		
C23.	Gnaeus Papirius Aelianus		144–155		
C24.	Gnaeus Julius Verus		155–158		

C25.	Longus or Longinus		?158–160?		name incomplete
C26.	Marcus Statius Priscus		160–161		
C27.	Sextus Calpurnius Agricola		161–166		
C28.	Caerellius Priscus		166–170		period uncertain
C29.	Lucius Ulpius Marcellus		170–175		first term
C30.	Quintus Antistius Adventus		175–183		period uncertain
(C29)	Lucius Ulpius Marcellus		183–185		second term
C31.	Publius Helvius Pertinax	126	185–192	193	same as B16
C32.	Decimus Clodius Albinus[b]		192–197		declared emperor; see B18
C33.	Virius Lupus		197–202		
C34.	Marcus Antius Calpurnianus		202–203		acting governor only
C35.	Gaius Valerius Pudens		203–205		
C36.	Lucius Alfenus Senecio		205–211?		

Hereafter the province of Britannia was divided into Britannia Superior in the south, with its capital at London, and Britannia Inferior in the north with its capital at York.

Britannia Superior

C37.	Gaius Junius Faustinus	?211–222?
C38.	Titus Julius Pollienus Auspex	?223–226
C39.	Rufinus	?
C40.	Marcus Martiannius Pulcher	?
C41.	Titus Desticius Juba	?253–255

Britannia Inferior

C42.	Gaius Julius Marcus	?211–215?
C43.	Marcus Antonius Gordianus	?215–218?
C44.	Modius Julius	?218–219?
C45.	Tiberius Claudius Paulinus	220
C46.	Marius Valerianus	221–223?
C47.	Claudius Xenephon	223
C48.	Maximus	?224–225
C49.	Claudius Apellinus	*between* 222–235
C50.	Calvisius Rufus	*between* 222–235

Ref.	Ruler	Born	Reign	Died	Notes
C51.	Valerius Crescens Fulvianus		*between 222–235*		
C52.	Tuccianus		?236–237?		
C53.	Maecilius Fuscus		*between 238–244*		
C54.	Egnatius Lucilianus		*between 238–244*		
C55.	Nonius Philippus		?241–242?		
C56.	Octavius Sabinus		*between 260–269*		

From 270 onwards records of Roman governors become sparse, whilst other information suggests that Britain was claiming increasingly greater independence. Over the next few years we see a succession of Romans who declared themselves as emperors within Britain, some moving on to claim the purple in Rome, others failing disastrously. (See listing on page 83 from B51 on).

Governors and Vicarii

Britain was restored to the Empire after Allectus and a new governor installed. The administration was further complicated however by the creation of separate civil and military governors few of whose names are recorded. Britain was divided into four provinces, as shown in Map 2, each with a provincial governor. The following are the few known remaining provincial governors who seemed to exercise control over parts of Britain.

C57.	Aurelius Arpagius	296–305	governor of Britannia Secunda
C58.	Flavius Sanctus	*c*350s	
C59.	Lucius Septimius	*c*360s	probably governor of Britannia Prima

There are no records of other governors and by 383 Magnus Maximus had declared himself emperor in Britain. For the remaining thirty years of Roman administration Britain become increasingly more independent.

[B1] **CLAUDIUS** Emperor of Rome, 24 January 41–13 October 54.
Born: *Lyons, 1 August 10BC. Died(poison?): Rome, 13 October 54, aged 64.*
Although Julius Caesar had successfully invaded Britain in 54BC and exacted tribute, the island was not integrated into the Roman world as a province until the campaign by Tiberius Claudius Caesar in AD 43. The invasion was led by Aulus Plautius who successfully defeated the combined British armies under CARATACUS and TOGODUMNUS. Although CARATACUS continued a guerilla warfare for another decade, and the full conquest of Britain (with the exception of what is now Scotland and Wales) would take another forty years, Britain was absorbed into the Roman Empire. Claudius spent sixteen days on the island, and in that time ensured that the basis would be established for certainly one, and subsequently two further client kingdoms, those of COGIDUMNUS in southern Britain, PRASUTAGUS in the east and later CARTIMANDUA in the north. Claudius never returned to Britain, but as its conqueror for Rome may be regarded sufficiently as its overlord. He established a governorship by Rome with Aulus Plautius the first governor. Claudius became the figurehead of oppression amongst the British. After his death he was deified by the Romans and a temple in his honour was built at Camulodunum (Colchester). This became the focal point for the first attack when the British rebelled under BOUDICA

in 60 and the temple was destroyed. Claudius was one of the few Roman emperors to visit Britain, though others include HADRIAN and SEVERUS. Several later emperors were declared by their troops in Britain and a few identified themselves specifically as emperor of Britain (see ALBINUS, CARAUSIUS and ALLECTUS).

[B11] **HADRIAN** Emperor of Rome, 11 August 117–10 July 138.
Born: Rome, 24 January 76. *Died*: Baiae, nr Rome, 10 July 138, aged 62.
Publius Aelius Hadrianus, the adoptive son of the Emperor Trajan, was the first Roman emperor to visit Britain after its conquest by CLAUDIUS, nearly eighty years earlier. A strong military tactician, he was the first emperor to seriously consider the nature of the Empire's defences and spent ten years touring the frontier. He spent the summer of 122 in Britain. At this time the British "could not be kept under control", as Hadrian's biographer termed it, though the full extent of this is not clear. The Brigantes may have been in revolt or the province of Britain may have been under threat from the Celts to the north. Hadrian commanded the construction of a wall across northern Britain, which served not only as a defence against the northern Celts but also enabled the Romans to keep the Brigantes under stricter control. The wall extends for 73 miles but took less than ten years to complete. Hadrian did not return to Britain, but he left a mark on the land which has never been forgotten. He also, ostensibly, established what would later become the boundary between England and Scotland. His successor was ANTONINUS PIUS.

[B12] **ANTONINUS PIUS** Emperor of Rome, 10 July 138–7 March 161.
Born: Lanuvium, 19 September 86; *Died*: Rome, 7 March 161, aged 74.
Although Antoninus Pius never set foot in Britain he left his mark by ordering the settlement of southern Scotland. This began soon after Antoninus became emperor in 138, under the new governor Quintus Lollius Urbicus. It took Urbicus four years to subdue the local tribes, in particular the Selgovae and Votadini. Once this was achieved, the wall established by HADRIANUS was abandoned and new defences constructed forty miles north running thirty-seven miles between the Forth and the Clyde. Construction began in 143. Although its construction – a stone base surmounted by turf – was inferior to Hadrian's, its shorter length and concentration of manpower made it a stronger defence. However, within a decade of its completion problems amongst the Brigantes meant that forces had to be concentrated back on Hadrian's wall. This limited the defence of the Antonine Wall and for a period around 160 it was abandoned. After the Brigantian rebellion had been curbed the Wall was re-occupied but only for a short period. It was found harder to defend with the onslaught of tribes from the south as well as the north and eventually, around 185 it was abandoned and the frontier reset at Hadrian's Wall. Antoninus Pius, consequently, was the only Roman emperor to control part of Scotland and certainly ruled over the largest part of Britain.

[B18;C32] **ALBINUS** Emperor in Britain, April 193–19 February 197.
Decimus Clodius Albinus was the first example of a British governor to be declared emperor by his troops. During the reign of emperor Commodus (180–192) the troops in Britain became unhappy with their treatment by Rome and lost respect for Commodus, the most depraved emperor since Nero. When Commodus was murdered, troops around the empire took the opportunity to declare their own

successor. Whilst Publius Helvius Pertinax, a former governor of Britain, was declared emperor in Rome, three other pretenders were announced. Amongst these was Albinus, who had been appointed governor in 192, who declared his bid for the title in April 193. The strongest of the claimants was Septimius SEVERUS who marched upon Rome and was declared emperor in June 193. Severus wrote to Albinus appointing him as Caesar, which in effect meant successor. Albinus accepted and stayed in Britain while Severus turned his attentions to the other claimant Pescennius Niger in Syria, whom he defeated and killed in 194. Albinus now became aware of Severus's plans to dispose of him, which became abundantly evident when Severus tried unsuccessfully to have him poisoned. Severus proclaimed his son, BASSIANUS (later known as Caracalla), Caesar in late 195 in defiance of his earlier promise to Albinus. This led to all-out civil war. Albinus's troops proclaimed him Augustus in 195. Albinus, supported by his three British legions and the legion in Spain, crossed into Gaul and established a base at Lyons. The final showdown took place just outside Lyons on 19 February 197. The battle first favoured Albinus, but the sheer weight of numbers forced Albinus into defeat. He fled into Lyons, but realising it was hopeless, he committed suicide. The fate of Albinus set in train a sequence of events that changed the administrative and economic face of Britain.

[B20] **SEPTIMIUS SEVERUS** Emperor of Rome, 1 June 193–4 February 211.
Born: *Lepcis Magna (Libya), 11 April 145.* **Died**: *York, 4 February 211, aged 65.*
A powerful but short-sighted emperor, Severus was noted for his treachery. He was also the first Roman emperor to die in Britain. Severus received the purple of Rome during a period of civil war when he disposed of three other claimants, including Clodius ALBINUS. Severus was unhappy over the degree of support the British legions had accorded Albinus and determined that no one should have such authority again. He thus decided to split the Empire into smaller provinces, reducing the power base of governers. He set into motion the reorganization of Britain into two provinces, Britannia Inferior in the north, based at York, and Britannia Superior in the south, governed from London, but with legions are Chester and Caerleon. This did not come fully into effect until the start of Caracalla's reign in 211, and it was probably one of the reasons for Severus's decision to visit Britain in order to plan this reorganization whilst settling the total conquest of Britain once and for all. He was also troubled by the hostility between his sons, Caracalla and Geta, and Severus decided to take them both with him on his campaign. They arrived in Britain in 208. Geta was left in charge in London, whilst Severus and Caracalla travelled north to York and from there up to the Hadrianic and Antonine walls. During 209 Severus established firm bases around Carpow in Fife before heading up the eastern coast attempting unsuccessfully to draw the native tribe (the Maeatae) out into full battle. There were many local skirmishes in which Severus was always successful and by the end of the year he had established a peace agreement in exchange for land, but this was short lived and in the following summer (210), Caracalla led a punitive expedition into the heart of Maeatae and Caledonian territory. The slaughter that followed was still indecisive. There was no surrender and the result was an even more entrenched hostility to Rome. When Severus, who had long been ill from gout, died at York in February

211, Caracalla soon abandoned Scotland and returned to Rome to consolidate his position there. This was the last attempt to conquer the northern Celts.

[B21;P80] **CARACALLA** or **BASSIANUS**, Emperor of Rome 4 February 211–8 April 217.
Born: Lyons (France), 4 April 188. **Died** (murdered): Carrhae (Mesopotamia), 8 April 217, aged 29.
Bassianus was the name used by Geoffrey of Monmouth in his History for Caracalla. Geoffrey invented an almost fictional account of Caracalla's life in Britain raising him to the role of a British king. According to Geoffrey SEPTIMIUS SEVERUS had two sons: Geta was the son of a Roman wife, but Bassianus was the son of a British woman and was thus more popular amongst the Celts of Britain. Although Severus appointed Geta to succeed him, the native British chose Bassianus. After Severus's death in 211 the two brothers fought and Geta was killed. Thereafter Bassianus ruled Britain until deposed and killed by the usurper CARAUSIUS. This is a considerable time leap as Caracalla was murdered in 217, seventy years before Carausius's revolt. Geoffrey's use of Bassianus for Caracalla can be easily explained. Caracalla was not his real name. It was a nickname derived from the type of cloak that he wore. His imperial name was Marcus Aurelius Severus Antoninus Pius, but his natal name was Lucius Septimius Bassianus. This last name came from that of his maternal grandfather, Julius Bassianus, the high priest of Emesa in Syria. Bassianus never ruled as king in Britain. He and Geta were sons of the same mother. They accompanied her and their father's remains back to Rome in 211 and Caracalla never returned to Britain. Ten months after returning to Rome Caracalla murdered Geta. He was not quite the despot some historians have made him, and he was popular with his troops, but his initial popularity rapidly waned and he was murdered whilst in Mesopotamia on 8 April 217, four days after his twenty-ninth birthday.

[B51;P81] **CARAUSIUS** Emperor of Britain, 286–293.
Mauseus Carausius was a Gallic soldier who had been put in charge of the coastal defences along the shores of what is now France, Belgium and Holland. His base was at Boulogne. At that time the coast was being raided by various Germanic tribes. Carausius, though of lowly birth, was a capable soldier and sailor, popular with the army. He was also not averse to a little plunder himself. Carausius would wait until after the raids, capture the boats, and then keep some of the booty to himself. The Emperor Maximian became aware of this and ordered Carausius's arrest and execution. In response Carausius declared himself emperor. At this time Carausius was probably in his mid to late thirties, though details of his life and background are meagre. It is not clear whether he promptly escaped to Britain or first entrenched himself in Boulogne, but it is likely that he spent some months in Gaul towards the end of 286 before settling in Britain. Either way he maintained an enclave at Boulogne even after he established himself in Britain. Here he was not only supported by his army, but had control of the entire fleet and the use of the new coastal defences set up around southern and eastern Britain during that period. An attempt to capture Carausius in 289 was unsuccessful and Maximian suffered heavy losses. Maximian transferred the problem to his newly appointed Caesar, CONSTANTIUS, who succeeded in regaining Boulogne after a siege of some months

during the summer of 293. This weakened Carausius and, later that year, he was assassinated by his "treasurer", ALLECTUS.

Although details about Carausius are few (the Romans did not care to record the deeds of their enemies) the archeological evidence is that Carausius did much to improve and extend defences and civic buildings in the south-east. There is no doubt that he was popular amongst his troops, until his defeat and downfall, and he was clearly also popular amongst the general populace. This may be because he was of Gallic origin, and thus as much Celtic as he was Roman. There are even those that claim he was king of the Silures, though there is no evidence to support this.

[B52;P82] **ALLECTUS** Emperor of Britain, 293–296.
Allectus is recorded as "treasurer" of the self-styled Emperor CARAUSIUS, which probably means that he had the equivalent of consular rank and was in charge of finances and other civic duties. Allectus managed affairs in Britain whilst Carausius dealt with the defences. By this means Allectus would have ensured the soldiers were promptly paid and thus guaranteed their support when, after Carausius suffered a set-back at the hands of CONSTANTIUS, Allectus murdered Carausius and proclaimed himself emperor. He remained in power for a further three years during which time Constantius strengthened the Roman fleet and prepared for a major invasion. Allectus was not the soldier or tactician that Carausius had been, and was defeated by Constantius's dual attack from east and west. Allectus was killed in battle near Farnham in Surrey by ASCLEPIODOTUS. Although this marked the end of the brief British Empire, it set a precedent for the future as the Roman Empire weakened and a native British nobility prepared to rule itself.

[B53;P85] **CONSTANTIUS** Emperor of Western Rome, 1 May 305–25 July 306.
Born: Illyricum, 31 March 250; Died: York, 25 July 306, aged 56.
Gaius Flavius Valerius Constantius had been appointed Caesar (and successor) by Maximian in 293AD and had played the major role in quelling the revolution of CARAUSIUS and his usurper successor ALLECTUS. Despite the concern over the British revolt, there were problems elsewhere in the Empire and Constantius did not return to Britain until 305, shortly after he had become emperor, when he headed a campaign against the Caledonian Celts (whom, for the first time, the Roman historians called Picts). Constantius, accompanied by his son CONSTANTINE, achieved some success over the Celts, but not enough to subdue them or bring them into the Empire. His campaign was cut short by his death, possibly of leukemia, in York. His troops immediately proclaimed his son Constantine as emperor.

[B55;P86] **CONSTANTINE** (I) Emperor of Rome, 25 July 306–22 May 337.
Born: Naissus, 27 February 272; Died: Ankyrona, 22 May 337, aged 65.
Gaius Flavius Valerius Constantinus, better known as Constantine the Great, was one of the most important Roman emperors, not least because he made Christianity an official religion of the Roman empire. History, or more properly myth, has linked him more closely with Britain than is correct. There are those histories that say he was born in York, but he was born in eastern Europe, in the province of Moesia, in modern day Bulgaria. He was the illegitimate son of CONSTANTIUS by Flavia Helena, who some claim was a British noblewoman, the daughter of king

COEL, but these stories are all apocryphal. Constantine remained for only a brief time in Britain after the death of his father before moving his base to Gaul. A power struggle continued for some eighteen years before Constantine was at last declared sole emperor of Rome in 324. Nevertheless it was during Constantine's reign that the administrative reforms established by Diocletian (286–305) were implemented in Britain. This established four provinces. The northern province, Britannia Secunda, remained much the same as before, its boundaries set by Hadrian's Wall to the north and a line between the Mersey and the Humber to the south. Its capital was at York. Britannia Prima comprised all of western Britain from Wales down to Devon and Cornwall, including Gloucestershire, Wiltshire, Somerset and Dorset. Its capital was at Cirencester. The remainder was divided approximately in half. Flavia Caesariensis covered the Midlands and Norfolk, with its capital at Lincoln; Maxima Caesariensis covered all of the south-east and what is now called the Home Counties, with its capital in London. Because special coins were minted in about 310 and 315 it has been suggested that Constantine revisited Britain at that time, perhaps to inspect troops and agree the administrative arrangements, but otherwise his subsequent links with Britain were tenuous.

[B56;P92] **CONSTANTINE II** Emperor of Britain and Gaul, 9 September 337– Spring 340. *See* CONSTANS *below for details.* It is this Constantine whom Geoffrey of Monmouth makes the father of CONSTANS, AURELIUS AMBROSIUS and UTHER PENDRAGON and leads us into the legend of ARTHUR.

[B57] **CONSTANS** Emperor of Rome, 9 September 337–January 350.
After the death of CONSTANTINE the Great the Roman Empire was divided between his three sons. Constantine II received Britain, Gaul and Spain, but his greed in conquering the rest of Europe led to his early death in 340, and his younger brother Constans took over all of the western provinces. Constans paid a surprise visit to Britain during the early winter of 343. It is not recorded why, but for an emperor to risk a winter crossing it must have been serious, yet it was apparently not to quell an uprising. The orator Libanius, who recorded the event, stated that the administration in Britain was stable. Constans probably thwarted plans for a rebellion before it happened and the real facts were deliberately silenced. Constans never returned to Britain and was murdered in 350. Geoffrey of Monmouth makes Constans the son of Constantine II who is made king around the year 410 or 420 by VORTIGERN but is soon murdered by Vortigern's agents.

[B64;P88] **MAGNUS *MAXIMUS* or MACSEN *WLEDIG* (*LEADER*) or MAXIMIA-NUS** Emperor of Western Rome (Britain, Spain, Gaul), 25 August 383–28 July 388. The period from 367 to 383 had been an unsettling one in Britain. The island became increasingly subject to attacks, both from Germanic tribes and from Picts and Irish. By 367 the problem was at such a height, with the death of the Roman duke, Fullofaudes, that the emperor Valentinian sent an army into Britain under the command of Theodosius the Elder, a Spanish general. Magnus Maximus, another Spanish soldier, accompanied Theodosius. Within two years Theodosius had brought matters under control and established a new administration. However, the British nobility now felt the poorer, and the strict rule of the young new emperor, Gratian, caused unrest in Britain. In 383 the Roman army in Britain declared Maximus emperor. Maximus had stayed on in Britain after Theodosius's campaign and had established himself with considerable authority and popularity. It is probable that he had attained the title of duke. In 382 he had achieved a strong victory over another uprising of Picts. Within months of the soldiers declaring Maximus emperor, he raised an army and sailed to France where he engaged Gratian in battle outside Paris. After five days Gratian fled. Soldiers caught and killed him at Lyons on 25 August 383, though not under the orders of Maximus. Maximus was rapidly accepted as emperor in the West, a position acknowledged by Theodosius the Younger, who was emperor in the East. Maximus held his court at Trier on the Moselle.

Maximus was clearly a popular emperor, despite the fact that he had to levy high taxes to sustain his army. He was Christian and was highly respected by the Church, though his strict catholic outlook led to him ordering the death of heretics, particularly the Gnostic Priscillianists in Spain. By 386 he became increasingly certain that he needed to move into Italy which nominally was still under the control of the youth Valentinian II. He prepared his way carefully and, by January 388, was successfully installed in Rome. Now feeling under threat Theodosius brought his better trained forces against Maximus who, after a few engagements, was defeated and captured. Although Theodosius was prepared to be lenient, Maximus was killed by a group of soldiers on 28 July 388. His son, Victor, whom he had made Caesar, was captured in Gaul and killed.

Maximus left a remarkable legacy in British folklore. He was readily adopted into the fabric of British history where he became Macsen *Wledig*, the latter a title reserved for a few leaders who emerged from the landed gentry. He is reputed to have married Elen, or Helen, the daughter of Eudaf (or Odes, or OCTAVIUS) the Ruler of the Gewisse in southern Wales, and his own daughter Servia or Severa, married VORTIGERN, the later high king of Britain. Through his children Macsen became credited as the father of the later rulers of Gwent and Glamorgan, including ERB and the fabled ARTHUR, and Britain's first high king, OWAIN. Such was the impact of Maximus's achievement in attaining the throne of Rome, that many British rulers endeavoured to claim descent from him. What is uncertain now is how many of these genealogies are rigged or whether there is some essence of truth. Maximus did live in Britain for sixteen years before being raised to the Purple, and he was evidently extremely popular.

The legacy of Maximus's campaign was, however, to weaken an already weakening Britain. Although he did not withdraw all the forces from the island, he certainly withdrew a substantial number. There is no doubt that as a seasoned campaigner he would not have left the island undefended, and this is probably where the origins of other royal families arose. It is probable that Maximus installed some strong commanders in the territory between the Hadrianic and Antonine Walls who became the forebears of later rulers. These would include Quintilius, or Cinhil, the grandfather of CERETIC of Alclud, and Padarn of the Red Cloak, grandfather of CUNEDDA. It is also possible that Maximus established the arrangement of a strong Irish leadership, under EOCHAID in Demetia (south-west Wales), and the colony of Britons in Armorica (Brittany) in Northern France. His period as emperor was brief, but his impact on the emerging kingships in Britain was considerable.

[B66] **EUGENIUS** Emperor in Britain and Gaul, 392–394.

In the years after the death of MAGNUS MAXIMUS, the young emperor Valentinian II sought to regain power, but he soon met his death, probably by order of Arbogast, a military commander who then set himself up as king in Gaul. Arbogast raised a colleague, Eugenius, an administrator and former teacher of rhetoric, to be emperor in the West. Eugenius was really only a puppet ruler; Arbogast was the man with the power. Arbogast was also a pagan, allowing pagan practices to flourish again in Britain and Gaul. It is certain that neither Arbogast nor Eugenius ever came to Britain, but later tradition has made Eugenius, OWAIN, the son of Magnus Maximus. Since Maximus's family were living in Gaul during his emperorship, the connection is tempting. Within two years, though, Eugenius was defeated in battle against Theodosius and executed.

[B68] **MARCUS** Emperor in Britain, 406.

By the start of the fifth century Roman authority at the borders of its empire was crumbling, and the armies at the frontier occasionally raised their own officials as emperors. This practice was especially prevalent in Britain, but seldom successful. Marcus was one of the least successful. Toward the end of 406, when the Germanic hordes had crossed the Rhine and were invading the Empire, the British declared a Roman official, Marcus, as emperor. However, they soon found he was not the man they expected and murdered him within a matter of weeks.

[B69] **GRATIAN** Emperor in Britain, January-May 407.

Soon after the murder of Marcus, the British raised a second official to the Purple. This was Gratian, who was a Briton, and probably a senior nobleman from one of the local royal families. However, he too was found wanting and after four months he was murdered, probably in May 407. Their third attempt was slightly more successful with CONSTANTINE III.

[B70] **CONSTANTINE III** Emperor of Britain and Gaul, 407–411.

After the soldiers had raised MARCUS and Gratian to the authority of emperor and then just as quickly despatched them, it would have needed a strong and ambitious man to take on that responsibility. But in Constantine they found just that man. It was becoming apparent that in seeking their own emperor the British had some design on taking over the whole Roman Empire (or at least the Empire in the West) rather than see its destruction by the Germanic armies which, at the close of 406, had crossed the Rhine and were laying claim to Gaul. That may have been a long term ambition, but in the immediate future Britain had need to defend itself. Constantine rapidly established defences in Britain, and then crossed into Gaul, rebuilding the Roman defences and guarding the passes. In 408, he established his authority over Spain. By 409 Honorius, the emperor in Rome, was forced to recognize Constantine as Augustus. Constantine established his capital at Arles.

The next twelve months, however, saw everything fall apart. Honorius, at one point prepared to make a deal with the Visigoth king Alaric whose forces now controlled Gaul, changed his mind, and in 410 Alaric entered and sacked Rome. Seeing the change in fortune, Gerontius, Constantine's general, changed allegiances and raised a further general, Maximus, as a rival emperor. Their forces gained Spain and parts of Gaul, and Constantine found himself besieged in Arles. Cut off from

Britain he was unable to protect the island. The British nobility wrote to Honorius seeking help against the barbarians, but Honorius had enough problems of his own and his response was to tell the British to defend themselves. The British took this as an opportunity to rid themselves of Roman officials, many of whom left the island, with cohorts of the army, to Gaul and Spain. Constantine was abandoned and, a few

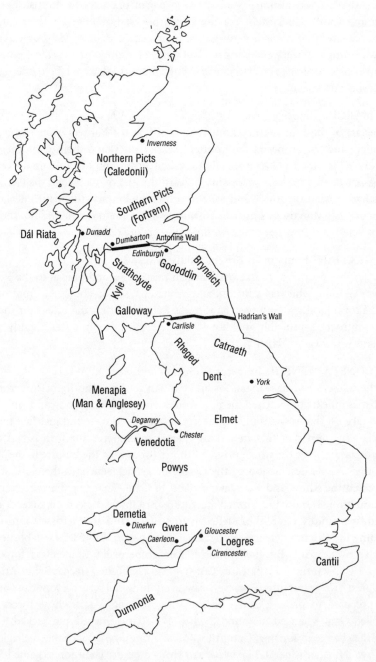

Map 3 **The emerging Post-Roman Kingdoms**

months later he surrendered and was executed on 18 September 411. He was the last Roman to rule Britain.

British tradition has made something more of Constantine. He was the brother of Alan, king of Brittany and grandson of EUDAF, the father-in-law of MAGNUS MAXIMUS. He was apparently proclaimed king of the British soon after Maximus's death in 388, and it was as king that he led the Romano-British forces into Gaul in 407. This is within the realms of possibility and provides a reason for the selection of Constantine, but the evidence is thin.

D. THE BRITISH KINGDOMS

DA. NORTHERN BRITAIN (from Yorkshire to the Clyde)

As Britain emerged from the Roman Empire it fell to the leading noblemen and generals to maintain law and order. A number of leaders began to establish themselves in various corners of Britain The first were along the northern frontier, where Coel the Old carved out a kingdom ruled by "the Men of the North". Their domain stretched from the northernmost Roman wall (that of Antoninus Pius) down to what is now Yorkshire. After Coel's death his kingdom was split between his descendants and it rapidly sub-divided, weakening the realm. The kingdoms were gradually reduced by the Saxons, although the British kingdom of Strathclyde survived much longer as a unit, and is treated separately on page 183. It is difficult to be clear about who ruled which kingdom so the following covers all the known Men of the North in as close chronological sequence as possible along with their likely territories. Map 3 shows the approximate location of these kingdoms.

Ref.	Ruler	Born	Reign	Died	Notes
DA1.	Coel *Hen* ("Old King Cole")		c410–c430	c430	all of northern Britain; see P84
DA2.	Tutagual		fl 400–c420s		Galloway and Kyle
DA3.	Garbaniawn or Germanianus		c430s–c450s		southern Votadini (Bryneich)
DA4.	Cunedda		c420–c450		northern Votadini (Gododdin); moved to North Wales, see ED1 on page 141
DA5.	Ceneu or Cenen (also Keneu)		fl 450s–470s	c470s	Rheged and Catraeth (equal to Cumbria and York)
DA6.	Ceretic		fl 450s–470s		Strathclyde, see FB1 on page 183
DA7.	Lewdwn or Leudonus		fl 470s–490s		northern Votadini
DA8.	Gurgust		fl 480s–500s	c500s	Rheged
DA9.	Bran *Hen* (*the Old*)		fl 500s		Votadini (may be Gododdin and Bryneich)
DA10.	Pabo or Pappo		fl 500s–c530	c530	central Yorkshire
DA11.	Morcant *Bulc*		fl 510s–540s		Votadini
DA12.	Cathen		fl 510s–540s		Galloway and Kyle
DA13.	Merchiaun *Gul*		fl 510s–540s	c540s	Rheged

2. Celts (2) – Men of the North

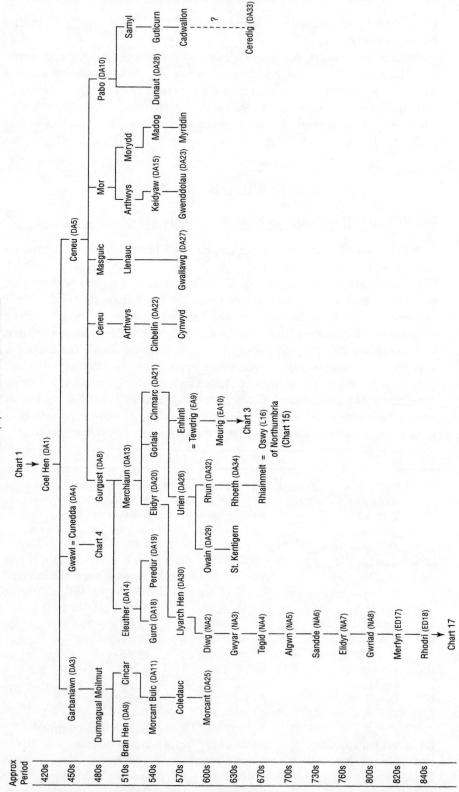

Ref.	Ruler	Born	Reign	Died	Notes
DA14.	Eleuther or Elidyr		*fl* 530s–550s	*c*550s	Catraeth and York; murdered
DA15.	Ceidiaw or Keidyaw		*fl* 540s–550s		Galloway or Rheged?
DA16.	Rhun		*fl* 550s–560s		Galloway and Kyle; lost kingdom to rulers of Rheged
DA17.	Outigern		*fl* 540s–550s		Votadini
DA18.	Gwrgi or Gurci		*fl* 550s–580	580	Catraeth/York; killed in battle
DA19.	Peredur		*fl* 550s–580	580	Catraeth/York; killed in battle
DA20.	Elidyr		*fl* 540s–*c*560	*c*560	Rheged; killed on a raid
DA21.	Cinmarc or Kynmarch		*fl* 560s–*c*570	*c*570	Rheged
DA22.	Cinbelin or Kynvelin		*fl* 540s–570s		northern Votadini
DA23.	Gwenddolau		*fl* 560s–570s	573	Galloway; killed in battle
DA24.	Clinog or Clydno *Eitin*		*fl* 560s–580s		northern Votadini
DA25.	Morcant		*fl* 580s–590s		Votadini?
DA26.	Urien or Urbgen	*c*540	*c*570–*c*590	*c*590	Rheged
DA27.	Gwallawg		*fl* 570s–590s	*c*595	Elmet; though this name may also apply to a ruler of Galloway and the Clyde
DA28.	Dunaut		*fl* 570s–595	595	central Yorkshire
DA29.	Owain		*c*590–*c*595	*c*595	Rheged
DA30.	Llywarch *Hen*		*c*560–595	640	retired to Powys
DA31.	Mynyddog or Mynydawc		580s–595		northern Votadini
DA32.	Rhun		*fl* 600s	*c*630	Rheged; retired to the priesthood
DA33.	Ceredig		*c*595–625	*c*625	Elmet; expelled; see P103
DA34.	Rhoeth		*fl* 620s		Rheged

[DA1;P84] **COEL *HEN* (THE OLD)** Ruler of the northern Britons, *c*410s-*c*430s
Whether the nursery rhyme about Old King Cole has any connection with the real
King Coel is unlikely, but that a real King Coel existed is indisputable, although
records of him survive only from later songs and genealogies. He was almost
certainly a native Briton whose forebears had probably been high-ranking individuals amongst the Romano-British nobility. He was likely to be either from the
British tribe of the Brigantes or, more likely, the Votadini. In the late fourth century
and early fifth century the northern frontier of the Roman empire, which had
retrenched along Hadrian's Wall, came under fierce attack from the Picts to the
north. Following the withdrawal of support from Rome in 410, the British were left
to fend for themselves. In such events leaders emerge, and it was under these
circumstances that Coel emerged. Whether he was a *dux bellorum*, as John Morris
has suggested, is not proven, but there is little doubt that he met the need for strong
leadership to protect the northern British against the Picts as well as from incursions
by the Irish who, over the last century, had made regular forays into the Galloway
territory of what is now Scotland. Coel has become the name associated with

whichever leader first took control during this period of considerable unrest. Gildas and others record this as a period of civil wars, invasions and ultimately famine. It lasted for about a generation from some time after 410 to around 450. That period also saw the arrival of Saxons or other Germanic adventurers who probably came as mercenaries to help in Coel's army rather than as invaders. Some may have received land in payment. It has been conjectured that HENGEST's lieutenant OISC (sometimes described as his son) could have been the leader of these Germans, perhaps of a second and more significant wave that came across in the 440s or 470s.

The extent of Coel's "kingdom" is uncertain. It is possible that it extended as far south as York, perhaps to a line between the Humber and the Mersey, and possibly as far north as the Antonine Wall between the Forth and the Clyde. This is a vast territory, too much for one man to govern, and covering more than one tribe. Coel would almost certainly have appointed a number of commanders, perhaps the leaders of the individual tribes. Whether or not these were related to him as later genealogies suggest can neither be proved nor disproved. One son, GARBANIAWN (or Germanianus), ruled the southern Votadini, the territory known to the British as Bryneich, which became Bernicia under the Angles. Coel's son-in-law, CUNEDDA, ruled the territory of the northern Votadini, also known as the Gododdin, a realm later known as Lothian (from the ruler Lewdwn or LEUDONUS). Another son, Cenen or CENEU, seems to have taken command of the lands south of Bryneich, around York, firmly in the territory of the eastern Brigantes, which later became known as Deira but at this time probably known as Catraeth. To the west was CERETIC who commanded the territory of the Clyde, including Galloway and probably down into Cumbria, the territory of the Novantae and Selgovae. It is difficult to say for sure how definite these commands were. Coel might have moved his commanders about or, more likely, perhaps during or soon after his death the old tribal enmities returned with leaders fighting for supremacy. Whatever the case, their final power bases almost certainly formed the core of later (mostly short-lived) British kingdoms. Coel's own headquarters are variously stated as being at York or in the area around Ayr, which is now called Kyle, possibly named after him. Coel seems to have dominated this area for perhaps twenty years, possibly up until the year 430 or beyond. One legend has it that he died fighting the Irish near Ayr.

There is certainly no truth in the stories perpetuated by Geoffrey of Monmouth that Coel was the duke of Colchester, and that his daughter Helena married the Roman emperor CONSTANTIUS. It seems that Colchester later adopted Coel as its own patron, because of the similarity of names. It is true that later generations of rulers in northern Britain claimed themselves as "sons of Coel". Whether this was literal, or whether it meant they had inherited the lands that he ruled, we cannot be sure. The most famous amongst them are DUMNAGUAL (or Dyfnwal), MORCANT, ELEUTHER, PEREDUR and PABO.

[DA2] **TUTAGUAL (I)** Galloway, *fl* 400–c420s. The earliest reference to Tutagual, known as Tuduvallus to the Romans, is in the *Life of St Ninian* written by Abbott Aelred in 1165. According to Aelred, when Ninian returned to Rheged in around 390 he established a church at Whithorn in Galloway. Soon after he was able to cure the local king, Tuduvallus, who had been smitten with blindness because of his haughty and evil ways. Thereafter he was converted to Christianity.

[DA3] **GARBANIAWN** or **GERMANIANUS** Ruler of the southern Votadini, in Bryneich around c430s to 450s. The later genealogies treat him as the son of COEL and the father of Dumnagual *Moilmut*. Nothing more is known about either of them, but it is likely that their main fort was at Bamburgh, and that most of their lives would have been spent in fighting the Picts and the increasing onslaught of the Angles and Saxons who began to harry the eastern coasts during Garbaniawn's reign. He may be the same as Geoffrey of Monmouth's Gorbonianus, whom he records as a benign and peaceful king.

[DA4] **CUNEDDA** Ruler of northern Britain but subsequently founder of the Venedotian kingdom of Gwynedd. *See full entry under Gwynedd on page 141.*

[DA5] **CENEU** or **CENEN** Ruler of the southern Votadini or of the Brigantes in Yorkshire, probably 450s to 470s. It may have been him who faced the settlement of Deira by SOEMIL. *See under* AELLE *and* COEL HEN *for details.*

[DA6] **CERETIC** Founder of the dynasty of Strathclyde. *See full entry on page 183.*

[DA7] **LEUDONUS** A ruler of the northern Votadini, south of Edinburgh, in the final decades of the fifth century. His capital was at Traprain Law. His name, which is also rendered as Lewdwn in Celtic, may have given itself to the district of Lothian. He was probably the original of the Arthurian King Lot. Certainly their dates would overlap. In one story ARTHUR helped Lot regain his kingdom, although in the main legend Lot was one of the rulers who was openly against Arthur. There is almost certainly a core of truth here of dispossessed warrior lords forming alliances to regain their kingdoms. Leudonus may well have had clashes with the dynasty of MORCANT who seems to have established himself in the area in later years. Leudonus is also recorded as the grandfather of St Kentigern.

[DA8] **GURGUST** *THE RAGGED* Rheged, *fl* 480s–500s.
Gurgust, which is a Latinised spelling of GWRGI, is listed in the genealogies as a grandson of COEL and the great-grandfather of URIEN. In the great upheaval of the century after Roman rule, it seems likely that Gurgust inherited most of the Brigantian territory from his father Ceneu, particularly the area of Rheged and the west, though it seems that the central part of the territory went to his brother PABO.

[DA9] **BRAN** *HEN* (**the** *OLD*) Chieftain of the Votadini, *fl* 500s. Bran's name is recorded amongst the genealogies of the Men of the North and it is likely that he ruled the area of the Votadini soon after LEUDONUS. From his nickname, "the Old", we must assume that he was either old when he became chieftain, or succeeded in surviving for longer than most during these turbulent times. That suggests that he came to some agreement with the Angles, who by now were settling along the eastern coastline and Bran's time may therefore have been one of relative calm. Since his reign would coincide with that of the legendary ARTHUR, he may well have been part of that period of prosperity.

[DA10] **PABO** or **PAPPO** central Yorkshire, *fl* early 500s.
Pabo was the brother of GURGUST and the grandson of COEL. He was called "the Pillar of Britain" which presumably means he was a strength to the British in the dark days of invasion from the Picts, Irish and Saxons, as well as the in-fighting

between the British tribes. Just where he ruled is not entirely clear. It has been suggested that he controlled the Pennines throughout Yorkshire, though it has also been suggested that he ventured west into Rheged and may have controlled parts of Cumbria. In all probability Pabo controlled central Brigantia whilst Gurgust controlled the west. Although he divided his territories between his sons DUNAUT and Samyl, it seems that his nephew, MERCHIAUN, must have taken over Cumbria. The dating of Pabo is difficult. His son, Dunaut, is recorded in the *Welsh Annals* as dying in 595, and he was also present at the Battle of Arthuret in 573. Assuming that Dunaut was probably then in his thirties, would suggest that Pabo lived from around 510 to 550. However, if he were genuinely the grandson of Coel, who is traditionally dated to around the year 430, Pabo's father CENEU would have lived probably from around 430–480, which would place Pabo into the period roughly 460–520. He has been associated with the Welsh saint Pabo who died in about 530 and who is buried at Llanbabo in Anglesey. It is possible that Pabo retired there in his old age, perhaps in his sixties.

[DA11] **MORCANT *BULC*** seems to have ruled the Votadini, south of Edinburgh in the early years of the sixth century. The name means "defender at the sea edge" and is the ideal name for the rulers along the cliff forts of north-east Britain. The genealogies show him as descending from Germanianus, the son of COEL, though this may not be a direct descent. He probably ruled a tribe who had some authority down the north-east coast of England, perhaps north of the Tyne, in the territory which became Bernicia. His nickname means "lightning", which suggests he may have been a warlord with an ability to strike fast in raids and battles. Bulc was a proud and well established nickname amongst the Celts, and comes from the same word as the name of the tribe Belgae.

[DA12] **CATHEN** Galloway and Kyle, *fl* 510s–540s.
Recorded as the grandson of TUTAGUAL and probably a cousin of the ruler of Alclud (*see* RHYDDERCH). The name Cathen appears in the *Life of St Kentigern* as the military adviser of King Morken (*see* MORCANT) of Cambria. This may be the same person. It is possible that Morcant overran Galloway and Cathen became his vassal king. Cathen's dynasty was soon lost to history as it appears that his grandson, RHUN lost the territory to the rulers of Rheged, most likely in conflict with GWENDDOLAU.

[DA13] **MERCHIAUN *GUL* (the *LEAN*)** Rheged, *fl* 510s–540s.
Merchiaun appears in the old genealogies of the Men of the North as the son of GURGUST and brother of ELEUTHER. He may well be the same as the elder MORCANT of the Votadini, although they are shown as cousins. We may imagine that there was considerable territorial conflict between the descendants of COEL as old tribal rivalries erupted. Merchiaun seems to have carved out for himself a kingdom in southern Cumbria, south of Carlisle, including what is now the Lake District and parts of Lancashire. This would have brought him into conflict with PABO and his son DUNAUT. Merchiaun's kingdom became one of the most powerful of the North, particularly under Merchiaun's grandson URIEN. He was succeeded by his son ELIDYR.

[DA14] **ELEUTHER** or **ELIDYR** Catraeth and York, *fl* 530s–550s.
There were two kings of the North with this name. Although the names are the same (the Roman and Celtic equivalents) over the years they have become known

separately in order to avoid confusion (*see* ELIDYR). Eleuther (also known as Eliffer) was the son of GURGUST. In the inter-dynastic rivalries amongst the sons and successors of COEL in the fifth and sixth centuries, Eleuther seems to have inherited or claimed the lands around York and Catraeth (modern Catterick). He is known as "Eleuther of the Great Army", from which we can presume he was a powerful defender of his lands, particularly against the increasing waves of Angles who were settling in Northumbria in the mid sixth century (see IDA and AELLE). Eleuther was father of PEREDUR.

Geoffrey of Monmouth must have detected a whiff of these historical facts in his own *History* although they got lost beneath the delight of his own imagination. His Elidurus the Dutiful was one of the five sons of the heroic and unfortunate Morvidus, who was killed by a sea-monster. His eldest son, Gorbonianus, was a benign king under whose reign Britain prospered, but after his death his brother, Archgallo was a tyrant. He was deposed and his brother Elidurus made king in his place. After five years Elidurus encountered Archgallo wandering lost in the forests of the north and he forced his nobles to swear allegiance to Archgallo and accept him again as their king. Archgallo was a changed man and ruled wisely for ten years from his kingdom at York. After his death Elidurus returned to the throne but now faced an insurrection from his younger brothers Ingenius and PEREDURUS who dethroned Elidurus, imprisoned him in London, and then shared the kingdom between them. Ingenius died seven years later and Peredurus ruled alone, a good king who was fondly remembered. After his death, Elidurus was released and restored to the throne. He must by now have been very old. He was succeeded by an unnamed nephew, and thereafter Geoffrey rattles through the names of over thirty kings, few of whom are known amongst the historical records, although the much later ruler Samuil was probably his cousin SAMWL. The fact that Geoffrey has Elidurus ruling from York rather than London suggests he was basing him upon the real king of this name.

[DA15] **CEIDIAW** Galloway and Kyle (?), *fl* 540s–550s.
Ceidiaw (or Keidyaw) is remembered only as the father of GWENDDOLAU. We may presume that he helped conquer the lands around Galloway and Kyle, and possibly into northern Rheged sometime in the middle of the sixth century. He may have usurped the kingdom of RHUN. It is interesting to speculate whether he was the origin of either Geoffrey of Monmouth's Cador of Cornwall or of the legendary ARTHUR's seneschal Cei or Kay.

[DA16] **RHUN** Galloway and Kyle *fl* 550s–560s.
Rhun or Rhain is the name of several British and Welsh princes. It seems to be related to the Irish *Rón* meaning "seal" and the Norse *Ragn* meaning "counsel", both names referring to the holder's wisdom and authority. This Rhun was the grandson of CATHEN, descended from DUMNAGUAL and related to the rulers of Strathclyde. Little is known of him except that he was the loser in the battle for his territories which passed to CEIDIAW and his son GWENDDOLAU.

[DA17] **OUTIGERN** Votadini and Bryneich, *fl* 540s–550s.
The similarity between the words Outigern and VORTIGERN may suggest it is a title rather than a personal name. The only reference to Outigern is in the chronicles of

Nennius, where he states that in the first half of the sixth century Outigern fought bravely against the English. The Angles were then settling along the north-east coast and a strong colony already existed in Bernicia under IDA. We may deduce that after Ida deposed the native chieftain MORCANT, who went on to carve out a kingdom to the west, Outigern took over as chief of the British in Bernicia. His fate is not known, but it is likely he died in battle. The struggle against the English was continued by first PEREDUR of York, and then URIEN and OWAIN of Rheged.

[DA18] **GWRGI** or **GURCI** Catraeth and York (?), *fl* 560s–580s.
Gwrgi was the son of ELEUTHER and brother of PEREDUR. The two brothers may have either jointly ruled, or split their kingdom, in which case Gwrgi almost certainly inherited the lands around Catraeth (modern Catterick). The two brothers are always recorded together and are reckoned amongst the last defenders of the British against the invading Angles in north-eastern Britain.

[DA19] **PEREDUR** York, *fl* 560s–580.
Peredur was one of the great heroes of the north, in the battles between the British and the invading Angles. His exploits passed into the legends around king ARTHUR, and his name later became inextricably linked with that of Sir Perceval. The real Peredur was the son of ELEUTHER and brother of GWRGI. Eleuther seems to have established a strong kingdom in the territory around York, and with his sons developed one of the stronger defences against the Angles, who had been invading and settling in Northumbria since the middle of the sixth century (*see* AELLE *and* IDA). The brothers also had to face expansion from British opportunists who were fighting over their own territories in northern Britain in the lands either side of Hadrian's wall. In the century since the death of COEL only a few strong kings had emerged with sufficient authority to sustain and develop their lands. In most cases the kings were "tyrants", as later chroniclers recalled them, leaders of war-bands who took what lands they might and, in the absence of money, traded in people. The slave trade between northern Britain and Ireland was what so angered St Patrick (*see* CERETIC). Peredur was one of the stronger kings who sought to establish authority and a rule of law across northern Britain. He was thwarted in his plans firstly by the renegade chieftain GWENDDOLAU. His father, CEIDIAW, had invaded northern Rheged and the lands around Galloway, and seemed to be expanding into the territory of the Brigantes. Peredur and Gwrgi faced Gwenddolau and defeated him at the famous battle of Arfderydd, also known as Arthuret, which is dated to 573AD (though there is no reason to presume that date is wholly accurate). Defending their territories on both flanks must have been very difficult to Peredur and Gwrgi, and serves to emphasise what strong rulers they were. However they met their fate in 580 when they marched against the army of the Angles in Bernicia at Caer Greu, an unidentified site. Both Peredur and Gwrgi were killed. Peredur's son, Gwgaun, who may also have fought in the battle and survived, is recorded as not taking up his inheritance. He may well have fled to any of the remaining British kingdoms, possibly either Rheged or Elmet, but his fate is not known. After Peredur's death, York came under the rule of the Angles.

The Arthurian Peredur has become so entwined with the story of the Holy Grail that it is difficult to sift out any genuine historical facts about him. Geoffrey of Monmouth lists the rule of a Peredurus in his *History*, although places the king to at least 200 or even 300BC. In his story Peredurus is the brother of Elidurus whom he deposes, ruling benignly in his stead, so much so that he was the best remembered of the sons of Morvidus. The general feeling remains that Peredur was revered as a strong king and one of the last great defenders of Britain. *See also* PEREDUR *of Dumnonia, page 118.*

[DA20] **ELIDYR** or **ELEUTHER** *THE HANDSOME* Rheged and/or Man, *fl* 540s–*c*560.

Elidyr was the son of MERCHIAUN who became king of Rheged some time in the mid sixth century. He almost certainly also inherited the kingdom of the Isle of Man, though it is possible that he ruled only Man, and that the kingdom of Rheged was divided between him and his brother CINMARC. Elidyr had married the sister of RHUN, king of Gwynedd, whose capital was on the Isle of Anglesey. The islands of Man and Anglesey have long been regarded as part of a single unit, known as the Mevanian Islands to the Romans, and probably inhabited by related Celtic tribes since before the Roman conquest. On the death of MAELGWYN, Elidyr believed he had a claim on Anglesey and so invaded the island in about 560. He was killed in the conflict. His brother Cinmarc and other kings of the North raided Anglesey in revenge for Elidyr's death, but this only angered Rhun more who marched on the northern Britons to teach them a lesson which they never forgot. Elidyr should not be confused with his namesake who is usually called ELEUTHER.

[DA21] **CINMARC** or **KYNMARCH** Rheged, *fl* 560s–*c*570s.

The son of MERCHIAUN and the father of URIEN. We can imagine that in Cinmarc's time, if not earlier, the rulers of Rheged established an overlordship of the Isle of Man. Cinmarc is known to have had a substantial fleet of ships for in around the year 560 he and his contemporaries, RHYDDERCH and CLYDNO, raided Anglesey in revenge for the death of his brother ELIDYR at the hands of the Welsh king RHUN. They did a lightning strike and returned, but this incurred the wrath of Rhun whose march across north England in revenge passed into legend.

[DA22] **CINBELIN** or **KYNVELIN** Goddodin, *fl* 540s–570s.

Cinbelin (the name is a variant of Cunobelinus or Cymbeline) was the son of DUMNAGUAL. After his father's death, Cinbelin established himself in the territory of the Goddodin amongst the northern Votadini, with his base at Traprain Law near Dunbar. He apparently inherited the major part of his father's army which was probably required on the eastern front to combat the growing number of Angles establishing themselves in Bernicia, and the consequence of the infighting amongst the ejected Britons, led by MORCANT. One ancient chronicle suggests that Cinbelin was a Brigantian chieftain who took an army north and imposed himself upon the Votadini. If this is true then the genealogies must be wrong. There is probably just enough weight of evidence to favour the genealogies. Cinbelin's son, CLYDNO, further established himself as a force amongst the Goddodin.

[DA23] **GWENDDOLAU** Galloway and northern Rheged, 560s–573.

Gwenddolau was the son of CEIDIAW, one of a number of renegade chieftains who sought to gain land for themselves amongst the emerging kingdoms of northern Britain, particularly the land between the Walls. Gwenddolau's campaign was eventually thwarted by a confederate army led by PEREDUR of York who defeated and killed Gwenddolau at the battle of Arfderydd or Arthuret, north of Carlisle, in about the year 573. What has kept Gwenddolau's name alive is the name of his court adviser, Myrddin or Merlin. Merlin is supposed to have gone mad with grief after his lord's death and fled into the Caledonian forest where he lived like a wild animal.

[DA24] **CLYDNO (or CLINOG)** *EITIN* Votadini, *fl* 560s–580s.
Clydno succeeded his father, CINBELIN, as ruler of the Gododdin, acquiring the name *Eiten* (Edinburgh) to distinguish him from his uncle, CLYDNO, who was ruling Alclud, at the other end of the Antonine Wall. Clydno appears as an ally of RHYDDERCH (who was his cousin's son) against the rebellious dynasty of MORCANT and his sons. Clydno was also involved in the expedition led by Rhydderch with CINMARC of Rheged against RHUN of Gwynedd. Though they scored an initial success, Rhun's remarkable march against the northern Britains in about the year 560 put a stop to any ambitions they had in that direction. Soon afterward, their energies were directed towards stemming the invasion of the Angles along the north-east coast of Britain. It is not clear what the relationship is between Clydno and Mynyddog *Mwynfawr*, who seems to have succeeded him. At this time the kingdom of the Gododdin became suffocated by the Bernician kingdom under ATHELRIC.

[DA25] **MORCANT** If the genealogies are correct this ruler was the grandson of Morcant *Bulc*, and lived in the latter half of the sixth century. He is probably the same as the avaricious king Morken who appears in Jocelyne's *Life of St Kentigern* and who is described as ruling the Cambrian kingdom in the territory of the Clyde in the early years of Kentigern's ministry, around the 580s. Morken had probably expanded the kingdom of his grandfather so that it stretched between the Votadini of Edinburgh across to the territory of the Alclud. This would have brought him into conflict with URIEN of Rheged which resulted in Morcant killing Urien. There does not seem to have been any retribution for this unless we read something more into the legends of St Kentigern. Kentigern had asked Morken for provender for the new community he had established at Glasgow. Morken refused saying that, if Kentigern's god was so powerful, He could provide. Following Kentigern's prayers the river Clyde flooded destroying all of Morken's corn. Morken was furious and determined to expel Kentigern from his lands, but he seems to have been smitten with some ailment of the foot from which he died, and which plagued his descendants thereafter. The relationship between Urien and Morcant has caused some commentators to speculate that Morcant may be the original of Mordred whose similar lust for revenge and power resulted in the death of ARTHUR.

[DA26] **URIEN** Rheged, *c*570–590.
Urien is one of the better attested rulers of the North Britons in the period between the end of the Roman Empire in Britain and the emergence of the Saxon kingdoms of England. He ruled the territory known as Rheged, which equates roughly to Cumbria and Lancashire and possibly part of Galloway. Urien inherited the kingdom from CINMARC around the year 570, probably just after the battle of Arthuret in which the northern renegade GWENDDOLAU was killed. Urien is not specifically named as being at that battle, and he may therefore have benefited from the victory of PEREDUR, DUNAUT and his father Cinmarc. This gave Urien authority over the region north of Carlisle into the old kingdom of Galloway. This brought

him into conflict with the expansionist regime of MORCANT of the Votadini, who had been expelled from his lands to the east by the Angles of Bernicia and was carving out for himself a kingdom south of the Clyde.

In 580, or soon after, the Angles defeated and killed PEREDUR of York and his brother leaving the old British kingdoms of York and Catraeth exposed. The main conflict was with THEODORIC of Bernicia. Urien appears to have recovered the lands of Catraeth, around Catterick and Richmond, but was then defeated by Theodoric and had to seek refuge back in his homeland. It seems that Urien then succeeded in convincing the other British kings RHYDDERCH, GWALLAWG and Morcant to forget their differences and unite to defend their lands against the Angles. A vast confederate army swept across the Cheviots and down on the Angles. Although their main fort was at Bamburgh, the focus of the ensuing battle was on the headland opposite Lindisfarne, where Urien and his army succeeded in trapping the English on the island. The weight of the siege went in favour of the British and the Bernicians were nearly annihilated. However, during the siege, one of Morcant's men, called Lovan, slew Urien. The motive was probably jealousy. Bamburgh was the site of Morcant's original kingdom and it seemed he wanted the victory and the spoils to be his. Unfortunately with the death of Urien the strength evaporated from the army and they departed, even on the edge of victory. Urien's battle was continued by his son OWAIN.

Urien was so famous in his day that his exploits have been compared with those of King ARTHUR. Like Arthur he commanded forces who fought the Picts and Saxons. Like Arthur his kingdom was regarded as one of plenty where no man suffered. There are those that believe Urien was the original Arthur. His adventures form part of the later Arthurian legends, where he appears as the husband of Morgan Le Fay. Urien's family is also well remembered. His sister, called variously Enhinti or Efrddf, who may have been a twin, reputedly married king TEWDRIG of Gwent and was the mother of King MEURIG. In addition to his successor, Owain, Urien was the father of Rhun, who entered the Celtic church and is recorded as baptising EDWIN of Northumbria during his exile in Powys. Interestingly, although the genealogies list Urien's grandfather as MERCHIAUN, tradition also cites his mother's father as BRYCHAN who was the founding ruler of Breichiniog. There probably were considerable links between the British of the North and the British of Wales during the fifth and sixth centuries, which were, however, severed (other than by sea) once the English kingdoms established themselves across the north and in the Midlands. Urien's cousin LLYWARCH, who briefly ruled part of southern Rheged early in Urien's career went into self-imposed exile in Wales and became renowned as a poet.

[DA27] **GWALLAWG or GUALLANC** Elfed or Elmet, *fl* 570s–590s.
Gwallawg is usually identified as a king of Elmet in the late sixth century who allied with URIEN of Rheged, RHYDDERCH of Alclud and MORCANT of Galloway in their desperate stand against the Angles settled in Bernicia. Elmet was a small British kingdom at the southern end of the Pennines, near Leeds, and thus would have formed an enclave to the south of Rheged, and perhaps part of the kingdom established by Samwl son of PABO in the 550s or 560s. However, the genealogies show Gwallawg as a son of Llenauc, whose name was the origin of Lennox in the

area north of the Clyde. There was a Gwallawg or Gwallauc recorded as a "judge", presumably ruler, of the area known as Elvet near Stirling. Since the Gwallawg who joined forces with Urien and Rhydderch had a fleet of ships, he is much more likely to have been the ruler of Stirling than Leeds. Gwallawg was at the seige of Lindisfarne in 590 but, after the death of Urien, joined with Urien's enemies to try and destroy his sons and his kingdom. Gwallawg's fate is not known but he is likely to have been killed by OWAIN, Urien's son, soon after.

[DA28] **DUNAUT** *the STOUT* Pennines and central Brigantia, *fl* 570s–595.
Dunaut was the son of PABO and great-grandson of COEL, if we can trust the ancient genealogies. On the basis that Dunaut lent his name to the territory around Dent in the Yorkshire Dales, we may believe that he inherited that part of his father's domain. He is identified as fighting alongside his cousins PEREDUR and GWRGI against GWENDDOLAU at the battle of Arthuret in 573. The *Welsh Annals* record his death in the year 595. Both these dates are very late for someone recorded as only three generations removed from COEL, so we must assume that a generation or two are missing. His family fled to Powys where his son, Deiniol, founded the monastery at Bangor. Another of Dunaut's sons is believed to be the bard Aneirin.

[DA29] **OWAIN** MAP **URIEN** Rheged, *c*590–*c*595.
Owain was the son and successor of Urien who took over after his father's treacherous murder while fighting the Angles of Bernicia. Owain continued the battle against THEODORIC and his successor ATHELRIC. He allied himself with the Gododdin king MYNYDDOG and together they sought to reunite a confederate British army to defeat the Bernicians. The resultant host, which numbered in its thousands (some records say tens of thousands) met the English under ATHELFRITH at Catraeth (Catterick) in 595, give or take a year. The result was total annihilation for the British. Even allowing for poetic licence the later ballad of the battle, which cites there was only one survivor amongst the British, indicates how total the victory was for the English. Owain fell in the battle and with his death the kingdom of Rheged was extinguished. Owain's uncle LLYWARCH retired to live in Powys as a court poet where Owain's own brother, Rhun also settled as a priest. Owain is remembered in Arthurian legend as Sir Yvain, though his adventures there have little relation to his harsh struggle for British survival.

[DA30;NA1] **LLYWARCH** *HEN* Rheged and Man, *c*560–595.
Llywarch was the son of ELIDYR who was killed in about the year 560. It is not clear how old Llywarch was at this time. He may still have been a youth. Elidyr had married the daughter of MAELGWYN of Gwynedd, so it is possible that Llywarch was Maelgwyn's grandson and related to the royal family of Gwynedd and Powys. Although he succeeded to the kingdom of Rheged it is unclear exactly where the boundaries of his territory were. It is possible that he governed southern Rheged whilst his uncle CINMARC and cousin URIEN ruled northern Rheged. His authority may also have extended to the Isle of Man, though this was conquered by Aedán of Dál Riata in 582. Cinmarc may, in any case, have ruled until Llywarch came of age. Llywarch may later have settled into a role as vassal king once Urien came to power. He was more of a scholar and poet than a ruler and it seems that once the power of Rheged waned after the death of Urien and later Owain, Llywarch retired to his

relatives in Powys, in North Wales, where he was court poet. He is said to have lived to a great age, dying perhaps as late as 640 when he must have been well into his nineties. It is probable that he died earlier but that his name lived on amongst other court poets who may have used his name on their work. Llywarch's poetry, or least what can be attributed to him, included tributes to Urien, and a lament upon the deaths of Llywarch's own sons in battles against the Angles. Llywarch's descendants are supposed to have ruled Man (see DIWG).

[DA31] **MYNYDDOG or MYNYDAWC *MWYNFAWR* (*the RICH*)** Gododdin, 580s–595.
Mynyddog was one of the last great rulers of the Men of the North to muster an army against the Angles of Bernicia. After the siege of Lindisfarne, where URIEN was murdered, the British army scattered. Urien's son OWAIN endeavoured to regroup the army and, with the help of Mynyddog, whose wealth was fabulous in his day, he succeeded in gathering together a force which confronted the Angles at Catraeth. Alas, the British were destroyed. The events of the battle are recorded in the famous poem Y *Gododdin* attributed to Aneirin. It is not clear whether Mynyddog was involved in the battle – it has been suggested that he was too old to fight. If so, one wonders for how long Mynyddog ruled the Gododdin. He may have been a successor to OUTIGERN who had endeavoured to fight back the Angles a generation earlier, but whose forces had been depleted by the renegade MORCANT who sought to establish a new Votadinian kingdom to the west, or he may have been the successor to CLYDNO EITEN. It is not known how long Mynyddog survived after Catraeth.

[DA32] **RHUN MAP URIEN** Rheged, *fl* 600s.
Whether Rhun ever succeeded to the kingship of Rheged is uncertain. He was the younger brother of OWAIN and may well have already entered the church by the time Owain fell at Catraeth. He may briefly have returned in order to defend the kingdom against being overwhelmed by the Bernicians but if he ruled at all it is likely to be only as a client king to ATHELFRITH. This was probably of only a short duration for we read of Rhun being resident in Powys a few years later, where he is supposed to have baptized the young EDWIN of Northumbria. Rhun may therefore have left the kingdom to his son RHOETH.

[DA33] **CEREDIG** Elmet, expelled 619 or 625.
Ceredig is recorded as the last king of Elmet, in the southern Pennines around Leeds, who was expelled from his domain by EDWIN of Northumbria in either 619 or 625 (scribal error may have miscopied a date which is now difficult to confirm, but the earlier date is more likely). How long Ceredig had ruled and who his predecessors were is not known. An earlier ruler of Elmet, GWALLAWG, is more likely to have been a ruler of a similarly named territory (Elvet) around the Clyde and Forth near Stirling. PABO's son, Samyl, established his own kingdom in the southern Pennines around the year 560, so it is possible that Ceredig was Samwl's grandson. The genealogies show the descendants of Samwl as Guticun (or Gutigern) and Catguallian (or Cadwallan) but nothing more is known of them. Cadwallan and Ceredig are such common Celtic names that it is difficult to distinguish the exploits of one from another.

[DA34] **RHOETH** MAP **RHUN** Rheged, *fl* 620s.

Rhoeth was almost certainly only a client-king of Rheged if he ruled at all in anything but name. He was probably a prince in exile in North Wales in his youth, following the death of his uncle OWAIN at the battle of Catraeth, but may have been restored to his kingdom sometime after 600 when his father, RHUN, entered the church. If such was so, then he would have ruled as a vassal to king ATHELFRITH of Northumbria. His lands would almost certainly have been confiscated again by EDWIN of Northumbria, although since Rhoeth's father had baptized Edwin, the Northumbrian may have shown rather more respect for the prince of Rheged than he did for the rulers of the other British kingdoms that he overran in the early part of his reign. It is recorded that Rhoeth's daughter, Rhiainmelt, which means 'Queen of the Lightning', married the later Northumbrian king OSWY. It is likely that during Oswy's reign, Rheged was annexed, perhaps to protect it against the expansionist regime of OWEN MAP BILI of Strathclyde.

DB. SOUTHERN BRITAIN (England south of Yorkshire)

Southern Britain, the part which romantic legend has called Loegres, must also have divided into its former tribal status after the Roman departure, but it was less evident than in the north, where the defences were strongest against the Picts, Irish and Saxons. Southern Britain retained, to a degree, the heart of the former Roman administration and it is possible to see that there was an attempt, at least for a while, to maintain a more cohesive administration amongst the southern tribes probably based at the heart of the wealthiest Roman centres around Cirencester and Gloucester, where the tribes of the Dobunni, Silures and Cornovii mingled. It was probably from here that the primary leaders of southern Britain emerged in what would later be the British kingdoms of Gwent, Powys and the Gewisse, and it was from here that the high king, or Pendragon, emerged. The following list is a close approximation of the high kings during the immediate post-Roman period before new kingdoms began to establish themselves. The Welsh Triads identify the first high king as Owain, though his existence is not otherwise recorded. The dates used are those most commonly associated with the rulers, but are in themselves dubious. Reference should be made to individual entries for further clarification.

Ref.	Ruler	Reign	Died	Notes
DB1.	Owain	c411–c425	425	see P87; existence dubious
DB2.	Vortigern (or Vitalinus)	c425–c466	c466	deposed 455–460; restored but deposed again and probably murdered; see P94
DB3.	Vortimer (or Natalinus) *May be the same king as Natanleod*	c466–c471	c471	poisoned or killed in battle; see P95
(DB2)	Vortigern (*restored*)	c471–c480	c480	could be a different ruler using the same title of Vortigern; would have ruled in opposition to Ambrosius Aurelianus
DB4.	Ambrosius Aurelianus	c466–c496	c496	see P96

Tradition lists Uther Pendragon as the successor of Ambrosius but his existence is uncertain. Brychan [EG1] may also have been High King at this time.

DB5.   Arthur   *c*496–*c*537   *c*537   see P98
DB6.   Constantine of Dumnonia *fl* 530s   *c*540   see also DC9 and P99

Hereafter the role of senior king passed to Maelgwyn of Gwynedd [ED4] and continued in Wales.

[DB1] OWAIN Alleged High King of Britain, *c*411–*c*425.

The very existence of Owain is dubious – he is known only from the Welsh Triads. Yet it seems necessary to bridge the gap between the withdrawal of Britain from the Roman Empire under its own last claimant to the imperial throne, CONSTANTINE III, and the rise to power of local kings COEL and VORTIGERN. Tradition has made Owain the son of MAGNUS MAXIMUS, and synonymous with EUGENIUS, a former claimant to the Roman purple who survived briefly between 392 and 394. Since Eugenius was dead by 411, he cannot be the same Owain that tradition states was elected as the first High King of Britain since the arrival of the Romans, but tradition may have confused fact with fancy and Eugenius is the most likely candidate for Owain. Even if he did not exist he is a convenient personification for government in Britain after the removal of Roman authority. There was a strong need for some form of continuing control. Not only was there the threat from the Germanic armies in Gaul, but the Picts posed a constant threat to the north and the Irish to the west. According to Gildas, it was a period of civil war and famine. Owain's period as governor, king or administrator was thus fraught with problems, and there is no evidence that he was able to tackle them successfully. He has been associated with AMBROSIUS.

[DB2;P94] VORTIGERN High King of Britain, *c*425–*c*466; *c*471–*c*480.

Vortigern is a title, not a name, and means "High King". Its Welsh equivalent was Gwrtheyrn Gwrthenau, or Vortigern the Thin. It is possible that his real name was Vitalinus, or that this was his father's name, and evidence of his existence has been found in the archeological remains of a villa near Gloucester. Although the later literary tradition has blackened Vortigern's reputation, making him something of a traitor to the British, in the years after his death Welsh leaders were proud to claim their descent from him. It seems that his successors through PASCENT ruled mid-east Wales around Wroxeter, and four centuries after his death, CYNGEN AP CADELL of Powys claimed he was a direct descendant. It is difficult to extract the fact from fiction, but the essence is as follows. Vortigern came to power some time around the year 425. He was probably the first post-Roman ruler to be declared High King of Britain, though this title may also have been bestowed upon OWAIN the son of MAGNUS MAXIMUS or upon AMBROSIUS *THE ELDER*. Tradition states that Vortigern married a daughter of Magnus Maximus called Servia. For over twenty years Vortigern led the organization and defence of Britain. Some of this may have been in conjunction with COEL *HEN* of Northern Britain, who seems to have been his contemporary. Vortigern was probably the High King at the time of the visit of Germanus in 428 or 429, who came at the request of the British church to root out and destroy the followers of Pelagius. This was a period of continued civil war, famine and raids from the Picts, Irish and Saxons. The first significant Saxon raid is recorded as happening at about the same time as Germanus's visit, in 429. At some stage Vortigern seems to have caused the enmity of Ambrosius the Elder for the two clashed in battle at Guoloph or Wallop in Hampshire in 437. Vortigern's endeavours to defend Britain became increasingly difficult and eventually, around the year 449, he and his council of elders took the decision to buy the help of Saxon mercenaries who had been displaced from their lands in Jutland. These mercenaries, under HENGEST, helped the British drive back the Picts and, in return, Vortigern gave them the Isle of Thanet in which to settle. Over the next five years the Saxon settlement grew in power and in 455 they rebelled. Later tradition states that Vortigern had become infatuated with Hengest's daughter Rowena, and had been given her in marriage in exchange for more land. The British now feared the Saxon might. VORTIMER, Vortigern's son, overthrew his father and embarked upon a war with the Saxons. He was, however, killed in battle (though other sources say he was poisoned), and Vortigern returned to rule. He was, however, now an old man, and unable to wield the authority he did in earlier years. It is possible that this later Vortigern is a different king, the son or grandson of Vortigern I, who assumed the title of High King. Around the year 466 AMBROSIUS AURELIANUS appears as rival warlord. He drove Vortigern into Wales where he remained a ruler around Powys (*see page 156*).

In addition to Vortimer and Pascent, Vortigern was the father of Cattegirn, who was killed fighting the Saxons, and Faustus, who became a bishop in Gaul. Faustus was rumoured to be the child of an incestuous relationship between Vortigern and his daughter. There are many other legends associated with Vortigern, most notably his role in the discovery of Merlin, when he wanted to know why the fortress he was trying to build in Snowdonia kept collapsing. Merlin stated that it was built upon a site where two dragons fought and he predicted Vortigern's fate to be burned alive in his tower by Ambrosius.

[DB3;P95] **VORTIMER** or **GWRTHEVYR** Son of VORTIGERN and allegedly High King of Britain from about 466–471. He rebelled against his father's association with the Saxons and for a while was elected High King in replacement of his father. He was apparently killed in battle against the Saxons, though other tales say that he was poisoned by his stepmother, Rowena, the daughter of HENGEST.

[DB4] **AMBROSIUS** This may be the name of two high kings of Britain, because the period of Ambrosius's activities is too long for one person. **Ambrosius the Elder** may be synonymous with OWAIN (*c*411–*c*425). This was a difficult period with civil wars and famine, and raids from the Irish, Picts and Saxons. It is more than probable that in the first few years no single powerful ruler emerged, whilst the old British tribal chieftainships resurfaced and faction fought faction. Gildas records that Britain was ruled by "tyrants", which suggests powerful people who usurped authority. One of these was COEL HEN, who ruled in the north, but in southern Britain two names gradually emerge – VORTIGERN and AMBROSIUS. Ambrosius is noted by Gildas as having parents and grandparents who wore the purple, which suggests they were among the claimants to the Roman throne. It is possible, but unlikely, that he was the son of CONSTANTINE III, but it is more credible that he was in some way descended from MAGNUS MAXIMUS. Ambrosius was regarded as a virtuous and stable ruler, not one warped by the influence of power. It seems that he and Vortigern were rivals and they clashed in battle at Guoloph (or Wallop in Hampshire) in 437. Vortigern's power was only temporarily curbed, however, and it was not until the reign of Ambrosius thirty years later that Britain had its first really effective ruler. This is too long a life span for one man, so either the dates are wrong, or there is a second Ambrosius, probably the son of the first. This Ambrosius we shall call **Ambrosius Aurelianus** [*see also* P96], known to the Welsh as Emrys Wledig. One tradition suggests that Ambrosius had sought refuge in Brittany and returned to help the defence of Britain. It is possible that the elder Ambrosius retired to Brittany, unable to quash the power of Vortigern, and that his son returned, sometime around 466. It is also likely that Ambrosius the Elder was killed during the fighting with Vortigern, possibly before 450. Ambrosius the Younger rallied together the armies of the chieftains of Britain and they accepted him as their leader against the Saxons. There were Saxon incursions at many places around Britain, most notably under HENGEST in Kent, AELLE in Sussex and OISC along the Northumbrian coast. Ambrosius's activities seem mostly to have been confined to the south, whilst CENEU, LEUDONUS and GURGUST tackled the raids in the North. It is not known how long Ambrosius ruled or what became of him. His main period of activity seems to have lasted for about fifteen years, or 466–481. Tradition passes on his authority to either UTHER PENDRAGON or ARTHUR. Uther's existence is itself very questionable, and Arthur's reign varies between twenty-five and forty years. It is possible that Ambrosius's authority continued for another fifteen years, from about 481–496. It has been suggested that his son or grandson was HONORIUS or Ynyr who ruled in Gwent, whilst another grandson may have been the notorious AURELIUS CANINUS.

[DB5;P98] **ARTHUR** Semi-legendary king of Britain, *fl c*500.
The greatest folk-hero of Britain about whom almost all we know is legend. More has been written about Arthur than almost any other king of Britain, but much of this serves only to confuse. The real name of this king and the period when he lived are both in doubt. There is no contemporary evidence of his existence and what does exist, dating from the late seventh century and after, may already be confused and could be referring to more than one person. The usual sources for information about Arthur are the *British History* of Nennius and the *Welsh Annals*. In both cases texts survive from only the ninth or tenth centuries. The years in the *Annals* were assigned later by calculation back from known dates. It states that in the year 516 Arthur fought at the battle of Badon for three days and nights and the Britons were the victors. For the year 537 it states that Arthur and Medraut both fell at the battle of Camlann. Nennius calls Arthur a *dux bellorum* or leader in battle, not a king in his own right, and lists twelve battles that Arthur waged against the Saxons at the time of Octha or OISC of Kent, culminating in the great victory of Badon (which Nennius states lasted only a day). In addition the near contemporary historian Gildas, who does not refer to Arthur, states in his *De Excidio* that the battle of Badon occurred in the year of his birth, forty-four years earlier. Gildas's life can be approximately dated and the writing of *De Excidio* is usually given as between 540 and 550, which would place Badon in about 500, a sixteen year variance from the Annals. Most historians agree with this dating, although John Morris places Arthur earlier with a span of reign from 475 to 515.

We can conclude from this that a battle leader called Arthur lived at about the year 500 and during this period succeeded in rallying the kings of Britain against the invading Saxons, soundly defeated them at Badon and, for about twenty years, had a period of relative calm, before he was killed in a second wave of onslaught. To draw further conclusions is to lean toward the creative fantasy of later romances.

Other records suggest something more of Arthur's existence. It seems he was the latest in a series of British defenders who had been fighting against the Saxons and other invaders (notably the Irish and the Picts) since the fall of Roman authority in Britain in the year 410. The principal of these was AMBROSIUS AURELIANUS who preceded Arthur, but who arguably may be the real Arthur. One wave of retreating British fled to Brittany in Gaul under their leader, who went under the title RIOTHAMUS but who was probably CYNAN. The Arthurian legend would thrive in Brittany which remained closely attached by trade and culture with Cornwall, which explains why Cornwall features so heavily in the later legends. Both these "defenders" lived in about 460, which suggests that Arthur's appearance must have been about the year 480 onward. This makes him a contemporary of both Oisc of Kent and AELLE of Sussex who are likely to be the two Saxon aggressors against which Arthur fought at Badon. We can assume (but only assume) that this Arthur lived mostly in southern Britain, while his contemporaries CERETIC, BRAN and LEUDONUS dominated the northern defence.

That is all we can say about the fifth-century Arthur. In all likelihood he was not a king in his own right, but a Defender of the Realm. However, it is quite possible that some of the adventures attributed to Arthur come from later kings or warriors either bearing the name Arthur (which would lead to obvious confusion) or undertaking deeds so similar to Arthur's as to merge into one in folk memory. Two obvious connections are with ARTHWYR, king of Dyfed and his namesake the king of Gwent, both of whom ruled around the end of the sixth century, a hundred years later than Arthur. Not much is known about either of these kings and, indeed, Arthwyr of Gwent may not even have reigned. Both seem to have fought Irish and Saxon incursions into southern Wales, and their exploits may have merged with legends of the earlier Arthur. In addition some legends grant Arthur a son called NOWY or Noe, and Arthwyr of Dyfed had a son with that name. This may account for why so many of the Arthurian legends are based in Wales.

The most likely candidate is Artiur, the eldest son (or in one source, grandson) of AEDAN MAC GABHRAN who was the heir to the kingdom of Dál Riata but who died in battle sometime in the mid-590s. It was predicted by Columba that Artiur would not reign and would predecease his father and he did indeed die at the battle of Camlann, by Hadrian's Wall, fighting the Picts. It is possible that Artiur fought alongside his father at the battle of Arthuret in 573 and that he had twenty years of fighting in which he established his name. This is the same period of PEREDUR of York and URIEN of Rheged, both valiant kings whose deeds passed into legend and became associated with Arthur. Writing about the year 600 in *Y Gododdin*, the poet Aneirin waxed enthusiastic about the former valour of the army of Arthur, comparing it to the less glorious performance of the British at Catraeth in 595 which must have happened after Artiur's death.

Historically that is as far as we can go. The myth, created by Geoffrey of Monmouth in his *History of the Kings of Britain* (1136), mixes possible facts with blurred memory and Geoffrey's own creativity to create a single character, Arthur, who exists alongside the other heroes whose real exploits were grafted onto

Arthur's. In addition Geoffrey mixed in the life of the fourth century MAGNUS MAXIMUS, to portray Arthur setting out to conquer Rome. He also describes his need to return home because of the treason of his deputy Mordred. This may be an association with the northern king MORCANT. It is likely that all of Arthur's most famous knights were originally rulers or sons of rulers in Britain, though in some cases their names have long since become distorted by their French versions. Peredur, Urien and OWAIN are the obvious ones, but there are almost certainly true identities to be found behind Cei, Bedwyr, Gwalchmai and even Lancelot, spread throughout Wales, Scotland, Cornwall and Brittany. Similarly his wife Guinevere has been associated with Gwenhwyfar, a princess of the royal line in Brittany or, more likely, a Pictish princess through whom royal inheritance could pass.

The folk memory has made Arthur and his heroes a composite of very many historical people. It is ironic that the real Arthur was probably not a king in his own right, a legacy that passed on to those subsequent heirs to the throne named Arthur who did not become kings either (*see under* JOHN *and* HENRY VII).

[DB6;DC9;P99] **CONSTANTINE** or **CUSTENNYN** Dumnonia and High King of Britain, *fl* 530s.
Although legend credits Constantine with inheriting the high kingship, it is doubtful if this was the case and he almost certainly remained ruler of Dumnonia in south-west Britain. See the full entry under DC9 below.

DC. THE SOUTH-EAST AND SOUTH-WEST

The south-east was the first area to be dominated by the Saxons, especially Kent and Sussex. Within a century after Roman rule the British in what became England were forced further west into either Wales or Dumnonia (Devon and Cornwall), which became known as the West Welsh (the word Welsh being derived from the Saxon for foreigner). The Dumnonian king list is one of the hardest to reconcile. It is complicated by legend, the connection between its own kings and those in south Wales, and its relationship to Brittany in France, as some kings ruled both kingdoms. The British Dumnonia originally covered Cornwall, Devon, Dorset and Somerset, though by 710, only Cornwall (Kernow) remained. The post-Roman kings of Dumnonia may have been descended from the Cornovii who migrated from Wales in the early fifth century. There were probably several cases of kings ruling at the same time, and the following list is only indicative and not definitive. For the Dumnonian family tree see Chart 1 on page 67.

Ref.	Ruler	Reign	Died	Notes
Cantii (Kent)				
DC1.	Gwyrangon	*fl* 450		
Dobunni (Severn Valley)				
This may also be the territory of the High Kings listed in DB above.				
DC2.	Aurelius Caninus	*fl* 530		see P100
DC3.	Coinmail, Farinmail and Condidan	*fl* 577		defeated at Dyrham

Ref.	Ruler	Reign	Died	Notes

Dumnonia

DC4.	Cynan map Eudaf (Octavius)	*fl* 420s		
DC5.	Gadeon map Cynan	*fl* 450s		
DC6.	Docco	*fl* 470s	*c*473	
DC7.	Gwrwawr map Gadeon	*fl* 480s		
DC8.	Tudvawl map Gwrwawr	*fl* 500s		
DC9.	Custennyn (Constantine) map Tudvawl	*fl* 530s	*c*540	see also DB6
DC10.	Erbin map Custennyn	*fl* 540s		
DC11.	Geraint map Erbin	*fl* 550s		killed in battle
DC12.	Hoel or Riwal	*fl* 550s–570s		also king in Brittany (SA10)
DC13.	Cunomor or Mark	*fl* 550s–570s		
DC14.	Drust or Tristan	*fl* 570s		
DC15.	Cador map Geraint	*fl* 580s		
DC16.	Peredur map Cador	*fl* 600s		
DC17.	Tewdwr or Theudo map Peredur	*fl* 620s		

Kingship at this point uncertain

DC18.	Judhael	*fl* 650s		
DC19.	Erbin	*fl* 690s		
DC20.	Geraint	*fl* 700s	710	killed in battle

After 710 Dumnonia (except for Cornwall) was under the control of Wessex.

Kernow (Cornwall)

Kings of Cornwall between Geraint and Doniert are not known

DC21.	Doniert or Dungarth	*fl* 870s	875	drowned
DC22.	Ricatus	*fl* 900?		
DC23.	Hoel	*fl* 920s		
DC24.	Cynan or Conan	*fl* 930s		

Probably the last native ruler of Cornwall, though his descendents survived as ealdormen, having probably married into local Saxon families. Cador (fl 1066) was one such and his son, Cadoc, had a daughter who married Henry I's illegitimate son Reginald, who became the first earl of Cornwall. Hereafter the kingdom became part of the Norman earldom of Cornwall.

[DC1] **GWYRANGON** British king of the Cantii, *fl* 450.
The king who ruled the tribe of the Cantii in Kent at the time that the High King VORTIGERN invited the Saxon HENGEST to Britain to help in the battle against the Picts and Irish. Vortigern gave Gwyrangon's lands to Hengest in return for Hengest's daughter in marriage (or in return for services rendered). The response by Gwyrangon is not recorded, but he likely became one of the kings who turned against Vortigern and regarded him as a traitor.

[DC2;P100] **AURELIUS CANINUS** Dobunni, *fl* 530.
Aurelius Caninus was one of the tyrants whom Gildas berates in the *De Excidio Britonum* for his wicked ways. Caninus had, apparently, waged civil wars with his

fellows and indulged in rape and adultery. Unfortunately we do not know where Caninus ruled. Since Gildas's diatribe seems to work geographically around southern Britain and Wales, Caninus probably ruled amongst the Dobunni of the Severn Valley in Gloucestershire. Gildas does not tell us much about him, but he does say that his father and brothers died young, indeed Caninus probably inherited the kingdom by killing them himself. It is possible that he was a grandson of AMBROSIUS AURELIANUS, as Gildas refers to the degeneration of his descendants. Gildas is not clear as to how long ago this happened, but it was probably a good few years, as Gildas also suggests that Caninus had so plundered the lands about him that he had nothing to show for his efforts. Attempts have been made to identify Caninus with Cynan, a prince of the ruling family of Powys, but the link is far from definite, and probably unlikely. It is more likely that Caninus ruled a small kingdom in the region of Gloucester or Wiltshire and would have been one of the kings defeated by the invading Saxons. He might be one of the Cynans of the Dumnonian royal family, especially as Geoffrey of Monmouth makes him a nephew of the Dumnonian king CONSTANTINE. Geoffrey allots him a rule of only three years, from about 546–549. He regarded Aurelius as a brave and worthy king spoiled only by his delight in civil war, having murdered his uncle (Constantine's brother) to gain the throne. There was a COINMAIL defeated by CEAWLIN at Dyrham in 577 who may have been Caninus's son.

[DC3] **COINMAIL** Dobunni, *fl* 577. [DC3] **CONDIDAN** Dobunni, *fl* 577. [DC3] **FARINMAIL** Somerset(?) *fl* 577.
The three British kings defeated by the West Saxons CUTHWINE and CEAWLIN at Dyrham in 577. The names of these kings must have been important to have been remembered by the chroniclers. If the *ASC* list of towns captured is in the same sequence, Coinmail may have ruled Gloucester, Condidan ruled Cirencester and Farinmail ruled Bath. It is tempting to think that Coinmail may have been the son of AURELIUS CANINUS and thus a descendent of AURELIUS AMBROSIUS. It is possible that Condidan could be the same as or related to CADOR of Cornwall, whilst Farinmail may have been a Cornovian chieftain of the Dumnonii.

[DC4] **CYNAN (I)** Dumnonia, *fl* 420s. Although listed in the genealogy of the kings of Dumnonia, he may not himself have ruled in that territory. He is shown as the son of Eudaf the Old (*see* OCTAVIUS) which, if true, would place him a generation or two earlier. In all probability the reference means only "descended from" Eudaf rather than a direct son, though this obviously leaves us uncertain as to when Cynan lived. He was probably part of the Cornovian migration that moved from mid-central Wales into Devon and Cornwall during the early and mid fifth century. His descendants remained in that area, though some migrated further into Brittany in north-west France, led by another Cynan known as Meriadoc, who may have been his son or grandson. It is interesting that another Cynan, known to Gildas as AURELIUS CANINUS ruled in northern Dumnonia, somewhere on the route that Cynan must have taken, and it is possible that he was also a descendent.

[DC5] **GADEON** or **ADEON** Dumnonia, *fl* 450s.
Variously shown as the brother or, more likely, son of CYNAN, Gadeon was involved with him in establishing the Cornovii in Dumnonia and driving out the Irish

settlers. He was a contemporary of RIOTHAMUS, the leader of the British settlers who migrated from Wales and Dumnonia into Brittany, and this is likely to be his brother or nephew Cynan Meriadoc. Gadeon would also have been involved in the migration but he is more closely connected with Dumnonia and probably became the first leader of the settlers there. His son was GWRWAWR.

[DC6] **DOCCO** Dumnonia, *fl* 470s.

The name of a British chieftain associated with the early settlement of Dumnonia in the middle of the fifth century. He was probably a contemporary of GADEON but is said to have lived to an old age and died around the year 473.

[DC7] **GWRWAWR** Dumnonia, *fl* 480s.

Listed in the genealogies as the son of GADEON and father of TUDVAWL. He was one of the chieftains ruling in Dumnonia at the time of the first Saxon incursions, though we know nothing more about him.

[DC8] **TUDVAWL** Dumnonia, *fl* 500s.

Tudvawl, which is another Celtic variant of Tutagual or possibly Tewdwr, was the son of GWRWAWR and father of the more famous CONSTANTINE. He was a chieftain of Dumnonia of the main royal line, but we know nothing about him.

[DC9;DB6;P99] **CONSTANTINE** or **CUSTENNYN** Dumnonia and High-King of Britain, *fl* 530s.

A name too commonly associated with the history and legends of king ARTHUR and thus one where fact and fancy merge. According to Geoffrey of Monmouth, Constantine was the son of Duke Cador of Cornwall who accepted the kingship from his cousin Arthur at the time of his death, which Geoffrey dates as 542. Constantine faced an uprising by the sons of Mordred, whom he overthrew. He continued a vendetta against them, killing them both when they sought sanctuary within the church. For this Constantine was punished and struck down by God. He was succeeded by his nephew, AURELIUS CANINUS, who murdered Constantine's brother. Geoffrey may have some facts at the core of his narrative as Gildas also recalls Constantine, and he was a contemporary of his. He calls him a "tyrant whelp", who had abandoned his lawful wife many years previously and become a cruel despot. Gildas also refers to the murder of two royal princes. He entreats Constantine to repent, stating that he knows he is still alive. This last statement suggests that perhaps Constantine had abdicated or been deposed and was in exile, possibly in Brittany. He was succeeded in Cornwall by his son ERBIN.

[DC10] **ERBIN** MAP **CUSTENNYN** Dumnonia *fl* 540s.

He was the son of CONSTANTINE, though he is overlooked in Geoffrey of Monmouth's narrative. His name appears in the genealogy of the Dumnonian kings where he is identified as the father of GERAINT. Interestingly a second Erbin who lived two centuries later was also the father of a GERAINT and it is possible the chroniclers became confused. There is another pairing of ERBIN and GERAINT in Strathclyde. If he existed Erbin would certainly have been one of the Britons who confronted CERDIC as he sought to establish territory in Britain. In all likelihood he met his death in battle against the Saxons.

[DC11] **GERAINT (I)** Dumnonia *fl* 550s.

He was the son of ERBIN and grandson of CONSTANTINE. There is a problem dating Geraint's reign however. He is remembered in a remarkable Welsh poem which recalls his heroic fight and death at the battle of Llongborth or Longport, where the poet fancies he saw "ARTHUR's heroes" cut with steel. It is not likely that the poet intended Geraint to be a contemporary of Arthur's, though the oral tradition may mean that some of Arthur's own men were still alive and fighting alongside Geraint. This may be the same battle recorded in the *ASC* under the year 501 when the unlikely named Port arrived with his sons and slew a noble young British king at the battle of Portsmouth. This would place him contemporary with Arthur but would make it difficult to be the grandson of Constantine who was Arthur's successor. We know that the *ASC* dates for this early period are notoriously inaccurate and that because the annalists often computed using the Easter cycle of dates (when Easter repeats itself on a cycle of nineteen years) it is possible that the battle of Longport took place in 520 or more probably 539 or 558 (annalists were notorious at pushing dates back in time to establish historical precedent). Geraint's existence is a good example of how difficult it is to relate ancient (and usually non-contemporaneous records) to a logical chronological sequence. He was the father of several missionaries, notably St Cyngar or Congar who founded churches in Brittany suggesting that many of Geraint's descendants migrated to Gaul at this time.

[DC12;SA10] **HOEL, HYWEL** or **RIWAL** Dumnonia, *fl* 550s–570s.

Hoel was the name of three rulers of Armorica (Brittany). The first was regarded as a great king, ruler of the Britons in both Brittany and Dumnonia in Britain, and a friend of ARTHUR's. He was the son of Budic and grandson of Theodoric, and was thus related to TEWDRIG of Gwent, but was also related to the British Dumnonian line of ERBIN and GERAINT. Hoel ruled in Brittany, but returned to help his fellow British in Dumnonia, and very likely in Wales, against the invading Saxons. Following the death of GERAINT it seems that Hoel became the leader for a while. Geraint was supposed to have died young so his son, CADOR, may not yet have been of an age to rule. Hoel ended his days in Brittany however where he became notorious for the death of several kinsmen. He was succeeded in Brittany by CUNOMOR.

[DC13;SA8] **CUNOMOR(US)** or **MARK** Dumnonia, *fl* 550s–570s.

Like HOEL, Cunomor was a ruler in both Brittany and Britain. He is remembered as a cruel king. Nothing is known of his real life, though the legend may be close. He learned that he would be killed by one of his sons, so he executed each wife as she became pregnant. One wife remained hidden until after the birth. When Cunomor found out he beheaded his wife and left the child to die, but it survived (*see* JUDHAEL). Some scholars have identified him with Kynvawr or CONSTANTINE (certainly they were both tyrants and wife-killers). The connection to the Arthurian King Mark of Cornwall may be because of a misplaced association with Kynmarch or CINMARC, the contemporary British king of Rheged. A stone pillar outside Fowey in Cornwall is engraved "Drustaus filius Cunomori" which has also caused scholars to link him with the TRISTAN of Arthurian legend. In this legend it is Mark who is the wronged king as his nephew, Tristan, falls in love with Mark's bride-to-be Iseult. One version of the legend states that when Mark eventually discovered the truth he killed Tristan. If, as the Fowey Stone suggests, Mark was Tristan's father and not his uncle, it makes the relationship with the wife (stepmother?) even more potent. It has been suggested that as Drust or Drest is a Pictish name, that the legend derives from a Pictish source, especially as in the Welsh version of the tale Mark's name is Tallwch, suggestive of Talorc. There are two cases in Pictish history when a king called Talorc was succeeded by a nephew called Drust, the most timely being TALORG MAC MORDILEG and DREST MAC MUNAIT, whose reigns are exactly contemporary with Cunomor's.

[DC14] TRISTAN or DRUST Cornwall or Dumnonia, fl 570s.
Tristan, sometimes called Tristram, is immortalised in the Arthurian tragedy of Tristan and Isolde, the doomed love affair between Tristan and his father's wife to be. Tristan almost certainly existed as his name is commemorated on the ancient stone which once stood at Castle Dore in Cornwall, but now stands by the road outside Fowey. Whether this Tristan actually ruled in Cornwall or Devon is not certain, as the legend may have been derived from contemporary Pictish sources. Tristan is identified as the son or nephew of CUNOMOR whom see for further details.

[DC15] CADOR MAP GERAINT Dumnonia, fl 580s.
Son of the legendary hero GERAINT. In Arthurian legend he would seem to be the same as Duke Cador, a valiant hero and supporter of ARTHUR, who helps defeat the Saxons, and who was the father of CONSTANTINE. However, if Constantine and Custennyn of the genealogies are one and the same then this Cador was the great-grandson of Arthur's Duke (which is possible). He would have been in the thick of the fighting against the West Saxons who were striving to advance west during this period. Cador may just possibly be the same king as CONDIDAN who was defeated at Dyrham in 577. He was the father of PEREDUR. This suggests a connection with the PEREDUR of York and it is possible that there are confused genealogies, as Geoffrey of Monmouth refers to Cador's defeat of the Saxon Baldulf at York. Possibly some of Cador's feats have become confused with CEIDIAW of Galloway.

[DC16] PEREDUR Dumnonia, fl 600s.
Peredur's name appears amongst the genealogies of the Dumnonian king-list as the son of CADOR and the father of TEWDWR. It is interesting that he is a virtual contemporary of PEREDUR of York, which does raise a question of possible duplication by the chroniclers. Geoffrey of Monmouth refers to a Peredur son of Peredur who attended ARTHUR's court, and elsewhere he refers to Cador defeating the Saxon Baldulf at York. All this is suggestive of confused genealogies.

[DC17] TEWDWR Dumnonia fl 620s.
The son of PEREDUR and grandfather of JUDHAEL. Although not named in the chronicles it is likely that it was against TEWDWR that CYNEGILS of Wessex imposed such crippling casualties in his efforts to conquer the west. Over two thousand British fell at the battle of Beandun in Dorset in 614. This may account for the gap in the genealogies at this point, as only a daughter of Tewdwr is recorded, not a son. Either he had no son, or the son was killed in battle before he sired an heir.

[DC18;SA17] JUDHAEL Dumnonia fl 650s.
This unusual British name, which may be a variant on Idwal, appears in two places. Once in the Dumnonian king-list, where he is the last descendant from Eudaf *Hen* (*see* OCTAVIUS), and once in the legend of CUNOMOR where, as Judwal, he is the son

who survives his father's attempts to kill his offspring before they are born. It is worth noting that he is almost contemporary with IDWAL of Gwynedd, and there may be a connection between them. Judhael is almost certainly the same as Judicael, king of Brittany, who offered his allegiance to the Merovingean king Dagobert and established the boundaries of Brittany in about the year 635. Thereafter he was allowed to rule within his own kingdom. Whether he also had domain over Cornwall or Gwent is uncertain, but his son ERBIN seems to have ruled in south-western Britain.

[DC19] **ERBIN (II)** Dumnonia *fl* 690s.
It is possible that this Erbin was confused with the earlier one because of the presence of two GERAINTs in the Dumnonian record.

[DC20] **GERAINT (II)** Dumnonia *fl* 700s.
Like his predecessor of the same name, this Geraint was also the son of Erbin which has given cause for some confusion. He was probably the last king of Dumnonia. The *ASC* records that in the year 710 INE of Wessex and Nunna or NOTHHELM of Sussex fought against Geraint. It does not record that Geraint was killed. We heard of Geraint a few years earlier when bishop Aldhelm wrote to him encouraging him to adopt the Roman form of Christian worship rather than the Celtic. It may have been Geraint's failure to do so that Ine used as an excuse to attack. From that year it is probable that Dumnonia ceased to exist as a separate kingdom, though Geraint may have continued to lead a resistance movement against the Saxons, as there was continual problems in Devon and Cornwall over the next century. The royal family may therefore have continued to exist, but no more names are known until that of DONIERT.

[DC21] **DONIERT** or **DUNGARTH** Kernow, *fl* 870s.
Doniert's death is recorded in the Welsh Annals in 875, where it is noted that he drowned in the River Fowey on Bodmin Moor. By this year EGBERT of Wessex had already conquered Cornwall but presumably had allowed the native rulers to continue to reign, provided they paid tribute to him. There is a Celtic cross erected near Bodmin Moor in Cornwall known as King Doniert's Stone and on which is inscribed, DONIERT ROGAVIT PRO ANIMA ("Doniert ordered this for the good of his soul") and presumably once stood at a Celtic church.

[DC22] **RICATUS** Kernow, *fl* 900?
A king of Cornwall whose name has survived from the cross preserved at Penlee House near Penzance. By this period the West Saxon kings had subjugated the Cornish and although the native royal line persisted and no doubt occasionally rebelled against the Saxons, they made little imprint on the might of EDWARD THE ELDER and ATHELSTAN.

[DC23] **HOEL** Kernow, *fl* 920s.
In July 927 ATHELSTAN summoned a meeting at Eamont Bridge in Cumbria where he called together the kings of Scotland and Strathclyde to pay him homage and to swear they would not support the Norse king GOTHFRITH. Amongst the kings at Eamont was Hywel of the West Welsh, a phrase usually reserved for the Cornish. Although most scholars suggest this was HYWEL DDA of Wales, it is possible that it refers to a Hoel of Cornwall, a name we know was common in that area. The year

before Athelstan had led a punitive expedition against the Cornish, pushing them back into Cornwall and setting up a force of Saxon earls as reeves to control them. Whether Hoel was the leader of this revolt is not clear, but it is possible that Athelstan took him as hostage and he had remained with Athelstan in his campaigns in the north. Five years later there was a further uprising in Cornwall, which Athelstan dealt with with equal effectiveness. It may be that Hoel was killed during this rebellion.

[DC24] **CYNAN (II)** Kernow *fl* 930s. A ruler of Cornwall, in succession to HOEL, who may have been involved in a rebellion against ATHELSTAN in the late 930s. He is the last known native ruler of Cornwall, though his descendents survived in the area as ealdormen.

Map 4a **The Welsh Kingdoms – Gwent and Glywysing**

E. THE WELSH KINGDOMS (400–1291)

The native British retained a degree of autonomy in Wales throughout the Roman occupation. Little is recorded about them that can be established as firm historical fact though it is possible that the Silures, Ordovices and Demetae continued to be ruled by tribal chieftains within the Roman administration. Towards the end of this period an influx of Irish from the west and British from the east began to test these tribal boundaries and new ones emerged based, initially, on the old tribes, but subsequently developing into four main kingdoms – Gwent, Gwynedd, Powys and Deheubarth. The following lists all of the main kingdoms and most of the sub-kingdoms.

EA. GWENT and GLYWYSING

The rulership of south-east Wales is complicated by the many sub-divisions of the land due to partible succession. Essentially there were two main kingdoms: Gwent and Glywysing, both descended from the Silures. Petty chieftains responded to the stronger rulers, sometimes from Gwent and sometimes from Glywysing but it was not until the tenth century that the two kingdoms effectively united under the name Morgannwg. The following lists the primary rulers. In almost all cases lands were sub-divided between sons and brothers, resulting in many sub-kings who are not listed here.

Ref.	Ruler	Reign	Died	Notes
EA1.	Erb	*fl* 420s		Gwent
EA2.	Nynniaw	*fl* 450s		Gwent
EA3.	Teithfallt	*fl* 480s		Gwent
EA4.	Glywys	*fl* 490s		founder of Glywysing
EA5.	Honorius or Ynyr	*fl* 510s		Gwent
EA6.	Gwynllyw	*fl* 520s		Glywysing
EA7.	Iddon	*fl* 540s		Gwent
EA8.	Cadoc or Cadog	*fl* 550s		Glywysing
EA9.	Tewdrig or Theodosius	*fl* 550s	?584	Gwent; abdicated but killed in battle
EA10.	Meurig or Mouric	*c*580–*c*615	*c*615	Gwent and Glywysing
EA11.	Cynfeddw	*fl* 610s		possibly sub-king in Gwent
EA12.	Arthwyr or Athrwys ap Meurig	*c*615–*c*630		probably ruled Gwent
EA13.	Morgan *Mwynfawr* (*the Generous*)	*c*630–*c*665	665	Gwent and Glywysing; may have died in battle

Although Morgan is reckoned to have been succeeded by his son Ithael, there remains a gap in the chronology which is difficult to fill.

EA14.	Ithael	*c*715–*c*745		Gwent and Glywysing
EA15.	Ffernfael ap Ithael	745–775	775	Gwent
EA16.	Rhys ab Ithael	745– ?		Glywysing
EA17.	Arthwyr ap Ffernfael	775– ?		Gwent
EA18.	Arthfael ap Rhys	*fl* 800		Glywysing
EA19.	Ithael ab Arthwyr	? –848		Gwent

3. Wales (1) – **Gwent and Glywysing**

Of all the Welsh genealogies this is the most confusing. The following chart is as accurate an interpretation of the texts as possible but still includes a degree of conjecture. The chart includes rulers of Ergyng and Brittany.

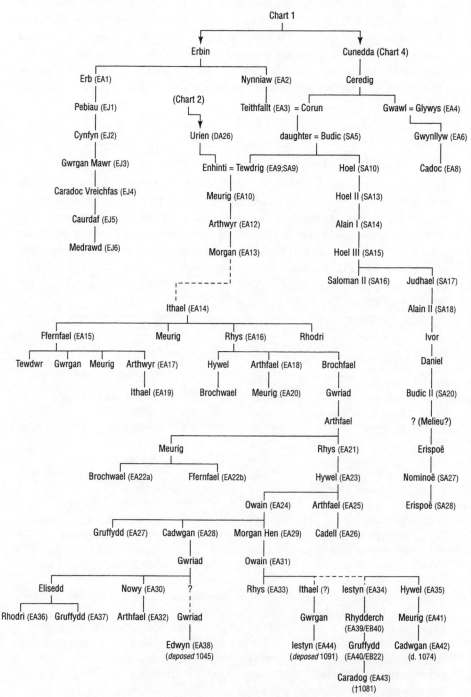

Ref.	Ruler	Reign	Died	Notes
EA20.	Meurig ab Arthfael	*fl* 830s		Gwent
EA21.	Rhys ab Arthfael	*fl* 830s		Glywysing
EA22a.	Brochwael ab Meurig	*fl* 880s		Gwent
EA22b.	Ffernwael ab Meurig	*fl* 880s		Gwent; ruled jointly with above
EA23.	Hywel ap Rhys	*c*840–*c*885	885	Glywysing
EA24.	Owain ap Hywel	*c*885–*c*930	930	Glywysing
EA25.	Arthfael ap Hywel	*fl* 920s		Gwent
EA26.	Cadell ap Arthfael	*fl* 930s	942	Gwent
EA27.	Gruffydd ap Owain	930–934	934	Glywysing; Gower from 928; killed in battle
EA28.	Cadwgan ap Owain	930–950	950	West Glywysing; killed in battle

On the death of Cadwgan his brother, Morgan, united Gwent, Gower and Glywysing and created the single kingdom Morgannwg, later called Glamorgan. Details of this kingdom are given in Part 2 on page 325.

[EA1] **ERB** Gwent and Ergyng, *fl* 420s.
The genealogies list Erb or Yrb as the son of Erbin, an earlier chieftain in the Gwent area, and grandson of OCTAVIUS. Erb is the first historically attested king of this territory, as a charter survives where he granted land to St Dubricius, probably close to the end of his life as he observed that "ambition and the power of the world are perishable." The dating of Dubricius has never been resolved, his life lying somewhere between the years 475 and 612. Erb was the father of PEBIAU who inherited Ergyng (*see page 162*). Gwent passed to his brother NYNNIAW.

[EA2] **NYNNIAW** Gwent, *fl* 450s.
It is difficult to be accurate about the chronology of these early kings, but Nynniaw is shown as a contemporary of CUNEDDA and must therefore have lived about the middle of the fifth century. He may well have been named after the holy man St Ninian, a Celtic missionary amongst the Picts who died in 431. There is no record to say whether Nynniaw modelled himself upon his namesake but it is very possible.

[EA3] **TEITHFALLT** or **TEWDFALCH** Gwent, *fl* 480s.
The son of NYNNIAW, he married Corun the daughter of CEREDIG the son of CUNEDDA. His name is a Celtic version of Theodosius and may have been adopted to reflect the glory still attached to a Roman commander called Theodosius, who restored peace in Britain in the period 367–371 after quelling an uprising of Picts and Irish. Teithfallt might even have been distantly related to him. He was succeeded by his son TEWDRIG, though parts of Gwent at this time were also shared with Honorius or Ynyr.

[EA4] **GLYWYS** Glywysing, *fl* 490s.
The traditional founder of the kingdom of Glywysing, to the west of Gwent, Glywys no doubt carved this out from the lands of Demetia held by the Irish, then ruled by the powerful AIRCOL. He was almost certainly helped in this enterprise by CEREDIG, and married his daughter Guaul. Since Glywys's neighbour, TEITHFALLT of Gwent, had also married a daughter of Ceredig, we can imagine that the sons of CUNEDDA were active in south Wales, not only endeavouring to drive out the Irish but

establishing alliances with the native princes. Glywys passed his newly-won king-dom on to his son GWYNLLYW.

[EA5] **HONORIUS** or **YNYR** Gwent, *fl* 510s.

Honorius is a name recorded as a ruler in Caerwent in southern Gwent, also known in Celtic as Ynyr. It is tempting to think that he may have been a descendant of a Roman general once stationed at Caerleon. It is certainly likely that he came to power because of his ability to defend Gwent from the Saxons who, at the start of the sixth century, were beginning to emerge as a problem in the Severn valley. It has also been suggested that Ynyr may be the same person as Emrys or AMBROSIUS of legend; or more likely a son or grandson. If so then Ynyr was one of those Gildas referred to as "greatly inferior" to their forebear. According to one tradition Ynyr was married to Madrun, the daughter of VORTIMER. Their son IDDON also ruled in Gwent.

[EA6] **GWYNLLYW** or **GUNLYU MILWR (the WARRIOR)** Glywysing, *fl* 520s.

The son of GLYWYS and great-grandson of CUNEDDA. He gave his name to the *cantref* of Gwynllwg to the west of Gwent. Gwynllyw is remembered by the Welsh as a saint, but only for the asceticism of his later life. As his epithet implies, his early life was spent in battle, almost certainly fighting the Irish settlers in Demetia and the Saxons in the east. It is quite possible that Gwynllyw was involved in the battle of Badon, which defeated the Saxons and allowed a period of relative peace. Gwynllyw married Glwadys, a daughter of BRYCHAN – she must have been one of the younger girls as Gwynllyw's grandfather, CEREDIG, had also married one of Brychan's daughters. They had at least three children of whom the eldest, CADOC, became one of the most renowned saints in Wales. It was he who admonished his father for his violent ways, so that Gwynllyw later turned his back on worldly affairs and became a hermit.

[EA7] **IDDON** Gwent, *fl* 540s.

The son (or grandson) of Ynyr or Honorius, and thus probably descended from a Roman family. Iddon is recorded as having a victory over the Saxons in the Wye valley. His reign is difficult to date, and he may have ruled as late as the 580s or 590s, in which case his victory was probably against CEAWLIN of the Gewisse, but it is more likely to have been an earlier skirmish against either CERDIC or CYNRIC. Not all of Iddon's life seems to have been worthy. Late in life he granted much land to the church in expiation "of his evil deeds", though what these were is not described.

[EA8] **CADOC** Glywysing, *fl* 550s.

The eldest son of GWYNLLYW, who apparently spent part of his early life as the secular ruler of Glywysing. It is likely that he assumed the responsibility after his father abdicated to become an anchorite, but it is unlikely that Cadoc remained a ruler for long. Legend has it that Cadoc found it difficult to defend Glywysing against the oppression of MAELGWYN HIR and his son RHUN as well as from the Saxons to the east in the days after Camlann, and prayed to God to send a new king. The answer appeared in the form of MEURIG AP TEWDRIG. Cadoc's greatest achievement was the foundation of the Celtic monastery at Nantcarfan (now Llancarfan). He travelled widely, throughout Brittany and Cornwall as well as Wales, and he is believed to have ended his days in Italy.

[EA9;SA9] **TEWDRIG** Gwent (and later Glywysing), *fl* 550s–*c*584.

The name Theoderic (and its Celtic equivalent Tewdrig) were popular in the sixth century and this blurs identification of some individuals. This Tewdrig may have been the son (or grandson) of TEITHFALLT, who ruled Gwent at the end of the fifth century, or he may have been the son of Budic, a Celtic ruler of Brittany, who was expelled after the death of his father (in 556) and returned to Wales, where he had spent much of his youth engaged in aiding the British in their battles against the Irish in both Wales and Cornwall. Whichever the case, he ascended the throne with considerable prestige gained from his youthful valour. He built upon that prestige by marrying Enhinti, the sister of URIEN of Rheged, who was already becoming regarded as the most powerful British king. Tewdrig continued his exploits in Wales and Cornwall, and through his actions firmly established Gwent as the most powerful nation in south Wales, driving back the Irish of Demetia and increasing the territory of Glywysing. Towards the end of his long life he retired to become an anchorite, apparently living in a cave or cell near Tintern. However, he emerged a few years later to help his son, MEURIG, in an offensive against the Saxons who were making great advances around Gloucester. The Saxon annals record a Saxon withdrawal from the Wye around the year 584, and this may be the year of Tewdrig's death. He was mortally wounded in battle and died three days later. He ordered that he be buried where he died and a church established there. The traditional burial place is Mathern, near Chepstow.

[EA10] **MEURIG** AP **TEWDRIG** Gwent and Glywysing, *c*580–*c*615.

Meurig was the name of three kings of Gwent and surrounding territories. The name is the same as the French Maurice and tends to refer to someone who is dark-skinned, like the Moors. The first of that name became ruler of Gwent when his father, TEWDRIG, retired to become an anchorite. However, both father and son led a Welsh army against the Saxons and soundly defeated them at Tintern around the year 584 (*see* CEAWLIN *and* CUTHA). Tewdrig had had a dream that if he fought alongside his son they would have a victory which would result in peace for thirty years. Meurig was also the answer to St CADOC's prayers, since he wished to hand the rulership of Glywysing over to someone more able than he. Meurig thus became the first ruler of a combined Gwent and Glywysing, which were the equivalent of modern Glamorgan and formed the later kingdom of Morgannwg. Meurig's power grew. He married into the royal family of Gower and subsumed that kingdom into his own. The last king of Ergyng, GWRFODDW, died during Meurig's reign, and that kingdom became part of Glywysing. He also overthrew, once and for all, the domination of the Irish kingdom of Demetia, and it is possible that he installed his own son, ARTHWYR, as their ruler. Tewdrig's dream of a peaceful reign had translated into one where Meurig suffered no oppression, but dominated others. He was almost certainly an impulsive man with a strong temper. A deed exists whereby Meurig paid atonement for killing CYNFEDDW.

[EA11] **CYNFEDDW** Southern Gwent, *fl* 610s.

A sub-king to MEURIG AP TEWDRIG. They were evidently constantly in conflict. The two finally met at Llandaff and swore on the relics of the saints to keep the peace, but soon after Meurig, by deceit, succeeded in killing Cynfeddw. It is possible Cynfeddw was a son or relative of IDDON, a former king of Gwent. It is also interesting to speculate that this Cynfeddw may be the same as the father of CADFAEL who became king of Gwynedd in 633, though there is no evidence to support the connection.

[EA12] **ARTHWYR** Gwent (?), *fl* 620s.

On the death of his father, MEURIG AP TEWDRIG, Arthwyr appears to have inherited the sub-kingdom of Gwent. Considering the fame attached to both his father and grandfather, and which would also be attached to his son MORGAN *MWYNFAWR*, it is surprising that so little is recorded about Arthwyr beyond a few grants of land. Some historians are not even sure that he actually reigned. However, because of his name, others have claimed that this is the fabled King ARTHUR, though it is extremely unlikely that this Arthwyr could claim such noble and valorous deeds. Such were more likely to apply to his namesake, ARTHWYR of Dyfed. It is possible but unlikely that the two Arthwyrs are one and the same (even though their genealogies differ) and that he was installed as ruler of that kingdom after his father defeated the Demetian ruler PEDR. If they are the same, then Arthwyr may be accorded greater glory, as he would have ruled all of southern Wales from Dyfed to Gwent and would be remembered in legend for driving out the Irish and holding the Saxons at bay.

[EA13] **MORGAN** *MWYNFAWR* AP **ARTHWYR** Gwent and Glywysing, *c*630–*c*665.

His nickname means "the Generous", but this must have been earned late in life, for all the evidence of his reign is of a ruthless and calculating ruler. It is possible that in the first half of his reign Morgan combined forces with ARTGLYS of Ceredigion in an effort to overthrow Dyfed (*see under* GWLYDDIEN). Morgan was also locked in a power struggle with his uncle Frioc, who probably inherited parts of Gwent from MEURIG AP TEWDRIG. Morgan and Frioc swore an oath before the Bishop of Llandaff that they should each keep the peace and that should one kill the other they must resign their kingdom and become a pilgrim. In due course Morgan did kill Frioc, probably in battle. The Welsh annals record "slaughter in Gwent" in the year 649. Morgan was tried and judged by the elders of Glamorgan. Because the kingdom was then under considerable threat they agreed that Morgan should remain king, provided he paid atonement. Thereafter Morgan became very generous to the church for the good of his soul. The threat to the British was from CENWEALH of Wessex, who was expanding his territory west into Dumnonia and threatening the borders of Gwent, where the Mercian kingdom was also becoming established. The area around the Cotswolds became a cauldron of activity for the next twenty years, and Morgan almost certainly sided with the Mercians against the West Saxons. However, it was the West Saxons who made the gains. In the year 665 the Annals record the second battle of Badon, and also note that Morgan died that year. It is not clear if he died in that battle, but it is probable. He would, by then, probably have been nearly sixty. After his death there is a gap in the chronology of Gwent, though the records show he was succeeded by his son ITHAEL.

[EA14] **ITHAEL** AP **MORGAN** Gwent and Glywysing, *c*715–*c*745.

During his reign there was considerable destruction carried out by the Saxons along the Welsh border, which Ithael did his best to check. The power of Gwent, which had increased with each sole powerful king, was fragmented after Ithael's reign by the division between his six sons. The premier rulers were Meurig, RHYS and FFERNFAEL.

[EA15] **FFERNFAEL** AP **ITHAEL** Gwent, 745–775.
Ithael's combined territory of Gwent and Glywysing was divided amongst his sons. Ffernfael became ruler of Gwent, which was ruled by his descendants for the next two generations, whilst his brothers RHYS, Meurig and Rhodri shared Glywysing. The hostilities previously recorded on the Welsh border had halted during Ffernfael's day, probably because of the civil war that had broken out within Mercia and its continued rivalry with Wessex. Ffernfael was succeeded by his son ARTHWYR.

[EA16] **RHYS** AB **ITHAEL** Glywysing, 745– ?
Rhys apparently ruled Glywysing jointly with his brothers Meurig and Rhodri, although the presence of charters bearing solely Rhys's name suggests that he was the senior ruler. It is not clear when he died, and the chronology of Glamorgan at this period is uncertain. It is possible that Rhys was ruling toward the end of the eighth century. He was succeeded by his son ARTHFAEL.

[EA17] **ARTHWYR** AP **FFERNFAEL** Gwent, 775– ?
Records of activities in Gwent at this time are few, but Arthwyr was almost certainly the ruler at the time of the construction of Offa's Dyke. His lands and those of BROCHFAEL AP ELISEDD of Powys probably provided the majority of the labour, but exactly how the building of this Dyke was organized is still uncertain. One has to conclude that Arthwyr, Brochfael and Offa's administrators were able to work closely together for each other's mutual benefit. Arthwyr was succeeded by his son ITHAEL.

[EA18] **ARTHFAEL** AP **RHYS** Glywysing, *fl* 800.
By the time of Arthfael, Glywysing had been subdivided amongst many brothers and cousins so that each was ruling only a relatively small cantref of land. Although Arthfael tends to be identified as the senior king, it is unlikely that he had much authority over his brothers Hywel and Brochfael, his nephews Brochwael and Gwriad, his cousins Tewdwr, Gwrgan and Meurig, and his uncles Meurig and Rhodri, all of whom seem to have been ruling at about this same time, in addition to his cousin ARTHWYR in neighbouring Gwent. This partible succession continued under his sons Meurig and Rhys, both of whom ruled around the 830s–840s. It was not until the time of Rhys's son, HYWEL, that Glywysing began to recover some of its former status.

[EA19] **ITHAEL** AB **ARTHWYR** Gwent, *fl* 830s and died in 848.
He was the last of the line of FFERNFAEL AP ITHAEL, and after his death the throne of Gwent passed to Meurig ab Arthfael and his sons BROCHWAEL and FFERNWAEL.

[EA20] **MEURIG** AB **ARTHFAEL** Gwent, *fl* 830s.
[EA21] **RHYS** AB **ARTHFAEL** Gwent, *fl* 830s.
These two brothers ruled jointly. Little is recorded of their reign, though it seems certain that the division of territory amongst sons and cousins may have seriously weakened Gwent's status but not its military power and jointly they continued to defend the land against the incursion of Danes and Mercians.

[EA22] **BROCHWAEL** and **FFERNWAEL** Gwent, *fl* 880s.

Two brothers, the sons of Meurig ab Arthfael, who are listed together by Asser in his *Life of Alfred.* suggesting that they ruled jointly. They probably needed their combined strength as they suffered from conflict on at least two fronts, possibly three. Asser records that they sought the support of ALFRED against persecution by ATHELRED of Mercia who was hostile to the Welsh and took any opportunity to harry their border. In addition the Danes were driven out of England into Wales in the year 894 and the Annals record that they laid waste to much of Gwent and Glywysing. The rest of Wales was oppressed by ANARAWD and his brothers in Gwynedd, and there is no reason to assume Gwent felt any less vulnerable. The number of documents surviving in the name of Brochwael suggest that he may have been the senior ruler or that he outlived his brother. In later life Brochwael quarrelled with Bishop Cyfeiliog of Llandaff, to the point where Brochwael was threatened with excommunication. The result was that Brochwael condescended to agree to Cyfeiliog's terms and made extensive land grants. Brochwael may have lived into the early 920s.

[EA23] **HYWEL** AP **RHYS** Glywysing, *c*840–*c*885 (may also have ruled Gwent).

There is considerable confusion amongst the chronology and genealogy of the rulers of Glamorgan during the ninth century. Hywel ap Rhys is noted upon the scene in the mid-ninth century, but was of uncertain origin. He was probably the son of RHYS AB ARTHFAEL, and therefore the cousin of BROCHWAEL AB MEURIG of Gwent, but this is far from certain. It seems that early in Hywel's reign there was a dispute over the accession with Gwallwn ap Ceidrich, whom Hywel eventually slew. For this act Hywel was excommunicated and was forced to do penance by the Bishop of Llandaff. Hywel is one of the kings named by Asser as seeking help from ALFRED THE GREAT sometime during the 880s because of oppression from ATHELRED of Mercia. This alliance is always possible (though recent historians have cast doubt on it), not because of internal politics, but because of increasing threats from the Danes. The date of Hywel's death is also uncertain. There is a record of a Hywel ap Rhys who died in Rome in 884 or 885 at an improbably great age. However, Hywel's name is also attached to land grants negotiated with Bishop Cyfeiliog of Llandaff in the early tenth century. It is possible, allowing for the uncertainty of the ninth century, that Hywel had a son called Rhys and a grandson who was also Hywel ap Rhys who ruled in Glywysing in the early tenth century, but the latter would have been a minor king.

[EA24] **OWAIN** AP **HYWEL** Glywysing, *c*885–*c*930.

It is not certain when Owain succeeded his father HYWEL AP RHYS. His reign seems inordinately long for the period although his son, MORGAN, also ruled for over forty years, and Hywel was recorded as living to a remarkable age, so it is possible that Owain was of a long-lived family. He was probably ruler of Glywysing at the time of the Danish onslaught of 896 that devastated much of south-east Wales, and brought Owain into closer association with the West Saxon rulers of England. Owain is also recorded as having submitted to ATHELSTAN in the year 927. Owain had three sons, GRUFFYDD, CADWGAN and Morgan, who initially shared Glywysing but it was re-united by Morgan.

[EA25] **ARTHFAEL** AP **HYWEL** Gwent, *fl* 920s.

Arthfael succeeded his father HYWEL AP RHYS in the territory of Gwent. He may have ruled as early as 885, and he was certainly alive in the 920s when his name is appended to various grants agreed with Bishop Cyfeiliog. He was probably ruling Gwent at the time of the great Danish raids of 896 and 915 which drove the Welsh into a closer relationship with the West Saxons.

[EA26] **CADELL** AP **ARTHFAEL** Gwent, *fl* 930s.

Cadell succeeded his father, ARTHFAEL AP HYWEL, probably around the year 930. His death is recorded in the year 942. He does not appear to have had any children (or none who survived him) and, on his death, Gwent was absorbed into Morgannwg and came under the rule of MORGAN HEN.

Map 4b **The Welsh Kingdoms – Ceredigion and Seisyllwg**

[EA27] **GRUFFYDD** ᴀᴘ **OWAIN** Glywysing, 930–934.

Gruffydd succeeded to Gower as part of his share of Glywysing as early as 928. His short reign was one of constant conflict with ʜʏᴡᴇʟ ᴅᴅᴀ of Ceredigion against whom Gruffydd died in battle. Gower remained in dispute between Hywel and Gruffydd's brothers ᴄᴀᴅᴡɢᴀɴ and ᴍᴏʀɢᴀɴ.

[EA28] **CADWGAN** ᴀᴘ **OWAIN** West Glywysing, 930–950.

Cadwgan ruled West Glywysing as his share of his patrimony with his brothers ɢʀᴜꜰꜰʏᴅᴅ and ᴍᴏʀɢᴀɴ. Gruffydd was killed in battle against ʜʏᴡᴇʟ ᴅᴅᴀ of Ceredigion in 934, and Cadwgan and Morgan faced constant conflict against Hywel who extended his domain over Southern Wales. Although Cadwgan attended the court of ᴇᴀᴅʀᴇᴅ in 949, he became involved soon after in a border skirmish with the English in which he was killed. After his death Morgan ruled all of Gwent and Glywysing and in later years the combined kingdom became known as Morgannwg after him. For details see page 325.

EB. CEREDIGION and SEISYLLWG

Ceredigion was one of the sub-kingdoms allegedly established by Cunedda's son Ceredig. It probably formed around a previous Ordovician kingdom. Its early history may be indistinguishable from Gwynedd in the north whilst in the south it originally formed part of the kingdom of Dyfed. Its independence did not start to emerge until the reign of Seisyll ap Clydog. The family tree for the rulers of Ceredigion is included in the chart on page 140. Map on page 129.

Ref.	Ruler	Reign	Died	Notes
EB1.	Ceredig	fl 470s		
EB2.	Iusay	fl 500s		
EB3.	Serguil	fl 530s		
EB4.	Bodgu ap Serguil	fl 560s		
EB5.	Artbodgu ap Bodgu	fl 600s		
EB6.	Artglys ap Artbodgu	fl 640s		
Kingship during this period is uncertain				
EB7.	Clydog ap Artglys	fl 730s		
EB8.	Seisyll ap Clydog	fl 770s		

Seisyllwg

EB9.	Arthgen ap Seisyll	? –807		
EB10.	Dyfnwallon ap Arthgen	807– ?		
EB11.	Meurig ap Dyfnwallon	fl 850s		
EB12.	Gwgon ap Meurig	? –871	871	drowned

After Gwgon's death Rhodri the Great annexed Seisyllwg to the kingdoms of Gwynedd and Powys. After his death his kingdom was split and Seisyllwg passed to his son Cadell.

EB13.	Cadell ap Rhodri	878–909	909	
EB14.	Clydog	909–920	920	

After Clydog's death his brother Hywel, who had inherited Dyfed after his father's conquests in 904, combined Seisyllwg and Dyfed to form the new kingdom of Deheubarth which occupied most of South Wales except for Glamorgan. Hywel also annexed Gwynedd in 942 making him the ruler of all West Wales. See page 332 for continuation.

[EB1] **CEREDIG** Ceredigion, *fl* 470s.

Ceredig is the eponymous founder of Ceredigion, and supposed son of CUNEDDA. His existence, though, is subject to doubt, and his name may have been assumed by working back from the name of the territory. If he existed, he must have been a younger son of Cunedda, as EINION inherited the heartland of Venedotia (Gwynedd), while Ceredig inherited the coastal territory of west Wales. He probably ruled it as a sub-kingdom of Gwynedd, assuming it existed as a kingdom at all at that time. There is some archaeological evidence to suggest that the southern part of Ceredigion was culturally part of Dyfed and thus had closer Irish connections. Ceredig is recorded as marrying Eleri, the daughter of BRYCHAN, which, if true, would place him closer to the early sixth century. Two of Ceredig's daughters married the native rulers of Gwent and Glywysing (*see* TEITHFALLT and GLYWYS) suggesting that Ceredig was keen to develop alliances in south Wales. It is just possible that this Ceredig bears some relation to CERETIC, the ruler of Alclud, for although the latter is clearly identified with Dumbarton, both would have had opportunities to undertake slave trading in Ireland.

[EB2] **IUSAY** Ceredigion, *fl* 500s.

Iusay is recorded as the son of CEREDIG, but whether he actually ruled in Ceredigion or merely serves as a genealogical link is uncertain. His reign coincided with that of AIRCOL *LAWHIR* of Demetia who almost certainly ruled the southern half of Ceredigion. Iusay, if he had any role at all, might have been as a defender of Gwynedd against the Irish of Demetia.

[EB3] **SERGUIL** Ceredigion, *fl* 530s.

Serguil was the son of IUSAY and grandson of CEREDIG. At this time Ceredigion was a frontier zone between Gwynedd, then ruled by MAELGWYN, and Dyfed, ruled by VORTEPOR, and there was not room for much in between.

[EB4] **BODGU** Ceredigion, *fl* 560s.

Nothing is known about Bodgu's life. He was the son of SERGUIL and the father of ARTBODGU. He ruled (assuming he had any authority at all) at the time of RHUN, the mighty lord of Gwynedd, and it is more probable that Bodgu served as a frontier vassal king.

[EB5] **ARTBODGU** AP **BODGU** Ceredigion, *fl* 600s.

Fifth in line of descent from CEREDIG. At this time Ceredigion was almost certainly ruled from Gwynedd; but, during Artbodgu's reign, Ceredigion seems to emerge as having some identity of its own, distinct from Gwynedd to the north and Dyfed to the south, and it might be that he was the first to start seriously carving out a kingdom of his own. His son was ARTGLYS.

[EB6] **ARTGLYS** Ceredigion, *fl* 640s.

Artglys lived at a time when Gwynedd underwent an internal struggle between its ruling dynasty and the usurper CADFAEL. Consequently Ceredigion could seek some independence, and the archeological evidence indicates that around the early seventh century Ceredigion began to develop its own culture. Artglys probably started what his son CLYDOG continued and which developed particularly in the reign of SEISYLL.

[EB7] **CLYDOG** AP **ARTGLYS** Ceredigion, *fl* 730s.
Clydog is known only as the father of SEISYLL who united Ceredigion with Ystrad Tywi.

[EB8] **SEISYLL** AP **CLYDOG** Ceredigion and Seisyllwg, *fl* 770s.
Ruler of Ceredigion who, at some stage in the late eighth century invaded Dyfed and took control over those *cantrefi* which are known collectively as Ystrad Tywi. This expanded kingdom he named Seisyllwg after himself and it formed the basis of the future Deheubarth. The length of Seisyll's reign is uncertain but it is possible he ruled for some time, perhaps as long as forty years, as there is some suggestion that he was around in the 730s. In fact Seisyll's existence is only known by reference back from his son, and his predecessors are known only from the king lists.

[EB9] **ARTHGEN** AP **SEISYLL** Ceredigion and Seisyllwg, ? –807.
Arthgen inherited the newly expanded kingdom of Seisyllwg from his father, though it may have been Arthgen who gave it its new name in honour of his father. He was still recorded as king of Ceredigion, however, at the time of his death.

[EB10] **DYFNWALLON** Ceredigion, 807– ?
Dyfnwallon was the son of ARTHGEN. His reign commenced in 807, but it is not certain how long he ruled and he may have survived into the 830s. At this time MERFYN *FRYCH* of Gwynedd was beginning his territorial expansion and Dyfnwallon must have had problems in retaining his independence. He was succeeded by his son MEURIG.

[EB11] **MEURIG** AP **DYFNWALLON** Ceredigion, *fl* 850s.
Meurig was a contemporary of RHODRI *MAWR*, the king of Gwynedd who, during Meurig's reign annexed the neighbouring kingdom of Powys. Meurig would have struggled between keeping his independence and having the help of Rhodri against the Viking invaders harrying the Welsh coast from the 850s. Meurig's solution was to marry his daughter Angharad to Rhodri. Soon after Meurig's death, his own son GWGON drowned, and Rhodri annexed Ceredigion.

[EB12] **GWGON** Ceredigion, ? –871.
The last king of Ceredigion in male descent from CEREDIG. His sister, Angharad, married RHODRI *MAWR*, who began to interfere in the affairs of the kingdom. Either through Rhodri's connivance or by other means, Gwgon drowned in 871, and Rhodri annexed the kingdom to Gwynedd and Powys. Only after Rhodri's death, in 878, was the kingdom reformed as Rhodri's inheritance was partitioned, and it was passed to CADELL AP RHODRI.

[EB13] **CADELL** AP **RHODRI** Seisyllwg, 878–909.
The younger son of RHODRI *MAWR*, Cadell inherited Ceredigion and Ystrad Tywi while his brother ANARAWD inherited Gwynedd and Powys. The previous dynasty of Ceredigion had died out with GWGON when Rhodri annexed the kingdom, but

there were no doubt factions of the royal family who strove to regain power. Cadell and Anarawd combined forces to ensure that they suffocated any opposition. By the early 890s, they had not only forced Ceredigion into submission, but had become a menace to HYFAIDD, king of Dyfed, and ELISEG of Brycheiniog. The hositility worsened as the threatened kings sought the help of ALFRED of Wessex, which Anarawd and Cadell countered in 894, by bringing in the Danes of York, a disastrous move as the Danes ravaged Gwynedd and Anarawd in turn had to seek aid from Alfred. In 895, however, Anarawd and Cadell began another campaign against Seisyllwg and forced it into submission. It was probably only at this time that Cadell effectively became ruler of the kingdom,

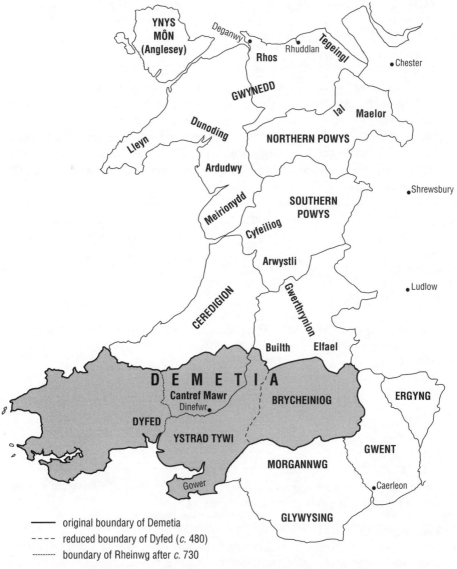

Map 4c **The Welsh Kingdoms – Demetia and Dyfed**

but always under the overall control of Anarawd. Cadell went on to conquer Dyfed in 905, eliminating the previous ruling family. Cadell held his land by force, in complete contrast to his son, HYWEL, whose abilities made him the greatest ruler the Welsh ever had.

[EB14] **CLYDOG** AP **CADELL** Seisyllwg, 909–920.
When Cadell died in 909 his kingdom was shared between his sons. Clydog, the elder, received Seisyllwg, whilst HYWEL received Dyfed. It was the younger brother who would prove the most able ruler, and to a large degree the two brothers ruled both kingdoms jointly. Clydog and Hywel appeared together at the convention of 918 to demonstrate their fealty to EDWARD *THE ELDER*. Clydog was probably only in his forties when he died in 920 and the whole kingdom passed to Hywel. Details of Hywel's new kingdom are on page 330.

EC. DEMETIA and DYFED

The kingdom of Dyfed, in the far south-west of Wales, was originally the tribal territory of the Demetae, and the kingdom was first known as Demetia. When Roman authority waned it was settled by the Irish, who traced their descent from Artchorp in the fourth century, who was descended from the Irish High Kings. Details of the kings and their reigns are sparse. The Demetian rulers are distantly related to the Scottish settlers of Dál Riata and their genealogy is shown in Chart 8 on page 194. The Map is on page 133.

Ref.	Ruler	Born	Reign	Died	Notes
EC1.	Eochaid		*fl* 400		son of Artchorp
EC2.	Corath		*fl* 420s		
EC3.	Aed		*fl* 450s		
EC4.	Tryffin		*fl* 480s		
EC5.	Aircol *Lawhir* (*Longhand*)		*fl* 500		
EC6.	Gwrthefyr, or Vortepor		*c*515–*c*540		see P101
EC7.	Cyngar		*fl* 550s		
EC8.	Pedr		*fl* 570s		
EC9.	Arthwyr		*fl* 590s		
EC10.	Nowy		*fl* 610s		
EC11.	Gwlyddien		*fl* 640s		
EC12.	Cathen		*fl* 670s		
EC13.	Cadwgan		*fl* 700s		
EC14.	Rhain		*fl* 730s		

Rhain's kingdom was severely diminished by conquest by Seisyll of Ceredigion and the remnant became the smaller kingdom of Rheinwg.

Rheinwg

EC15.	Tewdws or Tewdwr		*fl* 770s		
EC16.	Maredudd	*c*745	? –*c*797	*c*797	

EC17.	Rhain (II)	c767	c797–808	808	
EC18.	Owain ap Maredudd	c770	808–811	811	
EC19.	Tryffin ap Rhain		811–814	814	

Details of Dyfed's rulers vanish at this time, possibly as the result of Viking raids. No more rulers are recorded until the time of Owain's grandson, Hyfaidd.

EC20.	Hyfaidd ap Bledri	fl 880s–893	893	
EC21.	Llywarch ap Hyfaidd	? –904	904	drowned
EC22.	Rhodri ap Hyfaidd	904–905	905	beheaded
EC23.	Hywel *Dda* (*the Good*)	905–950	950	

Hywel Dda inherited Seisyllwg after his brother's death and combined the two kingdoms as Deheubarth. See page 330 for full details.

[EC1] **EOCHAID** Irish chieftain of Demetia, *fl* 400.

The name ascribed to the chieftain of the Déisi, in Leinster, who led settlers across from Ireland at about the end of the fourth century to establish themselves in south-west Wales and in parts of Cornwall. By all accounts the settlement was peaceful; there is no evidence, archeological or written, of wars, though these certainly developed in later years. Eochaid is recorded as the son of Artchorp, who was ruler of the Déisi in the lands around present-day Waterford and Tipperary.

[EC2] **CORATH** Demetia, *fl* 420s.
[EC3] **AED** Demetia, *fl* 450s.

Corath was the son of EOCHAID and ruler of the Demetian Irish in south-west Wales in the first quarter of the fifth century. Although nothing is recorded of his reign it is certain that Corath must have established his power base across much of south Wales towards the territory of Gwent and probably north towards Venedotia. It was almost certainly the expansion during his reign and that of his son Aed that brought CUNEDDA to North Wales to contain the Irish advance.

[EC4] **TRYFFIN (I)** *FARFOG* (the *BEARDED*)ruled in the 480s.

He was presumably the son of AED, although it is with him that the names of the rulers shift from Irish to a Romanized Celtic. Tryffin may be no more than the Celtic translation of Tribune. Since his son, AIRCOL, is the Celtic form of Agricola, and his grandson, VORTEPOR, was known as the Protector, rather than King, we must recognize that some other influence may have been at work at this time. Tradition states he married the daughter of Clotri, a British lord of Dyfed, descended from MAGNUS MAXIMUS. Although the Roman Empire had long abandoned Britain by the 470s, attempts to sustain the Roman culture and civilisation continued, particularly in the former Roman heartlands of Gloucester and south-east Wales. It is possible that this influence reached into Demetia, and that one branch of the ruling family became strongly Romanized and found themselves as senior officials in the army of AMBROSIUS AURELIANUS and subsequently ARTHUR. It is recorded that CUNEDDA and his sons drove the Irish out of north Wales, and pushed them back in the south. It is likely that at this time Demetia was split into two, with the territory of Brycheiniog being separated to the east, and Demetia taking the form of later Dyfed on the south-west peninsula.

[EC5] **AIRCOL *LAWHIR* (*LONGHAND*)** Demetia/Dyfed, *fl* 500.

The son of TRYFFIN. Although descended from Irish settlers, Aircol and his father clearly came under Roman influence as evidenced by their names. It is thus likely that they served in the armies developed under AMBROSIUS AURELIANUS and ARTHUR to defend Britain after the end of Roman rule from the invading Picts and Saxons. Aircol is also remembered as a strong patron of the church, granting lands to St Teilo. He was succeeded by his notorious son Gwrthefyr or VORTEPOR.

[EC6;P101] **VORTEPOR or GWRTHEFYR** Demetia/Dyfed, *c*515–*c*540.

Vortepor is remembered from the writing of Gildas in *The Ruin of Britain* who rebuked the ruler for his evil ways, stating that he was the bad son of a good king (AIRCOL) who had committed murder and rape, possibly even of his own daughter. It does not seem that Vortepor was entirely bad, as Gildas likens him to a leopard, "spotted with wickedness". Since he lived during the relative peace and calm of the last golden age of Britain (between Badon and Camlann; see ARTHUR) and was accorded the title of Protector, it seems likely that he was a once strong and powerful ruler who had grown wicked in his old age because of the lack of action. A memorial inscription to Vortepor survives and originally stood in the church of Castell Dwyran, which was presumably the ancestral home of the rulers of Dyfed. Since Vortepor was a contemporary of ARTHUR it is surprising that he does not emerge in the Arthurian legends. At that time the ruler of Dyfed is recorded as Stater, a name that means nothing in the genealogies. Geoffrey of Monmouth regarded Vortepor as a frugal and peaceful king who ruled all of Britain after he had successfully defeated the Saxons.

[EC7] **CYNGAR** Dyfed, *fl* 550s.

The son and successor of VORTEPOR. No other details are known, though it is certain that he would have faced conflict from the sons of MAELGWYN who endeavoured to expand the power of Gwynedd at this time.

[EC8] **PEDR** Dyfed, *fl* 570s.

Successor of CYNGAR. Nothing is known of his reign, but he was a contemporary of RHUN of Gwynedd and may have been a vassal to Rhun's all-powerful kingdom. He would also have faced attack by MEURIG AP TEWDRIG of Gwent who is recorded as having eventually overthrown the Demetian overlordship in southern Wales. If so, then Meurig may have deposed Pedr and installed his own son, ARTHWYR, as ruler.

[EC9] **ARTHWYR** Dyfed, *fl* 590s.

The successor of PEDR, Arthwyr is listed amongst the genealogy of Dyfed. The timing would make him a contemporary of ARTHWYR of Gwent and it is possible (though unlikely) that the two were one and the same, and that Arthwyr (one of the candidates for the real King ARTHUR) had extended his kingdom to cover all of South Wales and into Dyfed. If this were so he would have displaced the dynasty of Eochaid, and this is not recorded. Moreover the Arthwyr of Gwent is firmly recorded as the son of MEURIG. Arthwyr of Dyfed was a tyrannical ruler and it is memories of him that created the darker side of the legendary Arthur.

[EC10] **NOWY** or **NOE** Dyfed, *fl* 610s.

The king-lists of Dyfed show that ARTHWYR was succeeded by Nowy, or Noah. The legendary ARTHUR also had a son called Nowy who died fighting in the West. Nowy was a strongly religious king; he bestowed much land to the church. The exact length of his reign is uncertain, but it is possible he survived well into the 600s. His daughter, Sanan, was the mother of ELISEDD of Powys, who lived in the early 700s.

[EC11] **GWLYDDIEN** Dyfed, *fl* 640s.

The successor of NOWY. It was during his reign that the Welsh annals record "the hammering of the region of Dyfed" in the year 645. This was probably an onslaught from ARTGLYS of Ceredigion who may have been assisted by the ambitious MORGAN AP ARTHWYR of Gwent, seeking to regain his father's kingdom. Gwlyddien's reign may, therefore, have been short. He was succeeded by CATHEN.

[EC12] **CATHEN** Dyfed, *fl* 670s.
[EC13] **CADWGAN** Dyfed, *fl* 700s.

It was during the reign of Cathen that ARTGLYS began to establish himself in Ceredigion and we can imagine that some conflict occurred between the two kingdoms that continued throughout the reign of his son Cadwgan to his grandson, RHAIN.

[EC14] **RHAIN** Dyfed, *fl* 730s.

Fourteenth in descent from EOCHAID and ruler of the Gaelic settlement of Dyfed, Rhain suffered repeated attacks from the rulers of Ceredigion, particularly CLYDOG and his son SEISYLL. Early in his reign, probably in the 730s, it seems that Seisyll succeeded in conquering the territory later known as Ystrad Tywi which thereby came under his rulership as part of the newly named Seisyllwg. Likewise Rhain's reduced kingdom was named, in comparison, as Rheinwg, but the name does not appear to have superseded the more common Dyfed.

[EC15;EG6] **TEWDWS** or **TEWDWR** Dyfed, *fl* 770s.

Little is known of his reign. There is a record of the invasion of Dyfed by OFFA of Mercia in 778, and Tewdws may have been killed during that raid. He was succeeded by his son MAREDUDD. It is possible he is the same Tewdws ap Rhain who claimed sovereignty over part of the kingdom of Brycheiniog in rivalry to his kinsman ELWYSTI AB AWST and who subsequently murdered Elwysti. This may account for the confusion over the territory known as Rheinwg between Dyfed and Brycheiniog.

[EC16] **MAREDUDD** AP **TEWDWS** Dyfed, ? –*c*797.

Little is known of Maredudd's reign. His death is recorded in the Cambrian Annals in 796 or 797. This coincides with a raid upon Dyfed by the Mercians and he may well have been killed in the conflict. He was succeeded by his eldest son RHAIN.

[EC17] **RHAIN (II)** Dyfed, *c*797–808.

Rhain was ruler at a particularly difficult time. Power struggles to the north in Gwynedd and to the east in Gwent, made Dyfed's borders vulnerable, and the coast was becoming increasingly subject to Viking raids. It is likely that the reason both for the short reigns of Rhain's successors and for the lack of information is destruction caused by the Vikings, who in fact may have briefly overrun the kingdom. Rhain was succeeded by his brother OWAIN.

[EC18] **OWAIN** AP **MAREDUDD** Dyfed, 808–811.
There are no details about Owain's brief rule in Dyfed, but it is likely the country became subject to increasing Viking raids and that Owain was killed. He was succeeded by his nephew, TRYFFIN (II).

[EC19] **TRYFFIN (II)** Dyfed, 811–814.
The last recorded ruler of Dyfed before a brief hiatus. It is likely that the Vikings raided Dyfed during this period and Tryffin may have been killed in one such raid. No other king is recorded until the time of HYFAIDD AP BLEDRI.

Map 4d **The Welsh Kingdoms – Gwynedd**

[EC20] **HYFAIDD** AP **BLEDRI** Dyfed, *fl* 880s–893.

Hyfaidd emerges as one of the kings of south Wales mentioned by Asser in his life of King Alfred. It seems that Hyfaidd, threatened by the sons of RHODRI THE GREAT, sought the help of ALFRED THE GREAT. Doubt has since been cast on Asser's biography, although there is no reason to doubt the existence of Hyfaidd and the general thrust of the narrative. Hyfaidd is the first named king of Dyfed since the death of TRYFFIN (II) in 814. Whether Dyfed was overrun by Vikings in the intervening sixty or seventy years, or whether their raids destroyed all records of Hyfaidd's predecessors is not clear. It seems that Hyfaidd claimed the Demetian kingdom through his descent from OWAIN AP MAREDUDD, whose daughter was Hyfaidd's mother. The continued Viking threat would have led the Welsh princes and Alfred to unite against a common foe, and the increasing threat of ANARAWD and his brothers (particularly CADELL) may have added to the need for an alliance. Hyfaidd's death is recorded in 893. He was succeeded by his son LLYWARCH.

[EC21] **LLYWARCH** AP **HYFAIDD** Dyfed, ? –904.
[EC22] **RHODRI** AP **HYFAIDD** Dyfed, 904–905.

Llywarch was the last recorded ruler of Dyfed. He was deposed and ritually drowned by CADELL AP RHODRI of Gwynedd and his brother, RHODRI, who probably briefly proclaimed his kingship, was soon after beheaded. Llywarch's daughter Elen married HYWEL DDA, and through that marriage Hywel inherited the kingdom. Thereafter Dyfed was incorporated into Deheubarth (*see page 330*).

ED. VENEDOTIA and GWYNEDD

Gwynedd covered the territory of the Ordovices, but the kingdom established by Cunedda brought together migratory British from elsewhere in Britain. The territory was originally known as Venedotia, a name which mutated to Gwynedd over the next two centuries. The heart of Gwynedd was originally at Deganwy, but shifted to Anglesey and at one time included the Isle of Man. It became the most powerful kingdom of Wales. The family tree on page 140 shows the main line of Gwynedd descent together with the other sons of Cunedda.

Ref.	Ruler	Born	Reign	Died	Notes
House of Cunedda					
ED1.	Cunedda		*c*450s–*c*460s		see D4
ED2.	Einion		*c*470s–*c*480s		
ED3.	Cadwallon *Lawhir* (*Longhand*)		*c*500–*c*534	*c*534	
ED4.	Maelgwn *Hir* (*the Tall*)	*c*497	*c*520s–*c*549	*c*549	died in a plague; see P102
ED5.	Rhun *Hir*	*c*520	*c*549–?580s		
ED6.	Beli		580s–*c*599	*c*599	
ED7.	Iago		*c*599–*c*613	*c*613	
ED8.	Cadfan		*c*615–*c*620	*c*625	see P104

Edwin of Northumbria overran Gwynedd between 620 and 627

Ref.	Ruler	Born	Reign	Died	Notes
ED9.	Cadwallon	c590s	c620–634	634	in exile 620–627; killed in battle; see P105
ED10.	Cadfael		634–c655		usurper; later deposed
ED11.	Cadwaladr		c655–c682	c682	died in a plague; see P106
ED12.	Idwal		c682–?720	?720	
ED13.	Rhodri *Molwynog*		c720–c754	c754	

4. Wales (2) – **The sons of Cunedda**

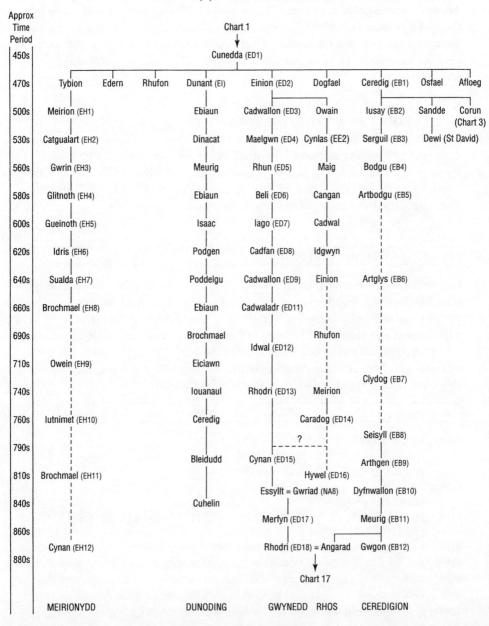

ED14.	Caradog	c754–c798	c798	killed
ED15.	Cynan	c798–816	816	may have ruled from 813 only
ED16.	Hywel	814–825	825	
ED17.	Merfyn *Frych* (*the Freckled*)	825–844	844	son of Gwriad of Man (NA8)

Merfyn's son, Rhodri, succeeded to the kingdoms of Powys in 855 and that of Seisyllwg in 872, becoming king of all North Wales. Under him and his successors Gwynedd entered its period of greatness which is dealt with in Part 2, starting on page 344.

[ED1;DA4] **CUNEDDA** Lothian (Gododdin), 430s; North Wales, 450s–c460s.

Cunedda is one of the founding fathers of the Welsh royal dynasties, which means he has attracted as much tradition as history. There can be little doubt that he really existed, but how much of his life we can consider genuine is difficult to say, although there is nothing to dispute the generally accepted story. The name Cunedda is better known today as Kenneth, and it derives from the Celtic Counodagos, meaning "good lord", and is related to the later name Cinead, meaning "born of fire". Both of these derivations may be significant in Cunedda's case, as his genealogy (if it is correct) makes him the grandson of Padarn Beisrudd, which translates as Paternus of the Scarlet Cloak. Paternus was almost certainly a Roman official of high rank who, sometime around the year 388 was placed in command of the troops in the area of the Votadini or the Gododdin, in what later became Bernicia and Lothian. It is not quite certain whether Paternus had authority over the whole of this territory, or whether his domain was either south or north of the Wall. This command probably continued through Paternus's son, Eternus, to Cunedda who, around the year 430, effectively became the leader of the tribes of the Votadini, although he may not have been native to them. At this time Cunedda would have been heavily involved in the wars against the Picts who were threatening the lands south of Hadrian's Wall. During this period Cunedda married Gwawl, the daughter of COEL HEN.

Around the year 450 the problems throughout Britain became acute. Famine ravaged the land and Britain was beset by further invasions from the Saxons to the east and the Irish to the west. At this time, perhaps under instruction from the high king of the British (*see* VORTIGERN), Cunedda and his family moved south, leaving his eldest son, Tybion, in control in the north. Cunedda's role was to protect Wales from the invasions of the Irish. He established himself in north Wales, in the territory of the Venedotians, which became the core of the later kingdom of Gwynedd. Cunedda succeeded in holding the Irish incursions at bay, although he was never able to drive them out of Demetia, in south-west Wales. It is not certain where Cunedda established his base, though the old Roman fort at Chester is the most likely.

We know little about Cunedda himself, although his name may suggest a powerful lord with an aristocratic bearing. He certainly needed to be authoritative to command respect from the beleaguered Romano-British forces, though the degree of his success was plainly limited. A battle poem celebrating his successes calls him Cunedda the Lion, which is probably testament to his strength and courage. Although his dates are subject to degrees of uncertainty, he was probably born around the year 400 and may have lived into his 60s. Later tradition ascribed him nine sons, from whom territories of northern and central Wales derived their

names, though it was not until the tenth century that the genealogies linked these to
Cunedda. It is thus difficult to know for certain how many children Cunedda had
and how these were linked to later generations of rulers. CEREDIG and EINION have
separate entries.

[ED2] **EINION** *YRTH* Venedos (Gwynedd), *c*470s–*c*480s.
Little is recorded of Einion's period of authority. As one of the sons of CUNEDDA he
must have been highly respected, and the fact that he inherited the core territory of
North Wales, may suggest he was the senior of the sons who accompanied Cunedda
to Wales. With the help of his brothers, especially CEREDIG, and his nephew
MEIRION, Einion was able to build upon the conquests of his father and carve out
the territories which became the later kingdoms of Gwynedd, Ceredigion and
Meirionydd. He was the father of CADWALLON *LAWHIR*.

[ED3] **CADWALLON** *LAWHIR* [*LONGHAND*] Gwynedd, *c*500–*c*534.
A grandson of CUNEDDA and father of the notorious MAELGWYN, Cadwallon
succeeded his father EINION as ruler of the Venedotian territory in north Wales.
We can derive some understanding of Cadwallon from his name and nickname.
Cadwallon became a common Welsh name, especially amongst rulers, because it
translates as "battle leader", though this is its first appearance amongst the post-
Roman rulers. *Lawhir* means longhand, and almost certainly refers to a physical
attribute rather than meaning his power extended over a large area. As his son,
Maelgwyn, was also known as the Tall, we can imagine that Cadwallon was a tall
and powerful leader who held his territory by the regular deployment of troops
around North Wales. It was during Cadwallon's reign that ARTHUR gained his
victory over the Saxons at Badon. Although we do not know that Cadwallon was
present at that battle, we can presume that he was involved in earlier skirmishes
against the Saxons, most likely in the territory around Chester and down through
the Welsh marches. Although he would have benefited from the peace that followed
Badon, Cadwallon had to remain on the alert to defend his western borders from
continued threats from the Irish. One noted episode remembered by the Welsh
bards is that Cadwallon led his army into Anglesey to defeat the Irish and claim the
island, which later became his base. It is possible that Cadwallon was succeeded by a
brother, whose name we do not know, who was subsequently murdered by
Maelgwyn.

[ED4;P102] **MAELGWYN** *HIR* (**the** *TALL*) Gwynedd, [520s?] *c*534–*c*549.
Maelgwyn was one of the most powerful rulers of early sixth century Britain, so
much so that he has been regarded by some as the original of king ARTHUR,
especially as Gildas, who rebuked Maelgwyn severely in his *Ruin of Britain,* called
him the "dragon of the island", a reference to the title of Pendragon or high king.
Others have tried to associate Maelgwyn with Lancelot, although the links are
purely circumstantial. Nevertheless, with Maelgwyn, we have a king whose reign
coincides with the height of Arthur's fame and who was certainly the senior king
amongst the British after Arthur's death. Maelgwyn's nickname, *Hir,* means Tall,
and his name, *gwyn,* means fair, so we can picture him as a tall, powerful, blond
man, probably quite handsome (since he won over women later in his life).
Geoffrey of Monmouth (who calls him Malgo) specifically refers to his handsome

features, but also states that he was homosexual. Gildas's name for him, Maglocunus, means Great Hound which is probably descriptive not only of his strength and power but of his tenacity and single-mindedness.

Maelgwyn's life was turbulent. Called by Gildas "first in evil", he was regarded as a vicious tyrant, but he also had a period of repentance during which he turned to the church, before he once again took up a life of tyranny. Gildas records that in his youth he killed his uncle. This may have been Owain or Eugene, the father of CYNLAS, who became a rival with Maelgwyn over the territories within Gwynedd. It is possible that Maelgwyn had been too young when his father died to inherit directly but that a year or two later, perhaps still only in his late teens, he took control by force. Having established himself in Gwynedd he then seems to have been smitten by his conscience, for he is alleged to have become a monk. It was quite common amongst the Celtic nobility for older brothers to become secular rulers and the younger brothers to enter the church. Maelgwyn may have been a younger brother who rebelled against the church in his youth but later saw the error of his ways. This suggests, however, that Maelgwyn stepped down as ruler and there is no evidence that this happened. What evidence there is suggests that rather than enter the church, Maelgwyn paid for his past deeds by bounty to it. He is reputed to have founded the bishopric of Bangor and to have built or strengthened other churches. However, this period of grace lasted only a limited time before Maelgwyn returned to his evil ways. He married, but soon his passions turned to his nephew's wife. Maelgwyn murdered his wife and nephew and took his nephew's wife as his own. There is also reason to believe that he married a Pictish princess. He established a rich and powerful court at Deganwy, to which he attracted many bards whom he ensured wrote copiously of his triumphs and achievements. He was recognized as both a great patron of the arts and as a lawgiver, though some of this was probably his own propaganda! Those who despised Maelgwyn may have felt he eventually received just retribution, as he died of a plague (probably cholera) which was then sweeping Europe.

Somehow the traditional span ascribed to Maelgwyn's reign does not seem long enough for all of this to happen, and certainly not for Maelgwyn to have had a son old enough to succeed him after his death if Maelgwyn only married after becoming king. The implication is that Maelgwyn may have usurped only part of Gwynedd in his youth when the territory was divided between EINION's sons. This may have happened as early as 515, when Maelgwyn was perhaps about eighteen. He may then indeed have retired to a monastery during the early 520s before returning to secular life in the late 520s, at which time he would have married. Upon his father's death in 534 Maelgwyn would have made a claim for total rulership, killing the nearest claimant, his nephew, and marrying his wife, who it seems had encouraged Maelgwyn in his plans. His son and successor, RHUN, was almost certainly a child of the first marriage. Maelgwyn was also the father of BRUDE, who was chosen by the Picts to be their leader. By the time of his death Maelgwyn was firmly established as the primary ruler of the British, and a natural successor to ARTHUR.

[ED5] **RHUN** *HIR* Gwynedd, c549–?580s.
Rhun was the son and successor of MAELGWYN. He was probably in his late twenties when his father died of the plague. The early part of Rhun's reign shows that he

could claim to be the most powerful king of his day in Britain, and that he could even have established himself at the head of a pan-British kingdom. Sometime after his father's death, presumably around 560, ELIDYR, the ruler of Rheged, who had married Rhun's sister, believed he had claim to Gwynedd, and more especially the island of Anglesey. At this time Elidyr almost certainly ruled the Isle of Man as well and the islands of Man and Anglesey have a long historic association. Elidyr's attempt at conquest, however, failed, for he was killed by Rhun. Elidyr's cousins from the north, particularly RHYDDERCH *Hen* and CLYDNO *Eiten* who ruled Strathclyde and Lothian, were wary of Rhun's power. Rhun's half-brother, BRUDE, had recently been elected ruler of the Picts, which meant that Rhydderch and Clydno were trapped between a growing dynastic power to north and south. Rhydderch and Clydno along with Elidyr's brother CINMARC, sailed down to Anglesey and sacked the town of Arfon (now Caernarvon) on the mainland. Instead of building upon their advantage they now retreated, clearly feeling they had taught Rhun a lesson. But the opposite happened. Rhun gave them a demonstration of his power. Mustering forces from all over north Wales, Rhun led an army, probably the greatest force that had been seen since the days of ARTHUR, and marched from Wales up through Rheged (Lancashire) and across the Pennines to York. In all that march, which lasted several months, Rhun was unopposed. In effect he exercised authority over all of north Wales and northern Britain and, in alliance with Brude, extending into the lands of the Picts. Rhun could have sought to establish a major kingdom. But he did not have a sufficient power base back in Wales to sustain such rule, and though his authority was recognized, he did not take control of the territory. Instead he made peace with PEREDUR of York, apparently marrying his cousin Perwyr, and then returned to Gwynedd. The expedition, which probably took place in the early 560s, lasted about a year, and passed into Welsh legend. It is therefore surprising that nothing more is heard of Rhun although he ruled for perhaps another twenty years. One can conjecture that during that period he established Gwynedd as a prosperous and strong kingdom not threatened by any outside powers. Rhun was succeeded by BELI AP RHUN, who was either his son or nephew.

[ED6] **BELI** AP **RHUN** Gwynedd, 580s–c599.
Little is known about the reign of Beli, the son or nephew of RHUN, even though he inherited a powerful and stable kingdom. It may be pertinent that although his forebears, Rhun, MAELGWYN and CADWALLON were all noted for their height and strength, no such name attached itself to Beli, possibly an undistinguished ruler who reigned during a period of relative peace and thus failed to pass into legend. He was succeeded by his son IAGO.

[ED7] **IAGO** AP **BELI** Gwynedd, c599–c613 (or 615?).
The name Iago is the Welsh equivalent of Jacob or James. Although little is recorded about Iago ap Beli, it was during his reign that the power of the Angles in Mercia grew under PYBBA and his son PENDA. Later evidence suggests that the Welsh and the Mercians became allies, and it may be that Iago entered into some form of agreement with Pybba that the latter would not attack him in return for support for Mercia when needed. This was especially important because of the growing power of ATHELFRITH of Northumbria. In 604, Athelfrith had driven EDWIN out of

Northumbria and the young king sought refuge at the courts of Iago and SELYF of Powys. Athelfrith, determined to be rid of Edwin turned his wrath against the Welsh; it seems that the Mercians provided little assistance. Athelfrith slaughtered the monks of a monastery at Bangor and then his forces defeated and killed Selyf at the Battle of Chester. It is not recorded that Iago took part in this battle; in fact it is suggested that Iago may already have abdicated as king and died that same year in a monastery. He was succeeded by his son CADFAN.

[ED8;P104] **CADFAN** AP **IAGO** Gwynedd, c615–c620.

Cadfan is remembered as a wise king, which suggests that not only did he administer the laws justly to his subjects, but that he also succeeded in maintaining peace at a time of growing hostility between the Welsh and the Angles, especially the Northumbrian king ATHELFRITH. Despite Athelfrith's victory at the Battle of Chester, Cadfan continued to shelter EDWIN, the Northumbrian prince whom Athelfrith was intent on killing. When Athelfrith was himself killed in battle four years later, Edwin was restored to his throne. He did not show any particular favouritism to his saviours, however; he became intent on conquering other Celtic lands, including Elmet, Rheged and Man, and was eventually killed by Cadfan's son CADWALLON.

[ED9;P105] **CADWALLON** AP **CADFAN** Gwynedd, c620–634.

Cadwallon was the son of CADFAN, but whereas his father chose wise counsel whereby to govern, Cadwallon preferred the spear and sword. The story of Cadwallon and EDWIN of Mercia is one of those remarkable relationships in history. Legend has it that both were of about the same age although in reality Edwin was older. When Edwin was driven out of Northumbria by ATHELFRITH he was given refuge in the courts of Gwynedd and Powys. This brought Athelfrith hammering on the door of Gwynedd and an enmity between the two kingdoms. One might think that when Edwin was restored to the throne of Northumbria in 617 all would be well between them, but not so. We may conjecture that as youths Edwin and Cadwallon had grown apart and become rivals, and that rivalry developed into a fury in later years. Once restored to the throne Edwin determined to conquer Britain. He soon captured the British kingdom of Elmet and deposed its king CEREDIG. With the death of Cadfan, Edwin invaded North Wales, driving the Welsh back toward the sea. Cadwallon, unprepared, fled to the islet of Priestholm, off Anglesey, and from there escaped to Ireland. His exile lasted about seven years, during which time Edwin's authority spread over all of northern England and Wales and the Isle of Man. Around 626 Edwin was converted to Christianity and ceased his conquests. Cadwallon returned from Wales and was restored to his kingdom, though as a vassal to Northumbria. But Cadwallon would have none of that. He entered into an alliance with PENDA, the new warlord of the Mercians who had his eyes firmly set on power, and the combined armies entered into a prolonged war with Edwin. It is unclear when this war began, but probably not until around the year 630 or 631. A Welsh poem recalls that Cadwallon fought fourteen battles and sixty skirmishes which, even allowing for exaggeration, is too much for one year. Edwin had a strong hold on the land and his power would not be overturned in a short period. The climactic battle came at Haethfeld, or Hatfield Chase, just north of Doncaster, in October 633 when the combined powers of Cadwallon and Penda were too much for the Northumbrian army. Edwin was killed, as were most of his family and many of his nobles. Cadwallon had regained the old kingdom of his forebears, for it was from Northumbria that CUNEDDA had come two centuries before.

However Cadwallon was no administrator and not especially used to kingship. Had he followed his father's ways he might have restored a strong British kingdom in the north and changed the fortunes of the Saxons. Instead Cadwallon chose to ravage and destroy Edwin's kingdom. For a whole year the land was laid waste. Cadwallon also killed Edwin's successors EANFRITH and OSRIC, but he was taken by surprise by OSWALD, the son of the former aggressor Athelfrith. Oswald attacked Cadwallon at dawn while the Welsh leader was encamped at Heavenfield, near Hexham, by Hadrian's Wall. So unprepared was Cadwallon's army that it fled, almost without fighting, for five miles. Cadwallon was killed in the affray.

Cadwallon could have been a great king. He was remembered as such by the Welsh because, for one brief period, he re-established the might of the British against the Saxons. Had he been a wise king he could have restored British might and glory. But he lost this chance, and the British never again regained such power. At his death he was only in his late thirties. His son, CADWALADR was too young to take power, and Gwynedd was lost to an adventurer called CADFAEL.

[ED10] **CADFAEL *CADOMEDD* AP CYNFEDDW** Gwynedd, 634–c655.
On the death of CADWALLON in battle, Cadfael seized the throne of Gwynedd. We know little about him. One imagines he was a cousin or other relative of Cadwallon, although the Welsh triads remember him as one of three kings "who were sprung from villeins", suggesting he was not of royal stock. It is just possible that his father was the CYNFEDDW murdered by MEURIG of Gwent. Cadfael may have been raised in the court of Gwynedd and been given some degree of authority when Cadwallon went to war with EDWIN of Northumbria in 630 or 631. He may even have featured earlier during Cadwallon's exile, as Edwin probably had some native administrator installed in Gwynedd during his period of overlordship. The name by which he is known may not have been his given name, as Cadafael or Cadfael means "battle seizer", which suggests it was a nickname given after he took control by force and perhaps held it by force. Whatever his origins, he clearly had strong control of Gwynedd as he remained in power for over twenty years. He evidently sustained the alliance with Mercia which had been forged by Cadwallon and his forebears, and this almost certainly helped keep Cadfael in power, as his reign coincides with the authority of Penda. Cadfael was not fondly remembered by the Welsh, and his fate seems suitably ignominious. He fought alongside Penda in the fatal battle of Winwæd in 655 where Penda fell. Cadfael fled the battlefield, thus earning his second nickname, *Cadomedd* or "Battle Shirker". We do not know what happened to Cadfael after the battle. He may have died soon after, possibly killed by CADWALADR, or he may have fled into exile.

[ED11;P106] **CADWALADR *FENDIGIAD* (the *BLESSED*)** Gwynedd, c655–c682.
Cadwaladr was perhaps the last great British hero, remembered in Welsh texts almost like another ARTHUR. He was the son of CADWALLON, and was still a boy when his father was killed in battle. He was presumably raised in exile either in Ireland, or in one of the neighbouring Welsh kingdoms. The native Venedotians of

Gwynedd did not like their usurper king CADFAEL; they hailed Cadwaladr as a promised saviour to deliver them from his yoke and to conquer the English again, echoing the achievements of Cadwallon. Unfortunately he did not live up to their expectations. In 658 he led an army against the West Saxons at Peonne in Somerset and was soundly defeated. Thereafter he seems to have spent his years establishing peace and prosperity in Gwynedd, rather than attempting to conquer the English. He established at least three religious foundations in Gwynedd and became highly regarded as a good and pious ruler. Indeed he was remembered as a saint in the Welsh church. He is the last British king recorded by Geoffrey of Monmouth in his *History of the Kings of Britain*, and his death seems to mark the end of the last chapter of British resistance against the Saxons. This is probably more a choice of convenience than of events at the time, for many great Welsh kings were yet to follow, but it is true that Wales never again mustered a king able to challenge the Saxons who, by the time of Cadwaladr's death, were firmly entrenched in England. The date of Cadwaladr's death is uncertain. All histories agree that he died in a plague but whether it was the one of 663/4 or the one of 682 is not clear. The latter seems more likely, otherwise the reigns of his successors IDWAL and RHODRI would be improbably long.

[ED12] **IDWAL *IWRCH* (*ROEBUCK*)** AP **CADWALADR** Gwynedd, *c*682–*c*720.
After the death of CADWALADR the history of the Welsh ruling houses enters a dark period for over a century until the emergence of MERFYN *FRYCH* and RHODRI *THE GREAT*. Idwal's nickname, *Iwrch* or 'roebuck', suggests that he was probably small and elegant in stature, and almost certainly young when he came to the throne. Like his father, therefore, he was probably not warlike, but preferred to rule wisely and pay countenance to the church. Nevertheless it is evident that during Idwal's reign the Welsh sought to protect their lands from the encroaching power of Mercia to the east. Powys was more vulnerable, and their rulers were weaker, so in the early years of the eighth century (probably between 704 and 709), Idwal would have joined when the opportunity offered in a series of raids on Mercian territory during the comparatively weak reign of COENRED. The result was the construction by the Mercians, of Wat's Dyke, which ran from the southern end of the Dee estuary down towards Oswestry. This formed a line of demarcation between Mercian and Welsh territory and was not ostensibly intended as a defence. Idwal may not have lived to see the completion of the Dyke. He was succeeded by his son RHODRI *MOLWYNOG*.

[ED13] **RHODRI *MOLWYNOG*** AP **IDWAL** Gwynedd, *c*720–*c*754.
We know little of his reign, or even when he came to the throne. His reign, however, coincides with that of ATHELBALD of Mercia who, by 736, was styling himself King of Britain. Athelbald had seen the completion of Wat's Dyke between the borders of Mercia and Powys, but this had been more as a statement of frontier than of defence, and we can imagine that Athelbald continued to force and exercise his authority into Wales. Although it is far from clear, Rhodri may well have retreated to establish his stronghold on the island of Anglesey, which had always been the seat of power in Gwynedd and which was the site of power struggles between Rhodri's children or grandchildren. There were no other strong Welsh chieftains at this time and we can imagine Rhodri and his family clinging proudly to their heritage, which they could trace back to CUNEDDA and COEL. It is not clear who succeeded Rhodri as

there is an uncomfortable timespan to fill before we encounter Rhodri's later successors, HYWEL and CYNAN, fighting for the throne. It has been suggested that he was succeeded by a distant cousin, CARADOG AP MEIRION.

[ED14] **CARADOG** AP **MEIRION** Gwynedd, c754–c798.
The eighth century has few records to illuminate the lives of the Welsh royal families. It is likely that during this period the royal house of Gwynedd withdrew to their stronghold on Anglesey. It is also probable that Gwynedd was ruled by two related houses, descendants of CUNEDDA, one of whom held Anglesey and the other ruled *cantrefi* (the equivalent of the Saxon hundred) on the mainland. The main Gwynedd *cantrefi* were Llyn, Arfon, Arllechwed and Rhos. Caradog was the ruler of Rhos and claimed descent from EINION's son Owain. By the late eighth century Caradog had the upper hand, though quite when he gained control is hard to say. It may have been much later than 754, when RHODRI ap Idwal died. Caradog was almost certainly ruler in 768, the year in which Elfoddw, the bishop of Gwynedd, persuaded the Welsh church to adopt the church of Rome's method of calculating Easter, which had been the main rift between the Roman and Celtic churches since the Synod of Whitby under OSWY of Northumbria in 664. Although this was a decision of the church, it would have needed support from a strong secular king and Caradog was the only king of any stature at that time. Caradog faced increasing encroachment from the Saxons who were invading Powys during this period. Caradog seems to have met his death from the Mercians under CENWULF, although other records state that he was strangled. His successor, HYWEL, is identified as his son in some genealogies.

[ED15] **CYNAN** *DINDAETHWY* AP **RHODRI** Gwynedd, 798–816.
It is not exactly clear who ruled Gwynedd in the last years of the eighth century. There were almost certainly a series of power struggles between collateral lines of descent from CUNEDDA and his successors, especially after the death of CADWALADR when Gwynedd entered a period under weaker rulers whose power was overshadowed by the might of the Saxon kingdom of Mercia. Evidently many young princes believed they were the ones who could restore Gwynedd to its old glory, and Cynan was one of these. Although it is not clear when he came to power, certainly by the year 813 it is recorded that he was waging a civil war with HYWEL, who was either his brother or a distant cousin. Hywel gained the upper hand in 814, but Cynan won back control in 816, only to die later that year. Cynan almost certainly sought help in his war from GWRIAD, the ruler of the Isle of Man, who had married Cynan's daughter Essyllt. Essyllt became the mother of MERFYN *Frych* who established a new dynasty in Gwynedd and began the re-establishment of Gwynedd's power.

[ED16] **HYWEL** Gwynedd, 814–825.
The name Hywel is the Welsh version of HOEL, both names meaning "eminent". Hywel has variously been identified as the son (or grandson) of RHODRI ap Idwal or the son of CARADOG ap Meirion. Whichever was the case, he appeared on the scene in a dynastic struggle with his brother or distant cousin CYNAN AP RHODRI over the rulership of Gwynedd, and in particular over the heartland of Anglesey. Hywel managed to wrest control from Cynan in 814 but two years later was ousted.

However Cynan died later in 816 whether from natural causes or murder is not known, and this left the way open for Hywel to take over complete control. We may imagine that both claimants were old in years as Rhodri had died some sixty years earlier. Hywel either left no children or all had died in the many skirmishes during these dark days for, after his death, power was taken by Cynan's grandson MERFYN FRYCH.

[ED17] **MERFYN** *FRYCH* (*THE FRECKLED*) Gwynedd, 825–844.
Merfyn came to power following the death of HYWEL ap Caradog, and his accession marked the end of a period of turmoil in Gwynedd's affairs and the start of a new dynasty. Merfyn was the son of GWRIAD, the king of the Isle of Man, through whom he could claim descent from LLYWARCH HEN. His mother was Esyllt, the daughter of CYNAN ap Rhodri, who was descended from the main line of Venedotian kings since the days of CUNEDDA. Merfyn married Nest, the daughter of CADELL AP BROCHFAEL of Powys, thus uniting the two great North Wales royal families. Someone of Merfyn's strength of character was needed at this time. The seas around Wales, Man and Ireland were being patrolled by Viking pirates. Merfyn must have been regarded as having authority over the seas – his name means "sea ruler", not a great surprise for someone descended from the rulers of Man, who relied upon their marine skills for their livelihood. But Merfyn was obviously also a skilled negotiator and statesman. His alliance with Powys meant that the two kingdoms presented a powerful front to the Saxons in the east. Merfyn thus established a stable, if uneasy peace. It was during the early part of Merfyn's reign that the *History of the Britons* was completed. This is attributed to Nennius, a cleric and scholar of Gwynedd who may well have been requested by Merfyn to establish a history of Britain. Some evidence suggests that Nennius had already started on this, either for his own interests or perhaps at the instigation of Hywel ap Caradog, but it seems almost certain that it was Merfyn who recognized the project for its true worth and promoted it. Interestingly it was not used as a way of demonstrating the power and might of Merfyn, as he is not mentioned anywhere in the *History*. Nevertheless it demonstrates that during Merfyn's reign scholarship was encouraged, which is always the sign of a strong but compassionate king. Merfyn passed these and other qualities on to his son RHODRI *Mawr* who would become king of all North Wales – see page 344.

EE. POWYS AND THE MARCHES

The kingdom of Powys was carved out of the lands of the Cornovii and Decangii in eastern and north-eastern Wales. At the height of its power, during the late sixth century, its boundaries stretched beyond the current border of Wales into Cheshire, Shropshire and Herefordshire, the territory known today as the Marches. It struggled to retain its independence since it was under threat from the might of Gwynedd to the west and the encroachment of the Mercians to the east. The identity of its early rulers is uncertain because there were almost certainly several tribes along the borders of Wales with no single dominant ruler. For related kingdoms see Gwerthrynion [EF] and Brycheiniog [EG].

Ref.	Ruler	Reign	Died	Notes
EE1.	Cadell or Catel(lus)	*fl* 450		

Powys was partitioned between Cadell's sons and the sons of Cunedda and Vortigern. Rulers probably included Owain ap Einion, Cattegirn, Brittu and Pascent, but precise details are uncertain.

EE2.	Cynlas ab Owain, or Cuneglasus	*fl* 530s		
EE3.	Cyngen	*fl* 550s		
EE4.	Brochfael *Ysgythrog* (*of the Tusks*)	*fl* 570s		
EE5.	Cynan *Garwyn* (*the Cruel*)	*fl c*600		

— Border of Powys

---- Border of Powys in 6th Century

Map 4e **The Welsh Kingdoms – Powys**

5. Wales (3) – **Early Powys**

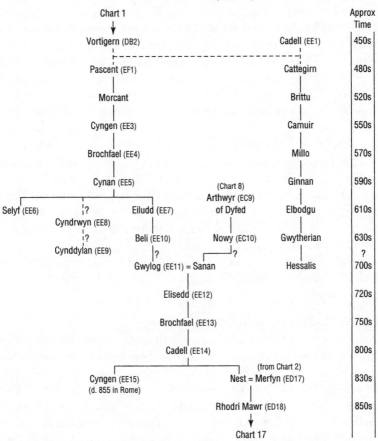

	Approx Time
Chart 1	
Vortigern (DB2) Cadell (EE1)	450s
Pascent (EF1) Cattegirn	480s
Morcant Brittu	520s
Cyngen (EE3) Camuir	550s
Brochfael (EE4) Millo	570s
Cynan (EE5) (Chart 8) Arthwyr (EC9) of Dyfed Ginnan	590s
Selyf (EE6) ? Cyndrwyn (EE8) Eiludd (EE7) Elbodgu	610s
? Cynddylan (EE9) Beli (EE10) Nowy (EC10) Gwytherian	630s
Gwylog (EE11) = Sanan Hessalis	700s ?
Elisedd (EE12)	720s
Brochfael (EE13)	750s
Cadell (EE14)	800s
Cyngen (EE15) (d. 855 in Rome) (from Chart 2) Nest = Merfyn (ED17)	830s
Rhodri Mawr (ED18)	850s
Chart 17	

EE6. Selyf ap Cynan   ? –615   615   killed in battle
EE7. Eiludd ap Cynan   615– ?

At this stage Powys fragmented into North and South.

Southern Powys (Shropshire) – Pengwern
EE8.   Cyndrwyn *the Stubborn*   *fl* 620s
EE9.   Cynddylan   c640–c655   c655   killed in battle

Northern Powys (Chester, Clwyd)
EE10. Beli ap Eiludd   *fl* 630s
Rulers between Beli and Gwylog are uncertain
EE11. Gwylog ap Beli   *fl* 700s
EE12. Elisedd ap Gwylog   c725– ?
EE13. Brochfael ap Elisedd   *fl* 760s
EE14. Cadell ap Brochfael   ? –808   808
EE15. Cyngen ap Cadell   c808–c853   855   died in Rome

After Cyngen's death Powys passed to his nephew Rhodri Mawr and formed part of the kingdom of Gwynedd until the death of Bleddyn ap Cynfyn in 1075. For its continuation under Rhodri turn to page 344, and for its re-emergence as an independent kingdom turn to page 364.

[EE1] **CADELL** or **CATELLUS** Powys, *fl* 450.

The founder of the first dynasty of Powys. Legend has it that he was a slave, possibly a herdsman, of king Benli. Benli refused to give St Germanus shelter during a storm, but Cadell offered him refuge and food. Inevitably Benli's castle was struck by fire, and Germanus appointed Cadell as king in his place. Behind the legend is probably a genuine story of a young man who defeated a tyrant king and supplanted him. That king was probably a ruler of the Cornovii in central Wales and Shropshire, and later legends suggest that this may have been VORTIGERN. Cadell almost certainly had problems holding his kingdom, as much against the expansionist regime of EINION AP CUNEDDA to the west as against the sons of Vortigern, of whom PASCENT was ruling in Builth, and another, Cattegirn, seems to have re-established himself in Powys after Cadell's death. It seems likely that after Cadell's death his lands were apportioned between his sons and the sons of Vortigern and CUNEDDA. Nothing is entirely certain of the main line succession in Powys until the emergence of CYNGEN, the father of BROCHFAEL, although it is possible that Gildas's CUNEGLASUS also ruled in this area.

Geoffrey of Monmouth lists a Catellus as ruling Britain and he may have picked this name up from the historical Cadell, but Geoffrey's bears no relation to his historical namesake.

[EE2] **CUNEGLASUS** Powys and Rhôs (?), *fl* 530s.

Cuneglasus is one of five rulers of Britain whom Gildas attacks for their wickedness in his *Ruin of Britain*. Cuneglasus seems to have been evil since his youth, not only in his murder and conquests (he clearly led a large warband) but in the rejection of his wife and the desire to marry her sister who, though also regarded as villainous, had apparently turned to God. Little is said to help us identify Cuneglasus, though the reference to him as "driver of the chariot of the Bear's stronghold", makes one wonder whether he had at one stage fought alongside ARTHUR (*arctos* in Latin can mean the Great Bear). He was certainly a contemporary of Arthur and, with the peace that emerged following Badon, Cuneglasus may have carved out for himself and his warriors a kingdom in mid/north Wales in the lands between Powys and Gwynedd – one suggestion has been the *cantref* of Penllyn. Attempts have been made to link him with Cynlas, the son of Owain and grandson of EINION AP CUNEDDA, which is possible, as the dates would be about right. If so, Cynlas was not of the main line of Powys, and his descendants, starting with CARADOG AP MEIRION would later succeed to the kingdom of Gwynedd.

[EE3] **CYNGEN** Powys, *fl* 550s.

With the first of this name the history of Powys emerges from the mists of time. The genealogies place Cyngen fourth in descent from CADELL through PASCENT. He lived in the mid sixth century before the rise of Mercia and it is likely that his kingdom extended beyond today's borders of Wales into what is now Shropshire and Herefordshire. His capital may well have been at Pengwern, the original site of Shrewsbury. The extent of his kingdom, though, is uncertain. His son was BROCHFAEL.

[EE4] **BROCHFAEL *YSGYTHROG* (*OF THE TUSKS*)** Powys, *fl* 570s.

The first ruler of Powys to establish himself in the bardic memory, where his name became synonymous with his kingdom. This suggests that it was Brochfael more than any of his predecessors who carved out a recognizable kingdom from the mass of petty chieftainships that no doubt existed in eastern, northern and central Wales. Apparently his capital was at Pengwern, the Celtic fortress that became Shrewsbury, and his lands almost certainly extended north toward Chester and possibly westward as far as Builth. Brochfael must have maintained good relations with his neighbours, especially RHUN of Gwynedd and the long-lived MORGAN of Morgannwg, to have developed his kingdom without a history of bloodshed. In addition to his son CYNAN, Brochfael was the father of St Tysilio, whose cult spread throughout Wales and whose mission probably helped bond the emerging kingdoms of Wales for at least a brief period. It was Tysilio who established the ecclesiastical centre of Powys at Meifod.

[EE5] CYNAN GARWYN (the CRUEL) AP BROCHFAEL Powys, fl c600.

The son of BROCHFAEL. His nickname means "the Cruel", but he was also renowned for his White Chariot. Whether this was a chariot of state for ceremonies, or whether he drove this into battle, is not stated, but it was probably the latter as, during Cynan's reign, the Mercians began to establish themselves in central and western England.

[EE6] SELYF AP CYNAN Powys, ? –613 (or 615?).

The son of CYNAN AP BROCHFAEL whose kingdom stretched down through the Welsh Marches from Chester to Shrewsbury, and possibly further south. His name is recorded in the annals because he was killed in the battle of Chester that marked the victory of ATHELFRITH of Northumbria over the Welsh princes of Gwynedd and Powys. Athelfrith's anger was directed toward EDWIN of Northumbria who had sought refuge amongst the Welsh kingdoms. It seems that Powys acted as a haven for several dispossessed rulers at this time. RHUN the son of URIEN of Rheged came to Powys as a monk. This suggests that Selyf was a benign and compassionate ruler. The fact that he is sometimes called Solomon may also indicate his wisdom. His death cast Powys into a period of turmoil before the emergence of CYNDDYLAN as its next strong ruler.

[EE7] EILUDD AP CYNAN Powys, 615?–?

The brother of SELYF, Eiludd presumably survived the battle of Chester and endeavoured to regain control of Powys. Since little is heard of Powys at this time it is possible that Eiludd ruled only as a client king of CADFAN of Gwynedd. This period of Powys's history is uncertain but it is probable that following the death of Selyf, his family were unable to sustain the large kingdom created by his grandfather, BROCHFAEL, and that Eiludd ruled only Northern Powys, whilst a scion of the family, perhaps a cousin, CYNDRWYN ruled Pengwern to the south.

[EE8] CYNDRWYN the STUBBORN Southern Powys (Pengwern), fl 620s.

Cyndrwyn is only known as the father of CYNDDYLAN and by his nickname, which suggests that he stubbornly held the southern lands of Powys, around Shrewsbury, during the period after the death of SELYF AP CYNAN at Chester in 613. This was the period during which Powys's English neighbours began to coalesce into the kingdom of Mercia under their powerful king PENDA, who was at war with the Northumbrian ruler EDWIN and later OSWALD. Cyndrwyn seems to have allied himself to Penda, which for a period was Powys's salvation.

[EE9] **CYNDDYLAN** Powys, c640–c655.

Cynddylan was the son of CYNDRWYN and first enters history around the year 642 at the battle of Maserfelth where PENDA of Mercia killed OSWALD of Northumbria. He is depicted as an ally of the Mercians, which fits into the general picture of the period when, since the Battle of Chester in 613, the Welsh of Gwynedd and Powys had seen the Northumbrians as their enemies. It is nevertheless a strange situation that the Mercians, who were basically Angles, the same as the Northumbrians, were seen as allies to the Welsh even though they potentially posed the greater threat and would, eventually, overrun much of eastern Wales. It is more than possible that Penda had entered into an alliance to use the power and wrath of the Welsh princes to his own ends, and it worked in his favour. It is also possible that the two families intermarried, given the development of Penda's dynasty (see CEOLRIC). Cynddylan apparently had a brother called Morfael who governed territory as far east as Lichfield, which must have been the frontier between the Welsh kingdoms and the Mercians. There is some hint in the records that Cynddylan and Morfael were engaged in battles against the British which, if true, suggests that Cynddylan may have been more pro-Mercian than the British felt appropriate. Cynddylan supported Penda throughout his career, and it appears that he died at the same battle in which Penda met his death, at Winwaed in 655. Mercia was overrun by the Northumbrians and the eastern part of Cynddylan's kingdom was forfeit. When the Mercians regained the ascendance under WULFHERE there were no alliances to protect eastern Powys and the lands fell to the English. Cynddylan's traditional burial place is at Baschurch in Shropshire.

[EE10] **BELI** AP **EILUDD** Powys, fl 630s.

Beli features in the ancestry of ELISEDD of Powys, but the ancient genealogy provides us with a confusion over dates. If Beli was genuinely the son of EILUDD, and nephew of SELYF, then he must have lived in the decade or two after the Battle of Chester in 613. This would make him a contemporary with CADWALLON of Gwynedd, and there is little doubt that the rulers of Gwynedd and Powys at this time would have united in their campaign against the Northumbrians. Like Cadwallon, Beli was probably driven into exile by EDWIN. However, his son GWYLOG married the daughter of NOWY of Dyfed, and Nowy is a generation earlier than Beli, which would place him into at least the 590s if not earlier. This would make it impossible for Beli to be the grandfather of Elisedd who lived around 725. These anomalies are far from being resolved.

[EE11] **GWYLOG** Powys, dates uncertain (fl 700s?).

Gwylog is shown both as the father of ELISEDD who lived about 725 and as the son of BELI who lived about 620, and these dates are incompatible. Gwylog also married Sanan, the daughter of NOWY of Dyfed, which would place Gwylog back around the period 620 or even earlier. Clearly the genealogies are at fault. This is not surprising. The period from the Battle of Chester in 613 to the recovery of the lands of Powys under Elisedd in 725 was a dark age for the Welsh when many were driven into exile by the Northumbrians and Mercians, apart from the brief period of triumph of CYNDDYLAN who does not feature anywhere in the genealogies. We must conclude that at least two generations of Powys' rulers have been lost and that during these years the land was probably dominated by the rulers of Gwynedd.

[EE12] **ELISEDD** (or **ELISEG**) Powys, 725–?

Elisedd was remembered by his great grandson, CYNGEN AP CADELL, a century later, for having rebuilt Powys and recovered lands from the English. He erected a stone column, now known as "Eliseg's Pillar" which commemorated his descent, tracing it all the way back to VORTIGERN. The genealogy provides us with some dating problems, but we must assume that Elisedd lived sometime in the early/mid eighth century. This coincides with the reign of the Mercian king ATHELBALD, a turbulent period where the Mercians generally had the upper hand but where some victories went to the underdogs. We can imagine that Elisedd succeeded in regaining lands along the Welsh/Mercian border from this powerful king, which made his victories all the more significant. It is possible that Elisedd ruled (or was active as a battle leader) earlier, because there are Welsh border incidents recorded during the reign of the Mercian king CENRED, around the year 708. The fact that the Pillar was erected at Llangollen, well inside the later Welsh border, shows that these territorial gains were not permanent.

[EE13] **BROCHFAEL** AP **ELISEDD** Powys, *fl* 760s.

The son of ELISEDD, little is known of his reign, except that it would have paralleled that of Mercia's greatest king, OFFA. Whatever lands Elisedd had gained in the first half of the century, Brochfael probably lost in the second half. Offa undertook many raids into Wales during his reign, some as far west as Dyfed, and Powys was little more than a doorstep to his mighty army. Although the dates of Brochfael's reign are not known, it is possible he reigned for a considerable period. It was during his reign that Offa's Dyke was constructed, a remarkable feat of engineering which must have taken many men many years. It is a sign of Offa's power that it could be achieved at all, and it is probable that it was the men of Powys and of Glywysing who were pressed into service to complete the work. It served as much as a line of demarcation as a defence, and as such shows that Offa effectively agreed a border between the Welsh and the English which would help sustain peace. Brochfael would therefore have benefitted from the Dyke in the short term, though in the long term it spelled the end for Powys. Brochfael was succeeded by his son CADELL.

[EE14] **CADELL** AP **BROCHFAEL** Powys, ?–808.

Ruler of Powys during the oppressive reign of the Mercian CENWULF. Cadell died before Cenwulf's main drive into Wales, and he may have benefitted from the comparative peace that followed the construction of Offa's Dyke. However, in the last year of Offa's reign, the Mercians penetrated into Rhuddlan, and this was a signal of the fragile relationship that would exist between Welsh and Mercians for the next thirty years. Cadell was succeeded by CYNGEN.

[EE15] **CYNGEN** AP **CADELL** Powys, *c*808–853.

The last king of the first dynasty of Powys. He succeeded his father, CADELL, at a time when the Mercians under CENWULF and later CEOLWULF were making a concerted drive into Wales. Their efforts were concentrated in North Wales, though they also penetrated as far south as Dyfed. In 823, Beornwulf (penetrating into Gwynedd) captured the Welsh citadel at Deganwy, and claimed that the whole of Powys was in his hands. Beornwulf was killed soon after, and Mercia's power declined under a series of rival claimants until it fell easy prey to the power of

EGBERT of Wessex. From 826 to 830 Mercian energies were directed elsewhere and this would have given Cyngen an opportunity to regain his lands. It was probably at this time that he erected the stone column now called "Eliseg's Pillar" both as a tribute to his own achievement and to that of his forefathers. It was a proud declaration of the antiquity of Powys. It did not last for long. In 830 Egbert sent his army into Powys to subdue Cyngen and, although the record is quiet on the matter, Cyngen may have had to recognize Egbert as overlord. The next twenty years saw the rise in power of RHODRI who succeeded to Gwynedd in 844. Rhodri's mother was Cyngen's sister Nest and, although Cyngen had three sons of his own, it probably became evident in Cyngen's later years that Rhodri had every intention of claiming Powys as his inheritance. In 853 the Mercians under BURGRED, with the help of ATHELWOLF, began a new offensive into Wales, and again overran Powys. Although they were not able to penetrate into Gwynedd, it seems that Rhodri was content to sacrifice Powys whilst defending his own lands. In 853 Cyngen retired and went on a pilgrimage to Rome, where he died two years later. Records suggest he was a sad and embittered man. He was also old, having ruled for forty-five years. It is not clear whether his sons pre-deceased him, or whether they died soon after, for there is no record of them attempting to claim the throne of Powys. Instead Rhodri annexed it to Gwynedd and it remained part of the frontier between England and Wales, constantly changing hands, until the death of BLEDDYN AP CYNFYN in 1075 (*see page 364*).

THE MINOR KINGDOMS

EF. GWERTHRYNION – BUILTH

This small kingdom was in the centre of Wales bounded by Powys, Ceredigion and Brycheiniog. Like Powys, it developed from lands once ruled by Vortigern in the mid fifth century. The name is derived from Vortigern's real name, Gwrtheyrn. The extent to which it remained an autonomous kingdom is not clear. It may at various stages have been subject to Powys, Brycheiniog, Gwent, and Gwynedd.

According to Nennius, after Vortigern it was ruled by his son Pascent (*fl* 460s) and then successively by Briacat (*fl* 490s), Idnerth (*fl* 510s), Meurig (*fl* 540s), Paul (*fl* 560s), Elaeth (*fl* 590s), Eldat (*fl* 610s), Moriud (*fl* 640s), Gwyddgant (*fl* 660s), Pascent (*fl* 690s), Tewdwr (*fl* 710s) and Ffernfael, or Fernmail (*fl* 740s). Apart from Pascent, nothing is known about these rulers beyond their names.

[EF1] **PASCENT** Gwerthrynion, *fl* 460s.
Pascent is listed as the third son of VORTIGERN, who inherited the heartland of his father's lands in mid-south Wales, around Builth. There was, by all accounts, fighting between Pascent and his brothers as well as rival kings, especially EINION AP CUNEDDA and CADELL, but in time Pascent established a kingdom which would survive for a further twelve generations until the last ruler, Ffernfael, in the mid eighth century. Nothing is known of these later kings who must all have been tenacious, clinging to their mountain fastness and surviving against all comers. One gets the impression more of a warrior band than of a formal kingdom. They may well have become vassal mercenaries to the Mercian kings who made incursions

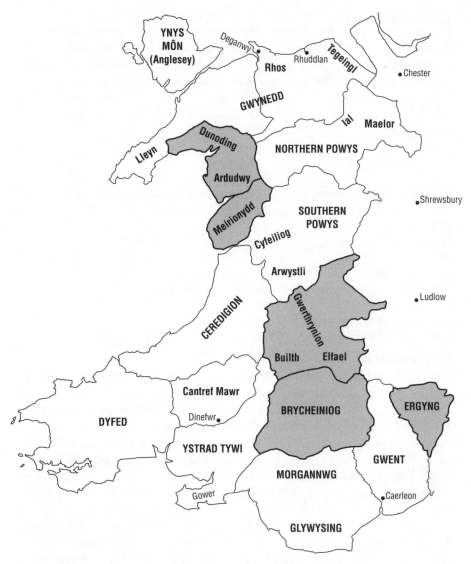

Map 4f **The Welsh Kingdoms – The Minor Kingdoms**

from the east during the seventh century. One of Pascent's descendants also bore the name and ruled in the late seventh century.

Pascent does not figure as a good character in the traditional tales. He fled to Germany after his father's defeat by AMBROSIUS AURELIANUS, returned, fled again to Ireland where he was able to raise an army but was again defeated. He then resorted to subterfuge and bribed a Saxon woman to poison Ambrosius.

EG. BRYCHEINIOG

Brycheiniog's origins are lost in legend and are also associated with Vortigern. The territory was initially part of southern Powys but later formed part of northern Gwent. It was named after its first and most famous ruler, Brychan.

Ref.	Ruler	Reign	Died	Notes
EG1.	Brychan	*fl* 520s		
EG2.	Rhun *Dremrudd* (*the Red-Eyed*)	*fl* 550s		
EG3.	Awst	*fl* 580s		

Here the king list becomes corrupt. Brycheiniog may have been overrun by Dyfed and remained part of that kingdom until the time of the second Awst.

EG4.	Awst	*fl* 750s		
EG5.	Elwystl ap Awst	*fl* 770s		murdered
EG6.	Tewdwr or Tewdws ap Rhain	*fl* 770s		May be same as EC15 of Rheinwg

Brycheiniog may have been ruled from Dyfed for the next century.

EG7.	Tewdwr	*fl* 870s		
EG8.	Elise ap Tewdwr	*fl* 890s		
EG9.	Tewdwr ap Elise	*fl* 925		may be the last ruler

[EG1] **BRYCHAN** Brycheiniog, *fl* 520s.
The semi-legendary founder of the kingdom of Brycheiniog was the son of Anlach, an Irish prince, and Marchell, traditionally the daughter of TEWDRIG, king of Gwent, though the chronology does not support this. Although born in Ireland, Brychan returned with his parents to Bannau, near Brecon, where he was raised. It seems he was a wayward youth, and certainly produced many illegitimate children. He raped the daughter of the king of Powys (called Benadel in legend) and thus had to serve the king as hostage. He eventually succeeded as king of Garthmadryn, which later became known as Brycheiniog. Historically, Brychan was a contemporary of VORTEPOR of Dyfed. There were strong Irish connections throughout south and east Wales, but it was at about the time of Brychan that Brycheiniog became separated from Dyfed as a distinct kingdom. It is also pertinent that this probably occurred soon after the peace achieved by ARTHUR at Badon, thus allowing Brychan a period of relative calm in which to establish his kingdom. Tradition states that Brychan married three times, one of his wives being the daughter of VORTIGERN. He had thirty-six children. Amongst them were St Cynon, Gwladys (the mother of St Cadoc), Tydwall who became the mother of BROCHFAEL *YSGYTHROG* of Powys, Eleri who married CEREDIG, Cludwyn, who subdued much of south Wales, and RHUN, who succeeded his father. Another son, also called Brychan, moved north to the territory of the Picts and settled in the area around Brechin, named after him.

[EG2] **RHUN DREMRUDD (*THE RED-EYES*)** Brycheiniog, *fl* 550s.
The eldest legitimate son of BRYCHAN, Rhun succeeded to his father's kingdom some time in the mid-sixth century. His brother Cludwyn is noted for having invaded territories throughout south Wales, which may suggest conflict with the rulers of Dyfed, from whom Brycheiniog was a breakaway kingdom, and with

MORGAN, the ruler of Morgannwg, who was also expanding his territories. Since Brycheiniog did not expand and establish itself as a significant kingdom it is possible that during Rhun's reign it was either overrun by the rulers of Dyfed or temporarily became subject to them, as the king list of Brycheiniog becomes confusingly interlinked with that of Dyfed. The next known king of Brycheiniog was AWST, who ruled nearly two centuries later.

[EG3] **AWST** or **AUGUSTUS** Brycheiniog, *fl* 580s.
The name of at least two kings of Brycheiniog. The first was probably a son of RHUN AP BRYCHAN and ruled toward the end of the sixth century. It seems that he was something of a renegade and was called to order by the new bishop of Llandogo, Oudoceus. Awst's sons were Eliud and Rhiwallon. Rhinwallon may have ruled briefly before the kingdom was overrun by Dyfed.

[EG4] **AWST** Brycheiniog, *fl* 750s.
The second Awst was the the first known king of Brycheiniog after more than a century. It is possible that he took advantage of weakening power in the kingdom of Dyfed to reassert his authority in Brycheiniog. This was short-lived as after his death the territory was divided between his own son ELWYSTL and that of his nephew, TEWDWR AP RHAIN.

[EG5] **ELWYSTL** AB **AWST** Brycheiniog, *fl* 770s.
The son of AWST, Elwystl was forced to share his kingdom with his cousin TEWDWR AP RHAIN and who was subsequently murdered by Tewdwr.

[EG6;EC15] **TEWDWR** or **TEWDWS** AP **RHAIN** Dyfed and Brycheiniog, *fl* 770s.
Ruler of Dyfed who also claimed sovereignty over part of the kingdom of Brycheiniog in rivalry to his cousin ELWYSTI AB AWST and who subsequently murdered Elwysti. This may account for the confusion over the territory known as Rheinwg between Dyfed and Brycheiniog. Tewdwr remained a common name amongst the rulers of Brycheiniog over the next two centuries, including the father [EG7] of ELISE AP TEWDWR.

[EG8] **ELISE** AP **TEWDWR** Brycheiniog, *fl* 890s.
Elise is recorded by Asser as one of the Welsh rulers who was driven by ANARAWD of Gwynedd to seek support from ALFRED THE GREAT. Although Asser's biography of Alfred is suspect, there is no reason to doubt that he has faithfully recorded the identities of the Welsh rulers. This is the first identification of a ruler of Brycheiniog for a century. He was succeeded by his son TEWDWR. It was during Elise's reign (in 896) that the Vikings devastated parts of Brycheiniog and Gwent and this was probably another, if not a stronger, reason for Elise to seek help from Alfred.

[EG9] **TEWDWR** AP **ELISE** Brycheiniog, *fl* 925.
The last historically attested king of Brycheiniog, who was forced to grant some of his lands in compensation for having stolen funds due to the church. The genealogies stop with Tewdwr's son and it is probable that Brycheiniog thereafter came under the authority of MORGAN HEN of Gwent (*see page 325*).

EH. MEIRIONYDD

Meironydd was a small *cantref* on the western seaboard of Wales. It was never a fully autonomous kingdom, existing as a vassal state to Gwynedd. The rulers were reputedly descended from Meirion, the grandson of Cunedda. The genealogy of the kings is shown on Chart 4 on page 140.

Ref.	Ruler	Reign	Died	Notes
EH1.	Meirion	*fl* 490s		
EH2.	Catgualart	*fl* 510s		
EH3.	Gwrin *Farfdrwch* (*of the Ragged Beard*)	*fl* 530s		
EH4.	Glitnoth	*fl* 570s		
EH5.	Gueinoth	*fl* 600s		
EH6.	Idris or Iudric	? –632	632	killed in battle
EH7.	Sualda	*fl* 640s		
EH8.	Brochmael	? –662	662	killed in battle
EH9.	Egeniud or Owein	662– ?		
EH10.	Iutnimet	*fl* 690s		
EH11.	Brochmael (II)	*fl* 710s		

Although the genealogies show Brochmael as the father of Cynan the next four or five generations are not known.

| EH12. | Cynan | *fl* 870s | 880 | killed in battle |

Merioneth was absorbed into Gwynedd; the territory often inherited by younger sons of the king.

[EH1] MEIRION or MARIANUS Meirionydd, *fl* 490s.

The semi-legendary founder of the kingdom of Meirionydd; traditionally the grandson of CUNEDDA. His father, Tybion, apparently stayed in the north when Cunedda and his other sons moved into Wales. Meirion followed at some later date. Although Meirionydd was culturally part of Powys, it became one of the vassal kingdoms to Gwynedd, through the sons of Cunedda, and although it retained its own dynasty for three centuries, it is not clear how independent it remained. Most of its kings left little mark on the history of Wales, although of special significance are GWRIN, IDRIS, BROCHMAEL and CYNAN.

[EH2] CATGUALART Meirionydd, *fl* 510s.

The son of MEIRION. His reign coincided with that of CADWALLON LAWHIR, to whom he was almost certainly a vassal.

[EH3] GWRIN FARFDRWCH (*of the RAGGED BEARD*) Meirionydd, *fl* 530s.

The grandson of MEIRION and, as a contemporary of MAELGWYN HIR, likely to be a vassal king of Gwynedd. This is the same king identified by Geoffrey of Monmouth as Gurguit Barbtruc [P24], though he had displaced him to some time around 300BC. According to Geoffrey, Gurguit was a wise and clement king who nevertheless waged war on his neighbours when they defied him. Gurguit fought the Danes, chased them back to their home country and subdued them. On his return he encountered thirty boats full of Spanish exiles looking for a homeland. Gurguit led them to Ireland, which was then deserted, and there they became established.

What truth we can deduce from this is hard to say. Gwrin may well have been a wise king but faced with considerable onslaught from his neighbours and from Irish pirates. It was during Gwrin's reign that St Cadfan came to Wales and established churches at Tywyn and Bardsey.

[EH4] **GLITNOTH** *GARAHNHIR (LONGSHANKS)* Meirionydd, *fl* 570s.
The son of GWRIN FARFDRWCH. Nothing is recorded of him in the annals, but it is possible he is treated by Geoffrey of Monmouth as GUITHELIN [P25], a temperate and liberal king whose wife, Marcia, apparently developed an extensive Code of Laws subsequently used by King ALFRED. Although Geoffrey is totally confused, it is not beyond the bounds of possibility that Glitnoth, who was a contemporary of RHUN HIR of Gwynedd, did seek to establish some kind of law code for the Welsh courts, though no record of it survives.

[EH5] **GUEINOTH** Meirionydd, *fl* 600s.
A contemporary and possibly a vassal king of IAGO AP BELI of Gwynedd. He was the father of IDRIS.

[EH6] **IDRIS** or **IUDRIC** Meirionydd, ? –632.
One of the few kings of Meirionydd whose name lives on in the dark and sinister mountain of Cader Idris, or Throne of Idris. The name Idris means impulsive ruler, suggesting that Idris was probably headstrong. He may well have used Cader Idris as the site for a fort during the many battles and sieges that would have raged through Meirionydd at this time. Idris's death is recorded in a battle on the banks of the river Severn in 632. This probably happened soon after the Battle of Haethfeld, when OSWALD returned from exile in Ireland to claim his right to the throne of Northumbria and, en route, became engaged in skirmishes with the Welsh and West Saxons. The fact that Idris was operating so far to the east suggests that he was serving in a confederate Welsh army, probably under the leadership of CYNDRWYN of Powys.

[EH7] **SUALDA** Meirionydd, *fl* 640s.
The son of IDRIS – nothing is recorded of Sualda's reign, though it is contemporary with the rise to power of CYNDDYLAN and we can imagine that Sualda served as a client king in Cynddylan's army. He was succeeded by his son BROCHMAEL.

[EH8] **BROCHMAEL** Meirionydd, ? –662.
The successor to SUALDA, he was killed in battle in the year 662. The Welsh annals confuse him with BROCHFAEL YSGYTHROG of Powys who lived a century earlier.

[EH9] **OWAIN** (or **EGENIUD**) AP **BROCHMAEL** Meirionydd, 662–?
Succeeded to Meirionydd on his father's death, though details of his reign are not known. It is likely that Meirionydd was still a vassal kingdom of Gwynedd, then under the control of CADWALADR.

[EH10] **IUTNIMET**, Meirionydd, *fl* 690s.
The end of the seventh century is one of the darkest periods of Welsh history and little is known in any detail about the rulers of even the largest kingdoms. It was at this time that the West Saxons and Mercians were at the height of their power and seeking to control the borders and rich lands of Wales and, in particular, the Severn

valley. We can only imagine that Iutnimet's reign was one either of constant defence against the Saxons or of seeking to work with them.

[EH11] **BROCHMAEL** AP **IUTNIMET**, Meironydd, *fl* 710s or 840s.
Brochmael's exact dates are uncertain. His is the only name in the genealogies between Iutnimet and Cynan, though this covers nearly two centuries. If Brochmael lived later, then his reign might have coincided with the Danish and Viking invasions of Wales which increased through the mid ninth century. If so then he would certainly have fought alongside RHODRI MAWR against the Danes and might have been killed in one such raid.

[EH12] **CYNAN** AP **BROCHMAEL** Meirionydd, *fl* 870s.
The last recorded independent ruler of Meirionydd. He was killed in battle in 880, almost certainly by Cadell, the brother of ANARAWD of Gwynedd. Thereafter Meirionydd formed part of Gwynedd.

EI. DUNODING

This kingdom was just north of Merioneth and covered the territories around the north-east of Cardigan Bay which subsequently became subject to Gwynedd. It received its name from Dunant (*fl* 460s), a son of Cunedda. The genealogy of the kings is shown on chart 4 on page 140.

The king list details Dunant's successors as Ebiaun, Dinacat, Meurig, Ebiaun (II), Isaac, Podgen, Poddelgu, Ebiaun (III), Brochmael, Eiciawn, Iouanaul, Ceredig, Bleidudd and Cuhelin. The dynasty may have remained relatively autonymous until the time of Rhodri Mawr in the mid ninth century. Nothing is known about these kings and we must treat them as little more than vassals to the kings of Gwynedd.

EJ. ERGYNG, or NORTHERN GWENT

A small but rich kingdom on the borders of Wales and England around Hereford, known better by the later name of Archenfeld. This was also the location of the peoples known as the Gewisse who later became subject to the West Saxons (see page 296). The genealogy of these kings is shown on chart 3 for Gwent (page 122).

The first king may have been Pebiau (*fl* 490s), the son of Erb of Gwent, and the territory remained in Pebiau's family for the next five generations passing through Cynfyn (*fl* 510s), Gwrgan *Mawr* (*fl* 530s), Caradoc *Vreichfas* (*fl* 550s) and Caurdaf (*fl* 570s) to Medrawd (*fl* 590s). One final ruler of Ergyng is recorded: Gwrfoddw (*fl* 610s or earlier), after whose death Ergyng came under the rule of the kings of Gwent but was later absorbed into the Saxon kingdom of the Magonsæte.

[EJ1] **PEBIAU** *CLAFORAWG* (*the DRIBBLER*) Ergyng, *fl* c500.
Pebiau inherited Ergyng from his father ERB of Gwent and established a dynasty that was the main power in south-east Wales during the following century. Dating Pebiau is difficult because of conflicting information. The charters in the *Book of Llandaff* suggest he was a contemporary of St Dubric, but other genealogies show

Pebiau as the grandfather of Dubric through his daughter Yrddil. Dubric's date of death is shown variously as 520, 550 or 612 and he is believed to have lived into his sixties so that we may date Pebiau's birth perhaps eighty years earlier, i.e. 440, 470 or 532. One charter notes that Pebiau had married a daughter of King Cystennyn. If this is the same as CONSTANTINE of Dumnonia, then it would favour the later date and place Pebiau in the 550s. Unfortunately Pebiau is also shown as the great-grandfather of Onbrawst who married MEURIG of Gwent, who was born about 560. The same reckoning of 20–25 years per generation would place Pebiau's birth at about 490 which may be more accurate if another of his grandchildren, CARADOC VREICHFRAS, was also a contemporary of King ARTHUR's as tradition believes.

Pebiau was apparently also known as *Claforawg* (or *Spumosus* in Latin), both of which refer to his affliction of constantly frothing at the mouth. Like all of the kings at this time they spent much of their life in conquest and in older age grew conscious of the hereafter and turned to the church for salvation. Pebiau's atonement was rather different. He discovered his daughter was pregnant and ordered that she be drowned, but she kept floating back to the shore. He then ordered she be burned, but the next morning they discovered her alive with her child, who became St Madle and who, as an infant, cured Pebiau of all his ailments.

[EJ2] **CYNFYN** Ergyng, *fl* 510s.
Son of PEBIAU and father of GWRGAN MAWR.

[EJ3] **GWRGAN *MAWR* (*the GREAT*)** Ergyng, *fl* 530s?
Gwrgan must have been a battle-leader of note to have become known as the Great, though nothing of his exploits survives. If his assumed dates are correct then Gwrgan would certainly have been in battle against the Saxons, and probably fought against CERDIC. It is important to note that the territory of the Ergyng has also been identified as the Gewisse, and Cerdic was called king of the Gewisse. Cerdic may therefore have been a renegade prince of Ergyng, possibly even Gwrgan's son or brother, who joined in league with the Saxons. Gwrgan's son was CARADOC VREICHFAS.

[EJ4] **CARADOC *VREICHFAS*** Ergyng and Gwent, *fl* 550s?
It is difficult to be sure about the date of Caradoc's life. He was the great-grandson of PEBIAU and probably lived during the middle of the sixth century. His nickname means "of the strong arms", suggesting he was a strong and valiant hero. He is remembered as the founder of the royal dynasty of Gwent, though this would date him too early. Unless there are two heroes of the same name, the genealogies that show him as the father of Eudaf *Hen* (see OCTAVIUS) are almost certainly in error, as this would place him a century or two earlier (see CARADOCUS of Geoffrey's *History*). No historical facts of Caradoc's life remain, though we can imagine he was a noted warrior, probably involved in the fight against the Saxon invaders. It is interesting to speculate on the similarity of names between Caradoc and CERDIC, the chief of the Gewisse, claimed as the ancestor of the West Saxons. Ergyng was known as the territory of the Gewisse, and it is just possible that Cerdic and Caradoc may have been one and the same. Cerdic/Caradoc may have led an army of Saxon mercenaries to help fight against other Saxon marauders and as a consequence carved out his own kingdom in Wiltshire, not many miles from Ergyng, his

homeland. In Welsh legend Caradoc is shown as a contemporary of ARTHUR. His wife, Gurguint, was the sister of CADOR of Cornwall.

[EJ5] **CAURDAF** Ergyng, *fl* 570s?
The son of CARADOC VREICHFAS. Nothing is recorded of his exploits though he lived at the time of considerable battles against the Saxons. It is possible he was one of the three kings defeated at Dyrham in 577, though his name does not compare with either COINMAL or CONDIDAN. It is certain that his lands would have been affected by that victory. He may also have been at the battle of Tintern in 584.

[EJ6] **MEDRAWD** Ergyng, *fl* 590s.
One of the last kings of Ergyng, the son of Caurdaf and grandson of CARADOC VREICHFAS. Medrawd was killed in battle, and it has been suggested that he was the historical person behind Mordred of Arthurian legend. Medrawd was second cousin or ARTHWYR of Gwent. Though there is no record that he fought against Arthwyr, there could have been territorial disputes and the association of names later could have become linked to the Arthurian legend.

[EJ7] **GWRFODDW** Ergyng, *fl* 610s.
The last recorded king of Ergyng, after whose death the kingdom passed to the kings of Gwent and may have later formed part of the Mercian kingdom of the Magonsæte. Gwrfoddw is recorded as celebrating a great victory over the Saxons, who had been fighting for territory along the borders of Ergyng for the last forty years.

F. THE PICTS AND SCOTS

FA. PICTS

Pict is a generic name created by the Romans for the tribes of northern Britain. They were from an older wave of Celtic settlers, and not the same as the Belgic tribes of southern Britain who had moved across from the continent in the first or second century BC. The early history of the Picts is lost in legend. The king-lists usually start with a legendary ancestor called Cruithne. He and his sons came from Ireland and settled in Alba (Scotland) probably in the first or second centuries BC. The various provinces of Scotland are named after his seven sons. These, with their later names, were Círech (Angus and Mearns), Fótla (Atholl and Gowrie), Fortriu (Strathearn and Menteith), Fíobh (Fife), Cé (Mar and Buchan), Moireabh (Moray) and Cat (Caithness). Cat remained in Scotland whilst his brothers went to France. It was from Cat that the line of Pictish high-kings descends. Another legend states that Gub, king of the Picts, was banished from Ireland and his son, Cathluan (who is probably the same as Cat), became the first high-king of the Picts. The king-lists vary, and it is highly probable that some of the kings ruled concurrently in different provinces rather than in succession. The Picts were not a single unit. Over time two strong divisions emerged. The Southern Picts or Maetae (where the kingdom became called Fortrenn or Fortriu) based around Forteviot, and the Northern Picts, or Caledonii, with their capital at Inverness. The following list contains rulers from both territories.

Map 5 **The Picts**

The legendary or semi-historical kings are listed with an alpha reference (i.e. *a*, *b*, *c* etc.). Those with a biographical entry are marked [b]. The numerical sequence begins with the first historical authenticated king of the Picts. The following begins with Ged, the son or successor of Cat or Cathluan and is based on the lists printed by Marjorie Anderson in *Kings and Kingship in Early Scotland* (Lists B and D). *See also List FD (Moray) on page 413.*

Ref.	Ruler	Reign	Died	Notes

Legendary or Semi-historical rulers

Ref.	Ruler	Reign	Notes
FA*a*.	Gede or Gilgidi	reigned 50 years	
FA*b*.	Tharan or Tarain[b]	reigned 100 years	
FA*c*.	Merleo	reigned 15 years	not present in all lists
FA*d*.	Deocillimon or Duchil	reigned 40 years	
FA*e*.	Ciniod mac Artcois[b]	reigned 7 years	not in all lists
FA*f*.	Deort or Duordegel	reigned either 50 or 20 years	
FA*g*.	Blieblith	reigned 5 years	not in all lists
FA*h*.	Deototreic or Tethothrect	reigned 40 years	
FA*i*.	Conbust or Usconbust	reigned 20 years	

6. Celts (3) – **The Picts**

An accurate genealogy of the Pictish kings is almost impossible because of the matrilinear succession and the lack of certainty over mothers' or fathers' names. The following is a close approximation based on such evidence as exists but includes much that is conjectural. It excludes the semi-legendary rulers

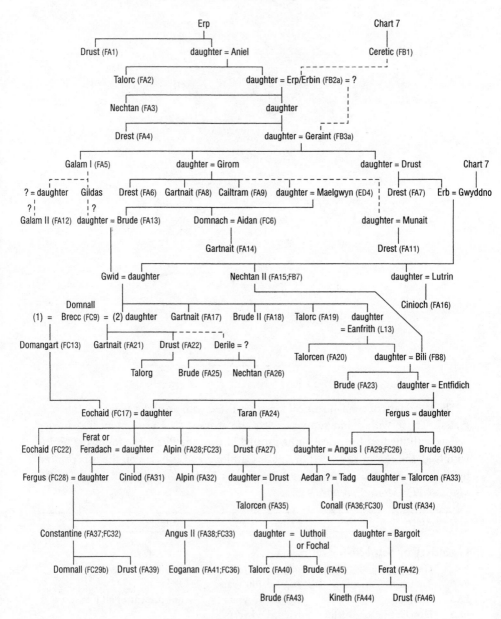

Ref.	Ruler	Reign	Died	Notes
FAj.	Crautreic or Karanochrect	reigned 40 years		
FAk.	Deordiuois	reigned 20 years		not in all lists
FAl.	Uist	reigned 30 years		not in all lists
FAm.	Caruorst	reigned 40 years		not in all lists
FAn.	Gartnait *Bolgh*[b]	reigned either 4 or 9 years		

One list suggests that after Gartnait Bolgh had reigned 4 years he was succeeded by four further kings, each called Gartnait, who reigned 9 years in total.

Ref.	Ruler	Reign	Died	Notes
FAo.	Breth or Brude mac Muthut[b]	reigned 7 years		not in all lists
FAp.	Vipoig Namet or Vipoguenech	reigned 30 years		also called Poponeuet
FAq.	Fiachu or Fyahor *Albus*	reigned 30 years		

Some lists merge the previous two kings into one king who reigned 30 years.

Ref.	Ruler	Reign	Died	Notes
FAr.	Canatumel or Canutulachama	reigned 6 years		some lists say reigned 5 years or 1 year; also called Tonaculmel
FAs.	Donarmahl or Douernach *Uetalec*	reigned 2 years		
FAt.	Feradach or Feodak *Finlegh*[b]	reigned 2 years		probably same as king called Wradechuecla
FAu.	Gartnait or Gauiach Diuberr[b]	reigned 40 or 60 years		
FAv.	Talorc map Achiuir[b]	reigned 25 years also called Balarg		

Historical rulers

Ref.	Ruler	Reign	Died	Notes
FA1.	Drust	424–53		
FA2.	Talorc	453–7		
FA3.	Nechtan *Morbet*	457–68		
FA4.	Drest *Gurthinmoch*	468–98		
FA5.	Galanan (or Galam I) *Erilich*	498–513		see also FB3c (Caw of Strathclyde)
FA6.	Drest	513–33		deposed between 521–9
FA7.	Drest	513–29		ruled jointly with above
FA8.	Gartnait	533–40		
FA9.	Cailtram	533–41		
FA10.	Talorg	541–52		
FA11.	Drest	552–3		
FA12.	Cennalath (or Galam II)	553–7	579	
FA13.	Brude (I)	556–84	584	possibly killed in battle
FA14.	Gartnait	584–602		
FA15.	Nechtan (II)	602–21	621	
FA16.	Cinioch or Ciniath	621–31		
FA17.	Gartnait	631–5		
FA18.	Brude (II)	635–41		
FA19.	Talorc	641–53		
FA20.	Talorcen	653–7		
FA21.	Gartnait	657–63		

Ref.	Ruler	Reign	Died	Notes
FA22.	Drust	663–72		expelled
FA23.	Brude (III)	672–93		
FA24.	Taran	693–7		expelled
FA25.	Brude (IV)	697–706		
FA26.	Nechtan (III)	706–24	732	abdicated
FA27.	Drust	724–6	729	driven out; killed in battle
FA28.	Alpin	726–8	736	driven out; became king of Dál Riata in 733 (see FC23); possibly killed
(FA26)	Nechtan (III) (restored)	728–9	732	
FA29.	Angus (Oengus)	729–61	761	King of Dál Riata from 736 (see FC26)
FA30.	Brude (V)	761–3	763	
FA31.	Ciniod	763–75	775	
FA32.	Alpin	775–9		
FA33.	Talorgen or Talorcen	779–81	781	
FA34.	Drust	780–2		
FA35.	Talorcen	782–5		
FA36.	Conall	785–9	807	deposed; became King of Dál Riata in 805 (see FC30)
FA37.	Constantine	789–820	820	King of Dál Riata from 811 (see FC32)
FA38.	Angus or Oengus II	820–34	834	also king of Dál Riata (see FC33)
FA39.	Drust	834–7		ruled jointly with Talorc
FA40.	Talorc	834–7		ruled jointly with Drust VIII
FA41.	Eoganan (or Ewen)	c837–9	839	king of Dál Riata (FC36); killed in battle
FA42.	Ferat or Uurad	839–42		
FA43.	Brude (VI)	842	842	
FA44.	Kineth	842–3		
FA45.	Brude (VII)	843–5		
FA46.	Drust	845–7	847	killed in battle

Thereafter the Southern Picts were absorbed into the kingdom of Alba under Kenneth macAlpin (see page 379). For a period the Viking Thorstein (NB2a) established a kingdom in the northern Pict territory of Caithness and Sutherland (see page 437). It is likely that a Pictish kingdom continued in the north in Moray (see page 413).

LEGENDARY OR SEMI-HISTORICAL RULERS

[FA*b*] **THARAN** or **TARAIN** was one of the earliest legendary rulers who is assigned an impossible reign of one hundred years. It has been suggested that this first ruler was really a memory of Taranis, the Celtic god of thunder. The only known altar to Taranis in Britain was at Chester where the Romans absorbed the cult into their non-Christian worship in the first or second century AD. This suggests that worship of Taranis may have been quite widespread throughout the Celtic world at that time and it is not impossible to assume that the Picts king-lists refer to this cult holding sway over the Pictish world for a century at this time.

[FAe] **CINIOD** MAC **ARTCOIS** An early pre-historical king of the Picts, recorded as the son of Artcois and the successor of Deocillimon. No date is accorded to his reign of only seven years, but if he existed at all he probably lived at the beginning of the third century AD, and could therefore be related to ARGENTOCOXOS.

[FAn] **GARTNAIT** *BOLGH* is one of the prehistorical kings about whom we have no other written data. His reign length is given variously as four or nine years, with one king-list suggesting that he was succeeded by four other kings called Gartnait who reigned nine years in total. He probably lived around the first quarter of the fourth century and was almost certainly involved in the increasing ferocity of raids upon Hadrian's Wall at that time.

[FAo] **BRETH** or **BRUDE MAC MUTHUT.** Brude was the name of seven historical rulers of the Picts, plus this quasi-legendary king. Brude, Bruide, Breth or Bridei as it is sometimes spelt, means "strength", and was particularly apt for at least two of the rulers. It is almost certainly the name known by Geoffrey of Monmouth which he interpreted as BRUTUS. It first appears as the name of a quasi-historical king who apparently ruled for seven years but about whom nothing else is known. If he existed then he would have reigned about 330.

[FAt] **FERADACH** A semi-legendary king who preceded GARTNAIT (II) and therefore probably ruled in the second half of the fourth century. He had the epithet *Findlaech*, the first of the Pictish kings to sport that name. It means "white hero" and suggests not only that he was brave but that he also had fair skin, which was unusual for the dark-haired dark-skinned Picts. It's possible that Feradach may have been albino. Despite his heroic nature, he is only ascribed a reign of two years which suggests that he perished in some internecine squabbles of the period.

[FAu] **GARTNAIT** or **GAUIACH DIUBERR** succeeded FERADACH and probably ruled at the end of the fourth century, although the reign ascribed to him of either forty or sixty years is unlikely. He was succeeded by TALORC MAP ACHUIR.

[FAv] **TALORC** MAC **ACHIUIR** Although treated as one of the pre-historical kings (meaning his name appears nowhere other than the king-lists), he ruled immediately before DRUST MAC ERB and, if his reign length is correct, we may then assign him to the period 400–24. This Talorc may well have been associated with St Ninian and his religious house at Whitehorn, and therefore may also be linked with TUTAGUAL the British king of Galloway.

HISTORICAL KINGS

[FA1] **DRUST** MAC **ERP** Picts, 424–53.
Drust is the name of at least 10 kings of the Picts. It is sometimes rendered as Drustan, or more popularly TRISTAN or Tristram in the Arthurian legends. Its meaning is uncertain but probably derives from the Celtic word *drude* for druid and suggests that the name may originally have been reserved for the pre-historic priestly rulers of the Celts.

The earliest Pictish king for which we can establish some historical basis bore this name. His death is recorded in the *Annals* of Clonmacnoise in the year 449, though the accuracy of this source is uncertain. If Drust did rule at this time, then he may well have been the Pictish king with whom CERETIC of Alclud entered into an arrangement for capturing youths from Ireland to sell into slavery in Pictland. One of the king-lists refers to Patrick's ministry to Ireland beginning in the tenth year of Drust's reign – the actual year was 435. Drust was well known in Irish legend as the hero of a hundred battles. It is difficult to know over how much of Pictland Drust had authority (there were almost certainly several Pictish kings ruling at any one time), but it is probable that Drust is remembered for being one of the Pictish kings who harried the British across Hadrian's Wall in the years after the withdrawal of Roman support. We can imagine that at some stage Drust and COEL HEN ("Old King Cole") came to blows.

[FA2] **TALORC** MAC **ANIEL** who died in 457, probably ruled for four years, sandwiched between two giants of the early Pict world, DRUST MAC ERP and NECHTAN *MORBET*.

[FA3] **NECHTAN** *MORBET* Picts, 457–68.

Nechtan is the name of three kings of the Picts. The original Nechtan was a river god from Celtic legend and the name seems to have been applied to kings with strong marine associations. This is reinforced by the epithet of the first king called Nechtan, styled *Morbet*, meaning the "speckled sea", and it is likely that he was heavily involved with the invasion forces of the Saxons and Angles. It was during Nechtan's reign that the British brought over Saxon mercenaries to help in their battle against the Picts, and a number of these forces were based on the coast of north-east Britain around the Firth of Forth. The Picts probably conducted many sea raids on the Saxons and British across both the Forth and Clyde. Nechtan is also associated in some lists with having founded the church at Abernethy, but this was more likely the work of the second NECHTAN who ruled a century after. Nechtan is recorded as the son of Erp, which causes confusion with the second Nechtan who was the son (or grandson) of another Erp or Irb.

[FA4] **DREST** *GURTHINMOCH* Picts, 468–98.

Although nothing is recorded of Drest beyond his name and length of reign it is pertinent to note that he was king of the Picts not only at a time when there was relative peace between the Picts and the British, but also when the Irish Dál Riatan princes, Fergus, Angus and Loarn, landed in Argyll and Kintyre and established their kingdoms. Since Drest ruled for thirty years it is unlikely that he was a weak king, and we may therefore deduce that he was a rather more skilled in the arts of diplomacy than his predecessors. However, from the date of his death it is possible that he was killed in territorial disputes with the Irish.

[FA5] **GALAM** or **GALANAN** *ERILICH* Picts, 498–513.

Ruler at the time when DUMNAGUAL HEN established his strong kingdom of Alclud between the Walls. He is believed to be a cousin of Dumnagual, originally called CAW, great grandson of CERETIC and briefly king of Strathclyde before he abdicated to assume the Pictish kingship (probably under strong pressure from Dumnagual). He was apparently very religious and was probably deposed because of his religious views by DREST MAC GIROM. He subsequently settled in Anglesey.

[FA6] **DREST** MAC **GIROM** Picts, 513–21 and 529–33, jointly with DREST MAC DRUST, *whom see for details*. He was succeeded by his two brothers GARTNAIT MAC GIROM and CAILTRAM MAC GIROM.

[FA7] **DREST** MAC **DRUST** Picts, 513–16 and 521–9.
Drest would have been ruler of the Picts when the first major wave of Saxons and Angles came across from northern Germany to settle in Bernicia and the area of the Gododdin. Almost certainly Drest would have led combative raids against these settlers. He may well have also had conflicts with the former British occupants of Bernicia, under MORCANT *Bulc*, who were now being driven out of their homeland and seeking new territories. Drest also had internal battles with DREST MAC GIROM, who unseated him for five years, but whom he then deposed for nine years. Drest mac Girom resumed the kingship after Drest's death.

[FA8] **GARTNAIT** MAC **GIROM** Picts, 533–40. He was the successor of DREST MAC GIROM, and ruled jointly with his brother CAILTRAM MAC GIROM, *whom see for details.*

[FA9] **CAILTRAM** MAC **GIROM** Picts, 533–41.
Successor of DREST MAC GIROM, who ruled jointly with his brother GARTNAIT MAC GIROM, whom Cailtram outlived by one year. There were usually several Pictish kings ruling at once over the various local tribes, and it was rare for the Picts to select a high king with authority over all of the tribes, although they occasionally recognized a king with special abilities. It is therefore more likely that Cailtram and Gartnait ruled separate parts of Pictland, one to the south, in the tribal area sometimes called the Maetæ, and the other to the north in the more traditional area of Caledonia.

[FA10] **TALORG** MAC **MORDELEG** (sometimes called **GOLORG**) Picts, 541–52.
At this time IDA is said to have established himself as ruler of the Bernician Angles from his fortress at Bamburgh. It is hard to imagine this would happen without Talorg being involved either in negotiations with Ida or, more likely, in conflict.

[FA11] **DREST** MAC **MUNAIT** Picts, 552–3.
Ruled for only a year, which suggests he was slain in battle, probably against the British. This was a period when the Gododdin, under DUMNAGUAL *Hen* and CINBELIN were struggling for their own survival against the Angles to the south and the Picts to the north.

[FA12] **GALAM (II)** or **TAGALAD** *CENNALATH* Picts, 553–7.
The last recorded king of the Picts before the election of BRUDE MAC MALCHEON. Although he ruled jointly with him for one year there is evidence to suggest that Galam was either deposed or resigned, since he seems to have lived for a further twenty years. The election of Brude suggests that the Picts wanted a strong king able to defend their lands against the encroachments of the Saxons and Scots, and for this they went to a British prince. We can only deduce from this that Galam, and probably several of his predecessors, had been weak kings successively defeated in battle.

[FA13] **BRUDE (I)** MAC **MAELCHEON** Picts, 556–84.

Most historical king-lists of the Picts start with Brude, ignoring his many predecessors. Brude's appearance was a departure from precedent. It was traditional amongst the Picts to elect their king from within a select aristocracy who were sons of Pictish princesses. Brude, however, is generally acknowledged to have been the son of MAELGWYN, the ruler of Gwynedd (though this identification is not definite). If we accept this, then it is clear that Maelgwyn must have married a Pictish princess, which gave Brude his authority, but it also meant that Brude brought with him considerable strength. Maelgwyn was regarded as the most powerful ruler in Britain and his son, RHUN, continued to enforce that authority.

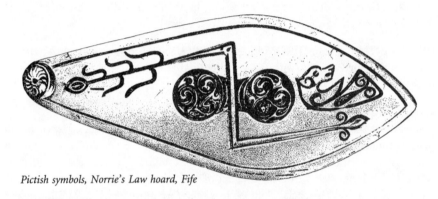

Pictish symbols, Norrie's Law hoard, Fife

Brude took over a kingdom that had suffered considerably in the last decade, particularly at the hands of the Scots of Dál Riata, and their king GABHRAN. Initially Brude shared the kingdom with his predecessor, GALAM, but after a year Galam was deposed. As we cannot be absolutely sure of dates at this time it is possible Brude's position was strengthened when his half-brother, Rhun, marched on the north to seek revenge for the raid on Anglesey by ELIDYR of Rheged, who was assisted by CLYTNO of the Goddodin. Rhun's army marched to the very shores of the Forth and it is possible that one of the results of this was the deposing of Galam. Rhun's army may also have assisted Brude in his fight against the Dál Riatans. Within the first two years of his reign Brude had successfully defeated Gabhrán and driven the Scots back into their kingdom. Gabhrán died either in that conflict or soon after, and his son and successor, CONALL, was not inclined to pick any further fights with Brude.

After these initial conflicts to establish his authority, Brude dominated the Picts by his strength of character and his wisdom. There was a further major change with Brude. He could claim descent from Christians but it is unlikely that he was a practising Christian himself, merely sympathetic to the faith. The Picts were pagans, steeped in their centuries-old druidic culture. St Columba used the opportunity of Brude's sympathies, however, to help convert the Picts to Christianity. In 565 Columba travelled across northern Pictland to Brude's capital at Inverness. Adomnán's life of Columba provides a dramatic telling of this journey and of the reception that Columba received. Brude apparently ordered that the gates of his castle be closed against Columba, but Columba made a sign of the cross upon the gates and as he laid his hand upon them they burst open. Thereafter Columba was apparently set in contest against Brude's chief druid, Broichan, to see who could achieve the most through the power of their religion. Columba's achievements apparently converted Brude and Columba baptized him and hundreds of his people in Loch Ness. This colourful account is probably more fantasy than fact, but there can be little doubt that the sheer passion of Columba would have impressed Brude and that he was happy to give Columba freedom to preach the Christian message across his lands. He would also have formally authorised Columba to build his monastery on Iona.

Brude ruled the Picts for nearly thirty years and proved one of their most powerful and gifted kings. He maintained peace during a period of otherwise significant hostilities to the south, and was acknowledged as sole ruler not only by all of the Pictish chieftains on the mainland, but those amongst the Orkneys and the Western Isles. Brude's temper must have been roused in 580 when the Dál Riatan king, AEDAN MAC GABHRAN, marched through Pictland in an expedition against Orkney, and it is likely that the end of Brude's reign saw a continued rise in hostilities throughout the land. The southern Picts, who remained the most hostile to Brude, continued to rebel occasionally and it is likely that Brude was killed in a battle against them in the year 584, when he was around the age of sixty. It seems that after his death the Picts repeated their election procedure by selecting as their new king the son of another powerful ruler, this time GARTNAIT, son of their old enemy Aedán mac Gabhrán.

[FA14] **GARTNAIT** MAC **DOMECH** Picts, 584–602.
He was the successor of the mighty BRUDE (I), and is believed to be the son of the Scottish king AEDAN MAC GABHRAN by the Pictish princess Domech or Domelch. Gartnait probably ruled the Northern Picts from the stronghold at Inverness and, as with past Pictish rulers, had little control over the southern Picts or Maetæ who continued to stir up trouble with the Dál Riatan Scots. If the Picts had hoped that Gartnait would be able to sustain peace with his father, then these hopes were dashed, as Aedán continued to war against the Maetæ with disastrous results. In a battle waged in about 590, Aedán lost two of his sons. Although there were representatives of the Picts at the famous battle of Catraeth in 595 celebrated in Y Gododdin (see OWAIN AP URIEN), Gartnait himself was not present. While this may have seemed wise in retrospect, it did not show Gartnait as supportive of the Celtic cause. Overall Gartnait's reign has to be assessed as a comparative failure.

[FA15] **NECHTAN** (**II**) Picts, 602–21.
Scholars have attempted much genealogical untangling with Nechtan on tempting but tenuous evidence. It has been suggested that he was the grandson of his predecessor GARTNAIT MAC DOMECH, which would have made Nechtan very young when he was elected to the kingdom, almost certainly too young to be respected by the elders and chieftains or to serve as a strong king. It has also been suggested that he is the same NECHTAN who ruled Strathclyde in succession to RHYDDERCH HEN [see (3) below]. This is more probable. They were contemporaries and it is very likely that Nechtan sought to extend the Pictish territories back into Strathclyde when the old king died, but whether the Pictish Nechtan and Rhydderch were cousins, as other genealogies suggest, is unresolved. Nechtan is remembered as a strongly religious king and the first openly Christian king of the Picts. He founded the churches at Abernathy and Kildare. This would suggest that from Nechtan's

time on all Pictish marriages must have been Christian, although this did not stop the rule of matrilinear succession. This became significant to the later kings of Northumbria and their relationship with the Picts. After the death in battle of ATHELFRITH of Northumbria, his son EANFRITH sought refuge amongst the Picts. He was presumably made welcome at Nechtan's court even though Eanfrith was not himself Christian. It has been suggested that Eanfrith's mother, Bebba, was herself Pictish, or certainly British, and might possibly have been a sister or daughter of BRUDE (I). That Nechtan accepted Eanfrith at his court, despite the significant antagonism between the Picts and the Angles, says much for Nechtan's magnanimity and perhaps is one example of why he was later called Nechtan *Mawr*, 'the Great'. Eanfrith subsequently married the sister of the later Pictish king GARTNAIT MAC GWID and his own son, TALORCAN became king of the Picts in 653.

[FA16] CINIOCH (or CINIATH) MAC LUCHTREN Picts, 621–31.

Cinioch's reign coincides with that of EDWIN of Northumbria and there must have been considerable tension between Cinioch's court, where EANFRITH, the son of Edwin's predecessor, ATHELFRITH, lived. Eanfrith was clearly accepted amongst the Picts for he married a daughter of Gwid, one of the valiant chieftains who fought alongside OWAIN AP URIEN at Catraeth in 595. When Edwin set out upon his conquest of northern Britain it is rather surprising that he did not attempt to root out Eanfrith, especially as he did turn upon his old allies in Gwynedd. One can only imagine that in weighing up the consequences the Picts were seen as harder to attack than the British, even though the terrain of both lands was similar. Edwin cannot have imagined he could equal the Pictish war machine, and this must be some indication of the power and authority now wielded by Cinioch, since BRUDE and NECHTAN established some degree of unity amongst the Picts.

[FA17] GARTNAIT MAC GWID Picts, 631–5.

Gartnait was one of three brothers who ruled consecutively. They were all sons of Gwid, who is probably the same Gwid who fought at the battle of Catraeth in 595. The brothers must all have been comparatively old at this time, but as the sons of a valiant old chieftain they must have been considered highly suitable. In fact their reigns are remembered only for continuing border skirmishes between the Britons of Strathclyde, the Scots of Dál Riata and the Angles of Northumbria.

[FA18] BRUDE (II) MAC GWID Picts, 635–41.

Brude had some success during his short reign in the constant warfare between the Picts and the Scots of Dál Riata. He defeated DOMNALL BRECC in 638 at Glenn Mureson, soon after Domnall's disastrous campaign in Ireland, which resulted in the Picts having greater control over the Scots for the next generation. However Brude met his match in the British king of Strathclyde, OWEN MAP BILI, whose power grew during this period and who checked the authority of the Picts. Brude died, possibly in battle, in 641, and was succeeded by his brother TALORC.

[FA19] TALORC MAC GWID Picts, 641–53.

If Talorc's father was the Gwid noted for his heroism at Catraeth in 595 then Talorc must have been into his late forties when he was elected to the kingdom in succession to his brothers GARTNAIT and BRUDE. Talorc faced growing hostility in the south where on the one side the conflict between the Strathclyde Britons and the

Dál Riatan Scots saw encroachment upon Pictish lands. The death of the Scottish king DOMNALL BRECC in 642 solved one problem; the growing might of his opponent, OWEN MAP BILI, created another, though only briefly, as Owen had died by 645. On the other side the Northumbrian English had systematically conquered the territory of the Gododdin and had laid siege to Edinburgh. It was only the death of OSWALD in 642 that stopped the advance upon the north whilst his successor, OSWY, sought to consolidate the expanded kingdom of Northumbria and protect himself against the advance of Mercia. There was thus a brief respite in the frontier warfare in the borders, which may account for Talorc's slightly longer reign.

[FA20] **TALORCEN** MAC **ENFRET** Picts, 653–7.
Talorcen was the first half-English ruler of the Picts. His father, EANFRITH, was the brother of the Northumbrian king OSWY. During his exile in Pictland Eanfrith had married a Pictish princess, probably around the year 620, which would make Talorcen in his early thirties. It is unlikely that he was automatically elected by the Picts. More likely that he was imposed by Oswy. But Talorcen had all the right credentials – the son of a Pictish princess and a king, and the grandson of two great warriors (Gwid and ATHELFRITH) who had fought each other at the battle of Catraeth in 595. Early in his reign Talorcen defeated and killed DUNCHAD, king of the Dál Riatan Scots, at the Battle of Strath Ethairt. With Talorcan in control in the north and, effectively, his own vassal, Oswy could rightly claim to have dominion over the Picts during his reign. Although Talorcen is not recorded as dying in battle, this may account for his death at such a young age.

[FA21] **GARTNAIT** MAC **DONUEL** Picts, 657–63.
Gartnait succeeded TALORCEN MAC ENFRET who had been established as Oswy's client king over the Picts. This arrangement continued under Gartnait and his brother DRUST, though it galled the Picts. It has been suggested that these brothers were the sons of the Dál Riatan king, DOMNALL BRECC, who had been killed in 642. If this is so then the new king of Dál Riata, DOMANGART, who succeeded in 660, was their half-brother. This did not, however, lead to harmonious relations and the conflict between the Picts and the Scots continued to worsen.

[FA22] **DRUST** MAC **DONUEL** Picts, 663–72.
Drust succeeded his brother GARTNAIT at a time of growing hostility between the Picts and the Scots under Drust's half brother DOMANGART, and a growing resentment by the Picts of their domination by the Northumbrian English under OSWY. Drust, like his two predecessors, had been installed as client king, denying the Picts their independence. These were dark days for the Picts. In 668 Domangart succeeded in establishing his domination over the Western Isles north of Argyll, and in particular over Skye, expelling many of the Picts to Ireland. Drust seemed incapable of a response. When, in 670, Oswy of Northumbria died, the Picts rebelled. How much of this rebellion was led by Drust and how much was aimed at him is not clear, but by 672, after such a massacre of a Pictish army by the new Northumbrian king EGFRITH that their bodies blocked two rivers, Drust had been expelled. What became of him after that is not known. Power amongst the Picts was seized by BRUDE MAC BILI.

[FA23] **BRUDE (III)** MAC **BILI** Picts, 672–93.

Brude came to power during the rebellion of the Picts following the death of OSWY of Northumbria – exactly when is uncertain, but it is likely to have occurred after, not before, the massacre of the Picts by Oswy's successor EGFRITH in 672. The previous Pictish king, DRUST, had been expelled and Egfrith had replaced him with his own non-Pictish subregulus, BEORNHETH. The Picts would have none of this and elected their own ruler. Their choice was another of mixed blood. Brude was the son of the Strathclyde ruler BILI MAP NECHTAN and the daughter of EANFRITH (Egfrith's uncle). Brude and Egfrith were thus second cousins, but Brude also claimed British and Pictish blood. Since Bili had died young in 633 we must assume that Brude was at least forty when he became king, possibly older.

After the massacre, Egfrith believed he had taught the Picts a lesson and turned his attention to troubles in the south with Mercia. The Anglian church, however, continued to stamp its authority over the Picts, completing in 678 a new church at Abercorn on the borders of Pictland and ordaining Trumwine as bishop to the Picts. Brude was himself highly religious, a friend of Adomnán, who became abbot of Iona in 679. Adomnán supported the Roman church in its recognition of the dating of Easter and he spent many of his years preaching to the Picts to convert them to Christian ways. For the moment, therefore, Brude left the church at Abercorn alone.

In the meantime Brude continued to establish his authority amongst the Picts after a period of some fifty years when no high king had ruled and the Picts had reverted to squabbling tribes. Over the next ten years Brude systematically rebuilt the kingdom of the Picts, finally, in 683, conquering the Orkneys and beseiging the Dál Riatan fortress at Dunadd. Egfrith became concerned over Brude's power and, in May 685, decided to crush him, going against all the advice of his council. The two armies met at Nechtansmere, which is modern-day Dunnichen Moss, near Forfar. The battle was over in moments. The Northumbrians were slaughtered and Egfrith killed. Brude hammered home his victory by pursuing the Northumbrian forces back across the Forth and re-establishing Pict-controlled territory in Lothian. This included taking over the Anglian church at Abercorn, the abbot fleeing to Whitby where he spent the rest of his days. Brude now ruled unchallenged all the territory north of the Clyde and Firth. He also held in check the Dál Riatan Scots in the south-west, and asserted authority over the lands around Lothian and Dunbar. It was not only Brude's but the Picts' finest hour, for their fortunes would never be as healthy again.

An interesting anecdote is related in the Life of Adomnán about the death of Brude. His body was conveyed to Iona for burial where Adomnán prayed over the body all night. In the morning the body apparently showed signs of recovery at which point the monks warned Adomnán that such a miracle would set too high a standard. Brude was thus allowed to die. If this anecdote is true it suggests that Brude had passed into a coma before death. When he died he was probably in his early sixties. He was remembered as one of the greatest rulers of the Picts.

[FA24] **TARAN** MAC **ENTFIDICH** Picts, 693–7.

Unlike his powerful legendary namesake, the historical Taran ruled only four years and was then expelled from the kingdom by his successor, BRUDE MAC DERILE, and later sought exile in Ireland. Evidently he did not live up to the standards set by his predecessor, BRUDE MAC BILI. He is recorded as the son of Entfidach, who may well have been an Irish chieftain.

[FA25] **BRUDE (IV)** MAC **DERILE** Picts, 697–706.

Brude deposed his predecessor, TARAN, early in 697. Whether this was because Taran was a weak ruler, or whether there was inter-dynastic rivalry amongst the Picts is unclear. As so often happens, there was unrest in the wake of a powerful ruler (BRUDE MAC BILI) and it was a while before another strong ruler emerged. It has been suggested that this Brude was the grandson of Brude mac Bili but, if that were the case, Brude would at most have been in his early twenties. It is more likely that Brude came from a collateral line, possibly descended from a daughter of DOMNALL BRECC and thus the nephew of DRUST MAC DONUEL. Brude had a half-brother or cousin, Talorg mac Drust which suggests that their mother may also have married the earlier king, DRUST MAC DONUEL. Whatever his ancestry Brude soon established himself as a strong king commanding respect. He was one of those present at the Synod of Birr in Ireland later in 697 when Adomnán proposed his *Law of the Innocents*, protecting the elderly, children, women and the clergy from the ravages of war. That Adomnán brought this forward at that time suggests that the reign of Taran may have been particularly bloodthirsty. To establish his authority Brude led an army against the Northumbrians in Lothian in 698, slaying their sub-king Beorhtred and confirming Pictish control of that territory. Brude died in 706 when he must still have been comparatively young.

[FA26] **NECHTAN (III)** MAC **DERILE** Picts, 706–24 and 728–9.

Nechtan succeeded his brother BRUDE at a time when the Pictish kingdom was at its most powerful. Both his brother and the earlier BRUDE MAC BILI had re-introduced Pictish rule to the south of the Forth in Lothian, and this remained a battlefield for at least the first five years of Nechtan's reign. In 711 there was a decisive battle between the Maetæ Picts and the Northumbrians on the plain of Manaw in Lothian where the Picts were slaughtered. After this Nechtan negotiated for a peace treaty with OSRED, king of Northumbria, which remained in force for several decades. Nechtan needed this security to the south. The Pictish kingdom was again fragmenting with the old rivalries breaking out. In 713 Nechtan faced a rebellion from his half-brother, Talorg, and there is record of other disquiet at this time. Nevertheless Nechtan did not wish to rule by the sword. He was an intensely religious man and had accepted the Christian faith. Rather than be subordinate to the Anglian church, Nechtan wished to be recognized in his own right as head of the Roman church amongst the Picts. Nechtan welcomed the ministry of Curetan, one of the bishops of Adomnán, who continued to spread Christianity to the Picts in the first decades of the eighth century. Nechtan was baptized by Curetan and ordained that a church be built, "in the Roman fashion", at Restenneth in Angus. In 716 the remarkable bishop, Egbert, succeeded in converting the monks on Iona to celebrate Easter in accordance with the Roman calendar, but adherents to the Celtic church remained. Nechtan then brought his authority to bear and expelled the Celtic adherents from Iona in 717. Nechtan's reign really marked the conversion of the Picts from a pagan to a Christian people, a century and a half after the arrival of Columba.

Nechtan's role as head of the church clearly affected his secular role in the latter half of his reign. It is quite likely that many of the Pict chieftains, whilst accepting Christianity, wanted a strong warrior leader, not an evangelical one. By the year 724 there came a leadership crisis. Nechtan retired to a monastery. This may have been by choice, but more likely he was forced into retirement by his elected successor DRUST, because Nechtan sought to regain the kingdom two years later and this time was imprisoned by Drust. Later that same year, however, Drust was himself deposed by ALPIN who then remained in authority for two years. During this time it is probable that Nechtan remained imprisoned but by 728 he had gained his freedom and defeated Alpin at the battle of Moncrieffe Hill. Nechtan now resumed the role of king, but the peace over which he had presided in the previous decade was shattered. Nechtan faced continued opposition from a further claimant, Onuist or ANGUS, who defeated Nechtan at the battle of Monith Carno in 729. At this stage Nechtan either admitted defeat or was forcibly retired to his monastery where he died three years later. After a few more battles Angus assumed the throne.

[FA27] **DRUST** Picts, 724–6.

When Drust deposed NECHTAN in 724 it started a wave of anarchy that lasted for five years and eventually resulted in the emergence of ANGUS as the next powerful ruler of the Picts. Drust, whose patronym is not known but who may well have been EOCHAID's son, succeeded in holding the kingship for nearly two years, but it was a period full of battles against at least two other claimants, ALPIN and Angus (a third, Gartnait, may in fact be identifiable with Drust). In 726 Nechtan also returned to fight for the throne, but Drust defeated and imprisoned him. Soon after Alpin defeated Drust and drove him into exile, but a year later Drust returned and fought three closely contested battles with Angus. At length Drust was killed at the battle of Druim Derg Blathuug, leaving Angus the sole victor.

[FA28;FC23] **ALPIN** ruled Picts, 726–8; Dál Riata, 733–6.

When DRUST deposed NECHTAN for rulership of the Picts in 724 he cast the kingdom into a period of anarchy where other tribal chieftains fought for supremacy, including those of neighbouring kingdoms. The kingdom of Dál Riata was also in the midst of a dynastic struggle between the descendents of Fergus and those of Loarn. Through the various marriages and inter-marriages of his forebears Alpin had as much claim on the Pictish throne as he did on that of Dál Riata. Quite what happened is not clear, but it is evident that there was intense squabbling for both thrones amongst some seven or eight contenders. In the space of the year 726 DUNGAL was deposed from Dál Riata and DRUST, whom he supported, from rulership of the Picts. Alpin probably supported his own brother EOCHAID for the kingship of Dál Riata, whilst he fought against Drust and ANGUS for the Pict throne. Alpin defeated Drust and claimed rulership of the Picts which he held for nearly two years, despite further opposition from Drust and Angus. By 728, Angus proved the more powerful contender and defeated Alpin at the battle of Monid Croib where Alpin's own son was killed. Alpin endeavoured to hang on to the kingdom, but he was again defeated, this time by Nechtan at Moncrieffe Hill, and Alpin fled back to the safety of his brother's kingdom. When Alpin's brother Eochaid died in 733, Alpin assumed rulership of Dál Riata, but he was faced with opposition from MUIREDACH of the dynasty of Loarn. For three years civil war raged

between the Scots which was only concluded when Angus, now in charge of the
Picts and growing in might, invaded Dál Riata and convincingly defeated both
Alpin and Muiredach. From 736 until 750 the kingdoms of the Picts and the Scots
were united. Alpin's fate is not known – he either died in battle or fled to Ireland.

[FA29;FC26] **ANGUS (I)** ruled Picts 729–61; Dál Riata 736–50.
The name Angus is of ancient Celtic origin. It usually appears as Oengus and is
rendered as Unuist in Pictish. The name means "unique" or "sole choice", and it
has been suggested that it derived from the original Greek Aeneas. The first Pictish
king of that name was well deserving of its significance. He emerged as the victor
from the civil war that raged in Pictland from 724 to 729 when DRUST deposed
NECHTAN and various factions then entered the fray to vie for supremacy. One of
those was ALPIN, whom Angus defeated, and when Angus defeated Drust at the
battle of Druim Derg Blathuug in August 729 he became sole ruler. Alpin, in the
meantime, had fled to Dál Riata, which was also being torn apart by an inter-
dynastic conflict. Angus took advantage of this struggle and their weak rulers to
dominate that kingdom. From 731 to 736 there were a series of raids and battles in
the territories of Dál Riata and Loarn. Angus had a personal feud against an earlier
Dál Riatan king, DUNGAL, who had been deposed but who continued to live in
Loarn. Angus's brother, BRUDE, battled against Dungal for two years, at the end of
which Dungal committed a mortal sin by invading the Irish island of Tory where
Brude was in sanctuary. The next year (734) Angus invaded Loarn and captured the
fortress of Dunolly. Dungal was wounded and fled to Ireland.

Having secured Loarn (though not actually assuming the kingship), Angus
turned his attention to Dál Riata and, in 736, with a series of raids and concerted
attacks, Angus stormed the fortress of Dunadd. Alpin either died in this battle or
fled to Ireland. MUIREDACH the rival king also seems to have fled the kingdom –
while his son, EOGAN, is recognized as briefly holding the throne, presumably as a
vassal to Angus, to all intents Angus ruled Dál Riata, though he does not seem to
have claimed the kingship. But there is no other recorded king until AED FIND in
750, and as Angus imposed the laws of the Picts upon the Scots, we may just as
easily regard him as the first king of the Picts and the Scots.

Angus continued to hunt down and destroy any member of the Dál Riatan royal
family who crossed him, as well as any potential Pictish claimants to the throne. In
739 it is recorded that he killed Talorgen, the tribal king of Atholl, whilst in 741
there was a further punitive raid upon Dál Riata when the sons of FIANNAMAIL were
killed. From 744, Angus turned his attention to the rulers south of the Clyde, clearly
seeking domination of the whole of northern Britain. This was a mistake. In 750,
TEUDEBER MAP BILI the king of Strathclyde defeated Talorgen, Angus's brother, at
the Battle of Mugdock. This seems to have weakened Angus's control and it is
possible that there was a rebellion amongst the Picts that year for there is a record
that Angus lost control of his kingdom and did not regain it until two years later.
However suspect this reference might be, it was at this time that AED FIND took
advantage of Angus's lapse in power, to regain control of Dál Riata. In order to
exact retribution upon the Strathclyde Britons, Angus joined forces with EADBERT
of Northumbria. In 756, after savage fighting, their combined forces captured the
citadel of Dumbarton and in effect destroyed the Strathclyde dynasty. However the

British army descended on the Northumbrian and Pictish forces on their return from the siege and slaughtered them. Angus remained in power for a further five years but it is clear by this time his authority had waned, and it is possible he was ruler only of the Southern Picts. He was succeeded by his brother BRUDE.

[FA30] **BRUDE (V)** MAC **FERGUS** Picts, 761–3.

There does not seem to have been a smooth succession following the death of ANGUS (I) in 761. His brother assumed the throne of the southern Picts, but he cannot have been much younger than Angus and was almost certainly in his fifties. It may have been as a caretaker role while a more suitable ruler was elected. However, dynastic struggles continued and when Brude died after only two years, the kingship passed to his nephew CINIOD who had probably already regarded himself as the rightful heir.

[FA31] **CINIOD** MAC **FEREDACH** Picts, 763–75.

Ciniod's father, Feredach, was the brother of DUNGAL, the former ruler of Loarn and Dál Riata, whom ANGUS had captured when he invaded Loarn in 736. It has generally been accepted that Feredach subsequently married Angus's sister (or sister-in-law) so that his son had a right of claim on the Pictish throne through their rule of matrilinear succession. If this is so then Ciniod must have been in his mid- twenties when he assumed the kingship. Ciniod presumably contined to act as if he had control over Dál Riata, which Angus had conquered in 736 but where AED FIND had resumed control in 750. Although little is recorded about Ciniod's actions, we can assume he was sufficiently oppressive for Aed Find to venture into Pict territory in 768. The result of the battle between him and Ciniod is not recorded but was presumably sufficiently decisive for Aed to claim he had thrown off the yoke of the Picts. With Ciniod the Pictish kingship enters a period of decline. His reign was followed by a series of weak kings who were almost certainly not recognized by all of Pictland.

[FA32] **ALPIN** MAC **FERET** Picts, 775–9.

One of the several minor kings of the Picts who ruled after CINIOD. It is unlikely that Alpin's claim was recognized by all of the Pictish tribes or, indeed, that it was recognized consistently by any of them. His reign is reckoned as either three or five years, which may either be a copyist's error, or an indication of the ebb and flow of his authority. It is likely that he did not maintain authority over the southern Picts and that his rule there was taken over by TALORGEN MAC DRUST.

[FA33] **TALORGEN** or **TALORCEN** MAC **DRUST** Picts, 779–81.

One of the five kings who vied for the kingship following the death of CINIOD. This Talorgan is probably the one described as Black Talorc (*Dubthalorc*), who is recorded as ruling the Southern Picts and who died in 781.

[FA34] **DRUST** MAC **TALORGEN** Picts, 781–2.

One of five claimants to the Pictish kingship on the death of CINIOD. He reigned for only a year, probably as ruler of the Northern Picts, and most likely died in battle or was driven into exile.

[FA35] **TALORCEN** MAC **ANGUS** Picts, 782–5.

If Talorcen's father is the same as the ANGUS who ruled the Picts from 729–761, then this was the first case in Pictish history of a son subsequently ruling after his father.

Talorcen was probably already into his fifties by then and must have staked his claim to the throne as much on the strength of his father's name as on his own abilities. However he did little to prove himself and died after a reign of only four years.

[FA36;FC30] **CONALL** MAC **TADG** Picts, 785–9; Dál Riata, 805–7.
He was the last of the minor claimants to the Pictish throne whose short reigns spanned a period of fourteen years between the death of CINIOD in 775 and the emergence of CONSTANTINE in 789. Nothing is known about Conall's reign other than that he was defeated by Constantine in battle in 789 and fled to the kingdom of Dál Riata where he sought refuge with DOMNALL. After Domnall's death in 805 Conall assumed the kingship of Dál Riata. There is no reason to assume he usurped the throne, although his claim is vague and he does not fit easily into the genealogical hierarchy. The stronger claimant, CONALL MAC AEDAN, laid siege to Conall and killed him in battle in 807.

[FA37;FC32] **CONSTANTINE** MAC **FERGUS** Picts, 789–820; Dál Riata, 811–20.
Although Constantine was the son of the Dál Riatan king, FERGUS MAC EOCHAID, he apparently did not inherit the throne on his father's death in 781. All kinds of reasons have been proposed for this (*see under* DOMNALL *for details*), but the upshot is that Constantine set out and challenged CONALL MAC TADG for the throne of the Picts. We must assume that Constantine had a Pictish mother to allow his aceptance by the Picts. Constantine and Conall met in battle in 789 where Conall was defeated and fled for sanctuary, surprisingly to Dál Riata. Constantine was elected as king of the Picts and was their first powerful king since ANGUS, who had come to the throne sixty years earlier. The Picts needed a strong king, as it was during Constantine's reign that the Vikings began their harrying of the western coast. Records are incomplete for this period, but there is no denying the horror implied by the entry in the *Annals of Ulster* for 794 which stated: "Devastation of all the islands of Britain by the heathen." The Viking raids continued annually with particular acts of plunder recorded at Skye in 795 and in the Hebrides in 798. It is quite probable that the Vikings began to settle in the Western Isles from this period, using them as a base for their pillaging of the coast of Ireland and Pictland (although it was another forty to fifty years before the settlements were sufficiently large or established to warrant their own rulers). Constantine could do little about this. The Vikings attacked quickly and moved quickly around the islands and inlets. It was impossible for the Picts to fight them on land, and difficult to defeat them at sea, where the Vikings had superiority. Instead Constantine sought to strengthen the heart of his territory. In the early 800s he built a new citadel for himself at Forteviot in Perthshire, and nearby established a new church at Dunkeld. Some of the monks from Iona transferred there after the repeated attacks on Iona by the Vikings in 795, 802 and 806, although the majority of them migrated to Kells in Ireland. A few remained to face the wrath of the Vikings, who were seeking the relics and treasures of Columba but never found them. These were eventually brought to Dunkeld under KENNETH MACALPIN, forty years later.

Meanwhile, Constantine looked again to consolidate his kingdom. In 805 Domnall had died and Constantine's old adversary, Conall, claimed the throne of Dál Riata. He was soon defeated and killed in battle by CONALL MAC AEDAN who took over the kingship in 807, but he died in 811. Constantine now claimed the title which had probably been rightfully his since 781. He was only the second king since ANGUS to rule the Scots and the Picts at the same time, and he was the first to pass that joint rulership on to his successor, his brother ANGUS II. Constantine must have been nearly sixty when he died in 820. He had done more than any previous king to unite the Picts and the Scots, which became easier when faced with the common menace of the Vikings. His reign was a major step toward the unification of Scotland.

[FA38;FC33] **ANGUS (II)** MAC **FERGUS** ruled Scots and Picts, 820–34.
The first ruler to inherit the kingship of both the Scottish Dál Riata and the Picts when he succeeded his brother CONSTANTINE. Full details of his reign are given under Alba on page 207.

[FA39] **DRUST** MAC **CONSTANTINE** Picts, 834–7.
[FA40] **TALORC** MAC **UUTHOIL** Picts, 834–7.
Co-rulers and amongst the last rulers of the Picts before the disastrous battle with the Vikings in 839. *See under* EOGANAN MAC ANGUS *for details, page 207.*

[FA41;FC36] **EOGANAN (or EWEN)** MAC **ANGUS** Picts and Scots, 836 or 837–9.
When ANGUS II died in 834 the combined kingdom of the Picts and the Scots was then shared between the various claimants to the throne. Eoganan was but one of several rivals and their details are provided under Alba on page 207.

[FA42] **FERAT** or **FERADACH** Picts, 839–42.
[FA43] **BRUDE (VI)** MAC **FERAT** Picts, 842.
[FA44] **KINETH** MAC **FERAT** Picts, 842–3.
[FA45] **BRUDE (VII)** MAC **FOCHEL** Picts, 843–5.
[FA46] **DRUST** MAC **FERAT** Picts, 845–7.
When the Pict aristocracy was all but annihilated in the battle with the Vikings at Forteviot in 839, it left a vacuum that was soon filled by one of the few surviving earls. Ferat (or Uurad in Pictish) was the son of Bargoit, who is not otherwise known from the genealogies though he may have been a nobleman who married a sister of CONSTANTINE and ANGUS II. Ferat was allowed to keep the throne whilst KENNETH MACALPIN established his power in Dál Riata, but by 842 Kenneth extended his feelers toward Fortrenn. Ferat probably died in that year (or his death may have been arranged) for Kenneth to move into power, but Ferat's sons, Brude and Kineth, immediately claimed the throne. Brude died within a month, almost certainly murdered. Kineth held on to the throne for a year before another claimant, Brude mac Fochel, made his own bid. This Brude ruled for two years before he was deposed by another of Ferat's sons, DRUST. Drust succeeded in holding the kingship into a third year before he was eventually overcome and killed by Kenneth in a decisive battle at Forteviot, which established Kenneth as overall monarch of Scotland and finished the line of Pictish kings.

The Pictish kingship almost certainly continued subversively in the north, but to all intents with Kenneth Pictland was absorbed into the single kingdom of Alba. Details of its kings start on page 379.

FB. STRATHCLYDE

This kingdom was based on the British tribal division of the Damnonii around Alclud, or Dumbarton. At its greatest extent it included Kyle, Galloway and northern Rheged.

Ref.	Ruler	Reign	Died	Notes
FB1.	Ceretic or Coroticus	fl 450s–70s		same as DA6

After Ceretic's death the kingdom was subdivided between his sons and grandsons.

Ref.	Ruler	Reign	Died	Notes
FB2a.	Erbin	fl 470s–80s		probably inherited Alclud and Galloway
FB2b.	Cinuit	fl 470s–80s		probably Manau Gododdin
FB3a.	Geraint	fl 480s–90s		probably Alclud
FB3b.	Tutagual	fl 490s–500s		probably Galloway and Kyle
FB3c.	Caw map Geraint	fl c490s		abdicated; may be same as Galam of Picts [FA5]
FB3d.	Dyfnwal or Dumnagual (I) *Hen*	fl 510s–30s		initially Manau, but reunited Strathclyde
FB4.	Clydno or Clinoch	fl 530s–40s		probably Alclud and Manau
FB5.	Tutagual	c559–80		reunited Strathclyde
FB6.	Rhydderch *Hen* (*the Old*)	c580–612	612	may have ruled as early as 560
FB7.	Nechtan	612–21	621	may be same as FA15
FB8.	Bili (I)	621–33		
FB9.	Owen or Eugene (I)	633–c45		
FB10.	Gwraid or Gureit	c645–58		
FB11.	Dumnagual (II) or Dyfnwal	658–94		
FB12.	Bili II	694–722		
FB13.	Teudebur	722–52		
FB14.	Dumnagual (II) or Dyfnwal	752–60		
FB15.	Owen or Eugene (II)	760–c80		
FB16.	Rhydderch II	fl 790s		
FB17.	Cynan	? –816	816	
FB18.	Dumnagual (IV)	816– ?		
FB19.	Artgal	? –872		
FB20.	Rhun	872–?7		
FB21.	Eochaid	?877–89	?890	also king of Alba (FC42); deposed

Hereafter Strathclyde was merged with the kingdom of the Scots. It was initially ruled by Donald II (FC43) but, under Constantine, Strathclyde became a sub-kingdom governed by a member of the royal family, usually the heir. Details continue on page 375.

[FB1;DA6] **CERETIC** Alclud (Strathclyde), *fl* 450s–70s(?).
Ceretic is the earliest ruler we know of the territory later called Strathclyde. This had as its core the tribe of the Damnonii, and it is likely that Ceretic was of that tribe. His pedigree suggests his forebears were Roman officials who had been placed in authority over the Damnonii. His grandfather is recorded as Cinhil (possibly the

Map 6a **Scotland 500–1200 – Strathclyde**

Roman Quintillius) the son of Cluim (or Clemens), who was probably a Roman general established in command at the Clyde during the reign of MAGNUS MAXIMUS in the late fourth century. It is also just possible that this Ceretic is the same as CEREDIG, the son of CUNEDDA, and that he may not only have established a kingdom in Alclud, but subsequently joined his father in North Wales where his descendents ruled Ceredigion.

Ceretic's strict area of rule may not have extended far from his rocky fortress of Dumbarton, but his influence certainly extended far afield. He is known because St

7. Celts (4) – **Strathclyde**

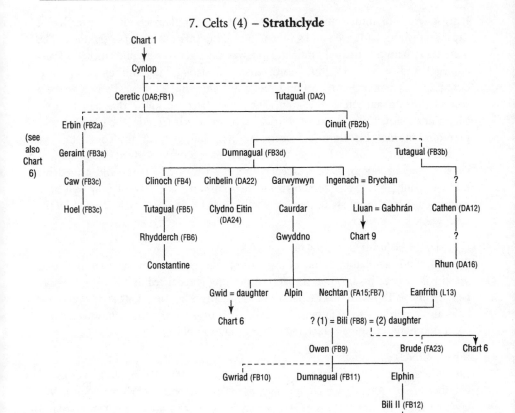

(see
also
Chart
6)

Patrick wrote to him, some time about 450, to complain about his practice of capturing young Irish men and women and selling them as slaves to the Picts. The slave-trade between Ireland and Scotland was extremely profitable (in lieu of any coinage) and it was on this wealth that the strong kingdom of Alclud was established. It is not recorded that Ceretic did anything about it. Patrick wrote a second time to admonish the king. The only effect we know this had is from Muirchu's colourful account of Patrick's life in which Ceretic apparently had a premonition that his time had come and, in full view of his court, he was transformed into a fox and ran away. This may have a double-edged interpretation. Ceretic may, at length, have quailed before the wrath of Patrick and ceased his trading openly, but foxes are known for their cunning, and Ceretic may well have continued it in a more sly fashion. We will never know. He was succeeded by his sons ERBIN and CINUIT.

[FB2a] ERBIN Strathclyde, *fl* 470s–80s.

Erb or Erbin is alluded to as one of the sons of CERETIC. He almost certainly shared the kingdom with his brother CINUIT, but nothing is recorded of his reign. He may be the same as Erp who was the father of the Pictish king NECHTAN MAC ERP. Since he is also recorded as the father of GERAINT it is possible that there has been some confusion between these rulers and those of Dumnonia.

[FB2b] CINUIT Strathclyde, *fl* 470s–80s.

Cinuit was the son of CERETIC and his successor to the small kingdom of Dumbarton or Alclud, which he may have shared with a brother ERBIN. We know little about him and his existence may be subject to doubt, merely serving as a link between Ceretic and DUMNAGUAL, who firmly established the Alclud dynasty.

[FB3a] GERAINT Strathclyde, *fl* 480s–90s.

The son of ERBIN, though his rule in Strathclyde is uncertain. He may have shared the kingdom with his cousin TUTAGUAL. It is possible the genealogists have confused him with GERAINT of Dumnonia or with a Pictish chieftain GARTNAIT. He was the father of CAW.

[FB3b] TUTAGUAL Galloway, *fl* 490s–500s.

The brother of DUMNAGUAL. The two probably shared the kingdom between them at the outset although Dumnagual soon imposed himself as the overlord. Little is known of Tutagual's reign but we may imagine him a strong supporter of his brother.

[FB3c;FA5?] CAW Strathclyde, *fl* c490s.

Caw is a name frequently listed in the old records, primarily because he was the father of Gildas, although there remains some dispute as to whether this is the same Gildas who wrote *The Ruin of Britain*. His name is an anglicization of the Roman Caius, and we may imagine that he still endeavoured to retain an element of Roman law in his territory. In tradition his sons, especially Huail, rebelled against ARTHUR. Huail was killed and Caw was eventually driven out of Strathclyde, probably by DUMNAGUAL HEN. There is some evidence to suggest that through his descent from a Pictish princess Caw claimed the kingship of the Picts, choosing his Pictish name

GALAM or Galanan, and that he ruled them for some years before being driven out again. Perhaps his adhesion to the Roman ways and his strong Christian views were no longer in favour. Either way he eventually settled in northern Wales, probably Anglesey, where his descendents became renowned holy men.

[FB3d] DUMNAGUAL or DYFNWAL *HEN* (*the OLD*) Strathclyde, *fl* 510s–30s.

Folk tradition suggests that Dyfnwal, the grandson of CERETIC, was a strong and powerful ruler. Whether he is the same as Dumnagual, identified in the genealogies as also the grandson of COEL and son of Garbaniawn, is difficult to say. Both names are Celtic versions of Domhnall (later Donald), which means "ruler of the world", and Dumnagual may have seemed just that in the dark days after the withdrawal of support by Rome.

His name also appears, however, as a ruler of the Gododdin, or northern Votadini, which suggests that he conquered that tribe later in his period of power. This would mean that Dumnagual exercised power along the length of the Antonine Wall between the Forth and the Clyde, and possibly had influence over all lands between that and Hadrian's Wall. Dumnagual is also credited with having taken a census of his people in order to determine how to levy taxes. This suggests that Dumnagual reigned during a period of relative peace and prosperity, and this is possible as his reign coincides pretty closely with the peace of ARTHUR's reign between the battles of Badon and Camlann. It also suggests that Dumnagual was sufficiently powerful to exercise such authority. Since the early part of his reign must have been spent making territorial gains, we can only assume the period of administrative reform came at the end of a comparatively long reign. His nickname, Dumnagual *Hen* (the Old) may well suggest, therefore, that he lived to a great age and enjoyed a long reign, and not that he was Dumnagual from the Old Days, i.e. "of Old". However, his "golden age" was to be short-lived. At his death his kingdom was divided between CLYDNO, who inherited the western half, and CINBELIN, who inherited the east. Although these two retained their kingdoms, they came increasingly under attack from the Angles and from the other Britons that were displaced (*see* MORCANT).

[FB4] CLYDNO or CLINOCH Alclud, *fl* 530s–40s.

The son of DUMNAGUAL and uncle of CLYDNO EITEN. On his father's death Clydno's seems to have inherited the western part of his father's kingdom. It is not clear whether an elder brother, Gwyddno (or Guithno) ruled with him, perhaps as king of Galloway for part of his reign. He may well have been dispossessed of his kingdom by MORCANT and his sons who seem to have established themselves in this area at this time.

[FB5] TUTAGUAL (II) Strathclyde, *c*559–80.

Tutagual's reign must have been one of constant struggle against his fellow Britons. At that time the British dynasty of MORCANT had been expelled from Bernicia by the Angles (*see* IDA) and had sought to establish itself in the west. This conflict lasted throughout the rest of the sixth century. Tutagual's father, CLYDNO, was in all likelihood dispossessed of his kingdom and may have fled to Ireland. Tutagual would have spent much of his time seeking to reclaim his kingdom. Although he succeeded in this, the hold was tenuous.

[FB6] **RHYDDERCH** *HEN* (*the OLD*) Strathclyde, c580–612.

Rhydderch inherited an insecure kingdom from his father TUTAGUAL. During his father's conflict with MORCANT, it is possible that he kept his sons safe in Ireland. The *Life of St Kentigern* tells us that Rhydderch was baptized in Ireland. Thus, when he was able to inherit his father's kingdom he set about ridding the land of the pagan influence of MORCANT. He welcomed the return of Kentigern and sought to spread Christianity throughout the land. Joceline's story that Rhydderch actually offered Kentigern his kingdom may be something of an exaggeration, but may show how tenuous a hold Rhydderch felt he had on his kingdom so that he was keen to share it with another of strong mind, as an equal partnership of the spiritual and secular. Rhydderch's Christian practice seems to have become exceptional in his time for he was also called Rhydderch *Hael*, "the Generous", yet it is unlikely that he ruled with any particular prosperity.

Some chronological enigmas arise with the start of Rhydderch's reign. He is listed amongst those who sailed with CINMARC to take revenge upon RHUN of Gwynedd for the death of Cinmarc's brother ELIDYR. If this is so, then Rhydderch must already have been reigning around the year 560. He may, at that stage, have been installed as a sub-prince of Alclud, perhaps in northern Rheged. He was probably quite young at that time. Rhydderch later joined the coalition of forces commanded by URIEN of Rheged against the Angles of Bernicia in 580. It is suggested that Rhydderch did this reluctantly. In fact at some stage Rhydderch is alleged to have consulted St Columba as to whether he would die in battle. Columba's response, though he did not wish to predict the future, reassured Rhydderch that he would die comfortably in bed. Nevertheless, Rhydderch would have been unhappy leaving his kingdom unprotected whilst he joined the confederate army of Urien. AEDAN MAC GABHRAIN of Dál Riata was growing in strength and throughout the 580s led armies into various territories of the Picts and British, including the Isle of Man, which he seems to have taken from Rheged in 582. Consequently immediately after the siege of Lindisfarne in 590, where, but for the treachery of Morcant, the British might have defeated the Angles, Rhydderch hastily returned to Alclud and remained ensconced there. Aedán did invade the Alclud territories at least twice, but Rhydderch succeeded in keeping his kingdom on both occasions. It seems that Aedán was more interested in establishing a forward base from which to keep the Bernicians under check.

The last years of Rhydderch's reign are less well documented. It is recorded that he and Kentigern died in the same year, which is usually recorded as 612, when he must have been in his seventies. It is not clear whether Rhydderch had any sons. He is credited with one called Constantine, and though some chronicles suggest he succeeded to Rhydderch's kingdom, it is more likely that, if he existed, Constantine had already retired to a monastery. Most likely he has been confused with later CONSTANTINES who ruled in Scotland.

[FB7] **NECHTAN** Strathclyde, 612–21.

After the death of RHYDDERCH *Hen* the kingdom of Strathclyde suffered a setback. In line with traditional Celtic inheritance the kingdom would have been divided amongst his sons, but it appears that Rhydderch either had no sons or the one son suggested for him, Constantine, had entered the church. At a time when Strathclyde

was under threat from the Angles of Northumbria to the east and the Scots of Dál
Riata to the north, the kingdom needed a strong king to survive. But it is not clear
who did inherit. The king lists suggest the name Nechtu, a grandson of DUMNAGUAL
and a distant cousin of Rhydderch's. At this same time there was a NECHTAN [FA15]
who was a powerful king of the Picts, and it has been suggested that the Strathclyde
Britons looked to the Picts for their leadership. This is always possible. The Picts
themselves had chosen a British leader fifty years earlier in BRUDE, son of
MAELGWYN. But if these two Nechtans are the same there remains a genealogical
puzzle to untangle. After Nechtan's death the Strathclyde kingdom passed to his
younger son BILI.

[FB8] **BILI** MAP **NECHTAN** Strathclyde, 621–33.
The history and succession of the kingdom of Strathclyde is not easy to follow in the
early seventh century and names in genealogies do not always respond to kings.
NECHTAN, who has been identified as both king of Strathclyde and the Picts, was
apparently succeeded in Strathclyde by his son Bili. We do not know as much about
Bili as we would like. He became ruler of Strathclyde soon after the succession of
EDWIN to the Northumbrian kingdom and, over the next ten years, Edwin set out
for total conquest of the north. He overran the kingdoms of Elmet, Powys,
Gwynedd, Rheged and Man. Why he did not overrun Strathclyde too is not
clear. It is unlikely to be because of the strength and valour of Bili, otherwise his
name would be sung in the songs of old. It is possible that Edwin already regarded
Strathclyde as his own territory, following the earlier conquests of ATHELFRITH,
although that is open to conjecture. It is more likely that Athelfrith and NECHTAN
had reached a peaceful agreement whereby the Strathclyde Britons paid homage to
Athelfrith. The Scottish kingdoms during Edwin's reign were in the strong hands of
the Pictish king CINIOCH and the Dál Riatan king EOCHAID and these were a
sufficient barrier to Edwin. Instead Edwin turned his sights on Wessex, seeking first
to conquer all of England. Edwin was finally defeated by the Welsh under
CADWALLON at the Battle of Hatfield Chase in 633. It is not recorded that Bili
took part in that battle, but it is possible, since he died at about that time. If the
genealogies are correct Bili had two powerful sons. OWEN MAP BILI succeeded him in
Strathclyde and restored the kingdom to its former glory, whilst, BRUDE later
became overlord of the Picts. Bili almost certainly died young, as his brother and
sons outlived him for many years.

[FB9] **OWEN** MAP **BILI** Strathclyde, 633–c45.
Owen was the son of BILI MAP NECHTAN and inherited the kingdom of Strathclyde at
a time when the land was under threat from all sides. Owen, who must have been
quite young on his accession, seemed to have the ability to withstand any
opposition and rebuilt the strength of Strathclyde. His only check was in expanding
eastward where he was stopped by OSWALD of Northumbria. His crowning
achievement came when he defeated the king of the Dál Riatan Scots, DOMNALL
BRECC, at the battle of Strathcarron in Stirlingshire in 642. This decisive victory
terminated the domination of the Scots and re-established Strathclyde, albeit
briefly, as the leading force north of the Wall. It is not recorded what became of
Owen or when he died. Had he died in battle, or been murdered, one would have
expected this to be recorded in song, and, as he was still young we must assume he

died of an illness or injury. He was succeeded by GWRAID or Guret, who may have been an uncle or cousin.

[FB10] **GWRAID** Strathclyde, *c*645–58.

We know nothing about the reign of Gwraid or Guret of Strathclyde, other than the record of his death in 658. He was presumably the successor of OWEN MAP BILI, who had restored Strathclyde to something of its former glory, but whether he usurped that authority or inherited it is not known. He was succeeded by DUMNAGUAL (II).

[FB11] **DUMNAGUAL or DOMHNALL (II)** Strathclyde, 658–94.

It is possible that Dumnagual was not the only ruler of Strathclyde at this time, but records are uncertain. The length of his reign, whilst possible, is unlikely in this difficult period when Strathclyde struggled for survival against the growing power of the Northumbrians to the east and Picts to the north. One would otherwise expect it to be remembered in song or annals. It is likely that, despite the brief supremacy of Strathclyde under OWEN MAP BILI, it had again become a client kingdom of Northumbria. Dumnagual may have ruled jointly with, or been succeeded by, his brother Elphin. The only certainty we have is that Elphin's son, BILI (II) became king in 694.

[FB12] **BILI (II)** MAP **ELPHIN** Strathclyde, 694–722.

Bili's reign consisted of trying to keep the kingdom of Strathclyde in one piece as it increasingly became part of the battle ground between the Picts, Scots and Northumbrians. Bili was one of the provincial kings who witnessed the *Law of Innocents* promulgated by Adomnán, the bishop of Iona, at the Synod of Birr in Ireland in 697, which endeavoured to protect the clergy, women, children and the elderly from the constant warfare of the seventh century. Bili was drawn into battle at least twice against the Scots and on both occasions defeated, but he still retained his kingdom, almost certainly as vassal to whichever was the strongest power at the time. It fell to Bili's son, TEUDEBUR, to strike back against oppression.

[FB13] **TEUDEBUR** MAP **BILI** Strathclyde, 722–52.

Teudebur, like most of his predecessors since the time of RHYDDERCH HEN, lived under the successive domination of Northumbrians, Picts or Scots. During Teudeber's reign the ascendance was with the Picts under their powerful king, ANGUS, who dominated northern Britain during the period 730–750. However in 750 it was Teudebur who had the strength and skill to overcome the Picts at the battle of Mygedawg, believed to be Mugdock, a few miles east of Dumbarton. Angus survived the battle but his brother, Talorgen, was killed. So thorough was the British victory that the power of the Picts was halted. This did have its disadvantage unfortunately, because the Picts had, over the years, kept the Northumbrians at bay. Now EADBERT of Northumbria brought his forces to bear upon the Strathclyde Britons and by 752 had conquered and annexed the territory of Kyle. Teudeber died that same year probably killed in the hostilities.

[FB14] **DUMNAGUAL (III)** Strathclyde, 752–60.

The son and successor of TEUDEBUR, after whose death Dumnagual entered into an alliance with EADBERT of Northumbria, which resulted in Strathclyde losing the territory around Kyle to the south. This did not guarantee the British any peace.

ANGUS, king of the Picts, had his own cause for revenge upon the British who had defeated him in battle in 750. Angus and Eadbert combined forces in 756 to attack Dumbarton. It is some sign of the strength of the British and in particular the invincibility of the Rock of Dumbarton that it took this combined force to defeat them. Nevertheless, at that stage the Northumbrians took over the kingdom of Strathclyde and for the next century it remained a vassal state, its rulers uncertain.

[FB15] **OWEN** MAP **DUMNAGUAL** Strathclyde, 760–c80.

[FB16] **RHYDDERCH (II)** Strathclyde, *fl* 790s.

[FB17] **CYNAN** MAP **RHYDDERCH** Strathclyde, *d* 816.

[FB18] **DUMNAGUAL (IV)** Strathclyde, ruled 816–?

We know nothing of these four kings beyond their names in the genealogies. They were almost certainly subordinate to Northumbria and it is not certain whether they had any authority as kings or even vassals.

[FB19] **ARTGAL** Strathclyde, *d* 872.

We do not know when Artgal assumed the vassal administration of Strathclyde, but it was probably during the 850s. This coincided not just with the reduction in power of Northumbria, which had been on the decline for half a century, but also with the rise in power of the Scots under KENNETH MACALPIN and the start of the Viking raids on the western Scottish coast. None of these were to work in Artgal's favour. Though he no doubt strove to regain British supremacy over Strathclyde he was overcome by the Vikings, who stormed Dumbarton in 871, abducting many of the inhabitants into slavery. Although Artgal escaped captivity, he was murdered in the following year through the treachery of CONSTANTINE (I), king of the Scots. After Artgal's death, Strathclyde became subsumed into the expanding kingdom of the Scots.

[FB20] **RHUN** MAP **ARTGAL** Strathclyde, 872–8.

It is unlikely that Rhun ruled Strathclyde other than in name. He probably existed as a vassal ruler with no authority. The Strathclyde British no doubt looked to Rhun for salvation, but without success – by this time Rhun was almost certainly too old. He had earlier married the daughter of KENNETH MACALPIN, and their son, EOCHAID, would briefly re-establish the name of Strathclyde.

[FB21;FC42] **EOCHAID** MAP **RHUN** Strathclyde (and Alba), ?877–89.

Eochaid was the last native ruler of Strathclyde. He succeeded his father RHUN possibly before 878, in which year AED, the king of the Scots, was slain by his cousin GIRIC. Eochaid was probably quite young and he allied himself with Giric, who became his foster father. They ruled Scotland jointly. In theory Eochaid remained ruler of Strathclyde as part of Scotland, but in practice for a brief period the kingdom regained its independence. The alliance allowed Giric to extend the Scottish territories further south into the Northumbrian territory of Bernicia, and Strathclyde extended its borders south into Cumbria. In 889 both Giric and Eochaid were expelled from the kingdom by DONALD II (Eochaid's second cousin). Thereafter Strathclyde (the southern part of which was also known as the kingdom of Cumbria) was absorbed into Scotland, but was ruled by a sub-king or mórmaer, usually the heir to the throne. Its importance as an ancient kingdom was thus recognized. It is believed that Eochaid and the remaining royal family of Strathclyde fled to northern Wales, to the court of ANARAWD AP RHODRI, where Eochaid died soon after.

Details of the remaining rulers of Strathclyde continue on page 375.

FC. DÁL RIATA SCOTS

The original "Scots" were the Irish who came from the Dál Riatan homeland in northern Ireland and settled in Argyll. They gradually took over most of Argyll, Galloway and the southern Hebrides until the Viking invasions pushed them inland to conquer the kingdom of the Picts. The Scots developed a genealogy taking their pedigree back to 330BC, based on their Irish ancestry. These earlier kings almost certainly existed but probably as no more than chieftains amongst the Scottish islands and coastal fringes. They are listed in the appendix on page 719. These include the more historically attested rulers of the settlement attributed to Cairbre *Riata*, son of the Irish high king Conaire *Moglama* (see T121) in the mid third century, and from whom the name Dál Riata was derived.

Ref.	Ruler	Born	Reign	Died	Notes
FC1.	Fergus (I) Mor (*the Great*)	c440	c498–501	501	
FC2.	Domangart		501–7	507	
FC3.	Comgall		507–38	538	
FC4.	Gabhrán		538–58	558	
FC5.	Conall		558–74	574	
FC6.	Aedán	c533	574–608	608	first king to be anointed
FC7.	Eochaid *Buide*	c583	608–29	629	
FC8.	Connad *Cerr*		629	629	killed in battle after reign of 3 months
FC9.	Domnall *Brecc*		629–42	642	killed in battle
FC10.	Ferchar		637–50	650	shared kingdom with Domnall
FC11.	Dúnchad		650–4	654	killed in battle
FC12.	Conall *Crandomna*		650–60	660	ruled jointly with Dúnchad
FC13.	Domangart (II)		660–73	673	
FC14.	Maelduin		673–88	688	
FC15.	Domnall Donn		688–95		killed (in battle?)
FC16.	Ferchar *Fota* of Loarn		695–7	697	usurped the throne
FC17.	Eochaid (II)		697	697	murdered after a brief reign
FC18.	Ainbcellach of Loarn		697–8	719	usurper; expelled within a year.
FC19.	Fiannamail		698–700	700	killed in battle
FC20.	Selbach of Loarn		700–23	730	abdicated in favour of his son
FC21.	Dúngal		723–26	after 736	expelled
FC22.	Eochaid (III)		726–33	733	
FC23.	Alpin		733–6	736	king of the Picts (FA28); possibly killed

FC24.	Muiredach	733–6	736	
FC25.	Eogan	736–9		
FC26.	Angus or Oengus (I)	736–50	761	king of the Picts (FA29)
FC27.	Aed *Find* (*the Fair*)	750–78	778	
FC28.	Fergus mac Eochaid	778–81	781	

Map 6b **Scotland – Dál Riata**

8. Celts (5) – **Dál Riata and Dyfed – The Irish Connection**

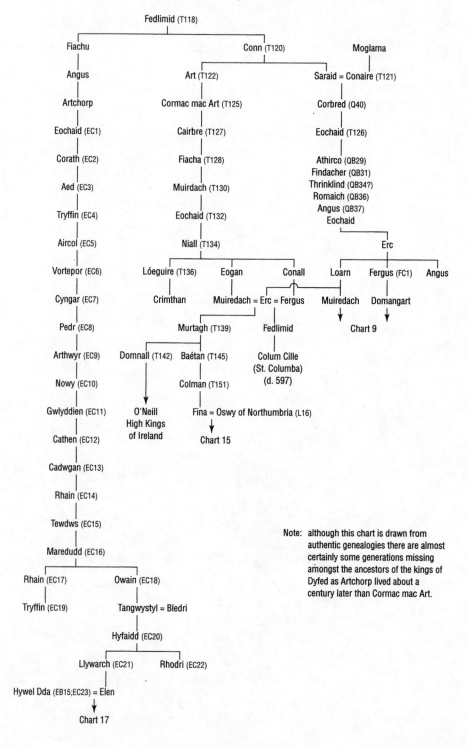

Note: although this chart is drawn from authentic genealogies there are almost certainly some generations missing amongst the ancestors of the kings of Dyfed as Artchorp lived about a century later than Cormac mac Art.

9. Scotland (1) – Dál Riata

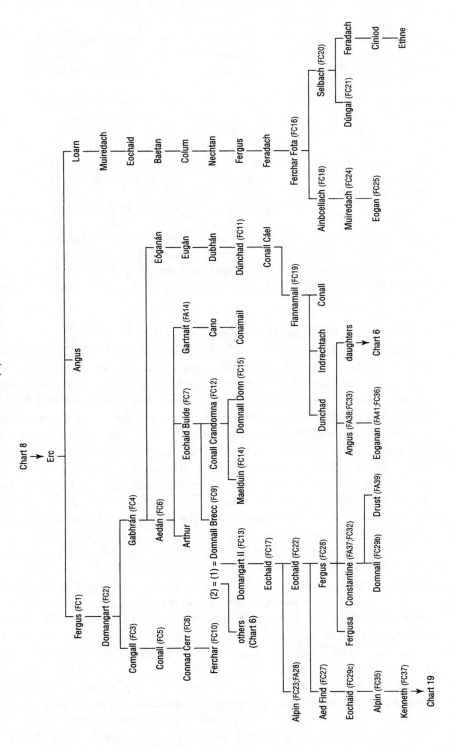

Ref.	Ruler	Born	Reign	Died	Notes
FC29a.	Donncorci		?781–91	791	possibly shared kingdom
FC29b.	Domnall		781–805		possibly shared kingdom
FC29c.	Eochaid (IV) the Poisonous		781– ?		possibly shared kingdom
FC30.	Conall mac Tarl'a (or Tagd)		805–7	807	king of the Picts (FA36); killed in battle
FC31.	Conall mac Aedán		807–11		
FC32.	Constantine		811–20	820	king of the Picts (FA37)
FC33.	Angus (II)		820–34	834	king of the Picts (FA38)
FC34.	Aed mac Boanta		834–9		
FC35.	Alpin		834	834	sub-king of Galloway; killed in battle
FC36.	Eoganan (or Uen)		c837–839	839	king of the Picts (FA41); killed in battle

With the death of Eoganan, Kenneth macAlpin united the Picts and the Scots and the infant kingdom of Scotland (at first known as Alba) emerged. Listing continues on page 379.

[FC1] **FERGUS MOR (the GREAT)** Dál Riata, c498–501.

Traditionally the founder of the Dál Riatan dynasty of Argyll and Kintyre. Fergus and his brothers Angus and Loarn, the sons of Erc, came from the Dál Riatan homeland in northern Ireland sometime around the year 498 to establish their domain along the western headlands of Scotland. It is certain that Irish/Gaelic settlers had established themselves in these territories for several centuries (see CAIRBRE), living jointly with the native Picts. It was quite natural that as the settlements grew they would look to their Irish rulers for guidance, and it was also natural that, as inter-dynastic squabbles over territory in Ireland led to increasing friction, someone would strike out to claim new lands. There is no record that Fergus and his brothers had to conquer their territory and it is only in later generations that the conflict arose between the Irish Scots and the Picts. It is not clear whether the three brothers carved out their territories in their own lifetime, or whether this happened in subsequent generations, but in principle it seems that Fergus took the primary share of Kintyre and central Argyll, Loarn took the territory to the north around Loch Linnhe and Glencoe, and Angus settled on the island of Islay. Fergus is supposed to have brought with him the Stone of Destiny upon which all the high kings had been ordained at Tara for centuries. The Annals record the death of Fergus in the year 501, and he was succeeded by his son DOMANGART. Since Domangart died within a few years we may assume they were both old. It is unlikely that he would have achieved the epithet "the Great", or indeed have been known as Fergus, which means "man of power", if he had died young. The Irish annals record the death of his father, Erc, in 474. Moreover we find amongst the tales of the life of St Patrick that he visited the court of Erc and prophesied that Fergus would be the father of a nation. Since Patrick died in 461 and Fergus was already an adult we may deduce that he was born perhaps five years either side of 440.

[FC2] **DOMANGART** (**I**) Dál Riata, 501–7.

The son of FERGUS MOR, Domangart was probably already in his late forties or early fifties by the time his father died. He had married an Irish princess called Fedlim the Fair. Domangart's name was not included amongst contemporary records and seems to be only a later genealogical insertion, so it is uncertain whether he actually ruled as king. If anything the record suggests that he entered the church. It is more likely, considering that Fergus died soon after the arrival in Scotland, that his brothers Loarn and Angus took over authority, perhaps shared with Domangart, and that the real kingship did not start until the time of Domangart's sons, COMGALL and GABHRAN. His brief reign is recorded as "turbulent" without further comment, though this as likely refers to struggles within the Dál Riatan territory (probably amongst his cousins) than to any external conflict.

[FC3] **COMGALL** Dál Riata, 507–38.

Son of DOMANGART, and the founder of the Comgall dynasty of Scots kings, usually known as the Cenél Comgall, which shared the Scot's rulership with Comgall's brother, GABHRAN, head of the Cenél Gabhráin. Comgall ruled for over thirty years, a remarkable span for such a period. Although little is recorded about him we can deduce at least two things from this length of reign. Firstly Comgall must have been comparatively young when he inherited the throne, perhaps in his twenties. Secondly, he must have been able to establish himself as a strong king to resist any aggression from the Picts, who were themselves suffering from considerable internecine strife, and in defending his territory against the Angles who were settling on the eastern coast. Perhaps we can speculate that the Scots had been accepted by the Picts and allowed to settle in a relatively enclosed area whilst the Picts were involved in their own struggles. Moreover Comgall's reign coincided with that of the strong ruler of Alclud, DUMNAGUAL, whom Comgall was unlikely to challenge. It was only when Comgall's brother sought to expand the Dál Riatan territory that conflict emerged.

[FC4] **GABHRAN** Dál Riata, 538–58.

The successor of COMGALL as the fourth king of the Irish Scots. If the genealogies are correct, Gabhrán's father, DOMANGART, had died in 507, so that Gabhrán was probably then quite young. During his reign, Comgall had succeeded in establishing a strong Dál Riatan kingdom in the area of Argyll and Kintyre. It seems that Gabhrán endeavoured to expand that kingdom westward into the territory of the Picts, taking advantage of the inter-tribal battles between not only the Picts and the British, but also those two cultures and the invading Angles. Gabhrán was initially successful, and he seems to have established a rapport with a northern British enclave of the Gododdin in the Mearns around modern Brechin. The name of the territory of Gowrie is apparently a corruption of Gabhrán or Gafran. Gabhrán married Luan, the daughter of Brychan of the Gododdin and granddaughter of DUMNAGUAL HEN. However, Gabhrán's expansion was curbed in 558 soon after the succession of BRUDE MAC MAELCHON as ruler of the Picts. After a series of battles, the Scots were routed and forced back into their core territory. Gabhrán's death is recorded in the same year, but whether that was a consequence of the battles, or another reason, is not known. He was succeeded by his nephew CONALL MAC COMGALL.

[FC5] **CONALL (I)** MAC **COMGALL** Dál Riata, 558–74.

Conall seems to have inherited some of the pacifism of his father, COMGALL, as he was clearly not a warrior chieftain like his uncle GABHRAN. Early in his reign, in 563, Conall welcomed the arrival of Columba, to whom he was distantly related. Columba, who was himself entitled to election to the high kingship of Ireland, had devoted himself to spreading the Christian message, and Conall welcomed him as an ally against the pagan Picts. Conall is recorded as having given Columba the island of Iona on which to establish his monastery and Conall probably saw in Columba not only an ally but an agent who could help establish peaceful relationships between the three main tribes of northern Britain: the Gaelic Scots, the Picts and the Britons of Strathclyde, then ruled by RHYDDERCH HEN. This Columba achieved and the period of Conall's reign was relatively peaceful. The only tension was within Conall's own family, an inter-dynastic challenge to Conall's authority. In 568 he led an expedition against his cousins, the Cenél Angus, in Islay, in league with Colmán the Little, king of the Southern O'Neill. His success established him as sole ruler of the Dál Riatan Scots and paved the way for his powerful successor, AEDAN MAC GABHRAN.

[FC6] **AEDAN** MAC **GABHRAN** Dál Riata, 574–17 April 608.
Born: c532/3, "near the Forth"; *Died*: Kilkerran, 17 April 608, aged about 75. *Buried*: Kilkerran.
Married: at least three wives, names unknown, and had at least seven sons and several daughters.
Aedán was the first significant ruler of the Dál Riatan Scots and one of the most powerful rulers in sixth century Britain. Aedán probably had eyes on the succession even before the death of his cousin CONALL, even though Conall's own son Donnchad and Aedán's brother Eoganan had prior claims. Aedán had set out to prove himself a powerful warlord. It is likely that he regained some of the territory in Gowrie gained by his father thirty years earlier but lost by Conall. Scant evidence suggests that he served as a chief of the Gododdin Britons for a few years prior to 574, commanding the lands around Aberfoyle, the region where he subsequently granted land to St Berach for a monastery. It was probably in this capacity that he was present at the battle of Arfderydd in 573 (*see* GWENDDOLAU *and* PEREDUR), as has been suggested. After Conall's death a squabble broke out between the children of Conall and GABHRAN over the succession that was finally settled by Columba. Columba preferred the more pacifist and learned Eoganan but, after a vision, in which Columba was scourged by an angel, he ordained Aedán as king. This was the first time that a Christian king was apparently selected and ordained by God. It was, in effect, the start of what later developed into the belief of the divine right of kings that caused the downfall of CHARLES I.

Early in Aedán's reign, in 575, the Irish high king, Aed mac Ainmerech, called a meeting at Drumceat in Derry to determine the position of the Dál Riatan peoples who still lived in the original homeland of Fergus in Ulster. It was agreed that whilst Aedán retained authority over them, and could thus collect taxes and tribute, those people were ultimately answerable to the Irish high king for military support. It was a compromise, probably engineered by Columba, which clarified the authority of the respective kings and showed that the Dál Riatan rulers were still ultimately answerable to the Irish high king. It is pertinent that the ruling did not recognize any authority over Dál Riata of Baetán, the king of Ulster in which the territory fell, but instead showed a direct relationship between Aedán and the Irish high king. This gave Aedán considerable authority and doubtless aggravated the relationship between Aedán and Baetán. Although it is not recorded, it has been suggested that Baetán may have undertaken raids upon Dál Riatan territory in Kintyre and that over the next few years there were hostilities between the two factions. It is possible that a record in the annals in the year 582 refers to Aedán ejecting Baetán from the Isle of Man. Whether this means that Aedán extended his authority from that year to Man is not clear. By Aedán's reign the Pictish king, BRUDE, was old and had become more tolerant of his neighbours. It was nonetheless an affront by Aedán in 580 when he undertook a raid on the Orkneys, whose piratical inhabitants had no doubt been plundering Dál Riatan territory, most likely Iona. Although it is not recorded, it is likely that the Scots and the Picts must have clashed in numerous skirmishes and that Aedán generally won the advantage. It is possible that after Brude's death in 584, his successor, GARTNAIT, was a son of Aedán's through his marriage with a Pictish princess. Although this may have given Aedán authority over the northern Picts, it had little effect over the southern Picts, or Maetæ. In or around the year 590 Aedán was drawn into battle with them. Although he won, he lost two of his sons, Artuir (*see* ARTHUR) and Eochaid *Find*, a fact apparently predicted by Columba.

Aedán also turned his might against the British kingdoms of Alclud, ruled by RHYDDERCH *HEN*, and the Gododdin, ruled by MYNYDDOG, and these internecine squabbles almost certainly played into the hands of the Bernician Angles under ATHELFRITH who, by the late 590s, was seeking to extend his territory into the land between the Walls. In 603 Aedán led an army of Scots and Irish against the Bernicians at Degsastan, in Lothian. Although the Angles claimed the victory there were heavy losses on both sides, and Aedán lost another son, Domangart. The records suggest that Aedán may have abdicated soon after this defeat and retired to a monastery at Kilkerran, where he died. His son, EOCHAID *BUIDE* had, apparently, already been nominated as his successor by Columba. Despite his failures, Aedán established Dál Riata as a major force in northern Britain.

[FC7] **EOCHAID *BUIDE* (*THE YELLOW-HAIRED*)** Dál Riata, 608–29.
According to Admonán's *Life of Columba*, Columba identified Eochaid as the successor to AEDAN MAC GABHRAN, even though he was one of Aedán's younger sons, recognizing that the elder sons would be killed in battle. This prophecy happened before the battle against the Maetæ in around 590, at which time Eochaid was still young enough to sit on Columba's lap, which suggests he was probably born around the year 583 or 584. Although he ruled for twenty years nothing specific is stated in the surviving records about his reign, but we can infer certain actions by later events. Firstly, at his death, Eochaid is styled "king of the Picts". Although he is not incorporated in the Pictish king-lists, this does not preclude Eochaid conquering certain Pictish territory, probably to the north of Dál Riada in the western highlands, and possibly also re-establishing an overlordship in the territory of his father's conquests around Aberfoyle. It was during Eochaid's reign, in 617, that ATHELFRITH of Northumbria died, and his children sought refuge from

EDWIN in the lands of the Picts and the Scots. It seems likely that OSWALD and OSWY found refuge on Iona. They grew to manhood under Eochaid's protection and they also became involved in Eochaid's campaigns in Ireland. There was continued trouble between Eochaid and the rulers of Ulster, where the Irish territory of Dál Riata was. This came to a head after the death of Eochaid, but it is almost certain that Eochaid was involved in battles and skirmishes with the rulers of Ulster over his homeland territory. There is a possibility that his son and successor, CONNAD CERR, was appointed a sub-king over the Irish territory, perhaps around the year 627. The problems were not resolved in Eochaid's day, and we can regard him as a king who managed to hold the Dál Riatan kingdom together during a period of considerable conflict.

[FC8] **CONNADD *CERR*** Dál Riata, 629.
Conadd is listed variously in the old annals as the youngest son of CONALL MAC COMGALL or of EOCHAID *BUIDE*. Although there are points in favour of either case it is more likely that he was either a direct son (or a fostered son) of Eochaid, whom he succeeded in 629. Eochaid's reign was beset by problems with the rulers of Ulster over the Dál Riatan homeland in Ireland. It seems possible that Connad was appointed as sub-king or governor over the Irish territory from about the year 627 in which year he is recorded as having a victory over Fiachna, king of the Ulaid in Ulster, at the battle of Ard Corann. When Eochaid died in 629 Connadd succeeded to the whole territory of the Dál Riata, but he remained in Ireland and was killed, after only three months, at the battle of Fid Eoin, where he fought on the side of the Northumbrian Angles against the Ulaid. He was succeeded by his brother, DOMNALL BRECC.

[FC9] **DOMNALL *BRECC* (*THE SPECKLED* or *POCK-MARKED*)** Dál Riata, 629–42.
His reign saw the Scots of Dál Riata lose much of what they had gained during the reign of Aedán mac Gabhrán. The early part of his life saw him heavily involved fighting in Ireland alongside the Irish high king, also called Domnall, but by the year 629 the complicated hostilities in Ulster had caused a change in allegiance. Over the next eight years there was open conflict between the Scottish Dál Riata and the kings of the O'Neill, with Domnall siding with the Ulster king of the Dál nAraide. This proved a disastrous alliance and resulted in total defeat for Domnall at the battle of Mag Rath in County Down in 637. This was taken as the fulfilment of a prophecy uttered by St Columba, forty years earlier, that the Dál Riatan Scots would retain power and authority provided they remained in alliance with the kings of the O'Neill. After Mag Rath Domnall *Brecc* not only lost his authority in Ireland, but seems to have lost much of his authority in Scotland. From 637 he was forced to reign jointly with his nephew FERCHAR, the son of CONNAD CERR. It is not clear whether Ferchar retained any authority over the Dál Riata of Ireland or whether, as is more likely, he became recognized as overlord of the Dál Riata in Scotland, with Domnall relegated to the ruler of only part of Dál Riata in Kintyre and Argyll. No doubt over the next five years Domnall sought to re-enforce his authority, but he met with failure after failure. In 635 and 638 he was defeated in battles against the Picts, and in 642 he was killed in battle at Strathcarron, near Falkirk, by OWEN MAP BILI of the Strathclyde Britons. It would be another one hundred and fifty years before the Scots re-established themselves as a significant force in Northern Britain.

[FC10] **FERCHAR** (I) Dál Riata, 637–50.

He was the son of CONNAD CERR and seems to have been elected as king of the Dál Riata after the defeat of DOMNALL BRECC at the battle of Mag Rath in Ulster in 637. It is not clear, but it is likely that Ferchar was appointed as overlord of the Scottish Dál Riata either as superior to Domnall, or certainly as his equal, perhaps retaining some say in the position of the Dál Riata peoples who still lived in Ulster. Whilst it may have been hoped that he might curb some of Domnall's excesses, this does not seem to have happened. Domnall continued to battle against the Picts and the British and was eventually killed in battle in 642. Ferchar now ruled alone, but the conflict with the Picts continued, with the main battlefield appearing to be the Isle of Skye. When Ferchar died in 650, the kingdom was again divided between his uncle CONALL CRANDOMNA and a distant cousin, DUNCHAD.

[FC11] **CONALL** (II) *CRANDOMNA* MAC **EOCHAID** Dál Riata, 650–60.

He succeeded FERCHAR to a divided kingdom, sharing it with a distant cousin, DUNCHAD, after whose death in 654, Conall ruled alone. The once powerful kingdom of Dál Riata had suffered defeats during the reign of Conall's brother DOMNALL BRECC from which it would take generations to recover. Although Conall survived Dúnchad, we may believe that Conall continued to remain subservient to the Picts under TALORCEN and GARTNAIT.

[FC12] **DUNCHAD** Dál Riata, 650–4.

Dúnchad is rather a mystery man in the Scottish regnal lists. He is identified as the son of Dubhán, a name which means "little dark one" and which has been interpreted as a nickname. However Dúnchad itself (which is an early form on Duncan) also means "dark warrior" which suggests that this family perhaps came from a more swarthy branch of the Dál Riatan family, probably one more closely related to the Picts. To be elected to the Scottish kingship, Dúnchad must have had a share of Dál Riatan blood, and it has been suggested that he was descended from either Eóganán, the elder brother of AEDAN MAC GABHRAN, or from Aedán's son Conaing, brother of EOCHAID BUIDE. It is further possible he was descended from Aedán's Pictish son, GARTNAIT. Whoever he was, his reign (which he shared with CONALL CRANDOMNA) was short-lived. Involved in regular skirmishes against the Picts, he became embattled with their king TALORCEN (a client of the Northumbrians), and was killed at the battle of Strath Ethairt in 654.

[FC13] **DOMANGART** (II) Dál Riata, 660–73.

The son of DOMNALL BRECC, Domangart became sole ruler of the Scots in 660 after the kingdom had been divided since the disastrous defeat of his father at Mag Rath in 637. His reign was marked by a consolidation of the kingdom, giving it something of its former strength, but although Domangart made advances against the Picts amongst the Western Isles and Highlands, particularly around Skye, it is not recorded that he made any significant territorial gains to the east. It may be significant that the Irish missionary Maelrubai succeeded in establishing his own monastery at Applecross, in Pictish territory, in 673, perhaps under Domangart's sovereignty. For a period, then, Domangart may be seen as having stemmed the tide of disaster that followed his father's reign. He was succeeded by his cousin, MAELDUIN.

[FC14] **MAELDUIN** Dál Riata, 673–88.

When Maelduin, the son of CONALL CRANDOMNA, inherited the kingdom of the Scots in 673 it had been to some extent restored by his cousin, DOMANGART (II), to something of its former status following a generation of division. Little is recorded of Maleduin's reign, or that of his brother and successor DOMNALL DONN, and it is evident that their own ability to expand was held in check by the strength and power of the Northumbrian king EGFRITH and, after 685, by the Picts' king BRUDE MAC BILI.

[FC15] **DOMNALL *DONN*** Dál Riata, 688–95.

He succeeded his brother, MAELDUIN, as king of the Scots in 688. We know little of his reign, though can imagine that any attempts at territorial expansion were held in check by the might of the Pictish king BRUDE MAC BILI. We can further conjecture that during Domnall's reign, perhaps even earlier, inter-dynastic rivalry broke out within the Scottish royal family, between the two main dynastic lines of the descendants of COMGALL and GABHRAN, the sons of DOMANGART (I), and the descendants of Loarn, brother of FERGUS MOR. Although the descendents of Loarn had established territory to the north of the main Dál Riatan lands, they did not seem to figure amongst the successors to the kingship. However, in the late seventh century, the head of the Loarn family, FERCHAR FOTA, came to the fore as a contender for the kingship of Dál Riata. The obituary of Domnall *Donn* states that he was "killed" but this does not say whether this was in battle or whether he was murdered. Either way, it seems likely that his death came as a result of the dynastic struggle with the Cenél Loarn.

[FC16] **FERCHAR (II) *FOTA* (*THE LONG*)** Dál Riata, 695–7.

He was the *ri* or head of the tribe of Loarn, eighth in descent from Loarn the brother of FERGUS MOR, who first settled the territory of the Dál Riata in Scotland two centuries earlier. Until the year 695 the kingship of the Dál Riata had passed traditionally down through the sons of Fergus, but by 695 a challenge to the throne came from Ferchar. Exactly what happened is not clear, but we can surmise that Ferchar, possibly frustrated by the continuing weakness of the Dál Riatan kings and the continued domination by the Picts, challenged the king DOMNALL DONN, leading to Domnall's death in 695. Ferchar then had a two year battle with the natural successor, EOCHAID, son of DOMANGART (II), before Ferchar's death in 697.

[FC17] **EOCHAID (II) *CROOKED-NOSE*** Dál Riata, 695?-7.

On the death of DOMNALL DONN, the kingship of Dál Riata was disputed between Eochaid, the son of DOMANGART (II) and FERCHAR FOTA, head of the Loarn branch of the family of Erc. As most king lists identify Ferchar as the successor to Domnall and not Eochaid, we may presume that Eochaid was either expelled or held captive. Ferchar died in 697, possibly of natural causes, but also possibly as a result of the inter-dynastic struggle. Eochaid succeeded in claiming the kingship, but only for a brief period – within a few months, he was murdered by Ferchar's son AINBCELLACH. He remained in authority long enough to lend his name to Adomnán's *Law of the Innocents* which was promulgated during 697.

[FC18] **AINBCELLACH** Dál Riata, 697–8.

In 697 Ainbcellach, son of FERCHAR (II) of Loarn, murdered EOCHAID (II), but his claim on the kingship was short lived for, within a year, he was captured by

FIANNAMAIL and taken in chains to Ireland. Ainbcellach presumably benefited from the succession of his brother SELBACH, though clearly there remained hostility within the family. In 719 Ainbcellach attempted to dethrone Selbach but he was defeated and killed at the battle of Findglen.

[FC19] **FIANNAMAIL** Dál Riata, 698–700.

The grandson of DUNCHAD. In the civil war between the descendants of FERGUS MOR and those of Loarn that broke out in 695, Fiannamail briefly gained the ascendance by capturing and expelling AINBCELLACH of Loarn. However, within two years Fiannamail was killed in battle. This may have been by Ainbcellach's brother SELBACH or in some other battle, possibly involving Ainbcellach in Ireland.

[FC20] **SELBACH** Dál Riata, 700–23.

Son of FERCHAR FOTA who succeeded in restoring a period of relative stability to the kingship of the Scots of Dál Riata after a five year civil war. Selbach claimed the throne after the death of FIANNAMAIL in battle, but his authority did not go unchallenged. He faced opposition both from the traditional ruling house of the Cenél Gabhrán and from within factions of his own house, the Cenél Loarn. This rivalry continued for the best part of twenty years, with Selbach eventually defeating his own brother, AINBCELLACH, in 719. However, since Selbach had succeeded in rebuilding the family fortress at Dunollie in 714, we may imagine that most of the hositility had ceased by that time. Selbach also faced a major challenge in a sea battle in 719 against Dúnchad *Becc*, who was styled king of Kintyre. He was possibly a son or cousin of Fiannamail. Although Dúnchad was victorious, Selbach retained the kingship and outlived Dúnchad, who died in 721. Perhaps satisfied that he had firmly established a new dynastic control over the kingship, Selbach retired to a monastery in 723 in favour of his son, DUNGAL. However, when Dúngal was expelled three years later, Selbach returned in an attempt to regain the kingdom. His battle against EOCHAID (III) was inconclusive and the records do not show whether Selbach believed he retained any authority. He survived for a further three years and died in 730.

[FC21] **DUNGAL** Dál Riata, 723–6.

Dúngal inherited the throne when his father, SELBACH, abdicated in his favour. However his authority did not go unchallenged and, in 726, he was deposed by EOCHAID (III). Dúngal's father tried to regain the throne, but without success. However Dúngal lived on. He tried again to reclaim the throne after the death of Eochaid in 733, but was defeated by his cousin MUIREDACH. During these years Dúngal had also become enmeshed in dynastic affairs amongst the Picts. He strongly supported DRUST (VI), who had also been deposed in 726, and this incurred the anger of ANGUS, who gained the throne of the Picts in 729. Dúngal was captured and imprisoned by Angus in 736. What became of him subsequently we do not know.

[FC22] **EOCHAID (III)** Dál Riata, 726–33.

Eochaid was the son of EOCHAID (II), who was murdered in 697. At that time the younger Eochaid was probably still an infant but by 726, after the retirement of SELBACH and the succession of DUNGAL, Eochaid must have been nearly thirty. He successfully deposed Dúngal and restored the kingship of Dál Riata to the original Cenél Gabhrán ruling family. Selbach sought to recover the kingship in the following year, but was defeated. Eochaid's hold was, however, tenuous. During this same period there was another inter-dynastic civil war for the throne of the Picts in which Dúngal became involved. This brought the wrath of ANGUS (I) against the Cenél Loarn which was further aggravated when, in 728, ALPIN, another of the Pictish claimants, sought refuge amongst the Dál Riata. It has been conjectured that Alpin may have been a brother or half-brother of Eochaid. Whether or not Alpin subsequently shared the kingdom with Eochaid is not clear, but certainly upon Eochaid's death in 733 (and since he was only in his late thirties his death may be suspicious) he claimed the throne. It would be nearly twenty years before Eochaid's son AED FIND reclaimed the throne of Dál Riata and succeeded in restoring the kingship to something of its old glory.

[FC23;FA28] **ALPIN** ruled Picts, 726–8; Dál Riata, 733–6.

[FC24] **MUIREDACH** ruled Dál Riata, 733–6

The decade from 726 to 736 was one of constant warfare not only within the rival families of the Dál Riata, but also amongst claimants to the throne of the Picts. This came to a head in 733 following the death of EOCHAID (III). His brother (or half-brother) ALPIN, who had briefly claimed the kingship of the Picts, now claimed the throne of Dál Riata (*see page xx*). He was challenged by Muiredach, the son of AINBCELLACH and cousin of the earlier king DUNGAL, who was still active in the struggle for the throne, in support of the Pictish king DRUST. ANGUS, who finally defeated the other claimants and gained the throne of the Picts, turned his anger against Dál Riata, needing to silence both Alpin, his former rival, and Dúngal, who had plotted against him. The war raged for three years, and in 736 Angus defeated (and possibly killed) Alpin, and captured Dúngal. Muiredach was defeated in battle by Angus's brother, but it is not certain that he was killed. At least one annal records the death of Muiredach in 771, which might mean that Muiredach fled to Ireland.

[FC25] **EOGAN** ruled Dál Riata, 736–9.

Son of MUIREDACH who claimed the title of king of Dál Riata in 736, but who almost certainly ruled with no authority. He was either a king in exile, or ruled as a vassal to ANGUS (I), king of the Picts, who became overlord of the Scots in 736. He is probably the same king identified by Boece as EUGENIUS VIII.

[FC26;FA29] **ANGUS (I)** ruled Picts 729–61; Dál Riata 736–50.

Angus was king of the Picts and full details of his reign will be found on page xx. He succeeded in defeating the rival claimants to the kingship of Dál Riata in 736 and imposed his authority over all of southern Scotland. In fact he was probably also recognized as overlord by the Northern Picts and over Strathclyde, so that Angus may be regarded as the first true ruler of what would later be called Scotland. Angus sustained his authority until 750 when he was weakened by a series of problems which allowed AED FIND to gain control of Dál Riata. The Britons of Strathclyde also fought back and in 756 Angus found his authority restricted to his original heartland of the Southern Picts, whom he continued to rule until 761. Nevertheless, for some twenty years Angus was one of the most powerful rulers in Britain.

[FC27] **AED FIND (the FAIR)** ruled Dál Riata, 750–78.

The name Aed is of ancient Celtic origin. It is derived from Aodh, the Celtic sun god, and means "fire". Aed *Find* was the son of EOCHAID (III) and was probably a child when his father died in 733, and when ANGUS, king of the Picts, defeated the ruling families of Dál Riata and claimed overlordship in 736. In the subsequent fourteen years there were several skirmishes between the Scots and the Picts, in one of which it is suggested that the sons of FIANNAMAIL were killed. By 750, however, we may presume that Aed was in his twenties. In that year Angus was defeated by TEUDEBUR of Strathclyde. Aed seized the opportunity and re-established himself in Dál Riata. His claim seems to have gone unchallenged, as Angus had enough problems to contend with. Eventually, in 768, Aed led an army against Angus's successor, CINIOD. Although the battle at Fortriu was inconclusive it resulted in acceptance by Ciniod of Aed's authority in Dál Riata. He established a period of stability amongst the Scots that had been unknown since the reigns of AEDAN and EOCHAID BUIDE over a hundred and fifty years before. This enabled Aed to govern his kingdom and establish a set of laws which were incorporated as the laws of Alba by DONALD (I) a hundred years later. In addition to his nickname "the Fair", Aed was known as Aed *Airechtech*, "of the assemblies".

[FC28] **FERGUS** MAC **EOCHAID** ruled Dál Riata, 778–81.
Fergus succeeded his brother AED FIND as ruler of the Dál Riata. By then he may well have been in his late forties and had lived long in the shadow of his powerful and successful brother. He left no mark and died three years later. The kingship then seems to have been disputed between two unidentifiable successors, DONN-CORCI and DOMNALL. Fergus was the father of CONSTANTINE, the first true king of the combined kingdom of Scots and Picts.

[FC29a] **DONNCORCI** ruled Dál Riata, ?781–91.
A ruler known only by his obituary entered in the *Annals of Ulster* in 791. Whether he shared the kingship of the Scots Dál Riata with DOMNALL, or whether he ruled just part of the kingdom is not known. It is possible he could be identified with Eochaid the Poisonous (*see below*).

[FC29b] **DOMNALL** ruled Dál Riata, 781–805.
Domnall is recorded in the genealogies as a son of CONSTANTINE, who became king of the Picts in 789. For a son to inherit a kingdom before his father is difficult enough to imagine during this troubled time, especially when by even the most generous calculation, Domnall could have been only in his early teens. It is more likely a scribal error confusing this Domnall with a later son of CON-STANTINE (I) who became DONALD II a hundred years later. This calls into question the very existence of this Domnall, although someone ruled for the period 781–805. The period up until 791 has, in some lists, been allocated to the otherwise unknown rulers DONNCORCI and EOCHAID. This period saw the first Viking invasions on the Western Isles, starting in 795, and focussing on Iona. It required a strong king to combat them and one whose exploits would have been remembered by the annalists. This is not the case with Domnall, though it is the case with Constantine. What we may imagine, therefore, is that Constantine probably ruled the Picts and Scots jointly from perhaps as early as 781, but that perhaps he placed his son, Domnall, who could then have been in his early twenties, in command in parts of Dál Riata. Domnall's reign apparently ended in 805 when the Viking raids were at their height, and it is possible that Domnall was

killed during one such raid. This interpretation, though, has to be read alongside Constantine's treatment, in 789, of CONALL MAC TADG who fled to the kingdom of Dál Riata to seek refuge, which would have been difficult had Constantine been king of both territories.

[FC29c] **EOCHAID (IV) *THE POISONOUS*, ruled Kintyre?, 781–?**
The existence of this king is dubious. He is named amongst the forebears of KENNETH MACALPIN, and was purportedly the son of AED FIND and the father of ALPIN through his marriage to Fergusa the daughter of FERGUS MAC EOCHAID. The start of his reign is assigned to 781, the same year that the mysterious DOMNALL came to power and it is entirely possibly that two rival factions emerged in Dál Riata, and that Eochaid ruled part of the kingdom, possibly only Kintyre. If he did rule as early as 781, he would have been very young, but he could have survived against his rivals for several years. He earned the nickname Eochaid the Poisonous, which apparently related more to his vicious tongue than his murderous abilities. However it is virtually impossible that he would have survived until as late as 834 to pass the kingdom on to his son ALPIN, and we must regard Eochaid's rule as plausible but suspect. By the same token, Eochaid equates to the legendary Achaius who is attributed with having established an accord with Charlemagne of the Franks (and thus the origins of the "Auld Alliance") and also with founding the original Noble Order of the Thistle. If either of these have a basis in fact then Eochaid must have had a stature greater than the record of his existence suggests.

[FC30;FA36] **CONALL MAC TADG ruled Picts, 785–9; Dál Riata, 805–7.**
Conall was one of the minor claimants to the Pictish throne who ruled from Forteviot between 785 and 789 but was driven out by CONSTANTINE in 789. He fled to Dál Riata where he sought refuge with DOMNALL, after whose death in 805 Conall assumed the kingship. The real heir, CONALL MAC AEDAN, laid siege to Conall and killed him in battle in 807.

[FC31] **CONALL MAC AEDAN ruled Dál Riata, 807–11.**
Conall defeated CONALL MAC TADG in 807. Some records refer to them as brothers, and it is possible they were half-brothers, with Aedán as their father, and Tadg as the Pictish mother. Their descent amongst the Dál Riatan ruling family is unclear. He was succeeded by CONSTANTINE.

[FC32;FA37] **CONSTANTINE MAC FERGUS Picts, 789–820; Dál Riata, 811–20.**
Although Constantine was the son of the Dál Riatan king, FERGUS MAC EOCHAID, he did not apparently inherit the throne on his father's death in 781. This may have been because his mother was a Pictish princess and he was thus the son of a second wife. Whatever the reason Constantine successfully challenged for the Pictish kingship in 789, defeating Conall mac Tadg (*see page xx*).

Constantine was a powerful warrior king, able to withstand the devastating raids by the Danes and Vikings which wracked the western seaboard during his reign. These raids drove the Scots of Dál Riata further inland to seek safety. The Picts and the Scots gradually found themselves siding together to face a common enemy. It helped for them to be ruled by the same strong king. Constantine was able to claim the Dál Riatan kingship in 811 after the death of CONALL MAC AEDAN. He was only the second king since ANGUS to rule the Scots and the Picts at the same time, and he was the first to pass that joint rulership on to his successor, his brother ANGUS II. His reign was a major step toward the unification of Scotland.

[FC33;FA38] **ANGUS (II)** MAC **FERGUS** ruled the Scots and Picts, 820–34.

He was the first ruler to inherit the kingship of both the Scottish Dál Riata and the Picts when he succeeded his brother CONSTANTINE. He must by then have already been middle aged, perhaps even into his early fifties. He continued the work of his brother in strengthening and defending the kingdom against the Vikings, whose attacks on the western coast became more sustained and violent as each year passed. They sought not only young men and women to take into slavery, but also plunder from the holy places. One of the most chilling attacks was on Iona in 825. Most of the brothers had left for Kells in 814, but a small body remained guarding the relics of Columba. In 825 the Vikings assaulted the island for the fifth time trying to find Columba's tomb. The abbot Blathmac refused to reveal its whereabouts and, as a result, he was torn limb from limb. Angus continued to fortify the churches in the east of his kingdom and tradition states that he established the church at St Andrew's in Fife, where the saint's relics were transferred by Regulus (although the founding of St Andrew's has also been attributed to the earlier ANGUS). When Angus died the kingdom was divided between his sons and nephews who ruled jointly. Although they had Pictish names, it seems less likely that the rule of matrilinear succession applied in all cases, and it must be seen that by the reign of Angus, the old kingdom of the Picts had all but been subsumed into a greater kingdom of the Scots, although this was not formally recognized for another six years.

[FC34] **AED** MAC **BOANTA** ruled Dál Riata, 834–9.

One of the successors of ANGUS II, listed as inheriting the kingdom of Dál Riata, which he later ruled together with EOGANAN MAC ANGUS (*whom see for details*).

[FC35] **ALPIN** ruled Galloway, 834.

The existence of Alpin as a king is questionable. His name is known because of his son KENNETH MACALPIN, and he is usually presumed to be a sub-king of Galloway. The genealogy that makes him a son of Eochaid and grandson of AED FIND may have been a later invention to grant Kenneth a pedigree. If he existed at all, he is supposed to have been killed while fighting the Picts. Galloway at this time was still part of the kingdom of Strathclyde, though this had been subsumed within Northumbria for several generations.

[FC36;FA41] **EOGANAN (or EWEN)** MAC **ANGUS** ruled Picts and Scots, 836 or 837–9.

When ANGUS II died in 834 the combined kingdom of the Picts and the Scots was then shared between the various claimants to the throne. There are no records to show whether this was the choice of the ruling class, or a series of rivals, but it is likely it was deliberate. Firstly the normal rule of Celtic succession was for the new kings to be elected, and not inherit automatically – the selection was usually made before the previous king died so that there was a recognized heir. The old rule of partible succession, whilst continuing in Wales, had largely died out in Scotland, but it was still common for the younger princes to become sub-kings of territories. With the threat of the Vikings to the west, it may well have been agreed that it was better to subdivide the land between four kings by agreement than to have an internecine battle that further weakened the kingdom. It is not clear who inherited which territory precisely, although AED MAC BOANTA initially claimed the territory of the Dál Riata, Drust inherited part of the territory of the Picts (probably that of the Southern Picts) and TALORC MAC UUTHOIL the remainder, though as some king-lists run their names together as Drustalorg, it is possible that they genuinely shared the throne of the whole kingdom. A fourth claimant, Eoganan (or Owen), the son of Angus II, did not seem to come into his inheritance until 836 or 837. This may be because he was younger than the others (though this is unlikely) or that he had originally chosen not to become king until the pressure of the Viking raids caused him to be elected high king in 837, as he does appear as ruler of both Dál Riata and the Picts in that year. In that year the other rulers almost certainly become subservient to him.

At this time another prince of Dál Riata, Cinioth or KENNETH MACALPIN, the ruler of Galloway, was negotiating with the Vikings of Ireland to help him in his own plans. In 839 a major Viking force landed in Galloway and marched inland. Near St Fillans they met the Pictish army under Eoganan. The battle was a disaster for the Picts. Almost all the Pictish royal family and aristocracy were killed, and this paved the way for Kenneth to establish himself as king. Under Kenneth the kingdom of the Scots and the Southern Picts was formally united. Its history is continued on page 379.

THE SAXON KINGDOMS

The Saxons began to settle in Britain in the second quarter of the fifth century. The *Anglo-Saxon Chronicle* proclaims the descent of all of the kings from Odin, but it is likely that many of the ancestral names are genuine. Chart 10 shows not only the descent of the Anglo-Saxon kings but their relationship to the ancestors of other Danish and Norse rulers in Britain. The earliest Saxon kingdom was in Kent, but elsewhere other roving bands of warriors gradually carved out territory for themselves, particularly in Wessex and Northumbria. The following are in order of the establishment of each kingdom. Some kingdoms, especially Mercia, had sub-kingdoms which, for a brief period, held a degree of autonomy.

G. KENT

KENT (Kent, and at times parts of Surrey)
Kent was settled by the Jutes, who also settled on the Isle of Wight, although the two kingdoms are seldom linked or associated. Although the kingdom's origins are lost in legend, Kent was the first substantially independent kingdom to emerge and the first to introduce Christianity to the English. Kent was often ruled by two kings, one for East Kent and one for West Kent – divided by the river Medway.

Ref.	Ruler	Born	Reign	Died	Notes
GI.	Hengest	c420	455?–?488	?488	
G2.	Oeric, Oisc (or Aesc)		?488–c516	c516	killed in battle (Badon?)

10. The Scandinavian Ancestry of the Anglo-Saxon-Danish Kingdoms

The traditional genealogy of the Anglo-Saxon settlers in Britain is probably correct for several generations back but then largely mythical unless you accept a common ancestor who adopted the name of the Nordic deity Odin and who would have lived sometime in the late second century.

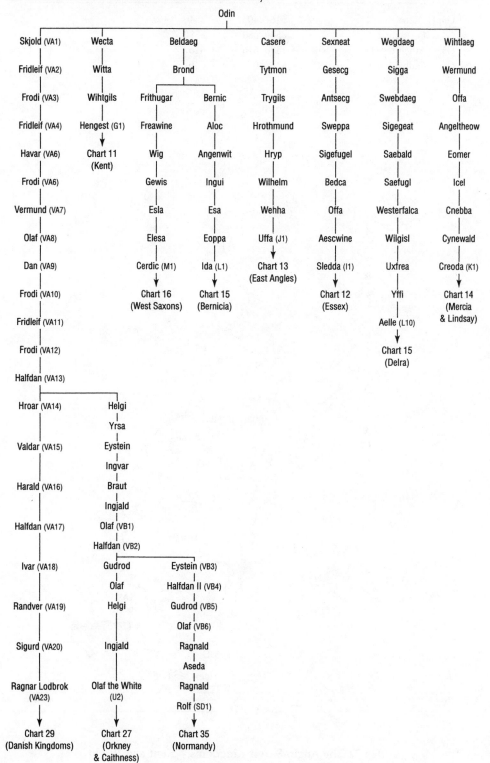

Ref.	Ruler	Born	Reign	Died	Notes
G3.	Octha		516–c40	c540	
G4.	Eormenric		c540–c80	c580	
G5.	Athelbert (I)	c552	c580–616	616	
G6.	Eadbald	c582	616–40	640	

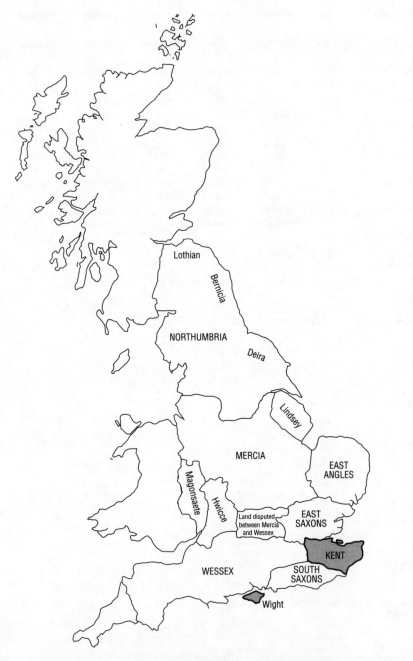

Map 7a The Anglo-Saxon Kingdoms – Kent and Wight

G7.	Eorcenbert	c624	640–64	664	
G8.	Egbert (I)	c641	664–73	673	
G9.	Hlothhere	c644	673–85	685	killed in battle
G10.	Eadric	c663	685–6	686	killed during conquest by Caedwalla
G11.	Caedwalla of Wessex		686–7	688	Kent conquered by Wessex; see M11
G12.	Mul		686–7	687	burned to death
G13.	Sigehere of Essex		687–8	688	king of Essex; see I9
G14.	Oswine		688–90	?	
G15.	Swaefheard or Sweafred		689–692	c707	later king of Essex; see I12
G16.	Wihtred	c670	691–725	725	
G17.	Athelbert II		725–48		ruled jointly with Eadbert,
			c754–62	762	then retired; returned after Eardwulf's death
G18.	Eadbert (I)	c697	725–c62	c762	ruled with Athelbert II and then Eardwulf
G19.	Ealric		725– ?	?	ruled jointly with step-brothers
G20.	Eardwulf	c730	c748–54	754?	ruled jointly with father Eadbert
G21.	Sigered		759–63	after 778	
G22.	Ealhmund		762–4	784	deposed and later restored
G23.	Heaberht		764–c71	771?	
G24.	Egbert II		764–c84	c784	
G22.	Ealhmund (restored)		c784–c785	785	restored but then killed
G25.	Eadbert II Praen		796–8	after 811	deposed and imprisoned
G26.	Cuthred (of Mercia)		798–807		

Kent was ruled directly by Cenwulf and Ceolwulf of Mercia from 807 to 823.

| G27. | Baldred | | 823–5 | | |

Hereafter the kings of Kent were sub-kings to Wessex, a title usually offered to the heir presumptive.

G28.	Athelwolf		825–39	858	see M19
G29.	Athelstan		839–52?	852?	may be the same as J17
G30.	Athelbert		855–60	865	see M21

The title seems to have ceased after Athelbert, during the Danish wars, but was briefly restored for the son of Edward the Elder:

| G31. | Edwin | c902 | c920–33 | 933 | drowned |

[G1] **HENGEST** Saxon & Jutish war leader, 455?–?88.

Despite the romantic tradition that Hengest, or Hengist, was the first king of Kent, we have no contemporary evidence of his existence and little but tales told by bards of later generations vying with other courts to establish a precedence of conquest in Britain. The story of the arrival of Hengest does contain a degree of logic, and is probably based on fact, but whether Hengest existed as a person is far from certain. The dates attributed to his arrival are also suspect and subject to the same questioning as under CERDIC. Nevertheless, despite this uncertainty there is a certain continuity and logic to the threads of tradition related to Hengest's life which allow us to assemble a possible biography.

11. Anglo-Saxon Kingdoms (1) – Kent

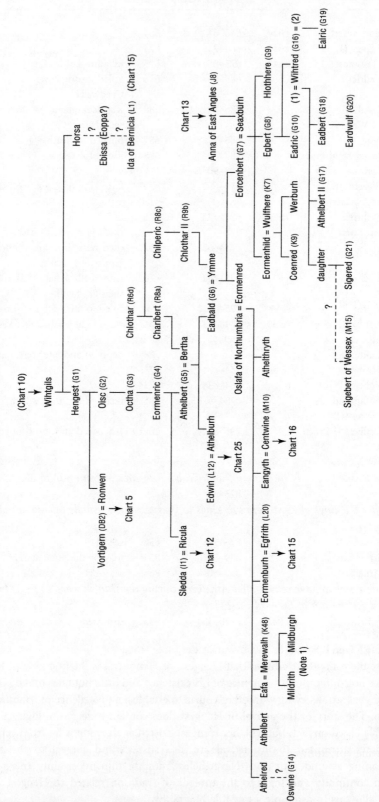

Note 1. By an earlier marriage Merewalh had two sons, Merchhelm and Mildfrith

The traditional story is that with the fall of Roman imperial rule, the heartland of Britain came under threat from three sources: the Irish, the Picts and the Saxons. The time came when one of the high kings, VORTIGERN, decided to pit at least one against the other and he invited Hengest and his warriors to aid in the fight against the Picts. The date usually attributed to this is 449 but it has been suggested to be as early as 428, or as late as the 470s, the later date being the more likely. Hengest and his brother Horsa (both names mean horse, Hengest being more strictly stallion) agreed to help provided they could bring over more warriors. Traditionally they landed at Ebbsfleet, by the Isle of Thanet, but this may not have been the site of their first landing. Older chronicles refer only to their landing in the east and, since the battle was against the Picts, it is probable that Vortigern arranged for them to meet him much further north, perhaps as far as the territory of the Gododdin (see CUNEDDA). The mercenaries did their job well. It is suggested that Hengest remained at his base and despatched his son OISC in charge of a contingent to fight the Picts, whilst his cousin (or nephew), Ebissa, took the fleet to battle the Irish. In return for this Hengest bargained for land, and Vortigern gave them the island of Thanet, in east Kent.

Long-eyed Celtic mask,
Aylesford, Kent

It is tempting to connect this Hengest with the Hengest the Half-Dane referred to in the epic poem *Beowulf.* Here we see Hengest as an exiled Frisian prince who rebels against the Danish hegemony and becomes the leader of a band of mercenary warriors. It is not a large step to presume that Hengest and his band fled Frisia and made their way to Britain, perhaps Kent, where trade had long existed with the continent.

Another legend states that Vortigern became infatuated with Hengest's daughter, Hrothwine (or Ronwen), and Hengest was prepared to give her in marriage to Vortigern in exchange for land. Vortigern thereupon handed Hengest the land of the Cantii, then ruled by a Briton called GWYRANGON. This was unlikely to be the whole of Kent as we know it today, but the land around Canterbury and the marshland towards Thanet. This area certainly has the oldest archeological evidence of Germanic settlement in Britain, suggesting that tradesmen and craftsmen from the northern coast of Saxony had been settling there throughout the fifth century.

After six years, during which time Hengest consolidated his new kingdom, and established his forces, the Jutes struck out for more land. There were a series of battles, at one of which Horsa was killed (traditionally at Aylesford, near Maidstone), where the British were driven out of Kent and into London, and Hengest thereafter claimed the whole of Kent. They possibly conquered land further west into Sussex and as far as the Isle of Wight, since the people of Wight claimed a common stock with those of Kent.

The *ASC* refers to a few further battles over the years as Hengest establishes his control over south-eastern Britain, by which time his own success encouraged others to chance their arm in Britain so that by the end of the fifth century the conquests of AELLE and Cerdic are being recorded. Hengest's death is recorded in 488 which must have placed him into his late sixties at least. Geoffrey of Monmouth, whose history is always suspect but tempting, states that Hengest was killed and buried at Knaresborough.

Whilst there is no great reason to doubt Hengest's existence, it is also dangerous to read too much into the written record. The balance of evidence would suggest he was a real warrior who, by subterfuge, laid claim to Kent in the mid-late fifth century and opened the way to other Germanic conquerors.

[G2] OISC, OERIC (or AESC) ruled *c*488–*c*516.

The later kings of Kent styled themselves as Oiscingas, meaning of the tribe or family of Oisc, from which we can deduce that Oisc was, to a large degree, the founder of the kingdom. He is treated in the chronicles as either the son or grandson of HENGEST, but dates and events are uncertain and mixed with tradition. Oisc is elsewhere called Oeric or Eric, surnamed Oisc, which suggests that Oisc was a nickname. Elsewhere, though, Oisc is referred to as the son of Octha and the grandson of Hengest. This confusion serves to underscore the vagueness of historical data at this period. Even the dates are uncertain, but may be regarded with a degree of accuracy as by this time other Saxon and Frisian hopefuls were staking their claims on British soil, in particular AELLE in Sussex and possibly CERDIC in Hampshire or Wiltshire. It is quite likely that Oisc had already established a kingdom in Kent. As the part of Britain closest to the continent, Kent already had a long tradition of trade with the European mainland, and communities of these tradesmen were establishing themselves in Kent during the fifth century. If the stories about Hengest are correct, the Kentish lands were bought from the British in return for services rendered. Thus we may reasonably regard Oisc or Eric as the first to rule Kent as an established king rather than a conquering warlord. Hengest had sent Oisc to command the armies of the north, and Oisc may have been a leader of a northern Saxon or Jutish contingent who returned to Kent after Hengest's death.

Details of his reign are sparse, but we can imagine it was one of safeguarding the small Frisian and Saxon enclave against the Britons who, under AMBROSIUS and later ARTHUR, sought to repel them. What is significant is that Oisc is the only English king named at the battle of Badon where Arthur was victorious. Since Aelle was, at this time, regarded as the sovereign English ruler, Oisc was evidently fighting under his command, but Arthur destroyed the Saxon armies and we may presume that Oisc was killed. The date of Badon would therefore define the date of his death though, as the entry on ARTHUR explains, that date remains open to question. Oisc's death no doubt left the kingdom of Kent in disarray and it took some while for it to become re-established. This explains the lack of real continuity in the line of succession of kings, despite the attempts of later genealogists to re-define it.

[G3] **OCTHA** ruled c516–c40.

[G4] **EORMENRIC** (or **IURMENRIC**) died c580.

Eormenic is recorded variously as the son or grandson of OISC. As Oisc died at Badon around 516 Eormenric is unlikely to have been his son, and therefore we may assume another, presumably Octha, ruled between Oisc's death and Eormenric's succession. This is by no means definite, however, as Oisc's death would have left Kent in some turmoil, perhaps without a clear successor. Whilst Oisc claimed descent from the Jutes or Frisians of northern Saxony, the name Eormenric is more closely associated with the Frankish royal family, descendants of Clovis, and from the mid sixth century many Frankish treasures and remains are found in Kentish archeological sites. Eormenric may, therefore, have been an offspring of the Frankish royal family who married into the lineage of Oisc. This would certainly account for the close relationship between the two families, particularly that of Eormenric's son ATHELBERT, who entered into an arranged marriage with Bertha, the daughter of the king of Paris. This family alliance also brought much prominence and wealth to the Kentish royal family, and was significant for bringing Christianity to the Saxons. For all that we know little about Eormenric it is evident that his role in developing Kent as a kingdom and bringing wealth to the Saxon domains was significant. His reign probably extended from at least 560–80, and may have begun even earlier. It is possible that it was during his reign rather than that of his son's, that the nobility of Kent strove to move further westward and came into conflict with the West Saxons. A battle is recorded in the *ASC* in the year 568 between CEAWLIN and Athelbert, a date that is chronologically impossible for these two monarchs, so either the date is wrong or the kings are. Since Athelbert succeeded Ceawlin as *bretwalda*, we might assume the earlier date had some significance and relates to conflict between the Kentish and West Saxon kingdoms as both fought for domination.

[G5] **ATHELBERT** (I) ruled c580–24 February 616.

Born: c552; Died: 24 February 616; Buried: Canterbury.

Married: (1) c578, Bertha (c560–c602), dau. Charibert, king of Paris; (2) second wife unknown.

Athelbert is the first Anglo-Saxon king about whom we have some strong historical facts, although even these are inconclusive about the length of his reign or of his life. The *ASC* records his birth as being in 552, which could be right, though if he died in 618 he would be aged 66 and not 56 as suggested by Bede (Bede's reference is ambiguous and the 56 years has been interpreted as the length of his reign rather than his life). Other evidence, particularly that related to his marriage to Bertha, narrow the limits of his reign, but still give us a picture of a strong and wealthy king.

Athelbert was the son of EORMENRIC whose alliance with the Merovingian Franks had brought both stability and wealth to the kingdom of Kent. Athelbert's sister,

Ricula, had married the king of Essex (*see* SLEDDA), over whose territory Athelbert was overlord. Athelbert soon became regarded as the *bretwalda* or overlord of the other Saxon domains. This extended over the kingdoms of the East Angles, Lindsey, Mercia, the Middle Angles and to some extent the West Saxons. Athelbert's reign coincides with the first great period of Saxon domination after the death of ARTHUR and the expulsion of the remnant British Celts from the heartland of Britain. Although battles continued in the north and west, Kent remained comparatively free of conflict, and this allowed Athelbert to increase the wealth and influence of his kingdom. It is possible that early in his reign he had some expansionist skirmishes with CEAWLIN of the West Saxons – though the date recorded in the *ASC* (568AD) is wrong if it refers to Athelbert, it might refer to his father or to an incident early in Athelbert's reign (say around 583) which was a setback for Athelbert but only a temporary victory for Ceawlin.

From a coin

It was thus especially significant that Athelbert was the first Saxon king to embrace Christianity. He already had sympathy with the religion because his wife was Christian and part of the marriage arrangement was that her chaplain, Liudhard, should accompany her. Liudhard was allowed to restore the old Roman church of St Martin's at Canterbury which had stood for some two centuries. Athelbert was initially cautious in welcoming the mission of Augustine who was sent by Pope Gregory I to convert the Saxons. Augustine landed at Thanet in 597 and was met by Athelbert under an oak tree which the Saxons venerated and which he believed would cancel any magic the Christians might practice. Athelbert recognized the sincerity of Augustine but declared he could not abandon the religion of his fathers. Nevertheless he allowed Augustine and his colleagues to establish a house at Canterbury, where they used Liudhard's church of St Martin's, and within a short period many hundreds of Athelbert's subjects were baptized. Athelbert himself was not baptized until 601, but thereafter he became fervent in his support. He actively encouraged Augustine to establish another church, in west Kent at Rochester, and a third in London, the original St Paul's. It was a sign of Athelbert's authority as *bretwalda* that he was able to organize a meeting between Augustine and the Celtic church, at a place later known as Augustine's Oak on the borders of Gloucestershire and Somerset, as part of Augustine's plan to bring the Celtic church under Roman authority. Unfortunately it failed because of Augustine's arrogance and, by association, it dented Athelbert's power.

With the help of Augustine, Athelbert established a set of law codes, which formed the basis of those later developed by OFFA and ALFRED. These had the innovation of giving particular protection to the church, but were otherwise probably developed from existing Frankish laws. They went into immense detail, bringing in a system of monetary fines (rather than payment in kind, such as livestock), allowing people to pay in instalments, and establishing the level of fine in accordance with the severity of the crime. The king was reckoned as overlord so that if any crime were committed within his kingdom, the perpetrator had to recompense the king as well as the victim (or victim's family). The law also gave considerable protection to women and allowed a wife to leave her husband if there was good cause, although the husband had the final say as to who kept the children. These laws not only restored a form of governance and administration to Britain, but with the emphasis on monetary compensation, also reinstituted a financial system. Coins were based on the Frankish design and Athelbert established a mint at Canterbury to produce his own coinage. He introduced the silver *sceat* as the common basis of coinage, the nearest equivalent to a penny, as a twentieth part of the gold *solidus*, or shilling.

Under Athelbert Kent became not only the most sophisticated, but in all probability the safest of Saxon kingdoms in England, and that in turn allowed it to become the wealthiest. This would have made it the envy of the other Saxon kings, particularly in the emerging states of Wessex and Mercia, so that it needed a strong monarch to sustain it. Athelbert was such a strong monarch, which was why he was acknowledged as *bretwalda* for much of his reign (probably from about 588), but he needed strong successors if his kingdom's power was to remain. Unfortunately that did not happen. His son, EADBALD, was a different character; he turned his back on Christianity and the power of Kent faded. Nevertheless, the Christian message was sustained by Athelbert's daughter, Athelburh, who married EDWIN of Northumbria, and introduced Christianity to the northern Angles. Athelbert was later venerated as a saint. A small cult developed in Kent, probably soon after the king's death, but the main centre of his worship developed in the thirteenth century. Not only was he the first Saxon saint in Britain he was, more significantly, the first Saxon king to be so venerated.

[G6] **EADBALD** ruled 24 February 616–20 January 640.
Born: *date unknown but probably around 582*; **Died**: *20 January 640, aged about 57.*
Buried: *Canterbury.*
Married: *(1) 616, name unknown, widow of Athelbert; (2) date unknown (before 624, perhaps 620), Ymme (or Emma) of the Frankish royal household.*
Although the son and successor of ATHELBERT, Eadbald did not embrace the Christian church, and indeed aggravated the relationship further by marrying his stepmother, flouting the rules of Pope Gregory. We do not know when Eadbald's mother, Bertha, died, other than that it was some time after 601AD. We must assume that his stepmother and wife was herself not a Christian, or that she lapsed, and that she was a young wife of Athelbert's old age. Eadbald is later recorded as having married a Merovingian princess called Ymme, identified by some as the daughter of the Neustrian Mayor Eorcinwald, or as the daughter of the Austrasian king Theodebert. She was probably already a Christian and therefore could not have been Eadbald's first wife. Eadbald was probably in his thirties when he inherited the kingdom of Kent and he must also have been a lapsed Christian. It would be strange for his father to convert to Christianity without making the same provision for his son, unless we are to assume that Athelbert was making only a token gesture. Bede records that because of his lack of devoutness he was visited by bouts of madness and infirmity, which may be an early Christian interpretation of epilepsy.

Eadbald later returned to Christianity, baptized by either Augustine's successor, Laurentius, or the later archbishop, Justus. As Laurentius died in 619AD, we must assume this happened within only a year or two of Eadbald's succession, though in view of the turbulent days for the Christian church, it is more likely to date it to around 624AD when Justus returned from his exile in France to claim the see of Canterbury. According to Bede, Eadbald was affected when he was shown the evidence of some miraculous scourging upon the body of Laurentius that had occurred whilst he dreamt one night. This may have placed the fear of God in Eadbald and been enough for him to put aside his pagan wife, possibly further influenced by another apparent miracle achieved by Bishop Mellitus. Around 623AD a fire broke out in Canterbury, probably caused deliberately, which threatened to destroy the whole church. Mellitus was carried into the flames at which point the direction of the wind changed and the church was saved. Eadbald was probably influenced by his counsellors and advisers at court in the early days of his reign, and only later exerted his own authority as the fervour and determination of the early Roman missionaries was demonstrated. Eadbald's sister, Athelburh was a confirmed Christian, and her marriage to EDWIN of Northumbria about 625 was crucial in the conversion of that kingdom, and of the future of Christianity, as it was a condition of the marriage arrangement that Edwin place no hindrance in the path of Athelburh's worship. Nevertheless, the new Christian church went through a difficult period in Kent and, even after Eadbald's conversion, he was unable to sustain the church in London. This demonstrates that Eadbald had neither the authority nor strength of his father, and he was not acknowledged as *bretwalda*, or overlord, a title that passed to REDWALD of the East Angles. Nevertheless Eadbald must have been a reasonably strong king, as he retained his throne for 24 years. It is possible that he did this through his alliance to other kings of growing power, for later evidence suggests that after the death of Edwin, he changed his allegiance to Edwin's successor Oswald. Athelburh, who had returned to the protection of her brother's household, thereupon sent her two infant children to Francia for safety. Nevertheless we must assume that by the time of his death Christianity had taken a strong hold in Kent. Eadbald's children and grandchildren became fervent Christians. He was succeeded by his younger son EORCENBERT.

[G7] **EORCENBERT** ruled 20 January 640–14 July 664.
Born: *c624 or earlier.* **Died:** *14 July 664.* **Buried:** *Canterbury.*
Married: *c640, Seaxburh, dau. Anna, king of the East Angles.*
It is uncertain whether Eorcenbert was the son of Eadbald and his second wife Ymme, or of his first wife, the unnamed widow of ATHELBERT. To have been old enough to succeed Eadbald in 640, Eorcenbert cannot have been less than sixteen, and quite possibly older. It may be that his mother died in giving birth to him. He was the first Saxon king to be raised as a Christian, and on his accession ordered that the idols of the pagan worshippers be destroyed throughout Kent. He strengthened the laws of his grandfather to ensure that his decrees be taken seriously, and he also gave royal assent to the observation of fasting in Lent. He effectively outlawed pagan worship in Kent, although small enclaves persisted as shown by the survival of such names as Woodnesborough (or Woden's Barrow) near Canterbury. Eorcenbert also appointed the first Saxon archbishop of Canter-

bury after the death of Honorius, the last of Augustine's companions, in 653. This was Frithuwine of the West Saxons, who took the name of Deusdedit (dedicated to God).

Eorcenbert married Seaxburh, the daughter of ANNA of the East Angles, who must also have been young at that time. During their reign she established the nunnery at Minster, on the Isle of Sheppey, to which she retired as abbess after her husband's death in 664. In 679, on her sister's death, she became abbess of Ely, and her own daughter, Eormenhild (or Irmengeld), the widow of king WULFHERE of Mercia, succeeded as abbess of Minster, and later at Ely.

Eorcenbert's observation of Lent brought with it conflict over the strict dating of Easter. Because the Roman and Celtic churches calculated the time of the Easter feast differently it meant that at times Easter might be celebrated twice in any one year. This led to king OSWY of Northumbria calling the Synod of Whitby to determine whether the Celtic or Roman approach should be paramount. Eorcenbert sent his bishop Deusdedit, who clearly favoured the Roman method, and this view prevailed. Deusdedit died of a plague soon after Whitby, and it seems that the same plague caused the death of Eorcenbert who was only in his forties. He died on the same day as Deusdedit, and was succeeded by his son EGBERT.

We can be fairly certain that during Eorcenbert's reign Kent continued to develop as a prosperous kingdom, and farmsteads and hamlets grew into villages and towns. Most of the long established villages in Kent can be dated to the middle of the seventh century.

[G8] **EGBERT** (I) ruled 14 July 664–4 July 673.

He was born sometime around 641, and began his reign with the clearly un-Christian act of ordering the death of his cousins, Athelred and Athelbert, the sons of his father's elder brother, Eormenred. The reason was almost certainly to ensure his right of succession, although this hardly seemed to be challenged by his contemporaries. Nevertheless, at this time there was not an immediate right of succession from father to eldest born son, and Egbert was evidently ensuring he had no opposition. Unfortunately for Egbert the two young princes soon became the centre of a small cult, and this caused a rift in the Kentish royal household that Egbert was keen to mend. Eafa, the sister of the murdered brothers, demanded a blood price from Egbert, and in reparation he granted her land near the isle of Thanet where a second monastery was built (now Minster-in-Thanet) and consecrated in 675, with Eafa as the first abbess. Egbert also founded a church at Reculver, and granted land for another abbey at Chertsey, which shows that his authority extended as far as Surrey, at least in matters of the church. Soon after he became king he consulted the Northumbrian king OSWY over the selection of a successor to Deusdedit, the archbishop of Canterbury. The cruel start to Egbert's reign ended up being extremely profitable for the church, an uneasy balance which would continue for the next thousand years. Egbert died young (he can only have been in his early thirties), probably from an illness, and was buried at Canterbury. He was succeeded by his brother HLOTHHERE.

[G9] **HLOTHHERE** ruled 4 July 673–6 February 685.

Although a difficult name to pronounce in modern usage, Hlothhere is the Saxon version of the Frankish Clothair, the name of the Merovingian king who was his maternal great-grandfather. The name emphasises the connections between the early kings of Kent and those of the Franks. The start of Hlothhere's reign was one of turmoil. He had no immediate right of accession to the throne. His brother, EGBERT, had left two young sons, EADRIC and WIHTRED, who came under the care of their grandmother, Seaxburh. Egbert's sister had married WULFHERE of Mercia who, during this period, was systematically dominating England. Wulfhere took the opportunity of Egbert's death to bring Kent under his influence, not with a show of force, but by peaceful means. He established FRITHUWOLD as a sub-king in western Kent and Surrey and, as the uncle of Eadric and Wihtred, claimed to rule in their name until they were old enough to succeed to the throne. Thus, for a period of about a year, during which time Seaxburh served as regent and no doubt negotiated actively with Wulfhere, Hlothhere did not feel he had the authority to claim the throne. However the Kentish people, themselves fiercely independent, having had over a century without battle or domination, rose up against Wulfhere in support of Hlothhere. The latter probably entered into some kind of agreement to rule as regent until Eadric was old enough to claim the throne. Hlothhere set about reconsolidating the kingdom of Kent, first establishing himself at the core of the kingdom, around Canterbury. By 675, with the death of Wulfhere, Hlothhere grew in confidence and reclaimed central and mid Kent, around Rochester, so that he was in control of all lands to the east of the Medway. However in 676 Wulfhere's successor, ATHELRED, sent an army into Kent which pillaged and desecrated wherever it struck, including the destruction of the church at Rochester. Athelred was actually a very religious king (he later became a monk), so he strongly regretted his actions against the church. The strength of the church in Kent therefore saved the kingdom, for Hlothhere was able to further establish his authority, not just in Kent but over parts of London and Surrey, which had been conquered by the Mercians.

Having consolidated his kingdom, Hlothhere proved to be a fair and forward-thinking monarch. Along with Theodore of Tarsus, the powerful archbishop of Canterbury who had established his own pre-eminence over Britain, Holthhere not only started on a building programme in Kent, restoring churches and manor houses, but also introduced a new law code, significantly updating that of Athelbert's. The code was not issued until late in Hlothhere's reign, in 685, but was developed over a period of years. Significant amongst these laws was the imposition of tolls, which brought money into the royal coffers from the process of trade at the major ports of Kent, including London. Such had been the practice for several years, but the right now became established in law and further enhanced the profitability of Kent as a major trading route.

From 679 Hlothhere recognized Eadric not only as his successor but almost as co-ruler, for both names begin to appear on charters and official documents. Eadric, however, was ambitious and probably felt it would be many years before his uncle (who was perhaps fifteen to twenty years older than Eadric) would die. In collusion with the South Saxons, who were themselves supported by the Mercians, Eadric raised an army against Hlothhere. The king was wounded in battle and died soon afterwards. In the light of what happened subsequently, especially the ferocious onslaught of the West Saxons under CAEDWALLA, it is probable that Holthhere's days were numbered in any case. Nevertheless with his death Kent lost a remarkable and unjustly forgotten king, and the kingdom was plunged into a period of alien domination from which it never fully recovered.

[G10] EADRIC ruled 6 February 685–31 August 686.

Eadric was the son of EGBERT and believed himself the rightful heir to the Kentish throne. His uncle, HLOTHHERE, agreed to accept Eadric as his successor, and introduced him gradually into joint rule from about 679 onwards, when the prince was probably about fifteen or sixteen. Eadric, however, was impatient, and in 685 raised an army of South Saxons and defeated Hlothhere in battle. The Kentish people, whilst accepting Eadric, did not support or respect him. He was young, and almost certainly arrogant and hot-headed. Nevertheless, he was of the Kentish royal line, and a better option than subjugation by the Mercians or West Saxons. However, in August 686, CAEDWALLA, who was re-restablishing the kingdom of the West Saxons, invaded Kent, and installed his own brother, MUL, as king. Eadric either died in the battle or fled, as he was never heard of again. His brother, WIHTRED, eventually succeeded to the throne after four years of domination by the West Saxons and East Saxons.

[G12] MUL ruled 686–7.

Mul was the brother of the West Saxon king and conqueror CAEDWALLA. As a usurper Mul was not accepted by the Kentish people and, at the earliest opportunity, they rose up in revolt. Mul and his companions were driven into a building near the church at Canterbury which was set on fire, and Mul burned to death.

After Mul's death Kent was ruled by Sigehere of Essex (see page 235).

[G14] OSWINE ruled 688–90.

In the period after the death of EADRIC, Kent became the political battleground for several ambitious kings. SIGEHERE, the king of the East Saxons, who had supported CAEDWALLA of Wessex, retained a nominal authority after the murder of Caedwalla's brother MUL. King ATHELRED of Mercia tried a different policy to offer the Kentish peoples one of their own royal family as king, provided they acknowledged Athelred as overlord. It was a short-term expedient. The new king was Oswine, whom some believe was the son of Athelred, whose murder EGBERT had arranged, and great-grandson of EADBALD. Indeed, had the rule of primogeniture been practised by the Saxons, Oswine had a better claim to the throne than WIHTRED. Despite this, and despite Oswine's generous bequests to the church, mostly to his aunt Eafa at Minster-in-Thanet, the Kentish people did not readily accept a king who was little more than a puppet of Mercia. Sometime in the spring of 690 Oswine must have fled the kingdom, probably to escape another uprising. Although the East Saxon king, SWAEFRED, continued to issue charters in his name as king of Kent during 690 and even as late as 692, by 691 Wihtred was being supported as the legitimate king of Kent.

[G15;I12] SWAEFRED or SWAEFHEARD ruled West Kent 689–92; East Saxons, 693–c707.

Swaefred succeeded Sigehere of Essex as king of West Kent and for at least two years operated as if he were the senior king. On Sebbi's death, however, Swaefred was elevated to senior king of the East Saxons. For full details see page 236.

[G16] **WIHTRED** ruled 691–23 April 725.
Born: *date unknown, but c670.* **Died**: *23 April 725, aged about 55.* **Buried**: *Canterbury.*
Married: *(1) pre-694, Cynegyth; (2) c696, Athelburh; (3) after 697, Werburh.*
Wihtred was the son of EGBERT and brother of EADRIC. Following Eadric's death or deposition in 686, Kent became the battleground of a number of usurper and client kings, subject to the power struggles of Mercia and Wessex. During this period Wihtred remained in sanctuary, protected by the church, and in the guardianship of his aunt, Eormenhild, the widow of WULFHERE of Mercia. Wihtred finally emerged to challenge the claimants to the throne late in the year 690, or early in 691, when he was aged probably not much more than 20. He rapidly received the support of the Christian church, which surprisingly had done little to support the earlier claimant OSWINE, also descended from the Kentish royal family. For a period Wihtred ruled jointly with SWAEFRED of Essex, but in 693 Swaefred's father SEBBI died, and Swaefred became preoccupied with establishing himself in Essex. Wihtred was soon able to settle terms with him and negotiate his own sole rule. Furthermore in 694, Wihtred bought his peace with INE, king of Wessex, by paying over a substantial sum in recompense for the murder of MUL by the Kentish people. With Ine, Wihtred established the boundary between Kent and Surrey which has remained almost unchanged to this day. Ine and Wihtred also consulted over a new set of laws, Ine being impressed with those established by Wihtred's predecessors, and Wihtred in turn wishing to update and embellish those of his uncle HLOTHHERE. Wihtred, a strong supporter of the church, but also a severe judge of misdemeanours, made his punishments more strict. His support for the church became most evident in his decree, probably issued in 708, that the church should be exempt from taxation, a principle that was subsequently taken up by other kings and remained fundamental in English law.

Having established an enviable authority Wihtred settled down to rule Kent during a period of continued prosperity. He preferred to rule from his villas in mid-Kent such as Bearsted, near Maidstone, rather than from around Canterbury. When he died in 725, after a reign of nearly thirty-five years, he had established an inviolable bond between the kingdom of Kent and the Christian church. He can be seen as a strict king, an intelligent strategist, but severe rather than avuncular. Rather surprisingly he left the kingdom in the hands of three sons, ATHELBERT, EADBERT and EALRIC.

[G17] **ATHELBERT II** ruled 23 April 725–748 (retired); returned c754–62.
Despite the apparent length of his reign, little is known about him. On the death of WIHTRED the kingdom of Kent was divided between his three sons and Athelbert ruled jointly with his brother EADBERT and half-brother EALRIC. Nothing more is heard of Ealric, and it seems that whilst Athelbert was the eldest and remained the senior king, Eadbert ruled west Kent, and Athelbert east Kent, with the rich lands around Canterbury. Eadbert tried once to usurp his authority in 738, but this was soon suppressed. However, by about 748, Athelbert seems to have retired from public affairs, leaving the government of Kent to Eadbert and his son EARDWULF. This suggests that whilst Athelbert was initially a resolute king, in later years he tired of the demands and retired to his estates. He reappeared briefly in 762 to authorise

a charter, but apparently died later that year when he was in his late sixties. The fact that Athelbert's reign can appear so uneventful, even to the point of his retirement, is testament to the isolation of Kent, even during the period when ATHELBALD of Mercia claimed overlordship of all southern England. Athelbert may have acknowledged this out of prudence, but Athelbald's impact on Kent appears to have been negligible. It was his successor, OFFA, who would have the more significant effect. There is no record that Athelbert married and he retired almost certainly in the belief that the dynasty would continue through his nephew Eardwulf.

[G18] **EADBERT** (I) ruled 23 April 725–c762.
He was probably born about the year 697, and succeeded to the kingdom jointly with his brother ATHELBERT II and half-brother EALRIC. Ealric is not heard from again, and it seems the others split the kingdom between them, with Eadbert taking west Kent. Although Athelbert was the senior partner, around 748 he retired from public life leaving Eadbert to rule jointly with his son EARDWULF. Eadbert seems to have been the more ambitious of the brothers and, at one time, had attempted to increase his authority. Although Athelbert quashed this then, later he evidently let Eadbert take control. From 748 Eadbert succeeded to east Kent and Eardwulf to west Kent. During the reigns of Eadbert and Athelbert Kent's prosperity grew, and the peace allowed not only trade to develop but also agriculture and industry. The earliest working water-mills came into Kent during their reign and work began in draining the marshes at Romney and Walland, initially for salt panning, but then for pasture. It seems likely that Eadbert outlived Athelbert but only by a few months. It also seems likely that his son, Eardwulf, had died young. With the death of Eadbert the dynasty of the Oiscingas, apparently came to an end. Eadbert was alone of all the major Kentish kings in being buried at the church at Reculver rather than Canterbury.

[G19] **EALRIC** ruled 725.
A son of WIHTRED, also spelt as Alric, who, according to Bede, succeeded to the kingdom of Kent jointly with his half-brothers ATHELBERT and EADBERT. However there is no record of his name on any official documents and we may suppose that he either died young, within a few months, or retired (willingly or otherwise) from public life. Nothing more is known of him or whether he had any offspring.

[G20] **EARDWULF** ruled 748–54?.
The son of EADBERT, with whom he ruled jointly once he had come of age, which suggests he was born around the year 730. Eardwulf ruled west Kent while his father took over from his brother ATHELBERT in east Kent, but it is not clear when he ceased to rule. His name last appears on a letter in 754. An undated charter has been assigned to 765, but this is unlikely. Whether Eardwulf died young or abdicated is not known. He was the last recorded of the male line of Oiscingas, or descendents of OISC, who had ruled Kent more or less uninterrupted for over 250 years. He seems to have been succeeded in west Kent by SIGERED.

[G21] **SIGERED** ruled perhaps 759–63 or 764.
With the death of EADBERT, Kent was without an immediate successor. Earlier in Eadbert's reign, perhaps at the time of the death of his son EARDWULF, a possible successor seems to have been found in Sigered. We know little about him, though it

has been temptingly suggested that he was the brother of SIGEBERT, a sub-king in Wessex, both of whom may have been sons of an unnamed daughter of WIHTRED. This would have made Sigered Eadbert's nephew. However Sigered's rule did not long outlast Eadbert's death, for in 764 OFFA of Mercia invaded Kent, and we soon find him issuing charters in the name of client kings which overturned those issued by Sigered. We must assume that Sigered was deposed rather than killed, as his name reappears on a charter in 778 during the reign of EGBERT II. His fate thereafter is not known. Offa replaced him as king of Kent by HEABERHT.

[G22] **EALHMUND** ruled 762–4, and again c784–c5.
It has been suggested that Ealhmund was the same as the earlier Eanmund, whose name appears confirming a charter of SIGERED, the king of West Kent. If this is so then Ealhmund was the more senior king. He has been associated with Ealhmund, the father of the famous EGBERT of Wessex – if this is so, then we know that he was descended from Ingeld, the brother of INE. It is quite probable that his father or grandfather had married into the Kentish royal family, thus establishing his claim on the Kentish kingdom. Ealhmund was, however, deposed by OFFA of Mercia when he invaded Kent in 764. He would have been a young king at the time, probably in his early twenties, with no power to oppose Offa. He almost certainly went into exile, but later became allied with EGBERT II, the king who had displaced him but who in turn rebelled against Offa. When Egbert died, sometime in the early 780s, Ealhmund returned to the kingship. For a second time he faced the wrath of Offa, which this time was more violent and conclusive. Ealhmund was almost certainly killed, and Kent came directly under Offa's rule until the revolution of EADBERT PRAEN in 796.

[G23] **HEABERHT** ruled 764–c71.
A Kentish noble, whose name may more properly be Eadbert, whom OFFA of Mercia installed as one of his client kings (co-jointly with EGBERT II) instead of the reigning king SIGERED. He was probably related distantly to the former Kentish royal family, but the connection is not known. Interestingly his name appears on some extremely rare silver pennies, the first of their kind, minted at Canterbury in imitation of coins minted in France. Offa took up this idea and established the penny as the basic coin across England.

[G24] **EGBERT II** ruled 764–c84.
He was a client king set up by OFFA of Mercia following his intervention in 764. His descent is not known, though his name suggests a relationship to the Kentish royal family, whose male line had died out with EARDWULF. Egbert seems initially to have been subordinate to Offa's other client king, HEABERHT, and it is tempting to consider that Egbert may have been his son or nephew. However after Heaberht's passing around 771, Egbert became sole king of Kent. He was still acknowledged as such briefly by Offa, but within a year or two Offa was operating as if he was sole ruler of Kent and the rest of southern England, in fact as the ruler of all England. The fiercely independent Kentish people rebelled. Egbert's smaller force faced the might of Mercia at the battle of Otford, near Sevenoaks, in 776. The battle apparently involved great slaughter, but it seems that the victory was Egbert's which, considering that the Kentish people had previously had little cause to take

to arms, shows how valiantly and determinedly they must have fought. Offa left Kent alone for nine years. Sometime in that period Egbert died. It is not certain when, but it was probably around 783 or 784, because Offa no doubt sought revenge as soon as Egbert was off the scene, and he exacted it on Egbert's successor EALHMUND.

Ealhmund restored 784–5 – see above.

[G25] EADBERT II *PRAEN* ruled 796–8.

He was probably the last independent descendent of the Kentish royal family, through the female line from OISC. He may have been the nephew of EALHMUND, though his true descent is not known. After Ealhmund's death, around 785 or earlier, Eadbert was probably forced into the priesthood and exiled in France, but in 796, with the death of the Mercian overlord OFFA, Eadbert renounced his orders and seized the Kentish throne. He deposed Athelheard, the pro-Mercian archbishop of Canterbury who had been installed by Offa, and this led to a rift between Eadbert and the church which might otherwise have been sympathetic to his claim. The new Mercian king, CENWULF, did not immediately rush into conflict. Instead he established himself militarily whilst negotiating with the pope, Leo III, over the situation at Canterbury. At length Cenwulf could claim the support of the pope, and with that he descended on Kent, destroying the kingdom and capturing Eadbert. Cenwulf installed his brother CUTHRED as king. Eadbert was imprisoned and blinded, and had his hands chopped off, but he was not killed. He remained imprisoned until, as an act of clemency, Cenwulf freed him in 805 or soon after. His fate is unknown but it is likely he ended his days at Winchcombe Abbey in Gloucestershire. Kent remained under Mercian domination until the reign of EGBERT of Wessex.

[G26] CUTHRED ruled 798–807.

Cuthred was installed as king of Kent by his brother, CENWULF, king of Mercia, after he reconquered Kent from the claimant EADBERT PRAEN. Cuthred was never anything other than a client king, and had to refer all official documents to Cenwulf for authorisation. He maintained the Kentish folk in total subjugation, though he continued to ensure that trade prospered in order to benefit from the revenues. It was during Cuthred's reign that the first Viking raids on Kent began. After Cuthred's death Cenwulf resumed the kingship until his death in 821.

Kent was ruled directly by Cenwulf and Ceolwulf of Mercia until 823 (see page 259).

[G27] BALDRED ruled 823–5.

Baldred was probably an ealdorman or earl of Kent or Sussex who took advantage of the chaos following the death of CENWULF and allied himself to Wulfred, the archbishop of Canterbury, and BEORNWULF of Mercia. With that support, Baldred briefly operated as king of Kent, probably more in name than in authority, which remained vested in Wulfred. Baldred, however, was soon chased out by EGBERT of Wessex, who incorporated Kent into his kingdom. Thereafter Kent became the sub-kingdom of the heir apparent to the throne of Wessex, and was ruled in turn by ATHELWOLF and ATHELBERT of the West Saxons (*see pages 316 and 318*).

Only two other sub-kings ruled Kent without succeeding to the West Saxon throne.

[G29;J17?] **ATHELSTAN** ruled 839–c52.

The *ASC* records that on the death of EGBERT, Wessex passed to his son ATHELWOLF, while Kent (which included Essex and Sussex) passed to his son Athelstan. The phrasing is ambiguous and some authorities regard this Athelstan as the eldest son of Athelwolf. That is possible, though as Athelwolf's marriage is usually dated to 830, Athelstan would have been nine years old, and it is very unlikely that a king would entrust the command of such vulnerable territories to an infant, even as a token of future inheritance. Athelwolf may have married earlier, but the more likely interpretation of the *ASC* is that Athelstan was a younger son of Egbert's, perhaps born around the year 800, and thus in his late thirties. There is a suggestion that this Athelstan may previously have reigned in East Anglia from 825 and, though this cannot be proved, it would make sense. In 851 Athelstan and his ealdorman Ealhere, met a Danish fleet off the coast of Sandwich in Kent, and won. The Danes were the masters of the sea, and to defeat them in a naval battle was a remarkable achievement. Athelstan is not mentioned again after this battle, though there is no suggestion that he died in the conflict. He probably died a year or two later.

[G31] **EDWIN** sub-king of Kent, c920–33.

There is a suggestion that Edwin was made the sub-king of Kent by his father EDWARD THE ELDER. He was his oldest surviving legitimate son (born about the year 902), if we accept the belief (not necessarily proven) that his half-brother ATHELSTAN was illegitimate. Granting him the kingship of Kent was recognizing him as the heir to the throne. Since he did not succeed, we may assume that Edwin was content in his own kingdom and did not wish to rule England. Nevertheless Athelstan may have regarded him as a potential problem or, perhaps in later years (if we assume the date of his death is properly recorded and not an error for 923) he became a threat. He drowned at sea while crossing to Flanders and there was a strong rumour that the boat had been made unseaworthy at Athelstan's orders. Edwin's body was recovered and buried at St Bertin's Abbey in Flanders.

GA. ISLE OF WIGHT

Although the ASC would suggest Wight was occupied by the West Saxons it was, in fact, more closely associated with the Jutes who also occupied Kent. The full record of its kings does not survive.

Ref.	Ruler	Reign	Died	Notes
GA1.	Stuf	534– ?		joint rulers
GA2.	Wihtgar	534–44?		joint rulers
The ruling house uncertain for the next century.				
GA3.	Arwald	? –687	687	killed by Caedwalla of Wessex (M11)

Wight thereafter came under Saxon rule. Part of the island was given to Beornwine, nephew of Wilfrid, the former Bishop of York, in order to convert the islanders to Christianity.

[GA1] **STUF** and [GA2] **WIHTGAR** Isle of Wight, 534–44 or 554–64.

According to the *ASC*, CERDIC conquered the Isle of Wight in the year 530 (more likely 549) and upon his death in 534 (554) his son CYNRIC gave the island to his kin Stuf and Wihtgar, who may have been father and son. An earlier entry shows that Stuf and Wihtgar had landed in Hampshire sixteen years before. This is probably all stuff and nonsense. Wihtgar is in all likelihood a concocted name derived by the annalists writing three centuries later by working back from the name of Wight and assuming its first ruler gave it his name. Since Wight had been settled by Jutes rather than Saxons it is unlikely that they had any connection with Cerdic, and if anything the island's rulers were descended from the nobility of Kent. Wihtgar is given a ten year reign, but no more mention is made of Stuf or his successors. Wight was a prize possession and was conquered in turn by the Mercians (*see* WULFHERE) and West Saxons (see CAEDWALLA). The island's only historically attested king was ARWALD. Their fame (legendary or otherwise) was clearly important as ALFRED *THE GREAT*'s mother claimed descent from them.

ARWALD [GA3] Isle of Wight d. 687.

Arwald is the only historically known king of the Isle of Wight. He was, unfortunately, the last of his line, because he, and many of his people, were slaughtered by CAEDWALLA of Wessex. The story, according to Bede, was that Caedwalla had agreed to convert to Christianity and as a sign of his faith determined to wipe out the pagans of Wight, who were a Jutish people. All this sounds like another excuse in the constant struggle between Wessex and Mercia. A few years earlier WULFHERE of Mercia had become overlord of the South Saxons and had taken control of Wight and handed it over to his sub-king, ATHELWALH. His death in 685 was an opportunity for Caedwalla to claim territory from Mercia. In all likelihood Arwald was a young king, possibly related to the South Saxons and the Jutes of southern Hampshire. Arwald's younger brothers escaped the island into Hampshire and were converted to Christianity on the mainland. This did not save them for Caedwalla still had them executed, but apparently they faced death safe in the knowledge of their salvation. Such was the end of the kingdom of Wight.

H. SOUTH SAXONS

The original Saxon settlement was based around Pevensey and was contained on the north by the vast forest of the Weald. The first named rulers of the South Saxons were invading warlords who did not established a kingdom. The kingdom of Sussex did not emerge until the early seventh century and the record of its first kings has not survived.

Ref.	Ruler	Reign	Died	Notes
H1.	Aelle	491–c516	c516	killed in battle (Badon?)
H2.	Cissa	491–c516	c516	killed in battle (Badon?)

No further rulers are known between c516 and c660, when the kingdom became subject to Mercia.

Ref.	Ruler	Reign	Died	Notes
H3.	Athelwalh	c660–c85	685	killed in battle
H4.	Berthun	685–6	686	killed in battle

Overrun by Wessex; later kings are poorly documented and were all client kings of Wessex or Mercia

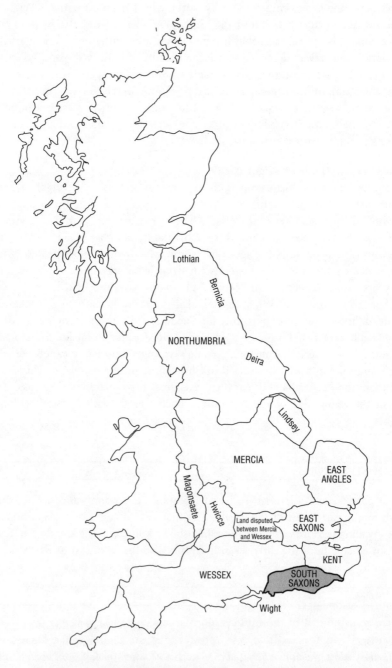

Map 7b **The Anglo-Saxon Kingdoms – South Saxons**

H5.	Nothhelm or Nunna	c692–c725	c725	
H6.	Wattus	fl 692		
H7.	Athelstan	fl 714		
H8.	Athelbert	c725–c50		may be same as G17
H9.	Osmund	c758–c72		

After Osmund the status of kingship was demoted to the equivalent of duke.

H10.	Oswald	fl 772		
H11.	Oslac	fl 772		
H12.	Ealdwulf	765–c91		may have ruled with Elfwald after 772
H13.	Elfwald	c772– ?		ruled with Ealdwulf

Hereafter the kings were relegated to "dukes" and the kingdom became part of Mercia, and subsequently Wessex.

[H1] **AELLE** or **ÆLLI** ruled c491–c516.

The leader of the Saxons who, according to the *ASC*, landed on the south coast, at Selsey Bill, in the year 477 and drove the native British into the great forest of the Weald. Aelle came with his three sons, Cymen, Wlencing and CISSA. It is another eight years before we hear more of him. In 485 he had a decisive victory over the British at the river Mearcraedes, a location as yet unknown, but possibly the Arun. The rivers name identified it as a boundary, and probably remained so for the next century. Six years later (491), Aelle and Cissa massacred the British who had taken refuge in the Roman fort of Anderida near Pevensey. Thereafter the native British were wiped out in Sussex. The archeological and linguistic evidence suggests that the surviving British fled from the area, probably west toward Devon and Cornwall, or into Wales, and the Saxons took complete control over the land. No more is heard of Aelle, although Bede would identify him as the first *bretwalda*, or overlord of the Saxons. Bede's source for this is not known and, on first reflection it seems strange. There were only a few scattered Saxon colonies in Britain at this time, mostly in Kent and possibly Wiltshire, plus the Angles in East Anglia and Deira. Bede may have meant no more than that Aelle was the first of the Saxon race to establish himself in Britain and as the elder representative was entitled to be acknowledged as the first *bretwalda*. But this does not seem sufficient. It is tempting to think that Aelle did serve as a battle leader uniting the forces of the West Saxons and Jutes in their defence against the British. His dates coincide with those of the legendary ARTHUR, and it is possible that Aelle was Arthur's main adversary. If this is true then it may have been Aelle who led the confederate Saxon forces at the Battle of Badon where he and his sons and Oisc of Kent were killed. The fact that there is no further reference to the South Saxons for almost two hundred years suggests they were soundly defeated and retreated to their coastal bases around Pevensey and Alfriston.

[H2] **CISSA** ruled c491–c516.

Identified as one of the three sons of AELLE who conquered the south coast around Pevensey at the end of the fifth century. Cissa's name is apparently the origin of Chichester, and the archeological evidence suggests that Saxon colonization of Chichester did not happen until about a century after Aelle. Cissa may, therefore, also be the name of a third or fourth generation descendant of Aelle who eventually extended the realm of the South Saxons from its heartland around Alfriston toward the west in the first decades of the seventh century. There is a battle recorded in the *ASC* between the West Saxons under CEOLWULF and the South Saxons in 607, and this may have been part of the advance of Cissa towards the west.

[H3] **ATHELWALH [ÆTHELWEALH]** ruled *c*660–*c*85.

The first South Saxon king to be definitely identified since AELLE. It is not certain whether he was a descendant of a line of well established kings, or a client king installed by WULFHERE of Mercia who had conquered England as far south as Sussex and the Isle of Wight by the year 661. The *ASC* records that Wulfhere took Wight and the lands of the Meon Valley in Hampshire from the West Saxons and gave them to Athelwalh. These lands were still pagan, and the arrangement was probably part of a deal to convert the inhabitants. Wulfhere had recently converted Athelwalh, probably at the time of Athelwalh's marriage to Eafa or Eaba, the daughter of EANFRITH of the Hwicce. It is probable that Athelwalh was then at Wulfhere's court, in all likelihood summoned to agree an alliance, and that part of the deal for his continued kingship of Sussex was to convert to Christianity. Although Eafa was Christian, Athelwalh does not seem to have been particularly active in converting his fellow Saxons, and he certainly did nothing with the people of the Isle of Wight. In around 680, Wilfrid, the exiled bishop of Northumbria, came to Sussex and was granted land at Selsey where he later established a monastery. It was under Wilfrid that the real conversion of the South Saxons began. During this period Athelwalh must have had an uneasy relationship with the West Saxons. In 685, CAEDWALLA, an exiled Wessex prince, invaded Sussex and Kent in an endeavour to establish a new kingdom for himself. His main wish was probably to recover Wight and the Meon Valley but his ambitions soon grew beyond that. Caedwalla killed Athelwalh in battle, but he was driven out of the kingdom by two ealdormen BERTHUN and Andhun.

[H4] **BERTHUN** ruled 685–6.

After the renegade West Saxon CAEDWALLA killed ATHELWALH in 685, he was driven out by the king's ealdormen Berthun and Andhun; but a year later, when Caedwalla had established himself as king of the West Saxons, he returned and conquered Sussex, killing Berthun. It is possible that Sussex was divided at this time between East and West, as has remained traditional ever since, and that Andhun continued to hold authority over East Sussex. However, by 686 Caedwalla's authority seemed complete and the South Saxons were reduced to subjection. After Caedwalla's death his successor INE installed two client kings in Sussex, NOTHHELM and WATTUS.

[H5] **NOTHHELM** or **NUNNA** ruled *c*692–*c*725.
[H6] **WATTUS** *fl* 692.

Little is known of Nothhelm. When his name appears on charters it appears in close relationship with INE of the West Saxons and it is likely that he was a client king installed by Ine who had authority over the South Saxons. He may even have been related to Ine, as the *ASC* called him his kinsman. In 710 Nothhelm and Ine defeated GERAINT, the British king of Dumnonia. Nothhelm may have ruled only in West Sussex as he is a contemporary of another South Saxon king, Wattus who probably ruled East Sussex.

[H7] **ATHELSTAN** *fl* 714.

A client king established in East Sussex by INE of Wessex probably in succession to Wattus. In the year 722 it is recorded that the South Saxons gave refuge to a West Saxon exile, Ealdbert, and Ine invaded Sussex to root him out. The South Saxons, who had put up with Ine's tyranny for over thirty years, rebelled and a war raged between them for the next three years until Ealdbert was killed. Ine abdicated soon after, and it may be that in these final years Athelstan established a degree of independence.

[H8] **ATHELBERT** ruled *c*725–*c*50.

Although recorded as a king of the South Saxons, it is possible that after the death of the West Saxon overlord, INE, and his client king NOTHHELM, the South Saxons strove to regain their independence and, for a period, East Sussex may have recognized ATHELBERT of Kent as overlord. By the 730s Wessex had again fallen under the domination of Mercia, whose king ATHELBALD also sought to regain authority over Sussex, but may have only established it over West Sussex. It was not until the reign of OFFA that Mercian client kings were again established over Sussex.

[H9] **OSMUND** ruled *c*758–*c*772

The eighth century was a dark period in the history of Sussex. Names of native kings are uncertain but it is likely that Osmund was a client ruler in West Sussex, recognizing the overlordship of OFFA, whilst EALDWULF was ruler in East Sussex, and may not have recognized Offa's authority. Possibly conflict broke out between Osmund and Ealdwulf and Offa eventually stepped in to resolve the issue. In 772 he formally annexed Sussex and it ceased to exist as a separate kingdom. It was ruled thereafter by "dukes" who were appointed by Offa. What happened to Osmund after 772 is not clear, but he may have been succeeded by his sons Oswald and OSLAC.

[H10] **OSWALD** *fl* 772; and
[H11] **OSLAC** *fl* 772.

After 772, when OFFA imposed his rule, the native kings lost their authority and became called "dukes". Thereafter the kingdom of Sussex ceased to exist in any formal sense. This is what happened to Oswald and Oslac who were regarded as "dukes" of the South Saxons. Their relationship to Ealdwulf is not certain, but it seems likely that whilst Ealdwulf was regarded as the senior "duke" in East Sussex, Oswald and Oslac held authority in West Sussex.

[H12] **EALDWULF** ruled *c*765–*c*791, and
[H13] **ELFWALD** ruled 772– ?

Ealdwulf was probably the last official "king" of Sussex. In 772 OFFA of Mercia, who held authority over Sussex, asserted his control over its internal affairs. In all likelihood there was some internal strife in Sussex, perhaps between East and West, over support for Offa. Ealdwulf's rival was almost certainly OSMUND. Ealdwulf continued to rule jointly with Elfwald, who may have been installed by Offa to keep Ealdwulf in check. The date of their deaths is not known, though Ealdwulf seems to have disappeared from the record after 791.

I. EAST SAXONS

The original kingdom of the East Saxons was bigger than modern-day Essex stretching into Hertfordshire and Bedfordshire and even into parts of Middlesex and Berkshire. London was part of the kingdom. The East Saxons were initially subordinate to Kent, but subsequently gained their independence and for a brief period ruled Kent, before becoming subject to Mercia and later Wessex. Aescwine is usually identified as their first king, but he was in all probability a governor imposed by Eormenric or Athelbert of Kent.

Ref.	Ruler	Reign	Died	Notes
I1.	Sledda	c580s–c600		
I2.	Saebert	c600–c616		
I3.	Sexred	c616–23	623	killed in battle
I4.	Saeward	c616–23	623	killed in battle
I5.	Saexbald	c616–23	623	killed in battle
I6.	Sigebert (I) *Parvus (the Little)*	623–c50		
I7.	Sigebert II *Sanctus (the Good)*	c650–c3	c653	murdered
I8.	Swithhelm	c653–63	663	
I9.	Sigehere	663–88	688	also king of Kent (G13)
I10.	Sebbi	663–c93	693	abdicated and retired to a monastery
I11.	Sigeheard	693–c707		
I12.	Swaefred or Swaefheard	693–c707		earlier king of Kent (G15)
I13.	Offa	707–9	c710	abdicated and became a monk
I14.	Saelred	709?–46	746	
I15.	Swebert	709–38	738	
I16.	Swithred	746–59		
I17.	Sigeric	759–98		
I18.	Sigered	798–825		

Thereafter Essex became part of the kingdom of Wessex.

[I1] **SLEDDA** ruled c580s–c600.
Sledda was the son of Aescwine, who was recorded by Henry of Huntingdon as ruling over the East Saxons from as early as 530. Aescwine's name, though, is closer to those of the Kentish royal house and the fact that Sledda married Ricula, the sister of ATHELBERT of Kent, suggests that Aescwine was a Kentish nobleman, probably related to Athelbert, who helped extend the Kentish domain north of the Thames, probably in the 560s or 570s, and was established as an ealdorman or governor there. His son's marriage was probably arranged by Athelbert's father EORMENRIC, and may have taken place shortly before 580, probably as part of the arrangement for installing Sledda as a ruler north of the Thames, subject to Athelbert. The traditional date for his accession is 587. His territory would have covered not only modern Essex but Hertfordshire and Middlesex. Nothing else is recorded of Sledda's reign or of his death which must have been before 604, when his son SAEBERT is recorded as ruling.

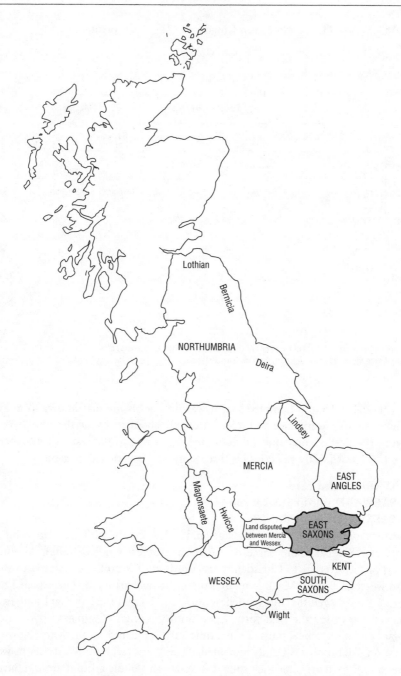

Map 7c **The Anglo-Saxon Kingdoms – East Saxons**

[I2] **SAEBERT** ruled *c*600–*c*16.
Saebert was the son of SLEDDA and nephew of ATHELBERT of Kent who was also
overlord of Essex. Athelbert had been converted to Christianity and it was he who
founded the see of London at St Paul's in 604, installing Mellitus, one of
Augustine's missionaries, as its first bishop. Nothing more is said of Saebert's

12. Anglo-Saxon Kingdoms (2) – **East Saxons**

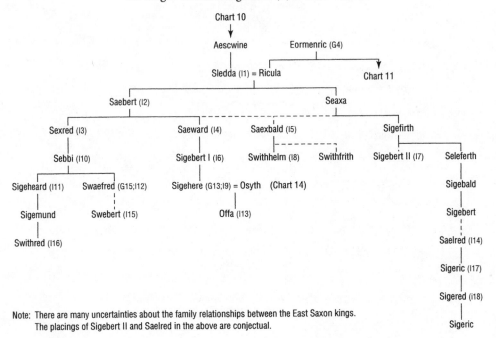

Note: There are many uncertainties about the family relationships between the East Saxon kings.
The placings of Sigebert II and Saelred in the above are conjectual.

reign, though it should be noted that it was during his life that REDWALD of East
Anglia came to prominence and it was probably about this time that the division
between the East Saxons and the East Angles was put to the test. After Saebert's
death Essex was jointly ruled by his three sons who reverted to paganism.

[I3] **SEXRED** ruled c616–23;
[I4] **SAEWARD** ruled c616–23; and
[I5] **SAEXBALD** ruled c616–23.

Saeward succeeded his father SAEBERT and ruled jointly with his two brothers
Sexred and Saexbald (the name of the third brother is not definite). Although
Saebert had converted to Christianity, Saeward and his brothers reverted to their
pagan worship. Bishop Mellitus refused them the Eucharist and they expelled him
from St Paul's. Mellitus and his fellow missionaries returned to Gaul and Essex
remained pagan for the next forty years, until the reign of SIGEBERT THE GOOD.
Saeward and his brothers must at some time have come into conflict with REDWALD
of East Anglia, but this is not documented. Their battles with the West Saxons were
however (see CYNEGILS), as they sought to establish middle ground around Surrey
and northern Hampshire All three brothers were apparently killed in battle against
the West Saxons in 623.

[I6] **SIGEBERT (I)** *PARVUS* (*THE LITTLE*) ruled 623–c50.

He was probably the son of SAEWARD and continued supporting pagan worship.
Nothing is known about him. His name is presumably related to his size rather than
his authority, for it is unlikely he would have ruled for twenty-seven years had he
been a weak king, particularly as his reign coincides with the rise to power of the

Mercian ruler PENDA. It was during his reign, in 635, that Penda invaded East Anglia. Since Essex was not invaded, despite the growing importance of London, we can imagine that Sigebert and Penda (both pagans) had already formed some alliance.

[I7] **SIGEBERT (II)** *SANCTUS* (*THE GOOD*) ruled c650–c3.

He may have ruled part of Essex earlier. His relationship to his predecessor is not clear but they were probably cousins or second cousins. Sigebert was on friendly terms with OSWY of Northumbria who convinced Sigebert of the importance of Christianity. Oswy was a regular visitor to Sigebert's court, which reminds us that they were distantly related, and that Oswy probably visited Sigebert en route to Kent. But though this relationship was almost certainly not just social – Oswy was seeking alliances in his conflict with PENDA of Mercia, who was still a pagan – it is evident that the two kings enjoyed each other's company. Sigebert visited Oswy's court and returned with an abbot from Lindisfarne, Cedd, who re-established Christianity in Essex. Unfortunately this was also Sigebert's undoing. Sometime after his conversion he was murdered by a kinsman who had been excommunicated and had become furious at Sigebert's desire to forgive everyone in the true Christian spirit. He was succeeded by his cousin SWITHHELM.

[I8] **SWITHHELM** ruled c653–63.

It has been suggested that Swithhelm was one of the brothers responsible for murdering his predecessor, SIGEBERT THE GOOD. If this was so then it was a miraculous repentance, for the murderer had been excommunicated because of an unlawful marriage and a persistence in pagan ways. Swithhelm was baptized by Cedd, the bishop to the East Saxons, in the royal court of Rendlesham in East Anglia. It seems an unlikely event for a murderer, particularly a regicide. Swithhelm apparently ruled jointly with his brother Swithfrith, but nothing more is said of their reign. It seems likely, however, that after the rise to power of WULFHERE in Mercia in 658, Swithhelm changed his allegiance from Northumbria to Mercia.

[I9;G13] **SIGEHERE** ruled East Saxons 663–88; Kent, 687–8.

Although Sigehere's predecessors, SIGEBERT (II) and SWITHHELM, were both Christians, it is evident that the faith was still not deeply embedded amongst the East Saxons. In 664, soon after Sigehere succeeded to the kingship, there was a plague. Unable to believe that there was salvation hereafter, Sigehere turned his back on Christianity and re-opened the pagan temples, although his co-ruler SEBBI remained steadfast in the faith. WULFHERE of Mercia, to whom Sigehere had almost certainly sworn fealty, sent his bishop Jaruman to reconvert Sigehere, in which he was successful. It was at this time that Eorcenwald, who would later become Bishop of St Paul's, founded a monastery at Barking for his sister, Athelburh, which became noted for its miracles. Sigehere married Osyth, the niece of Wulfhere, and daughter of FRITHUWOLD of Surrey. Their son was the golden youth OFFA of Essex. Sigehere benefitted from his association with Mercia, but when CAEDWALLA of Wessex began his rampage across southern England, Sigehere also supported him. Evidently Sigehere was as happy to run with the hare as with the hounds. After Caedwalla conquered Kent he first installed his brother MUL as king, but Mul was promptly murdered. Caedwalla died soon after and Sigehere stepped into the vacuum. He ruled both Essex and Kent (probably only West Kent) in his final year, and almost certainly secured the succession of his second cousin, SWAEFRED, in Kent.

[I10] **SEBBI** ruled 663–93.
Sebbi ruled jointly with his cousin SIGEHERE, but whereas Sigehere returned briefly to paganism during the plague of 664, Sebbi remained true to the faith. In fact he was so devout that many believed he was more suited to the church than to secular rule. He also remained loyal to the kings of Mercia, whilst Sigehere switched sides when necessary. Part of the battle between Wessex and Mercia was for control of London, and the key to this was the Church of St Paul's which came under the secular authority of Essex. Sebbi's devoutness ensured that the church remained secure under his control. In his final year Sebbi fell painfully ill, and he resigned from the throne and retired to a monastery. Bede reports that on his death bed Sebbi had a vision which allowed him to die in peace. Furthermore, Sebbi's tomb was apparently too short, but when they came to lay Sebbi to rest they discovered the tomb had miraculously lengthened. Because of these events Sebbi became venerated as a saint. He was buried in St Paul's. His sons, SWAEFRED, who had already been made king of Kent, and SIGEHEARD succeeded him.

[I11] **SIGEHEARD** ruled 693–c707.
During the comparatively long reigns of SEBBI and SIGEHERE it seems that allowances were made for the growing princes to rule as sub-kings over parts of the kingdom. Sigeheard was attesting charters alone in Middlesex before the death of Sebbi, and seems to have remained in that part of the kingdom while his brother, SWAEFRED ruled first Kent, then Essex. We do not know when Sigeheard died, but it must have been by 707 when OFFA came briefly to the throne.

[I12;G15] **SWAEFRED or SWAEFHEARD** ruled West Kent, 689–92; East Saxons, 693–c707.
It is not certain whether Swaefred and Swaefheard are variant spellings of the same king or were brothers. The weight of evidence suggests they were the same king. Swaefred succeeded Sigehere in West Kent, which was then a client kingdom to Mercia, and the arrangement must have been sanctioned by the Mercian king ATHELRED. On Sebbi's death, however, Swaefred (or his brother Swaefheard?) was elevated to senior king of the East Saxons. We do not know when Swaefred or his co-ruler SIGEHEARD died, but it must have been by 707 when OFFA came briefly to the throne.

[I13] **OFFA** ruled 707–709.
Offa was the saintly and golden child of SIGEHERE and his wife Osyth, the niece of WULFHERE of Mercia. According to Bede the youth was "so lovable and handsome" that everyone yearned for him to become king, but no sooner had he become so he turned his back on the secular life, and joined his cousin CENRED of Mercia on his pilgrimage to Rome, where he became a monk and retired to a cloistered life. Bede may not have been telling the whole story, even though it was within his living memory. There were probably power struggles within the ruling family. A distant cousin, SAELRED, came to power and doubtless sought to dispose of potential rivals. Offa may not have been suited to kingship in any case, though it is evident, in Bede's memory at least, that he was sadly missed.

[I14] **SAELRED** or **SELERED** ruled 709?–46; and
[I15] **SWEBERT** ruled 709–38

Details of the later East Saxon kings are sparse. Despite the apparent length of Saelred's reign we know little about him. He came from a more distant branch of the ruling family and it is possible that there was a power struggle when he came to the kingship. During his reign, and that of his co-ruler Swebert, London increased in importance as a port. Essex remained subordinate to Mercia, and gradually during the reign of ATHELBALD of Mercia, the Mercians took over more control of London and the Thames. Power struggles re-emerged later in Saelred's reign, for the ASC records that in the year 746 he was slain. It does not say whether this was the result of an internal struggle or of a deterioration in Saelred's relationship with Mercia. He was succeeded by a distant cousin, SWITHRED.

[I16] **SWITHRED** ruled 746–59.

During Swithred's reign the East Saxons lost control of London to the Mercians, and Swithred established a new capital at Colchester. The East Saxon kingdom now took on a closer form to the modern county of Essex. By the end of Swithred's reign OFFA was firmly entrenched as ruler of Mercia and Essex had become little more than a client kingdom.

[I17] **SIGERIC** ruled 759–98.

Sigeric's reign coincides almost exactly with that of OFFA's of Mercia. As there is no evidence of hostility between the two kingdoms, and as Sigeric retained the title of king, we must deduce that the two monarchs were on good terms. Essex had long had a strong relationship with Mercia and this clearly continued. Although Mercia had taken control of London, both as its major port and, from Offa's reign, as its mint, it is possible that Offa continued to rely on officials from Essex to run the city. Sigeric was the son of SAELRED, who had been murdered in 746, and it is interesting to note that from Sigeric on, the ruling family shifted solely to his line and away from the original ruling group. Perhaps Sigeric was the victor of a dynastic struggle between families. If so, then he secured a strong position. It is unlikely that he was young when he came to the throne, and was probably in his late twenties, which means he would have been in his late sixties when he abdicated in 798 to undertake a pilgrimage to Rome. No more is recorded of him and he presumably died there soon after.

There was a later Sigeric identified as a "minister" in Essex, witnessing charters issued by WIGLAF of Mercia during the 830s, demonstrating that even after the kingdom had been absorbed into Wessex, the strong administrative relationship between Essex and Mercia continued.

[I18] **SIGERED** ruled 798–825.

The last king of Essex. After 811 his title as king was demoted by CENWULF of Mercia to that of "duke" or ealdorman. Sigered was the son of the elderly SIGERIC and was probably already in his thirties or forties when he became king. He must have been close to his sixties when, in 825, EGBERT of Wessex, through his son ATHELWOLF, conquered Kent and forced Essex into submission. There is no evidence to suggest that Sigered was killed, but he may have abdicated. His son, Sigeric, seems to have continued in control as the "minister" of the county.

J. EAST ANGLIA

The kingdom of the East Angles covered modern Norfolk, Suffolk, and parts of Cambridgeshire and Bedfordshire. Although this kingdom acknowledged the sovereignty of Mercia at different times it remained fiercely independent until overrun by the Danes.

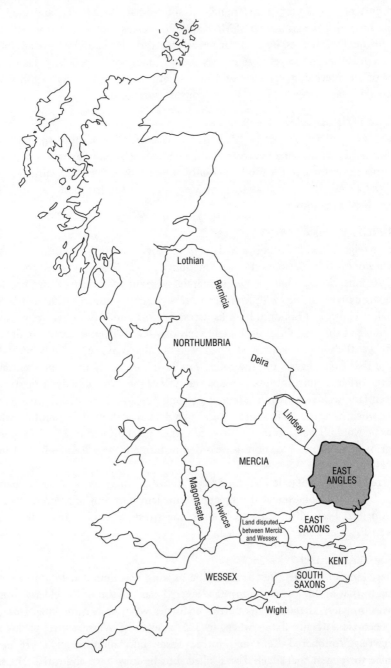

Map 7d **The Anglo-Saxon Kingdoms – East Angles**

13. Anglo-Saxon Kingdoms (3) – **East Angles**

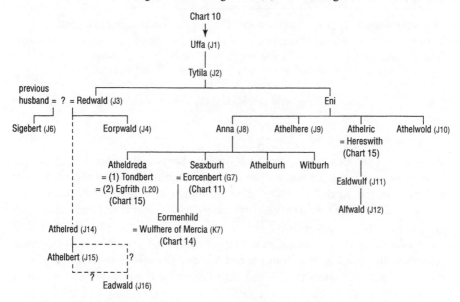

Note: The relationship between many of the East Anglian rulers is uncertain.
1. Sigebert (J6) is noted as a half-brother of Eorpwald but not as a son of Redwald so was probably a stepson from his wife's earlier marriage, probably amongst the East Saxon dynasty.
2. Egric (J7) is noted as a "kinsman" of Sigebert. He was probably a paternal cousin.
3. Athelred was descended from Redwald but his forebears and his relationship to Beonna (J13) is not known.

Ref.	Ruler	Born	Reign	Died	Notes
J1.	Uffa		571–c8		
J2.	Tytila		c578–c99		
J3.	Redwald		c599–c625	c625	
J4.	Eorpwald		c625–c32	c632	murdered
J5.	Ricbert		c632–c34		
J6.	Sigebert		c634–c38	c641	retired to a monastery; killed in battle
J7.	Egric		c638–c41	c641	killed in battle
J8.	Anna		c641–c53	c653	killed in battle
J9.	Athelhere		c653–5	655	killed in battle
J10.	Athelwold		655–c63	c663	
J11.	Ealdwulf		c663–c713	c713	
J12.	Alfwald		c713–c49	c749	
J13.	Beonna		c749–c61		
J14.	Athelred		c761–90		
J15.	Athelbert		790–4	794	beheaded

Overrun by Mercia 794–6

| J16. | Eadwald | | c796–c9? | | |

Overrun by Mercia c799–823? Technically became subject to Wessex after 829 but the following kings retained a high degree of independence.

| J17. | Athelstan | | c823–37 | ?852 | may be the same as G29 |

Ref.	Ruler	Born	Reign	Died	Notes
J18.	Athelweard		837–50?		may have ruled jointly with below
J19.	Beorhtric		852–4		
J20.	Edmund	c841	854–69	869	killed in battle
J21.	Oswald		c870		

Hereafter colonized by Danes who established their own kingdom of East Anglia (see page 466 for details).

[J1] **UFFA** or **WUFFA** ruled c571–c8.

The eponymous ancestor of the East Anglian kings, who were known as the Uffingas or Wuffingas. He was the son of Wehha who is sometimes regarded as the first ruler of the Angles. Nothing much is known of either leader. It has been conjectured that they may have been of Scandinavian rather than Germanic origin, but there is little to substantiate this. They must have settled in eastern England in the middle of the sixth century, at the time of a major Germanic invasion, giving rise to the kingdoms in Northumbria and Mercia. These were different peoples to those who were already settling in southern England and establishing territories in Hampshire and Kent. Those who created the East Anglian kingdom are amongst the least known, because subsequent Viking invasions destroyed most of the records. Nevertheless the East Anglians must have quickly established a firm hold on their lands for they soon became wealthy.

[J2] **TYTILA** ruled c578–c99.

The son of UFFA and father of REDWALD. We know nothing of Tytila but the *ASC* records that in the year 597 CEOLWULF of Wessex "made war against" the Angles. Though this was probably the Mercians, there is no reason to doubt that Ceolwulf's ambitions would have brought him up against Mercia's neighbours who, at that time, had probably still not firmly established their identity. The Devil's Dyke near Newmarket was as likely to have been a defence erected at about this time against the West Saxons as against the East Saxons. Tytila may even have died in a defence of the Dyke, which has been dated to about the end of the sixth century.

[J3] **REDWALD** ruled c599–c625.

Redwald was listed by Bede as a *bretwalda*, or overlord, of the English, who rose to power during the reign of ATHELBERT of Kent. It has been suggested on tempting but flimsy evidence that the magnificent burial site found at Sutton Hoo, near Rendlesham, which contains some of the greatest treasures of the Saxon age, was the tomb of Redwald. Even though this is not certain it does demonstrate the richness and power of the East Anglian kingdom during Redwald's reign, one that is unlikely to have happened over night. Redwald must have inherited a strong power base from his father TYTILA to allow him to develop and establish his kingdom. Nevertheless most of our knowledge of Redwald comes from Bede. He was a pagan who was converted to Christianity at the court of Athelbert in Kent but who, under the influence of his wife, reverted to his pagan ways. Apparently he maintained a temple with both a Christian and a pagan altar. Bede's view of Redwald was probably influenced by these dual standards when he stated that he was "noble by birth though ignoble in his deeds", but we may presume that as

Redwald asserted his authority over southern England in the early years of the seventh century, that he used fair means and foul to gain the ascendancy. Because of his power EDWIN, the exiled prince of Northumbria came to Redwald's court for refuge. ATHELFRITH of Northumbria sought to bribe Redwald to murder Edwin, which is also indicative of how Redwald was regarded, but apparently Redwald's wife rebuked him, saying that to murder a guest was dishonourable. In any event, Redwald used this to his advantage. In 616, Athelbert of Kent died, and Redwald took the opportunity to grab power. He raised an army and marched against Athelfrith, whom he defeated and killed on the banks of the River Idle, probably near Bawtry south of Doncaster. Redwald restored Edwin to the Northumbrian throne. During the next decade Redwald was regarded as the senior monarch

*Motif from a purse lid,
Sutton Hoo*

amongst the English, which means he probably exerted authority as overlord over Kent and Mercia. By the early 620s his power was being eclipsed by Edwin. We do not know for sure when Redwald died. The suggested date of 620 is almost certainly too early, based on the evidence of his son's death, and the general view is that he died around 624 or 625. He was succeeded by his son EORPWALD.

[J4] **EORPWALD** ruled c625–c32.

He was originally a pagan until converted to Christianity by EDWIN of Northumbria. Soon after he was murdered by RICBERT because of his Christian beliefs. It was not until the reign of his half-brother, SIGEBERT, that Christianity took a stronger hold on the East Angles.

[J5] **RICBERT** ruled c632–c4.

Ricbert is identified by Bede as the pagan who murdered the recently converted king EORPWALD. What Bede is not clear about is whether Ricbert then assumed the throne; he only states that "the kingdom remained in error for three years." It suggests there may have been a non-Christian usurper, and that he in turn was deposed when Eorpwald's brother SIGEBERT returned to claim the throne. If Ricbert did reign then he must have been a member of the ruling family, probably a cousin of Eorpwald's.

[J6] **SIGEBERT** ruled c634–c8.

[J7] **EGRIC** ruled c638–c41.

Sigebert was the brother of EORPWALD and probably the stepson of REDWALD. Bede records that he sought refuge in France to escape the wrath of Redwald. Sigebert was a devout Christian, and a disagreement may have arisen over Redwald's continued pagan worship. East Anglia remained pagan, for although Eorpwald was converted by EDWIN of Northumbria, he was murdered soon after. Sigebert eventually returned to England after ten or more years in exile and succeeded in claiming the throne in about the year 634. Sigebert had sufficient religious zeal to set about converting the East Anglians, in which he was helped by bishop Felix, who was sent to Sigebert by Honorius, archbishop of Canterbury. Felix established his bishopric at Donmoc, which is usually treated as Dunmow, but may have been Felixstowe. Sigebert also ensured that monastery schools were established in East Anglia. Sigebert eventually retired to a monastery after five years, leaving the kingdom in the hands of his kinsman EGRIC, whom we are told was already ruling in part of the land. Possibly some of the division between the North Folk and South Folk was already starting. Sigebert apparently remained in the monastery for several years, but around 640 or 641 East Anglia came under attack by PENDA of Mercia. The East Angles pleaded with Sigebert to lead them into battle. Remaining true to his Christian beliefs Sigebert went into battle with only a staff, and was cut down and killed, along with Egric. Sigebert's holy death caused him to be venerated as a saint.

[J8] **ANNA** ruled c641–c53.

Anna was the nephew of REDWALD and came to rule East Anglia when his cousins SIGEBERT and EGRIC were killed in battle. He was probably about thirty at the time. Penda did not press home his advantage and Anna must have sufficiently restored the defences of his land, because a few years later, in about 645, CENWEALH of Wessex found refuge in East Anglia when Penda drove him out of Mercia. Anna had probably not expected to rule and it seems likely he had planned to dedicate himself to the Church as he was renowned for his Christian devotion. He converted Cenwealh to Christianity and raised four daughters, all of whom became saints. The most famous of these was Æthelthryth or Atheldreda, who late in life founded the abbey of Ely. She was married twice, the second time to EGFRITH of Northumbria, but she retained her virginity. Her name later devolved into Audrey. She loved necklaces and later fairs held in her honour on St Audrey's day used to sell necklaces and scarves many of which were cheap and shoddy and were called "tawdry" after St Audrey. Her sister Athelburh became abbess of Faremoutiers-en-Brie in France, while a third sister, Seaxburh, became the wife of EORCENBERT of Kent, founded the monastery of Minster-in-Sheppey and later became the abbess of Ely. Her daughter, Eormenhild (Anna's granddaughter), married WULFHERE of Mercia. Around the year 650 there was another fierce Mercian attack on East Anglia and Anna was briefly expelled from the kingdom. At this time the Mercians destroyed one of the new monasteries, possibly Burgh Castle in Norfolk. Penda gained considerable ground over the previously autonomous Middle Angles (who lived between Mercia and East Anglia) and established his son PEADA as king over them. Although Anna regained his kingdom he died in a third onslaught by the Mercians.

[J9] **ATHELHERE** ruled c653–15 November 655.

After the death of ANNA in battle against the Mercians, PENDA imposed his sovereignty over the East Angles. Although Athelhere, Anna's brother, was not a puppet ruler, he did regard Penda as his overlord and he led his own contingent alongside Penda in the battle of Winwæd in which both he and Penda were killed.

[J10] **ATHELWOLD** ruled c655–c63.

Brother and successor of ATHELHERE. With the death of PENDA the Mercian power over East Anglia was temporarily curbed, and it seems more likely that Athelwold came under the sphere of influence of Northumbria. Certainly Essex, which had been closely allied with Mercia, suffered a setback and it is possible that Athelwold sought to exercise some authority over Essex. Their king SWITHHELM was baptized at Athelwold's court at Rendlesham, north of Ipswich. However the rapid return to power of Mercia under WULFHERE must again have threatened East Anglia, although Athelwold benefited from the marriage of his niece's daughter, Eormenhild, to Wulfhere. We do not know Athelwold's age, though he was probably quite old when he died. He was succeeded by his nephew EALDWULF.

[J11] **EALDWULF** ruled c663–c713.

Ealdwulf was the son of Athelric, a brother of ANNA, whilst his mother Hereswith was the daughter of a nephew of EDWIN of Northumbria. He is recorded as reigning for fifty years, the longest known reign of any Saxon ruler, and yet virtually nothing remains to tell us who he was or what he achieved. To have ruled for so long during these turbulent times tells us that he must have been able to develop a good working relationship with both Mercia and Northumbria. That he was descended from the Northumbrian royal family might have made him beholden to their kings, especially EGFRITH, but this would have made him a natural enemy of his close neighbours the Mercians, whose ruler WULFHERE was intent on dominating all of Saxon Britain. Since Wulfhere did not conquer East Anglia we can only deduce that he made an alliance with Ealdwulf that worked to their mutual benefit. A long reign, with minimum warfare, usually means a prosperous country and it is probable that trade in East Anglia flourished during Ealdwulf's day. This is emphasised with the gradual introduction of coinage into East Anglia late in his reign. Yet it is surprising that if this were so, his name is not better recorded in documents outside East Anglia. He must have been into his seventies when he died.

[J12] **ALFWALD** ruled c713–c49.

The son and successor of EALDWULF. Since Ealdwulf ruled for fifty years, Alfwald must either have been a younger son (elder brothers, if he had any, may already have died) or was comparatively elderly when he came to the throne, although since he also reigned for at least thirty-six years he is unlikely to have been much older than forty. We know nothing of Alfwald's reign. Felix, the author of the *Life* of St Guthlac, dedicated the book to Alfwald; whilst Alfwald is identified as the author of a letter of support to St Boniface. These small facts tell us that Alfwald was a devoted Christian, but so were all of the later kings of East Anglia. Like his father before him, Alfwald must have worked in alliance with Mercia to sustain his independence, but it seems that Mercian authority was imposed from about 740 on. East Anglian prosperity remained.

[J13] **BEONNA** ruled *c*749–*c*61.

Beonna was the successor of ALFWALD, but we do not know his relationship. His name is more suggestive of the Middle Angles than the East Angles and he may have been either a usurper or a more distant relative. Initially Beonna shared the kingdom with Hun and Alberht, two otherwise unknown kings, but Beonna emerged as the dominant ruler. Not only were coins minted in his name, but they were of increased silver content, suggesting that the prosperity of East Anglia grew during his reign. Like his predecessors, Beonna seems to have remained on good terms with Northumbria yet continued to withstand the growing might of Mercia. How they achieved this is not known, but it must almost certainly be linked to the agricultural and trading prosperity of East Anglia, from which Mercia must also have benefited.

[J14] **ATHELRED** ruled *c*761–*c*90.

A descendant of REDWALD and successor of BEONNA, although the relationship between these later East Anglian kings is not known. Athelred reigned throughout the rule of OFFA of Mercia and it is inconceivable that Offa would not have overrun East Anglia had there not been a strong alliance between the two kingdoms.

[J15] **ATHELBERT** ruled 790–4.

The son and successor of ATHELRED. All we know about him comes from twelfth-century sources and is unreliable as history. There is no doubt that Athelbert came into conflict with OFFA of Mercia, but quite what happened that led to Offa ordering Athelbert's execution is not known. The core of the story is that Athelbert was visiting Offa's royal villa at Sutton Walls in Hereford, apparently seeking marriage of Offa's daughter Alfthryth. Maybe the two rulers clashed over negotiating an alliance, but it is extremely unusual for a king to order an execution of a fellow king, short of betrayal or treachery. Anything on this scale you would expect to find in surviving Mercian documents, but the written record remains silent. However, the fact that he was subsequently venerated as a saint, not just in East Anglia, but in Hereford and Gloucestershire, suggests that he must have sought to strike some blow for freedom from the oppression of Offa. Later tradition suggests that Offa suspected him of reconnoitring Offa's defences prior to an attack. His body was buried at Marden, by the river Lugg but was later translated to Hereford, where the cathedral is dedicated to him. After his death Offa assumed control of East Anglia.

[J16] **EADWALD** ruled 796–9?

After the death of OFFA of Mercia it appears that Eadwald managed to regain the kingdom of East Anglia. It looks unlikely that he kept the kingdom for long, as CENWULF sought to re-establish Mercian authority. Eadwald had sufficient control to mint coins in his name around the year 798, but Cenwulf was using the East Anglian mint by 805. How much authority Eadwald retained in the years between is not certain, but it was probably limited. We do not know who Eadwald was, though it is likely he was a close relative of ATHELBERT. East Anglian control was wrestled from the Mercians by ATHELSTAN in 825.

[J17;G29?] **ATHELSTAN** ruled 825–37.

The *ASC* records that in 825 the king of the East Angles turned to EGBERT of Wessex for help in overthrowing the Mercian domination and later that year the East

Angles killed BEORNWULF, the Mercian king. The East Anglian king is not named, but it is likely it was Athelstan. The suggestion is that he may already have been a client ruler under Mercia for some years and at some uncertain date succeeded EADWALD. The number of coins minted in Athelstan's reign, however, suggests he may have increased his authority earlier, most likely after the death of CEOLWULF of Mercia in 823. Although East Anglia became subject to Wessex after 829, it does not appear that EGBERT or ATHELWOLF imposed their authority, and Athelstan and his successors continued to reign with a degree of autonymy. It has been suggested that Athelstan was the son of Egbert, which is a tempting idea as it would explain why East Anglia retained such a high degree of independence. It may also mean that he is the same ATHELSTAN who ruled Kent after 839.

[J18] **ATHELWEARD** ruled 837–50; and
[J19] **BEORHTRIC** ruled c852–4
Athelweard ruled East Anglia subject to the overlordship of ATHELWOLF of Wessex. We know nothing about him beyond his coinage, and even the length of his reign is uncertain, though it has been suggested that he was the son of his predecessor ATHELSTAN. It is possible that he continued to reign until the year 854 and that he then shared the kingdom with Beorhtric who, from his name, may have been a Mercian or Middle Angle (possibly a relative of BEORHTWULF of Mercia). These kings seem to have remained independent of Wessex, despite Athelwolf's sovereignty, but almost all record of them was eradicated by the Viking invasion of 869 when Athelweard's successor EDMUND was slain.

[J20] **EDMUND** ruled 854–69.
The last independent king of the East Angles. He was born about the year 841, and his coronation is recorded as happening on Christmas Day 854, though he would have been only thirteen. Because so few records exist of the East Anglian monarchy, there is no further mention of him until 865. In the winter of that year (865/6) the Danes settled in East Anglia. At that stage they evidently made peace, were allowed to set up winter quarters, and were even given horses. The Danes now used this as a base to harry the lands to the north and west. By 869, when they returned to establish winter quarters at Thetford, Edmund determined to expel them. Their force, under IVARR, was too great and in the ensuing battle at Hellesdon, Edmund was captured, his men slain, and East Anglia overrun. Edmund was apparently flayed, tortured and killed. One legend states that he was beheaded, and his soldiers found the head guarded by a wolf, which is why one of Edmund's symbols is that of a wolf. When, in 915, his body was removed from Hellesdon and buried at Bedricsworth (which later became known as Bury St Edmunds), it was found to be incorrupt, and a cult grew around his memory. Within a century he was regarded as one of England's patron saints, a position he held until well into the fifteenth century when he was gradually displaced by St George. After Edmund, the Danes who dominated East Anglia were ruled first by Ivarr and then by GUTHRUM, but it seems they allowed the native royal family to exercise some administrative control over affairs. The name ATHELRED on some East Anglian coins is probably that of ATHELRED of Wessex but may just possibly be a native ruler.

[J21] **OSWALD** ruled *c*870.

After the death of EDMUND, the Danes imposed their authority over East Anglia, though it seems they allowed the native royal family to exercise some control. The name Oswald appears on some local coinage, although the name is not typical of East Anglian royalty. He may have been an official imposed upon the East Anglians from York, where the Danes had also established themselves, or he was a representative of a lesser line of the East Anglian royal family. His authority must have ceased by 879 when ALFRED of Wessex made GUTHRUM king of East Anglia under his baptized name of Athelstan.

For the Danish kingdom of East Anglia turn to page 466.

K. MERCIA
(including Hwicce, Lindsey and the Magonsæte)

Mercia was one of the three major kingdoms of Anglo-Saxon England. Its kings were Angles. Its earliest rulers almost certainly ruled a much smaller territory around Tamworth and Lichfield. At its greatest extent Mercia covered all of central England south of the Humber and north of the Thames, and held authority over territories south of the Thames, especially Sussex and Kent. Its ruler Offa was the greatest of all English kings before Alfred the Great.

Ref.	Ruler	Born	Reign	Died	Notes
K1.	Creoda or Crida		*c*585–*c*93		may be the same as K39
K2.	Pybba		*c*593–*c*606		
K3.	Ceorl		*c*606–*c*26		
K4.	Penda	*c*604	*c*626–55	655	may have shared rule for a period; killed in battle.
K5.	Eowa		*c*635–42	642	co-ruler and possible rival claimant
K6.	Peada	*c*629	*c*653–6	656	murdered

Peada was sub-king of the Middle Angles and briefly sub-king of Southern Mercia after 655, Oswy of Northumbria held authority over Mercia between 655 and 658.

Ref.	Ruler	Born	Reign	Died	Notes
K7.	Wulfhere	*c*640	658–75	675	
K8.	Athelred	*c*642	675–704	716	abdicated and retired to a monastery
K9.	Cenred or Coenred		704–9		abdicated and went to Rome as a monk
K10.	Ceolred		709–16		died of madness (or possibly poisoned)
K11.	Athelbald		716–57	757	murdered by his own soldiers
K12.	Beornred		757		
K13.	Offa		757–96	796	
K14.	Egfrith		Jul–Dec 796	796	ruled jointly with his father from 782
K15.	Cenwulf or Coenwulf		796–821	821	
K16.	Ceolwulf (I)		821–3		deposed

Map 7e **The Anglo-Saxon Kingdoms – Mercia and sub-kingdoms**

K17.	Beornwulf	823–6	826	killed during a revolt
K18.	Ludeca	826–7	827	killed during a revolt
K19.	Wiglaf	827–9		expelled by Egbert of Mercia
		830–9	839	regained the kingdom
K20.	Wigmund	c839–40?	840	may have been only sub-king

14. Anglo-Saxon Kingdoms (4) – Mercia and Lindsey

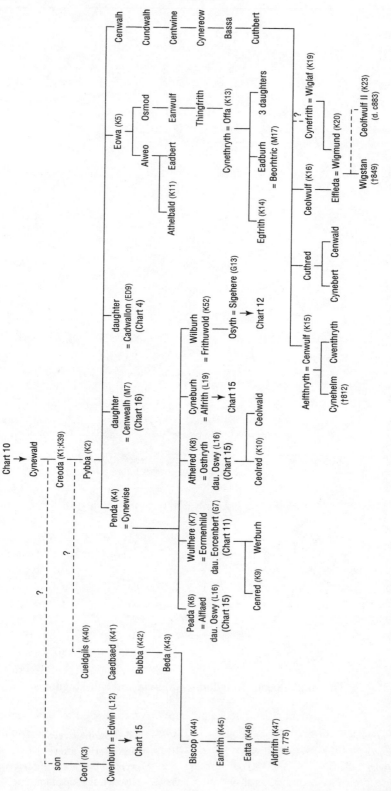

Note:
1. Although they claimed relationship to the Mercian royal family it is not known where Beornred (K12), Beornwulf (K17) and his son Beornred was the father of Beorhtric (M17) who married Eadburh and that Beornwulf was his son or nephew, but this is unproven. It is possible that Beornred was the

2. The descent of Aldfrith of Lindsey from Creoda is unproven but possible.

Ref.	Ruler	Born	Reign	Died	Notes
K21.	Beorhtwulf		840–52		
K22.	Burgred		852–74?		expelled and retired to Rome
K23.	Ceolwulf II		874–c83	c883	

Hereafter Mercia came under the control of Wessex. Alfred established the title of "Lord of the Mercians" whose holders ruled with sub-regnal authority.

Ref.	Ruler	Born	Reign	Died	Notes
K24.	Athelred		c883–911	911	
K25.	Athelflaed	c869	911–18	918	
K26.	Elfwynn	c898	918–19?		deprived of her lands

In 919 Edward the Elder of Wessex took control of Mercia. He installed his son Athelstan as king of Mercia in 924, but after his brother's death, Athelstan united Mercia and Wessex.

[K1] **CREODA** or **CRIDA** ruled Mercia (and Lindsey?), c585–c93.

Creoda is usually cited as the first king of Mercia, though precisely what that means needs some clarification. The later genealogies show that Creoda was the son of Cynewald, son of Cnebba, son of Icel, from whom the rulers of Mercia are known as the Iclingas. One concludes from this that Icel was probably the first of this family of Angles to land in Britain, but where this was and where they settled has not been determined. There is some possibility that they originally settled in East Anglia, particularly around the Wash, and later generations made their way further inland. This would bring them up not only against remnants of the British in the middle of Britain but against the West Saxons who had settled in the south and were driving northwards. The *ASC* records that Creoda died in 593, the same year as CEAWLIN of Wessex, and though it does not say that they fought each other, it suggests that there were some clashes between the Angles migrating west and the Saxons moving north. Creoda was probably the first of the Iclingas to establish a hold on the territory that later developed into Mercia, but it is unlikely that this was of any significant size. Its location was likely to be in the south-west Midlands around Lichfield. It is possible one of Creoda's children interbred with the British royal family of Lindsey and established a dynasty there (*see* K39 *below*).

The name also appears in the genealogy of the West Saxons as a son of CERDIC and father of CYNRIC. The name is almost certainly included in error, though it does help explain some of the chronological anomalies in the sequence of early Saxon kings. Although there could be more than one Creoda, the name is of Angle origin, not Saxon, and is unlikely to feature in the pedigree of the Gewisse.

[K2] **PYBBA** or **PIBBA** ruled c593–c606.

Pybba was the son of CREODA and father of PENDA. The dating of his reign is difficult because of the presence of another known ruler of Mercia, CEORL, whose name does not feature in the genealogies. His achievements are thus a little uncertain. All we can deduce is that Pybba must have continued to build upon the success of his father in establishing the territory of the Angles in the Cotswolds and, in all likelihood, began to forge some relationships with the British rulers of Wales and the Marches (the words Marches and Mercia come from the same source). Among these almost certainly must have been BROCHFAEL YSGYTHROG of Powys and MEURIG of Gwent, because of the later alliance between the Welsh and the Mercians, against the Northumbrians and West Saxons, which could not have been established if the earliest rulers settled in their territory through use of force. Whether Pybba died in 606 or was deposed by Ceorl is not known.

[K3] **CEORL** or **CEARL** ruled c606–c26.

Ceorl is identified by Bede as king of the Mercians at the time of EDWIN of Northumbria's exile. Edwin married Ceorl's daughter Cwenburh who was the mother of the future king EANFRITH. However, Ceorl's name does not feature in the later genealogy of the Mercian rulers. We can conclude that he was either a usurper or, more likely, a collateral relative. If our assumption over dates is correct then when PYBBA died, his son and heir PENDA was still an infant, and Ceorl, who may have been Pybba's brother or cousin, thus ruled instead. Edwin must have stayed at Ceorl's court for some while, possibly a year or two, and his marriage with Cwenburh may have formed part of an alliance with the Mercians against the Northumbrian ruler ATHELFRITH. The latter had a major vendetta against Edwin, as he sought him out wherever he found refuge, and it is likely that Athelfrith advanced against Mercia sometime around the year 615, forcing Edwin to move on to REDWALD of East Anglia. Redwald was then the most powerful of the southern kings of the English, and probably exercised some authority over the Mercians. How long after 615 Ceorl lived is not known, but he must have been dead by 626 when Penda emerged on the scene.

[K4] **PENDA** ruled c626–15 November 655.
[K5] **EOWA** ruled c635–5 August 642.

Penda was one of the most bloodthirsty and ambitious of all the early English kings, and it was under him that the kingdom of Mercia became established as a force to be reckoned with. Although he was the son of PYBBA he does not seem to have directly succeeded his father, possibly because he was still an infant when his father died. There has been much dispute about Penda's age, length of reign and when he came to power, but one of the likeliest interpretations of the data is that he died when he was about fifty after a reign of thirty years, and since his death at the battle of Winwæd is fairly conclusively dated to 655, he must have been born about 604 or 605. Although CEORL ruled during Penda's infancy, there was nothing to stop Penda having become a sub-king part of Mercia once he reached adulthood, probably around 622. If this happened he is most likely to have been placed in charge of western Mercia, perhaps in the territory of the Hwicce or bordering on Powys, as he was most closely connected with these areas in later years. It would also have allowed him to cement some of the relationships with the British that he had enjoyed early in his reign and upon which he relied so heavily to establish his power base. It is not entirely certain whether Penda's succession was automatic. He is likely to have been challenged by the son of Ceorl, and the lack of any reference to this does not suggest it did not happen. He also had a brother, Eowa, who at some stage was reckoned as a king of the Mercians.

Penda's first victory came in the battle of Cirencester in 628 when he took on the power of the West Saxons under CYNEGILS. Although the West Saxons were not soundly defeated, the *ASC*'s reference to the two parties coming to an agreement suggests that Penda had the upper hand. It is probably at this time that the territory of the Hwicce passed from West Saxon to Mercian control. It may also be that part of the agreement was a marriage arrangement between Penda and Cynewise, whose name suggests she was almost certainly a Saxon and possibly a sister of Cynegils. Penda had in all probability used Welsh soldiers in this battle, either those of CADWALLON of Gwynedd or those of the exiled prince CYNFEDDW of Gwent. Certainly within a few years Penda had formed a strong alliance with Cadwallon, who had a ferocious antipathy toward the Northumbrians, and in 633 the combined forces of Mercians and Welsh killed EDWIN of Northumbria at Hatfield. Edwin's sons, the grandsons of Penda's predecessor Ceorl, who may have held some claim on the Mercian kingdom, also died in the battle. Cadwallon continued to press home his advantage, devastating Northumbria over the next year, but as Penda was not involved in that slaughter we must conclude that he took advantage of the chaos in the north to consolidate his kingdom in the south. He took with him Eadfrith, the son of Edwin, as a hostage and possibly with the intention of installing him as a puppet ruler in the north at some later stage. However, a few years later, he had him murdered, just one of many examples of Penda's disregard for Christian attitudes. He was a confirmed and very ardent son of Woden.

The sequence of events within Penda's reign is not entirely clear, particularly in the period between 633 and 642. During this decade Penda sought to subdue the East Angles whose former king REDWALD had been *bretwalda*. Penda killed the East Anglian kings SIGEBERT and EGRIC in battle. He probably came to an agreement with SIGEBERT THE LITTLE of the East Saxons who continued to rule, but as vassal. It is also possible that during this period tension developed between Penda and his brother Eowa. Later records suggest that the Mercians were divided between those north of the Trent and those to the south. It is possible that Eowa established himself as king of the northern Mercians whilst Penda continued to consolidate his hold on the south and east. He also strengthened his alliance with the Welsh under CYNDDYLAN of Powys so that in the year 642 Penda led a major force against the Northumbrian king OSWALD at Maserfield, later known as Oswestry. Both Oswald and Eowa were killed. Penda did not immediately press home his advantage into Northumbria, possibly learning from the earlier disaster of Cadwallon, but he established a formidable frontier between the Mercians and the Northumbrians, because it was a year before OSWY was able to recover Oswald's body from the battlefield. It does seem that a few years later Penda led a force into the north in an attempt to conquer Northumbria, but, unable to take the royal city of Bamburgh, he tried to destroy it by fire. Through the prayers of Bishop Aedán of Lindisfarne, according to Bede, the wind changed direction and threatened the Mercians so that they fled the field. It is unlikely that this alone would trouble Penda, but he probably realised Bamburgh was too well defended and retreated.

In the meantime Penda turned his attention again to the West Saxons. He had continued to live in an uneasy alliance with Cynegils, who had married Oswald of Northumbria's daughter, which probably frustrated Penda. He had sought to establish a stronger alliance by allowing the marriage of his own sister to Cynegils's son CENWEALH. However, in 645 Cenwealh abandoned his wife, and this caused Penda to take revenge. He drove Cenwealh out of Wessex and into exile with the East Anglian king ANNA. The records do not show that Penda installed himself as ruler of Wessex, and Cenwealh seems to have returned unchallenged to his kingdom three years later, but it does seem likely that during those three years

Penda exercised authority over the West Saxons. Penda subsequently taught Anna a lesson too, probably for giving refuge to Cenwealh, by driving him out of his kingdom sometime around 650. Even though Anna regained his lands, Penda later killed him in battle around 653. By now Penda believed he had sufficient authority to install his son PEADA as king of the Middle Angles. He also set about establishing further alliances through marriages. He married his daughter, Cyneburh, to ALFRITH, the son of Oswy of Northumbria. Another daughter Wilburh married the ealdorman FRITHUWOLD, who was later installed as king of Surrey. He also established a sub-kingdom of the Magonsæte in Shropshire, installing MEREWALH, who may have been another son, as king. It is also possible that Penda established the kingdom of the Hwicce around Worcester and Gloucester. With these client kingdoms and alliances, Penda had a firm hold over the lands south of the Humber; he also had an alliance with the Deirans. If he could conquer the Northumbrians he would be lord of all England. It was probably this ambition, more from delight in war and conquest than in systematic empire-building, that caused Penda to continue to devastate the north throughout the early 650s. Each time Oswy offered terms, including fabulous riches, Penda refused. Penda did take Oswy's son, EGFRITH, as hostage, and it was probably this as much as Penda's endless slaughter, that finally drove Oswy to the offensive. Bede states that Penda's army included thirty "dukes", or ealdormen, and though this may seem an exaggeration, he almost certainly outnumbered Oswy's forces quite significantly. Penda was supported by the rulers of the East Angles, Middle Angles, Powys and Gwynedd, probably augmented by Irish mercenaries, as well as Oswy's nephew ATHELWALD. By the sheer weight of numbers Penda should have won, but perhaps it was its very size that made his army difficult to control. Oswy had advanced south towards Leeds, and the two armies met on the banks of the river Winwæd, which is probably the river Went, just south-east of Leeds. The date was Sunday, 15 November 655. There had been torrential rain and the river was in full flood. Apparently the battlefield turned to a sea of mud and this worked against Penda's large army. By superior tactics Oswy succeeded in weaving through the Mercian forces and Penda, along with many of his client kings, was killed.

Penda lived and died a pagan, dedicated to his Nordic religion, yet in his later years he tolerated Christianity within his realm. All of his known children became Christians, including his successor Peada, and his daughters Eadgyth and Eadburh, who were later venerated as saints. Because of his paganism, Bede, from whom we learn the most about Penda, regarded him as a villain and a murderer. There is little doubt that Penda had no time for Christian virtues, but it does mean that our picture of him is one-sided. We have to recognize that a king who could almost single-handedly create a formidable nation out of virtually nothing and, by the end of his reign, command an army of thirty legions, had a tremendous gift as a commander and warrior. His death threw Mercia into disarray for a few years until his son, WULFHERE, emerged as the new power in the land.

[K6] **PEADA** ruled Middle Angles, c653–6; Southern Mercia, 655–6.
The son of PENDA. His father made him king of the Middle Angles around the year 653, probably on the death of ANNA of East Anglia in battle against Penda. The Middle Angles were a rather ill-defined set of peoples, who existed between the

authority of Mercia to their west and the East Angles, and seem not to have established a ruling family of their own. They were subsequently absorbed into Mercia, but their existence was briefly acknowledged with the kingship of Peada. Peada was regarded as a noble youth by Bede, but there is no reason to believe that he was much less of a pagan than his father. Peada accepted baptism because it was a condition placed by oswy of Northumbria on the marriage of his daughter Alflæd to Peada. Peada only agreed on the urging of Alflæd's brother ALFRITH, who seemed on good terms with Peada. Soon after Peada was drawn into his father's war against Oswy and was probably present at the disastrous battle of Winwæd in which Penda and many of his allies were killed. Oswy now commanded authority over northern Mercia, but allowed Peada to rule in the south. However, five months later, at Easter 656, Peada was murdered, apparently by the treachery of his wife, and probably at Oswy's instigation. Peada was probably no more than twenty-six at the time.

[K7] **WULFHERE** ruled 658–75.
After the death of PENDA of Mercia at the battle of Winwæd, oswy of Northumbria held authority over Mercia. Bede reports that after three years of Oswy's overlord-ship the ealdormen of Mercia rebelled and rallied behind Wulfhere, Penda's young son, whom they had kept concealed. Bede does not clarify Wulfhere's age, but presumably he had come of age in the time since his father's death, which means he was then either sixteen or eighteen. His actions and authority suggest that he was at least eighteen or even older. Wulfhere was soon able to regain Mercian indepen-dence, probably while Oswy was preoccupied with the rebellion of his own son ALFRITH. Wulfhere set about re-establishing Mercian authority over southern England and was able to take this even further than his father. The main difference between Wulfhere and Penda was that Wulfhere was a Christian and did not seek to establish his authority by conquest. Warfare was a last resort. Instead Wulfhere systematically developed alliances and agreements with his fellow kings in the south, with most of them either recognizing him as overlord or becoming sub-kings in the true sense. His first alliance may have been his marriage with Eormenhild, the daughter of EORCENBERT of Kent, which probably happened around the year 660. Kent had been the first Christian kingdom and had strong alliances with North-umbria. Bringing Wulfhere into their fold must have seemed a major coup, but by the same token, Wulfhere could now command some of the authority of the church at Canterbury in his own dealings. He used this authority to subjugate Essex under king SWITHHELM, and this almost certainly allowed Wulfhere access to the port of London, which was now growing in importance. This allowed Wulfhere to install Wine, the expelled bishop of the West Saxons, in London in 670. Although Wulfhere did not exert the same authority over the East Angles, there is no record of conflict between them. Wulfhere did take control of Lindsey, the kingdom to the north of East Anglia, and in controlling Essex he effectively hemmed East Anglia in, and probably forced their king EALDWULF into an alliance.

Sometime around 660 Wulfhere must have expanded Mercia to the west, filling the vacuum in Powys left by the death of CYNDDYLAN, and thus bringing Shropshire and Herefordshire under Mercian control. It may have been at this time, rather than during Penda's reign, that the sub-kingdoms of the Magonsæte and Hwicce were established, under MEREWALH and EANFRITH. Wulfhere then moved south, imposing his authority over Sussex and either installing ATHELWALH as king or at the least ensuring Athelwalh recognized his overlordship. This advance was Wulfhere's main offensive. He drove the West Saxons out of Sussex and eastern Hampshire, but never exploited this by conquering the West Saxons in the heartland of their domain. Wulfhere extended his power east, establishing his brother-in-law FRITHUWOLD in 670 as king of Surrey, which at that time almost certainly extended west around London. Surrey had originally been under the control of Wulfhere's other brother-in-law EGBERT of Kent, but it seems that by 670 Wulfhere was now exercising greater authority over Kent. In 673, on the death of Egbert, Wulfhere stood as guardian to Egbert's young sons EADRIC and WIHTRED, effectively ruling Kent through them. It was under Wulfhere's aegis that the first general synod of the English church was summoned by Archbishop Theodore at Hertford on 24 September 672. This reorganized the episcopal structure of the church into smaller, less tribally-based dioceses, which in turn led to a change in the administrative base of England, through the use of these dioceses as administrative centres.

This was the height of Wulfhere's power. He was probably in his mid-thirties by then and could claim authority over all of southern England apart from Wessex and Dumnonia in the south-west, and East Anglia. It was then that pride and ambition got the better of him. In 674 he raised a confederate army of the southern kingdoms to march on Northumbria, ruled by EGFRITH. Egfrith had been a hostage in Penda's court around the year 655 and may have known the teenage Wulfhere. Egfrith's army proved too powerful, and Wulfhere was put to flight. It was his first major defeat, and was followed rapidly by an overthrow of his authority in Kent, when the men of Kent rose against him under HLOTHHERE. Wulfhere now threw his might against the West Saxons but he was again defeated in 674, by AESCWINE. It may be that Wulfhere was wounded in this battle, or that he developed an illness, but he died soon after, early in 675. Despite these later failures, he exercised more authority over England than any previous king and left a powerful legacy to his brother ATHELRED.

[K8] **ATHELRED** (I) ruled 675–704.

We learn nothing of Athelred during OSWY's overlordship and his brother's supremacy, but he may well have dedicated much of his time to the church, since he is remembered as a devout and pious man. He probably did not expect to rule Mercia, and must have been surprised at his brother's sudden death in 675. Athelred was probably in his early thirties. At about that same time he married Osthryth, the daughter of OSWY of Northumbria and the sister of EGFRITH. The two were devoted to the church and were probably well matched, but it did not stop Athelred warring against Egfrith and defeating the Northumbrian king decisively at the battle of the Trent in 679. Osthryth's brother ELFWINE was killed in the battle, and he was so beloved by both kingdoms that the grief over his death nearly led to a blood feud between the Mercian and Northumbrian royal families. This was only resolved when Archbishop Theodore negotiated the appropriate compensation. Although Northumbria did not come directly under Mercian control, this defeat ended the Northumbrian supremacy of the seventh century and made Mercia the major power in the land. Athelred was not especially aggressive, although he had already in 676 shown his power, both to HLOTHHERE of Kent and to any other insubordinate vassal, devastating Hlothhere's kingdom and sacking Rochester.

For the rest of his reign Athelred held the appropriate overlordship of England (though Bede never acknowledged this) and established a workable relationship with INE of Wessex. Athelred's main interests were religious. He and Osthryth founded the monastery at Bardney in Lindsey where Osthryth brought the remains of her uncle OSWALD, despite local opposition. It was also during Athelred's reign, in 679, that Archbishop Theodore created the bishoprics of Worcester and Hereford. Athelred was a friend of the much exiled bishop Wilfrid, and he gave Wilfrid sanctuary at Leicester when he was expelled from Northumbria in 691.

Tragedy struck Athelred in 697 when his wife was murdered by Mercian noblemen, allegedly because she had been implicated in the murder of PEADA forty years earlier. Osthryth had almost certainly already taken up the life of a nun by this time and was no longer married to Athelred, as there is some suggestion that he took a second wife. Nevertheless in 704, Athelred abdicated in order to enter the monastery at Bardney, where Osthryth was buried. He became abbot and still held some temporal influence, as two years later he summoned his successor CENRED, telling him to remain on good terms with the elderly bishop Wilfrid. Athelred lived until 716, when he must have been in his mid-seventies.

[K9] **CENRED or COENRED** ruled 704–9.
The son of WULFHERE, he succeeded his uncle ATHELRED. Cenred's reign has generally been regarded as ineffectual. He managed to hold the kingdom together although during his reign the Welsh made some territorial gains in the west. Like his uncle he was devoted to the church and in 709 he and the East Saxon king OFFA both abdicated in order to journey to Rome, where they became monks. Cenred and Offa were not only cousins but close friends, and neither seemed to enjoy the secular life. It is possible that power struggles in both the East Saxon and Mercian royal houses encouraged them to depart. Cenred was succeeded by his cousin (Athelred's son), CEOLRED.

[K10] **CEOLRED** ruled 709–16.
Ceolred's age on his succession is not known but he was believed to be the son of Athelred's second wife, which means he may only have been in his late teens when he ascended the throne. He was remembered in later years for his profligacy and wickedness, suggesting perhaps a spoilt youth who misused his power. During his comparatively short reign he seems to have abused the church, which consequently left a poor view of his life. In 715 he fought against INE of Wessex at Adam's Grave, on the Wiltshire Downs. The outcome of the battle is not recorded. However in 716 Ceolred is reported to have been overcome by madness and died at a banquet. It is possible that he may have been epileptic, but an equally possible explanation is that he was poisoned, and everyone was glad to see the end of him. He was buried at Lichfield. One record suggests he was succeeded by Ceolwald, probably his brother, but there is no other evidence of his existence. Instead a second cousin, ATHELBALD succeeded to the kingship.

[K11] **ATHELBALD** ruled 716–57.

Athelbald was the grandson of PENDA's brother EOWA, and the son of Alweo. He succeeded his second cousin CEOLRED after what may have been a dynastic coup. Athelbald had possibly sought to gain the throne earlier, during the reign of CENRED, but when Cenred abdicated, Ceolred took control and banished Athelbald into the Fenlands. Athelbald succeeded in gaining power upon the death of Ceolred, and it is possible that Athelbald had a hand in that death. Once king, Athelbald seems to have wielded authority similar to that of WULFHERE and ATHELRED, holding in check all his neighbouring kings. He had good relations with SAELRED of the East Saxons (through whom he gained increased authority over London and the commercial trade along the Thames), ALFWALD of East Anglia and WIHTRED of Kent. In 726 he is believed to have supported ATHELHEARD of Wessex in his claim to the throne so that thereafter that king was beholden to Athelbald. Athelbald succeeded in gaining land (the modern Berkshire) from Wessex in 730, and three years later Athelbald led a successful expedition into Somerset.

Athelbald had greater trouble with the Welsh. The rulers of Powys under ELISEDD were intent upon recovering lost lands in Shropshire and Herefordshire and though it is possible some of their efforts took place during the reign of Cenred, the aftermath continued into Athelbald's day. It was during the latter half of Athelbald's reign that work began on what became known as Wat's Dyke, the predecessor to Offa's Dyke, a major earthwork to denote the boundary of the Welsh and English.

In 740, Athelbald devastated Northumbria and burned York while EADBERT was fighting the Picts. That same year Athelheard of Wessex died and his successor CUTHRED felt less obliged to Athelbald. Throughout his reign Cuthred fought against Athelbald, but with little effect, and on at least one occasion, in 743, Cuthred was forced to join with Athelbald in his battles against the Welsh. Only in 752 did Cuthred achieve a notable victory over Athelbald at the battle of Beorhford.

All records suggest that Athelbald was a violent and wicked king for all that he professed Christianity. He is supposed to have used the church finances to his own ends, and forced the monks to work on his own royal building programme. There is little doubt that by Athelbald's day Mercia was an extremely wealthy kingdom and having gained authority over his neighbours, Athelbald used his wealth in ungodly ways. He never married but delighted in fornicating with nuns, and encouraged a profligate life-style amongst the monks. In 746 he was admonished by the West Saxon bishop Boniface, who beseeched him to repudiate his ways for fear he would die a violent death. This had no affect upon Athelbald, who continued as usual. Eventually in 757 his sins caught up with him and he was murdered at Seckington by his own bodyguard. He almost certainly suffered from a dynastic coup, the same fate that befell his predecessor and allowed him to come to power. He was buried at Repton. After a short period of civil war, Mercia came under the rule of its greatest king, OFFA.

Athelbald's reign was important for another reason. The extent of his authority caused him to identify himself in a charter of 746 as king of the "gens Anglorum". It was from that time that his subjects began to call themselves Aenglisc, or English. It is thanks to his authority that the English became English and not Saxons, even though the latter was still the name used by the Celts (as in Sassenachs).

[K12] **BEORNRED** ruled 757.

Little is known of Beornred beyond his name. He usurped the Mercian throne after the murder of ATHELBALD and it is possible that he had engineered the rebellion of Athelbald's troops. Beornred was almost certainly a Mercian ealdorman distantly related to the Mercian royal house. Although he was driven out of Mercia by OFFA within a few months, his descendants may have later reclaimed the throne (*see under* BEORNWULF *and* BEORHTWULF).

[K13] **OFFA** ruled 757–26 July 796.

Offa was the first Saxon king for when there is some truth in the claim that he was "king of the English", even though he had trouble holding on to parts of his kingdom. He came to power in the civil strife that followed the murder of ATHELBALD, and the brief reign of BEORNRED. He was the son of Thingfrith and claimed descent from EOWA, the brother of PENDA, and was a distant cousin of Athelbald's. It took Offa some time to gain his control over Mercia and during this period of uncertainty Mercia's hold over the surrounding kingdoms, especially Wessex (under CYNEWULF) and Kent, was reduced. The sub-kingdoms of Mercia, particularly Hwicce and Lindsey, also seem to have bid for autonomy. The king of the Hwicce, EALDRED, may well have combined forces with the Welsh, perhaps ELISEDD of Powys or his son BROCHFAEL, as there is a record of a Welsh victory at Hereford in 760. The lack of reliable contemporary records cloud Offa's activities, but the evidence of Offa's later years suggest that early in his reign he used a combination of military strength and negotiating skills to bring Mercia and its subordinate kingdoms back under his control. The *ASC* says nothing of Offa between 757 and 777, but a few other records do suggest how Offa's power grew. We may imagine that he had firmly re-established a hold on Mercia and its satellite kingdoms by about the year 760, when his energies then became re-directed against the Welsh. The Welsh threat was almost certainly not resolved at that time, and Offa may have gained a temporary respite through allowing Elisedd or Brochfael territorial gains. He then took advantage of uncertainty in the kingdom of Kent where a series of claimants following the death of ATHELBERT II in 762 weakened the hold of the native dynasty and allowed expansion by Essex under king SIGERED. Offa

From a document
in Trinity College, Dublin

used his own strength and skills to support a new claimant, HEABERHT, whom he established as a co-ruler in 764. His control over Kent was important, not only because of the trade route out of London along the Thames, but also because of the connection with Canterbury. The Kentish kings had a strong link with the kings of Francia, and it may be at this time that Offa began his own connection with the Frankish court where Charlemagne came to power in 768. It is probably at this time that Offa married Cynethryth, likely to have been a Frankish princess. She must have matched Offa with a strong character, because not only did he later add her image to his on his coinage, but she incited Offa to a number of rash acts, such as the suggested marriage of their son EGFRITH to Charlemagne's daughter, and the later murder of Athelbert of East Anglia. Cynethryth may be the first woman who could rightly claim to be regarded as queen of England.

Offa almost certainly established alliances with ATHELRED of East Anglia and SIGERIC of Essex during this period, so that by the early 770s he had re-established the power base of Mercia. However he did not have things all his own way. In 776 there was an uprising in Kent. EGBERT II, who found his authority was being increasingly ignored by Offa, took control, defeating the Mercians at the battle of Otford. Offa was unable to regain power over Kent, and soon found his energies diverted in conflict with Cynewulf of Wessex. Here Offa was more successful, defeating Cynewulf at the battle of Bensington in 779 and regaining much lost territory. Nevertheless it was not until after Cynewulf's death and the succession of BEORHTRIC in 786, that Offa could claim Wessex was subservient to him. Soon after this we find Offa successfully reimposing his authority on Kent. From 777 on he also conducted raids deep into Welsh territory, and it is probably in the 780s that he negotiated a border between the Welsh and the English and began construction of what is now known as Offa's Dyke. This remarkable earthwork, which runs almost complete for 150 miles from the estuary of the river Dee in the north to Tidenham on the Severn in the south, required extensive power and authority to construct, and remains the single biggest man-made legacy from the Saxon period. It could not have been achieved without co-operation from the Welsh rulers of Gwent and Powys, but it is likely that by this time these rulers had recognized Offa's supremacy.

It is from the mid-780s that Offa may be regarded as the most powerful Saxon ruler who had yet ruled England. He maintained that authority, however, by a policy of bloodshed and manipulation. Although he had re-established control over Kent he was still opposed by Jaenberht, the archbishop of Canterbury. The pope sent two legates to England to ensure that papal codes were being followed, and a legatine council was held in 786 in Mercia. Offa's role was strongly supported by Pope Hadrian I, who granted Offa authority to establish a separate archiepiscopal see at Lichfield. It was there, in 787, that the first (and only) archbishop of Lichfield, Hygeberht, crowned Offa's son, Egrifth, as King of the Mercians. This was an unprecedented move amongst the Saxons, and demonstrated that Offa regarded himself as king of all the English. His authority was recognized by Charlemagne, though their relationship remained sensitive. Around 789 Charlemagne entered into an agreement that his son Charles would marry Offa's daughter, but when Offa made this dependent on Offa's son Egfrith marrying one of Charlemagne's daughters, the Frankish king was so enraged that he broke off trading relations with England. They were only restored after some intense negotiations amongst the clergy, and the planned marriage never materialised. It served to suggest that whilst Offa had become the most influential of the Saxon rulers, he was not necessarily regarded as an equal on the stage of Europe. It would be true to say that Offa was a vain and ambitious king, who could be cruel and vindictive when he needed to be – his ordering the execution of Athelbert of East Anglia was proof of that – but who also sought to be wise and practical. He developed a new code of laws, which unfortunately has not survived, and he introduced the silver penny, which would remain the basis of the English coinage for the next five hundred years.

Offa sought to emulate Charlemagne and certainly hoped that his son would ultimately come to rule all of England, and possibly all of Britain. He had paved the way for his son's succession by ensuring that likely rivals amongst the royal family were put away. Although he must be regarded as a great ruler, he was almost certainly not beloved by his subjects, which is why he never became remembered as Offa the Great. The kingdom that he created would soon falter under his successors.

[K14] **EGFRITH** ruled July-December 796.
Egfrith was the son of OFFA and his queen Cynethryth. He was crowned as King of the Mercians at Lichfield in 787 while his father still ruled. This was more a recognition of Egfrith as heir rather than an official succession, for Offa continued to exercise complete authority, but it allowed Egfrith to witness charters and prepare for governance. Offa clearly groomed his son for kingship, perhaps recognizing in him similar qualities to his own. Chief amongst these was a vicious streak that had enabled Offa to prepare the ground for Egfrith's unrivalled succession by disposing of other claimants. However, when Offa died, in July 796, Egfrith survived him by only 141 days. The cause of his death is not known, and it is easy to believe it may not have been entirely natural. With his passing Offa's planned mighty dynasty ended. Egfrith was succeeded by a distant relative, CENWULF.

[K15] **CENWULF** or **COENWULF** ruled Mercia 796–821; Kent, 807–21.
Cenwulf came to power after the death of OFFA's son EGFRITH. He claimed descent from Cenwalh, a younger brother of PENDA and EOWA, though even in his day the authenticity of this pedigree was dubious. The sudden death of Egfrith, though apparently of natural causes, must be suspect and Cenwulf's ambition was itself so patently clear that one may conclude that he engineered his succession. It has been suggested that Cenwulf was related to the former royal family of Hwicce. This kingdom seems to have disappeared as a separate entity at just the time Cenwulf appeared (see EALDRED), both with their power base at Winchcombe. Whether Cenwulf was a successor to Hwicce or usurped that kingdom as a stepping stone to bigger territory is conjectural. The Northumbrian abbot Alcuin, who was an advisor at the court of Charlemagne, believed Cenwulf was a tyrant and usurper and admonished him for having disposed of his first wife in favour of another. Cenwulf had sufficient sense to bide his time upon succession to ensure papal acceptance not only of his position but a judgement on the expulsion by EADBERT PRÆN of Kent of Athelheard, the archbishop of Canterbury. Pope Leo III's response enabled Cenwulf to invade Kent, capture, mutilate and imprison Eadbert, and install his own brother CUTHRED as king. Cenwulf similarly imposed his authority on East Anglia, where

EADWALD had endeavoured to regain independence. We do not know of Eadwald's fate, but it may have been no less vicious than Eadbert's. In 799 Cenwulf concluded a peace treaty with Wessex, whose king BEORHTRIC had been installed with the support of Offa. It is testament to Cenwulf's power that he was able to re-establish Mercian authority so quickly. At this time he went so far as to style himself as king and "emperor", the first after Charlemagne to claim that title since the end of the Roman Empire. He next turned his venom against the Welsh, heading raiding parties into Powys and Gwynedd in one of which, in 798, the Welsh king CARADOG AP MEIRION was killed. He also seems to have supported an insurrection against the Northumbrian king EARDWULF, for in 801 Eardwulf led a campaign against Cenwulf which eventually resulted in peace terms.

Cenwulf remained unhappy that the primary archiepiscopal see in England was at Canterbury and he sought the pope's permission to transfer it to London. This was refused, but by 803 Cenwulf was on more amicable terms with archbishop Athelheard, and was sufficiently satisfied with his relationship with Canterbury to arrange for the see at Lichfield to be demoted to a bishopric. He came to regret this, because his relationship with the new archbishop, Wulfred, who was appointed in 805, rapidly deteriorated. Much of the argument was over the secular control of church lands. Mercia owned much land in Kent, particularly at Minster-in-Thanet and Reculver, which Wulfred believed belong to Canterbury. This brought Cenwulf and Wulfred into conflict, all the more so after Cenwulf installed himself as king of Kent after the death of his brother in 807. Their quarrel was held in abeyance for a few years but in 815, after Wulfred returned from Rome where his authority was upheld by the pope, Wulfred again sought to regulate the control of church lands. Cenwulf was so furious that he expelled Wulfred from the kingdom and refused him re-entry. Pope Paschal I allowed Cenwulf to continue his control, and though Wulfred returned, he did not regain his position until after Cenwulf's death. In the meantime Cenwulf had resumed his offensive in Wales, leading raids as far south as Dyfed, and taking advantage of dynastic struggles in Gwynedd to plunder that territory. Cenwulf's ambition was such that he probably intended to subdue the Welsh (certainly in Powys) and impose his authority over them. However, he died in 821, whilst preparing for a new offensive in northern Wales. Cenwulf was a strong king with a vicious and uncontrollable temper, some of which seems to have been inherited by his daughter Cwenthryth, who was abbess of Winchcombe in Gloucestershire, where Cenwulf was buried. Legend claims that Cwenthryth was instrumental in the murder of her brother Cynehelm (d. 812), who was heir to the throne, and though the folk tale surrounding this is more fanciful than factual, it seems likely that an ambitious streak continued in Cenwulf's daughter.

[K16] **CEOLWULF (I)** ruled Mercia and Kent, 821–3.

He was the brother of CENWULF whom he succeeded late in 821. There was an auspicious coronation on 17 September 822, but within a few months he was deposed and ousted from the kingdom by a rival claimant, BEORNWULF. Just why Ceolwulf was dethroned is not clear. He was old, probably in his early fifties, and after years in the shadow of his brother, he may have been seen as a weak king. Certainly the few surviving records show that there was considerable discord in Mercia in Ceolwulf's day. His successor was a much more vigorous king.

[K17] **BEORNWULF** ruled 823–6.

Beornwulf was probably the key player in the dethronement of CEOLWULF (I), whom he succeeded in the summer of 823. We know little of Beornwulf, but it is likely he was related to the rival royal family of the Middle Angles, previously represented by BEORNRED. Early in his reign Beornwulf showed his authority by a powerful campaign against Powys, which may have been started by Ceolwulf. The dating of the campaign is uncertain, but by 823 Powys was under Mercian control (*see under* CYNGEN AP CADELL). Beornwulf supported the election of BALDRED as king of Kent. However, EGBERT of Wessex also had designs on Kent which had been ruled by his father EALHMUND. In 825 the emerging power of Egbert caused Beornwulf to confront him at Ellendun (now Wroughton, near Swindon), where Beornwulf was defeated. Beornwulf's power began to weaken. Egbert hammered home his success in Kent and Essex and this led to a revolt in East Anglia under ATHELSTAN. When Beornwulf endeavoured to crush the rebellion he was killed.

[K18] **LUDECA** ruled 826–7.

Ludeca was a leading ealdorman of Mercia who assumed the kingship when BEORNWULF was killed. Southern England was now in an uproar. EGBERT of Wessex had taken control of Kent and Essex, and the East Anglians had seen this as an opportunity to reassert their independence. Ludeca led a second offensive against them a few months later but was himself killed.

[K19] **WIGLAF** ruled 827–9; 830–9.

Wiglaf was a Mercian ealdorman who claimed the kingship after the death of LUDECA. There is a possibility that Wiglaf's wife, Cynefrith, was related to the Mercian royal family, and he had almost certainly married her some years before. In fact Wiglaf was probably well into his forties when he came to the throne. He did not suffer the same immediate misfortune of his predecessor, but in 829 EGBERT of Wessex invaded Mercia and deposed Wiglaf. Egbert's success, though, was short-lived, for in 830 Wiglaf regained the throne. Many have wondered how Egbert's supremacy could have so easily been overturned, and it seems likely that the Frankish support that he had previously been receiving had now faded. Egbert did not seek to reimpose his authority over Mercia, and while the previous Mercian supremacy was never regained, Wiglaf did succeed in recovering a degree of control over Essex and thus over London. Wiglaf further sought to tie his dynasty in to the old ruling house by marrying his son WIGMUND to Elfleda, the daughter of CEOLWULF (I) and the only surviving heiress. Wiglaf's ability to sustain the kingdom of Mercia is impressive. He was buried at Repton, the church of the former king ATHELBALD, to whom he may thus have been related.

[K20] **WIGMUND** ruled c839–40?

It is only local tradition in Evesham that holds Wigmund ever reigned as king. It is possible his father, WIGLAF, made him sub-king in the former territory of the Hwicce, but this is not confirmed. His death must have occurred either soon before or soon after Wiglaf's, because BEORHTWULF sought to marry his son Beorhtric to Wigmund's widow Elfleda, in order to secure his succession. Wigmund was buried at Repton, as was his son Wigstan.

[K21] **BEORHTWULF** ruled 840–52.

Beorhtwulf seems to have assumed the kingship on the death of WIGLAF or possibly his son WIGMUND. Wigstan, the son of Wigmund was supported by the people as heir, but Wigstan was devoted to the church and did not wish to rule, but instead declared his mother Elfleda as regent. According to the later *Life of St Wigstan* Beorhtwulf sought to marry his son Beorhtric to Elfleda to legitimise their link with the ruling family, but Wigstan refused. The result was that in 849 Wigstan was murdered. Much of this may be later embellishment to glorify the memory of Wigstan. Beorhtwulf claimed to be a cousin of Wigstan, and may have been descended from BEORNWULF, who had deposed Elfleda's father CEOLWULF (I). Beorhtwulf may have recognized ATHELWOLF of Wessex as his overlord, as a joint coin was minted. Throughout his reign Beorhtwulf was preoccupied with conflict with Powys, whose king CYNGEN AP CADELL strove to regain territory in Shropshire and Herefordshire. At the end of his reign Beorhtwulf's forces were defeated by a Viking invasion of London in 851, though the Vikings moved on into Surrey rather than Mercia.

[K22] **BURGRED** ruled 852–74.

Burgred succeeded BEOHRTWULF, though the relationship between the two is uncertain. From the outset Burgred remained a close ally, and probably client king, to ATHELWOLF of Wessex, whose daughter Athelswith, Burgred married at Easter 853. In that same year, Burgred relied upon West Saxon forces to complement his own in an offensive against the Welsh of Powys, which almost certainly resulted in the fall of the king CYNGEN AP CADELL. Conflicts continued between Burgred and the Welsh, when Cyngen's nephew, RHODRI MAWR, claimed authority over Powys. The forces of Rhodri and Burgred clashed again in 865 when Mercian troops invaded Anglesey, the heartland of Gwynedd. Although Burgred claimed the victory, he was unable to defeat Rhodri's own forces and had to retreat because of the Viking threat. The Vikings had invaded Wessex in 851, and this common enemy had further united the Mercians and West Saxons. By 864 the Viking army under IVARR was harrying eastern England and, in 867/8, they wintered at Nottingham. Burgred was unable to dislodge them, even with a reinforcement of West Saxon soldiers, and was forced to enter into a peace treaty. The Vikings continued to tighten their hold over Northumbria and East Anglia and, in 874, wintered at Repton, one of the royal houses of Mercia. Again Burgred was unable to dislodge them, and this time he was expelled. He retired to Rome where he died.

[K23] **CEOLWULF II** ruled 874–c83.

Ceolwulf was the puppet king of the Vikings under HALFDAN and GUTHRUM, who installed him after they ejected BURGRED. Later chroniclers claimed Ceolwulf had royal descent, and it has been conjectured that he may have been the son of WIGMUND and Elfleda, and thus a grandson of CEOLWULF I. Some records attribute Ceolwulf a reign of only five years, but this five years might run from 877 when the Danes partitioned Mercia and gave a portion to Ceolwulf for his loyalty. Some might regard Ceolwulf as a traitor, but he did in fact protect Mercia from an all-out invasion. After Guthrum's defeat by ALFRED, Ceolwulf found he still retained part of Mercia – the heartland around Worcester – which he continued to rule subject to Alfred. The impressive joint coinage issued by the two kings is at least some evidence of Ceolwulf's position. It is not entirely clear whether Ceolwulf died or abdicated. If he was a younger brother of Wigstan he may well have been in his sixties by 883 and thus died of old age. Indeed his age may have been a key reason why the Vikings accepted him as their client ruler, because he was too old to cause trouble, yet his royal pedigree made him acceptable to the Mercians.

[K24] **ATHELRED (II)** ruled c883–911.
He succeeded CEOLWULF II. His pedigree is not known; his name suggests he may have come from either Mercian or West Saxon stock. Although he issued many charters in his own name, which imply a royal status, by the time of his reign Mercia was subject to ALFRED, and Athelred was at most a client king. He became better known under the title "Lord of the Mercians", though he was also styled ealdorman, the title used in the *ASC* in 886 when Athelred was entrusted with the city of London. It was likely that by this time Athelred had already married Alfred's daughter ATHELFLÆD. Athelred was noted for his hostility to the Welsh and there were many border battles. At one stage BROCHWAEL of Gwent was alleged to have sought aid from Alfred to stop Athelred's oppression. Athelred fortified Worcester and developed Gloucester, which was their seat of residence. Athelred continued in power after the death of Alfred, but his position seemed less secure during the reign of EDWARD THE ELDER. He had a debilitating disease in his final years and left much of the government to Athelflæd. He died in 911.

[K25] **ATHELFLÆD** "Lady of the Mercians", 911–12 June 918.
Athelflæd was the eldest child of ALFRED THE GREAT. In or about 884, when she was about sixteen, she married the Mercian ealdorman ATHELRED, who had been created "Lord of the Mercians" by Alfred. Athelflæd often signed charters jointly with Athelred and by 900 had started to take over the administration as Athelred's illness drained his strength. Athelflæd had inherited much of the resolve of her father, and continued her husband's campaigns against the Welsh. She also led the defence against the Vikings who, having established themselves in the north and east, now began to settle in the Wirral. Athelflæd negotiated with their leader, Ingimund, to control the settlement, but in 905 the Vikings attacked Chester, causing Athelflæd to fortify the town. Athelflæd recognized that the Vikings might destroy the Saxon relics in the north and wherever possible she sought to salvage objects of veneration. These included the relics of OSWALD of Northumbria which were translated to Gloucester in 909. When Athelred died in 911, Athelflæd continued to rule, though subject to her brother, EDWARD THE ELDER of Wessex. Athelflæd created new fortified boroughs against the Welsh and Vikings, including those at Bridgnorth and Bromsgrove, and she sought to assist the Scots and Strathclyde Britons against the Norse of Dublin and York. Athelflæd was one of the great warrior queens of England and was highly respected by her enemies. She died at Tamworth on 12 June 918, probably aged about fifty. Although she was succeeded by her daughter ELFWYNN, it is evident that she expected ATHELSTAN, the eldest son of Edward the Elder, whom she had fostered and raised, to become king, which he eventually did.

[K26] **ELFWYNN** or **ÆLFWYNN** "Lady of the Mercians", 918–19.
The daughter of ATHELRED and ATHELFLÆD, she succeeded to Mercia on the death
of her mother. She was only about twenty, and it is likely that her uncle EDWARD
THE ELDER did not feel such a young girl could control Mercia and in the following
year he deprived of her lands. Nothing more is known of her, and she probably
ended her days in a nunnery. It is likely that Edward determined to keep Mercia as
an administrative unit because upon his death he bequeathed Mercia to his eldest
son ATHELSTAN.

HWICCE

*Although a Mercian sub-kingdom, roughly equivalent to the territory of Worcestershire,
Hwicce seems to have been a much venerated territory. Its boundaries were roughly
equal to the territory of the Dobunni at the Roman conquest, and was almost certainly
the heartland of the British revival after the end of Roman authority and the home of
Ambrosius Aurelianus and possibly Arthur. It may thus have held much greater
historical and even religious significance in the seventh century than is remembered
today.*

Ref.	Ruler	Reign	Died	Notes
K27.	Eanfrith	650s?–c74		
K28.	Eanhere	c674–5?		
K29.	Osric	c675–c85		
K30.	Oswald	c685–c90		
K31.	Oshere	c679–c99		
K32.	Athelbert	fl 700		
K33.	Athelweard	fl 710		
K34.	Athelric	fl 720		
K35.	Osred	fl 730s		
K36.	Eanbert	fl 759		brothers who ruled jointly
K37.	Uhtred	fl 759		brothers who ruled jointly
K38.	Ealdred	c759–c90		brothers who ruled jointly

Thereafter Hwicce came directly under Mercian rule.

[K27] **EANFRITH** ruled c650s–c74; and [K28] **EANHERE** ruled c674–5?
Eanfrith and his brother Eanhere are the earliest known rulers of the sub-kingdom
of Hwicce, which was established in the mid seventh century. Throughout its
existence it was a satellite of Mercia, although it had relative autonomy. It may have
been established by PENDA, though it probably owes its existence more to
WULFHERE. The territory may already have had its local rulers who acknowledged
the overlordship of Mercia and perhaps, because of assistance they gave the
Mercians, were elevated to kingship. It has been suggested that Eanfrith was
descended from the Bernician royal family but apart from a certain coincidence
of names and dates the evidence is far from conclusive. The kingdom of the Hwicce
seems to have had almost a reverence amongst the Saxons as it is often referred to in
special terms, and it may have held some significance amongst the early rulers. It is
also probable that the peoples of the Hwicce were a mixture of Saxons, Angles and
Britons. Eanfrith's daughter, Eafa, married ATHELWALH of the South Saxons, a
marriage alliance which was seen as sufficiently important for Athelwalh to

recognize Wulfhere as his overlord. Eanfrith may have ruled jointly with Eanhere, but the two brothers apparently died within a year of each other in about 674/5. Their successor was OSRIC.

[K29] **OSRIC** ruled c675–c85. [K30] **OSWALD** ruled c685–c90. [K31] **OSHERE** ruled c679–c99.

These three brothers ruled parts of Hwicce jointly. It was during their reign, in 679, that the bishopric was established at Worcester by ATHELRED of Mercia. It is likely that the territory of the see equalled that of the Hwicce kingdom. Osric established the monastery of St Peter at Gloucester and another at Bath, whilst his brother Oswald founded Pershore Abbey (689), and the third brother Oshere, established minsters at Ripple, Inkberrow and Withington. Osric seems to have died first in around 685, Oswald ruled through to about 690, and Oshere may well have survived as long as 699. It is possible that Osric came into conflict with the Welsh rulers of Gwent whose history is vague at this time, but border skirmishes were common. There is uncertainty about Oshere's date of death, but the manner of it is recorded as "bitter and cruel". Since the Hwicce formed a difficult border territory between the West Saxons, the Mercians and the Welsh, it is not surprising that it was often subject to conflict. It was Oshere's sons who ruled after him.

[K32] **ATHELBERT** ruled fl 700. [K33] **ATHELWEARD** ruled fl 710. [K34] **ATHELRIC** ruled fl 720.

Sub-kings of the Hwicce during the reigns of ATHELRED and CENRED of Mercia. It is probable that they ruled jointly and may thus all have been children of OSHERE or his brothers. Apart from a few charters and land grants nothing is known of their reigns which extended through to the 720s.

[K35] **OSRED** ruled fl 730s.

Sub-king to ATHELBALD of Mercia. It is not clear whether Osred was still ruler when OFFA became king, but if he was there is a suggestion that he aided Offa in overthrowing the rival claimant BEORNRED.

[K36] **EANBERT** ruled fl 759. [K37] **UHTRED** ruled fl 759.

Eanbert appears as a ruler of the Hwicce early in the reign of Offa. It is possible, in the uncertainty at the start of Offa's reign, that Eanbert, along with his brothers Uhtred and Ealdred, sought to claim greater autonomy, but their close connection with Mercia meant that they soon returned their fealty.

[K38] **EALDRED** ruled c759–c90.

The last recorded ruler of the Hwicce. He came to the kingdom jointly with his brothers Eanbert and Uhtred early in the reign of OFFA of Mercia, and may have briefly sought to claim greater autonomy. Ealdred presumably outlived his brothers, as only his name appears attached to Offa's charters in the territory of the Hwicce towards the end of his reign, by which time Offa had relegated his position to that of ealdorman. After his death, some time around 790, there were no further recorded kings of the Hwicce. However, CENWULF, who subsequently became king of Mercia emerged from the territory of Hwicce and may have been a scion of the royal family.

LINDSEY

Roughly equivalent to Lincolnshire, the territory of the Coritani at the time of the Roman conquest. This kingdom is one of the least well documented and only the genealogy of Aldfrith provides any details on the Lindsey royal family (see page 248). We cannot assume that all of his ancestors were kings and we do not know for certain their dates. Lindsey may once have been an independent kingdom, possibly Celtic, but it was subject to Northumbria from c620–58 (though may have been relatively independent from 642–51), to Mercia from c658–c75, to Northumbria c675–9, and Mercia again from 679, whereafter its kings were reduced in authority to "dukes" or ealdormen. Little is known about them and only those of any significance are accorded a biographical entry below (marked [b]*).*

Ref.	Ruler	Reign	Died	Notes
K39.	Critta or Crida[b]	fl 580s		may be the same as K1
K40.	Cueldgils	fl 600?		
K41.	Caedbaed[b]	fl 625?		
K42.	Bubba	fl 650?		
K43.	Beda	fl 675?		
K44.	Biscop	fl 700?		
K45.	Eanfrith	fl 725?		
K46.	Eatta	fl 750?		
K47.	Aldfrith[b]	fl 775?		

[K39] CRITTA or CRIDA *fl* 580s.

It has been conjectured by John Morris that Critta is the same as Creoda, the founder of Mercia [K1], although their ancestry differs. Creoda's travels from East Anglia to the Midlands may well have taken one of his children to Lindsey where they interbred with the local Celtic royal dynasty, since Critta's grandson is named CAEDBAED. Such a close family connection would explain Mercia's desire to control Lindsey, and would further explain the enmity between Mercia and Northumbria, who conquered Lindsey at about the time of Caedbaed.

[K41] CAEDBAED *fl* c625.

Caedbaed's name appears in the genealogy of ALDFRITH. It is an anglicization of Catuboduos, a Celtic name, and it is possible that Caedbaed's father or grandfather married into an existing Celtic royal family. Details, however, are not known. Caedbaed would have been in power at the time that EDWIN of Northumbria conquered most of northern England and laid claim to several former Celtic kingdoms, including Lindsey and Elmet. It is probable that during Caedbaed's day Lindsey was settled by Angles from both Northumbria and Mercia. It may also have been during Caedbaed's reign, or that of his successor Bubba, that Paulinus came to Northumbria in 630 to convert the Angles to Christianity.

[K47] ALDFRITH or EALDFRITH *fl* 775?

Usually identified as the last recorded king of Lindsey, though there is some dispute whether he retained the status of king or was "duke" or ealdorman by that time. The identification of this Aldfrith with the witness of a charter of the Mercian king OFFA around the year 786 is now seriously in doubt. It is possible that Aldfrith or his predecessor had earlier sought to wrest Lindsey away from Mercia when Offa came to power in 757, but Offa had regained control by the 770s. A period of independence may explain the existence of a genealogy of Aldfrith which states his ancestors through eight generations back to Critta or CREODA, the first reputed ruler of Lindsey.

MAGONSÆTE

Roughly equivalent to northern Herefordshire and southern Shropshire, the territory of the Cornovii at the Roman conquest. The Magonsæte thus shared some of the territory of the Welsh Powys and certainly Ergyng. It is possible that the territory was once the homeland of the Gewisse, from whom some of the West Saxon kings were descended (see page 296).

Ref.	Ruler	Born	Reign	Died	Notes
K48.	Merewalh	c625	c650–685		
K49.	Merchhelm		685–?700		
K50.	Mildfrith		fl 700s		

The kingdom was probably overrun by Powys around the year 710

[K48] **MEREWALH** or **MERWALD** c650–685.

Merewalh is a fascinating mystery in early Anglo-Saxon history. He is identified as the first king of the Magonsæte and as a son of PENDA. This last causes some problems, not least because the name is not consistent with others of the Mercian royal household. Merewalh means "illustrious Welshman". It is known that Penda allied himself with the Welsh, particularly CADWALLON and later CYNDDYLAN, in order to further his own ends. It is very possible that Merewalh (his Celtic name is not known) was a member of a Celtic royal household, maybe even a relative of Cynddylan, who fought bravely alongside Penda and who married one of Penda's daughters and was thus his son-in-law rather than son. His valour and support were rewarded by the kingship over the Magonsæte, which would have included land in eastern Powys recently gained by Penda. Merewalh was apparently already married by this time, but in 660 he was converted to Christianity and it may have been then that he married Eafa, the cousin of WULFHERE's wife Eormenhilda, and a princess of the Kentish royal family. In 679 the bishopric of the Magonsæte was created at Hereford. Merewalh had two sons by his first marriage, MERCHHELM and MILD-FRITH, who succeeded him, a third son from his second marriage Merefin, and three daughters, Mildrith, Mildburh and Mildgyth. His daughters all entered the church: Mildburh became the abbess of Much Wenlock, a monastery founded by Merewalh, while Mildrith joined her mother in founding the monastery at Minster-in-Thanet in Kent in 673, to which she succeeded as abbess when her mother died in 694. Merewalh died in 685 and was buried at Repton.

[K49] **MERCHHELM** fl 690s.

The eldest son and successor of MEREWALH. Nothing is known of him although his name, which means "helmet of the Mercians", suggests that he was a strong and valiant warleader, perhaps in his youth, fighting alongside his father and WULFHERE. His name vanishes from charters by about the year 700. He was succeeded by his brother MILDFRITH.

[K50] **MILDFRITH** *fl* 700s.

Mildfrith is the last recorded king of the Magonsæte, the son of MEREWALH. Nothing is known of him and his name vanishes from charters after about the year 706. His half-sisters Mildburh and Mildrith lived until around the year 730 and, though Mildfrith was probably born before the year 660, he was not likely to have been over fifty when he died. He may, therefore, have been killed in battle. His name means "mild and peaceful", and he may originally have been destined for the church and not noted for his strength in battle. Around the early eighth century the Welsh rulers of Powys, particularly ELISED, began to rebel against the Mercian domination of the border and there were several raids into Mercian territory. It is possible that the land regained by Elised was that of the Magonsæte and that Mildfrith was killed in the conflict. The kingdom was never restored although the name remained for several centuries associated with the bishopric of Hereford.

OTHER MERCIAN SUB-KINGDOMS

Ref.	Ruler	Reign	Died	Notes
Chilterns				
K51.	Dida	c670–5		
Surrey				
K52.	Frithuwold	673–c5		

His son Frithuric may also have ruled briefly as a client king.

[K51] **DIDA** Chilterns, *c*670–5.

Dida is mentioned briefly in the chronicles as a sub-king of the Mercian territory around Oxford, which was in constant dispute with the West Saxons. He was almost certainly a Mercian noble raised to the rank of sub-king by WULFHERE. It is not known how long he retained that authority. He is recorded as the father of St Frideswide of Oxford, and therefore may have been related to the sub-king FRITHUWOLD of Surrey.

[K52] **FRITHUWOLD** Surrey, *c*673–5.

Frithuwold is named in one of the earliest surviving English charters as "sub-king of the province of the men of Surrey". He was a client king to WULFHERE of Mercia, whose sister Wilburh he had married. He was probably of the nobility of the Middle Angles, and his name and that of his kin is associated with the swathe of land from what is now Buckinghamshire through to Leicestershire. Though it does not seem that his client kingdom extended that far, he certainly held lands there, as his daughter Osyth was born at Quarrendon near Aylesbury. He was probably also related to St Frideswide (*see* DIDA) who was buried at Oxford in 727. Frithuwold was associated with the abbey at Chertsey and he and his family all seem to have been dedicated to the church. It is not known whether his son, Frithuric, also ruled as a client king, but his grandson, OFFA (I), was briefly king of Essex. Frithuwold may have been the father of Frithugyth, the wife of ATHELHEARD of Wessex.

L. NORTHUMBRIA (including BERNICIA and DEIRA)

Some of the first Angles to reach Britain settled in Deira, in the lands south of the Tyne, and subsequently overran the British kingdom of Bernicia between the Tyne and the Tweed. Although the two kingdoms were united as Northumbria, the rivalries remained fierce throughout Northumbria's existence. At its greatest extent

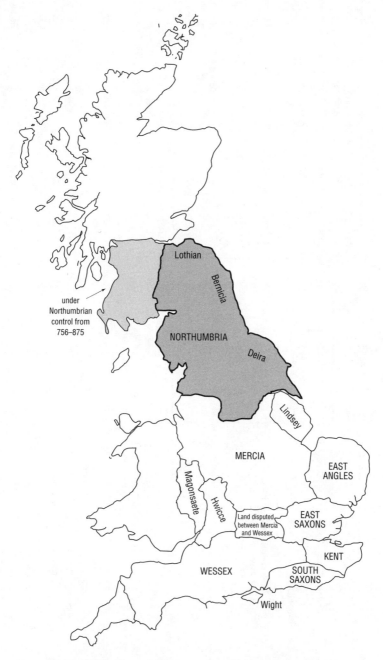

Map 7f **The Anglo-Saxon Kingdoms – Northumbria**

15. Anglo-Saxon Kingdoms (5) – **Bernicia, Deira and Northumbria**

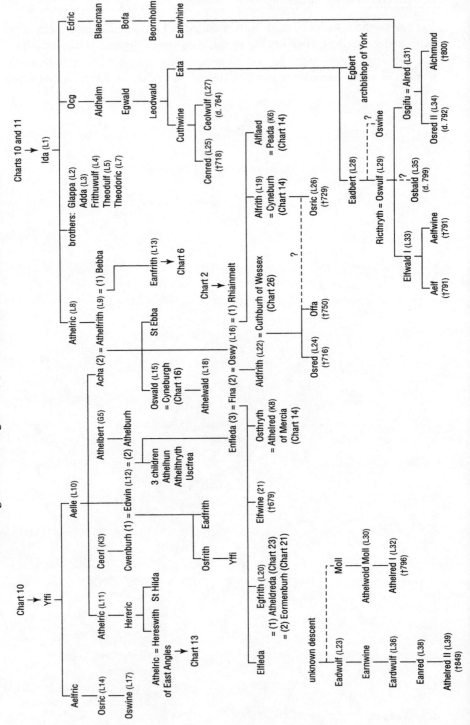

Northumbria stretched as far as the Forth and across all of northern England, absorbing Rheged, Strathclyde and Galloway.

Ref.	Ruler	Born	Reign	Died	Notes
Bernicia					
L1.	Ida		c557–c69	c569	tradition cites reign as 547–59
L2.	Glappa or Clappa		c569–c574		
L3.	Adda		574?–81?		
L4.	Frithuwulf or Freothulf		c573–80?		
L5.	Theodulf		573?–74?		
L6.	Hussa		c580–c7		
L7.	Theodoric		584?–91?		
L8.	Athelric		587?–93?		killed in battle
L9.	Athelfrith		593–604		

In 604 Athelfrith drove Edwin of Deira into exile and united the two kingdoms.

Ref.	Ruler	Born	Reign	Died	Notes
Deira					
L10.	Aelle		569?–99?	599?	tradition cites reign as 559–89
L11.	Athelric		c599–c604	604?	murdered?
Northumbria					
(L9)	Athelfrith		604–16	616	killed in battle
L12.	Edwin or Eadwine	c585	616–33?	633?	killed in battle
kingdom briefly split					
L13.	Eanfrith		633?–5?	635?	ruled Bernicia, killed
L14.	Osric of Deira		633?–4?	634?	killed in battle
kingdom reunited					
L15.	Oswald	c605	635?–42	642	killed in battle
L16.	Oswy	c611	642–70	670	

during Oswy's reign there were several sub-kings (•) of Deira

Ref.	Ruler	Born	Reign	Died	Notes
• L17.	Oswine		643–51	651	murdered
• L18.	Athelwald		651–5	655?	killed in battle or fled
• L19.	Alfrith	c635	654–64?	?	killed, exiled or died of plague?
L20.	Egfrith	c645	664–85	685	king of Northumbria from 670; killed in battle
• L21.	Elfwine	661	670–9	679	sub-king of Deira; killed in battle
L22.	Aldfrith	c640	685–704	705	
L23.	Eadwulf		704–5	?	expelled after two months
L24.	Osred (I)	c696	705–16	716	murdered or killed in battle
L25.	Cenred		716–18	718	possibly murdered
L26.	Osric	c698?	718–29	729	slain
L27.	Ceolwulf		729–37	764	deposed and restored in 731; later retired to a monastery
L28.	Eadbert		737–58	768	abdicated to enter the church
L29.	Oswulf		758–9	759	murdered
L30.	Athelwold *Moll*		759–65	?	deposed
L31.	Alred		765–74	?	deposed

Ref.	Ruler	Born	Reign	Died	Notes
L32.	Athelred (I)		774–9		deposed and later restored
L33.	Elfwald (I)		779–88	788	murdered
L34.	Osred II		788–90	792	deposed
(L32)	Athelred (I) restored		790–6	796	murdered
L35.	Osbald		Mar–Apr 796	799	deposed and later became a monk
L36.	Eardwulf		796–806		driven into exile
L37.	Elfwald II		806–8		deposed
(L36)	Eardwulf restored		808–11	811	
L38.	Eanred		811–43	843	
L39.	Athelred II		843–9	849	briefly deposed in 844; restored but later murdered
L40.	Redwulf		c844	c844	killed in a Viking raid
L41.	Osbert		849–66	867	expelled; killed in the Viking invasion
L42.	Aelle (II)		862–7	867	initially ruled jointly with Osbert; killed in the Viking invasion

During Aelle's reign the Vikings settled in Northumbria establishing their kingdom at York (Jorvik) which corresponded with Deira and is covered in Section NC below (see page 456). The kingdom of Bernicia remained in Saxon hands though it was subservient to Danish overlords.

Bernicia

L43.	Egbert (I)		867–72	873	expelled
L44.	Ricsig		872–6	876?	
L45.	Egbert II		876–88?	?	may have been ejected by Scots
L46.	Eadulf or Eadwulf		888?–913	913	

After Eadulf's death the earldom of Bamburgh remained in his family's hands until 1041. The earls were Ealdred (913–30), Uhtred (930–49), Oswulf (949–63), Eadulf Evilcild (963–94), Waltheof (994–5), Uhtred II (995–1016), Eadulf Cudel (1016–19), Ealdred II (1019–38), Eadulf (1038–41). Thereafter it was absorbed into the earldom of Northumbria.

Dunbar or Lothian

After Oswy's death the Picts rebelled against the Northumbrian overlordship. Egfrith established an hereditary sub-kingdom in Lothian, similar to one of the Welsh Marcher lords.

L47.	Beornheth		670–85	685	killed in battle
L48.	Beorhtred		685–98	698	killed in battle
L49.	Beorhtfrith		698–after 711		

[L1] **IDA** Bernicia, c547–c59 or c557–c69.

Ida was identified by Bede and later annalists as the ancestor of the Northumbrians and the first king of Bernicia, whose reign began in 547. All of these statements need challenging, for all that they have a core of truth. Bede, normally a scrupulous chronicler, reached the date by totalling the reigns of kings down to his time and then subtracting them from the last date of accession. This omitted the possibility of reigns running simultaneously, which almost certainly happened in the break-up after Ida's death, and if this is so then it would bring Ida's reign forward a decade or two, perhaps into the 560s. It has also been suggested that Ida was the son of Ebissa the son of OISC, recorded in his own genealogy as Eobba and Ossa. Elsewhere Oisc and Ebissa are identified as cousins, but there is a tradition that, after the two had fought the Picts sometime in the 480s, Oisc returned to Kent where he established his own ruling dynasty while Ebissa remained in the North. Later genealogists may have got confused, but the dates would be right for Ida to be a grandson of Oisc, regardless of where Ebissa fits into the picture. The general background is that Germanic settlers had begun to make their home along the Northumbrian coast by the late fifth century, possibly earlier. One of these, Soemil (see under AELLE) succeeded in making Deira, the land north of the Humber, an English colony. A generation or two later Ida set sail from the Humber northward and succeeded in capturing the old British fortress of Din Guairi, now called Bamburgh. He is supposed to have defeated a British chieftain called OUTIGERN, and may have driven out another British prince who was either MORCANT himself or more likely Morcant's father Coledauc. We know nothing more about Ida other than that he was successful in holding fast to Bamburgh, but probably had little opportunity to develop his hold on land around the fortress. Nennius records Ida's wife's name as Bearnoch, but this is remarkably similar to Brynaich, the Celtic name for Bernicia, and so may not be accurate. It could mean, though, that Ida married a Celtic princess. He is variously recorded as having from three to twelve sons, and after his death (which may have been as late as 569) the conquered territory seems to have been disputed between them. It is likely that this forced his sons to travel further afield, and that the shaping of Bernicia and conquest of the native Celts happened during this period.

[L2] GLAPPA Bernicia, c569–c574.

Glappa or Clappa is usually identified as succeeding IDA, though he is not recognized as one of his sons. His reign is also variously assigned as lasting either one year or five. This may be accounted for by the fact that he reigned five years in total but only one of these alone. It is possible that he either usurped control of Bernicia after Ida's death or served as regent until Ida's eldest son ADDA was of age. We will probably never know the precise record.

[L3] ADDA Bernicia, c570–7 or c574–81.

Adda (pronounced Atha) is listed as the eldest son of IDA who reigned over Bernicia for seven years. It is not clear whether he succeeded Ida immediately or whether there was a period of confusion after Ida's death during which GLAPPA took command. If Adda was Ida's eldest son one would imagine he was already sufficiently senior to assume control, but this may not be so. If not, then he must still have been in his mid-twenties when he died, suggesting that he died in battle. The short reigns of all of the rulers between Ida and ATHELFRITH suggest that most died violently, and it is a fact that only four or five of Northumbria's ruling kings died naturally. Adda is sometimes identified as the victor at the battle of Caer Greu, in Bernicia, where he defeated PEREDUR. Since this battle is usually dated to 580 it would support the later dates for Adda's reign.

[L4] **FRITHUWULF** or **FREOTHULF** Bernicia, 573?–80?

One of the rulers of Bernicia between IDA and ATHELFRITH. He was not a son of Ida, but may have been an opportunist from Deira who settled in Bernicia after Ida's conquest. Nennius specifies that Frithuwulf was ruling at the time of Augustine's mission to England in 597, but this is unlikely, unless he was not killed in 580 but was deposed, and was known to still be alive, possibly the chief of a local warband in 597.

[L5] **THEODULF** Bernicia, 573?–74?

Theodulf is listed as ruler of Bernicia only by the chronicler Florence of Worcester, and as he also lists THEODORIC he was evidently not confusing the two. Theodulf ruled only one year, but just when this was between the death of IDA in 569 and the accession of ATHELFRITH in 593 cannot be certain. The above date follows Florence's listing and assumes Theodulf succeeded GLAPPA. It is entirely possible that Theodulf ruled much later and was the king called Ulph killed by OWAIN of Rheged sometime after 590.

[L6] **HUSSA** Bernicia, c580–c7.

The exact dates of Hussa's reign are not known. He ruled for seven years and is not identified as a son of IDA. If the sequence of kings listed by the chroniclers is correct then Hussa ruled toward the end of the sixth century. He is sometimes identified as the king besieged by URIEN of Rheged at Lindisfarne, but that was more probably THEODORIC. There is no doubt, though, that Hussa would have been involved in many battles against the British during his reign. His son, Hering, is identified in the *ASC* as leading an English host against the Scots in 603. This may also suggest that Hussa was the son of an earlier Hering or Hyring whom another chronicler (John of Eversden) identified as ruling before Ida, suggesting that there were at least two English warbands in Bernicia at this time.

[L7] **THEODORIC** Bernicia, 584?–91?

Theodoric is identified as a son of IDA. However he clearly did not succeed immediately after Ida's death as he is only accorded a reign of seven years, and as he is identified as the king whom URIEN and his sons besieged on Lindisfarne, which happened about the year 590, we must assume that Theodoric only began to reign during the 580s. Urien's son OWAIN continued his battle against the English and killed one of the kings soon afterwards. Although this king is referred to as Ulph (and thus may have been THEODULF), it might also have been Theodoric.

[L8] **ATHELRIC** Bernicia, 587?–93?

Athelric is identified as the second son of IDA, but as he did not rule until twenty years or so after his father's death, he may have been either an infant when his father died or happy to leave the ruling to others until affairs became so difficult that he stepped into the breach. This may have been after the death of HUSSA, probably in battle against the British. If so, then Athelric may have ruled jointly with THEODORIC for a few years and taken up the campaign against the British under OWAIN of Rheged after Theodoric's death. Two different pictures of Athelric emerge from the records. According to the Welsh tradition, if Athelric is to be identified with Fflamddwyn, the traditional enemy of Owain, then he was a Firebrand, perhaps a man of hot temper and raging courage, characteristics he would have passed on to his son. However, William of Malmesbury calls Athelric "a pitiable prince", already advanced in years, who would have been forgotten had he not had such a valiant son. These two portraits cannot match, so we are left with there either being two Athelrics, or that Fflamddwyn was not Athelric but Theodoric. In fact there may well be two Athelrics, as some chronicles refer to an ATHELRIC, king of Deira, the son of AELLE. Another interpretation is that Athelric was driven out of Bernicia by Theodoric or another, and that he succeeded to Deira upon Aelle's death, but this is less likely. The more likely interpretation is that the Bernician Athelric was the courageous Firebrand, and that he was killed in battle against Owain two years after Theodoric's death.

[L9] **ATHELFRITH** Bernicia, 593–604; all Northumbria, 604–16.
It is with Athelfrith that the real history of the kingdom of Northumbria begins, and it is a remarkable story of bloodshed and revenge. Athelfrith was the son of ATHELRIC and grandson of IDA and he succeeded his father as ruler of Bernicia when his father was killed in battle against OWAIN of Rheged. Athelfrith therefore pursued Owain, eventually defeating and killing him at the battle of Catraeth in 595. Athelfrith's skill in battle suggests he was no novice and we must imagine he was in his mid-to-late twenties at least by this time. Later annalists would record Athelfrith with two epithets. Some called him Athelfrith the Ferocious, an apt description of this powerful warrior; but others called him Athelfrith the Artful, which suggests that he sometimes used wile, cunning and doubtless deceit to achieve his ends. The battle of Catraeth was so decisive that it wiped out the threat of the Gododdin once and for all. It allowed Athelfrith to advance north into the territory of the Votadini, quelling British opposition. It was probably at this time that he took as his wife a British or Pictish princess, Bebbe, after whom Bamburgh is named. Athelfrith's dramatic rise to power no doubt brought concern to the ageing Dál Riatan king AEDAN MAC GABHRAIN, who may have sought to parley with Athelfrith. Around the year 598 one of Aedán's sons, Bran, was killed by the Northumbrians in suspicious circumstances – possibly an example of Athelfrith's deceit. In 603 Aedán took the offensive and led a mighty confederate Scottish/Irish army against the English at Degsastan, in Lothian. Apparently losses were great on both sides, but Athelfrith claimed the victory, and soon after Aedán abdicated. Athelfrith did not lay claim to Dál Riata, but for the time being the north was his, with Bernicia extending far into the territory of the old Votadini. Instead he turned his attention south and in 604 he invaded Deira, south of the Tees, killing the king, ATHELRIC. He also tried to kill Athelric's brother EDWIN, but the young prince escaped and fled into exile. To legitimize his claim to the Deiran kingship, Athelfrith took as his second wife Edwin's sister, Acha (we have no idea whether Bebbe was still alive). Athelfrith now controlled the whole of eastern Britain from Lothian in the north to the Humber in the south, and he may even have exercised some authority over Lindsey, south of the Humber. It could have been the threat of Athelfrith that caused CREODA or PYBBA to move further inland, establishing the kingdom of Mercia south of the British kingdom of Elmet, as yet unconquered by the Northumbrians.

Little is recorded of Athelfrith's activities during the next few years. With such an expanded kingdom he must have spent some time establishing a strong adminis-tration and fortification. There were probably many border skirmishes but none of these are recorded. However by 613 Athelfrith was on the move. He was determined to ferret out the escaped prince Edwin who had sought sanctuary at the courts of the kings of Gwynedd and Powys. Athelfrith used this as his excuse to advance across the Pennines toward Chester. A party of monks from the monastery at Bangor-on-Dee advanced to parley with Athelfrith, but his army wiped them out. He then defeated the Welsh under SELYF AP CYNAN at the battle of Chester. The date of this battle is sometimes given as 615. Edwin escaped from Wales to Mercia and from there to East Anglia. Athelfrith apparently tried to bribe REDWALD to murder Edwin, but to no avail. Since Redwald was himself very rich (if the burial treasures at Sutton Hoo are his own), it suggests how much wealthier Athelfrith had become. Instead Redwald brought together an army and advanced against Athelfrith. Considering the might of Athelfrith and his achievements in battle, this was a major risk for Redwald and suggests that he was not doing it simply to support Edwin, but to protect his own kingdom. By now Athelfrith had almost certainly mastered Lindsey and was an immediate threat on Redwald's borders. The two armies met on the banks of the river Idle near Doncaster. This time Athelfrith, perhaps too sure of his invincibility, had brought a smaller army, and though they threw their might at Redwald, the East Anglians stood fast. Athelfrith was separated from his bodyguard and was cut down. After twelve years Edwin was restored to his kingdom. Athelfrith may be seen as a vindictive and violent king, but it was his conquests which established Northumbria as the major English kingdom, which it would remain for the rest of the seventh century. His sons EANFRITH, OSWALD and OSWY would later all become kings.

[L10] **AELLE** Deira, 569?–99? (sometimes given as 559–89).
Aelle is often shown as the founder of the Deiran royal house, but this is almost certainly not so. Considerable confusion surrounds Aelle, aggravated by a lack of contemporary records and scribal errors amongst the later documents. Because Aelle came to rule upon the death of IDA it is sometimes stated that he was the son of Ida, an easy error when the annals record Aelle's father as Yffe, a name which could, in Old English, be transcribed as Ida. It is also similar to UFFA, who was ruling East Anglia at that time, but there is no reason to suppose those two rulers were directly related. The Northumbrians were also Angles and names derivative of their early hero Offa were common. Aelle's pedigree shows that he was descended from Soemil, who is identified as the first of the Germanic invaders to establish Deira as an English colony distinct from the British. This was probably as early as 450 and his descendants held onto it against constant opposition from the rulers of Catraeth, such as CENEU, GURGUST and ELEUTHER. We can imagine that Aelle was the first to firmly establish independence from the surrounding Britons and that he expanded the kingdom into York around the year 580, when PEREDUR and his kin were killed. By 590 Aelle must have ruled a prosperous kingdom as he is recorded as selling slaves as far afield as Rome. This gave rise to the delightful story of Pope Gregory, seeing the slaves in the market and, being concerned that such beautiful people were heathens, asked where they came from. Being told they were Angles, he twisted the word into Angels, and it was from that moment that he determined they should be converted to Christianity, which gave rise to Augustine's mission in 597. We must conclude, therefore, that Aelle was still alive around 595 or 596, when the

event occurred, and could not have died in 588 or 589 as recorded by the *ASC*. The chronicler Reginald of Durham recorded that Aelle was murdered by ATHELFRITH of Bernicia, which is possible if he had ruled to 599, but unlikely to be earlier. However Reginald is probably in error, as Aelle was succeeded by his son ATHELRIC who was probably Athelfrith's victim. Aelle was also the father of EDWIN.

[L11] **ATHELRIC** Deira, *c*599–*c*604.
The son of AELLE. He should not be confused with ATHELRIC of Bernicia, the son of IDA. The Deiran Athelric was remembered by William of Malmesbury as an old and pitiable king. He reigned for five years and was almost certainly murdered by ATHELFRITH of Bernicia.

[L12] **EDWIN** or **EADWINE** Northumbria, 616–33.
Born: *possibly Goodmanham, near Driffield, 585 or 586;* **Died**: *(killed in battle) Hatfield Chase, near Doncaster, 12 October 633 or 634, aged 48.* **Buried**: *York, but relics later translated to Whitby.*
Married: *(1) c615, Cwenburh, dau. Ceorl of Mercia; 2 children; (2) c625, Athelburh, dau. Athelbert of Kent; 2 children.*
Although remembered as a saint, Edwin was a vindictive ruler whose life was one of revenge and betrayal. He was the son of AELLE, king of Deira. Edwin was only about thirteen when his father died, and his elder brother ruled, but in 604 ATHELRIC was murdered by ATHELFRITH of Bernicia who invaded Deira and took control of both lands. He would have killed Edwin if he could, but Edwin escaped and spent the next ten years in exile. His first flight was to Wales where he found a home at the courts of IAGO AP BELI of Gwynedd and SELYF AP CYNAN of Powys. Edwin was supposed to have befriended CADWALLON, Iago's grandson, who was about four years his junior, but this friendship soon turned to one of intense animosity. In 613 or soon thereafter Athelfrith came searching for Edwin and invaded Powys, killing Selyf at the battle of Chester. Edwin escaped to Mercia where he befriended CEORL and married his daughter Cwenburh. This was probably a political alliance, but Ceorl may not have been the strong king Edwin needed for by 615 he had fled again, this time to the court of REDWALD of East Anglia. Athelfrith tried to bribe Redwald into killing Edwin or handing him over, but Redwald, who professed to be a Christian king, was dissuaded by his wife. Instead Redwald raised an army and marched against Athelfrith, killing him at the battle of the river Idle in either 616 or 617. Edwin was thus restored to the kingdom of Deira and, indeed, all of Northumbria.

After settling into his kingdom Edwin turned his attention to the conquest of the north. First, in about 619, he descended on the British kingdom of Elmet, around Leeds. He expelled the king, CEREDIG, even though Ceredig had sheltered Edwin's nephew Hereric and his wife from the wrath of Athelric. One story states that Ceredig poisoned Hereric and that Edwin's invasion was to exact retribution, but since Ceredig would have expected such a reaction it would seem a suicidal act on his part. It seems more likely that Edwin sought to eradicate the remaining British kingdoms, and this may be because of some treatment he had from Cadwallon during his days in exile. Next Edwin conquered Rheged, which may still have been ruled by either RHUN or his son RHOETH, and this gave him the gateway to the Mevanian islands of Man and Anglesey and brought him into contact with his former friend Cadwallon, who had just become king of Gwynedd. Edwin's army drove the Welsh back to the tip of Anglesey, and Cadwallon was forced to flee to Ireland. By about the year 620 or 621 Edwin was master of the north, ruling from Lothian, just south of Edinburgh, down as far as Leeds, and across all of England and northern Wales. At this time Ceorl was probably still king of Mercia and, as Edwin's father-in-law, there would have been peace between the two nations. Redwald of East Anglia probably died at about this time, and Edwin had no strong relationship with his son EORPWALD. Instead, around the year 624, Edwin sought an alliance with Kent, which under ATHELBERT had been the strongest Saxon kingdom. He negotiated to marry Athelbert's daughter Athelburh, from which we must assume that his first wife had died. Athelburh was Christian, and the marriage was dependent upon the Northumbrians being converted to the faith. Athelburh brought Paulinus with her to the north. Edwin was not himself an immediate convert. In fact it was not until he was nearly murdered that he considered the option. In 626 Cwichelm of Wessex sent one of his thanes, Eumer, to assassinate Edwin, and he nearly succeeded, wounding the king. On the same day, Athelburh gave birth to a daughter, Enfleda, and joyous at this happy and safe delivery, Edwin agreed to become Christian if Paulinus's God granted him victory against the West Saxons. Edwin's punitive raid upon Wessex was successful, and he exacted retribution upon those who had plotted against him, although Cwichelm still lived. Although Wessex did not become subservient to Northumbria, Edwin had showed them his power, and there is no doubt that by the year 626 Edwin was the strongest ruler of Britain. It is certainly from that date, if not earlier, that he would become regarded as *bretwalda*, or overlord. After this victory Edwin consented to his baptism. The Celtic and English annals disagree over who baptized Edwin. Whilst Bede states it was Paulinus, the Celtic record states it was Rhun of Rheged. There is no way that Edwin would have been baptized by anyone other than Paulinus in 627. It is, of course, quite possible that while Edwin was in exile at the court of Iago and his son CADFAN, that Edwin would have been baptized by the exiled Rhun, who then lived in Powys. Although Edwin in this case would have subsequently lapsed, he probably had become sympathetic towards the new faith, hence his agreement to Paulinus's coming to Northumbria, but he would join it on his own terms. Edwin now sanctioned the conversion of the Northumbrians and established a bishopric at York. He also negotiated with the Pope to raise York to an archbishopric for the Angles. The fact that the Pope approved this is an indication of the authority that Edwin held. York was now established as Edwin's capital. For the next few years Britain experienced a remarkable period of peace and prosperity. Bede recalled that a woman and child could traverse Edwin's Northumbria unmolested.

However Edwin's past was soon to haunt him. Around the year 630 Cadwallon returned to power in Gwynedd. He entered into an alliance with PENDA, the new ruler of Mercia, in a series of raids and attacks on Northumbrian land. Eventually the two great armies met at Hatfield Chase, just north of Doncaster, in October 633 (or 634). The battle was noted for Cadwallon's ferocity and the day was his. Edwin was killed, along with his eldest son Osfrith, whilst his second son Eadfrith was taken as hostage by Penda, and later murdered. Edwin's army was scattered and Cadwallon marched on through Northumbria devastating the land. Edwin's wife

Athelburh fled with her two children, Enfleda and Uscfrea, back to Kent, along with Paulinus. Northumbria was split asunder. Edwin's cousin OSRIC inherited Deira, but Bernicia returned to the family of Athelfrith (*see under* EANFRITH *and* OSWALD). Edwin subsequently became regarded as a martyr and a small cult grew up around his memory. He was in fact a ruthless, cunning and vengeful king who manipulated people and events to his own advantage. His strength nevertheless established Northumbria as a Christian kingdom and, though this lapsed briefly after his death, the creation of the see of York ensured that Christianity would prevail in the north.

[L13] **EANFRITH** Bernicia, 633 (or 634)-634 (or 635).
The eldest son of ATHELFRITH and his British wife Bebbe, Eanfrith was probably born around the year 596. When his father was killed in 616, Eanfrith and his brothers fled. Eanfrith made his way to the land of the Picts, probably the relatives of his mother, and he married a Pictish princess. His son TALORCEN later became king of the Picts, whilst through a daughter he became the ancestor of several more Pictish kings. There is some evidence to suggest that Eanfrith began to ally himself with other British exiles, notably CADWALLON of Gwynedd, whom EDWIN of Northumbria had driven into Ireland. When, in 633 (or 634) Cadwallon killed Edwin at the battle of Hatfield Chase, Eanfrith immediately stepped into the kingship of Bernicia. Unlike Edwin, who had been a Christian convert, Eanfrith remained a pagan, which was probably welcomed by many of his subjects. Eanfrith apparently endeavoured to reach a peace treaty with Cadwallon who, for over a year, ravaged the north. After eighteen months Eanfrith, in company with twelve thanes, met with Cadwallon, but the Welsh king killed him. He was succeeded by his brother OSWALD.

[L14] **OSRIC** Deira 633 (or 634)-634 (or 635).
Osric succeeded his cousin EDWIN after the latter's death in battle against CADWALLON of Gwynedd. He was the son of AELLE's brother Aelfric, and although he had probably become Christian following Edwin's conversion around 626, Osric reverted to paganism in the crisis that followed Edwin's death. Cadwallon continued to ravage the north, and it was Osric that led the attack against him. Although he succeeded in besieging Cadwallon in a fortress in the following summer, Osric was unable to contain the Welsh army, which broke out and surprised his men. Osric was killed in the mayhem. He had ruled for less than a year. For the next year Deira had no ruler, although EANFRITH probably sought to maintain control from Bernicia.

[L15] **OSWALD** Northumbria, 635?-5 August 642.
Oswald was the son of ATHELFRITH and EDWIN's sister Acha. He fled into exile along with his brothers EANFRITH and OSWY when his father was killed in battle by Edwin. Oswald and Oswy found their way to Scottish Dál Riata, along with their sister Ebba. Since their father had been responsible for defeating the former Dál Riatan king AEDAN twenty years earlier, there was evidently a change of heart amongst the Scots to protect Athelfrith's children, and this says something for the Christian perspective of EOCHAID BUIDE. The children were apparently left in the care of the monks of Iona where they were baptized into the Christian faith. It is interesting to speculate whether Oswald's name was given to him by the monks at that baptism

rather than bestowed by his father. The name means "godlike ruler". Since Athelfrith was pagan his use of the name would be entirely different to that of the monks who may have prayed that Oswald would later become king of Northumbria and bring the Christian message to the land. Oswald was about twelve at the start of his exile and he remained under the protection of Eochaid for the next twelve years, accompanying the king on his battles into Ireland to protect the Dál Riatan homeland. There is little doubt that in these later years Oswald befriended CADWALLON of Gwynedd who had also been driven into exile in Ireland by Edwin. However, after 633, when Cadwallon had killed Edwin in battle, the Welsh king entered upon a wholesale devastation of Northumbria, subsequently killing Oswald's brother EANFRITH. By now Oswald was established back on the British mainland, probably in Lothian, supported by an army of Scots and possibly Picts. He took advantage of Cadwallon's over-confidence and surprised him near Hexham in sight of Hadrian's Wall. Bede records how Oswald prayed to God on the dawn of the battle, planting a cross in the battle field, which thereafter was known for centuries as Heavenfield, now believed to be Hallington.

Oswald reunited Bernicia with Deira and thus re-established his father's kingdom of Northumbria. His acceptance by the Deirans may have been because he was Edwin's nephew, the son of Acha, Edwin's sister. He was the first Northumbrian king to succeed to the throne as a Christian and one of his first acts was to summon Aedán from Iona to establish the Christian church in Northumbria. Aedán was given the island of Lindisfarne off the coast from Bamburgh, where he established a Christian community. Because Aedán was not fluent in English, Oswald, who had learned Gaelic in exile, had to translate for him, it was this unity of king and abbot that helped establish Christianity amongst a nation that had remained predominantly pagan, despite Edwin's previous conversion. Oswald had introduced Celtic Christianity as distinct from the Roman tradition previously preached by Paulinus, who had fled from York after the death of Edwin and had become the first bishop of Rochester in Kent.

Bede regarded Oswald as *bretwalda* or overlord of the Saxons, though this is surprising. It is unlikely that Oswald succeeded in holding much authority beyond Northumbria, although he evidently entered into an alliance with CYNEGILS of Wessex whose daughter Cyneburh he married, and to whom he stood as godfather at Cynegils's baptism about 639/40. He probably supported the succession of ANNA in East Anglia after his predecessors had been killed in battle by the Mercian king PENDA. Oswald's design seems to have been to create an alliance of rulers around Penda and thus to contain him. It does not look, though, that Oswald's alliance stretched as far as Essex and Kent. In fact he would have held some animosity against EADBALD of Kent who had given refuge to Edwin's children, though it seems that Oswald and Eadbald must have reached enough agreement for Edwin's widow, Athelburh, to despatch her son Uscfrea to Dagobert, king of the Franks, for safety.

Oswald seems to have spent some time strengthening his borders to the north. Although he now had strong connections with the Dál Riatan Scots and, through his deceased brother Eanfrith, with the Picts, the relationship with the British of Strathclyde was less harmonious. Their new king, OWEN MAP BILI, was rapidly rebuilding the former strength of that kingdom. The annals suggest that, around the year 638, Owen and Oswald must have clashed in the territory around Stirling and

Edinburgh, where Oswald's army won the day. However, the weight of Oswald's activities were pitched against Penda. In the battle for East Anglia, around the year 640, Penda had laid claim to Lindsey which Oswald sought to recover. There is some question as to whether at this time Oswald won over EOWA, Penda's brother, who was probably ruler of northern Mercia. Nevertheless, Oswald and Penda continued to clash and in 642 their armies met at Maserfield, where Oswald was captured and killed in a savage pagon ritual. The king's body was dismembered and the parts hung on various stakes on a tree – after which the place has become known as Oswald's tree, or Oswestry. It was a full year before OSWY was able to recover the relics. The body was buried at Bardney in Lindsey, and was later translated to Gloucester. The head was buried on Lindisfarne, whilst his right hand which Aedán had prophesied would never perish because of Oswald's generosity to the poor, was preserved on display in Bamburgh. Soon after many people began to claim that the spot where Oswald fell held special properties and could cure people, even a horse, of their ailments. Within a few years Oswald was being venerated as a saint, his feast day being August 5th, when he died.

[L16] **OSWY** or **OSWIU** Northumbria, 5 August 642–15 February 670.
Oswy fled with his brother OSWALD into exile in Dál Riata in 616 or 617 and was raised by the monks of Iona. Oswy was born around the year 611, and in his infancy was baptized into the Christian faith. It is likely that while he was in exile Oswy had a couple of romantic affairs. Around the year 634 he married Rhiainmelt or Riemmelth, the daughter of RHOETH of Rheged. This was a significant alliance between the English and a former major British kingdom, and may be seen as part of Oswald's strategy in the north, where he also seems to have reached an agreement with OWEN MAP BILI of Strathclyde. Oswy had at least one son by Rhiainmelt, ALFRITH, but his wife must have died within a few years, perhaps even in childbirth, as she is no longer mentioned. A year or two after her death Oswy took part in the Dál Riatan dynastic squabbles in Ireland and there he became involved with Fina, the daughter of the former high king Colman. It is not recorded that they married, yet no scandal seems to have been attached to the relationship even though Fina bore Oswy a son, the future king ALDFRITH.

We hear little of Oswy during the reign of Oswald, though there is little doubt that he would have assisted his brother in his campaigns, quite possibly in the north. It is possible that Oswy administered much of Bernicia on Oswald's behalf, while Oswald campaigned in the south. It is unlikely that Oswy was at the battle of Maserfield in 642, when Oswald was killed, as Oswy would almost certainly also have met his death. Although Oswy immediately inherited the kingdom of Bernicia, it seems that he had problems in keeping a hold on Deira, which may well have remained a disputed zone between PENDA and Oswy. It was a year before Oswy could recover his brother's remains from the battlefield and bury the body at Bardney in Lindsey. By this time OSWINE, the son of Edwin's cousin OSRIC, had succeeded in installing himself as king of Deira. This may have been part of a special arrangement for in 642 or 643, Oswy married his cousin, Enfleda, the daughter of Edwin. Although Oswine recognized Oswy as his overlord the relationship between the two seems to have been severely strained, with Oswy the more intractable. By the year 651 the two kings were at loggerheads, and though both raised an army,

Oswine refused to fight and instead sought refuge at Gilling. He was betrayed and killed on Oswy's orders. Enfleda was furious over this and insisted that Oswy build a monastery at Gilling in expiation. Oswy installed his nephew, ATHELWALD, as king of Deira, but he soon came under the influence of Penda, who was still seeking Oswy's downfall. Penda had been harrying Northumbria for several years since Maserfield, and around the year 644 had advanced as far as Bamburgh, but a change in the wind direction saved the town from the threatened conflagration. Evidently by the year 653 Penda and Oswy sought to make alliances through marriage. Oswy's son ALFRITH was married to Penda's daughter Cyneburh, while Penda's son PEADA, sought to marry Oswy's daughter Alflæd. A condition of Peada's marriage was that he be baptized into the Christian faith, which Peada accepted. Following this Oswy began to send Christian missionaries throughout Mercia. Penda may have seen this as a subversive infiltration of his people and, though he was not against Christianity, he clearly would not have supported its spread if it weakened his hold over his kingdom. Moreover in 653 Oswy's nephew TALORCEN became king of the Picts, possibly at Oswy's instigation. This, combined with his alliance with Dál Riata and Strathclyde gave Oswy a formidable strength in the north. To counter this Penda raised a mighty army with over thirty contingents and marched north, forcing Oswy to retreat perhaps as far as Stirling. A peace agreement was achieved, in November 655, and Penda took Oswy's son EGFRITH as hostage. As Penda was returning south, Oswy, and a smaller army, overtook him at the river Winwæd, near Leeds, where Oswy defeated and killed Penda and many of his allies, including his nephew Athelwald.

It was from 655 that Oswy could lay claim to being *bretwalda*, or overlord of the Saxons in England. He established Peada as king of the southern Mercians but a year later, possibly at Oswy's instigation, Peada was murdered. Oswy now ruled all of Mercia. He established his son ALFRITH as ruler of Deira and with his nephew as king of the Picts, Oswy could lay claim to being overlord of all of northern Britain and as far south as the Thames, and also held close alliances with CENWEALH of Wessex and EORCENBERHT of Kent. Even though WULFHERE succeeded in recovering Mercia in 658, Oswy's authority was still considerable, and it was this that enabled him to make one of the most significant decisions of his day.

Ever since his marriage to Enfleda, Oswy had become aware of the differences between the Celtic church, into which he had been baptized, and the Roman church to which Enfleda belonged. Although both professed Christian teachings there was a clash over the calculation of Easter. Because this differed every year, Oswy could be celebrating Easter while his wife was still fasting in Lent. Oswy might have continued to suffer this, but matters became a problem when in 658 Alfrith became an ardent supporter of the Roman church, expelling Eata and Cuthbert from the monastery at Ripon and installing the Roman proponent Wilfrid. There was now a split within Oswy's own kingdom and he needed it resolved. In 664 he called a synod at Whitby, where he had recently established a new monastery. What factors influenced Oswy are unclear: whether he was won over by the silver tongue of Wilfrid, or whether he realised that he needed the support of Rome and the continent rather than the Picts and Scots, but Oswy found in favour of the Roman church. This decision was fundamental and resulted in a significant ecclesiastical reorganization over the next few years which, despite Oswy's probable intention, favoured the rulers of southern England more, especially Wulfhere and Cenwealh. It seems likely that by the time of Oswy's death, aged 58 according to Bede, his overlordship had already waned, and Northumbria would never again exert quite the same power. Nevertheless Oswy was one of the few kings of Northumbria to die naturally and not be killed or deposed. Bede records that he died of an illness. He was succeeded by his son Egfrith. His wife, Enfleda, retired to the monastery of Whitby, where her daughter Elfleda had been brought up and in 680, upon the death of the incumbent abbess Hilda, Enfleda and her daughter became joint abbesses. Enfleda died in about 704, aged about eighty.

[L17] **OSWINE** Deira, 643–20 August 651.
The son of OSRIC, Oswine had fled into exile in Wessex when his father was killed during CADWALLON's devastation of the north. During the confusion that followed PENDA's defeat of OSWALD at Maserfield, Oswine gained the support of the people of Deira and claimed the throne. He acknowledged the overlordship of OSWY of Bernicia, who had succeeded Oswald as ruler of Northumbria, but it appears that Oswy had trouble securing his authority in Deira. Bede, who was often over zealous in his description of saintly kings, called Oswine "tall and handsome, pleasant of speech, courteous in manner, and bountiful to nobles and common alike." He was such a pious and humble monarch that Bishop Aedán of Lindisfarne was convinced he would not live long, because "this nation does not deserve to have such a ruler." And so it came to be. Oswy raised an army against Oswine and, seeing he was outnumbered, Oswine disbanded his own army to avoid bloodshed. He sought refuge in the home of a supporter who betrayed him and he was murdered by the local reeve. The church at Gilling was built at the site of the crime, although Oswine was buried at Tynemouth.

[L18] **ATHELWALD** Deira, 651–5.
The son of OSWALD, the saintly king of Northumbria. It is uncertain whether Athelwald was made king of Deira by his uncle OSWY following the murder of OSWINE, or whether Athelwald claimed it in his own right. Athelwald was a confirmed Christian and he gave land to Bishop Cedd, who established a monastery at Lastingham high up on the Yorkshire moors. It is evident that there was no love between Oswy and Athelwald, and the latter received the support of PENDA of Mercia, even though Penda had cruelly slaughtered Athelwald's father at the battle of Maserfield. Athelwald supported Penda when the latter raised a vast army in the autumn of 655 to advance on Oswy's kingdom. Although peace was agreed, Oswy followed Penda back through Northumbria and engaged him in battle at the river Winwæd where many of Penda's supporters died. It is not clear whether Athelwald was amongst them, for Bede reports that he withdrew from the battlefield. If he survived, he must have known he could no longer be safe following Oswy's victory and have fled into exile. No more is heard of him.

[L19] **ALFRITH (ALCHFRITH or EALHFRITH)** Deira, 655–64?
The son of OSWY of Northumbria and his British queen Rhiainmelt of Rheged. After the death or disappearance of ATHELWALD at the battle of Winwæd, Alfrith was made king of Deira by Oswy. He must have been about twenty at that time, and had already shown his battle prowess at Winwæd. Alfrith was married to Cyneburh the

daughter of PENDA, and was on friendly terms with her brother, PEADA, whom Alfrith convinced to adopt the Christian faith. Alfrith's relationship with his father seems to have fractured after the death of Peada in 656, and this has given rise to an image of Alfrith as something of a hot-headed youth. The relationship is more likely to be one of "like father like son", both sharing an obstinacy that refused reconciliation. In 658 Alfrith welcomed to Deira the young bishop Wilfrid, who had studied at Lindisfarne before travelling to Canterbury and then Rome. Wilfrid became converted to the Roman orthodoxy and convinced Alfrith of its importance. Alfrith appointed Wilfrid as bishop of Ripon, expelling the incumbent bishop Eata. This further frustrated Oswy, who now had both Celtic and Roman Christian teachings in his kingdom. It led to the Synod of Whitby, held in 664, at which Oswy found in favour of the Roman church. As a result Wilfrid was appointed bishop of York. One might imagine this would cement the relationship between Oswy and Alfrith, but not so. Wilfrid travelled to Paris to be consecrated and while he was away Oswy appointed Chad in his stead. Nothing more is heard of Alfrith and one could surmise that Oswy's act caused Alfrith to rebel against his father and he died in the insurrection. However Bede would probably have reported such an upheaval. An alternative explanation is that Alfrith died as a result of the plague which swept England during 664 and it was following his death that Oswy took the opportunity to install Chad in Wilfrid's place. Whatever happened, EGFRITH succeeded as ruler of Deira.

[L20] **EGFRITH** Deira, 664–70; Northumbria, 15 February 670–20 May 685.
During Egfrith's reign the authority previously held by Northumbria over England waned. He was the son of OSWY and Enfleda, the daughter of EDWIN. He was born about the year 645, because he was only ten when taken as hostage by PENDA during his invasion of the north in 655. In 660, aged only fifteen, Egfrith was married to Etheldreda, the daughter of ANNA of East Anglia and already a widow. She was about twelve years Egfrith's senior, but was devoted to the church and vowed to

From a coin

retain her virginity. The marriage was clearly a political move to ally Northumbria and East Anglia. After Egfrith succeeded to the Northumbrian throne, the two separated and Etheldreda became the founding abbess of Ely. Egfrith became sub-king of Deira following the death or expulsion of ALFRITH sometime in or just after 664. On his father's death he was raised to the throne of Northumbria in preference to his elder but illegitimate brother, ALDFRITH, whilst a younger brother, ELFWINE, was installed in Deira.

Egfrith's campaigns in the early part of his reign were successful though violent. In 672 the Picts expelled their ruler DRUST and threw off the yoke of the Northumbrians who had installed client rulers, with EANFRITH'S son TALORCEN becoming king in 653. Egfrith sent a punitive expedition into Pictland and won such a major victory that his army could cross a river on the bodies of the massacred Picts. Although Egfrith regarded the Picts as conquered and subservient, he established a new sub-kingdom in Lothian and installed his ealdorman BEORNHETH as ruler. He also established an Anglian bishop over the Picts by installing Trumwine in Abercorn in 681. Meanwhile the Picts' new king BRUDE MAC BILI bided his time and would prove Egfrith's nemesis. Soon after Egfrith defeated an army sent against him by WULFHERE of Mercia. Wulfhere was at the height of his power, and Egfrith's victory was significant.

In between these two victories, Egfrith took a new queen, Eormenburh, the cousin of EGBERT of Kent. Eormenburh became notorious for her hatred of bishop Wilfrid of Northumbria, and her feelings persuaded Egfrith to have him imprisoned and later expelled, in the year 680. In the meantime Egfrith continued to dominate the north. Throughout the first decade of his reign he had systematically driven the British out of Rheged, establishing settlements for the English. However in 679 Egfrith was overwhelmed by ATHELRED of Mercia in a battle on the banks of the river Trent. Egfrith had clearly underestimated the Mercians. Having defeated them easily five years earlier, and with Athelred married to his sister Osthryth, Egfrith must have believed he would have no problems from the south. Although this dented his authority it seemed to make Egfrith more determined and egotistical. His onslaught against the British of Rheged had only served to drive the British into Ireland where they became mercenaries for the Irish royalty and began harrying the English coast. In 684 Egfrith sent a punitive expedition against the Irish, devastating the kingdom of Brega in Leinster. It has also been speculated that Egfrith's expedition was to reduce the Irish support for his elder half-brother Aldfrith. Despite advice not to invade, Egfrith was victorious. It may be that now he was over-confident for in 685 he led a great army back into Pictland, but was lured beyond safe limits and he and many of his men were slaughtered by Brude mac Bili at the battle of Nechtansmere. Brude pursued the surviving army back into Lothian and recovered some of the lands previously held by Egfrith. Northumbria's strength was severely weakened and it never regained the military power it had exercised during the seventh century. After Egfrith's death Eormenburh retired to the abbey of Carlisle. The date of her death is not known. Surprisingly Egfrith's body was conveyed to Iona for burial. Although an enemy of the Picts, his blood relationship to the royal line evidently allowed him this final honour.

[L21] **ELFWINE** Deira, 670–9.

The youngest son of OSWY of Northumbria, born about the year 661 and elevated to the title of king of Deira (aged nine) when his brother EGFRITH became king of Northumbria. The title indicated that he was heir to the throne, but Elfwine never succeeded as he was killed in the battle of the Trent against the Mercians in 679. Elfwine was so beloved by both the Northumbrians and the Mercians that his death nearly resulted in a blood feud between the two royal houses, until Archbishop Theodore negotiated compensation.

[L22] **ALDFRITH** Northumbria, 20 May 685–14 December 704.

Aldfrith was the illegitimate son of OSWY and the Irish princess Fina. The date of his birth is unknown, but John Marsden's analysis that it must have been about 640 is convincing. Because of his illegitimacy, Aldfrith was overlooked in the succession to the throne which had passed through his half-brothers ALFRITH, EGFRITH and ELFWINE. During these years Aldfrith devoted himself to study, initially in Ireland and subsequently at Canterbury and Malmesbury before settling on Iona in 684, where he indulged in poetry and the study of riddles. It was only following the sudden death of Egfrith with no natural heirs that the Northumbrians turned to Aldfrith, upon the pleading of his half-sister Elfleda. Aldfrith was the first scholar-king of Northumbria, which might have seemed a suicidal choice with the threat of ATHELRED of Mercia to the south and BRUDE MAC BILI of the Picts to the north, but the contrary was the case. His reign was one of comparative peace in which art and learning flourished. Aldfrith released the hostages captured by Egfrith during his campaign in Ireland in 684 and made peace with the Irish. There was a campaign against the Picts late in his reign, in 698, but it was probably led by Aldfrith's thane BEORHT and not Aldfrith himself. Aldfrith spent much of his time encouraging scholarship and art throughout Northumbria. It was during his reign that the beautifully illuminated Lindisfarne Gospels were compiled as well as many other literary and ecclesiastical treasures. It has been conjectured that Aldfrith himself may have written one of the great works of the age, *Beowulf*, and though this may never be proven, it was certainly the peace and intellectualism of Aldfrith's reign that allowed such works to emerge.

From a coin

Aldfrith had an altercation with the ever-present bishop Wilfrid. Aldfrith had summoned him back from exile to Northumbria in 685, and he was established first as bishop of Ripon and then as abbot of Lindisfarne when Cuthbert died in 687. However the two men could never see eye to eye. Aldfrith had been raised amongst the Celtic church and was totally sympathetic to the abbots of Iona whilst Wilfrid was an ardent Roman who felt it his mission to rid the Roman churches of the Celts. By 690 Aldfrith had had enough and expelled Wilfrid again. It was not until after Aldfrith's death that Wilfrid was reinstated in Northumbria one final time.

Aldfrith married Cuthburh, the sister of INE of Wessex, around the year 695. He had at least two sons, possibly more, and was succeeded by the eldest, OSRED. Cuthburh retired a few years before Aldfrith's death to the convent at Barking in Essex and, after 705, she founded Wimborne Minster in Dorset. Aldfrith died at Driffield after a long illness at the age of sixty-four, having established the monasteries of Northumbria as the greatest seats of learning in England. He was the last great king of the Northumbrians.

[L23] **EADWULF** Northumbria, December 704–February 705.
A thane who usurped the Northumbrian throne after the death of ALDFRITH but within two months was driven out of the kingdom by the supporters of OSRED. It is possible that his descendants later laid claim to the throne (*see* ATHELWOLD MOLL).

[L24] **OSRED (I)** Northumbria, February 705–716.

The son of the scholarly ALDFRITH. Born late in the king's life, he was not yet nine when his father died. The throne was usurped by the thane EADWULF but he was expelled within two months by the combined efforts of BEORHTFRITH, the sub-king of Lothian, and Wilfrid, who became the boy's foster-father. Beorhtfrith effectively acted as regent and commander of the army during the boy's minority, whilst Wilfrid, now restored to the see of Hexham, looked after the boy's spiritual learning. Perhaps young Osred learned too much of Wilfrid's haughtiness and single-mindedness, combined with the egotism of his uncle and grandfather, for he grew into a wayward youth. Wilfrid died in 710 and we hear no more of Beorhtfrith after 711, by which time Osred had probably assumed authority and had no one to curb his wanton tendencies. His one remaining good influence was John, bishop of York and founder of the monastery at Beverley, to which Osred gave generously. But elsewhere he was known for his violence. He had no Christian morals, but frequently raped nuns and murdered or exiled many of the Northumbrian nobility. He was apparently brave and courageous in warfare, though this may have been due to his delight in battle and bloodshed. After four years of his personal tyranny, his kinsmen rose up against him and he was killed in a rebellion led by his distant cousin CENRED.

[L25] **CENRED** or **COENRED** Northumbria, 716–18.

Cenred claimed descent from IDA through a younger son called Ocg. Neither he nor his descendents seem to have left any record of their activities, but there is no reason to doubt their existence for all that genealogies could be fabricated for convenience. Cenred was specifically the son of Cuthwine, and in 716 he appears to have led the rebellion to depose the obnoxious young king OSRED. To this end he seems to have been aided by Osred's own brother, OSRIC (*though see Osric's entry for a possible alternative explanation*). Cenred was presumably the senior partner, since Osric was still in his teens, and it may be for that reason that Cenred took over the kingdom. His age is not known, but allowing the traditional estimate of twenty-five years per generation means he was probably in his thirties or forties. He may have been one of the nobles under threat from Osred who, towards the end of his reign, seemed to be systematically eradicating the nobility as (presumably) they turned against him. Regicide, no matter how disliked the king, is still a terrible crime and Cenred does not seem to have shaken off his guilt, which is the only act for which he is remembered. He ruled for only two years. A later chronicler, John of Fordun, remarked that both Cenred and Osric "polluted the air by their foul end" which suggests that they both died violently. His brother was the much troubled king CEOLWULF.

[L26] **OSRIC** Northumbria, 718–29.

Osric is identified as the younger brother of OSRED and son of ALDFRITH. Since Osred was born in about 696, it is unlikely that Osric was born much before 698, and would thus have been twenty when he inherited the throne. Two years earlier he had been involved with CENRED in the uprising that resulted in the death of Osred. It has been suggested that he may have been the son of ALFRITH, OSWY's eldest son, who had either died or vanished into exile soon after 664. This has a plausible ring, especially as this would make Osric older, probably in his late fifties, and could even reverse the accepted scenario, placing Osric as the architect of the rebellion in order to place Cenred on the throne. Although Osric ruled for eleven years, nothing is recorded of his reign. Bede is noticeably quiet on this period, perhaps because it was within living memory and therefore did not need to be recorded, but just as possibly because the events were too unpleasant and too close to home to remember. It seems unlikely, however, that Osric could have avoided some involvement in the civil war which erupted within the Pictish royal house and which resulted in the rise to power of ANGUS, with whom either Osric or his successor, CEOLWULF, negotiated a treaty. The *ASC* records that Osric was slain, but it is not clear whether he died in battle or was assassinated.

[L27] CEOLWULF Northumbria, 729–37.

Ceolwulf is recorded as the brother of CENRED and son of Cuthwine, though he seems to have been made of entirely different material to his brother. It is likely that Ceolwulf was much younger than Cenred, perhaps born around the year 700, and during the tyranny of OSRED he may well have gone to Ireland for safety, as he is remembered in the Irish Annals by the Celtic name, Eochaid. Probably Ceolwulf was always intended for the church. He was a studious and literary man, and perhaps his nomination as successor to OSRIC may have been in the hope that Ceolwulf would restore some of the golden age achieved by the previous scholar king ALDFRITH. The times were different to those of Aldfrith, however, with Northumbria a much weakened kingdom fraught with internal problems. Within two years of his succession Ceolwulf was deposed, imprisoned and forcibly tonsured, thus disbarring him from the kingship. This may also be part of a groundswell of opinion against the church, for 731 was a year of troubles as other churchmen were deposed and some killed. It is perhaps ironic that in this very year Bede completed his *Ecclesiatical History* which he dedicated to Ceolwulf and handed to him about the middle of the year. Ceolwulf must have been deposed soon after but only briefly, as if to be taught a lesson, for he was restored to the throne before the end of the year. Who deposed him is not recorded, but we can imagine that some of the rebels who subsequently supported Osred's brother Offa against EADBERT may have been involved, resenting the favours being offered the church and desiring the glorious days of Northumbria's past conquests. Ceolwulf may have suffered because England was in a period of relative peace compared to the constant warfare of the previous century. It was a false spring, as troubles would follow in the succeeding generations. Ceolwulf rode out the troubles and the remaining years of his reign with comparative calm. In 735 Rome restored York to archiepiscopal status, and Egbert, Ceolwulf's cousin, was elevated to archbishop, the first since Paulinus. The significance of this event is often overlooked during the reign of Northumbria's latterday kings, yet it established the position of Northumbria as independent of southern England in its ecclesiastical affairs and by extension elevated the status of its king. Although it established York as a major seat of learning, Ceolwulf did not take sufficient advantage of its status, and in fact soon after, toward the close of 737, he abdicated, this time of his own volition, and retired to the monastery at Lindisfarne. He was apparently exceedingly generous in his bequests to the monks as they were subsequently able to partake of wine and ale whereas previously they had subsisted solely on milk and water. He remained in his monastic retreat for over twenty years, dying in or about 764, and though he may have advised on temporal matters he is not recorded as becoming involved in subsequent state affairs. He was subsequently venerated as a saint. He was succeeded as king by his cousin EADBERT.

[L28] **EADBERT** Northumbria, 737–58.

Eadbert's reign saw the return of the first successful warrior king of the Northumbrians since EGFRITH sixty years earlier. The Northumbrians liked nothing better than a strong war leader, and Eadbert's reign was consequently long remembered, particularly as it followed a period of uncertainty and rebellion. Eadbert was the cousin of CEOLWULF and brother of Egbert, the new archbishop of York. Although he shared with these relatives a love of the church, he was also a man of the world not afraid to confront his enemies and defend his frontiers. From the start of his reign Eadbert seems to have become involved in a series of battles with the Picts who, under their own new strong warleader ANGUS, were broadening their frontier and had already taken control of Dál Riata. It is possible that Eadbert's battles were not against Angus. The Picts were never a strongly united race and much of Angus's fighting was against rival factions within the Picts. It is more than likely that this spilled over to the south as displaced Pictish lords struggled to regain land, and this would have commanded Eadbert's attention as he protected his frontier. The opportunististic ATHELBALD of Mercia took advantage of this situation to invade Deira in 740, setting fire to York. Eadbert was able to repulse this onslaught, though not until Athelbald had inflicted much devastation upon Northumbria. At this same time Eadbert ordered the execution of Eanwine, the son of EADWULF, who had made a peremptory claim on the throne over thirty years earlier. Eanwine had presumably taken advantage of Eadbert's absence to plot a rebellion, and may even have conspired with Athelbald. This shows that inter-dynastic factions were rife in Northumbria, but that, for the time being at least, Eadbert had their measure. A period of comparative calm followed, much owing to the strength of Angus in controlling the Picts and Scots, allowing Eadbert to consolidate his kingdom. However in 750 further internal strife occurred which challenged his authority. Offa, believed to be the youngest son of ALDFRITH (though by now he would have been about fifty) made a bid for the throne and had to escape to the sanctuary of Lindisfarne. Eadbert incurred the wrath of the church by violating this sanctuary, not only in capturing Offa, but by imprisoning the bishop, Cynewulf, presumably for harbouring Offa. It is unlikely that Eadbert could have achieved this had he not had the support of his brother, the archbishop of York.

That same year, the Strathclyde Britons rebelled under their king TEUDEBUR and defeated Angus at the battle of Mugdock. This seriously weakened the Pictish king and the British saw this as their opportunity to regain the glory of old. However, without the Picts as a barrier, the British now faced the might of Eadbert's army, which swept across the borders and by 752 had conquered and annexed the territory of Kyle, as part of a peace agreement with the new king of Strathclyde, DUMNAGUAL. However this treaty was of short duration as four years later in 756, Eadbert combined forces with the Picts under Angus and attacked Dumbarton. For the next century the kingdom of Strathclyde was a vassal state to Northumbria.

Eadbert had to a large degree re-established Northumbria's superiority in northern Britain, and had even extended the borders. By 757 he must have felt that the kingdom was in good shape. The rebellious sons of past claimants had been vanquished and to the south Mercia was in turmoil following the death of Athelbald. As Eadbert was probably now approaching his sixties, he abdicated in favour of his son OSWULF and retired to the abbey at York. He lived until the year 768 and it is unfortunate that no one has recorded whether he played any part in holding the kingdom together after the murder of Oswulf within a year. Indeed at that time both Eadbert and Ceolwulf were still alive, and it would be hard to believe that they were not in some way consulted over the events of the next few years.

[L29] **OSWULF** Northumbria, 758–24 July 759.
The son of EADBERT who came to the throne after his father's abdication. Eadbert must have believed he was handing over a safe kingdom, but he had underestimated the inter-dynastic feuds which he had capably handled but which his son mismanaged. Within a year Oswulf was murdered at Market Weighton. The perpetrators were probably descendents of EADWULF, whose son Eanwine Eadbert had killed in 740. A week after Oswulf's murder ATHELWOLD MOLL was elected king.

[L30] **ATHELWOLD MOLL** Northumbria, 5 August 759–30 October 765.
Athelwold's genealogy is not recorded so he almost certainly did not claim descent from IDA, but his cognomen Moll may be related to another of that name, identified as the brother of a king, who was involved in a dispute over church land. This king was quite probably EADWULF who had usurped the throne in 704, who may have had a brother called Moll. If so, then Athelwold could be that brother's son or, more likely, grandson. It seems very likely that there was a long-running dispute between Eadwulf's family and the dynasty of Ida, perhaps even earlier than 704, probably with its roots in the dealings of OSWY in the 650s and 660s, and possibly related to the houses of Bernicia and Deira. Athelwold may well have been involved in the murder of OSWULF in 759, for two weeks later Athelwold was elected king "by his own people". Retaining kingship under such conditions is always difficult unless the king has outstanding qualities. Athelwold was certainly capable but demonstrated nothing special; in fact many may have regarded the plague that swept through northern Britain in 760 as a bad omen. He did quell a revolt two years later when Oswine, who may have been a younger brother of Oswulf, raised an army against Athelwold. The opposing forces met in the Eildon Hills in August 761 in a battle that lasted for three days before Athelwold emerged victorious. He must have felt relatively secure after this for he married a certain Etheldreda the following year. However matters worsened. A devastating winter of 763/764 brought the kingdom to its knees and by 765 a council of elders deposed Athelwold and drove him into a monastery. No more is known of him. The leader of the elders may well have been ALRED who succeeded him as king.

[L31] **ALRED** Northumbria, 30 October 765–Easter 774.
Alred was the son of Eanwine and claimed descent from IDA's son Edric. This cadet line is not otherwise known although the name of Alred's grandfather, Beornholm, may suggest some connection with BEORNHETH's dynasty. Alred was elected king after ATHELWOLD MOLL was deposed. He sought to ally himself further with

EADBERT's dynasty by marrying Osgifu, the daughter of OSWULF, in 768. Alred was closely associated with the church and in particular the programme of missionary work in Europe. He also made contact with Charlemagne, probably in advance of the overtures of OFFA of Mercia. However by 773 there were increased disturbances in Northumbria and possibly a falling out between Alred and the new archbishop of York, Athelbert, who was a distant relative. The nature of the disagreement is not recorded but it seems to have been related to the missionary work in Frisia and possibly a clash between the Saxons and the Angles of Northumbria. Whatever the cause, Athelbert was able to call a council which deposed Alred in 774 and despatched him and his household into exile to the court of the Pictish king CINIOD. Although no more is heard of him one of his sons, OSRED, ruled briefly whilst another, Alchmund, was venerated as a saint. He was succeeded by ATHELRED (I).

[L32] **ATHELRED** (I) Northumbria, Easter 774–779 and again 14 September 790–28 March 796.

The son of ATHELWOLD MOLL, but unless he was the child of an earlier marriage, or an illegitimate son, he cannot have been more than eleven years old when elected king to replace ALRED. The suggestion is that Athelred was the puppet of more senior nobles unwilling to take the crown themselves. These would almost certainly be the relatives of Athelwold, who may still have been alive himself. Whatever machinations went on behind the scenes, Athelred eventually made up his own mind for, in March 778, he ordered the execution of three ealdormen by two high reeves. The likelihood is that the ealdormen had plotted against him and that the two reeves, Athelbald and Heaberht, were amongst Athelred's supporters. However support for Athelred waned thereafter, for by early 779 he was driven out of the kingdom by ELFWALD, the son of OSWULF.

Nevertheless support did not entirely fade away. Indeed it grew stronger over the next decade and, in 790, Athelred was able to stage a recovery following the expulsion of OSRED II. He was now in a more commanding position and used his strength to destroy his enemies. First he ordered the murder of a local ealdorman, EARDWULF, though the latter miraculously escaped and fled into exile. Then, early in 791, the sons of ELFWALD, who had claimed sanctuary in York Minster, were lured out and murdered. This may have caused some disquiet amongst Athelred's supporters for Osred was recalled in 792 to reclaim the throne, but he was betrayed and murdered. Athelred must have felt secure at this stage for he married Elfleda, the daughter of OFFA of Mercia, and there is no doubt that Offa would not have married his daughter to anyone other than a strong king. Nevertheless it was in Athelred's day that the first Viking ships arrived off the coast of England. In 793 they plundered the monastery on Lindisfarne, looking for the treasures of St Cuthbert. Abbot Alcuin, then residing in France, wrote to Athelred stating that the Viking attack was a punishment from God for the degeneration of the Northumbrian kingdom. In other kingdoms the presence of a common enemy might have united the factions, but not in Northumbria. The dissent between the royal families of Deira and Bernicia had now become too deeply rooted. In March 796 Athelred was murdered by Ealdred, a supporter of OSBALD, who ruled briefly before he in turn was overthrown.

[L33] **ELFWALD (I)** Northumbria, 779–23 September 788.

The son of OSWULF, who came to power following the deposition of the teenage ATHELRED in 779, presumably with the support of Archbishop Athelbert of York, whose role had become significant in deciding the fate of kings. However Athelbert retired from the archbishopric in 780 and there was immediately a reaction against Elfwald. His patron, Beorn, was murdered by OSBALD and Athelheard, supporters of Athelred. Elfwald weathered this storm, but civil unrest increased to the extent that in 786 a papal legate, George of Ostia, was sent to inquire into the state of health of the archbishopric at York. George was disappointed with what he found and believed that the Northumbrian kingship had degenerated. He issued a decree about the legitimacy of the royal dynasty and its relationship with the church which was confirmed by Elfwald. This included a reference to the sanctity of the kingship which was an earthly representation of the church. Unfortunately Athelred's supporters did not follow this decree, for two years later, in September 788, Sicga, who had once been Elfwald's adherent, murdered him at his royal residence near Chesters-on-the-Wall. Elfwald was buried at Hexham where a cult grew up about him and he became venerated as a saint because a light had been seen shining over the spot where he had been murdered. His murderer later committed suicide.

[L34] **OSRED II**, Northumbria, September 788–790.

The son of ALRED was probably born about the year 770 so was scarcely eighteen when chosen to succeed his murdered cousin ELFWALD. Support for him did not last long and within less than two years he was deposed, apparently by the same nobles who elected him. Osred was banished and fled to the Isle of Man. He attempted to regain the throne in 792 but was captured and killed on 14 September. He was buried at Tynemouth.

[L35] **OSBALD** Northumbria, 28 March-24 April 796.

Osbald was a one-time supporter of ATHELRED, who seems to have turned against his king in the second part of his reign and was even implicated in his murder. Osbald's parentage is not recorded, and by his time the inter-dynastic fighting between the royal families of Bernicia and Deira had become so complicated that he could have belonged to any one of four or five branches, but the likeliest is some connection with the family of EADBERT, whose son OSWULF had been murdered forty years earlier. Support for Osbald was the briefest of all in these volatile years, for within only twenty-seven days he was abandoned in favour of the exile EARDWULF. Osbald escaped to Lindisfarne where the monks escorted him to Pictland for safety. Osbald later entered the church and died in 799. He was buried at York.

[L36] **EARDWULF** Northumbria, 24 April 796–806; 808–11.

Eardwulf was yet another claimant to the Northumbrian throne in the years of civil strife that plagued the eighth century. We know little of his lineage except that he was the grandson of another Eardwulf or Eadwulf, who might have been to the earlier usurper EADWULF and may have been the son of the Eanwine executed by Eadbert in 740. Eardwulf had been lucky to escape with his life in 790 when ATHELRED ordered his death, presumably because Eardwulf had plotted against him. Eardwulf was left for dead but recovered and fled into exile. Eardwulf seems to have rapidly endeared himself to the church, though not necessarily to his fellow nobility for several plots against his life plagued the early years of his reign. The most serious led to the battle of Billington Moor in May 798, apparently against supporters of OSBALD, who was still in exile, but Eardwulf was victorious. Eardwulf became estranged from the new archbishop of York, Eanbald, partly because Eanbald reprimanded the king for his adulterous lifestyle (he had abandoned his wife and taken a mistress), but also because many of Eardwulf's enemies sought sanctuary from the church, giving the impression that Eanbald was supporting them. The first five years of Eardwulf's reign were thus very tense. Matters came to a head in 800 when Eardwulf ordered the execution of Alchmund, the son of ALRED, who had apparently been plotting against Eardwulf with the support of the Mercians. Eardwulf led a punitive expedition against CENWULF of Mercia in 801 which resulted in long-drawn out hostilities, only resolved by the negotiation of bishops of Mercia and Northumbria. Eardwulf's strength seemed to rely on the good relationship he had with the Frankish king Charlemagne. When he was deposed by ELFWALD (II) in 806 he fled to the court of Charlemagne and was able to rely on an escort provided by both Charlemagne and Pope Leo III who restored him to his kingdom in 808. Eardwulf seems to have been the first to die peacefully as king since ALDFRITH a century before. He established a short-lived dynasty, as he was also the first king since EADBERT to be succeeded directly by his son EANRED, the last great ruler of the Northumbrians.

[L37] ELFWALD II Northumbria, 806–8.

His ancestry is not known and though his name suggests a link with the first ELFWALD, that cannot be taken for granted. He successfully deposed EARDWULF in 806, but was himself overthrown two years later when Eardwulf returned triumphant with an escort from Charlemagne and Pope Leo. His fate thereafter is not known, though Eardwulf's earlier record for revenge suggests that Elfwald would have been lucky to have escaped with a pardon.

[L38] EANRED Northumbria, 811–43.

Eanred was the son of EARDWULF. His father's reign and the establishment of political alliances with the court of Charlemagne had given the Northumbrian kingdom the first opportunity for stability in over a century. Eanred's reign of thirty-two years is the longest recorded of any Northumbrian king and speaks volumes for his own abilities and how he must have been regarded. By now the Northumbrians must have tired of decades of inter-dynastic struggles which had plagued the eighth century. Eanred clearly established sufficient authority to check them. How he did this is unfortunately not recorded but we can imagine that Eanred involved his ealdormen more directly in his government and vested greater authority in them. He is remembered as a highly diplomatic king. Although Eanred submitted to the overlordship of EGBERT of Wessex in 829, this seems to have interfered little with his government, probably because the return to power of WIGLAF of Mercia and ATHELSTAN of East Anglia effectively drove a barrier between Wessex and Northumbria. Eanred's attention was directed more to the north where the kingdom of the Picts was disintegrating before the increasing power of the Dál Riatan Scots. When KENNETH MACALPIN assumed authority in 840 he raided Northumbrian territory and Eanred was driven to re-establish his frontier.

Though this pressure may have weakened his control over the kingdom in his final years, it does not detract from the remarkable reign of Eanred, which held some of the glitter of Northumbria's former glory.

[L39] **ATHELRED II** Northumbria, 843–49.
[L40] **REDWULF** Northumbria, c844.

Athelred was the son of EANRED. Although he inherited a relatively stable kingdom, it seems likely that Eanred's personal standing had held previous dynastic rivalries in check. Soon after Athelred's accession his authority was challenged by REDWULF, who was probably a distant relative. Redwulf usurped the throne and Athelred was temporarily deposed. Redwulf may have proved a more powerful king than Athelred but his reign was abbreviated when he was killed repulsing a Viking raid in 844 or soon after. Athelred returned to the throne but was murdered in 849 by supporters of another rival faction under OSBERT.

[L41] **OSBERT** Northumbria, 849–66.

Annals vary over the length of Osbert's reign, from thirteen to eighteen years. The latter is the more likely, though it may have been calculated to the time of his death, a year after his expulsion. His pedigree is not known, and though his name suggests a link to rulers of the previous century it is not possible to link him with any one family. Since his brother was possibly called AELLE, it seems likely that he was from a Deiran royal family. Little is known of his reign except that he faced increasing threats from the Vikings as well as raids from the Scots king KENNETH MACALPIN into Lothian. Perhaps because of these pressures, Aelle joined him as co-ruler in 862, though records are uncertain on this. Whatever the case, by 866 Osbert had quarrelled with the church and confiscated lands from the community of Lindisfarne. This was clearly the final straw and Osbert was deposed, not necessarily by Aelle, although that is the favoured story. He was still called king by the *ASC* when Osbert and Aelle fought against the Vikings at York, where both were killed.

[L42] **AELLE (II)** Deira, 862–21 March 867.

The last independent king of Northumbria. He is sometimes identified as the brother of OSBERT, though the *ASC* states that he was not of royal blood. He came to power in the year 862, and may have ruled jointly with Osbert for the next four years. They divided the kingdom between them with Osbert ruling Bernicia and Aelle in Deira. In 866 Osbert was ousted from the kingdom and Aelle ruled alone, but within a few months the two were united in facing the onslaught of the Danes. The first invasion came from Ragnar Lodbrok, whom Aelle killed. His sons, IVARR and HALFDAN, returned for revenge and took York in November 866. Aelle escaped but there was a second battle in March 867. There was overwhelming slaughter in which both Osbert and Aelle died. Thereafter York and the kingdom of Deira fell into Danish hands. The Vikings ruled Deira directly but installed a puppet king, EGBERT in Bernicia.

[L43] **EGBERT (I)** Bernicia, March 867–872.

Nothing is recorded of his activities which must have been confined to administering the kingdom subject to Viking demands. His authority lasted for five years until the Northumbrians revolted in 872 under RICSIG and Egbert fled into exile in Mercia, where he died the following year.

[L44] **RICSIG** Bernicia, 872–6.

A Northumbrian nobleman, probably of royal descent, who rebelled against the Viking domination of Bernicia in 872 and expelled their client king EGBERT. It seems that Ricsig succeeded in maintaining his independence from the Vikings even though his campaign brought the Viking army back to Northumbria to contain his revolt. The Vikings agreed to re-installing archbishop Wulfhere at York, but they did not place a client king on the throne of Deira. Instead by 876 they settled in Deira, parcelled out land, and established their own kingdom of Jorvik under HALFDAN. It was in 876 that Ricsig's reign ceased, but it is not clear whether he died or was overthrown. He was succeeded by EGBERT II.

[L45] **EGBERT** (II) Bernicia, 876 till 878 and possibly 888.

Egbert was no client king, but it is possible he was more amenable to working with the Vikings than Ricsig. The greater threat to Egbert was from the north where the combined forces of GIRIC and EOCHAID of the Scots succeeded in driving the Angles out of Lothian and northern Bernicia and reclaiming the land for the Celts. Egbert may have exercised authority over Deira, as the Danes were without a king from 877 to 883, and he may have continued to rule the Bernician Angles, if only indirectly through the church. It is uncertain if Egbert was himself expelled from Bernicia by 888 or whether he ruled for a few more years. He was eventually succeeded by EADULF.

[L46] **EADULF** or **EADWULF** Bernicia, 888 (or later)-913.

Eadulf's pedigree is not known, though he may have been related to EGBERT II. Eadulf ruled Bernicia between the Tyne and the Tweed, a territory which remained an English enclave and was not overrun by either the Vikings or the Scots. Eadulf established a strong alliance with ALFRED THE GREAT, who would have needed the support of Eadulf in his campaign against the Vikings. Although Eadulf is described by the *Annals of Ulster* as "king of the northern Saxons", he probably acknowledged the overlordship of Alfred and his son EDWARD THE ELDER. By the end of his reign he was regarded as ealdorman, but he established a dynasty of earls who controlled Bamburgh until the Norman conquest. Although his sons Uhtred and Ealdred were expelled from Bamburgh by the Viking king RAGNALD in 914, they regained their lands in 920. The last of the dynasty was Osulf, who was killed in 1067.

LOTHIAN

[L47] **BEORNHETH** Lothian, 670–85.

[L48] **BEORHT** or **BEORHTRED** Lothian, 685–98.

Beornheth was a sub-king of Lothian appointed by EGFRITH of Northumbria to help guard the northern approaches against the Picts, who had rebelled against Northumbrian sovereignty under BRUDE MAC BILI. He was a good man to have, strong, valiant and loyal. He helped to win a mighty victory against the Picts in 672 and held the borders for the next thirteen years. He accompanied Egfrith on his fateful expedition against the Picts in 685 and was killed at the battle of Nechtansmere. His son, Beorht or Beorhtred, had already served Egfrith well in leading his campaign into Ireland in 684, where he ravaged the kingdom of Brega and sought out British pirates. It is likely that Beorht and his father were involved in Egfrith's campaign against the British of Rheged throughout the 680s. Beorht was himself killed fighting the Picts in 698. His son BEORHTFRITH continued the dynasty.

[L49] **BEORHTFRITH** Lothian, 698–711 or after.

The son of BEORHT, Beorhtfrith continued to serve ALDFRITH as valiantly as his father. He was a sub-king, rather like a Marcher Lord, defending the northern frontier of Northumbria against the Picts. In 704, on the death of Aldfrith, Beorhtfrith held the kingdom safe against the usurper EADWULF and protected Aldfrith's son OSRED until the arrival of Bishop Wilfrid. Thereafter Beorhtfrith served as regent and commander of Northumbria. He inflicted a major defeat on the Picts on the plains of Lothian in 711. He is not mentioned again in the annals after that date. Wilfrid had died shortly before and Osred entered his majority. It is possible that Osred later exiled Beorhtfrith as he did other Northumbrian nobles who came to dislike his ways. Because of Beorhtfrith's loyalty it is quite possible that some of the later claimants to the Northumbrian throne were his own descendents.

M. WEST SAXONS – Gewisse and Wessex

It was not until the late seventh century that Wessex began to take on a unified shape. The West Saxons were a number of tribes who conquered territory across the south of Britain. The main concentration was in Wiltshire and Hampshire, but there was another core of settlers along the Berkshire Downs. There was considerable rivalry first with the British and then the Mercians for territory in Gloucestershire and the Severn valley. Later the West Saxons began to push further west into Somerset and Dorset. With territory fragmented and covering such a spread of ground there would have been several kings at any one time, not necessarily related, though later genealogists sought to contain them in a single family tree. In fact the West Saxons were a confederacy of tribes and adopted the name Gewisse, which means confederate but which originally related to a British tribe or tribes in the area known as Ergyng or Archenfield. It was not until the reign of Ine that these tribes became united. Under Egbert they would become the dominant kingdom, and the West Saxon dynasty became the rulers of England. This section traces these rulers down to the time of Alfred the Great and the Danish invasion.

Ref.	Ruler	Born	Reign	Died	Notes
M1.	Cerdic		538?–54?	554?	
M2.	Cynric		554?–81?	581?	
M3.	Ceawlin		581?–8?	589?	ruled with Cutha; deposed
M3a.	Cutha		*fl* 570s–80s		sub-king of the Gewisse
M4.	Ceol		588–94	594	
M5.	Ceolwulf		594–611	611	
M6.	Cynegils		611–43	643	ruled with Cwichhelm
M6a.	Cwichhelm		*c*614–*c*36		sub-king of the West Saxons
M7.	Cenwealh		643–72	672	in exile 645–8
M7a.	Cuthred I		645–8	661	Cuthred served as vassal king under Penda
M8.	Seaxburh (Queen)		672–3		the only recorded Saxon queen

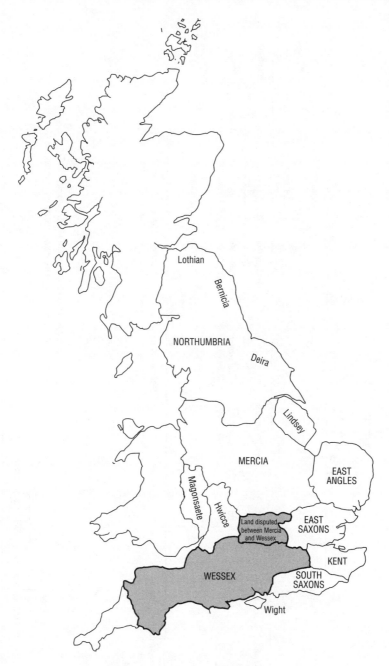

Map 7g **The Anglo-Saxon Kingdoms – Wessex**

Wessex was fragmented amongst many sub-kings during the period 672–82. These included Cenfus, Cenred and Baldred at the outset plus the following three kings in later years and almost certainly other claimants.

M9.	Aescwine	674–6	676	
M10.	Centwine	676–85	?	abdicated and became a monk

16. Anglo-Saxon Kingdoms (6) – The West Saxons

The genealogies of the early West Saxon kings are very suspect and relationships between rulers cannot be taken for granted.

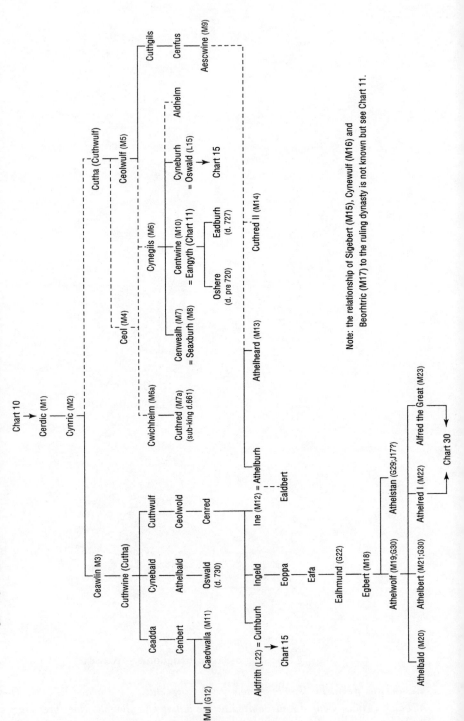

Note: the relationship of Sigebert (M15), Cynewulf (M16) and Beorhtric (M17) to the ruling dynasty is not known but see Chart 11.

Ref.	Ruler	Born	Reign	Died	Notes
M11.	Caedwalla	c659	685–687	688	also ruled Kent and Sussex; died on pilgrimage in Rome
M12.	Ine		688–726	728	abdicated and retired to Rome
M13.	Athelheard		726–40	740	
M14.	Cuthred II		740–56	756	
M15.	Sigebert		756–7		expelled and murdered
M16.	Cynewulf		757–786	786	murdered
M17.	Beorhtric		786–802	802	
M18.	Egbert	771?	802–39	839	became bretwalda in 829
M19.	Athelwolf	c795	839–55	858	retired; see G28
M20.	Athelbald	c831	855–60	860	
M21.	Athelbert	c833	860–5	865	also sub-king of Kent; see G30
M22.	Athelred (I)	c837	865–71	871	died as a result of wounds in battle
M23.	Alfred (the Great)	849	871–99	899	

By the time of Alfred the West Saxons had imposed their authority over the rest of England, but the nation had again become riven by the Danish invasions and the fight for Britain began. For the kings from Edward the Elder onwards turn to page 469.

[M1] **CERDIC** Gewisse or West Saxons, 519–34 or 538–54.

Cerdic is something of a mystery. The traditional story, as told in the *ASC* by the ninth century annalists seeking to find a pedigree for their great Saxon kings, was that Cerdic, the son of Elesa, and his son CYNRIC came to Britain with five ships and landed at Cerdicesford and on that day fought the British. Six years later they "obtained" the kingdom of the West Saxons, Cerdic ruling for fifteen years. The dates ascribed are contradictory and unlikely. The introduction to the *ASC* states they arrived in the year 494 and that six years later, or 500, they "conquered" the kingdom of Wessex. The later annals, however, assign the year 519 to the birth of Wessex. The latter year is the more likely (otherwise Cynric is exceedingly old by the time he dies) if we accept the six year period before gaining Wessex that would place their arrival in around 513/514, the year the annals describe another pair of Saxons (STUF and WIHTGAR) arriving, also at Cerdicesford, and also putting the British to flight. Possibly the annalists confused dates or Saxons in their desire to grant Wessex an ancient pedigree. It is possible that in reckoning their dates backward (based on the Easter cycle of feasts which repeats every nineteen years) they counted back from 519 instead of forward, which would start Cerdic's reign in 538, a more satisfactory date. This revised dating robs us of the opportunity of Cerdic clashing with ARTHUR. The original dates for Cerdic's reign (494–516) allow us to assume that Cerdic was killed at Badon (*see under* AELLE).

Even more confusing, though, is that Cerdic is a British name, not Saxon, the same as CEREDIG and CARADOC. Since no independent records survive to prove Cerdic's existence we have to draw conclusions. It has been suggested that Cerdic may have been a British chieftain, governing as an administrator (not a hereditary monarch) after the Roman fashion in the land around Salisbury: Wiltshire and Somerset. It is even possible that he or his relatives had married into the Saxon nobility, as the Saxons were already making incursions into Britain. Perhaps, with Saxon support, Cerdic proclaimed himself king and established a dynasty around the year 519 (or 538). The Britons would now regard him as a traitor, so the battle ascribed to him against the British in the year 527 (or 546) may well be true. A clue to this is in the name of Cerdic's tribe. He was known as the chief of the Gewisse (the name of Wessex did not come into existence for another two centuries). This name relates to his great-grandfather Gewis, another British name, but more significantly the Gewisse was originally a tribe or group of tribes which existed in the area around Shropshire and Herefordshire, running into the territory of Ergyng. The word Gewisse came to be used to describe a confederate army which may have consisted of Celts and Saxons and which had no fixed territory but roamed throughout the territory of Wiltshire and Somerset. However Cerdic may well have been a prince of the Gewisse in Wales, probably in Ergyng, which may have made him a relative of GWRGAN or CARADOC VREICHFAS. He may have been expelled from Ergyng because of his Saxon sympathies and with an army of Gewisse he may have fled across the English Channel to Brittany, where other British tribes had migrated, and from there he returned a few years later attempting to regain his lands but with an army of Saxon mercenaries. Cerdicesford, where he reputedly landed, is in Hampshire, near the head of the Solent. However no archeological evidence supports this. This area contains more remains of the Jutes (who had settled on the Isle of Wight) than the Saxons, whose archeological remains are more to the west, in Somerset and Wiltshire.

It is just possible that Cerdic has nothing to do with Wessex. The *ASC* states that in 530 (which may be 549), Cerdic and Cynric obtained the Isle of Wight and slew men at Wihtgarasburh. The Isle of Wight was occupied by Jutes not Saxons. It has been suggested that Wihtgarasburh is in fact Wigtown in Galloway, and that Cerdic led his Saxon forces into battle in the north. Only later did his descendants move south, but so great a hero had Cerdic become that his name became associated with the later established kingdom. It is conjectural, but not without possibility, as it does help explain the anomalous years following his death (*see under* CYNRIC). Cerdic died either in 534 or 554 and is believed to be buried at Cerdicesbeorg in the northern part of Hampshire, near Stoke-in-Hurtsbourne, though it is also suggested he died and is buried in Northumbria. *See also* KEREDIC.

[M2] **CYNRIC** West Saxons, 534–60 or 554–71 (or 581).
The son (or possibly grandson) of CERDIC, the supposed founder of the kingdom of Wessex. Cynric is closely associated in the *ASC* with his father from the year 494 to his death in 560, but even assuming he was just of age (16) in 494, this would make him 82 at the time of death, an unlikely age, since he was still battling the British only a few years before. The West Saxon regnal lists refers to CREODA as the son of Cerdic and father of Cynric, which would help explain the anomaly. Allowing a normal Saxon generation of about 20 years would bring Cynric's age at death down to a more acceptable 62. We also need to allow for the possible miscalculation of dates by the annalists (*see under* CERDIC *for details*) which introduced a 19–year discrepancy. This shifts Cynric's reign to around 554–581. Whether he did rule for 26 years must also be subject to doubt, especially as his son is also accorded a long reign. There may be some lost kings during this period, or some reigns overlapping.

The *ASC* records two battles for Cynric, one at Searoburh (Old Sarum) in 552 (probably 571) and one at Beranburh (Barbury Castle) four years later. Both of these are consistent with establishing and sustaining a kingdom around Wiltshire. Cynric was succeeded by his son CEAWLIN.

[M3] **CEAWLIN** West Saxons, 560–92 or 571 (or 581)–88.
With Ceawlin, the third named king of Wessex, we reach firmer historical ground. There is more support for his reign than for those of his predecessors CYNRIC or CERDIC, though the problem over dates remains. According to the *ASC* he succeeded to the kingdom in 560 and reigned for 32 years. However the West Saxon regnal list only affords him seventeen (or seven) years (versions vary). Since the *ASC* gave an equally lengthy reign to Cynric, this is suggestive either of other forgotten kings, with the reigns of the known kings extended to fill the gaps, or of prolongation of reigns to establish a more ancient pedigree, something later Wessex annalists were likely to desire once Wessex became the primary power. He may already have ruled jointly with his father for part of his reign, especially if his father lived into his sixties. This overlap would explain the discrepancy of the two long reigns and allow us to reduce Ceawlin's solo reign to a more credible period.

Ceawlin's reign includes a catalogue of battles. He is recorded as fighting with his father at the battle of Beranburh in 556 (which may adjust to 575). In 568 (or 583) he teamed up with fellow Saxon CUTHA to fight on a united front against ATHELBERT, the new king of Kent, who was expanding his frontiers, which suggests that Ceawlin was stretching his own borders to the east. His other battles, especially at Dyrham, in 577 (this date may be accurate) were to the west and consolidated his kingdom around Wiltshire and Somerset. Dyrham was a decisive battle where Ceawlin defeated the British kings of Gloucester, Cirencester and Bath and (presumably) took over their land (*see* COINMAIL, FARINMAIL and CONDIDAN). These towns took several generations to recover from the battle. Bede lists Ceawlin as the second Saxon *bretwalda*, a form of high king, following the death of AELLE. In these early years the title is meaningless, but if it was conferred by any general agreement it probably came as a result of this victory, which allowed Ceawlin to establish a fixed West Saxon kingdom as distinct from his roving war-band.

Events went poorly for Ceawlin thereafter. Although he won another victory over the British at Fethanlea in 584, it was not without cost, and his ally Cutha was slain. Fethanlea is usually placed in Oxfordshire, but there was another decisive battle against the British near Tintern on the Wye which both sides identified as a victory (*see under* MEURIG AP TEWDRIG). A few years later it was recorded that there was "great slaughter" at Adam's Grave, east of Devizes, and Ceawlin was "expelled". The records do not say whether this battle was against the British or (more likely) against fellow Saxons, as this was the period of the great influx of Mercian Angles. In the following year Ceawlin "perished", though the records do not say how. If he had died valiantly in battle the annals would have been only too keen to boast of the fact, so one must assume Ceawlin met a rather ignominious death. He was succeeded by CEOL.

[M3a] **CUTHA** West Saxons, *fl* 570s–80s.
The name Cutha seems to be an abbreviation used for two different Saxon war-leaders, Cuthwine and Cuthwulf. The use of the abbreviated version in Saxon

annals and genealogies makes it difficult to distinguish between the two individuals or to make any accurate relationship about their identity. Cuthwine is usually identified as the son of CEAWLIN, and Cutha or Cuthwulf is named as Cuthwine's son, but elsewhere Cutha is identified as Ceawlin's brother. John Morris has suggested that both Cuthwine and Cuthwulf were warleaders of the Eslingas, a tribe of Saxons who operated in the territory around Bedford and Buckinghamshire, and were not related to Ceawlin. The dating of their activities is confused by errors in the *ASC* chronology, particularly in relation to ATHELBERT of Kent, but revising the dates disrupts what was evidently a clear sequence of events. In the year 568 (in *ASC* chronology) Cutha joined forces with Ceawlin to drive back Athelbert who was expanding his frontiers west and north. Three years later Cutha defeated the Britons along the north Thames between Bedford and Oxford, driving them further west. In that same year Cutha (Cuthwulf?) died. The other Cutha (Cuthwine?) along with Ceawlin defeated the British at Dyrham in 577, a decisive battle which probably saw the first firm foundation of the West Saxon kingdom. Cutha's last battle was at Fethanlea in 584, when he again fought alongside Ceawlin but was killed. This battle is usually located in Oxfordshire, but it may equally apply to an as yet unidentified site near Tintern, where it is also recorded in 584 that MEURIG of Gwent defeated a Saxon army so convincingly that they did not attempt to trouble the Welsh across the Wye for another thirty years. This may well be the battle where Cutha fell. He was never identified as a king, but as a war leader his victories were decisive in carving out the territory of the West Saxons. He may have been the father of CEOLWULF who became king in 594.

[M4] **CEOL** West Saxons, 588–94.
Ceol (whose name is also recorded in error as Ceolric in the *ASC*) was almost certainly a usurper who claimed the kingdom of the West Saxons from CEAWLIN. Later genealogies tried to make him the nephew of Ceawlin, which is possible, but the reliability of these records is suspect, especially in relation to a period of major uncertainty. Ceol's name is similar to an early (and equally uncertain) ruler of Mercia (*see* CEORL) who was endeavouring to carve out his patch of British soil and would have clashed with the West Saxons (*see also* CREODA *whose reign parallels Ceol's*). Ceol probably defeated Ceawlin in battle at Adam's Grave, near Devizes, and held his territory for a few years (six according to the *ASC*). The *ASC* does not record Ceol's death, so it is possible that after six years he lost his gains to CEOLWULF, recorded in the annals as his brother, but almost certainly the son of CUTHA, Ceawlin's former ally and ruler of the neighbouring Eslingas.

[M5] **CEOLWULF** West Saxons, 594–611.
Ceolwulf's ancestry is unclear from the variant references in the *ASC*. Allowing for the possibility that there was more than one Ceolwulf, he is described variously as the brother of CEOL, the son of CUTHA (which may be Cuthwine or Cuthwulf) and the son of CYNRIC. Although the genealogists strive to show a descent from CERDIC, this may not have been the case. After the overthrow of CEAWLIN and the brief reign of the usurper CEOL, it is possible that Ceolwulf regained the kingdom through a show of strength. If he was the son of Cutha, his father would have been a renowned soldier whose son would have been a welcome leader of the Gewisse. The *ASC* is not too certain about Ceolwulf's activities. He seems to have fought against everyone,

including the Picts and the Scots: the annalists may here have confused this Ceolwulf with later rulers of Mercia and Northumbria. We have already conjectured that Cerdic may have been involved in battles against the Picts sixty years earlier, but it is a much harder to imagine Ceolwulf active in the north at a time when he was struggling to consolidate his territories in the south. The one possible solution to this may relate to the Pictish king NECHTAN, who also came to rule Strathclyde and possibly part of Rheged. It is just possible that some of Nechtan's troops reached as far south as Chester and that Ceolwulf's forays along the Welsh border took him this far north. He would certainly have been fighting the Angles of Mercia at this stage under PYBBA, and Pybba may even have called upon British or Pictish support as his son later called upon assistance from the Welsh. The one clearly recorded battle of Ceolwulf's is against the South Saxons in 607. He is not identified as the victor, and we may assume that this formed part of the advance of the South Saxons towards the West (see CISSA). Ceolwulf was succeeded by CYNEGILS.

[M6] **CYNEGILS** or **CYNGLIS** West Saxons, 611–43.
[M6a] **CWICHELM** Joint ruler of the West Saxons from 614 or earlier to 636 or later.
Cynegils's exact ancestry is unclear but it seems likely that he was the son (or nephew) of CEOLWULF and grandson of CUTHA. The confusion over his pedigree has caused some commentators to suggest that there were two Cynegils, which may also account for the length of his reign, though the latter may be explained if Cynegils was young when he was elected leader. Cynegils is shown as fighting alongside Cwichelm in 614, and Cwichelm is elsewhere identified as Cynegils's son, but this is probably a false attribution. Cwichelm may even have been older than Cynegils and seems to have been a joint king of the Gewisse, probably ruling a separate grouping to the north of the Thames, where Cynegils ruled to the south. The battle of 614 was at Beandun, a site as yet unidentified, though Bindon, near Axmouth on the Devon-Dorset border, has been suggested. The scale of this victory was immense – the *ASC* records that over two thousand Welsh [British] were killed, and it is probable that the Celts of Dumnonia were supported by contingents from Wales (see TEWDWR). If Bindon is the correct location then it must have given the Saxons firm control over Dorset and probably Somerset. We can imagine that for the next few years Cynegils and Cwichelm fought to consolidate their victory along the borders of Dumnonia across the whole south-west peninsula and along the Severn Valley. Dorset, Somerset and Wiltshire was probably wholly Saxon by 625, and Cwichelm evidently had greater designs on territory to the north and east. It was probably his forces, or those of another group of the Gewisse, that attacked the East Saxons south of London in 623, killing the sons of SAEBERT. In 626 Cwichelm despatched a thane to assassinate EDWIN of Northumbria. He was unsuccessful, and Edwin sent a punitive army which devastated parts of Wessex and killed a number of war leaders. This must have weakened Cwichelm's defenses for in 628 he and Cynegils were defeated by PENDA of Mercia at the Battle of Cirencester, and thereafter the territory around Gloucester and Cirencester passed into Mercian hands. For the time being Cynegils and Cwichelm had to be satisfied with their territories in the south. In 634 Pope Honorius I despatched a new envoy to Britain. This was Birinus. It has never been

fully explained why he was sent when the missionaries who had arrived with Augustine were still present. Possibly the Pope felt they needed additional support, as their efforts were concentrated in the south-east. Birinus came to the West Saxons and found that the Christian faith had not reached them at all. The date of this mission may be a few years later, because OSWALD of Northumbria was present when Birinus baptized Cynegils, and Oswald is unlikely to have left Northumbria in 634 or 635 within only a few months of regaining his kingdom. Oswald married Cynegils's daughter Cyneburh, and it may have been a condition of that marriage that Cynegils become a Christian. It is possible, of course, that Oswald himself requested Birinus in order to learn more about the Roman church – Oswald was already a Christian convert from his years of exile on Iona. The wedding and his conversion probably took place around 639 or 640 rather than 635. Cwichelm, it seems, was not converted until the following year (636 or 641) the same year in which he died. Cynegils gave Birinus land at Dorchester, south of Oxford, demonstrating that at this stage he still commanded land north of the Thames which was not yet subject to Mercia. Conversion did not happen all at once. Cuthred, Cwichelm's son, who probably succeeded his father as king of northern Wessex, was not converted until 639 (643?), whilst CENWEALH, who succeeded Cynegils, was not converted until much later. Cynegils's reign marked the start of the transition for the Gewisse from a group of roving war-bands to an established kingdom.

[M7] **CENWEALH** West Saxons, 643–5; 648–72.
The son and successor of CYNEGILS. His name means "bold (or keen) Welshman", which suggests his mother was British. The "keenness" was reflected in his later actions. He was a headstrong youth, as he refused to accept conversion to the Roman Christian faith under Birinus who had come as missionary to the West Saxons in or after the year 634. Cenwealh had also been married to the sister of PENDA of Mercia, probably as part of a political alliance during the late 630s. However, early into his reign, probably about the year 645, Cenwealh abandoned his wife in favour of another. This infuriated Penda who sent an army against Cenwealh and drove him out of the kingdom. He fled into exile in East Anglia where he subsequently accepted Christianity from the devout Anglian king ANNA. Cenwealh was restored to his kingdom after three years, though what he did to make amends to Penda is not recorded. Though it is not stated who ruled Wessex during his exile, it was likely to be CUTHRED, the son of Cwichelm. In 648 Cenwealh gave Cuthred three thousand hides of land (between 300 and 450 square miles) at Ashdown (on the Berkshire Downs), probably by way of compensation. Now that Cenwealh had converted to Christianity, he wished to promote it amongst the West Saxons. When Birinus died in 650, Cenwealh invited the Frankish monk Agilbert to take over the see at Dorchester. Unfortunately Agilbert did not know the Saxon language and Cenwealh, ever impatient, got fed up trying to understand him, and in 660 he created a new diocese at Winchester, appointing Wine as the bishop. Agilbert had not been consulted over this and so left Wessex. Wine also fell out with Cenwealh sometime before 670 and entered into negotiations with WULFHERE of Mercia to buy the see of London. Wessex was thus without a bishop. Cenwealh appealed to Agilbert, who was now bishop of Paris, and though Agilbert refused to

return he sent his nephew Leuthere. These episodes demonstrate that Cenwealh was an impulsive, impatient man, with strong passions once his mind was made up, but with little regard for the consequences.

Throughout the latter part of his reign Cenwealh was increasingly over-shadowed by Mercia, which grew in power and encroached upon former West Saxon territory. It seems that after his exile Cenwealh had needed to re-establish his authority for in 652 he is recorded as fighting at Bradford-on-Avon, possibly against the British of Dumnonia, though the Welsh under MORGAN MWYNFAWR were also involved. One chronicler referred to this battle as a civil war suggesting Cenwealh was defending himself against other West Saxons, which is quite a possibility considering what happened after his death. The battle seems to have been indecisive, and we can imagine that his control over his territories was weakened. However he recovered and in 658 was victorious over the British at Penselwood, driving them back across the river Parret into Somerset. Three years later he defeated them again at Postbury, so that by 661 he could claim to have regained controlled over Somerset. However, by that same year, Wulfhere controlled all of the lands to the north of the Thames, possibly including the abbey at Dorchester, which is why Cenwealh created a new one at Winchester. Cuthred is recorded as dying in 661, the same year that Wulfhere invaded his territory at Ashdown, and it is likely that Cuthred died in the conflict. Another sub-king, Cenberht, also died in 661. By the end of 661 Wulfhere's army had invaded as far as the Isle of Wight which he took from the West Saxons and gave to the South Saxons. It has been suggested that these events were not all telescoped into one year but the result of a series of incursions by Wulfhere, but it is certain that by the mid-660s Cenwealh's territory had been seriously reduced by Wulfhere and his authority limited. Although he still remained on good terms with a number of kings and church officials, particularly in Northumbria, when Cenwealh died he left a kingdom weaker than when he came. As a result the government of the kingdom fractured under a number of sub-kings, whilst Cenwealh's queen, SEAXBURH, endeavoured to maintain control.

[M7a] CUTHRED (I) West Saxons, 645–8.
He was a sub-king, son of Cwichhelm, who ruled over northern Wessex and may well have exerted wider authority over the Gewisse during the period of PENDA's overlordship. He was rewarded by CENWEALH with three thousand hides of land in Berkshire which presumably remained his "kingdom" until his death in 661, possibly in battle against WULFHERE.

[M8] SEAXBURH Queen of the West Saxons, 672–3.
Seaxburh is unique in being the only queen regnant identified in the Saxon regnal lists. These exceptional circumstances are not explained in the annals and need some consideration. She was the widow of CENWEALH and, unless he married again, we must assume that she was the wife he took in the year 645 when he abandoned his first wife, the sister of PENDA. She was probably in her late forties at least when he died, possibly older. Bede records that on the death of Cenwealh, sub-kings assumed control and divided the kingdom up amongst themselves until reunited by CENTWINE ten years later. The regnal lists however do not identify multiple kings, and it is not necessarily correct to state that the four kings named between Cenwealh and INE necessarily ruled concurrently. The picture painted is more

one of civil strife, common in many Saxon kingdoms, of rival claimants fighting over the throne. It is probable that in these circumstances Seaxburh endeavoured to hold together some form of central power with the support of Leuthere, the bishop of Winchester. There were any number of *athelings* (princes) in Wessex at this time aspiring for kingship. Amongst the more powerful were Cenred, the father of INE, who seems to have had territory in or around Dorset, Cenfus, the father of AESCWINE, who ruled somewhere in northern Wessex, and Baldred who ruled for many years in parts of Somerset. How long Seaxburh survived is not recorded, but Aescwine seems to have usurped authority after a year. It is strange that no children are recorded to Cenwealh and Seaxburh, and they may have had none, but it is possible that Seaxburh remained as regent for an infant son, who may have died or been killed by one of the rival claimants. Seaxburh's death is not recorded, but she probably retired to the monastery at Winchester.

[M9] **AESCWINE** West Saxons, 674–6.

One of the many sub-kings who partitioned Wessex amongst themselves after the death of CENWEALH. One chronicle records that Aescwine's father, Cenfus, also claimed the kingship. Both claimed descent from Ceolwulf, the son of CYNRIC (who may be the same CEOLWULF who ruled seventy years earlier). Aescwine's name may have survived because he alone amongst the claimants defeated WULFHERE of Mercia, late in 674 or early 675. The battle was doubtless over territory just north of the Thames. Aescwine ruled for only two years, yet he must have been a young man, so we must deduce he died of an illness or was mortally wounded or killed in battle. He was succeeded by CENTWINE.

[M10] **CENTWINE** West Saxons, 676–85.

Centwine is identified as a son of CYNEGILS and brother of CENWEALH, and if so he must have been in his forties when he claimed rulership of the West Saxons. This may seem a little too old for one who was regarded as a strong king by bishop Aldhelm, and who was victorious in battle, but it is about the right age for one who eventually abdicated and became a monk perhaps ten years later. In truth Centwine's origins are uncertain. If he was one of the many sub-kings who, according to Bede, divided the kingdom between them after Cenwealh's death, then he was the one who united the kingdom again, as Aldhelm recognized him as the king of the West Saxons. Aldhelm recalls three major victories of Centwine's, though over whom he does not state. The *ASC* records only one, in 682, when Centwine "drove the British as far as the sea", which probably means a major campaign into Devon. Another victory may have been against his rival CAEDWALLA, who was driven into exile probably around the year 680. Although Bede makes no reference to Centwine, the king had connections at the Northumbrian court through his wife Eangyth, the niece of EORCENBERT of Kent. Her sister, Eormenburh, was the wife of EGFRITH of Northumbria. Eormenburh's hatred of Bishop Wilfrid meant that when he was expelled from Northumbria, Eangyth convinced Centwine not to allow him into Wessex, and he found his way instead to Sussex where ATHELWALH granted him land at Selsey. Centwine is believed to have had at least two children: the abbess Eadburh (known affectionately as Bugga) who later went on a pilgrimage to Rome, and a son Oshere, who died some time before 720. Centwine was a great benefactor of the church, especially Glastonbury Abbey, and retired (willingly or by force is not clear) to become a monk in his final years. It has been suggested that he was related to St Aldhelm, who might have been his brother.

[M11;G11] **CAEDWALLA** West Saxons, 685–8; Kent 686–8.
Caedwalla's name is an anglicized form of the Celtic CADWALLON: CADWALADR, son of the Welsh prince of that name, had died only a few years before. To be named after someone who so recently had sought to destroy the Northumbrian kingdom suggests a very strong British connection in Caedwalla's parentage. The *ASC* gives his descent from CERDIC and though in many instances such connections are suspicious, Caedwalla's may be true, since CERDIC was also probably British. Caedwalla's father, Cenberht, had been a sub-king of CENWEALH's who had died during WULFHERE's advance into Wessex in 661. Caedwalla was two years old then and living in refuge with the remnants of his family in the great Forest of the Weald. He is likely to have been one of the claimants who sought to regain territory after the death of Cenwealh, and was expelled by CENTWINE around the year 680. Caedwalla was now a king without a kingdom and became notorious for his roving war-band of mercenaries which plundered the border territories of Wessex and Mercia. Although he was a pagan and remained so until his final years, he seems to have befriended Bishop Wilfrid who had come to Sussex in 680 and established a monastery at Selsey. Thereafter Caedwalla would use the excuse of the church, and as defender of Christianity, in his later purges, particularly of the Isle of Wight. It is likely that Caedwalla became involved in the feud between EADRIC of Kent and his uncle HLOTHHERE, as Caedwalla doubtless saw this as an opportunity to manipulate power. In early 685 Caedwalla's war-band descended on Sussex, laying the land to waste and killing its king ATHELWALH. He was driven out by two dukes, BERTHUN and Andhun.

At this time CENTWINE abdicated and retired to a monastery. It is not certain that Caedwalla forced him to abdicate, but Caedwalla seized the opportunity and was proclaimed king. Other sub-kings still ruled, but there is no record that they showed any opposition to Caedwalla who, probably by sheer force, held the position of power. He used this to oppose the Mercian menace which had killed his father, driven him into exile and usurped the West Saxon lands in the east. In the summer of 686 he returned to Sussex, killed Berthun and placed the kingdom under West Saxon control. His warband swept through into Kent, defeated Eadric and took control. Caedwalla placed his brother MUL in charge as king of Kent (he may also have had this authority over the South Saxons, though that is not recorded). He then invaded the Isle of Wight, killed their king ARWALD, allowed the two younger princes to be converted to Christianity and then executed them. Caedwalla was intent upon wiping out the Jutes of Wight and embarked upon a campaign of slaughter, which he saw as a war of Christianity against the pagans. At this stage he had determined to become baptized but had still not officially accepted the Christian faith. During this campaign Caedwalla was severely wounded, but this did not stop him returning to Kent to exact revenge for his brother whom the Kentish people had burned to death. His injury seemed mortal, and late in 688 he abdicated the throne in order to undertake a pilgrimage to Rome. He was baptized by Pope Sergius on Easter Day 689, and died ten days later on 20 April. He was buried in Rome.

Caedwalla was a complex character and far more than the "bloodthirsty young heathen" he has been described. He clearly was sympathetic to the Christian faith, for all that he used it to further his own ends, and he was recognized for his faith by many of the church leaders, including Wilfrid and Eorcenwald, the bishop of London. He endowed the church with land on the Isle of Wight, founded the monastery at Farnham in Sussex and supported monasteries elsewhere in Wessex, Kent and even Essex. He was the most powerful ruler in southern England since CEAWLIN, and it was due to his conquests that Wessex became the third power in the land, after Northumbria and Mercia. This power base was developed by INE.

[M12] INE West Saxons, 688–726.

Ine was the first true *king* of the West Saxons, as distinct from a war-leader. He not only firmly established Wessex as a kingdom but introduced a code of laws and a strong administrative system to govern the land. The genealogies show his descent from CUTHA, though the links back to CERDIC may be more forced. Ine's name is singular, but is almost certainly an affectionate diminutive of a longer name (probably Cuthwine or Cenwine). Wine was a common suffix in Saxon names and means "friend". It was the name of the bishop of Wessex from 660–4, and Ine may have been named after him, as he was probably born at about that time. He was the son of Cenred, who was one of the sub-kings ruling a fragmented Wessex following the death of CENWEALH in 672. Cenred's territory seems to have been to the west, around Dorset, and it is likely that he continued to rule jointly with his son at the outset. Ine came to power following the abdication of CAEDWALLA. He probably did not succeed immediately as there would have been several claimants, and it is likely that initially he ruled with other sub-kings until he established his claim. He did this rapidly, however, for by late 688 he was already in the process of developing his law code, which was formulated over the next five years. Ine was the first to codify a set of laws for the Saxons, although Athelbert of Kent had produced one for his kingdom (Jutes and Franks) ninety years earlier. This was the key part of his re-organization of Wessex that enabled him to manage it as an single kingdom rather than a collection of sub-units, which had been the nature of the old Gewisse. By the time he had issued his law code, in 694, he had almost certainly eradicated the sub-kingdoms but had developed in their place a series of shires which coincide to a large degree with the modern counties, and these were administered by ealdormen or reeves who, in most cases, would have been the former sub-king. It needed a strong king to impose these changes and the memories of Ine that survive suggest that he was a harsh and unforgiving king (despite his name) who ruled with an iron hand and would brook no challenge. He continued to treat the South Saxons harshly in the early years of his reign, enslaving the common populace and imposing upon them his own client king, NOTHHELM, who was apparently related either directly or through marriage. He also exacted compensation from WIHTRED of Kent for the murder of Caedwalla's brother MUL. Ine established a firm relationship with Wihtred. Between them they agreed the boundary between Kent and Wessex which remained the Kentish boundary for over a thousand years. He also sought Wihtred's advice over his law code, drawing upon that already established in Kent. By 694 Ine was well in control of his realm and the next decade saw him seek to develop its economic and ecclesiastical prosperity. He created a new episcopal see at Sherborne, under Bishop Aldhelm in 706, with Daniel installed as the new bishop of Winchester. Ine also created a new town at Hamwic (Southampton) which became a centre for trade and crafts, and one of the largest towns in Saxon England. By the early years of the eighth century Wessex was a prosperous and well organized kingdom, firmly governed.

Ine's law code sought to be fair to the native British population even though they were regarded as inferior to the Saxons. There was almost certainly strong intermarriage between the two races, including within the royal family, and it seems likely that, working with Aldhelm, Ine endeavoured to bring the British of Dumnonia under his control. The British were already Christians but of the Celtic church. Following the Synod of Whitby in 664 the Anglo-Saxons had followed the Roman church, most notably in its calculation of the date of Easter. Soon after 706 we find Aldhelm in communication with GERAINT of Dumnonia, exhorting him to adopt the Roman church. Geraint refused, and Ine probably used this as an excuse to invade Devon. There were probably a series of raids and forays during 709 and 710 in which Ine was supported by Nothhelm, but in 710 Geraint was killed at the battle of Longport, and Devon fell under West Saxon rule. It was never extensively colonized by the Saxons, remaining predominantly British, but ceased to be a separate kingdom. Ine was never able to push his control into Cornwall. He was defeated by the Cornish in 722 at the river Tamar, and thereafter withdrew his forces.

Ine seems to have established a good alliance with the Mercians under ATHELBALD and CENRED as there is no evidence of any major hostilities during their reigns. However their successor CEOLRED was an ambitious young hothead with more recklessness than sense. In 715 his forces clashed with Ine's at Adam's Grave in Wiltshire. The cause of the battle is not recorded, but doubtless Ceolred was attempting to expand control over territories ever in dispute with Wessex, and Ine soon taught him a lesson. Despite his power, Ine's control over internal affairs clearly weakened in later years. The full facts are not clear and the tantalising clues in the ASC and later chronicles only provide hints. It seems likely, however, that by 721 Ine was facing internal dissension amongst claimants to the throne. In that year he killed a certain Cynewulf, and probably sent into exile Ealdbert, who may have been involved in Cynewulf's plot, or may have been another claimant. Support for Ealdbert must have been strong, though, for in 722 he was besieged in Taunton by Ine's queen, Athelburh, who destroyed Taunton in the process. For the queen to be involved suggests something close to home, and it may be that Ealdbert was Athelburh's own son. Ealdbert escaped, however, and sought refuge in Surrey and Sussex. Ine should have been able to rely on his client king in Sussex, ATHELSTAN, to hand Ealdbert over, but such was not the case. Ealdbert must have found support in Sussex, and the South Saxons used this as an opportunity to fight for independence. This civil war continued for three years until Ine defeated and killed Ealdbert in battle in 725. Ine was now in his sixties, and this campaign must have taken its toll. Moreover if Ealdbert was his son, his rebellion and death was a bitter blow to Ine's succession. It may have been this that caused Ine to abdicate in the following year and retire to Rome as a pilgrim. He died there two years later. Bede records that Ine abdicated in order to leave the kingdom "to younger men", but he did not leave it in safer hands, and it would be nearly eighty years before Wessex again saw a ruler of the stature of Ine.

[M13] **ATHELHEARD** Wessex, 726–40.

When INE abdicated in 726, he left behind a kingdom to which he had given shape and form but which in its final years had become wracked by internal dynastic strife, and this continued. Ine had evidently not nominated a successor or, if he had, it was disputed between two athelings, Athelheard and Oswald. Oswald's pedigree given in the *ASC* shows his descent from CEAWLIN (or probably more accurately CUTHA), but Athelheard's ancestry is not known. A copy of an ancient charter (later found to be forged, but which may contain some truth) noted that Athelheard was the brother of Ine's wife. If this is true Athelheard may have been middle-aged. ATHELBALD of Mercia used this dynastic division to impose his authority over Wessex. He supported Athelheard's claim, and thereafter the West Saxon king was beholden to Mercia. The later West Saxon chroniclers who composed the *ASC* must have regarded this as a sign of weakness, because they troubled to record the date of Oswald's death in 730, suggesting that they supported him. Oswald probably continued to contest the throne until his death which would have further undermined Athelheard's control. It is likely that Athelheard's wife, Frithugyth, was also Mercian, related to Athelbald's sub-king, FRITHUWOLD. Athelheard therefore appears as a weak king dominated by his Mercian patron. This allowed Athelbald considerable leeway. In 733 he invaded Somerset, captured Somerton, and brought much of western Wessex directly under Mercian control. Athelbald also took control of Berkshire, always a disputed territory, much of Wiltshire, extending Mercia's borders south of the Thames and into the West Saxon heartlands, and of Sussex. Athelheard seemed powerless against this. In fact Athelheard had to support Athelbald in his campaigns against the Welsh. Little else is known of Athelheard's reign. In 737 it is recorded that his wife Frithugyth journeyed to Rome with bishop Forthhere of Sherborne, but nothing else is said about this.

[M14] **CUTHRED (II)** Wessex, 740–56.

He was related to his predecessor ATHELHEARD, though if Symeon of Durham's suggestion that they were brothers is true, then he must have been elderly when he ascended the throne, because Athelheard was also supposed to be the brother-in-law of INE. According to the *ASC*, Cuthred "resolutely made war against ATHELBALD of Mercia", who had imposed his overlordship on Wessex. Although this entry is given in the first year of Cuthred's reign it is not evident that Cuthred did rebel immediately, though he may have made it known that he was not as weak a king as his brother. In 743 it is recorded that Cuthred fought alongside Athelbald against the Welsh. Athelbald had for many years had border problems with the Welsh and had started construction of Wat's Dyke, so it is probable that Cuthred was genuinely fighting against the people we now call the Welsh. But the origin of that word "welisc" meant "foreigners" in the Saxon tongue and was equally applied to all the native British. Cuthred's battle against the "Welsh" may have been against the British in Cornwall, and that is almost certainly what is meant by a similar entry in 753, when Cuthred alone is mentioned. Although Ine had conquered Devon, he had not conquered Cornwall, and there were almost certainly border skirmishes and local insurrections throughout the eighth and ninth centuries. Cuthred may have been able to contain the conflict, but he made no progress towards conquering Cornwall. In the second half of his reign he had to face the inevitable uprisings by claimants to the throne. The *ASC* records, without explanation, that in 748, Cynric, prince of Wessex, was slain, and that in 750 Cuthred fought against Athelhun, "the presumptuous ealdorman"! Although Cuthred weathered these storms it shows that his control at home was not absolute, and it may have been this that caused him to assert himself against Athelbald. Bede records that in 750 Cuthred "rose against Athelbald", and this was the start of hostilities that culminated in the battle of Beorhford in 752, where Cuthred defeated Athelbald. From then on he must have reclaimed his independence from Mercia and gained control again over lands in Berkshire and Wiltshire. By the time he died in 756, Cuthred must have been comfortable in the knowledge that he had restored the status of the West Saxons, though he did not realise that this would be short-lived. He does not seem to have nominated an heir and he was succeeded by SIGEBERT.

[M15] **SIGEBERT** Wessex, 756–7.

Sigebert's name suggests an Anglian ancestry and though he is recorded as the brother of a West Saxon prince, Cyneheard, it is likely that his mother was an Angle. Sigebert may therefore have had Mercian connections, and been supported in his election to the West Saxon kingship by ATHELBALD. However, early in 757, the *witan* (or council) of Wessex, led by CYNEWULF, voted Sigebert out of the kingdom for "his unlawful acts", suggesting that while he had been in power he had misused his authority. He retained control of Hampshire, where he still had the support of the ealdorman Cumbra but, probably in a fit of rage, Sigebert killed Cumbra and was driven into the great Forest of the Weald, where he was stabbed to death by a herdsman. Nearly thirty years later Sigebert's brother, Cyneheard, would obtain his revenge on Cynewulf.

[M16] **CYNEWULF** Wessex, 757–86.

The relationship of Cynewulf to the West Saxon royal dynasties is unclear, but it seems that in 757 he was a powerful man in the council (or *witan*) of the West Saxons for he led the elders in expelling SIGEBERT from the kingship. For this degree of authority he must already have been regarded as senior, and possibly in his thirties, yet he must have been young enough that he could still have a mistress thirty years later, which was the cause of his downfall. At the start of his reign Cynewulf was still regarded as subservient to ATHELBALD of Mercia, even though CUTHRED had defeated him a few years earlier and reclaimed much lost territory. However, within a few months Athelbald was murdered and the ensuing civil strife in Mercia allowed Cynewulf to take the initiative and regain lands in Berkshire and Wiltshire. Although the new Mercian king, OFFA, became the greatest in the land, and may have been regarded as such by Cynewulf, he never exercised any direct authority over Wessex. Cynewulf attended his court in 772, but that seems to be more as a royal visitor and not as an attendant client king. It was not until 779 that Cynewulf and Offa clashed at Bensington, and though Cynewulf was defeated, and thereafter must have regarded Offa as sovereign, he never submitted to Mercian overlordship. Much of Cynewulf's reign seems to have been occupied in battles against the British of Dumnonia, though Cornwall remained unconquered. The British clearly did not accept Saxon sovereignty in the West Country, and even by the time of the Domesday Book, three centuries later, the extent of Saxon occupation of Devon was limited. Cynewulf's reign was long – twenty-nine years

– and though he did not institute reforms like his predecessor INE, he did make considerable grants of land, not only to the church, but also to his "counts", who were lay people outside the royal family. Such practice did not seem to happen before Cynewulf.

In the latter years of his reign Cynewulf began to experience trouble from Cyneheard, the brother of Sigebert, whom Cynewulf had deposed. Cynewulf agreed to expel Cyneheard from the kingdom but before he could do so Cyneheard surprised Cynewulf at the manor of his mistress and killed him. The manor was soon surrounded by Cynewulf's men, and Cyneheard was killed. The story is told at length in the *ASC* and was clearly a popular heroic tale of its day – though it is not entirely clear who was the hero! He did not leave an heir and was succeeded by BEORHTRIC.

[M17] **BEORHTRIC** Wessex, 786–802.

After the murder of CYNEWULF, Beorhtric was elected as king. He seems to have been strongly supported by OFFA of Mercia, and Beorhtric subsequently married Offa's daughter Eadburh in 789. Offa was at the height of his power, and although Beorhtric retained the title king, he does not seem to have been able to act of his own accord. All charters in Wessex are in Offa's name, whether or not Beorthric also witnessed them. Eadburh also appears to have been a dragon of a wife, wielding the authority that came with being Offa's daughter, and it is as likely that she held the true control in Wessex. She passed into legend for her cruelty, so much so that a folk-tale grew up about her having poisoned Beorhtric and fled to the court of Charlemagne. Charlemagne offered her marriage either to himself or to his son and, when she chose his son, he told her she could have neither and cast her on to the streets. She was supposed to have ended her days as a beggar. None of this is likely, but it serves to show what hatred there was for the memory of Eadburh, so much so that for the next few generations the West Saxons refused to recognize the wife of the king as a queen. Some time during his reign Beorhtric's authority was challenged by the young atheling EGBERT but Beorhtric was able to call upon Offa to get Egbert exiled in France. Probably the most ominous entry in the *ASC* for Beorhtric's reign occurred in 789, the same year as his marriage to Eadburh. In that year three Danish ships appeared off the Devon coast at Portland. The local reeve went to meet them, believing them traders, but they killed him. This was the first recorded visit by a Viking ship. Their raids would dominate British history for the next three hundred years.

Offa died in 796 and this must have considerably weakened Beorhtric's position. There was a state of uncertainty for a short period in Mercia's affairs, and it seems that relationships between Wessex and Mercia cooled. It is likely that there was pressure on Beorhtric to reassert his independence and to reclaim lost territories. Some border skirmishes doubtless occurred, not necessarily instigated by Beorhtric, and the West Saxons were probably involved in the fight for independence in Kent. It was three years before Beorhtric regained a good relationship with CENWULF when the two signed a peace treaty. The power and vindictiveness of Cenwulf was such that Beorhtric was still regarded as a subordinate. He remained so until his death, three years later, at which point Egbert returned from exile to assume the kingship. It was with Egbert that the whole focus of power in England would change.

[M18] **EGBERT** Wessex, January(?) 802–July(?) 839.

Most chronologies of the kings of England start with Egbert, chiefly because he was the first West Saxon king to exercise authority over most of England. This is a somewhat biased West Saxon perspective, for although Egbert's descendants went on to become kings of England, Egbert himself exercised no greater authority than some of his predecessors, particularly OFFA of Mercia and others claiming the title *bretwalda*. Nevertheless, it is with Egbert that the chain of events begins that brings us to a united England.

From Rider's History of England

Egbert was the son of EALHMUND, almost certainly the same Ealhmund who was briefly king of Kent in 784. He claimed descent from Ingeld, the brother of INE of Wessex, and through him back to CERDIC the founder of the West Saxon kingdom, though the authenticity of this descent is dubious. Egbert's birth date is sometimes cited as 775, and it is unlikely that he was born much earlier than that. However, some chroniclers claim that Egbert contended for the throne of Wessex after the murder of CYNEWULF in 786, but that Offa's influence gave the kingship to BEORHTRIC. If Egbert was actively competing at that time he is likely to have been older than eleven, though possibly no more than fifteen or sixteen, which would push his birth year back to 770 or 771. The *ASC* claims that Egbert spent three years in exile at the court of Charlemagne in Francia, but it is not clear when those three years were. Some have speculated that the *ASC* is in error and that his exile in Francia lasted for thirteen years. It is difficult to reconcile these dates with the likely chain of events. It seems that after Egbert first contended for the throne in 786 he retreated to the court of Offa. He was a troublesome youth, and Beorhtric believed that all the time Egbert was in England he would be a problem. It was in 789, at the time that Beorhtric was negotiating with Offa over his marriage to Offa's daughter, that Beorhtric suggested Egbert should be handed over to him. Egbert, realising his life might be in peril, prudently left Mercia and probably left England all together. As the son of Ealhmund, whose Kentish ancestry gave him strong Frankish connections, he may have been welcome at the court of Charlemagne even though at that time, Offa had angered Charlemagne by seeking to marry his son to one of Charlemagne's daughters, and Charlemagne broke off all trade relations with England. But it is as likely that Egbert did not go directly to Francia but arrived

there after some travels possibly around the year 792. In truth we know little of
Egbert's wanderings. At Charlemagne's court he would have encountered other
exiled princes, as well as the great scholar and teacher Alcuin, whom Charlemagne
had placed in charge of his school in Aachen. Egbert may well have accompanied
Charlemagne on some of his campaigns, and he would certainly have learned the
science of military tactics as well as the art of kingship. He probably married whilst
at Charlemagne's court as his wife is recorded as Eadburh (or Redburga),
Charlemagne's sister (or more probably niece) and his first-born ATHELWOLF was
probably born there, around 795. 796 may have been the next milestone in Egbert's
life. Alcuin left Aachen and became Abbot of Saint Martin, Tours, and that same
year saw the death of Offa. Egbert may have used this as an opportunity to return to
Britain and seek to regain his authority. The period between 796 and 799, when
Beorhtric eventually restored relations with CENWULF of Mercia is not well
documented, and it is possible that Egbert sought to regain the kingship of
Wessex at that time. Even though he was unsuccessful it would have brought
him back to the attention of the *witan*, or council, of Wessex with whom he must
have remained in contact. He is very likely to have become involved in the uprising
in Kent led by his cousin EADBERT, and may well have remained in Kent until
Eadbert was deposed in 798. Egbert may then have returned to France and it is to
this final three years that the *ASC* refers before Egbert was recalled from exile in 802,
after the death of Beorhtric, to succeed to the kingdom of Wessex.

Even though the *ASC* is predominantly a West Saxon document produced in the
time of ALFRED, Egbert's grandson, it is rather surprising that so little is recorded of
the early years of Egbert's reign. Considering the later authority that he wielded one
might imagine that he spent his early years in conquest, but this does not seem to be
the case. One may conjecture from this that Egbert was not readily accepted by all as
king and the inter-dynastic squabbles which troubled the West Saxon line for
generations may have occupied much of Egbert's initial years as he sought to
establish himself. He probably had the support of Charlemagne in this endeavour,
and quite possibly the Pope as well. There is no doubt that once Egbert set out on
his campaign of conquest, he did it from a firm base, and it would not be surprising
that it took him ten years to establish. Egbert needed to re-organize his army so that
it could move quickly and lightly, under strong command. He also needed to re-
organize his administration so that it could handle the greater demands Egbert
would place on it. Primarily he needed to gain the support of the church, and there
is little doubt that Egbert developed a strong alliance with Wulfred, the radical
archbishop of Canterbury. It is noticeable that Egbert's first bid for power came
after Wulfred had visited Rome and gained the support of the pope for his reforms.
With a strong archbishop amongst his supporters, and one who rapidly became
alienated from Mercia (see under CENWULF), Egbert had much going for him.

It had probably served as a good omen that on the very day Egbert came to
power, the *ASC* records that Athelmund, an ealdorman among the Hwicce of
Mercia, invaded Wiltshire at Kempsford and was confronted by Weohstan of
Wiltshire. Both ealdormen were killed in the conflict but the West Saxons were
triumphant, and this may have been seen as a good sign. Egbert's first strike came in
815 when he decided to ensure that he had only one border on which to advance. In
that year he invaded Cornwall and devastated the kingdom, bringing it under his

authority. He allowed client kings to rule, and they would take any opportunity to oppose Saxon sovereignty, but to all intents and purposes from 815 the kingdom of Kernow had lost its independence. There were doubtless skirmishes between the Saxons and Cornish over the next ten years but the only one recorded was at Camelford in 825 when Egbert had again to subjugate the Cornish. Perhaps aware that Egbert was engaged in the south-west, BEORNWULF, the new king of Mercia, invaded Wessex. The chronicles suggest that Egbert was taken by surprise, but his years of preparation now paid off. The two armies met at Ellendun on the Marlborough Downs in Wiltshire and the victory went to Egbert. Whether planned or not, this seemed to be the opportunity Egbert had waited for, and he capitalised on it with a vengeance. He despatched a large army under the command of his son Athelwolf, ealdorman Wulfherd and Ealhstan, the bishop of Sherborne, into Kent, driving out the local king BALDRED. Egbert had claimed his patrimony and avenged his father's death. Surrey and Sussex had submitted to Athelwolf en route, and when Baldred escaped into Essex, the East Saxons rapidly submitted to Athelwolf's army. ATHELSTAN, king of East Anglia, promptly appealed to Athelwolf for support in fighting Mercia and with the aid of the West Saxons, Athelstan gained his freedom from Mercia. It has been suggested that this Athelstan was a son of Egbert, set up to lead the East Angles in their fight for independence. Although unconfirmed it is a tempting theory, because it would explain the otherwise apparent independence of the East Angles during Egbert's reign and beyond. Over the next two years the West Saxons no doubt continued to support the East Angles in their fight against the Mercians. Beornwulf was slain and the kingship of Mercia was in crisis until the emergence of WIGLAF. Egbert invaded Mercia directly in 829 and defeated and deposed Wiglaf. Egbert continued with his army of conquest north into Northumbria, but EANRED met and submitted to Egbert at Dore. From 829 Egbert was recognized as *bretwalda* or overlord and, because his dominion included Cornwall, hitherto unconquered, it is fair to say that Egbert was the first king of all England. Nevertheless, his client kings still exercised considerable authority, and there is some question as to whether Wiglaf's return to power in 830 was as a client to Egbert or whether he had regained control over Mercia. It is likely that after 830 Egbert lost some of his support from the Frankish Empire, due to its internal problems, and this weakened authority allowed Wiglaf to reassert himself, even though nominally accepting Egbert as his overlord. There must have been some agreement between them because in 830 Egbert led an army through Mercia into north Wales to subdue the resurgent CYNGEN AP CADELL. His devastation was so effective that Cyngen may well have been forced to regard Egbert as his overlord, despite Cyngen's recent display of pride in erecting the Pillar of Elisedd in commemoration of his victories.

After 830 Egbert's reign was dominated by the raids of the Danes. In 835 the Vikings devastated Sheppey in Kent, and in the following year they landed at Carhampton (or Charmouth) in Devon. Egbert gathered together his army and almost defeated the Danes, but with the dying rays of the sun the Danes turned the battle and Egbert had to admit defeat – the only recorded defeat of his reign. The Danes began to establish themselves in Devon and, by 838, had combined forces with the Cornish to declare an all-out war on the Saxons. Egbert's army was now better prepared. He no doubt had spent the time studying the battle tactics of the

Danes. The forces met at Hingston Down, near Callington, on the Devon-Cornwall border, and Egbert inflicted a resounding defeat upon the enemy. It is unlikely that Egbert took a direct part in this battle. He was now in his late sixties, and his earlier defeat may have been an indication of his failing strength. He no doubt planned the battle tactics like an army general, but the army was probably commanded by one of his ealdormen, or possibly his son Athelwolf.

Egbert died the following year after a reign of thirty-seven years and seven months, probably in his sixty-ninth year. He was succeeded by Athelwolf. He also had a daughter, Edith (Eadgyth) who became a nun at Polesworth Abbey in Warwickshire.

[M19;G28] **ATHELWOLF** Kent, 825–839, 856–858; Wessex, July(?) 839–855.
Born: *France (probably the court of Charlemagne, Aachen), c795;* **Died**: *13 January 858, aged about 62.* **Buried**: *Steyning (Sussex) but later moved to Winchester Cathedral.*
Married: *(1) c830, Osburh (died c852), dau. Oslac of Hampshire: 5 children; (2) 1 October 856 at Verberie-sur-Oise, France, Judith (c843–post 879), dau. Charles the Bald, king of the Franks: no children.*
Athelwolf was the son of EGBERT, whose subjugation of most of England from 825 onward became the foundation of the future kingdom of England. Although usually listed amongst the kings of England, Athelwolf remained king of Wessex only. These territories incorporated Sussex, Kent and Essex, which Athelwolf had conquered on his father's behalf in 825 and of which Athelwolf was duly appointed sub-king. Athelwolf appointed his brother (or son) ATHELSTAN as sub-king of these territories when he became king of Wessex. However, Athelwolf did not directly rule East Anglia, Mercia or Northumbria, all of which had their own kings who acknowledged Athelwolf as their overlord. Athelwolf's direct ascent to the throne of Wessex was a rare event in the West Saxon kingdom. Over the past three centuries the kingdom had passed either to the next most appropriate local chieftain as confirmed by the council or *witan* or, in a few cases, by conquest. Wessex had been a fairly loose knit confederacy of smaller kingdoms, and succession did not pass directly from father to son. Egbert's rigorous readministration of the kingdom had ensured his eldest son would inherit and that there would not be the inter-dynastic squabbling that had weakened other kingdoms. The ability to appoint younger sons to sub-kingdoms helped this process. Elsewhere the leading chieftain of the shire became the ealdorman, a position of considerable privilege second only to the king. In Athelwolf's time we find that the ealdormen became of major importance in helping defend the kingdom from the Danes, whose raids increased considerably during the 840s. Athelwolf or his ealdormen succeeded in defeating the Danes on almost every occasion. The raids reached a peak in the years 850/1 when there were three assaults spread across the south. The sequence may not be as the *ASC* records, but it suggests that first an army landed in Devon which was defeated by the local ealdorman. A further army arrived off the Kent coast near Sandwich, where Athelstan and his ealdormen fought a sea battle, defeating the Danes and capturing nine of their ships. The Danes spent that winter in Thanet. Then, early in 851, a major force arrived in over three hundred ships which sailed up the Thames and attacked inland. It first defeated BEORHTWULF of Mercia and then turned its

attention south of the Thames, where it met Athelwolf and his son ATHELBALD at a place called Acleah, somewhere in Surrey (usually associated with Ockley, though not all authorities agree). If the number of ships is correct (and not miscopied as 350 instead of 35) then the Danish force must have numbered nearly 10,000 men. The *ASC* notes that this was the greatest slaughter of the Danes that was known up to that time and was evidently a significant battle.

A few years of peace followed, and we may imagine that after the battle of Acleah Athelwolf had agreed some form of peace arrangement with the Danes, or that they sought easier places of conquest. The following year (852) Beorhtwulf of Mercia died, and a new king, BURGRED, appeared. He was almost certainly a vassal of Athelwolf's, possibly even one of his ealdormen. At Easter 853, Burgred married Athelwolf's daughter Athelswith, and later that year Athelwolf aided Burgred in his battle against the Welsh where they subjected CYNGEN AP CADELL to a major defeat.

Athelwolf's life was soon after tinged with sadness as his wife died, probably at the end of 853 or early 854. By all accounts Athelwolf loved her deeply. The character of this king is somewhat perplexing. Many of the chroniclers recorded his bravery in battle, and there is no reason to doubt that he was anything other than courageous; but he was a very religious man and from his youth had apparently been devoted to the church. He probably accepted his role as king as a consequence of his heritage and his role in battle as a necessary evil, but there is no reason to assume he relished fighting. In 855, even though it is recorded that the Danes had wintered in Sheppey in Kent, and thus still represented a threat, Athelwolf abdicated the throne. He first donated a tenth of his estate to the church, a measure that was bound to endear him to later chroniclers, and then set off on a pilgrimage to Rome with his youngest son ALFRED. He left the government of England to his two eldest sons, Athelbald and ATHELBERT, supported ably by his council of ealdormen. He must have been convinced that he had left England in safe hands. He was himself now approaching sixty and would have been too old to fight. The *ASC* records that he spent a year in Rome and on his return spent some time at the court of Charles the Bald, king of the Franks, whose daughter Judith he married. This was clearly a political alliance as Judith was no more than thirteen, but it had its repercussions. At the ceremony, the officiating archbishop, Hincmar of Rheims, placed a crown upon Judith's head, thereby making her a queen. This position had been outlawed by the West Saxons sixty years earlier because of the wickedness of BEORHTRIC's wife Eadburh. It may have been this action that alienated the ealdormen of Wessex for when Athelwolf returned to England later that year (856) he was welcomed but they would not accept him as king. This has been described as a civil war, but it is unlikely to have been that destructive. Athelwolf almost certainly did not want the rigours of kingship, and was quite happy to retire to Sussex as the sub-king of the Kent, Sussex and Essex territories. He died there some eighteen months later.

[M20] **ATHELBALD** Wessex, 855–20 December 860.
Athelbald was the eldest son of ATHELWOLF (unless the mysterious ATHELSTAN was also Athelwolf's son), and was probably born about the year 831 or 832. He is first mentioned as fighting alongside his father at the battle of Acleah in 851, where they defeated a host of Danes. On his father's abdication in 855, Athelbald became king of Wessex, supported by Ealhstan the bishop of Sherborne, and with his younger

brother ATHELBERT as king of Kent. There is no doubt that Athelbald was a strong and determined king, probably more ambitious than his father, inheriting some of the grit of his grandfather EGBERT. When the following year Athelwolf returned, perhaps unexpectedly, from his pilgrimage to Rome, Athelbald refused to concede the kingdom to him, and Athelwolf retired to Kent. After his father's death, Athelbald caused a scandal by marrying his step-mother, Judith, the daughter of Charles the Bald, king of the Franks. Since Judith had been crowned queen, Athelbald may well have believed that this confirmed further authority on his position and upon his likely children. He was twenty-seven and Judith was only fifteen, and there was every likelihood of a long reign and many children. However the church frowned on the marriage and within a year it was annulled. Judith returned to Francia where, six years later, she married Baldwin, count of Flanders. Their son, Baldwin, married Elfreda, the daughter of ALFRED THE GREAT. Athelbald lived only another year after this, dying in December 860, probably of an illness. He was buried at Sherborne Abbey.

[M21;G30] **ATHELBERT** Kent, 855–856, 858–860; Wessex, 20 December 860–865/6. Athelbert was the second son of ATHELWOLF, and succeeded to the sub-kingdom of Kent (which included Essex and Sussex) in 855, when his father abdicated and ATHELBALD (his elder brother) succeeded to the kingdom of Wessex. It is possible that Athelbert succeeded to the sub-kingdom earlier, whenever their uncle ATHELSTAN died, but there is no record of the date. When Athelwolf returned from Rome in 856, Athelbald refused to concede the kingdom of Wessex, so Athelwolf retired to Kent, where Athelbert seemed more amenable to bow to his father's authority in that land. It was probably no more than a token gesture, as Athelwolf was already in his sixties, and Athelbald now held authority over all of southern England. When Athelbald died in 860 Athelbert succeeded to Wessex and does not seem to have appointed a new sub-king in Kent. During his reign the Danes returned with a vengeance. Sometime soon after his accession a Danish army landed either via the Thames or on the south coast and advanced as far as Winchester before two contingents of Saxons defeated them. Towards the end of his reign a more organized force arrived under the command of Ragnar Lodbrok. His fleet had been harrying the east coast of England, particularly Northumbria, and in the winter of 864/5 they stayed in Thanet. Although the Saxons made a pact with them, the Danes plundered east Kent, before advancing back up the east coast. Athelbert died towards the end of 865 (or possibly early in 866), aged about thirty-two. He was buried at Sherborne Abbey He had not married and was succeeded by his brother ATHELRED.

[M22] **ATHELRED** (I) Wessex, 865/6–23 April 871.
The third son of ATHELWOLF, he was born about the year 837. His father had bequeathed Wessex to Athelred in his will, should ATHELBALD die childless, but Athelred had probably not expected to become king. He had little time to think about the consequences, for from the start of his reign he was confronted with a series of Danish raids and invasions, which had become considerably more aggressive since the co-ordinated attacks of IVARR THE BONELESS and his brother HALFDAN. These two Danes lived in Dublin from where they co-ordinated their fleet, but they became incensed when their father Ragnar Lodbrok, who had been

harrying the eastern coat of Britain for the last year, and had wintered during 865/6 in East Anglia, was killed in York by AELLE. The two brothers now brought all their forces to bear upon England. They conquered York in November 866, rebuffing a counter-attack by AELLE in March 867. Deira became a Viking kingdom (Jorvik). The army marched south and occupied Nottingham. BURGRED of Mercia sought Athelred's help in dislodging the Danes but this proved impossible, and they were forced to negotiate. The Danes returned to York in 868 and then sailed south to East Anglia in 869, where the local king EDMUND was killed. By 870 they were prepared to advance on Wessex. They were now joined by another army under the leadership of GUTHRUM. This was a major invasion force. If the Danes could conquer Wessex, England would fall to them. The first battle was at Reading, where the Danes occupied a royal villa. The ealdorman Athelwolf, who had bravely fought the Danes on several previous occasions, met them again at Englefield, where he put a raiding party to flight. However, a few days later the Danes caught the Saxons by surprise and Athelwolf was killed. Athelred and his brother ALFRED had just arrived at this point and only narrowly escaped. The Saxon forces regrouped at Ashdown in Wiltshire, which was the site of the next engagement. The Saxons celebrated this as a victory, because they killed many of the Danish earls including one of their kings, Bacseg, but the Danes were able to regroup just two weeks later for the battle of Basing, and this time the Danes were victorious. The winter of 870/871 was a harrowing one in England as the Danes sacked and plundered their way through the countryside. The next major engagement was in early 871 at Meredune, believed to be Martin in Hampshire. This was another indecisive battle, with considerable slaughter on both sides, and the advantage going first to the Saxons but ultimately to the Danes. Athelred was seriously injured in the battle and died of his wounds a few weeks later at Witchampton, near Wimborne, where he was buried. The nation had no time for mourning, although the shock of Athelred's death must have reverberated about the kingdom. He had married Wulfrida in 867 or 868 and had two infant sons (*see* ATHELWOLD), but their future looked bleak. As the spring of 871 came to England the fate of the Saxons rested in the hands of one man: Alfred.

[M23] **ALFRED *THE GREAT*** Wessex, 23 April 871–26 October 899.
Born: Wantage (?), c847; Died: Winchester (?), 26 October 899, aged 52(?). Buried: Winchester.
Married: 868, Ealhswith (d.902) of Mercia – 5 children.
Although Alfred is certainly the best known of the West Saxon kings, much of what we think we know about him is myth, created by later writers in veneration of the saviour of the Saxons who alone held back the onslaught of the Danes and who established a period of prosperity in England. In that sense he shares something of the role in folk memory of king ARTHUR. Alfred was also a man of learning and did much to establish a history and chronology of his time, and was responsible for starting (or reforming) the *ASC*, but that does not mean we have to trust everything that was written about him at the time. This includes his *Life* written by Bishop Asser which some claim to be a forgery and which certainly has many anomalies. Contrary to our image of him as a strong and valiant king, he was something of a hypochondriac, being struck down with or threatened by mystery diseases, and a long sufferer of piles.

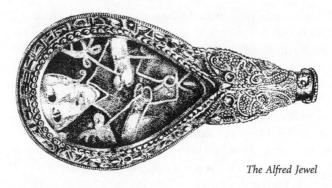

The Alfred Jewel

Alfred was the fourth son and fifth child of ATHELWOLF. His mother is recorded as Osburh, though he may have been the son of a second, unknown, marriage as there is a gap of several years between Alfred's birth and those of his elder brothers. Alternatively Alfred may have been older than we are led to believe, a point which may be attested by his ill health in his final years. Little is known of his childhood – as the youngest son with three elder brothers he was not thought likely to become king – so even the place of his birth is not certain. Asser's reference to Wantage is generally accepted but not definite, and somewhere like Wimborne is more probable. It is also unlikely that, as a child, Alfred was sent to Rome on his own and consecrated by the pope as future king. It is likely that he accompanied his father on his pilgrimage to Rome from 854–855 and spent some time at the court of Charles the Bald, king of the Franks. Alfred became fascinated with the Frankish world, the court of the descendants of Charlemagne, and modelled his own court on it, which included his passion for scholarship. Alfred was probably being groomed for the church, as his father was intensely religious.

Although Alfred's name begins to appear on authenticated charters around the year 861, he does not step onto the stage of history until around 865 and 866 when we find him in harness with his brother ATHELRED in battle against the Danes who had been harrying England for decades but were now showing greater strength of arms. At best Athelred and Alfred held the Danes at bay, but in 871 Athelred died of wounds and, though he had two infant sons (see ATHELWOLD), it was Alfred who was declared successor. Alfred had already proved his battle prowess, particularly at Ashdown in 870, but there was no time to celebrate his succession – there is no record of his coronation, despite the claim that he was crowned at Kingston upon Thames. Within a month of his succession Alfred was in pitched battle with the Danes at Wilton, a day which Alfred thought he had won but the wiliness of the Danes with a false retreat caught the English off guard. Battle followed battle that first year, the outcomes swinging both ways till, at the end of the year, Alfred bought peace with the Danes. The Danes settled north of the Thames, where peace was also bought with the Mercians, and for a period Alfred could consolidate his army. It was also during this time that Alfred began to develop a navy in order to meet the Danes on their own terms.

In 876 a new generation of Danish warrior leaders, of whom the most significant was GUTHRUM, began further incursions into Wessex. His army descended on Alfred's camp at Wareham, but Alfred was prepared and defeated the Danes, buying extra time. The Danes also suffered defeat in a naval campaign off the coast at

Swanage, but in the winter of 878 they caught the English by surprise at Chippenham, taking over the royal court, and forcing the English to flee into the surrounding marshes at Athelney, in Somerset. It is to this period that belong the legends of Alfred burning the cakes and disguising himself as a harper to spy in the camp of Guthrum. Other Danish forces were called to the area, including a Danish fleet established in the Bristol Channel, endeavouring to blockade Alfred. However, Alfred's forces in Devon defeated the fleet and then, with his local knowledge, Alfred was able to outwit the Danes and led his army out of Athelney to Selwood. There he strengthened his forces, marched on the Danes and defeated them at the battle of Ethandune (probably Edington). The Danes submitted and, more significantly, Guthrum agreed to be baptized a Christian. Peace was declared with the treaty of Wedmore.

The next eight years, 878–885, were a period of peace in Wessex. It was now that Alfred became regarded by all the Saxons of England as their overlord, but he was never king of all England, as the Danes still held the greater part of the north and east. He spent this period reviewing the administration, fortification and legal system of the Saxons. He created a series of twenty-five fortified boroughs around his kingdom, such as Oxford and Hastings, and extensively refortified London. He developed seats of learning across southern England, and introduced his law code, extensively revising that of INE. This code was administered by a number of local reeves (or sheriffs) and judges, and Alfred reviewed their activities in his own series of visits. This forced the local administrators to read to ensure the books were properly kept. Alfred also decreed that all the sons of freemen should learn to read and write, firstly in English and, for those destined for high office, in Latin.

Apart from a brief skirmish with the Danes in 885, peace held until 893 when another war with the Danes of East Anglia erupted and lasted until 897. The Danes caused havoc across Mercia and into Wales, but were unable to penetrate the fortifications of Wessex. Alfred re-organized the navy into a major fleet, for which he is remembered as the father of the English navy. Alfred's strength eventually drained the Danish vitality and their army faded away. Although they would return again and again, Alfred had established a kingdom which, for the next few decades, was invincible.

Alfred had married in around 868 at a time when he had not expected to become king. His wife, Ealhswith, was the daughter of a Mercian nobleman and, through her mother, descended from the Mercian royal line, so that Alfred's sons could claim the royal blood of both Wessex and Mercia. He had five children (possibly six; one may have died in infancy) including ATHELFLEDA, who became the Lady of the Mercians, and Elfreda, who married Baldwin, count of Flanders, whose mother was Judith, Alfred's own stepmother. From Elfreda was descended Matilda, who became the wife of WILLIAM I. Alfred was succeeded by his son EDWARD. In later centuries, when Alfred earned the epithet "the Great", it was not solely because he held the Saxon nation together against the Danes, but because he improved the strength, culture and quality of his realm. Although this golden age also owed something to his son and grandson, Alfred was truly the most impressive of the Saxon kings.

2. THE FIGHT FOR BRITAIN

This part covers the kingdoms of Britain from the period of the first Danish settlements around the year 900AD. It covers not only the Saxon, Welsh and Scottish kingdoms but the emerging Danish and Norse kingdoms, including the Danish conquest under Swein and Canute, and the subsequent Norman conquest under William of Normandy, which was also part of the Viking world. Although the Normans established a new culture in England, which began to spread into Wales and Scotland over the next two hundred years, Britain was still a divided country constantly at war with itself. England was riven by several civil wars after the Norman Conquest in addition to the constant battles with Scotland and Wales. Edward I would eventually conquer Wales and integrate it into England in 1284, and he thought he could do this with Scotland, but without success. Scotland was also a land divided, and the Norse continued to have sovereignty over the islands of the Hebrides and the Orkneys right through this period. The Hebrides and Man were eventually handed over to Scotland in 1266. Soon after Scotland entered a succession crisis with the death of the infant queen Margaret and became easy prey to Edward I. Although he installed John Balliol as puppet king, Balliol soon rebelled and the War of the Succession continued through the guardianship of William Wallace and the eventual restoration of independence under Robert the Bruce. With the end of this period, therefore, we see the end of the Scandinavian fight for Britain, and the country stabilising under two main kingdoms, England (with Wales) and Scotland.

It is divided into the following, the reference numbers maintaining the continuity from Part One.

E. The Welsh Kingdoms
   EA. Morgannwg and Glamorgan
   EB. Deheubarth
   ED. Gwynedd
   EE. Powys

Covers the struggle for the unification of Wales, particularly between the principal kingdoms of Deheubarth and Gwynedd, up to the final conquest of Wales by England.

F. The Scottish Kingdoms
   FB. Strathclyde and Cumbria
   FC. Scotland
   FD. Moray (the Highlands)

Covers the gradual unification of Scotland after Kenneth macAlpin, with the absorption of Strathclyde and Moray into the kingdom. The sections ends at the time of the War of Succession when

Scotland almost lost its independence to England.

N. The Scandinavian Kingdoms
   NA. The Western Isles – Hebrides and Man
   NB. The Earldom of Orkney
   NC. Jorvik (York)
   ND. East Anglia

Covers the settlement of England and Scotland by the Danes and Norse, who at one point commanded almost half of Britain in addition to territory in Ireland.

England
   M. Saxon and Danish rule
   O. The Normans and early Plantagenets

E. THE WELSH KINGDOMS

The ninth century saw the many small Welsh kingdoms uniting under a series of strong monarchs, amongst them Hywel the Good and Rhodri the Great. Although partible succession meant that their strong kingdoms were weakened by division amongst sons, the good that they did became more permanent and two strong kingdoms emerged in Wales – Gwynedd in the north and Deheubarth in the South. In the south-east Gwent and Glywysing merged to form the stronger kingdom Morgannwg, which remained independent, whilst in the east along the Marches the kingdom of Powys re-emerged under a series of powerful kings. Although these kingdoms acknowledged the supremacy of the Saxon kings they still retained a high degree of independence. This was considerably eroded after the Norman conquest

Map 8a **The Later Welsh Kingdoms – Morgannwg**

when the Marcher Lords, established by William the Conqueror, began their subjugation of Wales. Morgannwg was the first to fall to the Normans, followed by Deheubarth. Powys and Gwynedd were harder to conquer but their time came, and in 1284 Wales ceased to be a separate "country".

EA. MORGANNWG and GLAMORGAN

Under Morgan the Old the former kingdoms of Gwent and Glywysing were united as Morgannwg. The individual kingdoms retained their identity to some degree and Morgannwg continued to be fragmented under successor kings, although there was now more propensity to unity, especially in facing the advance of the Danes and later the Normans. See Chart 3 (page 122) for the family tree.

Ref.	Ruler	Reign	Died	Notes
continued from page 123				
EA29.	Morgan *Hen* (*the Old*) ab Owain	930–74	974	Morgannwg
EA30.	Nowy ap Gwriad	*fl* 950s		Gwent
EA31.	Owain ap Morgan	974– ?		Glywysing
EA32.	Arthfael ap Nowy	*fl* 970s	*c*983	Gwent; probably murdered
EA33.	Rhys ab Owain	*fl* 990s		Glywysing (part)
EA34.	Iestyn ab Owain	*fl* 990s	*c*1015	Glywysing (part)
EA35.	Hywel ab Owain	*c*990s–*c*1043	1043	Glywysing (part)
EA36.	Rhodri ap Elisedd	983–*c*1015	*c*1015	Gwent
EA37.	Gruffydd ap Elisedd	983–*c*1015	*c*1015	Gwent
EA38.	Edwyn ap Gwriad	1015–45		Gwent; imprisoned and blinded by Meurig
EA39.	Rhydderch ab Iestyn	*c*1015–33	1033	Glywysing and Deheubarth (*see* EB20); killed in battle
EA40.	Gruffydd ap Rhydderch	1033–55	1055	Glywysing and Deheubarth (*see* EB22); killed in battle
EA41.	Meurig ap Hywel	1045–55		Gwent
Morgannwg and Gwent were taken over by Gruffydd ap Llywelyn of Gwynedd, 1055–63.				
EA42.	Cadwgan ap Meurig	1063–74		Morgannwg
EA43.	Caradog ap Gruffydd	1075–81	1081	Gwent 1063–74; usurped Morgannwg; killed in battle
EA44.	Iestyn ap Gwrgan	1081–91	?1093	deposed; died in a priory

Glamorgan (Morgannwg) and Gwent were taken over by the Normans in 1091 under the control of Robert Fitzhamon. The descendants of Caradog ap Gruffydd became lords of Caerleon until they were deprived of their lands in 1270; the descendants of Iestyn ap Gwrgan became lords of Afan until deprived of their lands in 1282.

[EA29] **MORGAN** AB **OWAIN** later known as **MORGAN HEN (THE OLD)**, ruled 930–74.

Morgan first shared Glywysing with his brothers GRUFFYDD and CADWGAN but, following their deaths he became ruler of all of Glywysing by the year 950. By then he had also absorbed Gwent from his cousin CADELL AP ARTHFAEL who died in 942, making Morgan ruler of all of Morgannwg or Glamorgan. The first decade of

Morgan's reign was one of conflict with HYWEL DDA of Deheubarth who was intent on consolidating and extending his kingdom, but the two kings subsequently came to respect each other. Each shared an admiration for the English court and would frequently be found attesting charters signed by ATHELSTAN. Morgan continued this relationship after Hywel's death in 950, with EDMUND and EADRED, but it noticeably cooled under EDGAR, who regarded himself as ruler of all England, and treated the Welsh princes as his vassals. It is not recorded that Morgan was present at Edgar's assembly in Chester in 973 when the rulers of Wales and Scotland paid homage. By then Morgan was in his late seventies or even early eighties, and he died soon after. During the 950s Morgan may have granted rulership of Gwent to NOWY AP GWRIAD. Morgan had five sons, and the rest of his domain was shared amongst them, though the senior ruler appears to have been OWAIN.

[EA30] **NOWY** AP **GWRIAD** Gwent, *fl* 950s.
Nowy may have been granted Gwent by MORGAN AB OWAIN sometime after the death of CADELL AP ARTHFAEL in 942, but it is as likely that he took the land by force. Nowy is recorded as murdering Arcoed ap Dissaith about the year 948. Seven years later, in 955, Nowy's kin broke into a church and killed a deacon in revenge for the death of a relative. Evidently Nowy's family had a vicious streak, as Nowy's son, ARTHFAEL, is also recorded as killing his own brother, Elisedd. Nowy's descent is uncertain. It has been suggested he may have been the grandson of CADWGAN AP OWAIN, which would have made him the great nephew of Morgan. Although Morgan lived to a great age, it is unlikely that Cadwgan's grandson could have come into power while his grandfather was still alive in 950, unless he was very young, in which case he would still have been relatively young when he died some time in the 960s or 970s.

[EA31] **OWAIN** AP **MORGAN** Glywysing, 974–?
Owain was probably the eldest of MORGAN HEN's five sons, and seems to have inherited the major part of his father's domain on Morgan's death in 974. An election of kings is recorded in the year 983 when land was also apportioned to Owain's brothers Idwallon, Cadell and Cynfyn. Glywysing was further apportioned amongst Owain's sons Rhys, Iestyn and HYWEL, which meant that the land had no strong leadership during the troublesome period when it was under threat by the Danes, who raided in strength in 988, and by the rulers of Gwynedd and Deheubarth, who also sought to gain lands in Glamorgan. Throughout Owain's reign there were disputes over the territories of Gower and Brycheiniog.

[EA32] **ARTHFAEL** AP **NOWY** Gwent, *fl* 970s.
Arthfael inherited the vicious family streak (*see under* NOWY AP GWRIAD) and murdered his brother, Elisedd. Arthfael was excommunicated, and no doubt in fear that this meant he would not inherit his father's lands, he atoned with much penance. He eventually succeeded his father, some time in the 970s, but clearly did not rule long. He was probably murdered by the sons of Elisedd, RHODRI and Gruffydd, who succeeded him in 983.

[EA33] **RHYS** AB **OWAIN** Glywysing (part only), *fl* 990s, co-ruler.
[EA34] **HYWEL** AB **OWAIN** Glywysing *c*990s–*c*1043, co-ruler.

[EA35] IESTYN AB **OWAIN** Glywysing (part only), *fl* 990s, co-ruler.

Hywel inherited part of Glywysing from his father OWAIN AP MORGAN and ruled alongside his brothers Rhys and Iestyn, who pre-deceased him. Hywel's reign was remarkably long considering the constant threats to his rule, both externally, from the Danes, who harried the coast of Wales throughout this period, and from LLYWELYN AP SEISYLL, who reunited Gwynedd and Deheubarth and set out to conquer all of Wales. After Llywelyn's death in 1023, Hywel's nephew, RHYDDERCH AP IESTYN set out on his trail of conquest, taking over Deheubarth and proclaiming himself ruler of all South Wales. Hywel seems to have taken little part in this and one must assume he was forced into the background as a vassal king. Sometime before his death, in 1043, his son MEURIG took over the administration. Some records suggest that Hywel died at the age of 110, which is very unlikely, even allowing for the noted longevity amongst his forebears. He was probably in his eighties.

[EA36] RHODRI AP **ELISEDD** Gwent, 983–*c*1015.
[EA37] GRUFFYDD AP **ELISEDD** Gwent, 983–*c*1015.

Rhodri and his brother Gruffydd succeeded to Gwent after the death (or murder) of ARTHFAEL AP NOWY, who had murdered their father. Their reign paralleled that of the rise to power of LLYWELYN AP SEISYLL, who united Gwynedd and Deheubarth and sought to extend his authority in Glamorgan. There were also power struggles within their own family for, in about the year 1015, Rhodri was overthrown by EDWYN AP GWRIAD, who was probably a second cousin.

[EA38] EDWYN AP **GWRIAD** Gwent, 1015–45.

Edwyn's father bears the same name as NOWY AP GWRIAD's but it is unlikely that the two were brothers, as Edwyn lived up to a century later. In all likelihood Edwyn's father was a grandson of Nowy's father, which would make Gwriad either the brother of cousin or ARTHFAEL AP NOWY. Arthfael had killed his brother Elisedd and Elisedd's sons RHODRI and Gruffydd later overthrew Arthfael. Edwyn probably in turn overthrew Rhodri and Gruffydd. The fact that he bore an English name suggests that his father was on good terms with the Saxon rulers, but whether Edwyn was able to continue this same relationship once CANUTE usurped the English throne is not known. Edwyn had also to face the power struggles within Wales of LLYWELYN AP SEISYLL and RHYDDERCH AB IESTYN, but he fell victim to another's ambitions when he was blinded and imprisoned by MEURIG AP HYWEL. He probably died soon after.

[EA39;EB20] RHYDDERCH AB **IESTYN** Glywysing, *c*1015–33; Deheubarth, 1023–33.

With the death of LLYWELYN AP SEISYLL in 1023 Gwynedd and Deheubarth were again split. IAGO AP IDWAL reclaimed Gwynedd, but Deheubarth was usurped by a claimant to the kingdom of Gwent, Rhydderch ab Iestyn, whom some genealogies identified as a descendant of HYWEL DDA's son OWAIN, but who was more probably descended from MORGAN HEN's son OWAIN. Genealogies were easily blurred in order to prove authority. He came to power first in Glywysing probably around 1015 after the death of his father IESTYN AB OWAIN, and he soon took advantage of the death of Llywelyn to storm through Deheubarth and lay claim to the whole of South Wales. Although his hold over Deheubarth was tenuous, he was a popular ruler who restored some of the pride and dignity to the people of South Wales which they had not experienced since the days of MAREDUDD AB OWAIN. After ten years, Rhydderch was slain in battle by HYWEL AB EDWIN, the grand-nephew of Maredudd. He was succeeded by his son GRUFFYDD.

[EA40;EB22] **GRUFFYDD** AP **RHYDDERCH** Glywysing, 1033–55; Deheubarth, 1047–55.

After the death of RHYDDERCH AB IESTYN, Deheubarth was claimed by HYWEL AB EDWIN, whilst Rhydderch's son Gruffydd succeeded to his patrimony in Glywysing. He long planned to recover all of South Wales and he must have been a saviour to Deheubarth against the oppressive GRUFFYDD AP LLYWELYN, after the latter had defeated Hywel ab Edwin at the battle of the river Towy in 1044. It took three years of intense war before Gruffydd ap Llywelyn was eventually driven out of Deheubarth and in his anger he laid waste to parts of Dyfed and Ystrad Tywi. The reign of his father was fondly remembered in Deheubarth, and Gruffydd gained much popular support. He played to this and is remembered as much in legend as in history for his ingenious battle ploys. The best of these was in 1049 when the Danes posed a threat upon the Welsh shores. Gruffydd first ensured that all possible plunder was removed from the coast and hidden in the inland woods. He showed the Danes that there was no spoil to be had, but he offered to show them richer lands to the east. He then led the Viking fleet towards the lands of Gwent (now in the hands of MEURIG AP HYWEL) and the neighbouring English territory of Gloucester, where they plundered to their hearts' content. Gruffydd further led the Danes up the Severn attacking English settlements. The English never forgave Gruffydd and, in 1053, they captured and executed his brother Rhys. Gruffydd led a retaliatory attack on Westbury-on-Severn later that year. Gruffydd's reign, however, was now in its twilight. In 1055 he was attacked again by Gruffydd ap Llywelyn and this time was defeated and slain. The victor from the north at last claimed Deheubarth for which he had fought for twenty years. He held it until his death in 1063 when Glamorgan was regained by CADWGAN AP MEURIG.

[EA41] **MEURIG** AP **HYWEL** Gwent, 1045–55.

The evidence suggests that Meurig grew impatient at the longevity of his father, HYWEL AB OWAIN, and longed to assume power. His father began to include him as a signatory to grants in the 1040s, but Meurig's impatience caused him to invade Gwent in 1045 and capture EDWYN AP GWRIAD, who was blinded and imprisoned. Meurig installed his son CADWGAN as ruler of Gwent and took over the kingship of Glywysing. At this time Meurig was really a vassal king to GRUFFYDD AP RHYDDERCH, who had reclaimed Deheubarth and styled himself king of South Wales. Gruffydd was a popular king and evidently disliked Meurig, as he tricked a Viking raid into leaving Glywysing untouched and led it into Gwent, which it devastated. Meurig was finally driven out of Gwent by GRUFFYDD AP LLYWELYN of Gwynedd who, in 1055, declared himself king of all Wales. Meurig's son, Cadwgan, was later able to reclaim Morgannwg after Gruffydd's death.

[EA42] **CADWGAN** AP **MEURIG** Gwent, 1045–55; Morgannwg, 1063–74.

Cadwgan was first installed as ruler of Gwent by his father, Meurig, who usurped authority there in 1045 by killing EDWYN AP GWRIAD. Cadwgan may still have been quite young at that stage, probably in his twenties. He and his father were driven out of south-east Wales in 1055 by GRUFFYDD AP LLYWELYN, but after Gruffydd's death in 1063 Cadwgan succeeded in recovering the territory of Morgannwg, whilst CARADOG AP GRUFFYDD claimed Gwent. Despite attempts by HAROLD II to subdue the Welsh, Cadwgan held on to his kingdom, but the position changed radically under the Normans. William Fitzosbern, who was made earl of Hereford by WILLIAM THE CONQUEROR, made a major incursion into southern Wales from 1067 to 1070 and took over most of Gwent. Although the records are silent on the matter, Cadwgan probably died in one of the skirmishes, but his place was soon filled by the dispossessed Caradog.

[EA43] **CARADOG** AP **GRUFFYDD** Gwent, 1063–74; Morgannwg, 1075–81.
The son of GRUFFYDD AP RHYDDERCH, who had ruled all of South Wales until killed in battle against GRUFFYDD AP LLYWELYN of Gwynedd. Caradog was probably still a youth when his father died, but by the time Gruffydd ap Llywelyn died in 1063, Caradog was probably into his early twenties, and he was determined to recover his father's lands. He settled in upper Gwent, where in 1065 he undertook an audacious raid on HAROLD II's hunting lodge without reprisals. He was not, however, secure in Gwent for, following the Norman invasion of England, the marcher lords, particularly William Fitzosbern of Hereford, began their incursions into Wales. Fitzosbern undertook a major offensive around 1067 and claimed Gwent by conquest. Soon after, CADWGAN AP MEURIG, who had established himself as ruler of Morgannwg, died, and Caradog, driven out of his own lands, usurped Morgannwg. He had already, in 1072, slain MAREDUDD AB OWAIN of Deheubarth, but had been unable to lay claim to the kingdom because Maredudd's brother RHYS came to the fore. In 1078 Caradog defeated and killed Rhys, but then faced a new rival, RHYS AP TEWDWR. Early in 1081 Caradog finally drove Rhys out of Wales and for a few brief months bathed in the glory of ruling most of South Wales. However, Rhys returned with substantial forces and defeated Caradog at the battle of Mynydd Carn in Dyfed. Caradog almost certainly died in the battle, as he is not heard of again. His son, Owain, was created lord of Caerleon by the Normans, and his descendants held the title until the year 1270.

[EA44] **IESTYN** AP **GWRGAN** Morgannwg, 1081–91.
The last independent ruler of Morgannwg. He was an opportunist, a descendant of OWAIN AP MORGAN but a relatively minor prince until he assumed power after the death of CARADOG AP GRUFFYDD. Tradition states that Iestyn had worked himself into the favour of Robert Fitzhamon, the Norman lord in Gloucester, with promises of help against RHYS AP TEWDWR of Deheubarth. There may well be some truth in this, but Iestyn did not benefit much from it. Fitzhamon was able to establish himself in a castle in Cardiff and from there systematically conquered and claimed Glamorgan. Iestyn was eventually driven out of the kingdom in 1191 and sought refuge in a priory at Llangenydd in Gower, where he died at an uncertain date, probably 1093. His descendants, however, were raised to the title of lords of Afan.

EB. DEHEUBARTH

Deheubarth came into existence in 920 when Hywel Dda combined the former kingdoms of Dyfed and Seisyllwg. Occasionally rulers of Deheubarth gained control over Gwynedd and vice versa. The Normans conquered Deheubarth in 1093, though descendants of the ruling family were allowed to hold authority over Cantref Mawr ("the Great Cantref") and Ystrad Tywi and from this base the former kingdom of Deheubarth briefly re-emerged in the twelfth century under Maredudd ap Gruffydd and the Lord Rhys. Thereafter Norman control was re-exerted and Deheubarth ceased to exist as a kingdom after 1234.

Map 8b **The Later Welsh Kingdoms – Deheubarth**

17. Wales (4) – **Gwynedd and Deheubarth**

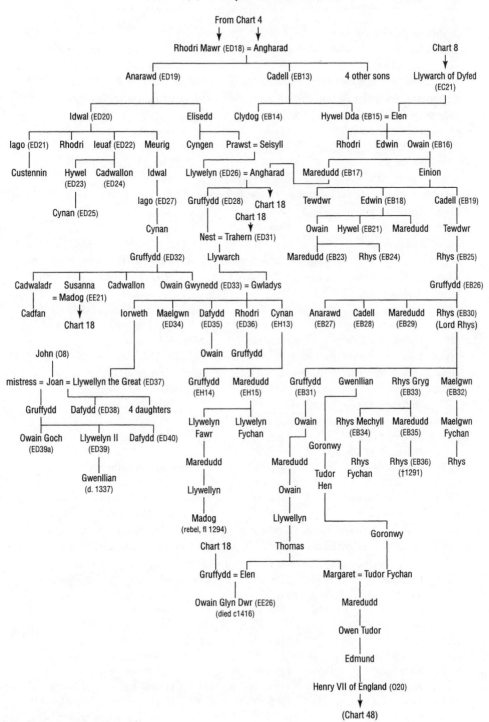

Ref.	Ruler	Born	Reign	Died	Notes

continued from page 130

| EB15. | Hywel *Dda* (*the Good*) | *c*882 | 920–50 | 950 | also ruled Gwynedd and Powys, 942–50 |

After Hywel's death Gwynedd regained its independence. Hywel's three sons split the kingdom of Deheubarth, but after Rhodri died in 953 and Edwin in 954, Owain was able to reconsolidate it.

| EB16. | Owain ap Hywel | | 954–86 | 988 | retired |
| EB17. | Maredudd ab Owain | | 986–99 | 999 | also annexed Gwynedd from 986 |

After Maredudd's death the combined kingdoms of Gwynedd and Deheubarth were ruled from Gwynedd by Cynan ap Hywel from 999–1005.

| EB18. | Edwin ab Einion | | 1005–18 | | |
| EB19. | Cadell ab Einion | | 1005–18 | | |

In 1018, Llywelyn ap Seisyll of Gwynedd, who married into the Deheubarth royal family, laid claim to Deheubarth and ruled until his death in 1023. Gwynedd and Deheubarth were then overrun by Rhydderch ab Iestyn of Gwent, who styled himself king of Deheubarth.

| EB20. | Rhydderch ab Iestyn | | 1023–33 | 1033 | also ruled Gwent (EA39); killed in battle |
| EB21. | Hywel ab Edwin | | 1033–44 | 1044 | killed in battle |

Hywel was overthrown by Gruffydd ap Llywelyn of Gwynedd in 1044 and, in the ensuing power struggle, Rhydderch's son Gruffydd laid claim to Deheubarth.

| EB22. | Gruffydd ab Rhydderch | | 1047–55 | 1055 | also ruled Gwent (EA40); killed in battle |

Conquered by Gruffydd ap Llywelyn of Gwynedd from 1055–63.

EB23.	Maredudd ab Owain ab Edwin		1063–72	1072	killed in battle
EB24.	Rhys ab Owain ab Edwin		1072–78	1078	killed in battle
EB25.	Rhys ap Tewdwr		1078–93	1093	briefly overthrown in 1081 and 1088; killed in battle

Deheubarth was overrun by the Normans in 1093, remaining in their possession until 1155. Territory was granted to Rhys's son Gruffydd in 1116, and further land was progressively regained after the grand revolt of 1136/37.

EB26.	Gruffydd ap Rhys	*c*1090	1116–37	1137	ruled only Cantref Mawr; killed in battle
EB27.	Anarawd ap Gruffydd	*c*1116	1136–43	1143	murdered
EB28.	Cadell ap Gruffydd		1143–51	*c*1175	seriously injured and incapacitated
EB29.	Maredudd ap Gruffydd	*c*1130	1151–5	1155	rebuilt old kingdom of Deheubarth
EB30.	Rhys ap Gruffydd	*c*1133	1155–97	1197	in 1158 submitted to Henry II and dropped title of king, being known as The Lord Rhys
EB31.	Gruffydd ap Rhys		1197–1201	1201	

EB32.	Maelgwyn ap Rhys	c1170	1199–1230	1230	gained control of Ceredigion, though lost the northern part in 1207
EB33.	Rhys *Gryg* (*the Hoarse*)		1216–34	1234	ruled Cantref Mawr (from 1204) and neighbouring territory; died of wounds

After the deaths of Maelgwyn and Rhys the princes of Deheubarth were effectively minor lords subject to Gwynedd and ruling small commotes and cantrefs in Ystrad Tywi and Ceredigion with no real authority. Rhys ap Maredudd below was the last to make a stand in the South and was briefly proclaimed lord of Ystrad Tywi.

EB34.	Rhys *Mechyll*	1234–44	1244	ruled Cantref Mawr only
EB35.	Maredudd	1244–71	1271	ruled Cantref Mawr only
EB36.	Rhys ap Maredudd	1271–83	1291	ruled Cantraf Mawr only; executed for treason

[EB15;EC24] **HYWEL DDA (*the GOOD*)** AP **CADELL** ruled Dyfed, 905–50; Seisyllwg, 920–50 – the two kingdoms combined as Deheubarth after 920; also ruled Gwynedd and Powys, 942–50.

Arguably the greatest of the Welsh rulers, and certainly the only one to be called 'Good'. By the time of his death he was king of all of west Wales. His date of birth is not recorded, but it was probably around 880/2. He was given Dyfed by his father CADELL AP RHODRI who had conquered it in 905, deposing the last king RHODRI AP HYFAIDD. Although Hywel ruled this as sub-king to Cadell, it was an early sign of Hywel's abilities that Cadell should entrust his new kingdom to his younger son. Hywel consolidated his rule in Dyfed by marrying Elen, the daughter of LLYWARCH AP HYFAIDD. When Cadell died in 909, Hywel's brother CLYDOG inherited Seisyllwg, but to all intents Hywel ruled Dyfed and Seisyllwg jointly with CADELL. Upon Cadell's death in 920, Hywel combined the two kingdoms to which he gave the new name of Deheubarth.

Hywel is recorded as a regular visitor to the court of the kings of England. On some occasions, as in 918 and 927, these were meetings called by the Saxon kings in order to reaffirm their suzerainty and to seek fealty from the other rulers of Britain. On at least one occasion, in 934, Hywel had to prove that fealty by accompanying ATHELSTAN in his punitive expedition against CONSTANTINE II of Scotland. On none of these occasions would Hywel have relished this subordination, but he was sensible enough to know that he had neither the need nor the strength of arms to defeat the English and that he could benefit by working with them. This affiliation brought respect from the English kings and a recognition of Hywel's authority. At other times he seems to have attended the English courts as a friend, often to witness charters, and took the opportunity to study how the administration and jurisdiction operated. Though it may go too far to say he was an Anglophile, he did christen one of his children with an English name, Edwin, and the English ability to organize clearly appealed to him. He had the good sense to understand what worked well and could respect the English way of life. This was further amplified after his pilgrimage to Rome in 928. It had a marked effect upon him, not simply in the religious sense, but in recognizing the benefits that could come to a well organized kingdom, which he witnessed in France and Rome.

Hywel benefited from his association with the English. In 942 his cousin, IDWAL AP ANARAWD of Gwynedd, was killed in battle against the Saxons. His sons were expelled from the kingdom and the dominion of the land passed to Hywel. He was now ruler of most of Wales, with the exception of the south-east. He took this opportunity to organize and consolidate the many tribal laws of the land. Soon after 942, probably around 945, he called a great conference at Ty Gwyn ("the White House") in Dyfed (near the modern town of Whitland), with representatives from every parish. The conference met for six weeks during which time we must imagine that all of the laws were codified and differences debated. It is unlikely that within that six weeks all differences were resolved, but it provided the basis for developing a series of three law books, which represented the respective laws of Gwynedd, Deheubarth and Morgannwg. These law books established such authority that it was later said none of the laws could be amended without gathering together a similar assembly. By codifying these laws, which was apparently done under the masterful direction of a lawyer called Blegywryd, Hywel did more towards unifying the Welsh as a nation than any other ruler had sought to achieve by conquest and domination. Even when after Hywel's death his kingdom was again partitioned amongst his successors, his laws lived on, and remained the cornerstone of Welsh administration. So paramount was Hywel in his role as king and lawgiver that he was also the first and only Welsh prince to issue his own coinage. Since it was issued from the mint at Chester, Hywel must have consulted with the English over its production.

When Hywel died in 950, probably in his late sixties, he left behind a legacy that would long be remembered as a golden age in Welsh history. After his death Deheubarth was split between his three sons, Rhodri, Edwin and OWAIN, whilst Gwynedd regained its independence under IAGO AB IDWAL.

[EB16] OWAIN AP HYWEL Deheubarth, 950–86.

HYWEL DDA's three sons inherited Deheubarth in south Wales and split it between them, but it was important that they remained united for immediately they were under attack from IAGO AB IDWAL, who was determined to regain Gwynedd and avenge the death of his father and the loss of his inheritance. The sons of Idwal and the sons of Hywel met in battle at Nant Carno, in Arwystli. The victory went to Iago and Ieuaf and they reclaimed Gwynedd and Powys. The two sides continued to battle for the next three years, with Idwal and Iago usually proving the stronger. Eventually, by 954, Owain and his brother left the bellicose northern brothers alone. In fact Owain was soon on his own. Rhodri died in 953 and Edwin in 954, both still young. As they had no heirs, Owain's claim to the throne was strong. It may have been this, and the strife to the north, that caused Owain to order the organization of the Welsh chronicles and genealogies, tracing not only his paternal and maternal descent but those of other dynasties. This work was completed by about 977.

Although Owain left Gwynedd alone after 954, in 960 he led a punitive attack against the kingdom of Morgannwg. Border skirmishes continued and in 970 Owain's son Einion laid waste to the Gower peninsula which had been occupied by the men of MORGAN *hen*, a tactic which was repeated in 977. Indeed, Owain's sons Einion and MAREDUDD seemed more proficient as soldiers than their father. Einion was more prone to involvement in petty scraps, including a territorial dispute with

Alfhere of Mercia who, supported by HYWEL AP IEUAF of Gwynedd, invaded Einion's lands in 983. It was a similar skirmish, this time with the men of Gwent, that led to Einion's death in battle in Gower in 984. It may have been this incident that caused Owain to decide to step down as ruler and leave the administration in the hands of Maredudd, although Owain remained king in name until his death in 988.

[EB17] **MAREDUDD** AB **OWAIN** Deheubarth and Gwynedd, 986–99.

By the time OWAIN AP HYWEL reached his late sixties, he left the administration of Deheubarth in the hands of his two surviving sons, Einion and Maredudd. Einion was killed in a border skirmish in 984, and soon after Maredudd seems to have assumed more or less full control. He began his reign with a devastating raid on Gwynedd, achieving what his father and uncles had never been able to do. He slew the king CADWALLON AP IEUAF, and again united Gwynedd and Deheubarth. Maredudd was clearly an able and skilled warrior and tactician. In 987, when Vikings attacked Anglesey, Mardedudd ensured the safety of the refugees and paid for the return of the hostages. He even allowed the Vikings to settle in part of Anglesey, and evidently experienced little trouble from them thereafter, for he was able to use Viking forces for a punitive raid on Morgannwg in 992. He took advantage of the general weakness of the new Saxon king ATHELRED II and tackled Mercian encroachment into Wales, especially settlements in the territory of Radnor, driving the Saxons back across the recognized border. Unfortunately his strength as a soldier was regularly challenged by domestic problems from his nephews Tewdwr, EDWIN and CADELL AB EINION, who sought to gain some of Maredudd's southern territories for themselves. He had to rebuff onslaughts from them in 991 and 994 – Tewdwr was killed on the second occasion. Maredudd held his command and ruled with power and authority for thirteen years, earning recognition for a while as the "most praiseworthy king of the Britons". After his death, however, his kingdom fell asunder with a host of claimants to the throne, the strongest of whom, LLYWELYN AP SEISYLL, initially won Gwynedd and later, through marriage to Maredudd's daughter Angharad, also claimed Deheubarth. Maredudd's nephews, Edwin and Cadell ab Einion also ruled southern Wales for a time, more in name than in authority.

[EB18] **EDWIN** AB **EINION** Deheubarth, 1005–18.
[EB19] **CADELL** AB **EINION** Deheubarth, 1005–18.

After the death of MAREDUDD AB OWAIN, his combined kingdoms were ruled by CYNAN AP HYWEL until his own death in 1005. Then Edwin and Cadell, the sons of Maredudd's brother Einion, managed to reclaim some of the lands in Deheubarth. They were aggressive brothers who had sought to gain a share of the kingdom from the earliest opportunity, challenging Maredudd for territories in southern Wales in 991 and 994. Their hold on authority was tenuous and they were challenged by Aeddan ap Blegywryd, a usurper of uncertain origin, though it is tempting to wonder if he was a relative of Blegywryd, HYWEL DDA's lawyer. Aeddan succeeded in deposing Edwin and Cadell. Their exact fate is unknown, and they may have been killed at this time, for they are not mentioned in any later records. Aeddan was himself soon overthrown by Llywelyn ap Seisyll who again reunited Gwynedd and Deheubarth. Edwin's son HYWEL was to later regain the throne in 1033.

[EB20;EA39] **RHYDDERCH** AB **IESTYN** Glywysing, c1015–33; Deheubarth, 1023–33.

With the death of LLYWELYN AP SEISYLL in 1023, Gwynedd and Deheubarth were again split. IAGO AP IDWAL reclaimed Gwynedd, but Deheubarth was usurped by a claimant to the kingdom of Gwent, Rhydderch ab Iestyn. Although his hold over Deheubarth was tenuous, he was a popular ruler. After ten years, Rhydderch was slain in battle by HYWEL AB EDWIN, the grand-nephew of Maredudd. *For full details of Rhydderch see page 327 under Morgannwg.*

[EB21] **HYWEL** AB **EDWIN** Deheubarth, 1033–44.

Hywel was the son of EDWIN AB EINION who had ruled Deheubarth twenty years earlier. Hywel, and his brother Maredudd, succeeded in regaining the kingdom of Deheubarth after they defeated RHYDDERCH AB IESTYN in 1033. The next decade was one of constant border battles. Maredudd was killed in 1035 and Hywel ruled alone. His main foe was GRUFFYDD AP LLYWELYN, the powerful ruler of Gwynedd who sought to regain Deheubarth as part of the kingdom ruled by his father, LLYWELYN AP SEISYLL. Hywel, however, proved a particularly strong opponent. A series of skirmishes continued over the years. In 1039 Gruffydd succeeding in claiming Ceredigion, but Hywel remained in control of Dyfed and Ystrad Tywi. The two forces met again in 1041, when again Gruffydd was victorious and this time captured Hywel's wife, but Hywel retained his lands. The next year Hywel had to face a force of Vikings landing in northern Dyfed, whom he succeeded in defeating. Sometime after, probably in late 1043, Gruffydd forced Hywel out of the kingdom, but Hywel soon returned, this time with the support of a Viking fleet. The battle took place at the estuary of the river Towy. Gruffydd was the victor and Hywel was killed. However, no sooner had Gruffydd ap Llywelyn gained control of Deheubarth than he found new opposition from GRUFFYDD AB RHYDDERCH.

[EB22;EA40] **GRUFFYDD** AB **RHYDDERCH** Glywysing, 1033–55; Deheubarth, 1047–55.

Following the death of RHYDDERCH AB IESTYN, his son Gruffydd succeeded to Glywysing, but determined to recover all of South Wales. Gruffydd was able to take advantage of the defeat of HYWEL AB EDWIN in 1044 to increase his authority, and three years later GRUFFYDD AP LLYWELYN was driven out of Deheubarth. Thereby Gruffydd ab Rhydderch became king of all South Wales. He was extremely popular, and a valiant hero. Unfortunately his reign was all too short. In 1055 he was defeated and slain by Gruffydd ap Llywelyn of Gwynedd who gained Deheubarth and held it until his death in 1063 when it passed to MAREDUDD AB OWAIN AB EDWIN. *For full details of Gruffydd see page 328 under Morgannwg.*

[EB23] **MAREDUDD** AB **OWAIN** AB **EDWIN** Deheubarth, 1063–72.

Unlike his namesake and great grand-uncle, this Maredudd was a rather ineffectual king. He was the nephew of HYWEL AB EDWIN who had been killed in 1044, when he and his brothers had been driven into exile. In 1063, however, after the death of GRUFFYDD AP LLYWELYN, Earl Harold (later HAROLD II) ensured that the new rulers of Wales would be loyal to him and not likely to cause much trouble. Maredudd was restored to his family's patrimony on the basis that he would not raid Saxon territory. Maredudd was happy to accept this, but three years later everything changed as WILLIAM THE CONQUEROR swept into England. William's men soon made inroads into Gwent, which fell to them by 1070. Because Maredudd had not interfered, he was granted manors in England provided he left well alone. The more fiercely independent of the Welsh princes regarded Maredudd as a weakling and a traitor. In 1072 CARADOG AP GRUFFYDD, who was intent on carving out a kingdom for himself, attacked Maredudd along with a force of Norman soldiers, and killed him at the river Rhymni. Deheubarth passed to Maredudd's brother RHYS.

[EB24] RHYS AB OWAIN Deheubarth, 1072–78.

Brother and successor of MAREDUDD AB OWAIN AB EDWIN. Rhys was a weak king, who was ineffectual in defending Ceredigion from the ravages of the Normans who attacked it in 1073 and 1074. His only retaliation was against the much beloved king, BLEDDYN AP CYNFYN of Gwynedd, whose murder Rhys engineered in 1075, a death that was regarded as an outrage. If Rhys sought to benefit from this death he was misguided. In 1078 TRAHERN AP CARADOG of Gwynedd invaded Dyfed and defeated Rhys at Goodwick. Trahern seems to have taken great delight in hounding Rhys through the rocks and cliffs of Dyfed like a frightened deer. Rhys escaped only briefly with his life for, a few months later, he and his brother Hywel were killed by their nemesis, CARADOG AP GRUFFYDD, who had previously killed their brother Maredudd. Caradog, however, did not succeed to the throne of Deheubarth, which was claimed by Rhys's second cousin, RHYS AP TEWDWR.

[EB25] RHYS AP TEWDWR Deheubarth, 1078–93.

Rhys was one of the more memorable of the later kings of Deheubarth, and the last of any significance. He claimed the rulership after the death of RHYS AB OWAIN, his second cousin. He had a good claim to the throne, being fifth in descent from HYWEL DDA, but he needed to prove himself against the ever vigorous CARADOG AP GRUFFYDD, his third cousin and also fifth in descent from Hywel Dda. Caradog mustered his forces in 1081 and pressed Rhys back to the coast, until Rhys was forced to seek refuge in the church at St David's in Dyfed. Rhys combined forces with the exiled GRUFFYDD AP CYNAN of Gwynedd and the two defeated and killed Caradog at the decisive battle of Mynydd Carn. Rhys was now firmly in control of Deheubarth, and a strong ally of Gruffydd, who had likewise regained Gwynedd. Later in 1081, WILLIAM THE CONQUEROR led an expedition into southern Wales. Ostensibly a visit to the shrine of St David, William used it to free Norman prisoners isolated in various remote castles. There is little doubt that William and Rhys met and agreed a treaty whereby Rhys was allowed to rule in Deheubarth without any threat from the Normans provided he kept the peace and paid an annual tribute of forty pounds. This arrangement continued satisfactorily up to and beyond William's death in 1087.

Rhys was able to rule in relative calm and prosperity for a few years, but by 1088 conflict returned to the kingdom. In that year he was attacked by MADOG AP BLEDDYN and his brothers with such ferocity that he was forced to seek refuge in Ireland. He soon raised the help of a Danish fleet with which he returned and defeated his enemies, killing Madog and his brother Rhiryd. In 1091 Rhys's authority was again challenged, this time from within his own kingdom, when the nobility in Dyfed offered the crown to Gruffydd, the son of MAREDUDD AB OWAIN, who had been killed in 1072. Gruffydd had been in exile in England all these years, and would have done well to stay there. He and his supporters met Rhys at the estuary of the river Towy, on the borders of Dyfed and Ystrad Tywi, where Rhys was the victor and Gruffydd was slain.

During these latter years the Normans, now ruled by WILLIAM II who exercised less control over them, had been battling their way along the Welsh border, making gains in Gwent and Brycheiniog. In April 1093 Rhys became involved in a skirmish with the Normans at Aberhonddu in Brycheiniog where he was killed. The exact nature of his death is uncertain and there are hints of treachery. His death, though, was a fatal blow to southern Wales. Until then William Rufus had respected Rhys's authority while the tribute had been paid. With his death, the agreement was annulled, and the Normans flooded into Morgannwg and Deheubarth. It was from this point that the independence of Wales was gravely eroded.

Rhys had married Gwladys, the daughter of Rhiwallon ap Cynfan of Gwynedd, sometime around 1080. Their son, GRUFFYDD, briefly regained rulership within Deheubarth, though only in the territory of Cantref Mawr, whilst his grandson, RHYS, formally dropped the title of king. His daughter Nesta, was known for her beauty and had many lovers. She married Gerald of Pembroke, with whom she had several children, and became the grandmother of Giraldus Cambrensis, but she was also the mistress of HENRY I by whom she had at least one son. In 1109 she was abducted by OWAIN AP CADWGAN, for which reason she became known as Helen of Wales. It is tempting to think that Nesta served as a model for Guinevere in the Arthurian stories that began to emerge in the twelfth century, as many would remember her beauty and escapades.

[EB26] GRUFFYDD AP RHYS (I) Cantref Mawr, 1116–37.

The younger son of RHYS AP TEWDWR, who was only three when his father was killed in 1093. He was given sanctuary in Ireland. During those years the Normans made considerable advances into southern Wales, establishing their fortifications and their authority. They had also forced GRUFFYDD AP CYNAN of Gwynedd into becoming their vassal. It was against this background of Norman domination that Gruffydd ap Rhys reappeared on the scene in 1113, footloose and disinherited but determined to gain a hold on his father's lands. Initially he did nothing but stir up discontent but within a couple of years HENRY I saw the problems he might cause and set out to capture him. Gruffydd sought refuge with his father's former ally, Gruffydd ap Cynan, but Gruffydd already knew the power of Henry I and was not prepared to face it again. He was ready to hand the young Gruffydd over, but the prince escaped across Cardigan Bay. His patriotic zeal was now enflamed and he was soon able to raise an army (or more appropriately a rabble) of young malcontents. At the start of 1116 they began a series of attacks on Norman castles. He achieved enough successes to raise Welsh hopes and, with a much enlarged army, he led a raid on Ceredigion. It was evident that Gruffydd had no control over this larger force and its size worked against it. The skilled castellan at Aberystwyth was able to use his greater experience and put the army to flight. Gruffydd was forced to seek refuge in Ystrad Tywi.

It is to Henry's credit that he did not hound Gruffydd down and imprison him, though he made several attempts to capture him. Henry found the young hothead impulsive but in the end agreed that he could have the lordship of Cantref Mawr, "the Great Cantref" in Ystrad Tywi. Although he styled himself king, it was a title without authority, and an ignominious end to a once great kingdom. Nevertheless, having regained some territory, Gruffydd seemed happy to settle down. He upset his Norman neighbours in 1127, which caused him briefly to seek refuge in Ireland, but he soon returned. He married Gwenllian, the daughter of Gruffydd ap Cynan, though he already had two children, presumably of an earlier marriage or liaison. With Gwenllian he had six children, including RHYS, who inherited Cantref Mawr.

The death of HENRY I in 1135 gave signal to the Welsh of new hopes. Small insurrections soon flared into a major revolt. While Gruffydd rode into Gwynedd hoping to rally forces along with Gruffydd ap Cynan and his sons, Gwenllian led her own force against the castle at Kidwelly, where she met her death. Gruffydd joined in the invasion of Ceredigion in 1137 and led his own force down into Dyfed. His initial engagements, mostly against the Fleming settlers, were victorious, but he was finally cut down and killed. His sons continued the rebellion in the south: ANARAWD, the eldest, followed by CADELL, but it was not until the time of the younger son, RHYS, that Deheubarth regained any independence.

[EB27] **ANARAWD** AP **GRUFFYDD** resistance leader of Deheubarth, 1136–43.
Anarawd was the eldest son of Gruffydd ap Rhys, though he was still only a little over twenty when his father was killed. Anarawd had already proved himself in 1137 by slaying the local Flemish tyrant in Dyfed, Letard, which proved a popular killing. The next year Anarawd and his brother CADELL joined forces with OWAIN GWYNEDD and his brothers in their concerted attacks on the Norman castles in Ceredigion. Although a Viking force also came to their assistance, the engagement was stopped by a truce. Nevertheless, by the end of 1138 Anarawd felt safe in his role as leader of the people of Deheubarth in Dyfed and Ystrad Tywi. In 1143 Anarawd was murdered by the men of Owain Gwynedd's brother Cadwaladr, which led to Cadwaladr's expulsion to Ireland.

[EB28] **CADELL** AP **GRUFFYDD** resistance leader of Deheubarth, 1143–51.
Cadell took over as the leader of the peoples of Dyfed and Ystrad Tywi in 1143 after the murder of his brother, ANARAWD. He continued the fight to drive the Normans out of Wales and regain the lands of Deheubarth. His greatest victories were in Dyfed, but he also regained ground in Ceredigion from the rulers of Gwynedd. Cadell seemed poised to make even greater gains when, in 1151 he was caught by surprise whilst hunting by a Norman raiding party. Severely wounded he was left for dead. Although he recovered he was left scarred and crippled and unable to lead his forces. He handed the leadership over to his younger brothers, under the command of MAREDUDD. In 1153 he left for a pilgrimage to Rome and nothing more was heard of him until 1175 when his body was returned to the abbey at Strata Florida for burial.

[EB29] **MAREDUDD** AP **GRUFFYDD** ruled parts of Dyfed and Ystrad Tywi, 1151–5.
Maredudd was barely twenty when his elder brother CADELL was ambushed and severely wounded and was no longerable to lead the resistance movement against the Normans. Despite his youth, Maredudd led his forces with considerable skill and wisdom. Unlike his elder brothers and his father, Maredudd was also just, not

intent on wholesale slaughter. He rapidly earned a reputation for his fairness and clemency. Had he lived long enough he may have proved a remarkable leader. Unfortunately, having regained Ceredigion in 1153, and in the same year recovered lands in Gower and across Carmarthen Bay at Tenby, so that he had virtually rebuilt the old kingdom of Deheubarth, Maredudd died, aged only twenty-five. It is not recorded that he died violently, so we must assume that he died of an illness. He was succeeded by his brother RHYS.

[EB30] **RHYS** AP **GRUFFYDD** – *THE LORD RHYS* Deheubarth, 1155–97.
Born: *c1132 in Ireland.* **Died:** *28 April 1197, aged about 65.* **Buried:** *St David's Cathedral.*
Married: *(date unknown), Gwenllian, dau. Madog ap Maredudd of Powys; 9 children, plus at least 9 illegitimate.*
In the eighteen years since the death of GRUFFYDD AP RHYS, his sons had progressively reclaimed and rebuilt much of the old kingdom of Deheubarth, recovering lands from the Normans and from the rival kingdom of Gwynedd. Rhys had been only four when his father died, but by the age of thirteen he was involved with his brothers in various engagements so that he was already battle hardened when the early death of his brother MAREDUDD catapulted Rhys into power in 1155.

He came to power at the same time as HENRY II of England, who felt he needed to repair the damage caused in both England and Wales during the last twenty years. He soon tested Welsh resistance by a campaign into North Wales in 1157 that saw the submission of OWAIN GWYNEDD. Rhys held out for a year with a display of bravado, but when Henry put it to the test in 1158, Rhys was forced to submit. His parley with Henry was costly. Rhys was forced to hand back all of the captured castles to the Norman families and was left in control of only Cantref Mawr and a few outlying territories. Deheubarth was again split asunder as if the last twenty years had been for nothing. Perhaps even more ignominious was that Rhys agreed to drop the title of king, demonstrating his total submission to Henry's authority. Ever after he was always known as *Yr Arglwydd Rhys* – "The Lord Rhys". Such a decision was not easily accepted. Rhys's nephew, Einion ap Anarawd, rebelled and slew the garrison at Castell Hywel. Henry returned with a show of force and Rhys had to capitulate. However, soon after Henry returned to France, Rhys attacked several castles in Dyfed, most notably Carmarthen, which resulted in a major Norman force being despatched by Henry's illegitimate son, Reginald, earl of Cornwall. The scale of the opposition drove Rhys back into his stronghold of Cantref Mawr from which the combined forces of five Norman earls, plus the assistance of the rulers of Gwynedd, were unable to displace him. A truce was finally called and, for the next three years, Rhys remained quiet.

Then, in 1162, Rhys began again on a series of raids, taking the castle at Llandovery. When Henry returned to England in early 1163 his first mission was to penetrate into South Wales. Henry caught up with Rhys in Ceredigion. Quite how or why Rhys submitted is not clear, but there was no struggle, and Henry took Rhys away as prisoner. It is a demonstration of Henry's belief in his own strength and authority that, after a few months, he released Rhys after he had paid homage to Henry at Woodstock in July, along with MALCOLM IV of Scotland and Owain

From a picture in the
National Library of Wales

Gwynedd. Rhys remained obdurate. While he had been prisoner, his nephew Einion had been murdered. The murderer was being sheltered by Roger de Clare, earl of Hertford. Once back in Wales, Rhys immediately led an army in Ceredigion destroying any Norman stronghold he found as he progressed. This was the last straw for Henry. He planned to raise a major army and subdue Wales once and for all. The threat of this at last brought the various factions in Wales together into a major uprising. At the same time Henry had his own domestic problems over Thomas Becket, and his campaign of 1165 failed dramatically. Rhys seized this as an opportunity to regain all of his lost lands and within a year had rebuilt much of Deheubarth. He never was able to regain much of the land in Dyfed or along the southern coast, but most of Ceredigion and northern Ystrad Tywi was under his direct rule, and many surrounding territories were ruled by client kings.

For a period the Norman lords despaired, many of them turning their attention to Ireland to expand their power. This further annoyed Henry whose next expedition to Wales in 1170 was not to subjugate the Welsh but to bring his Norman lords back to heel. It seems that during the 1160s both sides had learned their lessons. In 1171 and 1172 Henry and Rhys held a series of meetings out of which Rhys emerged as Henry's recognized "justiciar" in Deheubarth, a role which demonstrated that Rhys acted with the authority of Henry and had power over the administration of the law, and that meant power over the lesser rulers in South Wales. Rhys actually styled himself "Prince of South Wales". It was a turning point in Welsh affairs. From then on, for the second half of his reign, Rhys put aside his rebellious past and assumed the rôle of a governor, negotiator, peace-maker and king's man. He even sent a force to support Henry during the revolt of his sons in 1173. Rhys saw the benefits of Norman England and even began to imitate the Norman way of life and administration. But he did not neglect Welsh culture. He rebuilt the castle at Cardigan and, upon its completion in 1176, inaugurated there the first official *eisteddfod*. He also founded or rebuilt a number of abbeys, of which Strata Florida was the most striking example.

Unfortunately most of Rhys's achievements were built on shifting sands. They relied primarily on his own strength and stamina and on the relationship that he developed with Henry II. After Henry's death in 1189, Rhys found it difficult to receive any co-operation from RICHARD's government, and the protection he was allowed from the ambitions of the marcher lords also evaporated. Tensions again began to mount, intensified by unrest between Rhys's own sons. The result was that Rhys once again had to take to arms to defend himself. The main Anglo-Norman opponent was William de Breos, lord of Radnor and Builth. Initially Rhys showed his strength, but by 1194 the in-fighting within the family began to take its toll. The main trouble-maker was one of Rhys's younger sons, MAELGWYN, who was imprisoned and later handed over to Breos by his own brother GRUFFYDD. When Rhys secured Maelgwyn's release, it only led to more in-fighting between Maelgwyn and Gruffydd. Rhys was caught in the middle and in 1194 found himself captured and imprisoned by Maelgwyn. He was soon released, but found that other sons, RHYS GRYG and Maredudd, had captured Deheubarth's royal stronghold at Dinefwr. Rhys was incensed. Showing something of his old strength and verve he regained his castles and, in 1196, led a major campaign against the Normans. During the last few years William de Breos had succeeded in regaining some of his old territories, but in a remarkable campaign Rhys stormed and captured many of de Breos's castles and razed Norman towns to the ground. Rhys went out in a blaze of glory. He died the following spring. He was the last great ruler of southern Wales, and certainly one of Wales's greatest rulers. From out of almost nothing he rebuilt Deheubarth, and held it against overwhelming odds for over forty years. Unfortunately, as was ever the case with a strong king who ruled for so long, the rivalry between his sons soon pulled the kingdom apart.

[EB31] **GRUFFYDD** AP **RHYS** (II) Cantref Mawr, 1197–1201.
Born: *date unknown, possibly mid-1150s.* *Died*: *25 July 1201, probably in late forties.*
Buried: *Strata Florida Abbey.*
Married: *1189, Matilda, dau. William de Breos; 2 sons.*
Gruffydd was the eldest son of RHYS AP GRUFFYDD, "The Lord Rhys", but had little of his father's strength and verve. Inter-filial rivalry had broken out long before Rhys's death, particularly between Gruffydd and his younger brother MAELGWYN. Gruffydd should have been in a strong position on his father's death. He inherited the heartland of Deheubarth, Cantref Mawr in Ystrad Tywi, but he was soon under attack by Maelgwyn who had inherited Ceredigion. Maelgwyn had joined forces with GWENWYNWYN of Powys and within months they had captured and imprisoned Gruffydd. Gruffydd was set free several months later and over the next year succeeded in gaining most of Ceredigion from Maelgwyn. Maelgwyn negotiated with the English King JOHN over ownership of the lands and was restored to most of Ceredigion. In July 1201, Gruffydd's brother, Maredudd, who had inherited Cantref Bychan in Ystrad Tywi, was killed. Gruffydd succeeded in gaining the lands, but he was overcome with a fever and died three weeks later.

[EB32] **MAELGWYN** AP **RHYS** Ceredigion, 1199–1230.
Born: *c1170.* *Died*: *late in 1230 at Llannerch Aeron, aged about 60.* *Buried*: *Strata Florida Abbey.*
The sixth son of RHYS AP GRUFFYDD, Maelgwyn was a violent and aggressive youth whose actions contributed towards the dissolution of the south Welsh kingdoms after his father's death. Maelgwyn initially rallied to the Cross in 1188 and was overcome with crusader zeal, but this enthusiasm soon waned and shifted instead to fighting against his brothers for territorial gain. He was imprisoned by his father in

1189 and subsequently passed by his brother GRUFFYDD to the Anglo-Norman lord William de Breos. When released in 1193, Maelgwyn sought revenge upon Gruffydd and, in the process captured and imprisoned his own father. As a result, in 1194, Maelgwyn was banished into exile, but he returned promptly upon his father's death in 1197 to claim Ceredigion as his inheritance. Although Maelgwyn initially defeated and imprisoned Gruffydd, with the aid of GWENWYNWYN of Powys, Gruffydd was able to turn the tables and in 1198 drove Maelgwyn out of Ceredigion, apart from a couple of castles. Maelgwyn turned to King JOHN of England for support and, by treaty, John confirmed Maelgwyn as lord of Ceredigion in 1199. In effect Maelgwyn had sold Ceredigion to John for the privilege of being its lord.

Over the next few years Maelgwyn benefited from the deaths of his brothers Maredudd and Gruffydd, and he engineered the death of a third brother Hywel Sais. With the death of Gruffydd, Maelgwyn laid claim to Ystrad Tywi and, with the aid of Gwenwynwyn, captured the castles at Dinefwr, Llandovery and Llangadock in 1203. At that stage Maelgwyn could claim to rule much of the lands of his father. However, this all soon began to crumble. In 1204 his brother RHYS GRYG and his nephews Rhys and Owain, the sons of Gruffydd, drove Maelgwyn out of Ystrad Tywi. Later that year he was expelled from Dyfed by William Marshal, earl of Pembroke. In 1208 Maelgwyn faced a further threat as events elsewhere in Wales led to the fall from power of Gwenwynwyn and the rise of LLYWELYN THE GREAT. Maelgwyn now lost the northern territories of Ceredigion to his nephews Rhys and Owain, who were supported by Llywelyn, and Maelgwyn was forced into the lands south of the river Aeron. Maelgwyn continued to support whichever side might benefit him. In 1211 he supported John in his war against Llywelyn, but gained nothing from this so shifted his support to Llywelyn. Llywelyn continued to distrust Maelgwyn, but at the Council of Abderdovey in 1216 he did receive the lands of northern Dyfed and parts of Ystrad Tywi, in addition to his lands in Ceredigion. After the death of his nephew Rhys in 1222, Maelgwyn was allotted part of his lands in northern Ceredigion.

In these latter years Maelgwyn ceased to force territorial claims, seeming relatively content with his lot and remaining loyal to Llywelyn. Although Maelgwyn mellowed, his life was indelibly stamped by the rash aggression of his youth, which showed him as a treacherous opportunist liable to make more enemies than friends. That he reached old age is more a sign of his abilities to back the right side at the right time.

His son, Maelgwyn *Fychan* (*the Younger*), who succeeded him as lord of Ceredigion, died in 1257 and was in turn succeeded by his grandson, Rhys *Ieuanc*. Despite their titles they were lords of small commotes in northern Ceredigion, subject to the overlordship of Gwynedd. Rhys *Ieuanc* (also known as Rhys *Fychan*) surrendered to EDWARD I in 1277, thus escaping imprisonment, but was dispossessed of all title, and spent the rest of his days serving in the English army. He died in 1302.

[EB33] **RHYS *GRYG* (*the HOARSE*) AP RHYS** ruled Cantref Mawr, 1204–34; and most of Ystrad Tywi, 1216–34.

[EB34] **RHYS *MECHYLL*** ruled Cantref Mawr, 1234–44.

[EB35] **MAREDUDD** AP **RHYS** *GRYG* ruled Cantref Mawr, 1244–71.

[EB36] **RHYS** AP **MAREDUDD** ruled Cantref Mawr, 1271–83.

In the general rebelliousness of Rhys's sons in the early 1190s, Rhys *Gryg* (also known as Rhys *Fychan*, or Rhys the Younger) the fourth son of RHYS AP GRUFFYDD who was probably born in the 1170s, claimed the territories of Cantref Mawr and Cantref Bychan in Ystrad Tywi, including the ancestral castle of Dinefwr. His father soon reclaimed the lands and Rhys was imprisoned. Rhys remained supportive of his brother, GRUFFYDD, but after the latter's death in 1201, the heartland of Deheubarth, Cantref Mawr in Ystrad Tywi, was claimed first by MAELGWYN AP RHYS and then, in 1204, by Rhys. Rhys initially sided with King JOHN, who in 1211 aided Rhys in his battles against his nephews, the sons of Gruffydd, who had taken sides with LLYWELYN THE GREAT of Gwynedd. Later that year, however, Rhys realised the grand plans of John and, with his brother Maelgwyn, transferred their support to Llywelyn. Thereafter Rhys remained loyal to Llywelyn. In 1216 he was confirmed in his position as lord of Cantref Mawr and most of the other territories in Ystrad Tywi. Little else is recorded of Rhys's lordship of Ystrad Tywi. However in 1231, during the great rebellion against the Normans, Rhys was found fighting alongside his brothers. He was involved in the long and unsuccessful siege of Carmathen Castle in the winter of 1234, where he was mortally wounded. He died soon after at Llandeilo Fawr and was buried at St David's Cathedral.

His territories passed to his son, Rhys *Mechyll* [EB34]. None of these later princes of Cantref Mawr can be regarded as significant rulers of parts of Wales. After Rhys *Mechyll's* death in 1244, Cantref Mawr came under the lordship of his brother, Maredudd [EB35], who remained in power until 1271. Maredudd stayed loyal to the English king HENRY III, which led to him having to forfeit lands to LLYWELYN AP GRUFFYDD of Gwynedd. His son, Rhys [EB36], was a proud and disappointed man. With the accession of EDWARD I, Rhys proclaimed his loyalty and endeavoured to reclaim some of his former patrimony. The result was humiliating. In 1283 Edward forced Rhys to quitclaim his castle at Dinefwr and he was publicly humiliated by Edward. In 1287 Rhys led a rebellion which saw him regain lands around Ystrad Tywi, but it was short-lived. By January 1288 he was in hiding. He was eventually betrayed and in April 1292 was arrested, tried for treason and executed. With his death the old royal line of Deheubarth was effectively extinguished.

ED. GWYNEDD

Gwynedd was always the primary kingdom of Wales, even though it had moments when it was dominated by rulers from the south. It had several great rulers during its early years but the first to earn the title "the Great" was Rhodri ap Merfyn who by 871 had inherited Powys and Seisyllwg, in addition to Gwynedd, and was effectively ruler of all northern and western Wales.

Ref.	Ruler	Born	Reign	Died	Notes
continued from page 141					
ED18.	Rhodri *Mawr* (*the Great*)		844–78	878	driven out by Vikings; killed in battle

Rhodri succeeded to the kingdoms of Powys in 855 and Seisyllwg in 871, becoming king of all North Wales

| ED19. | Anarawd ap Rhodri | 878–916 | 916 | |
| ED20. | Idwal *Foel* (*the Bald*) | 916–42 | 942 | killed in battle |

Idwal submitted to Edward the Elder of England from 918–37. Gwynedd was ruled by Hywel Dda of Deheubarth (see EB15) from 942–50.

ED21.	Iago ab Idwal	950–79	?	deposed
ED22.	Ieuaf ab Idwal	950–69	988	deposed and imprisoned
ED23.	Hywel ap Ieuaf	974–85	985	killed
ED24.	Cadwallon ap Ieuaf	985–6	986	slain

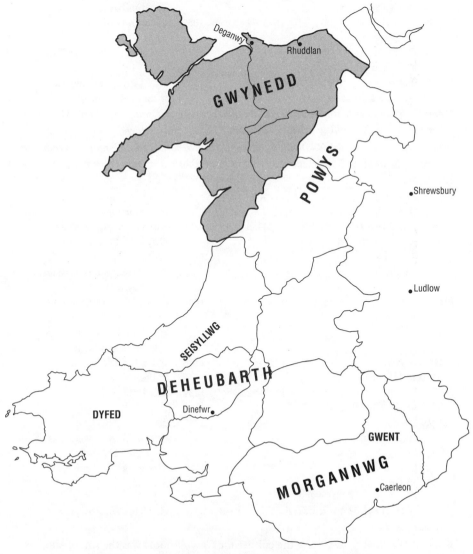

Map 8c **The Later Welsh Kingdoms – Gwynedd**

Ref.	Ruler	Born	Reign	Died	Notes
Gwynedd was ruled by Maredudd ap Owain of Deheubarth (see EB17) from 986–999.					
ED25.	Cynan ap Hywel		999–1005	1005	
ED26.	Llywelyn ap Seisyll		1005–23	1023	also ruled Deheubarth from 1018
ED27.	Iago ap Idwal ap Meurig		1023–39	1039	murdered
ED28.	Gruffydd ap Llywelyn		1039–63	1063	ruled Deheubarth from 1055; recognized as sovereign ruler of all Wales; murdered.
ED29.	Bleddyn ap Cynfyn	*c*1025	1063–75	1075	murdered
ED30.	Rhiwallon ap Cynfyn		1063–70	1070	co-ruler with Bleddyn; killed in battle
ED31.	Trahern ap Caradog		1075–81	1081	killed in battle
ED32.	Gruffydd ap Cynan	*c*1055	1081–1137	1137	regained territory briefly in 1075
ED33.	Owain Gwynedd	*c*1100	1137–70	1170	styled Prince of Gwynedd from 1157

Upon Owain's death his lands were divided between his sons, of whom Maelgwyn inherited Anglesey. Civil war broke out from 1170–4, from which emerged two victors who eventually divided the kingdom between them. Another son, Cynan, succeeded in retaining his land at Merioneth and briefly re-established a ruling dynasty there (see EH13).

Ref.	Ruler	Born	Reign	Died	Notes
ED34.	Maelgwyn ab Owain		1170–3	?	fled to Ireland; returned but imprisoned.
ED35.	Dafydd ab Owain Gwynedd	*c*1135	1170–95	1203	East Gwynedd; ruled all of Gwynedd 1174–5; deposed
ED36.	Rhodri ab Owain Gwynedd		1170–90	1195	West Gwynedd; deposed, though temporarily regained Anglesey in 1193
ED37.	Llywelyn *the Great*	1173	1195–1240	1240	acceded to East Gwynedd in 1195 and gradually rebuilt the kingdom; became effective ruler of Wales from 1216
ED38.	Dafydd ap Llywelyn	*c*1208	1240–6	1246	styled himself "Prince of Wales"
ED39.	Llywelyn (II) *the Last* ap Gruffydd	*c*1225	1246–82	1282	killed
ED39a.	Owain *Goch* ap Gruffydd		1246–55	1282?	deposed by his brother; later reinstated by Edward I as co-ruler, 1277–1282?
ED40.	Dafydd ap Gruffydd		1282–3	1283	deposed and executed for treason.

[ED18] **RHODRI *MAWR* (*THE GREAT*)** ruled Gwynedd, 844–78; Powys, 855–78; Seisyllwg, 871–78.

The first Welsh king to receive the epithet *the Great*, Rhodri was the son of MERFYN FRYCH and, through his mother, the grandson of CADELL AP BROCHFAEL of Powys.

Rhodri thereby succeeded to the kingdom of Gwynedd on the death of his father, and to the kingdom of Powys on the abdication of his uncle, CYNGEN AP CADELL. Through his marriage to Angharad, the daughter of MEURIG of Seisyllwg, Rhodri also came to rule that territory when Angharad's brother GWGON drowned in 871. By the end of his reign Rhodri ruled the greater part of Wales, the most united under a single monarch since the days of MAELGWYN.

If there was any time when Wales needed a strong king, it was then. Rhodri's kingdom was under attack from the Danes to the west and the Saxons to the east. In 853 BURGRED and Mercia combined forces with ATHELWOLF of Wessex in a major assault against the Welsh. Though they overran Powys, they were unable to defeat Rhodri and withdrew. In 855 the first Viking attack occurred on the coast of Anglesey. Rhodri marshalled his defences and, in the following year, he met a Danish fleet in battle and slew their leader, Gorm. The victory was celebrated not only in Wales, but across England and in Francia, which was also subject to Danish attacks. The Danes continued to harry the coasts of England and Ireland, and later returned to Dyfed in southern Wales, but left Anglesey alone for twenty years. This indicates that Rhodri had established significant defences to discourage any invasion. Rhodri again faced an onslaught from the Mercians in 865, when Burgred invaded as far as Anglesey but had to withdraw because of the Viking threat to his own kingdom.

For Rhodri to sustain his defences on both east and west borders shows a high degree of strategic skills and an ability to command considerable support and loyalty. There is no doubt that Rhodri gave back to the Welsh a belief in themselves and a chance to show their strength. If this had been achieved earlier and sustained by RHUN and CADWALLON, the native British might well have regained much of the island, but they were never able to sustain it beyond the reign of one ruler. With Rhodri there came a ruler who changed the culture and thinking of his people, a change which outlasted him and formed the basis for the establishment of modern Wales.

Unfortunately for Rhodri his abilities let him down after a powerful reign of over thirty years. In 877 the Danes renewed their raids on Anglesey, this time with a stronger power base in Dublin and the Western Isles. They succeeded in breaking through Rhodri's defences and he fled for safety into Ireland. He returned to Gwynedd in the following year to face an onslaught from CEOLWULF II of Mercia, himself a vassal king of the Danes, and Rhodri died in battle.

[ED19] **ANARAWD** AP **RHODRI** Gwynedd, 878–916.

As RHODRI's eldest son, Anarawd inherited the greater part of his father's kingdom, namely the heartland of Gwynedd and Anglesey and the kingdom of Powys, although the indication is that his brother Merfyn became at least a sub-ruler in Powys. Another brother, CADELL, became ruler of Seisyllwg. They found strength by acting in unison rather than in opposition and thereby became the major force across Wales. In 880 or 881 Anarawd and his brothers gave the Mercians such a sound beating at the battle of the Conway that they treated it as revenge for the death of their father. Quite what happened next in Anarawd's reign is difficult to say for historians have relied upon the testimony of Asser in his *Life of King Alfred*, purportedly written during Anarawd's reign by a fellow Welshman, but which has since had doubt cast upon its reliability. Reliance upon it for facts about Anarawd is dangerous. The assumed wisdom, however, is that around the year 885 Anarawd entered into an alliance with the Danes of York, who had just established their kingdom under GOTHFRITH. This, however, backfired, as the Danes of East Anglia (*see* ERIC) ravaged Gwynedd in 894. Anarawd then turned to ALFRED THE GREAT for help. Alfred apparently obliged, although he insisted that Anarawd be re-confirmed a Christian (but whether Alfred stood as his god-father is something we must treat with caution). Supported by West Saxon soldiers, he attempted to conquer Dyfed and Glamorgan, sending their kings pleading to Alfred for support. The extent to which Alfred involved himself in Welsh affairs, especially at a time when he needed to defend himself against the new Danish incursions, was probably limited. It is likely that Alfred, recognizing the military skill of Anarawd, entered into an alliance with him in opposition to the Danes, and that when the Danes invaded Wales, Anarawd called upon Alfred's soldiers to help defend him and then, in turn, used those soldiers to try and conquer South Wales.

What Anarawd did during the next twenty years is not known. Wales was still subject to attacks by the Danes, which Anarawd succeeded in repulsing. His brother Merfyn died in 904 and Cadell in 909. By this time Anarawd must have been well into his sixties but he remained master of his domain until his death.

[ED20] **IDWAL** *FOEL* (*THE BALD*) AB **ANARAWD** Gwynedd, 916–42.

The son of ANARAWD AP RHODRI, Idwal inherited the pride of his father which was, ultimately, to be his undoing. Fiercely independent, Idwal was the most reluctant of the Welsh rulers who submitted to the English king EDWARD THE ELDER in 918, and though he was present at ATHELSTAN's court several times over the next decade we can imagine that this was more out of necessity than desire. He was also present at the meeting called by Athelstan at Hereford in 926 where the river Wye was established as the border between England and South Wales. At this same meeting Athelstan is recorded as exacting a huge annual tribute from the Welsh princes, though it is uncertain how often this was paid. Unlike his distant cousin HYWEL DDA, who saw the advantages of certain aspects of English life and used them to develop his own kingdom in Deheubarth, Idwal distanced himself from them. Probably the final straw came in 934, when Idwal was forced to accompany Athelstan in his campaign against the Scots. Athelstan was pitting Celt against Celt, and though the Celts had often fought against each other in their own lands, it had not been at the instigation of the Saxon overlords, who were still regarded as invaders. Thereafter Idwal bided his time and, after the death of Athelstan, took up arms against his young son, EDMUND. However Edmund was no pushover. Although struggling to maintain his father's kingdom, he succeeded in fighting battles on several fronts and defeated Idwal, who died in the battle along with his son, Elisedd. Two other sons, IAGO and IEUAF, were expelled, and the territory of Gwynedd passed to Hywel *Dda*. Idwal was known as Idwal the Bald, and though this is not necessarily an indication of his age, it is likely that Idwal was nearly, if not actually, into his sixties when he entered into his final battle against Edmund. Evidently it was rare for Welsh rulers to lose their hair, as no others acquired this nickname (although two Scots rulers of the next generation did).

[ED21] **IAGO** ab **IDWAL** Gwynedd, 950–79.

[ED22] **IEUAF** ab **IDWAL** co-ruler of Gwynedd, 950–69.

The joint rule of Iago and his brother Ieuaf is a good example of how battles between the Welsh royal dynasties stopped Wales from establishing itself as a formidable force for any consistent period. There were just too many princes striving for power and too few strong kings to maintain authority.

When IDWAL AB ANARAWD died, his sons Iago and Ieuaf were driven from the kingdom by HYWEL DDA who then ruled most of southern and northern Wales. However upon Hywel's death, war broke out between his sons (OWAIN, RHODRI and EDWIN) and Iago and Ieuaf. Between them Iago and Ieuaf were able to regain Gwynedd and, in a series of battles between 950 and 952, drove Hywel's sons back into their southern territories, ravaging Dyfed and Ceredigion in the process.

The two brothers then turned on each other and waged a civil war for the next seventeen years. In the end Ieuaf was imprisoned in 969. Whether he spent the rest of his life in prison is not clear, though he lived until 988. Ieuaf's son HYWEL continued the battle with Iago. Although both attended the council called by the the English king EDGAR at Chester in 973 to acknowledge Edgar as their overlord, the two factions continued to fight and the next year, 974, Hywel managed to briefly expel Iago from Gwynedd, though Iago soon re-established himself. The pair played off against each other whatever forces they were able to command, Hywel some-times using English troops, sometimes Vikings, and Iago likewise. In the end, in 979, Hywel gained the upper hand. Iago had been using Viking mercenaries whom Hywel succeeded in buying off, and the Vikings captured Iago. Hywel had him imprisoned. His fate thereafter is unknown, but it is unlikely that he lived much beyond 979. He was probably well into his late fifties by then. Iago's son Custennin tried to avenge his father, but Hywel slew him in the following year.

Iago and Ieuaf inherited a certain stubbornness and hot-headedness from their father, and a pride that would not allow them to settle their differences and work together. As a result they destroyed each other and the power of Gwynedd which would not recover for another hundred years.

[ED23] **HYWEL** ab **IEUAF** Gwynedd, 974–85.

The son of Ieuaf ab Idwal, he continued his father's battle against IAGO AB IDWAL in an attempt to gain sole control of the kingdom of Gwynedd. After Ieuaf was imprisoned in 969, Hywel assumed his authority and attended the council called by the English king EDGAR in 973 of all the vassal kings of Britain to acknowledge him as their overlord. Hywel must have spat bile over the ignominy of having to row Edgar along the river Dee along with his fellow kings. In the following year, Hywel succeeded in deposing Iago and driving him out of the kingdom, but the battle continued, each side deploying or purchasing various mercenaries or soldiers as might be available among the English and Vikings. Although Iago re-established himself in 978, Hywel eventually managed to engineer his capture by Viking troops and Iago was imprisoned. Hywel then slew Iago's son Custennin who was attempting to regain the kingdom. Hywel thereby became sole ruler of Gwynedd in 980. His father, Ieuaf, was still alive at this time and it is not clear whether Hywel left him in prison or freed him. Certainly there is no record that Ieuaf either regained the throne or was consulted as any form of authority. Hywel now sought to capture the southern kingdom of Deheubarth and, in league with Alfhere of Mercia, the senior English ealdorman who had his sights on increased power, Hywel invaded Deheubarth in 983. The battle was inconclusive and, with the death of Alfhere later that year, Hywel lost his support. Thereafter everything went downhill for Hywel and attempts to regain English support went awry in 985 when Hywel was tricked and slain.

[ED24] CADWALLON AB IEUAF Gwynedd, 985–6.

Cadwallon succeeded his brother HYWEL AB IEUAF after the latter's murder in 985. Although Cadwallon's father, Ieuaf ab Idwal was still alive, it is interesting that he did not regain the throne. He would have been old at this time, probably in his sixties and may, through years of imprisonment, have become ill and degenerate, but it may also be indicative of the lust of the royal line of Gwynedd to gain power at whatever cost. Although little had been written about Cadwallon prior to his gaining the throne, we can assume that he took his part in his brother's struggles against his uncle, IAGO AB IDWAL. Cadwallon's control over affairs, however, was short-lived, for within a year he was slain by MAREDUDD AB OWAIN of Deheubarth who avenged the attack by Hywel on his kingdom three years previously. Maredudd united Gwynedd and Deheubarth for the first time since the reign of RHODRI the Great, a century earlier and, for a brief period, sanity returned to the land under a strong rule. Cadwallon's nephew, CYNAN AP HYWEL eventually succeeded to Gwynedd on Mareddud's death.

[ED25] CYNAN AP HYWEL Gwynedd and Deheubarth, 999–1005.

Cynan briefly regained the throne of Gwynedd after the death of MAREDUDD AP OWAIN. He was the son of HYWEL AP IEUAF who had waged a long and debilitating war with IAGO AB IDWAL and between them had brought the kingdom of Gwynedd to its lowest ebb. Its fortunes had been saved briefly by Maredudd and, after the death of Cynan, after an inglorious reign, were further restored by LLYWELLYN AP SEISYLL.

[ED26] LLYWELYN AP SEISYLL Gwynedd, 1005–23; Deheubarth, 1018–23.

If Llywelyn's pedigree is correct, he must have been quite old when he took over the throne of Gwynedd. He claimed to be the grandson of Elisedd, the younger son of ANARAWD ap RHODRI and, if that is so, he must have been in his forties when he claimed the throne after the death of CYNAN AP HYWEL. Fortunately Llywelyn was no ordinary usurper. For fifty years, since the death of HYWEL DDA, Gwynedd had suffered from the internecine battles between the sons and grandsons of IDWAL FOEL, apart from a brief respite under MAREDUDD AP OWAIN, whose daughter, Angharad, Llywelyn married. Although Idwal's dynasty persisted and intermittently regained the throne after Llywelyn's death (*see* IAGO AP IDWAL AP MEURIG), Llywelyn established his own dynasty that would help rebuild the strength of Wales.

Llywelyn easily established himself in Gwynedd, but the throne of Deheubarth was shared by his cousins, EDWIN and CADELL, who were killed by the usurper Aeddan ap Blegywryd in 1018. Llywelyn defeated Aeddan and his sons, and thus re-established the combined kingdoms of Gwynedd and Deheubarth. He also defeated another potential claimant, Rhain ap Maredudd (possibly the same as Llywelyn's brother-in-law) in 1022. With his years of conquest we learn little about Llywelyn the man or his strength as an administrator but we can imagine, from the legacy continued by his son GRUFFYDD, that Llywelyn was a strong and well organized with a clear vision for the unification of Wales, that his son was able to put into effect.

[ED27] **IAGO** AB **IDWAL** AB **MEURIG** Gwynedd, 1023–39.
The inter-dynastic rivalries of the descendants of RHODRI *MAWR* continued after the death of LLYWELYN AP SEISYLL, when his distant cousin, Iago ab Idwal, great-great grandson of ANARAWD AP RHODRI reclaimed the throne of Gwynedd. It seems that his struggle for the throne lasted for perhaps ten years as he battled another claimant, RHYDDERCH AB IESTYN, who succeeded in gaining the throne of Deheubarth. Iago did not eventually settle in Gwynedd until the death of Rhydderch in 1033, but his grip on the country was weak and after six years of inconsequential but oppressive rule, Iago's own men turned on him and he was murdered. Gwynedd passed into the more determined hands of GRUFFYDD AP LLYWELYN. Iago's own son, Cynan, sought refuge in Ireland from where his son, GRUFFYDD AP CYNAN, sailed to reclaim the throne nearly forty years later.

[ED28] **GRUFFYDD** AP **LLYWELYN** Gwynedd and Powys, 1039–63; Deheubarth, 1044–47 and 1055–63; from 1055 also regarded as sovereign of all Wales.
Born: *date unknown but probably around 1000*. **Died**: *5 August 1063*.
Married: *c1057, Eadgyth (i.e. Edith) (c1042–after 1070), dau. Alfgar, Earl of Mercia; 3 children*.
Like the see-saw between the descendants of Augustus to be emperor of Rome, so the pendulum swung between the varied and many descendants of RHODRI *MAWR* for the kingship of Gwynedd. The descendants of IDWAL *FOEL* were fairly weak and usually destroyed each other by internecine battles. The other line, descended from Idwal's brother Elisedd, was stronger but had less opportunity to gain the throne. When they took it they were often dominant, as in the case of Gruffydd's father LLYWELYN AP SEISYLL, but the most decisive of them all was Gruffydd himself. This may seem strange for a man who, in his youth, had displayed little ambition but, matured by the instruction of his father, Gruffydd turned into a virtual war machine. He seized power in Gwynedd when IAGO AB IDWAL AB MEURIG was murdered, and was generally welcomed by the populace who had enjoyed the reign of his father. Gruffydd first turned his ferocity against the Mercians who constantly harried the borders of Wales and in 1039 won a decisive victory at the battle of Rhyd-y-Groes, near Welshpool, where he slew Edwin, the brother of Earl Leofric of Mercia. The victory was so decisive that for a period the Saxons stopped all hostilities across the border. This allowed Gruffydd to turn his attention to South Wales with a sustained onslaught on HYWEL AB EDWIN of Deheubarth. The battles were intense with heavy losses on both sides and much despoiling of the land, especially around Ceredigion. After two resounding defeats, Hywel recruited an army of Vikings from Ireland and there was a climactic battle at the estuary of the river Towy in 1044, where Hywel was slain. Gruffydd's victory was brief, though, for within a few months he was challenged by GRUFFYDD AB RHYDDERCH, another of the princely descendants of Rhodri *Mawr*. For two years the battles continued, and when warfare did not succeed treachery was brought into play, and in 1047 over a hundred of Gruffydd ab Llywelyn's soldiers were slaughtered through deceit on the part of Gruffydd ap Rhydderch's brothers. In revenge Gruffydd laid waste to parts

of Dyfed and Seisyllwg. He also went into an alliance with Swein, the new earl of Mercia, in order to have Saxon support for his claim on Deheubarth, but even this did not succeed and, for a while, Gruffydd ceased his campaigning in the south.

He turned his attention again to the eastern Marches, and sought to gain further land beyond Offa's Dyke. He entered into an alliance with Alfgar, the son of Earl Leofric of Mercia, taking advantage of rivalry between Leofric's family and that of Earl Godwin of Wessex whose son, Swein, Gruffydd's former ally, had been forced into exile in Byzantium. At about this time Gruffydd married Alfgar's daughter, Eadgyth (who would later become the wife of HAROLD II), who was aged about fifteen. A series of raids began in 1052 and between them Gruffydd and Alfgar gained much territory along the Marches. Saxon border patrols were overwhelmed even as far south as Westbury in Gloucestershire. In 1055 the town of Hereford was sacked and burnt.

Gruffydd was now at the height of his powers, for in 1055 he at last had his victory over Gruffydd ab Rhydderch, whom he slew in battle, and thereafter claimed the kingdom of Deheubarth. In 1056 the bishop of Hereford, Leofgar, led an army against Gruffydd but he was soundly defeated. By this time Gruffydd claimed sovereignty over all of Wales, although it was a tenuous claim that he could hold only by show of force, and not as a ruler in the normal sense. Nevertheless the English respected this authority and, in 1057, they at last sought a treaty with Gruffydd. After lengthy negotiations, led by Harold Godwinson and Earl Leofric, an agreement was reached, and Gruffydd swore his fealty to king EDWARD the Confessor.

One might think Gruffydd would settle down and enjoy his power and attempt to administer the rule of law across Wales, but he continued to work in alliance with Earl Alfgar, helping him to regain his lands after he was temporarily dispossessed in 1058. However, after Alfgar died in 1062, Gruffydd became vulnerable. In his old age Gruffydd let down his guard and, late in 1062, Harold Godwinson mounted a surprise attack on Gruffydd's court at Rhuddlan, destroying Gruffydd's fleet. Gruffydd escaped, but he was now a refugee. Harold, with his brother Tostig, mounted a combined attack on Wales in 1063, forcing the Welsh army into submission. Not only did Harold exact tribute and hostages but he demanded that the Welsh abandon Gruffydd. Gruffydd's own men turned on him and he was slain by Cynan ap Iago in August 1063, his head sent to Harold as a sign of the victory. Thereafter his kingdom was sub-divided by Edward and allocated to various princes. MAREDUDD AB OWAIN AB EDWIN inherited Deheubarth, whilst BLEDDYN AP CYNFYN and his brother RHIWALLON shared Gwynedd and Powys.

[ED29] **BLEDDYN** AP **CYNFYN** Powys and Gwynedd, 1063–75.
*Born: c1025; **Died:** (murdered) probably at Powis Castle, 1075; aged 50.*
Married: (1) name unknown, 2 sons; (2) name unknown, dau. Brochwell ap Moelyn of Anglesey; 2 sons, 2 daughters; (3) Haer, dau. Cillin ap Blaidd Rhudd of Gest; 1 son; (4) Morien, dau. Idnerth ap Cadwgan, 2 sons.
Although Bleddyn was a puppet ruler, installed along with his brother RHIWALLON, by EDWARD THE CONFESSOR after the death of GRUFFYDD AP LLYWELYN, he was a good one, and benefited the inhabitants of north Wales considerably, to the extent that after his death he was remembered as "the comfort of Wales". Bleddyn and

Rhiwallon were the half-brothers of Gruffydd, whose mother had remarried after the death of her first husband LLYWELYN AP SEISYLL. Her second husband, Cynfyn ap Gwerstan, may have been half Saxon, for the name Gwerstan may only be a Welsh form of Werestan, a Mercian name where the *Were-* prefix was common. If this were the case, it would account for Gruffydd's sympathetic attitude toward certain Mercian families, and might explain why Edward selected Bleddyn and Rhiwallon as vassal kings. They were, in fact, strong allies, for after the deaths of Edward and HAROLD II, they remained supportive of the Mercians in their battles against the Normans, especially during 1067 and 1068, when they ravaged Herefordshire. Because of their actions the Normans had to take the Welsh seriously, and WILLIAM THE CONQUEROR established two castles at Shrewsbury and Chester under the control of two of his most powerful barons, to contain the Welsh extremists.

Bleddyn and Rhiwallon were then faced with an internal revolution as the young sons of Gruffydd ap Llywelyn, Maredudd and Idwal, who were only in their late teens, challenged for the throne. The battle of Mechain in 1070 was decisive, for there Maredudd, Idwal and Rhiwallon fell, leaving Bleddyn the sole ruler of Gwynedd and Powys.

There followed a brief respite in Bleddyn's life, when he undertook many activities for which he was most fondly remembered. He was a generous king, bestowing much upon the churches and the populace and was also the first king in over a hundred years to revise and develop the laws of HYWEL *Dda*. Unfortunately, this period was short-lived for, in 1073, the Normans under Robert of Rhuddlan, began their advance through North Wales, defeating Bleddyn in a surprise attack. Much weakened, Bleddyn became easy prey for RHYS AB OWAIN of Deheubarth who betrayed Bleddyn in 1075, leading to his murder. Bleddyn's descendants, however, became the main ruling family of Powys (*see page xx*)

[ED30] **RHIWALLON** AP **CYNFYN** co-ruler of Powys and Gwynedd, 1063–70. *See* BLEDDYN AP CYNFYN *for details.*

[ED31] **TRAHERN** AP **CARADOG** Gwynedd, 1075–81.
Trahern was a prince of Arwystli in southern Powys who took his opportunity at the death of BLEDDYN AP CYNFYN to seize control in Gwynedd. He was challenged by GRUFFYDD AP CYNAN, a more direct claimant to the throne and a grandson of IAGO AB IDWAL AB MEURIG, who succeeded in defeating Trahern at Dyffryn Glyngin in Merioneth, but Trahern bounced back trouncing Gruffydd at the battle of Bron yr Erw and sending him into exile in Ireland. After establishing himself in Gwynedd, Trahern took on RHYS AB OWAIN of Deheubarth and defeated him at the battle of Goodwick in 1078. Rhys died soon after. Trahern regarded that as revenge for the death of Bleddyn, whom he claimed as a first cousin, although the relationship was possibly more distant than that. RHYS AP TEWDWR claimed succession to Deheubarth, and Trahern failed to force home his claim. Instead Rhys was temporarily deposed by another pretender to the throne, CARADOG AP GRUFFYDD, which forced Rhys into exile. He met with Gruffydd ap Cynan and the two combined forces to invade Wales and reclaim their respective lands. At the climactic battle of Mynydd Carn in 1081 both Trahern and Caradog were killed. Although Trahern's descendants continued to rule in Arwystli, Trahern might have rested more

peacefully had he known that his great-great grandson would come to the throne of Wales and be remembered by all as LLYWELYN THE GREAT.

[ED32] **GRUFFYDD** AP **CYNAN** Gwynedd, 1081–1137.
Born: c1055. *Died*: 1137, aged 82. **Buried**: Bangor Cathedral.
Married: c1095, Angharad (c1080–1162), dau. Owain ab Edwin; 8 children.
The longest reigning of all Welsh rulers, Gruffydd was born in Ireland in about the year 1055. His father, Cynan, who was in exile in Ireland, was the son of IAGO AB IDWAL AB MEURIG, which made Gruffydd seventh in direct descent from RHODRI *Mawr*. His mother, Ragnhildr, was a daughter of Olaf, the son of Sitric III, king of Dublin. Gruffydd thus had mixed Celtic and Norse blood.

On the death of BLEDDYN AP CYNFYN in 1075, Gruffydd challenged TRAHERN AP CARADOG for the throne of Gwynedd. He had some initial success, winning the cantref of Llyn and defeating Trahern at a battle in Meinonydd. Gruffydd then made two serious errors. Firstly he attacked the castle of Robert of Rhuddlan, who had supported Gruffydd in his claim for the throne. Although Gruffydd did not take the castle, he lost Robert's support and this was vital when the men of Llyn rebelled against the Vikings whom Gruffydd had employed in his army and left in charge in Llyn. Trahern used this opportunity to attack Gruffydd at Bron-yr-Erw, near Clynnog, and Gruffydd was forced to flee back to Ireland.

His next opportunity came in 1081. In that year RHYS AP TEWDWR of Deheubarth was put to flight by his rivals. Rhys and Gruffydd joined forces to regain their respective thrones. They met their enemies at the battle of Mynydd Carn and were victorious, Gruffydd overthrowing Trahern. Unfortunately Gruffydd had not long settled into his homeland when he was captured by the Normans and imprisoned at Chester for at least ten, perhaps twelve years. During that time the Normans established themselves firmly across north Wales, building castles at Bangor, Caernarvon and Aberlleiniog. When Gruffydd was given a conditional release he soon became involved in resistance, leading a rebellion against the Normans in 1094. For four years Gruffydd maintained an uneasy authority in Gwynedd, ensconced in his stronghold of Anglesey, but in 1098 the Normans, under WILLIAM II, led a two-pronged attack from their castles at Chester and Shrewsbury. The Welsh were soundly defeated and Gruffydd found himself trapped on Anglesey from which, eventually, he made his escape back to Ireland. When Gruffydd returned, in the following year, he reached an agreement with the Normans and was allowed to rule Anglesey as a vassal king. Over the next few years, for good behaviour, he was allowed to extend his lordship across the Conway into parts of old Gwynedd. While he was still alive his sons continued to extend their control over the lands so that, by the time of his death in 1137, in his early eighties, Gruffydd's Gwynedd was restored to its former self. HENRY I made a show of strength in 1114, though Gruffydd and his sons retained their lands in return for Gruffydd accepting the authority of the Normans. If anything Gruffydd and Henry seemed like-minded and each was prepared to tolerate the other. Gruffydd showed no further hostility to the Normans and instead spent his time rebuilding the old glory of Gwynedd. He had a particular passion for music and stories of old, and has earned a reputation as a patron of the bardic tradition, laying down the basis for the modern *eisteddfod*. His court poet was the legendary Meilyr Brydydd.

When Gruffydd died his reign had spanned over sixty-two years, of which nineteen were spent either in exile or in prison. He was clearly a survivor, and his strength, willpower and, ultimately, his tenacity, brought him the respect of the Normans, who allowed him to re-establish the kingdom of Gwynedd, when they could have dominated it. During the height of his reign, from 1100 to around 1120, Gruffydd rebuilt the pride and culture of the northern Welsh. He passed this legacy on to his son, OWAIN Gwynedd.

[ED33] **OWAIN *GWYNEDD* AP GRUFFYDD** Gwynedd, 1137–70.
Born: *Angelesey, c1100.* **Died:** *28 November 1170, aged 70.* **Buried:** *Bangor Cathedral.*
Married: *(1) Gwladys, dau. Llywarch ap Trahern; 2 sons; (2) Christina, dau. Gronw ap Owain; 2 sons. Owain had at least 6 illegitimate children by two or three other women.*
Owain ap Gruffydd originally earned the surname Gwynedd to distinguish him from another prince with the same name who became known as OWAIN CYFEILIOG, but the name was even more apt, as Owain built upon the achievements of his father, GRUFFYDD AP CYNAN, to establish Gwynedd as a power in the land, one which aroused respect, and not a little concern, in the English king HENRY II. By the end of his reign, Owain was being called Owain the Great.

At the start, though, it seemed as if Gruffydd's achievements might be split by the inevitable enmity arising among the sons of strong monarchs, as his lands were partitioned between his various heirs. But in fact the sons acted with one accord, realising that between them they had the strength to dominate Wales. This had started to happen even before Gruffydd's death. Owain and his elder brother Cadwallon (who died in 1132) had systematically extended the borders of Gwynedd to incorporate the territories of Meirionydd, Rhos, Rufoniog and Dyffryn Clwyd, thereby establishing their power throughout northern and north-west Wales. On the death of Henry I in 1135 there was a general uprising amongst the Welsh princes to regain their territory from the Normans, taking advantage of the political uncertainty in England which resulted in the civil war between STEPHEN and MATILDA. None was more powerful or better placed to gain from this anarchy than Owain. In 1136, the Norman lord Richard de Clare (whose father had been given the lands of Ceredigion in 1110) was ambushed and killed by Welsh renegades. Soon after there was a significant battle at Crug Mawr, in northern Ceredigion, where the Welsh slaughtered a large Anglo-Norman army. Owain and another brother, Cadwaladr, used these opportunities to invade Ceredigion, taking the northern territories, and extending their hold the following year. Their attempts to break into Dyfed in 1138 failed, but Cadwaladr sought to consolidate his hold upon Ceredigion, which he maintained until 1143. Then Cadwaladr's involvement in the murder of ANARAWD AP GRUFFYDD led to his expulsion from Wales and his exile in Ireland for a year until he was temporarily restored by his brother in 1144.

Meanwhile Owain was gradually extending his control over the territories of northern Wales, taking over one district at a time so that by 1149 almost all of the old kingdom of Powys was under his control, and the boundaries of Gwynedd once again extended from Anglesey to the estuary of the Dee. Although Owain continued to plan for further territorial expansion, the next few years saw a period of

From a picture in the
National Library of Wales

strengthening his existing domain, and it was as much his qualities as a politician as an expansionist which made him one of Wales's greatest rulers.

His only setback occurred in 1157. By then HENRY II had come to the throne and restored political strength in England. Pope Adrian IV had granted Henry authority over the whole of Britain in 1155, and with this as his passport, Henry despatched his forces into Wales. Although Owain lost some ground, Henry did not force the king into submission. Nevertheless Owain was sensible enough to know that he needed to negotiate with Henry. Henry agreed to cease any further incursions into Gwynedd, provided Owain accepted Henry as his overlord. Henry had also taken under his wing, Owain's brother, Cadwaladr, who had been exiled in England, and had become an ally of the Norman earls of Chester and Shrewsbury. Henry required that Owain accept Cadwaladr as his partner in government in Gwynedd, which Owain did becoming, at last, reconciled to his renegade brother. Owain accepted all these terms freely. His great strength was in recognizing the benefits that came from being allied to Henry II and his great Angevin empire. It meant that the Welsh prince was regarded as a significant feudal monarch rather than as a tribal chieftain, and it was through Owain that the sovereignty of Gwynedd was recognized. Owain was regarded as the premier ruler in Wales, and was officially styled "Prince of the Welsh" (subject to Henry as overlord), though he was still called king of Wales by his subjects. Henry publicised this at a ceremony in July 1163 at Woodstock, where all the Welsh rulers and the Scottish king assembled to pay homage to Henry. Amongst their numbers was RHYS AP GRUFFYDD who was still hostile to Henry, and it required Owain's authority and skills as a negotiator to convince Rhys that he should submit to Henry.

Although he maintained his fealty to Henry for the rest of his life, this did not stop Owain ensuring that the rights and status of the Welsh were acknowledged by the Normans. The ceremony of 1163 unsettled many of the Welsh princes, seeing it as domination by the Normans, and in 1164 a series of uprisings broke out all over Wales. Henry decided that a show of force was necessary and brought together a mighty army from France, Scotland and Ireland, but he mismanaged the whole operation. Owain united the Welsh armies and stood fast at Corwen, on the river

Dee, awaiting the Norman onslaught. It did not happen: undone by the weather, the terrain, and the sheer size of his force, Henry retreated, taking only a few hostages. The Welsh drove home their advantage, with Owain and Cadwaladr regaining the territory they had lost ten years earlier and re-establishing the borders of Gwynedd.

Owain had a somewhat ambivalent relationship with the church. Whilst he was strongly religious he had no wish to be dictated to – a trait he shared with Henry II! He incurred the displeasure of the church when, as his second wife, he took his cousin Christina. Such a close marriage was not regarded as lawful in the eyes of the church, but Owain did not falter, and indeed his deep love for his second wife became legendary. Owain saw the authority of the see of Canterbury over the Welsh church as just as much a sign of domination as his submission to the Norman king, and whilst he saw the advantages in the latter, he did not so willingly concede the necessity for the former. He refused to accept the authority of Canterbury in appointing his local bishops, especially at Bangor, where he did not replace the bishop for thirteen years.

At the time of his death in 1170 Owain was thus master of all of North Wales, the premier prince of Wales, and was held in high regard throughout Europe. If his sons had had similar qualities, they might have avoided the civil war that broke out between them upon Owain's death and, once again, sundered the kingdom. It was left to his grandson, LLYWELYN THE GREAT, to restore the kingdom to its final days of glory.

[ED34] **MAELGWYN** AB **OWAIN** Anglesey, 1170–73.
On the death of Owain Gwynedd the lands were partitioned between his sons. The elder son, Iorweth *Drwyndwn* (*Flatnose*), who had the senior claim on the territories of his father, only inherited two small *cantrefi*, suggesting he and his father were at odds. The main inheritance went to MAELGWYN, who inherited the heartland of Gwynedd, Anglesey, when the lands were partitioned on Owain's death. However, the island became little more than a prison, as Maelgwyn was besieged by his brothers DAFYDD and Rhodri until both Maelgwyn and Iorweth fled to Ireland in 1173. Although Maelgwyn returned in 1174, he was captured and imprisoned. Nothing more is known of him, and in all likelihood he died in prison.

[ED35] **DAFYDD** AB **OWAIN** co-ruler Gwynedd from 1170, sole ruler 1174–5; thereafter east Gwynedd, 1175–95, when deposed.
Born: *c1135;* **Died:** *May (?) 1203, at Hales, Shropshire, aged about 68.*
Married: *August (?) 1174, Emma de Laval, half-sister of Henry II; 2 children.*
On the death of the great OWAIN GWYNEDD, his kingdom was partitioned amongst his sons. Whereas the sons of the previous generation had worked together to support Owain, his own sons worked against each other. Upon Owain's death in 1170 the sons teamed up into opposing factions. Dafydd and his brother RHODRI, the younger sons of Owain's second marriage, joined forces against Hywel, Owain's eldest son though himself illegitimate. They met at the battle of Pentraeth on Anglesey where Hywel was killed. They next turned their attention to MAELGWYN, who had inherited the main heartland of Gwynedd, Anglesey itself. After three years, Maelgwyn was driven out of Anglesey into exile in Ireland. Although he

returned, he was imprisoned and probably died soon after. Dafydd and Rhodri next attacked Iorweth, who had inherited Arfon, and whether he died or was expelled is not clear, but he had vanished from the scene by 1174. In that same year the last remaining brother, Cynan, died, although he had established sufficient claim upon Meirionydd for his family for Dafydd and Rhodri to leave alone. The two remaining brothers now turned on each other, and Dafydd defeated and imprisoned Rhodri. By the summer of 1174, therefore, Dafydd was sole ruler in Gwynedd. Dafydd had something of the entrepreneurial flair of his father, and in 1174 he sought marriage to HENRY II's half-sister, Emma, whose first husband, Guy de Laval, had recently died. Henry reluctantly agreed, for this gave Dafydd a greater royal profile than Henry perhaps wished. In fact the outcome was satisfactory for both of them. Dafydd, had he been able to rule alone, would probably have proved a capable and likeable king. Unfortunately, within a few months of Dafydd's marriage, Rhodri escaped from prison and succeeded in driving him out of Anglesey and into eastern Gwynedd. There, with Norman support, Dafydd was able to remain, but Gwynedd was now apportioned between him and Rhodri. Dafydd continued to benefit from his links with Henry II as, in 1177, he was granted estates at Ellesmere and Hales (hence Halesowen) in Shropshire, in return for unconditional fealty to the king. He also extended his castle at Rhuddlan, which became one of the most glorious castles of the age. Dafydd was known as a patron of the arts, encouraging the court poets, unlike his brother Rhodri, who was altogether different.

Both their fortunes suffered, however, from 1190 on. Rhodri was expelled from Anglesey by Cynan's children, Gruffydd and Maredudd whilst, in 1194, Dafydd was expelled from East Gwynedd by Iorweth's son LLYWELYN. He clung tenaciously to three castles but was effectively deposed in 1195. When Llywelyn's power grew, he imprisoned Dafydd for a year, from 1197–1198, and only released him on condition that he went into exile. Dafydd retreated to his estates in Shropshire where he died in 1203.

[ED36] **RHODRI** AB **OWAIN** Gwynedd, 1170–4; west Gwynedd, 1175–90.
Rhodri was one of the younger sons of OWAIN Gwynedd. He initially joined forces with his brother DAFYDD in order to expel their elder brothers from their territories, which had been sub-divided amongst all of Owain's sons upon his death. This they succeeded in doing, although Rhodri was in turn defeated an imprisoned by Dafydd in 1174. He escaped from prison the following year and drove Dafydd into East Gwynedd, so that Rhodri gained the main part of Gwynedd, including the original heartland of Anglesey. He remained there in power until 1190, when he was defeated and expelled by his nephews, Gruffydd and Maredudd ap Cynan. He fled to Ireland, but later negotiated with RAGNALD, king of the Isle of Man, for support to help him regain the throne. Anglesey and Man had once been regarded as a single unit (the Mevanian Islands) and the rulers of Man always had eyes on Anglesey as a lost part of their domain. Ragnald almost certainly believed his aid might have long term benefits for his kingdom. Such hopes were short-lived, however, for although Rhodri succeeded in penetrating back into Anglesey in 1193, he was soon ousted again by his nephews, now further aided by LLYWELYN AP IORWETH. He probably fled back to Ireland or Man, where he died in 1195. He is apparently buried at Holyhead.

[ED37] **LLYWELYN** *FAWR (THE GREAT)* AP **IORWETH**

Gwynedd (east Gwynedd from 1195) 1200–40; incorporating Powys from 1208; overlord of Deheubarth from 1216; regarded as prince of Wales from 1210.
Born: *Dolwyddelan, Nantconwy, c1173.* **Died:** *11 April 1240, aged about 66.* **Buried:** *Aberconwy Abbey.*
Married: *1205, Joan, illeg. dau. King John of England; 5 children. Llywelyn had at least one illegitimate child.*

If there is one Welsh prince everyone knows (or think they know) it is Llywelyn the Great, although some of his exploits often get confused in the public consciousness with those of his grandson, known as LLYWELYN THE LAST. Llywelyn rightly deserved the epithet *the Great*, the most of all the Welsh rulers, almost solely for his leadership and statesmanlike abilities. Certainly he had no finesse or cultural qualities, but he was the man that Wales needed to pull it out of the Dark Ages and make it a united country. He was an ideal successor to GRUFFYDD AP CYNAN and OWAIN GWYNEDD.

His rise to power was meteoric. His father, Iorweth *Drwyndwn,* had died soon after Llywelyn's birth and he was raised with his mother's relatives in Powys. By his late teens he had joined forces with his cousins, Gruffydd and Maredudd ab Cynan in their opposition to their uncles RHODRI AB OWAIN and DAFYDD AB OWAIN. Llywelyn soon got the upper hand over his cousins, so that when Dafydd was deposed from East Gwynedd in 1195 Llywelyn claimed the territory as his own. Although technically he initially shared it with his uncle, Dafydd was soon squeezed out of the land, imprisoned in 1197, and then banished altogether in 1198. In 1200, his cousin Gruffydd, who had ostensibly become the ruler in West Gwynedd, died, and Llywelyn promptly annexed that territory. In 1201 and 1202 he deprived Maredudd of his lands in Llyn and Meirionydd respectively, so that by 1202 he had reunited all of Gwynedd.

Llywellyn learned from his predecessors that it was important to stay on cordial terms with the king of England. Soon after JOHN came to power, he and Llywelyn entered into a detailed agreement. This enforced John's overlordship of Wales, and stated the terms by which Llywelyn and his own lords must render fealty; but it also recognized the authority of Welsh law and stated on what basis cases might be tried. This agreement, the oldest to survive between an English and a Welsh monarch, while definitely constituting an imposition of English overlordship, nevertheless recognized the relevance and need of Welsh law and government and thus gave Llywelyn a power in his own land that was unequalled by any previous English-Welsh relationship. Llywelyn sought to cement this accord further by marrying Joan, an illegitimate daughter of John's, in 1205. He also accompanied John on his punitive expedition against the Scots in 1209.

In the meantime Llywelyn took what opportunities presented themselves to expand his authority in Wales. His closest rival was GWENWYNWYN, the prince of Powys, who also had expansionist desires, but he overstepped the mark in 1208, literally, by several ill-disposed attacks on the marcher lands. King John reacted swiftly and deprived Gwenwynwyn of all of his lands. Llywelyn promptly annexed southern Powys and used this as a means to march into and lay claim to southern Ceredigion. He then claimed overlordship of the other lesser lordships in southern Wales and, by 1210, was declaring himself as prince of all Wales.

This insubordination angered John who sent two expeditions into Wales in 1211. The first suffered from poor organization but the second was highly successful, penetrating far into the stronghold of Gwynedd. East Gwynedd was placed again under Norman control, and John cleverly engineered the isolation of Llywelyn by ensuring the support of the other princes. Exacting tributes were demanded and severe retribution taken on the hostages John took, including Llywelyn's illegitimate eldest son. For a few months Llywelyn was vulnerable. There was even a rival movement which sought to bring his cousin, Owain ap Dafydd, to the throne, but at the moment of crisis Llywelyn found unanimous support amongst his countrymen. In 1212 Llywelyn regrouped his forces and prepared to face the might of John's army, which he had convened with a view to total conquest of Wales.

It could have been the biggest invasion force since the Norman conquest of England but, at the last moment, John changed his plans. Domestic problems amongst his barons, which culminated in John's signing of the *Magna Carta*, meant that he turned his attention from Wales. This was not a retreat, but the Welsh regarded it as a victory. Llewelyn had not been afraid to face the might of the English, and the English had backed down. Thereafter Llywelyn felt able to recommence his onslaught against the Norman-controlled territories, regaining East Gwynedd and lands in the Marches, as well as commanding fealty from the remaining Welsh princes in Powys and Deheubarth. By 1216 Llywelyn was prince of all Wales in fact as well as title, as confirmed by the Treaty of Worcester in 1218.

Border skirmishes continued for several more years, mostly with the new regent of England, William Marshal, one of the marcher lords and the new earl of Pembroke, until his death in 1219. From 1216 to 1234 lands and castles frequently changed hands, but it was as much a period of testing as of outright hostility. The two parties came to understand each other and, with the Pact of Middle in 1234, an agreement was reached by both sides which assured a modicum of peace.

Llywelyn was determined that all he had achieved would not be broken asunder after his death so, as early as 1208 he ensured that his newly born legitimate son, DAFYDD, was recognized as his heir. He also determined to revoke the Welsh law of partible succession, which had been the ruin of previous attempts to unite Wales. Under that rule a landowner had to divide his inheritance amongst his sons. Llywelyn sought to introduce the rule of primogeniture so that his eldest legitimate son inherited. Although this caused a family rift between Llywelyn's eldest illegitimate son, Gruffydd, and his nominated successor, DAFYDD, Llywelyn succeeded in gaining total acceptance. Dafydd was recognized as heir not only by HENRY III in 1220, but by the Pope in 1222, and in 1226 Llywelyn required that all the senior Welsh lords swore fealty to Dafydd as the next prince of Wales. Never had Wales been so united as under Llywelyn the Great. Had someone of his stature existed in previous generations, especially prior to the Norman conquest of England, it is entirely possible that the Welsh could have regained their native Britain. Unfortunately, Llywelyn achieved it at a time when England had increasingly powerful monarchs, and although he left a much improved legacy to his son and grandson, they had to face England's strongest monarch yet – EDWARD I.

[ED38] **DAFYDD** AP **LLYWELYN** ruled, 11 April 1240–25 February 1246.
*Born: c1208; **Died:** Aber, 25 February 1246, aged 37. **Buried:** Aberconwy Abbey.*
Married: 1230, Isabella de Breos; no children.

Despite every effort taken by LLYWELYN *the Great* to ensure that his son enjoyed unchallenged authority as "Prince of the Welsh", the short reign of Dafydd brought all to naught. The cause of this problem was Dafydd's selfishness and indecision. On his accession Dafydd met the English king, HENRY III, who was his uncle (for all that they were about the same age), and acknowledged him as overlord at a ceremony at Gloucester in May 1240. Here Dafydd paid homage to Henry and swore his fealty, and in return Henry crowned Dafydd with the diadem of authority. However, Henry also demanded that the lands regained by Dafydd's father during the last years of his reign be returned, as these were not part of the territories agreed between Llywelyn and John as the principality of Wales. Dafydd had clearly not expected this requirement and instead of agreeing, and thereby enjoying peace, he delayed for a year. By then Henry felt enough time had passed, and he gathered together a force and invaded Wales. Dafydd was unable to stop him and, in August 1241, he surrendered. Under the terms of the Peace of Gwern Eigron, Dafydd was forced to return the lands in dispute and release his prisoners, who included his elder half-brother Gruffydd and Gruffydd's son Owain. Henry, to ensure that war did not break out between Gruffydd and Dafydd, took Gruffydd under his wing and held him in the Tower of London, where his family had free access. He thus served as an ideal hostage. Dafydd knew that if he did anything against Henry's wishes, Henry would release Gruffydd and support him as prince of Wales in Dafydd's place. Dafydd could do little. Had Dafydd realised that the stalemate worked as well for him as for Henry, he would have settled down and acted sensibly. For two years he did turn his attentions inward and spent some time reviewing the Welsh laws. Then, in March 1244 everything changed. Gruffydd, in attempting to escape from the Tower of London, had fallen and died. Dafydd immediately instigated a new conflict, gaining land along the Welsh Marches. He also submitted a case to the pope, appealing against the oppressive domination of the English, which Innocent IV considered sympathetically. Henry III brought an army against Dafydd at Deganwy in the summer of 1245, but this time the success went to Dafydd. Any hopes to capitalise on that success, however, crumbled in February 1246 when Dafydd died of an illness. He left no heir. He was succeeded by Gruffydd's son Llywelyn.

[ED39] **LLYWELYN (II)** AP **GRUFFYDD** (*LLYWELYN THE LAST*)

Gwynedd (west Gwynedd from 25 February 1246, effectively 30 April 1247) June 1255–11 December 1282; styled prince of Wales from 1258.
*Born: date unknown, but probably c1225. **Died:** 11 December 1282, aged about 57. **Buried:** Cwm Hir Abbey.*
Married: 13 October 1278 at Worcester, Eleanor, dau. Simon de Montfort; 1 daughter.

Llywelyn was the last native ruler of Wales. The sudden death of his uncle, DAFYDD AP LLYWELYN, just as events had turned in his favour, gave HENRY III of England an unexpected advantage. He was able to sweep through Wales, meeting no organized resistance and, one by one, the minor princes submitted to him. The Treaty of Woodstock on 30 April 1247 concluded the affair and saw Llywelyn and his elder brother OWAIN, the senior princes of Gwynedd, also submit to Henry. The Treaty was severe. Henry invoked many clauses from previous agreements and reclaimed vast areas of Wales directly for the crown, including some territory that had been lost since the reign of OWAIN GWYNEDD, a century earlier. These lands were incorporated as part of England in perpetuity. Moreover, whilst Henry still respected Welsh law, the Treaty brought with it certain obligations which required the recognition of English law. Any lasting vestige of Welsh autonomy was quashed. Owain and Llywelyn were allowed to administer Gwynedd, which now consisted of Anglesey and the few *cantrefi* on the adjacent mainland, as vassals to Henry. Moreover Henry actively supported other young claimants to the remaining Welsh territories, probably in the hope that internecine wars would wear down Wales and enable Henry to mop up the remnants and take control of the whole country.

However, it did not work out that way. Llywelyn had more political acumen than Henry gave him credit. Over the next eight years he entered into a series of secret alliances with neighbouring princes ensuring their support. Then, in June 1255 he met his brothers Owain and DAFYDD in battle at Bryn Derwin. They were defeated and imprisoned and Llywelyn became sole ruler of Gwynedd. The following year Llywelyn called in his support and his new alliance conquered East Gwynedd, ejecting its English lords. Over the next two years, Llywelyn swept through Wales reclaiming all the territory lost to Henry. Although Henry attempted a punitive expedition in August 1257, it failed dismally and Henry, already in serious trouble at home with his barons, was forced to reach an agreement with Llywelyn on 17 June 1258 which granted him authority over the conquered lands. At that point Llywelyn declared himself "Prince of Wales", and the native princes transferred their fealty from Henry to him. Under the Peace of Montgomery, agreed with Henry III in 1267, Llywelyn was recognized as the sovereign of Wales. Wales (which at this time still excluded some of the territories in the south) for the first and only time had become a single sovereign state. In the decade leading up to 1267, Llywelyn had allied himself to Simon de Montfort, and this resulted in considerable gains as Llywelyn took control of much land in the Welsh Marches. Llywelyn contracted to marry de Montfort's daughter, Eleanor, in 1265 but the marriage was delayed, first when de Montfort died, and then when the new king, EDWARD I, detained Eleanor at Windsor. The marriage eventually took place in 1278. They had one daughter, Gwenllian, but unfortunately Eleanor died in childbirth in 1282.

After de Montfort's death, as Llywelyn endeavoured to consolidate his principality into a more unified whole, it became increasingly apparent that his territories were held together more by fear and the strength of his own personality than by any inherent loyalties. His actions to sustain law and order became increasingly severe, and respect for the prince visibly evaporated. Also the lack of an heir fuelled factionalism. In 1274 a plot against his life by his brother Dafydd and GRUFFYDD AP GWENWYNWYN of southern Powys was uncovered that resulted in the two conspirators fleeing to England. Llywelyn promptly overran Gruffydd's lands. That year saw a new king on the throne of England, Edward I, who openly supported the two princes. Edward did not initially plan to enter into conflict with Llywelyn – the two in fact had a high degree of respect for each other. However, Llywelyn's failure to attend Edward's coronation in 1274 or pay homage to Edward, despite several demands, angered Edward irretrievably. Moreover, Llywelyn's high-

From a picture in the
National Library of Wales

handedness towards the church in wanting a share of revenues caused as much dissension among church officials, as other actions did among his lords and subjects. The last straw came when Llywelyn refused to pay homage in 1276, despite Edward travelling to Chester. In reaction Edward stopped Llywelyn's bride-to-be, Eleanor de Montfort, travelling to Wales and detained her at Windsor. Llywelyn's hot-headedness and pride made it impossible for him to climb down and the two were set on a collision course. In November 1276 Llywelyn was declared a rebel and hostilities began. Edward knew he could soon turn the dissension amongst the Welsh to his advantage. His first test of the Welsh borders in 1276 saw resistance crumble immediately in northern Powys where its prince, Llywelyn ap Gruffydd ap Madog promptly changed his allegiance to Edward. Edward's progress through Wales was systematic and clinical. Within a year Llywelyn was forced to submit and, under the Treaty of Aberconwy, he was relegated to ruling only the heartland of Gwynedd, west of the Conway. Although he retained the title "Prince of Wales", it was meaningless. He was also forced to share that kingdom again with his brother Owain, who was resettled in the cantref of Llyn in 1278.

Although humiliated, Llywelyn maintained his dignity. He treated Edward with the utmost respect and endeavoured to maintain amicable relations, while also seeking to regain his hold on Wales. Over the next four years he began to re-cement relationships with the various princes across Wales. In some cases he was successful; in others woefully unsuccessful. Territorial disputes, especially with Gruffydd ap Gwenwynwyn, who had been restored by Edward in southern Powys, began to fray Llywelyn's temper. Throughout this period Wales was in uneasy humour, uncertain over the degree to which they should support Llywelyn or respect Edward. In the end it was the inevitable unrestrained irresponsibility of Llywelyn's brother Dafydd that sealed the fate of Wales. Dafydd, in league with Llywelyn ap Gruffydd ap Madog of Powys, ravaged the borders around Oswestry in March 1282. Whether or not Llywelyn was himself aware of the revolt, he was soon caught up in it and had no other choice but to become its leader. Edward was outraged and, though he had to react swiftly, he planned his strategy with cool deliberation, marshalling forces that would be powerful enough to resolve the matter once and for all. It was a much harder struggle than in 1277, but Edward was relentless. Victory would almost certainly have been his, even if Llywelyn himself had not been killed in December 1282. He was killed, not in a pitched battle, but in a scuffle by an opportunist who did not realise at the time who he was. The war continued for four more months under the command of Dafydd, but in April 1283 he surrendered at Castell y Bere and was imprisoned. In October he was executed for treason. With the Statute of Wales, issued on 19 March 1284, Wales passed under the government of England. All the local princes were dispossessed, and the political face of Wales was changed for ever, the old kingdoms replaced by new counties and a provincial administration run by a governor-general.

Llywelyn's daughter, Gwenllian, was sent to a nunnery where she remained till she died in 1337. Dafydd's daughters were likewise consigned to nunneries while his two sons were imprisoned for the rest of their lives: Llywelyn died in 1288; Owain, some time after 1305. Alone of all the royal family, Rhodri ap Gruffydd, who had sold his inheritance to Llywelyn as early as 1272, lived on as a lord of the manor in Surrey and in Cheshire, dying in 1315. His grandson, Owain ap Thomas ap Rhodri, who lived much of his life in France, held pretensions to invade Wales and reclaim the principality. He received a modicum of support at the time, and there were even rumours of an invasion between 1369 and 1372, but his plans came to nothing and he was assassinated in 1378. The only successful attempt to regain the principality came under OWAIN GLYN DWR in 1400.

[ED39a] **OWAIN *GOCH* AP GRUFFYDD** Co-ruler of Gwynedd, 1246–55; restored to part of Gwynedd, 1277–c82. Probably died about 1282. *For details see* LLYWELYN THE LAST *above.*

[ED40] **DAFYDD AP GRUFFYDD** ruled 11 December 1282–25 April 1283. Executed for treason, 3 October 1283. Styled himself "Prince of Wales", and the last defender of Gwynedd. *See above under* LLYWELYN THE LAST *for details.*

EE. MEDIEVAL POWYS

For over two hundred years Powys formed part of the kingdom of Gwynedd. It was re-established as a separate kingdom by the sons of Bleddyn ap Cynfyn soon after 1075 and although it was later divided into Northern and Southern Powys it remained independent for two centuries until eventually possessed by England.

Ref.	Ruler	Born	Reign	Died	Notes

continued from page 151

House of Bleddyn

Ref.	Ruler	Born	Reign	Died	Notes
EE16.	Madog ap Bleddyn		1075–88	1088	
EE17.	Iorweth ap Bleddyn		1088–1103	1111	imprisoned; restored 1110, but murdered
EE18.	Cadwgan ap Bleddyn		1088–1111	1111	murdered
EE19.	Owain ap Cadwgan		1111–16	1116	captured 1114–15; murdered

| EE20. | Maredudd
ap Bleddyn | 1116–32 | 1132 | |
| EE21. | Madog
ap Maredudd | 1132–60 | 1160 | |

After Madog's death the kingdom was divided into North and South.

Northern Powys

| EE22. | Gruffydd
Maelor (I) | 1160–91 | 1191 | Powys was shared with Owain
Fychan (to 1187) and Owain
Brogynton (to 1188). |
| EE23. | Owain | 1191–97 | 1197 | ruled jointly with his brother
Madog |

Map 8d **The Later Welsh Kingdoms – Powys**

18. Wales (5) – Medieval Powys

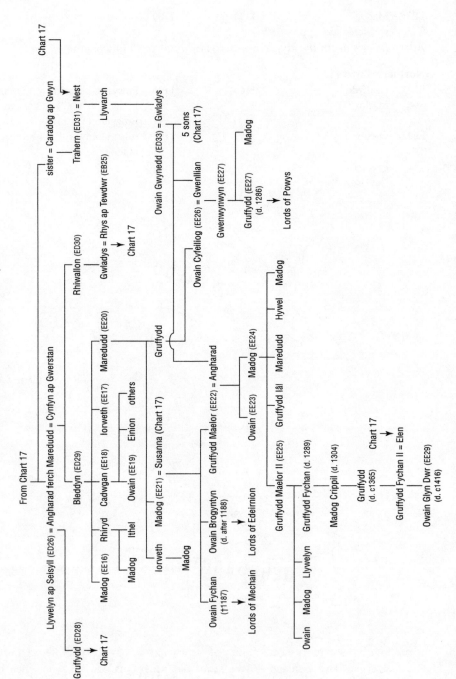

Ref.	Ruler	Born	Reign	Died	Notes
EE24.	Madog ap Gruffydd		1191–1236	1236	initially ruled jointly with his brother
EE25.	Gruffydd Maelor II		1236–69	1269	

After Gruffydd Maelor's death his lands were partitioned amongst his sons, and Powys was never again reunited. His youngest son, Gruffydd Fychan (d.1289) had a son called Madog Crippil (d. c.1304) whose grandson, Gruffydd Fychan, was the father of Owain Glyn Dwr (see below).

Southern Powys

Ref.	Ruler	Born	Reign	Died	Notes
EE26.	Owain Cyfeiliog	c1125	1160–95	1197	retired to a monastery
EE27.	Gwenwynwyn		1195–1216	1216	dispossessed and died in exile

Lands came under the rule of Llywelyn the Great of Gwynedd, 1216–40.

Ref.	Ruler	Born	Reign	Died	Notes
EE28.	Gruffydd ap Gwenwynwyn	c1215	1240–86	1286	in exile 1257–63 and 1274–7

After Gruffydd's death Powys came under the sovereignty of England. Gruffydd had already given up his title as king to become a lord of the Marches, a title maintained by his family until 1421.

Wales

Ref.	Ruler	Born	Reign	Died	Notes
EE29.	Owain Glyn Dwr (Glendower)	c1354	1400–12	c1416	declared Prince of Wales

[EE16] **MADOG** AP **BLEDDYN** Powys, 1075–88.

The eldest son of BLEDDYN AP CYNFYN. On the death of his father Madog and his brothers took advantage of the war of succession that was happening throughout Wales, in particular the rivalry between RHYS AB OWAIN of Deheubarth and TRAHERN AP CARADOG of Gwynedd and, by around 1080, had succeeded in claiming for themselves the old kingdom of Powys. It seems they shared the land between them, though Madog and his full brother Rhiryd, were regarded as the premier rulers. In 1088 the brothers attacked RHYS AP TEWDWR of Deheubarth, driving him into exile in Ireland. Their triumph was short-lived, for Rhys raised a Danish fleet and returned victorious. Madog and Rhiryd were killed in the ensuing battle.

[EE17] **IORWETH** AP **BLEDDYN** Powys, 1088–1103; 1110–11.

One of the younger sons of BLEDDYN AP CYNFYN who came to power jointly with his brother CADWGAN after the death of his elder brothers MADOG and Rhiryd in 1088. Iorweth was easily influenced and became involved in a number of raids and uprisings, sometimes at the behest of his countrymen, sometimes at the bidding of the Normans. He was involved in the rebellion of Robert of Montgomery in 1102, which failed due to his own desertion. He expected to be honoured by HENRY I with lands in Powys and Ceredigion which, instead, went to Cadwgan, and when he received no other lands, Iorweth became openly hostile. He was arrested and imprisoned in 1103. His release in 1110 was only in the hope that he might be able to control the family disharmony amongst the sons and grandsons of Bleddyn and prove a better ruler than Cadwgan. The main malcontents were OWAIN AP CADWGAN and his cousin, Madog ap Rhiryd, whom Iorweth succeeded in driving into Ceredigion and from there into exile in Ireland. However, this fortune did not last for long. Madog returned and, in 1111, murdered Iorweth. Control of Powys and Ceredigion passed back briefly to Cadwgan.

[EE18] CADWGAN AP BLEDDYN Powys, 1088–1111.

One of the seven sons of BLEDDYN AP CYNFYN who each laid claim to territory in Powys or elsewhere. Cadwgan joined with his half-brothers in their attack upon RHYS AP TEWDWR in 1088 and narrowly escaped with his life when Rhys returned to the offensive. MADOG and Rhiryd were killed. Cadwgan and his brother IORWETH now shared the kingdom between them. This was the period when Wales was under pressure from the Norman earls, to whom WILLIAM II had given free rein in their designs upon Wales. GRUFFYDD AP CYNAN, the primary ruler of Gwynedd, was imprisoned, and it was Cadwgan who led the Welsh rebellion of 1094 to shake off the Norman yoke. He achieved a major victory at Coed Yspwys in northern Wales (its exact site is unknown) in 1094. Gruffydd escaped from prison later that year and he and Cadwgan joined forces for a major offensive. Victory went with the Welsh until 1098, when the Normans directed their forces to capturing Anglesey. Gruffydd and Cadwgan were forced to flee to Ireland where they remained in exile for a year. Cadwgan was evidently respected by the Normans for his abilities and above all sensibilities – he did not have the extremes of other members of his family – and he benefited from this. The new Norman overlords granted Cadwgan the rule of Powys and Ceredigion, which he retained over the next decade. However, rather than being able to build upon his power, Cadwgan found himself head of a family that he could not control. Not only his brothers, especially Iorweth and MAREDUDD, continued to cause trouble, but his own sons, particularly OWAIN (see below). Cadwgan suddenly found himself besieged by his own nephews (sons of Rhiryd) and by other sons of chieftains hopeful for a share of the pickings. Cadwgan was driven out of Ceredigion in 1109, but soon made his peace with the English king and was restored in 1110. However, Owain's excesses continued, this time with the murder of a Flemish nobleman. Once again Cadwgan was deprived of his kingdom, and Owain was banished to Ireland. Although Cadwgan had one last chance in 1111, when his lands were again restored to him after the murder of Iorweth, within months he also fell victim to his nephew Madog, and was murdered at Welshpool. Although he was succeeded by his wayward son, Owain, the real master of Powys was his brother Maredudd.

[EE19] OWAIN AP CADWGAN Powys, 1111–14; 1115–16.

Owain was probably the single most disastrous factor in stopping the rise to power of Powys at the start of the twelfth century. He was the son of CADWGAN AP BLEDDYN, a capable enough ruler but one who had no control over his son. From 1106 onwards, Owain caused problem after problem. In that year he murdered two sons of TRAHERN AP CARADOG, starting an inter-dynastic feud. In 1109 he abducted Nesta, the daughter of RHYS AP TEWDWR and wife of Gerald, castellan of Pembroke, which caused a major political conflict between HENRY I of England and Cadwgan. Owain then embarked upon banditry in Dyfed, capturing victims for the Irish slave trade, before committing a major felony by murdering a prominent member of a local Flemish family. At last in 1110 Owain was banished to Ireland; he was pardoned and returned in 1111, but was soon obliged to go back to Ireland. Within months, his father was murdered by Madog ap Rhiryd, and Owain returned to Wales to claim his inheritance. He was awarded the kingship of Powys, sharing a small part of the lands with his cousin, Madog. It seems that once he was in power Owain's character changed. He had achieved his ends and now sought to rule strongly but fairly. This did not stop him imprisoning Madog in 1113 and blinding him. In 1114 Henry invaded Wales as a punitive expedition against GRUFFYDD AP CYNAN. In the process he captured Owain and took him with him back to Normandy. It seems that Henry took to Owain. For all the excesses of his youth, he must have been a likeable rogue, with his own code of honour. Henry knighted him and returned him to his kingdom in July 1115. The next year, Owain was fighting on behalf of Henry and suddenly found himself ambushed and killed by Gerald of Pembroke and his Flemish archers, both of whom Owain had so badly wronged a few years earlier.

[EE20] MAREDUDD AP BLEDDYN Powys, 1116–32.

One of the younger sons of BLEDDYN AP CYNFYN who somehow survived the trials and tribulations of his brothers and nephews and eventually, in 1116, came to inherit most of Powys. He was a weaker ruler than his brothers, and certainly than his nephew OWAIN AP CADWGAN, though he had been no less a hothead in his youth. In 1103 he had been handed over to the English Crown by his brother IORWETH, but escaped from prison in 1108. When HENRY I invaded Wales in 1114 and captured Owain, Maredudd paid homage to the king and ruled as steward until Owain was restored the next year. In 1116, after Owain's murder, Powys was shared out amongst his brothers, but Maredudd was able to exercise authority as overlord, and gradually rebuilt the kingdom. Nevertheless, Maredudd remained in power primarily because of his fealty to Henry I. When Henry again invaded Wales in 1121, Maredudd was unable to defend himself and fled into Gwynedd. GRUFFYDD AP CYNAN was not prepared to annoy Henry by harbouring Maredudd, and Maredudd had to buy his peace with 10,000 cattle. Powys came increasingly under pressure from Gwynedd, during the ruthless expansion of Gruffydd's son Cadwallon, but with his death in battle against Powys at Llangollen in 1132, peace was temporarily restored. Maredudd must have lived well into his sixties. He married twice and had at least four children. He was succeeded by his eldest son, MADOG.

[EE21] MADOG AP MAREDUDD Powys, 1132–60.

The last ruler of all of Powys. The start of his reign saw him in a position of considerable authority. He had allied himself with the Normans and succeeded in being on good terms with both HENRY I and STEPHEN, thus protecting his boundaries to the east. He had married Susanna, the daughter of GRUFFYDD AP CYNAN, in order to build an alliance to the west, which improved after the death of Gruffydd's ambitious son Cadwallon. However, by the 1140s, Gruffydd's successor, OWAIN, was again expanding the power of Gwynedd and was successfully encroaching upon Powys by claiming one commote after another as he progressed eastward through North Wales. This came to a climax in 1149 when Madog, supported by Ranulf, earl of Chester, met Owain in battle at Coleshill. The day went to Owain, and Madog lost the cantref of Iâl, the heartland of Powys. Madog had expanded his own kingdom elsewhere by taking the manor of Oswestry and surrounding lands during an opportunist moment in the English civil war, but in effect, by the end of 1149, much of Powys was in the hands of Owain Gwynedd. In this same year, Madog passed Cyfeiliog to his nephews OWAIN and Meurig, for safe keeping. Madog remained under the oppression of Gwynedd for eight years, until 1157 saw HENRY II in control in England and determined to resolve the problems over Wales. Madog's support for Henry in this operation held him in good stead, for Madog was restored to authority in Powys, although he had to hand back the manor and lands of Oswestry. Madog ruled peacefully for the rest of his reign and his death in 1160 was much mourned. Madog is remembered in the Arthurian romance, *The Dream of Rhonabwy*, where he is portrayed as a mighty and powerful lord. For much of his reign he was, but only because of the patronage of the English. After his death his land was divided amongst his sons GRUFFYDD MAELOR, Owain *Fychan* and Owain *Brogyntyn*, his nephew OWAIN CYFEILIOG and his brother Iorweth *Goch*.

[EE22] **GRUFFYDD** *MAELOR* **(I)** AP **MADOG** Northern Powys, 1160–91.
On the death of MADOG AP MAREDUDD, Gruffydd inherited his share of the kingdom, along with four others. His domain was predominantly the cantref of Maelor, in north-eastern Powys, and Iâl, the main heartland of Powys. He later added Nanheudwy, but it was not until the death of his brother, Owain *Fychan* in 1187, that he added the remaining territories that made up Northern Powys. At that stage he also came into possession of lands in England, east of Oswestry. He remained in good favour with the English court under HENRY II and the only challenge to his authority came in 1177 with an attack by Hugh, earl of Chester, who overran Maelor and surrounding territories with the help of DAFYDD AB OWAIN. However, this conquest was short-lived and the balance restored by Henry's decree. Gruffydd was remembered for his generosity. He gave freely to his friends and relatives; gave many gifts to the church and was renowned for his wonderful banquets. The church did not seem to give much in return. Gruffydd was prevailed upon to divorce his wife Angharad, the daughter of OWAIN GWYNEDD, who was his distant cousin. This did not, however, disinherit his two sons, MADOG and OWAIN, both of whom succeeded him.

[EE23] **OWAIN** AP **GRUFFYDD** *MAELOR* Part of Northern Powys, 1191-7.
[EE24] **MADOG** AP **GRUFFYDD** *MAELOR* Northern Powys, 1191–1236.
On the death of Madog's father, Northern Powys was divided between his two sons Madog and Owain. Owain died in 1197 and Madog was able to re-unite Northern Powys, which in later years became known as Powys Fadog after him. Madog was initially supportive of his neighbouring king, LLYWELYN AP IORWETH, but became increasingly wary as Llywelyn's power rose. Madog owed his status and position to the good relationship his father and grandfather had established with the English Crown and Madog was not about to lose that, especially when JOHN came to the throne in 1199 and showed himself as a king not to be trifled with. Thus, when Llywelyn sought to establish a Welsh confederacy against the Normans, Madog remained in the English camp, despite the dire straits that placed him in. This remained so until 1215, when John's domestic problems caused him to release his hold over Wales and, at that stage, Madog switched to Llywelyn. It was a shrewd move. When the Treaty of Worcester was agreed in 1218 Madog was confirmed in his position, even though he had to acknowledge Llywelyn as supreme prince of

Wales. Madog was a strong supporter of the church and, in 1201, he established a Cistercian abbey at Llyn Egwestl, in the Valley of the Pillar of ELISEDD, known as the Valley of the Cross. It was in this abbey that Madog was buried in 1236. On his death, his lands were again divided amongst his five sons, of whom GRUFFYDD was the senior.

[EE25] **GRUFFYDD** *MAELOR* **(II)** AP **MADOG** Northern Powys, 1236–69.
Upon the death of MADOG AP GRUFFYDD the lands of Northern Powys were again sub-divided, leading as ever to disharmony and inter-filial rivalry. Gruffydd remained the senior prince amongst the brothers, though soon lost some lands when one brother, Maredudd, murdered another, Gruffydd Iâl, and LLYWELYN THE GREAT forfeited Maredudd's lands. Like his predecessors, Gruffydd was torn between his loyalties to Gwynedd and to England. After Llywelyn's death in 1240, Gruffydd sided again with England, and this briefly worked in his favour, though DAFYDD AP LLYWELYN later sought vengeance against him. However, it was not until the rise of LLYWELYN THE LAST that Gruffydd found his loyalties truly tested. In 1256 Llywelyn routed Gruffydd and drove him briefly out of his kingdom but he was soon restored, and thereafter remained loyal to Llywelyn, fighting with him throughout the ensuing struggle.

Gruffydd died in 1269. His lands were again partitioned between his sons, and this time there was no strong one amongst them to act as overlord. Powys effectively came under the control of Llywelyn, who approved the partition. The senior brother, who received the heartland of Iâl was Gruffydd *Fychan* (*the Younger*). He died in 1289, but his great-grandson, also called Gruffydd *Fychan*, was the father of OWAIN GLYN DWR.

[EE26] **OWAIN** *CYFEILIOG* AP **GRUFFYDD** Southern Powys, 1160–95.
Born: c1125. **Died:** *Strata Marcella, 1197, aged about 72.* **Buried:** *Strata Marcella.*
Married: *(1) Gwenllian, dau. Owain Gwynedd; 2 sons; (2) name unknown, dau. Rhys ap Gruffydd.*
Owain was the son of Gruffydd ap Maredudd, who had died in 1128. The young child came under the wing of his uncle, MADOG AP MAREDUDD, who treated him as one of his own. In 1149 he conferred upon him the commote of Cyfeiliog, by the name of which he always became known, to avoid confusion with OWAIN GWYNEDD. On the death of Madog in 1160, Owain remained in control of Cyfeiliog, while the remainder of Powys was shared out amongst Madog's sons and his brother Iorweth. This effectively neutered Powys as a power. However, Owain was soon to join forces with his foster brothers, particularly Owain *Fychan*, and succeeded by 1167 in having established a united kingdom of Southern Powys. Owain was a capable warrior. In 1153 he had defended Cyfeiliog against RHYS AP GRUFFYDD, who remained his sworn enemy, even though he later married his daughter. He also joined forces with Owain Gwynedd in 1165 to face the might of HENRY II's army in a threatened invasion that never happened. Such unity amongst the Welsh princes was rare, and soon after Owain Gwynedd and Rhys ap Gruffydd both attacked Owain seeking to regain territory. What he lost Owain soon regained with English help for, by 1167, Owain had sworn fealty to Henry II

Although clearly an able soldier, Owain was also a religious man, a poet, a keen wit, and a very enlightened ruler. He was much admired by Henry II and always welcome at his court. Owain benefited from this relationship and, after 1167, settled down to ensure Powys thrived and prospered. With the death of Owain Gwynedd in 1170, ending the squabbles that rent that kingdom asunder for twenty years, Owain was able to enjoy a period of calm, especially as Rhys ap Gruffydd had also put aside his armour and allied himself to Henry II. The period 1170–1190 was thus one of relative prosperity in Wales that enabled Powys to grow and Owain to indulge in his delight for poetry and the arts. It is almost certain that the tales that subsequently were collected together as the *Mabinogion* began to take their final shape at this time, though there are no surviving manuscripts earlier than the 1230s. Despite his strong religious views, Owain was also a pragmatist. In 1188, Baldwin, the new archbishop of Canterbury, toured Wales recruiting finance and support for the Crusade. Owain, alone amongst the princes, refused his support and was excommunicated. This did not seem to concern him unduly. By 1195, when he was about seventy, he abdicated in favour of his son GWENWYNWYN and retired to his monastery at Strata Marcella, which he had established in 1170. There he died and was buried.

[EE27] **GWENWYNWYN** Southern Powys, 1195–1216.
The last great ruler of Powys. The son of OWAIN CYFEILIOG and grandson of OWAIN GWYNEDD, Gwenwynwyn had an impressive pedigree, a strong character and a patriotic fervour that caused him to step rapidly into the power vacuum left by the deaths of DAFYDD AB OWAIN in 1195 and RHYS AP GRUFFYDD in 1197. A series of raids along the English border in 1196 and the annexation of Arwystli in 1197 gave Gwenwynwyn a strong power base from which he launched his claim for overall control of Wales. Raids into Ceredigion brought him control over those territories, but increasingly roused the ire of LLYWELYN AB IORWETH, whose ambition for the Welsh hegemony was as powerful as Gwenwynwyn's. The two would remain rivals for the next ten years, although Gwenwynwyn's authority was weakened in August 1198 when English forces defeated him at Painscastle. Nevertheless the next year, with the accession of JOHN to the English throne, saw Gwenwynwyn benefitting from the favour of the English king, with the grant of lands in Derbyshire. Later that same year Llywelyn established a rapport with John and the two Welsh lords became locked in intense rivalry. In August 1202 Llywelyn planned an all-out raid on Powys, but was temporarily persuaded to an amicable treaty. Gwenwynwyn eventually overstepped the mark in 1208 when he recommenced raids in mid Wales to take advantage of the fall from grace of William de Breos, the senior marcher lord. John reacted immediately. Gwenwynwyn's forces were soon overcome, and the Welsh prince was summoned to Shrewsbury in October where John confiscated his lands and only allowed him his freedom upon rendering twenty hostages. Llywelyn promptly overran Ceredigion and Powys, and Gwenwynwyn found himself a prince dispossessed. John eventually restored Gwenwynwyn to his lands in southern Powys in November 1210, but under such strict conditions that Gwenwynwyn was virtually a pawn. Unable to suffer this for long, in 1212 he swallowed his pride and threw in his lot with Llywelyn. The next four years saw Llywelyn's rise to overall power in Wales with Gwenwynwyn as a staunch supporter, paying him formal homage in 1215. But all this came to naught in early 1216 when John restored Gwenwynwyn to his manor in Derbyshire. Llywelyn saw this as a

treacherous act and immediately invaded Powys, driving Gwenwynwyn into exile. He is heard of no more after June 1216 and presumably died about that time.

[EE28] **GRUFFYDD** AP **GWENWYNWYN** lord of Powys, 1240–86.
Powys remained in the hands of Llywelyn until his death in 1240. Soon afterwards Gwenwynwyn's son, Gruffydd, who had been only a year old on his father's death, was granted the lordship of Southern Powys by HENRY III, but on very strict terms. Gruffydd held these lands intermittently during a constant power struggle with LLYWELYN AP GRUFFYDD, finding himself again in exile in 1257, imprisoned in 1263 – in which year he changed his allegiance to Llywelyn – and in exile again in 1274. Although reinstated in his lands in 1277 he held them only under the authority of the English king and, after his death in 1286, all lands passed to the English crown.

[EE29] **OWAIN GLYN DWR** or **GLENDOWER** prince of Wales, 1400–16.
The last Welsh national to claim the title "Prince of Wales". He was descended on his father's side from MADOG AP MAREDUDD, the last ruler of a united Powys, and on his mother's side from RHYS AP GRUFFYDD, the Lord Rhys of Deheubarth. Later chroniclers would also find a distant link with the families of OWAIN GWYNEDD but, even without that, after the murder of Owain ap Thomas in 1378, whose pretensions to the Welsh throne in 1372 had caused an upsurge of Welsh pride and nationalism, Owain Glyn Dwr was certainly the primary contender to the principality of Wales. Little is known of his early life. He was born around 1354 and on his father's death in 1370, inherited estates in Powys and Meirionydd. Sometime around 1383 he married Margaret, the daughter of David Hanmer, a justice of the King's Bench, and it is likely that up to this time, Owain had been receiving legal training. He also served a military apprenticeship, between 1383 and 1387, in northern England, Scotland and France. He settled down to the life of a country squire, building himself fine new houses and estates at Sycharth and Glyndyfrdwy.

From a portrait in
the National Library of Wales

Although the next decade gave no indication of Owain's future intentions it is evident that he was held in high regard by the Welsh and that increasingly he became the voice for their complaints of ill-treatment by their English overlords. It seems that it was a boundary dispute with his English neighbour that suddenly caused tempers to flare. Everything came to a head on 16 September 1400 when Owain's supporters declared him prince of Wales. There was now a new king on the English throne, HENRY IV, and perhaps this was seen as an added opportunity to settle old scores.

After an initial show of power in late 1400, which was followed by an equally quick punitive expedition by Henry IV, Owain went into hiding for several months. During this period, although English agents were searching for him, he was able to maintain a guerilla campaign. Encouraged by Owain's acts other rebellions broke out across Wales, the most momentous being the capture of Conway Castle in April 1401. By August 1401 Owain's forces were tightening their grip over north-west Wales, and a further expedition by Henry IV only strengthened national resistance and brought support to the Welsh from Scotland and Ireland. In June 1402 Owain made a further show of force at the battle of Bryn Glas, where he overwhelmed an English levy and put fear into the marcher lords. The leader of that levy, Edmund Mortimer, was captured and won over to the Welsh cause, marrying Glyn Dwr's daughter Katherine. Owain soon began to win over other factions from England, most notably the PERCY family, who held the earldom of Northumberland and, by the end of 1403, he was receiving support from the French. Owain's successes came to their peak in 1404 when he summoned a parliament at Machynlleth, on the borders of Powys and Meirionydd, and soon after he contracted a Franco-Welsh alliance. The support of the French resulted in major gains in south Wales during 1405. It was in July 1405 that Owain held his second parliament. He had also, by now, gained the support of the Welsh church through his own support in the long-running dispute over the autonomy of St David's.

By this stage, however, Owain's ambitions seem to have grown unrealistically. It seems that during 1405 his alliance with Henry Percy, earl of Northumberland, and Edmund Mortimer reached the stage where they were plotting the overthrow of Henry IV and the division of England and Wales between them. Such plans required significant forces, support and finances. These were all available in some measure but not sufficiently co-ordinated and, by the end of 1405, Owain's fortunes began to founder. Northumberland was the first to suffer defeat and he withdrew his forces. Further promised support from the French and Scots did not materialise and by late 1406 Owain was in retreat before a more organized offensive by the English king. With the death of the earl of Northumberland in 1408, Owain's English support evaporated. Gradually castle after castle was regained by the English, the last two – Aberystwyth and Harlech – falling from Owain's hands in 1409. Edmund Mortimer died in the siege of Harlech, and Owain's wife and several of his children and grandchildren were captured. Thereafter Owain and his son Maredudd remained in hiding. There were occasional skirmishes thereafter in the mountain fastness of north-west Wales, and Owain was never betrayed, but the revolt was over and Wales was subdued. It is possible that his final days were spent in a remote part of Herefordshire. It is presumed Owain died either late in 1415 or early in 1416. It was not until April 1421 that Owain's son, Maredudd, accepted a pardon. Owain's resting place is not known, allowing him to pass into legend like ARTHUR as a saviour who might one day return.

THE SCOTTISH KINGDOMS

FB. STRATHCLYDE and CUMBRIA

In 889 the once British kingdom of Strathclyde was merged with the kingdom of the Scots. It retained a degree of autonomy and it later became the practice that the heir to the Scottish throne was made king or prince of Strathclyde. This practice was not always consistent and there remained a few rulers of Strathclyde who were not subsequently elevated to the Scottish throne. The following covers all of the Scottish rulers of Strathclyde with full biographies only of those who were not also kings of Scotland. See Map 9 and Chart 19 on pages 380 and 381.

Ref.	Ruler	Born	Reign	Died	Notes
continued from page 183					
FB22.	Donald mac Aed		908–*c*25	934	retired
FB23.	Owen *Caesarius*		*c*925–37	937	probably killed in battle
Probably ruled directly by the Scottish kings Constantine and Malcolm, 937–45.					
FB24.	Donald mac Donald		937–45	?	deposed and blinded
FB25.	Indulf		945–54	962	became king of the Scots 954 (FC46)
FB26.	Dub or Duff		954–62	966	became king of the Scots 962 (FC47)
FB27.	Donald mac Owen		962–73	975	abdicated in favour of his son
FB28.	Malcolm mac Donald		973–97	997	
FB29.	Malcolm mac Kenneth	*c*954	990–5		deposed
	(*restored*)		997–1005	1034	became Malcolm II of Scotland (FC54)
FB30.	Owen *the Bald*		1005–18	1018?	
FB31.	Duncan		*c*1018–34	1040	became king of Scotland 1034 (FC55)
FB32.	Malcolm mac Duncan	*c*1031	1034–58	1093	became Malcolm III of Scotland (FC58)
FB32a.	Maldred mac Duncan	*c*1003	1034–45	1045	Regent; probably killed in battle

When Malcolm inherited the Scottish throne Strathclyde was fully integrated into his kingdom. Malcolm seems to have styled his son Edmund as prince of Cumbria, though his cousin's son Dolfin was earl of Cumberland before 1092 when he was expelled by William II of England, and Cumbria was taken from Scotland.

[FB22] **DONALD** MAC **AED** Strathclyde, 908–24/5.
He seems to have been the first king appointed to the new sub-kingdom of Strathclyde after its integration into the kingdom of Scotland. Evidently CON-STANTINE II was endeavouring to form a good relationship with the Strathclyde

Britons whose last independent king, EOCHAID, had been driven out by DONALD II. Strathclyde thus maintained a degree of autonomy but its king was appointed by the king of the Scots and was usually the heir to the Scottish throne. Donald was Constantine's younger brother. Constantine's concern at that time was the Viking threat to Scotland, and having a strong steward in charge of the Strathclyde frontier was all important. Donald's role was thus more one of defender of the kingdom than of a ruler. His reign was almost entirely one of conflict with the Vikings which resulted, though, in the treaty between Constantine and RAGNALL of York in 918. Donald was present at the subsequent meeting between EDWARD *the Elder* and Constantine where Edward sought to have the support of the Scots against the Norse. Some time after this Donald either stepped down as ruler of Strathclyde or was replaced. Although he lived on until 934, his cousin, OWEN MAC DONALD, is recorded as king of Strathclyde in 927. There is some suggestion that Donald's continued support of the Norse kings of York angered the new Saxon king ATHELSTAN when he came to power in 924, and that Constantine thus replaced Donald with the newly recognized heir to the throne.

[FB23] **OWEN *CAESARIUS* (III)** Strathclyde, 925–c37.

Owen came to power at the same time as the new Saxon king ATHELSTAN, and it may be that CONSTANTINE II of Scotland replaced the former Strathclyde king, DONALD, as part of an overall agreement, which also allowed Constantine to establish the Strathclyde kingdom as an appanage for the heir to the Scots throne. Owen was the son of DONALD II and under the normal Celtic rule of succession was accepted as the next king. If ATHELSTAN expected Constantine and Owen to be subordinate he was mistaken for, although the two were present at the meeting at Eamont Bridge in July 927, they continued to support the Norse claimants to the kingdom of York. It is also apparent that Athelstan sought to ensure that the two kings banished idolatry from Scotland, particularly in Strathclyde and Galloway where many of the local British, already becoming intermingled with the Norse, had lapsed into paganism. Constantine and Owen continued to snub Athelstan and in 934 Athelstan led a punitive force into Scotland. Constantine retaliated and in 937 a combined force of Scots, Norse and British met the Saxons at Brunanburh. It was a Saxon triumph and Owen was probably killed in the battle, as he was not heard of again. He is believed to be buried in Penrith.

[FB24] **DONALD MAC DONALD** Strathclyde, 937–45.

It is not entirely clear what happened after the death of OWEN at the battle of Brunanburh. It seems likely that the kingship of Strathclyde was disputed between the rightful heir, who was subsequently MALCOLM I of Scotland, and the sons of DONALD MAC AED, who had apparently established themselves in Strathclyde by the early 940s. There names are not recorded, and the suggestion in the slightly confused chronicle of Florence of Worcester that one may have been called Donald may in fact be a confusion with their father. Strathclyde was riven with Scottish, British and Norse factions and was a potential powder keg. The Saxons were also concerned about this territory because it formed part of the link between the Norse of Dublin and of York. The reign of EDMUND of Wessex was filled with his campaign against the Norse which eventually resolved itself in 943. Two years later Edmund invaded Cumbria, and deposed the sons of Donald, blinding them. Their fate, thereafter, is not known. Edmund handed Cumbria over to Malcolm, who had become king of Scotland in 943. He inaugurated INDULF, CONSTANTINE's son, as the king.

[FB25;FC46] **INDULF** Strathclyde, 945–54; Scotland, 954–62.
See page 388 for Indulf's later reign. His reign in Strathclyde would have been especially difficult because of the intense action in the neighbouring kingdom of York (*see under* ERIK BLOODAXE, OLAF SITRICSSON *and* EADRED *of Wessex for details*).

[FB26;FC47] **DUFF** or **DUB** Strathclyde, 954–62; Scotland, 962–6.
The son of MALCOLM I. When he was nominated as king of Strathclyde, he inherited a kingdom much enlarged by the victories of INDULF over the English in Lothian. Duff thus ruled a kingdom which stretched from the Clyde to the Firth, south to the Tweed on the east coast and the Ribble on the west. He held this land as heir to the throne of Scotland, and not in his own right, but it still formed a substantial kingdom. When Indulf retired to a monastery in 962, Duff inherited the throne of Scotland and he passed on the kingdom of Strathclyde to his cousin, DONALD MAC OWEN. This enraged CUILEAN, the son of Indulf, who expected to be the next heir, and led to a civil war between Cuilean and Duff. *See page 388 for further details.*

[FB27] **DONALD** MAC **OWEN** Strathclyde, 962–73.
The son of OWEN, king of Strathclyde, and grandson of DONALD II, Donald was chosen as ruler of Strathclyde (and hence potential successor to the Scottish throne) by DUFF over CUILEAN, who regarded himself as the rightful heir. The civil war that broke out seems to have taken place mostly between Cuilean and Duff, resulting in the death of Duff in 966. Cuilean then turned his might on Strathclyde but was killed in battle by Donald's son Rhydderch. Having established a right to the throne of Strathclyde, Donald, who was at heart a peaceable king, made every effort to retain it for his children, rather than it pass on to the heir to the Scottish throne. He no doubt hoped that his children might indeed become kings of Scotland. At the convention at Chester held in 973 by the English king EDGAR, Donald was present along with his son, MALCOLM, who was regarded as king of the Cumbrians. Evidently Donald had instigated a right of succession within his own kingdom, with Malcolm ruling the land of Cumbria which had been given to the Scottish king MALCOLM I in 945. No doubt at this convention Donald sought agreement to Malcolm's rights over the whole kingdom of Strathclyde, to which KENNETH II must have agreed, for in 973 Donald abdicated in favour of his son and retired to a monastery. He died two years later whilst on a pilgrimage to Rome.

[FB28] **MALCOLM** MAC **DONALD** sub-king of Cumbria and Strathclyde, 973–97.
Malcolm inherited Strathclyde from his father, DONALD MAC OWEN who retired in 973. Malcolm seems to have existed on peaceful terms with KENNETH II of Scotland, though in 990 Malcolm's right to the kingdom was challenged by Kenneth's son Malcolm (the future MALCOLM II of Scotland). The two ruled jointly for five years, until Malcolm mac Kenneth was deposed in 995 on the death of his father. It is perhaps pertinent that Malcolm mac Donald did not endeavour to claim the throne in 995 during the dynastic struggle between CONSTANTINE III and KENNETH III. He died in 997 and was succeeded by his brother OWEN THE BALD. Some records confuse this Malcolm with a Malcolm son of DUFF, whose death is recorded in 990,

though there is apparently some doubt as to whether that Malcolm actually existed. It is not impossible that a son of Duff laid claim to the kingship of Strathclyde at this time, and that three Malcolms may have been just too much for later chroniclers to cope with.

[FB29;FC54] MALCOLM II MAC KENNETH

Sub-king of Cumbria and Strathclyde, 990–5, 997–1005; king of Scotland, 1005–34. Malcolm's kingship of Strathclyde was one of rivalry with MALCOLM MAC DONALD as detailed in the previous entry, and was more a battle about the new rules of patrilinear succession than about personal animosities. Malcolm eventually succeeded to the Scottish throne as MALCOLM II and details are provided on page 390.

[FB30] OWEN *THE BALD* Strathclyde, 1005–18?

Owen was the brother of MALCOLM MAC DONALD. He managed to secure the kingship of Strathclyde sometime after Malcolm mac Kenneth succeeded to the Scottish throne as MALCOLM II. Just when is uncertain as Malcolm would certainly have wanted to pass the Scottish throne on to his own children, but Malcolm had three daughters and no sons and his grandson, DUNCAN, was too young to inherit Strathclyde. Owen, therefore, seems to be something of a second choice, serving almost as a regent to Malcolm in the event of the king's premature death, although Malcolm secured the right of succession for Duncan once he had come of age. That probably happened in 1018, or soon after, but it is not clear whether Owen stepped down at that time, or may have died. It is probable that he was killed in or died soon after the battle of Carham, in which Owen fought alongside Malcolm against the Northumbrians. Owen was probably in his fifties or even his sixties by then, and stood aside in favour of Duncan. Nothing more is heard of him after 1018.

[FB31;FC55] DUNCAN (I) *THE GRACIOUS* Strathclyde, c1018–34; Scotland, 25 November 1034–15 August 1040.

Duncan was the grandson of MALCOLM II. His period of rule as King of Strathclyde was of little consequence. He inherited the Scottish throne in 1034. *For full details see page 392.*

[FB32a] MALDRED regent of Strathclyde, 1034–45.

Maldred was the younger brother of DUNCAN. When Duncan inherited the throne of Scotland in 1034 his son Malcolm (MALCOLM III) was too young to rule Strathclyde as heir, so Maldred served as regent. Maldred's support to Duncan was vital in the early years of his reign when the Northumbrians, under Earl Eadulf, sought to reclaim the territory in Bernicia and Lothian that MALCOLM II had claimed. The Northumbrians also ravaged Strathclyde, but Maldred succeeded in repulsing them. This happened during 1038. It was probably at this time that Maldred sought to unite his family with the Northumbrians by marrying Edith, the half-sister of Eadulf. Their son, Gospatrick, became earl of Northumbria sometime around 1068, and also styled himself king of Cumbria. When Duncan was killed in 1040, Maldred would have had a claim on the throne, but he seems not to have sought it. Instead he allied himself with Siward, earl of Northumbria, as guardians of the infant Malcolm. Maldred had to face an onslaught from THORFINN, earl of Orkney, who sent his forces south in 1042 against Crinan (Maldred's father) and plundered parts of Strathclyde and Cumbria. Thorfinn was eventually rebuffed by the forces of Maldred and Siward. Maldred seems to have died in 1045 alongside his father Crinan in a rebellion against MACBETH at Dunkeld.

[FB32;FC58] **MALCOLM** *CANMORE* (*BIGHEAD*)
Sub-king of Cumbria and Strathclyde, 1045–58 (officially from 1034); King of Scotland, 17 March 1058–13 November 1093. Crowned: Scone Abbey, 25 April 1058. Malcolm was the young son of DUNCAN I who in his youth was spirited for safety to England, while his uncle MALDRED served as regent. An excellent strategist, Malcolm was able to win back Strathclyde and Cumbria in 1054 with the help of his uncle, Siward, earl of Northumbria. Malcolm used his position to continue his war against MACBETH and LULACH and after their defeat he gained the Scottish throne. From that point on Strathclyde and Cumbria were formally incorporated into the kingdom of Scotland and there were no further sub-kings. *Full details of Malcolm III's reign are on page 395.*

FC. SCOTLAND

In 848 Kenneth macAlpin united the kingdoms of the Picts and the Scots which later became known as Scotland. At this stage the kingdom was centred at Forteviot in southern Scotland and Kenneth and his successors held little authority over the Highlands which were still dominated by the Cenél Loarn and the Picts who later emerged as the separate "kingdom" of Moray (*see page 413*). Further north the Vikings settled in Orkney and their authority spilled over into Caithness (*see page 437*).

It was centuries before Scotland became united. Only in 1265 did Norway cede the sovereignty of the Western Isles and Man to Scotland and, though the earldom of Orkney passed into the hands of a Scottish family it remained Norwegian territory for another two centuries. It was ironic, therefore, that at the time that Scotland began to feel it had control over its affairs, Alexander III should die with only an infant successor and her death left the country with a succession crisis. The country fell into the hands of the English king Edward I. This section therefore follows the Scottish kingship through from the creation of Alba under Kenneth macAlpin to its fight for freedom at the time of John Balliol and William Wallace.

Ref.	Ruler	Born	Reign	Died	Notes

continued from page 196

The House of Alpin

Ref.	Ruler	Born	Reign	Died	Notes
FC37.	Kenneth (I) macAlpin		840–58	858	
FC38.	Donald (I)		858–63	863	murdered or killed in battle
FC39.	Constantine (I)		863–77	877	killed in battle
FC39a.	Olaf *the White*		866–71	872	also king of Dublin (U2); overlord of Picts and Scots
FC40.	Aed		877–78	878	killed in battle
FC41.	Giric		878–89	?	deposed; ruled jointly with Eochaid

Ref.	Ruler	Born	Reign	Died	Notes
FC42.	Eochaid		878–89	889	also king of Strathclyde (FB21); deposed

Hereafter the kingdoms of the Picts, Dál Riata and Strathclyde were united under one monarch, the first to be honoured as **king of Scotland.**

Ref.	Ruler	Born	Reign	Died	Notes
FC43.	Donald II		889–900	900	killed in battle
FC44.	Constantine II		900–43	952	abdicated to become a monk
FC45.	Malcolm (I)		943–54	954	killed in battle

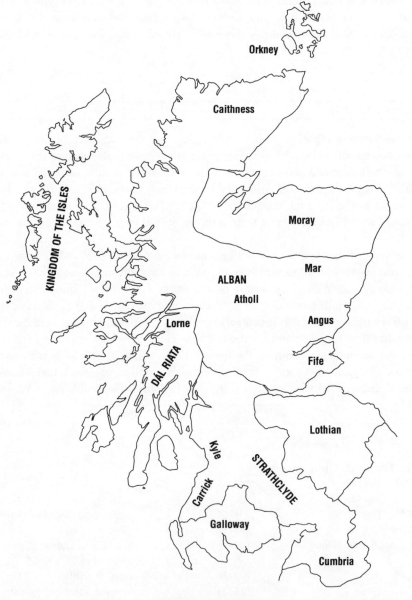

Map 9 **Scotland 500–1200**

19. Scotland (2) – Kings of the Scots: Alpin to Macbeth

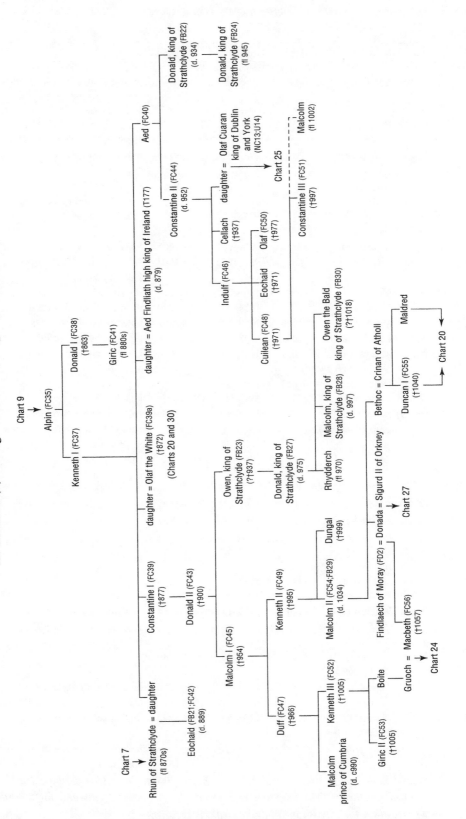

Ref.	Ruler	Born	Reign	Died	Notes
FC46.	Indulf		954–62	962	abdicated to become a monk; slain by Vikings soon after; see also FB25
FC47.	Duff or Dub		962–c66	c966	driven into exile and slain; see FB26
FC48.	Cuilean *Ring* (or Colin)		c967–71	971	killed in battle
FC49.	Kenneth II		971–95	995	murdered
FC50.	Olaf		971–7	977	rival claimant; killed in battle
FC51.	Constantine III *the Bald*		995–7	997	killed in battle
FC52.	Kenneth III		997–1005	1005	killed in battle
FC53.	Giric II		997–1005	1005	sub-king ruled with above; killed in battle
FC54.	Malcolm II	c954	1005–34	1034	see also FB29
FC55.	Duncan	c1001	1034–40	1040	murdered; see also FB31
FC56.	Macbeth	c1005	1040–57	1057	killed in battle; see FD5
FC57.	Lulach *the Fool*	c1031	1057–8	1058	killed in battle; see FD6
FC58.	Malcolm III *Canmore* (*Bighead*)	c1031	1058–93	1093	killed in an ambush; see also FB32
FC59.	Donald III *Bane*	c1033	1093–4		deposed, but later restored
FC60.	Duncan II	c1060	May–Nov 1094	1094	killed in battle
(FC59)	Donald III *Bane* (restored)	c1033	1094–7	1099	ruled northern Scotland; deposed again, blinded and imprisoned
FC61.	Edmund		1094–7	?	ruled southern Scotland; deposed and retired to a monastery
FC62.	Edgar	c1074	1097–1107	1107	
FC63.	Alexander (I) *the Fierce*	c1077	1107–24	1124	
FC64.	David (I) *the Saint*	c1084	1124–53	1153	
FC65.	Malcolm IV *the Maiden*	1141	1153–65	1165	
FC66.	William (I) *the Lyon*	c1143	1165–1214	1214	William submitted to English under Henry II from 1174–1189.
FC67.	Alexander II *the Peaceful*	1198	1214–49	1249	
FC68.	Alexander III *the Glorious*	1241	1249–86	1286	killed in riding accident
FC69.	Margaret, *Maid of Norway*	1283	1286–90	1290	died at sea

Interregnum from 26 Sep 1290–17 Nov 1292 during which Edward I served as overlord

| FC70. | John (Balliol) | c1250 | 1292–6 | 1313 | abdicated |

Second interregnum from 10 Jul 1296–25 Mar 1306 during which period Edward I claimed the throne. The kingdom was governed by several regents and for a while wrested from the English by William Wallace.

FC70a. William   *c*1274   1297–8   1305   Governor: briefly held
        Wallace   control

The year after William Wallace's death Robert the Bruce laid claim to the throne of Scotland and began a new chapter in the country's history. This is continued on page 546.

[FC37] **KENNETH** MACALPIN Scots, 840–58; and Picts, 847–58.

Kenneth's origins are obscure, and his fame rests more on the subsequent development of his dynasty than any significant actions during his own reign. Although he must have come from some branch of the ruling Cenél Gabhrán faction, his exact antecedents have never been satisfactorily identified, though a twelfth-century genealogy makes him the great-grandson of AED FIND, through his son EOCHAID. This is, of course, possible, but it is surprising that someone who shot to power so quickly had not otherwise already featured in the activities prevalent during the previous decade where a high ranking and ambitious prince is bound to have made his mark. The story that he succeeded his father as a sub-king of Galloway is again possible, but unlikely. What seems more likely is that Kenneth was a prince of the Cenél Gabhrán but was not necessarily resident in Dál Riata for all of his early life. He may have lived part of the time in Ireland, or elsewhere amongst the Western Highlands. It has been suggested that his father married not only a Pictish princess (Kenneth's mother) but a Norse princess, and that Kenneth thus already had strong connections with the Vikings. The Irish annals record that in 836, Gothfrith macFergus, a Gaelo-Norse half-breed, who had established himself as king of Oriel in northern Ireland and who apparently also had dominion over some of the Hebrides, visited Kenneth in Argyll in order to discuss the Viking attacks on western Scotland. Could Kenneth have negotiated some form of treaty with the Vikings which worked to their mutual benefit? In 839 the Vikings advanced through Dál Riatan territory into the heart of the land of the Picts and, in the ensuing battle at Forteviot, killed many of the Scots' and Picts' nobility. In the chaos that followed Kenneth claimed the kingship of Dál Riata. Kenneth held power by his own strength and cunning. There must have been others who believed they had a greater right to the throne or who, for whatever reasons, distrusted Kenneth, and his first few years must have been bloodthirsty, as he rid himself of his enemies and secured his right to the throne. None of this is recorded, because Kenneth subsequently became such a revered ruler that his past and origins were whitewashed to an extent, but some of his character comes through in the tale about how he deceived the Picts. Apparently he invited the Pictish nobility, then ruled by DRUST MAC FERAT, to a feast. Kenneth had already dug pits around the benches and weakened the bolts holding the benches together, so that once the Picts had become drunk it was easy to release the bolts, cast the Picts into the hidden trenches and slaughter them. Whatever the real events, tradition records that Kenneth conquered the Picts by deceit and slaughter. By 847 he had united the old kingdoms, establishing them as a single entity. To do this he must have considerably subdued any remaining Pictish nobility for never again did they lay claim to their throne. Kenneth called his combined kingdom Alba, or Albany, and by the time of his grandson DONALD II, thirty years later, it was already being called Scotland. Kenneth not only established his capital at Forteviot, the previous capital of the Picts, but he also established Dunkeld as the spiritual capital of Alba by removing there some of the relics of St Columba from Iona.

Kenneth's reign was violent but successful. Having taken over control of the Picts he still warred against the Angles to the south and the British of Strathclyde, and he retained an uneasy peace with the Vikings. He relied heavily on his own strength of character, though he also cemented his authority with neighbours and allies by inter-dynastic marriages through his daughters. One married OLAF, the King of Dublin; another married Aed *Findliath*, who became High King of Ireland in 862, whilst a third married RHUN, prince of Strathclyde. Kenneth's violent life evidently took its toll for he died of an illness, in February 858. His age is uncertain but he was probably in his late forties. He was succeeded by his brother DONALD.

[FC38] **DONALD** (I) Picts and Scots, 858–63.
He was the brother (or possibly half-brother) of KENNETH MACALPIN and was probably of a similar age. It has been suggested that his mother may have been Norse. His reign was brief, but he continued the work begun by his brother in cementing the kingdoms of the Picts and the Scots. He imposed the laws of the Scots, developed (or more likely revised) by AED FIND, upon the Picts, and this almost certainly made him unpopular. The Picts might not have been an especially united race but they were bonded by their laws and customs, though there is some evidence that this was breaking down by the early ninth century. Nevertheless, it is possible that this blatant subordination of the Picts aroused hostilities as there is some suggestion that Donald was murdered at Scone, or that he was killed in battle. He was succeeded by his nephew, CONSTANTINE.

[FC39] **CONSTANTINE** (I) Picts and Scots, 863–77.
Son of KENNETH MACALPIN and successor of DONALD I. His reign was dominated by battles against or connivances with the Vikings who had settled in Ireland and who constantly harried the western coast of Scotland. In 866 a major Viking raid, under their king OLAF, reached as far as Forteviot and resulted in the taking of hostages and considerable plunder. Olaf seems to have remained in Pictland and it has been suggested that he even demanded homage from Constantine, so that Olaf may have considered himself ruler of the Picts. By 870 Constantine was evidently in league with Olaf, who had married Constantine's sister. The two of them conspired, along with the other Viking leader, IVARR THE BONELESS, to attack Dumbarton, resulting in the fall of the British kingdom of Strathclyde. Two years later Constantine betrayed the exiled king of Strathclyde, ARTGAL, who was defeated and killed by the Vikings. Constantine's treachery did not benefit him in the same way it had his father. In 875 he was defeated by a Viking army led by Ivarr's brother, HALFDAN. This same army killed Constantine two years later in battle at Crail, when it was returning from York to Dublin. Constantine was buried on Iona. He was succeeded by his brother AED.

[FC39a;U2] **OLAF** or **ANLAF GOTHFRITHSON,** *THE WHITE* Dublin, 853–71; overlord of Picts and Scots, 866–71.

Olaf established himself as king of the Norse Vikings in Dublin in 853. Within four years he was in league with the leader of the Danish Vikings, IVARR THE BONELESS, and the two used Dublin as the base for raids not only along the Irish coast but throughout the western isles and sea lochs of Scotland. In 866 he embarked on a major campaign across Scotland, seeking to establish a right of access from the Clyde to the Forth which would allow the Viking longships to be transported across land rather than to risk the vulnerable trip around the north Scottish coast. Olaf not only defeated the king of the Picts and Scots, CONSTANTINE (I), but he demanded tribute from him. Olaf may thus be regarded as the overlord of the Picts and Scots from 866 to 871. His authority over Constantine allowed the free passage of Vikings across Pictland and this facilitated the Danish conquest of York and East Anglia. Olaf's impact upon Britain was therefore significant. Olaf married at least three times. His first wife was Aud the Deep-Minded, the daughter of KETIL FLATNOSE, by whom he was the father of THORSTEIN THE RED. He also married the daughter of KENNETH MACALPIN and finally a daughter of CONSTANTINE (I). The historical record is vague about Olaf's fate. One record suggests that he became involved with RAGNALD in the battle to clear the Orkneys of Norse pirates and was killed at the battle of Hafrsfiord in 872. Another suggestion is that Olaf returned to Norway to assist his father and brother in the civil war that eventually resulted in establishing a united kingdom of Norway. If so, then he is almost certainly the same Olaf who was buried in the ship at Gotstad, one of the rich archeological finds in Scandinavia. He was hailed as the greatest ruler of the western seas.

[FC40] **AED** *WHITEFOOT* Picts and Scots, 877–78.
The son of KENNETH I. During his reign the combined kingdom of Picts and Scots was in danger of crumbling under two destructive forces. On the one hand the Vikings had dominated the land and had all but treated Aed's brother, CONSTANTINE, as their puppet ruler. On the other side Aed's cousin GIRIC also claimed the throne. Giric's challenge was successful for he killed Aed at the battle of Strathallan.

[FC41] **GIRIC (I)** Picts and Scots, 878–89.
[FC42;FB21] **EOCHAID** MAP **RHUN** Strathclyde and Scots, 878–89.
Giric was the son of DONALD I, who defeated his cousin AED to claim the Scottish throne. He was assisted in this by EOCHAID, king of Strathclyde, who seems to have shared the kingship with Giric, though this probably means he retained a vassal kingship in Strathclyde (*see page xx*). The two formed a strong bond, for they succeeded in ridding Scotland of the stranglehold of the Vikings, and they drove the Angles out of Bernicia, ejecting EGBERT II. Giric was thus the first to rule a kingdom whose borders equated roughly to those of modern-day Scotland. Giric and Eochaid were defeated, however, by their cousin DONALD II and driven from the kingdom. The fate of Giric is not known but he may have fled with Eochaid and other dispossessed Strathclyde Britons into northern Wales.

[FC43] **DONALD II** Scotland, 889–900.

The son of CONSTANTINE I he usurped power by deposing his cousins GIRIC and EOCHAID and took over a kingdom that extended from the farthest north of Britain down to Bernicia and Strathclyde, borders roughly equal to the modern-day Scotland. He was the first ruler to be termed *Rí Alban*, or king of Scotland. However during his reign he lost some territory to the Norse who, having already established themselves amongst the Western Isles, now sought to dominate the north. The earldom of Orkney was created at around this time, and THORSTEIN THE RED laid waste to Caithness and Sunderland establishing his own kingdom in the north. Donald placed his emphasis on integrating the former British kingdom of Strathclyde into Scotland. Having deposed Eochaid, its last king, he also expelled the nobility. In all likelihood many left of their own accord, not wishing to live under Gaelic rule, and they moved south to live with their closer relatives in north Wales. Either Donald, or more likely his successor, CONSTANTINE, established Strathclyde as a sub-kingdom ruled by the heir to the throne. This at least sustained its identity for another century before its final merger into Scotland. Donald died in battle at Forres and was buried on Iona.

[FC44] **CONSTANTINE II** Scotland, 900–43.

One of the longest-ruling of Scottish monarchs, the first to rule for more than forty years (it would have been over fifty had he not abdicated to enter the church). The son of AED, he must have been an infant when his father died in 878, although (as he had a younger brother) he was probably at least two years old, so he was probably in his early twenties when he succeeded his cousin DONALD II. The length of Constantine's reign and his strength of character allowed him to establish Scotland as a unified kingdom. His first concerns were against the Norse who, in 902, had been driven out of their kingdom in Dublin. Their ruler in exile, RAGNALL, clearly intended to establish a new kingdom in the area of Strathclyde and Cumbria, and the years 903 and 904 were ones of regular skirmishes between the Scots and the Norse. In 903 the Norse raided as far east as Dunkeld, but at this stage the Norse army seems to have withdrawn, though must always have remained a threat, for in 910 Ragnall succeeded in invading York and establishing himself as ruler. It was against this background that Constantine perceived a need to strengthen his defences around Strathclyde and Cumbria, and he established the sub-kingdom of Strathclyde in 908, with his brother DONALD as its ruler. The Norse threat continued, however. Ragnall, now established in York, sought to expand his kingdom into neighbouring Bernicia and, on the death of EADULF in 913, Ragnall expelled his successor Ealdred who fled to Constantine's court. Constantine fought two major battles against the Norse, in 914 and 918, both at Corbridge. Although the Scots suffered defeat on both occasions, it was not without heavy losses to the Norse. Ragnall was anxious not to lose his links with Dublin, which kingdom he had regained in 917, so in 918 the Norse and Scots entered into a peace treaty. Constantine then allied himself with the Norse against the Saxons of Wessex, resulting in the famous pact with EDWARD THE ELDER in 920. It is very unlikely that on this occasion Constantine regarded Edward as his overlord, despite the record of the *ASC*. It is more likely that each side acknowledged the other's authority and status. This pact was subsequently renewed with ATHELSTAN at Eamont Bridge near

Penrith in July 927, a meeting which followed Athelstan's defeat of Gothfrith of Dublin, who had invaded Northumbria to claim the throne of York. Athelstan gained Constantine's agreement not to support Gothfrith, but Constantine reneged on this in 934 when he supported Gothfrith's son, OLAF, the new king of Dublin, in his claim on the throne of York. The most flagrant sign of Constantine's support was when he gave one of his daughters to Olaf in marriage. This incensed Athelstan, who invaded Scotland as far north as Edinburgh and inflicted losses upon Constantine. He apparently also took one of Constantine's sons (probably Cellach) as hostage. Constantine's support for Olaf, however, remained steadfast and, in 937, Olaf invaded Northumbria. The armies met the Saxons at Brunanburh, where Olaf and Constantine were dealt a crushing defeat by Athelstan, regarded as one of the greatest Saxon victories. Cellach died in the battle, as probably did OWEN of Strathclyde. However, when Athelstan died two years later, Olaf ventured again to claim York and this time succeeded. Olaf's alliance with Constantine increased the latter's power.

In 943, when he must have been about sixty-five, Constantine abdicated. He was clearly still able and active, but he must also have recognized that it was time for new blood. In 943 EDMUND of Wessex had resolved his problems with the Norse kings of York, which weakened Constantine's command of northern Britain. He retired to the monastery at St Andrews. During his reign Constantine had had a mixed relationship with the church. He had allied himself with the pagan Norse, had tolerated the reversion to pagan practices in Galloway and Kyle, and had delayed long in the baptism of his son Indulf. Yet as early as 906 he had agreed, with Bishop Cellach of St Andrews, to uphold the authority of the Scottish church, and he had also been a friend of St Catroe, escorting him on his mission through Scotland in during the 940s. It is possible that his meeting with Catroe provided a good excuse to abdicate.

There is a long-held belief that Constantine came out of retirement in 948 to join with Malcolm in an invasion of England. Since he would have been at least seventy years old by then, it seems very unlikely, though it is possible that Constantine encouraged Malcolm in the enterprise. Constantine died in 952 at the monastery of St Andrews, and was almost certainly buried there.

[FC45] **MALCOLM (I)** Scotland, 943–54.

He was the son of DONALD II and inherited the Scottish throne on the abdication of CONSTANTINE II. It is possible he may have been nominated as king of Strathclyde on the death of OWEN in 937, but records are uncertain on this, though there seems to have been some inter-dynastic strife in Strathclyde during this period (*see under* DONALD MAC DONALD). At this time OLAF SITRICSON, the Norse king of York, whom Malcolm supported, had been driven out of York by EDMUND of Wessex in 943 and had sought refuge in Strathclyde as leader of the exiled Vikings of Dublin. Malcolm gave him shelter, but Edmund continued to pursue the Norse and in 945 he invaded Cumbria and Strathclyde, driving out Olaf and deposing the sons of Donald. Edmund gave Malcolm Cumbria on the basis that he would support Edmund in defending northern Britain against the Vikings. This greatly enlarged the Scottish realm, of which Strathclyde was a part, and though Malcolm handed the kingship of Strathclyde to his heir, INDULF, he still retained overlordship and this extended his authority down through what is now Lancashire, almost as far as the Mersey. The kingdom of York remained a problem, for in 947 ERIK BLOODAXE established himself as king in York. His rule was no more favoured by Malcolm than by EADRED of Wessex, so in 948 Malcolm led an army into York, in support not so much of Eadred but of Olaf Sitricson, who was able to use the banishment of Erik as his opportunity to regain the kingdom of York, which he held for three years.

Malcolm experienced problems at both ends of his kingdom. The expulsion of Erik Bloodaxe, whose family found its way back to Orkney, caused further disquiet in the north. The earls of Orkney also ruled over land in Sutherland and Caithness which brought them into conflict with the mórmaers (or earls) of Moray. These (the Cenél Loarn) were descended from the brother of FERGUS mac Erc, the first king of Dál Riada, and their forefathers had, for a period, ruled Dál Riada (*see under* FERCHAR FOTA). Their descendents therefore believed they had equal claim to the high kingship of Scotland and the rulers of Moray were often designated as kings of Alba (they eventually claimed the throne with MACBETH). The friction caused by the earls of Orkney began to unsettle the men of Moray and this drew Malcolm into battle against them. At the battle of Fetteresso, near Dunnottar, in 954, Malcolm was slain. He was probably nearly sixty at the time of his death. He was buried on Iona, and was succeeded by his second cousin, Indulf.

[FC46;FB25] **INDULF** Strathclyde, 945–54; Scotland, 954–62.
Indulf was the son of the long ruling CONSTANTINE II and thus may already have been in his forties when MALCOLM II made him ruler of the newly enlarged kingdom of Strathclyde and Cumbria. This kingdom was usually ruled by the heir to the throne, but it also brought with it the demands of defending the realm against the Vikings. Indulf's reign in Strathclyde would have been especially difficult because of the intense action in the neighbouring kingdom of York (*see under* ERIK BLOODAXE, OLAF SITRICSSON *and* EADRED *of Wessex for details*). This did not cease when Indulf took over as king of Scotland following the death of Malcolm. In the same year Erik was expelled from York and murdered on his way back to Orkney by the treachery of Osulf, high-reeve of Bamburgh. With the fall of the Norse kingdom a vacuum opened up in the territories of Northumbria, which allowed Indulf to press to reclaim his lands around Edinburgh and Lothian which had long been in English hands. Indulf almost certainly pushed his borders down at least as far as the Tweed, which is where the modern boundary of Scotland lies. These lands were incorporated into the kingdom of Strathclyde. Indulf was a religious man and, in 962, when he was probably around sixty, he abdicated and retired to a monastery (probably St Andrews, where he was later buried). He was soon forced out of retirement to meet his death in battle against the Danes at Findochty on the northern coast of Banff in the heart of Moray. Indulf was presumably fighting alongside the men of Moray against the Danes, but it is an unlikely alliance, and the reason for Indulf fighting so far north must be questionable. He was succeeded by DUFF.

[FC47;FB26] **DUFF** or **DUB** Strathclyde, 954–62; Scotland, 962–6/7.
The son of MALCOLM I. When he was nominated as king of Strathclyde, he inherited a kingdom much enlarged by the victories of INDULF over the English in Lothian. Duff thus ruled a kingdom which stretched from the Clyde to the Forth, south to

the Tweed on the east coast and the Ribble on the west. He held this land as heir to the throne of Scotland, and not in his own right, but it still formed a substantial kingdom. When Indulf retired to a monastery in 962 Duff inherited the throne of Scotland and he passed on the kingdom of Strathclyde to his cousin, DONALD MAC OWEN. This enraged CUILEAN, the son of Indulf, who expected to be the next heir, and led to a civil war between Cuilean and Duff. Duff was initially victorious, but in 966, perhaps in league with the men of Moray, Cuilean succeeded in driving Duff out of the kingdom. He was slain in Moray by the governor of Forres Castle. Somehow his body was collected by his kin and conveyed all the way to Iona for burial, a remarkable journey considering the troubled times.

[FC48] **CUILEAN *RING*** Scotland, 966/7–71.

Cuilean (or Colin) claimed the Scottish throne by expelling DUFF from the kingdom. It seems the war of succession was not solely about the Scottish throne, but about rulership of Strathclyde, which Cuilean might have expected to inherit upon the succession of Duff. That did not happen and Strathclyde passed to DONALD MAC OWEN. After Cuilean gained the Scottish throne, he still seems to have yearned after Strathclyde, which contained the rich and fertile lowlands. He was unsuccessful and was killed in battle against Donald's son, Rhydderch. He was succeded by KENNETH II.

[FC49] **KENNETH II** Scotland, 971–95.

The son of MALCOLM I, Kenneth came to the throne during a period of inter-dynastic rivalry over the succession. There were at least three other factions at work: the rulers of Moray, who continued to cause trouble in the north though they had, as yet, made no serious claims on the Scottish throne; the rulers of Strathclyde, who were normally seen as heirs to the throne of Scotland and whose own heir, Rhydderch, had killed Kenneth's predecessor, CUILEAN; and finally the descendants of AED, whose family alternated in the kingship. At the same time as Kenneth's succession, his distant cousin, OLAF, brother of Cuilean, claimed the throne. Olaf's claim did not seem to be recognized by the English. It was Kenneth who attended the convention at Chester in 973, on the succession of EDGAR, along with other Celtic princes, and promised their fealty to the English. At this meeting Edgar confirmed Kenneth's right to the lands of Lothian, which had been captured by INDULF twenty years earlier and which now became accepted as part of the Scottish realm. It was a crucial meeting in the development of defining the state of Scotland.

Kenneth was keen to preserve Scotland as a united kingdom, and endeavoured to rid the succession of dynastic rivalry by agreeing with the Scottish magnates that the succession should become patrilinear, passing from father to son, rather than alternating between dynasties. This seems to have been only partly accepted, for it would take at least a generation before the dispossessed princes passed away and the process became accepted as the norm. For six years the rivalry continued between Kenneth and Olaf before Olaf was slain in 977. However the rivalry over succession only passed on to the next generation with Olaf's nephew, CONSTANTINE, and Kenneth's great-nephew, GIRIC, eventually conspiring against Kenneth to cause his downfall and murder. He died in rather mysterious circumstances at Finella's Castle near Fettercairn. Nevertheless it was Kenneth's descendants who subsequently regained and retained the Scottish throne.

Little else is recorded of Kenneth's reign, other than that he also got involved in a dynastic dispute between the earl of Orkney, LIOT, and his brother Skuli, whom Kenneth seems to have made earl of Caithness. This was an interesting development because it suggested that the earls of Orkney recognized that Kenneth had authority over all the mainland territory of Scotland, whereas otherwise they owed their allegiance to the king of Norway. This, and the fact that he retained the throne for over twenty years amidst such opposition says much for his strength of character and abilities. He remained friendly with the kings of Strathclyde, whom he could so easily have overthrown in favour of his own son, should he have so wished. This suggests a king who was strong-willed but tolerant, qualities that were passed on to his son, MALCOLM II.

[FC50] **OLAF** Scotland, 971–7.
The son of INDULF and brother of CUILEAN, Olaf established a rival claim to the throne during the earlier years of KENNETH II's reign. The claim seems never to have been recognized formally, though at his death he was recorded as king of the Scots. Even his base of operations is uncertain, though was probably in the Scottish Highlands. He was killed in battle by Kenneth in 977.

[FC51] **CONSTANTINE III** *THE BALD* Scotland, 995–7.
The son of CUILEAN, Constantine was one of the rival claimants to the throne during the reign of KENNETH II, and it is almost certain that he conspired along with GIRIC II to cause Kenneth's death in 995. His nickname suggests Constantine may already have been into his forties or fifties by this time, and although he had married, he had no children. His reign was brief. His former ally, Giric, almost certainly turned against him once his father, KENNETH III, agreed Giric's own right of succession, and the two defeated and killed Constantine in battle at Rathinveramon. He was buried on Iona.

[FC52] **KENNETH III** Scotland, 997–1005.
[FC53] **GIRIC II** Scotland, 997–1005.
Kenneth was the son of DUFF and may already have been in his forties or fifties when he wrested the throne from CONSTANTINE III. It is possible that because of his age Kenneth agreed that his son GIRIC rule jointly with him, though he also recognized his cousin, MALCOLM, as king of Strathclyde and Cumbria, the title usually held for heirs to the throne. So, although Kenneth evidently sought to secure the future kingship for his son, there was already built-in tension. In 1005 both Kenneth and Giric were killed at Monzievaird, near Loch Earn, by Malcolm.

[FC54;FB29] **MALCOLM II** MAC **KENNETH**
Sub-king of Cumbria and Strathclyde, 990–5, 997–1005; king of Scotland, 1005–34.
Born: c954. Died: 25 November 1034, aged 80, at Glamis Castle. Buried: Iona.
Married: c980 (date and spouse's name unknown): 2 or 3 daughters.
Malcolm's father, KENNETH II, was keen to secure a patrilineal right of succession to the Scottish throne to avoid the inter-dynastic squabbles that threatened to weaken the kingdom. He was not especially successful in this, but in 990 he sought to establish his son as his heir by proclaiming him king of Strathclyde and Cumbria. Since MALCOLM MAC DONALD was still king of Strathclyde (unless records that suggest he died in 990 are correct) the kingdom was clearly divided, and Malcolm

mac Kenneth probably ruled Cumbria. When Kenneth was killed in 995, Malcolm was also deposed from Strathclyde, by the rival faction of CONSTANTINE III, but upon his death in 997, Malcolm regained Strathclyde. This was an unhealthy situation, as the new king of the Scots, KENNETH III, was evidently seeking to establish right of succession for his own son GIRIC II, who was made either co-ruler or a sub-king, possibly also in Strathclyde. The two rulers tolerated each other for eight years then, in 1005, Malcolm defeated and slew Kenneth and Giric at the battle of Monzievaird. Malcolm was not only a strong and ambitious ruler, he was a strategist and an opportunist. His long reign allowed him to expand and consolidate his kingdom, though some of his actions, not least the slaying of Kenneth and Giric, sowed seeds of discontent that would result in the killing of his grandson DUNCAN by MACBETH thirty years later. Malcolm first endeavoured to establish his rulership over Bernicia, extending his lands beyond the Tweed. He was severely defeated by Uhtred of Northumbria in the siege of Durham in 1006 and it was twelve years before Malcolm again tested the lands to the south. He did, however, ensure an ally in the kingdom of Strathclyde. This kingdom was traditionally ruled by the heir to the throne. Malcolm had only daughters and his grandson, Duncan, was too young to rule, so Malcolm appointed OWEN as ruler of Strathclyde. Owen was almost certainly older than Malcolm, and as the youngest son of DONALD of Strathclyde had probably never entertained aspirations to kingship, so this elevation made him a strong friend and ally to Malcolm and helped strengthen the lands to the south.

In the meantime Malcolm sought to make an alliance with the Norse earls of Orkney and, in 1008, he married his daughter to SIGURD II. The main reason was to have the Norsemen as allies against the men of Moray, who for the last fifty years had worked against the main Scottish royal line, and Malcolm granted Sigurd lands as far south as Moray. Malcolm seemed to be seeking Sigurd's recognition of Malcolm as his overlord, even though the earls of Orkney were subjects of the kings of Norway. In Malcolm's eyes, though, this gave him authority over Moray, Caithness and Sutherland. The arrangement soon worked in Malcolm's favour for, in 1014, Sigurd was killed at the battle of Clontarf in Ireland and while his sons by an earlier marriage squabbled over the succession, Malcolm proclaimed his young grandson, THORFINN, as earl of Caithness, even though he was only five. The young boy seemed to be much loved by the nobility of Orkney and by the king of Norway, so that he soon obtained claims on parts of Orkney until he became sole earl in 1030. With this support in the north Malcolm believed he had stifled the problems in Moray (even if only temporarily).

In 1018, following the annexation of Lothian two years earlier, Malcolm turned his attention to Bernicia and, with Owen of Strathclyde's help, he defeated Earl Eadulf at Carham on Tweed. Immediately afterward Malcolm bestowed much bounty on the church at Durham and claimed overlordship of southern Bernicia. In that same year he installed his grandson, Duncan, as king of Strathclyde. Malcolm was now in his early sixties, and the first king to rule the territory of Scotland as we know it today. He might have sought to rest upon his achievements. However, he needed to be ever vigilant. The rulers of Moray continued to fight for control and began a series of raids and skirmishes from the north; one of these, in 1027, resulted in the burning of Dunkeld. At the same time, CANUTE had established himself in

England and was intent upon ensuring he had no opposition from the north. In 1031 records suggest that Canute "invaded" Scotland, although there is some doubt as to whether he led an army, or simply made a royal visit. The latter seems more likely because, had Canute succeeded in marching north with an army and defeating Malcolm, he would almost certainly have continued with a campaign to conquer Scotland, of which he was capable. In all likelihood Canute's main aim was to secure a friendly alliance with Malcolm who, now in his mid-seventies, could in any case offer little resistance. However, either now, or soon after, Canute did reclaim Bernicia and Cumbria, with the result that the borders of Scotland as we know them today were finally established.

In his old age Malcolm did what he could to secure the throne for Duncan. In 1032 he endeavoured to slaughter the family of Kenneth III's grand-daughter Gruoch by surprising them in their fortress at Atholl and burning it to the ground. GILLECOMGAIN was killed but Gruoch, his wife, and their son LULACH escaped. A few months later he arranged the murder of Kenneth III's great-grandson Malcolm, who was still only an infant. The next year Malcolm died, probably in his eightieth year. Later historians claimed he was murdered as part of the continuing inter-dynastic struggle, and this is just possible, though unlikely. He was the last male heir of KENNETH MACALPIN. Malcolm had lived long enough for Duncan to inherit the throne, although his future was far from certain.

[FC55;FB31] **DUNCAN (I)** *THE GRACIOUS* Strathclyde, 1018–34; Scotland, 25 November 1034–15 August 1040.
Born: c1001; **Died** *(killed in battle) Pitgaveny, 15 August 1040, aged 39.* **Buried:** *Iona.* **Married:** *c1030, Sybilla, sister (some records say dau.) of Siward, earl of Northumbria: 3 sons and possibly one daughter.*
Duncan was the son of Bethoc, the daughter of MALCOLM II, and Crinan, mórmaer (or earl) of Atholl and abbot of Dunkeld. Although Malcolm had done everything to eliminate all other rival claimants amongst the immediate descendants of KENNETH MACALPIN, he had not quashed the rival Loarn dynasty which ruled Moray. They offered little, if any, allegiance to the kings of Scotland, and certainly had little respect for Duncan. He might have inherited his grandfather's ambition, but he was not his equal as a strategist or commander. Duncan was fortunate in that soon after he inherited the throne, England was in turmoil following the death of CANUTE and an argument over the succession, whilst to the north THORFINN, earl of Orkney, was also facing an internal challenge. Had Duncan struck at those moments he might have succeeded in expanding his kingdom along the lines that Malcolm had planned. However, Duncan left it for some years, and instead found himself facing an attack by Eadulf of Bernicia in 1038, in revenge for the conquest of Durham by Malcolm twenty years earlier. Eadulf was driven back only by the help of Duncan's brother, MALDRED. In 1040 Duncan was ready to fight back although he chose to do it on both fronts and, by this time, Thorfinn of Orkney had regained his authority. Early in 1040 Duncan marched on Durham whilst his nephew, Moddan, led an army north to Caithness. Moddan found himself out-numbered and rapidly retreated whilst Duncan's assault on Durham was nothing short of incompetent and his army suffered heavy losses. Duncan now decided, rather late, to concentrate his forces on one front, and set out to encounter

Thorfinn. He was out-manoeuvred on every front, narrowly escaping with his life in a sea battle, whilst Moddan was killed at Thurso. Duncan retreated into Moray, where any sensible commander would realise he was in unsafe territory. Although the men of Moray had for years battled against the Norsemen, they had no wish to support Duncan. The mórmaer of Moray, MACBETH, allied himself with Thorfinn and slaughtered Duncan's army at Pitgaveny on 15 August 1040. Duncan was killed in the battle. His death was not mourned. The historical Duncan is nothing like the victim portrayed in Shakespeare's *Macbeth*. He was seen as a ruthless and incapable king. His son, MALCOLM (III) was still only an infant and was not considered eligible to inherit the throne. It took the Scottish council only a short while to accept Macbeth as king.

[FC56;FD5] **MACBETH** Moray, 1032–57; Scotland, 15 August 1040–15 August 1057. *Born: c1005; Died (killed in battle): Lumphanen, 15 August 1057, aged 52. Buried: Iona.*
Married: c1033, Gruoch, widow of Gillecomgain, mórmaer of Moray: no children.
The Macbeth of history was rather different from the tragic character portrayed by Shakespeare. He was the son of FINDLAECH, the mórmaer of Moray of the line of Loarn, a collateral branch of the rulers of Dál Riata who now ruled much of what was soon to become Scotland. His mother, Donada, was the daughter of MALCOLM II of Scotland. Not much is known about his youth. His father was murdered when Macbeth was fifteen or so, and the mórmaership was taken by Macbeth's cousins MALCOLM and subsequently GILLECOMGAIN. It was after the latter's murder in 1032 that Macbeth, now twenty-seven, inherited the title. Whilst his predecessors had been hostile to Malcolm II and had actively sought to usurp the throne, Macbeth was less belligerent. Malcolm's successor, DUNCAN, Macbeth's cousin, however, was a far less competent king. He bungled his first attempts at invading Northumbria to the south and Caithness to the north at the same time in 1040, and so concentrated all his forces on the north, against the earl of Orkney, THORFINN. Duncan's forces were outmanoeuvred at every turn. Thorfinn's forces were supplemented by those of Macbeth as Duncan retreated, so that it was Macbeth who encountered Duncan at Pitgaveny in August 1040, where Duncan was killed. Later accounts that Macbeth murdered Duncan are total fabrication. Duncan's eldest son, MALCOLM (III) was only nine and he and his brother were hurried away to the English court for safety. Macbeth was the next in line to the throne and he was elected to the kingship apparently without contest or opposition.

Macbeth ruled strongly and wisely for the next fourteen years without any major mishap. Because of his close relationship with his half-brother Thorfinn, there was no conflict with the Norse of Orkney. If anything, Thorfinn knew he could rely on Macbeth's support when Thorfinn went on a punitive raid as far south as Man and North Wales in 1042. The only challenge to his rule came from his uncle Crinan, the father of Duncan and the mórmaer of Atholl. Crinan probably sought to place his second son, MALDRED, on the throne and in 1045 Crinan, then aged about seventy, staged a rebellion. The two factions met at Dunkeld where Crinan and Maldred were killed. For the next nine years there seems to have been no instability in Macbeth's reign. He was apparently a generous and pious ruler. He is described as a tall man with a ruddy complexion and fair hair. In 1050, he undertook a pilgrimage to Rome where it is recorded that he scattered gifts and money "like seed". This indicates that he must have had a sufficiently secure kingdom at that time, and by all accounts he was much loved by his subjects.

In 1054, however, Macbeth's world crumbled. By then Duncan's son Malcolm was twenty-three and regarded himself as the true heir to the throne of Scotland. He was supported in his efforts to regain the throne by EDWARD THE CONFESSOR, who placed Siward of Northumbria in charge of the invasion. Siward's forces advanced far into Scotland. Perhaps Macbeth sought to play the same tactics as BRUDE MAC BILI had against EGFRITH of Northumbria nearly four centuries earlier. But Siward had also learned not to venture too far into enemy territory without backup and he brought his fleet into the Firth of Tay. The two armies, both of considerable size, met at Dunsinnan on 27 July 1054. This is the battle commemorated in Shakespeare's play where Macbeth had been assured by the witches that he was safe until Birnam Wood came against him. Since the battle took place on an open field (and not with Macbeth hiding in his castle as portrayed by Shakespeare), it is unlikely that Siward's troops camouflaged themselves with greenery, though one cannot discount that such tactics may have been used in part of the battle. What is more likely is that Malcolm's troops, who were essentially the men of Atholl, wore sprigs of rowan in their caps as emblems, or carried branches of rowan as cudgels. It has also been suggested that the battle site was not Dunsinnan, just north of Scone, but a few miles further east at Dundee. It is worth reflecting upon the forces involved in the battle. Although it was essentially a Northumbrian (i.e. English) army versus a Scots, Siward's forces represented the Scottish heir Malcolm. The battle was, therefore, an internal Scottish conflict. Yet most of Siward's army was made up of Scandinavian troops, whilst Macbeth's army included many Norman soldiers. Normans had settled in England during the reign of Edward the Confessor, who had been raised in Normandy and had strong Norman sympathies. However his conflict with Earl Godwin had led him to expel many Normans from England in 1051 and some had taken refuge in Scotland. Although it is not stated that Thorfinn of Orkney assisted Macbeth, it is likely that Macbeth's army included levies from across northern Scotland and thus included soldiers from Caithness and Sutherland who would have been Norse. Thus the battle that decided Macbeth's fate was essentially fought between Scandinavian factions, primarily the old enemies of Danes versus Norse. Although Macbeth was overwhelmingly defeated he was not deposed, and there were sufficient casualties amongst Siward's forces for his army to retire. Malcolm laid claim to the southern kingdom of Strathclyde and used this as his base for further incursions into Scotland. There followed three years of civil war. Malcolm's strength grew and Macbeth was driven back further into his Moray base. However, during one such retreat Macbeth found himself cut off from his main army, and he was ambushed by Malcolm's forces at Lumphanan, west of Aberdeen. Tradition states that he made his last stand in the stone circle known as the Peel Ring where he and his bodyguard were butchered. Support for Macbeth remained strong for it was not Malcolm who was chosen to succeed him but his stepson LULACH.

Macbeth's reputation as a strong, wise and generous king has been overtaken by the image portrayed by Shakespeare. Shakespeare did not invent this, however. He drew his facts from the historical records available to him which had already been distorted mostly by Hector Boece, whose *History of Scotland*, published in 1527, contained many inventions, including the characters of Banquo, the three witches, and the image we have of Lady Macbeth. The real Macbeth was revered and given a royal burial on Iona. Apart from the brief reign of Lulach, Macbeth was the last truly Gaelic ruler of the Scots. With the subsequent succession of Malcolm (III), Scotland shifted toward a more Anglo-Norman outlook.

[FC57;FD6] **LULACH** *FATUUS* (*the FOOL*)

King of Scotland, 15 August 1057–17 March 1058. Crowned: Scone, November (?) 1057.
Born: *c1031;* **Died** *(slain): Essie, 17 March 1058, aged 27.* **Buried:** *Iona.*
Married: *Finnghuala, dau. Sinhill, mórmaer of Angus: 2 children.*
Lulach was the son of GILLECOMGAIN, mórmaer of Moray, and Gruoch, the granddaughter of KENNETH III. After his father's death, Lulach's mother married MACBETH and, after Macbeth's death at the hand of MALCOLM CANMORE, Lulach was elected king. There was evidently strong support in Scotland at this time for the Gaelic household which had descended through the mórmaers or stewards of Moray rather than the more anglicised faction which had been encouraged by MALCOLM II and was now actively promoted by Malcolm Canmore. Malcolm pursued his right to the throne and Lulach's short reign was almost entirely filled with their conflict. Malcolm eventually succeeded, ambushing Lulach at Essie, in Strathbogie, in March 1058. Lulach was subsequently remembered as Lulach the Fool or even the Simple, suggesting that he did not have all of his faculties. This is most unlikely. The later chroniclers must have believed he acted unwisely in his campaign against Malcolm, making foolish decisions that not only lost him his life, but lost Scotland its Gaelic inheritance. After Lulach, Malcolm III closed a door on Scotland's past and looked ahead into the Anglo-Norman world. Lulach's son, MAEL SNECHTA, however remained a rebel leader amongst the men of Moray.

[FC58;FB32] **MALCOLM III** *CANMORE* (*BIGHEAD*)

Sub-king of Cumbria and Strathclyde, 1045–58; king of Scotland, 17 March 1058–13 November 1093. Crowned: Scone Abbey, 25 April 1058.
Born: *c1031.* **Died:** *nr Alnwick, 13 November 1093, aged 62.* **Buried:** *Dunfermline Abbey (later removed to the Escorial, Madrid).*
Married: *(1) c1060, Ingibiorg (d. c1069), widow of Thorfinn, Earl of Orkney: 3 children; (2) c1069, Margaret (d. c1093), dau. Edward Atheling, son of Edmund II of England: at least 8 children.*
Many lists of Scottish kings begin with Malcolm III, even though he was the fifty-eighth in line since FERGUS established the kingdom of Dál Riata in Argyll, and the twenty-second since KENNETH MACALPIN had united the Scots and the Picts. The main reason for Malcolm's apparent status is that under his rule Scotland shifted dramatically away from its Gaelic past and moved toward the Anglo-Norman world of southern Britain. Malcolm had been raised in the Anglo-Norman court of EDWARD THE CONFESSOR. His father, DUNCAN, had been killed in battle against MACBETH in 1040, when Malcolm was eight or nine, and the young boy and his brother were hurriedly smuggled out of Scotland in fear of their lives. Macbeth was eventually killed in August 1057, and his stepson, Lulach, the following March. Five weeks later Malcolm was crowned as king of Scotland. His support was not total,

20. Scotland (3) – **Kings of the Scots: House of Dunkeld**

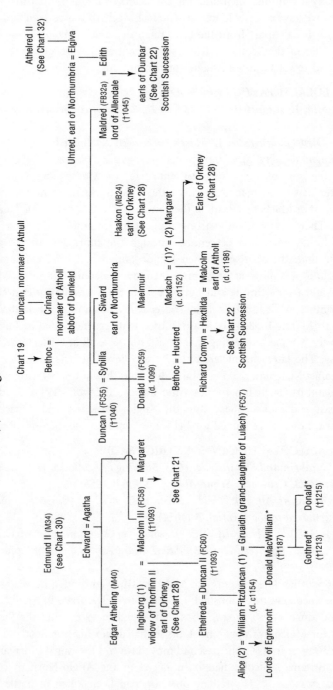

* All three killed in uprisings to regain the throne.

21. Scotland (4) – Kings of the Scots: Malcolm III to Margaret

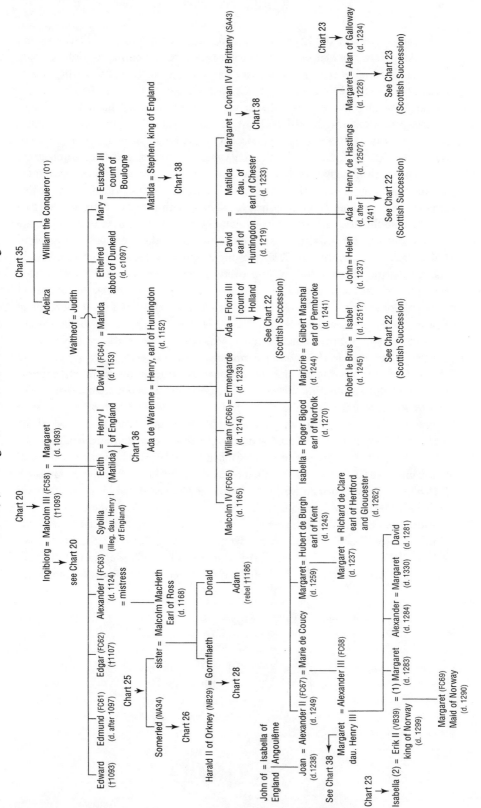

with many, especially the Highlanders, preferring their old ways and customs and not seeking to follow Malcolm. Nevertheless they accepted him as overlord because of his sheer physical power and menace. He was a swaggering bully who rapidly earned the nickname of *Canmore*, or Bighead.

Malcolm began his reign by establishing alliances. Amongst his father's former enemies was THORFINN, the earl of Orkney. It is not clear when Thorfinn died, but it is evident that he had not helped Macbeth in his fight for the monarchy, not because he did not support Macbeth (they were half brothers and allies) but because he was probably already very ill. He may have died as early as 1057 and was almost certainly dead by 1060. Malcolm married Thorfinn's widow, Ingibiorg, probably around the year 1060, and established an alliance with her sons PAUL and ERLEND who became the new earls of Orkney. Ingibiorg must by then have been in her late thirties, but she bore Malcolm three children before she died, probably around 1069. Malcolm's alliance with Orkney brought him into closer contact with Harald Haadraada, the king of Norway, and overlord of Orkney and the Western Isles. Malcolm was thus seen as an ally of Norway when, in 1066, Tostig, the brother of HAROLD Godwinson of Wessex, gained Haadraada's support for an invasion of England. The invasion force landed first at Orkney and sailed down the eastern coast of Scotland to the Humber estuary. Malcolm's motives are uncertain in this campaign. He was clearly a Saxon sympathiser, but evidently not a supporter of Harold Godwinson, whom he may have seen as a usurper in the south. His support for Tostig, who was nothing short of a rebellious thug, does not seem a wise choice and Malcolm would have gained little from a Norse victory beyond the possible annexation of Northumbria. He was more likely to have become a vassal of the Norwegian king. However, Harald and Tostig were killed at Stamford Bridge, and a few weeks later Harold Godwinson was killed at Senlac Hill by WILLIAM, duke of Normandy. At Christmas 1066 William was crowned king of England. Although Malcolm knew the Norman world – Edward the Confessor had been pro-Norman and there were many Normans at his court where Malcolm grew up as well as Norman soldiers in Malcolm's army – he was unsure what an alliance with the Normans would achieve. His initial sympathies were with the Saxons. EDGAR Atheling, the Saxon heir, joined in the unsuccessful rebellion against William in 1068, and subsequently fled to Malcolm's court to seek refuge. He was accompanied

by his sister Margaret whom Malcolm married the following year. This further consolidated the Scottish-Saxon alliance, but alienated Malcolm all the more from his Highland subjects, and made an enemy of William the Conqueror. It should be remembered, however, that in 1069 William's hold on England was far from secure and many believed that he would eventually be overthrown. Edgar was almost certainly convinced he would some day regain the throne of England, and Malcolm's move was part of his framework of alliances with neighbouring powers. Malcolm supported Edgar's unsuccessful attempt to regain England in 1069 along with Swein of Denmark. The next two to three years saw Malcolm supporting a series of raids throughout northern England, coming as far south as Cleveland. William was enraged, and in 1072 he invaded Scotland and sought the submission of Malcolm at Abernathy. The terms of the treaty meant that Malcolm could no longer harbour any of William's enemies, and Edgar Atheling again became an exile. William also forced Malcolm to recognize him as his overlord, and took his son DUNCAN as hostage. Later English kings would regard the Treaty of Abernathy as the date of their conquest of Scotland, though it is unlikely it was viewed as that at that time. Certainly it did not stop Malcolm raiding England in 1079, though this proved equally fruitless. William sent his son Robert to negotiate with Malcolm. This achieved little, though Robert decided to add to the fortifications of the north and built the New Castle at the estuary of the Tyne. William regarded Malcolm as an irritant at this time and certainly did not view him as a ruler of equal status. Malcolm, on the other hand, living up to his nickname, believed he was just as powerful.

Under the influence of his wife Margaret, to whom he was devoted, Malcolm changed steadily from the coarse ruffian of his youth to a mature individual who had strong respect for his wife's religious and cultural beliefs and interests. Margaret had been well educated in Hungary and England and was an avid Christian. It was under her direction that the abbey at Dunfermline was commenced in 1072, to equal the one Edward the Confessor had completed at Westminster just seven years earlier. Margaret also restored the monastery on Iona, and did much to bring the Celtic church in line with the Roman. Records suggest that from 1072 the archbishopric of York was given authority over the church of Scotland. Malcolm, who was not especially religious himself, seemed content to allow Margaret to undertake these reforms, surprisingly ignorant of their long-term affect. It is probably another example of his belief in his authority as absolute, but it is also a reminder that Malcolm truly loved Margaret and that their marriage was strong and happy.

Malcolm had evidently not forsaken his designs upon England. After the death of William I in 1087, Duncan was released and Malcolm again began planning an expansion of his territories. He was soon joined by Edgar Atheling, who recognized the opportunity, and in 1090 Malcolm invaded Northumbria. He was defeated by WILLIAM RUFUS and the terms of the Treaty of Abernathy were re-invoked. William continued to defend the north and in 1092 invaded Cumbria and built a fort at Carlisle. Malcolm and his son Edward came to meet William but were rebuffed. As they were returning north they were ambushed by Robert Mowbray, earl of Northumberland, near Alnwick and both Malcolm and Edward were killed. When Margaret, who was already extremely ill, heard the news four days later she pined away. It is an irony that Malcolm had replaced the old rule of tanistry by that of primogeniture, only to have his eldest son and heir die with him. The Scottish magnates had no idea what to do in such circumstances and civil unrest broke out. Five of his nine sons would eventually succeed him as king, though his immediate successor was his brother DONALD (III).

Malcolm had been temporarily buried near Tynemouth. Shortly afterward he and his wife were buried at the new Dunfermline Abbey. Following a papal inquiry in 1250 into the life and possible miracles of Margaret, she was canonized. During the Reformation their bodies were reburied at a specially built tomb in the Escorial, Madrid. In 1673 Margaret was named as one of the patron saints of Scotland.

Malcolm's reign was a clear transition from the Gaelic tradition to the acceptance of new values and beliefs. Although he was not supported in this by many of his countrymen he established a momentum that could not be stopped.

[FC59] **DONALD III** *BANE* (*THE WHITE*) sometimes called *DONALBAIN* Scotland 13 November 1093–May 1094 (deposed); restored 12 November 1094– October 1097.
Born: *c1033*. **Died**: *Rescobie, 1099, aged 66*. **Buried**: *Dunkeld Abbey, later removed to Iona.*
Married: *(name and date unknown): 1 daughter.*
Donald was the younger brother of MALCOLM III and for most of his life probably had no designs on the Scottish throne. He was almost certainly made mórmaer of Gowrie around the year 1060 but there is no record that he played any part in Malcolm's affairs. It is possible that the two brothers were estranged and that Donald did not support Malcolm's and Margaret's reforms. He lived in exile in Ireland and the Western Isles and thereby endeared himself to the pro-Gaelic party in Scotland. After the death of Malcolm and his heir Edward, it was Donald who was raised to the throne during the days of confusion over the succession. Donald was sixty, and although his hair had probably turned white (hence his nickname) he was evidently strong and hale of body. Donald and his supporters promptly expelled the Norman and Saxon refugees in Scotland. As a consequence Malcolm's eldest son, DUNCAN, who had hitherto also shown no interest in the kingship, but who had lived as a hostage at the courts of WILLIAM I and II of England for many years, came into the picture. He was supported by William II and his army defeated Donald and drove him out of Scotland. Duncan held the throne for only seven months before being defeated by Donald at the battle of Monthecin in November 1094, after which Donald was restored to the throne. However, Donald now divided the kingdom between himself and his nephew EDMUND, with Donald's rule amongst the heart of his supporters in the Highlands north of the Forth/Clyde valley. This arrangement survived for less than three years as another of Malcolm's sons, EDGAR, received greater support from William II and deposed Donald and Edmund in October 1097. Donald was blinded and imprisoned at Rescobie in Forfarshire, where he died some eighteen months later. He was buried at Dunkeld Abbey but later his remains were removed to Iona by his adherents. He was the last Scottish king to be buried there, and thus marks the end of the old tradition of Gaelic kings.

[FC60] **DUNCAN II** Scotland, May–12 November 1094.
Born: c1060. *Died* (*in battle*): 12 November 1094 at Monthecin, aged 33 or 34.
Buried: Dunfermline Abbey.
Married: c1090, Ethelreda, dau. Gospatric, Earl of Northumbria: 1 son.

Duncan was the eldest son of MALCOLM III and his first wife Ingibiorg, and was thus the half-brother of the earls of Orkney, PAUL and ERLEND Thorfinnson. He may at some stage have been regarded as the heir to the throne, especially as he was taken as hostage by WILLIAM I, during one of Malcolm's many incursions into Norman territory in 1072. This suggests that Malcolm must have later disinherited Duncan in favour of his children by his second wife, Margaret, because he had no qualms in invading England in 1079 regardless of Duncan's welfare. Duncan was not released from the English courts until after the death of William I in 1087, having spent at least fifteen years immersed in Norman life. He seems to have been on good terms with William's son (later WILLIAM II) who was of a similar age. Duncan stayed in England after his release, marrying the daughter of the earl of Northumbria, and showed little interest in the Scottish throne. However, after DONALD BANE usurped the throne following Malcolm's death, there was a period of hostility against the Norman and Saxon exiles who had sought refuge in Scotland. William Rufus wanted an ally on the Scottish throne and he encouraged Duncan to claim his birthright. Equipped with an army of Norman knights, Duncan invaded Scotland, defeated Donald and drove him into exile. Duncan, however, was not welcomed by the Scots who saw in him a Norman puppet. They forced him to dismiss the Anglo-Norman retainers upon whom he relied. Thus weakened he became easy prey to Donald Bane's resurgence, and Duncan was killed in battle at Monthecin (or Mondynes) south of Stonehaven in November, after a rule of less than seven months. It is somewhat tragic that neither Duncan nor Donald, who were nephew and uncle, had shown any interest in the Scottish throne until forced into action by their respective supporters. They were little more than pawns in the battle between Gaelic tradition and the encroaching power of the Normans.

[FC61] **EDMUND** southern Scotland, 12 November 1094–October 1097.

Edmund was the second son of Malcolm and his English wife Margaret, hence his Saxon name. He had probably never considered becoming king, since he had an elder brother and two elder half-brothers. It seems, though, that he had been created prince of Cumbria in his youth. This may have given him an air of superiority. Since he cannot have been born much before 1071, the title may not have been bestowed until his coming of age in 1086 or so. All three of Edmund's elder brothers had died by 1094, and with the death of the third, DUNCAN II, in November, Edmund was promoted to the kingship as part of an arrangement with his uncle DONALD III. Edmund was seen as acceptable by the Normans and was made king of Scotland south of the Clyde, whilst Donald ruled the Highlands. This arrangement was short-lived. Edmund incurred the wrath of William Rufus of England (WILLIAM II) by encouraging the rebellion of the earl of Northumberland and, in 1095, William nominated Edmund's brother, EDGAR, as king. With William's support, Edgar raised an army and defeated and deposed both Donald and Edmund. Whilst Donald was imprisoned, Edmund was despatched to Montacute Abbey in Somerset, where he became a monk. There is no record of his death, but he could have lived well into his sixties, dying sometime in the 1130s. He was probably buried at Montacute Abbey.

[FC62] **EDGAR** Scotland, October 1097–8 January 1107.
Edgar was the son of MALCOLM III and his second wife, Margaret, the sister of EDGAR THE ATHELING. In 1095 WILLIAM II declared Edgar king of Scotland, and it is likely that Edgar claimed lands in Lothian and Bernicia. No doubt skirmishes continued over the next couple of years, but in October 1097 Edgar succeeded in deposing both Donald and Edmund.

It is surprising that Edgar did not face a revolt from the Highlands, as he showed them little respect. Soon after his accession Magnus III of Norway led a major expedition to his territories in northern Britain. He deposed the earls of Orkney, PAUL and ERLEND, who were Edgar's step-brothers, and set off on a wave of conquest around the Scottish coast. Edgar quite happily gave Magnus sovereignty over the Hebrides. These islands were heavily populated by Norse or Gallo-Norse and seemed far removed from Edgar's world. Part of this arrangement, however, meant that the holy island of Iona came under Norwegian rule, which must have alienated many Scots.

Although Edgar was sensible enough not to encourage a wave of Norman settlement in Scotland, he increased his ties with England. He was already beholden to William II for gaining the throne, and was present at the coronation of HENRY I in August 1100. Three months later Henry married Edgar's sister Edith. This had been a move by Henry to tie himself closer to the Saxon kings, as Edith was the great-granddaughter of EDMUND II, but it also tightened the link with the Scottish king. Edgar preferred to stay in close contact with his Saxon and Norman colleagues. He remained in Lothian, living mostly in Edinburgh, and it does not appear that he ventured far beyond. He played the part of a Norman vassal to the letter and it is of little surprise that by this time the Norman kings of England began to regard Scotland, certainly the border territory, as their domain.

Edgar reigned for a little over nine years. He was only in his mid-thirties when he died early in 1107. He never married and was succeeded by his brother ALEXANDER.

[FC63] **ALEXANDER (I)** *THE FIERCE* Scotland, 8 January 1107–23(?) April 1124. A younger son of MALCOLM III and his English queen Margaret, he succeeded his brother EDGAR. It is possible that Alexander already ruled parts of Scotland as sub-king to Edgar who seemed to have little interest in Scotland beyond Lothian, and when Alexander succeeded to the throne it was intended that he share the kingdom with his brother DAVID. Alexander chose not to, and David threatened to invade the kingdom, but was never able to raise a sufficiently large army. It was not until 1113 that Alexander granted David territory in Strathclyde and the Borders. Upon his accession, Alexander married Sybilla, the fifteen year old illegitimate daughter of HENRY I. Henry was already Alexander's brother-in-law, as Henry had married Alexander's sister Edith. During the first phase of his reign Alexander was clearly Henry's vassal: he even accompanied Henry in his campaign into Wales against GRUFFYDD AP CYNAN in 1114. However, by the second half of his reign, Alexander had shifted back toward the heart of old Scotland, or Alba, and had taken up residence at Scone. It may be now that he earned his nickname of "the Fierce", apparently after the ferocious way he quelled an uprising by the men of Moray. It may have been through such an indomitable strength of character that Alexander began to win over the Highland Scots, despite considerable opposition. Alexander began a programme of castle construction, including the one at Stirling. His court became one of splendour – there is mention of Arab stallions and Turkish men-at-arms. Alexander also continued his mother's reforms in anglicising the Scottish church, and was the first to introduce coinage into Scotland. His reforms saw the introduction of the first sheriffs in Scotland as controller's of the king's peace. Thus, by the end of Alexander's reign, there had been a measurable shift toward uniting the older Scottish culture with the new Anglo-Norman world. Alexander had achieved this through his own strength and willpower, leaving a steady base for his brother David. Alexander died at Stirling Castle and was buried in Dunfermline Abbey.

[FC64] **DAVID (I)** *THE SAINT* Scotland, 23(?) April 1124–24 May 1153.
Titles: king of Scotland, earl of Huntingdon and Northampton (from 1113) and prince of Cumbria (1113–1124).
Born: c1084. Died: Carlisle, 24 May 1153, aged about 69. Buried: Dunfermline Abbey.
Married: 1113, Matilda (c1072–c1130), dau. Waltheof, earl of Northumberland, and widow of Simon de St Liz, earl of Northampton and Huntingdon: 4 children.
David was the youngest son of MALCOLM III and his English wife Margaret. He was about forty when he came to the throne, mature in his character, his outlook and his ability to govern. He had spent much of his youth, since the year 1093, at the court of HENRY I of England, who was his brother-in-law. Since his infancy he had been raised by Margaret with a respect for learning and the church, and it seems he had a tremendous respect for fair play, a trait let down only in his old age when he ultimately failed to uphold his promise of support for MATILDA. In 1107 David's elder brother ALEXANDER inherited the Scottish throne. Apparently their elder brother EDGAR had entreated that Scotland be divided between them, with David ruling the Lowlands south of the Clyde. Alexander did not honour this, and though David threatened to lead an army against him, it came to nothing. It was not until

From a
12th-century chapter

1113, when David married Matilda, and inherited vast lands in Northumberland, Northampton and Huntingdon, that Alexander relented and allowed David to become sub-king of the Lowlands. Since David also became earl of Huntingdon he was both a Norman baron and a Scottish king, which was immensely important in understanding the power that David was able to wield and the respect he had to be accorded by his peers.

When David became king in 1124 he continued the reforms started by his mother and brothers, but it was under David that it all came into shape. Chief of these reforms was the feudalisation of lowland Scotland. Tracts of land were given to Anglo-Norman barons in exchange for their loyalty and service. Amongst them were Robert de Brus, the ancestor of ROBERT BRUCE, who was given the lordship of Annandale, and Walter Fitzalan, who became High Steward of Scotland and thus the ancestor of the Stewart dynasty. This process was described by the disgruntled Highlanders as "invasion by invitation", and led to at least two revolts during David's reign (by ANGUS, earl of Moray, the grandson of LULACH, in 1130 who was killed at the battle of Strathcarro; and by Wimund, bishop of the Isles in 1140) and eventually the declaration of independence by SOMERLED of Argyll after David's death. Nevertheless, David's gradual reform brought a cohesiveness to Scotland that it had previously never enjoyed, particularly in the strength of the church and the world of learning. He founded the bishoprics of Aberdeen, Brechin, Caithness, Dunblane and Ross as well as the monasteries at Holyrood, Melrose, Kinloss, Newbattle and Dundrennan. He also forged strong links with Rome. Even during his life he had come to be regarded as a saintly king by his people, the epithet Saint David remained after his death, even though he was never formally canonized. It was David who really forged Scotland as a prosperous kingdom, introducing a strong coinage, and developing towns like Berwick, Edinburgh, Jedburgh, Stirling and Perth as major trading centres from which the king drew revenues. David also redrew the Scottish administrative map, creating the counties which remained until the reorganization of 1975. Justice was dispensed by a system of justiciars. In all these things David created the modern Scotland.

In military matters he was less strong and only partly successful. In 1127 he agreed, along with other English barons, to recognize Henry I's daughter, MATILDA, as the next ruler of England. He used this as an excuse in 1135, on the death of Henry and the succession of STEPHEN, to invade northern England, laying claim to Northumberland and Cumberland initially in the name of Matilda. The next three years saw considerable bloodshed in Northumberland where David's soldiers committed awful atrocities. Eventually David was defeated by the northern barons under Thurstan, archbishop of York, at Cowton Moor, near Northallerton, on 22 August 1138 at the battle of the Standard. David continued to press his claims in the north and Stephen, unable to fight his war on two fronts, eventually reached an agreement whereby David was granted the earldom of Northumberland provided he swore fealty to Stephen. The earldom was bestowed upon David's son, Henry, who was the king designate.

David switched sides again to support Matilda when she gained the upper hand in February 1141 and he ventured as far south as London for her coronation. However, he was expelled from London in September by Stephen's troops and only narrowly escaped back to Durham without being captured. Thereafter he remained on the sidelines, a nominal supporter of the Empress, but not engaging in further conflict. In 1149 he gained a promise from Matilda's son HENRY (II) that, should he become king, he would grant David the lands of Northumberland and Cumbria. When David died at Carlisle in May 1153 he almost certainly regarded himself as lord of all the lands from Caithness in the north to Cumbria and Northumberland in the south. Though these southern lands were never formally part of the kingdom of Scotland, David doubtless believed they would be.

Neither of David's own sons came to the throne. His firstborn, Malcolm, had been murdered in infancy, probably about 1114. Henry, who was groomed as the next king, died in 1152, aged thirty-eight. Henry's young son, MALCOLM, was promptly declared the king designate, though he was only twelve.

[FC65] MALCOLM IV *THE MAIDEN*
King of Scotland, 24 May 1153–9 December 1165. Crowned: Scone Abbey, June (?) 1153.
Born: 20 March 1141. **Died:** *Jedburgh Castle, 9 December 1165, aged 24.* **Buried:** *Dunfermline Abbey.*

Malcolm was the grandson of DAVID (I). He was catapulted into the limelight as king designate when his father, Henry, earl of Northumberland, died on 12 June 1152. Malcolm, then only eleven, was promptly taken on a tour of Scotland to witness, appreciate and above all understand the nature and problems of his realm. It seems that for all his youth, Malcolm inherited much of the wisdom and sense of fair play of his grandfather and was not overly influenced by other external factors. He kept his head in moments of crisis and ensured he received sound advice before making decisions. Nevertheless the mere fact of his age made him less able to deal with HENRY II of England. Although Henry had promised Malcolm's grandfather that he would bequeath Scotland the territories of Northumberland and Cumbria when he became king (which he did in 1154), he soon reneged upon this. In 1157 Henry met Malcolm at Chester and deprived him of these northern territories in exchange for the earldom of Huntingdon, which had been his grandfather's but had been lost in 1141. In 1159 both Malcolm and his brother WILLIAM were forced to accompany Henry on a mission to Aquitaine where Henry needed to punish the count of Toulouse. The Scots perceived Malcolm operating as the vassal of Henry, although Malcolm was only delivering his feudal obligations for the honour of Huntingdon. Nevertheless this led to a series of rebellions in Scotland amongst the Highlanders who resented not only the continued anglicisation of Scotland but the blatant subordination of Scotland to the English king. The first rebellion was in 1160 by Fergus of Galloway. Malcolm promptly put down this rebellion with the support of his Anglo-Norman barons, though it took two more expeditions before Fergus was eventually quashed. A further show of force in 1164 by SOMERLED of the Isles was equally effectively dealt with. Malcolm, for all his youth, proved himself stronger than many suspected.

Nevertheless Malcolm did not project the image of a powerful monarch. Slim, fair-haired and a declared celibate – for which he earned his nickname of "the Maiden" – Malcolm was devoted to the church, to which he made many endowments. He never married, despite earnest efforts by his mother to interest him in women, although it was rumoured he fathered an illegitimate child who died in infancy. When Malcolm died after a short illness at the age of twenty-three, he was succeeded by his brother William. Malcolm had had little chance of proving himself and we can only conjecture how his reign might have developed, had he lived. His dedication to the church might, in any case, have led to his abdication. His brother was to prove the much stronger king.

[FC66] WILLIAM the LYON
King of Scotland, 9 December 1165–4 December 1214. Crowned: Scone Abbey, 24 December 1165.
Titles: king of Scotland; earl of Northumberland (1152–1157).
Born: c1143. Died: Stirling, 4 December 1214, aged 71. Buried: Arbroath Abbey.
Married: 5 September 1186 at Woodstock Palace, Oxford, Ermengarde (d. 1234), dau. Richard of Beaumont-le-Maine: 4 children. William also had at least 9 illegitimate children.

William succeeded his brother MALCOLM IV at the age of twenty-two. He had been the earl of Northumberland since the death of his father, Henry, in 1152, but the earldom was lost in 1157 as part of Malcolm's dealings with the English king HENRY II. William's ambition to regain Northumberland became an obsession during his reign and strongly dictated the subsequent events – after an uneasy peace for the first eight years of his reign, it led him to join in the revolt of Henry II's sons in 1173. William had little command over his army and was captured in 1174 and taken in chains to Falaise in Normandy. There William was forced to pay homage to Henry, acknowledging him as his overlord. He thereby became the vassal of Henry, the terms of the treaty confirming that the Scottish barons also owed their allegiance to Henry. With the Treaty of Falaise Scotland theoretically passed into English hands. The Scots of Galloway immediately rebelled, led by Gilbert, the son of Fergus of Galloway. William, who had now returned to Scotland, was able to crush the rebellion with Norman support. He thereafter fortified Galloway with a series of burghs and castles, including those at Ayr and Dumfries, and thereafter Galloway was loyal to him. William now endeavoured to make northern Scotland subservient to him. Although he was always nominally their king, the Highlanders had remained effectively independent. In 1179, William advanced into the Highlands, establishing castles at Redcastle and Dunskeath. He was soon confronted by the opposition of Donald MacWilliam, who rebelled in 1181. This Donald was a legitimate claimant to the Scottish throne. On his father's side he was the grandson of DUNCAN II whilst, through his mother, he was a great-grandson of LULACH. Donald believed himself the king of the Highlands, and allied himself with HARALD II of Orkney in opposition to William. Donald's forces gained the upper hand for much of the next five years, taking control of Ross. It was more by chance than design that Roland of Galloway cornered Donald at Mangarnia Moor, near Inverness, on 31 July 1187 and killed him in battle. William founded burghs at Elgin and Inverness to further contain the north, but it was not until 1197 that Harald of Orkney gave William the opportunity to invade Caithness and regain the northern territories. Thorfinn, Harald's son, was taken hostage. Harald's stubbornness meant he refused to yield to William, and a further invasion of Caithness in 1202 caused William to react strongly. He blinded and castrated Thorfinn (from which wounds he died) and brought a mighty army into Caithness, against which

Harald was unable to raise anything its equal. Thereafter Harald submitted to William, recognizing him as his overlord in Caithness.

By this period William was in a strong position. In 1189 the new English king, RICHARD, desperate to finance his crusade, sold all rights in Scotland back to William for 10,000 merks (or about £6,700). This was known as the Quit-claim of Canterbury. It meant that by 1202 William was undisputed king and overlord of all mainland Scotland. One other turn of fortune for William had meant that in 1192 the Pope decreed that the Scottish church was answerable directly to him, and not subordinate to Canterbury or York, which further elevated William's status. William succeeded in maintaining a tense though cordial relationship with Richard's successor JOHN for all the latter remained the senior king. William held tightly to his control of Scotland, without being able to expand it into England. For some reason William chose not to marry until he was forty-three, and it was nearly twelve years before his first son, the future ALEXANDER II, was born. William's brother David had also married late, and these many years without a clear heir had only added to the unease in the north and encouraged claimants to the throne. One final rebellion in Scotland, in 1211, by Godfrey, the son of Donald MacWilliam, was easily quelled, and Godfrey was executed in 1213.

William's reign, one of the longest in Scotland by an adult king, was ultimately successful, for all its darker periods. Although he never extended his kingdom, he regained all that he lost and was a stronger king by the end of his reign. His soubriquet of "the Lyon" was added later. He was never known by that during his lifetime, and it is not believed to relate to his character, even though he was tenacious and strong in dealing with his subjects. It probably came from the symbol of the lion he used on his seal.

[FC67] ALEXANDER II *THE PEACEFUL*
King of Scotland, 4 December 1214–6 July 1249. Crowned: Scone Abbey, 6 December 1214.
Born: Haddington, East Lothian, 24 August 1198. Died: Isle of Kerrera, Oban, 6 July 1249, aged 50. Buried: Melrose Abbey.
Married: (1) 18 June 1221 at York, Joan (1210–38), dau. King John of England: no children; (2) 15 May 1239 at Roxburgh, Marie, dau. Enguerrand III de Coucy: 1 child. Alexander also had one illegitimate daughter.

Despite his nickname, earned more through his role as a codifier of laws than as a peace-keeper, Alexander ruled Scotland with an iron hand and maintained a guarded peace with England. Alexander faced the inevitable uprisings amongst the Highlanders, the first led by Donald, son of Donald MacWilliam who had rebelled during the reign of Alexander's father WILLIAM. The rebellion was soon quashed and Donald was killed in June 1215, his severed head put on display outside Alexander's court. Although there were further uprisings, they came to nothing, and the continued fortification of Scotland meant that Alexander had a reasonably firm control over the north, and over the lords of Galloway, who also retained pretensions of independence.

Although Alexander accepted the authority of the English king JOHN, he did not respect him, and readily joined the English barons in their uprising against him. John led an army against Alexander, plundering several towns along the Scottish border, but with little effect. Alexander was one of the signatories to the Magna Carta at Runnymede in 1215. His relationship with HENRY III was stronger, though cautious. Alexander married Henry's sister Joan, though she was barely eleven, a political marriage that bore no fruit. Although Henry claimed a sovereign authority over Scotland this was never accepted by Alexander and there were several diplomatic exchanges throughout his reign, usually involving money or proposed marriages. Eventually terms were reached in 1237 when Alexander gave up his claim on Northumberland.

Alexander's first wife died in March 1238. Alexander was now forty, and the marriage had been childless. He married again, but it was not until 1241 that a son (ALEXANDER III) was born. These years without an heir, especially after the death of Alexander's cousin, John, in 1237, had seen the rise to prominence of Robert le Brus, lord of Annandale. He was the husband of Alexander's cousin Isabella, the eldest surviving child of William the Lion's brother David. In 1238 it was agreed that in the absence of any direct heir from Alexander, Isabella's son, Robert le Brus, would become king. This rise to power of a Norman lord fuelled further discontent amongst the Highlanders. The most resistance came from the lords of Argyll, who still called themselves kings of the Isles, and it was while preparing for battle against EWEN of the Isles in 1249 that Alexander caught a fever and died. He was succeeded by his infant son.

[FC68] ALEXANDER III *THE GLORIOUS*
King of Scotland 8 July 1249–19 March 1286. Crowned: Scone Abbey, 13 July 1249.
Born: Roxburgh, 4 September 1241. Died: 19 March 1286, aged 44. Buried: Dunfermline Abbey.
Married: (1) 26 December 1251 at York, Margaret (1240–75), dau. Henry III of England: 3 children; (2) 1 November 1285 at Jedburgh, Yolande (d.1323) dau. Robert, Count of Dreux: no children.

Alexander was seven when he succeeded his father, and only ten when he was married to the daughter of HENRY III of England, but he went on to become one of Scotland's strongest kings, hence his nickname of "the Glorious". Even in his youth he was not overwhelmed by matters of state and refused to submit to Henry III as his overlord, except for his lands in England. Henry had a rather paternal feeling for Alexander and relationships were cordial and strong. It was through the good offices of Henry III that the dispute with EWEN, lord of the Isles, was resolved amicably in 1255, whenafter Ewen became a loyal supporter of the Scottish king. Ewen's cousin, DUGALD, remained obdurate, however, and encouraged the Norwegian king Haakon to enforce his claim upon the Hebrides. When Alexander assumed full control of government in 1261, he entered negotiations with Haakon in an attempt to buy sovereignty over the Islands. Haakon, probably against his better judgement, was talked into bringing an invasion force to Scotland in 1263 to claim the whole of the Hebrides and Man. His force was unsuccessful. There is a legend that one of the Norse, seeking to land quietly and catch the Scots by surprise, trod on a thistle and let out a cry, thereby warning the Scots. Thereafter the thistle became the emblem of the Scots. Haakon, now an old man, caught a fever and died. Negotiations continued with his successor, Magnus VI, and under the Treaty of Perth in 1266, Alexander acquired the whole of the Western Isles for four thousand merks (about

£2,700). Alexander now ruled a Scotland whose boundaries are the same as today's, except for the exclusion of Orkney and Shetland.

Alexander's reign was peaceful and prosperous, but personal disaster beset his final days. Alexander's eldest son and heir, also called Alexander, died in January 1284 at the age of twenty. Although married he had no children. Alexander's second son, David, had died a few years earlier, aged only eight. His daughter, Margaret, died in childbirth in April 1283, though her daughter, MARGARET, survived. Alexander rapidly married a new wife, Yolande of Dreux, in November 1285. One night, a little over four months later, whilst Alexander was returning to his wife at Dunfermline Palace after a routine council meeting in Edinburgh, his horse stumbled over a cliff near Kinghorn in Fife, and Alexander was killed. He was only forty-four. His strong realm was plunged into a period of darkness that would lead to war.

[FC69] **MARGARET, *MAID OF NORWAY*** queen of Scotland, 19 March 1286–26 September 1290.
Margaret was the eldest surviving child of Margaret, the daughter of ALEXANDER III, who had married Erik II, king of Norway in 1281. The infant Margaret was born in April 1283, so was less than three years old when her grandfather died in an accident. The child was then living at Bergen in Norway. The Scottish royal line was in crisis. The rule of primogeniture, which had been introduced by MALCOLM III, was still too new and untested by the Scots to know how it worked in circumstances like these. They turned to the English king, EDWARD I, for help. Edward decreed that Margaret was the rightful queen and that she would be married to his son, Edward. Although he maintained that Scotland would retain its independence, he was ensuring that the clerks inserted minor clauses that allowed him loopholes. It was one such that caused him to take possession of Man in the summer of 1290. In September 1290, Margaret sailed to Scotland, but the rough crossing proved too much for her weak constitution and she died on board ship in a storm off Orkney. There followed the first Interregnum, during which period a court under the direction of Edward I, decided the succession. It was to fall to JOHN Balliol.

[FC70] **JOHN [BALLIOL] *TOOM TABARD*, or *EMPTYCOAT***
King of Scotland, 17 November 1292–11 July 1296. Crowned: 30 November 1292.
Born: c1250. Died: 1313 in Normandy. Buried: St Waast, Normandy.
Married: before February 1281, Isabella, dau. John de Warenne, earl of Surrey: 3 (or 4?) children.
After the death of the infant queen MARGARET in September 1290, the Scots looked to EDWARD I of England to proclaim on the succession. It was a sign of the strength of the rule of law in Scotland which had been instilled over the last century and a half since the time of king DAVID, that the succession was decided by a foreign court, and not by strength of arms. The two main claimants to the throne came from the houses of Bruce and Balliol, both descendants of David through the female line. There were other contenders, but most were just stating a claim for future reference. Although Robert le Brus, the son of ALEXANDER II's cousin, had been named heir prior to the birth of ALEXANDER III, his right to the throne was not upheld by Edward's court. After two years of deliberation, consultation and procrastination, the court pronounced in favour of John Balliol. His mother, Devorguilla, was the daughter of Margaret, another cousin of Alexander II, and sister to Robert le Brus's

22. Scotland (5) – The Scottish Succession: 1290–1292

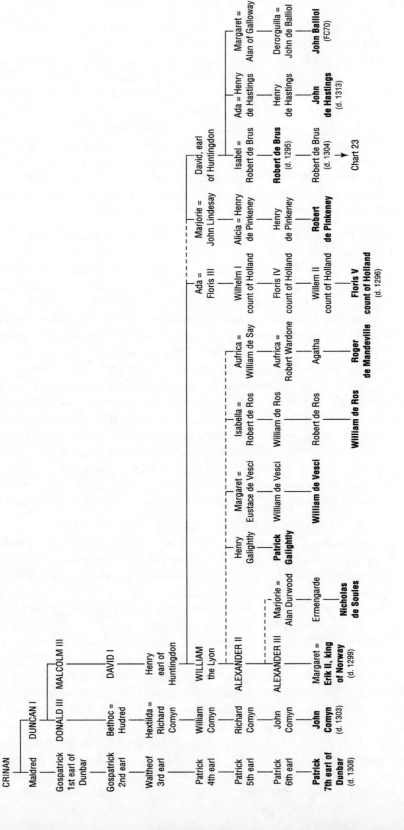

23. Scotland (6) – Scottish Succession: Galloway, Comyn, Balliol and Bruce

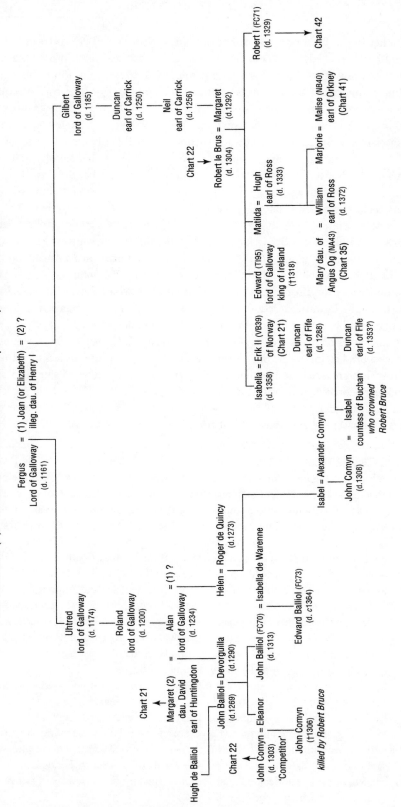

mother Isabel. John was crowned at the end of November 1292 and a month later paid homage at Edward's court at Newcastle. Edward tied John into such a formal state of fealty that Scotland was all but ruled by Edward. John found his position almost impossible. Edward declared that complaints against John by the Scots had to be heard in English courts. John objected, only to have three of his castles confiscated. He also faced increasing unrest from the other claimants to the throne, especially the Bruces, whilst Edward encouraged Erik II of Norway to reclaim the Hebrides because of failure to maintain payment of an annual fee of one hundred merks. The last straw came in 1295 when Edward insisted that the Scots help fund Edward's campaign against Philippe IV of France and that John join him in military service. John rebelled and joined forces with Philip. He brought together his army at Selkirk in March 1296. It was no match for Edward's superior forces. Edward sacked and plundered Berwick, massacring its inhabitants, whilst the forces of the earl of Surrey (his father-in-law) defeated John at Dunbar on 27 April. Soon after Edinburgh castle fell and John surrendered on 11 July 1296. John was stripped of his authority and imprisoned in the Tower of London, whilst Edward marched north in triumph. Edward seized the symbol of Scottish independence, the Stone of Scone, and brought it to London. John was eventually released in 1299 and spent his final years on his estates in France. He died in 1313. His son EDWARD would later make a brief claim on the Scottish throne, but made no more success of it than his father. John realised too late that he was merely a pawn of Edward's in his desire to conquer Scotland. However, it had not quite worked out as Edward planned. After John's surrender there followed a second interregnum, which saw the revolt of WILLIAM WALLACE and the eventual rise to power of ROBERT (I).

[FC70a] **WILLIAM WALLACE** Guardian of Scotland, October 1297–July 1298. When JOHN Balliol abdicated in July 1296 Scotland was again without a king. EDWARD I of England had marched through Scotland on a mission of conquest, but had subsequently retired south leaving the administration of Scotland in the hands of John de Warenne, earl of Surrey. Surrey had no desire to stay north of the border and left in charge two justiciars, Henry Cressingham and William Ormsby, both of whom sought to oppress the Scots. Although Edward's domination of the Scots seemed complete he had not extinguished their spirit. In August 1297 there were uprisings under the control of Sir William Wallace and Andrew Murray. These two joined forces and on 11 September thoroughly routed the English army at Stirling. Cressingham was killed; Murray was mortally wounded. Wallace had no pretensions to be king, but had a fanatical belief in Scotland having its own rightful monarch. He was thus declared and accepted as "Guardian of Scotland" on behalf of King John and "the community of the realm". The Scots accepted him as being in almost complete authority. For the next year he issued writs and made appointments in the name of the king. He also prepared for the inevitable battle that would ensue with Edward. This came at Falkirk on 22 July 1298, where Wallace's forces were annihilated. Wallace escaped. His whereabouts over the next few years are not wholly known, though he visited France. However, he was captured near Glasgow in August 1305. Tried for treason in London, he was hanged, drawn, beheaded and quartered, his remains sent to Newcastle, Berwick, Stirling and Perth as a lesson to all.

FD. MORAY

One of seven sub-kingdoms of the Picts (*see list on page 164*). By the ninth century it was ruled by a mórmaer, or earl, who was sometimes referred to as a king. The Cenél Loarn, a collateral dynasty of the kings of Dál Riata who believed they had equal right to the kingship, had migrated along the Great Glen away from the Viking raids. At the head of the dynasty were the descendants of Ainbcellach (FC18) who joined with the northern Picts in opposing the Scottish kingdom established by Kenneth macAlpin in the 840s. Usually referred to in the chronicles as the "men of Moray" this kingdom remained almost autonomous for three centuries and two of its rulers, Macbeth and Lulach, also ruled Scotland. The full list of rulers is not known. A Maelbrigte is mentioned as having been killed by Sigurd I of Orkney in 892, whilst a Donnchad mac Morgain was involved in a raid in Northern Ireland in 976. The following is incomplete and covers only the rulers after Donnchad mac Morgain.

Ref.	Ruler	Born	Reign	Died	Notes
FD1.	Ruairaidh or Rory		*fl* 980s		

Ruairaidh may have been succeeded by his elder son Maelbrigte.

Ref.	Ruler	Born	Reign	Died	Notes
FD2.	Findlaech or Finlay		990?-1020	1020	murdered?
FD3.	Malcolm macMaelbrigte		1020–29		
FD4.	Gillecomgain		1029–32	1032	murdered
FD5.	Macbeth	*c*1005	1032–57	1057	killed in battle; see FC56
FD6.	Lulach	*c*1031	1057–8	1058	killed in battle; see FC57
FD7.	Mael Snechta	*c*1051/2	1058–78	1085	deposed; retired to a monastery
FD8.	Aed or Heth		1078– ?	?	ancestry unknown; married Mael Snechta's sister
FD9.	Angus mac Heth	*c*1080	? -1130	1130	killed in battle

After 1130 Moray was formally absorbed into Scotland although factions continued to rebel including Malcolm macHeth (whose ancestry is much disputed but may have been Angus's brother or son but who is also believed to be related to Alexander I), who was the earl of Ross and was defeated and imprisoned in 1134 and not released until 1157. Malcolm's great-grandson, Kenneth, belonged to the last generation of rebels, being defeated in 1215. The MacHeths were the ancestors of the Clan Mackay.

[FD2] FINDLAECH or FINLAY Moray, 990?-1020.

The mórmaers of Moray regarded themselves as having equal title to the kingship of Dál Riata which, by the turn of the millenium, was starting to emerge as the dominant power in northern Britain and was taking the shape of Alba or Scotland. Their power meant that the kings of Scotland sought whatever means they could to subjugate them and, during the rule of MALCOLM II, this included developing a stronger bond with the Norse earl of Orkney, SIGURD THE STOUT. The mórmaer whose power concerned Malcolm was Findlaech, who had already showed much

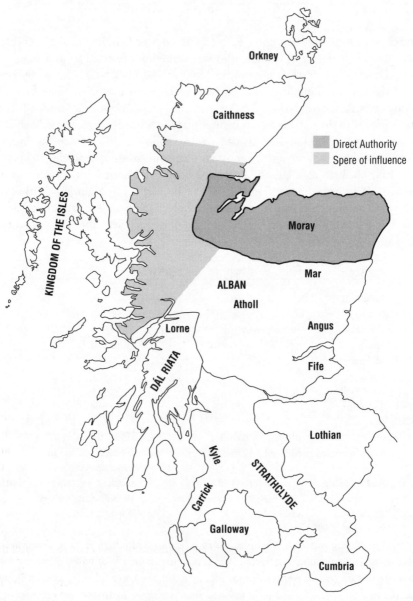

Map 10 Scotland – **Moray**

strength of character by challenging Sigurd to battle about the year 995. Although Sigurd won, it was not without significant loss. Findlaech was able to exercise considerable authority across northern Britain, disputing the borders of Orkney in the territory around Caithness and encroaching into Malcolm's territory around Ross and northern Atholl. Presumably as some form of peace arrangement, Findlaech married Malcolm's daughter Donada, possibly as early as the year 1000 when Malcolm was sub-king of Strathclyde. By this marriage Findlaech became the father of MACBETH. However, soon after Macbeth's birth a strange situation developed. Findlaech's and Malcolm's relationship must have become more tense

24. Scotland (7) – **The mórmaers of Moray**

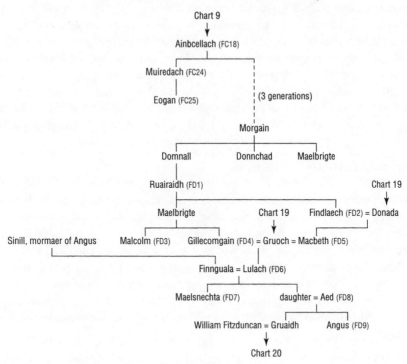

because Findlaech seems to have rejected Donada. We do not know the circumstances but by about the year 1006 Donada had been remarried to Sigurd of Orkney. Some records suggest that these were two different ladies of the same name and that Findlaech's wife was the daughter of KENNETH II and thus the aunt of the later Donada. Another interpretation has been that Sigurd's wife was another daughter of Malcolm's, not Donada. Either way, the improved relationship between Sigurd and Malcolm was a threat to Findlaech. Findlaech's power was further reduced when, during 1009 and 1010, Viking raids under SWEIN FORKBEARD began to intensify along the eastern coastline of Scotland and Moray. Findlaech found that he needed to call upon Malcolm's aid to rebuff the Viking menace.

In 1014 Sigurd was killed at the battle of Clontarf. This was an opportunity for Findlaech to increase his power across northern Britain. Although Malcolm was into his sixties he continued to scheme, and was looking after the fortunes of his grandson, the future THORFINN THE MIGHTY, whom he created earl of Caithness, territory which was only tenuously Malcolm's to bestow. The years after Clontarf saw the Orkney earls in some disarray and if any moment was ripe to attack Malcolm's power base it was then. For some reason Findlaech did not do so, and this doubtless caused a rift within the Moray hierarchy. In 1020 Findlaech was murdered by his nephews MALCOLM and GILLECOMGAIN.

[FD3] **MALCOLM** MAC **MAELBRIGTE** mórmaer of Moray, 1020–29.

Malcolm was son of Maelbrigte who may have been mórmaer prior to FINDLAECH. Malcolm was implicated in the murder of his uncle Findlaech in 1020 and was elected unopposed. It is possible that he believed he had prior claim to the stewardship, especially if his father had held the title, and that Malcolm had been too young to inherit the role when his father died. Since Findlaech remained in power for over twenty years, Malcolm was probably in his thirties when he came to power. He was more ardent than his uncle in seeking the throne of Scotland and throughout the 1020s made a series of raids on Scottish territory, including one that pillaged Dunkeld in 1027. Malcolm must have believed that the ageing Scottish king, MALCOLM, would soon die and that he would be able to challenge for the kingship. However it was Malcolm of Moray who died first, probably of natural causes, in 1029. He was succeeded by his brother, GILLECOMGAIN.

[FD4] **GILLECOMGAIN** Moray, 1029–32.
Son of Maelbrigte and brother of MALCOLM, with whom he was implicated in the death of their uncle FINDLAECH. Gillecomgain continued the raids against the Scots started by his brother, but in addition sought to work his way into the Scottish royal family. He married Gruoch, the granddaughter of KENNETH III, probably in 1029, when she was about fifteen. They had one son, LULACH, who would briefly rule Scotland. Gillecomgain continued to frustrate MALCOLM II of Scotland until, in 1032, Malcolm ordered a lightning raid on Gillecomgain's headquarters, which were set on fire. Gillecomgain and many of his household were killed, although Gruoch and her son escaped. Gruoch would soon marry Gillecomgain's successor, MACBETH.

*MACBETH succeeded to the throne of Scotland and is covered in detail on page 393, as is his short-lived successor **LULACH** (see page 395). Lulach's son, Mael Snechta, survived to become mórmaer of Moray.*

[FD7] **MAEL SNECHTA** or **MAELSNECHTAI** mórmaer of Moray, 1058–78.
The son of LULACH, the last of the Moray dynasty to rule Scotland. At the time of Lulach's death Mael Snechta was too young to rule, being perhaps six or seven, but he was evidently taken to safety from Scone to be raised secretly in the mountains of the north. His name means "servant of the snow", which may suggest either the weather conditions at the time of his birth or, more likely, his role as head man of the snowy north of Scotland. Whether MALCOLM III knew of his survival at the outset is not known, but he must have done by the time Mael Snechta came of age, in about 1068, as he would then have been formally invested as mórmaer (or to local sentiment – king) of Moray. Mael Snechta does not seem to have taken any hostile action against Malcolm directly, though he no doubt continued a guerilla warfare, harrying any of Malcolm's men who ventured north, and disrupted trade about the kingdom. Malcolm was eventually able to lead an army against him. Maelsnechta was defeated and driven into exile, spending his last years in a monastery, where he died, still comparatively young, in 1085. The Moray cause was not lost, as his sister's husband, AED, was raised to the mórmaership.

[FD8] **AED** or **HETH** mórmaer of Moray, c1078–?
We know nothing of Aed's background. He married the sister of MAEL SNECHTA and was elected mórmaer of Moray sometime after his brother-in-law was defeated and deposed by MALCOLM III in 1078. Malcolm had taken Mael Snechta's daughter captive, so it is possible that Aed was a husband forced upon her by Malcolm to

serve as a vassal king in Moray, but subsequent events make this unlikely. It is possible that Aed was a son of the mórmaer of Ross, and he may have been mórmaer of Ross in his own right. He remained a rebel until his death at some unknown date. It was probably he who led a raid into southern Scotland in 1116 and killed Lodmund, a grandson of Malcolm III. Aed may have been killed in the retaliatory expedition as no more is heard of him thereafter. He was eventually succeeded by his son ANGUS MAC HETH.

[FD9] **ANGUS** MAC**HETH** king of Moray, ?–1130.
Angus was the son of AED, also known as Heth, and grandson of LULACH. He was the last independent ruler of Moray. Nothing is recorded of his actions before 1130, though we can imagine he was a continual thorn in the side of the Scottish kings ALEXANDER I and DAVID I. It is just possible that Alexander may have had an illegitimate daughter by a sister of Angus, since there seems to have been some relationship between Alexander and the rebel Malcolm macHeth. In 1130 Angus and Malcolm led a huge army south into Scotland, intent on regaining the throne. At the ensuing battle of Strathcarro, Angus was defeated and killed and Malcolm was driven into hiding in the Highlands. He was eventually captured and imprisoned in 1134 and held in Roxburgh Castle until 1157 when he was released and restored to the earldom of Ross. David I took advantage of the death of Angus to formally integrate Moray into his kingdom. It was not the end of rebellion. William, the son of DUNCAN II, styled himself earl of Moray after Angus's death and his son, also called William, married Angus's sister Gruaidh. Their descendants, together with those of Malcolm macHeth, continued to rebel against the overlordship of the Scottish kings until the final confrontation in 1215 when Kenneth MacHeth and Donald MacWilliam were both killed in battle.

N. THE DANISH and NORSE KINGDOMS

Danish and Norse raids began in Britain at the end of the eighth century but it was fifty years before they established their own kingdoms. This included lands in Ireland (the kingdom of Dublin) and Normandy. Some kingdoms grew out of existing Scottish or English kingdoms as identified below.

NA. WESTERN ISLES – HEBRIDES and THE ISLE OF MAN

The Hebrides and the Isle of Man formed a kingdom known as the Western Isles to the Scots and the Southern Isles (or Sudreys) to the Norse. Identifying sovereignty over them is complicated. The islands were occupied by both the Irish and British during the various waves of invasion around the first centuries BC and AD. Legend attributes names to four early Celtic rulers of Man who may have some basis in fact – Dalboeth, Elathan, Alladh or Athas and Manannán. Manannán's name is most closely associated with the island. During the fifth century Man came under the control of the rulers of Rheged. It was conquered by Edwin of Northumbria in 620, but its rulership remained with the descendents of Llywarch Hen until it passed briefly to Wales and was then conquered by the Danes.

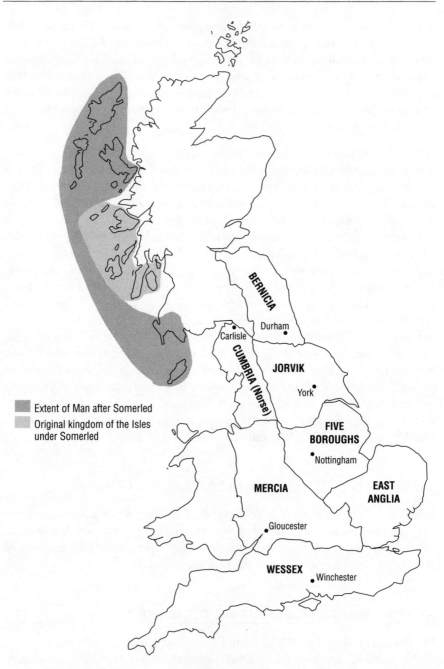

Map 11a **Kingdoms of Man and the Isles**

Ref.	Ruler	Born	Reign	Died	Notes
NA1.	Llywarch Hen		c560–95		see DA30

Man was conquered by Báetán mac Cairill of Ireland in 577 (see T147) and then by Aedán mac Gabhrán of Dál Riata in 582. It may have remained under Scottish domination until conquered by Edwin of Northumbria in 620.

NA2.	Diwg	*fl* 600s		
NA3.	Gwyar	*fl* 630s		Man overrun by Edwin of Northumbria
NA4.	Tegid	*fl* 670s		
NA5.	Algwn	*fl* 700s		
NA6.	Sandde	*fl* 730s		
NA7.	Elidr	*fl* 760s		
NA8.	Gwriad	*fl* 800s		

Gwriad's son, Merfyn Frych, became king of Gwynedd and Man in 825, but Man soon slipped out of his hands. By the 830s the Western Isles were being settled by Vikings and the Hiberno-Norse Gael-Gaedhil.

NA9.	Godred mac Fergus	*fl* 836–53	853	lord of the Hebrides
NA10.	Ketil *Flatnose* or Caitill *Find*	*c*853–*c*66	*c*870	

Olaf the White of Norway who became king of Dublin in 853 (see FC39a; U2) brought a degree of control to the Hebrides and Man and established his own jarls over the islands. Ketil Flatnose was the first, though he ruled more like a king. Others were Tryggvi (in the 870s) and Asbjorn Skerjablesi in the 880s. Asbjorn was slain by the children of Ketil Flatnose in around 899 and thereafter Man and the Western Isles were disputed between the Norwegian kings of Dublin and the Danish kings of York, until Ragnall established his authority across the North.

NA11.	Ragnall of York	*c*914–*c*21	*c*921	see NC9

Ruled by kings of Dublin and York, 920–940, who appointed sub-kings to the Isles. The only ones known are:

NA12.	Gebeachan or Gibhleachán	? –937	937	killed in battle
NA13.	Mac Ragnall	?937–42	942	killed

Probably came under authority of Olaf Sitricson of Dublin until 972 or so.

NA14.	Magnus Haraldsson	*c*972–7	977	killed
NA15.	Godred Haraldsson	977–89	989	killed in battle
NA16a.	Ragnald Godredson	*fl* 1000	1005	
NA16b.	Kenneth Godredson	1005– ?		
NA16c.	Swein	? –1034	1034	

Authority on the Western Isles was imposed by Sigurd the Stout of Orkney from 989–1014, but was regained by the kings of Dublin under Sitric Olafson from 1014–35. During this period Ragnald's brother Kenneth and Kenneth's son Swein continued to claim the title of king of Man until Swein's death in 1034. Thorfinn the Mighty of Orkney reconquered the Isles around 1038 and demanded tribute from Man if not directly administering it. Man and the Isles continued to be governed from Dublin subject to Orkney until soon after 1065.

NA17.	Margad Ragnallson of Dublin	1052–*c*61	1065	deposed; see U19
NA18.	Murchaid mac Diarmait of Dublin	1061–70	?	former king of Dublin

25. The Danish and Norse Kingdoms (1) – Kings of Man

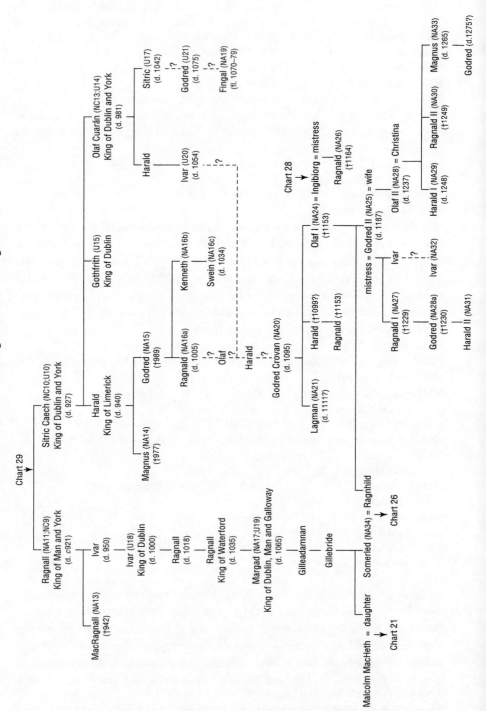

Ref.	Ruler	Born	Reign	Died	Notes
NA19.	Fingal Godredsson		1070–9		ejected by Godred Crovan

With the arrival of Godred Crovan the formal kingdom of Man and the Isles was created.

Man and the Isles

Ref.	Ruler	Born	Reign	Died	Notes
NA20.	Godred Crovan	?1040	1079–95	1095	also king of Dublin
NA21.	Lagman		1095–9	?1111	deposed; later went to Jerusalem
NA22.	Sigurd (I of Norway)	c1089	1099–1103	1130	see also NB23

Sigurd was installed as king of Orkney and the Southern Isles by his father Magnus III of Norway.

Ref.	Ruler	Born	Reign	Died	Notes
NA23.	Domnall mac Teige		1103–14?	1115	expelled and later killed
NA24.	Olaf (I) the Red	?1085	?1114–53	1153	murdered
NA25.	Godred II the Black		1153–58		expelled by Somerled (see NA34)

In 1156 Somerled established the separate lordship of the Isles, and he ruled the full kingdom of Man and the Isles from 1158–64. His dynasty is listed from NA34 (page 431) below. Thereafter Man included the Outer Hebrides under its jurisdiction until 1266.

Ref.	Ruler	Born	Reign	Died	Notes
(NA25)	Godred II (restored)		1164–87	1187	
NA26.	Ragnald		1164	1164	usurper, overthrown after 4 days
NA27.	Ragnald (I)		1187–1226	1229	killed in battle
NA28.	Olaf II the Black	1177	1226–37	1237	
NA28a.	Godred *Donn* (the Brown-Haired)		1230	1230	shared kingdom; slain
NA29.	Harald (I)	1223	1237–48	1248	shipwrecked and drowned
NA30.	Ragnald II		6–30 May 1249	1249	murdered
NA31.	Harald II		1249–50		deposed
NA32.	Ivar		1250–2		
NA33.	Magnus		1252–65	1265	submitted to Alexander III in 1264

Alexander III governed Man via a bailiff after 1265 until the island was seized by Edward I of England in 1290. See from NA49 (page 580) below. There was a brief rebellion in September 1275 when Magnus's son, Godred, seized the island and was declared prince by the Manxmen, but Alexander's forces soon quelled the uprising.

MANANNAN MAC **ALLADH** legendary king of Man, *fl* 500s.

Manannán is the legendary founder of the kingdom of Man from whom the island took its name. Manannán was the Celtic sea god, son of Llyr. However it seems likely that there was an historical Manannán, probably named after the god, who was the son of a royal Irish dynasty and who sometime around the end of the fifth century established himself in Man. There were almost certainly Irish settlers on the island at this time, and they probably had a local chieftain, but Manannán seems to have established himself sufficiently for many local sites to be named after him, especially Manannán's Chair and Manannán's Castle. The name Manannán has links with the Manau or Menapian tribe, which had settled in Lothian in southern Pictland, and Manannán may thus have been related to the kings of Lothian, such as his contemporary Lewdwn or LEUDONUS, after whom Lothian is named. Manannán's son, Mongan (who may be the same as another legendary king of Man called Mend), was supposed to be a contemporary of St Columba, whilst Manannán is also identified with the father of the famed Irish navigator St Brendan. Manannán himself was noted as a sailor. However, it is impossible to distinguish fact from legend other than to speculate about an early Irish king who established an independent kingdom on Man. His sons may have ruled the island for several generations but at some stage they either married into the family of the kings of Rheged or, more likely, were conquered by Rheged, probably under ELIDYR.

[NA1;DA30] **LLYWARCH HEN** Rheged and Man, c560–95.
Llywarch the Old was a son of the Men of the North, though also descended from the rulers of Gwynedd. He did not seem to have the temperament to be a king, and he retired at the earliest opportunity to be a poet at the court of the kings of Powys and Gwynedd. It is not certain that he ruled Man, though legend describes the island as belonging to his successors in the kingdom of Rheged. Man was also one of the Mevanian Islands, the other being Anglesey, and it is possible that even after he retired to Gwynedd, Llywarch retained authority over the two islands, at least until Man was conquered by Aedán of Dál Riata in 582. *See page 106 for more details.*

[NA2] **DIWG** Man, *fl* 600s.
Diwg is listed in the genealogies as the son of LLYWARCH HEN and as the ancestor of GWRIAD, the father of MERFYN FRYCH. Although tradition linked the descendants of Llywarch with the Isle of Man, it is not clear how far Gwriad's ancestors held authority over Man. It is probable that Diwg and his descendents held Man as vassals to the rulers of Gwynedd as a defence against the Irish throughout the seventh and eight centuries.

Nothing more is known of the descendants of Diwg beyond their names and approximate dates. The next historically attested ruler is Gwriad.

[NA8] **GWRIAD** or **GURIAT** Man, *fl* 800s.
Gwriad was a Welsh prince and descendant of LLYWARCH HEN who seems to have re-established himself on the Isle of Man sometime around the year 800 or later. As Man was predominantly Irish at this time, the presence of a Welsh chieftain suggests an interloper rather than a native ruler. Gwriad may have been of Powys descent, as it was in Powys that Llywarch *Hen* sought refuge after his self-exile from Rheged. Gwriad must have established himself with some degree of authority as he was in league with CYNAN AP RHODRI, who was seeking to claim the kingship of Gwynedd. Gwriad married Cynan's daughter Esyllt and their son, MERFYN, who was reputedly born on Man, later inherited Gwynedd. Gwriad left his mark on Man with the noted Guriat Cross originally placed on the north of the island, near Maughold. Merfyn was believed to have ruled both Man and Gwynedd, but

although Man probably remained in Welsh hands for several generations, it subsequently fell under Viking control.

[NA9] **GODRED** MAC **FERGUS** Man, *fl* 836–53.
Godred was probably the earliest leader of the *Gael-Gaedhil* or "foreign Gael" who were people of mixed Hiberno-Norse parentage. He was evidently the son of an Irish nobleman who had married a Norse lady. At the time of his first mention in the annals in 836 he was already lord of Oriel in northern Ireland, so he could have been in his early thirties. Since the first Viking raids were only in the 790s, he must have been the offspring of a very early settlement of the Norse amongst the Irish. At the time of his death he is referred to as *toiseach Innsi Gall*, which is "leader of the Gaelic Islanders", often interpreted as lord of the Hebrides. He had probably established himself as a leader of the Gaelic and Gaelo-Norse peoples who had settled in the southern Hebrides and the lands around Galloway, much of the old territory of Dál Riata. He assisted KENNETH MACALPIN in his claim for the kingship by acting as a go-between with the Vikings and securing mercenaries to support macAlpin's army. He was succeeded by KETIL FLATNOSE.

[NA10] **KETIL** *FIND* or *FLATNOSE* Western Isles, *c*853–*c*66.
Ketil *Flatnose* was one of the heroes of Norse Saga, the son of Björn Roughfoot, and one of the companions of the Norwegian king Harald Finehair on his expedition to the Scottish Isles in the ninth century. The legend probably bears some comparison with historical reality, although the king was not Harald, but OLAF THE WHITE, who established himself as king of the Norse in Dublin. Olaf married Ketil's daughter, Aud the Deep-Minded, probably at about the same time (*c*853). Ketil is probably the same as Caitill *Find* (Ketil the Fair), successor to GODRED MAC FERGUS as leader of the *Gall-Gaedhil*, a mixed Norse-Irish community that had grown in Ireland over the last fifty years. Ketil became rather too ambitious. He was charged by Olaf with ridding the Hebrides of Danish pirates, which he did successfully, but he set himself up as king of the Hebrides without Olaf's consent. Olaf was dissatisfied with Ketil and divorced Aud, who returned bitter to the Western Isles. Ketil remained as ruler, but had to submit to Olaf. In 866 Olaf embarked on his own conquest of Scotland and Ketil's authority further diminished. He died soon after, probably about 870. Subsequently his family left the Hebrides and established themselves as a dynasty of some importance in Iceland, where their name is remembered in the Icelandic sagas. Aud's son, THORSTEIN, established himself as the king of Caithness.

[NA11;NC9] **RAGNALL** or **RAGNALD** (I) York, 910–21; and Man, *c*914–*c*21.
Ragnall was a grandson of IVARR THE BONELESS who was amongst the many Vikings expelled from Dublin in 902. He spent the next few years harrying the western coast of Scotland and Strathclyde, and it may be that he established a base on Man or one of the Hebridean islands, but certainly did not wield the authority to call himself king. In 910 Ragnall seized the kingdom of York and began to carve out a kingdom across northern England. (*Full details about Ragnall are under York on page 462*). He probably declared himself king of Man in 914 when he defeated a rival Viking fleet off the coast of Man. Man became an ideal staging post between Dublin and York and became the key to Ragnall's power. Ragnall was eventually defeated by Edward the Elder in 920 and forced to recognize him as overlord. Nevertheless Ragnall's

hold on Man did not diminish, and it was ruled by the kings of Dublin for the next generation or two. It is believed that they appointed vassal kings to govern the island, of which Gebeachen is the earliest known.

[NA12] **GEBEACHAN** or **GIBHLEACHAN** Man and Western Isles, *d* 937.
Gebeachan is one of the kings identified as falling at the battle of Brunanburh in October 937, fighting alongside his overlord, OLAF GOTHFRITHSON of Dublin. It is not known how long Gebeachan had ruled the Isles. Olaf may have only recently invested him with that title following his victory over the Norse settlements in Ireland in August 937, but it is equally possible that he had ruled it since the death of SITRIC CAECH in 927. The Gaelic form of his name suggests that he was the leader of the *Gael-Gaedhel* Irish-Norse community once led by GODRED MAC FERGUS.

[NA13] **MAC RAGNALL** Man, ?937–42.
The Celtic chronicles mention a son of Ragnall who plundered the Irish coasts during 942 and sought refuge on an island. No more details are known, but since this pirate was identified as the son of a king, then he was probably a son of RAGNALL (I) of York, as he would be too old to be a son of RAGNALL (II). He may have been an illegitimate son, or one dispossessed by the rising power of SITRIC and his brother Gothfrith, and he resorted to piracy. He might have assumed control of Man after the death of GEBEACHAN at Brunanburh in 937. However, by 942 his raids had become a sufficient problem for the other Norse settlers to deal with him. He escaped them but was captured by Matudán, king of Ulster, who executed him.

[NA14] **MAGNUS** or **MACCUS HARALDSSON** Man and the Isles, *c*972–7.
[NA15] **GODRED HARALDSSON** Man and the Isles, 977–89.
Magnus and Godred were probably the sons of Harald Sitricson, making them grandsons of SITRIC CAECH, the king of Dublin and York. If so, then their father had been king of the Norse in Limerick until his death in 940, when Magnus may have been only an infant. Magnus was one of the kings present at Chester in 973 demonstrating his allegiance to king EDGAR. His brother, Godred, is also shown as ruling Man during and after Magnus's death, until he was killed by the Scots of Dál Riata in 989. Both brothers would have used Man for raiding mainland Britain and Ireland. Godred is recorded as raiding Anglesey in 979, during the reign of MAREDUDD AP OWAIN who used Godred's forces to support his own army. After Godred's death the island remained in dispute between the earls of Orkney and the kings of Dublin for the next century. Godred's son, RAGNALD GODREDSON, continued to call himself king of Man and was so recorded when he died in 1005.

[NA16a] **RAGNALD GODREDSON** Man, *d* 1005.
[NA16b] **KENNETH GODREDSON** Man, *fl* 1005.
[NA16c] **SWEIN** Man, *d* 1034.
Ragnald was the son of GODRED HARALDSSON. He was recorded as King of Man at the time of his death in 1005 though it is not clear whether he ruled under his own authority or as vassal to SIGURD of Orkney, who had imposed his authority over the Western Isles. It is likely that Man was sufficiently far south to escape much of Sigurd's control and that Ragnald and his brother Kenneth were able to rule Man with relative autonomy. Kenneth passed the kingship on to his son Swein, who died

in 1034 without an heir leaving the island vulnerable to the rule of Sitric of Dublin and subsequently THORFINN of Orkney.

[NA17;U19] **MARGAD RAGNALLSON** Dublin, 1035–8, 1046–52; Man and Galloway, 1052–c61; Galloway only 1061–4.

Also known as Echmarcach. His ancestry is uncertain but he was probably the son of Ragnall, the Norse king of Waterford who died in 1035, and could thus claim descent from RAGNALL, king of York and Man. He was first established as king of Dublin in 1035 after Sitric Silkenbeard was deposed but was himself deposed in 1038 by Ivar Haraldson, whom he in turn deposed to regain the kingdom of Dublin in 1046. When he was deposed again in 1052, he seems to have claimed the kingdoms of Man and Galloway during the conflict in Scotland of MACBETH's reign. He was defeated in 1060 or 1061 by MURCHAID MAC DIARMAIT, the king of Dublin, who brought Man under his control but Margad continued ruling in Galloway. He abdicated in 1064 and died the following year.

[NA18] **MURCHAID** MAC **DIARMAIT** Dublin and Man, 1061–21 November 1070.

Murchaid was the son of Diarmait mac Maíl, king of Leinster, who had conquered Dublin in 1052 and expelled the Norse king MARGAD RAGNALLSON who had fled to Man. In 1061 Murchaid led an army against Margad and expelled him from Man. Murchaid set himself up as king of Man and Dublin as sub-king to his father, who continued to rule until 1072.

[NA19] **FINGAL** Man and the Isles, 1070–9.

Fingal was the son of Godred Sitricsson (who had briefly claimed the Norse kingship of Dublin on the death of MURCHAID MAC DIARMAIT in 1070; *see* U21). Fingal was given the administration of Man and the southern Hebrides and seems to have survived the fall of his father in 1074. He was driven out by GODRED CROVAN, who conquered the islands in 1079.

[NA20] **GODRED *CROVAN* (*WHITE HANDS*)** Man, 1079–95; Dublin, 1091–4.

We know little about the background of Godred. He was Norse, and apparently raised on the Isle of Man (though not necessarily born there). His nickname, which he earned because of his habit of wearing white gauntlets into battle, is of Gaelic origin (*Crobhan*), suggesting links to the Irish-Norse colonies around Dublin. His family may have emanated from there and settled on Man during the conquests of THORFINN THE MIGHTY of Orkney, who established control over most of the western seaboard of Scotland and into the Irish Sea. This suggests he may have been born around 1040. He may even have spent his youth on the Orkneys as part of Thorfinn's summer army. It is probable that he was descended from GODRED HARALDSSON, who ruled Man a hundred years earlier. It is just possible that he was the grandson of Ivar Haraldson, king of Dublin from 1038–46, who died in 1054. Godred fought alongside the Norse king Harald Hardraada at the Battle of Stamford Bridge in September 1066. He survived and made his way to Man where he sought refuge. Man was nominally under the control of the king of Dublin, GODRED SITRICSON. His son FINGAL administered the islands and it was he that Crovan sought to defeat in three expeditions that he led against Man until his success in 1079. The islanders eventually welcomed him as their own. Just as EINAR (I) had in Orkney, Godred denied the islanders any udal rights, meaning that they owned the land as tenants to the king and not as an inheritance to their families. Godred thus claimed absolute authority over all of his domain. This extended throughout the Western Isles, including the northern Hebrides which he evidently conquered from the earls of Orkney (PAUL and ERLEND), who may not in practice have administered the islands. In order to govern this widespread diversity of islands, Godred established a parliament, the Tynwald, which consisted of thirty-two representatives. Sixteen of these came from Man itself, with the other sixteen from the four quadrants of the Hebrides with their bases at Lewis, Skye, Mull and Islay. The Hebrides were known to the Norse as the Sudreys or Southern Isles (with the Orkneys as the Nordreys). The name survives today in the bishopric of the islands, known as Sodor and Man. Man was nominally Christian when Godred conquered it, but Godred firmly established a local church under Bishop Roolwer or Rolf. Because of the extent of his kingdom Godred spent little time on Man, though he saw it as the centre of his government. His home was apparently on Islay, but he also spent much time in Dublin, which he succeeded in regaining from the Irish and which he governed from 1091–94. Godred died in 1095, probably in his mid fifties. His efforts had established a strong government across Man and the Isles and a dynasty that would rule for two centuries. He passed into the folklore of Man, where he became known as King Gorry or King Orry (the first G remaining as part of King). He was succeeded by his son LAGMAN.

[NA21] **LAGMAN** Man and the Isles, 1095–9.
Lagman was the eldest son of GODRED CROVAN, and inherited the kingship of Man and the Isles. His father had already granted him the lordship of the Northern Isles from 1091 when Godred established himself as king of Dublin. After Godred's death there was considerable rivalry for the rulership of Man and the Isles, and Lagman found himself in contention with DOMNALL MAC TEIGE and his own brother Harald. The sequence of events is unclear and it is not certain whether Harald's imprisonment, mutilation and subsequent death happened before 1099 or after. In 1099 Man was conquered by Magnus III of Norway, who established his young son SIGURD as king of Orkney and the Isles and he so remained until he returned to Norway in 1103. It may have been then that the rivaly between Lagman and Harald erupted. Either way, after Harald's death, Lagman was overcome with guilt and resigned the kingship, going on a pilgrimage to Jerusalem, where he died. The record of his death varies from 1097 to 1111, the latter seeming the more likely. This left the way open for Domnall mac Teige to claim the kingship.

[NA22;NB23] **SIGURD III** later known as *JORSALAFARI (THE CRUSADER)*, Man, Orkney and the Isles, 1099–1103.
In 1099, Magnus III, king of Norway, who had regained direct control over the Orkneys the previous summer, conquered Man and the Hebrides and installed his infant son, Sigurd III, as king, with HAAKON Paulson of Orkney as regent. Man was thus ruled from Orkney until 1103 when Magnus died and Sigurd returned to Norway. *For full details see page 451.*

[NA23] **DOMNALL** MAC **TEIGE** Man and the Isles, 1103–11/14.
There is some uncertainty over exactly when Domnall governed Man. One tradition goes that LAGMAN abdicated in around 1097 and, as his brother OLAF was too young

to rule, the Irish king of Dublin, Murchadh O'Brien, sent his son Domnall to serve as regent. An alternate interpretation of the slim records is that Lagman and Domnall remained rivals and after the brief reign of SIGURD, son of Magnus III of Norway, it was Domnall who gained the kingship of Man, and Lagman went on a pilgrimage to Jerusalem. Domnall was cruel and intolerant. He may have been expelled by a local rebellion after only three years or possibly as long as ten years. During his reign there were many attempts to gain the Manx throne, including two local chieftains Ottar and MacMarus who, according to legend, succeeding in killing each other in their battle for supremacy. By this time Olaf had come of age and assumed the kingship of Man.

[NA24] **OLAF (I) GODREDSON** called **OLAF *THE RED*** Man and the Isles, 1114–53. The son of GODRED CROVAN, he was too young on the death of his father and elder brothers to assume the title. This suggests he may well have been the son of a second marriage and was born late in Godred's life, perhaps around 1085/86. Because of his youth a regent was appointed (DOMNALL MAC TEIGE), whose rule was so oppressive that he was deposed. From 1099–1103 the Isles were under the direct control of Magnus III of Norway, who established his son SIGURD (III) as king of Orkney and the Isles, which included all of the Hebrides down to Man. During these years Olaf stayed at the court of HENRY I of England and learned about Norman administration. After Sigurd returned to Norway in 1103, Olaf strove to gain the kingdom of Man, though it seems that Domnall still held on to the title for some years and may not have been expelled until around 1111 or 1114. Olaf reigned in peace and harmony for forty years, a remarkable achievement considering the upheaval elsewhere throughout Britain. Part of the reason for this was Olaf's mastery of the seas around Man. He owned a powerful fleet, probably the most powerful in Britain. He served as a form of policing agent, but it also meant no one had the temerity to attack him. He succeeded in maintaining good alliances with all contemporary monarchs, and with the church. He established a Cistercian monastery in Man at Rushen in 1134. In 1140 his daughter, Ragnhild, married SOMERLED, the lord of Argyll who would subsequently usurp the kingdom of Man. By 1153 Olaf was approaching seventy and was too feeble to risk the journey to Norway to pay homage to his overlord, King Eystein III, so his son, GODRED (II) went in his stead. During his son's absence, Olaf's nephew, Ragnald, the son of Harald who had been murdered by Olaf's brother LAGMAN, grew impatient, believing he should have been king in Olaf's place. The impatience boiled into murder, and Olaf was killed.

[NA25] **GODRED II *THE BLACK*** Man and the Isles, 1153–8, 1164–10 November 1187.
Godred was not a peace-lover like his father, OLAF (I), though he did exercise wisdom from time to time. Godred was in Norway at the time his father was killed, paying allegiance to his overlord the Norwegian king. Although he returned promptly to Man, there must have been a space of several weeks to allow for him to receive the news and return. In that period no doubt his cousin, Ragnald, who had murdered Olaf, was establishing himself as the next ruler. Godred immediately had him executed and ensured he was recognized as king. He decided to stamp home his authority by conquering the kingdom of Dublin, which was then

ruled by Brodar Thorkellson. In raising his men he made promises to the various island chiefs upon which he subsequently reneged, so that although he was successful in his expedition to Ireland – he established an overlordship of Dublin – he was soon to lose that and much else. He was rapidly recognized as a despot and received little fealty from his chiefs. In 1155 Godred learned that his brother-in-law, SOMERLED, was building a major new fleet with the object of ousting him. He brought together his own fleet, and on 6 January 1156 the two parties met off the coast of Islay. Godred's navy should have won, but his men seemed less willing to fight on his behalf. Somerled's new vessels outmanoeuvred Godred's and, though he was outnumbered, Somerled gained the upper hand. Both sides suffered significant losses but Somerled won the day. He hammered home his advantage by entering into a treaty with Godred granting Somerled authority over all of the southern Hebrides, which amounted to the two quadrants founded by Godred's grandfather upon Mull and Islay, whilst Godred retained Man and the northern or Outer Hebrides – the quadrants of Skye and Lewis. Somerled thus became king of the Isles and was recognized as such by the king of Norway, though it was a few years before it was accepted by the king of Scotland. Godred was not happy with his diminished kingdom and this brought him into conflict with Somerled again in 1158. This time Somerled showed his new mastery of the seas and he drove Godred out of the kingdom. Godred retreated to Norway and was not restored to Man until after the murder of Somerled in 1164. Godred had to deal with his brother RAGNALD who claimed the kingdom, but he was promptly despatched. Godred retained the southern Hebrides so that thereafter he ruled only Man and the Outer Hebrides, which represented twenty-four chieftains at his Tynwald, the number which is retained by the Manx parliament today rather than the thirty-two established by GODRED CROVAN. Godred the Black ruled for a further twenty-three years in Man, having learned his lesson, and he was slightly less the despot than he had been, recognizing to a large degree HENRY II as his English overlord, as well as his Norwegian sovereign. After his death the rule of Man was disputed between two of his sons, RAGNALD (I) and OLAF (II).

[NA26] **RAGNALD OLAFSSON** Man 1164, for only four days.
He was the illegitimate son of OLAF (I). After the murder of SOMERLED and with GODRED II, his half-brother, in Norway, Ragnald seized Man. Godred was already returning home and promptly killed Ragnald upon his arrival. Ragnald's reign, although unofficial, is the shortest on record of any ruler in Britain.

[NA27] **RAGNALD (I)** Man, 1187–1230.
Ragnald was GODRED II's eldest son and, although illegitimate, seized the throne since his half-brother OLAF (II), the legitimate heir, was only ten. Ragnald himself may not have been much older, perhaps eighteen or slightly more. Ragnald had all the appeal of the Hollywood Viking – one tale about him states he spent three years on board ship. Though this is doubtless apocryphal, it does suggest that Ragnald preferred sea-roving and piracy to the due administration of his territory. Most of his reign seems to have consisted of annoying people and playing one king off against another. When his brother Olaf objected to his ill-treatment, he despatched him to WILLIAM THE LYON of Scotland, who kept him imprisoned for seven years. When Ragnald began to meddle in Irish affairs he offended the English king, JOHN,

who summoned Ragnald in 1206 to pay homage. And when Ragnald ignored his sovereign overlord, Inge II of Norway, he was summoned to pay homage to him in 1210. This further annoyed John, who invaded Man and demanded further fealty from Ragnald. Nevertheless Ragnald managed to ply the Irish seas for nearly forty years until, at length, Olaf caught up with him. In 1226 Olaf succeeding in forcing Ragnald to share part of the kingdom with him, but hostilities were still strong and split the island north and south. Ragnald sought support from his powerful allies in Galloway, whilst Olaf hurried to Norway seeking support from the king. In 1230 Olaf and Ragnald met in battle on the Tynwald Hill in Man, and Ragnald was slain.

[NA28] **OLAF (II) *THE BLACK*** Lewis, 1207, 1214–30; Man, 1226–37.

Olaf was the eldest legitimate son of GODRED II but was only ten years old when his father died in 1187. RAGNALD (I), Olaf's elder (illegitimate) half-brother seized the kingdom. Olaf spent most of his life trying to regain it. In 1207 he was granted Lewis in the Outer Hebrides, but was dissatisfied with this bleak and inhospitable territory. When he objected Ragnald had Olaf seized and handed to WILLIAM THE LYON of Scotland, who held him imprisoned until 1214. Upon his release Olaf was forced into a marriage with Lavon, the sister of Ragnald's wife, but within a short space of time the marriage was annulled on the basis that Lavon was too closely related to Olaf's mistress. Her sister was so affronted at this that she sent her son, GODRED DONN, to Lewis to murder Olaf, but Olaf escaped. Olaf subsequently married Christina, daughter of the earl of Ross, by whom he became the ancestor of the Macleod clan of Lewis and Skye. Olaf suffered Ragnald's abuses for a further ten years and then, in 1226, gathered together a fleet from amongst those chieftains who supported him, primarily from Skye, Lewis and Ross, and descended on Ragnald, who was forced to come to terms with Olaf. Olaf was now granted authority over all of the northern Hebrides, whilst Ragnald retained Man, but Olaf remained dissatisfied. He returned with his fleet, and in 1230 slew Ragnald in a battle at Tynwald Hill on Man. After forty years, at the age of fifty, Olaf had at last gained his inheritance. However, he now found himself caught between the opposing factions of the kings of England and Norway. In 1230 Olaf was summoned to Norway to pay homage to Haakon IV. Later that same year, when Olaf was forced to share half of his kingdom with Ragnald's son Godred *Donn*, Haakon IV sent a fleet to enforce Norwegian sovereignty over the whole of the Hebrides. He intended to place his own nominee, USPAK, as king of the Isles. The enterprise misfired somewhat, though it resulted in Lewis being laid to waste, and both Godred and Uspak being killed in battle. Olaf had been forced to support Haakon's venture, but HENRY III summoned Olaf to him, saying that it was Olaf's responsibility to police the waters of the Irish Sea against such marauders. Thereafter, regardless of Olaf's allegiance to Norway, he was forced to place fifty ships at the disposal of the English crown. This further annoyed Haakon, who summoned Olaf to Norway, but Olaf died when on the point of leaving. He was then aged sixty. His life must have been one of total frustration.

[NA28a] **GODRED *DONN* (*THE BROWN-HAIRED*)** Outer Isles, 1230.

He was the son of RAGNALD (I) and inherited many of his vicious qualities, though his life was not long enough to perfect them. His father had usurped the rule of Man and the Isles, and Godred had every anticipation of succeeding him, except that his uncle OLAF II insisted on claiming his rightful heritage. In about 1220, Godred's mother despatched him to Lewis to murder Olaf, but the uncle escaped and Godred exercised his wrath by despoiling the island. Years later uncle and nephew became reconciled, and in 1230 Godred was given Olaf's former share of the kingdom, the Outer Isles based on Lewis. In that same year king Haakon IV of Norway chose his opportunity to visit his kingdom in the Western Seas and install his own choice of king, USPAK. Godred rallied to support his uncle, but was killed in the conflict. He was probably in his early forties.

[NA29] **HARALD (I)** Man, 1237–48.

Harald found himself caught between his loyalties to Norway and England. On his accession, when he was only fourteen, he refused to acknowledge King Haakon IV as his overlord, so the Norwegian king promptly sent his agents to depose Harald and confiscate his revenues. Harald reconsidered his position and presented himself to Haakon in 1239 where he was so warmly received that Harald stayed at the court for two years, so it was a more mature eighteen-year-old who returned to Man in 1241. HENRY III of England, however, always in need of support, was keen to have access to Harald's fleet and commanding position. In 1246 he summoned him to his court and knighted him. Haakon would have none of that so summoned Harald back to his court, where he arrived in 1247. Again Harald was warmly received and given the hand of Haakon's daughter, Christina. All of this shows the importance that Man held to the Norwegian and English crowns. Unfortunately Harald and his new bride were drowned off Orkney on their return in October or November 1248.

[NA30] **RAGNALD II** Man, 6–30 May 1249.

After the death of Ragnald's brother HARALD (I) there was evidently a dispute amongst the claimants to the throne, the main two being HARALD (II), the son of GODRED DONN, and Ragnald. Haakon of Norway approved Ragnald who was duly installed on 6 May 1249. However, Harald continued to plot against him, and just over three weeks later Ragnald was assassinated by IVAR near Rushen church.

[NA31] **HARALD II** Man, 1249–50.

He was the son of GODRED DONN and sought to claim what he believed was his birthright. Even though RAGNALD II was the approved successor to HARALD I, Harald Godredsson succeeded in having him murdered after just three weeks. Harald usurped the throne, but he was promptly summoned to Norway, where he was deposed.

[NA32] **IVAR** Man, 1250–2.

A murderer and usurper. He murdered RAGNALD II in league with Ragnald's cousin HARALD Godredsson. It seems that Ivar took power after Harald's deposition. Although he is only described as "a knight" in the *Chronicle of Man*, he was almost certainly of royal descent with his own claim to the throne. He may well have been the son or grandson of GODRED II's son Ivar, and thus a second cousin to Harald II. Ivar's rule was challenged by EWEN, king of the Isles, but he was unable to impose his authority over Man. Ivar was finally overthrown two years later, by authority of Haakon IV of Norway, and Harald I's younger brother, Magnus, was elected to rule.

[NA33] **MAGNUS** Man and the Outer Isles, 1252–65.

The last independent Norwegian king of Man. He was the son of OLAF II and eventually succeeded his brother HARALD I after a period of dynastic rebellion. Unlike his elder brother, Magnus had no initial qualms about his loyalties, but he found himself entrapped in the conflict between England, Scotland and Norway for control of Man and the Western Isles. Magnus had already married a daughter of Eogan of Argyll, thus giving him Scottish allegiance, when he was summoned to Norway in 1253 to be confirmed as king. Magnus professed complete loyalty to Haakon IV. Soon after his return to Man, Magnus was summoned to the court of HENRY III of England who wanted to know if Magnus's fleet would be available to support Henry in times of need. Meanwhile ALEXANDER III of Scotland was negotiating with Haakon to purchase the Isles. Haakon would not concede and instead, when Alexander undertook raids against rebels in Skye, Haakon sent a punitive expedition to Scotland. The expedition was something of a failure, and Magnus was one of the few of Haakon's subjects who showed total support. Haakon died while wintering in Orkney in 1263, and his successor soon made overtures to Alexander about coming to an agreement over the islands. In 1264 Magnus was summoned to the court of Alexander III where the two kings agreed a truce. Magnus was allowed to remain king of Man alone, but the rest of the Outer Isles passed to Alexander. He took formal possession of them (including Man) after the Treaty of Perth in 1266. Magnus died in 1265, only in his thirties. Although he was the last formal king of Man the title was reinstated in 1333 for William de MONTACUTE. Magnus's son, Godred, seized the island in September 1275 and endeavoured to re-establish himself as king but he and his army were slaughtered by a Scottish army under the Crusader John de Vescy. It has been suggested that Godred survived the battle and fled into hiding in Wales, probably Anglesey, but he is not heard of again.

For the later English kings of Man turn to page 580.

KINGS OF THE ISLES

This kingdom was created by Somerled from the kingdom of Man and the Isles. It consisted of the eight island groupings centred on Mull and Islay. The holders were variously known as king or lord of the Isles.

Ref.	Ruler	Born	Reign	Died	Notes
NA34.	Somerled	c1105	1156–64	1164	murdered

After Somerled's death the kingdom was divided amongst three of his sons. The kingdom of the Isles was vested in his second son, Ragnald of Islay, but each son and grandson could style himself as king and often did. The following details the senior claimants only, who were the descendants of Ragnald and his brother Dugald.

Ref.	Ruler	Born	Reign	Died	Notes
NA35.	Ragnald		1164–c1210	c1210	
NA35a.	Dugald		1164–c92	c1192	lord of Lorne and Argyll
NA36.	Donald (I)		c1210–30	1247?	
NA37.	Duncan Mac Dougall	c1170	c1210–c47	c1247	

Ref.	Ruler	Born	Reign	Died	Notes
NA37a.	Dugald *Screech*	c1210–35?		1235?	joint claimant with Duncan
NA38.	Uspak or Gillespie		1230	1230	died of wounds
NA39.	Ewen Mac Dougall		c1248–66	c1270	strictly only held kingship 1247–9, but continued as vassal to Alexander III
NA40.	Dugald Mac Ruari (MacRory)		1249–66	1268	was appointed by Norse king over Ewen

Ewen submitted to Alexander III and his lands passed to the Scottish crown. Alexander later invested the titled Lord of the Isles in the MacDonald family, who held it for the next two hundred years (see page 536).

[NA34] **SOMERLED** king of the Isles, 1156–64.

Somerled was the son of Gillebride, thane of Argyll, and was descended from RAGNALL, the Danish king of York. He was born in Ireland (where his father had been exiled by the Scots king EDGAR) perhaps around the year 1105. His mother was Norse, the daughter of SIGURD II of Orkney, and she named the boy with a typical Norse nickname, which means "summer voyager". We know little of his early life, but he seems to have regained his heritage sometime before 1130, because he was already styled thane of Argyll when his sister married Malcolm, the illegitimate son of ALEXANDER I of Scotland. Somerled was a skilled negotiator from an early age and he had probably re-established himself with the Scottish king DAVID, for by 1138 he was in charge of the West Highland contingent of David's army. He also talked his way into the confidence of OLAF (I), king of Man, whose daughter, Ragnhild, he married in 1140. Throughout these years Somerled maintained a strong affection for the kingdom of the Gaels, not the rapidly anglicised or Anglo-Norman kingdom that King David had developed. Although it was the way of the future, Somerled rejected it. He was unable to convince David, but when the new and very young king, MALCOLM IV, succeeded to the throne in 1153, Somerled tried again. In 1154 Somerled and his nephews rebelled against Malcolm IV. At this same time Olaf of Man had died and his son, GODRED II, had returned to the Isles and was proving something of a despot. Somerled spent two years redesigning and rebuilding his fleet and then, in January 1156 met Godred in battle off Islay. Godred's fleet was the most powerful in Britain and he should have been the victor but Somerled's new design, which allowed him to out-manouevre his opponent, won him the day, though there were significant losses on both sides. As a result Godred and Somerled negotiated and agreed to divide the Isles. Somerled received the southern Hebrides, which consisted of the two main groupings of islands around Islay and Mull. Godred's continued intolerance caused Somerled to bring his fleet against him again in 1158 and this time Godred fled back to Norway. Somerled's claims were upheld and he became king of the Isles, a title accepted by both King Inge of Norway and eventually (in 1160) by Malcolm IV of Scotland. Somerled so ingratiated himself with the Scottish king that he earned the nickname, "sit-by-the-king". Nevertheless his attempts to sway Malcolm toward maintaining the Gaelic heritage remained thwarted. Somerled did try to have the Celtic church reinstated on Iona, and it was only his death that halted this development. In 1164,

26. The Danish and Norse Kingdoms (2) – **Kings of the Isles**

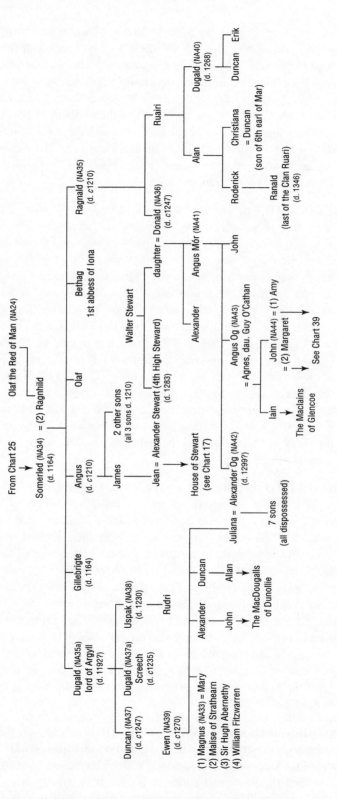

Somerled raised an army in the hope of forcing Malcolm into treaty. A force of 10,000 men sailed up the Clyde, from where Somerled took half the army on to Renfrew to parley with the king's representatives. Somerled was found murdered the following morning, but his killers were never identified. Somerled was buried on Iona but was apparently later reinterred by his son at Saddell Abbey on Kintyre.

After his death, Godred II regained Man and the northern Hebrides. The rest of Somerled's kingdom was divided between his sons. The eldest, DUGALD, took Lorne and Argyll, with the islands of Mull, Coll, Tiree and Jura. The second, RAGNALD, took Islay and Kintyre, which remained the focal point of the kingdom of the Isles. A third son, Angus, took Arran and Bute.

[NA35] **RAGNALD** king of the Isles, 1164–*c*1210.

The second son of SOMERLED who inherited his father's mighty fleet. Ragnald originally inherited only Islay and the Kintyre peninsula and shared Arran with his younger brother Angus who won it from Ragnald in 1192. His elder brother, DUGALD, inherited Lorne and the islands of Mull, Coll, Tiree and Jura, but after his death, around the year 1192, possession in these islands passed to Ragnald. From that time Ragnald began to style himself king of the Isles and lord of Argyll and Kintyre, effectively all of the original territory of Dál Riata. Although his brothers all had title to call themselves king (and did from time to time as they saw fit) it was Ragnald and his successors who were the primary line of kings of the Isles. Ragnald embodied a mixture of Norse and Gaelic values. He was a Christian with a great respect for the church – he founded monasteries and rebuilt churches destroyed by the Vikings. He brought the Cistercian monks to Saddell in Kintyre in about 1207, which is where he buried his father, and established an Augustinian nunnery on Iona. But with his powerful fleet he patrolled the seas along western Britain plundering when opportunity allowed.

[NA35a] **DUGALD** MAC **SORLEY** lord of Argyll, 1164–?92.

He was the eldest son of SOMERLED and on his father's death he inherited the territory of Lorne on the mainland and the islands of Mull, Coll and Tiree. It is only assumed he was the eldest son because in 1156 there had been a request by Somerled's earls that Dugald be created king of the Isles. Somerled had married in 1140, so this would have made Dugald about fifteen or sixteen. Unlike his brother Ragnald, little is recorded of Dugald's activities and it is likely that, despite his title, he behaved as a loyal vassal to the Scottish king, WILLIAM THE LYON. He appears to have been present with William at the time that the king paid homage to Henry II of England in 1175 at Durham. Nothing more is known of him, not even his date of death, though it is tempting to believe this may have happened in 1192 when rivalry broke out between Ragnald and Angus over control of the Isles. Dugald was the ancestor of the MacDougalls. Both his son DUNCAN and grandson EWEN became kings of the Isles.

[NA36] **DONALD** (I) king of the Isles, *c*1210–*c*30.

He was the younger son of RAGNALD and grandson of SOMERLED. He inherited the heartland of the kingdom of the Isles, which was Kintyre and Islay, from which his fleet controlled the western coastline of Scotland. He was at heart a pirate. He plundered Derry in 1212 and was involved in various uprisings, but he seems to have calmed down in later life. It is possible that his authority was curtailed by his cousins DUNCAN and DUGALD, who endeavoured to dominate the western seaboard in the first quarter of the thirteenth century. It is recorded that Donald made a pilgrimage to Rome and on his return made bountiful grants to the abbey at Paisley. His date of death is not known but it is believed to have been sometime between 1247 and 1269. He is generally regarded as the ancestor of the Clan MacDonald (*see* ANGUS MOR).

[NA37] **DUNCAN** king of the Isles, *c*1210–*c*47/48.
[NA37a] **DUGALD** *SCREECH* king of the Isles, *c*1210–35?
Duncan and his brothers Dugald and Gillespie (or USPAK) were the sons of DUGALD, son of SOMERLED. Duncan's name is recorded as early as 1175 and he was probably born in about 1170. His uncle RAGNALD inherited the lands, of which Duncan and Dugald gained possession after his death around 1210. Over the next twenty years Duncan and Dugald terrorised the western coast of Scotland as far south as Man, dominating the islands without effective challenge. They probably usurped the territories of their cousin DONALD, son of Ragnald. Their activities almost certainly added to the frustration of the dispossessed king of Man, OLAF (II) *THE BLACK*, who went to his overlord, Haakon IV of Norway, in 1230 to seek restitution. Haakon was already planning his own expedition spurred on by Gillespie, whom Haakon believed was the more capable ruler of the Isles and whom he was going to install as king. The expedition of 1230 was not very successful. Dugald was captured and Gillespie seems to have talked Duncan around to a more reasoned attitude. While the two of them were seeking to regain Bute as part of the Norse kingdom, Gillespie was killed, but Olaf was restored as king and may have been given authority over some of the southern Hebrides, as it appears that after 1230 Duncan was not allowed to call himself "king". He and Dugald operated only as "lords" of their respective territories – Mull, Islay and Kintyre. Dugald possibly died soon after, but Duncan was certainly alive in 1237 when he attested a charter. He also founded the priory of Ardchattan in Loarn. He died about the year 1247 when he was succeeded as Lord of Argyll by his son EWEN.

[NA38] **USPAK** king of the Isles, 1230.
Uspak was the Norwegian name of Gillespie, the son of DUGALD and grandson of SOMERLED. Haakon IV of Norway selected him as the rightful king of the Isles in place of his brothers DUNCAN and DUGALD, who were misusing their privileges amongst the islanders. Uspak set sail with OLAF II of Man, who had also come to Haakon's court to seek support for his claims. The expedition was ill-equipped, though it succeeded in achieving Olaf's desires. Uspak relied on negotiation with his brother Duncan and then all three brothers set out to recover Bute, which had fallen into Scottish hands some years earlier. This was less successful, as Uspak was wounded in the raid and died soon after. He was buried on Iona.

[NA39] **EWEN** MAC **DOUGALL** lord of Argyll and king of the Isles, *c*1248–66.
Ewen was the son of DUNCAN and great-grandson of SOMERLED. He inherited the lordship of Argyll sometime around the year 1248. At that time the king of Norway, Haakon IV, allowed the use of the title king of the Isles. Although Ewen and his second cousins DUGALD MAC RUARI, Alan Mac Ruari and ANGUS MOR all held

lordships within the Hebrides and may have regarded themselves as kinglets, they did not exercise overall authority. That was vested more in the king of Man, HARALD (I). In the year 1248 Ewen and Dugald visited the court of Haakon to apply for the title of king. Haakon vested it in Ewen. Soon after Harald of Man was shipwrecked and drowned, and Ewen was given authority to govern the full territory of Man and the Isles. Ewen returned to the Hebrides in 1249 where the Scottish king ALEXANDER II was preparing to commence hostilities against the western lords. The king caught a fever and died in July 1249, and Ewen and his cousins were safe for a while. However, Ewen was unable to convince the Manxmen to accept him as their king. How much he became involved in the intrigue between HARALD II and IVAR is not known, but when he returned to Haakon's court in 1252 to seek reinforcement of his title it was overturned in favour of MAGNUS, son of OLAF THE BLACK. Ewen stayed on a few years at Haakon's court as a mercenary sea captain but in 1255 returned to Scotland. He visited the court of the young Scottish king, ALEXANDER III who welcomed him and allowed him to retain his lordship of Argyll in return for a retainer of 60 merks (£40) a year. The English king HENRY III even interceded on his behalf. Thereafter Ewen remained loyal to Alexander. There is no doubt that Ewen was a loyal and sensible lord prepared to accept his position. His cousin, Dugald, on the other hand refused to become a Scot and remained staunchly loyal to Norway to the bitter end. He spent the period from 1253–62 patrolling the Isles as a robber baron, harassing the English, Scots and Irish fleets, and still claiming the title of king. During these years Alexander III sought to acquire the Isles from Norway without success. In 1263 Haakon sent his own fleet to teach the Scots a lesson and restake his claim to the isles. It was not successful. Ewen refused to fight and resigned his title in his island territories. After the Norse defeat at the battle of Largs in October 1263, Haakon retreated to Orkney, where he died of a fever. In the ensuing negotiations the Hebrides and Man passed from Norwegian control to Scotland. Ewen was granted the lordship of Lorn and remained a loyal subject of King Alexander. His exact date of death is not known but it was probably in the 1270s.

[NA40] **DUGALD** MAC **RUARI** king of the Isles 1249–66.
Dugald was the son of Ruari and grandson of RAGNALD, the son of SOMERLED. He was the second cousin of EWEN MAC DOUGALL and the two were intense rivals over the kingship of the Isles. Although they were both initially loyal to the king of Norway, Ewen later changed his allegiance to the king of Scotland. Even though Dugald had been set aside by Haakon IV of Norway in 1248, when Ewen was granted the kingship of the Isles, Dugald remained staunchly loyal. As a consequence when Ewen changed his allegiance in 1249, Dugald was proclaimed king by his men, a title confirmed by Haakon in 1252. Dugald acted as a pirate around the Scottish coast, constantly harrying the Scots' fleet and often slaughtering the crews. Dugald supported Haakon's invasion force, which came to Orkney and the Isles in 1263. Even after Haakon's death, Dugald continued to oppose the planned transfer of the Isles to Scotland and his ships frequently attacked Scottish ports and ships. He eluded attempts by ALEXANDER III to capture him and remained a free-booter until his death in 1268. He may be regarded as the last true Viking king of the Isles.

For the later Scottish lords of the Isles turn to page xx.

NB. ORKNEY

The earldom of the Orkneys was created by Harald king of Norway in the ninth century. Although its earls, or jarls, remained subordinate to Norway, they had considerable autonomy in Britain. Their territory included the northern (and sometimes the southern) Hebrides, known as the Sudreys, and usually included Caithness (and sometimes Sutherland) in mainland Scotland.

Ref.	Ruler	Born	Reign	Died	Notes
NB1.	Ragnald (I) or Rögnvaldur *the Wise*		c874–c5	894	returned to Norway; murdered
NB2.	Sigurd (I) *Riki* (*the Mighty*)		c875–92	892	died from bites from a dead head
NB2a.	Thorstein *Raudr* (*the Red*)		c875–900	900	established as king of Caithness and Sutherland; killed in battle
NB3.	Guthorm		c892–3	893	
NB4.	Hallad		c893–4		abdicated
Orkneys occupied by Danish pirates under Thori Treebeard and Kalf Skurfa.					
NB5.	Einar (I)		894–?920	?920	known as *Torf*-Einar
NB6.	Arnkel		?920–54	954	ruled jointly and became subordinate to Erik; both killed
NB7.	Erlend (I)		?920–54	954	in battle
NB8.	Erik Bloodaxe	c885	c937–54	954	also king of Jorvik at different times between 939? and 954; killed in battle
NB9.	Gunnhildr (*returned*)		954–5 976–7		widow of Erik *Bloodaxe*; ruled with her sons Ragnfred and Godred
NB10.	Thorfinn (I) *Hausakljúfr* (*Skull-splitter*)	c910	c947–77	977	
NB11.	Arnfinn	c942	977–?9	?979	murdered
NB12.	Havard	c944	?979–?81	?981	murdered
NB13.	Liot	c948	?981–?4		killed in battle
NB14.	Hlodvir	c946	?984–?7	c988	
NB15.	Sigurd II		?987–1014	1014	killed in battle
NB16.	Somerled		1014–15	1015	shared earldom
NB17.	Einar II		1014–20	1020	murdered
NB18.	Brúsi		1014–c30	c1031	handed his share to Einar 1018–20
NB19.	Thorfinn II *the Mighty*	c1007	c1018–c60	c1060	became primary earl from 1028
NB20.	Ragnald II	1011	1038–46	1046	murdered
NB21.	Paul (I)	c1038	c1060–98	1099	deposed and died in prison
NB22.	Erlend II	c1040	c1060–98	1099	deposed and died in prison
NB23.	Sigurd III	c1089	1099–1105	1130	See also NA22
Ruled as king of Orkney and the Isles, subject to his father Magnus III of Norway.					
NB24.	Haakon	c1071	1105–26	1126	previously Regent 1099–1105; co-ruled with Magnus
NB25.	Magnus (I)	c1075	1108–17	1117	executed

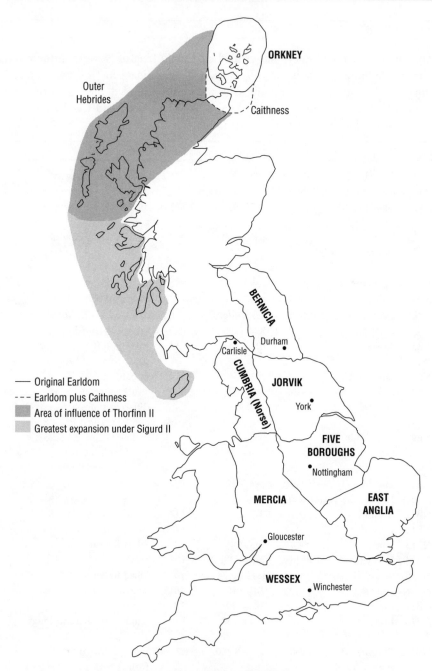

Map 11b **Earldom of Orkney**

Ref.	Ruler	Born	Reign	Died	Notes
NB26.	Paul II *the Silent*		1126–37	?1138	deposed and probably murdered
NB27.	Harald (I) *Slettmali (Smoothtalker)*		1126–31	1131	allegedly poisoned

27. The Danish and Norse Kingdoms (3) – Earls of Orkney (1)

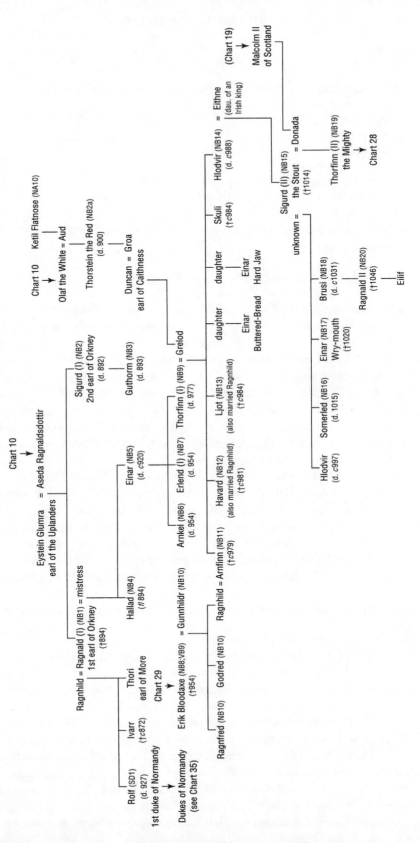

Ref.	Ruler	Born	Reign	Died	Notes
NB28.	Ragnald III	c1100	1137–58	1158	murdered
NB29.	Harald II Gamli (the Old)	1133	1139–1206	1206	
NB30.	Erlend III		1154–6	1156	killed in battle
NB31.	Harald III Ungi (the Young)	c1156	?1195–8	1198	killed in battle
NB32.	David		1206–14	1214	
NB33.	John (I)		1206–31	1231	murdered

John was the last earl of the house of Möre. With his death the earldom passed to a distant cousin and descendant of the earls of Angus. For these final Scottish-Norse earls of Orkney see page 541.

[NB1] RAGNALD (I) *THE WISE* earl of Orkney, c874–c5.

The jarl or earl of Möre on the west coast of Norway, who fought alongside the future king Harald Finehair in establishing a united Norway. Harald married Ragnald's sister Swanhilda. During this civil war many Norwegians were driven out of Norway and settled in the Shetlands and Orkney, called the Nordreys by the Norse (as distinct from the Sudreys, or Hebrides and Man), which they used as a base to attack Norway and Norse ships. The traditional view is that around 874 Harald sent Ragnald to the Hebrides to bring these islands under his authority. During the expedition Ragnald's son, Ivar, was killed. As a consequence, once Ragnald had conquered the islands, Harald granted them back to him in recompense for his son. The more recent view is that Ragnald may have set out earlier on the expedition to conquer the Nordrey pirates himself and worked in league with OLAF THE WHITE, who was the Norse king of Dublin. According to this view Olaf granted Ragnald the Orkneys around the year 871 or earlier. However, Ragnald had no desire to remain in the isles so in 875 (or earlier) Ragnald gave the islands to his brother SIGURD, and returned to Norway where he continued to fight on behalf of the king. This created enemies and around the year 894 he was burned alive in his hall by two of Harald's sons by another wife. Ragnald had three children by his wife Ragnhild. In addition to Ivar, who died, there was Rolf, who became the first Duke of Normandy, and Thori, who succeeded him as Jarl of Möre. He also had several illegitimate sons two of whom, HALLAD and EINAR (I) became later Earls of Orkney.

[NB2] SIGURD (I) *RIKI* (*THE MIGHTY*) earl of Orkney, c875–92.

He was the brother of RAGNALD (I), who was first granted the Isles but then gave them to Sigurd. Sigurd set out to establish himself a kingdom. In league with THORSTEIN THE RED, the son of OLAF THE WHITE, Sigurd began a systematic conquest of northern Scotland. Their conquests became the substance of many Norse sagas, all of which agree that these were the two mightiest warriors of their day. Between them they conquered the Picts of northern Britain, extending the border of their combined kingdom down through Caithness and Sutherland and into parts of Moray and Ross. Sigurd probably also laid claim to the northern Hebrides. The Scottish kings were too absorbed to the south in establishing their united kingdom and it is not even clear that DONALD II or his predecessors became involved in combatting the Norse conquests. This was left to the mórmaers, the earls of the Picts and the Scots. One of these was inadvertently the cause of Sigurd's death. Sigurd apparently flew into a temper when he was unable to negotiate terms with Máelbrigte, who was probably the mórmaer of Moray (and thereby an ancestor of MACBETH). He slew the mórmaer and hung his severed head from his saddle as a trophy. However the teeth of the head grazed against Sigurd's leg and gave him blood-poisoning from which he died. He was buried at Sydero on the shores of the Dornoch Firth. He was succeeded by his son GUTHORM.

[NB2a] **THORSTEIN *RAUDR* (*THE RED*)** ruled Caithness and Sutherland, c875–c900.

Thorstein was the son of OLAF *THE WHITE* and grandson of KETIL *FLATNOSE*. He stood to inherit a substantial kingdom, since Olaf was the king of Dublin, and Ketil was ruler of the Hebrides. However, Ketil displeased Olaf, and though he continued to rule, it does not seem that his heirs inherited his lands. Quite whether Olaf intended Thorstein to be his heir is not known, but by 872 Olaf had either been killed in battle or had returned to Norway. Ketil was now dead, and Thorstein decided to carve out his own kingdom. He joined forces with SIGURD THE MIGHTY of the Orkneys and together made themselves masters of much of northern Britain, certainly Caithness and Sutherland, and probably parts of Moray and Ross. Thorstein had married Thorida, the granddaughter of Cerball, king of Ossory in Ireland, and former ally of his father. He recognized the importance of political marriages as alliances following conquest. His daughter Groa married Dungad (or Duncan), the mórmaer of Caithness, who presumably recognized Thorstein as his overlord rather than the king of the Scots. Thorstein sought to extend his sovereignty further south into Scotland but he was lured into a trap and killed in the ensuing battle, probably around the year 900. After this his mother, Aud, decided she had no future in Britain. She gathered about her her family and friends and set sail for Iceland. Thorstein's son, Olaf, became the progenitor of a great dynasty in Iceland which was long remembered in the sagas.

[NB3] **GUTHORM** earl of Orkney, c892–3.

Guthorm seems to have been the only surviving legitimate son of SIGURD THE MIGHTY and inherited the earldom on his father's death. He ruled for less than a year, however, and may have died as a result of an exceptionally harsh winter. He was succeeded by his cousin, HALLAD.

[NB4] **HALLAD** earl of Orkney, c893–4.

Hallad was the eldest of the illegitimate sons of RAGNALD (I) and was granted the earldom of Orkney upon the sudden death of his cousin GUTHORM. Hallad was unable to control the raiding from Danish pirates or settle the complaints of farmers who came to Hallad to seek resolution. He abdicated his earldom and returned to Norway in ignominy. He was succeeded by his brother EINAR (I).

[NB5] **EINAR (I)** earl of Orkney c894–?920.

He was known as *Torf*-Einar because he introduced turf as a fuel to the islanders. He was the brother of the disgraced HALLAD who had been unable to control the Danish pirates in the western seas. Einar pleaded with his father to let him have the responsibility. He was given one longship and crew. He sailed first to the Shetlands to recruit more men and then advanced on the leaders of the Danish Vikings, Thori Treebeard and Kalf Skurfa, whom he killed, regaining control of the Orkneys. Soon after the Orkneys were invaded by Halfdan Haaleg, the son of the Norwegian king. Halfdan had already killed Einar's father, RAGNALD, and seemed intent on wiping out Ragnald's family. Einar escaped but conducted a surprise raid and captured Halfdan, whom he killed by carving an eagle shape out of his body in revenge for the death of his father. He sacrificed the remains to Odin. Harald Finehair brought his fleet to the Orkneys and exacted compensation from Einar for the death of his son, but he allowed him to retain his title as earl of Orkney. Although Einar is described as ugly, with one blind eye, he was remembered as a strong leader who protected his islanders, though in return confiscated their independent tenure and treated them as tenants. He apparently ruled much of the territory conquered by SIGURD and THORSTEIN, which included Caithness and Sutherland and parts of Ross. The date of his death is not recorded, though the sagas note that he ruled for a long time and died of a sickness. Allowing for the ages of his sons to succeed him he must have ruled to at least the year 920 or even later.

[NB6] **ARNKEL** earl of Orkney, 920 (or later)–54; jointly with
[NB7] **ERLEND (I)** earl of Orkney 920 (or later)–54.
The sons of *Torf*-EINAR, they ruled the earldom jointly, probably splitting the territory along the lines of the original arrangement between SIGURD (I) and THORSTEIN, with one ruling the Nordreys (Orkney and Shetland) and the northern Hebrides, and the other the mainland of Caithness and Sutherland. During their rule their earldom was taken over by ERIK BLOODAXE, the deposed king of Norway. They had to submit to his authority, and he installed himself as king of Orkney some time around 937. He used the Orkneys as the base for raiding the Scottish coast and islands, and Arnkel and Erlend accompanied him on his raids. Both brothers were eventually killed with Eric when they were ambushed on Stainmore in 954. This suggests they had installed themselves alongside Eric in his kingship of York. They were succeeded by their younger brother, THORFINN SKULL-SPLITTER.

[NB8;NC11;VB9] **ERIK** or **EIRIKR** *BLOODAXE* king of Norway, 933–c4; king of Orkney, 937–54; king of York, (?939–40?), 947–8, 952–4.
As his nickname suggests, Erik was the epitome of the modern-day image of the Viking – one who delighted in plundering, raping and slaughter. He was the favourite son of Harald Finehair, the first king of all Norway, and was probably spoilt. When he came to the throne after Harald's abdication in 933 he instigated a reign of terror that resulted in him being deposed in favour of his more mild-mannered half-brother, Haakon, who had been educated in England at the court of ATHELSTAN. Erik commanded a fleet of ships and a crew every bit as vicious as himself and set off to see what he could conquer. He came first to the Orkneys, governed by the descendents of his father's commander RAGNALD, ARNKEL and ERLEND, and immediately imposed his authority. Some authorities disagree on this early date for Erik's exile, preferring to place it a decade later. The difference is significant as it means Erik would not have been able to negotiate with Athelstan to be made a vassal ruler of York, as some records suggest he did in the summer of 939. This might have accounted for the invasion of York by OLAF GOTHFRITHSON in

November 939, to claim what he regarded as his birthright, but the record also suggests that Olaf entered York unopposed. If Erik had been installed as vassal king he was either absent, or had made good his exit before Olaf's arrival. Erik remained in Orkney, continuing his life of piracy until another opportunity presented itself in 947 after the death of EDMUND of Wessex, who had previously driven out the other Norse kings of York. Although the *witan* of York pledged their allegiance to Edmund's successor EADRED, Wulfstan, the archbishop of York, extended an invitation to Erik to become their king. Why Wulfstan should wish York to be ruled by such a bloodthirsty pagan is not clear, unless Wulfstan expected Erik to defeat Eadred and take over the English throne. To the Norse of York, however, Erik was welcome as a son of their royal house. No sooner was he ensconced, however, towards the close of 947, than Northumbria was invaded by Eadred, with limited success but enough to threaten devastation of the land unless they deposed Erik. At the same time OLAF SITRICSON, himself incensed at a rival claiming the throne he believed was his, had brought his army from Dublin to Scotland and allied with MALCOLM. The two invaded York and Erik was expelled. Eadred allowed Olaf to rule on the basis that he kept Erik at bay. However, in 954, through the machinations of Wulfstan, Olaf was himself expelled from York and Erik welcomed back. Eadred would have none of this and invaded Northumbria, capturing and imprisoning Wulfstan. It seems that during this second (or third) reign, Erik had brought with him Arnkel and Erlend from Orkney, and it suggests he retained as much interest in continuing a life of plunder from York as he had from Orkney, even though by now he was approaching his late sixties. However, with his main agent gone, support for Erik began to fade and in 954 he was driven from York. This time an army, led by Earl Maccus of Stainmore, lay in wait and ambushed Erik and his companions on their journey north, where most were killed. His wife, GUNNHILDR, and two of their sons survived and returned to Orkney to reimpose their rule.

[NB9] **GUNNHILDR** queen of Orkney, 954–5, 976–7.
[NB9a] **GODRED** or **GOTHFRITH** co-ruler of Orkney, 954–5, 976–7.
[NB9b] **RAGNFRED** co-ruler of Orkney, 954–5, 976–7.

Gunnhildr was the widow of ERIK BLOODAXE who bore him eight sons and one daughter. She was the daughter of Gorm the Old, the first king of united Denmark and their marriage had no doubt been a political alliance between Gorm and Erik's father, Harald Finehair of Norway. Nevertheless the two seemed well matched, for Gunnhildr supported her husband throughout his turbulent life. After his death at Stainmore in 954 she and her sons Ragnfred and Godred returned to Orkney with as much treasure from York as they could transport. There she established herself as queen with her sons taking over the earlship from THORFINN. They returned to Denmark in the following year. She lived well into her seventies, for she came back to the Orkneys in 976 when support for her brother waned in Denmark, but she left again in 977 to return finally to her homeland. Although she imposed herself as queen she no doubt used the islands as a quiet retreat, leaving the government to Thorfinn. Her daughter, Ragnhild, was married first to Thorfinn's son ARNFINN, and later to Arnfinn's other brothers HAVARD and LIOT after killing the first two.

[NB10] **THORFINN (I)** *HAUSAKLIFFER* (*SKULL-SPLITTER*) earl of Orkney *c*947–77.

He was the youngest son of EINAR (I) and was probably born about the year 910 or slightly earlier. The sagas recall that he ruled jointly with his brothers ARNKEL and ERLEND, though he is unlikely to have done so from the start, and may only have done so once all three had become vassals to ERIK BLOODAXE, who imposed his authority on the earldom in 937. Thorfinn's nickname suggests he was strong and powerful in battle, and he almost certainly joined his brothers with their new leader in their raids about the coast. Thorfinn's brothers do not seem to have married, but Thorfinn married Grelod, the daughter of the mórmaer of Caithness and granddaughter of THORSTEIN THE RED. He had five sons and two daughters. Whereas Thorfinn's elder brothers were closer companions of Erik's, and were with him during his final rule of York, Thorfinn remained behind in Orkney, and thus may have been the sole authority on the island for much of the time from 947 on. Even though he inherited the earldom after his brothers were killed alongside Erik in 954, he remained subservient to Erik's widow GUNNHILDR and her sons when they returned to Orkney that same year. It was at this time that Thorfinn's son ARNFINN married Gunnhildr's daughter Ragnhild. However, once they left in 955, Thorfinn finally became sole earl, though he had to relinquish that briefly to Gunnhildr and her sons when they returned in 976. Thorfinn lived to an old age, probably about sixty-seven, and was accorded a proud Viking burial in the Sound of Hoxa off South Ronaldsay.

[NB11] **ARNFINN** earl of Orkney, 977–?9.

Arnfinn was the son of THORFINN SKULL-SPLITTER. Through his mother he also inherited a right to the Scottish earldom of Caithness which his great-grandfather THORSTEIN had previously conquered. However, the right to Caithness was almost certainly claimed by his mother's kin of the family of Duncan, the mórmaer of Caithness, and from Arnfinn's day conflict grew between the Picts of Caithness and the Norse of Orkney over control of the mainland. In 954 Arnfinn had married Ragnhild, the daughter of ERIK BLOODAXE who, according to the *Orkneyinga Saga* was a scheming and wicked woman. She sought power and decided Arnfinn was not what she wanted, so she had him murdered at Murkle in Caithness. The date is not known, but it was probably only a year or two after he inherited the earldom. She then moved on to his brother, HAVARD.

[NB12] **HAVARD** earl of Orkney, ?979–?81.

Havard succeeded his brother ARNFINN who had been murdered by his wife, Ragnhild. Havard may have been involved in the murder, because he promptly married Ragnhild. However, he soon fell victim to her scheming as, once she realised Havard was not going to give her the power she wanted, she plotted with his nephew, Einar, that she would marry him and make him earl if he killed Havard. Einar was known by the delightful nickname of *Klining*, or "buttered-bread"! Einar murdered Havard at Stenness, on Orkney, though we do not know when. As with Arnfinn, Ragnhild probably wasted little time. It has been pointed out that as Havard was known as "Season-prosperous" and that he was good with harvests, that several years must have passed for him to earn that reputation. However, he may already have been known as that before he became earl, as he was probably nearly forty at the time. It only needed one good summer to continue the reputation. He may therefore have ruled only from about 979–980 or 981. Ragnhild did not fulfil her promise and instead contrived with another nephew, called Einar Hard-Jaw, to murder the first Einar in return for her hand. This was duly done, but then Ragnhild married LIOT instead who killed Einar for his crime.

[NB13] **LIOT** or **LJOT** earl of Orkney, ?981–?4.

Liot was the fourth son of THORFINN *SKULL-SPLITTER* and the next victim of Ragnhild's master scheme of power. He succeeded his brothers ARNFINN and HAVARD whom Ragnhild had previously married, and he now married her, killing her previous paramour, his nephew Einar. Liot was probably about thirty-five or slightly less. Ragnhild was now in her early fifties, but as the granddaughter of both Harald Finehair of Norway and Gorm the Old of Denmark she wielded tremendous power, and was looking for the man who could fulfil her dreams. Liot may have been that man, as he certainly did not avoid a fight. Liot's younger brother, Skuli, disputed Liot's claim to Orkney, and sought support from KENNETH II of Scotland, who made Skuli earl of Caithness. This shows that the earls of Orkney recognized the Scottish king's authority over mainland Scotland, despite their earlier conquest of Caithness. Skuli invaded Orkney but was driven back into Caithness. Liot followed him and reclaimed Caithness, driving Skuli south back into Scotland. Skuli raised an army with the support of Kenneth II and advanced again on Liot, but again Liot was victorious and Skuli was killed. Liot now openly claimed sovereignty over much of northern Scotland, so that Maelbrigte, the mórmaer of Moray, and ancestor of MACBETH, raised his army against Liot. They met at the battle of Skidmoor in Caithness. Maelbrigte was defeated but Liot died of his wounds. Nothing more is heard of Ragnhild after this. Liot was succeeded by his elder brother HLODVIR. It is possible that Liot's name was sufficiently well known across Britain for it to influence the Arthurian legends in placing Lot (LEUDONUS) as king of Orkney rather than of Lothian.

[NB14] **HLODVIR** earl of Orkney, ?984–?7.

Hlodvir was the last surviving son of THORFINN *SKULL-SPLITTER*. He may have been born about 946 and although we do not know the date of his accession it cannot have been much earlier than 983 or 984 to have allowed for the internecine struggles between his brothers. Hlodvir managed to keep out of the way of his scheming sister-in-law Ragnhild, probably because he was already married (to Ethne, the daughter of an Irish king, in about 966). We know nothing more about Hlodvir's reign, and he died, probably of an illness, in 986 or 987. He was buried at Hofn in Caithness. He had two daughters and one son, SIGURD, who succeeded him. One daughter married Gilli, the earl of the Hebrides, whilst the other married Havard, the steward of Caithness.

[NB15] **SIGURD II** *DIGRI* (*THE STOUT*) earl of Orkney *c*987–1014.

He was the only son of HLODVIR, but became one of the mightiest of the Orkney earls. The first few years were ones of either conquest, regaining lost lands or establishing authority. It happened rapidly for by 988 he was in battle against two Scottish earls who had killed his sister's husband, Havard, whom his father, Hldovir, had created steward of Caithness. Sigurd was victorious and reclaimed control over Caithness. He was subsequently challenged by FINDLAECH, the earl of

Moray, whom Sigurd defeated at the second battle of Skidmoor about 995. Sigurd had needed the support of his tenant farmers but they refused to fight without the return of their rights of independence which had been denied them by EINAR (I) ninety years earlier. Sigurd used his powerful fleet to establish authority over the Hebrides down as far as Man, though in the latter case he did no more than exact tribute. He appointed his commander, Gilli, earl of the Hebrides and gave him his sister in marriage in about the year 990.

One of the most important and famous episodes in Sigurd's life was his conversion to Christianity, albeit superficially. In 995, Olaf Tryggvasson was returning from England (where he had been involved in raids with SWEIN FORK-BEARD) to take up the kingship of Norway. Olaf had been converted to Christianity by the English king ATHELRED, and as the incoming sovereign over the Orkneys he visited Sigurd and encouraged him to adopt christianity. It took some encouraging as Sigurd was a proud son of Odin, but Olaf tricked him by threatening to sacrifice his son Hundi unless Sigurd accepted the faith. Sigurd conceded, but Olaf still took Hundi as hostage to ensure Sigurd remained faithful. Unfortunately Hundi died soon after, and Sigurd dropped his allegiance both to Olaf and to the Christian faith. Instead Sigurd now looked to the new king of Scotland, MALCOLM II, as a possible ally. Malcolm saw the advantage of having a powerful partner to the north as they could squeeze between them the troublesome rulers of Moray, who laid claim to the Scottish throne. It also meant that Sigurd recognized Malcolm's authority over the mainland of Scotland, thus strengthening Malcolm's position. Soon after 1005 Malcolm granted Sigurd authority over Caithness, Sutherland and Ross (not that it was necessarily his to grant) and gave Sigurd his daughter Donada, probably in the year 1006. Donada was the wife of Findlaech and the mother of MACBETH. Such arrangements infuriated the mórmaers of Moray but at this stage they were powerless to do anything. The power and authority of Sigurd is attested to by the events at the end of his life. In 1013 he was approached by Sitric Silkenbeard, the Norse king of Dublin, for help in his battle against the Irish high king, Brian Bóru. Sitric promised that if they were victorious, Sigurd would become high king of Ireland. Sitric needed Sigurd's support because it brought with it a vast army and navy from the scattered islands of Scotland. The battle took place at Clontarf on 23 April 1014. The Irish were victorious even though Brian Bóru was killed. It put an end to Norse ambitions in Ireland, and it also saw the death of Sigurd. Although he left the major part of his lands to his sons by his first marriage, it was his son by the daughter of Malcolm II, THORFINN THE BLACK who was to prove the greatest of the Orkney earls.

[NB16] **SOMERLED** earl of Orkney, April 1014–?1015.
The son of SIGURD II, he shared the earldom with his brothers BRUSI and EINAR but died about a year later, opening up a problem of territorial succession with his half-brother THORFINN. He was, apparently, a quiet and mild-mannered man, far from the traditional Viking.

[NB17] **EINAR II** *RANGMUND* (*FALSEMOUTH*) co-earl of Orkney 23 April 1014–14 October 1020.
Unlike his two elder brothers, Einar was ambitious and cruel and clearly wanted the whole of the Orkneys to himself. After SOMERLED's death in 1015, Einar inherited

his share and when their half-brother THORFINN objected, BRUSI bequeathed Einar his share provided he shared part of the earldom with Thorfinn. Einar was a notorious summer warrior and pirate, giving little concern to the welfare of his subjects, which task subsequently fell to Brúsi. Einar was regularly involved in battles in Ireland, and with the Norse kings of Dublin, but he suffered a significant defeat in 1018. This dented his pride and made him even more intolerable. In 1019 he killed the Norse earl Eyvind, who was stormbound on Hoy. This angered the Norse king Olaf, and it was almost certainly with Olaf's support that Einar was murdered the following year by Thorkel, Thorfinn's foster-father, while Einar was a guest at Thorkel's home in Sandwick. Einar's territories passed back to Brúsi.

[NB18] **BRÚSI** earl of Orkney, 1014–18, 1020–c30/1.
Son of SIGURD II, he initially shared the earldom with his brothers SOMERLED and EINAR. He was apparently a mild and peace-loving man who sought to be fair in all of his dealings, and he thus became the voice of sanity in the inheritance dispute that followed the death of Somerled in 1015, most of which is detailed under THORFINN. At one point he handed over his share of the inheritance to Einar on the basis that if he outlived Einar he would receive it back along with Einar's share. This happened after Einar's murder, and from 1020–8 Brúsi was the senior earl of Orkney, responsible for its defence and upkeep. He ruled wisely and was very popular with the Orcadians. After 1028 he handed the administration over the Thorfinn and by 1030, when he was about fifty, he retired all together. He died soon after, though the date is not recorded. His son was RAGNALD (II).

[NB19] **THORFINN II** known variously as *THE BLACK* and *THE MIGHTY*, shared part of the earldom of Orkney from 1018, most of it from 1028 and all of it from c1030 except for 1038–46, when he shared it with RAGNALD II.
Thorfinn's inheritance is complicated. He was the son of SIGURD II after his second marriage to Donada, the daughter of MALCOLM II of Scotland, and thus half-brother to MACBETH. When his father died at Clontarf in 1014, Thorfinn was only six or seven and was left in the care of the Scottish king. Malcolm confirmed Thorfinn as earl of Caithness, and installed him at Duncansby with a body of advisers and guardians. The leading official was Thorkel, known as the Fosterer. Malcolm clearly saw this as an opportunity to gain control over Caithness and possibly Orkney itself. It also gave him a powerful ally over the mórmaers of Moray. He thus supported Thorfinn as he grew into an intelligent but precocious young man, ambitious for power and wealth. Even at the age of eleven, possibly less, he became embroiled in a squabble over inheritance with his half-brothers, following the death of SOMERLED, who had left his territory to EINAR, who was every bit as ambitious as Thorfinn. Thorfinn, no doubt urged on by Malcolm, disputed Einar's share. Einar refused to budge, on the basis that Thorfinn already had Caithness, which was not part of the arrangement. Two years of negotiation ensued, mediated by the third brother, BRUSI. Eventually, in 1018, Brúsi bequeathed Einar his share of the land on the basis that Einar shared a third with Thorfinn. Einar did so, but refused to pay Thorfinn his share of the revenues. To settle the dispute Thorfinn travelled to the court of Olaf, king of Norway, in the summer of 1020. Olaf supported Thorfinn and gave both him and Thorkel a longship each. They returned to Caithness and prepared to embattle Einar until Brúsi negotiated a peace. Einar visited Thorkel at Sandwick,

28. The Danish and Norse Kingdoms (4) – Earls of Orkney (2)

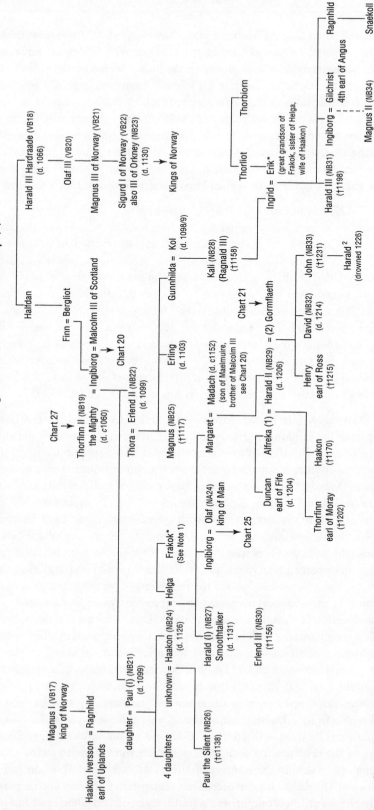

Note: 1. See connection between Frakok and her great-grandson Erik father of Harald III
2. After John's death in 1231 the earldom passed to Magnus II who it is conjectured was the nephew of Harald III

where he was promptly murdered. Thorkel was forgiven for this crime by King Olaf (who had no love for Einar) but he used it as an opportunity to claim a share of the Orkneys himself, so that by 1021, Brúsi, Olaf and Thorfinn each administered a third. Thorfinn negotiated to administer Olaf's third as a fief of the king, which was agreed, but Brúsi also earned the king's respect and was allowed the greater share of the earldom. From 1021 to 1028 therefore, Brúsi was the senior earl and administrator in Orkney, whilst Thorfinn retained one-third of that earldom, plus his own earldom in Caithness. Brúsi eventually handed over the majority of the earldom to Thorfinn in 1028, and all of it in 1030.

It was retaining his hold on Caithness that occupied most of his time from then on. The lands had long been under threat from FINDLAECH, MALCOLM and GILLECOMGAIN, the mórmaers of Moray. It is recorded that Thorfinn was in battle against them for much of his early adult life, though this changed when his half-brother MACBETH succeeded to the stewardship. By then Thorfinn's main adversary was the man the sagas call Karl Hundisson, who was probably the Scottish king DUNCAN (I), Thorfinn's cousin. Duncan/Hundisson invaded Caithness in 1040 with a view to conquest but was defeated by Thorfinn twice, resulting in Duncan's death. Thorfinn followed up this victory by not only reclaiming Caithness but Sutherland, Moray and Ross, so that he now dominated all of northern Scotland.

In 1038 Thorfinn was forced to share a third of the earldom with his nephew, RAGNALD, the son of Brúsi, who had been confirmed as earl by the king of Norway. Thorfinn tolerated Ragnald at first, in fact they seemed to work well together, and the two of them reconquered the Western Isles, which had been lost to the earldom since Clontarf. Thorfinn also exacted retribution upon Ireland for its support of Hundisson and in 1042 raided as far south as England, probably using the Isle of Man as his base. Thorfinn had no serious ambitions on England it was as much a show of strength, but it confirmed his authority. He and Ragnald now ruled over half of Scotland, including all of the surrounding islands. Unfortunately by 1045 the relationship between the two suffered when Thorfinn demanded Ragnald pay over the revenues from his third to help support the Norse earl, Kalf Arnesson, who had fled from Norway to seek refuge in the Orkneys. Thorfinn had married Kalf's niece, Ingibiorg, some years earlier. Ragnald refused and after a year of arguing, Ragnald went to Norway, received the support of King Magnus, and returned to the Orkneys with a fighting force. He defeated Thorfinn at first, but then Kalf Arnesson brought his soldiers into the picture and he and Thorfinn drove Ragnald back to Norway. Ragnald was reinforced by King Magnus, returned and caught Thorfinn by surprise, burning down his house. Thorfinn escaped to Caithness, but in his turn, came back and burned Ragnald's house. Ragnald was killed while escaping. Thorfinn reconciled himself with King Magnus and from then till his death was the sole earl of Orkney. He now underwent a conversion and, in 1048, went on a tour through the courts of Europe, culminating in a visit to the pope, who forgave him for his past sins. It is not stated that Thorfinn was baptized into the Christian faith, but after 1048 he was a professed Christian and, on his return to Orkney, he established an episcopal church beside his royal household at Birsay, with its first bishop Thorolf. With the help of Thorolf, Thorfinn completely reorganized the administrative and legal structure of his earldom. Surprisingly the exact date of his death, which followed a long illness, is not known. It is unlikely to be as late as 1065, as often recorded, because his widow Ingibiorg married MALCOLM III of Scotland and bore three children before 1069. He probably died between 1057 and 1060. Although his territories were always subject to the king of Scotland (on the mainland) and the king of Norway (Orkney and the Western Isles), Thorfinn seems to have governed with almost total autonomy, certainly towards the end of his life, and was ahead of his Scandinavian contemporaries in establishing a bishopric in his lands. Despite his early petulance and ambition, he became a wise and dedicated ruler, recognized throughout Europe, though today he is one of the forgotten great rulers of Britain. After his death his lands were shared between his two sons, PAUL and ERLEND (II).

[NB20] **RAGNALD II** earl of Orkney jointly with THORFINN II 1038–46.
Had Ragnald lived at another time he might have been better remembered, and achieved more, for he was a valiant earl, tall and strong, intelligent and gifted. He was the son of BRUSI and thus the nephew of Thorfinn. He was born in 1011, and remained at the court of the Norwegian king Olaf after 1021 in return for Brúsi's government of the Orkneys. Ragnald grew into a powerful young man who accompanied Olaf on many expeditions throughout Norway and into Russia. He fought alongside Olaf in the disastrous battle of Stikklestad in July 1030, from which he fled to Sweden and again to Russia where he joined the guard of the Russian Grand Duke Yaroslav. He eventually returned to Norway with the young king Magnus in 1036, when he was confirmed in his share of the earldom of Orkney. As detailed under the entry on Thorfinn, the two worked well together at the outset and between them conquered all of the Western Isles and ruled territory which stretched from Shetland in the north to Man in the south, with domain over much of the fiords and inlets of western Scotland. Unfortunately in 1046 he and Thorfinn became enemies over money issues (sparked off by a relatively minor matter over the upkeep of the refugee earl Kalf Arnesson, but probably more deeply rooted in territorial claims) and the ensuing dispute resulted in the death of Ragnald at the hands of Thorfinn's now aged foster-father Thorkel in December 1046. Early in their argument Ragnald defeated Thorfinn, and it is interesting to speculate whether Ragnald would have gone on to be a more stable and wise governor than Thorfinn became. Although Ragnald had a son, Eilaf, he never endeavoured to claim his inheritance.

[NB21] **PAUL (I)** joint earl of Orkney, c1060–98.
[NB22] **ERLEND II** joint earl of Orkney c1060–98.
Paul was the elder son of THORFINN II and inherited the earldom with his brother ERLEND (II). It is possible that both were installed as earls of Caithness in 1057, prior to Thorfinn's death, suggesting that the earldom may have become regarded as a title for the heir(s) apparent. We do not know for certain when Paul was born, but it was probably about 1038. Already by that date Thorfinn was professing his Christian beliefs by naming his first-born Paul, unless he was not christened until Thorfinn's visit to the pope in 1048. When the brothers inherited the earldom they ruled it jointly and did not divide the lands or revenues between them. It seems they worked well together and generally agreed in all their actions. Soon after their father's death, Harald Hardraada, the king of Norway, arrived in the Orkneys prior

to his invasion of England. He raised additional levies from amongst the earldom, which stretched as far as the Western Isles, and when he sailed for England in 1066, he was accompanied by both earls. Although Harald was defeated by HAROLD II of England at Stamford Bridge in September 1066, the two earls survived and returned to Orkney with Harald's son, Olaf, who remained with them during that winter before returning to establishing himself as king of Norway the following year. It is evident that they did not believe they had authority over all of the Western Isles, since they were not involved in the usurpation of Man by GODRED CROVAN in 1079. For most of their reign the two earls governed wisely and continued to develop and promote the bishopric of Orkney, but by the year 1090 or so a rift occurred between them over the ambitions of their respective sons, especially Paul's son HAAKON. Haakon was eventually banished from Orkney in 1093, and he stayed in Norway and Sweden for the next few years. It was he who encouraged Magnus III of Norway to visit his estates in the western seas and this planted the idea of Magnus installing his son, SIGURD (III), as king of the Orkneys, using the islands as an appanage for the heir to the throne. Magnus sailed to the Orkneys in the spring of 1098 and deposed the two earls, despite the care they had shown to his father Olaf. The earls were taken in captivity back to Norway where they both died within the year, Paul at Bergen and Erlend at Nidaros (Trondheim).

[NB23;NA22] **SIGURD III** later known as *JORSALAFARI (THE CRUSADER)*, king of Orkney and the Isles 1099–1105; king of Norway, 1103–30.
He was the son of Magnus III, king of Norway, and was created king of Orkney and the Isles in spring 1099 after the deaths of the incumbent earls PAUL (I) and ERLEND (II), whom his father had deposed. Magnus reconquered the southern Hebrides, which included the Isle of Man, in 1099 and included these in the kingdom. Sigurd was only about ten at this time, and the title was clearly seen as an honorary entitlement to the heir to the throne. His father returned to Norway in the summer of 1099 leaving Sigurd under the charge of Paul's son HAAKON, who had first encouraged Magnus to come to his lands in the Western Seas. Magnus returned in 1102 with a view to further consolidating his territories, particularly in Ireland. That year a political marriage was arranged between Sigurd and Blathmina, the daughter of Murchadh O'Brien, the Irish high king, although she was only five. Magnus died in Ireland in August 1103, causing Sigurd to return to Norway as king. He left Haakon in charge as his lieutenant, creating him the next earl of Orkney in 1105. In Man and the Isles, DOMNALL MAC TEIGE and OLAF THE RED assumed the kingship. Sigurd ruled as king of Norway until 1130.

[NB24] **HAAKON** earl of Orkney, 1105–26.
Haakon was the son of PAUL (I). He was probably born about 1070 or soon after and, as he came of age, he became involved in a succession dispute with his cousins, Erling and MAGNUS, the sons of ERLEND II. Haakon became such a problem that in 1093 he was banished and spent the next few years at the courts of the kings of Norway and Sweden. They evidently liked him for in 1098 Haakon convinced Magnus III, the king of Norway, that he should visit his territories to the west. Magnus used this as an opportunity to extend his hold over the Scottish islands. He deposed Paul and Erlend, sending them back to Norway in captivity. They died soon after, and Magnus created his own son, SIGURD (III) king of Orkney and the

Isles. Sigurd was only ten, so when Magnus returned to Norway in the spring of 1099, he left Haakon as regent. Sigurd returned to Norway in 1103 after the death of his father, leaving Haakon in charge and, in 1105, created him earl. Haakon was somewhat displeased when he cousin, MAGNUS, whom he quite possibly thought dead, reappeared in 1106 and was also made earl of Orkney two years later by Sigurd's co-ruler in Norway, King Eystein II. The two cousins ruled together amicably for a while since they both fought against a distant cousin called Duffnial, who laid claim to part of the Orkney estates. However, once he was defeated the old enmity returned and in the resultant conflict Magnus was imprisoned and executed (1117). One tradition states that Haakon later went on a pilgrimage to Rome to expiate his sins and he returned, like his grandfather, an older and a wiser man. He governed the Orkneys with good sense, established new laws which improved on THORFINN's, and ensured peace for the rest of his reign. He died in 1126. He was married twice, and children of both marriages – PAUL (II) and HARALD (I) – succeeded him.

[NB25] **MAGNUS (I)** later *SAINT MAGNUS*, earl of Orkney 1108–16 April 1117. He was the son of ERLEND II and from his youth was in a succession dispute with his cousin HAAKON. When Orkney was taken over by Magnus III of Norway, Magnus became his page, and accompanied him on his raids to the Western Isles, Wales and Ireland. However his Christian upbringing came to the fore and Magnus refused to fight in the battle of Anglesey Sound, in June 1098. He escaped to Scotland and sought refuge first with King Edgar and then the earls of Moray. Whether his survival was known to Haakon is not clear, but once Haakon had been created earl in 1105, Magnus returned to the Orkneys to stake his claim. Neither cousin could agree so Magnus sailed to Norway to seek dispensation from the joint rulers. King Eystein II bestowed the title of earl on Magnus in 1108 and an entitlement to his father's share of the lands. Haakon accepted the arrangement and for a while the two cousins co-existed amicably, even working together to fight off a distant cousin with his own claim on the title. During this period both cousins governed with an iron hand, being fair in their judgements, but stern when necessary. They suffered no opposition in their lands. However, by 1116 the friction between the two became intolerable and conflict erupted. Haakon eventually imprisoned Magnus on the small island of Egilsay where he had him executed on 16 April 1117 (some records say 1116). A cult grew around Magnus, who was supposed to have prayed for the souls of his executioners as he was killed. Miracles were soon attributed to his relics, and a church was erected in his name at Kirkwall by RAGNALD III, where his relics were translated. He subsequently became the patron saint of the Orkneys.

[NB26] **PAUL II** *THE SILENT*, earl of Orkney 1126–37.
He was the elder son of Earl HAAKON and initially ruled jointly with his half-brother HARALD (I) who plotted against him. Tradition suggests that Harald died from a poisoned shirt prepared for Paul, and after Harald's death Paul banished his stepmother Helga and her sister Frakok to Harald's estates in Sutherland. Paul ruled unopposed for the next four years until his cousin, Kali (RAGNALD III), claimed his share of the inheritance. Paul refused and, in 1136, hostilities erupted. Kali was defeated and retreated to Norway, but returned the following year with additional support and deposed Paul. Paul was sent to his sister's home in Atholl, where one

tradition states that Paul was imprisoned, blinded and later murdered, though the date is not known.

[NB27] **HARALD (I)** *SLETTMALI* (*SMOOTH-TALKER*) earl of Orkney 1126–December 1131, jointly with his half-brother PAUL II.
The son of Earl HAAKON, he took as his share of the inheritance the lands in Sutherland and Caithness. He was a friend of Sigurd, claimant to the Norwegian throne, and the two of them plotted to overthrow Paul. Although a peace was negotiated it was evident that Harald, together with his mother Helga and her sister Frakok, continued to plot against Paul. At Christmas 1131 they gathered at Orphir on Mainland. Tradition states that the two sisters had made a shirt dipped in poison for Paul, but Harald wore it by mistake and died. His son was ERLEND (III).

[NB28] **RAGNALD III** earl of Orkney 1137–20 August 1158.
The grandson of ERLEND II and nephew of MAGNUS (I). His given name was Kali, and it seems that early in his life he had no pretensions to the earldom. He served as a merchant, and it was during one of his trading expeditions, at Grimsby, that he became acquainted with Gillechrist, the brother of Sigurd I of Norway (see Earl SIGURD III). He returned to Norway where he became an official at Sigurd's court. Sigurd created Kali earl of Orkney in 1129, granting him the lands that had been held by Magnus, though Kali still remained in Norway. In March 1130 Sigurd died. Kali supported Gillechrist in his claim on the throne but they were defeated by Magnus IV, who deprived Kali of his earldom. However five years later Gillechrist deposed Magnus and came to the throne as Harald IV. In 1135 he reinvested Kali with the earldom, and Kali requested his share of the lands and revenues from his cousin PAUL II. Paul refused and in 1136 Kali set sail with a fleet to regain his inheritance. He was defeated in his battles that year and he returned to Norway, but in the next spring he set off with a larger fleet and this time deposed Paul who was sent in exile to his sister's in Atholl. Kali thus inherited all of the earldom and took the name Ragnald.

The Sagas describe Kali as a well set man, fair-haired and strong-limbed. He was apparently extremely likeable, as he had more friends than most and always dealt fairly whenever he could. Thus when two years later he was prevailed upon by the bishop of Orkney to grant lands in Orkney to Paul's nephew, HARALD (II), he agreed readily and he brought Harald to the islands in 1140, gave him half the lands, and created him earl, though he was aged only six. Kali was always an adventurer at heart and in 1151 he decided to undertake a pilgrimage to Palestine after the failure of the Second Crusade. He left Harald in control, supported by Thorbiorn, who was the grandson of Frakok, the aunt of earl HARALD I. He set sail with a fleet of fifteen ships. His travels took him to Spain, where he had many adventures, to the Barbary Coast and eventually to Acre, which he does not seem to have reached until 1153. After a year he travelled to Constantinople, spending the winter with the Emperor Manuel I, before returning home across Europe, visiting Rome and Norway, and arriving in the Orkneys in December 1155. On his return he discovered that Harald was at war with ERLEND (II), who had been made earl of Caithness by MALCOLM IV of Scotland. Kali initially supported Erlend, but afterwards Kali changed allegiance to Harald and together they defeated Erlend, who was killed in the battle. During this period Kali banished Thorbiorn who had murdered one of Kali's bodyguard, and Thorbiorn achieved his revenge two years later when he murdered Kali in Caithness.

[NB29] **HARALD II** *GAMLI* (*THE OLD*) earl of Orkney 1139–1206.

Harald was the longest serving earl of Orkney, although he was only six when RAGNALD III made him earl at the urging of the bishops of Orkney and Dunkeld. He was the son of Madach, earl of Atholl, whose wife Margaret was the sister of HARALD I, thus making Harald the grandson of HAAKON. Harald joined Ragnald on a trip to Norway in 1148, where Harald was confirmed in his earldom by king Inge. When Ragnald left on his crusade to Palestine in spring 1151 Harald, then aged 18, was left in full authority, supported by his first cousin (once removed) Thorbiorn. No sooner had Ragnald departed than Harald's cousin, ERLEND (III), the son of Harald I, claimed his share of the earldom. This dispute lasted for several years and in 1154 Erlend defeated Harald and ejected him from the earldom. Harald retained his share of the earldom of Caithness, however, and used this as his base in his unsuccessful attempts to regain the Orkneys. When Ragnald returned from his pilgrimage in 1155, he was initially supportive of Erlend until Erlend failed to return Ragnald's own share of the Orkneys. Ragnald then combined forces with Harald and, after a long struggle during the summer and autumn of 1156, with the advantage shifting from side to side, deposed Erlend and killed him. Ragnald was himself murdered two years later, leaving Harald the sole earl from August 1158.

For the next twenty years Harald ruled alone. He was evidently a popular ruler, as he was remembered by the sagamen as "a mighty chief, one of the strongest of men", but he was also hard-hearted as can be seen by his subsequent treatment of Earl HARALD III. Matters soured towards the end of his earldom. In 1194 Sigurd Magnusson used Orkney as the base for his insurrection against Sverre, the king of Norway. After Sigurd was killed, Harald was summoned to Norway to atone for allowing Sigurd to operate from Orkney. Harald was pardoned but he had to pay considerable fines and taxes to Sverre and was deprived of the Shetlands. In 1197 Harald encouraged his son, Thorfinn, to invade Moray, and this prompted WILLIAM *THE LYON* of Scotland to invade Caithness where he captured Harald and held him in prison. He was eventually restored to Orkney after Thorfinn surrendered himself. It was soon after this that he came into conflict with Harald III. Although he was the grandson of Ragnald III, who had always been kind and helpful to Harald the Old, Harald would not accept Harald the Young as his partner in the earldom. The dispute lasted for perhaps three years. Eventually Harald the Young prepared an invasion fleet but he was outfoxed by Harald the Old, who descended on his younger namesake and killed him at the Battle of Wick in 1198. Harald thereupon occupied Caithness. This angered William of Scotland, who confiscated Caithness and passed it in fief to RAGNALD Godredsson of Man. Harald recovered it in 1201, causing William to send his army north again. This time Harald reached terms with William, which meant him paying a quarter of his revenues on the lands over to the king. He agreed, because just at this same time Sverre of Norway had died, and Harald apparently refused to pay his fines to Norway thereafter. Harald died in 1206 aged about seventy-three. He had married twice and had eleven children. His eldest surviving son (since Thorfinn had died in 1202 and Haakon was killed in battle in Ireland in 1170), Henry, became earl of Ross, whilst the earldom of Orkney was shared between DAVID and JOHN.

[NB30] **ERLEND III** earl of Orkney 1154–21 December 1156.

He was the son of HARALD (I) and, with the encouragement of his devious great aunt Frakok, Erlend took advantage of RAGNALD III's absence on pilgrimage, to stake his claim on the Orcadian earldom. First he sought the permission of the Norwegian king, Eystein III, to administer Ragnald's share of the earldom, and though this was agreed, Erlend was unable to act upon it as HARALD II claimed he had sole authority in Ragnald's absence. Erlend visited the court of MALCOLM IV of Scotland where he secured the earldom of Caithness, in succession to his father. He then returned to Norway where Eystein made him earl of Orkney and gave him authority to depose Harald II, who had been appointed by Ragnald without Eystein's approval. Erlend attacked Harald at Kiarrek-Stadir at the end of September 1154 and forced him into surrender. Erlend now administered all of Orkney and although he agreed to share half with Ragnald when he returned from his crusade in 1155 he subsequently failed to surrender it. Harald and Ragnald combined forces and drove Erlend out of Orkney. However, he captured Thurso and used this as a base to strike back at Orkney, defeating Harald on 24 October 1156. Harald and Ragnald again combined forces and this time surprised Erlend at his retreat in a state of total drunkenness, and they killed him.

[NB31] **HARALD III INGI (the YOUNG)** earl of Orkney ?1195–8.

The grandson of Kali (RAGNALD III) through his only daughter Ingrid. At some date unknown Harald was invested with his grandfather's share of Orkney from Magnus V of Norway and of Caithness from WILLIAM THE LYON of Scotland. This was most likely when Harald came of age. His birth date is not known, though it was probably in 1155 or 1156, so he may have become earl in 1174 or soon after. However, he never pursued his claim to the territories and revenues of Orkney, remaining in Caithness; and when Magnus died in 1184, Harald visited his successor, Sverre, to have the grant of earldom reaffirmed. However, we do not know if Harald visited Sverre immediately, and it is more likely it did not happen until after the insurrection of Sigurd Magnusson in 1194, and may have been at the same time as HARALD II sought his pardon. This means it was probably soon after 1195 that Harald the Young sought to claim his inheritance, only to find that Harald the Old refused. He gathered together a fleet at his base in Wick, but Harald the Old wrong-footed him and descended on Wick with his own fleet. Harald the Young was killed in the ensuing battle, along with his brother and closest relatives. He was, in effect, the earl who never ruled.

[NB32] **DAVID** earl of Orkney, 1206–14; ruled jointly with
[NB33] **JOHN (I)** earl of Orkney 1206–31.

They were sons of HARALD II and their mother, Gormflaeth, was a niece of SOMERLED, king of the Isles. John's earlship was conditioned by the position of the Orkneys which placed him between activities in Norway and Scotland. At the start of their joint reign, John and David found themselves embroiled in the dynastic civil war in Norway with the Orkneys once again being used as a base for covert operations on the kingdom. Although neither earl seems to have been directly involved in the fighting they were accused of supporting the losing factions and in 1210 were summoned to Bergen, heavily fined, and forced to pay allegiance to the victorious king, Inge II. Only then was their earldom officially re-endorsed. David enjoyed it only till 1214 when he died, still quite young. John remained sole earl for the next seventeen years. Although he administered his lands wisely, he became embroiled in a variety of plots, schemes and uprisings. In 1222 the men of Caithness rose against their tyrannical bishop, Adam, and burned him alive in his home. ALEXANDER II of Scotland severely fined John, even though he had not been directly involved. The Orkneys continued to be used as a base for pirate raids on Norway, and John found himself again summoned to Norway in 1224 for reprimand. He had to leave his son, Harald, as hostage – unfortunately he was drowned two years later, and was the last direct heir to the earldom. John also became involved in 1230 in an enterprise by king Haakon IV, to substantiate Norwegian suzerainty over the southern Hebrides, which led John to support OLAF II of Man and USPAK of the Isles against Alexander II of Scotland. John eventually became embroiled in a territorial dispute on his own doorstep. At the close of 1231 HARALD III's nephew, Snaekoll, laid claim to part of Orkney, and during negotiations at Thurso, Snaekoll killed John. John was probably aged about fifty. He was succeeded by a distant relative MAGNUS II.

For the remaining earls of Orkney turn to page 541.

NC. JORVIK (YORK)

Jorvik, the Danish kingdom of York, was essentially the same as the old Saxon kingdom of Deira in Northumbria (*see page 269*). From 910 the kingdom was taken over by the Danish kings of Dublin.

Ref.	Ruler	Born	Reign	Died	Notes
NC1.	Ivarr *the Boneless*		866–73	873	also king of Dublin [U3]
NC2.	Halfdan Ragnarson		873–7	877	also king of Dublin [U5]; killed in battle
Kingdom ruled from Bernicia (see page 272)					
NC3.	Gothfrith		883–95	895	
NC4.	Sigfrid		895–c9	c899	
NC5.	Canute		c899–c900	c900	assassinated
NC6.	Athelwold		899–902	902	killed in battle
NC7.	Halfdan (II)		?902–10	910	co-ruler with Eowils; killed in battle
NC8.	Eowils		?902–10	910	co-ruler with Halfdan; killed in battle
York was taken over by the expelled Danish kings of Dublin, some of whom later became joint rulers.					
NC9.	Ragnall		910–c21	c921	also ruled Man [NA11]
NC10.	Sitric *Caech*		921–7	927	previously king of Dublin [U10]
Kingdom conquered by Athelstan of Wessex and ruled by him till 939					
NC11.	Erik *Bloodaxe*	c885	939?		this period as Athelstan's sub-king is spurious; restored in 947.

Map 12 **Danish and Saxon England**

NC12.	Olaf or Anlaf Gothfrithson	c919	939–41	941	also king of Dublin and of Danish Mercia ("the Five Boroughs") [U12]
NC13.	Olaf or Anlaf Sitricson *Cuaran*	c920	941–3		also king of Dublin [U14]; expelled; expelled again;
			949–52	981	returned to Dublin.

29. The Danish and Norse Kingdoms (5) – The Danish Kingdoms

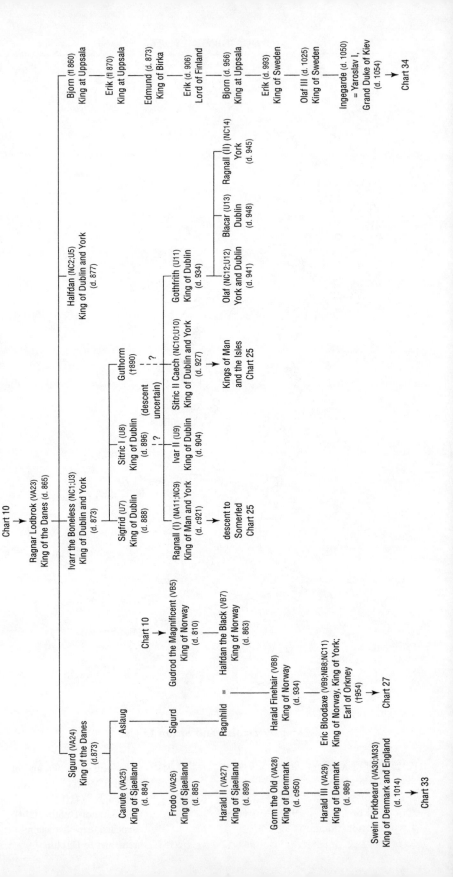

Chart 10

Ragnar Lodbrok (VA23)
King of the Danes (d. 865)

Ivarr the Boneless (NC1;U3)
King of Dublin and York
(d. 873)

Sigfrid (U7)
King of Dublin
(d. 888)

Sitric I (U8)
King of Dublin
(d. 896)

Guthorm (†890)

(descent
uncertain)

? ?

Ragnall (I) (NA11;NC9)
King of Man and York
(d. c921)

Ivar II (U9)
King of Dublin
(d. 904)

Sitric II Caech (NC10;U10)
King of Dublin and York
(d. 927)

descent to
Somerled
Chart 25

Kings of Man
and the Isles
Chart 25

Gothfrith (U11)
King of Dublin
(d. 934)

Olaf (NC12;U12)
York and Dublin
(d. 941)

Blacar (U13)
Dublin
(d. 948)

Ragnall (II) (NC14)
York
(d. 945)

Halfdan (NC2;U5)
King of Dublin and York
(d. 877)

Bjorn (fl 860)
King at Uppsala

Erik (fl 870)
King at Uppsala

Edmund (d. 873)
King of Birka

Erik (d. 906)
Lord of Finland

Bjorn (d. 956)
King at Uppsala

Erik (d. 993)
King of Sweden

Olaf III (d. 1025)
King of Sweden

Ingegarde (d. 1050)
= Yaroslav I,
Grand Duke of Kiev
(d. 1054)

→ Chart 34

Sigurd (VA24)
King of the Danes
(d.873)

Aslaug

Canute (VA25)
King of Sjaelland
(d. 884)

Sigurd

Chart 10

Gudrod the Magnificent (VB5)
King of Norway
(d. 810)

Halfdan the Black (VB7)
King of Norway
(d. 863)

Frodo (VA26)
King of Sjaelland
(d. 885)

Ragnhild = Harald Finehair (VB8)
King of Norway
(d. 934)

Harald II (VA27)
King of Sjaelland
(d. 899)

Eric Bloodaxe (VB9;NB8;NC11)
King of Norway, King of York;
Earl of Orkney
(†954)

→ Chart 27

Gorm the Old (VA28)
King of Denmark
(d. c950)

Harald III (VA29)
King of Denmark
(d. 986)

Swein Forkbeard (VA30;M33)
King of Denmark and England
(d. 1014)

Chart 33

Ref.	Ruler	Born	Reign	Died	Notes
NC14.	Ragnall (II) Gothfrithson	c921	943–5	945	killed in battle

York back under control of kings of Wessex, 945–8.

(NC11)	Erik *Bloodaxe*	c885	947–8		expelled
			952–4	954	restored; expelled again and slain

Kingdom regained by the English.

[NC1;U3] **IVARR the BONELESS** Jorvik, 866–73; Dublin, 871–3.

Ivarr was purportedly the son of the Danish hero Ragnar *Lodbrok* and brother of HALFDAN. The two brothers had allied with OLAF THE WHITE, the Norwegian king of Dublin as early as 857, using Dublin as a base for plundering the coasts of Ireland and Britain. From 864 Ivarr and Halfdan began campaigning across Britain. They had brought together what became known as the "Great Army" or "the Host", which was a formidable and almost invincible fighting machine. They invaded East Anglia in 865, and used it as their base. In 866, following the death of their father in a raid on York, Ivarr and Halfdan invaded Deira. Their victory was immediate and the last English kings of Deira were killed. Ivarr set up EGBERT (I) as his client king in Bernicia, but with his army now partly based in York, Ivarr was regarded as the power (if not the king) in that region. Over the next five years Ivarr and Halfdan continually harried the east coast of England. In the winter of 869 EDMUND of East Anglia attempted to stop them and was killed. In 871 Olaf the White returned to Norway and Ivarr took the opportunity to return to Dublin and claim the kingship. By the time he left Britain most of eastern England, from the Tees to the Thames was under Danish control. He left Halfdan in charge of the Great Army. On his death in 873 Ivarr was remembered as king of all the Scandinavians in Britain and Ireland. He also founded a dynasty that ruled Dublin (and for a period York) for the next two hundred years.

[NC2;U5] **HALFDAN RAGNARSON** Jorvik, 873–7.

Halfdan, the brother of IVARR THE BONELESS, took control of the "Great Army" in 871 and was effectively ruler of the Northumbrian Danes from that time. He returned to York in 872 to quell a revolt led by RICSIG, who had taken control in Bernicia. From that time the "Great Army" remained based in York. In 875, Halfdan combined his force with the "Summer Army" under GUTHRUM, and invaded Mercia, overthrowing king BURGRED at Repton and installing a client ruler CEOLWULF. Halfdan now controlled almost all the eastern half of England from the Tees to the Thames. However, in Halfdan's eyes the real jewel was the control of Dublin. Later in 875, he crossed Scotland, inflicting what damage he could upon the Picts, and upon reaching Dublin slew Eystein, the son of OLAF THE WHITE, who had been installed as king. Although Halfdan proclaimed himself king of Dublin, he was soon ejected by the Norse and he made his way back to York. It is at that time that the real kingdom of Jorvik may be said to commence, as Halfdan parcelled out land to his supporters who settled down to farm. Halfdan, however, was restless. He was a true warrior king. In 877 he sought to raise an army again to conquer Dublin. However this time many of his men were tired of battle and wished to settle and raise families. One record suggests that Halfdan was exiled from York. It was thus with a much smaller army that he ventured back across Scotland. He reached Ireland but was killed by the Norse at the battle of Strangford Lough. His dejected warband sought to return to York across Scotland where they were confronted by the army of CONSTANTINE (I), who was killed in the conflict. After Halfdan's death the Danes of Jorvik seemed content to be ruled by EGBERT (II) of Bernicia, and it was not until 883 that a new Danish king, GOTHFRITH, was elected.

[NC3] **GOTHFRITH** Jorvik, 883–24 August 895.

For some years the community of Danes who had settled in York under their leader HALFDAN seemed content to exist as farmers without their own leader. They were presumably subordinate to EGBERT of Bernicia, if they were subordinate to any king. However it seems that by the year 883 the church leaders in York felt that they needed a representative from amongst the Danes who could speak on their behalf and they arranged for the election of a king. Gothfrith emerged as their leader. He was apparently already a Christian and thus able to deal on equal terms with the church leaders. We know nothing more about him and can only question whether he was originally amongst Halfdan's "Great Army" or whether he settled in York later. If the former, then he may even have been amongst the leaders of the Danes who rejected Halfdan and refused to continue to fight, and so may have been the unofficial leader of the Danes since 877. The election of Gothfrith coincides with the return to Chester-le-Street in Durham of the monks who had been driven out by Halfdan, and it suggests a general attempt at reconciliation between the Angles and Danes. Gothfrith thus emerges as a king of the Danes only and not necessarily as the ruler of the Angles of Deira, who may have looked to Egbert for their governance or, more probably, took their instruction from the church. In 893 or 894 Gothfrith had to face the return to Northumbria of the pirate-earl SIGFRID who was pursued by Sitric, the Viking king of Dublin. Sitric harried the coast in revenge for Sigfrid's attacks on Dublin, but then retreated. The death of Gothfrith is recorded on 24 August 895 and he was given a Christian burial in York Minster. Sigfrid was elected to succeed him.

[NC4] **SIGFRID** or **SIGFRITH** Jorvik, 895–c9.

A Danish earl of Northumbria who was notorious in the ninth century chronicles for his piratical raids around the coast of England with his powerful fleet of forty ships. He attacked Wessex and Devon and, though he was routed by ALFRED's forces, it did not deter him from moving off and plundering again. In 893 he sailed from Devon to plunder the Irish coast, harrying the Norse settlements and incurring the wrath of the Viking king of Dublin, Sitric Ivarson. Sigfrid was evidently seeking to gain the kingdom of Dublin for himself – it is possible he may have been distantly related to Sitric. However, although he was welcomed by some factions in Dublin, Sitric succeeded in driving him out of Dublin and pursued him back to Northumbria, where Sitric raided and plundered Jorvik before returning to Dublin. One might think that the Danes of Jorvik would not have welcomed Sigfrid's antics, but upon the death of their king GOTHFRITH in 895, Sigfrid was elected his successor. Possibly they welcomed the more daring Sigfrid after a period of pacifism under his predecessor. Sigfrid was almost certainly also rich. Anyone who could control a fleet of forty ships and plunder almost at will must have had considerable wealth, and the Northumbrians may have welcomed a chance to enjoy such prestige. Sigfrid saw fit to issue a coinage, the first Danish money in York, in the form of a series of silver pennies. Sigfrid's reign, however, was brief. He died around the year 899. The circumstances are not known but, as he died before the invasion of CANUTE, he probably died of natural causes. At that same time ATHELWOLD was welcomed into the kingdom.

[NC5] **CANUTE** or **KNUT** Jorvik, *c*899–*c*900.
Canute was a Danish prince, who was probably driven out of Denmark when Gorm the Old established the Danish kingship and sought to establish himself in the Northumbrian kingdom of Jorvik. He arrived soon after the death of SIGFRID but found that he was repulsed by a Saxon king, ATHELWOLD. He attacked again, further along the coast at Scarborough, and this time found acceptance. According to the sagas, Canute had designs on the Viking kingdom of Dublin, but the records are divided on whether he got as far as Dublin, because after a reign of less than a year he was assassinated either while he was swimming or watching a sporting event.

[NC6] **ATHELWOLD** Jorvik, 899–902; East Angles, 902.
Athelwold was the son of ATHELRED (I) of the West Saxons and believed himself the true heir to the throne of Wessex. He had been born in 868 and had been too young to succeed when his father died in 871. After the death of his uncle ALFRED in October 899, Athelwold made a bid for the throne. He seized the royal manor at Wimborne where he was besieged by the soldiers of the new king, EDWARD (THE ELDER), but Athelwold escaped under cover of darkness and outran the levies, escaping into Northumbria. He must have arrived soon after the death of SIGFRID and, somewhat surprisingly, he was accepted by the Northumbrians – Danes and Angles alike – as their king. Athelwold soon found his position challenged by a dispossessed Danish prince, CANUTE, who landed at Cleveland, but Athelwold drove him back. However Canute was more successful on his second attempt and was accepted by the Danes as their king. It is not clear whether Athelwold remained king of the Northumbrian Angles during this period, but he almost certainly remained in the area. Canute was assassinated within the year, and although the record is silent on the matter, it raises the question of Athelwold's involvement. Athelwold was intent upon raising an army to regain his kingdom. At some stage he left Northumbria – it is not clear when – for by 902 he was amongst the Danes of East Anglia. It is possible he brought with him an army of Northumbrian Danes and joined forces with ERIC of East Anglia. Athelwold succeeded in bending the East Saxons to his will. In 902 Athelwold and Eric led a confederate army across the Thames to raid and plunder Wessex. Edward's army pursued Athelwold back into East Anglia without success, but just as Edward disbanded his army Athelwold made a surprise attack. The battle of the Holm, as recorded in the *ASC*, was long and bloody, and though the Danes regarded it as their victory, both their king and Athelwold were killed.

[NC7] **HALFDAN (II)** joint ruler of Jorvik, ?902–10.
[NC8] **EOWILS** joint ruler of Jorvik, ?902–10.
The period from the deaths of CANUTE and ATHELWOLD, around 900–902, and the deaths of Halfdan and Eowils (and possibly a third king, Ivarr) in 910 are uncertain ones in Danish Northumbria. There is no record of other kings during this period,

but we cannot be certain whether either king had ruled since 902, or whether there were no kings at all. If anything, Northumbria may have found itself overwhelmed with candidates following the expulsion of the Danes and Norse from Ireland in 902. Clearly there was upheavel in Northumbria, for in 909 ATHELFLAED of Mercia translated the relics of St OSWALD from Bardney to Gloucester for safety. EDWARD THE ELDER endeavoured to bring the Northumbrian Danes under his control and during 909 he harried the land for several weeks, but to little avail. The next year the Danes invaded Mercia and met Edward's army at Tettenhall, near Wolverhampton. Edward was victorious and the Danish kings were killed. This battle should have been decisive as it allowed Edward to lay claim to York, but within a few months RAGNALL of Dublin had taken advantage of the situation and secured York for the Norwegian Vikings.

[NC9;NA11] **RAGNALL** or **RAGNALD (I)** York, 910–21; Man, 914–21.
Ragnall was a grandson of IVARR THE BONELESS and was amongst the many Norse Vikings expelled from Dublin in 902. He spent the next few years harrying the western coast of Scotland and Strathclyde, and it may be that he established a base on Man or one of the Hebridean islands, but certainly did not wield the authority to call himself king. In 910 Ragnall seized the opportunity given by EDWARD THE ELDER's defeat of the Danish kings of York at Tettenhall to claim York as his own and allow the settlement of the homeless heirs of Ivarr. Ragnall began colonizing land along the Wear and broadened the old kingdom of Jorvik north in Bernicia. In 914 he drove out Ealdred of Bernicia who sought the aid of CONSTANTINE II of Scotland, but the combined Bernician-Scottish army was defeated at Corbridge later that same year. Ragnall rampaged his way across northern Britain, devastating Strathclyde. He rejoined his fleet, probably at Dumbarton, and towards the end of 914 soundly defeated a rival Viking fleet led by Bárd Ottarson of Waterford off the coast of Man. It may be in this year that Ragnall declared himself as king of Man as well as the southern Hebrides. During his absence, while he was helping his brother SITRIC regain Dublin, which they achieved by 917, ATHELFLAED of Mercia raised a confederate army against him, but her death in 918 weakened their resolve. A smaller army assembled by Constantine II was defeated again at Corbridge as Ragnall returned across Britain. Ragnall discovered that opposition against him had appeared amongst factions in York, probably amongst the former Danish settlers encouraged by the native English, but Ragnall swooped on York in 919 and regained it without difficulty. He was now firmly ensconced as king, holding control over all land from York to Cumbria, including Man. His tactics were to pitch the Danes against the English and he was assisted by Sitric in trying to goad the Danes into revolt. This failed. Instead of splitting the opposition, as Ragnall had hoped, he had combined them against him and in 920 Ragnall was forced to submit to Edward the Elder as overlord of England. Regaining York was thus a hollow victory, for though he was recognized as king within his kingdom, he could not act without the direct consent of Edward. He died early in 921, and was succeeded by Sitric.

[NC10;U10] **SITRIC** or **SIGTRYGG** *CAECH* (*THE SQUINT-EYED*) Dublin, 917–21; York, 921–7.
Sitric was the brother of RAGNALL and a grandson of IVARR THE BONELESS. With Ragnall and other Norse Vikings he was expelled from Dublin in 902 and he

probably accompanied Ragnall on his forays around the western coast of Scotland. Sitric may be one of the grandsons of Ivarr referred to in the Irish annals as defeating a Pictish king in 903 and 904. By 917, however, Sitric had regained Dublin and established himself as king. In 921, though, with the death of Ragnall, Sitric handed the kingdom of Dublin over to his brother Gothfrith, and succeeded as king of York. It is likely that Sitric included the Isle of Man as part of his York domain, but this is not certain. It may at some stage, and certainly by the time of his death, have passed to Gothfrith. Unlike Ragnall, Sitric did not recognize EDWARD THE ELDER as his overlord, but when Edward died in 924, Sitric realised that his successor, ATHELSTAN, who had been raised in Mercia and had strong support throughout middle England, was a much more dangerous adversary. Rather than fight, Sitric agreed a treaty with Athelstan at Tamworth on 30 January 926. Part of the arrangement included Sitric's acceptance of Christianity, and his marriage to Athelstan's sister Edith (Eadgyth). But within only a few months Sitric had renounced his faith and sent Edith packing to Polesworth Abbey in Warwickshire. Sitric died soon after, in March 927. The Irish annals record that he died young, yet by Viking standards he must already have been reaching middle age, and the youngest he could have been was in his mid-thirties. He was succeeded in Dublin by his brother Gothfrith, who endeavoured to regain York but was driven out by Athelstan. Sitric's son, OLAF, would eventually rule York twenty years later.

[NC11] **ERIK BLOODAXE** It is uncertain whether Erik did gain control of York in 939, no matter how briefly. His full entry is therefore given below when he returned to York in 947 and 952.

[NC12;U12] **OLAF GOTHFRITHSON** Dublin, 934–41; York and the Five Boroughs 939–41.
This ruler should not be confused with another Olaf Gothfrithson, an earlier king of Dublin who was known as OLAF THE WHITE. Olaf was the son of Gothfrith, king of Dublin, and nephew of RAGNALL and SITRIC, kings of York. His father had tried unsuccessfully to gain York in 927 and had been expelled by ATHELSTAN. Olaf doubtless kept up the hope of recovering the kingdom. Generally he emerges as a better commander and tactician than his father, despite his youth. Within three years of succeeding him as king of Dublin, he had achieved what had always eluded his father – the conquest of the rival Viking settlements along the east coast of Ireland, so as to become the king of a confederacy of Norse towns centred on Dublin. He was probably little more than eighteen at this time. He now had a strong power base from which to launch his campaign on York. In the autumn of 937 his fleet sailed for Britain. He succeeded in raising support from his allies in Scotland (CONSTANTINE II) and Strathclyde (OWEN III), and this vast army moved down the east coast of Britain to enter York. From there Olaf marched south into Mercia where he met the English army under Athelstan at Brunanburh, believed to be near Nottingham. This was one of the decisive battles of the Saxon period for had Olaf won, it would have shifted the Scandinavian-Saxon balance in England and Olaf would have had an opportunity to take overall command. As it was Athelstan's victory was complete; the Scandinavian, British and Scottish forces were devastated and Olaf only just escaped to his boat with his life. He sailed back to Scotland and eventually to Dublin to rethink his tactics. Within two years Athelstan was dead,

and Olaf immediately embarked on another invasion, even though winter was approaching. In November 939 he again successfully took York. Here he readily received the support of the Northumbrian *witan*, including Wulfstan, the archbishop of York, who accompanied Olaf on his march south into Mercia. Athelstan's brother EDMUND was only eighteen and, though already a seasoned warrior, was not the equal of his predecessor. Edmund besieged Olaf at Leicester but the king escaped. Eventually a truce was agreed between the two young kings with the aid of Wulfstan and Oda, archbishop of Canterbury. As a result Olaf became king not only of York but also of the Five Boroughs of Danish Mercia – Leicester, Lincoln, Stamford, Nottingham and Derby. His kingdom stretched across middle and northern England and across the Irish sea, including Man, to the confederate Viking towns of eastern Ireland. For a king then scarcely twenty-one it was a remarkable achievement. Had he lived longer he might have established himself more in the folk-memory of Britain, but he was killed the following year during a raid on Bernicia and Lothian, seeking the submission of the Northumbrian church. Despite his youth Olaf had married twice, first to a daughter of Constantine II, and secondly the daughter of Ormr, an Anglo-Danish earl in York. He had two sons who survived into their twenties but who died in Ireland. He was succeeded by his cousin OLAF SITRICSON.

[NC13;U14] **OLAF SITRICSON *CUARAN*** York 941–3 (with the Five Boroughs 941–2), 948–52; and Dublin, 945–8, 952–80.

He was the son of SITRIC CAECH but had been too young to inherit York after his father's death in 927, and indeed had been smuggled out of Britain to relative safety in Ireland by his uncle Gothfrith. He was known colloquially as Olaf *Cuarán* from the Gaelic for sandals, presumably from his habit of wearing these rather than more solid footwear. This may in its own small way give us an image of an Olaf who was rather more relaxed than his battle-mad brethren, and one that was testified by his ability to weather all storms and survive to a ripe old age, unlike any of his kin. He was still a fearless fighter, but did not have the military or political acumen of his father or his cousin, OLAF GOTHFRITHSON, though this did not seem to worry him. He no doubt fought alongside his cousin in his early campaigns, but he was left in charge of Dublin when Olaf Gothfrithson set out upon his second invasion of England in 939. Following Olaf's victory, Olaf *Cuarán* was summoned to York to help in the conquest of Bernicia, so he was already present in the kingdom when Olaf Gothfrithson died in 941. Olaf *Cuarán* was accepted as successor without argument. However his reign opened inauspiciously, for early in 942 EDMUND of Wessex regained the Five Boroughs and expelled the Norse from Danish Mercia. Recognizing Edmund's authority, Olaf submitted to him early in 943 and agreed to adopt the Christian faith. However, just like his father, he soon rejected it. It may have been this, or the sign of weakness in having lost the Five Boroughs, that caused the Northumbrian *witan* to eject Olaf later in 943. In all likelihood Wulfstan, the archbishop of York, who was a supporter of the Norse kings, had endeavoured to convert Olaf to Christianity, and Olaf's failure to keep the faith caused Wulfstan to seek his dismissal. Olaf sought refuge in Strathclyde, under king DONALD, where a significant Norse contingent lived. He was probably biding his time seeking an opportunity to recover York where his cousin, RAGNALL GOTHFRITHSON had been installed as king. However, in 945, Edmund led a further campaign against the Norse, which resulted in the death of Ragnall and the expulsion of Olaf from Britain. Olaf returned to Dublin where he deposed his cousin Blacar, who had been a rather ineffective caretaker king since 941. His next few years were full of rebuilding the Dublin kingdom which had been damaged by onslaughts from the Irish kings. Since the Irish were not united in their opposition, Olaf allied with one contingent to help fight another and in this he was successful until a disastrous defeat at Slane in 947. By then news had reached Olaf of the death of the English king EDMUND and the succession of his brother EADRED. Eadred had sought to subdue the Northumbrians who still defied Saxon rule, but though he was successful for a short period, York accepted ERIK BLOODAXE as their king. Olaf refused to consider a rival Norse king on the throne of his father, and late in 947 he re-mustered his fleet and sailed again to his Scottish allies to plan his attack on York. This time he was more successful. Eadred was more prepared to accept Olaf as king than the vicious Erik and, once Eadred had driven Erik out of York early in 948, Olaf resumed his kingship unopposed. Eadred allowed Olaf's rule on the basis that he would defend Northumbria against Erik. However, York was now divided. Archbishop Wulfstan and his party had given their support to Erik, and continued to do so. Despite his continuing opposition to Christianity, Olaf felt powerless against Wulfstan, who was the real ruler of Northumbria in his role as king-maker, and submitted to his bidding. Olaf was thus at a disadvantage in 952 when Erik returned in force to regain York. Despite the support of his Strathclyde and Scottish allies, Olaf found himself expelled from York again, this time by Erik. Olaf wintered in Scotland and returned to Dublin in 953 where he succeeded in re-establishing his control over the Norse settlements and remained there as king for the next twenty-seven years. Remarkably, for a man who had plundered and destroyed so many monasteries, he eventually accepted Christianity in 980 and retired to spend his final days on Iona. He died in 981, aged about sixty. His son Sitric *Silkenbeard* ruled in Dublin after him, but no more of the descendents of IVARR THE BONELESS ruled in York.

[NC14] RAGNALL (II) GOTHFRITHSON York, 943–5.

Ragnall was the son of Gothfrith, king of Dublin, and nephew of RAGNALL (I). He had probably been in York since his brother, OLAF, had regained Northumbria in 939. He is not likely to have been an older brother of Olaf's, which suggests that he was born around 920 or 921. In 943, after his cousin OLAF SITRICSON was expelled for refusing to accept Christianity, Ragnall was accepted as king. He was probably brought to power more by the authority of Wulfstan, archbishop of York, who had taken on the role of a northern king-maker, than necessarily by the general acceptance of the Scandinavians of York. There was a lapse of some months before Ragnall "made his peace" (as the chroniclers recorded) with EDMUND of Wessex, to whom he submitted late in that year, when he was also baptized. Olaf Sitricson retired to the hills of Strathclyde and during 944 and 945 no doubt plotted to recover the kingdom. Although there is no record, it is possible that some conflicts occurred between the two factions at this time, and it may have been this that prompted Edmund to bring his forces to bear upon the Norse kings. In 945 he attacked York and in the conflict that followed Ragnall was killed.

[NC11;NB8;VB9] **ERIK** or **EIRIKR** *BLOODAXE* Norway, 933–?4; Orkney, 937–54; York, (?939–40?), 947–8, 952–4.

Erik was a deposed king of Norway who set off to plunder the northern seas and established himself as king of Orkney in about 937. From there he set out to gain the kingdom of Jorvik, though whether he established a hold over the territory as early as 939 is still uncertain. (*The full story is told under Erik's entry under Orkney on page 442*). The people of York, who were a mixture of Danes, Norse and Angles, had a love-hate relationship with Erik. In particular Edmund of Wessex and his successor Eadred were determined to keep Erik out of York, fearful that this son of a Norwegian king would use York as a foothold to establish domain over the rest of Britain. Twice Erik was expelled from York but again he returned. The last time was to be his undoing. Erik's support had come primarily from Wulfstan, the archbishop of York, who in 954 was captured and imprisoned by Eadred. Erik was again driven from York, and this time he and many of his companions were slaughtered in an ambush on Stainmore. His wife, GUNNHILDR, and two of their sons survived and returned to Orkney to reimpose their rule.

ND. DANISH EAST ANGLIA

This kingdom covered the same territory as the old kingdom of the Angles dealt with on pages 238 to 246. The territory was awarded to Guthrum as part of the peace settlement with Alfred the Great.

Ref.	Ruler	Reign	Died	Notes
ND1.	Guthrum (baptized Athelstan)	879–90	890	
ND2.	Eohric or Yorrik	890–902		
ND3.	Guthrum II	902–16		

[ND1] **GUTHRUM (I)** baptized **ATHELSTAN**, ruled 879–90.

He was a Danish prince who was one of the leaders of the "Summer Army" which first appeared in England in 871 following the route of the Thames and plundering lands around Reading. This army occasionally joined forces with the "Great Army" led by IVARR THE BONELESS and his brother HALFDAN, as they did at Wilton in May 871. Guthrum is not named in that battle and we cannot be sure that he was a leader of the "Summer Army" for all of this period, though his seniority makes it probable. He first appears by name in 874 when the combined armies besieged Repton and drove the Mercian king BURGRED into exile. At the end of that year, Halfdan and Guthrum divided England between them, Guthrum taking the southern half. He wintered his army in East Anglia and in 875 began his conquest of Wessex. Over the next three years he was engaged in the now legendary war with ALFRED THE GREAT (*whom see for details*), which Guthrum nearly won until defeated at the decisive battle of Edington in May 878. Soon after that Guthrum submitted to Alfred and was baptized. Under the Treaty of Wedmore Guthrum was installed as king of the Danes in East Anglia, under his baptismal name of Athelstan. We hear little more of Guthrum. It seems that he fully accepted his role and settled down to establish his kingdom. The *ASC* does record that in 884 the Danes of East

Anglia broke the peace with Alfred, but it is not clear whether this was at Guthrum's instigation or because of the arrival of another Danish army, who plundered eastern England during that year and stirred up trouble. It may well have been the presence of Guthrum that re-established peace. Guthrum died in 890.

[ND2] **ERIC** or **EOHRIC** East Anglia, 890–902.
Eric succeeded GUTHRUM as ruler of the Danes in East Anglia. Eric had less reason than his predecessor to remain loyal to Alfred. Nevertheless he did not want to lose his kingdom, but instead he was happy to make the territory a safe haven for other Danish armies which sought to conquer England. This included the army under Hæsten, in 893, which not only established a base in East Anglia, but received reinforcements from the Anglian Danes. Likewise in 902 Eric gave support to ATHELWOLD, the renegade Saxon who was seeking to claim his birthright, and who raised an army of Danes in Northumbria before moving to Essex in 901 and East Anglia in 902. Eric joined Athelwold in his invasion of Wessex, but both kings were killed during the retreat. Eric was succeeded in East Anglia by GUTHRUM II.

[ND3] **GUTHRUM II** East Anglia, 902–16.
We know little about him, but it is evident that he remained a resistance leader aiding and abetting other armies intent on conquering England, just as had his predecessor. Although EDWARD THE ELDER agreed a peace treaty with Guthrum and the Northumbrian Danes in 902, this seemed to carry little weight. As the years moved on, the East Anglian Danes became more venturesome, particularly when a major Danish force moved into western England from the continent in 914. Over the next two years a number of armies from East Anglia raided Mercia, but with no co-ordinated control had little effect. Eventually Edward confronted them at Tempsford in 916 where he achieved a resounding victory. Guthrum was killed. There is no record of any successor king of the East Anglian Danes. By 917 the Danes had capitulated and accepted Edward as their king.

THE ENGLISH AND NORMANS (900–1284)

Although Alfred the Great held the Danes at bay and stopped a total conquest of England, they were granted land in East Anglia and Danish settlements rapidly grew. A foothold had been established. Danish and Norse raids continued and they were eventually victorious in 1013 when the English capitulated to Swein Forkbeard. After his death his son Canute became one of the great rulers of northern Europe. Even though Canute's sons were unable to sustain the scale of his empire, it was not the last England saw of the Northmen. Another branch of the ancient royal family, related to the earls of Orkney, had settled in Normandy, and their leader, William the Bastard, conquered England in 1066. The Northmen were ultimately victorious and drove the Saxons into serfdom. It was this generation of Northmen, William's sons and grandsons, that not only conquered England but dominated Wales and Scotland. Although Scotland was not quite conquered, Edward I died believing it was within his grasp, just like Wales, which he had dominated and absorbed into England in 1284. By the reign of Edward I Britain was fast becoming a united kingdom with the English king recognized as the sovereign lord. This section covers the English kings from Alfred the Great to Edward I.

30. The Saxon Kingdoms (7) – The House of Egbert

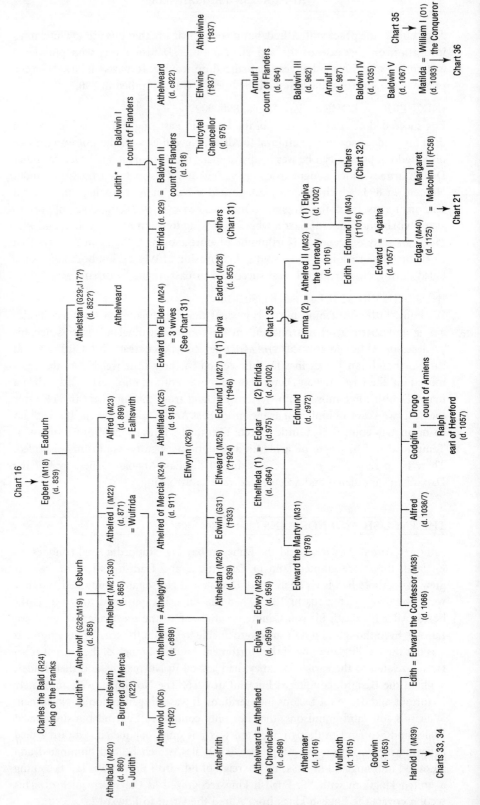

Ref.	Ruler	Born	Reign	Died	Notes

continued from page 299

M. Saxons and Danes

M24.	Edward *the Elder*	c871	899–924	924	
M25.	Elfweard	c904	924	924	ruled only 16 days
M26.	Athelstan	c895	924–39	939	

Athelstan was the first true king of the English, and was acknowledged as overlord by the Welsh princes. He also defeated the Scots and Norse in 937.

M27.	Edmund I	c921	939–46	946	killed trying to stop a brawl
M28.	Eadred	c923	946–55	955	died after a long illness

From Eadred on, the kings are justifiably called kings of the English.

M29.	Edwy or Eadwig *the Fair*	c941	955–9	959	
M30.	Edgar	c943	959–75	975	king of Mercia from 957

Edgar was the first king to be crowned king of the English in 973.

M31.	Edward the Martyr	c962	975–8	978	murdered
M32.	Athelred II the Unready	c968	978–1013	1016	
	Regent: Alfhere		978–83	983	ealdorman of Mercia

In 1013 the Danelaw submitted to Swein, king of Denmark.

M33.	Swein Forkbeard	c960	1013–14	1014	see VA30

Saxon rule restored

M32.	Athelred II the Unready	c968	1014–16	1016	
M34.	Edmund II Ironside	c989	1016	1016	died of wounds received in battle, or possibly murdered

Danish rule restored

M35.	Canute or Cnut	c995	1016–35	1035	also king of Denmark and Norway (VA32)
M36.	Harold (I) Harefoot	c1016	1035–40	1040	made regent in 1035 but seized the kingdom in 1037
M37.	Harthacanute	c1018	1035–42	1042	in Denmark from 1035; deposed 1037; restored 1040 died of a fit or poisoned; see also VA33

Saxon rule restored

M38.	Edward the Confessor	c1004	1042–66	1066	
M39.	Harold (II)	c1022	1066	1066	killed at the battle of Hastings
M40.	Edgar the Atheling	c1052	1066	1125	submitted to William the Conqueror

O. The House of Normandy

William of Normandy gained the throne of England by conquest. The Saxon royal family was overthrown and a new regime, not simply a new dynasty, was imposed which changed England forever.

O1.	William (I) the Conqueror	c1027	1066–87	1087	William II (SD7) of Normandy

Ref.	Ruler	Born	Reign	Died	Notes
O2.	William II *Rufus*	c1057	1087–1100	1100	killed in a hunting accident; possibly murdered
O3.	Henry I	c1068	1100–35	1135	see also SD9
O4.	Stephen	c1097	1135–54	1154	briefly deposed Apr–Nov 1141
O4a.	Eustace	c1131	1152–3	1153	crowned by his father but never acknowledged
O5.	Matilda	1102	Apr–Nov 1141	1167	not crowned

The House of Anjou, commonly known as Plantagenet

Ref.	Ruler	Born	Reign	Died	Notes
O6.	Henry II	1133	1154–89	1189	see also SB17, SC12, SD12
O6a.	Henry (III) *the Young King*	1155	1170–83	1183	crowned as Henry's successor
O7.	Richard I *Lionheart*	1157	1189–99	1199	see also SB18, SC13, SD13
O8.	John *Lackland*	1167	1199–1216	1216	see also SC14, SD14
O9.	Henry III	1207	1216–72	1272	minority until Jan 1227; see also SB19
	Regents during minority:				
	William Marshal		1216–19		
	Hubert de Burgh		1219–27		

For kings from Edward I onward, turn to page 587.

M. SAXONS AND DANES

[M24] EDWARD *THE ELDER*
King of the West Saxons, 26 October 899–17 July 924. Crowned: Kingston-upon-Thames, 8 June 900 (some sources say 31 May).
Born: *c871 or 872;* **Died:** *Farndon-on-Dee, 17 July 924, aged about 52.* **Buried:** *Winchester Cathedral.*
Married: *(1) c894 (though date unknown), Egwina (d. c901) "a noblewoman": 3 children; (2) c901/2, Elfleda (d. 920), dau. ealdorman Athelhelm: 10 children; (3) c920 Edgiva (905–968), dau. Sigehelm, ealdorman of Kent: 5 children. Edward may also have had an illegitimate child.*

Edward was the second son of ALFRED THE GREAT and was born about 871. His elder brother, Edmund, apparently died in infancy, though one tradition asserts he lived long enough to be crowned as heir apparent. In any case, the choice of his first two sons' names demonstrate Alfred's hopes for them. Both names mean "protector" (*mund*) or "guardian" (*ward*) of "riches", showing that Alfred hoped his sons would guard the prosperity of the nation for the future. Edward grew up firmly believing this. He was a soldier from childhood, not a scholar like his father and grandfather, and he knew, once his brother died, that it was in his hands that the future of the nation rested. He was a child throughout the wars that his father waged with the Danes, and they would have left a vivid impression on his mind. When the Danish problems arose again in 892 and 893 he commanded part of the army that captured the raiders. The Saxons were therefore already accustomed to him as their leader. However, after his father's death his succession did not go unchallenged. His nephew, ATHELWOLD, the son of ATHELRED, was dissatisfied with the terms of Alfred's will and felt dispossessed. He seized Wimborne manor and, though he was soon chased out of Wessex, he was accepted by the Danes and Angles of York as their leader and subsequently led a revolt amongst the Danes of East Anglia. He remained a thorn in Edward's side until he was defeated and killed in 902, after which Edward was able to seal a peace treaty with the Danes of the east. However the Danes of the north still defied Edward's sovereignty, ruling Jorvik as a separate Danish kingdom. Throughout 909 the Danes tested Edward's resolve with a number of border raids and skirmishes, and eventually Edward moved against them, raising a vast army. Edward harried Northumbria with little result. The following year he was tricked by the Danish fleet moving down the east coast, while the main Danish army moved across Northumbria and down into Mercia. Edward realised his error and chased the Danes, catching them at Tettenhall in August 910, where he inflicted upon them one of their most crushing defeats, resulting in the deaths of the two Danish kings HALFDAN and EOWILS. It was the end of the Danish hold on Jorvik, although soon after the Norse under RAGNALL moved in.

The Norse had been expelled from Dublin in 902 and were now landless. They first caused a nuisance in Wales and Scotland, but by 910 had become bold enough to enter Northumbria, and no sooner had Edward defeated one foe than another arrived. Rather than take them on instantly, Edward decided to work on one plan at a time. Since 905 Edward had been refortifying England. He rebuilt Chester and, along with his sister, ATHELFLÆD of Mercia, established a chain of fortified towns along the border with the Danelaw, including Runcorn, Tamworth, Stafford, Warwick, down to Hertford and over to Witham in Essex. Even before these forts were finished Edward was able to use them as a base to defeat a major Danish army which moved across England into Wales in 914, but no matter where the army tried to inflict major destruction, Edward was there, and the army eventually moved out of Britain at the end of the year. Most of the forts were completed by 915, and Edward progressively advanced into Danish territory. The Danes responded and from 916 on a series of skirmishes occurred across middle England. In almost all cases the English were victorious, with major successes at Leicester, Nottingham and Bedford. Early on the Danish king, GUTHRUM II, was killed, and thereafter there was no co-ordinated strategy from the Danes. Edward was able to pick off small bands of men one at a time. Eventually the Danes submitted. The year 920 saw the Danes of East Anglia and the Five Boroughs submitting to him.

In 918, during the war with the Danes, Athelflæd had died, and though her daughter ELFWYNN technically succeeded, Edward could not consider a young girl in charge during such a difficult period. Thus in 919 he assumed direct control over Mercia. With similar authority over the Danes of the east midlands, Edward now ruled over half of England. The Welsh princes, IDWAL FOEL, CLYDOG AP CADELL and HYWEL DDA, submitted to him, recognizing Edward as their overlord, for all that they remained sovereign princes. Even in the north, Edward's authority was recognized, though this was rather more tenuous. Ragnall of York had tried to goad the Danes into further revolt but by 920 they recognized that Edward was the victor. Ragnall realised his subterfuge would not succeed and recognized Edward as overlord; but his successor, SITRIC, did not. This must have alarmed CONSTANTINE II of Scotland and DONALD MAC AED of Strathclyde, both of whom had suffered from the Norse and now felt that they needed Edward's protection by acknowledging his supremacy. Thus, by the year 922, Edward was overlord of all of Britain except for the Norse settlements of York, Orkney and the Western Isles. It was a remarkable achievement for a man whose boyhood had been spent in hiding from the Danes. Edward was a fitting son of Alfred and it was important that a strong king followed him to maintain and build upon his successes. ATHELSTAN was such a king.

Edward was married at least three times, though the legitimacy of the first is in question. Of his many children, most were daughters, but of the sons who survived him, all of them – EDWIN, ELFWEARD, Athelstan, EDMUND and EADRED – succeeded him in some form within the kingdom. (*See Chart 31 on page 473.*)

[M25] **ELFWEARD** Wessex, 17 July-1 August 924.
Elfweard was the third surviving son of EDWARD THE ELDER, and some sources suggest that he was elected the heir to the throne of Wessex by the *witan*. If this is so, then it was a strange choice, as Elfweard had been a bookish boy. He had been born sometime around the year 904 and was supposed to be a hermit in Bridgnorth. If he was elected, he had little chance to assume the crown. He died – there is a suggestion that he may have been murdered, perhaps at the suggestion of his brother ATHELSTAN – sixteen days later at Oxford, presumably on his way back to Winchester, where he was buried.

[M26] **ATHELSTAN**
King of the English, 17 July 924–27 October 939. Crowned: Kingston-upon-Thames, 4 September 925.
Born: *c895.* **Died:** *Gloucester, 27 October 939, aged 44.* **Buried:** *Malmesbury Abbey, Wiltshire.*
Athelstan, arguably the most powerful of all Saxon kings, was the eldest son of EDWARD THE ELDER, though there is a question about his legitimacy. Edward may not have married Athelstan's mother Egwina, and though she was later described as "a noblewoman", the scandal-mongers of the day remembered her as a shepherd's daughter whom Edward took a fancy to in his youth and who bore him two or perhaps three children. Maybe it was because he was illegitimate that Athelstan was raised by Edward's sister, ATHELFLÆD, at her court at Gloucester in Mercia and not at Winchester. Some authorities make much of the fact that Athelstan was a favourite of his grandfather's, ALFRED, as if he preferred this child over the others and singled him out for succession; in fact Athelstan was the only grandchild Alfred knew, as all of Alfred's other grandchildren were born after his death. Nevertheless, because Athelstan was reared in Mercia he had a loyalty from the Mercians that his forebears had never received. When Edward died, the Mercians immediately proclaimed him their king whilst the West Saxon *witan* were still deliberating. No doubt, if Athelstan was illegitimate, there was an issue to resolve, and possibly Edward had suggested before his death that Athelstan would succeed him in Mercia whilst one of his legitimate sons would succeed in Wessex. EDWIN was already sub-king in Kent and the obvious choice but perhaps he declined (or, if his recorded death date is in error, he may have already been dead). There is a suggestion that ELFWEARD the hermit was summoned to Winchester as a possible candidate, but he died en route, and thereafter there was no other choice but Athelstan, but he was

31. The Saxon Kingdoms (8) – The Family of Edward the Elder

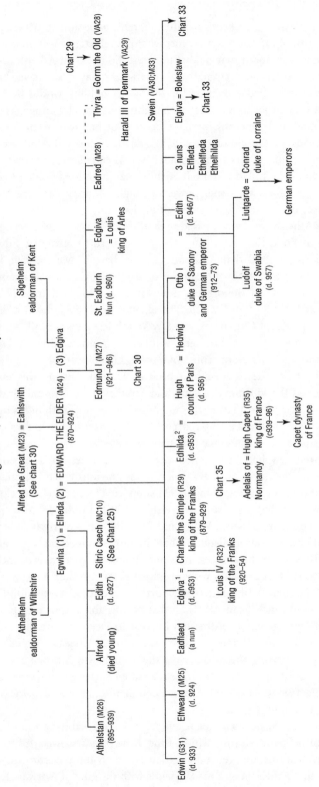

Notes: 1. Edgiva married secondly (c951) Herbert, count of Vermandois and had 2 further children: Stephen I, count of Vermandois (952–1021) and Agnes (b. 953)
2. Edhilda may have died in 938 and Hugh Capet may have been the son of a second marriage to Hedwig, sister of Emperor Otto I

not confirmed in Wessex until some months after his accession in Mercia. Even then he was not crowned for over a year. Just what the reluctance was amongst the West Saxons is not clear, and it may be that they just did not trust Athelstan. There is no doubt that Athelstan's strength of character may also have been a disadvantage, because he had a distrust for the Saxon nobility whom he treated with reserve, and they probably saw him as haughty and unwelcoming. Yet to his subjects he was kind and generous, perhaps because of his own origins. He was exceedingly generous to the church and delighted in giving gifts and receiving memorabilia. Like Arthur he was an avid reader but also a collector of treasures he later donated to the church. He was a tall, if thin, man with long golden hair and conveyed the image of a handsome, powerful knight. It may be something of Athelstan who lives on in our folk memory of Sir Lancelot.

No sooner was Athelstan ensconced as king than we find his authority recognized by SITRIC CAECH of York, the Norse king who had refused to recognize Edward's sovereignty. Sitric recognized that Athelstan's power base in Mercia gave him a much greater ability to attack Northumbria if necessary. Sitric and Athelstan thus agreed terms and as part of the arrangement Sitric was married to Athelstan's saintly sister Eadgyth on 30 January 926. The alliance with Sitric did not last for long, as he refused to accept Christianity, and by March 927 he was dead. Athelstan seized this opportunity. Sitric's brother, Gothfrith, who was king of Dublin, attempted to claim the throne of York, but Athelstan defeated him and, after showing him hospitality, despatched him back to Ireland. During this episode Athelstan summoned the kings of Scotland and Strathclyde to Eamont Bridge in July 927 and made them swear that they would not support Gothfrith in his designs upon the throne of York. Athelstan entered York, the first Saxon king to do so, since all previous kings before the Scandinavians had been Angles.

During 926 Athelstan had summoned the Welsh princes to a meeting at Hereford. Although the three primary rulers had previously paid homage to Edward, there had been a Norse uprising in 924 supported by the Welsh at Chester. Athelstan was determined to put a stop to Welsh hostilities in Mercia. At Hereford he laid down the boundary between Wales and England, particularly the southern stretch which had always been in dispute, where he now specified the Wye, and he exacted harsh tribute from the princes. It is not clear how far they ever met this demand, but it was evident that they recognized Athelstan's authority. HYWEL DDA in particular was fascinated by the Saxon court, appreciating its possibilities in Wales, and he learned much from Athelstan that he was able to put into practice. Immediately after this agreement, Athelstan hurried to Devon where the Cornish were again in revolt, probably under their king HOEL. Athelstan expelled the Cornish from Exeter. driving them back over the Tamar, which now became the boundary between Cornwall and England. He refortified Exeter and it seems he may have taken Hoel hostage to ensure the Cornish compliance, because Hoel was with him a year later at Eamont Bridge.

The alliance with the Scots lasted for seven years, a remarkable period of peace and prosperity in England during which time Athelstan reviewed his troops, improved his fortifications and generally settled down to the government of his subjects. It seems that Athelstan also made friends with the king of Norway, Harald Fairhair or Finehair, who sent gifts to Athelstan and also adopted the current vogue

From a coin

for fostering by sending his son, Haakon, then aged about seven, to Athelstan's court to benefit from understanding the English form of government. One consequence of this was that Haakon became such a welcome king in Norway that the elders deposed his brother, ERIK BLOODAXE, who immediately become a problem for Athelstan's successors. This was but one example of Athelstan's role in Europe. Because of a series of political marriages amongst his aunts and his own sisters, Athelstan was on close terms with many of the major rulers in Europe. These included Count Baldwin of Flanders, who had married his aunt Elfreda, Charles III of France, who had married his sister Edgiva, the influential Hugh, Count of Paris, who had married another sister, Edhilda, and Otto, duke of Saxony and subsequently German emperor, who had married a further sister, Eadgyth. There was another possible half-sister who married Gorm the Old, the first king of a united Denmark. All of this demonstrates that Athelstan was a key activist on the international scene, and though it is not recorded that he travelled abroad, his relationships improved trade and culture in England extensively.

In 934 Athelstan was incensed when the Scottish king CONSTANTINE married his daughter to OLAF GOTHFRITHSON of Dublin, which Athelstan saw as a flagrant breach of the Eamont treaty. He decided to give Constantine a lesson and in 934 he raised a huge army which increased in numbers as he marched north from Winchester, and he devastated Scotland en route as far north as Fordun. Constantine recognized Athelstan's power, but it only made him all the more determined to seek the support of Olaf as a defence against the English might. In 937, after the death of Gothfrith, Olaf combined his army with Constantine's. He took York and marched down into Mercia. Athelstan met him at Brunanburh, near Nottingham. It was one of the most decisive of all Saxon victories, and passed into legend. From then until his death two years later Athelstan ruled peacefully, the complete master of his realm. Athelstan's reign was remembered by later annalists as a golden age, and certainly there would be little like it again for many years to come. Athelstan died of an illness, probably a manifestation of the same malady which afflicted his family, many of whom died young. He was only forty-four. Athelstan had never married, and he was succeeded by his half-brother EDMUND.

[M27] EDMUND (I) *THE MAGNIFICENT*
King of the English, 27 October 939–26 May 946. Crowned: Kingston-upon-Thames, 29 November 939.
Born: *c921*; **Died**: *murdered Pucklechurch, 26 May 946, aged about 24.* **Buried**: *Glastonbury Abbey.*
Married: (1) *c940, Elgiva (d. c944/5): 3 children; (2) c946, Athelfleda dau. Alfgar, ealdorman of Wiltshire: no children.*
The name Eadmund in Saxon meant "protector of riches" giving an indication of Edmund's presumed role as guardian of the realm. Edmund was the half-brother of

ATHELSTAN, and the first child of EDWARD *THE ELDER*'s third marriage. He had been raised in Athelstan's household and once old enough had accompanied Athelstan in several of his campaigns, fighting heroically at Brunanburh in 937. As Athelstan had no children, Edmund succeeded him, even though he was only eighteen. His reign began inauspiciously, as the Norse king of Dublin, OLAF GOTHFRITHSON, regarded him as a weak successor and took the opportunity to regain his family's hold on York. This he did in little over a month after Edmund's succession, followed by his army's march down into Mercia, devastating countryside and towns, including Tamworth, before they were confronted by Edmund at Leicester. A rather ineffectual siege followed from which Olaf and his chief adviser, Wulfstan, archbishop of York, escaped. Talks followed which resulted in Olaf being allowed to retain the kingship over York, as well as rule over the Danish territories in East Anglia and the Five Boroughs. The Danes were none too pleased about this, as they were enemies of the Norse. Nevertheless, Edmund managed to recover from this ignominy. After only eighteen months, Olaf died. His successor, OLAF SITRICSON, was not quite his match. Edmund undertook a lightning strike across Mercia in 942 and recovered the Danish territories. Soon after Olaf was driven out of York, and was replaced by his cousin, RAGNALL GOTHFRITHSON, who was open to discussion with Edmund and more prepared to accept Christianity. Olaf took refuge in the kingdom of Strathclyde where guerilla warfare now existed between the Norse factions. Edmund took this as an opportunity to resolve the problem once and for all. In 944 he led an army into northern Britain. In the battle in York Ragnall was killed and York came back under Saxon control. The following year the army marched on Strathclyde. Olaf was driven out and back to Ireland. The king DONALD was also ejected, and Edmund conquered all of the Norse lands in Cumbria. These he handed to the new Scots king MALCOLM (I) on the basis that he would remain faithful to Edmund and not support the Norse.

From an ignominious start, Edmund's reign now looked highly successful. He had regained the territories that he had lost and was recognized as overlord by all the native kings. At twenty-four he should have been set for an auspicious reign, but then tragedy struck. In May 946 Edmund was celebrating the feast of St Augustine at Pucklechurch, north of Bath. During the feast he recognized a thief called Leofa whom Edmund had exiled six years earlier. Edmund asked his steward to arrest the man but a fight followed in which Edmund intervened and was stabbed. He soon died of his wounds. Edmund had two infant sons, EDWY and EDGAR, both of whom would become kings, but he was succeeded by his brother EADRED.

[M28] EADRED

King of the English, 26 May 946–23 November 955. Crowned: Kingston-upon-Thames, 16 August 946.

Born: c923. **Died:** *Frome, Somerset, 23 November 955, aged 32.* **Buried:** *Winchester Cathedral.*

Although Eadred was a physically weak king, almost unable to eat his food, he was every bit the warrior like his brothers EDMUND and ATHELSTAN and his father EDWARD (THE ELDER). Most of his short reign was involved with the Norse kingdom of York. Edmund had ejected the Norse kings and brought York under his control. At the start of his reign Eadred travelled north and sought the fealty of

Wulfstan, the archbishop of York, and of York's *witan* (council). Although they professed loyalty, within a few months they had appointed the Norse adventurer, ERIK BLOODAXE, as their king. Eadred regarded this as treachery and immediately raised an army and invaded Northumbria. He avoided attacking York but instead laid waste to the surrounding lands. On his return to Mercia his rearguard was attacked by Norse troops. Eadred was livid. His weak constitution had nevertheless created a man of iron will, vicious temper and little patience. His troops turned back on York and Eadred threatened to destroy the kingdom. The elders of York knew he was capable of it and they agreed to eject Erik. Satisfied, Eadred returned to Wessex. However, within months the former king of York, OLAF SITRICSON, returned and was re-installed. Rather than inflict another invasion Eadred bargained with Olaf, prepared to let him remain provided he patrolled the shores against other Norse and Danish pirates, particularly Erik Bloodaxe. The people of York did not seem to know what they wanted, and the internal politics of Wulfstan's party were becoming intolerable. In 952 Wulfstan ejected Olaf and brought Erik back into power. Infuriated Eadred invaded York in 954. Wulfstan was imprisoned. Erik was expelled, and on his way back to Orkney he was slain. The English, Norse and Danes of York readily accepted Eadred as their king and the Scandinavian kingdom of Jorvik was at an end. Eadred ruled it directly, whilst he allowed Oswulf a high degree of autonomy in ruling Bernicia as an earl. With the final expulsion of the Norse kings, Eadred could justifiably be called king of all the English. Like his brother, though, he would not live to enjoy his glory. He died in November 955, aged only 32 or so. Despite his valour in battle he was a strongly religious man, suffering his pains with piety. He apparently never married and after his death the throne passed to his even weaker nephews, EDWY and EDGAR.

[M29] EDWY or EADWIG *ALL-FAIR*

King of the English, 23 November 955–1 October 959. Crowned: Kingston-upon-Thames 26 January 956.
Born: *c941.* **Died:** *Gloucester, 1 October 959, aged 18.* **Buried:** *Winchester Cathedral.*
Married: *c957, Elgiva (descendant of Athelred I) (d 959): annulled, no children.*
Edwy was the eldest son of EDMUND I and with the untimely death of EADRED he ascended the throne at the age of only fourteen. The *ASC* states that Edwy succeeded to Wessex and his brother EDGAR succeeded to Mercia and Northumbria, but as Edgar was almost two years Edwy's junior, his succession was held in abeyance until he was older. In effect the two kings, and particularly Edwy, were advised by a strong council, which included Dunstan, the abbot of Glastonbury. Since these two were as headstrong as each other, and as intransigent, it led to considerable personal conflict. Edwy's relationship with Dunstan started poorly – apparently at his coronation Edwy disappeared from the council and was found consorting with a young lady – and got worse. Edwy could not work with Dunstan and had him banished from England in 957. All of Edwy's reign seemed to be a jockeying for position between himself and his council of elders, most of whom had the upper hand. Edwy himself never achieved anything. He married his childhood sweetheart, Elgiva, but this was annulled within a year on the grounds of consanguinity – they were third cousins. It suggests that the elders, particularly Oda, the archbishop of Canterbury, did not want Edwy to father children, perhaps

because of the continuing problem of health or, more likely, because these would threaten his brother's right to the throne, and it seems that by 959 the elders were now firmly behind Edgar. It thus may have come as a relief when Edwy died in October 959. He was only eighteen, and it has usually been accepted that he died of the inherent family malady, but the growing opposition to him may suggest he was helped on his way. Most of the churchmen who wrote Edwy's obituaries had less than fond memories of him, but his brother-in-law, who became Athelweard the Chronicler, believed he was much misunderstood. It was Athelweard who called Edwy "All-Fair", or "the Fair", a word which in Saxon did not just refer to his fair complexion, but which also meant pleasant and mild-mannered. Edwy comes across the centuries as an uncertain king trapped in a weak body surrounded by officialdom, knowing he could not live up to the glory of his forebears, but unable to find consolation, other than with his wife and mother-in-law. He was a sad and tragic king.

[M30] EDGAR *THE PEACEABLE*

King of the English, 1 October 959–8 July 975 (he was appointed king of Mercia and Northumbria from 957). Crowned: Bath Abbey, 11 May 973.
Born: c943. Died: Winchester, 8 July 975, aged 32. Buried: Glastonbury Abbey.
Married: (1) c960, Athelfleda, dau. Ordmaer, ealdorman of Hertford: either divorced c961 or died c961 or c964: 1 son; (2) c964, Elfrida (c945–c1002), dau. Ordgar, ealdorman of Devon, and widow of Athelwald, ealdorman of East Anglia: 2 children. Also had at least one illegitimate child.

The Saxon name Eadgar means "rich in spears", which was undoubtedly a recognition of his inheritance of military power. When Edgar's uncle EADRED died in 955, his brother EDWY became king in Wessex whilst Edgar was appointed to the kingship of Mercia and Northumbria. He was only twelve at the time and did not assume full authority until he was about fifteen, by which time he was welcomed, as Edwy was a weak and unpopular king. Edgar had been raised in East Anglia, in the household of Athelstan, the ealdorman of the old territory of the Danelaw which covered all of east Anglia and Danish Mercia. As such Edgar was already a popular prince amongst the middle-English and Danes and was readily accepted as king, whereas Edwy was seen as a weak and troublesome youth. By November 957 the Mercians and Northumbrians had renounced their allegiance to Edwy. Both kings were advised (or controlled) by a strong council which had led to conflict with Edwy who had expelled bishop Dunstan. When Edgar came of age he recalled Dunstan and was enthusiastic about his ideas for reforming the English church. When Edwy died in October 959, Edgar also became king of Wessex and as the archbishopric of Canterbury was vacant with the recent death of Oda, Dunstan was appointed to that see. With the support of the king, Dunstan introduced a major programme of monastic reform, not all of which was happily accepted at the time, but which brought Saxon England in line with developments on the continent. All secular clergy were ejected, and the church officials were granted considerable independence from the crown. The most extreme of these was the creation of the soke of Peterborough, where the abbot of St Peters had almost total independence. Many of the monasteries that had been destroyed during the Danish invasions were restored. It was only a period of peace that could allow such rebuilding and change. Edgar, for all that he was not a soldier or strategist to match his father or grandfather, was able to work alongside strong and well organized ealdormen in governing the kingdom and in ensuring its safety. All the time England seemed in capable hands, the Norse and Danes bided their time.

In 973 Edgar gave a demonstration of authority. Although he probably had a formal coronation when he became king of Wessex, Dunstan believed there was a need for a major ceremony similar to those of the King of the Franks and the German Emperor. The ceremony was delayed for some years because Dunstan was unhappy with Edgar's dissolute life. For all he supported the church reform Edgar was not a particularly religious man. There were rumours about his private life, which may have some base of truth. He had married a childhood friend, Athelfleda, early in life, but it seems that either she died in childbirth around the year 961 or the two became separated because of Edgar's amorous adventures with Wulfryth. Stories were later attached to the episode that Edgar had seduced a nun, but although Wulfryth later became a nun, the real story seems to be that he fell in love with a lady who bore him a child, but she either chose to enter (or was banished to) a nunnery and they probably never married. Edgar then became romantically entangled with Elfrida, who was already married, and again the scandalmongers hinted that the two might have planned the murder of her husband, Edgar's one-time foster-brother Athelwald in 964, in order to marry. Elfrida later came to epitomise the image of the wicked stepmother in her relationship with Edgar's youngest child, EDWARD (THE MARTYR). All of these shenanigans caused Dunstan to counsel Edgar to change his ways. Perhaps as he passed from youth into adulthood he became less reckless, and in 973 Dunstan agreed to a major ceremony at Bath. The coronation had double significance. For the first time a Saxon king was crowned as king of all the English, a title used by previous monarchs but never as part of their coronation. Edgar was thus the first genuine king of England. At the same time Elfrida was also crowned, the first queen of the English. This ceremony has remained essentially the same in content ever since. Following the coronation,

From a contemporary MS

Edgar put on a display of force. His army marched along the Welsh border from Bath to Chester, showing his authority over the Welsh, whilst his fleet sailed through the Irish Sea, also demonstrating his subjugation of the Norse who still held power in that area at Dublin and on Man. At Chester eight kings of Wales and the north assembled to make their submission to him. A later chronicler suggested that these eight kings then rowed Edgar along the river Dee with him at the helm. Strong though that image is, it is unlikely. It is more probable that there was a ceremonial voyage along the Dee with Edgar at the helm, and the other kings in submission. The coronation and ceremony were immensely significant. Although Edgar's position had been achieved by his predecessors, he was able to capitalise on it and demonstrate his authority over all of Britain with the exception of Orkney. Not all monarchs were present, the most noticeable absentee being OWAIN AP HYWEL of Deheubarth, though his absence was due to domestric strife rather than lack of respect. THORFINN SKULL-SPLITTER was not present, but as he owed his allegiance to the Norwegian crown, he might be excused – although, interestingly, MAGNUS HARALDSSON of Man and the Isles was present.

The ceremony marked the end of a peaceful and prosperous reign, and it was fortunate that the English could not see ahead as Edgar's was the last reign of peace and harmony. The Saxon world would thereafter start to disintegrate and within less than a century be almost wiped away.

[M31] EDWARD *THE MARTYR*

King of the English, 8 July 975–18 March 978. Crowned: Kingston-upon-Thames, 975.
Born: c962. **Died** (murdered): Corfe Castle, Dorset, 18 March 978, aged 16. **Buried:** Wareham Abbey, Dorset; later removed to Shaftesbury Abbey, Dorset. [What were believed to be Edward's relics were found during an archeological dig at Shaftesbury in 1931 and currently reside in the Midland Bank in Croydon.]

Edward was the young son of EDGAR and his first wife Athelfleda. Although he was the rightful heir there was opposition to his election as king, with much support for his half-brother ATHELRED (II). Athelred was only seven at this time and evidently the ealdormen who wanted him as king, wanted the power that went with it. Edward was thirteen, but old enough not to be trampled over. He was a precocious and ungovernable youth given to temper tantrums, and he soon had considerable opposition amongst his council. For the superstitious there were other signs and portents. In the autumn of his election there was a bright comet in the sky, always an ill omen. In the following year there was famine across England, presumably the result of a harsh winter and a wet summer. Some may have seen this as a message from God of dissatisfaction with the reform of the monasteries which had been carried out with such zeal under EDGAR's reign. Those who had been opposed to the reform used this as an opportunity to attack the church, and many monasteries were pillaged. By the end of 976 lawlessness seems to have broken out across the land. Dunstan alone stood firm in support of the king and of his reforms. There is a wonderful story of how Dunstan demonstrated his authority when he called a meeting of leading councillors at Calne, in the year 978. They met in an upper room and during the meeting the floor gave way so that many of the councillors were killed or injured, all save Dunstan who was standing on the one rafter that remained intact. It was proclaimed a miracle. Even if it was deliberately engineered Dunstan was taking a severe risk. He was aged about seventy by then.

That same year Edward was murdered. He was calling on his stepmother and half-brother at Corfe Castle in Dorset. As he arrived the household retainers went to greet him but then stabbed him to death as he dismounted from his horse. The attack had clearly been premeditated and before long Elfrida was implicated in the crime as the wicked stepmother. It is not likely that many missed Edward and his fits of rage, but within a decade people were saying miracles were occurring alongside his bones at Wareham, and Athelred declared him a saint and martyr.

[M32] **ATHELRED (II)** *THE UNREADY*
King of the English, 18 March 978–December 1013, 3 February 1014–23 April 1016. Crowned: Kingston-upon-Thames, 4 April 978.
Born: *c968.* **Died**: *London, 23 April 1016, aged 48.* **Buried**: *Old St Paul's Cathedral, London.*
Married: *(1) c985, Elgiva (c963–1002), dau. Thored, ealdorman of Northumbria: 13 children; (2) 5 April 1002, Emma (c985–1052), dau. Richard, duke of Normandy: 3 children.*

Athelred is remembered colloquially and half-jokingly today as the Unready, although the nickname was really a clever pun on his name, *athel* "noble" and *ræd* "counsel", meaning "noble counsel". Throughout his reign Athelred was ill-advised and if he made his own decision, he was as likely to change his mind, hence the nickname, *ræd-less*, or lacking counsel. He was a better administrator than history has given credit, but he was a hopeless king and leader.

He was the son of EDGAR and his second (or third) wife Elfrida. At the time of Edgar's death there were many who supported Athelred as the next king, but the *witan* elected his elder half-brother EDWARD. When Edward was murdered three years later, Athelred's supporters, who included his mother and the Mercian ealdorman Alfhere, ensured that Athelred came to the throne. He was still probably under ten, and Elfrida and Alfhere dominated the government of England. Alfhere had been the main opponent to Edward and led the anti-monastic movement which flared up following the death of Edgar. Alfhere believed that the monasteries were becoming too rich and powerful too quickly and that they could control the shires. Alfhere was implicated in the murder of Edward. Interestingly it was he who translated Edward's body from its hasty burial at Wareham to Shaftesbury, where it was buried amongst great ceremony and talk of miracles. Alfhere remained the most powerful ealdorman until his death in 983. He succeeded in shaping Athelred's policy toward reducing the power of the monasteries, although Athelred later over-turned this. Alfhere also had to face the impact of the first Danish raids for thirty years, which marked the beginning of the end for the Saxon kingdom. When he died, Alfhere was not much loved, being regarded as something of a bully.

After Alfhere's death Athelred endeavoured to exert his own authority and even his mother's considerable power waned, though she lived till 1002. There was a period in the late 980s when Athelred sought to reduce the power of the church, but he subsequently reverted to his father's interests and promoted the construction of new monasteries under the new order. He also endeavoured to update the laws of the country and reorganize local government. This culminated in the Wantage

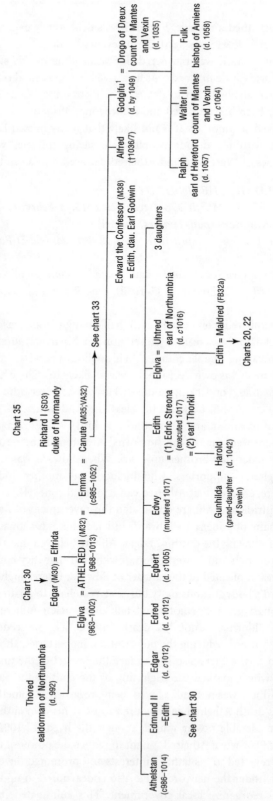

32. The Saxon Kingdoms (9) – The Family of Athelred II the Unready

Notes: 1. Godgifu married secondly Eustace II, count of Boulogne (d. 1093) and may have had a daughter

Code of 997 which, compared to past law codes, showed an unprecedented willingness to accept local customs, especially those amongst the Danes of eastern England. Many of the odd and curious anomalies that we have in our customs and codes of conduct in this country were enshrined under this Code. Had Athelred's reign been measured by his willingness and ability to reform and organize, he would have been remembered kindly, but his mettle was tested when the Danish raids returned and England was pushed to the limit.

The raids began in a comparatively small way as early as 980 and continued through to 982. Most of the raids were in the south west, but Southampton was severely damaged and London was attacked and burned in 982. Raids ceased for the next few years and perhaps Athelred was lulled into a false sense of security, for in 987 they began again, once more in the south-west and then, in 991, a major battle at Maldon in Essex. The Danish leader Olaf Tryggvason outwitted the East Saxon ealdorman Beortnoth, and the Saxons were killed to a man. The first payment of *danegeld*, or what amounted to protection money, arose following this battle, a policy instigated at the suggestion of Sigeric, the archbishop of Canterbury, who was one of Athelred's poor advisers. Olaf used this ploy as he moved around the south and east, plundering and destroying and then extracting payment. In 994, after the Danes had invaded London, Athelred paid 16,000 pounds in *danegeld*, but this time on the basis that Olaf would accept Christianity and never again raid Britain. Olaf kept his promise. He used the money to strengthen his fleet and finance his bid for the kingship of Norway. But his command was superseded by others who had made no such agreement, and so the raids continued. Each year the *danegeld* increased until the riches of England were savagely reduced. In addition the monasteries were plundered and destroyed and with armies being kept mobilised for most of the year men were unable to harvest. The country grew poorer, the men weaker, and spirits lower. The men had no equivalent of ALFRED or EDWARD (THE ELDER) or ATHELSTAN to look to for leadership. Athelred had never been tested as a battle commander and he had no idea what to do. He also had to face desertion from amongst his own ealdormen, whose actions in fleeing the command of battle further weakened their men's morale. Athelred seemed powerless to punish them. Instead he shifted from one mad scheme to another, none of which worked and all of which reduced the country's morale further. At one point in 1009, he demanded that a whole new fleet be constructed, but he was unable to find sufficient able commanders and had no battle plans to meet the Danes in the waters they controlled. The fleet spent more time anchored off-shore than in battle, and once it moved into battle it was destroyed. Athelred did nothing to save it but left it to its fate. The venture was a disaster and drained the country's resources further. In 1002 Athelred married Emma, daughter of Richard, duke of Normandy. The marriage was almost certainly to create an alliance whereby Richard stopped the Danes using Normandy as a base for raiding southern England. Richard no doubt played his part, but the plan was another of Athelred's ineffective tactics.

Probably his worst decision was the St Brice's Day massacre on 13 November 1002. He ordered the killing of every Dane who lived in England except the Anglo-Danes of the Danelaw. It is unlikely that the edict was carried out to the letter, but there was fearful slaughter across southern England which left a bitter stain on Athelred's character. Even if the resident Danes had supported him previously, they now turned against him. The massacre brought back to English shores the Danish commander SWEIN who had accompanied Olaf on earlier missions. Legend has it that Swein's sister and her husband had been killed in the massacre and Swein returned to exact revenge. Swein's campaign lasted from 1003 to 1007 when Athelred agreed a peace treaty with him and paid over an immense *danegeld* of 30,000 pounds. Swein returned to Denmark, but new commanders took his place and the raids and slaughter continued. The next major enemy was Thorkell the Tall, who arrived with a major army in August 1009 and left a wave of destruction across southern England. The low point of this campaign was the murder of Alphege, the archbishop of Canterbury in 1012. Thorkell had not condoned the murder and he subsequently offered his services to help protect England. Athelred had to raise a new tax, the *heregeld*, to pay for Thorkell's army, but this band of mercenaries was more effective than the English army because it had a strong, sound leader. Nevertheless, the whole of England had now become a battlefield, and the English were prepared to submit. Swein read the signs correctly when he returned to England. He landed in the Humber in August 1013, and the Northumbrians immediately submitted, followed soon by the Danes of Danelaw. Athelred waited with Thorkell's fleet in the Thames off London, so Swein marched on Bath, where the Mercians and West Saxons capitulated. By December 1013 London collapsed and Athelred fled to Normandy.

Swein died only three months later and Athelred was recalled, when Swein's son, CANUTE, returned to establish himself in Denmark. Athelred's return was conditional on that he governed "more justly than he had done in the past." Matters did not improve, however. Early in the fighting against Canute, in 1014 Athelred's eldest son and heir, Athelstan, was killed in battle. Early in 1015 Athelred executed the two leading thanes of the Danelaw, whom he regarded as traitors, which did not endear him to Mercia or the north. His son, EDMUND, gained the support of the Danelaw, and when Canute returned later in 1015, England was divided and the armies refused to move against the Danes unless the king himself commanded them. By now, though, Athelred was dying. Although he was only forty-eight, he had lived longer than many of his predecessors and was worn out by the fighting. He died on 23 April 1016, leaving Edmund to continue to battle for survival.

[M33;VA30] SWEIN, SWEYN or SVEN *FORKBEARD*
King of Denmark, c985–1014; King of England, 25 December 1013–2 February 1014.

Born: c960, Denmark. **Died:** Gainsborough, Lincolnshire, 2 February 1014, aged 54. **Buried:** Roeskild Cathedral, Denmark.
Married: (1) c990, Gunhilda (d. c1015), dau. of Duke Mieszko I of Poland, divorced c1000: 4 or more children; (2) c1000, Sigrid the Haughty (d. c1013), widow of Eric VIII of Sweden: up to 3 children.

Swein was the son of Harald *Bluetooth*, king of Denmark. He won the throne of Denmark as the result of a rebellion in 985 when he was probably in his mid twenties. He did not consolidate his hold on Denmark until his father's death in 986. He then turned his attention to richer pickings and combined his forces with those of Olaf Tryggvason of Norway to regain lost ground in England. His raids were amongst a massive wave of Danish and Norse incursions, but those of Olaf and Swein were organized as politically motivated campaigns of conquest. Swein's early raids were in the period 993 to 995. He returned in 1003 after his sister Gunhilda was apparently one of those killed in the St Brice's Day massacre of 1002. He returned annually, his army devastating the countryside. In 1006 they advanced as far as the Berkshire Downs. In past generations this territory had been fiercely defended by the West Saxons under ALFRED and others, and it had passed into Danish legend that any Viking army reaching that territory would never again see the sea. But there was no Alfred to rebuff Swein and he returned unmolested. It was clear England was for the taking, but ATHELRED agreed a truce with Swein in 1007, paying him a massive *danegeld*, and Swein returned to Denmark. When he returned in 1013 he knew that the English could take no more, following the total devastation caused by the army of Thorkell the Tall. Even though Thorkell had sold his services to Athelred for further sizeable payments, the English fighting spirit had reached its nadir. Swein landed at the Humber in August 1013, and the northern English and Danes of Danelaw immediately submitted to him. He marched across Mercia to Oxford and down to Winchester, where Wessex submitted. Unable to take London he marched on Bath where the Mercians and British of the west country submitted. Swein returned to his base in Lindsey, and learned that Athelred had fled to Normandy. The final resistance in London collapsed and on Christmas Day 1013 Swein was recognized as king of England. 225 years since the first Danish raid on Devon, and thousands of lives later, the Danes had conquered England. Swein did not live long to enjoy his prize. In his mid-fifties he was ill and exhausted from his campaigns and died six weeks later, following a fall from his horse. His son CANUTE would later regain the kingdom.

[M34] EDMUND II *IRONSIDE*

King of the English, 23 April-30 November 1016. Crowned: Old St Paul's Cathedral, April 1016.
Born: *c989.* **Died** *(murdered?): London, 30 November 1016, aged 27.* **Buried:** *Glastonbury Abbey.*
Married: *August(?) 1015, Edith, widow of Sigeferth, thane of East Anglia: 2 children.*
Edmund was the second son of ATHELRED (II) and became the heir to the throne after the eldest son, Athelstan, fell in battle some time in 1014. Edmund had already done his share of fighting, and had proved himself valiant, but once the heir he became even more determined. Angered at the weakness of his father, who had already been expelled from England by SWEIN in 1013, only to return a few months later promising to rule strongly and wisely, Edmund carved out his own plan to recover England. There was some respite during 1014 when CANUTE left England to gain the throne of Denmark, though Athelred used that time to exact retribution from those he believed had betrayed him. One of these was Sigeferth, a thane of East Anglia, who had been amongst the first to submit to Swein when he landed at Gainsborough in August 1013. Sigeferth was executed and his widow, Edith, imprisoned at Malmesbury. Edmund rescued Edith and married her. This action gained the support of the Danelaw of Mercia and the north, but divided Britain, with Athelred retaining support in the south. When Canute returned to England in September 1015 only Edmund's army was prepared. Athelred's men would not fight unless led by the king but he was seldom available (he was increasingly ill) and his

own ealdormen were always on the verge of desertion. Athelred died in April 1016 and Edmund was promptly declared king. There was no time for celebrations. Edmund and Canute's armies clashed at five major battles during the year. The outcome was rarely decisive, both sides claiming victory. Edmund succeeded in holding London against Canute's siege and he probably would have defeated the Danes at Sherstone had not one of his ealdormen (the ever-traitorous Eadric of Shropshire) tricked the Saxons into believing Edmund was dead. Canute defeated Edmund at Ashingdon, in Essex, on 18 October, but by this time both sides were battle-weary. One further engagement was fought near Deerhurst in Gloucester, at which point both parties agreed to negotiate. At the Treaty of Olney, signed at the end of October, Canute was granted Mercia and Northumbria, and Edmund remained in Wessex. Edmund returned to London. He had been seriously wounded at Ashingdon, and his continued fighting had not improved his health. Nevertheless his death, just one month later, still shocked the Saxon nation. There was talk of murder and the weight of evidence supports this. Later rumours of a particularly nasty disembowelling whilst on the privy have never been disproved. With his death Canute soon convinced the English to accept him as king. Edmund's sons were despatched from England, and other young Saxon princes were transferred to places of safety. Only one of them, Edmund's son Edward (the father of EDGAR ATHELING), would return.

[M35;VA32] CANUTE, CNUT or KNUT

England, 30 November 1016–12 November 1035. Crowned: London (Old St Paul's) 6 January 1017. Canute was also king of Denmark from 1018 and of Norway from 1028.
Born: Denmark, c995. Died: Shaftesbury, Dorset, 12 November 1035, aged about 40.
Buried: Winchester Cathedral.
Married: (1) c1014, Elfgiva (c996–c1044), dau. Alfhelm, ealdorman of Northampton: 2 children; (2) 2 July 1017, Emma, widow of Athelred II: 3 children.
The first Dane to be crowned as king of England. His subsequent rulership of Denmark and Norway made him the most powerful king of northern Europe. Canute had accompanied his father, SWEIN, on his conquest of England in 1013, when he was left in control of the Danish fleet in the north. Once his father had been elected king of England, Canute saw fit to entrench his position in the north and it was probably early in 1014 that he claimed marriage to Elfgiva, the daughter of Alfhelm, who had been ealdorman of Northumbria until his murder in 1006. Swein died early in 1014 and although the Danes elected Canute as their new king, the *witan* chose the return of ATHELRED whose forces drove Canute from the north. Canute was also concerned about establishing himself on the throne of Denmark, but by the time he had returned to his homeland his elder brother Harald was already ensconced as king. Canute returned to England late in 1015 and the next twelve months saw a wasting conflict between the Danes and the Saxons under EDMUND IRONSIDE. Neither side was the complete victor and in October 1016 Edmund and Canute divided England between them, with Canute taking Mercia and Northumbria. The following month Edmund died, many believed by the treachery of ealdorman Eadric. Canute was elected king of all England and was crowned early the following year.

From a coin

The records of Canute's early reign are limited and often prejudiced against him, as are most annals of a conqueror by the conquered. He comes across as a tyrannical king who systematically murdered or exiled most of the leading Saxon nobles, including those who had crossed to his side. The traitorous Eadric he had executed. However, he did not eradicate the Saxon nobility as this would serve him little purpose. England was by now a well established kingdom, whereas Denmark had only recently been united and Canute was young and untested in kingship, especially in a foreign land. He needed the support and help of those who understood England and the English. Initially he divided the land into four, granting territory to three of his earls by way of military commands, and keeping Wessex for himself. However, from 1018 he appointed Godwin as earl of Wessex and it was under Canute that Godwin became the most powerful earl in England. Canute also realised he needed to be on good terms with the church and went to great lengths to establish relationships with Wulfstan, the archbishop of York, and Lyfing, archbishop of Canterbury. It was with Wulfstan that Canute later issued his law codes, based heavily on those already promulgated by the Saxon kings. Canute was able to adapt these codes for use in Denmark. Finally Canute married Athelred's widow, Emma, in order to strengthen his right to the throne. By all accounts he was still married to Elfgiva, which has caused some commentators to presume she was his mistress. She was certainly more than that, some treating her as his "handfast" or common-law wife according to Scandinavian custom, whilst Emma was his formal wife and queen. By this arrangement it meant that the children of Emma were heirs to the English throne, whilst the children of Elfgiva had right of succession to the throne of Denmark. In 1018 Canute returned to Denmark where, after the death of his brother, he was accepted as king. He did not return to England until 1020, but even then required regular trips to Denmark to sustain the throne, particularly during the period 1022–3. In 1020 Canute held a major council at Cirencester. There seems to have been some unrest during his absence, and Canute dealt with this by banishing Athelweard, the ealdorman of the western provinces (the former Dumnonia). The reason for his exile is unrecorded, but we can imagine he had been plotting against Canute, perhaps to restore one of Athelred's sons to the throne, the likeliest one being Edwy. Some records suggest that Edwy had been murdered by order of Canute in 1017, but William of Malmesbury records that he survived and lived in the south-west of England, perhaps under the protection of Athelweard. It may be that Edwy was murdered after Athelweard's expulsion. The next year we find Canute at odds with Thorkell the Tall, another Danish earl who had sold his services to Athelred in 1013, but who had accepted Canute's overlordship and been made earl of East Anglia. Thorkell must have challenged Canute's authority, perhaps in his treatment of the Saxons. Thorkell, for all his early devastation of England, had married a Saxon and seems to have established a friendship. He possibly had more scruples than Canute and they disagreed over Canute's policy of government. Thorkell was banished. The two became reconciled in 1023 when Canute made Thorkell the regent of Denmark and the foster-father of his son HARTHACANUTE.

Canute's reign has all the hallmarks of a powerful king who was initially uncertain in his authority. The harsh measures at the start of his reign arose through his feeling of insecurity, though he was in fact more stable in England than in Denmark. The English had suffered nearly thirty years of privations under Danish raids, and all they wanted was a restoration of peace and prosperity. The degree of support that he had in England gave him the strong base from which to consolidate his rule of Denmark and, from 1028, to conquer Norway. From 1030 he installed his eldest son, Swein (then about sixteen), as king of Norway, with his mother Elfgiva, as regent. By the mid-1020s Canute had mellowed from his earlier tyrannical rule (which was probably exaggerated in any case by the chroniclers) to one of piety. He made considerable gifts to the church in the hoping of buying salvation for his soul. The famous (much later) story of Canute sitting in his throne on the beach and commanding the tide to turn may have an element of truth. Although the legend suggests that Canute wanted to demonstrate his authority over the waves – and by implication his power over the northern seas – the fact is that Canute was giving a demonstration of piety by proving that he did not have power over them. The event is traditionally sited at Bosham on the English south coast, but an earlier record, by Geoffrey Gaimar, does not refer to Canute's throne and places the episode in the Thames estuary. In 1027 Canute visited Rome and attended the coronation of the Emperor Conrad II whose son, Heinrich, would marry Canute's daughter Gunhilda in 1036. Canute visited Rome again in 1031.

Nevertheless, despite his piety, Canute sought to impose his authority not just over England but Scotland and Wales. He visited Scotland in 1031, probably not with an army of conquest, but in order to form a peace alliance with MALCOLM II who had taken advantage of unrest in England during Athelred's reign to impose his authority over Bernicia and parts of Northumbria. The agreement reached between Canute and Malcolm saw Bernicia restored to England and the English-Scottish border established more or less as it is today. The ASC records that three kings submitted to Canute in the north. In addition to Malcolm these were Mælbæth, who was almost certainly MACBETH, and Iehmarc, who was probably MARGAD RAGNALLSON, the Norse king of Dublin who had authority over Man and the Isles. THORFINN THE MIGHTY, earl of Orkney, was already subject to Canute as his Norse overlord. Canute's authority over Wales was more tenuous. There is some suggestion that RHYDDERCH AP IESTYN recognized Canute's authority, but that may have been an administrative convenience, judging from Rhydderch's love of power, and it is unlikely that Canute exerted any power in Wales.

The records and later folklore suggest that Canute came to love England, possibly more than his homeland. He was a monarch who had conquered and established the most powerful of all Scandinavian empires, and through his power and

33. The Danish and Norse Kingdoms (6) – The House of Godwin and the Danish Succession

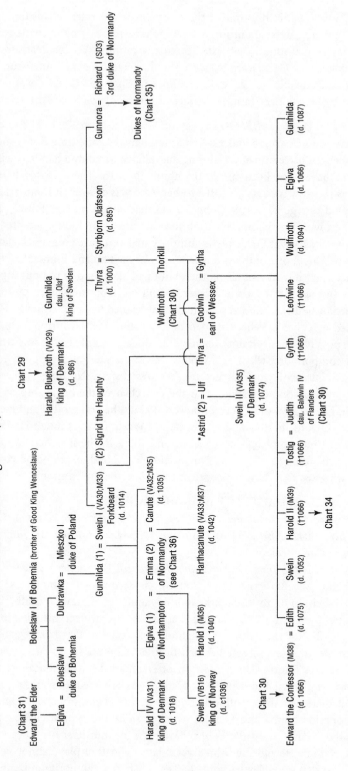

* Also married Richard II of Normandy (Chart 35)

authority was recognized as one of the most important rulers of his day. He died remarkably young, aged about forty. There is evidence that he knew he was dying and had a terminal illness that lasted for many months. Yet his death must have come suddenly as Harthacanute, who should have been his successor, was in Denmark and unable to stake his claim on England. Canute was therefore succeeded by his younger (and possibility illegitimate) son HAROLD (I).

[M36] **HAROLD (I)** *HAREFOOT* ruled 1037 (regent from 1035)-17 March 1040. He was the son of CANUTE and his first wife Elfgiva. At the time of his succession some challenged his legitimacy, claiming that Elfgiva was only a handfast wife. He is believed to have been born in Northampton in 1016. The accepted heir to the throne was HARTHACANUTE, his half-brother, who was delayed in Denmark. Harold was accepted as regent, to rule alongside Harthacanute's mother Emma, and Earl Godwin, but with Harthacanute's continued absence, Harold was accepted as king and crowned in 1037 at Oxford. His authority may not have gone unchallenged. In 1036 Prince Alfred, one of the younger sons of ATHELRED and Emma, had returned from exile, ostensibly to visit his mother, but in all likelihood to test out support for a possible bid for the throne. However he and his supporters were captured and imprisoned. Alfred was blinded so brutally that he died from the wounds. His death is recorded as either 5 February 1036 or 1037, the *ASC* favouring 1036, though either are possible as uncertainty remained in England until Harold was crowned; a situation compounded when Earl Godwin changed sides and supported Harold. Emma fled into exile to Flanders for her own safety. Nothing is recorded of Harold's reign beyond a dispute with the church over the ownership of lands at Sandwich. Like many young sons of powerful kings, he was spoiled and ineffectual. He died at Oxford in 1040 and was buried at Westminster, though Harthacanute exhumed the body and had it beheaded and flung in the marshes. He was later reburied, probably at St Clement Dane's church in London. He had a young son, Elfwine, who was raised on the continent and later became a monk.

[M37;VA33] **HARTHACANUTE or HARDICANUTE**
King of England, 12 November 1035–March(?) 1037, deposed; restored, 17 March 1040–8 June 1042. Also king of Denmark 1035–42. Crowned: 18 June 1040 at Canterbury Cathedral.
Born: *c1018.* **Died:** *8 June 1042 at Lambeth.* **Buried:** *Winchester Cathedral.*
Harthacanute was CANUTE's eldest son by his second wife Emma and was the designated heir in both Denmark and England. On Canute's death, however, Harthacanute was in Denmark and was forced to protect his kingdom from Magnus I of Norway who was fighting to reclaim the Norwegian crown. Harthacanute thus appointed his half-brother HAROLD (I) as his regent along with his mother Emma. The protection of Denmark kept Harthacanute busy for longer than anticipated and in 1037, Harold was crowned king in England. It is likely that there was some political coup, as Earl Godwin, originally appointed as regent alongside Emma and Harold, switched sides and supported Harold in his claim to the throne. Godwin may also have been the murderer of Prince Alfred, by order of Harold. Harold died three years later, and foul play cannot be entirely ruled out. At that time Harthacanute had established his authority in Denmark and was in fact on his way to England to recover his throne. He was staying with Emma,

who was in exile in Bruges. With Harold's death Harthacanute sailed on England with a large fleet and was immediately accepted as king. Harthacanute was especially vindictive to his half-brother. He had his body exhumed, beheaded and thrown into the marshes around Westminster. He was a harsh and intolerant king. Determined to defend his kingdom in Denmark, he raised an excessive tax in England to support his fleet at four times the rate of his father's. This led to rebellion in Worcester in 1041 which Harthacanute suppressed with vicious rage, almost destroying the town. It is to this period that the legend of Lady Godiva, or Godgifu, belongs. She was the wife of Leofric, earl of Mercia, who was forced to impose Harthacanute's tax across his domain. The people of Coventry could not afford it and Godiva therefore rode naked through the town to persuade Leofric to reduce the tax. Although this is wholly folklore, it does demonstrate the strength of opposition among the Saxon nobility to Harthacanute's taxes. This was further aggravated when Harthacanute ordered the murder of Eadulf, the ealdorman of Bamburgh. EDWARD (THE CONFESSOR) was recalled from exile and sworn in as Harthacanute's heir. Some records even suggest that he was anointed king. No one mourned when, in June 1042, Harthacanute died whilst drinking at a wedding party. Apparently he had a fit, but the possibility of poison cannot be ignored. He was an unpopular and much hated king. He had never married and with his death the kingdom passed back to the Saxons.

[M38] EDWARD *THE CONFESSOR*

King of England, 8 June 1042–4 January 1066. Crowned: Winchester, 3 April 1043.
Born: c1004, Islip, Oxfordshire; Died: Westminster, 4 January 1066, aged 61. Buried:
Westminster Abbey.
Married: 23 January 1045 at Winchester Cathedral, Edith (c1020–75) dau. of Earl
Godwin of Wessex: no children.

After the welcome death of HARTHACANUTE, there was no surviving male heir of CANUTE's line. His cousin, Swein, had believed himself heir, but his entitlement was overridden. In Scandinavia, Canute's domain was overrun by Magnus of Norway whilst England saw the return of the Saxon dynasty descended from EGBERT in the form of Edward, the only surviving son of ATHELRED (THE UNREADY) and his second wife, Emma, the daughter of Duke Richard of Normandy. Edward was half-Norman and had spent most of his youth (since the age of nine) in exile in Normandy. He thus grew up favouring Norman customs and, never having expected to become king, was also a rather idle and dissolute man. Upon his accession he realised he had a kingdom divided between Saxons, Danes and Norse with powerful earls of all factions. It is to Edward's credit that he succeeded in governing despite these differences. Critics of Edward accuse him of being a vacillating and indecisive king, like his father, but this may have been a façade for a cunning tactician, because Edward succeeded in ruling for over twenty-three years amidst much popular support. The fact that he was prepared to make strong decisions is evident from the start of his reign, when he confiscated his mother's property because she retained control over much of the Treasury. Emma was the most powerful and probably the richest woman in England, being the widow of two previous kings (Athelred and Canute), but her support for Edward had been limited. In fact she seemed to have almost disowned her marriage to Athelred and

From the Bayeux Tapestry

had become a strong supporter of the Danish court. Although Edward dispossessed her she was not sent into exile but remained in England. Charges were brought against her of involvement in the death of her sons by her first marriage and in supporting the Danish king Magnus. She seems to have bought her way out of this, although the more colourful records state that a trial by ordeal was arranged. Emma purportedly walked over nine red-hot ploughshares unscathed and at this show of innocence Edward restored all her lands and property and begged her forgiveness. She lived on at Winchester where she died on 6 March 1052, aged about sixty-six.

The power base in England at this time was with Godwin, earl of Wessex, and his many sons. It was Godwin's position that secured Edward his kingship, as the English Danes had previously recognized Canute's nephew Swein as successor. Godwin had married first the daughter of SWEIN (Canute's father) and after her death, Gytha, granddaughter of Swein's sister. Godwin regarded himself as a kingmaker (he had succeeded in raising HAROLD (I) to the throne and expected his son HAROLD (II) to become king in turn). To further cement this royal connection Godwin secured the marriage of Edward to Edith, the eldest child of Godwin and Gytha, in 1045. The marriage was apparently never consummated, and popular tradition has ascribed this to Edward's piety or effetism. Edward was to all intents married to the church. His single most lasting achievement was the construction of Westminster Abbey, which he financed personally and which was consecrated within a week of his death. Edward was not especially learned himself, but he loved to surround himself with knowledge and culture and encouraged scholarship throughout the country. With England benefitting from the first period of lasting peace for over seventy years, Edward's reign was the last glow of a Saxon golden age.

Edward had no reason to like Godwin, for all that he knew he needed his support. Godwin had been implicated in the murder of Edward's brother Alfred, who had been imprisoned and blinded in 1036/7 at the order of Harold I. Furthermore Godwin had twice changed sides, having come to power under Canute and supported Harthacanute before switching to Harold I, only to back Edward after Harold's death instead of the obvious successor Swein Ulfsson. Finally, the two had politically opposed ideals. Edward was primarily a Norman. He filled his court with Normans and appointed them to the most senior posts, whilst Godwin believed these posts should be given to the Saxon and Danish nobility. It was a conflict over Edward's favouritism to the Normans that led to an argument between Edward and Godwin in 1051. Edward, now feeling secure, banished Godwin and his sons, and despatched Edith to a convent. It was not a popular move as the Godwins were held in high regard by the English. It may have been partly to ameliorate this that Edward abolished the *danegeld* in 1051, the oppressive tax that Athelred had levied to pay the Danish pirates.

During this power vacuum, WILLIAM of Normandy visited Edward. William's father was Edward's cousin, and William knew that Edward had no formal heir and would not want the kingdom inherited by Godwin's sons. Although there is no record of any agreement at this time, it was later claimed that Edward then nominated William as his successor. However the following year Godwin and his sons invaded England. Edward was prepared to fight but the *witan* did not want a civil war. With bad grace, Edward pardoned Godwin and restored him and his sons to their earldoms. This made them more powerful than before. Godwin also secured his son Harold as senior amongst Edward's advisors, so much so that by 1053 Edward had more or less passed all administration over to Harold, leaving himself able to devote his energies to church matters and to hunting. Surprisingly during this period Edward supported the claim of MALCOLM (III) to the kingship of Scotland and gave his authority to an invasion of Scotland by Siward, earl of Northumbria, to depose MACBETH and place Malcolm on the throne. The initial onslaught was only partially successful but Malcom eventually succeeded to the Scottish throne in 1058 and his friendship to the Saxons would prove valuable to Saxon exiles in future years.

In the meantime Harold Godwinson grew from strength to strength. It was he who led most of the assaults against the Welsh who had harried the border territories for many years. During these campaigns Harold demonstrated his superior soldiery and skills as a general. Harold was increasingly looking like a successor to Edward, which Edward did not want. Even though he may have promised the succession to William, the anti-Norman feeling in England made this too dangerous a course to promote. Edward was thus relieved when he learned in 1054 that his nephew, known as Edward the Exile, was alive and well in Hungary. An embassy was despatched to recall him to England. As the son of EDMUND *IRONSIDE* he was the natural successor. His return was delayed but Edward finally arrived in England in August 1057. Within a few weeks he was dead, probably killed by order of Harold, though there is no evidence. Edward's succession plans were thwarted, although he now raised Edward the Exile's four-year old son, EDGAR, as his heir (atheling). Edward was forced to acknowledge that should he die before Edgar came of age, Harold would be regent. As a result the final years of Edward's reign were ones of increasing uncertainty. Edward still favoured William of Normandy as his successor, whilst the English increasingly favoured Harold, at least as war-leader if Edward died before the young atheling came of age. There was another claimant, Harald Haadraada of Norway, who already ruled Orkney and the Western Isles, and believed England was his by right. In 1065, Godwin's son Tostig was deprived of his earldom in Northumbria following his inept and tyrannical rule, and was banished to Flanders. He soon threw in his lot with Harald Haadraada, so that by the end of 1065, when it was clear that Edward was dying, the English throne was under considerable threat and needed strong leadership. Thus, when Edward died in that first week of January 1066, it was Harold who became the last king of the Saxons.

[M39] HAROLD II
King of the English 5 January-14 October 1066. Crowned: 6 January 1066 at Westminster Abbey.
Born: *c1022.* **Died** *(in battle): 14 October 1066, aged 44.* **Buried**: *Battle, Sussex; remains later removed to Waltham Abbey, Essex.*
Married: *(1) c1045, Edith Swanneshals (Swan-neck): 6 children; (2) c1066, Edith (Eadgyth) (b. c1042), dau. Alfgar, earl of Mercia, and widow of Gruffydd ap Llywelyn of Wales: 1 child.*

Harold is romantically portrayed as "the last of the Saxons" in the novel of that title by Lord Lytton. In some ways his heroic death at the battle of Hastings was a last ditch stand defending the old order against tyrannical oppression. On the other hand Harold was not the lily-white champion of virtue; he was a violent man with a vicious temper. He was the son of Godwin, earl of Wessex, and inherited his father's title in 1053, having previously been earl of East Anglia. He was exiled from England along with his father and brothers in 1051 when EDWARD THE CONFESSOR quarrelled with Godwin and used that as an opportunity to rid himself of someone who was becoming too powerful. Godwin and Harold nevertheless invaded England the following year. Had the family not been so popular and powerful and held in such high esteem by the English, any other king might have tried them for treason (Godwin was probably responsible for the death of Edward's elder brother Alfred, let alone this bold affront to the English crown). Edward, however, forgave Godwin (albeit unwillingly) and restored him and his sons to their earldoms. After Godwin's death, Harold, who was the eldest son, became the senior earl, and increasingly took over the administration and government of England, whilst Edward involved himself more in church affairs. By 1064 Harold was designated "Duke of the English", tantamount to heir apparent. Harold had almost certainly instigated the mysterious death of Edward the Exile, the real heir to the throne who had returned to England in 1057. Harold maintained a vicious campaign against the Welsh prince GRUFFYDD AP LLYWELLYN, whom he forced into submission first in 1057 and again in 1063, the latter campaign resulting in Gruffydd's death. Harold later married Gruffydd's widow, Edith, the daughter of the earl of Mercia, though Harold already had a wife, married according to the Danish law, also called Edith (known as Swan-neck), whom he truly loved and who bore him six children.

Sometime in 1065 Harold was at sea in the English channel when his ship was blown off course and he was driven on to the coast of Normandy. This has always been a curious episode, never fully explained. Harold purportedly agreed that Duke WILLIAM would be Edward's successor and paid homage to William. Knowing Harold's character this was unlikely, and could easily have been invented by William later, when no-one could disprove it. Whatever the circumstance, by the end of 1065 William, who had previously been made heir by Edward the Confessor, though again somewhat secretly, firmly believed he would be the next king of England. In November 1065 Tostig, Harold's brother and earl of Northumbria, was ejected from his earldom because of his callous misuse of authority. Harold

From the Bayeux Tapestry

attempted to mediate, but Tostig was forced to flee the country. During the winter he planned his invasion of England. On the night of January 4/5, 1066, King Edward died and Harold was proclaimed and crowned king. WILLIAM of Normandy regarded this as treachery and he too prepared to invade. The first to attempt it was Tostig with a fleet from Normandy. In May 1066 he harried the southern coast of England and round as far as Lindsey in the east, where he was defeated and fled to Scotland. He appealed to his cousin Swein in Denmark who was prepared to offer him an earldom, but not support for an invasion, so Tostig made his way to the court of Harald Haadraada, the king of Norway, and the most fearsome Viking of them all. Harald was initially unsure, knowing the strong defences of England, but Tostig convinced him and through the summer the Norwegians prepared their fleet whilst William of Normandy prepared his. Harold used the period to strengthen England's coastal defences. In September Harald Haadraada sailed with a mighty fleet of some two hundred warships, stopping first at Orkney where he gathered more supplies and men. He sailed with the earls PAUL and ERLEND down the coast to the mouth of the Tyne where Tostig waited with a further force of men from Scotland and Man. This massive force continued down the coast of Northumbria, pillaging and destroying as it went. It was met at Fulford on 20 September by an English army under earls Morcar and Edwin which was defeated. York agreed to surrender and the invaders withdrew to Stamford Bridge to await negotiators. There, on 25 September, they were surprised by the army of Harold Godwinsson which had undertaken a forced march north. The battle that followed was a total victory for Harold. Both the Norwegian king and Tostig were killed. But Harold had no time to relish his success. Two days later the wind that had stopped William sailing changed and his invasion began. Harold was forced to march south again at full speed, and the two armies met at Senlac Hill, north of Hastings on 14 October. With hindsight Harold should have waited. To engage two major invasion forces at either end of the kingdom within one month required superhuman ability. The astonishing thing is that Harold almost won. The Normans' technical sophistication was of limited use against the Saxon shield-wall with which they protected the position. A retreat by the Breton forces encouraged a pursuit that exposed the English to a cavalry counter-attack, but

34. The Bloodline of Harold II

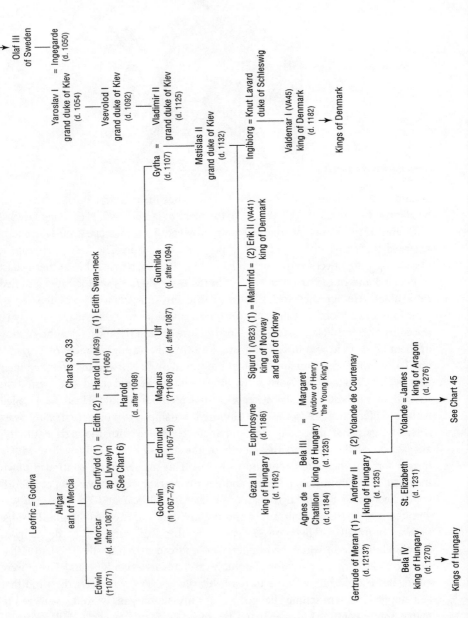

Chart 29 →

Olaf III
of Sweden

Yaroslav I = Ingegarde (d. 1050)
grand duke of Kiev
(d. 1054)

Vsevolod I
grand duke of Kiev
(d. 1092)

Vladimir II
grand duke of Kiev
(d. 1125)

Gytha =
(d. 1107)

Mstislas II
grand duke of Kiev
(d. 1132)

Ingibiorg = Knut Lavard
duke of Schleswig

Valdemar I (VA45)
king of Denmark
(d. 1182)

Kings of Denmark

Charts 30, 33

Leofric = Godiva

Alfgar
earl of Mercia

Gruffydd (1) = Edith (2) = Harold II (M39) = (1) Edith Swan-neck
ap Llywelyn   (†1066)
(See Chart 6)

Harold
(d. after 1098)

Morcar
(d. after 1087)

Edwin
(†1071)

Godwin
(fl 1067–72)

Edmund
(fl 1067–9)

Magnus
(?†1068)

Ulf
(d. after 1087)

Gunhilda
(d. after 1094)

Sigurd I (VB23) (1) = Malmfrid = (2) Erik II (VA41)
king of Norway   king of Denmark
and earl of Orkney

Geza II = Euphrosyne
king of Hungary   (d. 1186)
(d. 1162)

Bela III = Margaret
king of Hungary   (widow of Henry
(d. 1235)   'the Young King')

Agnes de = Andrew II = (2) Yolande de Courtenay
Chatillon   king of Hungary
(d. c1184) (d. 1235)

Gertrude of Meran (1) =

Yolande = James I
king of Aragon
(d. 1276)

See Chart 45

St. Elizabeth
(d. 1231)

Bela IV
king of Hungary
(d. 1270)

Kings of Hungary

the battle was decided by hard, attritional fighting. As dusk came on the lofted arrows were eroding the ranks of the Saxon axemen. Harold was not killed by an arrow in his eye, but he and his brothers died defending each other to the last.

Had Harold been the victor, it is a fascinating exercise in alternative reality to consider what might have become of England. Two such great victories would have made Harold secure in his kingdom, seemingly invincible. He was not young, but there is no reason why he could not have reigned another twenty years or so. In that time, unless he changed his ways, the real Harold would have been revealed – the sly and devious son of Godwin. The Saxons might have continued to rule for another century. But such was not to be. All but one of Harold's sons lived into the 1080s and beyond, though we lose track of them before their deaths. Although the English initially rallied around the young atheling, EDGAR, they soon capitulated to Duke William who ever after was known as William the Conqueror.

[M40] **EDGAR *THE ATHELING*,** 14 October–late November/early December 1066. Edgar was proclaimed king by the *witan* after the death of HAROLD II at Senlac Hill on 14 October 1066, though he was never crowned and submitted to WILLIAM (I) eight weeks later. He was only about thirteen or fourteen years old. He was the grandson of EDMUND IRONSIDE. His father, known as Edward the Exile, had been banished from England by CANUTE in 1016 when only a few months old. Rather than kill him on English soil, Canute's idea was to despatch him to Russia to be killed by the Viking dukes of Novgorod. This did not happen. Instead Edward made his way to Hungary and the court of King Stephen, where he remained until in 1054 EDWARD THE CONFESSOR learned he was alive and summoned him back to England. He returned in 1057 with his young children, but within days had died, probably murdered by order of Harold. Edward raised his nephew's children, Edgar, Margaret and Christina and nominated the young atheling as his heir. However he was too young at the time of Edward's death in January 1066 to defend the country against impending invasion, and his election as king after Harold's death was no more than a token of defiance. Edgar relied for his support upon Archbishop Stigand and upon Earls Edwin and Morcar and, when this weakened, Edgar was forced to submit to William at Berkhamstead in either late November or early December 1066.

William treated Edgar well. He kept him in his custody eventually taking him back to his court in Normandy. However, Edgar joined in the rebellion of the earls Edwin and Morcar in 1068 and, though defeated, he fled to the court of MALCOLM III of Scotland. The next year Malcolm married Edgar's sister Margaret, and agreed to support Edgar in his attempt to claim the English crown. Edgar now made common cause with Swein, king of Denmark and nephew of CANUTE, who believed he was the rightful king of England. Their combined forces invaded England in 1069. They captured York, but did not proclaim the independence of Northumbria. William marched on the north, devastating the land as he went. He paid the Danes to leave, whilst Edgar fled to Scotland. He remained in refuge there until 1072 when William reached a treaty with Malcolm which included the exile of Edgar. Edgar eventually made his peace with William in 1074 but he never fully gave up his dreams of regaining the throne of England. He supported Robert, duke of Normandy, against WILLIAM II in 1091 and again found himself seeking refuge in

Scotland. He also supported his nephew, EDGAR, in gaining the Scottish throne. In 1099 he set off on crusade, and was later taken prisoner at Tinchebrai in 1106 fighting for Duke Robert against HENRY I. He returned to England where Henry pardoned him, and he retired to his country estate in Hertfordshire. His niece Edith (renamed Matilda) had married Henry I in 1100. Edgar is believed to have travelled to Scotland late in life, perhaps around the year 1120, and was still alive in 1125, but may have died soon after, in his early seventies. By then he was forgotten by most and is remembered now only as the "lost king" of England.

O. THE HOUSE OF NORMANDY

[O1;SD7] **WILLIAM I** *THE CONQUEROR*, also called *THE BASTARD*
King of England, late November/early December 1066–9 September 1087.
Crowned: Westminster Abbey, 25 December 1066.
Titles: king of England, duke of Normandy and count of Maine.
Born: Falaise, Normandy, autumn 1028. *Died: St Gervais, Rouen, 9 September 1087,*
aged 59. *Buried: Abbey of St Stephen, Caen.*
Married: c1053 (at Eu), Matilda (c1031–83), dau. Baldwin V of Flanders, 10 children.
William the Conqueror, or William the Bastard as he was known in his day (though out of his hearing), was the illegitimate son of Robert I, duke of Normandy. The Normans were Vikings who had settled in northern France and had taken on the lifestyle of the French aristocracy, without losing that passion for conquest. William was descended from RAGNALD, the ancestor of the earls of Orkney.

Many histories would have you believe that Britain's royal history began with William, although his claim on the English throne was tenuous. He maintained that EDWARD THE CONFESSOR had promised him the succession as far back as 1051 during a period when Edward's relationship with Earl Godwin was low and Edward was looking for support. The connections between the Saxon and Norman royal families extended back to ATHELRED THE UNREADY who had married Emma the sister of William's grandfather, Richard II of Normandy. William was the son of Edward the Confessor's first cousin. Researchers have been unable to find any evidence of Edward's promise, at least amongst English documents, and its only provenance is amongst the Norman chronicles. William was later able to exact support for the claim from HAROLD Godwinson, earl of Wessex, who was at William's court in 1065, and the Bayeux Tapestry shows Harold offering fealty to William. Hence when Edward died in 1066 and Harold was crowned as king, William regarded him as a usurper and prepared to invade.

William had already demonstrated his strength as a commander and soldier. His life was one of almost constant warfare as he carved out for himself a position as one of the most powerful and, when necessary, ruthless rulers of his day. He had succeeded to the duchy of Normandy in 1035 when just seven or eight years old. His father had died while on a pilgrimage when only 27. His mother, Herleva or Arletta, was Robert's mistress. She was the daughter of a local tanner and, legend says, Robert spied upon her while she washed clothes at the river. During William's minority there was much rivalry at the Norman court as the aristocracy struggled for power. Three of William's guardians were assassinated and the young duke

35. The Danish and Norse Kingdoms (7) – The Dukes of Normandy

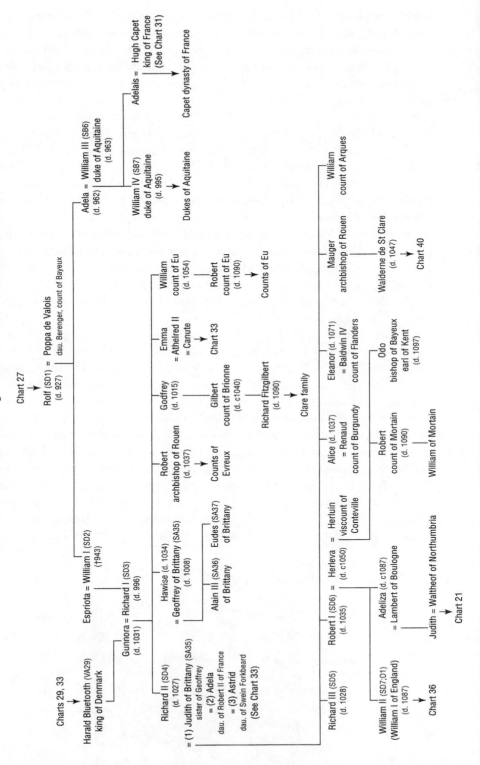

knew he needed to assert his authority as soon as he was able. That opportunity came in 1047 when his cousin, Guy of Brionne, rebelled and claimed the duchy. Guy had considerable support and William needed the help of Henri I of France to win the day after a tightly fought battle. This gave William his authority but it also imprinted upon him a streak of ruthlessness which caused him to retaliate viciously against anyone who challenged him.

William's authority increased when he married Matilda, the daughter of Baldwin V, count of Flanders, a powerful ruler whose acceptance of William as a suitable son-in-law showed that William had risen above the trials of his youth. William may also have seen in Matilda a further link with his claim on the throne of England as she was seventh in line from ALFRED the Great. The pope apparently opposed this marriage for some years on grounds of an earlier betrothal by Matilda, but it finally received his blessing in 1059.

During the decade of the 1050s William continued to consolidate his power, even to the point of incurring the enmity of his former ally, Henri I of France. William succeeded in rebuffing all attempts to invade Normandy and by 1062 had himself invaded Maine, on almost the same pretext as he would invade England four years later – that Herbert, count of Maine, had promised William the county if he died without heirs. William became count of Maine in 1063. William's other conquests meant that he had support from the surrounding powers of Anjou and Brittany, whilst the new king of France, Philippe I, was under the protection of William's father-in-law, Baldwin. This meant that when William prepared to invade England in September 1066 he was able to draw not only upon his own resources within Normandy, but upon those of his allies.

Nevertheless, this did not make William's conquest of England a certainty. He was up against one of the most aggressive armies of Europe under the command of Harold Godwinson. Harold's misfortune was that he had to face two invasions within one month. Harold's men already weakened by defeating the army of Harold Hardraada of Norway at Stamford Bridge on 25 September, faced a quick march back to fight William who had landed at Pevensey on 28 September. William took advantage of Harold's absence to develop his defences near Hastings and by pillaging the local farmsteads and hamlets. By so doing William succeeded in

From the
Bayeux Tapestry

drawing Harold toward him, whereas Harold's opportunity for success lay in drawing William away from his fleet and its supplies. The two armies met at Senlac Hill (now Battle), near Hastings, on 14 October 1066. Had Harold's army not been weakened he may well have won, but they were overpowered by William's cavalry. The Saxon army submitted after the death of Harold and his brothers.

For the next two months William's army moved strategically around the Kentish coast taking a circular route to London and seeking the submission of the English en route. They burned Dover, and laid waste to much of Surrey. The English, in the meantime, had elected EDGAR the Atheling as their new king, but he was only a boy of thirteen or fourteen, and unable to muster any forces to retaliate against William. The citizens of London prevented William crossing the Thames, so he sacked Southwark and moved west, crossing the Thames at Wallingford. Edgar submitted at Berkhamstead and the Normans then approached London from the north. Lud Gate was opened to the invader by a collaborator and, in the Battle of Ludgate Hill, countless Londoners were slain. William was crowned in Westminster Abbey on 25 December 1066, the ceremony conducted by Ealdred, archbishop of York. Cries of support from the Normans present were interpreted as an English rebellion and the guards promptly attacked the Saxons and set fire to nearby houses. William himself had to quell the panic. His reign began with terror and would remain a reign of terror for twenty years.

Although William was to style himself as king of England not all of England had accepted him as king. His dominion was primarily in the south, covering all of the old kingdoms of Wessex, Kent, Sussex and Essex, and stretching someway into Mercia. The powerful earls of Mercia and Northumbria, the brothers Edwin and Morcar, believed that William's design was only to conquer Wessex and accepted him as king within that domain, pleased that he had overthrown the Godwin family. They even hoped they would be accepted as kings in their territories. This short-sightedness sealed the fate of England, for had the brothers united their armies with those elsewhere in England and faced William before he became established, he might still have been defeated, but the old rivalries between Saxon families became their downfall and isolated rebellions were soon put down with the viciousness with which William became renowned.

William remained in England for three months after his coronation, during which time he appointed a wide range of Norman officials, and despatched the army to plunder the churches in order to pay his army. When he returned to Normandy in late February 1067 he took with him the most likely candidates to lead any rebellion in England, Edgar the Atheling, Stigand, the archbishop of Canterbury, and the earls Edwin and Morcar. During his absence in Normandy, where William displayed the spoils of his conquest and made most of his fame, his half-brother Bishop Odo endeavoured to impose Norman rule in England, but with minimal success. An attempted invasion by Eustace, count of Bolougne, who was Edward the Confessor's brother-in-law, was soon repelled, but the general unrest in England, especially in the north and west, continued to grow. William returned in December 1067 and began his systematic conquest of England in earnest. He turned his attention first to the west, at Exeter, where Harold's mother had taken refuge. The town submitted after a siege of eighteen days. William was comparatively lenient to the townsfolk, though he exacted payment. He also ordered the building of a castle and established a Norman noble, Baldwin of Brionne, as the local custodian. This became William's approach over the next few years. As he advanced upon his conquests he would build a castle from which a Norman duke or earl would maintain the peace in that territory. Initially the castles were hasty constructions of wood upon a motte-and-bailey site. It was only later that he and his successors began the construction of massive stone castles at key sites. These castles became the image of Norman power created not to defend England but to dominate it. In total 78 castles were constructed by William's order, the most famous being the Tower of London. By March 1068 William felt sufficiently secure in the south to bring his wife, Matilda, over to England where she was crowned queen. She remained in England for a year, accompanying William on his tour of conquest. Their last son, the future HENRY I was born at Selby in September 1068. She returned to Normandy in 1069 and remained there until her death in 1083.

It was during 1068 that William faced his first major opposition. Earls Morcar and Edwin rebelled, and Edgar the Atheling took refuge with MALCOLM III of Scotland – Malcolm married Edgar's sister Margaret the following year. The Saxons sought the support of the Welsh though clearly were not acting with any coherent plan for William was soon able to quash the rebellion by advancing on Warwick. William continued north, establishing castles at Nottingham and York. His original plans to govern northern England through the Saxon aristocracy now changed, as he believed Edwin and Morcar had forfeited their rights. From then on William redistributed the lands of the Saxons amongst the Norman and French aristocracy. The native English were not simply conquered, they were dispossessed. William was hated and despised by the English, but any attempt to display this feeling was countered by ruthless retaliation. When William returned briefly to Normandy in early 1069, faced with a revolt in Maine, the English attacked the Normans at Durham, killing many of them. They moved on to besiege the castle at York, but by then William had returned and he not only defeated the English but sacked the city.

The English resistance was far from over. Edgar the Atheling's followers joined forces with King Swein of Denmark. Swein had as much claim to the English throne as William, if not more. He was the nephew of CANUTE and maintained, like William, that Edward had named him as his successor. The English had learned to co-exist with the Danes. There had been Danish kings ruling parts of England for two centuries before Canute. The armies of Swein and Edgar, along with other northern rebels, recaptured York in September 1069. Again William marched on the north, this time destroying everything in his path. This harrying of the north was the most extreme example of despoiling and genocide that England has ever seen, and for which William was never forgiven by the English. He may have conquered them, but he never ruled them.

William succeeded in buying off the Danish force and they retreated in late 1070, after briefly returning for a second attempt. Pockets of resistance remained throughout the north, the west and especially in the Fenland of East Anglia, where the Saxon thane Hereward the Wake, perhaps the best known of the Saxon rebels, maintained the most ordered resistance to William. Hereward was joined by Earl Morcar whose brother, Edwin, had been treacherously murdered by his own men. William brought all his forces to bear upon the Isle of Ely where Hereward made the last major Saxon stand against the Norman might. William's power proved irresistible. Hereward escaped, but Morcar was captured and imprisoned, and other rebels were tortured and mutilated before their release.

The last to resist William was Edgar the Atheling who had fled back to the court of King Malcolm. In the summer of 1072 William marched into Scotland to demand that Malcolm cease aiding Edgar's insurrection. Malcolm agreed and, with the Peace of Abernethy, recognized William as his overlord. He also expelled Edgar from his court. Edgar, however, did not submit to William until 1074. By the end of 1072 William believed that his conquest of England was complete. Already he had replaced many of the Saxon officials with Normans, and these included the officials of the church. Probably his most significant appointment was of Lanfranc as archbishop of Canterbury. The Norman aristocracy were installed in lands across the length and breadth of England and their dominion established a feudal system in which all Saxons were increasingly treated as peasants. Although William had despoiled the land in order to subjugate the English, he had never intended to plunder it. Indeed, once he had established his authority he was keen for England to prosper so that he could benefit from the revenues. William returned to Normandy in 1072 and remained there for much of the next twelve years, needing to maintain his duchy against the opposition of the French and his former allies who were now fearful of his power. The administration of England was left in the hands of Richard Fitzgilbert and William de Warenne, two of William's most powerful barons.

William did not return to England for any significant period until 1085, when he brought over a massive army to defend the island against a planned invasion under Canute IV of Denmark. Canute, however, was murdered before the invasion began. William's restless army caused considerable hardship to the Saxons during this period. In addition William had to raise the land taxes in order to pay his sizeable army and this caused further disgruntlement. The problems that William had in knowing who owned what land and what its value was, so that he could levy the taxes, led to him ordering a major survey of England. The record of this survey, carried out with remarkable accuracy and speed during 1086, became known as the *Domesday Book*, and though its purpose was for William to ensure he had control over his taxes in England, the result is a rare and indispensable historical document. William, however, made little use of the document himself. He returned to Normandy at the end of 1086 where he became preoccupied with a local rebellion. In July 1087 William besieged the town of Mantes. As his horse jumped over a ditch William received an injury from the pommel of his saddle which ripped into his stomach. The wound became poisoned leading to peritonitis. William was carried back to Rouen in considerable pain. He lingered on for five weeks, and died in September. His body was returned to Caen for burial but apparently the tomb was not big enough – the king was a tall man, at least five feet ten inches. As a result, as the attendants forced the body into the tomb, the already decaying and swollen body burst open, letting out an intense smell of putrefaction that caused most to flee the site. Only a hardy few completed the burial.

William changed England irrevocably. His total domination had, within less than a generation, almost eradicated the Saxon aristocracy and imposed a feudal society run by a small handful of Normans. The language difficulties added further to the alienation, but perhaps the most significant difference was in the lifestyle. Although the Normans were descended from the Vikings, they no longer looked to the north

36. England (1) – The House of Normandy

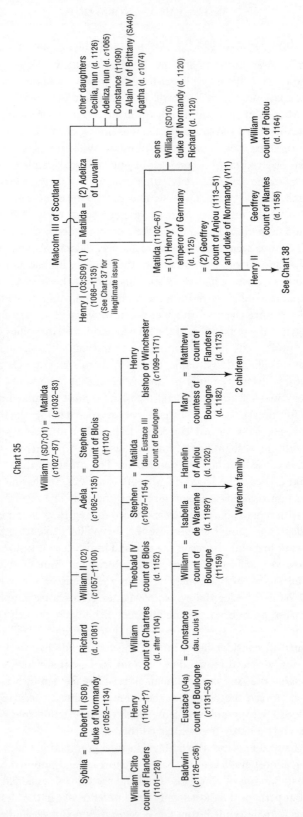

as their ancestral home, unlike the Saxons whose inheritance was from northern Europe. The Normans had taken on the more sophisticated lifestyle of the French, which brought with it the power, grandeur and aloofness of an upper-class existence. William used England as his playground, establishing the New Forest in Hampshire for his hunting. He had no liking for the English or, for that matter, for England, seeing it only as a rich source of revenues. Although his harsh rule brought peace to England, where man was apparently able to travel without fear of crime, this was only because the English lived in much greater fear of revenge and retribution from their Norman overlords. It created a rift between the nobility and the common man which remained in Britain for centuries.

William was devoted to his wife Matilda, and was much saddened at her death. They had ten children. The eldest, Robert, succeeded William as duke of Normandy and count of Maine even though he had been in open rebellion against his father in his latter years. The second son, Richard, died in his twenties in 1081 while hunting in the New Forest. Two other sons, WILLIAM and HENRY, succeeded William as kings of England. Of his six daughters, Adela became the mother of the future king STEPHEN.

[O2] WILLIAM II *RUFUS*

King of England, 9 September 1087–2 August 1100; Crowned: Westminster, 26 September 1087.
Born: *Normandy, c1057.* **Died:** *New Forest, 2 August 1100, aged about 43.* **Buried:** *Winchester Cathedral.*

The third and favourite son of WILLIAM the Conqueror, William was bequeathed the kingdom of England although many believed he might also inherit the duchy of Normandy. The duchy, however, went to William's eldest brother Robert. The two were always in open hostility, and had been during their father's lifetime, with William remaining loyal to his father. The consequences were divisive because barons who held lands in both Normandy and England found it impossible to know whom to support without fear of losing their lands on one side or the other. Much of William's reign, therefore, was spent in rivalry with Robert. It looked initially as if Robert's star might prevail, as barons rose in support of him in an insurrection in 1088 led by his uncle Odo. However Robert failed to capitalise on this support and William was quick to quash the rebellion, devastating Odo's estates in Kent. The rivalry between William and Robert was eventually solved to some degree in 1091, after a brief attempt at a coup by their younger brother Henry, which united William and Robert. William now showed his negotiating skills by reaching an agreement between all three brothers to their mutual benefit, and William even brought Robert to England to join him in an expedition against the Scots (*see* MALCOLM III). The position, however, was not fully resolved until 1096 when Robert decided to join the First Crusade. He pledged the duchy to William in exchange for money to raise his army. William was never officially duke, serving instead as his brother's regent, but he was more successful than Robert and won back lands in France that Robert had lost.

In fact William was a king for whom much seemed to go right. One might almost think that God smiled on him, though such a belief would have horrified the clergy who regarded William with total disdain. Because the chronicles of the time were written by monks, the opinion has passed down in history of William as a vicious and avaricious man who was "hated by almost all his people and abhorrent to God." It is difficult to get an objective picture of a man who had strong and powerful enemies amongst his own barons as well as within his own family. Some have claimed he was homosexual, his court being described as like that of the Roman emperor Caligula, with men dressed effeminately, if dressed at all. It is true that he never married, though there were later unsubstantiated rumours that he had an illegitimate son. He was portrayed as having a fiery temper, his face often flushed red, hence his nickname Rufus. The red face may be more an indication of his drinking and eating habits. He was stout, and despite being a man of action may well have had heart problems.

Despite all this William was a good soldier, who took a liking to England and endeavoured to rule justly. He attempted to conquer lands in Wales, and initially made considerable advances against the Welsh prince GRUFFYDD AP CYNAN but was eventually repulsed in 1094. A second onslaught in 1098 regained ground, and several of the Welsh princes recognized William as their overlord. During this period William established a line of castles along the Welsh marches.

William also continued an uneasy relationship with the Scottish king, MALCOLM III. William had spurned the Saxon prince EDGAR the Atheling, who returned to Scotland and, in 1090, encouraged Malcolm to invade England again, primarily with the purpose of regaining Scottish lands in Lothian and Northumbria, and defending Cumbria. William soon rebuffed Malcolm and succeeded in renewing the Peace of Abernethy. In fact Malcolm was friendly toward William and eventually despatched Edgar as a nuisance. William did not necessarily return that friendship for, in 1092, he seized the lands around Carlisle, establishing a castle there, and when visited by Malcolm for a parley, refused to see him. As the infuriated Malcolm returned to Scotland he was attacked and killed by the Normans in Northumbria. Malcolm's brother DONALD BANE claimed the throne in a period of violent upheaval against the Normans. William Rufus, however supported first DUNCAN II and EDGAR, the sons of Malcolm III, in overthrowing Donald. Edgar, whose reign was more stable, acknowledged the help and support of the Normans and realized that thereafter he was subservient to them. William thus stamped his authority on an expanding Norman base with tentacles creeping into Wales and Scotland.

Where William really roused the wrath of the clergy was in his dealings with them. He did not seem respectful of the church, unlike his father. Although he was held in check initially by Archbishop Lanfranc, when Lanfranc died in 1089, William did not bother to appoint a successor and, instead, took advantage of the revenues himself. In the eyes of the church, William was stealing from God. They urged that William appoint Lanfranc's student and friend, Anselm, as archbishop but William refrained. It was not until William was taken ill in 1092 and believed he was dying that he gave in. As Anselm was in England at that time, William offered him the archbishopric. Anselm at first refused but, under pressure from the clergy, he accepted. This was only the start of the problems between him and William. At this time there was a schism in the papacy. Urban II was the pope installed in Rome and he was supported by Anselm, but there was a rival anti-pope in Ravenna, Clement III. William remained uncommitted. In 1095 he called a council to judge the matter. William finally agreed to support Urban, but only

From Historia Anglorum

because he extracted acceptance from Urban that papal legates could not enter England without royal agreement. It was more an agreement of convenience than of loyalty. William in fact interpreted it as his freedom from the church. Although Anselm supported Urban, he refused to accept the way in which William had approached the issue, maintaining that church matters could not be judged in a secular court. William appealed to Urban, seeking for the pope to depose Anselm. A papal legate was despatched to England but no decision was made. In the end the relationship between Anselm and William became so impossible that Anselm went into self-imposed exile in 1097.

It was little wonder that the clergy so despised William, and they had good grounds, but they may have blackened his character a little too much. There have even been recent allegations that William was a devil-worshipper and practised the black arts, but there is no real evidence for this. What it boils down to is that William was a perfectly able and capable king who was successful in most of his campaigns, but whose temperament and affectations annoyed both the church and many of his barons.

This background consequently led to much speculation about William's death. He was hunting one summer's evening in the New Forest when he was killed by an arrow apparently shot at a fleeing deer. It was immediately claimed as an accident, the offending party being Walter Tirel. Tirel always proclaimed his innocence, stating that he was nowhere near the king when the arrow was fired, but Tirel was rapidly transported back to France. The conspiracist theory is that William was murdered, perhaps by order of one of the barons who supported his brother Robert. Duncan Grinnell-Milne, in his compelling piece of detective work *The Killing of William Rufus* (1968), was convinced that William's death was part of a master plan by his brother Henry to gain the throne. Certainly there were many relieved at the death of the king, and the verdict of accidental death was satisfactory to all (except Tirel who felt he was falsely accused), so no one investigated it further. William's body was hurriedly conveyed in a farm cart to Winchester Cathedral where it was peremptorily buried in the early hours of the next morning. Though there were official mourners, everyone seemed in much greater haste to return to Westminster. There is a strong feeling in reading about William's death and Henry's succession that William was a nuisance who was now out of the way and everyone could get back to the real purpose of government.

In retrospect William's reign is a minor episode in England's history, though had he lived he might have caused more problems in his relationship with the church. It remains a fact, though, that he was not only able to sustain his kingdom in England but that he reached workable relations with the kings and princes of Scotland and Wales as well as his brother in Normandy, which demonstrates an able administrator and king for all that he was opinionated, arrogant and ill tempered. England would have many rulers who were far worse than William.

[O3] **HENRY (I)** *BEAUCLERC*
King of England 3 August 1100–1 December 1135. Crowned: Westminster, 6 August 1100.
Titles: *King of England, Duke of Normandy (from 1106) and Lord of Domfront (from 1092).*
Born: *Selby, Yorkshire, September 1068; Died: St Denis-le-Fermont, near Rouen, 1 December 1135, aged 67. Buried: Reading Abbey.*
Married: *(1) 11 November 1100, Matilda (formerly Edith), dau. of Malcolm III of Scotland; 4 children; (2) 29 January 1121, Adeliza, dau. of Geoffrey VII, Count of Louvain; no children. Henry had at least 25 illegitimate children by eight or more other women.*

Henry was the fourth and youngest son of WILLIAM the Conqueror, and possibly the most ambitious. Although he was less quarrelsome than his elder brothers Robert, who inherited the duchy of Normandy, and WILLIAM, who became William II of England, he clearly had his eyes on ruling either England or Normandy or both as early as 1091. In that year, while Robert and William were fighting each other, Henry took control of several castles and made a bid for power. Realising that he had left his back unguarded William soon quelled his upstart brother, and did not take his eyes off him after that, keeping him always close at hand. William and Robert agreed that if either of them died childless, then the survivor would succeed. This effectively disinherited Henry who had long grudged the fact that he had not been able to inherit his mother's estates in England that she had bequeathed him upon her death in 1083. Instead his father believed that, as the youngest son, Henry would be destined for the church. As a result he had a good education, hence his nickname *Beauclerc*, meaning "fine scholar", since he was the first Norman king (and there had not been that many Saxon ones) who could read and write.

Henry was not satisfied with his lot and it has been conjectured that it was he who masterminded the death of William II, making it look like he was killed as the result of a hunting accident. If this is true then its timing was critical. In 1096 Robert of Normandy had joined the Crusade to the Holy Land and had pledged the duchy to William. By the summer of 1100 news reached England that Robert was returning, along with a new bride. Immediately upon the death of William a hastily convened council elected Henry as his successor. This despite the support that many barons had for Robert, who was on a crest of popularity following his victories in the Holy Land, even though his past record showed him as a weak ruler of Normandy. By the first week of September, when Robert had returned to Normandy, Henry had been elected and crowned. One of his first acts was to recall Anselm from his exile to the

From a coin

archbishopric of Canterbury, and with Anselm's support Henry's position was inviolable. He further cemented it by a political marriage to Edith, the daughter of MALCOLM III of Scotland and the niece of EDGAR the Atheling, thus establishing alliances with the elder Saxon aristocracy and with the Scots.

Robert raised a considerable army and invaded England in June 1101, cleverly misleading Henry whose army waited at Arundel while Robert landed at Portsmouth. It is possible that had Robert pressed home his advantage he could have defeated Henry's army. He might easily have captured Winchester, where the Treasury was held, but his army passed by that town. It stopped short of invading London, though this too was within his grasp. Instead the two armies met at Alton where Robert asked for negotiations. Clearly Robert lacked the opportunism that marked the success of his father and younger brother. Even worse, he was prepared to trust Henry. The result was that Henry agreed to pay Robert 3,000 marks annually and recognize him as the legal claimant to the throne in exchange for Henry remaining king while he lived. In the eyes of Henry and the barons possession was nine-tenths of the law, and Robert was the loser. A few years later, in 1106, Henry took control of the matter, invading Normandy and capturing his brother at Tinchebrai. Robert was brought to England and imprisoned for the rest of his life, which lasted another twenty-eight years: he was certainly over 80 when he died in 1134. Had he succeeded to the English throne in 1087, on the death of his father, he would have ruled for 47 years, one of the longest reigns of an adult monarch. However his weak nature suggests that he would have been overthrown by someone long before his death, and in all likelihood that would still have been his scheming brother Henry.

Whilst Henry was endeavouring to regain Normandy he had troubles at home with the church. Although he had recalled Anselm as archbishop of Canterbury, the relations between the two rapidly deteriorated. Anselm had fallen out with William Rufus because the latter had refused to acknowledge the authority of Rome and Anselm's rights in the reorganization of the church. Anselm reminded Henry of the papal authority in appointing clergy, since the pope had decreed as far back as 1059 that lay investiture was unlawful in the eyes of the Church. Henry would have none of this, and with other matters more pressing refused to consider it. By 1103 Anselm found his position untenable and he again went into exile. The pope threatened to excommunicate Henry and, fearful of how this would undermine his authority as king, Henry recalled Anselm and sought to negotiate a compromise. The result was that in 1106 Henry accepted clerical authority in investiture on the understanding that the clergy still recognized secular authority over the lands owned by the church. In this way Henry kept his revenues (which Anselm had maintained belonged to the church and thus to Rome) and it meant he could still agree who had possession of the property. (It was this loophole that allowed HENRY II to challenge Thomas

Becket sixty years later.) Nevertheless when Anselm died in 1109 Henry succeeded in keeping the see of Canterbury vacant for five years.

Once Henry had secured the dukedom of Normandy he had his hands full in keeping it. Since England was now relatively safe, he found he had to spend more time in Normandy. His queen Matilda officially served as regent during these absences, but increasingly the administration came under the capable control of Roger, bishop of Salisbury. Since Henry drew heavily upon the English revenues to finance his army in Normandy as well as his extensive building projects across England, Roger developed a system for controlling the exchequer. In effect he established the basis for what would evolve into the civil service.

Although Henry would enter into battle if necessary, he sought to pave the way by treaty or diplomacy first, and in this he was admirably skilled. One such act was the marriage in January 1114 of his eldest daughter Adelaide (who adopted the name MATILDA upon her marriage) to Heinrich V, Emperor of Germany, and she was crowned Empress on the same day. She was eleven years old; the Emperor was 32. Henry held Normandy against all opposition. His ultimate victory was the defeat of Louis VI of France in 1119. When peace was agreed with the pope's blessing, Henry was accepted unchallenged as duke of Normandy. Henry cemented this advance by marrying his eldest son William to Alice (who also changed her name to Matilda), the daughter of Fulk V, count of Anjou and Maine. William was only fifteen, Alice less than twelve. In 1120, as Henry's eldest son William came of age, he was made duke of Normandy, and stood in succession to the throne of England, even though Henry's eldest brother Robert and his son William were both still alive.

In the summer of 1120 Henry could be proud of his achievements. Through his own marriage and those of his children he had alliances with the strongest neighbouring royal families of Europe; others he had dominated by conquest or treaty. He had reached a satisfactory arrangement with the papacy and all looked well for the future. And then everything fell about him. In November 1120 his two eldest legitimate sons William and Richard drowned when the White Ship foundered off Barfleur while sailing from Normandy to England. He was left without a male heir, although his eldest illegitimate son, Robert Fitzroy, earl of Gloucester, now turned an eye to the throne. Henry's first wife, Matilda had died in May 1118, an event over which Henry did not seem especially concerned. He arranged a quick marriage of convenience to Adeliza, daughter of Geoffrey VII, count of Louvain. That marriage was childless, although Henry had several more illegitimate children, and Adeliza bore seven children to her second husband, William d'Albini, earl of Arundel, after Henry's death.

In 1125 Henry's daughter, Matilda, became a widow when the Emperor Heinrich died. She was twenty-three but had no children. In 1126, fearing he would have no further children, Henry made the barons swear an oath of fealty to Matilda as the heir-presumptive to the throne. The barons agreed, though the idea of being ruled by a queen was anathema to them. The position was further aggravated when, in May 1127, Henry arranged a second marriage for Matilda, this time with Geoffrey of Anjou, who was then only fourteen. The Normans had little affection for the Angevins and did not like to consider that Geoffrey might become their King. They began to turn their allegiance to Henry's nephew, William, the son of Duke Robert, who was known as William Clito. At this time, April 1127, he was supported by the

37. England (2) − **The illegitimate children of Henry I**

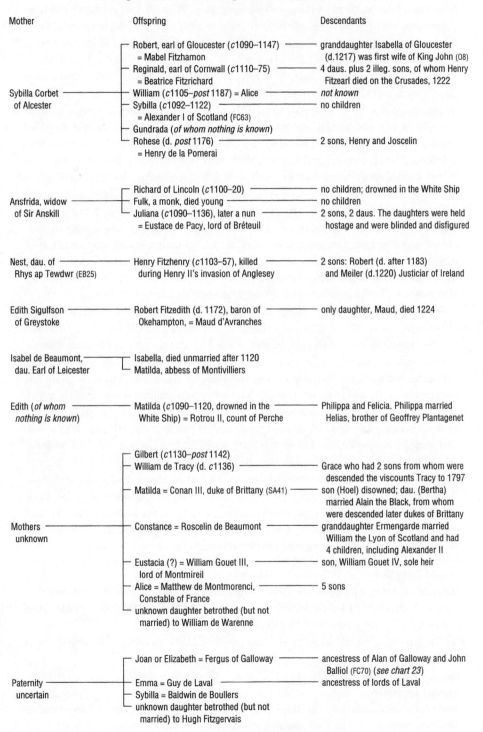

Mother	Offspring	Descendants
Sybilla Corbet of Alcester	Robert, earl of Gloucester (c1090–1147) = Mabel Fitzhamon	granddaughter Isabella of Gloucester (d.1217) was first wife of King John (O8)
	Reginald, earl of Cornwall (c1110–75) = Beatrice Fitzrichard	4 daus. plus 2 illeg. sons, of whom Henry Fitzearl died on the Crusades, 1222
	William (c1105–post 1187) = Alice	not known
	Sybilla (c1092–1122) = Alexander I of Scotland (FC63)	no children
	Gundrada (of whom nothing is known)	
	Rohese (d. post 1176) = Henry de la Pomerai	2 sons, Henry and Joscelin
Ansfrida, widow of Sir Anskill	Richard of Lincoln (c1100–20)	no children; drowned in the White Ship
	Fulk, a monk, died young	no children
	Juliana (c1090–1136), later a nun = Eustace de Pacy, lord of Bréteuil	2 sons, 2 daus. The daughters were held hostage and were blinded and disfigured
Nest, dau. of Rhys ap Tewdwr (EB25)	Henry Fitzhenry (c1103–57), killed during Henry II's invasion of Anglesey	2 sons: Robert (d. after 1183) and Meiler (d.1220) Justiciar of Ireland
Edith Sigulfson of Greystoke	Robert Fitzedith (d. 1172), baron of Okehampton, = Maud d'Avranches	only daughter, Maud, died 1224
Isabel de Beaumont, dau. Earl of Leicester	Isabella, died unmarried after 1120	
	Matilda, abbess of Montivilliers	
Edith (of whom nothing is known)	Matilda (c1090–1120, drowned in the White Ship) = Rotrou II, count of Perche	Philippa and Felicia. Philippa married Helias, brother of Geoffrey Plantagenet
Mothers unknown	Gilbert (c1130–post 1142)	
	William de Tracy (d. c1136)	Grace who had 2 sons from whom were descended the viscounts Tracy to 1797
	Matilda = Conan III, duke of Brittany (SA41)	son (Hoel) disowned; dau. (Bertha) married Alain the Black, from whom were descended later dukes of Brittany
	Constance = Roscelin de Beaumont	granddaughter Ermengarde married William the Lyon of Scotland and had 4 children, including Alexander II
	Eustacia (?) = William Gouet III, lord of Montmireil	son, William Gouet IV, sole heir
	Alice = Matthew de Montmorenci, Constable of France	5 sons
	unknown daughter betrothed (but not married) to William de Warenne	
Paternity uncertain	Joan or Elizabeth = Fergus of Galloway	ancestress of Alan of Galloway and John Balliol (FC70) (see chart 23)
	Emma = Guy de Laval	ancestress of lords of Laval
	Sybilla = Baldwin de Boullers	
	unknown daughter betrothed (but not married) to Hugh Fitzgervais	

French king, who had just made him count of Flanders. In January 1128 he married Giovanna, the daughter of the count of Burgundy. William was gradually rising in power and his right to the English throne was becoming increasingly recognized by the Norman aristocracy. Unfortunately William was wounded in a skirmish near St Omer in July 1128 and died five days later.

The barons now realised that there was little alternative but to Matilda becoming their queen, but they increasingly showed their opposition. Geoffrey, who became count of Anjou in 1129, recognized this and though he never seems to have considered himself having any claim on the throne of England, he did consider the duchy of Normandy and asked Henry if he would give him custody of the castles along the French coast. Henry refused, with the result that the relationship between Henry and Geoffrey deteriorated rapidly. It had not been helped by Matilda deciding she could not abide Geoffrey and deserting him to return to England. Henry, still with an eye on Matilda producing a grandson, sought to reconcile the two with some degree of success. Nevertheless, by 1135 Henry and Geoffrey were openly at war. Henry sailed to Normandy but soon after his arrival he became ill, apparently after eating some lampreys. The result was ptomaine poisoning and six days later Henry died. Despite having declared Matilda his heir, neither she nor the barons took up that position, and the throne was claimed by Henry's nephew, STEPHEN.

Henry was a highly capable king. Although he was frequently involved in warfare, either direct or diplomatic, most of this was over his lands in Normandy. For all of his long reign, after the first year, he maintained peace throughout England, though it was a peace at the cost of exacting taxes needed to maintain his army. This led to him establishing the crown exchequer, the basis of the future Treasury. With his many campaigns and international affairs, Henry had little time for anything other than pleasures of the flesh, although he did establish a royal menagerie at his manor at Woodstock, near Oxford, which is regarded as the first English zoo. It is ironic that, despite having fathered at least twenty-nine children, he was only able to leave one legitimate heir to the throne, and she was not seriously considered by Henry's barons until it became convenient to do so. For all of Henry's schemes and plans during his thirty-five year reign, the longest of any king of England since ATHELRED II, it all came to nought. Perhaps he schemed too much, for his efforts in his final years to find a successor meant that he found one too many, and within four years of his death, England was plunged into civil war.

[O4] STEPHEN
King of England, 22 December 1135–7 April 1141 (deposed); restored 1 November 1141–25 October 1154. Crowned: Westminster Abbey, 26 December 1135; and again Canterbury Cathedral 25 December 1141.
Titles: king of England, count of Mortain (before 1115) and count of Boulogne (from c1125).
Born: Blois, France, c1097. Died: Dover, 25 October 1154, aged 57. Buried: Faversham Abbey, Kent.
Married: c1125, Matilda (c1103–1152), dau. of Eustace III, count of Boulogne, 5 children. Stephen had at least five illegitimate children.
Stephen was the nephew of HENRY I. His mother, Adela, was the daughter of WILLIAM THE CONQUEROR, and inherited much of her father's strength and power,

dominating her husband Stephen, count of Blois, whom she despatched to the Crusades where he was killed in 1102. She had at least ten children of which Stephen was one of the youngest. He soon became a favourite of his uncle Henry who showered him with gifts of lands in England and Normandy, making him one of the richest men in Henry's kingdom. His younger brother Henry likewise gained lands and titles, and was consecrated bishop of Winchester in October 1129, still an influential post at that time. This meant that both Stephen and Henry had more influence than their elder brother, Theobald (whom Henry I did not like), who had succeeded to the county of Blois on his father's death and had a greater right of succession to the English throne than Stephen. In 1125, Stephen had married Matilda, the niece of Henry I's first wife Matilda and grandaughter of MALCOLM III of Scotland. She was also fifth in descent from EDMUND IRONSIDE. Stephen had thus married into the royal blood of Wessex. In 1126 Henry I had forced his barons to swear fealty to his daughter, the Empress MATILDA, as successor in the absence of another direct male heir. Stephen had been a party to this, but it was not popular amongst the Normans who did not like the idea of being ruled by a woman. On his uncle's death in December 1135, Stephen hastened to London from his estates in Boulogne. Although initially denied access through Dover by Matilda's half-brother Robert of Gloucester, Stephen's resoluteness brought him to Canterbury where he gained the support of William, the archbishop. Moving on to London he gained the immediate support of the city by granting it the status of a commune, with rights of collective self-government. Stephen was crowned within three weeks of his uncle's death. This took most barons by surprise. Some were mustering their support behind Theobald. However, rather than have a divided kingdom they soon switched their allegiance to Stephen and swore fealty to him both as king of England and duke of Normandy. Stephen was helped by his brother Henry who allowed Stephen access to the royal treasury at Winchester, so that Stephen was able to bribe many of his less ardent supporters. Theobald did not pursue his claim, but Matilda was outraged. She protested, even to the pope, but Innocent II supported Stephen on the basis that certain barons and clerics maintained they had heard Henry state on his deathbed that he wished Stephen to be his successor.

For the moment Stephen was secure. In fact initially Stephen was a popular king. He had an affable nature but a firm hand and rapidly commanded respect. He was fair in his judgements and seemed to have the common touch so that he was supported by the vast majority of the English. There were, however, disputes. DAVID I, the king of Scotland, invaded Northumberland and claimed the territory in the name of his niece, Matilda. In fact David's intentions were more to reclaim what he believed were his own territories by right of succession, and he used Matilda's cause as an excuse. Stephen's skirmishes against David were all successful, culminating in the battle of the Standard in August 1138. Stephen had less success in the Welsh Marches, the stronghold of Robert of Gloucester, Matilda's half-brother, and it was here that Stephen's weakness lay. Although Robert had given token allegiance to Stephen it is evident that the two remained distrustful of each other. Even though Robert accompanied Stephen in 1137 in his expedition against Geoffrey of Anjou, Matilda's husband, who had been making regular incursions into Normandy, he did not act outright against

Geoffrey and, by all accounts, began to support Geoffrey in his actions. In May 1138 Robert, who was then in Normandy, issued a declaration whereby he renounced his homage to Stephen. Stephen promptly forfeited Robert's lands and the only way Robert could regain them was by invading. Matilda now had an army to support her own claim to the English throne. Such were the roots of the first English civil war.

Once the rift was declared, Norman loyalties wavered and Robert was able to gain further support. It was during this period that Stephen's once sound judgement began to waver, but his determination caused him to make some ill-founded decisions that seriously weakened his position. First, in December 1138, he alienated his brother, Henry, by not supporting his claim to be archbishop of Canterbury, which went to the manipulative Theobald of Bec. Second, in June 1139, he arrested Roger, bishop of Salisbury and his nephews Alexander, bishop of Lincoln, and Nigel, bishop of Ely. These three, together with two of Roger's sons, had a tight control over much of the administration of England. It had come to Stephen's attention that all of them, under the leadership of Roger, were fortifying their castles in support of Robert of Gloucester. Stephen moved against them, arresting them on the grounds of threatening the peace. Henry of Winchester immediately denounced Stephen as infringing church authority, but Stephen's actions were subsequently upheld by the pope. In taking control of these bishops' castles Stephen had made a major military advance, but he had also made many enemies amongst their supporters. Third, after the battle of the Standard, Stephen gave the castle at Carlisle to the Scots. This enraged Ranulf, earl of Chester, since Carlisle and Cumbria had been part of the lands of his father, which had been forfeited following his father's insurrection against Henry I. Ranulf still regarded them as part of his heritage, and to have them given to the old enemy, the Scots, was more than he could bear. From then on Ranulf became an enemy of the king and though he allied himself to Robert of Gloucester's camp, it was more for his own personal revenge than for any support of Matilda.

In September 1139 Robert and Matilda made their move. Although Stephen had the ports barred, they arrived on the south coast and found refuge at Arundel which was under the control of Henry I's second wife, Adeliza, who had recently married William d'Albini, earl of Arundel. Stephen promptly marched on Arundel, but Robert had already left through minor and well-hidden by-ways to Bristol. Stephen pursued him without success, and it seems Robert may have been aided en route by Stephen's brother Henry. Certainly Bishop Henry successfully negotiated with Stephen to release Matilda under oath and he escorted her to Robert in Bristol. From the vantage point of history this seems a remarkably naïve action, though it emphasises Stephen's chivalric nature. Evidently Stephen believed there was little support for Matilda, and his main concern was Robert. Nevertheless, with Matilda by his side, Robert was able to draw upon her right of succession and held the equivalent of a separate court in the lands faithful to him, which were mostly the old heartland of Wessex in Wiltshire, Gloucestershire and Somerset. Soon William Fitzrichard, who held lands in Cornwall, sided with Matilda. This brought another of Henry's illegitimate sons, Reginald, earl of Cornwall and the full brother of Robert of Gloucester into the fray. Nevertheless, if Stephen had managed to contain the war within the south-west, he might have finished it quickly, and certainly his impressive energy gave him the upper hand during 1140. However his position was undermined when opposition broke out in East Anglia, focused on the support for the imprisoned Bishop Nigel of Ely. Trouble soon spread to Lincoln. Stephen had granted the Castle of Lincoln to William d'Albini, the husband of the dowager queen Adeliza. Ranulf of Chester believed he had a right to Lincoln and, although Stephen was prepared to accept this, and even granted the castle to Ranulf's half-brother William, Ranulf seemed less than satisfied. By Christmas 1140 the two brothers had seized Lincoln in their own name. The townsfolk rebelled and sent for Stephen's aid. Stephen laid siege to the town, although Ranulf had already escaped to gain the support of Robert of Gloucester. In this he was successful and Robert advanced with a large army upon Lincoln. Stephen was advised to retreat but he stubbornly refused. Victory here could well end the civil war. Moreover Stephen had promised help to the people of Lincoln and he was not about to let them down. Despite his smaller force, Stephen led his men into battle on 2 February 1141. It was the only major battle of the civil war and could have been decisive. Stephen fought bravely but he was outnumbered and his force was defeated.

Stephen was captured and imprisoned at Bristol. Although some remained loyal to Stephen they rapidly suffered as a consequence, and before long most turned their allegiance to Matilda, in the belief that Stephen would remain permanently imprisoned. Matilda and her forces gradually assumed control. They received the support of Bishop Henry in early March, and thereby had access to the royal coffers. She settled in London and began to rule as a queen, a title she occasionally used, though she more formally kept to her title of "empress" and sometimes as "Lady of the English". But she rapidly become unpopular and when she lost the support of Bishop Henry, the tide turned against her. Stephen's queen, also called Matilda, and her chief lieutenant, William of Ypres, remained forever faithful along with many of the people of Kent. The "Empress" was driven out of London and the planned coronation never took place. She took up residence in Oxford. However, in September Robert of Gloucester was captured during an incident at Wherwell. Now there was stalemate. Matilda was forced to accept an exchange of prisoners. Stephen was restored to the throne in November and enjoyed a second coronation on Christmas Day. The war was not won, but Stephen became more tenacious. England was divided, but Stephen retained the upper hand. In May 1142 Robert took a hazardous journey to Normandy to gain support from Matilda's husband, Geoffrey, but he was too busy trying to gain control of Normandy and refused assistance. Whilst Robert was absent Stephen pressed home his advantage and by December had Matilda under siege at Oxford Castle. She escaped at night and fled safely to Abingdon. It is worth noting that resident at Oxford at this time was Geoffrey of Monmouth who, just a few years earlier, had completed his *History of the Kings of Britain*. The book was dedicated to Robert of Gloucester.

The civil war would drag on for a further five years. Although Stephen continued to hold the advantage he could never rule in total confidence. A strong reminder of this came when the Empress's forces scored a notable victory over Stephen at Wilton. Stephen became less assured of his authority and frequently arrested people at a moment's notice on suspicion. Among these was the treacherous Geoffrey de Mandeville, constable of the Tower of London, who had been made earl of Essex. His support swung with the prevailing breeze and after his arrest his forces raised a rebellion in 1143, which Stephen was able to quash. For a while Robert and the "Empress" believed they might still have a chance, especially after Geoffrey of Anjou gained control of Normandy in January 1144, but to no avail. In 1145 Robert of Gloucester's son, Philip, transferred his allegiance to Stephen. Gradually Stephen wore down opposition, but in this process England was slowly being destroyed. In October 1147 Robert of Gloucester died, and a few months later Matilda left England. Her cause was taken up by her son Henry, the later HENRY II, but he did not have the resources to support a sustained war. Skirmishes continued throughout 1149, but nothing of any substance. The English civil war did not so much end as fizzle out. Stephen, though, was a shadow of his former self. The civil war had broken him. The strong, resolute, affable man of 1136, was now an ill, haunted, uncertain individual. His continued policies at home were thwarted by Theobald, archbishop of Canterbury, who refused Stephen's involvement in church affairs. Theobald found himself briefly exiled from England, but Stephen soon realised this worked against him. Stephen wanted to secure the succession for his son, EUSTACE, count of Boulogne, but he needed the approval of the archbishop to have him crowned. This Theobald refused to do. Although Stephen declared his son king of England in 1152, this was not acknowledged by the church. Stephen, now much saddened by the death of his wife in May 1152, became a broken man. In 1153 Henry of Anjou brought a force to England to establish his right to the throne. The engagements were all indecisive, not helped by Stephen's apparent lack of strength. Suddenly, in August 1153, Eustace died. Stephen's ambitions collapsed. He signed the Treaty of Wallingford with Henry in November 1153, acknowledging Henry as his heir and successor.

Stephen had less than a year to live. He spent most of these days in Kent, which had remained loyal to him, though he was in great pain from bleeding piles. He died of appendicitis at Dover in October 1154 and was buried alongside his wife and son at Faversham Abbey, which he had founded in 1147. Had Stephen's right to accession been unopposed there is no doubt that he would have ruled as a strong and popular king, but the civil war ruined the ambition and reputation of an otherwise capable, intelligent and brave king.

[O4a] **EUSTACE** The second son of STEPHEN, created count of Bolougne in 1147, and declared king of England in 1152 by his father. This was never acknowledged by the pope and Theobald, archbishop of Canterbury, refused to crown or anoint him. He was apparently a most unlikeable man, grasping and greedy. He had married Constance, daughter of Louis VI of France, when both were still young and, when he brought her to England, he kept her a virtual prisoner at Canterbury Castle. Eustace fought alongside his father during the invasion of Henry of Anjou (the later HENRY II) but died suddenly and unexpectedly, apparently of a fit or seizure, at Bury St Edmunds in August 1153, aged only twenty-two. The way was left open for Henry's succession.

[O5] **MATILDA** uncrowned queen of England, known as "Lady of the English". *Ruled 7 April–1 November 1141. Empress of Germany, 7 January 1114–23 May 1125.*

Born: *Winchester (or possibly London), August (?) 1102.* **Died:** *Abbey of Notre Dame, Rouen, 10 September 1167, aged 65.* **Buried:** *Bec Abbey, Normandy; later removed to Rouen Cathedral.*

Married: *(1) 7 January 1114, at Mainz, Germany, Heinrich V (1081–1125), emperor of Germany: no children; (2) 22 May 1128, at Le Mans Cathedral, Anjou, Geoffrey, count of Anjou (1113–1151): 3 sons.*

Matilda was the daughter of HENRY I and was christened Adelaide at birth. She adopted the name Matilda on her marriage in 1114 to the German emperor, Henry V. Since she was only twelve at this time it was clearly a political marriage and the young girl does not seem to have been especially happy. Raised in the strict atmosphere of the German court, Matilda acquired a haughty, almost arrogant nature, to some extent inherited from her father. She was used to having her own way and found it difficult to make friends. When her husband died in 1125, she returned to England to be acknowledged as heir to her father because of the death of her elder brothers some years earlier. Although the barons swore their fealty they did not relish the idea of being ruled by a woman, especially one who was now married a second time to the young count of Anjou. The Angevins were longtime enemies of the Normans in northern France, and if Matilda became queen her husband, Geoffrey, would almost certainly become king, and the Normans had even less desire to be ruled by an Angevin. As a result, when STEPHEN claimed the throne on Henry's death in 1135, the Norman barons soon rallied round him. It was not until May 1138, with the rebellion of Robert of Gloucester, an illegitimate son of Henry I and thus half-brother of Matilda, that Matilda's cause gained any significant support. Matilda and Robert landed in England, at Arundel, in September 1139. Robert escaped to Bristol and was soon joined by Matilda. For the next eight years England was in the grip of a debilitating civil war. (*The details are described under* STEPHEN). Matilda's hour came after the defeat of Stephen, at Lincoln, on 2 February 1141. Stephen's support wilted, all except from his own queen, also called Matilda. Within a month the "Empress" Matilda had secured the support of Henry, bishop of Winchester (Stephen's brother), which allowed her access to the royal coffers. She arrived at London a few weeks later and in April was declared "Lady of the English". She still preferred to be known as "Empress", but occasionally styled herself queen. Although preparations were in hand for her coronation, that never happened. Matilda rapidly made herself unpopular. First she raised a tax on all the nobility, and then she proposed to revoke the status of commune which had been granted to London by Stephen. This allowed London to collect its own taxes for its own benefits. Matilda wanted access to these taxes. Her support in London rapidly dwindled, and when Stephen's queen, Matilda, was able to bring her own forces from Kent, with William of Ypres, the "Empress" was driven out of London in June. She settled in Oxford, although she spent some weeks in the complicated siege within a siege at Winchester. It was during this and the following affrays in the surrounding countryside that Robert of Gloucester was captured and Matilda only narrowly escaped. Matilda needed Robert as head of her forces and as a consequence she had to trade for his release with the release of

Stephen from captivity in Bristol. Her advantage was lost and by November Stephen had restored himself as king. A year later Matilda found herself under siege at Oxford. She was able to escape from the castle by rope from an open window and then, cloaked in white as camouflage against the snow, she crossed the frozen river and made her way to Abingdon. Although her forces scored occasional victories in the ensuing months, it became a gradual war of attrition which fizzled out with the death of Robert of Gloucester in October 1147. Matilda returned to Normandy in the following spring and never returned to England. She continued to fight for the right of succession of her son, and indeed outlived Stephen to witness her son succeed to the throne as HENRY II. Although she ruled as uncrowned queen for less than a year, Matilda was the first queen of all England. Had she not been so arrogant and fiery tempered, she might have been remembered more for her successes than her failures.

[O6;SB17;SC12;SD12] **HENRY II**, *FITZEMPRESS or CURTMANTLE*
King of England 25 October 1154–6 July 1189. Crowned: Westminster, 19 December 1154.
Titles: king of England, duke of Normandy (from 1151), duke of Aquitaine (from 1152), count of Anjou, Touraine and Maine (from 1151).
Born: Le Mans, Maine, 5 March 1133; Died: Chinon Castle, Anjou, 6 July 1189, aged 56. Buried: Fontevrault Abbey, France.
Married: 18 May 1152, at Bordeaux Cathedral, Gascony, Eleanor (c1122–1204), dau. of William X, duke of Aquitaine, and divorcée of Louis VII, king of France: 8 children. Henry had at least 12 illegitimate children by five or more other women.

Henry was the eldest son of the empress MATILDA, who had briefly claimed the kingdom of England in 1141 during the extended civil war. His father was Geoffrey, count of Anjou, who became duke of Normandy in 1144. Geoffrey was frequently known as *Plantagenet* because of the sprig of broom he would wear in his cap, and this soubriquet subsequently became the surname of his descendants and the title of the royal house of England. Its official name, though, was the house of Anjou and it would dominate England for over three hundred and thirty years. It gave England some of its most powerful kings, including the first Angevin, Henry II.

Henry first attempted to continue his mother's war against STEPHEN after she had returned to Normandy in 1148, but Henry was a young squire of fifteen without sufficient resources to maintain such an effort. The next five years would see a significant change in him. When his father died in 1151 he inherited the duchy of Normandy as well as becoming count of Maine and Anjou. Eight months later he married Eleanor of Aquitaine, who was at least ten years his senior, the former wife of Louis VII of France whom Louis had divorced, ostensibly on grounds of consanguinity, but really because she had provided no male heir. This marriage

From a coin

infuriated Louis VII, especially when he had recognize the claim of Henry as duke of Aquitaine. Although Henry paid homage to Louis for his lands in France, he now effectively controlled more territory than the King himself. Louis sent forces against Henry as a show of power but Henry was able to contain them. In fact he felt sufficiently in control to accompany a small force to England in January 1153 in an effort to depose Stephen. In this he was unsuccessful, but Stephen was no longer disposed to fight, and most of the hostilities were between Henry and Stephen's son EUSTACE. In August 1153 Eustace died and this paved the way for Henry's succession which was sealed under the Treaty of Wallingford that November. By its terms Stephen continued to rule for as long as he lived but Henry was his undisputed successor. When Stephen died in October 1154, Henry succeeded to a considerable territory, subsequently called the Angevin Empire, though not known as that in Henry's day. At its peak it stretched from the Scottish border to the Pyrenees, and would include overlordship of Ireland.

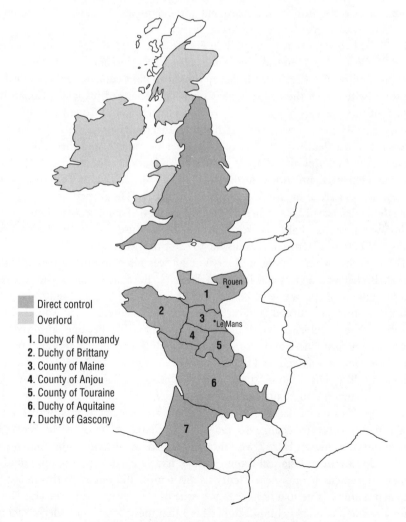

Direct control
Overlord

1. Duchy of Normandy
2. Duchy of Brittany
3. County of Maine
4. County of Anjou
5. County of Touraine
6. Duchy of Aquitaine
7. Duchy of Gascony

Rouen
Le Mans

Map 13 **The Angevin Empire under Henry II, c1174**

The energy with which Henry set about establishing his authority over his territories was awesome. This was helped by the papal bull issued in 1155 by the new Pope Adrian IV (the only English pope – Nicholas Breakspeare), which decreed that Henry had authority over the whole of Britain, including Scotland, Wales and Ireland. In the space of two years (1155–7) Henry had destroyed many of the castles established by barons during the civil war, and which he referred to as "dens of thieves"; he had negotiated terms with MALCOLM IV of Scotland, whereby Cumbria and Northumberland returned to English rule; and he had invaded Wales and brought the Welsh princes to heel. This last enterprise nearly cost him his life, however, when he was ambushed by the heir of Gwynedd, Cynan ab Owain. Henry's strength of character, his papal authority, and the immense resources upon which he could draw made him an impossible man to challenge, and by 1158 he had restored an order to England and its subservient kingdoms which it had not known to such a degree for many lifetimes. Wales would continue to be a thorn in his side for much of his reign, but he never considered it as much of a problem compared to other priorities. Subsequent campaigns of 1167 and 1177 served to remind successive Welsh rulers of his authority.

From 1158 to 1163 Henry was back in France. In July 1158 his brother, Geoffrey, had died. Geoffrey in 1150 had been made count of Nantes, one half of the duchy of Brittany, and on Geoffrey's death Henry sought to gain control. He was foiled by the speed with which the exiled duke, Conan IV, reclaimed his lands. Conan had been confirmed as earl of Richmond by Henry in 1156, and Conan was forced to acknowledge Henry's overlordship in Brittany. In 1166 Henry arranged a marriage between his son Geoffrey and Conan's daughter Constance, and thereafter Conan handed over the administration of Brittany to Henry to direct on behalf of the children. Henry's main thrust during 1159 and 1160 was against Toulouse, which he regarded as part of his wife's territory in Aquitaine. The French king, Louis VII, came to the defence of his brother-in- law, the count of Toulouse, and Henry had to withdraw rather than fight his French overlord. Toulouse and Aquitaine remained in dispute between Henry and Louis for the rest of their reigns.

The most notorious aspect of Henry's reign was his relationship with Thomas Becket. Becket was a personal friend of Henry's. Born in London, the son of a wealthy merchant, he was well educated and had trained as a knight before his father's misfortunes turned him to become a clerk, entering the household of Theobald, the archbishop of Canterbury, in 1142. He became an expert at canonical jurisprudence, and was appointed archdeacon of Canterbury in 1154 and chancellor of England in 1155. He fought alongside Henry in Toulouse and became wealthy. His election as the next archbishop of Canterbury in May 1162 came as a surprise to many, and was not universally accepted amongst other churchmen because of Becket's background and worldliness. It was probably this that caused Becket to change so radically in character in order to prove his devotion to the church. Henry, who thought he had an ally within the church who would help him in ecclesiatical disputes which had so plagued past kings, found he had an unpredictable opponent. Henry's short temper did not allow this to last for long and matters came to a head over the issue of clergy who broke the law. Henry maintained at a council held in October 1163 that these "criminous clerks" should be unfrocked and tried in a lay court. Becket maintained that they would be tried

38. England (3) – The House of Anjou (1) Henry II to Edward I

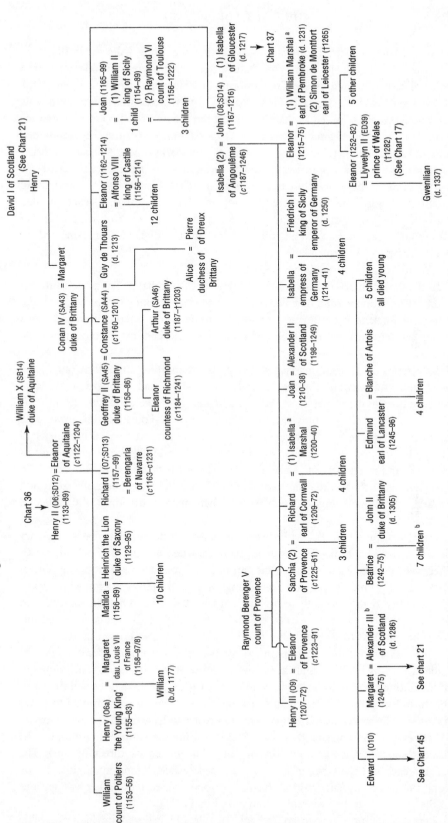

Notes: (a) William and Isabella Marshal were brother and sister

(b) Alexander III's second wife Yolande later married Arthur II, Duke of Brittany and eldest son of Beatrice and John

by ecclesiastical courts. Henry appealed to the new pope (Alexander III), who requested that Becket be more conciliatory. Henry now presented Becket with a series of terms, known as the Constitutions of Clarendon, which was where the council was held in January 1164. Becket argued tenaciously but eventually submitted. Henry believed he had succeeded but, soon after, Becket repented his change of heart and began lobbying the bishops. Henry was furious. He summoned him on various charges, including a debt of 44,000 marks (about £30,000) as owing since his days as chancellor. Becket was found guilty and his estates forfeited. He fled to France where he spent two years at the Cistercian abbey of Pontigny in Burgundy before the pope gave due attention to his cause. Becket pleaded personally before him in Rome, and Alexander restored him to the see of Canterbury. But Becket could still not return to England. He remained in France where he wrote letters of exhortation to the bishops, threatening excommunication unless they heeded his words.

In the meantime Henry had more pressing matters in hand. The pope's support and the Clarendon verdict had allowed Henry to start breaking down the old feudal system in England by ensuring that local baronial courts were subordinate to a strong central court. He re-established the jury system and introduced a new code of laws.

By a series of dynastic marriages Henry was establishing himself as one of the most powerful men in Europe. Already in 1160 he had arranged a marriage between his eldest surviving son, Henry, and Margaret, the daughter of Louis VII of France. Margaret was only two and Henry five, and Louis had not expected a confirmed marriage for many years after the betrothal agreement. But Henry had offered his support to the new pope, Alexander III, in 1160, whose succession was disputed, and in repayment, Alexander carried out the marriage. In February 1168 his eldest daughter Matilda was married to Heinrich the Lion, Duke of Saxony and Bavaria, whilst his youngest daughters were betrothed to the kings of Castile and Sicily.

Henry's dispute with Becket returned to haunt him in 1170. In that year Henry determined to have his eldest son formally crowned as king of England, which effectively elevated Henry himself into an imperial role. He needed the support of Becket and the pope in this, and begrudgingly accepted a reconciliation with Becket. However before this was fully resolved, Henry went ahead and had his son crowned (see HENRY – THE YOUNG KING) by the archbishop of York. Becket condemned this when he returned to England later that year. Becket was welcomed by the general populace as a hero: their champion against baronial oppression. Henry could not understand why Becket was always so quarrelsome. It was during one such moment of frustration that Henry uttered his notorious words: "Is there none will rid me of this turbulent priest?" Four knights, hearing these words and determined to prove themselves, immediately left Henry's court in Normandy, arriving at Canterbury on 29 December 1170 where they slew Becket within the cathedral. Although the murder shocked Christendom, it had not been at Henry's direct bidding. The knights each did their penance. Henry donned sackcloth, and apologised to the pope, but he soon weathered the storm. Everyone realised that Becket was best out of the way, though he was rapidly canonized in 1173.

Henry's attention turned to Ireland. He already believed he had ostensible authority over the country but plans for an earlier invasion in 1155 had been shelved. However in 1170 Richard Fitzgilbert, the earl of Pembroke, known as Richard Strongbow, had invaded Ireland at the request of the dispossessed king of Leinster, Diarmaid MacMurchada. Diarmaid had earlier appealed to Henry who had offered him his support, but gave him no direct help. Strongbow's forces however soon captured Waterford and Dublin. Strongbow married Diarmaid's daughter. Henry II became suspicious of Strongbow's intentions and brought his own army into Ireland in 1171. Henry's forces were too powerful for the Irish. They nicknamed them the *gaill glassa*, or "grey foreigners", from their armour which had not been seen before in Ireland. Henry soon established authority over eastern Ireland, especially the kingdoms of Leinster and Meath, whose rulers acknowledged his overlordship in the Treaty of Windsor in October 1175. Hugh de Lacy was made the first lord of Meath and remained as Henry's viceroy in Ireland, though his later aspirations to the kingship led to his assassination. Henry's youngest son, JOHN, was styled king of Ireland from 1177, though this was no more than an honorific as the hereditary kings of Ireland still ruled. John later adopted the more appropriate title lord of Ireland.

John's title was part of a settlement in a dispute between Henry and his children that rocked his final years. The "Young King" Henry was not satisfied with his authority in name only and wanted more. Although he was crowned a second time in August 1172, when he was created not only king of England but duke of Normandy and count of Anjou, he was still unsatisfied. His actions stirred Richard and Geoffrey into rebellion in 1173, which brought with it opportunists from elsewhere in the realm, including WILLIAM THE LYON of Scotland. William had long had designs on Northumberland and Cumbria which he believed were his inheritance. He invaded northern England in 1173 but was captured and taken prisoner to Henry in Normandy and forced to pay homage. The sons were supported by their mother Eleanor of Aquitaine, from whom Henry had drifted apart by the late 1160s. The problem intensified after 1180 when Louis VII was succeeded by Philippe II, a far less scrupulous monarch who was keen to shatter the Angevin Empire and agreed to help Henry's sons against their father. Henry's world which he had so painstakingly created was now in danger of collapsing. In June 1183 the "Young King" Henry died. Henry's third son, Geoffrey, was killed in an accident at a tournament in Paris in August 1186. Although this might have simplified the battle between Henry and his sons, it focused the attention on the rivalry between RICHARD, the eldest surviving heir and Eleanor's favourite, and John, the youngest and Henry's favourite. Henry had spent most of these latter years in France, visiting England only for official duties. It was in France that he faced the army of Richard and King Philippe, with whom was also his favourite son John. This broke Henry's spirit. He was already ill and prematurely aged. He no longer had the energy to fight and agreed terms with Philippe at Colombières on 4 July 1189. Two days later he died as the result of a massive haemorrhage, cursing his sons to the last. He was only 56 years of age. His widow, Eleanor, would live for a further fifteen years, dying at the remarkable age of 82, the oldest of any English queen consort until the twentieth century. She still continued to exert an influence over her scheming children, of whom Richard now inherited the throne of England.

[O6a] **HENRY, *THE YOUNG KING*.** The son of HENRY II, who was crowned as king of England in June 1170 to designate him as heir to the throne in the style of the French monarchs. Henry had been born on 28 February 1155 at Bermondsey Palace in Surrey, so he was only fifteen at the time of his coronation. He had already been married for nearly ten years to Margaret, the daughter of Louis VII of France. Louis had agreed the terms of the betrothal as far back as 1158 but had not expected such an early marriage. Henry II, however, used his influence with the new pope, Alexander III, to conduct the marriage and this brought with it certain castles in France as part of Margaret's dowry. Louis constantly objected to Henry's schemes and one-upmanship; Louis had no such skills. However he objected to the coronation of 1170 firstly on the grounds that his daughter had not been crowned queen at the same time but also that it was unlawful. The coronation should have been conducted by Thomas Becket, the authorised representative of the pope. Becket was still in exile in France at that time so the archbishop of York conducted the ceremony. Because of these antagonisms, Henry organized a second coronation at Winchester in August 1172 with the new archbishop of Canterbury and at which Margaret was crowned. The "Young King", as he was always known, had long been status conscious. There is the tale that at the banquet the father waited upon his own son, remarking that "No other king in Christendom has such a butler", to which the son retorted, "It is only fitting that the son of a count should wait on the son of a king." The young Henry was an ungrateful child and, encouraged by his mother, Eleanor of Aquitaine, he rose up in revolt against his father when the old king attempted to transfer three of Henry's key castles to John. The "Young King" sought his mother's help with the result that Eleanor was imprisoned. This led to the other sons coming into the fray, and the next decade saw an embittered rivalry between Henry and his sons. The "Young King" did not survive to inherit the throne, as he died of a fever at Martel Castle in Turenne on 11 June 1183, aged twenty-eight. His only child, William, who had been born in 1177, had lived only three days. His widow, Margaret, married Bela III, king of Hungary, in 1185. She died in 1197 at Acre in the Holy Land. The throne passed to RICHARD (I).

[O7;SB18;SC13;SD13] RICHARD (I) *LIONHEART*.

King of England, 6 July 1189–6 April 1199. Crowned: Westminster Abbey, 2 September 1189.

Titles: king of England, duke of Normandy and duke of Aquitaine (from 1172).

Born: Beaumont Palace, Oxford, 8 September 1157. Died: Chalus, Aquitaine, 6 April 1199, aged 41. Buried: Fontevrault Abbey, Anjou.

Married: 12 May 1191, at Limassol, Cyprus, Berengaria (c1163–after 1230), dau. of Sancho VI, king of Navarre: no children. Richard had one, possibly two illegitimate children.

Probably no other historical king of England has so much legend attached to him and so much reputation which is ill founded. We know Richard as the Lionhearted, or *Coeur-du-Lion*, the brave and intrepid champion of Christendom against the infidel, and he is one of our national heroes. And yet the truth is so very different.

Richard had little interest in England and certainly not in the administrative demands of government. In his youth he had not expected to become king, as his elder brother HENRY (*THE YOUNG KING*) was heir to the throne. In 1172 he was invested with the duchy of Aquitaine, the inheritance of his mother, Eleanor. Like all the sons of HENRY II, Richard seemed a less than grateful child. He was devoted to his mother and, when she was imprisoned, Richard joined in the rebellion of his brothers against their father seeking to gain more authority. Henry was still able to rebuff them at this time, but the relationship between father and sons soured over the years, with Richard's brother JOHN being the favourite. Richard had one passion in life. He loved to fight. The thrill of battle never left him. In his youth he had trained as a knight and was a champion of the tourney. His courage and strength soon became the wonder of Aquitaine where he spent several years in battle against the rebellious barons. His military skill was evident when he took the hitherto impregnable castle of Taillebourg in 1179. Richard was tall, with handsome features and tousled red hair. He seems to have attracted as much attention from men as from women and there is almost certainly some truth in the belief that Richard had homosexual inclinations.

After the death of his elder brother Henry in 1183 Richard became his father's heir. Henry hoped that Richard would pass Aquitaine on to John, but Richard had no such intention. Henry's efforts to gain land back from his sons for John only led to warfare between Richard and his father. In 1189 Richard joined forces with Philippe II of France and beat his father into submission. Henry died a few days later and Richard travelled promptly to England to be crowned, pausing briefly in Normandy to be acknowledged Duke.

Richard's coronation was marred by the persecution of the Jews that broke out in London and later in other cities, especially York. Two years earlier Saladin's forces had captured Jerusalem, and the cry went up across Europe to regain the heart of Christendom from the infidel. Henry II had originally been asked to lead the Crusade, and Richard had been anxious to take part, but with them both fighting each other nothing had happened. With Henry's death, Richard's one ambition now was to lead an army against the Saracens. His stay in Britain was brief, sufficient to raise finances and resources for the Crusade. This included the infamous Quit-claim of Canterbury whereby Richard sold all rights in Scotland back to WILLIAM *THE LYON* for ten thousand marks. He returned to France in December 1189 and would not set foot in England again for four years, and then

From Historia Anglorum

only for two months. Although king of England for ten years he spent only six months in his kingdom. He left the administration of England in the hands of William Longchamp, a loyal and capable chancellor whose short temper and arrogance caused considerable friction with other barons and for a period forced him to retreat to Normandy.

Richard combined forces with Philippe II of France and set off for the Holy Land in July 1190. The vast army encountered transportation difficulties when their fleet was delayed and they decided to winter in Sicily. Richard's sister Joanna was the recently widowed queen of Sicily and Richard was less than satisfied with her treatment by the new king Tancred. A skirmish broke out between the crusaders and the inhabitants of Messina which resulted in Richard capturing the town. This enabled him to negotiate favourable terms with Tancred, which not only brought the release of Joanna, but much needed funds for the Crusade. It was not a happy winter in Sicily, however. Richard and Philippe quarreled over Richard's planned marriage with Philippe's sister Alys. They had been betrothed for over twenty years, but during that time Alys had almost certainly become the mistress of Richard's father Henry. She was not exactly a shining example of virtue and Richard, who had little interest in the fair sex, declined to marry her. In the midst of this quarrel, Eleanor of Aquitaine arrived in Sicily with a new bride for her son, Berengaria of Navarre. Incensed, Philippe sailed on ahead to the Holy Land. Richard followed in April 1191, but en route the ship carrying his young bride and his sister was nearly captured by Isaac Comnenus, a Byzantine rebel who had usurped power on Cyprus. In the resultant battle Richard conquered Cyprus, which he subsequently sold to Guy de Lusignan, the exiled king of Jerusalem. While in Cyprus, Richard married Berengaria. There were to be no children of this marriage. Although Richard may have been homosexual (and he certainly had a fascination for Berengaria's brother Sancho) he had at least one illegitimate child, Philip, who became lord of Cognac, probably the offspring of a lady at court in Aquitaine, a child of Richard's youth.

Richard reached the Holy Land in June 1191 and his forces helped conclude the siege of Acre, which had been deadlocked since August 1189, and where the besiegers were themselves besieged by Saladin's army. Richard however fell out with Duke Leopold of Austria, whom he insulted. Both Leopold and King Philippe of France soon returned home. Richard killed the prisoners taken at Acre and marched down the coast to Jaffa, winning a victory at Arsuf en route. However his forces were unable to penetrate inland to Jerusalem and, in September 1192, Richard was forced to conclude a three-year treaty with Saladin. Although Richard's Crusade failed in its prime objective, his exploits were amplified in their telling so that his English and French subjects elevated him to the status of a super-hero. In fact he was an extremely arrogant, petulant king, with a vicious temper and a total lack of moral scruples.

Richard returned to Europe in October 1192 but his ship was wrecked in the Adriatic and he was forced to travel across land. When he entered the territories of his enemy Leopold of Austria he apparently disguised himself as a woodsman, but he betrayed himself because of his fine gloves and was handed over to the Emperor Heinrich VI, who demanded a ransom of 150,000 marks. Richard was held captive for fifteen months while negotiations ensued and the ransom was raised. The negotiations were conducted by Richard's new justiciar, Hubert Walter, who had accompanied him to Palestine and who had arrived safely home. Hubert not only succeeded in raising the ransom but also quashed the attempted revolt by John to gain the throne. John's ineptitude nevertheless lost him lands in northern France. It is to this period that the romantic legend belongs of Richard's minstrel Blondel travelling from one castle to another in Austria and singing Richard's favourite song until he heard Richard sing back in response from the castle of Dürrenstein. Like most legends it probably has a core of truth.

Richard was eventually released and returned to England in March 1194. Despite John's treachery, Richard forgave him, merely admonishing him for acting like a child. He devoted the remaining years of his life to regaining his lost territories in France. He left for France in May 1194 and never returned to England. He seemed little concerned about the problems that his absence had caused elsewhere in Britain, particularly in Wales where warfare had broken out between the various rulers, and also in the Irish Sea where RAGNALD of Man ruled as a pirate. Henry II had held these upstarts in check, but Richard showed no such interest.

Although Richard made peace with Philippe II on more than one occasion, war always broke out again. Nevertheless Richard reconquered all of his former territories and, in building new fortifications, left them stronger than before. He received an arrow wound during a skirmish at the castle of Chalus in the Limousin, and he died from the infection a few days later in April 1199. Richard spent his entire life as a warrior. He was an excellent soldier, fearless, brave and a great tactician, but he was useless at anything else. He left no heir, and had also spent a considerable fortune on his exploits. The English, in their usual way of preferring the legend to the facts, have long cherished the memory of a man who, in fact, had no interest in England other than as a source of revenue, and who was a ruthless fighting machine who made enemies of most of the royalty of Europe.

Berengaria survived Richard by over thirty years. She settled in Le Mans where she helped finance the construction of the Abbey of L'Epau where she was later buried. It is often stated that Berengaria was the only queen of England never to set foot in the country. She never did so during Richard's reign, but she made occasional visits after his death until she settled down as a nun at L'Epau.

[O8] JOHN *LACKLAND*

King of England: 6 April 1199–18 October 1216. Crowned: Westminster Abbey, 27 May 1199.

Titles: king of England, lord of Ireland (from 1177), count of Mortain (from 1189) and duke of Normandy (1199–1203).

Born: Beaumont Palace, Oxford, 24 December 1167 Died: Newark Castle, 18 October 1216, aged 48. Buried: Worcester Cathedral.

Married: (1) 29 August 1189, at Marlborough Castle, Isabella (c1175–1217), dau. of William, earl of Gloucester; divorced 1199: no children; (2) 24 August 1200, at Bordeaux Cathedral, Isabella (c1187–1246), dau. of Aymer Taillefer, count of Angoulême: 5 children. John also had at least twelve illegitimate children.

John was the youngest and favourite son of HENRY II and Eleanor of Aquitaine. His mother was forty-five when he was born and she had already given birth to nine children. As the youngest child John had no immediate inheritance, Henry's patrimony having already been divided amongst his other children. John thus earned the nickname *Lackland*. When Henry's eldest surviving son, HENRY (*THE YOUNG KING*), died in 1183, Henry hoped that RICHARD, who had now become the heir to the English throne, would transfer Aquitaine to John. Richard had no such intention. The conflict that followed, as brother fought brother and sons fought father, was an ignominious end to Henry's reign and revealed that John was as much a turncoat as the rest. It was John's treachery that hastened Henry's death. After Henry's conquest of eastern Ireland in 1175, John was invested with the honorary title of lord of Ireland, though it carried no authority or land. In 1185 John was despatched to Ireland to conclude the conquest, but instead he alienated the native kings by ridiculing their dress and appearance, and angered his soldiers by spending their pay.

John was clearly a spoiled child, but he did not waste his childhood. He had a good education and took a special interest in law and administration. He was the youngest male child by some eight years and there is little doubt that his elder brothers continued to treat him as a child. He did not get on with them particularly well and followed his own solitary pursuits. He became extremely petulant, but also shrewd, finding ways of achieving his own ends. His brothers, and others who knew him closely, found they could not trust him. When Richard left for the Crusades in 1190, he granted John sufficient territory in France in the hope it would keep him out of mischief, and ordered him not to set foot in England. But John's passion for power ruled his head and the moment Richard left, John determined to overthrow William Longchamp, whom Richard had left in charge. Richard heard of John's activities and sent Walter of Coutances to assist Longchamp. John was forced to retire to his estates but then paid homage to Philippe II of France, who had returned (ahead of Richard) from the Crusade in 1191. When Richard eventually returned to England in March 1194, John lost many of his lands in Normandy but Richard soon forgave him. Nevertheless with Richard close at hand, winning back his lands in France, John was not able to make more trouble. In fact he assisted Richard in his wars and Richard appointed him his heir.

When Richard died in 1199 John was accepted as king in England, but not by the Angevin territories in France, who preferred his nephew Arthur of Brittany. Arthur, and his sister Eleanor, were the children of John's elder brother Geoffrey, and had stronger claims, on the principle of primogeniture, to the throne than John did. John's subsequent actions did not help the situation. Little over a year after his coronation he divorced his wife and married Isabella of Angoulême. Their marriage was tempestuous – both highly-sexed and strong-willed, they were well matched – but the marriage was also the cause of John's downfall. She was already betrothed to Hugh de Lusignan, who complained to Philippe of France. He summoned John to answer the case but John refused, enabling Philippe to confiscate all of John's lands in France. In the ensuing conflict, which broke out in the spring of 1202, John defended his lands admirably, including a mercy dash to save his besieged mother. Unfortunately John made a singular error of judgement in capturing and imprisoning Arthur and his sister. Arthur was never heard of again, but by Easter 1203 there were strong rumours that his mutilated body had been seen in the river Seine. Blame attached itself to John, with many believing he had killed

From the Charter Roll
of Waterford

Arthur in a fit of rage. Arthur's fate unsettled the barons in Brittany, Normandy and Anjou, and their distrust of John increased. John found it difficult to defend his lands. He escaped to England in December 1203, leaving his Norman subjects to their fate. He succeeded in negotiating a truce for two years thus enabling him to hold on to most of Poitou, but by 1206 he was forced to surrender all of his territories north of the Loire.

John needed resources to re-establish an army to regain his French lands and though this was the main focus of his energies for the next few years he did not neglect the administration of England. It is unfortunate that John is remembered as a harsh king because to his subjects he was exceedingly fair, ensuring that the law was properly administered. In fact he was probably too fair, since he often angered his barons with his judgements against them in favour of their tenants. He further alienated the barons by levying severe taxes and strengthening the forest laws to increase his income. The most hated tax was scutage. This was levied on those barons who declined military service, which became increasingly common amongst those who had no lands in France and thus had no desire to fight abroad. Moreover many were less and less inclined to want to fight for John, and scutage became seen as an onerous punishment for their disloyalty. John did not seem to worry about annoying his barons. He had a good sense of humour and delighted in anything that ridiculed or deflated pomposity. This angered his barons even more, though John's common subjects found it a redeeming feature.

John's delight at challenging authority went a step too far, however, with the pope. In 1207 John rejected the new archbishop of Canterbury, Stephen Langton, and refused to accept the pope's injunction that Langton be re-installed. As a result in 1208 England was placed under an interdict that stopped all church services, and then John was excommunicated. This did not worry John because he used the opportunity to confiscate church revenues which provided much needed funds for his military endeavours. In the period 1208 to 1211 John undertook several successful campaigns throughout Britain, which bought him time with his restless nobles. Campaigns in Scotland, Ireland and Wales during these years brought the rebellious lords and vassals to order and demonstrated that John did possess military skills. In fact John's defeat of LLYWELYN THE GREAT in 1211 was perhaps his single most effective victory. He was able to exact severe tribute from these vassals to add to his growing treasury. John planned a further campaign in 1212 but by then other priorities took over. A rumoured murder plot, a threatened rebellion by his barons, a planned invasion by Philippe of France, and the threat of deposition by the pope made John reconsider his position. This was where he demonstrated his cunning. His negotiations with Pope Innocent III lifted the interdict on the basis that John would hold his lands as a fiefdom of the papacy. Innocent thereafter supported John in his actions against his barons, and even against Philippe.

John now had the finances and the papal support he needed. He had to capitalise on this by regaining his lands in France. His campaign, which began in July 1213, was initially successful. He routed the French fleet and won a number of battles. However, the following year, whilst campaigning in Poitou, John's allies were defeated at Bouvines in Flanders, which weakened John's position. He was forced to agree a peace treaty with France. In the eyes of the barons this was seen as a defeat. Their patience snapped. They rebelled openly and civil war broke out in May 1215. The hostilities were brief as John was betrayed and London fell within a month. John met the rebels at Runnymede on 15 June 1215, where he was forced to sign a charter, agreeing to restore many of the rights that the church and barons believed they had lost, not just during John's reign but that of Henry II. This later became known as the Great Charter or *Magna Carta*. It was not so very earth-shattering at the time, but it rapidly became the symbol of the success of the barons over their oppressive king. John soon denounced the charter as having been signed under duress and was supported in his actions by the pope. Civil war again broke out and this time the rebel barons declared Louis, the son of Philippe of France, as their king. Louis was able to land at Sandwich in May 1216 and advance on London unopposed. John was forced to retreat. Although he retained much of the West Country, the rest of England was opposed to him. While campaigning in the Fens, he crossed the Wash heading towards Lincoln but misjudged the tides. His treasures and crown jewels were lost, and it must have seemed like his kingdom was lost with them. He soon caught a fever, not helped by his over-eating, which led to dysentery, and he died a few days later aged only forty-eight. There was some suggestion that he might have been poisoned. He was succeeded by his nine-year-old son HENRY III. Queen Isabella retired to her estates in France where she married the son of her original lover, Hugh de Lusignan, and lived a further thirty years.

History has judged John rather more harshly than he deserves. He was a man who believed the world owed him something and created enemies by refusing to take authority seriously. But there were many who remained intensely loyal to him, otherwise there could not have been a civil war, and he certainly cared for England and the English more than his brothers or his father. It was from him, and not from his brothers, that two of England's greatest kings, EDWARD I and EDWARD III, were directly descended.

[O9;SB19] **HENRY III**
King of England: 18 October 1216–16 November 1272. Crowned: Gloucester, 28
October 1216, and again at Westminster, 17 May 1220.
Titles: *king of England, duke of Normandy (until 1259) and Aquitaine.*
Born: *Winchester Castle, 1 October 1207;* **Died:** *Westminster, 16 November 1272, aged*
65. **Buried:** *Westminster Abbey.*
Married: *14 January 1236, at Canterbury Cathedral, Eleanor (c1223–1291), dau. of*
Raymond Berenger, count of Provence: 9 children.

Henry inherited the English throne at a difficult time. He was only nine years old.
His father, JOHN, had died suddenly leaving an England riven by civil war, with
London and the south-east controlled by Louis, the son of the French king. Louis
had been invited to become the English king because of the dissatisfaction of the
barons with John's inept and autocratic government. In fact John had not been as
bad as the barons liked to insist, but with his death the main cause of the strife
passed. It did not take long for the appointed regent, William Marshal, and the
justiciar, Hubert de Burgh, to defeat the rebel barons and to bribe Louis into
departing. Young Henry had been crowned in a rather makeshift ceremony at
Gloucester Cathedral, where the royal family had fled. Because John had lost the
crown jewels in the Wash during his Lincoln campaign, Henry was crowned with
his mother's own bracelet or torque. Henry was fortunate in having William
Marshal as his regent. William was probably the most respected man in England.
He was a brave and valiant knight, the epitome of chivalry, and had loyally served
HENRY II, RICHARD and John. He vowed to carry the young king head-high on his
shoulders rather than submit to French domination. By the time Marshal died in
1219, he had restored law and order to the kingdom. Young Henry was crowned
again, this time with new regalia, at Westminster Abbey in May 1220. He was still
only twelve, and would not assume authority for another seven years. With the
passing of Marshal, Henry became the pawn of two men whose self aggrandisement
and poor advice would cause Henry's long reign to be regarded as weak and
ineffectual. These men were Hubert de Burgh and Peter des Roches. De Burgh, who
became regent after 1219, was an extremely able and talented soldier, and had
served under both Richard and John. He continued the struggle against the barons
and foiled the plot to capture Henry in 1223. However, de Burgh's actions in France
were less successful, with Aquitaine being lost in 1224, though Gascony, the
southern part of Aquitaine, was regained the following year.

Henry assumed direct rule in 1227, although Hubert de Burgh remained the chief
justiciar until 1232. By then he and Henry had fallen out because Henry needed
money to continue his campaigns to recover his territories in France and the royal
treasury was almost empty. Henry accused the justiciar of using the money for his
own endeavours and de Burgh was imprisoned. The main architect of de Burgh's
fall was his rival, Peter des Roches, the bishop of Winchester who, along with
Stephen Segrave, now become the equivalent of prime ministers in England. Des
Roches was from Poitou, which was no longer in English hands, thus the barons
became unsettled when des Roches filled most of the offices of his state with his
fellow Poitevins. England was coming under foreign rule. Edmund Rich, the
archbishop of Canterbury, along with William Marshal's son, Richard (who had
been declared a traitor because of his opposition to des Roches's government) led a

delegation of barons to entreat Henry to expell the Poitevins. Henry capitulated in
1234. He not only expelled the Poitevins, but dismissed Roches and Segrave and
took full government, into his own hands. Henry had come to realise that he
ignored the authority and power of his barons at his peril. Even though Henry had
reaffirmed the terms of the Magna Carta, he did not particularly abide by them. He
was essentially thoughtless in his views of the barons, and rather than follow their
counsel he began to fill his court with others, mostly from France. This process was
accelerated after Henry's marriage to Eleanor, the daughter of Raymond Berenger,
count of Provence, in January 1236 and the marriage of Eleanor's sister, Margaret,
to Louis IX, the king of France. Although this further angered the English barons it
had a remarkable effect upon English culture. France was at this time at the height
of literary and architectural art. French literature, especially the chansons and
romances des gestes, spilled over into England, and the many chivalric romances,
including those which built the stories of king ARTHUR and his knights, came into
their final form during Henry's reign. It also saw a massive increase in the building
and restoration of churches, castles and other religious houses in the Gothic art
form. Many of our great historic castles date in their existing form from this period.
This includes Westminster Abbey which was sumptuously restored and improved
for the coronation of Eleanor of Provence in 1236.

The seeds of discontent that grew between Henry and his barons were now firmly
sown and regularly watered. Not only did Henry fail to recognize the rights and
privileges of the barons, turning instead to his own court favourites for their
counsel and advice and showering them with honours, but he continued to place
onerous tax obligations upon his barons, including the infamous scutage. The
barons might have tolerated the latter had the money gone toward successful
military campaigns, but this did not happen. Although Henry was not a good
soldier, having lost most of his lands in France, he was a good negotiator. He
established a strong alliance with Scotland in 1237 under the Treaty of York, which
more or less established the existing boundary between England and Scotland;
whilst the Treaty of Woodstock in 1247 established a similar arrangement with the
Welsh princes. The reduction in border skirmishes meant that the marcher lords
and northern barons could turn their attentions again to matters of state, and they

*From a contemporary
document*

did not like what they saw. In 1250 Henry took the Cross, determined to undertake a Crusade. This may have been a diversionary tactic to raise the spirit of his nobles. It did not work, however, because Henry never did embark upon his Crusade. Instead, influenced by the pope, he used the money raised for the Crusade to support the pope in his battle against Manfred, the usurping king of Sicily. In return the pope nominated Henry's young son, Edmund (known as Crouchback because of his deformity), as the king of Sicily, in 1254. The enterprise was, however, doomed and the pope eventually deprived Edmund of the title and bestowed it upon Charles of Anjou, Henry's brother-in-law, in 1266. In the meantime Henry had concluded the Treaty of Paris in 1259 with Louis IX of France, whereby he renounced his rights in Normandy, Maine and Anjou, but retained Gascony as a fiefdom subject to Louis. As with his father, Henry was perceived by the barons as an inept king who taxed them to the hilt, ignored their counsel, and wasted resources on unsuccessful foreign campaigns. The Sicilian campaign was the final straw. Opposition to Henry was voiced first by the Marshal of England, Roger Bigod, earl of Norfolk, at the Council of Westminster in 1258, which was followed rapidly by what became called the Mad Parliament at Oxford. There Henry was forced to acknowledge a new charter known as the Provisions of Oxford, where he grudgingly agreed that the barons were allowed to select one half of the King's council, instead of the King having absolute discretion. Amongst these barons was Simon de Montfort, Henry's brother-in-law, with whom Henry's relationship had soured over the years. Simon was almost as high-handed and authoritarian as Henry, having caused an uprising in Gascony during his governorship. In 1260, when Henry returned from concluding the Treaty of Paris, he denounced de Montfort and overturned the Provisions of Oxford, obtaining papal support for his actions. The events of fifty years earlier repeated themselves and England slid into the abyss of civil war. Arbitration over the application of the provisions was made by Louis of France, who found in favour of the king in 1264. Hostilities broke out in April. The baronial army was supported by the Welsh princes under LLYWELYN AP GRUFFYDD. Henry's supporters were initially successful, capturing Simon de Montfort's son (also called Simon) at Northampton in April 1264, but the elder de Montfort fought back and, in the Battle of Lewes on 14 May, defeated and captured Henry. The king was forced to call a parliament at which he acknowledged the barons' demands. During the course of the next year the barons, under de Montfort, succeeded in gaining the king's assent to most of their proposals. However, in July 1265, Henry's son, Edward (later EDWARD I), escaped from custody and raised an army against de Montfort. At the ensuing battle of Evesham on 4 August 1265, de Montfort and his supporters were savagely defeated and Henry returned to power. He now overturned all of the acts forced upon him by the barons in the previous year and decreed grievous punishments against the barons and others who had sided with the revolution. Having exacted his revenge Henry became more conciliatory, granting certain privileges to the barons under the Treaty of Marlborough in 1267, and also recognizing Llywelyn as prince of Wales under the Treaty of Montgomery that same year. Henry retained his executive role and it would not be true to say that he granted the first parliament as we know it today. Nevertheless, the concessions of his final years went some way toward establishing a council of peers.

Now aged sixty, Henry began to suffer from approaching senility. He left much of the government to his son Edward and devoted his time to his pursuit of the arts, including completing the rebuilding of Westminster Abbey, which remains the greatest legacy of his day. He was apparently griefstricken at the death of his brother Richard in April 1272, and dementia overcame him. He died seven months later. He had been king for a remarkable fifty-six years, the longest reign of any English monarch up to that time, although ten of those years were in his minority. Despite that length of reign, Henry III is rather a forgotten king. More people are more likely to recognize the name Simon de Montfort and know of his rebellion than to know anything about Henry III. This serves to demonstrate the weakness of Henry's character and his inability to govern strongly, but he was not all bad. He believed in his absolute right to rule, and was unsympathetic to his barons, but he was pious, loving (a devoted family man) and preferred to seek peace wherever possible rather than wage war. Although that may have damned him in the eyes of his barons, it encouraged a remarkable flowering of art and culture in England which was his true legacy.

Under his son, Edward I, the power of England grew to dominate the whole of Britain. This story is continued on page 587.

3. UNITING THE KINGDOM

This part covers the final union of Great Britain. At the start of the period Edward I had integrated Wales into England but was unable to enforce the same arrangement with Scotland. There nationality was rekindled under Robert the Bruce who not only regained the kingship but also obtained the pope's assent for the anointing of kings, meaning that Scotland had a sovereign status equal to England. Edward I had gained the kingdom of Man back from Scotland and he created this as a separate fiefdom. After some years it passed to the Stanley family who ruled it for three hundred years. Similarly in Scotland the remaining Western Isles were granted to the Macdonald family, who ruled them first as kings and then as lords of the Isles. The Orkneys remained in Norwegian hands until 1469 when their sovereignty was given to Scotland.

It is perhaps ironic that, despite the long running enmity between England and Scotland and England's attempts to gain sovereignty over its northern neighbour, in the end it should be the Scottish king, James VI, who became king of England, when the heirs of Henry VIII died without an English successor. It was perhaps a hollow victory for Scotland, however, as James and his successors were rapidly seduced by the English court and all but abandoned Scotland. When Charles I was executed the Scots lost their king as well for, though they crowned Charles II as successor, Oliver Cromwell soon drove him out of Britain and completed his own domination of Scotland. With the Restoration of the monarchy the two kingdoms were considered as one in all but name, and in 1707 the Act of Union formally brought Scotland, England and Wales together into a United Kingdom. Catholic supporters of James II (VII) in Scotland continued to recognize his heirs, James Stuart and Charles Stuart, as the rightful kings of Scotland but the rebellion of 1715 and 1745 failed to restore them to the throne.

This section follows the unification of Great Britain from the reigns of Edward I and Robert the Bruce down to the present day. It is divided into the following sections, continuing the section numbers from Parts One and Two.

The Scottish Kingdoms
- NA. Lords of the Isles
- NB. The Earldom of Orkney
- FC. Scotland

England and Wales
- NA. The Kingdom of Man
- O. England and Great Britain

NA. LORDS OF THE ISLES

Sovereignty over both the Hebrides and the Isle of Man passed from Norway to Scotland in 1266. Man remained in Scottish possession until claimed by Edward I of England in 1290. The Hebrides formed a separate fiefdom known as "the Isles." Alexander III of Scotland invested the title "Lord of the Isles" in the MacDonald family, who held it for the next two hundred years.

Ref.	Ruler	Reign	Died	Notes
continued from page 432				
NA41.	Angus *Mór* (the Great) MacDonald	c1266–96	1296	
NA42.	Alexander (I)	1296–99	1308?	deposed
NA43.	Angus *Og* (the Younger)	1299–1330	1330	
NA44.	John (I)	1330–87	1387	
NA45.	Donald II	1387–23	1423	
NA46.	Alexander II	1423–49	1449	
NA47.	John II	1449–93	1503	imprisoned
NA47a.	Angus (III)	1480–90	1490	usurped power; assassinated
NA47b.	Donald *Dubh*	1545	1545	unsuccessful claimant

Title and lands were forfeited to the Scottish crown in 1493.

[NA41] **ANGUS MOR (THE GREAT)** king of the Isles from at least 1266–96.
Angus was the head of the Clan MacDonald and son of DONALD the grandson of SOMERLED. Little is known of his early life. He may have been an infant when his father died sometime before the year 1230 and he may not have come into his title until the 1240s when the rampaging of his father's cousins DUNCAN and Dugald had declined. Certainly by 1260 he was ruling the lands of his father as lord of Islay. Although Angus remained nominally loyal to the king of Norway for his island territories, it was evident that his support could not be wholly counted upon. When Haakon IV of Norway sent his fleet to the Western Isles in 1263 to restate his title to the territories, Angus only joined Haakon's forces after his son was taken hostage by the Norse. Haakon's expedition failed and he died on Orkney that winter. Angus's loyalties were severely tested. When, in 1264, ALEXANDER III sent a force under the earl of Mar to regain the lands and invade Man, Angus submitted, but his young son was taken hostage again (this time by the Scots), and Angus had to sign a declaration that his lands would be forfeit if he again changed his loyalties. In 1266 the Treaty of Perth saw sovereignty in the Hebrides pass from Norway to Scotland, and Angus became a vassal of Alexander III. Angus appears to have obtained the title of king of the Isles from Alexander and although he owed fealty to the Scottish king, Angus retained a considerable degree of independence. He rapidly established himself as the senior lord amongst the Islanders and was recognized as such even by his cousins from the more senior descent of Somerled, including EWEN MacDougall and Alan MacRory. By the time he died in 1296 he was known as Angus *Mór*, or the Great. His descendants would hold the title of lord of the Isles for the next two hundred years.

[NA42] **ALEXANDER (I)** king of the Isles, 1296–9.
He was the elder son of ANGUS MOR and came into his title just at the time of the abdication of JOHN Balliol. Scotland was thrust into the War of Independence.

39. The Danish and Norse Kingdoms (8) – Lords of the Isles

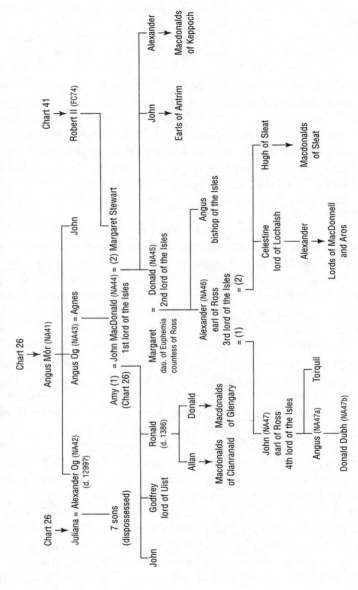

Alexander remained loyal to Balliol and thus to the English king EDWARD I, who vested Alexander with the office of administrator of the Western Isles. He was soon opposed by his fellow Islanders, including his brother ANGUS OG, and Alexander was driven out of the islands in 1299. His fate is uncertain though the *Irish Annals* suggest that he was killed in the battle. Others have suggested that he forfeited all his possessions and was imprisoned in Dundonald Castle, where he died around 1308. The former fate is the more likely.

[NA43] **ANGUS OG (*THE YOUNGER*)** king of the Isles, 1299–1330.
He was the younger brother of ALEXANDER (I) who was deposed because he favoured the English vassal king JOHN Balliol. Angus was elected the head of the Clan MacDonald and thereby king of the Isles. He was a strong supporter of ROBERT the Bruce and gave the king refuge during his flight from the English forces in 1306. Once Robert was established as king he confirmed Angus in his title as king of the Isles and gave him domain over all the southern Hebrides, a superior title to his cousins, the Clan MacDougall, who had supported the cause of Balliol. It was the start of the MacDonalds' almost total domination of the western Highlands.

[NA44] **JOHN (I)** lord of the Isles, 1330–87.
From his father, ANGUS OG, John inherited the islands of the southern Hebrides, primarily Mull and Islay, and the mainland territories of Kintyre and Argyll. Soon after his accession he further gained by charter from DAVID II the outer islands of Lewis, Harris, Skye and Colonsay. As a final coup he married Amy, the daughter of Roderick MacRory, and thereby inherited the lands of Garmoran and the remaining Isles. Thus by about the year 1340 he was lord of all of the Hebrides. John did not remain especially loyal to David, switching his support between David and EDWARD Balliol as he saw fit, until he realised that Balliol was prepared to sign away his independence and become a vassal to EDWARD III. At that point John switched sides, entering the independence party of the High Steward, Robert (the future ROBERT II). When John's first wife died he married Robert's daughter Margaret in 1350. Throughout this period, John's power increased. By 1366, when David levied a tax to help pay his ransom to the English king, the northern barons rebelled and John held out the longest. It required a special treaty at Inverness in 1369 for John to renew his support to David, and even then it was nominal. It was not until the death of David and the accession of Robert that John was able wholeheartedly to resume his loyalty to the Scottish crown, and from that point ceased using the title king of the Isles. Even so, Robert was wary of John's power and ensured that John entered into a series of agreements which fragmented future title in his lands between John's children by his two marriages, so that in future the two factions might be set against each other rather than against the throne. The western portion, which consisted of the Hebrides, Robert vested back to the children of his daughter Margaret as lords of the Isles.

[NA45] **DONALD (II)** lord of the Isles, 1387–1423.
The son of JOHN and grandson of ROBERT II of Scotland, Donald succeeded to the powerful lordship of the Isles established by his father's negotiations with the Scottish king. Although Donald did not use the title king, he was in many ways autonomous, choosing to offer such allegiance as he might as much to the English

king as to the Scottish or any other monarch. He presided from his own court at Eilean and issued his own judgements and decrees. On the mainland the power in the Scottish Highlands was vested in the earls of Ross. The earl at the time, since his marriage to Euphemia Ross in 1382, was Alexander, the son of ROBERT II popularly known as the Wolf of Badenoch. Between them Alexander and Donald commanded power in most of northern Scotland. Donald had married Mary, the daughter of Euphemia Ross by her first marriage. Mary was styled countess of Ross and, after Alexander's death in 1406, Donald claimed title to the earldom of Ross. This was initially denied him so, in 1411, Donald raised an army of some ten thousand men and marched across northern Scotland. He met little resistance en route until he reached the village of Harlaw in Aberdeenshire, in July 1411, where his army was opposed by that of Alexander Stewart, earl of Mar. There his force was checked. It could have been a decisive battle. Had he won, Donald might well have declared himself independent of the Scottish crown. But, unable to defeat Mar, Donald retreated and bided his time before resuming the conflict in the following summer. A rather ragged conflict continued sporadically until eventually Donald made peace with ROBERT STEWART, the regent. This conflict, whilst it demonstrated the support and comparative independence of the lords of the Isles, also dented their authority. They were seen as a savage and untamed tribe separate from the true Scots. Nevertheless, although their wick may have been trimmed, the candle still glowed and Donald's successors ALEXANDER and JOHN would continue to press the Scottish king.

[NA46] **ALEXANDER II** lord of the Isles, 1423–7 May 1449.
Through his mother Alexander inherited the earldom of Ross, as well as the lordship of the Isles from his father, DONALD (II). This made Alexander the most powerful lord in the Highlands. However he met his match in the new king of Scotland, JAMES I, who was as wily as he was intelligent. James summoned a parliament at Inverness in 1428 and promptly arrested fifty of the Highland lords as they assembled. Several he executed and the rest he forced into submission. Believing he had delivered a sufficient message, he set the others free, but Alexander immediately sought revenge and went on a rampage of wild savagery across the north of Scotland, culminating in the destruction of Inverness. James's army eventually captured Alexander and humbled him at court, after which he was cast into the dungeons of Tantallon Castle. The Highlanders did not settle, however, and war raged for a further two years until James's forces defeated the rebels. Eventually, in 1435, Alexander was released, pardoned and his titles restored to him. He lived in continued hatred of the king, but offered no further direct opposition. His son, JOHN (II), who succeeded him, revived the old hostilities.

[NA47] **JOHN II** lord of the Isles, 7 May 1449–May 1493.
[NA47a] **ANGUS OG**, self-proclaimed lord of the Isles, 1480–90.
[NA47b] **DONALD DUBH (THE BLACK)** claimed title of lord of the Isles, 1545.
John was as vehemently opposed to the kings of Scotland as his forebears. Since he inherited both titles of the earl of Ross and lord of the Isles he had considerable power and declared himself independent of the crown. In 1450, he entered into an alliance with the earl of Douglas and earl of Crawford, both of whom had cause to hate the Scottish king, JAMES II. He had humiliated John's father, and assisted in the

murder of the previous earl of Douglas. James sought to negotiate with William Douglas, but this ended in an argument in February 1452 when the king murdered the earl. Soon after Crawford was defeated and John, conscious of the power against him, decided to lay low for a while, though he continued to support James, the new earl of Douglas, in his war against the king. Douglas was defeated and fled to England, where he later found favour with the new king EDWARD IV. Douglas and John of the Isles entered into an agreement with Edward in February 1462. It is known as the Treaty of Westminster-Ardtornish (Ardtornish being one of the John's castles on the Sound of Mull). Under this treaty, James Douglas and John MacDonald became liegemen of the English king and would support him in his battle against the Scots. Should Edward conquer Scotland, then the land north of the Forth would be divided between John and Douglas. Bolstered by Edward's support, John declared himself independent of the Scottish crown, whose new king, JAMES III, was only nine. John effectively became king of Scotland north of the Clyde. The Scottish crown was in turmoil for a while, but it was the queen mother who realised that if Scotland came to terms with Edward IV, then the Westminster-Ardtornish treaty would be neutralised. It took two years of negotiation and wrangling before this happened, but by August 1464 John was forced to restore his allegiance to James III. The relationship between the Highlands and the Scottish king, however, did not improve and by 1473 John was back in open revolt. This time, however, he did not receive the support he hoped for and, in 1475, he was declared a traitor, his lands forfeited, and an army sent to capture him. It was only through the intervention of the earl of Argyll that John kept his life and was reinstated as lord of the Isles in 1476, though this was now as a peer of the Scottish parliament and not as an independent earl. He did however lose his other titles, including the earldom of Ross.

John's son, Angus, rebelled against this arrangement. In 1480, he usurped his father's authority, raised an army of Highlanders, and set off on a rampage across Scotland. He captured Inverness, where he declared himself king of the Isles. An army was sent against him, and the various encounters resulted in considerable bloodshed to the point where Angus was in retreat and only his father, John, retained a force in pursuit. Father and son met on the Ardnamurchan peninsula where there ensued the battle of Bloody Bay. John was defeated and Angus declared himself head of the Clan and ruler of the Isles. John retired to one of his castles and Angus reigned supreme amongst the Isles for the next few years. In 1490, while leading an army against Inverness, Angus was murdered by an Irish harper. John supported his nephew, Alexander, in his claim on the lordship, and in Alexander's efforts to regain the earldom of Ross. In 1491 and 1492 Alexander marched north to capture Inverness, and to plunder lands in Cromarty and Ross before being injured in battle and captured. It was as a result of this rebellion that JAMES IV abolished the title of lord of the Isles in 1493 and forefeited all lands to the Crown. John, now in his late sixties, retired to the Stewart court in Holyrood, and later to the abbey at Paisley, where he died in 1498. He was buried at Scone. His grandson, Donald, known as Donald *the Black* or Donald *Dubh*, had been held captive at Inchconnell Castle since his father's murder in 1490. In 1501 he was rescued by the MacDonalds and placed under the protection of his uncle Lord Torquil Macleod of Lewis. By 1503 Donald and his supporters were ready to lead a new insurrection and war broke out in the Highlands. It took two years before James IV was able to subdue the rebellion. Donald was recaptured in 1505 and imprisoned at Edinburgh Castle, where he was to remain for forty years. He succeeded in escaping in 1543 and rallied the support of the island chiefs. At a Council of the Isles held in 1545, Donald declared his allegiance to the king of England, HENRY VIII, and visited the English court to pay his allegiance. Unfortunately for Donald, he caught a fever on his return and died at Drogheda in Ireland. With him died the independent lordship of the Isles.

NB.ORKNEY (PART 2) *(continued from page 440)*

The Isles of Orkney remained a Danish/Norse possession until 1469, even though by the 1230s the earl was of Scottish descent. The earl continued to pay his homage to the Scandinavian king until the islands passed to Scotland as part of the dowry when James III married Margaret of Denmark.

Ref.	Ruler	Born	Reign	Died	Notes
House of Angus					
NB34. Magnus II			1231–9	1239	
NB35. Gilbert			1239–56	1256	
NB36. Magnus III			1256–73	1273	
NB37. Magnus IV			1276–84	1284	
NB38. John II		c1259	1284–1311	1311	
NB39. Magnus V			1311–c29	c1329	
NB40. Malise			c1329–?53	?1353	
NB41. Erengisl			1353–60	1392	may have lost the title in 1357

The title was in dispute after 1360. It was claimed by Erengisl's nephew Alexander de l'Arde but was removed from him and confirmed upon Henry St. Clair in 1363, though it was not formally granted until 1379. Although the islands remained nominally Norwegian until 1469, the loyalty of the earls was increasingly to the Scottish king.

Ref.	Ruler	Born	Reign	Died	Notes
House of St. Clair					
NB42. Henry		1345	1379–1400	1400	murdered; noted navigator who also ruled the Faeroes and Greenland; may have colonized north-eastern America in 1398
NB43. Henry		c1375	1400–20	1420	died of the plague
NB44. William		c1404	1420–71	1480	resigned earldom to the Scottish crown

[NB34] **MAGNUS II** earl of Orkney 1231–39.

Though he succeeded JOHN (I), their family relationship is unclear. Magnus was the son of the 4th earl of Angus, and it has been presumed that his mother was one of the sisters of HARALD III, though this is conjectural. It was during his earlship that the relationship between the kings of Scotland and Norway began to heat up over the possession of the Western and Northern Isles. Magnus seems to have kept a remarkably low profile, typical of the attitude of the Orcadians at this time who

40. The Danish and Norse Kingdoms (9) – Earls of Orkney (3)

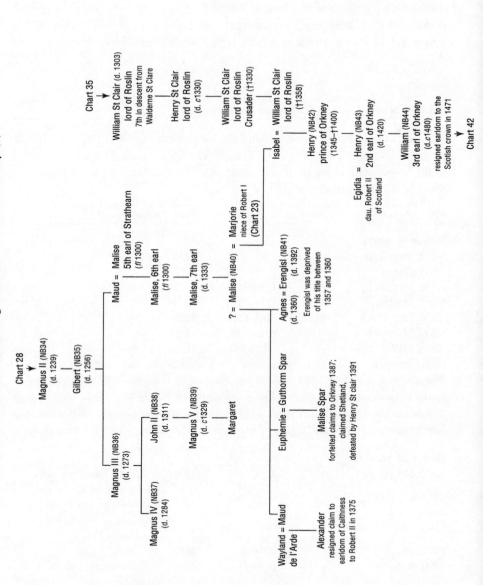

Chart 28 →

Magnus II (NB34)
(d. 1239)

Gilbert (NB35)
(d. 1256)

Magnus III (NB36)
(d. 1273)

Magnus IV (NB37)
(d. 1284)

John II (NB38)
(d. 1311)

Magnus V (NB39)
(d. c1329)

Margaret

Maud = Malise
5th earl of Strathearn
(fl 1300)

Malise, 6th earl
(fl 1300)

Malise, 7th earl
(d. 1333)

? = Malise (NB40) = Marjorie
niece of Robert I
(Chart 23)

Agnes = Erengisl (NB41)
(d. 1360)   (d. 1392)
Erengisl was deprived
of his title between
1357 and 1360

Euphemie = Guthorm Spar

Malise Spar
forfeited claims to Orkney 1387;
claimed Shetland,
defeated by Henry St clair 1391

Wayland = Maud
de l'Arde

Alexander
resigned claim to
earldom of Caithness
to Robert II in 1375

Chart 35 →

William St Clair (d. 1303)
lord of Roslin
7th in descent from
Walderne St Clare

Henry St Clair
lord of Roslin
(d. c1330)

William St Clair
lord of Roslin
Crusader (†1330)

Isabel = William St Clair
lord of Roslin
(†1358)

Henry (NB42)
prince of Orkney
(1345–†1400)

Egidia = Henry (NB43)
dau. Robert II 2nd earl of Orkney
of Scotland   (d. 1420)

William (NB44)
3rd earl of Orkney
(d.c1480)
resigned earldom to the
Scottish crown in 1471

Chart 42 →

were fiercely independent and tried not to get involved in external affairs. Magnus was probably about fifty at the time he inherited the earldom and so was approaching sixty when he died.

[NB35] **GILBERT** earl of Orkney, 1239–56.
The son of MAGNUS II. Little is recorded of his tenure. At this period the power of the crown in Scotland had increased and Gilbert's authority, inasmuch as it applied to his earldom of Caithness, was greatly reduced. Haakon IV of Norway still had pretensions over the Scottish Isles, but this came to a head in the time of Gilbert's successor, MAGNUS III.

[NB36] **MAGNUS III** earl of Orkney 1256–73.
It was during Magnus's earlship that the relationship between the kings of Scotland and Norway reached breaking-point over sovereignty of the Hebrides. When ALEXANDER III came of age in 1261 he undertook a series of actions guaranteed to provoke Haakon IV into action. The result was Haakon's punitive expedition of 1263. Magnus III was summoned to Bergen and placed in charge of a longship. The fleet sailed to Britain stopping first at Shetland and Orkney to gather forces. Much to Haakon's dismay, the men of Orkney refused to take part in the expedition and Magnus stayed behind with them when Haakon sailed on to the Hebrides and the eventual battle of Largs. In fact it was the dispute in Orkney that delayed Haakon's fleet and gave the advantage to the Scots. In the end the expedition was indecisive with both sides claiming levels of victory, but it was a major disappointment for Haakon. The fleet returned to Orkney when Haakon decided to winter, but he died of an illness that December. It had become evident that the inhabitants of the Western Isles, particularly the southern Hebrides, now owed their allegiance to Scotland, not Norway, and that the Orcadians themselves, whilst still acknowledging the sovereignty of Norway, were also strongly independent. Earl Magnus nevertheless accompanied the body of his king back to Norway. The negotiations with the new Norwegian king, Magnus VI, were initiated from Orkney and stretched over three years before the Treaty of Perth (1266), which still recognized Norwegian sovereignty over Orkney and Shetland, but returned the Hebrides to Scotland. Nothing more is known of Magnus's earlship, which now benefited from the general peace that reigned about Alexander's kingdom. He was eventually succeeded by his son MAGNUS IV.

[NB37] **MAGNUS IV** earl of Orkney 1276–84.
Evidently the new king of Norway, Magnus VI, had reservations about investing the earlship in the family of Magnus following their desertion from Haakon's expedition of 1263. It was three years before Magnus VI made his decision and he made sure that the new earl swore a strong fealty for the privilege. He was young, possibly no more than twenty, and the king may have waited until Magnus reached his majority before confirming the earlship. He remained earl for only eight years and may have died of an illness or accident. His last known official act was as a signatory to the declaration of 5 February 1284 that he and his fellow magnates would support the succession of MARGARET, Maid of Norway, to the Scottish throne in the absence of other male heirs. He was succeeded by his brother JOHN II.

[NB38] **JOHN II** earl of Orkney 1284–1312.

It was during his earlship that the child queen of Scotland, MARGARET, died near the Orkneys when her ship foundered on its way from Norway, in September 1290. Little else is recorded of his tenure except that he swore fealty to the new Scottish king, JOHN, and subsequently to EDWARD I of England. He was succeeded by his son, MAGNUS V.

[NB39] **MAGNUS V** earl of Orkney 1311–c29.

By the time of Magnus his authority was severely curbed by the growing power of the Scottish and English kings. His role, like that of his father and his successors, was increasingly one of support for the Scottish king, and his fealty to Norway, whilst still present, became increasingly distant. His precise date of death is not known and was sometime during the late 1320s. He left no son and was succeeded by a distant cousin, MALISE.

[NB40] **MALISE** earl of Orkney, c1329–?53.

He succeeded his distant cousin MAGNUS V, both of whom claimed descent from Earl GILBERT. He was the son of the earl of Strathearn and his life revolved more around that responsibility than his Orcadian inheritance. He was involved in the intrigue between the courts of England and Scotland and was twice accused of treason. By his reign the earldom had lost any independence it once held and, though still subject to the kings of Norway, was for all practical purposes part of Scotland. The exact date of Malise's death is not known but was probably around 1353. The earldom passed to his son-in-law, ERENGISL.

[NB41] **ERENGISL** earl of Orkney, 1353–?60. *Died* 1392.

The last non-Scottish earl of Orkney. He was the husband of Agnes, daughter of MALISE, though his own descent was Swedish. He had problems exercising any authority over the earldom, since he inherited it via his wife who died childless in 1360. Already by then his right to the title had been challenged by the king of Norway. Erengisl's title remained in dispute until his death and although he continued to style himself as earl throughout his life, he was effectively without authority from possibly as early as 1355, certainly from 1360, and definitively from 1379. In that year a new earl of Orkney was created. This was Henry ST CLAIR, the son of Malise's youngest daughter, Isabel. She had married William St Clair, the laird of Rosslyn. With Henry's investiture Orkney became ruled by a Scottish lord and the islands, for all practical purposes, became answerable to the Scottish crown even though they were still part of the possessions of Norway and remained so until 1470.

[NB42] **HENRY ST. CLAIR** earl of Orkney, 1379–1400. *Born* 1345.

The St. Clair family were lords of Roslin (or Rosslyn) in Midlothian. They were descended from Mauger, the uncle of WILLIAM THE CONQUEROR, and became one of the premier Scottish families. William St. Clair, 6th lord Roslin (d. 1303), was guardian of ALEXANDER III and became one of the Scottish envoys to France. His son, Henry (d. c1330), was the commander of the Knights Templar at the battle of Bannockburn. His son, William, was one of those charged with taking the heart of ROBERT I to the Holy Land – he and Sir James Douglas were killed when attacked by Moors in Andalusia. His son, also called William, married Isabel, daughter of

MALISE, the last hereditary earl of Orkney. After Malise's death, in about 1353, the title fell into dispute. It was claimed jointly by Malise's son-in-law ERENGISL, and two grandsons Alexander de l'Arde and Malise Spar. St Clair's own son, Henry, was only eight. Although Erengisl was invested with the title, he was soon deprived of it because of an alleged plot against the Norwegian crown. Alexander de l'Arde claimed the title in 1357 or 1358, in which year Henry's father was killed fighting with the Teutonic Knights in Lithuania.

It was not until 1363, when Henry came of age, that he staked his claim for the earldom of Orkney. He was confirmed in his right as earl of Orkney that year, when he attended the court of King Haakon VI of Norway upon the occasion of Haakon's marriage to Margaret of Denmark. However, before being fully invested with the title, Henry had to prove his loyalty to Norway. He was, after all, of a Scottish family, albeit descended from the Normans, and related to the Stewart dynasty. Indeed, after his return from the Crusades in 1366, Henry was appointed Lord Chief Justice of Scotland and Admiral. It was not until 1379, when Henry agreed to resign the earldom of Caithness, which had hitherto been closely associated with the Orkney earldom, that Haakon invested Henry with full sovereign powers in Orkney second only to the king himself. Henry became, in effect, prince of Orkney. He had almost absolute power amongst the islands and the northern seas. He built a massive castle and port at Kirkwall to harbour his fleet. He defeated and killed his cousin and rival, Malise Spar, who laid claim to the Shetlands in 1391. Henry, with approval from his new monarch, Queen Margaret of Norway, exerted his rule over Shetland and over the more northerly Faeroe Islands. By 1394 he had extended this authority to colonies in Greenland, and there is also strong evidence that in 1398 he financed and led an expedition which established Scottish colonies in Labrador and Newfoundland. This would make Henry the first European prince to rule territory in the New World, a full century before Columbus's expedition. Henry was killed upon his return to Orkney during a battle against English mercenaries and before he had time to provide details of his adventures to the west. He was succeeded by his son Henry.

[NB43] **HENRY** 2nd earl of Orkney, 1400–20.
Henry had a no less eventful life than his father, if somewhat less productive. His date of birth is not known but he was probably into his thirties when his father was murdered. It is not known whether Henry accompanied his father on his North American adventure, but as Henry inherited his father's position as Admiral of the Seas, he was almost certainly a sailor and navigator of equal competence. He was possibly less able as a soldier. He was captured at the battle of Homildon Hill in September 1402 and remained a prisoner for some while. Soon after his release he was charged with escorting the young prince James (JAMES I) to France for safekeeping in April 1406. James, who was only eleven, was unused to sea journeys and requested that they land. The ship and occupants were captured and Henry spent several more years in prison. Henry was released several times under safe conduct and eventually returned to Scotland helping in defence of the lands against the English onslaught. Henry also fought in France, on the side of the French, and was present at their defeat at Agincourt (1415). There is little doubt that Henry saw his allegiance first to the Scottish crown and did little to renew his loyalties to the

Norwegian crown, even though he held his title as a vassal to that authority. Henry died of the plague in 1420, probably aged about fifty. He was succeeded by his son.

[NB44] **WILLIAM** 3rd earl of Orkney, 1434–71. *Born c1404. Died* 1480.

William was only sixteen when his father died and thus not of an age to succeed to the earldom. King Erik of Norway used this as an opportunity to re-exert his authority in the Orkneys, and he appointed several governors to the islands from amongst the Sinclair family (as they now began to spell their name). It was not until 1434 that Erik invested William with the full title, though it was evident that William saw his loyalties first to the Scottish kings JAMES I and JAMES II. He was made Chancellor of Scotland and was the Scottish ambassador to France on several occasions. He was rewarded with the reinstatement of the earldom of Caithness in 1455 and established large estates throughout northern Scotland. The best was at his ancestral home at Roslin in Midlothian, where he undertook extensive rebuilding works from 1446 on. Sir William became the guardian of the Holy Relics of Scotland. In 1468 the marriage of JAMES III with Margaret of Denmark brought Orkney and Shetland to Scotland as part of the dowry. In 1471 William was asked to resign the earldom of Orkney and was given lands in Fife in compensation. William was more than content with this arrangement as the bulk of his revenues came from lands outside Orkney, and his main home was at Roslin. He settled there for the remaining nine years of his life, expending most of his resources on the completion of the castle.

FC. SCOTLAND – The Bruces and Stewarts *(continued from page 412)*

After two interregna, during which time Edward I sought to gain control over Scotland, Robert the Bruce declared himself king of Scotland, soundly defeated the English at Bannockburn and obtained sovereign status for Scotland. His descendants ruled Scotland for the next three hundred years until James VI became James I of England and paved the way for the final union of Scotland and England.

Ref.	Ruler	Born	Reign	Died	Notes
continued from page 383					
House of Bruce					
FC71.	Robert (I) the Bruce	1274	1306–29	1329	
FC72.	David II	1324	1329–32		deposed by Edward Balliol
			1332–3		restored but again deposed
			1336–71	1371	restored, most of 1334–1357 in captivity in England
FC73.	Edward (Balliol)	c1282	Aug–Dec 1332		deposed and expelled
			1333–4		restored but again deposed
			1335–6	c1364	restored and deposed again
House of Stewart					
FC74.	Robert II	1316	1371–90	1390	
FC75.	Robert III	c1337	1390–1406	1406	

Lieutenant of the Realm: David, duke of Rothesay (his son), 1398–1401.

FC76.	James (I)	1394	1406–37	1437	captive in England 1406–24; assassinated

Governor during imprisonment: Robert, duke of Albany, 1406–20; Murdoch, duke of Albany, 1420–4.

FC77.	James II	1430	1437–60	1460	killed during siege of Roxburgh

Regents during infancy: Joan (his mother), 1437–9; *Lieutenant:* Alexander Livingston, 1439–49.

FC78.	James III	1452	1460–88	1488	assassinated

Regents during infancy: Mary (his mother), 1460–3; Bishop James Kennedy, 1463–5; Alexander Boyd, 1466–9.

FC79.	James IV	1473	1488–1513	1513	killed in battle
FC80.	James V	1512	1513–42	1542	

Regents during infancy: Margaret (his mother), 1513–4; John, duke of Albany, governor, 1515–24; James, earl of Arran, chancellor, 1524–5; Archibald, earl of Angus, governor, 1525–8.

FC81.	Mary	1542	1542–67	1587	assumed authority in 1561; abdicated, imprisoned and executed

Regents during infancy: James, earl of Arran as governor, 1542–54; Mary, the queen mother, 1554–60.

FC82.	James VI	1566	1567–1625	1625	assumed authority 1580; became James I of England (*see* O26)

Regents during infancy: James, earl of Moray, 1567–70; Matthew, earl of Lennox, 1570–1; John, earl of Mar, 1571–2; James, earl of Morton, 1572–80.

FC83.	Charles (I)	1600	1625–49	1649	deposed and executed; also king of England (*see* O27)

Council of State existed 14 Feb 1649–16 Dec 1653, during which period the Commonwealth of England was not recognized and Charles II was elected king.

FC84.	Charles II	1630	1650–85	1685	also king of England (O28)
FC85.	James VII	1633	1685–8	1701	deposed; see James II of England (O29)

Interregnum from Dec 1688–Feb 1689 when William and Mary were recognized as monarchs.

FC86.	William II	1650	1689–1702	1702	also William III of England (O30); ruled jointly with Mary II
FC87.	Mary II	1662	1689–94	1694	also Queen of England (O31); ruled jointly with William III
FC88.	Anne	1665	1702–14	1714	

With the Act of Union in 1707, Scotland and England were formerly united as Great Britain

Stewart Pretenders

FC89.	James (VIII) the Old Pretender	1688	1701–16	1766	never reigned but was acknowledged rightful heir by the Jacobites; see page 671
FC90.	Charles (III) the Young Pretender	1720	1745–6	1788	acknowledged by a few supporters; see page 676
FC91.	Henry (IX)	1725	1788–1807	1807	never seriously pursued the claim; see page 681

41. Scotland (8) – Bruce to Stewart

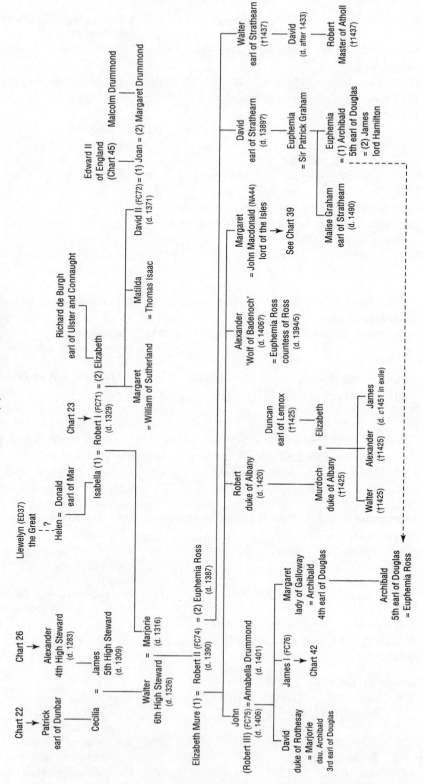

[FC71] **ROBERT (I)** *THE BRUCE*
Ruled 25 March 1306–7 June 1329. Crowned: Scone Abbey, 27 March 1306.
Titles: *king of Scotland; earl of Carrick (from 1292), lord of Annandale (from 1304).*
Born: *Turnberry Castle, 11 July 1274.* **Died**: *Cardross Castle, Dumbarton, 7 June 1329, aged 54.* **Buried**: *Dunfermline Abbey (though his heart was buried at Melrose Abbey).*
Married: *(1) c1295, Isabella, dau. Donald, earl of Mar: 1 child; (2) c1302, Elizabeth (d. 1327), dau. Robert de Burgh, earl of Ulster and Connaught: 4 children.*

The ancestor of Robert the Bruce was a Norman knight, also called Robert, who accompanied William the Conqueror on his invasion in 1066. This Robert de Bruis, who took his name from his family estates at Bruis near Cherbourg, received extensive lands in Yorkshire. His son, also called Robert, was made lord of Annandale by DAVID I of Scotland in 1124. This Robert's grandson, another Robert, married David's great-granddaughter Isabel in 1220. Their son, Robert le Brus (1210–1295) was at one time heir to the throne and competitor for the crown of Scotland against JOHN Balliol in 1292. His son, Robert (1243–1304) was the father of the famous Robert the Bruce, who succeeded him as lord of Annandale in 1304.

Robert had originally sworn fealty to EDWARD I of Scotland in 1296, when he inherited the title of Earl of Carrick. His father had sought the Scottish crown from Edward, but had been refused. Robert remained loyal to Edward until 1297, when he supported the revolt of WILLIAM WALLACE. After Wallace's defeat in 1298, Edward laid waste to Robert's lands. Nevertheless he made his peace with Edward and in 1299 Robert was made one of the four regents of Scotland. Robert's pride made it difficult for him to work alongside his co-regent John Comyn, the son of another competitor of 1292 and a descendant of DUNCAN III, but they needed to work together. In 1305 Edward had executed Wallace and was now preparing an ordinance for the governance of Scotland. Its independence would soon be a thing of the past. In February 1306 Bruce and Comyn met at Greyfriars church in Dumfries, endeavouring to resolve their rival claims to the throne and to plan a course of action against Edward. An argument followed in which Robert stabbed Comyn, who subsequently died. Robert knew he would be excommunicated and would thereby lose his right to the throne. Rather than flee, he acted on impulse and hurriedly gathered his supporters together and within six weeks had crowned himself king of Scotland. His support was far from complete. There were many who regarded him as a young hothead, but there were enough to rally round him as a symbol of Scottish kingship. Robert had been present at the execution of William Wallace and knew what would happen if he failed. He was therefore determined to succeed, regardless of the odds.

At first luck went against him. He was defeated by the earl of Pembroke who captured Perth and drove Bruce west into Atholl. Bruce was defeated again soon after by Comyn's uncle, Macdougal of Loarn, who forced Bruce further west, until he was driven out of Scotland and sought refuge on the Isle of Rathlin off the Irish coast. It is at this time that the memorable legend arose of Bruce hiding in a cave and, being inspired by a spider defiantly re-weaving its web against the weather, to resolve "if at first you don't succeed, try, try again."

Robert rallied. Early in 1307 he surprised the English at Carrick, who had garrisoned his own castle of Turnberry, and later that year defeated Pembroke at

Loudon Hill. Edward I marched against Bruce but died before reaching Scotland. The campaign was prematurely abandoned by his son, EDWARD II, and Bruce went from strength to strength. Over the next six years the English garrisons were driven out of Scotland. By 1314 only two castles remained in English hands: Berwick and Stirling. The governor of Stirling promised to hand over the castle unless the English sent reinforcements by 24 June. This galvanised Edward II into belated action. His forces arrived and engaged the Scottish at Bannockburn on 24 June 1314. This was one of the Scot's greatest victories. Edward's force of between 20,000 and 100,000 men were totally defeated by Robert's army of half its number.

Although skirmishes continued for the next decade, Robert's victory allowed a degree of respite in the hostilities. Robert even had time to support his brother, Edward, who had been made high king of Ireland in May 1316, but who was killed at the Battle of Dundall in October 1318. Edward Bruce was, for a time, recognized as Robert's heir. One might imagine the possibilities had Scotland's king also been high king of Ireland. After Edward's death the succession passed to Robert's infant grandson, the child of his daughter Marjorie and Walter, the steward of Scotland. Although this child later ruled as ROBERT II, Robert the Bruce eventually sired his own heir, DAVID II.

Robert still needed to make his peace with the pope, who had excommunicated him. By 1320 the Scots had compiled what became known as the Declaration of Arbroath, which not only established the sovereignty of Scotland but defined Robert's right to the throne. It has been described as "the most remarkable statement of nationalism in medieval Europe." It took Pope John XXII eight years to reach a decision. He eventually lifted his excommunication in 1328 and recognized Robert's right to the kingship. The same year saw the Treaty of Northampton between Robert and EDWARD III of England, which also recognized the independence of Scotland.

In the intervening years when not fighting, Robert had done his best to bring law and order back to a country rent by civil unrest. He instigated a major rebuilding programme and sought to re-establish trade. Scotland at last began to be restored. In early 1329 Robert prepared to set off for the Holy Land, but he died of leprosy before leaving Scotland. Although he was buried at Dunfermline, his heart was carried on the Crusade to atone for his sins and was eventually returned to Scotland and interred at Melrose Abbey. The young hothead and turncoat had become the saviour of Scotland and was long after remembered as "Good King Robert".

[FC72] DAVID II

Ruled 7 June 1329–August 1332 (deposed); restored 16 December 1332–March 1333 (deposed); restored 1336–22 February 1371. Crowned: Scone Abbey, 24 November 1331.

Born: Dunfermline Palace, 5 March 1324. Died: Edinburgh Castle, 22 February 1371, aged 46. Buried: Holyrood Abbey.

Married: (1) 17 July 1328, at Berwick, Joanna (1321–62), dau Edward II of England: no children; (2) 13 (?) February 1364, at Inchmahome Priory, Aberfoyle, Margaret (d. 1375), dau. Sir Malcolm Drummond; divorced 20 March 1370: no children.

David was the only son of ROBERT (I), the Bruce, and was only five when his father died. He had already been married to Joanna, the sister of EDWARD III of England, since July 1328. He was four, she was seven. Although they remained married for thirty-four years, they had no children and it was, apparently, a loveless marriage. This was symbolic of David's early life where, for much of the time, he was a puppet controlled by other forces. This made him a rather dissolute youth who took some while to live up to the expectations others had of him. Of particular significance, though, was David's coronation. Although he was only seven, and probably not that aware of the import, he was the first king of Scotland to be anointed with the symbol of papal approval, and to be crowned jointly with his wife. Nevertheless, it did him little good. Nine months later his forces were defeated by those of EDWARD Balliol (son of JOHN) who, supported by Edward III, had sought to regain what he believed was his rightful inheritance. Although Edward was crowned in September 1332, he was deposed three months later and David was restored. The overthrow of Balliol allowed Edward III to act. He invaded Scotland, defeating all opposition at Halidon Hill on 19 July 1333. At this stage David was taken for safety to the court of Philippe VI of France. Although he was restored to the throne in 1336, he remained in exile in France until it was felt safe for his return to Scotland in 1341, when he was seventeen.

An uneasy peace ensured for the next five years. By then the French were at war with the English and asked the Scots for assistance. David invaded England but was defeated by the forces of Archbishop William de la Zouche at Neville's Cross, near Durham, on 17 October 1346. David fought valiantly but was captured and held prisoner in England for the next eleven years. His nephew, ROBERT, remained steward of Scotland during this period when, to all intents and purposes, Scotland was subservient to England. Nevertheless, Edward's war with France meant his attention was elsewhere and the governance of Scotland continued unhindered. David was eventually released in 1357 under the terms of the Treaty of Berwick, whereby David had to pay Edward the staggering sum of 100,000 merks (about £67,000) in ten equal instalments. This was never fully paid, but David paid occasional instalments as and when it was necessary to stave off the ambitious Edward. David even proposed that Edward's second son, Lionel, should succeed him as king of Scotland, should David die childless. The Scottish Parliament rejected this proposal, and the death of Lionel in 1368 brought an end to the idea, but it was another factor in David's attempts to hold Edward at bay. Nevertheless whenever David sought to impose a tax to raise the instalments for the ransom he was met with outright rebellion, particularly from JOHN, the lord of the Isles. It required considerable negotiation, mostly by Robert the Steward, to restore an alliance. David did his best to re-establish the financial and civil strength of Scotland, despite the depredations of the Black Death which had severely reduced the population of Scotland and England whilst David was in captivity. Although David was never held in such esteem as his father, his final years showed that he was not totally the weak or inadequate king as he was later remembered. He just had the misfortune at living at the same time as Edward III, one of Europe's strongest monarchs. David was almost certainly infertile, for despite two marriages (he divorced his second wife, who had been his mistress) he died childless after a sudden illness, in February 1371, aged only 47. It brought an end to the short-lived house of Bruce. He was succeeded by his nephew, Robert, the first king of the Stewart dynasty.

[FC73] EDWARD [BALLIOL]

King of Scotland, 12 August 1332–16 December 1332 (deposed); restored March 1333–1336 (deposed briefly in 1334/5). Crowned: Scone Abbey, 24 September 1332.
Edward was the eldest son of JOHN Balliol, and never let his claim to the Scottish throne rest. His date of birth is not known. As his father married in or around 1281, he could have been born as early as 1283, though it is more likely that he was born in the 1290s. He spent much of his young adult life in exile in France, where his father died in 1313, but came to England in 1324 where he found considerable support amongst the "Disinherited" – the Scottish lords who lost their estates because of their support for the English against ROBERT *THE BRUCE*. Edward seized his opportunity for the Scottish throne on the accession of DAVID II, the infant son of Robert the Bruce. With the support of EDWARD III of England and the disinherited lords, Balliol invaded Scotland and on 12 August 1332 defeated the earl of Mar at Dupplin Moor in Perthshire. He was crowned the following month. However, in December, his army was surprised by the forces of Archibald Douglas and defeated at Annan. He only just escaped with his life. He fled to England but was restored a few months later in March 1333. The factions supporting Bruce and Balliol continued to fight. Edward III himself, who had watched the conflict with amusement from Berwick, now entered the fray. An army under Archibald Douglas was defeated with overwhelming slaughter at Halidon Hill, near Berwick, in July 1333. Douglas was killed, and Edward Balliol found himself more firmly ensconced as king. But it was not to last. Edward was deposed again in 1334, restored in 1335 and deposed for a third time in 1336. Thereafter he made no further claims on the Scottish throne, and surrendered all right of accession on 20 January 1356. He settled in his English estates, and little more is known about him. It is believed that he died around January 1364 at Wheatley, near Doncaster, probably in his seventies. He never married and with him the claims of the house of Balliol on the Scottish throne passed into history.

[FC74] ROBERT II

Ruled 22 February 1371–19 April 1390; crowned: Scone Abbey, 26 March 1371.
Titles: king of Scotland; earl of Atholl (1342–67), earl of Strathearn (1357?–69).
Born: Paisley, 2 March 1316. Died: Dundonald Castle, Ayrshire, 19 April 1390, aged 74. Buried: Scone Abbey.
Married: (1) 1336, with a second ceremony in 1348, Elizabeth Mure of Rowallan, Ayrshire: 10 children; (2) May 1355, Euphemia (c1330–87), dau. of Hugh, earl of Ross: 4 children. Robert had at least 8 illegitimate children.
Robert was the nephew of DAVID II, whom he succeeded. His mother, Marjorie, was the daughter of ROBERT the Bruce. She had died giving birth to Robert, following a fall from her horse. His father, Walter, was the sixth High Steward of Scotland, and a descendant of William Fitzalan, whose son Walter had received large estates from DAVID I along with the hereditary title of Steward of Scotland. Robert had been named the Bruce's heir if Bruce did not have a son of his own, but in the event David was born and succeeded. Although his nephew, Robert was eight years older than David, and grew into a tall, strong youth with good manners and a generous disposition. He was liked by all, and many wished that he had become king. He was twice the regent or guardian of Scotland during David's enforced absences. David,

however, regarded Robert as something of a traitor. Robert had withdrawn his forces from the battle of Neville's Cross in 1346 at which David was captured. Robert governed the kingdom for the next eleven years with as much weakness as he would when he subsequently became king, although the kingdom was plagued by the Black Death during this period.

When Robert succeeded to the kingship in 1371 he was nearly fifty-five and not the man he had been. He was described as red-eyed and enfeebled and was known as "Auld Blearie". Perhaps this was partly due to his amorous adventures – he fathered at least twenty children, possibly more. Because of this numerous progeny he was determined to clarify the succession and the very day after his coronation he declared who would succeed him and this was subsequently enshrined, in much more detail, in a statute issued two years later. This act was of more significance than might at first be apparent. Robert had married twice, and the marriage to his first wife, Elizabeth Mure, was not regarded by all as legitimate, because they were too closely related. Robert had to seek special papal dispensation to legitimise the children of his first marriage. The children of his second marriage, which was wholly legitimate, regarded themselves as the rightful heirs to the throne, and this remained a matter of conflict for the next eighty years. Clarification of the succession was probably Robert's most important act, as he had little ability to govern wisely, and soon ran down the effective government procedures and taxation established by David. The kingdom became poorer and ill-controlled with many crimes going unpunished. Lawlessness grew. Fortunately there was little conflict with the English, as Robert would certainly have had problems dealing with that. There was a vicious and destructive raid by RICHARD II in 1385, which included the burning of Edinburgh, leading to a number of border incidents, the most notable of which was the battle of Otterburn on 5 August 1388. Here the earl of March defeated and captured Henry Percy ("Hotspur"), the son of the earl of Northumberland. From about 1384, by which time Robert was growing senile, the general administration of affairs past to his son John, earl of Carrick (later ROBERT III). Unfortunately a kick from a horse in 1388 left John an invalid and increasingly incompetent, so that Robert's next son, also called Robert, took over the day to day government. Robert II's rule was therefore an inauspicious start to the Stewart dynasty. When he died in 1390, aged 74, he was the oldest of any Scots king since MALCOLM II.

[FC75] ROBERT III

Ruled 19 April 1390–4 April 1406; crowned: Scone Abbey, 14 August 1390.
Titles: king of Scotland; earl of Carrick (from 1368).
Born: *c1337.* **Died:** *Dundonald Castle, 4 April 1406, aged 68(?).* **Buried:** *Paisley Abbey.*
Married: *c1366, Annabella Drummond (c1350–1401), dau. Sir John Drummond of Stobhall: 7 children. Robert III also had one known illegitimate child.*
Baptized John, he assumed the name Robert on his succession, as he believed the name John brought ill luck, as shown by JOHN Balliol and the kings of that name of England and France. If only a change of name was so effective. Two years before his succession John, who had joined his father in the administration of government affairs in 1384, was kicked by a horse and became an invalid. His abilities to govern

were thus severely limited, and much of the administration was carried out by his younger brother, also called Robert. This Robert became better known as Albany when he was created duke of Albany in 1398. Albany was ambitious and took over almost complete control of the kingdom from the day of his brother's accession, but in 1393 the king decided to take the administration back into his own hands, with disastrous results. Robert III was about as incapable at governing as his father. The 1390s saw bribery and corruption throughout the Scottish lowlands, with money flowing from the government's coffers into the hands of the newly created barons (the many sons of ROBERT II) and their vassals. Even worse the rift widened between the Lowlands and the Highlands. The clans strengthened, with clan warfare becoming rife. Donald MacDonald (see DONALD II), lord of the Isles, ruled his lands as a separate kingdom. Robert III was unable to exercise any authority over them. They were more responsive to his younger brother, Alexander, the earl of Buchan and self-styled "Wolf of Badenoch", who became little more than a bandit leader. He married into the family of the lord of the Isles and to some extent became their proxy king in the North.

Robert III sank further into a state of depression, stating to his wife that he should be buried in a dungheap with the epitaph "Here lies the worst of kings and the most miserable of men." Annabella decided to take things into her own hands. She called a special council in April 1398 at which her eldest son, David, then still only nineteen, was made duke of Rothesay and "Lieutenant of the Realm". In his actions he still needed to consult with full council, but his primary adviser was his uncle, the ambitious Robert who, at that same meeting, was created duke of Albany. Unfortunately David was as inept as his father, being of a dissolute and licentious nature. When the new English king HENRY IV decided to invade Scotland in 1400, more as a show of strength than for any other reason, he was able to reach Edinburgh without much opposition. He lay siege to the castle but was eventually forced to retire through want of supplies. The Scots seemed powerless to respond. After Annabella died in October 1401, Albany had David thrown into prison at Falkland Palace in Fife where he left him to starve to death, though the word went out that he had died of an illness or, more accurately, "through the divine dispensation". Even after David's death Scottish fortunes did not revive. In September 1402 they made a expedition against the English to retaliate for the raid on Edinburgh, but were totally defeated by the earl of Northumberland at Homildon Hill.

David's younger brother, James, who was only seven, became the heir to the throne. It took his father some while to realise that he might be in danger from Albany but eventually, in late February 1406 the king entrusted the boy, then aged eleven, to the care of Sir David Fleming, to be smuggled out of Scotland to safety in France. Unfortunately everything went wrong. The sea and high tides limited shipping; Sir David was waylaid and killed; and when James was eventually hidden on a cargo ship by Henry St. Clair, it was attacked by pirates. The young boy was captured and taken to Henry IV, who promptly imprisoned him in the Tower of London. When news reached King Robert it was the last straw in a life of total ineptitude. He retired to his ancestral home at Rothesay and there pined away from grief.

ROBERT STEWART, DUKE OF ALBANY. Governor of Scotland, 1406–20.

Titles: earl of Menteith (from 1361), earl of Fife (briefly before March 1372), duke of Albany (from 1398).

*Born: c1340. **Died**: Stirling Castle, 3 September 1420, aged 80. **Buried**: Dunfermline Abbey.*

Married: (1) 1361, Margaret Graham, countess of Menteith (c1330–1380?): 7 children; (2) 1380, Muriella Keith (d. 1449): 5 children.

Robert was the ambitious and certainly most capable son of ROBERT II who sought to gain the crown of Scotland for himself and his own progeny. With the increasing senility of his father during the 1380s, Robert took on more of the country's administrative affairs, and after 1388, when his brother John was crippled following a kick from a horse, Robert became the senior administrator. He was not formally styled governor, even after the succession of his brother (as ROBERT III), for all that the power was almost wholly in his hands. The king sought to regain control of the government between 1393 and 1398 but that was a disaster and in April 1398 the king's son, David, was made "Lieutenant of the Realm", with Robert, now created duke of Albany, as his primary adviser. David was as inept as his father; this resulted in him being imprisoned in November 1401, and from April 1402 Robert was more or less in full control. Although the king's son, James, was now the heir, he was captured by pirates while being smuggled out of Scotland for safety in April 1406 and was handed over to the English king, HENRY IV, who imprisoned him in the Tower of London. Robert III died of grief soon after and, in June 1406, Robert Stewart was officially inaugurated as the governor of Scotland. Although he never held the title of king, he held the equivalent power, signing all the documents in his name and ensuring that his son, Murdoch succeeded him as governor. Nevertheless Robert realised that he was not all-powerful and could be toppled, so he sought to govern without alienating either the leading barons or the common folk. For the former, he allowed them ample use of the crown's revenues; and for the latter, he decreed that no taxes should be levied. As a result the kingdom grew poorer by the day and there was general lawlessness. Robert delegated the general administration of southern Scotland to Archibald, the earl of Douglas who had married Robert's niece Margaret, whilst northern Scotland was in the hands of Alexander, the earl of Mar and son of Robert's brother, Alexander, the notorious Wolf of Badenoch. Although Douglas was a capable soldier and administrator, Alexander Stewart was little more than a robber baron who held the Highlands under his sway. Robert did nothing to reduce his power and it would be fair to say that by the time of Robert's death, at the age of eighty, Scotland was in straitened and corrupt circumstances.

[FC76] JAMES I

Ruled 4 April 1406–21 February 1437. Crowned: Scone Abbey, 21 May 1424.

Titles: king of Scotland; duke of Rothesay and earl of Carrick (from 1404).

*Born: Dunfermline Palace, 25 July 1394. **Died** (assassinated): Perth, 21 February 1437, aged 43. **Buried**: Perth.*

Married: 2 February 1424, in Southwark, London, Joan Beaufort (d. 1445), dau. John, earl of Somerset, and great-granddaughter of Edward III: 8 children.

James was the second and much younger son of ROBERT III, born when his mother was in her early forties. When his elder brother, DAVID STEWART, died in prison in

March 1402, James became the heir to the throne. With increasing lawlessness in the land (because of the poor government of James's father and grandfather), Robert III decided to send James to France for safety in February 1406, under the safe-keeping of Henry ST. CLAIR of Orkney. However his ship was captured by pirates, who believed it was a cargo vessel, and realising the importance of their booty took him to the English king HENRY IV, who rewarded the pirates by allowing them to keep their ship. Henry declared that James did not need to go to France for his safety or education, both of which he could receive in England. James was promptly locked away in the Tower of London. Although his freedom was restricted, he was not totally deprived of his liberty as he spent most of his captivity with King Henry at Windsor and on his progress about England. As a consequence James gained not only an excellent education, but considerable knowledge of court administration and governance, almost certainly better than he would have received at home. James also accompanied HENRY V on military service in France, learning much about soldiery and military tactics. He also acquired literary skills. Not only is he the first Scottish king of whom evidence of his handwriting survives, he was also something of a poet. One of his poems, *The Kingis Quair*, is not only an autobiography of his years of captivity but records how he fell in love with his future wife. By the end of his captivity, the king was thirty. He had outlived Henry IV and Henry V, and was living during the minority of HENRY VI. The English had problems in their continuing conflict with France and saw an opportunity in restoring James to the throne as a way of stopping the Scottish support for the French. Under the Treaty of London, James was given his freedom, in return for a payment of 60,000 merks (£40,000) to cover the cost of his upkeep and education (a neat euphemism for a ransom). Before returning to Scotland James married his sweetheart, Joan Beaufort, the niece of RICHARD II and a granddaughter of John of Gaunt. James was eventually crowned king of Scotland in May 1424, at last king of a land he had not seen for eighteen years.

The country was in a pitiful state. Under the control of his uncle, ROBERT STEWART, the duke of Albany, Scotland had sunk into poverty and lawlessness, and it deteriorated more under Robert's son, Murdoch. To a man raised in the comparatively prosperous south, the condition of Scotland must have cut him to the quick. It was controlled, though not governed, by his cousin Murdoch and his wayward sons. James had been able to keep in touch with the Douglas family, whose earl, Archibald had married James's sister Margaret in 1390 or earlier. Archibald had endeavoured to govern southern Scotland and had by 1424 disassociated himself from Murdoch. It was Douglas who helped engineer James's release. James devoted all his energies to restoring the land. His first measure was to rid Scotland of its lawless governors. Within a month of his coronation James had imprisoned his cousin's son, Walter Stewart, who controlled the fortress of Dumbarton and was thus not only influencing the trade into the western Highlands and pocketing most of the revenues for himself, but was also controlling the despatch of forces to France, which James had agreed to stop under the Treaty of London. Over the next few months James imprisoned the earl of Lennox (Murdoch's father-in-law), Murdoch himself, Murdoch's wife Elizabeth and his son Alexander. Murdoch's youngest son, James, led a revolt in the area of Lennox and sacked Dumbarton. Although he escaped to Ireland where he remained in exile, his actions sounded the

42. Scotland (9) – The Stewart Succession

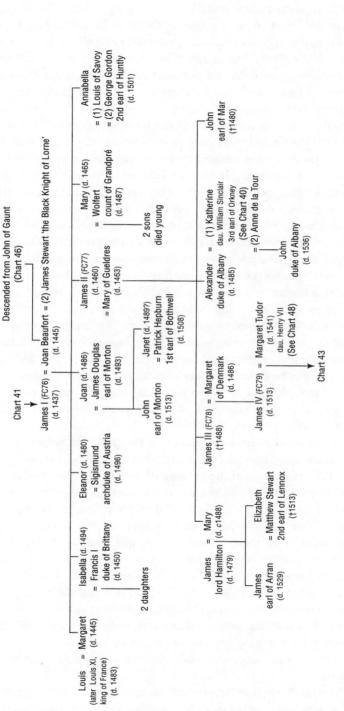

death knell for the other members of his family. Lennox, Murdoch, Walter and
Alexander were all executed at Stirling Castle on 24 and 25 May 1425.

James next sought to minimise the possibility of challenge from among his uncles
and cousins who were descendants of his grandfather's second marriage, which was
regarded as more legal than his first and thus may have represented a stronger legal
challenge to James's right to the throne. James deprived the young Malise Graham
of his right to the earldom of Strathearn, claiming it could not be passed on through
his mother, the only daughter of David, son of ROBERT II, who had died in 1389.
Malise was despatched to England as one of the hostages held against payment of
James's ransom. James recognized the seniority of his ageing uncle Walter, the
second son of Robert II's second marriage, who was earl of Atholl, and he created
him earl of Strathearn in July 1427. This was tantamount to recognizing Walter's
right of succession (and that of his sons Alexander and David) to the Scottish
throne. It would have dire consequences later in James's reign.

James next turned his attention towards the Highlands. The MacDonald clan had
assumed almost absolute power under DONALD II and ALEXANDER II, lords of the
Isles. The Highlanders did not regard themselves as the subjects of the Scottish king,
but were a law unto themselves, not that there were any laws to control them. In
1428 James called a meeting of clan leaders at Inverness. Once there he arrested
them, executing the more powerful ringleaders. This action, though, was a mistake.
For all that James was doing what he must, the way that he did it showed that he
was not a king to be trusted. At his worst he was cruel, vicious and vindictive, and
gave no inch to his enemies. Alexander of the Isles was released, but promptly led an
uprising and, although he was soon re-captured and forced to do obeisance to
James, the clan warfare continued for a few more years until an uneasy peace was
agreed in 1435.

In addition to curbing the powers of the clans and nobles, James sought to
reintroduce strong laws. He passed a considerable number during the first few years
of his rule, ranging from the banning of football (football hooliganism must be
older than we think!) and the introduction of licensing hours for drinking, to
organized fire-fighting and the control of tax collection. He briefly introduced
direct taxation in 1424, but it was so unpopular that he repealed it, though he
reintroduced it in 1431. He also developed trade with his close European
neighbours and, despite the Treaty of London, re-opened relationships with
France by renewing the Auld Alliance. His eldest daughter, Margaret, was betrothed
to the Dauphin of France in 1428, though the marriage did not happen until 1436,
when she was still only eleven. Other daughters were married to dukes and counts
of some consequence throughout Europe. It seemed for a while, though, that James
might not leave a male heir. It was not until October 1430 that his wife was
delivered of male twins, Alexander and James. Alexander soon died, but James
survived.

It was inevitable that James's ruthless actions in order to regain stability and
control in Scotland would make him enemies – in fact it made him few friends. In
addition, in the summer of 1436, a disastrous attempt to regain Roxburgh, from
which James was forced to retreat, lowered his prestige and demonstrated his lack of
control over his nobles, who had sought to create trouble at home while James was
away. James spent that Christmas at Perth. Legend has it that a local seer warned

him that he would not return south alive. While retiring for the night on 20 February, he and his wife were attacked by a group of assassins. His wife, who tried to protect him, was wounded, and James, who fled into an underground vault, was cornered and hacked to death. Ironically James had recently bricked off one end of this vault because tennis balls ended up down there and, in so doing, he had stopped off his means of escape.

The conspirators were led by Sir Robert Graham, the uncle of Malise Graham whom James had slighted at the start of his reign. Also involved in the plot were Walter Stewart, earl of Strathearn, whom James had once favoured, and his grandson Robert, whom Walter had hoped would be made king. The assassins were all caught, tortured and executed. Walter received his crown: a red-hot one of iron. James's widow, Joan, lived a further eight years and married a second time: to James Stewart, the famous "Black Knight of Lorne". The then lieutenant of Scotland, Alexander Livingstone, feared that they might abduct the child king (JAMES II) and so had them arrested in 1439 – they were released on condition that they would not attempt to retain custody of the child.

[FC77] JAMES II
Ruled 21 February 1437–3 August 1460. Crowned: Holyrood Abbey, 25 March 1437.
Titles: king of Scotland; duke of Rothesay (from 1431).
Born: Holyrood Palace, Edinburgh, 16 October 1430. Died (in battle): Roxburgh, 3 August 1460, aged 29. Buried: Holyrood Abbey.
Married: 3 July 1449, at Holyrood Abbey, Mary (1433–63), dau. Arnold, duke of Gueldres: 7 children. James also had at least one illegitimate child.

James was one of twins, the first born of which soon died. There must have been other problems at the birth for James bore a large birthmark which caused him to be known as James of the Fiery Face. He was only six when his father was murdered and for a while he remained in the care of his mother, Joan, until she remarried in 1439, when she was barred from having custody of the child or any dealings in day-to-day government. The new lieutenant of Scotland and the real power in the land was a relative unknown, Sir Alexander Livingstone, governor of Stirling Castle. The queen and her infant son had first sought refuge in Edinburgh Castle, governed by Sir William Crichton, and a wrangle broke out between Livingstone and Crichton as to who should have possession of the boy. These two officials remained in rivalry for several years, exercising authority over the boy and through him over the land. Crichton, in particular, became involved in the rivalry over the succession between the king and the Douglas family. The fifth earl of Douglas, Archibald, was James II's cousin, and he married Euphemia Graham, a great-granddaughter of ROBERT II. His sons, William and David thus had a strong title to the Scottish throne. When Archibald died in 1439, James was faced with the young upstart William, the sixth earl, a born trouble-maker. Crichton, acting on behalf of the king, invited the two brothers, William and David, to a feast at Edinburgh Castle on 28 November 1440. At the end of the meal a black bull's head was placed on the table as a symbol of death. The two brothers were then seized and subjected to a mock trial at which James pleaded for their release. They were, however, found guilty of treason and immediately executed. The Douglases were thereafter the sworn enemies of James and of Crichton and, as the family regained their power, they supported Alexander

Livingstone, engineering events from behind the scenes to effectively control the kingdom.

Throughout the 1440s, therefore, Scotland once again became a land of civil strife with rivalry between baronial factions. By 1449 the Livingstone family had control over almost all the key offices and castles. It was in that year that James II, now eighteen, assumed his full powers as king. Almost immediately, on 23 September 1449, he arrested most of the Livingstone officials. They were imprisoned and two of them were subsequently executed. Their fall from power was as sudden and mysterious as their rise. Soon after, William Douglas, the new earl, set off to France and Italy, probably to escape the king, who may have learned of the Douglas's assistance to the Livingstones. When William returned, in 1450, his relationship with the king remained cordial if distant, but James became incensed when he found that William had entered into an alliance with the earl of Ross, who was also the lord of the Isles (see JOHN II). Douglas was invited to dine with James on 22 February 1452, where James asked Douglas to break the alliance. Douglas refused, and James stabbed him in the neck. The attack was probably unpremeditated and the murder not planned, but its results were disastrous. William Douglas's brother, James, the new earl, withdrew his allegiance from the king and declared his allegiance to the English king HENRY VI. The Douglas family now united under a common cause against James II.

When conflict erupted it came as part of the English Wars of the Roses. James supported the Lancastrians while the Douglases supported the House of York, so that the war, which began with the battle of St Albans in May 1455, had its echo on Scottish fields. James, however, used his devious tactics in setting one noble house against another, and used his own strong support in the south to defeat the Douglases within a matter of months. James relied heavily on a new form of artillery, the cannon. These had only recently been introduced into Scotland, and James used his wife's connections in the Low Countries to acquire a monopoly on these giant guns. Castles had no protection against cannon power and soon fell to his siege train. It is likely that one of these cannon was the mighty Mons Meg, still on display at Edinburgh Castle. The power of the Douglases was destroyed once and for all. The earl survived but fled to England.

Over the next few years James aggressively revoked many of the acts and settlements agreed during his minority and removed many hereditary entitlements. Few earls were safe in their castles, as James reclaimed many of them as possessions of the crown. In effect the old feudal system was ended as many lands now became forfeit. James also updated many of the laws promulgated by his father and introduced many new ones, regulating dress and improving education. Glasgow University was established in 1451.

By the end of the 1450s James had a powerful hold over Scotland. He may not have been liked by many of his subjects, but he was respected. He could have had ahead of him a long and effective reign. But his delight in the power of the cannon which had won him his kingdom, was also his undoing. In August 1460 James was laying siege to Roxburgh Castle in support of Henry VI. His wife arrived on the scene and James was keen to fire a special salvo in her honour. As he ignited one cannon it exploded and killed him. James's heir, also called James, was only eight. It looked as if the events at the start of the last two reigns were to be repeated.

[FC78] **JAMES III**

Ruled 3 August 1460–11 June 1488. Crowned: Kelso Abbey, 10 August 1460.
Titles: king of Scotland; duke of Rothesay (from birth).
Born: *St Andrew's Castle, Fife, May 1452.* **Died** *(murdered): Milltown, 11 June 1488,*
aged 36. **Buried:** *Cambuskenneth Abbey.*
Married: *10 July 1469, at Holyrood Abbey, Margaret (1456–86), dau. Christian I of*
Denmark and Norway: 3 sons.

James was only eight when his father was killed in an accident, and once again Scotland found itself under the control of a council of regents. This was initially headed by his mother, Mary of Gueldres, a remarkably able woman, though she found herself opposed by James Kennedy, bishop of St Andrews. Scotland supported the Lancastrian cause in the English Wars of the Roses and it was to Scotland that the Lancastrian king, HENRY VI, fled after his defeat at Towton at the end of March 1461. The Scots gave him refuge and, in return, Henry restored Berwick to Scottish hands. It had been in English hands since 1296, and its recovery was a further boost to the regency following the recapture of Roxburgh the previous year. An attempt to aid Henry with military support was less successful as Scottish forces were defeated at Carlisle in June. A few weeks later EDWARD IV was crowned king of England. He soon entered into a treaty with the earl of Douglas and JOHN II, lord of the Isles, which was sealed in February 1462. This gained Edward the support of those rebels against the Scottish throne. Mary, the queen mother, realised that if Scotland entered into its own treaty with Edward, the agreement with Douglas and John would be worthless. Mary was strongly opposed in this by Kennedy and the two parties – known as the "Young Lords" headed by Mary and the "Old Lords" headed by Kennedy – almost rent the country apart. Mary did enter into negotiations with Edward, but was unable to bring these to a satisfactory conclusion before illness resulted in her early death on 1 December 1463, aged thirty. Meanwhile the Scots had been actively supporting Margaret of Anjou, Henry VI's wife, who had brought an army from France and was endeavouring to regain castles in northern England. However, when Edward agreed a truce with France in the autumn of 1463, the Lancastrian cause seemed hopelessly lost. Kennedy was forced to realise that the queen mother was right. Within days of her death, negotiations began between Kennedy and Edward IV that resulted in a truce. Henry VI was smuggled out of Scotland in March 1464 but, after two ignominious defeats, he was captured and imprisoned in the Tower of London. Soon after this John of the Isles realised his power had been annulled and although he technically resumed his allegiance to James III, he continued to rule as if independent of the crown.

Kennedy died in July 1465. Had he or the queen mother lived longer Scotland would have been spared the rise to power of the Boyd family, under the guiding control of Sir Alexander Boyd, the governor of Edinburgh Castle. He entered into an alliance with Gilbert Kennedy, the brother of the late Bishop Kennedy, and with Robert, Lord Fleming. Between them they were able to gain sufficient support from other members of the nobility to sustain their audacious plans. In July 1466, while the young king was hearing his accounts at Linlithgow Castle, Boyd and Fleming lured James out onto a hunt and kidnapped him, hiding him away at Edinburgh Castle. When Parliament was held that October James, who was still only fourteen, stated that his abduction had been made by royal agreement. Boyd was appointed guardian of the King and keeper of the royal fortresses. His elder brother, Robert, was already earl of Kilmarnock and now became the lord chamberlain. Robert's son, Thomas, married the king's elder sister, Mary, in April 1467 and was created earl of Arran. The consequent grants of land made him the senior lord of the country. For a little under three years the Boyds dominated the control of Scotland. Unlike the Livingstones, in the previous reign, the Boyds did not go for absolute power, preferring to drain the revenues for their own profit, and enjoy the use of their authority. Their fall was as sudden as their rise. The same Parliament that had acknowledged their authority had discussed the matter of the debt owed by Scotland to Norway for the annual rent due on the Hebrides which had been accumulating for over forty years. It was now becoming an embarrassment, and default could result in the restoration of the Hebrides to Norway. It had already been suggested some years earlier that Scotland would benefit from a marriage with the crown of Norway and negotiations began in 1468. It was Thomas Boyd who led these negotiations and, although the end result was of considerable benefit to Scotland, it did not help the Boyds. With the marriage of James III to Margaret of Norway in July 1469 the debt owing on the Western Isles was written off. King Christian agreed to pay 60,000 florins (£20,000) as a dowry. However, 50,000 of these were offset against Norway pledging its rights in Orkney to Scotland. When payment came to be made, Christian could not raise the 10,000 florins and instead further pledged his rights in the Shetlands to Scotland. By 1470, therefore, Scotland found itself in ownership of the Northern Isles, which had been in Norwegian hands for almost six hundred years, and in full ownership of the Hebrides. The last Norse earl of Orkney had died eighty years earlier and the earldom had been held by the ST CLAIR family. William resigned his earldom to the Crown in 1471, and was compensated with lands in Fife. St Clair's daughter, Katherine, married James III's brother Alexander in 1475. The kingdom of Scotland was now at its full extent.

With his marriage, James III assumed full regal authority and his supporters acted immediately. The Boyds were found guilty of treason and sentenced to death. Lord Boyd fled to England, where he remained in refuge but died within a year at Alnwick Castle. Thomas Boyd was warned by his wife Mary. He had been returning from Denmark but was able to set sail again. He was stripped of his title and remained in exile until his death in 1473. Alexander was less fortunate. He was arrested and executed in November 1469.

The reign of James III is a something of a paradox. The tradition passed down to us is of a dilettante who abandoned his nobles and the government of his people for his fascination for the arts and sciences. He is also portrayed as a weakling king who hid himself away in his castle and refrained from defending his country from the designs of the English. He was accused of being an anglophile, which was true, though was not necessarily as heinous as implied. James was rather more shrewd than he might at first seem. At the start of his reign he benefitted from a remarkable period of peace and prosperity which Scotland had not enjoyed for many years. The increased size and wealth of his realm, the relative calm with England and the reconciliation with John of the Isles, who was eventually brought to book in 1476, allowed James to explore other areas of interest. The fact that he tended to ignore the aristocracy in favour of artists and artisans should have been no bad thing. He encouraged learning: poetry, music, painting, astronomy, architecture and engineering all seem to have prospered during his reign. It should come as little surprise that he placed more trust in the middle class artisans than in the nobility who, hitherto, had given him little comfort. A case in point relates to the bishopric of St Andrews. In August 1472, due to the negotiations of the bishop, Patrick Graham, St Andrews was granted archiepiscopal status by the pope. This was a tremendous honour for Scotland, as this released it from the control of the archbishopric of York which had long claimed supremacy over Scotland. However Graham, who was a nephew of the former Bishop James Kennedy and was distantly related to James III, saw this as an opportunity to increase his authority over the king and certainly over all the clergy of Scotland. Opposition immediately arose against Graham, who was perceived as a megalomaniac. James III placed his court physician and astrologer, William Scheves, as head of this opposition faction. Scheves succeeded in making himself archbishop in 1478. Graham was deposed by papal bull on the grounds of heresy and simony and died insane soon after. The clergy seem prepared to accept Scheves, for all that he was not of noble birth, but Scheves turned out to be something of an adventurer and later turned against James III.

James's relations with England continued to remain cordial and, with the birth of his son (the future JAMES IV) in 1473, he entered into arrangements with Edward IV that once the prince reached his majority he would marry one of Edward's daughters. This was exceedingly beneficial for Scotland, though it was not necessarily perceived as such by all those north of the border. By the close of the 1470s James was being held in disdain by many of his subjects because of his anglophilia and because of his apparent abrogation of his kingly duties in favour of his pursuit of the arts. The nobility came to believe that these artisans, particularly the mason Robert Cochrane, were effectively running the government. James was even believed to have cultivated an interest in alchemy and the black arts. The Scottish aristocracy turned their allegiance to James's younger brothers, Alexander, duke of Albany, who was regarded as one of the greatest knights in Europe and the father of chivalry, and John, earl of Mar, another gifted knight and statesmen. It seems that these two brothers had all the knightly and kingly virtues in which James failed. Discovering the ambition of his brothers in the summer of 1479, James stripped them of their titles. Both were imprisoned at Craigmiller Castle in Edinburgh, where John died soon after, many believe murdered. Alexander escaped and sought refuge in France. Although James was temporarily rid of his ambitious brother, he was still surrounded by many disaffected barons who were increasingly dissatisfied at James's reluctance to confront Edward IV of England. Edward was openly plotting war against France, Scotland's old ally, and doing his best to ally himself with James's old enemies, including John of the Isles and James, earl of Douglas. Hostilities broke out on the English border in the spring of 1480. Attempts at reconciliation proved fruitless and by the close of 1481 Scotland and England were at war. Alexander, the king's brother, chose to side with Edward IV against James and, from June 1482 was openly styling himself as Alexander IV, king of Scotland. James was eventually forced to lead an army into England. However he took with him his court favourites, which angered the earls. While encamped at Lauder the earls, led by Archibald, earl of Angus, parleyed with the king and besought him to surrender his favourites and to cease circulation of the debased coinage which James had issued. James refused and, in anger, the earls seized the king's favourites, including Cochrane, and the king's musician, William Roger, and hanged them at the bridge into the town. James was arrested and imprisoned at Edinburgh Castle. Alexander marched on Scotland and concluded peace with England. Part of the price was that England regained Berwick in August 1482, which had been in Scottish hands for only twenty-one years. Thereafter Berwick remained English.

Alexander chose not to usurp the throne, even though he could almost certainly have counted on the support of the Scottish aristocracy and of the English king. Instead he released James from prison in October 1482. The two, for a while, were reconciled, but by early 1483 they were back in conflict. The death of Edward IV in April 1483 robbed Alexander of his English support and two months later James was able to drive Alexander out of Scotland. He eventually sought refuge in France, where he was killed while watching a tournament in 1485.

James's reign should have taken a turn for the better over the next few years. However, he was sadly affected by the death of his wife in July 1486 and thereafter increased his seclusion in his royal homes. Nevertheless he pursued, with singular dedication, the desire to formalise a marriage between his son and the royal house of England, even to the extent of suggesting a marriage between himself and Edward IV's widow. James pursued this throughout the short reign of RICHARD III and into the early years of HENRY VII. This apparent passion for England further angered the Scottish earls, who were already disaffected by James's continued mismanagement of financial affairs. Eventually, in the spring of 1488, the earls, led by Angus, Argyll and Gray, broke into open rebellion. James sought refuge in the north where he raised an army of supporters. The two factions met at Sauchieburn, near Bannockburn, on 11 June 1488. James's army was defeated and the king fled the battlefield. There are several stories of his fate, the most colorful of which is that he fell from his horse and was helped to safety by a local women drawing water from a well. He told her his identity and she went in search of a priest but, when she revealed James's whereabouts, a local opportunist found the king and killed him. More likely is that soldiers, pursuing James from the battlefield found his horse and soon discovered him in refuge, apparently at a local mill, where he was slain. It is not known who killed the king.

James III was in all probability a misunderstood king who severely miscalculated the power of his nobles. He was not as foolish as some made out since he succeeded in maintaining periods of considerable peace and prosperity in Scotland, despite the activities of his brothers and their supporters and the tactics of the English crown. Had he been less strong-willed and more conciliatory, he might have made a fine monarch.

[FC79] JAMES IV

Ruled 11 June 1488–9 September 1513. Crowned: Scone Abbey, 26 June 1488.
Titles: king of Scotland; duke of Rothesay, earl of Carrick and lord of Cunningham (from birth).
Born: 17 March 1473. Died (in battle): Flodden Field, 9 September 1513, aged 40.
Buried: possibly Sheen Abbey, Surrey, though his exact resting place is not known.
Married: 8 August 1503, at Holyrood Abbey, Margaret (1489–1541), dau. Henry VII of England (the marriage had earlier been performed by proxy on 25 January 1502): 6

children. James had at least seven illegitimate children, and it is claimed he was secretly married to Margaret Drummond, by whom he had one child and who was poisoned in 1502.

The reign of James IV saw Scotland (and Europe) emerge from the Middle Ages and enter a new age. This transition meant that although the young James (who was fifteen when his father was killed) took after his father in his patronage of the arts and sciences, it had become more acceptable and James was not pilloried because of it. It also helped that James was a strong king who did not ignore his nobles and, for the most part, earned their respect and support. His abilities as a politician and negotiator were appreciated and, despite the relative insignificance of his kingdom on the European stage, he could hold his own and maintain an influential voice. It was this which, by his own misfortune, would lead to his tragic death.

James was quick to bring his country back to order after the strife of the last year of his father's reign. In his first parliament, led by the earl of Argyll, they annulled all grants and enactments made by James III earlier that year and issued summons of treason against all those who still opposed the new king. Only three of these were dealt with summarily. The earl of Buchan was fully pardoned, whilst the lords of Bothwell and Montgrenane were stripped of their estates, but did not forfeit their lives. All others were pardoned and the heirs of those who had died at the battle of Sauchieburn were allowed to inherit their estates. Furthermore the absolution of the pope himself, Innocent VIII, was sought for all of those who had risen against James III on the basis of his interest in alchemy and the black arts. Within less than a year James had gained peace with most of his nobles, though matters were soured by the rebellion of Robert, Lord Lyle, the Justice General, and John Stewart, a distant cousin of the king, who had been created earl of Lennox. These two seemed dissatisfied with the share of the spoils, and they found unexpected support from Lord Forbes of Aberdeen. The insurrection broke out in April 1489 when the lords garrisoned their castles against the king. The sieges lasted throughout the summer but by October the castles had been taken and the lords' lands declared forfeit. With a remarkable act of clemency James later forgave the lords and restored their titles.

That same year saw a naval victory by Scotland against English ships which had been harrying the Firth of Forth. James's naval commander, Sir Andrew Wood, not only captured these ships, but defeated a punitive expedition sent by HENRY VII against James later that summer. This victory did much to raise the spirits of the Scottish populace. James used Wood in his activities amongst the Hebrides to help root out the rebellious supporters of ANGUS of the Isles. Angus was murdered in 1490, but his cousin, Alexander, was no less troublesome in the Isles. Eventually James took action against the aged MacDonald lord, JOHN (II), in May 1493. His lands were declared forfeit and he was summoned to appear before James IV and declare his submission. John complied and the title of Lord of the Isles ceased. Although hostilities remained amongst the Isles, James had dealt the final blow to the great adversary of his forebears. With such time as he was able James spent much of the 1490s visiting and taking measures throughout the Isles to restore order and loyalty. His actions were persistent and persuasive and he moved forward by occasional victories. For instance the flagrant opposition of Sir John of Islay, who stormed Dunaverty Castle in April 1494 and hanged James's new governor before the king's very eyes, was followed with swift retribution upon Sir John and his accomplices. The uprising of Alexander of Lochalsh in 1496 was similarly swiftly dealt with by James's supporters and Alexander was slain. There were still further rebellions, the main one being lead by Torquil Macleod, the lord of Lewis, who now regarded himself as the primary hereditary ruler of the Isles. He had taken under his wing DONALD *DUBH*, grandson of John of the Isles, who had escaped from prison in 1501 and by 1503 was prepared to lead his assault on the Scots king. It took three summers before Donald was captured, in 1505, but by then the measures that James took in order to subdue the Isles and guarantee the support of the chieftains were having effect. Firstly James had agreed to grant land by charter to the chieftains provided they gave him their fealty. Secondly, following Donald's rebellion, James established two sheriffs over the Isles to administer justice, while the government of the Isles was given to the Earl of Huntly in the north and the earl of Argyll in the south.

From a portrait in the National Gallery of Scotland

Throughout his reign James endeavoured to maintain peace with England, though in this he was fraught with dilemma. Since 1492 James had been aware of the endeavours of Perkin WARBECK, the pretender to the English throne who had begun his campaign in 1490. He rapidly gained the support of many princes of Europe, including James IV whom he first visited in 1495. James believed Warbeck's claims and, as a sign of his support, he not only wrote to the king of the Romans, Maximilian, offering his support if Maximilian should take action against Henry VII, but he married Warbeck to his cousin, Lady Catherine Gordon, in January 1496. In September 1496 James and Warbeck invaded Northumberland but the skirmishes proved fruitless and the two parties retreated after a little over two weeks. Warbeck became incensed at the way James had conducted the forces and Warbeck now fell out of favour. Although James continued to honour him as his guest for many more months, at the risk of war with England, Warbeck was eventually despatched from Scotland to France in July 1497. These hostilities, however, had led to a series of border skirmishes which remained until peace was eventually restored between England and Scotland in September 1497 through the medium of the Spanish ambassador Pedro de Ayala. Somewhat languidly James and Henry sought to strengthen this peace, reviving the aims of James's father in seeking a marriage between the royal families of Scotland and England. James was in his late twenties and his failure to marry and produce an heir was the cause of some consternation in Scotland. There were rumours that James had secretly married one of his mistresses, Margaret, the daughter of Lord Drummond, and that this would not complicate arrangements with the English, Margaret Drummond was poisoned, along with her two sisters, early in 1502. After three years of negotiation a marriage treaty was signed in January 1502 between James IV and Henry VII's twelve year-old daughter Margaret Tudor. The same day a formal peace treaty in perpetuity was signed between the two nations. This treaty also had papal blessing, so that if it were broken the transgressor would face excommunication. That this perpetuity was to last only eleven years was one of the unfortunate twists of fate. The official marriage between James and Margaret took place at Holyrood in August 1503. Through this union the crowns of Scotland and England would eventually be united under James IV's great-grandson one hundred years later.

Political endeavours aside, James continued to pursue his interests in the arts and sciences and encourage learning. Of great significance in this respect was his statute of 1496, which purports to be the first compulsory education act, making it incumbent upon all barons and gentlemen to send their sons to school from the age of eight, to remain there until they had mastered Latin. James had a fascination himself for all forms of study, especially medicine and dentistry. He apparently experimented in pulling the teeth of his own barber. The King's College at Aberdeen was founded in 1495, teaching among other subjects, medicine and in 1506 the Royal College of Surgeons was established in Edinburgh. Among the most colourful of James's doctors was John Damian, an alchemist, who was appointed abbot of Tongland in 1504. This eccentric experimented (like BLAEDUD) with flying and made his own wings, with which he plunged to his death from Stirling Castle in 1513. James was concerned about the morals of the nation. Among his many statutes was a ban on the playing of football in 1491, though he evidently enjoyed the game himself for there is a record that he purchased footballs for his own pleasure in 1497! To enforce his regulations James often accompanied the court justiciars, but from 1504 he established a permanent court in Edinburgh (or wherever the king held his court) which met daily and became the supreme court of justice in Scotland until superseded by the Court of Session in 1532.

James also encouraged the arts. The priest William Dunbar became Scotland's first equivalent of the poet laureate, receiving a pension from James in 1500 and thereafter penning poems for official occasions, notably *The Thistle and the Rose* to commemorate James's wedding in 1503. In 1507 the bookseller Andrew Myllar, financed by the king's clerk Walter Chapman, brought the first printing press into Scotland.

Although James now had a formal treaty with England, he also had a long-standing treaty with his old allies, France. This caused him another major dilemma when HENRY VIII prepared to do battle against France. Whom should James support? The war had come about because of the machinations of the pope, Julius II. Although James had supported the need for a holy war against the Turks, he was taken aback when he found that in 1511 Julius declared Louis XII of France a schismatic because he had dared to question the pope's actions. Julius formed a Holy League of Spain, Austria and England against France. James could not support this, finding that he too questioned the pope's decision. The Auld Alliance between

France and Scotland held good, but it meant that England and Scotland were again on opposing sides. Henry did not especially want war with Scotland, but James maintained that so long as Henry continued aggression against France there could be no peace between them. As part of his preparations, James strengthened his fleet and constructed the mighty battleship the *Great Michael*. At 240 feet long and with space for three hundred sailors, over a hundred gunners and a thousand soldiers, it was the largest ship yet built. Despite many efforts to ensure peace, border skirmishes and sea battles grew between the two nations until they could no longer avoid full hostilities. When Henry invaded France in June 1513, James declared war on England. The first major and decisive battle was at Flodden Field, just south of the border near Coldstream. Here, despite fighting valiantly, James was killed. With him died thirteen earls, fourteen lords, his twenty year-old son Alexander, whom he had made archbishop of St Andrews, and many hundreds of knights and soldiers. The English commander, the earl of Surrey, had also suffered considerable losses, and he did not follow up his victory by an incursion into Scotland. For the moment the battle was won.

There is an interesting aftermath. The historical account states that James's body was found on the battlefield by the English and was conveyed to Berwick and then to London, where it was kept at Richmond Palace for some time before being interred at Sheen Abbey. However rumours began to arise that James had not died at Flodden and that the body was that of a lookalike, or one so disfigured in the fighting to make identity uncertain. There was one rumour that James had survived the battle but was murdered soon after by Lord Home. Others maintained that James had gone on a pilgrimage to the Holy Land, from where he never returned. All of this is fanciful but was sufficient to provide James's widow, Margaret, who remarried in 1514, with an excuse to obtain a divorce from her second husband on the grounds that James had still been alive when the second marriage took place. The exact whereabouts of James's remains is still a mystery.

[FC80] JAMES V
Ruled 9 September 1513–14 December 1542. Crowned: Stirling Castle, 21 September 1513.
Titles: king of Scotland; duke of Rothesay (from birth).
Born: Linlithgow Palace, 10 April 1512. Died: Falkland Palace, 14 December 1542, aged 30. Buried: Holyrood Abbey.
Married: (1) 1 January 1537, at Notre Dame, Paris, Madeleine (1520–37), dau. François I of France; (2) 12 June 1538, at St Andrews Cathedral, Fife, Mary (1515–60), dau. Claude I, Duke of Guise-Lorraine: 3 children. James also had at least nine illegitimate children.

James V was only seventeen months old when his father died at Flodden. A special crown and sceptre was made for his coronation twelve days later. His whole reign, half of which was in his minority, was filled with attempts at diplomacy between France and the Papacy, most of which were successful, but which ultimately proved a disaster for the king.

Immediately upon his succession his mother, Margaret Tudor, set herself up as regent but, since she was English and the sister of the aggressor HENRY VIII, she scarcely commanded much support. The Scottish council preferred John, duke of

Albany, the son of JAMES III's brother, the chivalrous Alexander (*see* ALEXANDER IV), who was next in line to the throne. John had been born and raised in France – in fact he could not speak Scottish. The French king was not confident the Scots would continue to support him and did not sanction the return of Albany so for some months there was an uneasy stalemate. In April 1514 JAMES IV's posthumous son, Alexander was born. He became the new heir to the throne, which helped ease some of the tension between the factions which supported Stewart and Albany succession. Then in August 1514, Margaret Tudor married the untrustworthy Archibald Douglas, earl of Angus. Thus, under the terms of James IV's will she was excluded from her guardianship of the young king, and this increased the demand for a new regent. Since in that same month, France and England entered into a peace treaty, Louis approved the return of Albany to Scotland on the basis that he maintained the peace between Scotland and England.

Although there were suspicions that Albany had his own designs upon the Scottish throne he never evidenced this and in fact showed remarkable skill at handling a difficult situation. The only rebellion against him came from Alexander, Lord Home, who was already regarded as having played a dubious role at Flodden. He was promptly arrested and executed in 1516. Albany succeeded in administering justice and upholding the rule of law with admirable credit, though not without cost. Records show that he and his retinue drained the Scottish coffers and left the nation virtually bankrupt. Nevertheless, he was eventually accepted by the remaining Scottish factions once it was evident that Albany agreed that the French-Scottish alliance against England should be renewed. The new French king, François, was less supportive and when Albany returned to France to enter into negotiations in 1517 he found himself detained there for four years. During his absence the Council of Regents that he had established soon broke down leading to the notorious Cleansing of the Causeway in April 1520. This was a street fight between the Douglases (under the earl of Angus) and the Hamiltons (under the earl of Arran) which resulted in the Hamiltons being driven out of the capital.

In 1521 Henry VIII entered into an alliance with the emperor Charles V which reopened hostilities with France. The Anglo-French treaty was thus broken and François sought to renew his alliance with Scotland. Albany returned to Edinburgh with a treaty to be ratified by the Scots council. The Scots however had no desire to be merely the pawns of the French and it was a further two years of negotiations before the Scots agreed to support the French. Albany returned to Scotland in 1523 with men and finances, to find not only an antipathy to French soldiers in Scotland, but an increasing fear of attacking England. Past severe defeats began to make the Scots think twice about a renewed alliance with France. Albany returned to France in 1524 and never returned. He died there in 1536. The Douglases sought to take over control. The earl of Angus declared himself the new governor and keeper of the king. He effectively imprisoned James at Edinburgh Castle in 1526 while he and his family took over the official posts. This action was not supported by Angus's wife, Margaret Tudor, who succeeded in divorcing Angus in 1527. She eventually managed to make contact with her son who escaped from Edinburgh Castle in 1528 and was given refuge at Stirling Castle. Angus's lands were declared forfeit and he fled to England.

James was now sixteen and entered into his majority. The years of his youth had forced him into a position from which he could not retreat. He pursued his hostility to Angus with vitriolic vigor, though further conflict broke out before the Douglases were eventually banished from Scotland in November 1528. James's opposition to Angus, who had been the focus of the pro-English faction in Scotland, meant that any hope of reconciliation with England was limited. However James found that Henry had too much else to consider than to open hostilities with Scotland and a five-year peace treaty was concluded with England at Berwick in December 1528. This allowed James some respite to restore order to his fractured realm. He took action against the chieftains of the borders who were openly defying alliance to either Scottish or English monarchs. His punitive raids on the borders in 1529 and 1530 were decisive, especially the second, when he hanged nearly fifty rebels of the Armstrong clan of Liddesdale without trial. Although this restored peace to the Borders it brought further enmity from the Border folk toward James whom they felt they could no longer trust.

James next turned his attention to the Western Isles. Although the chiefs of the Isles had shown their allegiance to James's father, old rivalries had broken out during Albany's governorship and this erupted into full fury in 1528 when the Macleans took up arms against the Campbells for revenge for the murder of Lord Maclean by John Campbell, the brother of the earl of Argyll. Despite his youth James was able to use his authority and powers of diplomacy in negotiation with the Macleans by which he won the support of the chieftains of the Isles. James arrested and imprisoned Archibald Campbell, earl of Argyll, in 1531. These actions in the Highlands and Borders, while restoring peace, had also alienated James from many key nobles. When he needed their support in later years it was not forthcoming.

James re-opened negotiations with France and also with the pope. Clement VII's own relationship with Henry VIII had deteriorated beyond redemption and the pope was fearful that James might follow in his uncle's footsteps. Although James had no intention of doing this he nevertheless milked the situation for what it was worth, which resulted in his receiving an extensive annuity from the pope. This enabled James to replenish his bankrupt coffers and to re-establish a rule of law in Scotland by founding the Courts of Justice in 1532. Relations with England were tense, but as France was keeping peace with England and did not want to have to support Scotland in a war with Henry, the French were able to facilitate a new Anglo-Scottish peace treaty which was more lasting. James also sought to marry into the French royal house. He had long expected a betrothal to a daughter of the king of France, and when another planned marriage was rejected, James married Madeleine, the French king's sixteen-year-old daughter on 1 January 1537. The one objection to the marriage had been the young girl's weak constitution and the worst fears were proved right. Soon after she was brought to Scotland that summer she died, after a marriage of only seven months. James was distraught, but he soon entered into a new marriage alliance with Mary of Guise-Lorraine, whose first marriage to Louis de Longueville had also ended in 1537 with the duke's death. This girl was a more robust twenty-three year old and had borne her first husband two sons. James was to prove an unsuccessful father. His firstborn son, James, died after eleven months in April 1541. Three days later his second born son, Robert, died aged only eight days. That following November, James's mother, Margaret, died, and with her passing went the last family link between James and his uncle Henry.

At the same time James's relationship with his nobles was worsening. He remained an extremely popular king amongst the general public, and he was welcomed on a tour of Scotland during the summer of 1541 when the nation shared in his and his wife's grief.

By 1542 the relationship between England and France had worsened. A projected meeting between James and Henry VIII was stopped by François and the inevitable conflict became a reality. No formal declaration of war was made, but a series of border conflicts led to an incursion of Henry's men under the duke of Norfolk into Scottish territory in the summer of 1542. James's army followed Norfolk but refused to cross the border, again arguing that they were not going to do France's dirty work. James succeeded in raising another army but as it came to face the English army at Solway Moss in November 1542, James found his earls would not support him and the army broke into disarray. The English victory was easy. Scarcely anyone was killed, and James's army was routed.

It seems that after this defeat James lost the will to live. With no heir to the throne, no support from his nobles and no ability to fight the English, he took to his bed in early December and died a week later. Even the news of the birth of a daughter, the future MARY, Queen of Scots, did nothing to raise his spirits. He died of depression, aged only thirty. His defiant opposition to Henry VIII's Protestantism had established the course of conflict between his heiress, Mary, and the English crown that would prove both a disaster and ultimate success for the Scottish crown.

[FC81] **MARY** queen of Scotland and France
Queen of Scots, 14 December 1542–24 July 1567 (abdicated); Crowned: Stirling Castle, 9 September 1543. Queen consort of France, 10 July 1559–5 December 1560. Born: Linlithgow Palace, 8 December 1542. Died (executed): Fotheringhay Castle, 8 February 1587, aged 44. Buried: Peterborough Cathedral, later removed to Westminster Abbey in 1612.
Married: (1) 24 April 1558, at Notre Dame, Paris, François (1544–60), son of Henri II of France: no children; (2) 29 July 1565, at Holyrood Palace, Henry, lord Darnley (1545–67), son of Matthew Stewart 4th earl of Lennox: one son; (3) 15 May 1567, at Holyrood Palace, James, earl of Bothwell (1535–78): stillborn twins.
Mary was only one week old when her father, JAMES V, pined away from depression. Since Mary's elder brothers had both died in infancy, there must have been some concern that Mary might not survive. Although her mother, Mary of Guise, remained the child's protector, she was not made regent. That role fell to the heir presumptive, James Hamilton, second earl of Arran and great-grandson of JAMES II. Unlike past governors, however, Hamilton was not his own man and was easily influenced. The next five years saw Hamilton battered between the various pro-English and pro-French factions that dominated Scottish politics. The prize was in gaining a marriage treaty with the young princess. Hamilton entertained the hope that she would become the bride of his own son, James. HENRY VIII conspired to make her the wife of his son, the future EDWARD VI, by the Treaty of Greenwich, which was never ratified. When the Scots, under Cardinal Beaton, archbishop of St Andrews, ended this arrangement, English forces harried the Scottish borders in 1544 and 1545, which served only to strengthen the Scottish opposition to the English. Beaton was a fervid papist and ordered the burning of several heretics,

notably George Wishart in 1546. It was probably as a result of this that Beaton was murdered in May 1546, though whether sympathy with England or Protestantism contributed is not entirely clear. It was at this same time that John Knox was forced into exile following his own persecutions as a "heretic". He found refuge on the Continent but returned to Scotland in 1559 as its most fervent Protestant.

When Henry VIII died on 28 January 1547 the French began to exert a stronger influence in Scotland, particularly after the defeat of the Scots by the English Protector, the duke of Somerset, at Pinkie in September 1547. The Scots convinced Hamilton that the best place for Mary's safety was in France and she set sail in July 1548. For the next decade the Scots found themselves the pawn of French affairs, becoming embroiled in the war between France and Spain and consequently with England. Any chance of reconciliation with England, whose new queen MARY Tudor had reverted to Catholicism, was thwarted by the French hostilities. Scotland was powerless to conduct its own affairs, even after their queen, Mary, had decreed in 1554 that she wished to choose her own Governor. James Hamilton was replaced by Mary of Guise, the queen mother, who acted as much the agent for France as for Scotland. It was against this background that Mary was married to the French Dauphin, François, on 24 April 1558. She was fifteen; he was fourteen. The following year, when Henri II of France died in a tournament, Mary became queen consort of France and her husband, king François II. To many Scotland had now lost its sovereignty to the kingdom of France. Mary was believed to have made a secret treaty which made France a Scottish possession should she die without an heir. Considerable opposition to France grew in Scotland and although there was no outright rebellion it did allow the growth of Scottish reformists who supported English Protestantism. When the English queen Mary died in 1558, and it became evident that her successor, ELIZABETH, would follow her father's opposition to the pope and reintroduce the Church of England, the Scottish Protestants turned to England for support in driving out the French. Elizabeth, still not sure of her position, did not initially provide open support, but did not stop the action of her countrymen in their designs. A little earlier the French had recaptured Calais, the only English possession remaining in France, and set about the persecution of the English Protestants in France. Mary of Guise, the queen regent, carried out the same actions in Scotland. The Scottish Protestants and their supporters, who were now becoming openly hostile to the French, sought to depose the queen regent and install their own Regent. They first sought to follow James Stewart, Mary's illegitimate half-brother, but by December 1559 James Hamilton (sometimes called the earl of Arran), the son of the heir presumptive, escaped from captivity and this allowed his father, now known as the duke of Châtelherault, to return to Scotland and resume control. Civil war plagued Scotland over the next six months. Elizabeth of England eventually sent troops to support the Scots against the French. There were no decisive victories, however, and peace was only restored with the death of the queen mother in June 1560. Thereafter the Treaty of Edinburgh called for the peaceful retreat from Scotland of English and French troops. A parliament was called that September in the names of Mary and François II of France. Although an uneasy peace returned to Scotland, there were many loyalists who believed that Mary would remain in France and possibly abdicate her position as queen of Scotland. If she did, then the crown would fall to the Hamiltons, the younger of

From a contemporary portrait

whom was currently pursuing the hand of Elizabeth of England. All this changed, however, in December 1560, when the young French king died. Mary was suddenly without support in France as the new king, Charles IX, was under the power of his mother, Catherine de Medici. Mary determined to return to Scotland. The younger James Hamilton had already contacted Mary, reminding her of their childhood friendship. If they should marry, the Scottish lines of succession would come together and James would become the rightful king. Mary, however, rejected his suit. When she returned to Scotland in August 1561 she sailed to meet her half-brother, Lord James Stewart, at Leith rather than the Hamiltons at Dumbarton. Thereafter the younger Arran's mind began to fail and within a year he was incarcerated as insane.

Mary did not rush into marriage. Instead she worked with her councillors and church representatives to establish a moderate rule in Scotland acceptable by all. In this she achieved remarkable results. Her grace and good humour made her appeal to the general populace, and her desire to be seen about her kingdom increased her popularity. Mary, although at heart a Catholic, allowed religious freedom. She succeeded in walking this middle road by her sheer strength of character. Her supporters talked openly of her as the successor to the English throne and whilst they tried to unite Mary and Elizabeth in common views, Elizabeth's increasing antagonism toward Mary failed to bring about what could have been a strong union. The need for Mary to marry had caused some consternation amongst official circles but, in 1564, Mary fell in love with Henry, Lord Darnley, her second cousin and the next in line to the Scottish throne after herself. Although it seemed a natural match, it was unpopular amongst Mary's nobility. The marriage, which took place in July 1565, was enacted according to the Catholic rites and this ruffled the feathers of the reformers. Moreover, the rise to power of Darnley removed Châtelherault and James Stewart (now earl of Moray) from any likelihood of succession. Although these two nobles rebelled they were soon defeated by Mary who led her own troops into battle. The nobles, however, believed that Mary was neglecting their interests which were supplanted by her own court favourites, especially the court secretary and musician David Rizzio. Darnley also believed Mary was having an affair with Rizzio and, in March 1566, he and his fellow lords murdered Rizzio in front of

Mary. It is possible that the conspirators also intended to murder Mary, but she escaped, along with Darnley, with whom she became briefly reconciled.

However, Mary's position was now endangered. The birth of her son (the future JAMES VI) and his baptism by Catholic rites, further alienated the Protestants. Her reconciliation with Darnley was brief, and she began a new liaison with James Hepburn earl of Bothwell. Bothwell was disliked and distrusted by the other leading nobles, including Mary's own half-brother. Again she was blinded by passion. The two of them conspired to remove Darnley from the scene. This did not necessarily mean his murder, although a divorce might have meant the succession of Mary's young son becoming void. In fact Mary sought to reconcile herself again with Darnley when, on 10 February 1567, he was murdered under somewhat mysterious circumstances at his lodgings in the Provost's House near Holyrood. A tremendous explosion nearly destroyed the house, suggesting the conspirators had sought to murder both Darnley and Mary, except that Mary was not there and Darnley was found smothered in the grounds. The full facts behind the murder of Darnley were not satisfactorily resolved despite several convictions and the unseemly haste by which Bothwell divorced his wife, was acquitted of any part in Darnley's death, and then married Mary on 15 May, only added to the suspicion. Mary had now turned her back on the Catholic faith for she was married by Protestant rites. However, Mary's actions had discredited her in the eyes of many of her lords and her populace. A confederacy of lords united with the outward purpose of rescuing Mary from the traitor Bothwell, but with the real objective of replacing Mary with their own choice. Although Mary and Bothwell fled they were soon captured. Mary was despatched to the castle of Lochleven where, on 24 July 1567 she agreed to abdicate. While at Lochleven Mary miscarried of twins. Bothwell was stripped of all his titles and lands. He fled to Orkney and then to Norway where he remained in exile, dying in Denmark in 1578.

In May 1568 Mary escaped from Lochleven and rapidly raised a considerable army but it was defeated by the supporters of the young king at Langside on 13 May and Mary fled into England. She threw herself under the protection of Queen Elizabeth, but this resulted in Mary's imprisonment at Carlisle on suspicion of involvement in Darnley's murder. A commission which looked into Mary's affairs reached no clear conclusion. This did not wholly clear her name and Elizabeth, who had avoided speaking with Mary, consigned the Scottish queen to further imprisonment, for her own safety, in a series of castles – Bolton, Tutbury, Wingfield. Mary still had supporters, both in Scotland and England and there were many papists who yearned for the restoration of Mary and the overthrow of Elizabeth. While at Wingfield in 1569 she became romantically entangled with Thomas Howard, the Duke of Norfolk, who had investigated the Darnley enquiry on Elizabeth's behalf. Norfolk hatched a scheme with the Florentine financier, Roberto di Ridolfi, to free Mary, overthrow Elizabeth and restore Catholicism. The plan failed. Ridolfi escaped. Norfolk was imprisoned and executed. Mary was now doomed to finish her life imprisoned in a further series of castles and fortified houses: Chatsworth, Sheffield, Chartley and finally Fotheringhay. Throughout this period she managed to involve herself in various intrigues and plots against the English crown, becoming more and more dangerous. Amongst these was the plot of Antony Babington in 1586, who was encouraged by the Catholic priest John Ballard to head a conspiracy against Elizabeth. They were betrayed by double agents including Gilbert Gifford and Anthony Tyrrell. Letters from Mary to Babington were found. Ballard and Babington were executed. Mary was tried and convicted of treason. Elizabeth delayed from signing her death warrant for three months, but Mary was finally beheaded at Fotheringhay Castle on 8 February 1587. There were many who wondered why her son, James VI, now of age and in full sovereignty of Scotland had taken no action to save her. But James, who had never really known his mother, was plotting his own future and was in no mood to complicate matters further. Mary went to the executioner's block bravely and with honour – a victim perhaps of her own pride and recklessness, but ultimately a pawn in the power vortex of love, religion and politics.

[FC82] **JAMES VI**, also **JAMES I** [O26] of England.
Ruled 24 July 1567–27 March 1625. Crowned king of Scotland: Stirling Castle, 29 July 1567.
Full name and titles: James Charles, king of Scotland and (from 1603) England; duke of Rothesay (from birth), duke of Albany, earl of Ross and baron Ardmannoch (from 1567).
*Born: Edinburgh Castle, 19 June 1566. **Died**: Theobalds Park, Hertfordshire, 27 March 1625, aged 58. **Buried**: Westminster Abbey.*
Married: 23 November 1589, at Oslo, Norway, Anne (1574–1619), dau. Frederick II of Denmark and Norway: 9 children.
We tend to think of James VI more as James I king of England, overlooking the fact that he had been king of Scotland already for thirty-six years, twenty-three of those since he had taken the reins of government. He was the first king to rule the whole of Britain (only the Isle of Man retained a separate kingship but was subject to the Crown).

James was the only son of MARY Queen of Scots and Henry, Lord Darnley. Through both his parents he was the great-grandson of Margaret Tudor, sister to HENRY VIII of England, and he was thus heir to the English throne should ELIZABETH, the queen of England, have no children. He was just thirteen months old when his mother was forced to abdicate and, as with most of the Stewart kings of Scotland, their reigns began under a regency amid intense rivalry. James's was complicated by two factors. First his mother was still alive and her supporters, the papists, led by John Hamilton, archbishop of St Andrews, were still powerful amongst the Scots. Second, accusations were still flying over the murder of his father, Lord Darnley. Both his mother and his uncle, the earl of Moray, were implicated. Although both were eventually cleared of the charges, Moray (who almost certainly was a party to it) succeeded in casting the blame on to William Maitland of Lethington, who had been Mary's secretary of state. Maitland was thrown into prison but was never tried and though released later died in prison. Moray became regent of Scotland. He was the head of the pro-Reformation faction that opposed Mary. Although he had his enemies, Moray was a strong and able governor. Had he been conceived on the right side of the sheets he would have been a good king. He succeeded in subduing rebels in the Borders like no previous monarch, and it was primarily through his guidance that Protestantism spread throughout Scotland and took too strong a hold to fail. Nevertheless his enemies eventually got the better of him, and in January 1570 Moray was murdered by

James Hamilton of Bothwellhaugh, nephew of Archbishop Hamilton. Although the younger Hamilton was not brought to book, his uncle was. Elizabeth of England knew that Hamilton was the power behind a series of border incidents. She took advantage of the divisions between the Scottish nobility to encourage Matthew Stewart, earl of Lennox and James's grandfather, to attack and devastate Hamilton's lands. Lennox was promoted to the regency. Although he was becoming old and weak, he was still a passionate supporter of the King and in the ensuing months he captured Archbishop Hamilton who was tried, found guilty of complicity in the murders of Darnley and Stewart, and hanged. Over the ensuing months Lennox pressed home his advantage. His Protestant faction eventually won the day, though Lennox himself was shot and killed in a skirmish in Stirling in September 1571.

The next regent was John Erskine, earl of Mar, who governed for just over a year, but the real power behind the throne, and the next regent, was James Douglas, earl of Morton. Morton had his enemies but he established a firm and stable government. He was the strongest champion of the Protestant cause, to the extent of passing legislation that enabled justiciars to levy fines for non-conformity to the new faith. Although he was briefly ousted from the regency by the earls of Argyll and Atholl in 1578, he regained control for a further two years. The young king did not like Morton, who was cold and ruthless. James had been starved of parental affection for all of his childhood, and this allowed him to warm to the ebullient and avuncular Esmé Stuart, a cousin of his father's, who had been raised in France but who was also an heir to the throne. He came as an agent to Scotland in 1579 in the hope of converting the country back to Catholicism. Through his urbanity he soon won the affection of the young king and succeeded in overthrowing Morton who was charged with involvement in the murder of Darnley. Morton was arrested and executed in 1581. Stuart's true colours however now emerged and the threat of a popish plot caused the more extreme Protestant faction to react. William Ruthven seized James in August 1582 and refused to release him until James agreed to the banishment of Esmé Stuart. Once this was accomplished James was freed in June 1583. The episode, known as the Ruthven Raid, demonstrated what a powerful force Protestantism had become by the late sixteenth century, and how much the king was perceived as the figurehead in determining the direction of the church.

James's relationship with Esmé has caused some to regard James as homosexual, or at the least bi-sexual. It is quite likely as, starved of affection in his youth, James showered love and affection on anyone who showed him a personal interest. James had not been the most attractive of children. He was short and walked with a rolling gait that was suggestive of rickets. He had somewhat bulbous eyes and apparently had trouble swallowing so that he frequently drooled. This affliction also affected his speech which was, at times, slurred. How much of this picture of James was the product of his enemies is less easy to interpret, because much of it is recorded by later English chroniclers, some of whom found it difficult to understand James's broad Scottish accent. Other more dangerous rumours were spread about James. The most extreme was that he was a changeling child, swapped because Mary's had been stillborn. Some noticed a remarkable resemblance with John Erskine, earl of Mar. The remains of a newborn baby were found at Edinburgh Castle during

From a portrait by
Paul van Somer, 1620

renovations in the nineteenth century, but nothing was proved. The same rumours spread about JAMES II's only surviving son, the Old Pretender (*see* JAMES VIII).

Although James had exercised some authority in government since 1578, by 1583, at the age of seventeen, he decided he would no longer be the pawn of factions within his aristocracy. All those who attempted to control him, such as James Stewart, the new earl of Arran (and cousin of the previous earl, James Hamilton, former suitor of Mary, Queen of Scots), found their power rapidly curtailed. By 1586 James had established a government of moderates who moved along with his own wishes towards a firm relationship with England and a strong control over Protestant affairs. This did not stop James being an eternally nervous king, in regular fear of assassination, a consequence of his upbringing rather than of his current state. It also made him cautious in his foreign affairs. By 1586 he had reached an informal agreement with Elizabeth of England whereby he became her successor, and James would do nothing to endanger that. For that reason he remained silent while his mother was tried and executed in February 1587, and remained neutral during England's war with Spain and the invasion of the Spanish Armada in July 1588.

The death of Mary, Queen of Scots, reduced the power of the Catholic faction who now had no figurehead. Most of the Catholics were in the north of Scotland where Protestantism had barely reached. The Highlanders professed Catholicism, but many still held true to the old Celtic church, whilst others often practiced pagan worship. (Claims of witchcraft amongst the Highlanders were rife in the 1590s. James compiled a volume railing against witchcraft and satanism called *Dæmono-logie* (1597) and in 1603 introduced an act with the aim of abolishing its practice, though with little effect.) It was these northern Scots who still held dialogue with the Spanish and were a threat to Scottish uniformity – not that that was new in Scottish history. The Highlands and the Lowlands had seldom been one kingdom, for all they might have purported to be one country. Nevertheless, James could not have the north siding with Spain and creating a Catholic kingdom north of the

43. Scotland (10) – The Scottish – English Succession

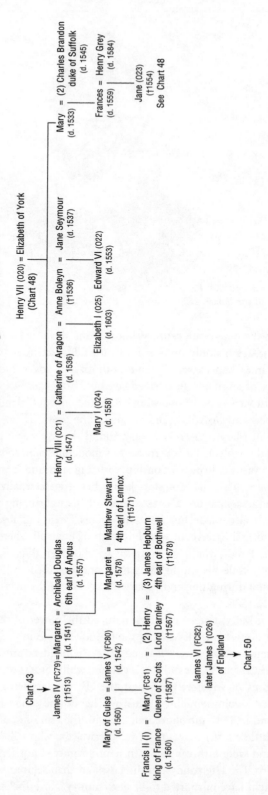

Clyde. In 1589 he quashed one potential rebellion when he discovered that the earls of Huntly and Errol had been in communication with Spain over a invasion. James treated the earls lightly. But in 1592 James became aware of similar plans again involving Huntly and Errol, this time in league with the earls of Angus and Bothwell. James bided his time, working matters to his own advantage until in 1594 he was able to surprise the earls and banish them from the kingdom.

At the same time he was increasingly nervous of the power of the Protestants, especially once Presbyterianism was introduced by Act of Parliament in 1592. These reformists regarded themselves as beholden only to God, not to the King. The King was as much a vassal of God as were they, and God's on Earth was spokesman the General Assembly. This meant that James VI effectively had no authority over the church, a matter of which Andrew Melville, the instigator of Presbyterianism, was prone to remind the king. James VI now worked one faction against another. In 1596 he recalled the northern earls and stated that these and other northern magnates should have their own equal representation on the General Assembly. Hitherto the Assembly had been composed almost entirely of earls from the south under the domination of Melville. Moreover, although Melville believed James could not abolish the General Assembly, James had statutory control over the holding of any assembly. He could thus control when the Assembly could meet and who was on it. In one quite masterful stroke he weakened the power of the Presbyterians and ensured the northern earls were no longer isolated. He was soon to remind Melville and his colleagues of his own belief in the authority of kingship. In 1599 he produced his book, *Basilikon Doron*, which espoused the divine right of kings. It was a direct challenge to Melville's Presbyterianism. Fifty years later it would lead to the death of James's son Charles.

After 1596 James was in complete control of his kingdom. Occasional skirmishes erupted, but nothing that seriously endangered his authority. The worst example was the Gowrie Conspiracy in August 1600 when it was alleged Alexander Ruthven, the brother of the earl of Gowrie, lured James to his house in Perth on some pretext only then to attack James. In the resultant fracas, Ruthven and the earl were killed. There has been some speculation over whether James fabricated this story to explain the death of Gowrie to whom James owed considerable sums of money, but the weight of opinion has settled in favour of James. Gowrie's primary opposition to James had been over his passion to unite England and Scotland, for which purpose James had planned to raise an army to ensure his succession.

James had used the authority of kingship to unite a kingdom more completely than any previous Scottish king. He still did not crack the inveterate obstinacy of the Highlanders who paid him mock allegiance but otherwise played by their own rules, but he had little interest in them anyway. By now Elizabeth of England was in her sixties, and her lack of an heir meant that it was only a matter of time before, barring accidents, James inherited the crown of England. He had married Anne of Denmark in 1589 and had a son and heir, Henry, born in February 1594, and a daughter, Elizabeth, in August 1596. Others would follow. No other king was so confident in his kingdom, and no other nation so expectant as Scotland. The news came on 26 March 1603 when a messenger arrived at Holyrood to inform the king that Elizabeth had died two days previously. Two days later another messenger arrived to say that the English Privy Council had decreed James was her successor.

On 5 April James left Scotland for England. Although he promised to revisit it often he only returned once in the next twenty-two years. Scotland may have gained a kingdom but it had lost its king.

The remainder of James's reign and the subsequent kings of England and Scotland are continued on page 647.

NA. KINGDOM OF MAN

In 1290 Edward I took possession of the island for England, placing it under the governorship of Richard de Burgh, earl of Ulster. John Balliol briefly reclaimed the island for Scotland from 1293–96; otherwise it remained under English control. During this period the most stable period of governorship was under Antony Bek, bishop of Durham, from 1298 to 1311. Robert the Bruce claimed Man again for Scotland in 1313. In 1316 the Irish ravaged the island and it remained a battlefield plundered and claimed by Ireland, Scotland and England until the powerful reign of Edward III. In 1333 Edward granted the island to William de Montacute in full possession, so that he became the first restored sovereign lord of Man for nearly seventy years.

Ref.	Ruler	Born	Reign	Died	Notes
continued from page 421					
NA49.	William de Montacute (i.e. Montague)		1333–44	1344	also created earl of Salisbury in 1337
NA50.	William Montague (II)		1344–92	1397	sold the island to William le Scrope
NA51.	William le Scrope		1393–9	1399	beheaded
NA52.	Henry Percy, earl of Northumberland		1399–1405	1408	deprived of lordship
House of Stanley					
NA53.	John	*c*1350	1405–14	1414	
NA54.	John II		1414–37	1437	
NA55.	Thomas	*c*1405	1437–59	1459	
NA56.	Thomas II	*c*1435	1459–1504	1504	created earl of Derby in 1485
On the death of Thomas II, his successor gave up the title of king and became lord of Man.					
NA57.	Thomas III	*c*1481	1504–21	1521	
NA58.	Edward	1509	1521–72	1572	
NA59.	Henry	1531	1572–93	1593	
NA60.	Ferdinando	*c*1559	1593–4	1594	
Succession in dispute 1594–1612; meanwhile Man returned to Elizabeth I and James I of England.					
NA61.	William I	*c*1561	1610–12	1647	Although the lawful ruler, William left governorship with his wife Elizabeth, and then his son James

NA62.	Elizabeth, countess of Derby	1575	1612–27	1627	
NA63.	James, Lord Strange	1607	1627–51	1651	executed

After the earl of Derby's death his wife briefly controlled the island, though she was deposed in a rebellion. Governorship passed to Lord Fairfax from 1651–60 until the restoration of the English monarchy, restored the Stanleys to the lordship of Man.

NA64.	Charles	1628	1660–72	1672	
NA65.	William II	c1655	1672–1702	1702	
NA66.	James II	1664	1702–36	1736	

House of Murray

NA67.	James Murray	c1690	1736–64	1764	2nd duke of Atholl
NA69.	John Murray	1729	1764–5	1774	

Murray sold the lordship to the British Crown in 1765 and the island came under British sovereignty.

[NA49] **WILLIAM DE MONTACUTE** king of Man, 9 August 1333–30 January 1344.
Montacute (*born* 1301; *died* 1344) was the son of the second Baron Montacute, who had served under EDWARD I in his wars against the Welsh and the Scots. The young William continued this service under EDWARD III, assisted in the arrest of Roger Mortimer in 1330 and was rewarded with some of Mortimer's lands. He was present at the siege of Berwick and the battle of Halidon Hill in 1333 where the Scots suffered a crushing defeat. In gratitude for Montacute's service Edward granted him full sovereignty of the Isle of Man which in effect re-established the island as an independent kingdom. The island people did not give in so easily and Montacute had to invade the island in 1341 when he was officially crowned king. William spent little time on the island. He was created earl of Salisbury in 1337 and Marshal of England in 1338, and fought in Flanders in 1340 where he was briefly captured.

[NA50] **WILLIAM MONTAGUE (II)** king of Man, 1344–92.
Born 1328. The second earl of Salisbury, was, like his father, another absentee king of Man. While still in his teens he became involved in a notorious case when, in about 1346, he married Joan of Woodstock, the granddaughter of EDWARD I, who was already married. The pope pronounced the marriage invalid on the grounds of bigamy. He spent much of his life serving EDWARD III in France and distinguished himself at Poitiers in 1356. He was not interested in the Island and, in 1392, sold both the land and the crown to William LE SCROPE, though he retained the title lord of Man until his death on 3 June 1397.

[NA51] **SCROPE, WILLIAM LE** king of Man, 1393–30 July 1399.
William (c1351–1399) was the son of Richard, the first Baron Scrope of Bolton, and one of a large northern family who produced a number of magnates in the fourteenth and fifteenth centuries. Like many of the knights of his day, Scrope spent much of his life fighting in France under EDWARD III before becoming vice-chamberlain of RICHARD II in 1393, the same year that he acquired the title and kingdom of Man from William MONTAGUE. Scrope remained a close ally of Richard

44. Kings and Lords of Man – **The House of Stanley**

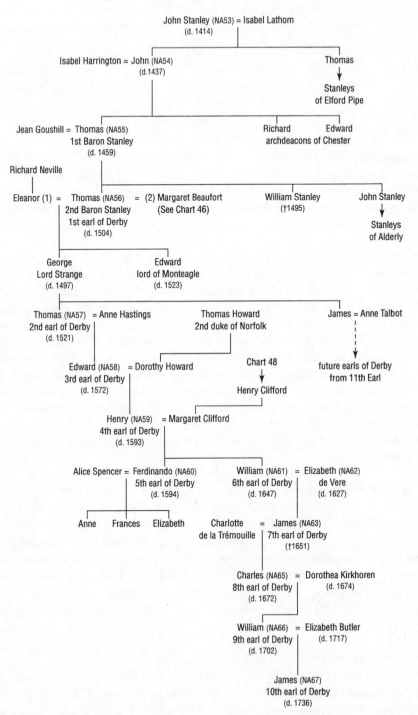

II, and assisted in the arrest and trial of the rebel barons. Scrope was richly rewarded, being created earl of Wiltshire, and taking possession of many of the lands of the earl of Warwick, who was made a ward of Scrope's on Man. Scrope and his allies were despised by the other nobles, and were closely associated with Richard II's tyrannies. He was so trusted by Richard that he made him executor of his will and left him as chief adviser to his uncle, Edmund, duke of York, who served as regent when Richard went to Ireland in 1399. When HENRY IV invaded, Scrope was captured at Bristol and promptly executed. On his death the kingdom was given to Henry PERCY, earl of Northumberland.

[NA52] **HENRY PERCY**, EARL OF NORTHUMBERLAND king of Man, 19 October 1399–April 1405.
The Percies were an important family in northern England whose ancestor, William de Percy, received lands in Yorkshire and elsewhere from WILLIAM I. Henry Percy (1342–1408) served under EDWARD III and was created earl of Northumberland and Marshal of England in 1377. Although he originally supported RICHARD II, he turned against him because of the king's increased violence and excesses and supported the invasion of HENRY IV in 1399. For this he received further honours including the kingdom of Man. Percy and his son, Hotspur, soon turned against Henry IV and plotted with Edmund Mortimer and OWAIN GLYN DWR to dethrone the king and share England and Wales between them. He was declared a traitor and deprived of his lands. He was killed in battle on 20 February 1408 at Bramham Moor. The Isle of Man passed to the STANLEY family.

[NA53] **JOHN STANLEY** king of Man, 4 October 1405–14.
The Stanleys were descended from Adam de Aldithley who accompanied William the Conqueror to England and whose descendants inherited land in Staffordshire and Derbyshire. The surname derived from Stoneley in Derbyshire. John Stanley, who was born in about 1350, supported HENRY IV at the time of the rebellion of the marcher lord Edmund Mortimer in 1403 and he was knighted and rewarded with the fiefdom of Man, which had been taken from Henry PERCY. In return Sir John's family had to provide two falcons at the coronation of each king of England. He never visited Man but spent his remaining years as lieutenant of Ireland. He was succeeded by his son, JOHN.

[NA54] **JOHN STANLEY** (II) king of Man, 1414–37.
John was the first "king" of Man to visit the island since WILLIAM DE MONTACUTE in 1341. He took an interest in the island's affairs and brought order to the chaos by codifying the old laws, abolishing church sanctuary, abolishing trial by combat and introducing trial by jury, and ensuring there were clerks to the justices keeping records of all proceedings. His influence lasted for generations as it was not until 1507 that another Stanley visited the island.

[NA55] **THOMAS** (I), BARON STANLEY king of Man, 1437–59.
Born c1406. Thomas was created Baron Stanley, 1456. He was lieutenant-governor of Ireland from 1432 to 1437 and later became a Member of Parliament for Lancashire, rising to Lord Chamberlain in 1455. He never visited Man but governed it through the administrators established by his father.

[NA56] **THOMAS II** king of Man, 1459–29 July 1504.

*Born c*1435. Thomas never visited Man, but he was one of the most prominent people in England in his day, mainly because of his remarkable ability for survival. Primarily a Lancastrian, and thus a supporter of HENRY VI, he nevertheless was able to switch sides comfortably to EDWARD IV, who made him chief justice of Chester, and back to Lancaster again with the restoration of Henry. He had married Eleanor, the sister of Warwick the King Maker, but survived the fall of the earl. In 1482 he married Margaret Beaufort, the granddaughter of John of Gaunt and widow of Edmund Tudor. He thereby became the stepfather of Henry Tudor. His only fall from grace came in 1483 when the future RICHARD III accused him of plotting against him and he was imprisoned, but he survived the punishment meted out to many of Richard's opponents, was released in 1484 and appointed Constable of England. He remained neutral at the battle of Bosworth (as he had on other occasions during the Wars of the Roses), but with his stepson's victory, Thomas found the crown on the battlefield and informally crowned Henry king. Thomas was made earl of Derby on 27 October 1485. He remained in the king's favour for the rest of his life though his brother, Sir William Stanley, became a supporter of the pretender PERKIN WARBECK and was executed in 1495.

[NA57] **THOMAS III** lord of Man and the Isles, 29 July 1504–23 May 1521.

*Born: c*1481. He succeeded his grandfather as earl of Derby and sovereign lord of Man since his father, George, had died the year before, believed poisoned at a banquet. In deference to HENRY VII, Thomas, the 2nd earl of Derby, relinquished his title as king of Man and became lord on his accession in 1504, though he retained full sovereign powers in fief. He became involved in a dispute between the islanders and the Scots, suppressing the latter in 1507. The port of Derbyhaven was named after him. A valiant soldier he accompanied Henry VIII in his French wars and was at the battle of the Spurs in 1513.

[NA58] **EDWARD** lord of Man and the Isles, 23 May 1521–24 October 1572.

Third earl of Derby. Edward's life (he was born in 1509) was unusually long for his day, but he succeeded in remaining on the right side of HENRY VIII, MARY and ELIZABETH. Interestingly, Henry's 1539 Act which suppressed the monasteries did not cover Man, but this did not stop the island's monasteries being closed and the property seized by the crown. Edward's lordship of Man was evidently nominal by this stage. Stanley was, in fact, a staunch Roman Catholic, and did not promote the Reformation in Man. As a consequence, although the monasteries were closed, it took over half a century before the new order began to pervade the island. Stanley never visited Man. He was lord lieutenant of Lancashire in 1552 and again in 1569. He suppressed uprisings in the north and was a prominent Privy Councillor, though in his final years the Queen became more than a little suspicious of him.

[NA59] **HENRY** lord of Man, 24 October 1572–25 September 1593.

Born 1531; fourth earl of Derby, known as Lord Strange until 1572. In his youth he was one of the courtiers to EDWARD VI and subsequently to Philip II of Spain. In 1555 he married Margaret Clifford, the cousin of JANE Grey. From 1574, when he was knighted, he was a commissioner for ecclesiastical causes and a member of the Council of the North. He was one of the peers who sat upon the trial of MARY,

Queen of Scots. During the rest of his life he did little to bring Man in line with the rest of the Reformation.

[NA60] **FERDINANDO** lord of Man, 25 September 1593–16 April 1594.
Born 1559; fifth Earl of Derby, known as Lord Strange from 1589. The son of the fourth earl, he was through his mother, fourth in descent from HENRY VII. When he succeeded to the lordship, he was approached by conspirators believed to be in the pay of Philip of Spain who were planning the assassination of the queen. They sought his interest in assuming the kingship but when he refused, with considerable indignation, he was allegedly poisoned by the conspirators. He was in his mid-thirties. He had three daughters but no son, so the earldom passed to his brother, William, but a dispute over the daughters' claims dragged on until 1610, during which time Man reverted to the Crown.

[NA61] **WILLIAM** lord of Man, 7 July 1609 (ratified 1610)–29 September 1642.
Sixth earl of Derby. *Born: c*1561. Although confirmed as lord of Man in 1610, after he purchased the title from his nieces, William left the government of the island to his wife, **Elizabeth** [NA62], who died in 1627, and then his son, James. He had previously been governor of Man on behalf of his father in 1593. His wife, Elizabeth, was the daughter of Edward de Vere, earl of Oxford. Interestingly both William and his father-in-law have been claimed by certain scholars to be the author of some, if not most, of the plays attributed to William Shakespeare. In Stanley's case there is interesting if circumstantial evidence that he could have written *Love's Labours Lost*, which was probably written in the late 1580s, and possibly also *The Tempest* (completed around 1611) where the Calf of Man may have served as the model for Prospero's Island. It is unfortunate that so little is known about the earl, who seems to have kept himself to himself.

[NA63] **JAMES, "THE GREAT STANLEY"**, lord of Man, 10 March 1627–15 October 1651.
Born 31 January 1607; seventh earl of Derby from 1642; Lord Strange from 1628. When the English Civil War erupted in 1642, the Isle of Man was as divided as the rest of England. James had appointed a Manx governor, Edward Christian, a sailor and soldier of fortune who had become rather too grasping and whom James demoted in 1639. However, he restored him to favour in 1641 and placed him in command of the troops on Man. There had been unrest in the island for several years because of the tithes that James imposed. Christian stirred these troops up in support of Cromwell, whereas James was a staunch Royalist. James visited the island in 1642 to resolve the dispute, which he did by reducing the tithes and imprisoning Christian. He also maintained that all of the islanders were tenants and none owned the land. James fought on the side of CHARLES I, but after the defeat at Marston Moor he retired to Man which he proceeded to fortify, succeeding in repulsing any Parliamentarian ships sent against it. Man remained a Royalist enclave until 1651, when James was lured from the island in the hope of supporting the army of CHARLES II. His Manx force was defeated at Wigan. James was captured, tried and executed as a traitor at Bolton. His wife, Charlotte, whom he married in 1626, would have held the island against the Parliamentarians when it was besieged in 1644, but she was betrayed by William Christian, who raised local Manx forces,

led by Illiam Dhone, against the countess and forced her surrender. The island was thereafter governed by Lord Fairfax until the restoration saw the return of the next earl of Derby.

[NA64] **CHARLES** lord of Man, 29 May 1660–21 December 1672.
With the Restoration, the new lord of Man, the eighth earl of Derby (*born* 19 January 1628), sought revenge upon William Christian who had usurped command. Christian was then in prison for debt, but he was released and brought to the island, where he refused to recognize any local court. He was therefore condemned without trial and executed by firing squad on 2 January 1663. Christian had appealed to CHARLES II but the news reached the king too late. He was repelled by this retribution and ensured that Christian's land was restored to his son and the other rebels were released. Some efforts were made during the earl's reign to improve education on the island though this was hampered by the adherence to the Manx language and the resolute opposition to English.

[NA65] **WILLIAM II** lord of Man, 21 December 1672–5 November 1702.
Born 18 March 1656; ninth earl of Derby. During William's reign on Man, a local coinage was introduced from 1679. William also tried to resolve the problem of land tenure arising as a result of the innovations of James STANLEY fifty years earlier, though this was not resolved until his brother's reign.

[NA66] **JAMES II** lord of Man, 5 November 1702–1 February 1736.
Born, 3 July 1664; tenth earl of Derby. It was James who at last resolved the land problem in Man with the Act of Settlement of 1704, known as the Manx Magna Carta, thanks to the work of the bishop of Sodor and Man, Thomas Wilson. The Act restored ownership of the land to the farmers in return for a lord's rent. Wilson was a strong character who believed that the church on Man should hold its former powers, allowing it the power of arrest. This resulted in 1716 in a dispute between Wilson and the lord of Man which caused considerable unrest and was never satisfactorily resolved. Wilson's domination of the island became almost tyrannical, though intended to be good for the souls of his flock. James had no surviving children and under the terms of the grant of his Lordship the sovereignty of the island passed to James MURRAY, duke of Atholl.

[NA67] **JAMES MURRAY** lord of Man, 1 February 1736–8 January 1764. Second duke of Atholl.
Born 1690. When James acquired the lordship he visited the island and presided over the annual Tynwald. He was welcomed by the islanders who were tired of the STANLEY regime. He passed a number of popular acts including the Act of Tynwald in 1737, known as the Manx Bill of Rights, which recognized the authority of the local parliament in fixing customs duties and, above all, ensured that everyone had the right of trial by jury. He was Lord Privy Seal from 1733–63 and thereafter Lord Justice General.

[NA68] **JOHN MURRAY** lord of Man, 8 January 1764–21 June 1765.
Third duke of Atholl. *Born* 1729. Nephew and son-in-law of James Murray. John was the last lord of Man with sovereign rights. The British government had become tired of the Island's position in a vast network of smuggling, which the previous

lords had encouraged because of the severe custom duties they had imposed on the island. The British government thereupon forced the sale of Man for £70,000. John's ducal rights as "lord of the manor", remained, but the sovereignty returned to GEORGE III. The duke died in 1774.

O. ENGLAND AND GREAT BRITAIN From Edward I to Elizabeth II

Civil war split England three times between the Norman Conquest in 1066 and the death of Henry III. With Edward I came the first strong king able to unite England and institute what became known as the Model Parliament in 1295. Edward also conquered Wales and with the Statute of Wales in 1284 incorporated it into England. Edward sought to do the same for Scotland, but found it harder to subdue the Scottish nation and died before the kingdoms were united. It would not be until 1603, with the death of Elizabeth I, that Scotland and England were ruled by the same monarch, and not until the Act of Union in 1707 that the United Kingdom was officially created.

Ref.	Ruler	Born	Reign	Died	Notes

ENGLAND

The House of Anjou (*continued from page 470*)

Ref.	Ruler	Born	Reign	Died	Notes
O10.	Edward I	1239	1272–1307	1307	
O11.	Edward II	1284	1307–27	1327	deposed and later murdered
O12.	Edward III	1312	1327–77	1377	assumed direct authority from October 1330
O13.	Richard II	1367	1377–99	1400	deposed and possibly murdered

House of Lancaster

Ref.	Ruler	Born	Reign	Died	Notes
O14.	Henry IV *Bolingbroke*	1367?	1399–1413	1413	
O15.	Henry V	1387	1413–22	1422	
O16.	Henry VI	1421	1422–61		declared of age November 1437; deposed March 1461
	(*restored*)		1470–1	1471	restored October 1470; deposed again April 1471; murdered

Protector during minority: John, duke of Bedford 1422–29.

House of York

Ref.	Ruler	Born	Reign	Died	Notes
O17.	Edward IV	1442	1461–70		deposed October 1470;
	(*restored*)		1471–83	1483	restored April 1471
O18.	Edward V	1470	Apr–Jun 1483	1483	deposed; one of the Princes in the Tower
O19.	Richard III *Crookback*	1452	1483–85	1485	killed in battle

House of Tudor

Ref.	Ruler	Born	Reign	Died	Notes
O20.	Henry VII	1457	1485–1509	1509	
O21.	Henry VIII	1491	1509–47	1547	
O22.	Edward VI	1537	1547–53	1553	

Protector during Minority: Edward Seymour, earl of Hertford, 1547–9.

Ref.	Ruler	Born	Reign	Died	Notes
O23.	Jane	1537	10–19 Jul 1553	1554	deposed after nine days; executed
O24.	Mary (I)	1516	1553–8	1558	
O25.	Elizabeth (I)	1533	1558–1603	1603	

ENGLAND AND SCOTLAND

House of Stewart

Ref.	Ruler	Born	Reign	Died	Notes
O26.	James (I)	1566	1603–25	1625	James VI of Scotland [FC82]
O27.	Charles (I)	1600	1625–49	1649	deposed and executed; see also FC83

Commonwealth declared May 19, 1649 under rule of a Lord Protector

	Oliver Cromwell	1599	1653–8	1658	
	Richard Cromwell	1626	1658–9	1712	abdicated

Commonwealth nullified May 1659; monarchy restored May 1660

Ref.	Ruler	Born	Reign	Died	Notes
O28.	Charles II	1630	1660–85	1685	see also FC84
O29.	James II	1633	1685–8	1701	abdicated; see also FC85

Interregnum 11 Dec 1688–12 Feb 1689 when government assumed by the Peers

Ref.	Ruler	Born	Reign	Died	Notes
O30.	William III	1650	1689–1702	1702	joint ruler with Mary II; see also FC86
O31.	Mary II	1662	1689–94	1694	joint ruler with William III; see also FC87

GREAT BRITAIN after Act of Union 1 May 1707

Ref.	Ruler	Born	Reign	Died	Notes
O32.	Anne	1665	1702–14	1714	see also FC88

House of Hanover

Ref.	Ruler	Born	Reign	Died	Notes
O33.	George I	1660	1714–27	1727	see also W2
O34.	George II	1683	1727–60	1760	see also W3
O35.	George III	1738	1760–1820	1820	see also W4

From 5 Feb 1811 the prince of Wales (future George IV) became "Prince Regent"

Ref.	Ruler	Born	Reign	Died	Notes
O36.	George IV	1762	1820–30	1830	see also W5
O37.	William IV	1765	1830–7	1837	see also W6
O38.	Victoria	1819	1837–1901	1901	

House of Saxe-Coburg-Gotha, changed to Windsor from 1917

Ref.	Ruler	Born	Reign	Died	Notes
O39.	Edward VII	1841	1901–10	1910	
O40.	George V	1865	1910–36	1936	
O41.	Edward VIII	1894	Jan–Dec 1936	1972	abdicated
O42.	George VI	1895	1936–52	1952	
O43.	Elizabeth II	1926	1952–		

[O10;SB20] EDWARD (I) *LONGSHANKS*

Ruled 16 November 1272–7 July 1307. Crowned: Westminster Abbey, 19 August 1274.

Titles: *king of England, Wales (from 1284), Man (from 1290), Scotland (from 1296), lord of Ireland, duke of Gascony (from 1254), earl of Chester (from 1254).*

Born: *Palace of Westminster, 17 June 1239.* **Died:** *Burgh-on-Sands, near Carlisle, 7 July 1307, aged 68.* **Buried:** *Westminster Abbey.*

Married: *(1) October 1254, at Las Huelgas, Castile, Eleanor (1241–90), dau. of Ferdinand III, king of Castile: 16 children; (2) 10 September 1299, at Canterbury*

Cathedral, Margaret (c1279–1318) dau. of Philippe III, king of France: 3 children.
Edward is reputed to have had one illegitimate child, although the claim is suspect.
Edward I is certainly the greatest of the Plantagenet kings of England and one of the
most important of all English kings. The soubriquets applied to him give some
indication of his abilities: "the Lawgiver", "the Hammer of the Scots", "the Father
of the Mother of Parliaments", "the English Justinian", let alone his personal
nickname of Longshanks, which was not derogatory. Edward was a tall man,
healthy, strong and immensely powerful, a born soldier.

He was the eldest son of HENRY III and Eleanor of Provence, born when his father
had already reigned for over twenty years. Thanks to his father's long reign, Edward
was able to ascend to the throne in the flower of his manhood. Thankfully he had
also matured, for his youth, whilst spent as part of a loving family, was also
tempestuous. In 1254, when only fifteen, he was married to Eleanor of Castile.
Eleanor was herself barely thirteen and was known as the infanta of Castile. To
English ears this sounded more like Elephant and Castle and gave rise to the name
of many inns and taverns, and through them the district in south London. It was a
political marriage in order to protect the southern borders of Gascony, England's
last possession in France. The governorship of Gascony had been in the hands of
Simon de Montfort whose autocratic rule had caused considerable unrest. Edward
was invested as duke of Gascony at the time of his marriage, and acknowledged his
fealty to the French king, the sainted Louis IX. However, Edward's command of
Gascony does not seem to have been any less turbulent than De Montfort's. It
appears Edward ruled with a strong hand and was not averse to severe retribution if
any of his subjects challenged his authority.

At the same time (1254) Edward had been invested with lands in Wales and
Ireland, and his first experience of warfare came in the uprisings in Wales when in
1256 the Welsh, under the leadership of LLYWELYN AP GRUFFYDD, rebelled against
the English imposition of a system of county administration. Peace was rapidly
concluded because Henry III was facing his own internal problems in the rebellion
of the barons. Edward initially sided with Simon de Montfort in producing the
Provisions of Westminster in 1259, but later supported his father in the war that
broke out in 1264. It was Edward who captured the younger Simon de Montfort at
Northampton, but it was also Edward's youthful rashness that led to his capture
alongside his father at the battle of Lewes later that year. Edward succeeded in
escaping his custody a year later and in August 1265 routed and killed the elder De
Montfort at the battle of Evesham. Henry's retribution on the disaffected barons
was severe and those who were disinherited fought back from a stronghold at Ely in
1267. It was Edward who overpowered the barons, and it was his military skill and
show of strength that helped bring a peace to England by 1269.

Edward was now thirty and, in 1270, set out on a long-awaited Crusade to the
Holy Land. Although his escapades were not entirely glorious, there was much
derring-do suitable for later retellings in adventure stories. Edward succeeded in
relieving Acre from one of its many sieges by the troops of the sultan of Egypt, and
won a victory at Haifa, but he was also wounded by a poisoned dagger wielded by
an Assassin. Had he died English history would have been significantly different,
and there would certainly have been a succession crisis with no adult heir. Edward
recovered, however; this was later said to be thanks to his wife who sucked the

45. England (4) – The House of Anjou (2) – Edward I to Edward III

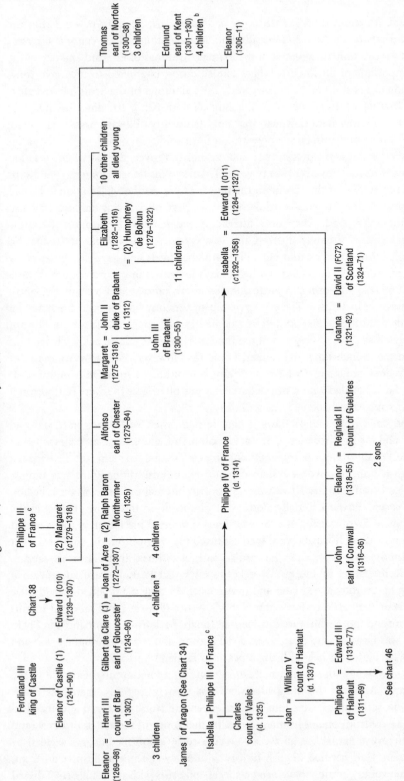

Notes: (a) Joan of Acre's children included Eleanor (1292–1337), who married Edward II's favourite Hugh le Despenser (†1326), and Margaret (1293–1342), who married Edward II's earlier favourite Piers Gaveston (†1312).

(b) Edmund's children included Joan, Maid of Kent (1328–85), the wife of Edward, the Black Prince (see chart 46).

(c) Philippe III of France was the father of Edward I's second wife and the grandfather of Edward II's wife.

poison from the wound. He was in Sicily on his way home when, in November 1272, he learned of his father's death. It is an indication of how confident Edward was in his English regents that he did not hurry home. Instead he travelled triumphantly through Italy as a Crusader hero and new king, and on through France to pay homage to the new French king, Philippe III. He eventually returned to England on 2 August 1274, with his coronation held seventeen days later.

The coronation was a momentous occasion, but a small cloud over it would cast a long shadow. Llywelyn ap Gruffydd, the prince of Wales, failed to attend to pay homage. Edward commanded him to attend his court on two later occasions and even travelled to Chester in 1276 to make it easier. When Llywelyn rebuffed him for a third time, Edward acted with lightning effect. He declared Llywelyn a rebel and thus anyone supporting him would be a traitor. When Edward brought his forces into Powys opposition immediately crumbled, and Edward was able to penetrate into Gwynedd and force Llywelyn into submission. Under the Treaty of Aberconwy in November 1277, Llywelyn retained the now hollow title of prince of Wales, and held authority over only Gwynedd, west of the Conway, and was forced to share that with his brother. Llywelyn, though humiliated, endeavoured to remain respectful of Edward to the extent that in October 1278 Edward allowed the long promised marriage between Llywelyn, and his cousin, Eleanor, the daughter of Simon de Montfort. This arrangement had been made in 1265, when Eleanor was only thirteen. Unfortunately Eleanor died in childbirth four years later, just at the time that actions by Llywelyn's brother DAFYDD caused a further rebellion in Wales and Llywelyn, possibly against his will, was forced back into the limelight. Edward, believing he had previously treated Llywelyn with surprising leniency, was furious. Although the Welsh offered more resistance than in 1278, Edward was able to call upon much greater resources than the Welsh. Victory was almost certain to be Edward's, but it was made more complete when Llywelyn was killed in a skirmish in December 1282. His renegade brother held out for a further four months but was arrested in April 1283 and executed for treason six months later. Edward was no longer prepared to tolerate the perpetual hostility from the Welsh. On 19 March 1284 the Statute of Wales was enacted, bringing Wales under the direct government of England. Wales now held the status of a colony of the Crown, and justice was administered by three sheriffs. Edward also set up a series of new lordships, some of which were granted to the dispossessed Welsh princes, but others to Edward's own barons. In June 1284 Edward celebrated his conquest of Wales by holding an Arthurian Round Table court at Nefyn. The festivities were so well attended that the floor of the court gave way under the strain. One of the legends attached to this period is that Edward promised he would grant them a prince who had been born on their own soil, and promptly presented to them his young son, Edward, who had been born in April 1284. Edward was not officially invested as prince of Wales until February 1301.

The Welsh exploits were but one chapter of Edward's early reign, though a significant one. Much of his energy was directed toward a survey of England and a reformation of feudal jurisdictions in the country's legal system. Soon after his coronation he despatched commissioners throughout his kingdom to establish who held what authority over what land and whether there had been any abuse of power. Hitherto barons holding lands in fief from the king had often administered the

From the Cotton MS,
British Library

king's laws within their territories, but many abused this privilege. In many cases barons claimed this had been their right since time immemorial, because they were unable to produce charters granting them such authority. Edward recognized that authority granted in the time of HENRY II (his great grandfather) was early enough to qualify as time immemorial, particularly given the unstable years of STEPHEN and MATILDA's civil war, but anything more recent had to be supported by written evidence. With this established Edward was able to put the collection of taxes and other revenues on a much firmer footing, and he was also enabled to reconstruct his authority and that of his barons in a more clearly codified set of laws. Edward needed clarity over his revenues to enable him to finance his extensive military campaigns. This time, however, he determined to appease the barons by gaining their assent to his tax collection. The combination of tax and legislative reforms in consultation with his peers was what brought about the evolution of government by Parliament. A Great Council had met since the time of JOHN, but it did not have the representative element of a formal Parliament. With his Statute of Westminster in 1275 Edward inaugurated reforms which led, over the next twenty years, to the establishment of a formal parliament. During this process Edward was quick to punish those who had abused their authority. In this way Edward endeared himself to the commoners of England, who saw him as their saviour. The one group to which Edward did not endear himself was the Jews. In 1278 he had passed an enactment which allowed all Jews in England to be arrested on the grounds of coin-clipping. Some 280 of them were hanged. The Jews had been one of the main alternative sources of income in England, but the Crusades had brought a reaction against them. While barons and royalty were keen to borrow their money, they had no desire to repay it and even introduced laws to stop the Jews claiming land in forfeit for non-payment. By Edward's reign the Jews were themselves becoming impoverished and the rising tide of nationalism in England increased the public antipathy to them. In 1290 Edward expelled all of the Jews from England, over sixteen thousand of them, on the grounds of usury. Thereafter the merchants became royal creditors, especially those from Venice and Lombardy in Italy.

Edward had long set his eyes on the conquest of Scotland. An opportunity arose in 1290 when MARGARET, the infant queen of Scotland (and Edward's great-niece) died. Edward had previously agreed with ALEXANDER III that the young queen would marry his son and heir Edward (later EDWARD II) which he hoped would lead to the union of England and Scotland. Margaret's death scuppered that plan, but Edward was now consulted by the Scottish magnates to adjudicate over the succession. In 1292, Edward eventually nominated JOHN BALLIOL, a fair decision, but also a weaker choice than the other primary candidate, ROBERT THE BRUCE, and one whom Edward could more easily dominate. Nevertheless over the next few years the Scots grew tired of John as a spineless pawn of Edward and incited him into rebellion in 1295. This came as a result of a difficult set of circumstances which now plagued Edward. In 1294 the French king Philippe IV had taken possession of Gascony. Edward had summoned a parliament to approve the collection of taxes for his campaign against France, but there was considerable resentment, especially north of the border where the Scots were expected to pay a tax for a war against the French, whom they regarded as their ally. At that same time, in October 1294, the Welsh took advantage of the French diversion to rebel, with Madog ap Llywelyn declaring himself prince of Wales. Edward was now facing rebellion on three fronts. It is evidence of his mastery of the situation that he was able to resolve all three in quick succession. From December 1294 to March 1295 he led his armies into Wales, defeated all opposition and slaughtered the main ringleaders. Back in England Edward summoned the first Model Parliament, which consisted of representatives of all three estates: the church, the barons and the shires and burghs. With the agreement of this parliament he was able to raise further revenues and enact plans for his campaigns in Scotland and France. Edward took his forces north, sacked and plundered Berwick in March 1296 and defeated John Balliol at Dunbar on 27 April. John surrendered two months later and was imprisoned in the Tower of London. Edward proudly seized the symbol of Scottish kingship, the Stone of Scone, which he brought south to Westminster, where it would remain for seven hundred years. Edward now believed he had conquered Scotland and left three magnates in authority. He needed to turn his attention to France. Parliament was less keen to raise further revenues for a French campaign, but regardless Edward sailed for France in 1297 and, through the intervention of the pope, was able to make a truce with France whereby he also regained control of Gascony. Thus in the space of two years Edward had held his possessions on two fronts and extended them on a third. The Scottish advance, however, was more chequered than Edward had anticipated. His three administrators proved unequal to their task and the tyrannical oppression of one of them, William Ormsby, had stirred the Scots back into revolt under WILLIAM WALLACE. Edward now led a further army north, defeating Wallace at Falkirk on 22 July 1298.

Over the next few years Edward sought the total subjugation of the Scots. His many campaigns, which culminated in the capture and execution of Wallace in August 1305, seemed to deliver Scotland firmly into his hands. And yet, even as he was in the process of confirming a constitution for Scotland another rebellion erupted, this time under Robert Bruce. Despite his age and increasing infirmity, Edward prepared for a further campaign. He marched north and was in sight of Scotland when he died of dysentery at Burgh-on-Sands near Carlisle in July 1307. Edward believed he had conquered the Scots and thus must have died disappointed at not seeing his vision complete. Nevertheless, unlike any ruler before him (and most since), he had the skill, strength and authority to undertake the task and failed ultimately only by his underestimation of the strength of the Scottish spirit.

Edward's first wife, Eleanor, had died in 1290 of a fever near Grantham while she was travelling north to meet Edward in Scotland. Edward had been devoted to her and was sorely grieved at her death. As her body was conveyed back to London, he established crosses at the sites where her body rested each night. There were originally twelve of these, of which the best known were at Waltham and Charing Cross. Eleanor had borne Edward sixteen children, the most from one legitimate union to any king of England. However few of these survived infancy and only four of them outlived Edward. Three of these were daughters, but the fourth was Eleanor's youngest son Edward. King Edward had remarried in 1299, this time to Margaret the sister of Philippe IV of France. It was another political marriage yet, although Edward was sixty and Margaret scarcely twenty, the match seemed to work, and Margaret bore Edward three more children.

Although Edward failed to conquer Scotland, his conquest of Wales has left its mark on Britain ever since, though possibly his most lasting legacy was the firm establishment of Parliament.

[O11;SB21] **EDWARD II**
Ruled 8 July 1307–25 January 1327 (abdicated). Crowned: Westminster Abbey, 25 February 1308.
Titles: *king of England and Scotland, lord of Ireland; prince of Wales (from 1301), duke of Aquitaine (from 1306).*
Born: *Caernarvon Castle, 25 April 1284.* **Died** *(murdered): Berkeley Castle, Gloucestershire, 21 September 1327, aged 43.* **Buried**: *Gloucester Cathedral.*
Married: *25 January 1308, at Boulogne Cathedral, Isabella (c1292–1358) dau. of Philippe IV, king of France: 4 children; Edward may also have had one illegitimate child.*

Edward II's reign was amongst the most despairing in history, cast into even greater notoriety because it was locked between the reigns of those two giants – his father, EDWARD I, and his son, EDWARD III. He was regarded as a weak king, not only through his lack of military ambition, but because of his total lack of interest in matters of state. He preferred gardening and basket-weaving to soldiery and government. Had he not been so easily influenced by his court favourites, he might have served better. The problem stemmed from his lonely childhood. Although he was the fourteenth of Edward's nineteen children, few of his brethren survived infancy and he never knew them. Of his elder sisters, three were married before Edward was six, while a fourth entered a nunnery around the time he was born. Only Elizabeth was close to Edward in age and would have been his closest childhood companion. Edward was already sixteen by the time his half-brother Thomas was born. Although his father was a devoted family man, his continued absence in his wars against Wales, Scotland and France left Edward to fend for himself, and the death of his mother when he was only six left him bereft.

As so often happens with lonely children (especially child heirs) they welcome anyone who shows them friendship and do not recognize when that friendship may be false, seeking only fame or riches. His closest childhood friend was Piers Gaveston, a rather handsome but affected knight from Gascony. The two of them led extravagant lifestyles, finding enjoyment in the disruption of ceremony and the annoyance of members of court, whom Gaveston delighted in calling by rude nicknames. Their inseparability and manner of dress caused the old king to believe they may have shared a homosexual relationship and Gaveston was banished from court on several occasions, but after the king's death, young Edward called Piers back. To the horror of the court magnates, Piers was made the earl of Cornwall (a title usually reserved for the king's sons), he was married to Edward's niece, Margaret, and when Edward went to France to collect his bride, Isabella, he made Piers regent. Piers made all the arrangements for the coronation, tried to outshine all others present by his manner of dress and had the highest honour of carrying the king's crown. Gaveston disgraced himself at the celebrations by his outward display of affection for Edward, which distressed the young queen. Gaveston further incurred the wrath of the court by bungling the banqueting arrangements resulting in a poorly cooked and late meal. The barons prevailed upon Edward to banish Gaveston, which Edward did by making him regent of Ireland in 1308, but within a year Gaveston had returned. Gaveston continued to abuse the barons with his wit and sarcasm, but probably what annoyed the barons more was that despite his foppishness, Gaveston was a good knight. He often arranged tournaments, only to defeat any knight who rode against him. One of these, the king's cousin, Thomas, earl of Lancaster, was incensed by this ignominy. Thomas was no man to upset. He was one of the most powerful in England, with vast estates and a huge private army. By nature he was vicious and haughty, caring only for himself. He led the opposition against the king and in the parliament of 1310 forced the king to agree to a committee of twenty-eight barons, known as the Lords Ordainer, who in effect governed the country. They forced Edward to agree to Gaveston's permanent exile. Edward made him lord of Man, but Gaveston could not stay away and turned up at the king's Christmas celebrations, as arrogant and obnoxious as ever. A group of barons, led by Lancaster, arrested Gaveston and executed him in June 1312 on the grounds that he was an enemy of the state. The barons soon realised Gaveston's execution was a mistake as it polarised opinion in England. There were those who believed the Lords Ordainer had acted unlawfully. The leader of this opposition was Hugh le Despenser, a long-time supporter of the king and a friend of Gaveston's. He and his son (Hugh the Younger) inveigled their way into the king's favour. By 1313, Hugh the Younger had become the king's chamberlain and closest adviser.

By this time Edward determined that he had to do something about Scotland. He had accompanied his father on several of his expeditions to Scotland in the early years of the century, and had been with his father on his final march north in 1307. The old king's last words had been to command young Edward to defeat the Scots. Edward had none of the military skills or leadership of his father and, though he tentatively crossed the border into Ayrshire, he rapidly retreated to the pleasures of the court, leaving ROBERT THE BRUCE to reclaim and rebuild Scotland. Edward led another brief foray to the Scottish borders in the autumn of 1310 and, meeting no opposition, regarded his expedition as a victory. However Robert merely bided his time and, on Edward's departure, returned to conquering castles and expelling the English. By the end of 1313 the only castle remaining in English hands was Stirling, which was under siege by Robert's brother. The governor of the castle, Sir Philip de Mowbray, declared that, if English reinforcements were not sent by 24 June 1314, he would surrender the castle to the Scots. Edward felt compelled to do something for the prestige of the English. On the eve of the appointed day he arrived at Stirling with one of the largest armies ever assembled in England. Although some estimates assigned it 100,000 men, it was probably closer to 20,000, but it still outnumbered the Scots two to one. Despite their numerical disadvantage, the Scots had spent months preparing for this battle and Bruce chose the site close to the Bannock Burn with precision. The English were forced into a course of action for which the Scots were ready, and almost from the outset the English infantry were thrown into chaos as they stumbled into prepared pits, whilst the cavalry were limited because of the surrounding bogland. The defeat was one of the worst ever to befall an English king. Edward fled from the battlefield, first trying to find shelter at Stirling Castle itself, probably one of the more extreme examples of stupidity from any English king, and then escaping by way of Dunbar back to London. Edward left Robert to his own devices, and though it was still another fourteen years before Scotland's independence was formally recognized, it was effective from the battle of Bannockburn.

Edward's reputation was at its nadir. England was torn between two opposing factions. The country was governed by the Lords Ordainer under Thomas of Lancaster, whilst the king's party was increasingly controlled by Hugh le Despenser. Although no official civil war broke out, there was a total state of anarchy with opposing factions fighting their own private battles, whilst the Scots plundered the north of England with almost complete freedom. To add to the problems England was laid low by a dire famine. It was only due to the negotiations of Aymer de Valence, earl of Pembroke, one of the more honourable and pragmatic nobles, that a form of reconciliation was made between the king and Lancaster in 1318. Had Edward seen fit to change his ways, matters might have improved, but Edward's conviction of his absolute authority only increased his intransigence. He listened only to his court favourites, the two Despensers, whom he showered in riches, and rebuffed his barons. Hugh the Younger had been created lord of Glamorgan and used the opportunity of further unrest amongst the dispossessed Welsh lords to establish an extensive domain in southern Wales. This development was opposed by Roger Mortimer, the most prominent of the marcher lords, who saw the Despensers' authority challenging his own in Wales. A confrontation in 1321 between Edward and Lancaster, supported by the Welsh marcher lords, caused Edward to temporarily agree to exiling the Despensers. This was more because Edward feared a rebellion among the Welsh being supported by a Celtic alliance with Scotland, and he needed to pacify the Welsh leaders. They hated Mortimer more than Despenser. It should not be forgotten that Edward had been invested as prince of Wales in 1301 which, at that time, was not solely an honorific title. The Welsh took it seriously, as did Edward, and in the years before he became king he administered Welsh affairs and pronounced upon petitions far more effectively than he was ever able to do as king of England. Wales was specially his own, and the Welsh recognized this. In 1322, this allowed Edward, for once, to become his own man and act with uncharacteristic resolution. He led an army against Roger Mortimer, whom he captured and imprisoned in the Tower of London in January 1322. He then led an army against Thomas of Lancaster, who was defeated at

Boroughbridge, captured and beheaded at Pontefract in March 1322. Flushed with success Edward continued north and laid waste to Scotland, his army reaching as far as Edinburgh before his luck ran out. He then retreated with all haste, pursued by a Scottish army, losing his baggage and plunder en route, but escaping with his life and a degree of dignity. Edward discovered further treachery along the Scottish borders where his warden of the Marches, Andrew Hartcla, had been conspiring with the Scots to allow them inroads to Cumberland. Hartcla was executed, and Edward agreed a truce with Scotland in May 1323.

The years 1321 to 1323 were the most decisive of Edward's life and showed his abilities when he put his mind to it. But he soon relapsed. The Despensers were recalled and they continued to create significant domains for themselves, especially in Wales, where they were allied with Rhys ap Gruffydd, who became sheriff of Carmarthen and was a strong supporter of the royal cause in Wales. The Despensers now caused the enmity of Edward's queen, Isabella. It seems that after the death of Lancaster, Isabella grew distant from Edward. It is difficult to say how close they ever were, since Edward had insulted Isabella at their coronation by his show of affection for Gaveston, but she had borne the king four children. The last, Joan, had been born in July 1321. Isabella now began openly to confront the king, spurred on almost certainly by Roger Mortimer, with whom Isabella became more closely acquainted at the Tower of London. The Despensers contrived with Edward to have Isabella deprived of her estates in 1324, but they underestimated her cunning. Relations with France were once again hostile and Isabella requested that she visit the king of France, her brother, to aid negotiations. Edward agreed. No sooner was Isabella in France than she was joined by Roger Mortimer, who lived with her openly as her lover. When her young son Edward arrived in France to pay homage for the lands of Ponthieu and Aquitaine, of which he was made respectively count and duke in September 1325, Isabella refused to allow him to return to England, in defiance of Edward's authority. She and Roger now raised an army to depose Edward and establish her son on the throne. The French king, Charles IV, with a remarkable display of honour, would not allow Isabella to conduct these affairs in France, especially with her open adultery with Mortimer, and she was exiled to Hainault, where the count allowed her to recruit an army of mercenaries from the Low Countries. Isabella and Mortimer sailed for England, landing at Harwich on 24 September 1326. Edward showed little resistance, retreating to his stronghold in Wales. Over the next two months his supporters were captured and executed, including the Despensers, and the king was eventually taken at Pen-rhys in the Rhondda on 16 December. He was held captive at Kenilworth Castle, where he was well treated by his cousin, Henry, the new earl of Lancaster and brother of the executed Thomas. Isabella called a parliament on 20 January 1327 to seek the deposition of Edward, but the parliament had no authority without the king's presence. Edward refused until he was given the ultimatum that his son's inheritance might also be forfeit, at which point he capitulated and abdicated in favour of his son on 25 January. Edward was now transported to Berkeley Castle in Gloucestershire, where his rescue was attempted by Rhys ap Gruffydd. Isabella and Mortimer feared that Edward might yet make a resurgence, and so Mortimer arranged for Edward's death. He did not want it to appear that violence had been committed against the king. He was hoping it might appear as a natural death, or suicide. However, attempts to starve the king did not work, and in the end Edward was held down while a red hot poker was inserted into his bowels. There were some rumours, however, that another victim was found to serve as a body whilst Edward was smuggled out of England and spent his final years as a hermit in Lombardy. The idea of the former ostentatious monarch being able to live as a hermit, regardless of his situation, beggars belief, however. He was buried at Gloucester Cathedral where a beautiful alabaster effigy was raised above the tomb by his son. Edward's death roused considerable sympathy amongst his subjects, especially the Welsh, and his memory was venerated for many years. It was not until 1330 that his death was avenged. Roger Mortimer was tried and executed, and Queen Isabella was placed in confinement at Castle Rising in Norfolk. She lived on for thirty years after her husband's death, dying on 22 August 1358 and was buried at Greyfriars Church at Newgate in London. Though a strangely matched couple, Edward and Isabella produced one of England's greatest kings, EDWARD III.

[O12;SB22] **EDWARD III**

Ruled 25 January 1327–21 June 1377. Crowned: Westminster Abbey, 1 February 1327.

Titles: king of England, duke of Aquitaine (from 1325), earl of Chester (from 1312), count of Ponthieu and Montreuil (from 1325), lord of Ireland, king of France (from 1340).

Born: Windsor Castle, 13 November 1312; Died: Sheen Palace, Surrey, 21 June 1377, aged 64. Buried: Westminster Abbey.

Married: 24 January 1328, at York Minster, Philippa (1311–69) dau. of William V, count of Hainault and Holland: 13 children. Edward also had at least three illegitimate children by his mistress Alice Perrers (c1348–1400).

Any king must have seemed an improvement after the embarrassing reign of EDWARD II, but England was fortunate in that his son, Edward III, was both a great king and a popular one. Although his reign was not as glorious as subsequent romancers and chroniclers liked to maintain, it was remarkable and one that England needed to restore its self-esteem and its position in Europe.

The start of Edward's reign was less momentous. He had been raised to the throne following the forced abdication of his father. He was only fourteen and was in the manipulative hands of his mother, Isabella of France, and her paramour, Roger Mortimer. They had detained Edward in France the previous year when he had gone to pay homage to the French king Charles IV for his lands in Aquitaine and Ponthieu, and it was under Isabella's standard that Edward returned to England in September 1326 to be proclaimed "Keeper of the Realm". Edward remained under the control of Isabella and Mortimer, though there was some saving grace in that the head of the regency council was Henry of Lancaster, a cousin of Edward's father and a more moderate man than most. The murder of Edward's father at the instigation of Mortimer shocked the nation, but the young king was in no position to do much about it at the time. Despite his youth he had led an army into northern England in the summer of 1327 to counter the attacks made by the Scots on the borders. After a month trying to track down the enemy amongst the wild country, Edward was forced to admit defeat and he returned dejected to York. Negotiations were opened with the Scots resulting in the Treaty of Northampton in May 1328

46. England (5) – Lancaster and York

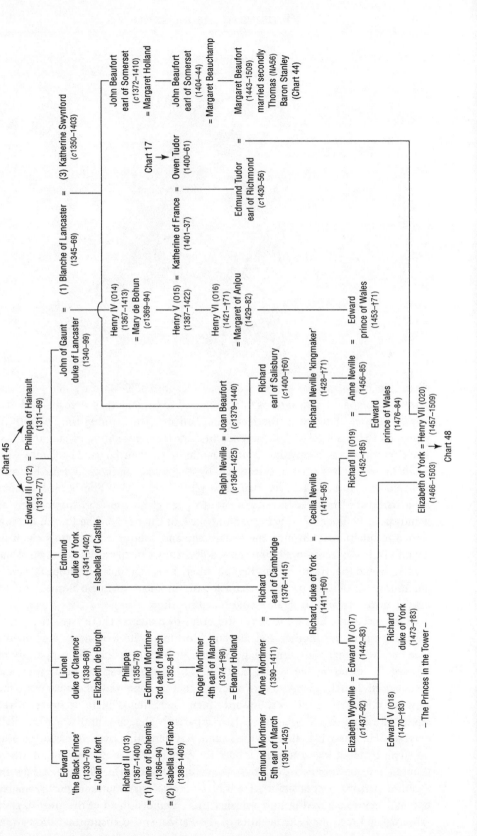

From the tomb,
Westminster Abbey

where the independence of the Scots was recognized. Edward's sister Joan was betrothed to ROBERT *THE BRUCE*'s infant son, DAVID (II), and they were married that July at Berwick. Edward in the meantime had married his long-time betrothed, Philippa of Hainault, who had travelled to York for the wedding in January 1328. Their marriage was happy and fruitful, far more so than England's alliance with Scotland which was always threatened by the uneasy *ménage à trois* between Scotland, England and France. That same year Charles IV of France died without an heir. Edward believed he had a more direct claim, through his mother, as grandson of Philippe IV of France and nephew of Charles IV. The French did not recognize inheritance through the female line and overturned Edward's claim in favour of Charles's cousin, Philippe de Valois. In any case there was no way that the French would be ruled by an English king, but that did not stop Edward's ambitions. He did not press his claim for the moment, but paid homage to the new king for his lands in France, and bided his time.

In the meantime Edward took control of his own affairs. There was a rising tide of feeling against his mother, Isabella, and Mortimer, who were now living openly together. Mortimer was continuing to seek retribution against the supporters of Edward II, including the young king's uncle, Edmund, earl of Kent, who was executed in March 1330. Edward decided that enough was enough. With the support of Henry of Lancaster, Edward's men (including William de MONTACUTE) seized Mortimer at Nottingham Castle, apparently dragging him from Isabella's embrace. He was tried and convicted, and was hanged, drawn and quartered at the new place of execution at Tyburn in London. He was the first of many thousands to be executed there over the next 450 years. On 20 October Edward assumed personal responsibility. He was to receive unanimous support from his barons. They recognized in him a quality that reminded them of the great days of Edward I. Edward used the facilities of the Parliament to ensure that the barons received a fair opportunity to contribute to debates, and he often took their advice. Whilst he remained superior, in the regal sense, he did not demean the barons.

Clearly none of this would have worked had Edward not proved himself an able soldier and king. His first opportunity came against the long standing enemy, Scotland. EDWARD BALLIOL maintained his right to the throne of Scotland against the family of Bruce and Edward supported his claim. In August 1332 Edward overthrew David II. Even though David was Edward's brother-in-law, Edward continued to support Balliol, and Balliol recognized him as his overlord at Roxburgh on 23 November 1332. Consequently, when Balliol was himself over-thrown a month later, Edward III responded, providing forces to support Balliol's endeavours to regain the throne. Edward's army won a crushing victory over the Scots at Halidon Hill on 19 July 1333. Here, for the first time, the strength of the English and Welsh longbowmen played their part in seriously weakening the Scots forces. Balliol was restored and a year later, in June 1334, gave to the English crown almost all of the border country between the Forth and the Tweed, which was immediately governed as part of England. The Scots however fought back. Balliol was deposed again, and although he soon regained the throne it became evident that Balliol could only rule with English support. When he was overthrown again in 1336, he gave up and David II was restored. Edward did not pursue rights to Scottish territory, because his attention shifted to France. France and Scotland had long been allies and Edward was only too aware that united the two could seriously damage England. Moreover the many Gascons living in England had a right of appeal in the courts to the French king, through Edward's fealty for his lands in Gascony. Edward recognized that these problems would be solved if his claim to the throne of France was upheld. He revived this claim in 1337 and declared his intentions to fight for it. This was the start of what became known as the Hundred Years' War. Supported by his barons, Edward crossed to Antwerp and invaded France in 1338. Philippe VI refused to fight, and the next eighteen months saw only minor and relatively unsuccessful skirmishes. However, in 1340 Edward won a major sea battle off the port of Sluys in Holland, and this emboldened him enough to declare himself king of France. He even challenged Philippe to decide the matter in single combat, but Philippe refused. For the next three years Edward was unable to make any advance, and the cost of maintaining his army and fleet became crippling. He reached a truce with Philippe in 1343, but that truce was conveniently broken in 1345. Now Edward's luck changed. His great general, Henry, earl of Derby, regained Gascony, and Edward followed up with a major invasion force. Landing in Normandy in July 1346, he harried his way through northern France with much pillaging and destruction, which galvanised Philippe into action. The two armies met at Crécy, near the Somme, on 26 August. Again it was the power of the longbow that gave the victory to Edward. His army moved on to Calais, to which he laid siege for several months until the citizens submitted, on the verge of starvation. Edward was prepared to sack and destroy the city but his queen, Philippa, who had accompanied him on the campaign, pleaded for their lives. While the siege was continuing Edward received excellent news from England. The Scots had sought to take advantage of Edward's absence by invading northern England, but their forces were routed by the archbishop of York at Neville's Cross

Edward III married Philippa, daughter of William V, Count of Hainault in 1328. The couple had thirteen children whose descendants would split the royal family into the factions of the Wars of the Roses and the Houses of Lancaster and York. The following chart lists all of these offspring and their key descendants.

Child and spouse	Grandchild	Descendants
1. Edward "the Black Prince" (1330–76) = Joan, Maid of Kent (1328–85)	(1) Edward of Angoulême (1365–72?) (2) **Richard II** (013)	*no children* *no children*
2. Isabella (1332–82) = Enguerrand de Coucy (1339?–97)	(1) Mary (1366–1404) = Henry of Bar (d.1401) (2) Philippa (1367–1411) = Robert de Vere, earl of Oxford (1362–92)	*no children*
3. Joan of Woodstock (1335–48) (*died of the Black Death*)		
4. William of Hatfield (d. 1337)		
5. Lionel, duke of Clarence (1338–68) =(1) Elizabeth de Burgh (1332–63) =(2) Yolande Visconti (*c*1353–86) (*no children*)	(1) Philippa (1355–*c*78) = Edmund Mortimer, earl of March (1352–81)	Their son, Roger (4th earl of March) was great-grandfather of **Edward IV** (017) and **Richard III** (019). Their daughter, Elizabeth (1371–1417), married Henry "Hotspur" Percy — they were the forebears of nine generations of earls of Northumberland.
6. John of Gaunt (1340–99) =(1) Blanche of Lancaster (1345–69)	(1) Philippa (1360–1415) = John I of Portugal (1357–1433)	8 children, the forebears of the Aviz Dynasty of Portugal. Their son John was the grandfather of Henry VIII's wife, Katherine of Aragon.
	(2) Elizabeth (1363–1426?) = John Holland, duke of Exeter (*c*1352–1400)	5 children including John, 3rd duke of Exeter whose son Henry (4th duke) married Edward IV's sister, Anne Plantagenet in 1447.
	(3) Henry Bolingbroke, later **Henry IV** (014) + 2 sons and a daughter, died young	**Henry V** (015) and **Henry VI** (016) (*see chart 46*).
=(2) Constance (1369–94), daughter of Pedro I, king of Castile	(4) Katherine (1372?–1418) = Enrique III, king of Castile (1379–1406)	3 children, of whom Juan (1406–54) became Juan II of Castile and whose daughter, Isabella, was the mother of Henry VIII's wife Katherine of Aragon.
=(3) Katherine Swynford (*c*1350–1403) Katherine was John's mistress before their marriage in 1396 and their children were later legitimised by the Pope.	(5) John Beaufort, earl of Somerset (*c*1372–1410) = Margaret Holland	Their son John (1404–44), duke of Somerset, had a daughter Margaret, who was the mother of **Henry VII** (020) (*see chart 46*). Their daughter Joan (d.1445) married James I (FC76), king of Scotland (*see chart 43*). Their son Edmund (*c*1406–55) duke of Somerset, was regent of France during minority of Henry VI and was held responsible for the loss of territory. He, and his son Edmund (*c*1439–71), were the heads of the Lancastrian faction in the Wars of the Roses.
	(6) Henry Beaufort (*c*1375–1447), bishop of Winchester	
	(7) Thomas, duke of Exeter (*c*1377–1427) = Margaret Neville	One son (Henry), died young.
	(8) Joan Beaufort (*c*1379–1440) = (2) Ralph Neville, earl of Westmorland (*c*1364–1425)	14 children of whom: ■ Richard (*c*1400–60) was the father of Richard Neville (1428–71), earl of Warwick, known as the "King-maker", whose daughter Anne (1456–85) married Richard III. ■ Cecilia (1415–95), who married Richard, duke of York (1411–60) and was the mother of **Edward IV** and **Richard III**.
7. Edmund, duke of York (1341–1402) =(1) Isabella (*c*1355–*c*92), daughter of Pedro I, king of Castile, and sister of Constance, wife of John of Gaunt	(1) Edward, duke of York (*c*1373–1415) = Philippa de Bohun (d.1431) (2) Constance (*c*1374–1416), = Thomas le Despenser (1373–1400) earl of Gloucester (*great-grandson of Hugh le Despenser, favourite of Edward II*)	no children; Edward was killed at the Battle of Agincourt. 5 children
	(3) Richard (1376–1415), earl of Cambridge = Anne (1390–1411), great-granddaughter of Lionel, duke of Clarence	Their son Richard, duke of York (1411–60) was the father of Edward IV and Richard III (*see chart 46*).
=(2) Joan Holland (c1380–1434) sister of Margaret Holland, wife of John Beaufort, son of John of Gaunt	*no children*	

8. Blanche (b./d. 1342)

9. Mary (1344–61/2) = John IV   *no children*
   (de Montfort), duke of Brittany
   (1339–99)

10. Margaret (1346–61) = John Hastings,
    earl of Pembroke (1347–75)   *no children*

11. Thomas (1347–8)

12. William (b./d. 1348)

13. Thomas (1355–97), duke of   (1) Humphrey (c1381–99),
    Gloucester = Eleanor de Bohun   earl of Buckingham
    (c1366–99)   (2) Anne (1383–1438), countess
         of Buckingham, married three times
         =(2) Edmund, earl of Stafford   3 children, of whom Anne married Edmund
         (1377–1403)   Mortimer, earl of March; and Humphrey,
         earl of Stafford, married Anne, daughter of
         Ralph Neville, earl of Westmorland.
         =(3) William Bourchier, count of Eu   5 children, of whom Henry became 1st earl of
         (d.1420)   Essex and married Isabella Plantagenet;
         and Thomas (1413–86) became archbishop of
         Canterbury.

in October 1346. David II was captured and taken as prisoner to England. A peace treaty was concluded in France and Edward returned to England.

The next few years may be seen both as the zenith of Edward's reign but also some of the darkest days in Britain. Edward, triumphant in his victory over France, and with David of Scotland his prisoner, established a court par excellence at Windsor Castle. Edward operated his Court on the model of the Arthurian Round Table. Arthur was his hero, and many of the incidents later related by Thomas Malory in his *Morte d'Arthur* have their counterparts in Edward's tournaments and chivalric quests. The world of Edward III was the world of Arthur. Edward planned to instigate an Order of the Round Table, which was eventually called the Most Noble Order of the Garter when he established it in 1348. It was the highest order of chivalry limited always to a select group of twenty-five or so knights. It was first bestowed upon Edward's eldest son, Edward, the Black Prince, and included among its illustrious ranks his second cousin, Henry, earl of Derby (later duke of Lancaster) (and grandfather of the future king HENRY IV), and Roger Mortimer, the grandson of his mother's lover. These honours and the opportunity to prove themselves to the king resulted in a rare camaraderie between the king and his nobles, one which helped sustain the successes of the first half of Edward's reign. Edward called to his court the greatest knights from throughout Europe who would prove their valour and strength in his tournaments. It was a period of considerable glory and prestige for England. However it was darkened by the Black Death, the name given to the virulent bubonic plague that swept through Europe, reaching its height in the north in 1348, and which was believed to have killed a third of the population of Britain (or almost a million people). Over two hundred people a day died in London alone for over two years. Edward's thirteen-year old daughter Joan died of it in Bordeaux in September 1348, as did his infant son Thomas, but although others of the court succumbed, the plague left the royal family surprisingly unscathed. Nevertheless it devastated the English economy and reduced the manpower on which Edward could call, but this was the same throughout Europe. It was through the remarkable ability of Edward's officials that the finances and administration of England were sustained through this period.

Philippe VI of France died in August 1350 and with the succession of his son, Jean II, hostilities broke out again with England. Jean, known as the Good, refused to acknowledge Edward's overlordship but likewise refused to fight until Edward's tactics of plunder and destruction drew the French out. A series of battles, of which the most decisive was at Poitiers in September 1356 under the command of the Black Prince, brought French government to the verge of anarchy. Jean II was taken captive to England. Unable to agree terms, Edward III invaded France in 1359, hoping at last to gain control. However, the continuance of the bubonic plague and a devastatingly severe winter weakened the English as much as the French and Edward was unable to strike the final blow. A treaty was nevertheless agreed at Brétigny in 1360. By this Edward's sovereignty was recognized over his former lands in France, primarily Aquitaine and Calais. In return Edward dropped his claim to the throne of France.

The year 1360 remains the peak of Edward's reign as the remaining sixteen years were ones of slow and sad decline. The plague returned with increasing virulence in 1361. The French king Jean was never able to raise his ransom (set at half a million pounds) and died in London in 1364. His son, Charles V, ascended the French throne and encouraged the French subjects of the English in Aquitaine to rebel. Although Edward tried to negotiate with France relations worsened. The great triumphs of the Black Prince faded as his health failed, and were replaced by the ignominious defeats of his brother John of Gaunt. The war became protracted and costly and, when the French plundered and burnt Portsmouth in 1369, English opinion began to turn away from the king. This was further aggravated when Edward drew upon church revenues in order to finance the conflict. By 1374 Edward had lost much of Aquitaine, and the French regained control over most of the English territories except Calais and a coastral strip in southern Gascony, near Bayonne.

Edward's health and spirit also failed. His wife, Philippa, died in August 1369 of an illness akin to dropsy. They had been married for forty years and by all accounts had remained very happy. Philippa had grown rather portly in her last years which added to her overall character as a friendly, homely, motherly woman whom the nation greatly loved. In her final years Edward had found himself drawn to Alice Perrers, one of his wife's chamber ladies, who became his mistress. Although she satisfied the old king's physical desires – in fact she bore him at least three children – she was also scheming and grasping and made his final years a misery. She was banished from the court in 1376. It was likely that she was the cause of the king contracting gonorrhoea. To add to the king's sadness, his eldest son, Edward the Black Prince, who had turned against his father's policies, died in June 1376. The king's final year was spent in much loneliness and sadness aware that the administration about him was crumbling. He died of a stroke at Sheen Palace in June 1377. He was succeeded by his grandson, RICHARD II. Although his reign is remembered for its great days of glorious knighthood and conquest, it was this and the Black Death that drove the country into poverty and near ruin and was the basis for the collapse of the Plantagenet dynasty in the next generation. Edward III cannot be denied the epitaph of a great king, but like so many other great kings he bequeathed little to his successors.

[O13] **RICHARD II**
Ruled 22 June 1377–29 September 1399 (abdicated). Crowned: Westminster Abbey, 16 July 1377.
Titles: king of England; prince of Wales, earl of Cornwall and earl of Chester (from 1376).
Born: Bordeaux, Gascony, 6 January 1367. Died: Pontefract Castle, on or about 14 February 1400, aged 33. Buried: initially Kings Langley, then removed to Westminster Abbey in 1413.
Married: (1) January 1382, at Westminster, Anne (1366–94) dau. Charles IV, Holy Roman Emperor and king of Bohemia: no children; (2) 4 November 1396, at Calais, Isabella (1389–1409), dau. of Charles VI of France: no children.

Richard was only ten when he ascended the throne. His father was Edward, known as the Black Prince, the son of EDWARD III. The Black Prince had been renowned throughout Christendom for his knightly valour. He had all the prowess of the Plantaganet line, but he also inherited their violent temper. Edward also proved himself a poor administrator and, for all that he was loved by the nation, he would probably have made a poor king. Richard's mother was also something of a character. She was Joan, the granddaughter of EDWARD I through his second marriage. Although she was known as the Fair Maid of Kent, she was older than Edward (she was 33, he was 31) and had already contracted a bigamous marriage to WILLIAM MONTAGUE, earl of Salisbury, and borne five children to her first husband, Sir Thomas Holland. She was a loving mother to Richard and his elder brother Edward, who died young, but was not the most virtuous. We have an image of the young Richard striving to live up to his responsibilities but surrounded by lecherous and grasping relatives all endeavouring to gain more than their fair share of the action. This no doubt made Richard all the more determined to assert his authority, a characteristic that would eventually cost him his life.

No formal regent was appointed on Richard's accession. Control of the government was initially assumed by Parliament, but this increasingly passed into the hands of his uncle, John of Gaunt, duke of Lancaster, who was the most powerful man in England and who also had claims on the kingship of Castile. Some contemporaries believed that Gaunt himself had pretensions to the throne but, if he did, these did not come to the fore and he remained one of the staunchest supporters of his nephew throughout his minority and into his kingship. Richard early proved his courage and strong spirit with the Peasant's Revolt of 1381. In 1377 the first poll tax had been introduced to help finance the wars with France and campaigns in Scotland, Wales and Ireland. It was unpopular but was tolerated, though the increases in the tax in 1379 and 1380 caused considerable unrest. In June 1381 one of the tax collectors was killed by Wat Tyler of Dartford in Kent because of the taxman's attack on Tyler's daughter. Tyler's colleagues came to his aid in defence and a force of around 100,000 evolved around Tyler as its leader to march on the capital. The rebels killed Simon of Sudbury, archbishop of Canterbury, and Robert Hales, the treasurer. The establishment had already raised the anger of the English common folk by proceedings against the religious reformer John Wycliffe, whose challenge to authority had gained popularity among the peasants. Richard appeased the rebels, promising to grant them their wishes. Although this satisfied many of them, a core remained with whom the king agreed to parley the following

From a painting in
Winchester Abbey

day at Smithfield. Here Wat Tyler became more presumptuous and raised his hand several times to the young king. Tyler was struck down by the Lord Mayor of London, William Walworth, and killed. The remaining peasants prepared to fight, but Richard risked placing himself in front of them and subdued their wrath. He led them out of the city, and many were attacked and killed by Sir Robert Knollys. Richard emerged from this with increased prestige, not only amongst his own barons, who respected his bravery, but surprisingly amongst the English common folk who held him in regard as their champion against oppression, even though he had in effect betrayed them, especially as he never instigated the reforms he promised. This success, though, influenced Richard's later life when he came to regard himself as a champion of England and one not to be dictated to by anyone, whether his barons or his subjects.

Nevertheless Richard's relationship with his court soon became divided. Much of this came at the instigation of Richard's close friend, his chamberlain, Robert de Vere, earl of Oxford, and of his advisor and later chancellor, Michael de la Pole. Richard bestowed much bounty upon these two colleagues which incurred the enmity of the court circle, whose opposition polarised around the leadership of Richard Fitzalan, earl of Arundel. By the mid 1380s Richard II's court had become divided along exactly the same lines as that of EDWARD II seventy years earlier. Richard even made the same mistake as Edward by seeking to gain glory by an expedition to Scotland in 1385. This had been occasioned by a show of might by a combined army of Scots and French, the French having allied themselves with Scotland against a common enemy. Although the army had caused havoc in Northumberland, it retreated against the might of Richard's army and though Richard marched through southern Scotland, laying waste as he went, the two armies did not once meet, and Richard retreated without a victory. The Scots bided their time for three years and then made further devastating raids on Northumberland. By that time Richard was in less of a position to respond because he was fighting for his own right to govern.

Richard had caused the final rift with his enemies in 1386, when he made Robert de Vere duke of Ireland with full powers of regency, and Michael de la Pole chancellor, without consultation with Parliament. When later that year John of

Gaunt, who had maintained the stability in government, sailed to Castile to defend his right to the throne, Richard's opponents took the opportunity to act against Richard. They were led by his uncle, Thomas, duke of Gloucester, with the earl of Arundel and Thomas Beauchamp, earl of Warwick. Together with Thomas Mowbray, earl of Nottingham, and Richard's cousin, Henry Bolingbroke, son of John of Gaunt, these five opponents became known as the Lords Appellant. Their private armies allowed them effectively to assume control of the country. They forced Richard to hand over his courtiers for trial. Richard did not, but retribution was still carried out. Some, like de Vere and de la Pole, escaped but had their lands forfeited, but others were rounded up and executed. For a while, although furious with the Lords Appellant, Richard complied with their wishes. Although he declared himself of age in 1389 and assumed full kingship, he carried out no vengeance upon the Lords Appellant, although he did dismiss most of the counsellors imposed upon him and replaced them with his own favourites. A relative period of calm followed over the next six years, during which time Richard successfully brought a settlement to the turbulence in Ireland in 1394 and concluded a twenty-eight year peace treaty with France in 1396. One major sadness was the death of Richard's wife, Anne of Bohemia, of the plague in June 1394. She was only twenty-eight. Richard was so grief stricken that he had the palace at Sheen, where she died, razed to the ground. They had had no children. Two years later, as part of his peace treaty with France, Richard married Isabella, the seven-year-old daughter of the French king Charles VI.

With troubles concluded abroad Richard believed he was now operating from a position of strength. In the summer of 1397 he had Gloucester, Arundel and Warwick arrested. Gloucester was despatched to Calais where he was murdered. Arundel and Warwick were tried before a parliament now firmly under Richard's control. Arundel was found guilty and executed. Warwick so prostrated himself before the king that he was reprieved but banished to the Isle of Man, under the lordship of WILLIAM LE SCROPE. As for Mowbray and Henry Bolingbroke, both had, in fact, been comparatively loyal to Richard. Many believed that Mowbray may have personally murdered Thomas of Gloucester. However in early 1398 they were both accused of treason and challenged to a trial by combat. Richard intervened before the contest. Mowbray was exiled for life and deprived of his lands, whilst Henry was exiled for ten years.

Richard now ruled as a total despot, assuming absolute power. He dominated his court and parliament and all lived in fear of his wrath. All of the viciousness and arrogance of the Plantagenet temperament become focused in Richard. He became the embodiment of the adage that absolute power corrupts absolutely. In his youth and when controlled by his parliament Richard had demonstrated both his courage and an ability to govern wisely, but this was now all laid aside in his desire for total control. For those who remained his favourites this was no problem as he continued to bestow his favours upon them. Richard was no warrior king, for all he was an able soldier, but like Edward II, Richard became a dilettante. He is credited with inventing the handkerchief, which may say much for his lifestyle, but there is no denying that his court encouraged the development of cultural pursuits. It was during his reign that Geoffrey Chaucer wrote his *Canterbury Tales* (1387). The rise of literature also brought with it the rise of criticism, and two other poets, William Langland and John Gower, both wrote remonstrances against Richard II's reign.

When John of Gaunt died in February 1399 Richard, instead of pardoning Henry Bolingbroke and allowing him to return to his estates, extended his banishment for life and forfeited his lands. He thereby made a dangerous enemy. In May 1399 Richard left for Ireland in order to quell the unrest. On 4 July Henry Bolingbroke landed in Yorkshire with a small army. The number soon swelled as Henry marched south. Richard returned to meet him but his support rapidly dwindled. Deserted, Richard was forced to submit to Henry at Flint on 19 August 1399. He was imprisoned in the Tower of London. Henry now used the precedent established by the deposition of Edward II to seek the abdication of Richard. It was complicated by the fact that Henry was not the direct heir. Richard was childless and the next in line to the throne was Edmund Mortimer, earl of March, who was descended from Edward III's son Lionel, the elder brother of John of Gaunt. However, Edmund was only eight, and there was no benefit following the revolution in installing an eight-year-old king. Parliament thus agreed that Henry should succeed. Richard II eventually consented to abdicate on 29 September 1399, and Henry came to the throne as HENRY IV.

Richard was removed to Pontefract Castle in Yorkshire, but several of his supporters sought his freedom and attempted to murder Henry IV and his family. Richard was clearly a danger while still alive. He was thus left to die at Pontefract, probably by starvation. There is no evidence of any physical murder. It was some years before Richard's body was removed from its original burial site at Kings Langley and buried in state at Westminster. Richard, like Edward II and later kings, especially CHARLES I, were capable monarchs who were corrupted by their own self-importance and arrogance and paid the price.

[O14] HENRY IV BOLINGBROKE

Ruled 30 September 1399–20 March 1413. Crowned: Westminster Abbey, 13 October 1399.

Titles: king of England, earl of Derby (from 1377), earl of Northampton and Hereford (from 1384), duke of Hereford (from 1397), duke of Lancaster, earl of Leicester and earl of Lincoln (from 1399).

Born: Bolingbroke Castle, Lincolnshire, 3 April 1367 (or 1366), Died: Westminster Abbey, 20 March 1413, aged 45. Buried: Canterbury Cathedral.

Married: (1) before 10 February 1381, at Arundel, Sussex, Mary (c1369–94), dau. of Humphrey de Bohun, earl of Hereford: 7 children; (2) 3 April 1402 (by proxy) at Eltham Palace, Kent, Joan (c1370–1437), dau. of Charles II, king of Navarre, and widow of John de Montfort, duke of Brittany: no children.

Henry was the first king of the House of Lancaster, but he was still a Plantagenet. Both he and RICHARD II, whose throne he usurped, were grandsons of EDWARD III. Henry's father was John of Gaunt, who had been the premier lord in England after the death of Edward III in 1377. Henry had been born at Bolingbroke Castle and was often called Henry Bolingbroke. His mother (whom he scarcely knew, as she died of the Black Death when he was three) was Blanche, the daughter of Henry, duke of Lancaster, and great-great-grandaughter of HENRY III. Bolingbroke was initially induced by his uncle, Thomas, duke of Gloucester, to oppose Richard's court favourites and he became one of the Lords Appellant, who effectively governed the country during the late 1380s. However he stepped down from this role a year later in 1389 and in subsequent years appeared as a supporter of the king. In 1390 Henry embarked on the first of his adventures, joining the Teutonic Knights on an expedition to Lithuania in the war over the Polish succession. Two years later Henry undertook a pilgrimage to Jerusalem, though his greater triumph was the grand journey he took through the courts of Europe on both the outward and return trips, where he was treated regally and evidently held in high esteem. At this time of his life Henry was still comparatively handsome, although he was rather short. He had inherited the Plantagenet red hair which, when he grew a beard, gave him a rather fiery appearance. In later life Henry developed a very severe form of eczema, to the extent that many believed he was suffering from leprosy, something he could have caught in his early travels. It is quite possible that the malady was stress-connected considering the difficult life Henry later led as king.

Henry was a good man for the king to have on his side, but Richard II did not seem to appreciate this. In 1398 Richard delighted in banishing Henry into exile on the grounds of past treasonable acts. The banishment was originally for ten years. In February 1399 Henry succeeded his father as Duke of Lancaster. King Richard chose to deprive Henry of his estates and extend the sentence to life. Henry invaded England in July and within six weeks Richard submitted to him. Henry succeeded in convincing Parliament of his eligibility to the throne (Edmund Mortimer, earl of March, had a prior claim, but he was only seven years old). Nevertheless it was an uneasy succession. For all that nearly everyone welcomed Henry over Richard, those who had supported Richard became concerned for their own lives and estates. Within months of his succession Henry found his life threatened in a rebellion organized by the earls of Kent, Salisbury and Huntingdon. Henry's retribution upon the earls and their supporters was swift and violent. It is likely that in its aftermath Henry also ordered the murder of the king who was starved to death, though the guilt of this continued to haunt Henry for the rest of his life.

Within a few months Henry faced a further revolt, this time in Wales, where OWAIN GLYN DWR was declared prince in September 1400. Although the initial revolt was swiftly put down by Henry, Owain was not caught and several years of guerilla warfare followed. Support for Owain grew, not only amongst the Welsh, but amongst the English barons who had their own axes to grind. Key amongst these were the marcher lords, the Mortimers, who believed that their heir, Edmund, was the rightful king of England. This heir's uncle, also called Edmund, was won over to the Welsh cause and married Glyn Dwr's daughter. Owain also found support from Henry Percy, the son of the earl of Northumberland. Young Percy, better known as Hotspur, was a vain and intolerant individual who never believed he had received just recognition for his border successes against the Scots. Moreover his wife was Mortimer's sister. In 1403 Hotspur threw in his lot with Glyn Dwr and Mortimer. Henry reacted quickly, before Hotspur and Mortimer could combine forces, and confronted Hotspur at the battle of Shrewsbury on 21 July 1403. Hotspur was killed and his uncle, the earl of Worcester, was captured and executed. Hotspur's father, Henry, earl of Northumberland, was spared, but he continued to plot against the king. By 1405 it became evident that Mortimer and Percy were planning to overthrow Henry and share England between them. Both

Thomas Mowbray, the Earl Marshal of England, and Richard Scrope, archbishop of York, became involved in the plot. The rebel army was defeated and this time Henry showed no mercy, though there was a great outcry when the archbishop was executed. Although the earl of Northumberland escaped to Scotland, he died in February 1408. Soon after Edmund Mortimer died during the siege of Harlech and the Welsh rebellion faded away.

At last by 1408 Henry felt reasonably safe. Two years earlier he had taken JAMES I of Scotland captive when the young heir to the throne was being sent to France for safety. James remained at the court of the English king for the next seventeen years and, with him as hostage, England's relationship with Scotland remained stable. Moreover threats from France diminished as the French became riven by its own civil war. Unfortunately for Henry his physical constitution gave way and for several years, between 1406 and 1409, there were concerns for his life. In addition to the stress of keeping his throne amid widespread opposition, Henry had struggled to sustain the administration and finance of England. Henry placed considerable demands upon his treasury, and Parliament often argued against him. Henry remained moderate throughout, careful to avoid a confrontation that might cost him his throne. He relied increasingly on his council to help him run his government. However, it became evident that his illness was taking its toll and that Henry was finding it difficult to govern. By 1409 his son, Prince Henry, was made chancellor in place of the king's favoured Thomas Arundel, archbishop of Canterbury. Arundel returned in 1411 amidst a quarrel between the King and his council, in which it seems it had been proposed that Henry abdicate in favour of his son. Henry refused. Rumours abounded that Prince Henry was going to take the throne by force, but that never happened. He had little time to wait. Henry's strange wasting disease took his life in March 1413, two weeks before his forty-sixth birthday. The valiant knight of twenty years earlier had been worn out by the stress of government and ill health. Nevertheless he had established a united kingdom, and passed on the throne to his son, HENRY V, who would become one of England's best known kings.

Henry had desired that he be buried at Canterbury Cathedral rather than Westminster Abbey. There is a story that while a ship bore his coffin down the Thames a storm erupted and the king's body was washed overboard. The sailors later substituted another body. When Henry's tomb at Canterbury was opened in 1832, the simplicity of the remains suggested that the story may have been true.

[O15;SB25] HENRY V

Ruled 20 March 1413–31 August 1422. Crowned: Westminster Abbey, 9 April 1413.
Titles: king of England; prince of Wales, duke of Cornwall, earl of Chester and prince of Aquitaine (from October 1399); duke of Aquitaine and duke of Lancaster (from November 1399).
Born: Monmouth Castle, 16 September 1387. Died: Bois-de-Vincennes, France, 31 August 1422, aged 34. Buried: Westminster Abbey.
Married: 2 June 1420, at Troyes Cathedral, France, Katherine (1401–37), dau. of Charles VI, king of France: 1 son (Henry VI).

Henry was the son of HENRY IV and from his youth demonstrated his abilities as a resourceful and valiant soldier. Even though he was only fifteen, Henry fought alongside his father in the war against the Welsh rebels under OWAIN GLYN DWR, and later against the English rebels, Henry "Hotspur" Percy and Edmund Mortimer. By the time he was eighteen Henry was heavily involved in working with his father's council of administrators. The young king was so admired that, when his father grew weak from a wasting disease, there was a call for the father to abdicate in his son's favour. This did not happen, and it is not proven that the prince wanted it to happen, but it is evident that in the king's final years he and his son disagreed over several matters. Chief amongst these was England's involvement in France. Henry IV had chosen to press again England's claims to French territories, and an opportunity had arisen in 1407 when civil war broke out in France during one of Charles VI's increasing bouts of insanity, between two factions – the Burgundians and the Armagnacs. Henry IV supported the latter but Prince Henry supported the Burgundians. Their dispute was never resolved, and the king's supporters used it as an opportunity to discredit the prince. However when Henry IV died in 1413, and Prince Henry became king, these disputes were rapidly resolved. Henry was quick to forget old grievances, even to the point of granting the last Plantagenet king, RICHARD II, a proper state burial at Westminster.

Henry focused his intentions single-mindedly on regaining the lands in France and galvanised Parliament into total support. His initial negotiations with the French proved fruitless – not surprisingly considering Henry's wish to have the whole of the old Angevin Empire restored. When negotiations ceased, Henry invaded on 11 August 1415. He successfully besieged Harfleur and then, on 25 October, confronted the French army at Agincourt. Although the French out-numbered the English three-to-one, their rash tactics against the English and Welsh longbowmen proved disastrous. The flower of French chivalry died on that day. It is reported that the French lost some six thousand men compared to four hundred English.

Although Agincourt was a major victory, it was not decisive because France did not immediately fall to Henry. But his success had caused the French to be extremely wary of Henry, and it earned Henry tremendous support in England. He also succeeded in gaining Sigismund, the Holy Roman Emperor, as his ally and together they won the support of John, duke of Burgundy. Starting again in August 1417, Henry pursued his campaign through Normandy which fell to him in the spring of 1419. A few months later the duke of Burgundy was murdered, and Henry found that his own claim on the French throne was now supported by all Burgundians in total defiance of the Armagnac party, adherents of the Dauphin, Charles. Henry signed the Treaty of Troyes with the Burgundians in May 1420, which recognized him as the heir to the French throne. To seal the alliance Henry married Katherine, daughter of the French king. Henry brought his bride back to England in February 1421 and spent the next few months in a triumphant tour of the land. It was soured slightly by the news of the death of his brother, Thomas, duke of Clarence, at the battle of Baugé in France in March. By June Henry was back in France, continuing his battle for the kingdom. The Dauphin's stronghold at Meaux fell to him in May 1422 after a long siege. Unfortunately Henry had become very ill during the winter, almost certainly with dysentery, and his health worsened during the summer. He died on 31 August 1422, aged only thirty-four. It was a cruel blow of fate. Less than six weeks later the French king died. Like Moses,

Henry was in sight of his kingdom but was denied entry into it. Nevertheless Henry bequeathed to his infant son a kingdom greater than any since the days of HENRY II.

Our image of Henry is probably drawn mostly from his portrayal by Laurence Olivier in the film version of Shakespeare's *Henry V*, but Olivier's own portrayal was based on a painting of Henry that shows a rather humourless, determined young man with a hard face, an over-large nose, thin eyebrows and a clipped monkish haircut. Although Henry's reign had been the shortest of any English king since the Norman conquest (even RICHARD I's was three months longer), it was one of the most successful. No other king gained such united support from his barons and no other king regained so much territory and held it. There is no way of knowing how Henry would have maintained his two kingdoms had he lived and his reign might have ended in failure, like EDWARD III's. But Henry was also a tireless administrator who, despite the pressure of his military campaigns, continued to respond to petitions from England and meet the needs and demands of his court. His ability to hold together his parliament despite the immense strain upon the treasury of his campaigns is further testimony to his abilities. Henry also remained fond of and on good terms with his step-mother, Joan of Navarre, even though she was accused of witchcraft in 1417 and imprisoned at Pevensey Castle. His ability to handle all of these eventualities and triumph in them all was remarkable. His early death was a tragic loss to England. His wife, Katherine, subsequently formed a romantic alliance with Owain Tudor, and most probably married in secret. By him she had four or five children, and died giving birth to the last in 1437. By her son Edmund, she was the grandmother of HENRY VII.

From a painting in the National Portrait Gallery

[O16;R55;SB26] **HENRY VI**

Ruled England 1 September 1422–4 March 1461 (deposed); restored 3 October 1470–11 April 1471 (deposed again). Crowned: Westminster Abbey, 6 November 1429, and again at St Paul's Cathedral, 6 October 1470. Also declared king of France, 11 October 1422. Crowned: Cathedral of Notre Dame de Paris, 16 December 1431.

Titles: king of England and France; duke of Cornwall (from birth).

Born: Windsor Castle, 6 December 1421. Died (murdered): Tower of London, 21? May 1471, aged 49. Buried: Chertsey Abbey, Surrey, but removed to Windsor Castle in 1485.

Married: 22 April 1445 at Titchfield Abbey: Margaret (1429–82), dau. of René, duke of Anjou and king of Naples: 1 son.

Henry VI is a prime example of the wrong king at the wrong time, and that made for a very tragic reign. Henry was the son of the strong, charismatic HENRY V whose single-mindedness in recovering the former Norman territories in France had led to him being recognized as heir to the French throne. Henry, however, died before he could benefit from his efforts. His son was almost nine months old when Henry died. Six weeks after inheriting the English throne, young Henry was also declared king of France with the death of Charles VI, his grandfather. Had Henry V lived he would have had the strength of character to take advantage of the situation, but with only an infant king, the new empire required something special to unite it. That something special was not there. In fact the empire soon became a victim of the same tensions that had threatened both thrones for as long as there had been kings: inter-dynastic rivalries, and hatred and suspicion of court favourites.

Although Henry was officially king of France, he never had much opportunity to rule it. In France Charles VI's nineteen-year-old son was also declared king as Charles VII. He held most of the southern provinces while Henry's regent, his uncle, John, duke of Bedford, governed the northern provinces for England. The battle for France dragged on, lacking the relentless drive and power of Henry V. Bedford endeavoured to consolidate the gains the English had made so that the benefits could be ploughed back to the crown and thus reduce the drain of the war on the English treasury. However this meant that any final victory was perpetually deferred. Neither Bedford nor the rather weak-willed Charles VII had sufficient skill to conclude the battle. The key to the fighting centred around Orleans which came under siege in 1427. This was the period of Joan of Arc who galvanised the French into action. Although she was only seventeen she led an army into Orleans and raised the siege in May 1429. The spirit of victory was restored to the French and a wave of national pride engulfed the country as they regained lands from the English along the Loire Valley. Charles was crowned king of France in June 1429. This concerned Bedford who urged on the coronation of young Henry. He was crowned king of England in November 1429, but it was another two years before he was crowned as king of France in 1431. He was the only king ever to be formally crowned in both countries. However, although it had been hoped this would instil a similar nationalistic fervour in the English, it achieved nothing. The French were gaining the upper hand and the English were losing all of the lands Henry V had gained. In 1435 the Duke of Burgundy, in whose name the English had first invaded France, reached an agreement with Charles VII known as the Treaty of Arras. From then on the English cause in France was lost; Charles entered Paris in 1436. Apparently when Henry learned of Burgundy's defection he cried. Although he retained the title of king of France, it held no authority. The conflict would continue for another eighteen years until the death of England's dashing champion John Talbot, earl of Shrewsbury, at Castillon in 1453. With that defeat England's Hundred Years' War with France came to an end. The only French territory remaining in English hands was Calais.

Henry did not declare himself of age until November 1437, just before his sixteenth birthday. Until then the protector of England had been his uncle, Humphrey, duke of Gloucester. No one seemed to like Gloucester, and he was not trusted with full regency powers, which had remained with Bedford until his death in 1435. The result was constant wrangles in Parliament as Gloucester endeavoured to exercise his authority. At times even the young king interceded to calm matters, although no one took much notice of young Henry. During his upbringing he had been told to behave himself and not believe himself to have absolute authority. By the time he took the reins of government he was already a pawn of the most powerful statesmen and was too weak willed to exert any power. This was not because he did not believe he should, it was mostly because he was not interested. People are not simply born kings, they have to be them, and Henry had no will to govern. As a result he invested power and authority in the hands of those he most trusted and, as Henry was amazingly naive, these tended to be the least scrupulous of people. Amongst them was William de la Pole, earl of Suffolk, and grandson of Michael de la Pole who had been one of RICHARD II's court favourites. Although de la Pole ingratiated himself into Henry's affections, and became his steward in 1435, he had good intentions since he was a peacemaker at heart. However, his solution for peace effectively meant the loss of France, and his chief opponent in this was Humphrey of Gloucester who was in favour of continuing the war of conquest. In other times, history might have been on the side of Suffolk, but in the years so soon after Henry V's great victories and with so many lives and resources expended, the English nation was not for sacrificing France. Nevertheless, because of his closeness to the king, Suffolk was able to plot his course for some years. It was through Suffolk's negotiations that Henry married Margaret of Anjou in 1444 with terms that should have brought peace. What many did not know until later was that one of the terms in order to extend the truce was that Henry would surrender Maine, to which he agreed. There was uproar when the truth was known to the extent that Henry no longer felt safe in London. Margaret of Anjou together with the Earl of Suffolk convinced Henry that his uncle was plotting an uprising. Humphrey of Gloucester was arrested and confined at Bury St Edmunds in February 1447, where he died a week later. Many believed that he was murdered, probably on Suffolk's orders. Suffolk, realising his unpopularity, switched from peacemaker to warmonger and invaded Brittany in 1449. This brought the conflict into Normandy which the French conquered by September 1450. Suffolk could not escape the loss of Normandy. Even before the war was concluded, Suffolk was arrested and impeached. Henry, hoping to save his life, had him banished, but his ship was intercepted at Dover and Suffolk was executed. Suffolk and his allies now became the scapegoat for all that had gone wrong both in France and with the mismanagement of English affairs. This was the main cause for the revolution led by John Cade in May 1450 which followed much the same course as the Peasants' Revolt of seventy years earlier, except that Henry VI did not show the bravery of the young Richard II. The revolt ran its course over the next two months before Cade's death. His rebellion was an opportunity to purge government, but Henry took little action. Instead he created further polarisation by appointing Edmund Beaufort, the Duke of Somerset (and Henry V's first cousin), as his closest adviser. Somerset had once been a good soldier, but his role as lieutenant of France had coincided with the loss of most of the English lands, and he was regarded as the focal point for English failure. He was also the sworn enemy of Richard, duke of York (who was Henry V's second cousin). York had been effectively banished to Ireland in 1447, because of his sympathy for Humphrey of Gloucester. However in August 1450 he returned to England, supported by his army, and demanded his place on the Council. The next few years were tense ones as the rivalry between Somerset and York grew: a rivalry that would erupt into the Wars of the Roses. Somerset had the upper hand to begin with, because of his direct link with the king, but matters changed after August 1453 when the king became afflicted by the first bouts of mental decline that would darken his later years. This was almost certainly inherited from his grandfather, the king of France, who also had bouts of imbecility. Exactly what was wrong with Henry is not certain, but he lost all memory and reason and would sit for weeks devoid of expression or awareness in a deep melancholia. The depression may have been triggered by the loss of France. It came just two months before the birth of Henry's first (and only) son, Edward. The king gave no sign of acknowledging the child and when, eighteen months later, Henry's reason returned, he had no idea where the child came from, believing it must have been born of the Holy Ghost.

Richard of York was made "Protector of the Realm" in March 1454 and promptly had Somerset arrested and imprisoned in the Tower. However, a year later, when Henry recovered, the king had Somerset released and York dismissed. York's entreaties to the king were ignored and the inevitable conflict broke out at St Albans on 22 May 1455. The battle was brief and Somerset was killed. That should have been an end of any hostilities, because Henry seemed prepared to be reconciled to Richard of York. When another bout of madness struck Henry in November 1455, Richard was again made protector but was again dismissed in February 1456. With Henry scarcely able to govern, his queen, Margaret, took up his cause. She despised the arrogant haughtiness of York and encouraged the new duke of Somerset, Henry Beaufort, against him. By 1458 the flames of war were being fanned across England between the Yorkists, supported by Richard Neville, earl of Salisbury, and his son, also Richard Neville, earl of Warwick, on the one side, and the Lancastrians, under the figurehead of Henry VI, but really led by Margaret of Anjou, supported by Somerset and Henry Percy, the third earl of Northumberland. With the battle of Ludlow in 1459 the Wars of the Roses began in earnest. At that battle the Yorkists were routed and Richard of York fled to Wales and then Ireland, while his supporters sought refuge in Calais. The following year the Calais element defeated the Lancastrians at Northampton, and Richard of York returned to England. He now formally placed his claim to the throne before Parliament in September 1460. The following month his right was acknowledged and he was declared the heir to the throne, in place of Henry's son Edward. Henry, his mind failing rapidly, agreed, but Margaret of Anjou was not so easily pacified. She raised a further army in the north and met the Yorkists at Wakefield on 30 December. York was killed in the battle, whilst Salisbury was captured and murdered. Margaret marched on London, defeating the earl of Warwick at St Albans early in 1461. Warwick managed to recruit another army, together with York's son, Edward, and they marched into London in triumph in March 1461. Edward declared himself king (as EDWARD IV). His forces marched north, following the retreating army of Henry and Margaret, and the two clashed at Towton near Tadcaster in Yorkshire. There, in the middle of a snowstorm, the Lancastrian army was defeated. Henry and Margaret fled to Scotland, where they were given refuge by the young king JAMES III. Henry bought support from the Scots by granting them Berwick, but the military aid he was given proved useless in the abortive battle at Carlisle. Edward was soon after crowned king of England. He outsmarted every move made by Margaret of Anjou, including her alliance with France, to try and regain the crown and, after three years, Henry became an embarrassment to the Scots. He was smuggled out of Scotland and spent a year in refuge in northern England, until he was betrayed and captured by English forces in July 1465 and imprisoned in the Tower of London.

Had Henry been of the same arrogant disposition of EDWARD II and RICHARD II, both of whom had been murdered in prison, Henry might have expected his days to be numbered. But following an amazing reversal in the fortunes of Edward IV, Henry suddenly found himself removed from the Tower on 3 October 1470 and reinstated as king. The earl of Warwick had changed his allegiance to Henry and even went so far, two months later, as to marry his daughter Anne to the king's son, Edward. Henry's 'readeption', as it was known, was not to last for long. Edward IV returned with an army in April and defeated and killed Warwick. The king was again captured and imprisoned. His wife's army arrived too late to save him. She and her supporters were defeated at Tewkesbury on 4 May 1471, where the young Prince Edward was killed. Margaret was also imprisoned in the Tower and on that same night, 21 May, Henry was stabbed to death. Just who killed him was never revealed, though his body was displayed in its coffin the next day as if he had died naturally, so as to avoid any later rebellion to restore him.

Margaret of Anjou remained in prison, first at the Tower, then Windsor and finally Wallingford, before being released to return to her father's estates at Angers in 1475. Her appearance had become as wretched as Henry's, exhausted by years of trial and tribulation. Had she been the queen of a stronger king, they would have made a remarkable pair and doubtless ruled with considerable effect, but Margaret had the misfortune to be married to a king who began weak and sank into mental decline. He should have been a younger brother and left government to John, duke of Bedford, who was much more able. Henry was more a scholar than a statesman. Although his reign led to the Wars of the Roses, he and his queen may best be remembered as the founders of King's College (1441) and Queen's College (1448) at Cambridge.

[O17] **EDWARD IV**
Ruled 4 March 1461–3 October 1470, deposed; restored 11 April 1471–9 April 1483. Crowned: Westminster Abbey, 28 June 1461.
Titles: king of England and France, earl of March (from birth), duke of York, earl of Ulster and earl of Cambridge (from 1460).
Born: Rouen, Normandy, 28 April 1442. Died: Palace of Westminster, 9 April 1483, aged 40. Buried: St George's Chapel, Windsor.
Married: 1 May 1464, at Grafton Regis, Northamptonshire, Elizabeth (c1437–92) dau. of Richard Wydville, 1st Earl Rivers: 10 children. Edward also had at least four illegitimate children.

Edward IV was the first king of the House of York though, like his predecessor HENRY VI, he was a Plantagenet. Both were descended from EDWARD III, Henry through Edward's son John of Gaunt, and Edward through a younger son, Edmund, duke of York(and in the female line through Lionel, duke of Clarence). Edward IV's father was Richard, duke of York, who, in 1460, had been declared heir to the throne, though he died soon after in battle at Wakefield. Edward, who was only eighteen, was able to rally support along with his cousin Richard Neville, earl of Warwick, and successfully invaded London. He was declared king on 4 March 1461, and just over three weeks later decisively defeated the forces of Henry VI at Towton, probably the bloodiest battle fought on English soil, and this secured his claim on the throne. Henry VI and Margaret of Anjou fled to Scotland, seeking sanctuary with JAMES III.

Edward IV was welcomed to the throne. Although he was young he had already proved himself an able soldier. Moreover he was tall (six feet three inches) and handsome with a dashing smile, golden brown hair and winning ways – he could, for instance, always remember the names of his knights and officials and something about them, which endeared him to the court. Nevertheless all the time Henry VI lived, Edward's claim on the throne could not be regarded as secure. He needed to rule wisely and ensure the support of his noblemen. He did this by limiting the previous practice of court favourites. Instead he placed the control of Crown lands under court officials, confiscating many of the lands previously bequeathed to Lancastrian sympathisers. He set about making England profitable through foreign trade, including his own commercial ventures, to the extent that he was eventually able to make the Crown solvent, rather than buried in debt as under previous kings. He did his best to make the Crown and government administratively efficient and financially sound, though it must be admitted that one reason he reduced administrative costs was in order for more money to be spent on himself and the image of the king so that his court was as resplendent as those in France and Burgundy.

Once Edward felt firmly established as king he left the work of defeating the remaining outposts of Lancastrian resistance, which were mostly in the north, to his cousins Richard and John Neville. Edward knew how much he owed to Richard Neville for his position as king and Neville was highly rewarded. He would later earn the reputation as Warwick, the King-maker. He was made the Chamberlain of England, as well as receiving many other honor and considerable land. He became the second most powerful man in England. After the battle of Hexham in May 1464, where the last important Lancastrian resistance was crushed, John Neville was given the earldom of Northumberland, the hereditary title of the Percy family. With the Nevilles supporting him, Edward's position was secure, and therefore Edward's next act was one of the greatest folly.

Edward was a highly-sexed man, and his actions were as much ruled by his lust as by his brain. Warwick, under his own initiative, had been working to secure an alliance with the French king Louis XI, who still supported Henry VI. The proposed treaty of friendship was to be sealed by the marriage between Edward IV and a French princess, Bona of Savoy. Warwick continued the negotiations throughout 1464 with a view to concluding them in October. Edward was not fully supportive of the negotiations as he favoured a treaty with England's older ally, Burgundy, which was itself at loggerheads with France. Edward's marriage was therefore a powerful bargaining tool. Yet Edward married in secret to an English lady and, to make matters worse, the marriage might even have been bigamous.

Although more rumour than fact, Edward had a reputation for taking many of the ladies of the court to his bed. All the time he was an honourable bachelor, and all the time this led to no consequences, everyone turned a blind eye. However, in May 1464, under the pretext of a hunting trip, Edward entered into a secret marriage with Elizabeth Wydville (often called Woodville), daughter of the 1st Lord Rivers, and the widow of Sir John Grey. The story went that Edward lusted after her but she would not submit without a promise of marriage. Edward agreed, probably not meaning it, but Elizabeth held him to his word. Edward was reputed often to make promises for sex with the ladies of the court, and this reputation would later be the downfall of his family. When news of his marriage leaked out – amazingly he kept it secret for four months – there was uproar. There was even a rumour that Edward had made a similar marriage compact with Lady Eleanor Butler a year or two earlier. How much of this was true has never been satisfactorily resolved, and the rumour was probably a fabrication built upon Edward's known philandering, but it was later a major weapon to be used against the legitimacy of his children by Elizabeth. What made matters worse was that Edward had married into a family of Lancastrian sympathisers: Elizabeth's father had married a second time to Jacquetta of Luxembourg, the widow of Henry V's brother John, duke of Bedford. Elizabeth's father, brother and her former husband had all fought on the side of Henry VI. Warwick was the most outraged at the marriage. It had humiliated him in the face of the French king and lost him his opportunity to gain lands and titles in France. Moreover it meant that the Wydville family now advanced in status and threatened to equal or even overthrow his stature as the second most powerful man in England.

Although Warwick continued to work with Edward and the Wydvilles over the next few years, he became increasingly exasperated at Edward's persistence in allying with Burgundy while Warwick tried to cement an alliance with France. Also when Edward thwarted Warwick's proposals of marriage contracts between his family and the king's, Warwick realised that differences between them were becoming irreconcilable. The last straw came when Edward married his sister, Margaret, to Charles, duke of Burgundy, in July 1468. Warwick withdrew his support from Edward and began to side with Edward's over-ambitious brother, George, duke of Clarence, who desired the kingship. Warwick was also supported by Louis XI, who promised Warwick lands in France if he successfully overthrew Edward. Warwick had not at this stage moved across to the Lancastrian cause, though he knew that Louis still supported Margaret of Anjou. Warwick's intention was to depose Edward and make George king in his place. In July 1469 Warwick succeeded in securing the marriage between George and and his daughter Isabella which Edward had so long opposed. Warwick now supported a series of uprisings that began in northern England. Although Edward was still a popular king amongst his subjects, his marriage had sullied his reputation and Elizabeth was never a popular queen. Warwick, on the other hand, was always a popular hero, seen by many as the nation's deliverer, and when in mid-July, Warwick issued a proclamation declaring that Edward must reform his ways or suffer deposition, Warwick received enormous support. Edward at first procrastinated, perhaps a little too sure of himself, and found himself trapped at Nottingham by a rebel army. A relief force was defeated and, although it allowed Edward's escape, Edward realised that his army was outnumbered. A battle was out of the question and, wisely, Edward dispersed his army and allowed himself to be captured by Warwick. Warwick imprisoned the king and sought to govern in his name, but was unable to find support in Parliament and, with government crumbling, he began to incur the wrath of the populace for imprisoning their sovereign. Warwick had no choice but to release Edward, who returned to London in October 1469 amidst much public acclaim. Although on the surface, Edward reconciled himself with Warwick and his brother George, Warwick knew that his authority was now limited. Grudgingly, if he was to achieve any restoration of his power, he needed to throw in his lot with Louis XI and Margaret of Anjou and defect to the Lancastrian cause. Supported by the Lancastrians, Warwick again fomented rebellion in the autumn of 1470, and their invasion fleet landed at Dartmouth in September. Edward was caught ill prepared. John Neville sent his army purportedly to support Edward but, at the last moment, declared his support for Henry VI. Edward suddenly realised that his forces were considerably outnumbered and his only recourse was to flee. He left England on 2 October seeking refuge with his brother-in-law, the Duke of Burgundy. Warwick seized the opportunity, brought Henry VI out of imprisonment in the Tower and restored him to the throne. Had Warwick withheld his zeal, Henry's restoration might have remained permanent, but urged on by Louis XI, Warwick and Louis declared war on Burgundy. Charles, who until then had not wished to be involved, was now compelled to grant Edward a fleet and an army, and on 11 March 1471 Edward returned to England. Edward's skills as a soldier and general now became apparent. Although outnumbered three to one, Edward's army soundly defeated Warwick's at the battle of Barnet, on Easter Sunday, where both Warwick and his brother John were killed. Edward marched victoriously into London and was restored to the throne. Six weeks later Edward defeated the army of Margaret of Anjou at Tewkesbury on 4 May, where Margaret's son, Prince Edward, was killed. Edward IV was once more firmly in command of his realm. To ensure there was no further rebellion in favour of Henry VI, Edward ordered that the old king be murdered, though the public message was that he had died naturally and his body was put on display to curb any rumours.

The second half of Edward's reign lacks the glory and excitement of the first, although it was more administratively sound. It was during this period that Edward was able to carry through the reforms he had started in the previous decade, which led to better executed offices of the Crown, more effective administration of the law, and generally profitable and safe trade throughout England. The Crown became self-financing, and the loss of burdensome taxes made Edward even more popular amongst his subjects. He exerted considerable diplomacy abroad, developing strong alliances with the dukes of Brittany and Burgundy and with the king of Aragon. In July 1475 Edward determined to recapture the former English lands in France but his own invasion army was not matched by the promised reinforcements from Burgundy, and Edward had no choice but to negotiate peace with Louis. This was almost certainly the better outcome for, despite Edward's superior generalship, continued conflict in France was bound to have financial repercussions that might have soured Edward's popularity. As it was, Edward's brothers Richard (see RICHARD III) and George both saw the peace treaty as an ignominious defeat. George, who still believed he should be king, began to plot against his brother. This time Edward had him arrested and tried for treason. Found guilty, George was executed in February 1478. The traditional story is that George was drowned in a butt of malmsey wine.

Edward was a great patron of the arts, and a pioneer patron of printing. Although he personally preferred the illuminated manuscript, he encouraged William Caxton in his pursuits, and in November 1477 helped finance the first book printed in England, *The Dictes and Sayenges of the Phylosophers*, which had been translated by the queen's brother, Anthony, Lord Rivers. Edward also financed major building works at Windsor Castle and Eltham Palace in Kent. Ultimately, however, he fell victim to his own love of food. His continued gorging had made him fat and lazy and the once virile and strong king had become stout and inactive. His health began to fail and he became subject to an increasing number of ailments. Just which one killed him has never been satisfactorily resolved. He died just before his forty-first birthday, probably of pneumonia, though it has been conjectured that he had contracted typhoid or may even have been poisoned. Certainly some attributed his death to a surfeit of food. Had he reigned longer Edward might well have been regarded as a great king. He was without doubt a strong one, and governed intelligently, though in his private life he was unwise and naïve, and his actions ultimately proved fatal to his dynasty.

[O18] EDWARD V

Ruled 9 April–25 June 1483, deposed, never crowned.

Titles: king of England; prince of Wales, earl of Chester and duke of Cornwall (1471–83), earl of March and earl of Pembroke (from 1479).

Born: *Westminster Abbey, 4 November 1470;* **Died:** *Tower of London, probably 3 September 1483, aged 12.* **Buried:** *Tower of London and subsequently Westminster Abbey.*

Edward did not live long enough to enjoy any of the benefits of kingship, only its hardships. He and his brother Richard, duke of York, are immortalised in history as the ill-fated "Princes in the Tower" whose deaths have become one of the best known historical mysteries.

The likelihood of Edward ever becoming king seemed doomed from the start. Although his father EDWARD IV was a popular king, his mother, Elizabeth Wydville, was not so universally liked. Possibly had Edward been their first born, he might have been old enough to take control himself at the time of his father's sudden and unexpected death. His eldest sister, Elizabeth, was then seventeen, and at that age Edward could have assumed royal authority. But he was his father's fourth child, and was born at the lowest ebb in Edward IV's reign, when the king had fled England and Elizabeth had sought sanctuary in Westminster Abbey. Although his father regained the throne, young Edward grew up in a family where there was considerable hostility between his father and his uncles, George, duke of Clarence, and Richard, duke of Gloucester (later RICHARD III). Nevertheless the child had a good education and a regal bearing and may, in due course, have made a fine king.

However upon his father's death, his uncle Richard rapidly manipulated events to establish himself as "Lord High Protector" of England. Young Edward was holding court as prince of Wales at Ludlow and travelled to London under the protection of his mother's brother, Earl Rivers. They were met at Stony Stratford by Richard, on his way to London from York. Thereafter he escorted Edward to London and, though professing absolute loyalty, he was already planning on assuming the kingship himself. Edward and his brother were installed in the Tower of London which, at that time, was still a royal residence and not solely a prison, but the young king's freedom was totally restricted and he never left the Tower again. Plans for his coronation were delayed and in June 1483 Bishop Stillington, almost certainly at the instigation of Richard, announced his belief that Edward IV's marriage to Elizabeth Wydville had been illegal because Edward already had a pre-contract marriage arrangement with Lady Eleanor Butler. As a consequence his children by his second marriage were illegitimate. Although no evidence for this first marriage was ever produced, such was Edward IV's reputation as a womaniser that it was easily believed, and Richard was able to gain the support of Parliament in declaring the young king illegitimate and he was summarily deposed on June 25th 1483. His period as king can scarcely be honoured with the description of a reign, since he had no opportunity to exercise any authority, but he was the true heir to the throne and as such had the shortest reign of any legitimate king after the Norman Conquest.

Rumours began almost immediately of the fate of Edward and his brother. The last they were seen was in July 1483, but there is circumstantial evidence to suggest that they lived for another four or five weeks. Over the centuries there has been considerable speculation as to what became of the Princes and who caused their deaths. Had they died naturally it would have been in Richard's interests to make it known. Some believe the boys survived Richard's reign and that they were subsequently murdered on the orders of HENRY VII. The fact that their fate remained such a secret allowed two pretenders to the throne to emerge during Henry VII's reign, Lambert SIMNEL and Perkin WARBECK, both of whom claimed that they were Edward's younger brother Richard. It was not until the year 1674 that the remains of two young children were found buried in the Tower of London. These were treated as the bones of Edward and Richard and were reburied in an urn in Westminster Abbey. More recent research on these bones, whilst inconclusive, was suggestive that they were the remains of the young Princes. The likely explanation of their deaths is the one given to Henry VII by Sir James Tyrrell, who declared under torture that he had smothered the two children by order of Richard III. Henry VII chose to maintain its secrecy because he had earlier shown favour to Tyrrell and it might be implied that Henry had sanctioned the death of the Princes.

Nevertheless the thorough research conducted by Alison Weir in her book *The Princes in the Tower* make it clear that the only person who could have been responsible for their deaths was Richard III.

[O19] RICHARD III *CROOKBACK*
26 June 1483–22 August 1485. Crowned: Westminster Abbey, 6 July 1483.
Titles: king of England; duke of Gloucester *(from 1461)*.
Born: Fotheringay Castle, Northamptonshire, 2 October 1452. **Died** *(in battle)*: Bosworth Field, Leicestershire, 22 August 1485, aged 33. **Buried:** Greyfriars Abbey, Leicester.
Married: Anne (1456–85) dau. Richard Neville, earl of Warwick, and widow of Edward, prince of Wales: 1 son. Richard had at least four illegitimate children.

Richard III has long been regarded as one of England's most villainous kings and, though many revisionists have sought to clear his name, the evidence continues to suggest that Richard was as conniving in his personal affairs as history dictates, but not necessarily any more conniving than many of his predecessors. He was certainly not the evil monster portrayed by Shakespeare in his play *Richard III* and, though he probably had a slight deformity in his shoulder, he was not a hunch-back.

Richard was the younger brother of EDWARD IV. His was apparently a difficult birth, and he seems to have been a delicate child, but grew through all of this into a strong and resourceful young man, albeit short. He was only nine when his brother became king, after a childhood where he was frequently moved to safe custody as the fortunes of his father, Richard, duke of York, waxed and waned during the Wars of the Roses. Five months after his brother became king, Richard was created duke of Gloucester. Although young, he was well aware of the actions of his elder brother George, duke of Clarence, who, encouraged by Richard Neville, earl of Warwick, rebelled against Edward in 1469, but Richard remained loyal to Edward. As Warwick rapidly fell from grace, starting in 1469 and culminating in his death at the battle of Barnet in 1471, Richard benefited, being granted many of Warwick's titles and much of his land in the north. By 1471 Richard was Constable and Lord High Admiral of England, chief justice of the Welsh Marches, chief steward, chamberlain of South Wales, Great Chamberlain of England and chief steward of the Duchy of Lancaster. In 1472, though still only nineteen, Richard married Anne Neville, the daughter of the earl of Warwick, herself a descendent of EDWARD III and the widow of Edward, prince of Wales, the son of HENRY VI. Their only child, Edward, was born early in 1476. Through this marriage Richard became entitled to half of the Warwick estates, which caused considerable acrimony with his brother, George, who felt that the reapportionment of Warwick's lands was unequal. During these years Richard strengthened his hold on the north of England governing it on Edward's behalf. He became known as "Lord of the North", ruling it as king in all but name. His chief residence was his castle at Middleham in Yorkshire, a strong yet comfortable castle which became known as the Windsor of the North. Richard accompanied Edward on his expedition to France in 1475, and the only show of dissension between Richard and Edward was over the peace treaty, which Richard held to be dishonourable. Nevertheless, Richard remained loyal to Edward during the continued defiance of George, resulting in George's execution. Richard strengthened his hold on the north and even turned his eyes towards Scotland. He conducted several campaigns against JAMES III resulting, in

1482, in regaining Berwick and advancing into Edinburgh. During all this period Richard was highly regarded by his peers and subjects, both as a just administrator and as a wise and strong general. To all intents Richard ruled northern England, which was recognized when he was granted palatine powers in the west March in 1483. Two months afterwards Edward IV died unexpectedly and his will named Richard as "Lord High Protector of the Realm" during EDWARD V's infancy.

Thereafter matters moved swiftly. Richard knew that he needed to assert his authority before the Wydvilles – the family of Edward's widowed queen – did so. Richard hastened down from York while the Wydvilles were bringing the young heir from Ludlow. Richard met them at Stony Stratford, took the young king under his protection, escorted him to London, and placed him in the Tower. The Tower was still a royal residence in those days, but it was also a strong fortress, and once there the king was entirely under Richard's power. Predictably the Wydvilles reacted, and Richard was able to represent their actions as being treasonable. Anthony Wydville, the queen's brother, was executed without trial. Richard meted out the same fate to Lord Hastings, once his loyal supporter and a staunch opponent of the Wydvilles. However when Hastings realised that Richard was seeking to claim the throne and depose Edward, he objected and was promptly arrested and executed. Richard now broadcast the belief that Edward V was illegitimate, because Edward IV had entered into a previous marriage contract. Parliament recognized this claim on 25 June, when the young king was deposed, and Richard was proclaimed king the next day. He had secured the throne quickly and quite ruthlessly in eleven weeks. By the standards of his day, while one might not condone his actions, one can understand them. The rivalry between the Yorkists and the Lancastrians were not at an end and England needed a strong ruler with full authority. Even acting as protector, Richard could not always count on the full support of Parliament. He thus needed to be rid of the young king. His main rivals were the Wydvilles whom Richard and most Yorkist supporters opposed, so it was crucial that they did not gain power. Seen in this light Richard's quick actions were those of a shrewd, calculating tactician who knew how to control and manipulate. Morals aside he was a very clever man.

With Edward V deposed, it remains questionable why the young king and his brother had then to be killed. Richard probably recognized that the Act of Parliament that had overthrown Edward's legitimacy could as easily be revoked and, so long as the princes were alive, they remained a threat to his overall control. It seems likely that Richard ordered their deaths in early September 1483 while he was on a state tour of the realm and outside the capital, but although rumours were rife about the fate of the princes, the real facts about their deaths did not come to light during Richard's lifetime.

Although secure on the throne, Richard had to deal with some residual rebellions. The main threat came from his once loyal supporter Henry Stafford, duke of Buckingham, who had entered an alliance with the Wydvilles and with Henry Tudor who, through his mother, was another descendent of EDWARD III and the last Lancastrian claimant. Buckingham's revolt was, however, ill planned and thwarted by rainstorms, and he was captured without battle and executed at Salisbury on 2 November 1483. Henry Tudor remained in Brittany but continued to ally himself with the Wydvilles and awaited his opportunity.

There is little doubt that Richard governed as a wise and competent king. This suggests two sides to his character. But though he may have been ruthlessly ambitious and duplicitous in his desire for kingship, he enjoyed the power of governance and treated his subjects fairly. He was highly regarded as a monarch by the English and by his contemporaries in Europe. Though it might seem hypocritical, Richard railed against the poor English morals and issued proclamations to uphold moral standards. Richard was, in fact, a very pious man, a staunch supporter of the church and generally loyal to his wife. He had fathered several illegitimate children before his marriage, but the records are unclear as to whether he continued to maintain mistresses afterwards. He was distraught when his young son, Edward, who had always had a weak constitution, died in April 1484, aged only eight. Richard's wife, Anne, was too weak to bear another child. She was consumptive and died within the year, in March 1485. Later stories implied Richard had poisoned her because of his plans to marry his niece, Elizabeth of York, in order to father a new heir to the throne. This never occurred, and it is not clear how serious Richard's plans were to this effect, and it may have only been to thwart Henry Tudor's plans to marry Elizabeth.

Henry Tudor's planned invasion happened in August 1485. The two armies met at Market Bosworth, just west of Leicester. Had Richard succeeded, his authority to rule would have been unchallenged. However the battle was soon over. Richard charged straight into the thick of it, intent upon killing Henry Tudor himself, and was killed in the close-fought action. His naked body was carried on a pack-horse to Leicester for burial. According to tradition Richard's crown was found on the battlefield under a hawthorn bush.

When his brief reign is viewed in the round, Richard was undoubtedly a worthy king. He was as capable of taking the kingdom forward into a new age as his ultimate successors. History as written has chosen to focus on the vicious and ruthless side of his character rather than a balanced view. Richard was certainly not someone to have as either your friend or your enemy, but he was a better king than many who had come before him and many who would come after. With his death the Plantagenet line came to an end. The nearest Yorkist claimant was Edward, the son of Richard's brother George, duke of Clarence. One of Richard's illegitimate sons, John, was captain of Calais but was murdered in 1499. Another likely illegitimate son, also called Richard, lived in anonymity in Kent until 1550 and is buried at Eastwell Church. Richard III was the last English king to die in battle.

[O20] HENRY VII
Ruled 22 August 1485–21 April 1509. Crowned: Westminster Abbey, 30 October 1485.
Titles: king of England; earl of Richmond (from birth).
Born: Pembroke Castle, 28 January 1457. Died: Richmond Palace, 21 April 1509, aged 52. Buried: Westminster Abbey.
Married: 18 January 1486, at Westminster Abbey: Elizabeth (1466–1503), dau. of Edward IV: 8 children. Henry allegedly had one illegitimate son, though this seems to have been disproved.
The first of the Tudor kings of England, Henry's claim to the throne was extremely tenuous. He was descended from EDWARD III's son John of Gaunt, but only through

his mistress Katherine Swynford. Their child, John Beaufort, was made duke of Somerset and his granddaughter, Margaret, was Henry VII's mother, giving birth when she was only thirteen. The Beaufort's claim on the English throne had once been declared illegitimate, but it was later legalised. Henry's more authentic claim was from the Welsh rulers. His father, Edmund Tudor, earl of Richmond, was eighth in line from RHYS AP GRUFFYDD, the Lord Rhys of Deheubarth, and through him Henry could claim descent from the Celtic princes of Wales and as far back as the pre-Saxon rulers of Britain. Rightly or wrongly Henry argued that the blood of ARTHUR flowed in his veins, and he even named his first-born son Arthur to emphasise that connection.

Nevertheless Henry was aware that his right to the throne by descent was not strong, there were at least a dozen others with a better claim – even assuming he knew that EDWARD V and his brother (the "Princes in the Tower") were dead. His real claim was by right of conquest. He had defeated RICHARD III at Bosworth and was a popular claimant. His uncle, the notorious Jasper Tudor, a colourful adventurer had been amongst the staunchest supporters of the Lancastrians in the Wars of the Roses. The Tudor name brought with it an aura of daring and excitement. The nobility had not fully supported Richard III, but neither were they especially supportive of Richard's nephew, Edward, earl of Warwick, who was then only ten years old, but who had the strongest claim to the throne by right of descent. Henry VII grew to resent Edward's existence and found reasons to have him imprisoned and later executed for treason in 1499. Henry strengthened his claim on the throne by marrying Elizabeth of York, the eldest daughter of EDWARD IV, thereby uniting the houses of York and Lancaster under the new dynasty. Richard III had declared Edward IV's children illegitimate, and one of Henry's first Acts of Parliament was to legitimize them again. It only serves to emphasise, however, the questionable entitlement that Henry had to the throne. He knew this and was forever fearful of other claimants. It is no coincidence that during Henry's reign two significant pretenders came forward, Lambert SIMNEL and Perkin WARBECK. Henry was gracious to the first, and patient to the latter.

Henry's childhood had been one of exile and estrangement. His father had died before his birth and his young mother remarried. Henry was raised by his uncle, Jasper, until Pembroke Castle fell to the Yorkists in 1461, when Henry's custody passed to William Herbert, soon created Baron Herbert and earl of Pembroke. Henry received a good education and was raised as a prospective husband for Herbert's daughter Maud, but all this changed when Herbert was executed for treason in 1469, and soon after Henry was reunited with his uncle Jasper, who was welcomed back at court with the restoration of HENRY VI in 1470. The king even recognized Henry Tudor as a likely heir. Fortunes changed again when Edward IV recovered the crown, and both Jasper and Henry fled Britain to seek refuge in Brittany. Despite attempts by Edward to find them they survived. Little is known of this period, but judging from Henry's later nature it was evident that he learned to survive by his wits and to trust no one. It was this wily but dashing soldier who defeated Richard III at Bosworth in 1485 and inherited the throne of England.

Yet Henry forever remained a nervous king. Despite his success over the various claimants to the throne, who remained troublesome throughout the first half of his reign, Henry was anxious to establish his authority amongst his peers in Europe. He

48. England (7) – The Tudor and Stewart Succession

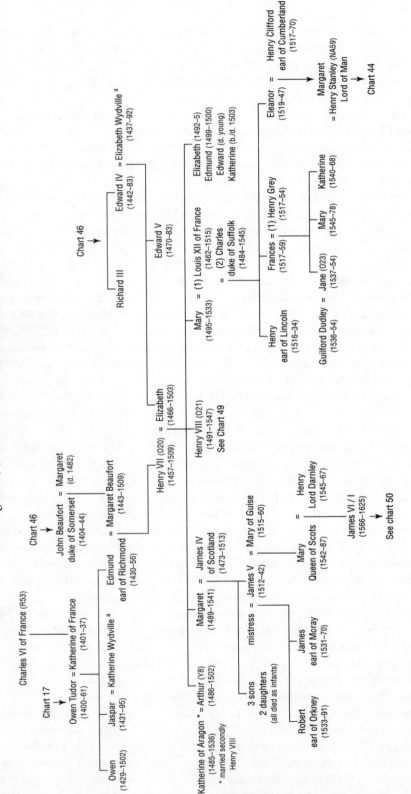

Note: (a) Katherine and Elizabeth Wydville were sisters

From a portrait dated 1505

received the backing of Pope Innocent VIII in 1486, who recognized his right to the throne and threatened excommunication to any who challenged that right. With the birth of his son, Arthur, in September 1486, Henry was keen to make a strong alliance with the rulers of Aragon, Ferdinand and Isabella, whose court was one of the richest in Europe. Their daughter, Katherine, had been born a few months earlier than Arthur, and negotiations over their betrothal began as early as 1489. They were eventually married in 1499.

The link with Spain became even more important following Columbus's discovery of a route to the Indies (or so was then believed) in 1492. Columbus claimed these islands in the name of Ferdinand and Isabella. Henry took considerable interest in trade and exploration, though he had failed to help finance Columbus's expedition. He certainly did not overlook a second opportunity and in 1496 authorised and financed a voyage of discovery by the Genoese sailor Giovanni Caboto, who set sail from Bristol in 1497 and discovered Newfoundland (five hundred years after the Vikings), though he also believed these to be the lands of the Great Khan. This was the dawn of the great voyages of exploration that would blossom in the sixteenth century and saw the great rivalry between England and Spain.

Henry was keen to avoid expensive wars and thus needed an alliance with England's centuries-old foe, France. Key to this was an alliance with Scotland. While pursuing one political marriage with Spain, Henry also negotiated another with Scotland. As early as 1487 plans were afoot to arrange no less than three marriages between the Scottish and English royal houses. The strength of JAMES III's friendship with the English angered many Scottish nobles and resulted in James's murder in 1488. Negotiations were not reopened until 1495, when the pretender Perkin Warbeck found favour with both JAMES IV of Scotland and the scheming German emperor, Maximilian I, who agreed to support the Scots against the English. This forced Henry to enter into discussions with Scotland with a view to encouraging Scotland to drop the Auld Alliance with France. Whilst James IV never agreed to this, a peace treaty was agreed between England and Scotland in 1502 and James IV married Henry's eldest daughter Margaret in August 1503. Henry had also negotiated an alliance with Maximilian in February 1496.

SIMNEL, LAMBERT. Pretender to the throne of England, crowned in Ireland as Edward VI of England on 24 May 1487. Simnel, who was aged only eleven or twelve, was a pawn in the dynastic struggles that had led to the Wars of the Roses and had not yet settled down at the start of the reign of HENRY VII. Simnel was of humble origin, and his real name is not known – contemporary records call him John, not Lambert, and even his surname is suspect. He was purportedly the son of an Oxford joiner and had been born in 1475. He was raised and educated by a local priest, Richard Simon, and through him came under the wing of John de la Pole, earl of Lincoln, the son of EDWARD IV's sister, Elizabeth. Lincoln had been nominated as his heir by RICHARD III and he believed he could use Simnel as a means to attain the throne. Henry VII's claim to the English throne was primarily by right of conquest, not by descent. There had been considerable secrecy during the reign of RICHARD III over the fate of Edward IV's sons, Edward (EDWARD V) and Richard, duke of York – the "Princes in the Tower". Also, on his accession, Henry VII had imprisoned Edward, earl of Warwick, another nephew of Edward IV. Simnel was the same age as Warwick, and only slightly younger than Richard of York. When Lincoln first put forward Simnel's claim it was as Prince Richard, but this was soon changed to Edward of Warwick. For his safety Simnel was taken to Ireland in late 1486, where there were many Yorkist supporters. Although Henry VII soon discovered the truth about Simnel and declared him an impostor in February 1487, bringing the real Warwick out of the Tower to prove he was alive, the support for Simnel grew and he was crowned in Dublin Cathedral as Edward VI. With Simnel as his figurehead, Lincoln led an invasion force into England in June 1487 but it was decisively beaten at the battle of Stoke on 16 June, where Lincoln was killed. Simnel, being still a minor, was pardoned by Henry who was kind to the boy. He allowed him to work in the royal kitchens and he was eventually elevated to the role of the king's falconer. He died in 1525, aged about fifty. He fared considerably better than the subsequent pretender, Perkin WARBECK.

Henry's ancestry meant he was held in high regard by the Welsh, and although he did not especially show them any favour, neither did he show them any hostility. In fact as his reign progressed, so members of the Welsh nobility were appointed to senior posts and granted territory in Wales, particularly the Marches. As a result the English domination of Wales by the marcher lords ceased. For the first time in generations, there was harmony between England, Wales and Scotland, with Henry's foreign negotiations bringing greater peace with his European counter-parts. This was perhaps Henry's greatest legacy. Although he was only continuing policies already initiated by Edward IV, the upsurge of trade and exploration at the start of Henry's reign, against a background of increased peace, prosperity, and also enlightenment, gives the feeling that, with the arrival of the Tudors, a new age had begun. Admittedly this was probably more evident in hindsight than at the time.

However the final years of Henry's reign were ones of personal sadness and increasing loneliness. His eldest son, Arthur, had died childless of consumption in 1502, aged only fifteen. Henry's wife Elizabeth died ten months later following the birth of their eighth child, who also died. Henry, who had never been a trusting or a happy king, became all the more surly, and retreated further into private life. Under his instruction Sheen Palace, which had been badly damaged by fire in 1497, was rebuilt and made all the more lavish as Richmond Palace, and it was here that he retired, keeping himself more to himself. His health failed and he had increasing bouts of asthma and gout. He died at Richmond Palace in 1509, aged 52.

Although Henry's reign is seen as the start of England's glory and the birth of Modern England, with the end of the Middle Ages, in truth his main achievement was in uniting a previously divided England and bringing harmony with Wales and Scotland, which provided a solid base upon which his successors, HENRY VIII and ELIZABETH, could build. Personally Henry was a sad king – faithful to his wife, but cautious with his affections and perhaps never truly enjoying the success that he achieved.

WARBECK, PERKIN. Pretender to the throne of England, who proclaimed himself as Richard IV in 1494. Like the earlier claimant, Lambert SIMNEL, Warbeck took advantage of the tenuousness of HENRY VII's claim to the English throne and the uncertainty over the fates of rightful heirs. He was in truth the son of a French official, John de Werbecque, and had been born at Tournai in Picardy in 1474. He subsequently gained work as a merchant's assistant and, while in Ireland in 1491, he gained the support of the Yorkists, first claiming to be Edward, earl of Warwick, then an illegitimate son of RICHARD III, and finally Richard, duke of York, the younger son of EDWARD IV and one of the "Princes in the Tower", whose fate was still uncertain. Warbeck may have already intrigued with Edward IV's sister, Margaret of Burgundy who, in November 1492, recognized him as her nephew and the rightful heir to the English throne. Warbeck travelled through Europe, gaining support and recognition, most importantly from Maximilian I, the new German emperor, who urged Warbeck to invade England. It was with Maximilian's encouragement that Warbeck proclaimed himself as Richard IV in October 1494 and returned to Ireland to raise an invasion force. Henry VII, however, had been quick to respond, and had succeeded in arresting most of the English nobility who supported Warbeck. For over a year Warbeck vacillated between Ireland and the Netherlands, seeking to gain support, every time finding himself bettered by Henry VII. He eventually turned to JAMES IV of Scotland who offered to help. James even married Warbeck to his cousin, Lady Catherine Gordon, daughter of the earl of Huntly, in January 1496. Their eventual invasion of England ended up as no more than a border skirmish in September 1496. By then Warbeck had already lost the support of the Emperor Maximilian and James IV. Warbeck emerged as a whinging, self-centred individual with a high opinion of himself but little ability. Warbeck's last refuge was in Cornwall, where the Cornish had rebelled against Henry VII's taxes. Warbeck raised a local force and in September 1497 besieged Exeter, but with little success. He fled and was captured a month later and imprisoned. Henry was lenient with Warbeck, allowing him to live at court, but when Warbeck sought to escape, he was imprisoned in the Tower, close to the real earl of Warwick. As was almost certainly intended, the two managed to communicate and plotted a conspiracy. As a consequence they were both charged with treason and executed. Warbeck was hanged at Tyburn on 23 November 1499, aged twenty-five.

[O21] **HENRY VIII**
Ruled 22 April 1509–28 January 1547. Crowned: Westminster Abbey, 24 June 1509.
Titles: king of England and (from 1542) of Ireland; duke of York (from 1494), duke of
Cornwall (from 1502), prince of Wales and earl of Chester (from 1504).
Born: Greenwich Palace, Kent, 28 June 1491. *Died*: Whitehall Palace, London, 28
January 1547, aged 55. *Buried*: Windsor Castle.
Married: (1) 11 June 1509, at Greenwich Palace, Katherine (1485–1536), dau.
Ferdinand II, king of Aragon; marriage annulled 23 May 1533: 6 children;
(2) 25 January 1533, at York Place (renamed Whitehall Palace), London, Anne
(c1500–36), dau. Thomas Boleyn, earl of Wiltshire; marriage declared invalid 17 May
1536: 3 children;
(3) 30 May 1536, at Whitehall Palace, London, Jane (c1508–37), dau. Sir John
Seymour; died in childbirth: 1 son;
(4) 6 January 1540, at Greenwich Palace, Anne (1515–57), dau. Johann, duke of
Cleves; marriage annulled 9 July 1540: no children;
(5) 28 July 1540, at Oatlands Palace, Surrey, Katherine (c1520–42) dau. Lord
Edmund Howard; executed 13 February 1542: no children;
(6) 12 July 1543, at Hampton Court Palace, Katherine (c1512–48), dau. Sir Thomas
Parr: no children.
Henry also had at least two illegitimate children, and probably more.

Henry VIII is probably the best known king of England and may even be the most
notorious (though there are plenty to compete for that title). Some may argue he
was also the most important king of England because of the status which he brought
to his kingdom along with the establishment of the Church of England. Certainly
his reign saw some of the most significant developments in England since the time
of EDWARD I.

Henry was not born to be king. He was the third child and second son of HENRY
VII and was groomed for the church, receiving a substantial classical education.
However, in April 1502 Henry's elder brother Arthur died of consumption and
Henry, still only ten, became heir apparent. Unlike his father, who was reserved and
surly, Henry was a happy child who delighted in all manner of sports and
entertainment. Not only did he master French and Latin, and become an excellent
rider and athlete, but he was a fine dancer and musician – the music of *Greensleeves*
has long been attributed to him. He also had a natural authority and self-command,
and enjoyed touring England and presenting himself to his subjects, which made
him a very popular prince and king. Although the nickname "Bluff King Hal" was
only accorded to him posthumously, it fitted his character well. Moreover unlike his
predecessors for the last one hundred years (and arguably longer), Henry was the
first to inherit a comparatively united kingdom, as an assured successor with every
right of inheritance to the throne. His father had established good relationships
with the leading countries of Europe, and with no foreign wars for some years, the
country's finances were strong. England was in the best shape financially, spiritually
and administratively that it had been for a long time.

Henry was two months off his eighteenth birthday when his father died. He was a
handsome, well proportioned youth, in love with life and the world. He happily
obeyed his father's dying wish that he marry his elder brother's widow, Katherine of
Aragon, in order to continue the alliance with Spain. They were married six weeks

later and two weeks after that there was a double coronation in Westminster Abbey at the height of Midsummer, with much feasting and merrymaking.

Henry was more interested in enjoying himself than bothering with the day to day affairs of government. He satisfied himself that his ministers could be trusted, and left the overall direction of affairs to William Warham, archbishop of Canterbury, Thomas Howard, earl of Surrey (later 2nd duke of Norfolk), who was the Lord Treasurer, Bishop Richard Foxe and, after 1514, to Thomas Wolsey. Henry rid the courts of Edmund Dudley and Sir Richard Empson, two key ministers in Henry VII's reign who were the architects of a strict tax regime and had become hated by the populace. Henry had them executed on the grounds of "constructive treason", as they had sought to arm their men as Henry VII lay dying.

Henry preferred to involve himself in European affairs, playing the role of an international magnate not confined to an English backwater. He supported his father-in-law, Ferdinand of Aragon, against the Moors in 1511, and joined Pope Julius II, along with Venice and Spain, in the Holy League against France, which was formed that October. This increased the friction between England and Scotland (France's old ally), which was exacerbated by border skirmishes and sea raids. JAMES IV of Scotland, who was Henry's brother-in-law, insisted that, if Henry remained part of the Holy League, the only outcome could be war between Scotland and England. Henry seemed undisturbed. In June 1513 Henry led an invasion force to Calais. James IV took advantage to invade England, something Henry had anticipated and so despatched Thomas Howard to counter. The result was the battle of Flodden on 9 September 1513, where James IV and the flower of Scottish nobility fell. Since the heir, JAMES V, was only a year old, Henry's sister, Margaret, became the Scottish regent. She did not receive the support of the Scottish aristocracy, but for a period, although skirmishes continued, the battle with Scotland was won, and Henry was victorious. He was also victorious in France, leading the successful sieges of Thérouanne and Tournai, whilst his forces defeated the French at the battle of the Spurs, at Guinegate, on 16 August 1513. The name of the battle signified the speed of the French retreat. Thomas Wolsey negotiated peace terms with France, one of the terms being the marriage of Henry's sister Mary to Louis XII of France in August 1514. The marriage was short-lived as Louis died only a few months later. Mary then angered Henry by running away with his close friend Charles Brandon, duke of Suffolk, and marrying in secret in February 1515. They were eventually pardoned, upon payment of an exacting fine, and they would subsequently become the grandparents of the ill-fated Lady JANE Grey.

Henry wanted to be the centre of the European stage. When the Holy Roman Emperor, Maximilian I, died in January 1519, Henry stood as a candidate to succeed him, having earlier been encouraged by Maximilian himself who regarded him as a good prospect. However, the electors selected from the controlling Hapsburg family. When Pope Leo X died in December 1521, Henry strove to have an English pope, nominating Thomas Wolsey but without success. Europe seemed a world closed to Henry and it frustrated him that a man of his abilities was denied greater influence in European affairs. It was probably this attitude that shaped his dealings with the new French king, François. In June 1520 Wolsey was able to engineer a summit meeting at Guisnes, near Calais, which became known as the Field of the Cloth of Gold because of the extravagance of the display, each party

From a portrait by Holbein

trying to outshine the other. Another peace treaty was negotiated, though it too was short-lived.

This period was one of change in Europe. Most significant, as far as England was concerned, was the reforming zeal of the German scholar and preacher, Martin Luther, who began a prolonged series of attacks upon the Papacy and the Catholic church, including his book *On the Babylonish Captivity of the Church* in 1520. Henry had remained a staunch supporter of the Pope and felt compelled to respond to Luther's attacks. Together with Thomas More and John Fisher, Henry wrote *Defence of the Seven Sacraments*, which became a best-seller throughout Europe. In recognition of his support the Pope conferred on Henry in 1521 the title of *Fidei Defensor*, or Defender of the Faith, a title which has been used by all subsequent English monarchs, regardless of their faith. Within a few years it would seem a singularly inappropriate title for Henry.

He was becoming increasingly concerned about the birth of an heir. His wife, Katherine, had borne him six children, but only one of these, MARY, had survived infancy. His eldest son, Henry, born in 1511, had died after only seven weeks. Their last born child died within hours of its birth in November 1518. By 1526, when Katherine had turned forty, it was evident that Henry would not have a son. It was unthinkable that he would be succeeded by a girl. He began to believe that the fault lay with him, and that he had committed a sin against the church in marrying his brother's widow, even though the marriage had received papal blessing. It was especially galling as in June 1519 Henry's mistress, Elizabeth Blount, who was only seventeen, had borne him a baby boy, who became Henry Fitzroy, duke of Richmond. Although illegitimate, Henry began to regard this boy as his likely heir if he was unable to produce a legitimate child. Also by 1527 Henry had become infatuated with the twenty-five-year-old Anne Boleyn, whose elder sister, Mary, had been Henry's mistress for some years. Anne refused to be simply his mistress and played for higher stakes. Wolsey entered into negotiations with the pope formally to annul Henry's marriage with Katherine. The new pope, Clement VII, was traditional in his outlook and a vehement opposer of Lutheranism. At first it looked as if he might accommodate Henry, but the pope then succumbed to the power of the Holy Roman Emperor, Charles V, who was the nephew of Henry's wife. Clement refused to accept that his predecessor's dispensation for Henry's marriage could have been in error, yet whilst he did not reject Henry's request outright, he procrastinated in every way possible, setting up a commission to review the issue. The affair dragged on for six years, during which time Clement was seen by more and more countries as a weak pope. The whole of Scandinavia broke with Rome and introduced Lutheranism, beginning in 1527. Henry's adviser, Thomas Cromwell, advised the same. His inability to resolve the matter had seen Wolsey fall from power. He was arrested for treason in November 1530, but died soon after. Cromwell now moved matters ahead and it was under his guidance that Henry became the Head of a separate Church of England with the authority to appoint his own archbishops and bishops. Thomas Cranmer, his newly appointed archbishop of Canterbury, pronounced on 23 May 1533 that Henry's marriage with Katherine was void. Henry had already taken this as read, as he had secretly wedded Anne Boleyn in January 1533, when she was already a month pregnant. The pope refused to accept the pronouncement, and in July 1533 he declared the divorce and remarriage void, and prepared to excommunicate Henry. The excommunication was suspended, but it was reaffirmed by Clement's successor, Paul III, who was however unable to gain the international support he desired to formalize the sentence. This merely served to force Henry further down his chosen road rather than allow for reconciliation. In fact Henry was at great pains to demonstrate that his argument was only against the pope, not the church. The significant change was that Henry was "Head of the Church" in his dominions, or (like the pope) God's representative. Otherwise, changes were limited, and Henry emphasised this with the publication of the *Act of the Six Articles* in 1539 which reaffirmed doctrines inherited from the Church of Rome. Nevertheless there were those who could not support Henry in his role as Head of the Church, such as Sir Thomas More and Bishop John Fisher, who refused to acknowledge this and were executed in 1535.

Henry's next move was to appoint a commission to report on the state of the monasteries. Cromwell had long believed that the monasteries were too powerful and were likely to lead any pro-Roman resistance to change. Following the report Parliament legislated in 1536 for the suppression of all small monasteries on grounds that they were uneconomic and, on the strength of this, dissolved all remaining monasteries in 1539. This caused considerable anguish throughout England, but especially in the north, where there was a rebellion known as the Pilgrimage of Grace. This rebellion was not just about the monasteries. Dissatisfaction had been fermenting for some time and the Acts of Dissolution were the final spark. Peasants were rebelling against the enclosure of common lands, which limited their ability to farm because of high rents. The rebellion began in Lincolnshire in October 1536 and spread through Yorkshire under the command of Robert Aske. Henry appeared conciliatory and defused the rebellion by promises, none of which he fulfilled, and some months later he had Aske and over two hundred of the rebels executed. This punishment was a salutory lesson to all and Cromwell's commissioners met little resistance as they moved from county to county closing the monasteries. The last to fall was Waltham Abbey in Essex in March 1540. Although the Crown benefitted considerably from the closure of the monasteries, since most of the profits arising passed to Henry who was always desperate for money for his foreign exploits, the ultimate beneficiaries were the local landed gentry who, once the monastery was closed and ransacked, acquired most of the land and remaining properties. It was the greatest shift in land ownership since the Norman Conquest.

Henry's early delight over Anne Boleyn's pregnancy soon faded when she gave birth to a girl, the future ELIZABETH (1). This was followed by two stillborn children. A fourth child was miscarried following a fall Henry had from a horse in January 1536 which left him unconscious and the shock brought on Anne's labour. Henry recovered, though the injury led to complications in his later years with a severely ulcerated leg. By now Henry had lost all interest in Anne – he even maintained he had been seduced by witchcraft. As a sign of this, Catholics later ascribed to Anne a shrivelled sixth finger. He readily believed charges of her infidelity and adultery and she was arrested, tried and found guilty of treason and executed on 19 May 1536. Just two days before Archbishop Cranmer declared Anne's marriage to Henry null and void, probably on the rather tenuous grounds that Henry had formerly had a relationship with her sister Mary.

During the previous two years Henry had become besotted with one of Anne's ladies-in-waiting, Jane Seymour, a not especially attractive lady but one who beguiled Henry with her coquettish ways. They were married eleven days after Anne's execution and the marriage was a happy one, albeit brief. Jane was never crowned queen because an outbreak of plague in London delayed the coronation and then Jane became pregnant. Henry was overjoyed when Jane gave birth to a boy, the future EDWARD VI, but Jane was seriously weakened by the birth and died twelve days later in the midst of Henry's celebrations. Because she had given him a son and heir, Jane remained the favourite of Henry's wives and after his death he was laid beside her in St George's Chapel, Windsor.

For his next wife Henry looked to Europe. Because of the papal bull isolating him, Henry was fearful that the French, the Habsburgs or both would invade England and depose him. As a consequence Henry sought a political marriage with Germany and, through the advice of Thomas Cromwell, settled on Anne, the sister of the duke of Cleves in Germany. Although Henry admired her portrait, he was horrified when he first met Anne in January 1540 but by then marriage arrangements had proceeded too far. Henry feared the backlash if he withdrew. Although they were wed on 6 January, the marriage was never consummated and both parties readily agreed to a divorce which went through seven months later. Henry was generous to Anne, because of her compliance, and the two remained good friends.

Unfortunately for Henry his next marriage, which was almost on the rebound, was to the beautiful teenage Katherine Howard, a cousin of Anne Boleyn's. He and Katherine were married within three weeks of the divorce and Henry delighted in his young bride, who seemed to put the spring back in his step, even though by now he was becoming grossly fat and ageing fast. Evidently Katherine soon tired of her husband, thirty years her senior, and turned to her former lovers. She was soon betrayed, charged with treason and executed on 13 February 1542. Henry had at first refused to believe the charges and never quite recovered from her loss. When he entered into his final marriage in the following year it was to an older lady, already twice widowed, Katherine Parr. By all accounts Henry was now after a companion rather than a lover, and in Parr he found a woman with whom he could converse on

49. England (8) – The Family and In-laws of Henry VIII

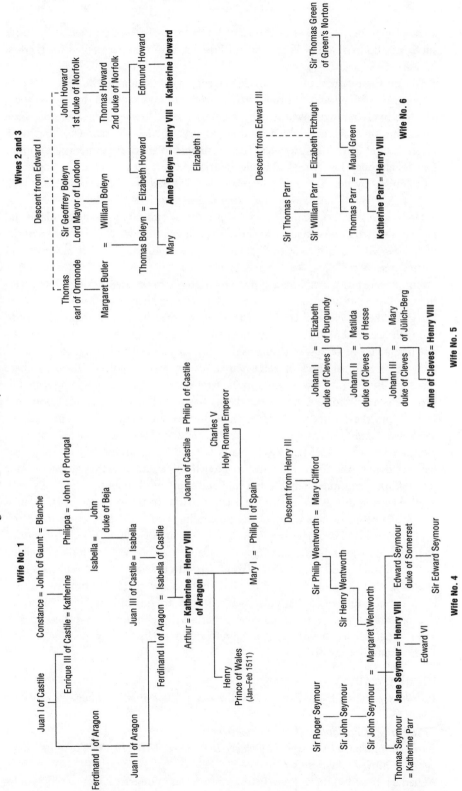

a wide range of subjects and who served as an excellent stepmother to his three surviving children, Mary, Elizabeth and Edward, who were reconciled for the first time in 1543.

During these tempestuous marriages Henry had not ignored the international scene, or indeed the state of Britain. He regarded the British Isles as his own empire, and had made a move towards consolidating it in 1536 with what has since been called the Act of Union, which officially incorporated Wales as part of England, rather than as a separate province. He was unable to enact the same legislation for Ireland, although his father had made the Irish parliament subject to the English. A rebellion led by the Fitzgeralds in Ireland in 1534 had been summarily dealt with and in 1542 Henry declared himself king rather than lord of Ireland.

Henry also kept a constant eye on the intrigues between France and Scotland and had even visited France to meet with the king, though the two could never reconcile their views. Relationships with Scotland soured. Henry regarded it as an affront when James V failed to keep a meeting at York in September 1541 and future meetings were postponed because of the interference of the French king. Henry grew tired of the Scots, and the last connections between them ended when his sister, Margaret, died in November 1541. The following year saw Henry prepared to go to war with Scotland and, although no formal declaration was made, hostilities broke out in a series of scraps and skirmishes with the upper hand going to the Scots. However a Scottish force of some ten thousand was soundly defeated by three thousand English at Solway Moss in November 1542. The Scots had appeared as such a disorganized rabble that the defeat was a double disgrace, and soon after James V pined away in despair. Henry now pursued a marriage alliance between his son Edward and James's infant daughter MARY and, under the terms of a peace treaty concluded in July 1543, Mary was to marry Edward in her tenth year. This treaty was never ratified by the Scots while the pro-French nobles did everything to undermine it. Hostilities continued between England and Scotland throughout the 1540s, with Scotland using this as an excuse the argue that the treaty was invalid. Henry had marginally better success with France, concluding a treaty with François in 1546.

Henry died on 28 January 1547, aged only 55, but a victim of his gross conduct. Despite the major reforms that he had made he was not a great initiator, relying instead on such great men as Wolsey and Cromwell whom he cast aside when no longer needed. At times he ruled like a despot, engineering everything to his own ends. Yet he could wield that power without it destroying him and it is true to say that no other English king could have undertaken such reforms and succeeded. It was through Henry, the first king to be referred to as His Majesty, that the modern English state was created.

[O22] EDWARD VI

Ruled 28 January 1547–6 July 1553. Crowned: Westminster Abbey, 20 February 1547.

Titles: king of England and duke of Cornwall.

Born: Hampton Court Palace, 12 October 1537. Died: Greenwich Palace, 6 July 1553, aged 15. Buried: Westminster Abbey.

As had happened so many times before, a strong and powerful king was followed by a weak one. Edward VI was the only surviving son of HENRY VIII and was only nine when his father died. His mother, Jane Seymour, had died giving birth, and though in his youth he seemed healthy, it became evident that he had a weak constitution. He had the potential to be a wise and powerful king, for he received an extensive education, and was raised with considerable care by his stepmother Katherine Parr. His childhood seemed to pass him by. Thrust into kingship and surrounded by scholarly men, Edward tried to run before he could walk, combining precocity with much of his father's stubborness and self-centredness.

Edward's uncle, Edward Seymour, duke of Somerset, was made "Protector of the Realm" during Edward's minority and started the reign with an invasion of Scotland to enforce the marriage treaty between Edward and MARY, Queen of Scots. Although he defeated the Scots at Pinkie in September he was unable to break the Scots' resolve and in fact drove them closer to a marriage alliance with France. Edward was surrounded by rival factions who sought to control the king's mind when he was still too young fully to understand the motives for his actions. It seems that he genuinely regretted having to agree to the execution of Thomas Seymour, who had become his step-father, on grounds of high treason in March 1549, and in 1552 he also agreed to the execution of the protector, Somerset, who had presumed on his authority and been ousted from power in October 1549. In his wake the over ambitious John Dudley, earl of Warwick (and soon to be created duke of Northumberland) came to power, operating as protector in all but name.

Edward had been raised a Protestant and at the outset of his reign Protestant reform continued at an even greater pace than before due to the unremitting zeal of the Protector Somerset. All shrine and pictures of saints were destroyed, many processions were banned and the number of official ceremonies reduced. The first English Prayer Book was issued in 1548. There was much Catholic discontent throughout England, though the only manifestation of it was a rebellion in Devon in the summer of 1549 against the *Common Prayer Book* and this was promptly dealt with by Lord Russell. At the same time, in East Anglia, there was a repeat of the problems which had given rise to the Pilgrimage of Grace in 1536, when local peasants, under the leadership of Robert Kett, a tanner, rebelled against the enclosure of common land. Kett gathered together a force of ten thousand men to blockade Norwich, but the rebels were defeated by John Dudley and Kett was hanged.

Edward founded a number of grammar schools throughout England which still bear his name, and he also established a workhouse for the poor at Bridewell and Christ's Hospital in London. It seems that the young king had a genuine concern to help the poor and needy as well as to promote education and learning. Although he was moulded into a zealous Protestant, he evidently promoted it with good intent. It was as much his concern as it was Northumberland's, that if he died young all the Protestant reform would be undone if his half-sister Mary, a staunch Catholic, came to the throne. He thus complied with Northumberland's plans in promoting Lady JANE Grey as his successor.

Edward's last year was one of much suffering. He contracted consumption and also suffered from congenital syphilis, passed on from his father. His death was a merciful blessing for him, but it would turn the country into a period of turmoil.

[O23] JANE *"THE NINE DAYS QUEEN"*
Proclaimed Queen of England, 10 July 1553. Deposed 19 July 1553.
Born: Bradgate Manor, Leicestershire, October 1537. *Died (executed)*: 12 February
1554, aged 16. *Buried*: Tower of London.
Married: 21 May 1553, at Durham House, London, Guilford (1536–54) son of John
Dudley, duke of Northumberland. No children.

Jane was the innocent victim of the schemes of her ambitious and recent father-in-
law to continue the Protestant faith in England after the death of EDWARD VI in
preference to the Catholic princess MARY (I). Jane was the granddaughter of Mary,
the sister of HENRY VIII, and under the latter's will, Mary's children had right of
succession only after the deaths of his own children and their heirs. Edward VI
signed an amendment to his father's will only a few weeks before his own death
which set aside his sisters' claims to the throne and nominated Jane. Just a month
earlier John Dudley, duke of Northumberland, who had assumed the role (if not the
title) of protector of the realm during Edward's minority, had arranged the
marriage of his son Guilford to Jane. Jane did not particularly like Guilford,
although their subsequent adversity drew them together.

Jane was formally offered the crown in accordance with Edward VI's wishes, and
declared queen, against her own better judgement, by the Council on 9 July 1553.
Jane did not want to be queen of England, but when she accepted the crown, she did
so recognizing it would help the Protestant reform. She was publicly proclaimed
queen the following day. She was an extremely well educated and well mannered
child who in other circumstances would have made an excellent queen consort. She
was obdurate that her husband would not be jointly proclaimed king. The nobility
were affronted by Northumberland's scheme. There was also overwhelming public
support for Mary. Jane retained the title of queen for just nine days. Northumberland's army was defeated, and he was arrested and beheaded. Jane and her
husband were also arrested and imprisoned in the Tower. Mary was prepared to be
lenient with them, recognizing their unfortunate position, but Jane's fate was sealed
when her father, Henry Grey, duke of Suffolk, became involved in Sir Thomas
Wyatt's rebellion against Mary. Jane refused to recant her Protestantism and on 12
February 1554 she was executed, having been found guilty of treason.

[O24] MARY (I), *"BLOODY MARY"*
Ruled England, 19 July 1553–17 November 1558. Crowned: Westminster Abbey, 1
October 1553. Also queen consort of Spain: 16 January 1556–17 November 1558.
Born: Greenwich Palace, Kent, 18 February 1516. *Died*: St James's Palace, London, 17
November 1558, aged 42. *Buried*: Westminster Abbey.
Married: 25 July 1554, at Winchester Cathedral, Philip (1527–98) son of Charles V,
Holy Roman Emperor. No children.

Mary was the eldest surviving daughter of HENRY VIII and his first wife, Katherine of
Aragon and, as such, she was despatched in 1525 to Ludlow Castle, styled Princess
of Wales. When Henry's marriage to Katherine was declared void by Thomas
Cranmer in 1533, Mary, who was then seventeen, was declared illegitimate. Mary,
who was a well educated child and a capable linguist and musician, was devoted to
her mother and hated the separation. She steadfastly refused to accept that the
marriage was not legitimate and indeed regarded her father's second marriage to

Anne Boleyn as bigamous and false. She had a violent and volatile relationship with her stepmother and disliked her young half-sister ELIZABETH. Mary remained obdurate throughout Henry's reign, refusing to accept the Protestant Reformation. Jane Seymour, Henry's third wife, worked hard to reconcile father and daughter, but the family were not fully reunited until Henry's last wife, Katherine Parr, who succeeded in bringing them all together, united, at last, in their support for the young EDWARD (VI). Mary's right to the throne was recognized in Henry's will, in succession to Edward. However Edward subsequently amended his father's will to disbar Mary from the throne for fear that she would undo all of the Protestant reforms enacted during Edward's brief reign. He nominated his cousin, JANE, as his successor, but although Jane was proclaimed as queen, she did not receive the support of her peers or the populace and was rapidly dethroned. Mary entered London in triumph on August 3, 1553 and was crowned two months later. Since neither Jane nor MATILDA had been crowned, Mary was the first genuine queen regnant of England. It is perhaps ironic that at the same time Scotland was also ruled by a Queen MARY, who was her first cousin.

As feared by the reformers, Mary did begin to reverse the legislation passed during her half-brother's reign and restore as much of the old order as she believed possible. She was cautious, because she did not want to provoke religious disorder and strove, instead, to find a balance. She reinstated some of the Catholic bishops and imprisoned certain zealous reformers, but she did not dare overturn her father's enactment which would have restored the Pope's supremacy. She did, however, pass an act which invalidated her father's divorce from Katherine of Aragon, restoring Mary's legitimacy and automatically bastardising Elizabeth.

Mary had never married; in fact she had come to regard herself as a spinster. It is true that she was not overly attractive and she had inherited congenital syphilis from her father which not only gave her a weak constitution, with regular headaches and poor eyesight, but gave her a form of rhinitis which meant that her breath was always foul-smelling. This hardly endeared her to anyone and if there was to be any marriage at all it would be a political one. Her choice settled on Philip of Spain, the son of the Holy Roman Emperor, Charles V. Parliament petitioned the Queen to reconsider and to seek a husband from within England, but Mary steadfastly refused. Her choice of Philip was extremely unpopular, with many believing that Philip would use the opportunity to enforce his own control over England and that Mary would become a Spanish puppet. A group of conspirators including Sir James Crofts and Sir Thomas Wyatt plotted against Mary but the intended *coup* was ill planned and only Wyatt's rebellion in Kent, which began on 25 January 1554, carried any force. It was, however, soon quashed, many of the ringleaders were captured, tried and executed. The Princess Elizabeth was also implicated in the *coup* and briefly confined to the Tower of London. Mary's marriage with Philip went ahead in July 1554. In accordance with Spanish tradition, Philip was granted the title of king. He is the only English king consort. Eighteen months later Philip's father abdicated, relinquishing to him the throne of Spain. Mary likewise assumed the title of Queen of Spain. It is also worth an aside here and noting that when Mary Queen of Scots married François, the French Dauphin in April 1558, he likewise became king consort of Scotland. Had Mary Tudor lived another eight months then England would have been ruled by a king and queen of Spain at the same time that

Scotland was ruled by a king and queen of France. Although Mary fell in love with Philip, the love was not reciprocated. Philip left for Spain in August 1555, returning to England only once between March and June 1557. His treatment of Mary was callous and left her heart-broken.

In November 1554 Cardinal Reginald Pole, the papal legate (and subsequently archbishop of Canterbury) announced that England had been absolved of papal censures and was restored to the Holy See. Whilst this was welcomed by many, in its wake came the papal requirement that all heretics must be burned at the stake. It was from this moment that Mary's reign of terror began, which earned her the title of Bloody Mary. Almost certainly much of it was not of her own desire, but between February 1555 and November 1558 almost three hundred victims perished cruelly in the flames. These included Thomas Cranmer, archbishop of Canterbury, and the famous example of Hugh Latimer, bishop of Worcester and Nicholas Ridley, bishop of London, who were burned outside Balliol College, Oxford. These executions were recorded and published, during Elizabeth's reign, by John Foxe in his best-selling *Acts and Monuments of these latter and perilous days* (1563), now popularly known as *Foxe's Book of Martyrs*.

Another conspiracy was hatched against Mary in December 1555, called the Dudley Conspiracy after one of its main architects, Sir Henry Dudley. The idea was to rob the finances from the Exchequer, depose Mary and Philip, and raise Elizabeth to the throne. It was also intended to secure her marriage to Edward Courtenay, a distant relative descended from EDWARD IV. However before the plot could be achieved news of it leaked out and by March 1556 most of the conspirators were either arrested or had fled to France. There were other plots, all of which failed, but England remained in a sorry state. The last blow to national pride came when Philip convinced Mary and the English Parliament to join Spain in its war against France. As a result of the conflict England lost Calais, its last possession in France.

Mary's husband had returned to Spain and never came back to her. Although she believed she might be pregnant, she had never conceived. Both of these facts caused a depression which added to her overall ill-health, and the loss of Calais as well as all of the Protestant persecutions caused Mary to regard her reign as a total failure. Her famous remark, "when I am dead, you will find Philip and Calais engraved upon my heart", was not without substance. She died in the early hours of 17 November 1558, her constitution further weakened by influenza. A few weeks earlier Mary had reluctantly conceded that her half-sister, Elizabeth, would be her successor.

[O25] **ELIZABETH (I)**
Ruled England 17 November 1558–24 March 1603. Crowned: Westminster Abbey, 15 January 1559.
Born: Greenwich Palace, 7 September 1533. Died: Richmond Palace, 24 March 1603, aged 69. Buried: Westminster Abbey.
Elizabeth was the only surviving child of HENRY VIII and Anne Boleyn. She was a disappointment to her father, who had anticipated a son and heir. She scarcely knew her mother, who was executed when Elizabeth was thirty-two months old, and the infant Elizabeth despatched to Hatfield Palace in Hertfordshire. She was also disowned by her sister, MARY, the start of a bitter rivalry that festered for twenty-five years. When Anne Boleyn's marriage to Henry was declared void,

Elizabeth became illegitimate, as had Mary before her, and was thus barred from inheriting the throne. It was only later, satisfied that he would be succeeded by his son EDWARD (VI), that Henry recognized Mary and Elizabeth as potential successors if Edward's line failed. Typically for Henry, however, he was prepared to recognize Elizabeth as the "heiress of a kingdom" in his negotiations with France over the possible betrothal of Elizabeth to Charles, duke of Angoulême, the younger son of the French king. Nothing came of this or of any other possible childhood proposals, but it was evident that the only real benefit Henry saw in his daughter was as barter in any political alliance.

Elizabeth was extremely well educated and was a precocious and intelligent child. She mercifully escaped the congenital syphilis passed by her father to his other children, and grew into a strong and healthy child who delighted in riding, hunting, archery and dancing and who became a proficient linguist. It was not until 1543 that Henry's last wife, Katherine Parr, brought all of the children together in a united household and proved an excellent stepmother. Whilst Elizabeth and Mary tolerated each other they never became close. Elizabeth always regarded herself as a rightful heiress. Though supportive of Edward VI, she was seen as a threat and a liability by Mary when she became queen in 1553. Elizabeth had been raised within her father's newly reformed Church of England while Mary remained defiantly Catholic. During Mary's reign there were terrible persecutions of the reformers after years of ardent Protestantism in Edward's reign. Mary even believed that Elizabeth had plotted against her in a number of conspiracies and had her sister confined first to the Tower of London and then to Woodstock, near Oxford. Thus, when Edward and Mary both died childless, it was with much relief and a belief by Elizabeth that "this is the Lord's doing," that she inherited the throne. Her accession was welcomed throughout the land.

Elizabeth had all the credentials for a strong queen. She inherited much from her father — her physical strength and resolution, her vicious temper, her cruelty, but also a delight in pomp, a passion for power and a general joy of life. From her mother, apart from her youthful beauty, she inherited a degree of insincerity and a tendency towards jealousy. She also had an interest in astrology, consulting the alchemist John Dee over the most propitious date for her coronation. His forecast evidently worked, for not only did Elizabeth go on to reign for nearly forty-five years, longer than any king since EDWARD III, and also live longer than any English monarch since PENDA, but her reign was undoubtedly the most glorious England had seen and one which firmly established England as a world power.

Elizabeth's first pressing responsibility was to resolve the religious division in England. She did not want a backlash against the Protestant persecutions of Mary's reign, but neither did she want the rampant Protestantism of Edward's. She sought to strike a balance, accommodating both religions, so that although Protestantism became the national religion, she did not regard it as wrong if there were those who wished to hear the Roman mass in private. But she disliked the more extreme Calvinist tendencies in Protestantism. Those who acted wisely would be safe in Elizabeth's realm, but she would not tolerate any who sought to test her will. Nevertheless, throughout her reign there were many Catholic conspiracies seeking to overthrow Elizabeth. This became worse after 1570 when the Pope, tired of seeking Elizabeth's compliance to the authority of Rome, issued a bull deposing her.

Since she took no notice of this, it only strengthened her role as "Supreme Governor of the Church of England" and meant that anyone who continued to practice Catholicism was effectively a traitor. Much against her own wishes, religious persecution returned after 1570 and this only aggravated the Catholic cause against her. This in turn widened the rift between England and Scotland and led to the darkest shadow cast over her reign, the treatment of MARY QUEEN OF SCOTS, her cousin and a claimant on the English throne.

The relationship between Scotland and England had been one of near constant hostility for a thousand years. Mary of Scotland was still in her teens when Elizabeth came to the throne, but as the queen consort of the king of France she exerted authority in two strong Catholic countries. Mary's mother, Mary of Guise, who was the queen regent in Scotland, was an even more ardent Catholic and it was her desire to place her daughter on the English throne. There were many Scots who feared that Scotland would become a puppet state of France, and the growing number of Protestants made Scotland a land divided. Elizabeth took advantage of this, secretly supporting the Scottish Protestants in their work against the two Maries. The Scottish rebels soon became too powerful to overlook and Mary of Guise sought aid from France. A French invasion became a probability, and advance troops landed in Scotland. Elizabeth was able to use this situation, albeit reluctantly, to enter into an alliance with Scotland in February 1560 (Treaty of Berwick), whereby England promised troops to help repel the French. Despite some rather scrappy fighting by the English, the French decided to negotiate, circumstances hastened by the death of Mary of Guise. The Treaty of Edinburgh was signed on 6 July. Five months later François II of France died and in August 1561 the widowed Mary returned to her native Scotland, much to the horror of the English who had hoped she would stay in France. Her power there had been eclipsed by the rise of Catherine de Medici, mother of the young king Charles IX, and Catherine had no love for the Guises. Whilst this helped Anglo-French relations, Mary's return to Scotland might have stirred up old rivalries. In August 1560 the Scottish Parliament had abolished the pope's authority and brought its Protestant church more in line with England's, but Mary remained a Catholic. To her credit, Mary was conciliatory and her charm captivated her Scottish subjects who soon welcomed her return. However, she refused to ratify the Treaty of Edinburgh, the terms of which would have denied her any possible succession to the English throne, and she actively sought to be regarded as Elizabeth's heir presumptive in the absence of any children. Plans for a meeting between Mary and Elizabeth nearly came to fruition in August 1562, but the eruption of civil war in France between the Catholic Guises and the Huguenots (Protestants) made the situation too tense. It was the closest Elizabeth and Mary ever came to meeting. Aggravatingly Elizabeth refused to name a successor, even after a near fatal bout of smallpox in October 1562, always maintaining that although she had no desire to marry, for the sake of the succession one day she would and produce an heir. Mary of Scotland, on the other hand, was actively in pursuit of a new husband and there was fear in England that if she married the heir of a strong Catholic country, she would have the power to invade England and oust Elizabeth. This was made all the more potent when negotiations opened between Scotland and Spain for the marriage between Mary and the heir, Don Carlos. These only ceased when Don Carlos was declared insane. Mary

From a portrait by Nicholas Hilliard, c1575

however lost her controlling hand when she fell in love with her cousin, Lord Darnley. The marriage proved unpopular and the subsequent events, including the murder of Mary's secretary, David Rizzio, the mysterious death of Darnley in February 1567 and Mary's affair with and rapid marriage to Lord Bothwell, brought about the fall from grace of Mary and her subsequent deposition. From July 1567 Mary was a captive, and in May 1568 she was driven out of Scotland and threw herself upon Elizabeth's mercy. Elizabeth was outwardly supportive but maintained she could not harbour Mary while the stigma of her involvement in the death of Darnley was unresolved. Mary remained in prison, first at Carlisle, and then in a series of castles in northern England. This continued for nineteen years with the inevitable consequence that Catholic factions used Mary as the figurehead for their cause. There were several conspiracies during this period (*see entry on* MARY *for details*) culminating in the Babington Plot in the summer of 1586. Plans were well advanced for the murder of Elizabeth and there were hopes of a Spanish invasion, when Babington was betrayed. Mary was aware of Babington's schemes and as a consequence was herself tried for treason, found guilty and, with much reluctance on Elizabeth's part, executed. At this same time Elizabeth had bestowed a pension upon Mary's son, JAMES VI, in effect recognizing him as her heir.

Just why Elizabeth did not marry is the matter of some conjecture. Her dedication to the throne and her people led her to say that she was married to the nation in much the same way as she believed her bishops were married to the church. She expressed a low opinion of any bishop who chose to marry. Her own haughtiness and belief in her absolute authority almost certainly meant she would have found it difficult to share government with anyone, for although she might remain queen, any husband, especially one of the proper status, could not have been denied his views. It was more a problem over whom to marry rather than whether to marry, and that problem was never resolved. It was not helped by the fact that Elizabeth's first love was almost certainly her favourite — Robert Dudley, earl of

Leicester, the brother of Guilford Dudley, husband of Lady JANE Grey. Dudley was already married, to Amy Robsart, whose mysterious death in 1560 caused many to believe that Dudley had murdered her. Thus tainted, Dudley was no suitable candidate as Elizabeth's husband, even though he pursued his suit for the next twenty years. He remained something of a philanderer and adventurer and died in 1588. Elizabeth was much saddened by his death for although she had other court favourites, such as Sir Christopher Hatton, the captain of the bodyguard, and, most notably, Robert Devereux, earl of Essex, the flame burned strongest for Dudley and he never left her heart.

Nevertheless Elizabeth recognized that a political marriage was necessary both for producing an heir and for strengthening England's position in Europe, but she constantly prevaricated over her choice, using it for political bargaining. For a period she had to be the most eligible spinster in Europe, and various royal families made their approaches. Early in her reign there had been negotiations with Philip II of Spain, the former husband of Elizabeth's sister Mary, but these were dropped when Elizabeth confirmed her opposition to papal sovereignty in 1559. The main contender then became Charles, the archduke of Austria, and younger son of the Holy Roman Emperor Ferdinand. He was an ideal candidate and, had Elizabeth been given more support from her brilliant and long-suffering adviser, William Cecil, the marriage might have happened. But Cecil counselled against it, Elizabeth became more involved with Dudley and negotiations collapsed in 1567 on religious grounds. By the time Elizabeth came to reconsider Charles in 1570 he was betrothed to another. Now approaching 37, Elizabeth's eligibility was failing. If she was going to marry she needed to marry soon. Negotiations opened with Henri, duke of Anjou, the younger brother of Charles IX, king of France (who had also been a suitor at one stage). Negotiations again failed on religious grounds (and possibly because of Henri's sexual practices – he was bisexual and a transvestite) and so Anjou's younger brother François, duke of Alençon, stepped into the frame. The age difference between the two was considerable, and it was not helped by the fact that the French persecution of the Huguenots aggravated the Anglo-French religious balance. Nevertheless Elizabeth apparently became enchanted with the diminutive young Duke, whom she nicknamed "frog" when she first met him in 1579. Though negotiations were erratic Elizabeth caused a sensation in November 1581, when she announced that she would marry him. This was really a ploy on Elizabeth's part to increase her bargaining power with the French as she was not that sincere in her proposals to marry. All came to naught in 1584 when Alençon died. He was the last serious suitor for by now Elizabeth was past the age of successfully bearing a healthy child. It is almost certain that despite her many favourites, Elizabeth remained a virgin all her life. She actually delighted in her virginity, deploying it as a strength, and became known as "the Virgin Queen". Walter Ralegh, another court favourite, named the territory in North America Virginia in her honour in 1584. Elizabeth refused to acknowledge that she was ageing. She wore a wig (as she had lost much of her own hair), whitened her face to hide the scarring from the smallpox, and even rubbed urine into her face to remove wrinkles. She could not hide her blackened teeth arising from her love of sugar.

During all these years England had been fighting an unofficial conflict with Spain. Philip II of Spain was infuriated by England's blatant piracy of Spanish ships from the New World. Spain and Portugal dominated the seas, and in 1580 Philip became king of Portugal as well as Spain, thus increasing his maritime and merchant strength. In 1493 the then pope had partitioned the New World between Spain and Portugal and now the bounty of the Americas was united in Philip. Spain had exerted an a exploitation of the New World, forbidding other countries access to the lands. In 1562 an English seaman, John Hawkins, had found a way round this by trading directly with the Spanish in Hispaniola over slaves. The venture proved profitable and two more followed, this time with Elizabeth as a shareholder, but the third expedition fell foul of the Spanish and only just limped home in early 1569. Hawkins's fellow captain, Francis Drake, now regarded it as open season on the Spanish and from 1572 he began to plunder Spanish enterprises in Central and South America. By 1577 Drake had been introduced to Elizabeth and she unofficially encouraged his activities against Spain. In December 1577 Drake set off on what would become his voyage around the world, plundering Spanish vessels in both South America and the East Indies. It has been estimated that the total value of Drake's booty was worth about £450,000, which would be many millions at today's rates. He returned to England in September 1580 and became a national hero. He was knighted in April 1581.

Philip's relationship with England continued to sour. England's support to the Netherlands against Spain was the final straw in 1585. After the execution of Mary Queen of Scots, Philip believed he had a divine right to invade England, a major heretical aggressor, and contended that he had a claim on the English throne, because he was distantly descended from EDWARD III. In July 1587 Philip secured a treaty with the pope approving the conquest of England, provided that the land was restored to Catholicism. The pope allowed Philip to choose whomever he wished as England's ruler. While these negotiations were in hand Drake led a punitive expedition into Spain, capturing and destroying many Spanish vessels. The culmination of all this was one of the most famous confrontations of all time when Philip sent his apparently invincible Armada against England in July 1588. Philip's venture was doomed by the weather even more than by the superiority of English seamanship and the better design of the English ships, which allowed them to hug the water and dart through the waves. By comparison the huge and imposing Spanish galleons were a liability in strong winds. Although Elizabeth had hesitated at first about the confrontation with the Armada, the defeat of Spain's might was one of the most important victories in English history. Conflict with Spain dragged on for another fifteen years. In April 1596 the Spaniards turned up on Elizabeth's doorstep by capturing Calais. A joint Anglo-Dutch offensive was made against Spain under the command of Essex. It captured and plundered Cadiz, destroying much of the fleet, and returning home rich with booty, little of which the queen saw as most of it ended up in the hands of the looters. Philip despatched a second Armada in October 1596, but this again fell foul of the weather as did, this time, the English fleet. This was the last major battle against Spain although hostilities continued beyond Philip II's death in September 1598, and even beyond Elizabeth's.

The end of the century saw England at the height of her power. Her great sea captains and explorers – Francis Drake, Walter Ralegh, Martin Frobisher, John Hawkins – meant that she effectively "ruled the waves". Literature blossomed – this was the age of Francis Bacon, William Shakespeare, Christopher Marlowe, Sir Philip Sidney and Edmund Spenser, whose *Faerie Queen* (first part, 1589; second part 1596) was dedicated to Elizabeth. Scientific study did not advance quite so quickly in England as it did in the Protestant parts of Europe, but there were some great physicists and speculative thinkers who emerged in Elizabeth's time, with Sir Francis Bacon again head and shoulders above them.

The last drama to be enacted during Elizabeth's reign was the revolution in Ireland and the subsequent fate of the earl of Essex. Hugh O'Neill, earl of Tyrone, had been in rebellion against the English for some years, and this reached a climax in August 1598 when O'Neill massacred an English force sent to relieve the fort at Blackwater. The Irish were now in open revolt and England sent in an army. The earl of Essex jumped at the opportunity to take command, hoping that this might restore his favour with the queen, who had been cold to him since Essex had quarrelled with her ministers William Cecil, now Lord Burghley, and his son Robert over the possibility that Elizabeth might negotiate for peace with Spain. This had followed an alleged assassination plot against the queen organized by Rodrigo Lopez, a Portuguese Jew supposedly in the pay of Philip of Spain, and involving Ferdinando STANLEY, king of the Isle of Man. Elizabeth had some suspicions that Essex had concocted the whole story in order to get back into her favour. Many did not believe that Essex was a capable commander, but the queen supported him and gave him all the men and finances he needed. Elizabeth would have been only too happy to be rid of Ireland, except that she feared it falling to a foreign power, especially to Spain. There had been other rebellions during her reign, that of Shane O'Neill in Ulster during the 1560s, the Fitzmaurice rising of 1569–73 and the Desmond rebellion of 1579–83. These received harsh retaliation from the English, slaughtering young and old alike and keeping the island savagely repressed. Elizabeth had hopes that Essex might similarly subdue the rebels, but instead he spent the summer of 1599 moving about the island and achieving little. He negotiated terms with O'Neill, after losing more than half his force to the unhealthiness of the Irish environment, and returned home without permission. Essex expected to be regarded as a hero, but instead the queen and the Privy Council showed him nothing but contempt. Essex was censured and humiliated. Essex sought his revenge upon the Council, but was caught and tried for high treason and executed in February 1601. Although Elizabeth was saddened by Essex's death, she was delighted when his successor in Ireland, Lord Mountjoy, succeeded in defeating Tyrone in December 1601 and in reaching an agreement with Spanish opportunists who had invaded Kinsale that September. Tyrone's eventual surrender was not received for another sixteen months.

Elizabeth died at Richmond Palace on 24 March 1603, aged 69. The final years of her reign lacked the vitality of her youth, unsurprisingly. Although she made no will, she had made it known that her cousin, James VI, was her lawful successor. She was thus technically the last queen of England. The combination of her reign and that of her father had made England one of the greatest powers in Europe. In November 1601 Elizabeth had made a speech before the House of Commons which became known as her Golden Speech. She used it as an opportunity to reaffirm her devotion to her people. "There is no prince that loves his subjects better, or whose love can countervail our love," she said, adding, "There is no jewel, be it of never so rich a price, which I set before this jewel: I mean your love." In this she was sincere. Elizabeth did truly love England, and in return she was greatly loved and sorely missed. Her reign was England's golden age.

[O26;FC76] JAMES I
Crowned king of England: Westminster Abbey, 25 July 1603.
For James's earlier life as king of Scotland see page 575. The following chronicles his rule when he became the first king of England and Scotland.

James was full of the joys of spring when he arrived in Westminster in April 1603. He had grand schemes to unite England and Scotland and establish a Great Britain. Unfortunately these plans failed. Although the Scottish Parliament, which had been left under the control of James's second cousin Louis Stuart (Esmé's son), passed an Act of Union in 1607, the English Parliament would have nothing to do with it, so that England and Scotland remained two discrete kingdoms. Nevertheless, to have two kingdoms ruled by one king meant that the border disputes that had cost so many lives for so many centuries now become a thing of the past. James rapidly found that governing England was not like Scotland. They did things differently. Although the English statesmen welcomed him as their new king, and one with a considerable reputation, he was nevertheless a foreigner, and one who spoke in a strange accent and brought with him favourites of his court. After Elizabeth's final few years, which had become rather dour and constrained compared to the earlier glories, James was invigorating, but he was also pompous, full of considerable self-importance, and paranoid about his safety. The English found him difficult to understand, and James took a while to become accustomed to the English Parliament and way of life. In fact he and his Parliament usually disagreed so strongly after a while that he regularly dissolved it in order to find other ways to meet his needs, especially for money. James disliked having to acquire the approval of Parliament to raise money for foreign activities.

All this uncertainty about James added to his increasing unease, which was not helped by Robert Catesby's Gunpowder Plot of 1604/5, when extremist Catholics sought to destroy James and parliament. In this respect James was sorely misunderstood. Although he was not Catholic, he was not as fervent a Protestant as the members of the Scottish Kirk that he had left behind – even if the Gunpowder Plot made him appear a near martyr for Protestantism. James worked long and hard at moderating Presbyterianism. When he came south James delighted in the Church of England, which had retained an Episcopalian structure and gave James ultimate authority over it, whereas the Presbyterian Assembly treated James as an equal and denied him control. In England James had more opportunity to impose his will. In 1605 he outlawed the Assembly and those who objected he arrested on grounds of treason. Andrew Melville was summoned to England and imprisoned in the Tower of London for mocking the English church. He was not released until 1611, when he left England for France and did not return. James had broken the back of the General Assembly and was able to impose his own system of diocesan bishops over the Scottish church. He also imposed moderation on the English puritans, whom he attempted to force to conform to the Anglican church. As the final stroke in his reforms of the church, James introduced his own Authorised Edition of the Bible, usually known as the King James's Bible, in 1611.

50. England (9) – The Stewarts

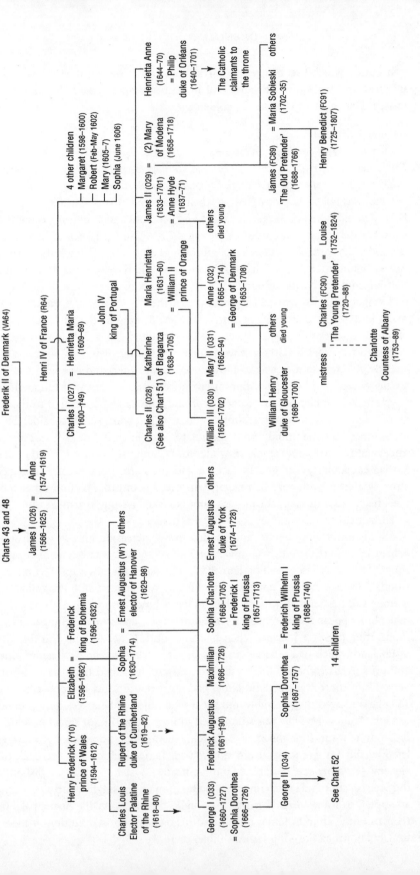

In other English affairs James fared moderately well. Ruling Scotland from a distance enabled him to work through others to achieve ends he might never have done at home. In 1608, through the earl of Argyll, he arrested the leading clansmen in the Hebrides and forced them into submission. A subsequent rebellion by the MacDonalds in 1614, hoping to revive the lordship of the Isles, was soon quashed, as was the rebellious lifestyle of James's second cousin, Patrick Stewart, earl of Orkney, who was eventually executed in 1615. James also began the plantation of English and Scottish protestants into Ulster from 1611 on.

In foreign affairs James had mixed fortunes. Scotland's original friendship with Spain allowed him to curtail England's war with Spain expeditiously, though relationships were never again the same. In 1607 the first English colony in North America was established by John Smith at Jamestown in Virginia. James's "kingdom" extended to Bermuda in 1609 and to New England in 1620 with the Pilgrim Fathers in the *Mayflower*. James endeavoured, through the marriages of his children, to establish a strong Protestant alliance throughout Europe. His crowning achievement was the marriage of his daughter Elizabeth to the Elector Palatine Frederick in February 1613 (from whom the Hanoverian kings of England were descended). He also hoped to marry his sons into the Spanish royal family. This was never likely, but even the possibility was thwarted when his son-in-law Frederick became king of Bohemia in 1618 and found himself at war with the Habsburg monarchy in Austria. Spain was the ally of Austria, and James came under pressure to support Bohemia against two of the greatest nations in Europe. He succeeded in maintaining his distance – mostly because the English Parliament would not vote him money for the enterprise – but his scheme of a Protestant alliance in Europe rapidly crumbled. By now premature senility was dulling his powers, and a series of poor decisions throughout the last fifteen years of his reign meant that this once ingenious and clever monarch became gradually more incompetent. It was not without good reason that he earned the reputation as "the wisest fool in Christendom", a phrase coined some years earlier by Henri IV of France. Some of the scandals in his later years included the murder of Sir Thomas Overbury in 1613 and the subsequent pardoning of the earl of Somerset and Lady Essex who were convicted of masterminding the poisoning; the execution in 1618 of Sir Walter Ralegh, whom James had long believed was conspiring against him; and the arrest and imprisonment of Sir Francis Bacon on the grounds of bribery and corruption. Despite these darker spots James showed himself to be forward looking. He became interested in scientific development, especially where it might aid the defence of the realm. He was the patron of several inventors including the remarkable Dutch scientist Cornelius Drebbel, who presented him with a purposted perpetual-motion machine. Drebbel is remembered for the development of the microscope and thermometer, but he should be better remembered for having developed the first submarine, which was really a submersible rowing-boat. He demonstrated it in the Thames in 1620 and even took James I for a trip, making him the first king ever to travel underwater.

By the end of his reign, with his intellect fading, James found himself under the strong influence of George Villiers later Duke of Buckingham, with whom James had become acquainted in 1614 and who rose rapidly to power. Villiers's schemes were often ill advised but James came wholly under his spell. James's final years thus saw him as a weak and dispirited monarch, a shadow of his former self. Nevertheless he had been an active king for over forty years, and in name had been a king almost all of his life. He had, in fact, ruled longer than any other Scottish king and had left a greater impact upon his nation of birth than any preceding him. Although it was only an accident of birth that caused him to become king of England, he nevertheless succeeded in governing both countries despite considerable handicaps and opposition, his ability to survive such trials and tribulations marks him down as one of the most remarkable and cunning of kings.

[O27;FC83] CHARLES (I)

Ruled 27 March 1625–30 January 1649. Crowned king of England at Westminster Abbey, 2 February 1626, and king of Scotland at Holyrood Abbey, 8 June 1633.
Titles: king of England, Scotland and Ireland, prince of Wales (1616–25), duke of Albany, marquess of Ormonde, earl of Ross, baron of Ardmannoch, duke of York (from 1605), duke of Cornwall and Rothesay (from 1612) and earl of Chester (from 1616).
Born: Dunfermline Palace, Fife, 19 November 1600. Died (executed): Whitehall Palace, London, 30 January 1649, aged 48. Buried: St George's Chapel, Windsor.
Married: 13 June 1625, at St Augustine's Church, Canterbury, Henrietta Maria (1609–69), dau. of Henri IV, king of France: 9 children.

Charles was the first king to succeed to the kingdoms of both England and Scotland. His father, JAMES VI of Scotland, had inherited the English throne (as JAMES I) on the death of ELIZABETH because of his descent from HENRY VII. Charles did not become the heir apparent until 6 November 1612 when his elder brother Henry died of typhoid. Charles also had an elder sister, Elizabeth, who survived him and from whom the later kings of England from GEORGE (I) are descended, although all his other brothers and sisters died in infancy. Charles himself was a weak child, backward and unable to walk or talk in infancy. He was left behind in Scotland when his father and family moved to London in 1603 and he followed a year later. He was nursed by Lady Carey who nurtured and strengthened him, so he could talk by the time he was four, though he never lost his stammer, and could walk by the age of seven. He was short (his final height was about five feet four inches), but grew into a more handsome figure than his father. He was devoted to his brother and sister and was much saddened at his brother's death and when, a few months later, his sister married the Elector Palatine of the Rhine and went to live at Heidelberg. Charles's teens were lonely years during which time he forced himself to become assertive, a trait important in a king but which was to become his downfall.

Charles was the first king to be raised within the Church of England. This religious divide made it impossible to marry the Infanta Maria of Spain, whom he visited incognito in 1623 with his friend George Villiers, who that year became the duke of Buckingham. Instead he married the French princess Henrietta Maria, but only on condition that she was allowed the free practice of the Catholic religion and to control the upbringing of their children. Their marriage happened two months after Charles succeeded to the throne. At first the marriage was unhappy: Henrietta was only fifteen and did not seem schooled in the art of courtship. She disliked Charles's childhood friend, the duke of Buckingham, and may have felt there was more than male bonding between them. Charles clashed with the large retinue that Henrietta had brought from France, which included a bishop, twenty-nine priests and over four hundred attendants. Within a year he had despatched these back to France. In 1628, Buckingham was murdered and it seems, with both these barriers removed, that their relationship warmed, and their first child was born in May 1629 (but died the same day). Henrietta always managed to maintain a controlling hand over Charles and exerted an increasingly unwise influence.

For the first three years of his reign Charles was heavily influenced by Buckingham whose exploits, which earlier might have seemed all a joke, became politically dangerous. Thanks to Buckingham, Charles found himself at war, first with Spain and then (in 1627) with France, with the intention of aiding the Huguenots. Buckingham led abortive and costly expeditions in both campaigns, and caused further international scandal by allegedly seducing the queen of France. Charles was also anxious to assist his brother-in-law Frederick to regain the Rhine Palatinate. Parliament did not like Buckingham and refused to grant Charles the finances for the wars. Charles consequently took what other avenues he could to raise money, including drawing on his wife's dowry and exacting loans from the wealthier peers. He also failed to pay soldiers. This attitude and his cavalier approach to Parliament, which he only called when he chose and then tended to ignore, incensed the Commons. They drew up a Petition of Right in 1628 to control Charles's excesses. Although he accepted it, he chose largely to ignore it. Charles's clash with Parliament continued beyond the murder of Buckingham in August 1628. In the end, when Charles adjourned Parliament in March 1629, he did not call another for eleven years, ruling in absolute authority and not seeking parliamentary sanction for his actions. He raised money through taxes and custom duties (known as "tonnage and poundage") as he chose, and also imposed forced loans and purchased knighthoods upon his wealthier subjects. Although he saved much expenditure by bringing the pointless wars to a close, he frequently did not pay members of the royal household, even though he continued to live in great luxury.

He further upset his subjects, particularly those in Scotland, when he attempted to bring the Scottish church in line with the Church of England, imposing a new service book on Scotland, and introducing his own prejudices within the church, especially a tendency – known as Arminianism – to oppose strict Calvinist views of predestination. This was associated with high church practices, which echoed much of the Catholic service. Charles worked with William Laud, the new archbishop of

From a portrait by
Daniel Mytens, 1634

Canterbury, and Thomas Wentworth, later earl of Strafford, who, in 1628, was created President of the North. Between the three they endeavoured to create an absolutism in church and state with Charles as the "most absolute prince in Christendom", ruling by divine right.

In some actions Charles might almost be justified. Wentworth's activities in Ireland after 1633, where he was lord deputy, were remarkable compared to past campaigns. Whereas previously the expenditure on Ireland had always oustripped any revenues received, Wentworth made the island profitable through his imposition of taxes and custom dues, his elimination of piracy, the introduction of a sound agricultural programme relying on the cultivation of flax, and the transformation of the army into an orderly force. This was done with a heavy-handedness that did not endear Wentworth to the king's subjects, but it was effective.

Attempts to run roughshod over the Scottish church, however, did not work so well. The Scots rejected Laud's new service book and declared defiant loyalty to the old Kirk. They formed a National Covenant in 1638 in opposition to Charles's policies. Following Wentworth's suggestion, Charles decided to impose his intentions by force. He raised an army in the spring of 1639, only to discover how little loyalty he commanded from his troops. Many of the English defected, not expecting to be paid and regarding the Scots as oppressed. The planned force of 30,000 ended up as only 8,000. Charles was easily defeated by the determined Scots in what became known as the First Bishops' War. Charles was in a predicament. He did not have the finances for a second campaign and had no alternative but to summon Parliament in April 1639. This Parliament, known as "the Short Parliament" because it was dissolved after only a few weeks, refused to grant Charles money unless he heard their grievances. Charles refused. Again he raised an army and again the Scots defeated him in the Second Bishops' War that August. Charles was again forced to call Parliament, and this time he was not allowed to dissolve it (hence it became known as "the Long Parliament"). Parliament chose Wentworth as the scapegoat for Charles's rule of tyranny, treating the understanding that Wentworth had promised to summon the army from Ireland to subdue the Scots as evidence of treason. Charles was forced to sign Wentworth's death warrant, and he was executed on Tower Hill on 12 May 1641.

Charles conceded some of Parliament's wishes, particularly over the ship-taxes he had imposed, but he would not give way on his reform of the Church of England. Charles attempted to rally support in Scotland but without success. However, when he returned to London he believed some support amongst Parliament was swinging his way. When John Pym presented his list of grievances against the king, known as the Grand Remonstrance, in November 1641, it did not receive universal support. Charles, encouraged by his queen, believed he could swing the balance in Parliament by removing the main opposition. In January 1642 Charles entered the House of Commons with an armed guard intending to arrest the five primary offenders. The five Members, who included Pym, had already escaped. This was the final straw. There was much public opposition to Charles's actions, so he withdrew from London. Negotiations over the next seven months failed to reach any agreement with the king totally intractable and Parliament increasing its demands. Civil war became inevitable and the king formally declared hostilities at Nottingham on 22 August 1642.

This was not the first civil war to divide England, and it was not the first to result in the deposition of a king, but because it was the first and only war in England to result in the abolition of the kingship, it has become known as *the* Civil War. The Royalists, or Cavaliers, generally had the upper hand in the early encounters, though they failed to strike decisively at the first main engagement at Edgehill on 23 October 1642 against the Parliamentarians, or Roundheads, under Robert Devereux, third earl of Essex (and son of ELIZABETH's favourite). As the conflict continued, so the Roundheads began to take the offensive, especially when Thomas Fairfax and Oliver Cromwell took command with their specially trained cavalry and restructured New Model Army. They achieved victories at Marston Moor in 1644 and particularly at Naseby on 14 June 1645. With his defeat Charles deliberated about his position for nearly a year before surrendering to the Scots, expecting greater clemency. For their part, the Scots expected Charles to meet their terms over his church reform, but when Charles defiantly refused, the Scots handed him over to the English. While Charles was held by the Scots at Newcastle, the English Parliament issued a set of terms which became known as the Propositions of Newcastle in July 1646. These terms were to agree to the Covenant, abolish episcopacy, authorise Parliament's control over foreign policy and the army and amend his reforms of the Church. Charles refused. When handed over to the English, Charles was confined to Hampton Court, where Fairfax and Cromwell sought to come to terms with him over a formal written constitution. Again Charles refused. Escaping from Hampton Court, he sought refuge on the Isle of Wight, where he was confined to Carisbrooke Castle. Charles now intriguingly played one party against the other, negotiating at once with both the Parliamentarians and the Scots. The Scots reached an agreement with Charles which became known as the Engagement, signed on 26 December 1647. Under its terms the Scots would restore Charles as their king provided he would accept Presbyterianism for a trial period. This would be imposed upon the English and the two kingdoms united – though in fact it was a Scottish takeover of the English Parliament. Although not all Scots were united over this agreement, it was sufficient for an army to invade England in July 1648, only to be decisively defeated by Cromwell in three engagements in August at Preston, Wigan and Warrington. Fairfax's army also rapidly subdued a Royalist revolt in southern England.

In January 1649 Charles was brought to trial for treason, on the grounds that he had fought against his subjects. Charles refused to recognize the court as having any authority over him and thus offered no defence. He remained dignified but disdainful of the proceedings. When the court delivered its verdict the 135 judges were split almost evenly, 68 finding him guilty and 67 innocent. Thus by a majority of just one, Charles was condemned to death. He was executed at Whitehall on 30 January. He wore two shirts so as not to shiver from the cold and give the impression he was afraid. The Scots were vehemently opposed to the execution of their monarch by the English parliament but following their recent defeat they felt powerless to react. They nevertheless transferred their allegiance to Charles's son, CHARLES (II), while in England the kingship was abolished.

Charles failed as a king in every respect except authority, and in that he presumed too much. He was an absolute dictator or autocrat who nevertheless, in practice, could not operate without the support of his Parliament. His dignity and defiance against the odds might make him a romantic figure were it not for his complete and utter intransigence and arrogance. Whilst he failed to pay his soldiers and supporters, he spent a small fortune on commissioning and acquiring works of art. Where Henry VIII and Elizabeth had the support of the people even though they acted in an almost similar way, Charles did not, because Charles worked against rather than for his subjects. It was left to his son to restore the humanity, if not the credibility, to the Crown.

[O28;FC84] CHARLES II

Ruled Scotland, 11 June 1650–3 September 1660 (fled into exile); restored 29 May 1660–6 February 1685. Crowned, Scone Abbey, 1 January 1651. Ruled England, 29 May 1660–6 February 1685. Crowned: Westminster Abbey, 23 April 1661.
Titles: king of England, Scotland and Ireland; duke of Cornwall and Rothesay.
Born: St James's Palace, London, 29 May 1630. **Died:** *Whitehall Palace, 6 February 1685, aged 54.* **Buried:** *Westminster Abbey.*
Married: 22 May 1662, in Portsmouth, Katherine Henrietta (1638–1705), dau. of John IV, duke of Braganza: 3 children (all stillborn). Charles had at least 16 illegitimate children by 8 mistresses.

Charles was the eldest surviving son of CHARLES (I) and Henrietta Maria. He was twelve when the Civil War broke out. Until then he had been raised in the stately magnificence of Charles's royal palaces and had received a good if not extensive education. He rapidly became skilled in the arts of war, fighting alongside his father in the early engagements and being made commander of his troops in the West Country in March 1645, when only fourteen. As the tide of the war changed, however, Charles wisely left England, settling first (1646) in France and then (1648) Holland, where his sister, Maria, the Princess Royal, had married Prince William of Orange. Charles had at least two sexual encounters during these years, and probably more. Rumours persist that he had fathered a son, James, while in Jersey in 1646 but of more significance was a second son, also called James, born in the Hague on 9 April 1649. The mother was Lucy Walter. The son, who became the duke of Monmouth, later claimed his parents were married and that he was the legitimate heir to the throne.

It was while living in the Hague that Charles learned of his father's execution. On 16 February he was proclaimed king in Jersey. A few days later the Scottish Parliament proclaimed Charles their king, provided he was prepared to accept the Scottish Covenant. This widened the rift between Scotland and England, where the new Parliament abolished the monarchy in March 1649. Charles really wanted to be king of England, and accepting the Scottish Covenant would have barred that route completely. Charles learned early on, therefore, that he needed to be cautious and devious. He was a remarkably pragmatic individual whose main aim was to enjoy himself, but he was prepared to fight and prove himself. He felt that everyone should be allowed to lead their own life, and thus he would bend with the wind and take whatever options best served his purpose. He therefore bided his time, exploring what other avenues might exist. He found Ireland closed to him by Cromwell's army while, in April 1650, an unofficial advance guard under the command of James Graham, the marquess of Montrose was defeated and Montrose hanged. Charles had to act so, in June 1650, he signed a treaty which he managed to keep sufficiently ambiguous but which effectively made him a covenanted king of the Scots. Twelve days later he landed in Scotland, a stranger in his own land. He was dubiously accepted as king but not allowed to exert any authority. He was more a figurehead than a sovereign, but his very presence posed immense danger, not only from rival factions in Scotland but from the English. A month later Cromwell led an army into Scotland. It was not overtly an invasion force, rather a move to explore the relationships between the two countries, but it left little doubt that Cromwell meant business if he met any opposition. However, as many past campaigners had found, Scotland is a difficult land to conquer without a massive support infrastructure and Cromwell's was disrupted by weather and disease. Nevertheless he engaged and overwhelmingly defeated a Scottish force at Dunbar on 2 September 1650, taking possession of Edinburgh and Leith. This was the downfall of the government of Covenanters under Archibald Campbell, marquess of Argyll, and the chaos that followed saw an untrusting but necessary alliance between the extremist factions who overthrew the anti-Royalists (known as the Remonstrants) and proclaimed Charles their king. He was crowned at Scone on 1 January 1651.

Cromwell continued to stamp his authority on Scotland, and in July 1651 Charles led a hopeful army south into England. He was met by Cromwell's army at Worcester on 3 September 1651 and soundly defeated. Charles was lucky to escape with his life. He fled into Shropshire and sought refuge at Boscobel House, where he was helped by the yeoman Richard Penderel. It was at this time that the famous episode happened of Charles hiding in an oak tree whilst Cromwell's soldiers scoured the woods. Charles disguised himself as a servant and a few weeks later made his escape to France. It was difficult for Charles to disguise himself as he had a most distinctive physique. He was tall, at last six feet three inches, which is surprising considering the shortness of his parents. He probably inherited the genes through his Danish grandmother.

He spent the next eight years on the continent, wheeling-and-dealing with whatever power might assist him. He was well placed, as during the next few years England found itself at war with first the Dutch (1652–54) and then Spain (1656–9). Charles took advantage of both conflicts to gain support for his own cause. These hostilities brought the English closer to the French as allies, which further helped Charles because of his own close affinity with the French. An Anglo-French force defeated the Spanish in northern France in 1658, as a consequence of which the Spanish surrendered Dunkirk to the English, who once again held territory in France.

During this period Cromwell's hold on England and Scotland grew. The Commonwealth was declared and, in 1653 Cromwell was made "Lord Protector". Though he governed through a Parliament, he was granted almost absolute powers and, indeed, in May 1657 Cromwell was offered the title of king. He refused but accepted the right of succession, so that his son, Richard, would be Lord Protector after him. For a brief period religious tolerance was observed throughout England and the Jews were readmitted, but towards the end of Cromwell's government there was a backlash against puritanism and extremism, and a return to a more Catholic practice. Nevertheless civic marriages were allowed and the registration of birth, deaths and marriages enforced.

*From a portrait by
Samuel Cooper*

Cromwell died on 3 September 1658. Richard Cromwell did not want the role of Lord Protector, and neither was he the man for the job. Had his elder brothers survived, the Protectorate might have continued, but Richard was unable to enforce any authority or control Parliament or the military and in May 1659 he resigned. England came under military rule and it was thanks to the authority of George Monck, who had been made governor of Scotland by Cromwell in 1654, that order was restored. Monck marched on London in January 1660, entering the city without opposition. He soon whipped up enthusiasm for the restoration of the monarchy and paved the way for Charles to return to England on 23 May 1660. Charles entered London six days later on his thirtieth birthday. He was crowned eleven months later with new regalia, the former crown jewels having been broken up during the Commonwealth.

Charles's restoration was dependent upon his religious intentions. When he signed the Declaration of Breda in April 1660, which laid down the terms of his restoration, he acknowledged religious tolerance, though he had trouble gaining any form of acceptance among the clergy and, by 1661, among his Parliament. Acts were passed against Jesuits and Quakers and Charles's efforts to reintroduce a modified form of the Church of England was rejected by an increasingly Puritanical parliament. A new English prayer book was introduced and Charles found most of his views ignored. The intolerance of the English Parliament pushed Charles back to his Catholic sympathies from his many years on the Continent. In 1662 he had married the Catholic Katherine of Braganza, the Portuguese Infanta. He negotiated in secret with Catholics and eventually, in 1672, he was able to carry through his Declaration of Indulgence, which suspended all penal laws against nonconformists and allowed private worship by Catholics. Charles himself was rumoured to be a secret Catholic and his brother, James, duke of York (JAMES II), openly professed his Catholicism. Feelings against Catholics continued to run strong resulting in the false Popish Plot of 1678. This was invented by Titus Oates, who spread rumours of an imminent rebellion by the Catholics to invade England from Ireland, overthrow the king and place James on the throne. The backlash against the Catholics was immense, with over thirty-five Catholics tried and executed on trumped-up charges. It was two years before Oates's plan was uncovered.

Early in his reign Charles was guided by Edward Hyde, the Lord Chancellor and head of government, who was made earl of Clarendon in April 1661. Clarendon was a staunch Royalist, ultra-conservative and anti-Puritan, who would have set the country back twenty years. He ultimately became the scapegoat for all the problems that beset Charles's early reign. The sale of Dunkirk back to the French in October 1662 was an unpopular move, as was the outbreak of war with the Dutch in March 1665, although Clarendon spoke against this. It need never have happened, and arose because of an impasse over merchant shipping routes and rights through the English Channel. As a precursor to this various Dutch trading posts and colonies were attacked and seized by the English, including New Amsterdam in the American colonies. This was captured by the distinguished sea captain, later admiral, Robert Holmes in August 1664 and renamed New York in honour of Charles's brother, the duke of York. Although the Dutch regained other territories, they never recovered New York. The war with the Dutch reached stalemate, because England suffered under the Great Plague which began to have its effects in London in April 1665 and was not assuaged until the Great Fire swept through London in September 1666. A treaty with the Dutch was eventually concluded in July 1667. Soon after Clarendon was dismissed and to avoid impeachment he fled to France, where he remained in exile. Clarendon's daughter, Anne, had married the duke of York secretly in 1659 and, through her, Clarendon became the grandfather of the future queens MARY II and ANNE (though he did not live long enough to know it). Clarendon's son, Laurence, who was Charles's Master of the Robes and later became the First Lord of the Treasury (1679) was the man who nicknamed Charles "the Merry Monarch". He also said the famous quip about Charles that "he never said a foolish thing and never did a wise one", to which Charles agreed, riposting "my words are my own, and my actions are those of my ministers."

Charles next came under the influence of a group of five advisers known as the Cabal from their initials: the Lords Clifford, Arlington, Buckingham, Ashley and Lauderdale. These advisers each looked after their own interests and so did not necessarily act in union. Indeed they had opposing religious views – Ashley (later earl of Shaftesbury) was an ardent Protestant, whilst Clifford was a Catholic. Clifford worked with Charles in his desire to wreak revenge upon the Dutch and helped negotiate a secret treaty with the French in May 1670, whereby the English would support the French against the Dutch in return for financial rewards and use of French ports. The treaty also provided that at some opportune time Charles would declare his reversion to Catholicism. Although Charles believed he was gaining ground, he effectively became a puppet of the French. A strong anti-French and anti-Catholic mood swept the country, aggravated in 1672 when the duke of York openly declared his conversion to Catholicism. Charles was forced to withdraw his Declaration of Indulgence and agree in 1673 to a Test Act, which excluded all Roman Catholics from official office. This excluded the duke of York from office, but did not stop James marrying the Catholic princess Mary of Modena. Parliament refused to sanction any finance to support the Dutch war, and Charles was compelled to act as mediator between the two countries which dragged on until the Peace of Nijmegen in 1678. One of the outcomes of this was that Charles's niece, the fifteen year old Mary, was married to WILLIAM (III) of Orange in 1677.

The Popish Plot encouraged by Oates showed the strength of anti-Catholic feeling in England. There was a strong fear that personal liberties would be infringed by royal whim and in May 1679 Parliament passed the act of Habeas Corpus, one of this country's most important items of legislation which protects the individual's freedom from unlawful imprisonment. This same Parliament, which was under Whig control under the leadership of the earl of Shaftesbury, introduced an Exclusion Bill which would deny the duke of York succession to the throne. By then the queen had had several stillbirths and miscarriages and Charles believed he would have no legitimate son, for all that he had sired many illegitimate ones. Charles prevented the bill's enactment by using his authority in the Lords. When Parliament met the next year the bill was introduced again, and passed, but Charles dissolved Parliament. A third Parliament met in Oxford in 1681 and the bill passed through the Commons and the Lords, but again Charles dissolved Parliament. Charles brought military pressure upon the Whigs to moderate their actions, and the country was fearful of another civil war. Charles entered a secret treaty with the French for their support in the event of a rebellion. It was in this atmosphere that the Rye-House Plot was uncovered in June 1683. It was a scheme devised by Lord William Russell, Algernon Sidney, Lord Capel and others to assassinate Charles and James on their departure from the races at Newmarket in March, and raise Charles's eldest surviving illegitimate son, the duke of Monmouth, to the throne. The plot was thwarted when a fire caused them to leave early. Sidney became the first victim of the infamous Judge Jeffreys, who tried him with minimal evidence and consigned him to the execution block. Jeffreys became a willing tool in serving Charles who wreaked revenge upon any likely conspirator.

With his own private army, with the Whig opposition dispersed, and with Judge Jeffreys happy to execute anyone who dared oppose the king, Charles's final years were unsurprisingly peaceful. While this suggests he ruled like a despot, he was in reality an amusing and likeable man with a great sense of humour. He was really a loveable rogue, a kind of "Chuck the Lad". He enjoyed many sports and pursuits, including horse-racing. He established the race-course at Newmarket in 1667 and even raced there as a jockey in the Twelve-Stone Plate in 1675 and won. He loved the theatre, which he re-established and patronised after it was banned during the Commonwealth, and loved the actresses even more. Two actresses became his mistresses. The better known was Nell Gwynne, who bore him two children. The eldest, Charles Beauclerk, survived and married the daughter of the earl of Oxford, and their descendants survive today. By Moll Davies, Charles had Mary Tudor, who married the earl of Derwentwater. Nell Gwynne also had a great sense of humour and the episodes between Charles and Nell in London often caused much jollity. One such was when Nell tried to outdo Charles's other mistress, Louise, duchess of Portsmouth, by wearing a more outrageous hat which was so huge that it threatened to overwhelm her when she appeared on the stage in the King's presence. It was at Nell Gwynne's urging that Charles established the Royal Hospital at Chelsea for army pensioners.

Charles was also a great patron of the arts and sciences. He loved discussing scientific issues and conducted his own experiments. His primary interests were in clocks and watches (he had seven clocks in his bedroom each of which chimed at different times) and in navigation. He was the first monarch to have a royal yacht, the *Royal Escape*. Not surprisingly these two interests come together in his patronage of the Royal Observatory at Greenwich in 1675 under the first Astronomer-Royal, John Flamsteed. Charles established the Royal Society in

51. England (10) – **The illegitimate children of Charles II**

Mistress	Offspring	Descendants
Lucy Walter of Haverfordwest (c1630–58)	James, duke of Monmouth (1649–85) = Anne Scott of Buccleuch (1651–1732)	the dukes of Buccleuch and Queensberry
Elizabeth Killigrew, *later* Lady Shannon	Charlotte Fitzroy (1650–84), =(2) William, earl of Yarmouth	Daughter, Stuarta Howard, who was lady-in-waiting to Mary of Modena.
Katherine Pegge	(1) Charles Fitzcharles (1657–80) = Bridget Osborne (d. 1718) (2) Katherine (1658–?1759), *nun*	} } *no children* }
Barbara Villiers (1641–1709), later duchess of Cleveland	(1) Anne Fitzroy (1661–1722) = Henry Lennard, earl of Sussex (2) Charles Fitzroy (1662–1730), duke of Southampton and Cleveland =(2) Anne Poultney (1663–1745) (3) Henry Fitzroy (1663–90), duke of Grafton = Isabella Bennett (d. 1723) (4) Charlotte Fitzroy (1664–1717) = Edward, earl of Lichfield (1663–1716) (5) George Fitzroy (1665-1716), duke of Northumberland = married twice (6) Barbara Benedicte, became Prioress (*she may have been the daughter of the duke of Marlborough*)	*no children* William (1697/8–1774), duke of Cleveland. No children; title extinct. the dukes of Grafton earls of Lichfield till death of Robert (13th and youngest son), 4th earl (1706–76), from a fall from a horse. *no children*
Nell Gwynne (1650–87)	(1) Charles Beauclerk (1670–1726) duke of St Albans = Diana de Vere (d. 1742) (2) James Beauclerk (1671–80)	the dukes of St Albans
Louise de Kérouaille (1649–1734) duchess of Portsmouth	Charles Lennox (1672–1723), duke of Richmond and duke of Aubigny = Anne Brudenell	the dukes of Richmond and Gordon
Mary (Moll) Davies	Mary Tudor (1673–1726) =(1) Edward, earl of Derwentwater (d.1705) =(2) Henry Graham of Levens (d. 1707) =(3) James Rooke	Their son James (1689–1716) was beheaded for his part in the rebellion of 1715; his brother Charles (1693–1746) was private secretary to the Young Pretender and was beheaded for his part in the rebellion of 1745. *no children* *no children*

Note: It has long been maintained that Charles had a son, James, by Margaret de Carteret of Jersey, but his paternity was never satisfactorily resolved.

London in 1660 with the view to "improving Natural Knowledge". This was the period when Isaac Newton formulated his theories on gravity; when Sir Christopher Wren undertook some of his greatest building works, including the present St Paul's Cathedral, on which work began in 1675; when Robert Boyle established the principles of scientific experimentation and developed modern chemistry out of ancient alchemy; when Richard Lower undertook the first blood transfusion between animals (1665); and when Edmund Halley correctly predicted the return of the comet now named after him (1682). Thanks to Charles's patronage, science received a boost which it had been denied under earlier rulers and saw the birth, in England, of a scientific reformation.

The first real newspapers appeared during Charles's reign, notably Roger L'Estrange's *The Public Intelligencer* in 1663 and the *London Gazette* in 1665. These were still controlled by royal licensing of the press and censorship of the press was re-introduced in 1680, lasting until 1695.

Some commentators on Charles's reign have called it "the worst reign in English history", which is a considerable exaggeration. The criticism is that Charles followed whatever course he deemed best to save himself, even if it meant selling his country and his religion to the French. Charles cannot be regarded as a good king, but neither was he an especially bad one, since he was never vindictive, had no wish to cause anyone any harm or anguish provided everyone was moderate. It was the extremists about him who, frustrated at Charles's lack of firm direction, forced issues that caused Charles to react unfavourably. Nevertheless the monarchy survived under him and beyond him. He died of a stroke while still comparatively young and was succeeded by his brother James.

[O29] **JAMES II**, also **JAMES VII** [FC85] of Scotland.
Ruled 6 February 1685–11 December 1688 (deposed); continued as king of Ireland until 1 July 1690. Crowned: Westminster Abbey, 23 April 1685.
Titles: king of England and Scotland; duke of York (from 1644), earl of Ulster (from 1659), duke of Normandy (from 1660).
Born: St James's Palace, London, 14 October 1633. Died: St Germain-en-Laye, near Paris, 16 September 1701, aged 67. Buried: Church of the English Benedictines, Paris. Married: (1) November/December 1659, at Breda, Holland, Anne (1637–71), dau. Edward Hyde, earl of Clarendon: 8 children; (2) 21 November 1673, at Dover, Kent: Mary (1658–1718), dau. of Alfonso d'Este, duke of Modena: 12 children. James also had at least seven illegitimate children by two mistresses.
James was the younger brother of CHARLES II and the son of CHARLES I. As the second son of the monarch he was granted the title duke of York, though this was not formally bestowed until January 1644. The English Civil War disrupted his education, which always remained moderate. He was just nine when he witnessed the battle of Edgehill (October 1642); he was then removed for his protection to the Royalist headquarters at Oxford where, apparently, he enjoyed the company of dwarfs. When Oxford was captured by the Roundheads in 24 June 1646, the young prince was taken prisoner and confined to St James's Palace in London, where he remained for nearly two years. In April 1648, disguised as a girl, and pretending to be playing hide-and-seek, he effected his escape and fled to Holland, joining his brother Charles with their sister Mary in the Hague. He frequently quarrelled with his brother and mother. Unlike Charles, who was good-natured and happy-go-lucky, James was rather dour and serious. This made him a better soldier than his brother and, in 1652, he was commissioned into the French army, serving under Turenne in the French wars in Spain and the Netherlands, being promoted to lieutenant-general. He had to resign this commission when France and England reached an alliance, but he subsequently served with Spain against France and England in 1658, and was noted for his courage.

During this period James had entered protacted negotiations with the duke of Longueville to marry his daughter, but these came to nothing. His mistress at this time was Anne Hyde, daughter of Charles's chief minister Edward Hyde, and lady-in-waiting to James's sister Mary. He entered into a private marriage contract with her in Holland in November or December 1659. When news leaked out relatives were horrified. Most refused to acknowledge the marriage, and even James denied it for a while. However, with the Restoration of the monarchy in May 1660, and Anne now heavily pregnant, James went through a public ceremony on 3 September 1660 in London. It was some years, however, before there was any real family harmony.

With Charles installed as king, James had a number of titles bestowed upon him. In addition to duke of York, he became the duke of Albany and was made an honorary duke of Normandy by the French king, the last English monarch to hold that title. He also became Lord High Admiral. He commanded the navy during the Anglo-Dutch war, defeating the Dutch at the battle of Lowestoft in June 1665. In 1664 the English had captured New Amsterdam in North America from the Dutch. It was presented to James and renamed New York after him.

In 1668 James and Anne converted to Catholicism but kept this secret until Charles was able to force his Declaration of Indulgence through Parliament in March 1672. Anne had died the previous year and James was soon negotiating to marry the ardently Catholic Mary of Modena. The Whig government under the earl of Shaftesbury was horrified and in March 1673 forced the King to withdraw his Declaration of Indulgence and to pass the Test Act, which banned Catholics from holding public office. James, who had served bravely again in the third Anglo-Dutch War at Solebay in May 1672, had to step down as Lord High Admiral. The Government also tried to pass an Exclusion Bill which would have removed James from the succession. Charles was able to thwart this on three occasions between 1679 and 1681, but this and the Popish Plot of 1678 where rumour spread of a plan to assassinate Charles and install James on the throne, caused a massive wave of anti-Catholic feeling. James prudently went into exile in Brussels, and thence to Scotland, in December 1679. He was greeted with considerable caution and trepidation. The Scots had been in upheaval over the last year against potential Catholic reform, and the presence of a Catholic heir in their midst did nothing to pacify them. James, however, remained the soul of discretion for the brief period he was there, and he was generally accepted. However on his return a year later, with the Exclusion Bills rejected, James became less moderate. In July 1681 he forced two bills through the Scottish Parliament. The Act of Succession made it clear that religious differences were no bar to the succession to the Scottish throne. The Test Act forced all those holding official posts to sign a document pledging their adherence to Presbyterianism, Episcopalianism and Catholicism. Few would comply and most resigned, James using this as an opportunity to purge government of any opposition. Over the next three years, even after he returned south, James continued to persecute the Covenanters and there are many stories (possibly not all true) of the atrocities committed by him and in his name.

These persecutions continued in Scotland after James became king in February 1685. Although he was proclaimed king, he never took the Scottish coronation oath and was the first king of Scotland not to be crowned in Scotland. In fact, he never visited it again. From the moment of his accession there was mounting opposition to James. Neither Scotland nor England wanted a Catholic monarch, especially one with such a cruel and vindictive streak. Two political exiles united with plans to invade their respective countries and oust the king. In Scotland this was Archibald Campbell, earl of Argyll, who invaded Scotland in May 1685, whilst in England it was James Scott, duke of Monmouth, Charles II's eldest illegitimate son, who arrived at Lyme Regis on 11 June 1685 and was proclaimed king at Taunton nine days later as the real James II. Both men were astonished that so little support rallied to their cause. Argyll was not joined by his clan. His small army was soon overpowered as it marched south. He was captured, imprisoned without trial and executed in Edinburgh on 30 June. Monmouth was defeated at Sedgemoor on 5 July and captured three days later. He was executed at Tower Hill in London on 15 July. The infamous Judge Jeffreys was sent on a Bloody Assizes circuit of the West Country, where many of Monmouth's followers were captured and executed.

James now imposed a reign of terror, determined to restore Catholicism in England and Scotland. He introduced a Declaration of Indulgence in April 1687 restoring rights to Catholics, and any protesters were imprisoned, including seven bishops, accused of seditious libel. His complete disregard for the wishes of Parliament and his evident intention to overthrow the Church of England at last galvanised his opponents into action. The last straw was the birth of a son, James (*see* JAMES VIII) on 10 June 1688 after a succession of stillbirths and daughters who had died in infancy. Until then it was possible the church might have tolerated James, as his heir presumptives, MARY and ANNE, were both Protestants, but the young James would be raised a Catholic and that prospect was too much. Rumours – false but declared in hope – that the new-born baby was a changeling and that James's child had died at birth, circulated rapidly and had sufficient credibility to allow the bishop of London and six supporters (known as the "Immortal Seven") to invite James's son-in-law, WILLIAM of Orange, to England to protect his wife's succession to the throne. William was himself alarmed at the return of England and Scotland to Catholicism, as it would confirm Britain as an ally of France against the Netherlands and in France's current mobilisation against Germany. On 29 September William sent a declaration to the English Lords accepting their offer and laying out his terms for a "free and lawful Parliament." Delayed at first by bad weather, William's army landed at Brixham on 5 November 1688 and was welcomed at Exeter. Over the next two weeks most of the major cities and bishoprics in England declared their support for William. James's army was first based at Salisbury, but in the light of William's advance he retreated to Reading and called a war council. His commander-in-chief, John Churchill, and others defected to William on the same day, and the next day James discovered that his daughter, Anne, had also defected. Realising he had been deserted, James called a Great Council and agreed to major concessions, including the dismissal of Catholics from office.

Negotiations, led by the marquis of Halifax, continued for a week, but they were little more than a delaying tactic. On 10 December James fled from London, discarding the Great Seal in the Thames. He was captured at Sheerness in Kent and returned to London, but William allowed him to escape again and he fled to France on 23 December. William accepted the government six days later.

James was installed at the château of Saint-Germain, near Paris and established a court-in-exile. With him was his eldest surviving illegitimate son and chief agent and negotiator, James Fitzjames, duke of Berwick, son of Arabella Churchill, the sister of John Churchill. There were still pockets of support for James, especially amongst the Irish Catholics and the Scottish Jacobites. Following a rebellion amongst the Irish in January 1689, James landed at Kinsale in Ireland and in May 1689 held a Parliament in Dublin which still acknowledged his authority. James raised an army in Ireland, including support from France, and governed for a year, passing a number of acts in favour of the Catholics. In June 1690 William brought his army to Ireland and defeated James at the battle of the Boyne on 1 July 1690. James fled back to France three days later. He continued to plot and scheme for the next seven years, including a further attempted invasion in 1692 and another planned for but not executed in 1695. He eventually devoted himself to religious pursuits after 1697 and apparently suffered a mental decline. He succeeded in obtaining recognition from France that his legitimate son, JAMES (the Old Pretender), should become king after the death of William III.

James's arrogance and viciousness cost him his crown, but surprisingly not his life. Continued support for him and his son amongst the Scots would result in two Jacobite rebellions over the next fifty years, and his descendants would remain pretenders to the Scottish and English thrones until 1807.

[O30] **WILLIAM III**, designated **WILLIAM II** of Scotland.
King of England and Scotland (jointly with MARY II*), 13 February 1689–8 March 1702. Crowned: Westminster Abbey, 11 April 1689.*
Full name and titles: king of England, Scotland and Ireland; Stadtholder of Holland, prince of Orange and count of Nassau-Dillenburg (from 1672).
Born: Binnenhof Palace, the Hague, Holland, 4 November 1650. *Died: Kensington Palace, 8 March 1702, aged 51.* *Buried: Westminster Abbey.*
Married: 4 November 1677, at St James's Palace, London, Mary, dau. of James II of England: 3 children, all stillborn.
William III was descended from the ancient house of Nassau in Germany and was the great-grandson of William the Silent, prince of Orange, who became Stadtholder (or chief executive) of the Netherlands in 1572. His father, William II, died just eight days before William was born. His mother, Maria Henrietta, was the daughter of CHARLES I of England and Scotland. He was thus the nephew of JAMES II, whose daughter, MARY (II), he subsequently married. William was deprived of his titles in Holland in his childhood because of his father's arguments with the regents of Holland, but he was restored in 1672 following the overthrow of the dictatorial John de Witt who had governed Holland, first in alliance with France and then, after war broke out with France in 1667, with England and Sweden. Young William led the Dutch against the French and succeeding in forcing a peace in 1678 in which all of the Dutch terms were agreed. As a precursor to this, in his negotiations with his uncle, CHARLES II, who was acting as mediator between France and the Netherlands, William secured a political marriage with England by marrying his cousin, Mary, in 1677.

When James came to the throne and began to pursue his active Catholic measures, William first distanced himself and then, afraid that James might actually tip the balance and secure a Catholic majority in Parliament, and thereby become an immediate ally of the French, decided to intervene. He responded to an invitation from seven English peers, invaded England in November 1688 and within eight weeks had succeeded in a bloodless *coup*. The English Parliament determined that by fleeing the country James had abdicated, whilst the Scots argued that he had forfeited the Crown by his pro-Catholic actions against the Scottish nation. Either way James was no longer recognized as king other than in Ireland. There was some support for a regency, but while James II was still active, and support grew in Ireland and Scotland, Parliament did not want an interminable interregnum. William, on his part, did not want to be solely seen as a king consort, and was prepared to return to Holland. The English did not want a vacant throne and Mary was uncomfortable about reigning alone, especially as it looked as if she had usurped her father's throne. As a consequence in February 1689 William was offered joint sovereignty with Mary. Although common in the time of the early Saxon rulers, there had been no joint rule in England for over eight hundred years, and none in Scotland since the time of EDMUND and DONALD in the eleventh century. A Declaration of Rights was issued which outlawed the way James II (and others) had exercised their royal prerogative. The next month a Mutiny Act was passed, to make the existence of an army in peacetime depend on the agreement of the House of Commons. The Commons also tightened the control over the royal expenditure with a Civil List Act. These measures restricted the royal authority considerably and because William needed the support of England for Holland he was prepared to accept these changes. They went a long way toward the modern form of constitutional monarchy.

William still needed to secure his authority across the realm. James II was causing problems in Ireland where he remained king and his army was besieging Derry. William sent troops into Ireland in August 1689 and followed himself in June 1690. He defeated James II at the battle of the Boyne on 1 July, which forced James to flee back to France. The Irish Catholics fought back but were defeated again, the following July, at Aughrim. Uprisings amongst the Scottish Highlanders were less easily dealt with, and the clansmen were given an ultimatum to swear their allegiance to the King by 1 January 1692 or face the consequences. When Alexander MacIan MacDonald failed to make the deadline the troops made an example of him, and nearly forty members of his clan, including women, children and MacDonald himself, were massacred at Glencoe on 13 February. This was a deep stain on William's character and few Scots forgave him, even after he sought to acquit himself with a public enquiry three years later. This brought the perpetrators to justice but no sentence was enforced.

The action was not typical of William, but not surprising either. He was a deeply serious man, boringly so, who tolerated no nonsense, had no sense of humour, and had little interest in Scotland. He was short (Mary was five inches taller, and generally larger all round), bad-tempered – a tendency exacerbated by his asthma – and obsessive about his desire to keep the French out of Holland. Everything drove him towards that goal, and apart from consulting with Parliament in order to raise finances for his foreign activities, William avoided government altogether, leaving this to his wife, Mary. Since Mary had no interest in government either, but merely followed her husband's wishes, Parliament had its own way much of the time. There were two attempts by Jacobites to overthrow William. The Lancashire Plot in July 1694 failed virtually before it began, while Sir John Fenwick's conspiracy to assassinate William and restore James was uncovered in February 1696.

William's war with France dragged on until 1697. There were victories on both sides, none overwhelmingly decisive, but often involving severe losses. Although William was victorious in the naval battle of La Hogue on 19 May 1692, which curtailed James II's efforts to invade England, the English and Dutch suffered major losses at Neerwinden on 29 July 1693. The Treaty of Ryswick in September 1697 brought a temporary and uncertain end to the hostilities. One of the outcomes of this war was the establishment of the Bank of England in 1694 to help organize the finances required to support the war.

Mary had died of smallpox in December 1694. The couple had not been well matched. William was often accused of having homosexual tendencies, though it was also known that Elizabeth Villiers was his mistress. Mary was frigid and in her youth had had a lesbian relationship. They were also ill-matched physically, Mary being much larger than William, who was probably embarrassed by the whole procedure. Though they strove for an heir, they had a succession of stillbirths. The public had tolerated William because of their respect for Mary and, after her death, his popularity diminished further. This only drove him more into his foreign negotiations, in which he delighted. From 1698 till his death he became embroiled in the problems over the Spanish succession.

A succession crisis in England emerged in 1700 with the death of his nephew William, ANNE's only surviving son. As a consequence an Act of Settlement was passed, which secured the Protestant succession to the throne, specifically the Hanoverian succession (see GEORGE I).

William died as the result of a riding accident. In February 1702 his horse stumbled on a mole hill and threw William, breaking his collarbone. A fever set in, followed by pleurisy and pneumonia from which he died. William may not have been a much-loved king, but he was more stable than James and, because of his general lack of interest in England, he allowed the strength of parliament to grow (even though he tried to by-pass it when he needed to). It was in his reign that parliamentary government began to emerge.

[O31;FC87] **MARY II Queen of England and Scotland.**
Ruling jointly with WILLIAM III [II of Scotland], 13 February 1689–28 December 1694. Crowned: Westminster Abbey, 11 April 1689.
Born: *St James's Palace, London, 30 April 1662.* **Died:** *Kensington Palace, London, 28 December 1694, aged 32.* **Buried:** *Westminster Abbey.*
Married: *4 November 1677, at St James's Palace, William III, prince of Orange: 3 children, all stillborn.*
Mary was the eldest surviving child of JAMES II and an heiress in her own right, though the Exclusion Bills which Parliament sought to introduce during 1679–81, which would have denied her father's accession to the throne, could in turn have denied her. Moreover when James did succeed, his fervent pro-Catholic acts might have closed the succession completely to Protestants, which would have denied Mary's accession again. It was James's Catholicism and his too close an alliance with France that caused Mary's husband, William of Orange, to challenge and ultimately

overthrow James. William and Mary became joint sovereigns of England (*see under* WILLIAM III *for details*).

Mary remained forever in the shadow of her husband and contributed little to government beyond her good humour. She was the more loved sovereign of the two, and her gay demeanour was much needed at court and in Parliament to lighten William's surliness. Nevertheless Mary had not been raised for government, and did not like it, preferring to defer to William except when he was out of the country. Mary had not welcomed the match with William. She had apparently wept when it was announced. Apart from his ill humour, he was short, almost hump-backed, and with little passion. Mary for her part had no especial liking for men either. The two had three stillborn children in the first two years of their marriage and nothing thereafter. She lived in Holland from 1677 to 1689, where she was much loved by the Dutch.

Mary fell out with her sister (and eventual successor) ANNE over John Churchill, the Earl of Marlborough. It was Churchill's defection to William in the rebellion of 1688 that had made William's accession so easy, and Churchill had served him valiantly since, but did not feel he had been suitably rewarded. Rumours emerged that Churchill was starting to plot against William. Churchill's wife, Sarah, was a longtime friend of Anne's, having been her maid of honour and lady of the bedchamber. When Churchill was arrested and imprisoned in 1692, Mary expected Anne to dismiss Sarah, but Anne chose not to, and Mary regarded this as an affront. The two were not reconciled within Mary's lifetime.

Mary was only thirty-two when she contracted smallpox and died in December 1694. The country mourned her passing far more than her husband's eight years later. Mary strove to improve the nation's morals, and instructed magistrates to be more active in enforcing the vice laws. She supported the Society for the Promotion of Christian Knowledge, which eventually took shape in 1698, and she had plans to build a hospital at Greenwich, which William carried through after her death.

[O32;FC89] ANNE

Ruled 8 March 1702–1 August 1714. Crowned: Westminster Abbey, 23 April 1702.
Titles: queen of England, Scotland, France and Ireland (became Great Britain, Ireland and France from 1 May 1707).
Born: St James's Palace, London, 6 February 1665; Died: Kensington Palace, London, 1 August 1714, aged 49. Buried: Westminster Abbey.
Married: 28 July 1683, at St James's Palace, George (1653–1708), son of Frederik III, king of Denmark: 19 children, of which 14 were stillbirths or miscarriages.

Anne was the second daughter of James, duke of York (later JAMES II) and through her mother, Anne, the grand-daughter of Edward Hyde, earl of Clarendon. She was comparatively poorly educated and preferred sport and riding to reading and art. In 1683, when she was eighteen, hot on the heels of a court scandal, when she was reputedly seduced by one of the courtiers, Lord Mulgrave, Anne was married to Prince George, brother of the Danish king Christian V. Whilst George had received a good education he seems to have absorbed remarkably little of it, as he was lacking in the most basic general knowledge and seemed to revel in being a nonentity. He was harmless, well-meaning and a good husband, and the pair made a pleasant couple, but no one wanted George as a possible future king. When Anne came to the throne in 1702, George was kept securely in the background. He certainly tried to do his duty in fathering an heir, but of nineteen children (including twins), fourteen were stillborn, and only one survived beyond infancy and he, William, died in July 1700, aged eleven, of hydrocephalus. Since each child arrived within scarcely a year of the previous one, Anne's body must have been exhausted – she was pregnant for at least thirteen of her twenty-five years of marriage. Anne was overweight, a condition that probably contributed to the lack of a healthy child, and she frequently needed to be carried in a chair (which may be why the sedan chair became so popular during her reign). She also suffered from gout and rheumatism, and must constantly have been in pain. How she maintained her generally bright and kindhearted demeanour is a tribute to her stoicism and conscientiousness. She may not have wanted to be queen, she may have been ill equipped for it, but she nevertheless sought to do her duty. She relied heavily on Sidney Godolphin, the Lord High Treasurer and nearest equivalent of the day of the Prime Minister.

Before she became queen, Anne fell out of favour with her sister MARY (II) over the relationship with the Churchill family. John Churchill was imprisoned in 1692 for possible acts against the king. John's wife, Sarah, was Anne's closest friend and lady of the bedchamber. They had virtually grown up together. Sarah was rather a masculine woman and it became common gossip that the two were having a lesbian affair. Anne refused to dismiss Sarah and, as a consequence, Mary cut off relations with her. They were never reconciled, but William made amends after Mary's death.

Early in her reign Anne demonstrated her interests in the Church and the needy by establishing a fund, known as Queen Anne's Bounty, which increased the stipends of poorer clergy. She also insisted upon the construction of more churches in London.

Anne's reign was dominated abroad by the War of the Spanish Succession. This had arisen because Louis XIV of France accepted the Spanish throne on behalf of his grandson Philip, instead of recognizing Charles of Austria as the successor, as had been agreed by the Partition Treaty of 1700. Britain, Austria, Portugal, Denmark and the Netherlands sided against France, Spain and Bavaria. War was declared in May 1702 and peace was not concluded until the Treaty of Utrecht in April 1713. England's hero in the war was John Churchill, whom Anne elevated to duke of Marlborough and gave a considerable income. His great victory was on 13 August 1704 at Blenheim, in Germany, where he stopped the French advance. When he came to establish his great estate at Woodstock, near Oxford, Churchill named it Blenheim Palace after his victory. Also of lasting consequence in the war was the capture by Admiral Sir George Rooke in July 1704 of Gibraltar, which has remained a British possession ever since.

Anne took an interest in the war but, like her subjects, grew tired of its inexorability. It forced her to take a stronger hand in her dealings with her government and even made her dismiss her chief ministers on more than one occasion. In this respect, while Parliament remained paramount and Anne had virtually become a constitutional monarch, she wielded sufficient authority to keep the government on its toes. She also believed that her actions reflected the mood of the nation as a whole. She wielded a similar authority against others in her life, eventually dismissing Sarah Churchill from her official duties in 1711, partly because the lady had become high and mighty, but mostly because she had been promoting Whig propaganda against Anne's own Tory preferences. Anne became lonely after the death of her husband in 1708, and her constant pain made her more moody and vindictive. Her closest friend was Lady Abigail Masham, the cousin of Sarah Churchill who remained with her in her final years. During this period Anne endeavoured to negotiate with her half-brother JAMES (the Old Pretender), imploring him to set aside his Catholic faith for the sake of the succession. The Act of Settlement of 1701 had conferred the succession on Anne's second cousin, Sophia, widow of the Elector of Hanover. She died six weeks before Anne, and the succession passed to her son, GEORGE I. By the time of her death in 1714 Anne had become so big she could not move and needed to go everywhere in a wheelchair. Her coffin was almost square.

The most significant change during Anne's reign was the Act of Union, effective from 1 May 1707, which united England and Scotland as one kingdom – Great Britain. This was personally encouraged by Anne who believed that the full economic and political union was the best development for both countries.

Anne's reign is often associated with the growth in tea and coffee houses, which themselves became the centres for developing businesses and commerce (the London Stock Exchange grew out of a coffee house). Trade grew considerably during this period, especially with the establishment of the South Sea Company in 1711, trading with South America, and the increased trade coming from India and the East. The new kingdom of Great Britain began to prosper as never before and the seeds of the British Empire were sprouting.

[O33;W2] **GEORGE (I)**
Ruled: 1 August 1714–11 June 1727. Crowned: Westminster Abbey, 20 October 1714.
Full name and titles: George Louis, king of Great Britain and Ireland, duke and elector of Hanover (from 1698).
Born: Osnabrück, Hanover, 28 May (7 June NS) 1660. Died: Osnabrück, Hanover, 11 June 1727, aged 67. Buried: Leinschloss Church, Hanover.
Married: 21 November 1682, at Celle Castle, Germany, Sophia Dorothea (1666–1726), dau. George William, duke of Brunswick-Lüneberg-Celle; marriage anulled 28 December 1694: 2 children. George also had at least three illegitimate children by Ehrengard Melusine von Schulenburg (1667–1743), who may subsequently have married George.
The Act of Settlement passed in 1701 formalised the succession should neither WILLIAM III and MARY II or ANNE have any surviving children. It was imperative that the line passed to a Protestant heir, and the act excluded all Catholics, which was why JAMES (the Old Pretender), a legitimate son of JAMES II was not allowed to rule. At the time the act was concluded, the nearest living Protestant heir was Sophia, the seventy-year-old daughter of Frederick, king of Bohemia and Elector Palatine of the Rhine. Her mother, Elizabeth, was the eldest daughter of JAMES I (at that time still JAMES VI of Scotland). Sophia died six weeks before Queen Anne in the summer of 1714 and the succession passed to her eldest son, George, who had succeeded his father, Ernst August, as duke and elector of Hanover on 23 January 1698. When George came to the British throne he was fifty-four, older than any previous English heir, though ROBERT II and DONALD III of Scotland had been older. Prior to 1701 there had been little thought that he would become king of England, and even during the last years of

52. Great Britain (1) – The Hanoverians

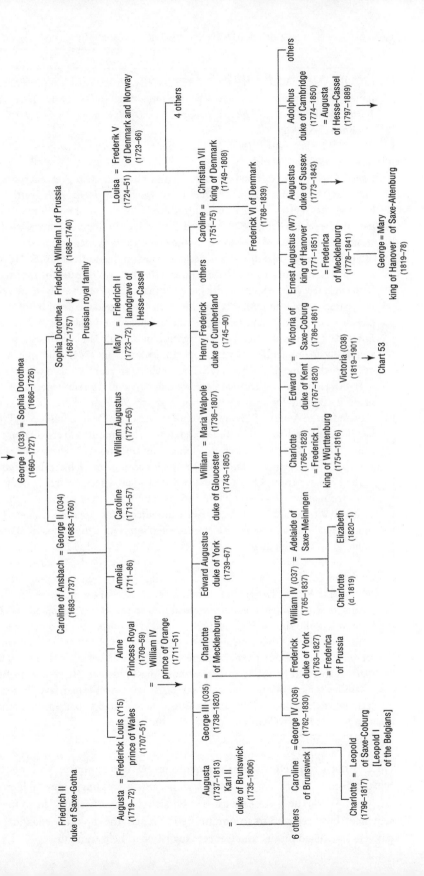

[FC89] **JAMES (VIII)** *THE OLD PRETENDER.* Proclaimed king in France as James III of England and James VIII of Scotland on 16 September 1701.

Born: *St James's Palace, London, 10 June 1688.* **Died**: *Rome, 1 January 1766, aged 78.* **Buried**: *St Peter's Basilica, Vatican.*

Married: *1 September 1719, at Montefiascone, Italy, Maria (1702–35) dau. Prince James Sobieski of Poland.*

James Francis Edward Stuart, known commonly as the Old Pretender, was the only surviving legitimate son of James II and Mary of Modena. At his birth many believed that he was a changeling, introduced into the royal bed in a warming-pan. In the rebellion of 1688 he preceded his father in flight to France, where he was raised. He received the support of the French king as successor to the thrones of England and Scotland, and was declared king on the death of James. He made an abortive attempt to land in Scotland in 1708, but was defeated by the English. In the next few years he served with great courage in the French army in the War of the Spanish Succession. All this time he yearned to regain the English throne. His cousin ANNE urged him to renounce his Catholicism and embrace the Church of England. He would then be the rightful heir. But James refused, sticking steadfastly to his faith. His next opportunity came in 1714, following Anne's death. By this time there were increasing Jacobite sympathies linked with concern over the Hanoverian succession (see GEORGE I). James's remoteness in France made it difficult for him to mobilise support. When rebellion broke out in Scotland on 26 August 1715, under John Erskine, earl of Mar, Louis XIV of France had just died, and James was indisposed. It took him months to cross France and gain a ship to Scotland, landing at Peterhead on December 22. The Jacobites were able to capture Perth, and James VIII held his court at Scone, but Edinburgh and Stirling resisted them. Over the next two weeks James's supporters at last got to know the man who had not set foot in Scotland for twenty-seven years. Although he had the regal bearing of the Stewart monarchy, and appeared balanced and sincere, he did not rouse them to Jacobite fervour. Quite the opposite. He was a rather gloomy individual resigned to failure from years of ill luck. His support, which at most had not exceeded 12,000, rapidly dwindled. Six weeks after his arrival in Scotland, James departed, slipping quietly out of the country and returning to France. He remained a refugee in Europe for the rest of his life, finally settling in Rome where the pope awarded him an income and demanded that he be known as the king of England. Only one other opportunity presented itself – in 1718 when Philip V of Spain agreed to support James. Another Spanish Armada set sail but, like the other two, it suffered in the bad weather and only a small force made it through to the Hebrides, without the Pretender. He retired to Rome where he took a bride, though it was far from a happy marriage. When the Jacobites rose again in 1745, James was too old and tired to bother and it was his son, Bonnie Prince Charlie who answered the call.

Queen Anne's reign efforts were made for James Stuart to convert to Protestantism, but the likelihood of George's succession became increasingly inevitable in the last few years. Whilst he had never learned English, he rapidly struggled to master key sentences, but preferred to communicate in French, the diplomatic language of the day. He also relied on his son, George Augustus, to help translate.

[FC90] **CHARLES [III]** *"BONNIE PRINCE CHARLIE"* or *"THE YOUNG PRETENDER"*. Proclaimed prince regent, 12 August 1745; defeated Culloden 16 April 1746. Styled himself Charles III, 1 January 1766–31 January 1788.
Born: *Rome, 31 December 1720.* **Died:** *Rome, 31 January 1788, aged 68.* **Buried:** *St Peter's, Rome.*
Married: *17 April 1772, at Marefischi, Ancona, Italy, Louise (1752–1824) dau. Gustavus Adolphus, Prince of Stolberg-Gedern (separated 1780): no children.*
Charles was the eldest son of James (*see* JAMES VIII) and regarded himself as the rightful claimant to the throne of Scotland (and to a lesser degree England). Unlike his father he was not a staunch Catholic, but supported the Jacobite cause. Also, unlike his lugubrious father, he had a good sense of humour and was a dashing, sporting individual. He was involved in the siege of Gaeta in 1734 and served well at Dettingen in 1743 in battle against GEORGE II. He made himself available to Louis XV of France who sought to use the Jacobite resistance in an invasion of England during the War of the Austrian Succession. Louis's expedition was prevented by bad weather and, in the end, Charles went it alone, losing one ship en route, and arriving in Eriskay in the Hebrides on 23 July 1745 with just seven companions. His resolve, passion and optimism soon fostered support amongst the Highlanders and he was declared prince regent on 12 August. A week later he raised his father's standard at Glenfinnan. His army grew. He entered Edinburgh without opposition and established himself at Holyrood. An army sent against him under the command of Sir John Cope was rapidly despatched. After a brief pause Charles marched south, reaching as far as Derby on 4 December, without opposition. At this point it seemed that England was his for the taking. George II was preparing to flee to France. However, although there was no resistance, Charles did not find any support amongst the English and it was considered prudent to return to Edinburgh. Thereafter the army became dispirited. The duke of Cumberland followed in pursuit, regaining ground and establishing a base at Inverness in February. By now Charles's lack of ability as a leader was showing, as his army became weakened and ill. The showdown between the two forces happened at Culloden on 16 April 1746. The Jacobites were soundly defeated by Cumberland. This was the last battle fought on British soil. Charles escaped. Aided by Flora MacDonald, and disguised as a spinning-maid, Charles remained a fugitive throughout the Highlands for five months, during which period Cumberland took revenge on any Jacobite nests remaining in Scotland. Realising his cause was lost Charles left Scotland in 18 September 1746 never to return. While in Scotland he had met the twenty-five year old Clementina Walkinshaw, who became his mistress and followed him to Europe. They had a daughter, Charlotte, born in 1753, who became duchess of Albany. Charles lost his verve and spirit and sank into drunkenness. He lost Clementine because of his cruelty, and had a short, unhappy and unfruitful marriage with Princess Louise of Stolberg-Gedern. His daughter, who was later legitimised, was his only companion in his final, sad years. He long regretted he had not died at Culloden with his supporters.

Before his elevation to king of England, George had already led an eventful life. He was the eldest child with five brothers and a sister. He outlived them all except his youngest brother Ernst. He had been a handsome youth, and still retained something of a cherubic if fat face, though his seeming inability to smile made him appear surly. He was not tall, but was fit and athletic, though he later became rather stout. He was well educated but delighted most in riding, hunting and military exercise. He first saw military service in 1675, and was involved in the Dutch and Turkish wars, distinguishing himself at Neerwinden in 1693. He developed a good relationship with John Churchill, the future duke of Marlborough, during the War of the Spanish Succession and commanded the Imperial Army on the Upper Rhine from 1707 to 1709. He was elevated to the College of Electors of the Empire in 1708 and became arch-treasurer of the Empire in 1710. He was resourceful and much respected, but was also highly ambitious, vindictive and used to having his own way. He had already demonstrated this by his treatment of his wife, which had become something of a scandal in Europe. He had married the beautiful sixteen-year-old Sophia Dorothea of Celle in 1682. The marriage was at first happy and they had two children: George Augustus and Sophia Dorothea. Sophia soon tired of her boorish husband, however, who seemed to have little respect for women, and she began an affair with Philip von Königsmark, a Swedish colonel of dragoons. When George discovered this in July 1694 he was furious. Sophia was imprisoned in the Castle of Ahlden for the rest of her life, forbidden to remarry and denied access to her children. Divorce proceedings were concluded in December 1694. Königsmark disappeared and it was widely believed that George had ordered his death. His body was supposed to have been discovered years later buried under the floorboards at the elector's palace. However, Königsmark had earlier had an affair with Clara, the Countess von Platten, and it was believed that she may have lured the Colonel to his death. This becomes even more sordid when we learn that Clara had also been the mistress of George's father, Ernst, and had borne him at least four children, one of whom, Sophia Charlotte, was rumoured to be George's mistress, even though she was his half-sister. It is more likely that the two simply enjoyed each other's company. Sophia Charlotte was not an attractive lady; in fact she grew to be excessively corpulent, so that when she and the king were seen together they were nick-named the Elephant and Castle. She became a naturalised British subject and was raised to the peerage as baroness of Brentford and countess of Darlington in 1722. George's one public mistress was Ehrengard Melusine von Schulenburg, an extremely thin lady whom the Germans called "the scarecrow" and the British dubbed "the Maypole". There is a strong belief that George may have subsequently married Melusine in secret, especially as in later years she was created Princess von Eberstein by the Emperor Charles VI who would not have done so had she not had some royal status. Robert Walpole also regarded her "as much queen of England as anyone ever was." She was generally known by the title duchess of Kendal which she was given in March 1719. George had already had two children by her before he divorced his wife, which only emphasises his hypocritical attitude when he discovered her affair. England's Queen Anne had taken a dislike to George when he visited her as far back as 1680 pursuing a possible marriage alliance, and from his subsequent sexual adventures one can only imagine what the outcome might have been for Anne and England had they married.

The English and Scots did not warm to George either when he paraded through London in September 1714. He had already taken nearly eight weeks to come to Britain, revelling in his new found glory in a series of parties across Europe. He was jeered by Londoners, who never quite took him seriously. By this time the power of the king was waning against the growing power of Parliament and, while the authority of the king retained a certain mystical aura, this was not what it had been before the Civil War and the English were already starting to regard the monarch as a figurehead. While they had taken Mary and Anne to their hearts, they did not like these foreigners who kept turning up to claim the throne – first William of Orange and then George of Hanover. This seriously damaged the acceptability of the monarchy in the eyes of the public. The Scots liked this "wee German laddie" even less. The Jacobite supporters of James II and his son James Edward Stuart grew in strength and in September 1715 the first Jacobite rebellion erupted at Braemar. It could have been far more serious than it was if the Old Pretender had not turned out to be such a discouraging pessimist. The rebellion fizzled out, but George still exacted a vicious penalty upon those who had taken part.

Despite what his amorous adventures might suggest (in fact they probably support it), George was shy and tended to keep out of the limelight when he could. He was not one for intellectual pursuits, though he did have a love for music and it was through George that the composer George Frederic Handel came to England. His *Water Music* was composed for a royal water-party on 22 August 1715, and George's love of Handel's work led to the foundation of the first Royal Academy of Music in 1720. George's shyness and inability to communicate well in English made him all the more blunt and short-tempered. He had been used to getting his own way in Hanover and could not adapt to the English parliamentary system where he needed to seek approval for his actions, especially when this affected his foreign policy and his wish to protect Hanover's interests. Because of the language problems, especially after the rift with his son in 1717 which meant the younger George no longer attended cabinet meetings to help translate, George needed another minister to represent him. This was the start of the post of Prime Minister, but it also reduced George's direct sphere of control. George had previously allied himself with Peter the Great of Russia and was keen to ensure that he benefitted from Peter's war with Sweden. To do so he needed to have control over his foreign policy and he could not do this with the Whig government that had come to power under Robert Walpole in 1715 after the failure of the Jacobite rebellion. In 1716 the Septennial Act had been passed, which postponed the opportunity of the Tories to return to power for four years. George distrusted the strong-minded and exceedingly able Walpole who would not sanction the funds George needed for his new campaign against Russia. George, however, rapidly appreciated that he could influence who led the Whigs. George set one faction against another within the party and succeeded in aiding the weak and malleable earl of Sunderland and Lord Stanhope to oust Walpole in 1717. George was now able to dictate his terms to Stanhope and gain an alliance with Holland and France against Russia. However in opposing Walpole he made a dangerous enemy. Walpole allied himself with George's son, George Augustus (later GEORGE II), who served as regent on his father's many forays back to Hanover. George despised his father because of his treatment of his mother, and would have been only too happy to depose him. He established a clique, known as the Leicester House Set, with the sole intention of frustrating the king's plans, and Walpole became part of the group. Walpole also became friends with Prince George's wife, Caroline, princess of Wales, an intelligent and influential lady who gave Walpole her stolid support. King George soon realised that he could not prevail against such opposition and was forced to be reconciled with Walpole. This was precipitated by the economic distaster known as the South Sea Bubble. The South Sea Company had been established in 1711, trading with the Spanish colonies in South America in anticipation of benefits that would arise from success in the War of the Spanish Succession. King George was made governor of the company in 1718 and it became fashionable to invest, especially once the Company took over the management of the National Debt in 1720. Senior officials in the company began to issue false stock to meet the demand and in September 1720 this bubble burst. Thousands of speculators found that their investment was worthless, including most of the country's leading nobility. When it was found that cabinet ministers and court officials had been involved in the dirty dealings it became a national scandal, threatening the Hanoverian dynasty. George was forced to rely on Walpole's skill in resolving the affair and restoring order. From then on Walpole was in supreme power and dominated English affairs. George's relationship with his politicians and the general state of English religious and cultural society at this time was lampooned by Jonathan Swift in *Gulliver's Travels* (1726).

Because of the supremacy of Parliament, George removed himself further from public affairs. It made the king less of a target, although the Jacobites still wished to restore the Stuart Pretender. In 1722 a plot was uncovered to do just that, known as the Atterbury Plot after one of its leading conspirators Francis Atterbury, bishop of Rochester. Where once he would have been executed, Atterbury was imprisoned and then banished, and all his possessions confiscated. Generally, though, plots against the king diminished because Walpole had him under control. George's excesses were by and large eradicated, although the relationship with Spain remained poor, resulting in a dispute over Gibraltar and a fruitless expedition against Spain's American colonies.

George liked to spend the summer and autumn in Hanover, and it was while travelling there in June 1727 that he died of a cerebral haemorrhage. His son and the British government were happy to leave him there and he was buried in the Leinschloss Church at Hanover, the first ruling British monarch to be buried abroad since RICHARD I. Although his brusqueness and pomposity caused him to be generally disliked, George had a considerable influence on the British parliamentary system and brought in (by default not design) the constitutional government that has dominated British politics ever since.

[O34;W3] GEORGE II

Ruled 28 May (11 June NS) 1727–25 October 1760. Crowned: Westminster Abbey, 11 October 1727.

Full name and titles: George Augustus, king of Great Britain and Ireland, duke and elector of Hanover, duke and marquess of Cambridge (from 1706), earl of Milford Haven (from 1706), duke of Cornwall and Rothesay (from 1714), prince of Wales and earl of Chester (from 1714).

Born: Schloss Herrenhausen, Hanover, 30 October (9 November NS) 1683. **Died**: Kensington Palace, London, 25 October 1760, aged 76. **Buried**: Westminster Abbey. **Married**: 22 August (2 September NS) 1705, at Schloss Herrenhausen, Hanover, Wilhelmina Charlotte Caroline (1683–1737) dau. of John Frederick, margrave of Brandenburg-Ansbach: 9 children (1 stillborn). George probably had one illegitimate child.

George was the only son of GEORGE I. He had been born in Hanover before the Act of Settlement had nominated the Hanoverian line of succession, but after this was passed in 1701, when George was seventeen, the youth was tutored in both the English language and the English way of life. He became a naturalised British citizen in 1705 and received a flock of British titles. There was a considerable rift between George and his father after the imprisonment of his mother in 1694, and the elder George refused to grant his son any local responsibilities. Even though he proved his valour at the battle of Oudenarde in 1708 in the War of the Spanish Succession, his father failed to recognize his abilities. This drove George more towards his future British subjects, and in later years he would state that he regarded himself as more British than German, even if he said it in a strong German accent.

George had a passion for the strict rules of etiquette and probity which at times became obsessive and made him irritating at official functions, but at least it meant he strove to get things right, which made him a more acceptable monarch to the British than his father — at least at the outset.

In 1705, when twenty-one, George married Caroline of Ansbach, who was just seven months his elder. It was a good match. Caroline more than matched George in intelligence and canniness, and also softened his German preciseness. She had an earthy charm and was attractive in a beguiling way rather than in her looks. Both partners recognized the need to flirt: George simply because of his sexual desires; Caroline as a way of influencing men of power. It was Caroline who became the power behind the throne, firstly during the reign of her father-in-law when, in the absence of a Queen, she took on the role of first lady as princess of Wales; and certainly when George inherited the crown.

When George's father became king, George and Caroline accompanied him to England and took up residence in London. George aided his father in understanding English, often translating at meetings of the cabinet or the Privy Council, and serving as regent during his father's regular summer returns to Hanover. However at the close of 1717 an argument erupted between George and his father over a misunderstanding that happened during the christening of the prince's latest son. The young George did not like the choice of the duke of Newcastle as godfather, and the duke misunderstood George's comments at the font as a threat. When the prince refused to apologise, the king first threatened to have the son imprisoned and then banished him from St James's Palace. George and Caroline set up home at Leicester House near St Martin-in-the-Fields and here established what became almost a rival court, often giving audience to the king's political enemies, most especially Robert Walpole. It was at Leicester House that Caroline used her wiles and influence to win over the men of authority whom she preferred. The consequences of this rift were significant. It meant that the king no longer felt comfortable at the cabinet meetings without his son and therefore handed over the management of them to his preferred minister, which was how the formal role of the Prime Minister emerged. It also meant that George and Caroline were able to have a trial run at their own cabinet meetings which were a solid grounding for the real thing.

What does seem surprising is that George, given the poor relationship with his father, should have been so hostile towards his own son, Frederick Louis. By all accounts he regarded Frederick as an imbecile, almost from birth, although Frederick was no such thing. George and Caroline left Frederick in Hanover when they came to England, and he was not allowed into England until 1728, when they did their best to ignore him. It rather irritated them both when they discovered that the young man, who they reluctantly created prince of Wales in 1729, became something of a favourite among London society. With little parental control Frederick became a dandy and a man-about-town, often going on the razzle and ending up drunk. He frequently gambled and built up huge debts that his father refused to acknowledge, let alone pay. Frederick had all the qualities of being a cultured man if his father had paid him any attention: he had a love of sport, art and the theatre. But his father liked none of those things and regarded his son as a wastrel. When Frederick died of a ruptured aneurysm in March 1751, aged 44, his father rather callously remarked that he was glad. It is quite likely that George had hoped Frederick might have died younger and that his heir would have been his younger and favourite son, William Augustus, duke of Cumberland, who shared his father's Germanic ruthlessness. However Frederick lived long enough to marry and father nine legitimate children, amongst them the future GEORGE III. Frederick also lived long enough to become a major thorn in George's side, always opposing his father's plans and siding with the opposition in government. Had he become king, he would have settled down and been moderate and compassionate, but his father brought out the worst in him. It was a real-life example of "like father, like son".

When George became king in 1727, England was under the strong political control of Robert Walpole. George had little need to interfere, but that did not stop him wanting to give the impression of being in charge. He sought to change his ministers much like his father, but his preferred minister, Sir Spencer Compton, admitted he was not up to forming an administration. George was thus forced to continue with Sir Robert Walpole, who accommodated George by voting him a larger share of the Civil List.

Like his father, George had a passion for war and it was all that Walpole could do to stop George involving himself in a number of hostilities throughout Europe, particularly the War of the Polish Succession. Matters began to change after the death of Caroline in 1737. George genuinely loved his wife and sorely missed her. He never remarried, but he now lived more openly with his mistress, Amalia von Walmoden. With Caroline's influence and support gone, Walpole's star began to wane. George's desire for war was granted when hostilities broke out with Spain in September 1739 and then with France in 1742 in the War of the Austrian Succession. Even though nearing sixty, George took the opportunity to lead an army into the field at Dettingen on 16 June 1743. This was the last occasion that a British sovereign would command an army in battle. He served valiantly, fighting beside his men, and it gave his popularity a boost.

Interestingly also serving in the battle of Dettingen, on the side of the French, was

Charles Edward Stuart, the Young Pretender (*see page 671*). Charles's desire to win back the Scottish and English thrones caused him to invade Scotland in 1745 and on a wave of popularity brought an army as far south as Derby. It was as a consequence of the Jacobite rebellion that the first recorded singing of the National Anthem occurred at Drury Lane on 28 September 1745, in a patriotic reaction to the rebels. George sent his second son, William, against Charles. William, duke of Cumberland, defeated the Scots at Culloden in April 1746 and followed this with a vicious culling of the Jacobites, which earned him the name of "Butcher Cumberland". This did not endear the duke or the king to the Scots. William was not, in fact, an especially good commander. At the battle of Fontenoy in France, the previous May, Cumberland had suffered a humiliating defeat and heavy losses. He was defeated again by the French at Laffeldt in 1747 and in 1757, when Britain became unnecessarily involved in the Seven Years' War, Cumberland was forced to surrender the Hanoverian army at Klosterseven. George was so humiliated by this that he stripped his son of his military commands.

Walpole had stepped down as prime minister in 1742 and George's attempts to appoint a capable one proved uneven over the next few years. Control passed mostly to Henry Pelham, who sanctioned the funds for George's wars but who was not an especially gifted administrator. In the end George was forced to consider William Pitt (the elder), who had been a supporter of his son Frederick and had formed a clique known as the "Patriot Boys", a kind of "brat pack" of the 1740s.

The war against the French had other consequences. In India, the daring adventures of Robert Clive at Madras (in 1746) and Arcot (in 1751) stirred the blood, and his subsequent achievements at Calcutta, Chandernagore and Plassey in 1756/7, saw the defeat of the French and the emergence of the British control of India. Soon afterwards, in Canada, General James Wolfe (who had served at Dettingen and Culloden) succeeded in capturing Quebec in September 1759 and fulfilling Pitt's plan to expel the French from Canada. There were further territorial gains in the West Indies and Africa. Thus as George's reign drew to a close, the British Empire was expanding on both sides of the globe. Had George lived another eight years he would have seen Australia added to the map. The 1750s thus saw an increase in national pride and a restoration, to some degree, of George II in the national affection although, as with his father, the British found it difficult to take any Hanoverian to their hearts.

George's reign must ultimately be seen as a success, though a clouded one at that, but certainly better than the results of either the Old Stewart Pretender or Bonnie Prince Charlie gaining the throne. George's successes outweighed his failures, thanks mostly to his choice of prime ministers, and Britain became prosperous and an increasing world power. George himself died in a rather undignified fashion – he had a heart attack while sitting on the lavatory.

[O35;W4] GEORGE III, *"FARMER GEORGE"*
Ruled 25 October 1760–29 January 1820 (declared unfit to rule 5 February 1811).
Crowned: Westminster Abbey, 22 September 1761.
Full name and titles: George William Frederick, king of Great Britain and Ireland (and nominally of France, a title relinquished in 1801), duke and elector of Hanover (king from 1814), duke of Cornwall and Rothesay, duke of Edinburgh, marquess of Ely,

earl of Eltham, viscount of Launceston, baron of Snowdon, prince of Wales and earl of
Chester (from 1751).
Born: *Norfolk House, London, 24 May (4 June NS) 1738.* **Died**: *Windsor Castle, 29*
January 1820, aged 81. **Buried**: *Windsor Castle.*
Married: *8 September 1761, at St James's Palace, Sophia Charlotte (1744–1818), dau.*
Charles, duke of Mecklenburg-Strelitz: 15 children. It is alleged that George had
previously married Hannah Lightfoot in secret on 17 April 1759, but this remains to be
proven.

George was the grandson of GEORGE II and the son of Frederick Louis, the Prince
of Wales, whom his grandfather despised so much. It seems that something of
both passed on to the new king. He had a strain of obstinacy, like his grandfather,
but in other matters he was flexible and conciliatory. He was the first of the
Hanoverian kings to be born and raised in England and to speak English without
a strong German accent, which helped the British warm to him. He had a binding
sympathy with the English and never visited Hanover, even though he remained
their ruler (and their king from 1814). He was good-hearted with a deep religious
conviction, lacking, at least in his youth, the vicious streak that had been
prominent in the first two Hanoverian kings. What George also lacked, however,
was sound judgement, a fault inherited from his father. He was too trusting and
was dominated by his mother. This contributed to some of the bad decisions that
darkened his reign.

George was well educated and did not have the wayward streak of his father. The
only skeleton in his youthful cupboard was his relationship with Hannah Lightfoot,
the daughter of a shoemaker from Wapping. George allegedly married Hannah in
secret in 1757 (or 1759, records vary) and she was supposed to have borne him
three children. Although documentation exists which purportedly proves the
marriage, it has been kept in the Royal Archives since 1866 and its authenticity
has not been proven. The likelihood of three children is remote. Although Hannah
may have been a momentary infatuation, George soon fell in love with Lady Sarah
Lennox, a daughter of the duke of Richmond and great-granddaughter of CHARLES
II by his mistress, the duchess of Portsmouth. George was advised that he should
not marry a British subject but should look to the eligible German princesses. The
final choice was the charming seventeen-year old Charlotte of Mecklenburg. The
coronation was delayed until after their wedding on 8 September 1761, so that a
joint coronation could be held two weeks later.

George was twenty-two when he was proclaimed king. He was keen to do what
was right and one of his first actions was to put out a proclamation against
immorality. He also wanted to get control back over the Government which had
gradually leeched power from the monarch over the last sixty years. George did not
like Pitt or the Whig philosophy. His preferred premier was John Stuart, earl of
Bute, who had been a close friend of his mother's and had assisted in his education.
Bute was a Whig, but being of Scottish descent, had Jacobite sympathies and was a
staunch royalist. He was not a good administrator so that while George got his way,
the country turned against Bute and he resigned in 1763. Bute remained in the
king's confidence for two more years, but in the meantime the king suffered a long
series of tedious prime ministers until he eventually found his man in Frederick,
Lord North, who became premier in 1770.

From a contemporary portrait

The first ten years of George's reign were thus difficult ones for him in getting to grips with the reins of government. Issues which in hindsight seem positive, such as securing peace with France and Spain in 1763, at the time were seen in a darker light. Bute was accused of receiving bribes from France, and the king was accused of selling out to the enemy. The Stamp Act introduced in 1765 met with considerable opposition and had to be repealed the following year. Throughout this period the king was subjected to constant abuse and libel from the renegade politician John Wilkes who published material which in previous generations would have led to his execution for treason. The strain on the king told and in early 1765 he suffered a physical collapse which may have been a precursor of his later mental affliction. Though not as severe as the bout of 1788 or the final decline of 1810, it was sufficient for Parliament to rush through a Regency Act. It was further fodder to George's opponents to denigrate him, and so much stigma has attached to him as king that it becomes difficult to see the real man and his achievements.

Lord North has likewise been criticised and is regarded by some as the worst of all prime ministers. To his premiership belongs the American War of Independence. The American revolution had its roots before North's administration. The colonies had been free of taxation, but also had no parliamentary representation. When a tax was re-imposed on molasses in 1764 and the stamp duty on legal documents and newspapers in 1765 there was an outcry. Although both of these measures were subsequently repealed, a new tax on tea, introduced in 1773, sparked off more antagonism and led to the Boston Tea Party in December 1773, when tea held in Boston Harbour was thrown overboard. The British closed the port at Boston and sent in troops, with the inevitable consequence that hostilities broke out on 19 April 1775 with battles at Lexington and Concord. The US Congress issued its Declaration of Independence on 4 July 1776 and thereafter George III became the figurehead for American hostility. George was intent upon bringing America to its knees and approved any measure that would cause the Americans the utmost distress, though the allegation that he would make them all slaves is an exaggeration. The worst defeat for Britain came at Saratoga on 17 October 1777, when

General John Burgoyne was forced to surrender his entire army. This action turned the balance of the war, as France now recognized the independence of the colonies and sent support. The last major battle was at Yorktown where George Washington, with the aid of the French, defeated Lord Cornwallis, who surrendered on 19 October 1781. The Treaty of Paris was signed on 3 September 1783. Whereas peace might have been concluded earlier and the colonies saved, George insisted on fighting to the bitter end and took the consequences. George's reputation suffered irreparably while Lord North resigned. It was some years before George again found a minister with whom he could work, William Pitt the Younger.

George clashed with Pitt over Catholic Emancipation. Such measures had been the downfall of past kings, especially JAMES II, and even the merest hint of equality had resulted in the Gordon Riots of June 1780 when the MP, Lord George Gordon, incited disorder throughout London, leading to widespread destruction of property and about three hundred deaths. The king remained remarkably calm during the riots and through his own resoluteness restored order. The memory of the riots burned bright for many years so that when Pitt tried to issue a Catholic Emancipation Act in 1801, George violently opposed it and Pitt resigned. Pitt's measure had been his way of controlling the Irish rebellion which erupted in 1798, encouraged by the success of the French Revolution. There had been unrest generally throughout Britain since 1795 and the king's popularity declined. Pitt introduced several repressive measures, including suspending *habeus corpus*, and sought to negotiate with France in 1797, which angered George. Despite efforts by later ministers George refused to entertain any consideration of emancipation for Catholics. For an exceedingly pious and generally good-natured man, this obstinacy verged on bigotry. Pitt was, however, able to force through the Act of Union between Great Britain and Ireland which came into force on 1 January 1801. On the same day George relinquished the anachronistic title of king of France, which all English kings had maintained since 1340.

A measure of the times is reflected in the two assassination attempts upon George by the public. Margaret Nicholson, a house-maid, threatened him with a dessert-knife on 2 August 1786, while James Hadfield fired a shot at the king at Drury Lane on 15 May 1800. Both would-be assassins were pronounced insane. George's reign was not short of its scandals. There was the trial of Warren Hastings for corruption and cruelty in the Indian administration, which ran from 1788 to 1795. There was the private and illegal first marriage of his son (the future GEORGE IV) to a commoner in 1785, followed by the immoral conduct of his legal daughter-in-law, Caroline of Brunswick, the wife he had forced upon his son, who deserted her in 1796. A committee of enquiry was set up in 1806 to undertake the "delicate investigation", as it was called, into Caroline's affairs. Caroline was eventually sent on a grand tour of Europe. There was the duel between the war secretary, viscount Castelreagh, and the foreign secretary, George Canning, in September 1809, in which Canning was wounded. Finally there was the assassination of the prime minister, Spencer Perceval, in May 1812, by John Bellingham. To set against this were the great victories of Horatio Nelson in the Napoleonic Wars, especially at Copenhagen in April 1801 and Trafalgar in October 1805, and the victories of Wellington in the Peninsular War, leading to the final defeat of Napoleon at Waterloo in June 1815. These victories abroad helped raise the morale of a country

[FC91] **HENRY [IX]** The last of the royal Stewarts, brother of Bonnie Prince Charlie [*see page 671*]. He was born in Rome on 6 March 1725. He never seriously pursued his title, although things may have been different had Charles succeeded in the rebellion of 1745. The Jacobites styled him the duke of York. After Charles's defeat, Henry became a cardinal in 1747 and, in 1761, bishop of Frascati. He received pensions from the Vatican and from Spain as well as income from two French abbeys. Although he styled himself Henry IX after his brother's death on 31 January 1788, it was only an honorific. He lost his fortune during the French Revolution, but was looked on kindly by GEORGE III who granted him a pension of £4000 in 1800. He died at Frascati on 13 July 1807, aged 82, and was buried in St Peter's Basilica in the Vatican.

where the nobility and middle classes were clearly benefitting from the nation's commercial prosperity, but where the ordinary man and woman were discovering how repressed and neglected they were. Most of the angst, however, was aimed at the Government and not directly at George who, despite his obstinacy and occasional lapse of judgement, remained popular amongst his subjects. In fact he was often viewed, especially by the middle classes, as their champion against the Government. He gave the royal assent to William Wilberforce's act to abolish the slave trade, which became law in 1807 (though it was another twenty-six years before slaves in the British colonies were granted their freedom).

George was a man of wide interests and intellect. He became fascinated in agriculture and botany, giving some of the land at Windsor over to farming, hence his nickname of "Farmer George". It was an appropriate epithet since the name George means "farmer" or "landworker", so George genuinely lived up (or down!) to his name. He wrote pamphlets on agriculture under the pseudonym of Ralph Robinson. He became more tolerant in his later years about the moral state of the nation, especially in the theatre and literature, just as the most sensational literature emerged. The gothic horror novel *The Castle of Otranto* (1764) by Horace Walpole and the salacious *The Monk* (1795) by M.G. Lewis, could never have been published in earlier times. Literature flourished during George's reign – this was the era of William Wordsworth, Samuel Taylor Coleridge, Percy Shelley and Lord Byron. There were many scientific advances during this period, which was the dawn of the age of invention. The best remembered were the perfection of the steam engine by James Watt in 1769 and the use of the steam engine by Richard Arkwright to perfect his spinning machine in 1790. These inventions laid the foundations of the Industrial Revolution but also led to such outbursts as the Luddite riots of 1811, a culmination of considerable unrest amongst textile workers to the new machines which would rob them of their livelihood, but which also ushered in a new class of industralists.

The last ten years of George's reign, however, were spent in sad decline. His recurrent bouts of "madness" became more severe. In November 1788 he suffered a particularly violent bout where he attacked the prince of Wales and began talking incessantly. He was forcibly restrained and removed to Kew where he underwent humiliating treatment by ignorant and not altogether well-meaning doctors. Remarkably he had recovered by April 1789, but there were further bouts in

1801 and 1804 and the final decline in November 1810, precipitated by the death of his youngest daughter Amelia. By then the king was also blind. His son was made "Prince Regent" with powers of sovereignty from 5 February 1811. The old king was confined to Windsor Castle, where he was more or less neglected, his hair and beard growing long and white. Just what lucid moments he had during these years is not known. Recent assessments have judged that George was not mad in the psychological sense but suffered from porphyria, a blood disease which upsets the body's chemical balance and can produce symptoms akin to madness. It has been called "the royal malady" and may have affected George's predecessors as far back as Charles VI of France. Charles's daughter, Katherine, married HENRY V and through her it passed on to HENRY VI. There are even suggestions that it may have afflicted the Saxon kings.

The two "facts" that most people remember about King George was that he was mad and that he ruled longer than any other monarch besides Victoria. In fact neither are true, as George's reign effectively ended when his son was made regent. What fewer people recall was that he had a genuine desire to do the best for his country during an especially violent period. The fact that he remained king, while the French monarchy was abolished, is some testament to how he was regarded and that he had learned how the manipulate the system of government.

[O36;W5] GEORGE IV

Ruled 29 January 1820–26 June 1830, with restricted powers as Prince Regent from 5 February 1811. Crowned: Westminster Abbey, 19 July 1821.
Full name and titles: George Augustus Frederick, king of the United Kingdom of Great Britain and Ireland, king of Hanover, duke of Cornwall and Rothesay, earl of Carrick, Baron Renfrew and lord of the Isles (from birth), prince of Wales and earl of Chester (from 1762).
*Born: St James's Palace, 12 August 1762. **Died**: Windsor Castle, 26 June 1830, aged 67.*
Buried: Windsor Castle.
Married: (1) 15 December 1785, at Park Lane, Mayfair, London, Maria Anne Fitzherbert (1756–1837) dau. Walter Smythe of Brambridge: no children; marriage not recognized under British law; (2) 8 April 1795, at St James's Palace, London, Caroline Amelia Elizabeth (1768–1821) dau. of Charles II, duke of Brunswick: 1 daughter. George also had at least two illegitimate children that he acknowledged, and probably many more.

George IV was the eldest son of GEORGE III, but in looks and manner he was more like his grandfather, Frederick, prince of Wales. He was tall and handsome in his youth, though became fat in middle age, and above all he was a spoilt child and a libertine. He had no care at all for his duties as prince of Wales or later as king, enjoying only the privileges and the money that came with them. His lifestyle resulted in many debts, which he managed to get the king and Parliament to pay. He had many mistresses and probably had more illegitimate children than he ever acknowledged. He was generally a profligate and ill-mannered man. Yet, like most such rascals, he could turn on the charm and dignity when he needed to, and he knew how to live and celebrate in style. London society therefore adored him, and today there is an idealised romantic view of the prince. The "Regency", strictly the period between 1811 and 1820 when he served as Prince Regent during his father's final mental decline, has become a by-word today for dazzling society gatherings and exciting court intrigue. It was also the period of the Napoleonic Wars, and the height of fame for Richard Brinsley Sheridan, Beau Brummell and the great poets and essayists of the day – Lord Byron, Robert Southey, John Keats, Percy Shelley, William Wordsworth, Leigh Hunt and many others. The period holds much fascination and interest, and this has influenced our image of the Prince Regent. In simple terms, had Parliament not been there to run the country, it is almost certain that George IV, seeking to operate outside the rules, would have brought the country to ruin and would quite possibly have been assassinated or deposed.

Much of George's life story is a catalogue of his romantic affairs, at least one of which endangered his succession to the throne. All of the Hanoverian monarchs were highly sexed, but George IV was probably the most profligate. It is not entirely clear why this should have been so. Unlike the relationship between GEORGE II and his son, George IV was not despised from birth. Quite the opposite. George III doted on him, and was reluctant for him to grow up. He was certainly spoiled but had an excellent education and was a quick learner. Perhaps this precocity, mixed with his good looks, made him too assured and confident of himself with a total disregard for how others viewed him. He was only sixteen when he had his first affair with the actress Mary 'Perdita' Robinson whom he saw in Shakespeare's *The Winter's Tale* in 1779. They remained together for a short while before George fell in love with another, and found he had to pay Mary a princely sum to keep her quiet. He worked his way through at least a dozen other mistresses over the next seven years, of varying degrees of high and low birth, and all costing him or the king a small fortune, until he encountered a young widow, Maria Fitzherbert, who was six years his senior. She became the one true love of his life. She refused to be his mistress, however, and George, in a typical immature tantrum, threatened to stab himself if she did not return his love. She eventually agreed to marry him. George knew that this was not possible. Not only was she already a widow (twice over) and pretty much a commoner (the grand-daughter of a baronet), but worst of all she was a Roman Catholic. The Act of Settlement of 1701 barred any Catholic from inheriting the throne, and it would effectively have barred George's accession. Moreover the Royal Marriages Act, which George's father had introduced in 1772, made any marriage by members of the royal family aged under twenty-five void unless it had received the formal approval of the king and the Privy Council. George acquired no such approval, but went ahead with the marriage anyway in December 1785. Under English law, George's marriage to Maria was void. The pope, however, regarded it as valid. George continued to have many more affairs, the most torrid of which was with the countess of Jersey. George III made every effort to control his son's debaucheries, for the prince, who now drank and ate to excess, was also becoming violent. He had spent to excess in building his own home at Carlton House in London, and as part of the arrangement for helping finance the debt, the king and Parliament insisted that George marry a proper wife. The King selected his niece, Princess Caroline of Brunswick. He must have been blind to her reputation, for not only was she not that attractive, and took little heed for her own personal hygiene, she was already supposed to have had one affair during her youth and, like George, she had wild tantrums. When the two first met three days before their wedding in April 1795, George felt sick at the sight of her and asked for a brandy, and Caroline called him fat and unhandsome. The Prince was drunk throughout his wedding ceremony and spent most of the wedding night in a stupor by the fire, but he must have done his duty, for nine months later to the day the Princess gave birth to their one and only child, Charlotte Augusta. George and Caroline separated soon after the birth and George denied Caroline any involvement in the raising of her daughter. Caroline established an orphanage in Kent in August 1797, whilst George went back to his mistresses. Mrs Fitzherbert returned to live with George for a while after 1800, still regarding herself as his lawful wife.

With the outbreak of the Napoleonic War, George applied several times for military service, jealous of the commands held by his brothers, but he was always refused. This was realistic, because the heir to the throne would no longer be put at such risk, but it was also pragmatic, as George had no military training and the government were fearful of what damage he might cause. Frustrated, George became mischievous at home. A dispute arose in 1804 over the custody of his daughter with the result that Charlotte was handed over to George III. Annoyed at this, Prince George cast aspersions over the conduct of his estranged wife, alleging that one of the orphans in her care, William Austin, was her own son. This led to a "delicate investigation" by Parliament in 1806 which, though it cleared Caroline of the charge, revealed that her conduct was far from becoming.

In 1810, George III sank into his final decline and George was made Prince Regent, with certain restricted powers. Nevertheless from 1811 he acted as if he was the sovereign. His extravagance, even though curtailed by Parliament, was still lavish. During this period the Royal Pavilion at Brighton was completely rebuilt on the mock-Oriental style designed by John Nash. Under instruction from the Prince, Nash also redesigned Central London, which is why Regent's Park and Regent Street are so named. The streets of the City of London were lit by gas from 1814. Waterloo Bridge was opened in 1817 and Southwark Bridge in 1819. The Prince Regent continued to entertain lavishly, especially after the victory of Wellington in the Napoleonic Wars, when England played host to the emperor of Russia and the king of Prussia in June 1814.

The Regency period however was not all glitter. Soldiers returning from war were not fully recompensed and did not find gainful employment. There was considerable unrest which found little sympathy from the government, especially from Lord Liverpool and Lord Sidmouth, who had previously dealt harshly with the Luddites. A gathering at Spa Fields in North London in December 1816, when manufacturers sought to present their views to the Prince Regent, turned ugly and was dealt with severely. Sidmouth used this as an opportunity to undertake what became called the Green-Bag inquiry in February 1817 when a series of secret committees looked into a number of alleged cases of sedition. As a result of this *habeus corpus* was suspended. A gathering in St Peter's Field in Manchester in August 1819 alarmed the authorities because of its size – the military dispersed the meeting, causing over four hundred injuries and eleven deaths. This incident became known as Peterloo (after Waterloo) and led to even more repressive legislation outlawing public assemblies. The populace were not happy and within only a few weeks of the Prince Regent becoming king in January 1820, a plot was unearthed, known as the Cato Street Conspiracy, to assassinate the members of the Cabinet and overthrow the Government.

George had other things on his mind, however. He had been grief-stricken when his only daughter, Charlotte, who had married in May 1816, died due to complications after childbirth in November 1817. He now had no heir to the throne, and his wife, Caroline, who was now approaching fifty, was past child-bearing age. In fact George did everything to keep Caroline out of the country. She had gone on a grand tour of Europe after the end of the Napoleonic Wars and was by all accounts romantically involved with an Italian courtier, Bartolomeo Pergami. However, on George's accession to the throne Caroline was determined to return and take her place as queen. George offered her £50,000 a year to stay away, but she brushed this aside and returned to Britain in June 1820. George introduced a parliamentary bill, called the Bill of Pains and Penalties, which was an enquiry into Caroline's conduct. Since Caroline appeared in the House of Lords, the enquiry has come to be regarded as her trial, though she never spoke in her defence. The bill was dropped and Caroline exonerated with much public rejoicing. George still refused to admit her and went to great pains to exclude her from his coronation in July 1821. George had ensured no expense was spared over this event which he planned for over a year and it remains the most extravagant coronation ever held in England. To George's relief, but also his shame, Caroline died just three weeks later on 7 August 1821 of inflammation of the bowels. The public had always been very supportive of the queen and voiced strong opposition to the king. A few weeks later George went on a royal progress through the kingdom, visiting Ireland and, at the urging of Sir Walter Scott, Scotland (the first Hanoverian to do so). He put on all his charm and elegance and was remarkably well received. One might question how much the populace were celebrating the continuance of the monarchy as distinct from the individual. The institution of the monarchy suffered considerably under George IV, but survived sufficiently due to the fond memory of George III to enter a golden phase under VICTORIA.

George's reign as king lasted for just over ten years and it advanced the country but little. George had a succession of prime ministers, most of whom he tried to oppose, especially as regards their foreign policy. Both he and the duke of Wellington vigorously opposed any political reform and it was only with reluctance on their parts that, at last, in April 1829 the Catholic Emancipation Act became law, restoring to Catholics the right to public office. It did not meet with the riots accorded earlier attempts to do this. There were greater troubles besetting the nation than religion, and it required a much stronger government than George IV and his ministers to tackle them. George died on 26 June 1830 of respiratory problems, aged sixty-seven. For all his dandyism and extravagance he was at the end a sad and lonely man, who had damaged the stature of the monarchy and whose only lasting legacy is the Brighton Pavilion. He was succeeded by his brother, WILLIAM IV.

[O37;W6] WILLIAM IV "THE SAILOR KING"
Ruled 26 June 1830–20 June 1837. Crowned: Westminster Abbey, 8 September 1831.
Full name and titles: William Henry, king of the United Kingdom of Great Britain and Ireland; duke of Clarence and St Andrews and earl of Munster (from 1789).
Born: Buckingham Palace, 21 August 1765. Died: Windsor Castle, 20 June 1837, aged 71.

Married: 13 July 1818, at Kew Palace, Adelaide Louise Theresa Caroline Amelia (1792–1849), dau. George, duke of Saxe-Meiningen: 6 children (4 stillborn). William also had at least eleven illegitimate children, ten by Dorothea Bland (1761– 1816).

William was the third son of GEORGE III and had not expected to become king. It was the death of GEORGE IV's daughter Charlotte in 1817, followed by the death of George's brother, Frederick (the "Grand Old Duke of York" of the nursery rhyme), in 1827 that made William the heir presumptive. Until then he had led a life fairly distanced from the extravagant carousel of his brother. William entered the Navy in 1779 at the age of fourteen and served at the relief of Gibraltar. He received few concessions initially because of his status, but served first as an able seaman, rising to midshipman and then rising through the ranks. He served under Nelson during 1786/7 in the West Indies, and was given the command of his own frigate, the *Andromeda*, in 1788 and the next year was appointed the Rear Admiral of HMS *Valiant*. He was made duke of Clarence in 1789 and thereafter regularly attended the House of Lords. He was made Admiral of the Fleet in 1811 and delighted in the official duties that imposed.

Like his brothers, William was an inveterate womaniser. During a visit to Hanover in 1784 he was supposed to have seduced and even entered into a secret marriage with Caroline von Linsingen. The marriage was unlikely (though it seemed to be a tradition amongst the Hanoverians) but the seduction was very likely and she bore him a son called William, who drowned in 1807. A typical sailor, Prince William had a girl in every port, but in 1790 William fell in love with the actress Dorothea Bland, better known by her stage name Dorothea Jordan. Although they did not marry, they lived happily together for twenty years. She bore him ten children who adopted the surname Fitzclarence. Their descendants live to this day. William suddenly abandoned Dorothea in 1811, probably because she had become an alcoholic and was no longer attractive. She tried to return to the stage, without success, and died following a mental collapse in France in 1816. William's callous treatment of her was out of character with his past actions, but probably a true representation of the real man.

William did not marry until after the death of his brother's heiress, the Princess Charlotte. He was fifty-two when he married the twenty-five-year-old Princess Adelaide, but despite the age difference the two became devoted to each other and she became a devoted stepmother to William's illegitimate flock. Unfortunately none of their children survived infancy.

William was nearly sixty-five by the time he became king and by then he had become a bad-tempered, miserly old man who delighted in being obstinate. He refused to have an extravagant coronation like his brother's, but insisted that it be simple, and he thereby abandoned much of the tradition that had accompanied the ceremony. He felt rather that he was a caretaker monarch, holding the throne for his niece VICTORIA and determined to survive long enough to avoid her mother, the duchess of Kent, becoming regent. He had no interests in art, science or literature, though he did establish a Royal Library at Windsor because it seemed strange without one.

His single most significant contribution to the advance of the nation came in 1832 when, against his own personal judgement, he supported Earl Grey and encouraged the Tory peers to abstain from voting against the Reform Bill, securing its passage. This was the start of modern democracy in Britain, reforming the representation of the people. This opened up the opportunity for a series of reforms, most of which would come to fruition in Victoria's reign. Others of importance were passed in 1833 – the Factory Act, against child labour, and the Abolition Act, which emancipated slaves in the British colonies. The Poor Law of 1834 was a well-intentioned piece of legislation, institutionalising the workhouse. Much of the administration of Britain was still at the level where it could transport the Tolpuddle Martyrs to Australia in 1834 for calling a trade union meeting of agricultural workers. Public reaction to their sentence added fuel to the growing Chartist movement for political and social reform. William found all of this reform rather distressing, as if the whole moral structure of the nation was collapsing. He died of pneumonia and cirrhosis of the liver on 20 June 1837, the last of the Hanoverian kings. Little did he realise that his successor, Victoria, would rule for the rest of the century and rule over the greatest empire the world had seen.

[O38] VICTORIA

Ruled 20 June 1837–22 January 1901. Crowned: Westminster Abbey, 28 June 1838.
Full name and titles: Alexandrina Victoria, queen of the United Kingdom of Great Britain and Ireland; empress of India (from 1 May 1876).
Born: Kensington Palace, 24 May 1819. Died: Osborne House, Isle of Wight, 22 June 1901, aged 82. Buried: Frogmore, Windsor.
Married: 10 February 1840, at St James's Palace, London, Albert (1819–61) son of Ernst I, duke of Saxe-Coburg-Gotha: 9 children.

Victoria might never have been born had not GEORGE IV's daughter, Charlotte, died following childbirth in November 1817. At that time there was no legitimate heir to the throne in the next generation amongst the descendants of GEORGE III. This sent George IV's remaining unmarried brothers scurrying to find wives and produce an heir. Edward Augustus, duke of Kent, married Mary Louise Victoria, the daughter of Franz I, duke of Saxe-Coburg-Saalfield on 29 May 1818. Edward was fifty years old and had not previously been married, though he did have several illegitimate children. Mary Louise (who was always known as Victoria) was thirty-one and had recently been widowed following the death of her husband, the prince of Leiningen, in 1814. She already had two children, Karl (1804–56), who became the next prince of Leiningen, and Anne (1807–72). Her brother was Prince Leopold, the husband of George IV's ill-fated daughter Charlotte. Leopold remained in London after his wife's death to help support his sister. Victoria's father, the duke of Kent, died on 23 January 1820 when she was only nine months old, so she never knew him, which was probably all to the good as he was a sadistic man with a vicious temper and no scruples. Uncle Leopold thereby became the mainstay of the family, helping his sister and providing a father figure to the young Victoria. She missed him tremendously when he became the king of the Belgians in 1831.

When George IV died in 1830, her uncle, WILLIAM IV became king and Victoria became the heir presumptive. When she was shown a genealogical chart, it brought home to her how close to the accession she was, and this occasioned her famous comment "I will be good." William IV died in the early hours of the 20 June 1837, so that Victoria learned she was queen in the middle of the night. Under the Salic Law, women could not rule the kingdom of Hanover which passed to her Uncle

53. Great Britain (2) – **Victoria to Elizabeth II**

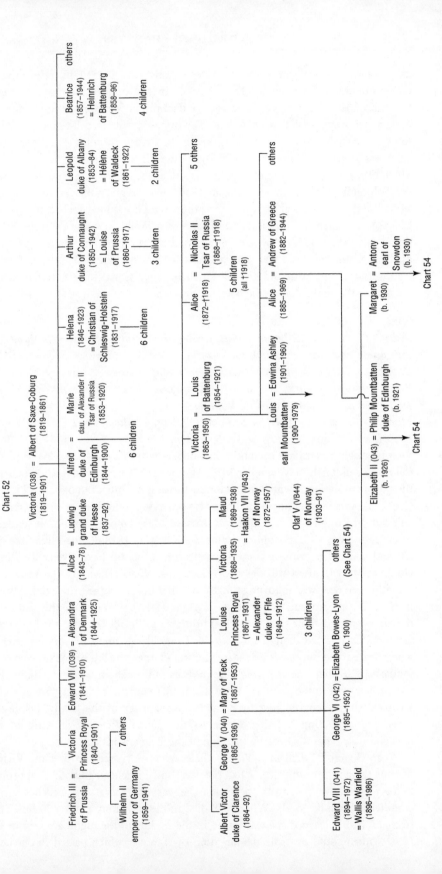

Chart 52

Victoria (038) = Albert of Saxe-Coburg
(1819–1901)   (1819–1861)

Friedrich III = Victoria
of Prussia   Princess Royal
              (1840–1901)

Wilhelm II
emperor of Germany
(1859–1941)

7 others

Edward VII (039) = Alexandra
(1841–1910)   of Denmark
                   (1844–1925)

Alice = Ludwig
(1843–78) grand duke
          of Hesse
          (1837–92)

Alfred = Marie
duke of   dau. of Alexander II
Edinburgh Tsar of Russia
(1844–1900) (1853–1920)

6 children

Helena
(1846–1923)
= Christian of
Schleswig-Holstein
(1831–1917)

6 children

Arthur
duke of Connaught
(1850–1942)
= Louise
of Prussia
(1860–1917)

3 children

Leopold
duke of Albany
(1853–84)
= Hélène
of Waldeck
(1861–1922)

2 children

Beatrice
(1857–1944)
= Heinrich
of Battenburg
(1858–96)

4 children

others

Victoria
(1868–1935)
= Haakon VII (VB43)
of Norway
(1872–1957)

Maud
(1869–1938)

Olaf V (VB44)
of Norway
(1903–91)

Louise
Princess Royal
(1867–1931)
= Alexander
duke of Fife
(1849–1912)

3 children

Victoria = Louis
(1863–1950) of Battenburg
            (1854–1921)

Alice = Nicholas II
(1872–†1918) Tsar of Russia
             (1868–†1918)

5 children
(all †1918)

5 others

Louis = Edwina Ashley
earl Mountbatten (1901–1960)
(1900–1979)

Alice = Andrew of Greece
(1885–1969)   (1882–1944)

others

Albert Victor
duke of Clarence
(1864–92)

George V (040) = Mary of Teck
(1865–1936)   (1867–1953)

Edward VIII (041)
(1894–1972)
= Wallis Warfield
(1896–1986)

George VI (040) = Elizabeth Bowes-Lyon
(1895–1952)   (b. 1900)

others
(See Chart 54)

Elizabeth II (043) = Philip Mountbatten
(b. 1926)   duke of Edinburgh
                     (b. 1921)

Chart 54

Margaret = Antony
(b. 1930) earl of
           Snowdon
           (b. 1930)

Chart 54

Ernst, and thereafter (in 1851) to her cousin George, who was just three days younger than Victoria. Had Victoria not been born, then her uncle and cousin would have become the next two kings of England.

At the time that Victoria became queen, the monarchy was not popular. The post-Napoleonic period had seen considerable distress amongst the English working folk and the country was well in need of reform. The high and wild living of George IV and his brothers had not helped respect for the monarchy and there had been several assassination attempts on him, as well as many riots across the country which had been put down with customary military zeal. The Whig government, with the reluctant aid of William IV, had succeeding in passing the Reform Act along with other much needed legislation, but it was still very early days and the Hanoverian dynasty, up until now, had shown little interest in such progress. There was a general attitude of "Why bother?" amongst both the royal family and many leading politicians. All this would change under Victoria, though at the outset the public could never have anticipated the scale of change that would happen or, for that matter, the length of reign that Victoria would have, a reign that would change the face of Britain and, to a large extent, the globe. In the first few years of her reign Victoria, as the symbol of a corrupt and profligate monarchy, was as unpopular as her predecessors. There were three assassination attempts in the first four years, the first on 10 June 1840, by Edward Oxford, and then two within a few weeks of each other in May and July 1842, when shots were fired at the queen.

Victoria had to face a scandal within the first year of her reign. During her youth she had always disliked Sir John Conroy, who was close to her mother (some felt too close) and who some believed wished to become the power behind the throne. When she became queen Victoria expelled Conroy, but believed that he continued to exert an influence through one of her mother's ladies-in-waiting, Lady Flora Hastings. She believed Conroy and Hastings had become lovers and that Hastings was pregnant with his child. In fact poor Lady Flora had cancer of the liver and the tumour had swollen her stomach. Victoria subjected Lady Flora to an examination which proved she was still a virgin, though Victoria retained her doubts. Lady Flora died soon after. This episode caused her considerable unpopularity and she was heckled at Ascot races. She was jeeringly called Mrs Melbourne because of her close association with the Prime Minister. Melbourne, who had himself been the subject of a scandal in 1836 over his friendship with the Honourable Mrs Caroline Norton (and had never really recovered from the association between his wife, Lady Caroline Lamb, and Lord Byron from twenty years earlier), was a close friend and adviser to Victoria in the first few years of her reign. He instructed her on political matters and provided an avuncular role in the absence of her Uncle Leopold. In 1839 Melbourne resigned and Victoria invited Robert Peel to form a government. As part of the arrangements Peel determined that the ladies in the royal household who had been Whig appointments should be replaced by Tory nominees. Victoria refused and Peel declined to form an administration. Melbourne returned. Victoria had flexed her muscles, albeit over a storm in a teacup and though she had won, she subsequently reconsidered the circumstances and allowed some changes when Peel was returned to power following the general election in 1841.

*From a painting by
Winterhalter, 1846*

Victoria met her future husband, Prince Albert, in 1836 when his father (the brother of Victoria's Uncle Leopold) brought him to London. She was immediately attracted to him and on their second meeting in 1839 Victoria asked him to marry her. The marriage took place on 10 February 1840. They were both twenty years old, with Victoria the senior by three months. Albert had not had a happy childhood. His parents had separated. Both his father and his brother were notorious womanizers, while Albert was the more studious, making the best use of his education. It was Albert and not Victoria who had the stronger moral values and he steadily impressed these upon her. Although they had nine children, Albert saw this more as his duty than as pleasure, whereas Victoria treasured the memory of their lovemaking.

Nevertheless Victoria was only too aware of the scandalous sexual adventures of her uncles as almost all of her cousins were illegitimate, and many of her uncles' mistresses still held a place in society. Albert believed that the royal family should set an example. Although at the start of their marriage Victoria maintained her role as the queen with Albert as no more than her husband, and not the master of the house, she soon deferred to his judgement, and Albert's strong moral standpoint was forced upon the government of the day. Ministers soon knew that any unbecoming conduct would be severely criticised by the queen. The stern views of Albert and the queen began to change the moral climate of the country, at least on the surface, though it repressed much. Nevertheless the queen was not such a prude as she is often portrayed, since she was prepared to accept that men might have affairs. She denied ever using the phrase "we are not amused", which was attributed to her late in life after seeing someone giving an impression of her.

Although they argued like any young couple, Victoria and Albert were ideally matched and intensely in love. Apart from their official residences in London and Windsor, the queen had Osborne House built for them on the Isle of Wight, which was completed in 1851. While it was under construction, the queen also purchased Balmoral House in Scotland in 1852. These became their two main country retreats.

Albert also took an interest in the social conditions of the country. It was his genuine concern for the condition of children and of workers that gave the reform movement a political acceptability that it had hitherto lacked. With the right ministers in place, especially Robert Peel at the outset, social reform gathered a pace during the mid-nineteenth century. The extent of social and cultural reform during

Victoria's reign was immense, much of it due to improved educational standards (especially after the Education Act of 1870), public health (with a series of acts in 1848, 1872 and 1875), and technology. In the last case it was Prince Albert's own initiative for Britain to hold a Great Exhibition in 1851, effectively the first World's Fair, for the display of technological knowledge and advances. The Exhibition was held in the famous Crystal Palace, designed and built by Joseph Paxton, which was later relocated to the park at Sydenham in South London. The Exhibition made a resounding profit which the Prince planned to spend on establishing the Victoria and Albert Museum in Kensington.

There is little doubt that the improvement in the working man's lot during the nineteenth century helped the monarchy by reducing social unrest. When Europe was wracked by a wave of revolutions in 1848, the British monarchy remained intact, although the Chartists took advantage of the general unrest to stage a demonstration. Britain had become a more democratic country than others in Europe and this process was strongly supported by Albert and to a slightly lesser degree by Victoria. She maintained that the European monarchs (many of whom were relatives) should stand together in mutual support. To this end she encouraged royal visits between monarchs, undertaking several herself. Her first had been to Louis-Philippe of France in September 1843, the first visit between an English and French sovereign since HENRY VIII visited François I in 1520. Her relationships with other European nations did much to stabilise Europe in the second half of the nineteenth century. Her involvement, for example, in keeping Prussia out of the war between Austria and Sardinia in 1857, and subsequently convincing her ministers to remain neutral, certainly stopped hostilities from escalating and brought a quick peace. She also strove to dampen down anti-Indian hysteria during the years of the Indian Mutiny (1857/8) and called for leniency in retribution in India. Victoria also urged neutrality in the American Civil War, although the incident over the British mailship *Trent*, which was boarded by the Federal Navy, taking prisoner two Confederate envoys on diplomatic business (later released), might have escalated into a British involvement in the war, had not Prince Albert intervened in a tactful rewording of the British government's despatch.

Albert was only ever "Prince Consort", the title of which was confirmed in 1857, although Victoria would have liked to have made him king. The two were a formidable pair and, through Albert, the nation became endeared to the monarchy. The whole of Britain was devastated by the death of Albert (probably from typhoid) on 14 December 1861, and Victoria was wracked by grief. She went so far as to consider suicide, and spent the rest of her life dressed in mourning. The Albert Hall and Albert Memorial were built in his memory.

After Albert's death, Victoria took a less prominent part in public affairs though she kept in touch with everything via her Prime Minister. Her relationship with her government had always been on a personal basis. Some prime ministers she could instinctively trust; and even though she did not like Robert Peel at first, she developed a high regard for him. She never trusted Lord Palmerston, although she eventually supported his action in the Crimean War of 1854/6. She instituted the Victoria Cross for valour in the Crimea; it was made from iron cast from the guns captured in the war. She never liked William Gladstone, whom she found patronising and obstinate, but she had her best relationship with Benjamin

Disraeli. Their views were similar and he knew how to flatter her. His greatest coup was making her empress of India in 1876. She sorely missed Disraeli when he died in 1881.

Throughout the second half of her reign, Victoria interceded in foreign affairs only in an effort to maintain peace and remain neutral. Generally she was successful, though at times this went to the brink as with the declaration of war between Russia and Turkey in 1877. Victoria and Disraeli's stand almost caused a war between Russia and Britain until terms were agreed at the Congress of Berlin in 1878. Victoria was horrified at the activities in the Sudan in 1883/4 and censured her ministers when they did not follow her orders and send relief to General Gordon in Khartoum in time to save him. Also throughout her reign there were continuing problems between Britain and Ireland. In 1886 Gladstone introduced a Home Rule Bill which would have restored the Irish parliament in Dublin and repealed the 1800 Act of Union. Victoria would have none of it and the discussion split Gladstone's Liberal Party, with the Unionists emerging on their own. A second attempt in 1893 was passed by the Commons but rejected in the Lords.

While there was every reason to hold Victoria in high respect for her abilities as a monarch, she came in for some criticism. The public believed her extended mourning for Albert was becoming unhealthy and affecting her judgement. She had found some consolation in a new shoulder to cry on, that of a Scottish estate worker and attendant John Brown, who was blunt and honest but caring. His concern for her welfare convinced Victoria that the working class often had better standards and morals than the aristocracy. This was not helped by the profligate behaviour of her son the Prince of Wales (*see* EDWARD VII). Her asssociation with John Brown was interpreted as something more serious than it was, with newspapers referring to her as "Mrs. Brown". She was in danger of reducing respect once more for the monarchy and there was even some discussion in 1871 of abolishing the monarchy, but it came to nothing. Brown remained her faithful attendant and stalwart until his death in 1883.

Towards the end of her reign Victoria was seen as the grandmother of Europe, and with her Golden and Diamond Jubilees in 1887 and 1897 there was much celebration. Through her daughter Victoria, who had married the future Friedrich III of Prussia, she was the grandmother of the future Kaiser Wilhelm II. Through her second daughter, Alice, her grandaughter (also called Alice) married Tsar Nicholas II of Russia. Her second son, Prince Alfred, was elected king of Greece in 1862 but declined the throne. His daughter Marie married King Ferdinand of Romania. There was scarcely a royal family in Europe who did not have some matrimonial link with Victoria, and most of them were present at her Diamond Jubilee. At that time the British Empire was also at its greatest extent and it would have seemed to Victoria's subjects that Britain ruled the world. It was not true, as would soon be seen, but it was a great feeling to the British while it lasted and brought the nineteenth century to a magnificent close.

When the queen died at Osborne House on 22 January 1901, she had not only ruled longer than any previous British monarch, but she could count more people as her subjects than any ruler ever. On her own she was not as great a queen as she was in partnership with Prince Albert, or with a strong prime minister, so it is difficult to rank her as a greater monarch than ELIZABETH I, but in terms of the changes that happened during her life, she must be accorded the most significant reign in British history.

[O39] EDWARD VII

Ruled 22 January 1901–6 May 1910. Crowned: Westminster Abbey, 9 August 1902.
Full name and titles: Albert Edward, king of Great Britain, Ireland and the British Dominions beyond the Seas, emperor of India, duke of Cornwall and Rothesay, earl of Carrick, lord of the Isles and Baron Renfrew (from birth), prince of Wales and earl of Chester (from 1841), duke of Saxe-Coburg-Gotha (1861–63).
Born: *Buckingham Palace, 9 November 1841.* **Died:** *Buckingham Palace, 6 May 1910, aged 68.* **Buried:** *Windsor Castle.*
Married: *10 March 1863, at Windsor Castle, Alexandra Caroline Marie Charlotte Louise Julie (1844–1925), dau. of Christian IX, king of Denmark: 6 children.*

Baptized Albert Edward, and always affectionately known as Bertie, he was the second child and eldest son of VICTORIA and Prince Albert of Saxe-Coburg. His parents were very strict with him as a child, determined that he would not become wayward and profligate like Victoria's father and uncles or Albert's father and brother, but it was to little avail. In fact they probably restricted him too much, as by his teens he had developed a cruel streak (which thankfully he lost), threw tantrums just as GEORGE IV did in his youth, and showed every tendency of rebelling against his parents. He grew out of this only because his good looks (he looked very much like his father and his maternal grandfather) allowed him to get his own way with women and he was able to enjoy himself as he pleased. His parents did not allow him to play any part in political affairs or undertake any state visits until much later in life, although he did tour Europe, Canada and America in his teens. Had they done so Edward might have taken his responsibilities more seriously because once he did become king, he became a skilled negotiator. Instead he suffered from the usual Hanoverian trait of parents not trusting their children and so, like his mother's great-grandfather, Frederick, prince of Wales, the new prince of Wales (which he was created when he was a month old) led the life of a playboy.

Although this made him a frustration to his parents, most people enjoyed his company and the nation took him to its heart, especially after the death of Prince Albert, when the queen went into mourning and became overly sombre. Prince Edward maintained a sense of humour and delighted in practical jokes and kept society bubbling. There was great national concern in 1871 when Edward became seriously ill with typhoid. The Queen, however, never forgave Edward for creating an incident in 1861 which she believed added to Prince Albert's stress and contributed to his early death. Prince Edward was in Ireland involved in army manoeuvres and as a joke a young actress was hidden in his tent. It was thought paramount that Edward should have a wife as soon as possible and on 10 March 1863 he married Princess Alexandra of Denmark. Edward had acquired a house and land at Sandringham in Norfolk in 1862, which became his and his wife's main country retreat. Alexandra was remarkably tolerant of her husband and her flexibility and good nature doubtless contributed to what is one of the longest marriages of any British monarch. They remained married for forty-seven years until Edward's death. Alexandra died on 20 November 1925 in her eighty-first year.

Although their marriage was happy and they had six children (though the last died after only a day in 1871), Edward remained a philanderer and enjoyed the company of many women. Perhaps his best known mistress was the actress Lillie Langtry (real name Emilie Le Breton), but he was regularly seen in the company of many different society ladies. Generally Edward kept these affairs discreet, although most people in society knew about them. Occasionally though they became more public. In 1870 the MP Sir Charles Mordaunt brought a divorce suit against his wife on the grounds of adultery. In her statement, Lady Mordaunt cited the prince of Wales as one of the co-respondents. During the course of the trial, at which the prince appeared as a witness, it become known that he frequently visited her alone when her husband was in the House of Commons, though nothing more was proved. Prince Edward never acknowledged any illegitimate children, though rumours were rife. Sonia, the second daughter of Alice Keppel, born in May 1900, was widely believed to be the Prince's. She became the grandmother of Camilla Parker Bowles.

Perhaps the most notorious incident attached to Prince Edward was the baccarat scandal of 1890. The prince had attended a house party at Tranby Croft in Yorkshire where they played the then illegal game of baccarat. One of the party, Sir William Gordon-Cumming, was accused of cheating but the matter was kept quiet, provided Sir William did not play cards again. However word leaked out and Sir William sued others of the party for slander. Again the prince appeared in court as a witness, and the nation expressed its outrage that the prince should be involved in an illegal gambling game. Such is society that it should express more concern over this than over Prince Edward's affairs.

In fact Edward's activities set the fashion in society – how he dressed, where he went, what he did. Society life revolved about him. He was primarily responsible for making Monte Carlo a fashionable location for the elite; he went big-game hunting in India; he loved horse-racing and regularly attended major society meetings – three of his horses won the Derby and another the Grand National. Edward also took an interest in yacht racing – the racing yacht *Britannia* was built for him in 1892. The public followed everything that he did: even leaving the bottom button on the waistcoat undone (because of his increased corpulence) became the height of fashion.

Although the queen denied Prince Edward involvement in political affairs, he still held his views. He caused sufficient family unrest in 1864 when the Schleswig-Holstein dispute erupted and Prussia declared war on Denmark. Victoria naturally supported Prussia, but Edward supported Denmark, his wife's country, and this view was shared by the Prime Minister. Edward further angered the queen when he welcomed the Italian revolutionary, Garibaldi, to England in April 1864, when he came to encourage further support for Denmark. In fact Edward proved himself far more tolerant and capable than ever his mother perceived. While she encouraged the nation to remain neutral when hostilities erupted elsewhere in Europe, Edward would, had he been allowed, have exerted his influence to resolve affairs. Instead the queen restricted him to state visits amongst peaceable nations and public ceremonies, such as the opening of the

Thames Embankment in 1871, the Mersey Tunnel in 1886 and Tower Bridge in 1894. He performed his public duties with considerable energy and aplomb and applied himself to a number of charity organizations and public committees. In particular he had concern over the condition of housing in Britain and was a member of the Royal Commission on Housing established in 1884. Edward also enjoyed himself helping with the preparations for his mother's Golden Jubilee in 1887 and Diamond Jubilee in 1897.

In January 1892 his eldest son, Albert, died of pneumonia. Albert (known as "Eddy" to the family) had always been an apathetic child and the prince believed him backward. It was later suspected that he suffered from syphilis of the brain. Rumours attached themselves to "Eddy" and his life style — it was alleged that he had secretly married Annie Crook sometime in the mid-1880s and that the Jack the Ripper murders were committed to silence those in the know, though no evidence but hearsay supports this.

One other cloud cast a shadow over Edward and that was an assassination attempt on 4 April 1900, when the prince was fired at while travelling through Brussels on his way to Denmark. The prince was unhurt. The cause was related to the Boer War in South Africa, which had soured relationships between England and its European neighbours.

Edward was welcomed as king in January 1901. Edward's coronation was delayed by six weeks because he developed appendicitis. The food, which had already been prepared, was distributed among the poor of London. The eventual celebrations, held on 9 August, were magnificent. It may not have been the most expensive ceremony, but it was almost certainly the largest, with representatives from all over the world. Although he ruled for fewer than ten years, his lifestyle made sufficient impression for the first decade of this century to be known as the Edwardian period. It was a period of fun and enjoyment. It was a time of major advancement in the welfare of society — trades unions were recognized, old age pensions and national insurance were introduced.

Edward took little interest in this. His time was spent becoming what the French dubbed "the uncle of Europe." He undertook regular visits to European monarchs, most of whom were his relatives, and helped Europe maintain a steady peace. All his life Edward had been a Francophile and it was primarily through his relations with France that England was able to conclude the *Entente Cordiale* alliance in April 1904. Edward became a major symbol of British strength and authority and was highly respected through Europe and the Empire. He was far more a humanist than any of his predecessors, something which he inherited from his father, and despite his reputation for the good life, was also charitable and philanthropic, sparing no energies in support of good causes. He upheld the best of the Victorian values and while not all of his views would accord with today's values (for instance, he opposed women's suffrage) his wish that everyone should lead a good life shaped and influenced English society for fifty years and still remains the image of the "good old days."

He died on 6 May 1910 of bronchial complications. His funeral was the last time the monarchy of Europe assembled together as four years later the Great War would rip Europe apart. Edward was succeeded by his only surviving son, GEORGE V.

[O40] **GEORGE V**
Ruled 6 May 1910–20 January 1936. Crowned: Westminster Abbey, 22 June 1911.
Full name and titles: George Frederick Ernest Albert, king of Great Britain and Ireland (only Northern Ireland after 1920) and the British Dominions beyond the Seas, emperor of India, duke of York, earl of Inverness and Baron Killarney (from 1892), duke of Cornwall and Rothesay (from 1901), prince of Wales and earl of Chester (from 1901).
Born: Marlborough House, London, 3 June 1865. *Died:* Sandringham House, Norfolk, 20 January 1936, aged 70. *Buried:* Windsor Castle.
Married: 6 July 1893, at St James's Palace, London, Mary Augusta Louise (1867–1953) dau. of Franz, duke of Teck: 6 children.

George V was the second son of EDWARD VII. Until his elder brother, Prince Albert, died in 1892, George had not anticipated he would be the next in line to the throne after his father. He had opted for a career in the navy, like WILLIAM IV, starting as a naval cadet at Dartmouth in 1877 and rising to the rank of commander in 1891. Unfortunately a bout of typhoid, followed by news of his brother's death, ended his naval career and he had to adjust to the prospect of becoming king. He had sufficient sense of duty to do this, though he did not welcome it, and neither did he like the additional political and language studies he had to do. He was not fond of intellectual pursuits, preferring, like his father, a sporting life. Unusually for the Hanoverian line, George was on very good terms with his father, but he did not copy him in any other way, especially the playboy role. George was rather shy, which he overcame by talking loudly in a booming voice, but he much preferred solitary pursuits and it was not unusual for him to hide away at Sandringham for periods of time, hunting, fishing and developing his collection of stamps of the British Empire. He was slightly below average height (about five feet seven inches) and had inherited his father's good looks and had captivating blue eyes.

George married his late brother's betrothed, Princess Mary of Teck, in 1893. He was twenty-eight; she was twenty-six. They had five sons and a daughter, Mary, who became the Princess Royal in 1932. Their two eldest sons became respectively EDWARD VIII and GEORGE VI. Their third son, Henry, duke of Gloucester, lived until 1974. The fourth son, George, duke of Kent, was killed on active service in the Second World War, when his plane crashed into a Scottish hillside in August 1942. Their youngest son, John, was an epileptic and was kept out of the public gaze at Sandringham, where he died in 1919 aged thirteen. Their marriage was not a love match but by all accounts George was faithful. An early allegation that he had married the daughter of Admiral Culme-Seymour before his marriage to Mary was rapidly squashed and the perpetrator of the story prosecuted and imprisoned. There was never more than minor gossip about George's love life and he was the first king since CHARLES I not to have any sexual scandal attached to his name.

Although Edward VII did his best to prepare George for the monarchy, both in terms of becoming acquainted with the political process, and in visits to foreign courts, George felt ill equipped for the political crisis that he was plunged into after his father's death in May 1910. The Liberals' budget of 1909, which had included provision for a super-tax to cover the cost of old-age pensions, had been rejected by

54. Great Britain (3) – The Royal Family

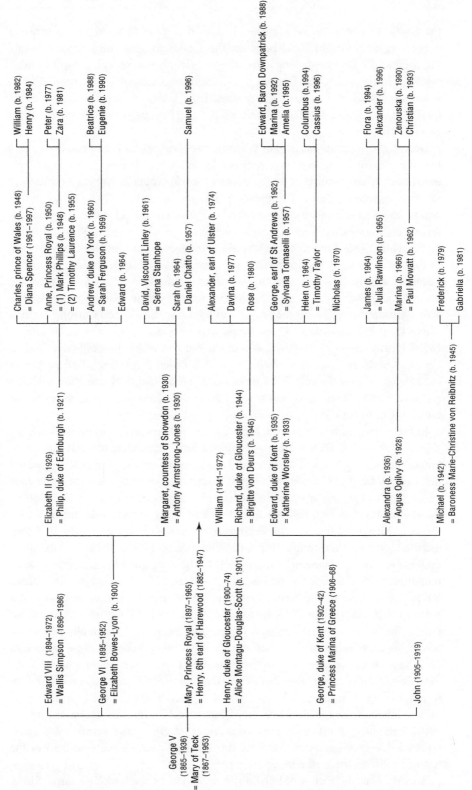

the House of Lords. Prime Minister Asquith had asked Edward VII to consider appointing additional Liberal peers to the House to vote the budget through. Edward had died before making a decision and George was now placed in a difficult position. In the end it was referred to a committee, followed by a general election where the increased Liberal majority caused the Lords to accept public opinion. George, however, did not like having been brought into party politics and made his views forcibly known.

George's coronation was held in Westminster Abbey on 22 June 1911, but he also had the idea of being crowned emperor in India, which neither his father nor grandmother had been. He and the queen sailed for India in November and were jointly crowned emperor and empress on 11 December 1911 at Delhi. It was on that occasion that Delhi became the country's capital. George VI did not repeat this second coronation, so it was a unique event.

It was also the last moment of glory of the old world, for soon after the situation in Europe worsened. The immediate problem was in Ireland. Asquith sought to introduce a Home Rule Bill (the third attempt; *see under* VICTORIA *for the first two*) and, though it was rejected twice by the House of Lords, the King was prepared to give it his support. However the lawyer and politician, Sir Edward Carson (the man whose cross-examination of Oscar Wilde had been the ruin of the playwright in 1895), refused to accept the provision of the Bill and in 1913 mobilised a force of Ulster Volunteers. The king, fearing civil war, called a meeting of all parties at Buckingham Palace in July 1914 to consider an amended Home Rule Bill that excluded Ulster. No decision was reached and discussions were set aside when war broke out in Europe.

In the years leading up to war, King George had repeatedly warned his cousin, Kaiser Wilhelm II, that if Germany showed any aggression towards Russia or France, Britain would come to their aid. He also expressed the hope that they would not have to be drawn in. Britain's past record suggested to Germany that they would remain neutral, so when the catastrophic sequence of events sparked off by the assassination of Archduke Ferdinand of Austria on 28 June 1914 escalated into war, Germany declared war on Russia and France and, to add to the problem, marched on France through Belgium. Britain, tied by its treaties to its allies, declared war on Germany on 4 August 1914. The King did what he could to keep morale high. He shared in the rationing, not wishing to be shown special treatment. He paid five visits to the Grand Fleet and seven visits to armies in France and Belgium. On one visit in 1915, he was thrown from his horse and fractured his pelvis. The King did what he could behind the scenes and the public seemed to accept his genuine patriotism, but when anti-German feeling became intense in 1917 he took the counsel of his government and changed his family name from Saxe-Coburg to Windsor. Even before the war had finished, there was revolution in Russia. George's cousin Alice had married Tsar Nicholas II and the couple, with all their children, were murdered on July 16th 1918. George was devastated by the news. The old Europe was crumbling and Victoria's descendants were being replaced. Kaiser Wilhelm survived the war but fled from Germany and spent the rest of his life in the Netherlands.

After the war, the matter of Ireland still needed to be resolved. The Easter Rising of April 1916 had done little to help the situation, the execution of the rebels Pearce,

Connolly and others only shifting support to the nationalists. King George opted for a conciliatory approach. The Government of Ireland Act of 1920 proposed for separate parliaments in Dublin and Belfast. The king and queen opened the Ulster Parliament in June 1921. Sinn Fein rejected the proposal for southern Ireland and it was not until the Anglo-Irish Treaty of 6 December 1921 that all of Ireland, except for Ulster, was recognized as the Irish Free State.

To George the old order continued to fade away. In 1924 the first Labour government was formed under Prime Minister Ramsay MacDonald. George was surprised to find the ministers easy to operate with. Unfortunately the Zinoviev letter, allegedly written by the head of the Communist International, encouraged armed revolution. The Labour Party was tainted with Communism and the letter contributed to their downfall. The General Strike of 1926 was further evidence of civil strife and potential revolution. The Baldwin government took a hard line with the strikers while the king had been prepared to be more conciliatory. It became evident as the years progressed and the strife grew that England was in the grip of a world depression. King George took a cut in his own pay via the Civil List. It was George who actively encouraged the idea of a National Government to tackle the problem, and this eventually came in under Ramsay MacDonald in 1931. It was this sense of needing to hold the nation together that caused George V to introduce two traditions in 1932. The first was his own personal distribution of Maundy Money on the Thursday before Easter. The tradition dated back to the time of EDWARD III in 1363, but since the Reformation had been conducted by the Lord High Almoner. His other innovation was to broadcast a Christmas Day message over the radio, which also continues to this day. These acts immediately brought the king to the hearts of people who otherwise had never seen him, let alone heard him, and it did more than any other action that he took to personalize the king. It undoubtedly contributed to his popularity, which he had never courted. He was overwhelmed at the enthusiasm and warmth accorded him at his silver jubilee in 1935.

In 1931 the Statute of Westminster made the change from the British Empire to the Commonwealth, with Parliament ceasing to control some of the overseas dominions directly. The King remained as Head of the Commonwealth and, in many cases, as head of state, but it was a further slide away from the old regime under which George had been reared and where he still felt most at home.

The king's health had declined in the last few years. In November 1928 he had suffered a near fatal bout of septicaemia, which weakened his constitution. He had been sent to Bognor Regis to recuperate. Thus, when he entered his final illness with a severe bronchial infection in January 1936, Queen Mary suggested he might again visit Bognor. This gave rise to his alleged but doubtless apocryphal last words, "Bugger Bognor!"

George V succeeded more than he ever realised in moulding together the disciplinarian approach of Victoria and Albert with the homely geniality of Edward VII to produce a monarch who stood for the best standards and principles of the nation. Few of his contemporaries fully appreciated the lengths to which he went to understand the problems of Britain and to promote stability and understanding throughout Europe. He succeeded far more than he failed, and the love he received from the nation was the testament to that.

[O41] **EDWARD VIII**
Ruled 20 January–11 December 1936. Never crowned.
Full name and titles: Edward Albert Christian George Andrew Patrick David, king of Great Britain and Northern Ireland, emperor of India, duke of Cornwall and Rothesay, earl of Carrick, lord of the Isles and Baron Renfrew (from 1910), prince of Wales and earl of Chester (from 1910); duke of Windsor (from 1937).
Born: *White Lodge, Richmond, Surrey, 23 June 1894.* **Died:** *Paris, France, 28 May 1972, aged 77.* **Buried:** *Frogmore, Windsor.*
Married: *3 June 1937, at Chateau de Candé, Maine-et-Loire, France, Wallis Simpson (née Warfield) (1896–1986): no children.*

Despite an abundant selection of Christian names (the last four being the four patron saints of Britain), the future Edward VIII was always known in the family as David. He was the son of GEORGE V and Mary of Teck. He inherited his family's handsome features, including the youthfulness of his mother and grandmother so that his face always had a boyish charm. Almost from the outset he reacted against the demands placed upon him. Like his distant predecessor EDWARD II he had little interest in state affairs, though unlike that same predecessor he also disliked the pomp and ceremony. He regarded his investiture as prince of Wales in 1911 as ridiculous and he rebelled against his father's discipline. He took after his grandfather, EDWARD VII, in preferring "the good life" and though his father tried to curb these tendencies he only aggravated them by continually treating Edward like a child. He was refused active service during the Great War, something that would certainly have been the making of him had he survived, and after the war, the king refused to involve him in political affairs. Instead, in the same way that Victoria treated "Bertie", so Edward was only entrusted with going on goodwill tours around the world. Edward enjoyed doing these, although they became exhausting, and over a period, throughout the 1920s, it came to look as if King George was doing all he could to keep Edward out of the country.

One side effect of all of this that would later have significant consequences was that the prince became attracted to the United States. Here was a country that accepted him for what he was and allowed him to speak his mind. He felt trapped and censured in Britain but alive and free in America. Edward and his father grew further apart. The prince embarked upon a series of affairs. He showed no interest in marriage, but seemed to have a liking for elder, already married women. He was evidently seeking that affection denied him by his parents. There were allegations that the Prince was a repressed homosexual, although his many affairs would speak against this. Nevertheless he was attracted to more masculine looking women. In January 1931 he first met Mrs Wallis Simpson, an American divorcée who had recently married for a second time. Edward fell in love with her, though it was never that clear how much she loved him – it was more the attraction of power. Nevertheless the two drew closer together and it was evident by 1935 that Edward had made his mind up to marry her. He never found the right moment to tell his father, because of his failing health.

In January 1936 the old king died and David became Edward VIII. Although he had no great desire to be king he was prepared to do his duty, but only if he could marry Mrs Simpson. Divorce proceedings were already going through between Mrs

Simpson and her husband, and the decree *nisi* was granted on 27 October 1936. During this period Edward and Mrs Simpson were almost inseparable but the British press remained silent on the matter. The American and European press, however, covered the news with relish, and it was only a matter of time before it would break in Britain. The king continued to believe that the nation would happily accept an American as queen. The government, the archbishop of Canterbury, and Edward's mother did not agree, believing that a marriage with a woman twice divorced, especially with both past husbands still alive, would be unconstitutional and wholly unacceptable. Edward remained determined. Mrs Simpson's decree absolute was set for 27 April 1937, fifteen days before the day planned for the coronation. It was not until November that Mrs Simpson realised the import of the constitutional dilemma – known as the Abdication Crisis – in which Edward was caught, and she offered to step aside. Edward would have none of it. On 16 November he gave the Prime Minister, Stanley Baldwin, an ultimatum that either he be allowed to marry or he would abdicate. Edward was supported by such stalwarts as Winston Churchill and Lord Beaverbrook, who were prepared to rally the country behind Edward, but he wanted none of that. If anything, this was the escape he was looking for. Edward was not cut out to be king and, though he would have suffered it for the nation, he would not do it alone. On 5 December 1936, Edward confirmed his intention to abdicate. The necessary papers were prepared and signed on 10 December and the next day, after making a moving broadcast to the nation, Edward sailed away to exile in France. There he and Wallis Warfield (she had reverted to her maiden name on 7 May 1937) were married on 3 June. A few months earlier, on 8 March, Edward had been made duke of Windsor, but the honorific of "Royal Highness" denied his wife, albeit legally she was entitled to be so addressed.

They remained living in France, mostly in Paris, for the rest of their lives, although they travelled extensively, mostly to the United States where they became the centre of high society. Edward wished to serve his nation during the Second World War but the closest he got was as governor and commander-in-chief of the Bahamas from 1940 to 1945. After the war rumours became rife that he had Nazi sympathies, though in fact he had visited Germany in 1937 in an effort to help stop the inevitable. Edward had such a high opinion of himself that he was blinded to his use by the Nazi propaganda machine.

Edward and his brother, who succeeded him as GEORGE VI, remained at a distance, though there were efforts at reconciliation by ELIZABETH II, who visited Edward just days before he died of cancer on 28 May 1972. His body was flown back to Britain and buried at Frogmore in Windsor. His widow survived for another fourteen years in a sorry state in their Paris home as senile dementia took hold. She died on 24 April 1986, in her ninetieth year, and was buried beside her husband at Frogmore.

Edward had let his heart rule his head, but since his heart was also telling him that kingship was not for him then he must have made the right decision. Although his reputation has suffered some brickbats over the years, he is still remembered as the king who sacrificed everything for love, and that romantic image will never fade.

[O42] **GEORGE VI**
Ruled 11 December 1936–6 February 1952. Crowned: Westminster Abbey, 12 May 1937.
Full name and titles: Albert Frederick Arthur George, king of Great Britain and Northern Ireland, emperor of India (until 22 June 1947), duke of York, earl of Inverness and Baron Killarney (from 1920).
Born: Sandringham, Norfolk, 14 December 1895. *Died*: 6 February 1952, aged 56. *Buried*: Windsor Castle.
Married: 26 April 1923, at Westminster Abbey, Elizabeth (b. 1900) dau. of Claude George Bowes-Lyon, earl of Strathmore and Kinghorne: 2 daughters.

Kings usually have many years to prepare for their role, unless they are usurpers, and even then they do it with intent. George VI had less than a week, and for much of that week he could not believe it was happening.

Albert Frederick Arthur George ("Bertie" to his family) was the second son of GEORGE V and had not expected to become king, certainly not within a few months of his brother, EDWARD VIII, succeeding to the throne. Edward's love for Mrs Wallis Simpson, however, which led to his abdication in December 1936, propelled George into the monarchy with scarcely a moment's notice.

Like his father, George VI had not been raised to be king. He was a rather delicate child who suffered from gastritis as a result of his nurse's neglect. It led to a duodenal ulcer in later years. He was shy and had a restricting stammer which he only overcame with hard work. He entered the Royal Navy in 1913, as a midshipman, and this was the making of him for, although he was sea-sick, he came to enjoy the naval life. He served with distinction during the First World War, being mentioned in despatches at the battle of Jutland. He served for a short period in the Royal Naval Air Service. He was created duke of York in 1920, of which he was excessively proud.

For all he was straight-laced and a stickler for protocol, George also had the common touch. In 1921 he set up the Duke of York's Boys' Camps which brought together working-class and public schoolboys in summer camps. They worked well and were held annually until 1939. He also became President of the Industrial Welfare Society and took a keen interest in the health and safety of the worker. He enjoyed sport, especially tennis, and made a brief appearance at Wimbledon in 1926 in the doubles with his wife.

He had met Lady Elizabeth Bowes-Lyon in 1922. She had originally been introduced to his brother Edward in the hope of making a match. Lady Elizabeth was attracted to the prince of Wales, but it was the duke of York who eventually won her hand, and the two were married in April 1923. Although not a member of a British or European royal family, Lady Elizabeth's family had a long and illustrious history, tracing its descent from John Lyon, secretary of DAVID II of Scotland who was made Lord Glamis in 1372 and who married Jean, a daughter of ROBERT II, in 1376. On her mother's side, Lady Elizabeth could trace descent from the Welsh prince OWAIN GLYN DWR. They were well matched and made a happy couple. They were blessed with two daughters, ELIZABETH in 1926 and Margaret in 1930.

Following their marriage George and Elizabeth settled into the Royal Lodge in Windsor Great Park. Although he continued to undertake special visits on behalf

55. Great Britain (4) – **The direct descent of Elizabeth II**

73 generations from Beli Mawr to Elizabeth II

A1.	Beli Mawr (*fl* 100BC)	EB13.	Cadell (d. 909)
A3.	Caswallon (*fl* 55BC)	EB15.	Hywel *Dda* (d. 950)
	Llyr (*fl* 20BC)	EB16.	Owain (d. 988)
	Bran *the Blessed* (*fl* AD 1)		Einion (d. 984)
	Beli (*fl* AD 20)	EB19.	Cadell (*fl* 1005–18)
	Amalech (*fl* AD 50s)		Tewdwr
	Eugein (*fl* AD 70s)	EB25.	Rhys (d. 1093)
	Brithguein (*fl* 100)	EB26.	Gruffydd (*c*1090–1137)
	Dyfwn (*fl* 120s)	EB30.	The Lord Rhys (*c*1133–97)
	Oumun (*fl* 150s)	EB31.	Gruffydd (d. 1201)
	Anguerit (*fl* 170s)		Owain (d. 1235)
	Amgualoyt (*fl* 200)		Maredudd (d. 1265)
	Gurdumn (*fl* 220s)		Owain (d. 1275)
	Dyfwn (*fl* 250s)		Llywellyn (d. 1309)
	Guordoli (*fl* 270s)		Thomas (d. *c*1343)
	Doli (*fl* 300)		Margaret
	Guorcein (*fl* 320s)		Maredudd ap Tudor
	Cein (*fl* 350s)		Owen Tudor (*c*1400–61)
	Tacit (*fl* 370s)		Edmund Tudor (*c*1430–56)
	Paternus (*fl* 400)	O20.	Henry VII (1457–1509)
	Edern (*fl* 430s)		Margaret Tudor (1489–1541) = James IV
DA4.	Cunedda (*fl* 450--460)	FC80.	James V of Scotland (1512–42)
ED2.	Einion (*fl* 470--480)	FC81.	Mary, Queen of Scots (1542–87)
ED3.	Cadwallon *Lawhir* (*fl* 500--520)	FC82.	James VI [James I] (1566–1625)
ED4.	Maelgwn (d. *c*549)		Elizabeth of Bohemia (1596–1662)
ED5.	Rhun (*fl* 560s)		Sophia, Electress of Hanover (1630–1714)
ED6.	Beli (*fl* 590s)	O33.	George I (1660–1727)
ED7.	Iago (d. *c*615)	O34.	George II (1683–1760)
ED8.	Cadfan (d. *c*625)		Frederick, Prince of Wales (1707–51)
ED9.	Cadwallon (d. 634)	O35.	George III (1738–1820)
ED11.	Cadwaladr (d. 682)		Edward, Duke of Kent (1767–1820)
ED12.	Idwal (d. *c*720)	O38.	Victoria (1819–1901)
ED13.	Rhodri *Molwynog* (*fl* 754)	O39.	Edward VII (1841–1910)
ED15.	Cynan (d. 816)	O40.	George V (1865–1936)
	Essyllt	O42.	George VI (1895–1952)
ED17.	Merfyn *Frych* (d. 844)	O43.	Elizabeth II (1926–)
ED18.	Rhodri *Mawr* (d. 878)		

of his father, George was not involved in any matters of government. On his accession he confessed that he had never seen a state paper and was at a complete loss as to what to do. His strong sense of duty carried him through. He wanted to emphasise the continuity of the monarchy and chose George as his regal name rather than Albert. The coronation already fixed for his brother went ahead as usual, but George simply stepped into his place. To the public it seemed as if George was well prepared, but it had been sheer pluck and determination that carried him through, along with the unstinting support of the queen.

One single affair dominated the world scene in 1937 and that was the growing menace of Nazi Germany. George supported his Prime Minister, Neville Chamberlain, in his policy of appeasement, not wishing to repeat another four years of war, but when all else failed to stop Hitler's intentions, George was also quick to show his support for the oppressed countries. No sooner was war declared on 3 September 1939 than the king broadcast a message to the Empire, encouraging them to show their allegiance. George's relationship with Winston Churchill, who became Prime Minister in May 1940, was initially remote, but they later became firm friends. The king and queen were determined to remain in residence in London, even during the dark period of the Blitz, and they both narrowly escaped with their lives when Buckingham Palace received a direct hit by six bombs in September 1940. The couple visited the worst hit areas in the East End and their genuine concern for the Londoners endeared them to the nation. He initiated the George Cross in 1940 as the highest award for heroism and gallantry shown by civilians, awarding it in 1942 to the island of Malta. The king kept a very public profile throughout the War, visiting factories and military sites, as well as the troops in North Africa in 1943. The victory celebrations on 8 May 1945 outside Buckingham Palace demonstrated just how much the royal family was the centre of Britain's hopes and aspirations.

George's affinity with his subjects made it easier to adapt to the Labour Government, which came to power in 1945 under Clement Attlee, than it had been for his father in 1924, even though he was not in total sympathy with their ideology. He advised caution in their policy of nationalisation. The king continued a strenuous round of public duties, including a tour of South Africa and Rhodesia in 1947. 1947 also saw the withdrawal of the British from India and the establishment of the independent nations of India and Pakistan. In 1951 George opened the Festival of Britain, intended as a celebration of postwar Britain like the Great Exhibition of Prince Albert's exactly one hundred year's before.

The king's health continued to deteriorate. He had an operation for blocked arteries in his legs in 1948, and in September 1951 part of his left lung was removed because of lung cancer. Although he recovered, he died in his sleep in the early hours of 6 February 1952, aged only 56. For the man who did not want to be king he had achieved wonders in restoring the popularity of the monarchy after the abdication crisis and in helping sustain Britain's morale through the dark years of the War. He was a courageous and extremely dutiful king.

[O43] **ELIZABETH II**
Ruled 6 February 1952 to date. Crowned: Westminster Abbey, 2 June 1953.
Full name and titles: Elizabeth Alexandra Mary, queen of the United Kingdom of Great Britain and Northern Ireland and of her other Realms and Territories; Head of the Commonwealth.
Born: 17 Bruton Street, London, 21 April 1926.
Married: 20 November 1947, at Westminster Abbey, Philip (b. 10 June 1921) son of Prince Andrew of Greece and Denmark.
Elizabeth was the eldest of the two daughters of GEORGE VI. She became heir presumptive on the abdication of her uncle EDWARD VIII in 1936, when she was ten, and thereafter she was groomed for her future role. Her childhood, and that of her sister Margaret, was part of a close-knit family. There were none of the problems or fractures that had marred earlier generations and to the public the royal family became the epitome of family life. The family even remained together at Buckingham Palace throughout the Blitz, though they later moved out to Windsor. It is a sharp contrast to the way the royal family would come to be perceived in the 1980s and 1990s. Elizabeth was determined to play her part in the war effort and, after an initial refusal, her father eventually allowed her to join the ATS (Auxiliary

56. Great Britain (5) – The descent of Elizabeth II from King Arthur

This chart shows the relationship of Elizabeth II to the two historic namesakes of King Arthur, Arthur of Dál Riata and Arthur of Dyfed

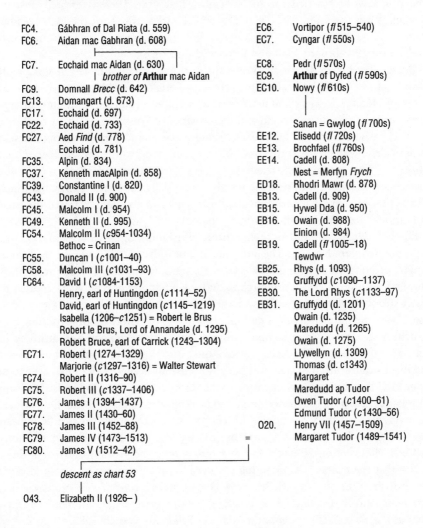

FC4.	Gábhran of Dal Riata (d. 559)		EC6.	Vortipor (*fl* 515–540)
FC6.	Aidan mac Gabhran (d. 608)		EC7.	Cyngar (*fl* 550s)
FC7.	Eochaid mac Aidan (d. 630)		EC8.	Pedr (*fl* 570s)
	brother of **Arthur** mac Aidan		EC9.	**Arthur** of Dyfed (*fl* 590s)
FC9.	Domnall *Brecc* (d. 642)		EC10.	Nowy (*fl* 610s)
FC13.	Domangart (d. 673)			
FC17.	Eochaid (d. 697)			
FC22.	Eochaid (d. 733)			Sanan = Gwylog (*fl* 700s)
FC27.	Aed *Find* (d. 778)		EE12.	Elisedd (*fl* 720s)
	Eochaid (d. 781)		EE13.	Brochfael (*fl* 760s)
FC35.	Alpin (d. 834)		EE14.	Cadell (d. 808)
FC37.	Kenneth macAlpin (d. 858)			Nest = Merfyn *Frych*
FC39.	Constantine I (d. 820)		ED18.	Rhodri Mawr (d. 878)
FC43.	Donald II (d. 900)		EB13.	Cadell (d. 909)
FC45.	Malcolm I (d. 954)		EB15.	Hywel Dda (d. 950)
FC49.	Kenneth II (d. 995)		EB16.	Owain (d. 988)
FC54.	Malcolm II (*c*954–1034)			Einion (d. 984)
	Bethoc = Crinan		EB19.	Cadell (*fl* 1005–18)
FC55.	Duncan I (*c*1001–40)			Tewdwr
FC58.	Malcolm III (*c*1031–93)		EB25.	Rhys (d. 1093)
FC64.	David I (*c*1084–1153)		EB26.	Gruffydd (*c*1090–1137)
	Henry, earl of Huntingdon (*c*1114–52)		EB30.	The Lord Rhys (*c*1133–97)
	David, earl of Huntingdon (*c*1145–1219)		EB31.	Gruffydd (d. 1201)
	Isabella (1206–*c*1251) = Robert le Brus			Owain (d. 1235)
	Robert le Brus, Lord of Annandale (d. 1295)			Maredudd (d. 1265)
	Robert Bruce, earl of Carrick (1243–1304)			Owain (d. 1275)
FC71.	Robert I (1274–1329)			Llywellyn (d. 1309)
	Marjorie (*c*1297–1316) = Walter Stewart			Thomas (d. c1343)
FC74.	Robert II (1316–90)			Margaret
FC75.	Robert III (*c*1337–1406)			Maredudd ap Tudor
FC76.	James I (1394–1437)			Owen Tudor (*c*1400–61)
FC77.	James II (1430–60)			Edmund Tudor (*c*1430–56)
FC78.	James III (1452–88)		O20.	Henry VII (1457–1509)
FC79.	James IV (1473–1513)	=		Margaret Tudor (1489–1541)
FC80.	James V (1512–42)			

descent as chart 53

O43. Elizabeth II (1926–)

Territorial Service) in 1945, where she learned how to handle and repair all manner of vehicles.

Princess Elizabeth first met her future husband in July 1939 during a visit to Dartmouth Naval College where he was a cadet. He was grandson of George, king of the Hellenes, and, through his mother, great-great grandson of Queen Victoria, and thereby Elizabeth's third cousin. His father had been banished from Greece during a military coup in 1922 and Philip was brought up by his uncle, Lord Mountbatten. Philip served with distinction in the Royal Navy during the Second World War, both with the Mediterranean Fleet and with the British Pacific Fleet in Southeast Asia and the Pacific. He was mentioned in despatches after the battle of Cape Matapan and received many decorations including the Greek War Cross, the Burma Star and the French Croix de Guerre.

When it became clear that Elizabeth and Philip would marry, it was necessary for Philip to renounce his rights to the Greek throne and he became a naturalised British subject as Philip Mountbatten, which was concluded on 28 February 1947. The couple were married on 20 November that year. He was created duke of Edinburgh on the same day. Their first son, Charles, was born on 14 November 1948. Princess Anne was born 15 August 1950, then, after a long gap, came Prince Andrew on 19 February 1960 and Prince Edward on 10 March 1964.

George VI's health deteriorated over the next few years but he felt in sufficiently good health in 1952 for Elizabeth to agree to undertake a world tour. She was at the Treetops Hotel in Kenya when news came of her father's sudden death in February. She returned hurriedly to Britain and was crowned at Westminster Abbey on 2 June 1953. The whole event was televised. The queen was to make much use of television in popularising the royal family and bringing her closer to the people. Her regular Christmas Day message was televised for the first time in 1957 and in 1969 she agreed to a television film being made about the daily routine of family life which displayed some remarkably rudimentary moments and also demonstrated the sense of humour Elizabeth inherited from her parents.

Elizabeth dedicated much of her time to establishing a closer bond to the Commonwealth of Nations. The independence of India in 1947 had seen the former Empire begin to crumble and its successor Commonwealth had a less clear identity. Elizabeth and the duke of Edinburgh undertook a number of state visits in order to foster stronger relationships. This was always difficult, especially during the 1950s and 1960s when much stronger national identities saw outbreaks of revolution and civil strife in many former colonies around the World. Problems and attitudes in Ghana, South Africa, Rhodesia, Canada and Australia, as examples, showed that Elizabeth's role as head of state was not always readily accepted and often criticised. Prince Philip's comments at the time of the Rhodesia crisis in 1963 caused friction with Parliament, and the prince needed to be reminded of his position. On balance, however, most of the Commonwealth countries respect the queen as a figurehead and recognize her constant efforts in striving to foster goodwill and harmony between fellow nations. It has been a demanding role, and possibly one that at times meant that the queen was becoming slightly removed from her own role towards her British subjects. Nevertheless, the constitutional role of the monarch had become so firmly established that despite a number of major foreign incidents, such as the Suez Crisis, Aden, and even the Falklands War in 1982, when Prince Andrew saw active service, they are seen as the responsibility of the government of the day and the queen's role, despite extensive consultation, is not seen by the public as paramount. Yet, despite this lack of association in Britain, other nations may use such events to praise or condemn the queen. This resurfaced in 1997 when the tour of India led to demonstrations seeking an apology from Britain for the massacre at Amritsar in 1919.

It was not until 22 February 1957 that the duke of Edinburgh was granted the title of "Prince". This followed a period of anguish when it was confirmed that the royal family would continue to use the surname Windsor, after Elizabeth's father, rather than Mountbatten. The Duke felt marginalised and, even though he respected his secondary role to the queen, he still strove to be recognized in his own right. It was as much Philip's desire as the queen's that the royal family should be seen as contemporary and not as a curious British anachronism. He made considerable use of the public relations media and became known for his outspokenness. He also encouraged the children to mix freely with other children, and insisted upon their education at public schools rather than privately at the Palace. The duke initiated the Duke of Edinburgh's Award Scheme in 1956 to encourage young people to tackle a wide range of challenges or experiences.

The queen was admonished by Lord Altrincham in 1957 for being "out of touch", a charge that has been levied by others in the intervening years despite the many measures the Queen has taken to become closer to her subjects. The main problem is that society has moved on, particularly since the 1960s, so if the queen is out of touch, it is only because the monarchy is not designed to follow fashion. If it did it would be criticised for losing its traditional values and the balance between those and being part of society is a difficult one to assess, especially when there is a high level of hypocrisy amongst the media in their dealings with the royal family.

Although there have been scandals galore in all generations about the love life of the monarchy, it has only been in this generation that the queen and her immediate family has had to face censure and vilification from the press and certain factions of the public, even though they have striven to maintain high standards, and certainly far higher than any monarch between CHARLES I and VICTORIA. This judgement began in 1955 with the press criticism of the suggested marriage between Princess Margaret and Group Captain Peter Townsend, the queen's equerry, who had been divorced. Margaret followed the teachings of the church and decided not to marry him. In 1960 she married Antony Armstrong-Jones, who became Lord Snowdon in 1961. They had two children, but marital problems began to emerge in the 1960s and the couple were eventually divorced in May 1978. The problems with the marriages of the queen's children were blown out of all proportion by the press. Perhaps the least criticised was Princess Anne, whose charitable work has caused her to be more highly respected, but also because her formidable character means she is well equipped to handle herself in difficult situations. Her marriage to Mark Phillips in 1973 ended in divorce in April 1992, when it was leaked that the Princess had developed an attachment to another former equerry, Timothy Laurence, whom she subsequently married. Prince Andrew's marriage in July 1986 to Sarah Ferguson soon had its difficulties and the couple were separated in March 1992 and divorced in May 1996. Sarah Ferguson's vivacity and extravagance was itself something of a threat to the image of the royal family and she was later criticised for bringing them into disrepute as a consequence of such antics as a royal edition of the popular television programme It's a Knockout in 1987. "Fergie", as she was popularly known, was not seen as acting with due decorum.

The major tragedy was the fairy-tale marriage with the unhappy ending between Prince Charles and Lady Diana Spencer. Charles had come under considerable pressure during the 1970s to marry, and his name had been duly linked to many famous people. His final choice of the twenty-year-old Diana, daughter of the eighth Earl Spencer, met with much enthusiasm, and the royal wedding on 29 July 1981 was a public holiday with street parties and great celebration. However over the ensuing years it became apparent that Diana was ill-suited to the pressure of life as a member of the Royal Family and her relationship with Charles, who became

57. Great Britain (6) – **The male line of descent of Prince Charles and Prince William**

The Prince of Wales is in direct male descent from the counts of Oldenburg from northern Germany, whose family included the kings of Denmark and Norway.

	Egilmar I, count of Oldenburg (*fl* 1100s)
	Egilmar II, count of Oldenburg (*fl* 1130s)
	Christian I, count of Oldenburg (d. 1167)
	Moritz, count of Oldenburg (d. *c*1209)
	Christian II, count of Oldenburg (d. 1233)
	Johann I, count of Oldenburg (*fl* 1250s)
	Christian V, count of Oldenburg (d. 1316)
	Johann Ii, count of Oldenburg (*fl* 1320s)
	Konrad, count of Oldenburg (*fl* 1340s)
	Christian VI, count of Oldenburg (*c*1360–*c*1420)
	Dietrich II, count of Oldenburg (*c*1390–1440)
VA59.	Christian I, king of Denmark, Norway and Sweden (1426–81)
VA62.	Frederik I, king of Denmark and Norway (1471–1533)
VA63.	Christian III, king of Denmark and Norway (1503–59)
	Hans, duke of Schleswig-Holstein-Sonderburg-Beck (1545–1622)
	Alexander, duke of Schleswig-Holstein-Sonderburg (1573–1627)
	August Philipp, duke of Schleswig-Holstein-Sonderburg-Beck (1612–75)
	Ludwig Friedrich, duke of Schleswig-Holstein-Sonderburg-Beck (1654–1728)
	Peter August, duke of Schleswig-Holstein-Sonderburg-Beck (1697–1775)
	Karl Anton August (1727–59)
	Friedrich Karl, duke of Schleswig-Holstein-Sonderburg-Beck (1757–1816)
	Friedrich Wilhelm, duke of Schleswig-Holstein-Sonderburg-Glücksburg (1785–1831)
	(*married Louise, great-granddaughter of George II of Great Britain*)
VA75.	Christian IX of Denmark (1818–1906)
	George I, king of the Hellenes (1845–1913)
	Prince Andrew of Greece (1882–1944)
	Prince Philip, duke of Edinburgh (b. 1921)
Y21.	Charles, prince of Wales (b. 1948)
	Prince William of Wales (b. 1982)

portrayed as an eccentric, "New Age" prince, began to crack. The couple separated in 1992 and were divorced in August 1996.

1992, with its rapid sequence of divorces and separations, brought a further decline in respect for the royal family, with a wave of support for abolishing the monarchy and establishing a republic. In the autumn of 1992, Windsor Castle was severely damaged by fire and there was increased criticism when it was learned that, because the castle and its priceless contents were not insured, the restoration work would have to be funded from the public purse. In response to the outcry the queen consented to pay income tax, and limited the scope of the Civil List. It was not surprising that in her annual speech at the Guildhall that year, the queen referred to 1992 as her "annus horribilis".

The queen and her relatives were not without personal threats and dangers. The most tragic of all was the murder of Lord Mountbatten by the IRA on 28 August 1979. In March 1974 a gunman named Ian Ball fired six shots at Princess Anne in his failed attempt to kidnap her. In June 1981 Marcus Sergeant fired six blanks at the queen while she was riding to the Trooping of the Colour, and in July 1982 there was the famous incident when Michael Fagan succeeding in breaching all security at Buckingham Palace and encountered the queen in her bedroom.

The tragic death of Diana, Princess of Wales in August 1997 saw such an upsurge in public sympathy, that it polarised attitudes between the traditional distant and stoic role of royalty and the apparently open and human approach adopted by Diana. The challenging encomium by Diana's brother Earl Spencer struck a chord with the public at large.

The role of the monarchy has become less appreciated than at any other time this century and respect is given to individuals rather than to the institution as a whole, which many now regard as outmoded. The challenge at the end of the twentieth century, as Britain becomes more deeply integrated with Europe, is for the monarchy to find a new place in the affections and confidence of the people.

THE WORLD ABOUT THEM: LEGENDARY AND EUROPEAN RULERS

1: LEGENDARY OR SEMI-HISTORICAL KINGS OF BRITAIN

Like all nations Britain has its share of myths, and from these come names of ancient kings and their deeds. The most famous of these king lists appears in *The History of the Kings of Britain* by Geoffrey of Monmouth completed in 1136. It provided the basis for the legend of King Arthur, as well as the source for stories about King Lear, Blaedud, Cymbeline and others. The following covers all of Geoffrey's kings, plus the legendary and semi-historical kings of the Picts and the Scots. Those which have separate biographical entries (either here or in their appropriate historical section as cross-referenced below) are marked [b].

P. BRITAIN

Long disowned by scholars, *The History of the Kings of Britain* by Geoffrey of Monmouth nevertheless contains the names of many kings who really existed, though he got most facts about them wrong. In many cases Geoffrey lists in sequence kings who may have ruled at the same time, so it is impossible even to guess at the dating of most of his rulers except where they impinge upon history. Some of the following names appear elsewhere, but all are included here to help guide through the tangled history created by Geoffrey.

Ref.	Ruler	Reign	Died	Notes
P1.	Brut or Brutus[b]	reigned 23 years		

After Brut's death Britain was divided between his three sons. Locrinus inherited the main part of Britain, which was called Loegres; Kamber inherited Cambria or Wales, and Albanactus inherited Albany or Scotland.

Ref.	Ruler	Reign	Died	Notes
P2.	Locrinus	reigned 10 years		son of Brutus; killed in battle
P3.	Gwendolen	reigned 15 years		widow of Locrinus; abdicated
P4.	Maddan	reigned 40 years		son of Locrinus and Gwendolen
P5.	Mempricius	reigned 20 years		son of Maddan; killed by wolves
P6.	Ebraucus	reigned 39 years		son of Mempricius; legendary founder of York
P7.	Brutus II, *Greenshield*	reigned 12 years		son of Ebraucus; contemporary of Solomon (*fl* 1000BC)
P8.	Leil	reigned 25 years		son of Brutus II; founded Carlisle
P9.	Rud Hud Hudibras	reigned 39 years		son of Leil; founded Canterbury, Winchester and Shaftesbury
P10.	Blaedud[b]	reigned 20 years		son of Rud Hud Hudibras; founded Bath; killed while trying to fly

Ref.	Ruler	Reign	Died	Notes
P11.	Leir or Lear[b]	reigned 60 years		son of Blaedud; founded Leicester
P12.	Cordelia[b]	reigned 5 years		daughter of Leir; imprisoned; committed suicide
P13.	Marganus	reigned 2 years		son of Goneril and Regan and nephew of Cordelia; ruled north of Humber only; killed in battle
P14.	Cunedagius	reigned 35 years		ruled 2 years south of Humber, then expelled his brother Marganus and ruled a united Britain for 33 years
P15.	Rivallo			son of Cunedagius
P16.	Gurgustius			son of Rivallo
P17.	Sisillius			ancestry not known
P18.	Jago			nephew of Gurgustius
P19.	Kimarcus			son of Sisillius
P20.	Gorboduc			ancestry not known

Civil war broke out between four chieftains: Cloten of Cornwall, Pinner of Loegres, Rudaucus of Kambria and Staterius of Albany.

Ref.	Ruler	Reign	Died	Notes
P21.	Dunvallo *Molmutius*	reigned 40 years		son of Cloten, king of Cornwall; created the Molmutine Laws
P22.	Brennius	co-reigned 5 years		son of Dunvallo; ruled north of Humber only; fled to France
P23.	Belinus[b]	co-reigned 5 years		expelled his brother Brennius; length of reign thereafter not stated
P24.	Gurguit *Barbtruc*[b]			son of Belinus
P25.	Guithelin[b]			ancestry not known
P26.	Marcia, as regent for Sisillius			widow of Guithelin
P27.	Sisillius II			son of Guithelin and Marcia
P28.	Kinarius			son of Sisillius II
P29.	Danius			son of Sisillius II
P30.	Morvidus			illegitimate son of Danius; killed by a monster
P31.	Gorbonianus			son of Morvidus
P32.	Archgallo			son of Morvidus; deposed; restored for a further 10 years
P33.	Elidurus or Elidyr *the Dutiful*[b]			brother of Archgallo; reigned 5 years then restored Archgallo; restored after Archgallo's death but deposed; restored a third time after Peredurus
P34.	Ingenius	reigned 7 years		brother of Archgallo; ruled south of Humber
P35.	Peredurus	reigned 7 years		brother of Archgallo; ruled north of Humber and then all of Britain after death of Ingenius

P36.	*unnamed*		a further son of Gorbonianus
P37.	Marganus II		son of Archgallo
P38.	Enniaunus	reigned 5 years	brother of Marganus; deposed
P39.	Idvallo		son of Ingenius
P40.	Runo		son of Peredurus
P41.	Gerennus		son of Elidurus
P42.	Catellus		son of Gerennus
P43.	Millus		ancestry not known
P44.	Porrex		ancestry not known
P45.	Cherin		ancestry not known
P46.	Fulgenius		son of Cherin
P47.	Edadus		son of Cherin
P48.	Andragius		son of Cherin
P49.	Urianus		son of Andragius
P50.	Eliud		
P51.	Cledaucus		
P52.	Clotenus		
P53.	Gurgintius		
P54.	Merianus		
P55.	Blaedud (II)		
P56.	Cap		
P57.	Oenus		
P58.	Sisillius III		
P59.	Beldgabred		
P60.	Archmail		brother of Beldgabred
P61.	Eldol		
P62.	Redon		
P63.	Redechius		
P64.	Samuil		
P65.	Penessil		
P66.	Pir		
P67.	Capoir		
P68.	Digueillus		son of Capoir
P69.	Heli (more likely Beli *Mawr*)[b]	reigned 40 years	son of Digueillis; see A1
P70.	Lud or Llud[b]		son of Heli; founded London; see A2
P71.	Cassivelaunus[b]		brother of Lud; see A3
P72.	Tenvantius[b]		son of Lud; same as Tasciovanus [A10]
P73.	Cymbeline[b]		son of Tenvantius; see A22
P74.	Guiderius[b]		son of Cymbeline; killed in battle
P75.	Arviragus or Gweyrydd[b]		son of Cymbeline; see A29
P76.	Marius[b]		son of Arviragus; see A33
P77.	Coilus or Coel[b]		son of Marius; see A35
P78.	Lucius[b]		son of Coilus; see A36
P79.	Sulgenius[b]		of unknown ancestry; united Britons against Severus of Rome; killed in battle
P80.	Bassianus[b] (i.e. Caracalla)		son of Sulgenius; killed; see B21

Ref.	Ruler	Reign	Died	Notes
P81.	Carausius[b]			usurper; murdered; see B51
P82.	Allectus[b]			deposed; see B52
P83.	Asclepiodotus[b]	reigned 10 years		formerly duke of Cornwall; elected king; killed in battle
P84.	Coel[b]			usurped the throne; see DA1
P85.	Constantius[b]	reigned 11 years		Coel's son-in-law; see B53
P86.	Constantine[b]			son of Constantius; see B55
P87.	Octavius or Eudaf *Hen* (the Old)[b]			usurper; abdicated; see B66 and DB1
P88.	Maximianus[b]	reigned 5 years		nephew of Coel; set off to conquer Gaul; killed in Rome; see B64
P89.	Caradocus[b]			possibly DA6 and FB1
P90.	Dionatus[b]			possibly DA28
P91.	Gracianus[b]			usurper; assassinated; see B63
P92.	Constantine II[b]	reigned 10 years		see B56
P93.	Constans[b]			son of Constantine II; see B57
P94.	Vortigern[b]			usurper; see DB2
P95.	Vortimer[b]			son of Vortigern; see DB3
P96.	Aurelius Ambrosius[b]			son of Constantine II; see DB4
P97.	Uther Pendragon[b]			brother of Aurelius
P98.	Arthur[b]			son of Uther; see DB5
P99.	Constantine III[b]			son of Cador of Cornwall and Arthur's cousin; see DB6 and DC9
P100.	Aurelius Conanus[b]			nephew of Constantine III; see DC2
P101.	Vortiporius[b]			see EC6
P102.	Malgo[b]			see ED4
P103.	Keredic[b]			may be same as DA33
Geoffrey now records an interregnum of unspecified period				
P104.	Cadfan[b]			see ED8
P105.	Cadwallo[b]			reigned 48 years; see ED9
P106.	Cadwallader[b]		689	reigned 12 years; fell ill from the plague and sailed to Brittany; see ED11.

[P1] **BRUT** or **BRUTUS** The legendary first king of Britain according to Geoffrey of Monmouth. In Geoffrey's *History*, Brutus is the son of Silvius who is the son of Aeneas's own son Ascanius. Aeneas was a prince of Troy who survived the war with the Greeks and fled to Italy along with other refugees from Troy. There they became the ancestors of the Roman kings. When Brutus grew into manhood he accidentally killed his father, as predicted by an oracle. He fled to Greece where he found other descendants of Trojan refugees enslaved by king Pandrasus. Brutus encouraged the Trojans to revolt, and bargained with Pandrasus that he might lead them out of Greece into a new land (shades of Moses in Egypt). Brutus also married the king's daughter, Ignoge. Directed by the goddess Diana Brutus sailed through the Mediterranean, collecting other Trojan descendants en route, and eventually made it to the island of Britain (then called Albion) where they landed at, of all places, Totnes. One of Brutus's followers, called Corineus, was made king of this territory (hence Cornwall is named after him). The Trojan settlers were attacked by giants who inhabited Albion. The giants were eventually killed including their leader, Gogmagog, whom Corineus cast over a cliff. Brutus then explored Britain (which is named after him) and decided to build his new capital along the Thames. He called it New Troy or Troia Nova, which became Trinovantum, the origin of the tribe of the Trinovantes who were descended from the Trojans. Brutus had three sons, each of whom inherited lands in Britain. The eldest Locrinus inherited what would later be called England, but which was then named Loegres after him. Kamber inherited Wales, or Cambria, whilst Albanactus inherited Albany, or Scotland. Brutus ruled for twenty-three years, and introduced a law code so that all lived peaceably. After his death he was buried within the city of New Troy.

Geoffrey dates Brutus as a contemporary of the Jewish High Priest Eli, who is traditionally dated to before 1100 BC. The traditional date for the fall of Troy is about 1180 BC. Allowing for a generation of around twenty to twenty-five years, a great-grandson of Aeneas would be living some fifty to seven-five years after the fall of Troy and consistent with the above dates. However recent archeological research has pushed the fall of Troy forward in time by perhaps two hundred and fifty years, to around the year 900 BC. Brutus, if he existed, would thus have lived around 800 BC, or roughly contemporaneous with the founding of Rome. This date is more consistent with that ascribed to the influx of the Celts across Europe and into Britain and Ireland. Although Geoffrey's Brutus is almost certainly a creation of his own imagination, there is no reason to disbelieve the concept of tribes of Celts settling in Britain at this period and one strong leader emerging. This leader may well have been called BRUDE, the usual Pictish name for their ruler, which means "strength".

Geoffrey's story of the descendants of Brutus is an enjoyable fantasy with all the intrigue of a family saga. Little of it has any historical value at all, and belongs more to a book on British mythology, but a few of the early names are worthy of reflection and are included in these biographies.

[P10] **BLAEDUD** or **BLADUD** Legendary king of Britain. Blaedud was the son of Rud Hud Hudibras. Hudibras had ruled for thirty-nine years so we can imagine Blaedud was fairly elderly when he came to the throne (even Geoffrey says he "finally" succeeded him, as if he'd waited a long time). If so, then Blaedud would have joined his father in his extensive building programme which included Canterbury, Winchester and Shaftesbury. Blaedud continued this by building Kaerbadum, or Bath. One legend states that Blaedud had leprosy and only the hot waters of the spa could ease his pain. Blaedud also introduced the worship of Minerva. He is called "a most ingenious man" who encouraged the study of necromancy. He also tried to fly and created for himself a pair of wings. However he fell to his death from the top of the Temple of Apollo in London. Geoffrey makes Blaedud a contemporary of Elijah in Israel, which would be about 920 BC. Allowing for the 250–year dating discrepancy amongst the archeological record (*see under* BRUTUS *for details*), we may more plausibly date Blaedud to about 650 BC. Despite this, Geoffrey's tale about Blaedud is fiction. Bath was founded by the Romans as *Aquae Sulis*. Blaedud was the father of LEAR.

[P11] **LEAR, LEIR** or **LLYR** Legendary king of Britain according to Geoffrey of Monmouth, whose *History* was also the basis for Shakespeare's play *King Lear*. He was the son of BLAEDUD and was the founder of Leicester. He reigned for sixty years and had no sons to succeed him, so decided to divide the kingdom between his three daughters Goneril, Regan and Cordelia. Although Goneril and Regan showed him signs of affection, and were married to the dukes of Albany and Cornwall, Cordelia was more cautious. In testing her father she upset him and was therefore banished to France where she married the king of the Franks, Aganippus. Lear continued to rule one third of the kingdom but found, after a few years, that his elder daughters wished to be rid of him. He eventually retired to France where he was reconciled with Cordelia and was able to return to England with a French army, which defeated the dukes of Albany and Cornwall and restored Lear (Geoffrey's story has a much happier ending than Shakespeare's version). When Lear died, he was buried in a vault under the river Soar at Leicester. Cordelia continued to rule Britain for five years, as the first queen of Britain, until her sisters' sons captured her. She killed herself in prison. The two nephews, Marganus and Cunedagius, divided the kingdom between them, north and south of the Humber.

Geoffrey seems to have adopted the name Lear from the Celtic deity Llyr or Lir, who was a god or ruler of the sea, and the father of MANANNAN and BRAN. Bran, which word probably means king as in the modern Welsh word *brenin*, may be the same as Brennius [P22], whom Geoffrey has ruling northern Britain over a century after Lear. Brennius was defeated by his brother BELINUS after five years and exiled to France, from where he continued to rule and waged war against the Romans. There was a genuine Celtic chief in Gaul called Brennus who invaded Rome around the year 390 BC. The semi-legendary Bran the Blessed, the archdruid of the British, lived about AD 50. He is supposed to have married Anna, a daughter of Joseph of Arimathea and was allegedly an ancestor of Cunedda. Bran was mortally wounded in his war against Ireland and he commanded that his head be buried at the White Mount in London, the present site of the Tower of London. Bran's head became a symbol of safety in guarding England against invasion. One legend states that Arthur dug it up and that signalled his doom. Bran's symbol was the raven, and the belief that England will be safe, provided the ravens stay in the Tower of London, is part of the same legend.

[P12] **CORDELIA** Legendary queen of Britain, according to Geoffrey of Monmouth, and daughter of LEAR, whom see for details.

[P22] **BRENNIUS** Legendary ruler of Britain, probably based on the leader of the Gaulish Celts, Brennus who sacked Rome in about 390 BC. The name is also rendered as BRAN. *See under* BELINUS *and* LEAR *for further details.*

[P23] **BELINUS** Legendary king of the British according to the *History* of Geoffrey of Monmouth. He was the elder son of Dunvallo Molmutius, the law-giver, and brother of BRENNIUS. The two shared the kingdom between them, with Belinus ruling the land south of the Humber, but he learned that Brennius was plotting against him. Belinus invaded the north and expelled Brennius, who fled to France. Later the two brothers became reconciled and combined in a war on Rome. At home Belinus was a great road and city builder. He was the founder of Kaerusk, or Caerleon as it became. He restored many cities in Britain destroyed during his civil war with his brother and in rebuilding the walls of London established Billingsgate or Belin's Gate, named after him. There is no historical foundation for Belinus, although Brennius may be the same as Brennus who lived about 390 BC. Belinus is more likely a corruption of the Celtic deity Beli or Bilé, the Celtic sun god, whose name lends itself to the feast of Beltaine. It appears as the name of several later kings including the many rulers called BELI or BILI and the noted early British rulers BELI MAWR and CUNOBELINUS.

[P30] **MORVIDUS** Legendary king of the British, according to Geoffrey of Monmouth. He was the father of five sons who succeeded him in turn. *See under* ELIDOR *and* PEREDUR *for details.*

[P74] **GUIDERIUS** Legendary British king listed by Geoffrey of Monmouth. Guiderius is the eldest son of CYMBELINE, born in the tenth year of his father's reign, or about AD 20. It was his failure to pay tribute to the Romans that led to the invasion by Claudius. Guiderius was killed in the first battle, and was buried at Gloucester. It may be that Geoffrey confused Guiderius with TOGODUMNUS or, more plausibly, that Guiderius (spelt as Gweirydd) was the real Celtic name of Togodumnus or his successor (according to Geoffrey) ARVIRAGUS.

[P79] **SULGENIUS** A legendary king of Britain according to Geoffrey of Monmouth. By Geoffrey's time scale he would have ruled about AD 200, and took over leadership following the unrest at the death of LUCIUS, who had no heir. This timing coincides remarkably with the revolution under the British governor ALBINUS, and Sulgenius may have been a high ranking Briton serving under Albinus who commanded troops in Britain. His name, however, is not otherwise recorded and Geoffrey's story of his original defeat by SEVERUS and his later death in a battle against Severus at York in 211 suggests that Sulgenius may have been a chief of the Picts, which would make him a contemporary of Conbust or Crautreic.

[P83] **ASCLEPIODOTUS** Identified in Geoffrey of Monmouth's *History* as a king of Britain who succeeded ALLECTUS in 295. Geoffrey makes him the duke of Cornwall, raised to the kingship by the British who disliked the usurper Allectus. Asclepiodotus defeated and killed Allectus and then laid siege to London, killing almost all of the Roman inhabitants. Asclepiodotus ruled for ten years, but it was during his reign that the persecution of the Christians began under Emperor Diocletian, which included the martyrdom of Alban. Geoffrey's chronology is probably right as he places Asclepiodotus between 295 and 305 (though Geoffrey states no precise dates), which is contemporaneous with Diocletian and a possible date for Alban's death. In all other facts, though, Geoffrey is as wrong as ever. Asclepiodotus was the praetorian prefect or second-in-command of the future emperor CONSTANTIUS. He brought his fleet around southern Britain to the Isle of Wight and marched into Hampshire whilst Constantius brought a second pronged attack on London. Asclepiodotus's army met and killed Allectus. Thereafter Constantius remained in Britain for some years rebuilding the state. Quite probably Asclepiodotus was in charge of much of this work, but he was never king and does not seem to have been made governor. That post was held by Aurelius Arpagius at this time. According to Geoffrey, in another of his flights of fancy, Asclepiodotus was killed in battle against Duke COEL of Colchester.

[P87] **OCTAVIUS** or **EUDAF** (or **EUDAV**) A shadowy semi-legendary ruler who almost certainly has some base in reality but who, like ARTHUR, has merged mostly into myth and fantasy. He appears in Geoffrey of Monmouth's unreliable *History*, where he usurps the throne after CONSTANTINE left England for Rome which, in Geoffrey's chronology, is about the year 308. Octavius was soon dethroned by the general Trahern and fled to Norway, but he returned with an army, defeated Trahern, and reigned thereafter for many years. Geoffrey suggests he reigned until the time of GRATIAN, but as that was a hundred years later we can rule that out. Even ruling until the time of Maximianus (*see* MAGNUS MAXIMUS) is pushing matters, as that is a gap of seventy-five years. Nevertheless, Geoffrey clearly believed Octavius ruled for many years in the middle of the fourth century, and Welsh tradition has just such a king at that time: Eudes or Euidaf, who was descended from LUCIUS. Euidaf was known as the duke or warlord of the Gewisse. The Gewisse is a name that we encounter again, particularly in connection with CERDIC. Its meaning is not entirely clear, as in Cerdic's day it was used to mean a confederacy of tribes. It may have meant that in Euidaf's day, since he seems to have commanded the British tribes focused on his own territory in southern Wales, around Gwent. Almost all of the later rulers of southern Wales claim descent from Euidaf. Tradition states that he married a daughter of Carausius, the Roman commander of the Saxon Shore, and had at least four children. Helena or Elen married Magnus Maximus, whose daughter Severa married VORTIGERN. His eldest son, Erbin, seems to have ruled in Gwent and passed the kingdom on to his son ERB. Another of Euidaf's sons, CYNAN, became ruler of Dumnonia, whilst Cynan's grandson Cynan Meriadoc (whom Geoffrey calls Octavius's nephew) became the first king of Brittany. Euidaf is sufficiently entrenched in Welsh tradition to be regarded as a real individual who held power in southern and central Wales around the period 350–80 and possibly beyond. His sons and grandsons enter the dawn of recorded history at the start of the fifth century.

[P89] **CARADOCUS** According to Geoffrey of Monmouth's *History*, a duke of Cornwall who supported MAXIMIANUS in his claim on the emperorship of Rome and encouraged the marriage between Maximianus and Helen, the daughter of OCTAVIUS. When Maximianus left Britain for Gaul and then Rome, Caradocus took over the kingship of Britain, but seems to have died soon after and was succeeded by his brother DIONATUS. This may all be an invention of Geoffrey's. There is no doubt that MAGNUS MAXIMUS (the real Maximianus) did leave behind commanders in Britain after he left and that some of these were the ancestors of later kings. Caradocus is one of the commonest names amongst the early British rulers, so Geoffrey has a reasonable chance of being right. He may have been the ruler of Ergyng, CARADOC VREICHFAS, or Geoffrey may have confused him with the later ruler of Alclud, CERETIC.

[P90] **DIONATUS** A legendary king of Cornwall and later of Britain mentioned by Geoffrey of Monmouth in his *History*. Dionatus was the brother of CARADOCUS and lived at the end of the fourth century. He apparently transported eleven thousand women from Britain to the new colony in Armorica (Brittany) as wives to the British settlers. However many of these were captured by the Huns and either murdered or transported to Germany. This legend has links with the story of St Ursula, believed to be the daughter of a British chieftain. Although betrothed to a pagan prince, she wished to remain a virgin and spent three years in worship and study on a ship. The ship was driven by a storm into the Rhine and Ursula and her companions were killed at Cologne when she refused to marry the leader of the Huns. Ursula's father may well have been a Dionatus or DONIERT or DUNAUT of Cornwall, as this was a popular British name.

[P91] **GRACIANUS** Geoffrey of Monmouth's version of GRATIAN in his *History*. His facts may be close to the truth. He records that Gracianus was a supporter of MAGNUS *MAXIMUS* who helped in the settlement of Britons in Armorica. When Magnus was murdered, Gracianus seized the British throne but ruled with such tyranny that he was soon murdered. Geoffrey may have confused the name with Gradlonus, also termed Gratian [SA2], who was an early chieftain in Brittany.

[P97] **UTHER PENDRAGON** Legendary king of Britain. Unlike other kings associated by Geoffrey of Monmouth with king ARTHUR who do seem to have some historical base, there is no origin for Uther, whose name is probably a straightforward misunderstanding by Geoffrey of a nickname. In Gaelic, *uther* means *terrible*, and Gildas referred to several notorious kings of this period as being vicious tyrants. The description might equally have applied to AURELIUS CANINUS, VORTIGERN or VORTIPOR as the likeliest candidates.

[P103] **KEREDIC** The name used by Geoffrey of Monmouth for a king who ruled in Britain between Malgo (MAELGWYN) and CADFAN, or 549 to 615. This is too long a period for one king's rule, especially as in Geoffrey's tale Keredic proved so hateful that the Saxons summoned a vast army of Vandals from Ireland, and they drove Keredic out of his kingdom. This suggests Keredic ruled for only a few years. Keredic is another version of the common Celtic name CERETIC, and Geoffrey was probably confusing more than one character in his story. Even so, it is not clear who he is talking about. The only ruler who fits into this period with this name is CERDIC who, though almost certainly of British descent, was the traditional founder of the West Saxon kingdom. Nothing that Geoffrey cites applies to our knowledge of Cerdic, but he may have linked his name with that of CEREDIG of Elmet, who was driven out of his kingdom by EDWIN of Northumbria. After Keredic's expulsion Geoffrey notes that the British were without a ruler of their own for many years until the rise of Cadfan.

Q. SCOTLAND

The Scottish kings later came to claim a pedigree that went back to 330BC and Fergus, son of Ferchard. The authenticity of this has no basis in fact, though the names in the list may well have existed in their Celtic forms among chieftains in northern Ireland and amongst the western islands of Scotland. The only details we have about them come from the records assembled by Hector Boece in *The History and Chronicles of Scotland* in 1527.

Ref.	Ruler	Reign	Died	Notes
Q1.	Fergus mac Feradach[b]	fl 330 BC		
Q2.	Ferithais			
Q3.	Maynus			son of Fergus; also called Maine
Q4.	Dorvidilla			son of Maynus; also called Dornadil
Q5.	Nathak			
Q6.	Rewtar			son of Dorvidilla; also called Reuther
Q7.	Rewtha			
Q8.	Therius			
Q9.	Josyn			
Q10.	Fynnane			
Q11.	Durstus			
Q12.	Ewin (Owen) I			
Q13.	Gillus			
Q14.	Ewin (Owen) II			
Q15.	Edeir			
Q16.	Ewin (Owen) III			
Q17.	Metellane			
Q18.	Caratak			
Q19.	Corbreid			
Q20.	Dardannus			
Q21.	Galdus			
Q22.	Lugtak			
Q23.	Mogallus			
Q24.	Conarus	fl 210		the same as Conaire Moglama (T121)
Q25.	Ethodius I			
Q26.	Satraell			
Q27.	Donald I			
Q28.	Ethodius II			
Q29.	Athirco	fl 275		also called Achir Cirre
Q30.	Nathalak			
Q31.	Findok	fl 300		son of Athirco; also called Findachar or Fionn Feicce
Q32.	Donald II			
Q33.	Donald III			
Q34.	Craithlint			also called Cruithluithe
Q35.	Fincormach			grandson of Findok; also called Senchormaich
Q36.	Romak	fl 310s		son of Fincormach; also called Romaich
Q37.	Angusiane	fl 330s		son of Romak; also called Angus and purportedly the great-grandfather of Fergus mac Erc
Q38.	Fethelmak	fl 350s		
Q39.	Eugenius I[b]	357–77		

Succeeded by Fergus mac Erc (see section FC on page 192)

There is an alternative version to the above which is more firmly rooted in reality. It lists the descendants of Cairbre *Riata*, the founder of the Scottish Dál Riatan dynasty, who almost certainly acted as heads of the settlements in Argyll and Kintyre until the arrival of Fergus.

Q40.	Cairbre *Riata*[b]	fl 220		led settlers to Argyll
Q41.	Finntain	fl 240s		
Q42.	Guaire	fl 270s		
Q43.	Cionga	fl 300s		
Q44.	Felim *Lamh-foidh*	fl 330s		
Q45.	Eochaid *Fortamal*	fl 360s		
Q46.	Fergus *Uallach*	fl 390s		
Q47.	Angus *Feartas* (the Fortunate)	fl 410s		
Q48.	Eochaid Mun-reamhar	fl 440s		
Q49.	Earc	? –474	474	father of Fergus [FC1]
Q50.	Loarn[b]	fl 500		ancestor of the Cenél Loarn and Men of Moray

[Q1] **FERGUS** MAC **FERCHARD** According to Scottish tradition, the first king of Scotland, settling there about 330 BC. From him all later kings of Scotland were descended, including FERGUS MOR mac Erc, the first acknowledged ruler of the Dál Riatan Scots. The Irish genealogies do record such a prince. He was the great-great grandson of Angus Tuirmeach, high king of Ireland in the 4th Century BC. We cannot dismiss his existence out of hand, nor can we rule out the possibility that he settled in the Western Isles or Highlands of Scotland and ruled a small community, but we cannot be certain that that same community was ruled continuously by his descendants thereafter. The name Fergus means "man of force" and, since this was the first appearance of that name in the Irish genealogies, we can assume that he was a formidable character and carved out some territory for himself. According to legend he was drowned while returning from Ireland. He was succeeded in turn by his sons Ferithais and Mayne. *See also* CAIRPRE RIATA.

[Q39] **EUGENIUS** or **EUGEN**, original form and variant of EOGAN or OWEN/ OWAIN. The name is also used extensively by Boece and others in their Scottish king lists though the names, as listed below, are not always synonymous with historical rulers.

Eugenius I ruled 357–77. Boece states that he was slain in battle against MAGNUS MAXIMUS, which is entirely possible as during this period Maximus was a general in the army of Theodosius, sent to Britain to quell the unrest. If he existed at all, therefore, Eugenius must have been the leader of Irish mercenaries fighting in Scotland and perhaps defending the Irish settlements against the Picts.

Eugenius II, ruled 420–51. Boece identifies him as a son of FERGUS MOR, but as he has the dates of Fergus wrong it is not possible to identify Eugenius or place him in an historical sequence.

Eugenius III, ruled 535–58. Another name which does not fit into the known historical sequence. Boece places him between Goranus (who may equate to GABHRAN), who was his uncle, and Congallus, who is probably the same as CONALL and who is identified as Eugenius's brother. He is identified as a just and fair ruler.

Eugenius IV, ruled 606–21. Identified as the son of AEDAN, this ruler is almost certainly synonymous with EOCHAID *BUIDE*.

Eugenius V, ruled 684–8. Identified as the brother of Malduinus, or MAELDUIN, and therefore he may equate to DOMNALL *DONN*.

Eugenius VI, ruled 688–98. Identified as the son of Ferchard II who was FERCHAR *FOTA* of the line of Loarn. However, since Boece also identifies him as the uncle of Amberkeletus (equal to AINBCELLACH), he may be a brother of Ferchar.

Eugenius VII, ruled 699–715. Identified as a brother of Amberkeletus (AINBCEL-LACH), though he cannot be SELBACH as Boece lists the latter separately as Solvatius, though much out of sequence. Boece states that an attempt was made to murder Eugenius, but by mistake they murdered his wife, Spontana.

Eugenius VIII, ruled 761–4. Identified as a son of Mordachus, that is MUIREDACH, and therefore he equates to the mysterious EOGAN. Boece tells us that he was a tyrant, given to the pleasures of the flesh, and was murdered by his nobles.

[Q40] **CAIRBRE** *RIATA* Dál Riata, *fl* 220. The founder of the kingdom of Dál Riata in Antrim. Cairbre was one of the sons of Conaire, the high king of Ireland. He lived in Munster but was forced north around the year 220 by famine. He and his followers settled in the north-easternmost point of Antrim where the Irish enclave of Dál Riata was established – the name means Riada's share. Apparently the settlers argued and Cairbre led a further band over the sea to Argyll and Kintyre and thereby founded the original Scottish kingdom of Dál Riata over which FERGUS MAC ERC later established kingship. Although most of the story is legend there is no reason to deny its possibility. Cairbre could also claim descent from FERGUS MAC FERADACH, an earlier legendary founder of the Scottish kingdom. Amongst Cairbre's descendants are several identified by Hector Boece as early kings of the Scots and, although the two lists do not coincide, there are sufficient connections to suggest Boece used the Irish genealogies as his source.

[Q50] **LOARN** *fl* 500. A prince of Dál Riata in Antrim and brother of FERGUS MOR who settled in the territories of Argyll and Kintyre in the late fifth century. Fergus, Loarn and a third brother, Angus, divided the territory between them. Loarn took the lands to the north of Argyll around Loch Linnhe, and this later extended into what became Moray. Descendants of Loarn, starting with FERCHAR *FOTA*, later claimed the throne of Dál Riata in Argyll. His best known descendant was MACBETH.

2: ASSOCIATED KINGDOMS AND AUTHORITIES

This appendix covers those kings or others in positions of authority who may not have been kings of Britain but who are of associated interest. These fall into two main categories. There are those other kingdoms in Europe where the rulers either had some dominion over Britain or where English rulers had dominion over these territories. Examples are the the kings of Norway and Denmark, the high kings of Ireland, the Viking kings of Dublin and the rulers of France, Brittany and Normandy. The second category are those titles which are more honorary than authoritative, though often not without power: the queen or king consorts of

England or Scotland, and the princes of Wales. Those who have biographical entries elsewhere in this book are cross-referenced to the relevant section.

R. FRANCE

France traditionally derives its name from Francio, a Sicambrian who lived in the first century BC. His descendants were kings of the Franks, a tribe that settled in the Roman province of Gaul. The tribe itself sub-divided into several groups, and it was from the northern or Salian Franks that the French kingdom would emerge. One of its rulers, Merovich, was the grandfather of Clovis, who established the basis for the kingdom of France; after him the early kings are known as Merovingians. The Franks had a close relationship with England, particularly the kingdom of Kent. After the dukes of Normandy became kings of England, the English held vast lands in France. The regular inter-marriage between the French and English kings resulted in Edward III assuming the title king of France in 1340, a title that was retained by English kings, no matter how anomalously, until 1801. Because of this close association, all of the French kings are listed.

Ref.	Ruler	Born	Reign	Died	Notes
Salian Franks					
R1.	Pharamond		*fl* 400	427	
R2.	Chlodian the Hairy	*c*395	428–47	447	
R3.	Merovich	*c*415	447–58	458	
R4.	Childeric (I)	*c*436	458–81	481	
R5.	Clovis (I)	*c*465	481–511	511	king of the Franks
On his death the Frankish kingdom was divided between Clovis's sons.					
R6a.	Chlodomir		511–24	524	ruled Orleans; killed in battle
R6b.	Theodoric (Thierry) I		511–34	534	ruled Austrasia (based at Rheims)
R6c.	Childebert (I)	*c*495	511–58	558	ruled Paris
R6d.	Chlothar (I)	*c*497	511–61	561	ruled Soissons; sole king from 558
R7a.	Theodebert (I)		534–48	548	Austrasia
R7b.	Theodebald		548–55	555	Austrasia
R8a.	Charibert (I)	*c*522	561–7	567	Paris; his daughter, Bertha, married Athelbert I of Kent
R8b.	Sigebert (I)	*c*535	561–75	575	Austrasia; murdered
R8c.	Chilperic (I)	*c*539	561–84	584	Soissons; murdered
R8d.	Gontran		561–92	592	Orleans, Burgundy and Aquitaine
R9a.	Childebert II	*c*570	575–95	595	Austrasia; plus Burgundy from 592
R9b.	Chlothar II	*c*584	584–629	629	Soissons; sole king of Franks from 613
R9c.	Theodebert II		595–612	612	Austrasia
R9d.	Theodoric (Thierry) II		595–613	613	Burgundy; plus Austrasia from 612

Ref.	Ruler	Born	Reign	Died	Notes
R10a.	Dagobert (I)	c600	623–39	639	Austrasia 623–634; Neustria 632–639
R10b.	Charibert II		629–32	632	Aquitaine
R10c.	Sigebert II	c630	634–56	656	Austrasia; murdered
R10d.	Clovis II	c634	639–56	656	Neustria and Burgundy
R11a.	Dagobert II		656–61		Austrasia; deposed
	(restored)		676–9	679	Austrasia, second term; murdered
R11b.	Chlothar III		656–73	673	Neustria
R11c.	Childeric II	c649	661–75	675	Austrasia; murdered
R11d.	Theodoric (Thierry) III		673–91	691	Neustria; plus Austrasia from 679

After the death of Theodoric III the kingdom of the Franks was reunited.

Ref.	Ruler	Born	Reign	Died	Notes
R12.	Clovis III	c682	691–5	695	
R13.	Childebert III	c683	695–711	711	
R14.	Dagobert III	c699	711–15	715	
R15.	Chilperic II		715–20	720	ruled Neustria only after 717 but was restored to all France in 720
R16.	Chlothar IV		717–20	720	
R17.	Theodoric (Thierry) IV		720–37	741	deposed
R18.	Charles Martel (the Hammer)	c690	737–41	741	Mayor of the Palace who assumed royal control
R19.	Childeric III		741–51	754	deposed and possibly murdered

Carolingian Dynasty

During the reigns of the last kings of the Merovingian dynasty, the power was assumed by the Mayors of the Palace of Austrasia, particularly Pepin of Heristal (635–714) and his son Charles Martel. Charles's son, Pepin, overthrew the Merovingian kings and established a new dynasty.

Ref.	Ruler	Born	Reign	Died	Notes
R20.	Pepin the Short	c714	751–68	768	
R21.	Carloman	751	768–771	771	Burgundy and southern France
R22.	Charles (I) the Great (Charlemagne)	c742	768–814	814	Austrasia only until 771; crowned emperor in 800

Charlemagne's empire also included most of Germany (Saxony, Alamannia and Bavaria) and northern Italy (Lombardy). Although Charlemagne planned to subdivide the kingdom between his sons, all but one pre-deceased him with the result that a united empire was continued.

Ref.	Ruler	Born	Reign	Died	Notes
R23.	Louis (I) the Pious	c778	814–40	840	
R24.	Charles II the Bald	823	840–77	877	his daughter Judith married Athelwolf of Wessex
R25.	Louis II the Stammerer	846	877–9	879	
R26a.	Louis III	c863	879–82	882	

R26b.	Carloman	c865	879–84	884	
R27.	Charles the Fat	839	884–7	888	grandson of Louis I and king of the East Franks; deposed
R28.	Odo or Eudes		887–98	898	count of Paris; elected when Charles the Fat deposed
R29.	Charles III the Simple	879	898–922	929	son of Louis II who regained control but was deposed and died in prison; he married Edgiva, daughter of Edward the Elder of England
R30.	Robert (I)	c865	922–3	923	count of Paris; brother of Odo; usurped control
R31.	Raoul		923–36	936	son-in-law of Robert I; king of Burgundy
R32.	Louis IV d'Outremer (Over the Sea)	920	936–54	954	son of Charles III; raised in England, hence his nickname
R33.	Lothair	941	954–986	986	
R34.	Louis V the Indolent	967	986–987	987	died in a hunting accident

Capet Dynasty

After the death of Louis V, the throne was assumed by the cousin of Louis IV, Hugh Capet, son of Hugh, count of Paris and his wife Edhilda, daughter of Edward the Elder.

R35.	Hugh or Hugo	c939	987–96	996	
R36.	Robert II the Pious or the Sage	970	996–1031	1031	
R37.	Henri (I)	1008	1031–60	1060	
R38.	Philippe (I)	1052	1060–1108	1108	
R39.	Louis VI the Fat	1081	1108–37	1137	
R40.	Louis VII the Young	1121	1137–80	1180	first husband of Eleanor of Aquitaine; his daughter, Margaret, married (1160) Henry the Young King of England
R41.	Philippe II Augustus	1165	1180–1223	1223	
R42.	Louis VIII the Lion	1187	1223–6	1226	married Blanche, the niece of John of England

When still heir, Louis was offered the throne of England in 1215 and was recognized as king by many of the barons.

R43.	Louis IX, St. Louis	1214	1226–70	1270	died of the plague
R44.	Philippe III the Bold or the Rash	1245	1270–85	1285	his daughter Margaret married (1299) Edward I of England
R45.	Philippe IV the Fair	1268	1285–1314	1314	his daughter Isabella married (1308) Edward II of England
R46.	Louis X the Stubborn	1289	1314–16	1316	

Ref.	Ruler	Born	Reign	Died	Notes
R47.	Jean (I)	1316	Nov 18–22	1316	born posthumously; died after seven days
R48.	Philippe V the Tall	1293	1316–22	1322	uncle of Jean I, served as regent until after the infant's death
R49.	Charles IV the Fair	1294	1322–8	1328	

Valois Dynasty

R50.	Philippe VI	1293	1328–50	1350	son of Charles, count of Valois, who was the son of Philippe III

Edward III believed he had a stronger title to the French throne and declared himself king of France in 1340.

R51.	Jean II the Good	1319	1350–64	1364	

Jean was held captive in England from 1356–60 and again from 1363 till his death.

R52.	Charles V the Wise	1337	1364–80	1380	regent during his father's captivity
R53.	Charles VI the Simple	1368	1380–1422	1422	

Although Charles ruled for 42 years, he was generally considered incapable and sank further into madness. For most of his reign his uncles Philip, duke of Burgundy and Louis, duke of Anjou, served as regents. His daughter Isabella married Richard II of England (1396) and her sister, Katherine, married Henry V (1420). It was believed to be through this marriage that Charles's insanity passed to the English king Henry VI. Charles was also the great-grandfather of Henry VII. Henry V of England had secured the succession to the French throne, but died before he could succeed. For the next thirty years there were rival kings of France.

R54.	Charles VII	1403	1422–61	1461	
R55.	Henry VI of England	1421	1422–61	1471	See also O16

Henry was crowned king of France in 1431 but did not assume full personal control until he was sixteen in 1437. By then most of his French lands were lost and his title held no authority, though it was retained by English kings for the next 370 years.

R56.	Louis XI the Spider	1423	1461–83	1483	married (1436) Margaret, daughter of James I of Scotland
R57.	Charles VIII	1470	1483–98	1498	
R58.	Louis XII, Father of the People	1462	1498–1515	1515	great grandson of Charles V; married (1514) Mary, sister of Henry VIII
R59.	François (I)	1494	1515–47	1547	great-great grandson of Charles V; his daughter Madeleine married (1537) James V of Scotland
R60.	Henri II	1519	1547–59	1559	died of wounds received in a tournament
R61.	François II	1544	1559–60	1560	married (1558) Mary, Queen of Scots
R62.	Charles IX	1550	1560–74	1574	

At the start of his reign Charles's mother, Catherine de Medici, acted as regent and retained control of most of the government throughout his reign and into his brother's, Henri III.

R63.   Henri III   1551   1574–89   1589   murdered

House of Bourbon

Henri III nominated his brother-in-law, Henri of Navarre, a distant relative, as successor on his death.

R64.   Henri IV   1553   1589–1610   1610   murdered; his daughter, Henrietta Maria, married (1625) Charles I of England

R65.   Louis XIII   1601   1610–43   1643
        Regent: Marie de Medici (mother) until 1617.

R66.   Louis XIV,   1638   1643–1715   1715
        the Sun King
        Regent: Anne of Austria (mother) until 1651.

R67.   Louis XV   1710   1715–74   1774   died of smallpox
        Regent: Philip, duke of Orleans (grandson of Louis XIII), until 1723.

R68.   Louis XVI   1754   1774–92   1793   deposed and executed following the French Revolution

R69.   Louis XVII   1785   1792–5   1795   never ruled but remained in prison where he died, probably poisoned

The Republic was declared in 1792, followed by the first Empire of Napoleon Bonaparte from 1804–15. Upon Napoleon's defeat the kingdom was restored by Louis XVI's brother.

R70.   Louis XVIII   1755   1815–24   1824
R71.   Charles X   1757   1824–30   1836   forced to abdicate; died of cholera in exile in Italy
R72.   Louis-Philippe   1773   1830–48   1850   forced to abdicate; died in exile in England

The Second Republic was declared in 1848, followed by the Second Empire under Napoleon III from 1852, before the republic was restored in 1870.

S. ANGLO-FRENCH TERRITORIES

SA. BRITTANY

The traditional story of the settlement of Brittany or Armorica by the British states that, after the death of Magnus Maximus in 388, his soldiers remained in Brittany under the leadership of Cynan Meriadoc. Cynan, or Conan, which means "chief", was a common appellation amongst the Celts of south-west Britain and it is not certain which Cynan may have been the first to establish authority over the British of Armorica. There was a second wave of settlers in the mid fifth century escaping the Saxon invasion, and a final settlement in the mid sixth century. Cynan's descendants later ruled in the region, although in true Celtic tradition the territory became divided amongst his successors and, for a short period, there were three small kingdoms: Dumnonia, Cornouaille and Broërech, each of which had chieftains, some of whom called themselves counts. The territory was reunited under

Waroc in the late sixth century. The last native Celtic king was Salomon after whose
death in 874 Brittany came under the control of the French count, Alain.

Ref.	Ruler	Born	Reign	Died	Notes
SA1.	Cynan Meriadoc		fl 450		may be same as Riothamus
SA2.	Gradlonus or Gratian		fl 480		son of Cynan
SA3.	Salomon (I)		fl 500		son of Gradlonus
SA4.	Aldroenus or Audren		fl 510		son of Salomon
SA5.	Budic (I)		fl 516–56?	556?	son of Aldroenus
SA6.	Chanao		fl 560		ruled Broërech
SA7.	Macliaw		fl 570		son of Chanao

*Macliaw also usurped Budic's kingdom after his death but was in turn deposed by
Theodoric*

SA8.	Cunomorus or Chonomor		fl 550	560	killed in battle
SA9.	Theodoric or Tewdrig		fl 570	584	also ruler of Gwent; see EA9
SA10.	Hoël or Riwal (I)		fl 570s		brother of Theodoric; also ruler of Dumnonia; see DC12
SA11.	Waroc		c577–94		son of Macliaw; united Brittany
SA12.	Canao		c594– ?		son of Waroc; ruled Broërech.
SA13.	Hoël (II)		fl 590s		son of Hoel I; murdered
SA14.	Alanus or Alain (I)		fl 600s		son of Hoel
SA15.	Hoël (III)		fl 610s		son of Alanus
SA16.	Salomon (II)		c620–32	632	son of Hoel III
SA17.	Judhael or Judicael		632–40	658	son of Hoel III; retired to a monastery
SA18.	Alanus (II)		fl 660s	690	son of Judhael
SA19.	Cunobertus		fl 680s		
SA20.	Budic (II)		fl 700s		
SA21.	Theodoric (II)		fl 720s		
SA22.	Raulhonus or Romulus		fl 740s		
SA23.	Daniel *Dremrost* (the *Red Eyed*)		fl 760s		grandson of Alanus II
SA24.	Aregstanus		fl 780s		
SA25.	Maconus or Morvan		fl 790s		

After Maconus the line passed to a new dynasty

SA26.	Frodaldus		795–826		
SA27.	Nomenoë		826–51	851	great-great grandson of Daniel
SA28.	Erispoë		851–7	857	son of Nomenoë
SA29.	Saloman (III)		857–74		

*After Saloman's death, Vikings overran Brittany and for over a decade the kingdom
was in chaos. Eventually the core of a separate kingdom (later duchy) was established
by Alain the Great.*

SA30.	Alain (I)		c888–907	907	held title king

Territory again overrun by Vikings.

SA31.	Raoul		922–3	held title king

Territory overrun by Vikings but subject to the Normans under William Longsword [W2].

SA32.	Alain (II) Barbetorte		936–52	952	established Duchy
SA33.	Drogo		952–58	958	

No clear successor left a power vacuum filled by the counts of Rennes, who claimed descent from Erispoë. The future dukes owed partial allegiance to the dukes of Normandy.

SA34.	Conan (I) le Tort	927	c970–92	992	killed in battle
SA35.	Geoffrey (I)	c980	992–1008	1008	
SA36.	Alain III	c997	1008–40	1040	
SA37.	Eudes or Odo	999	1040–56	1056	
SA38.	Conan II		1056–66	1066	killed in battle
SA39.	Hoël (IV) of Nantes		1066–84	1084	
SA40.	Alain IV	c1067	1084–1112	1112	
SA41.	Conan III le Gros	1089	1112–48	1148	

Conan's son Hoël was disinherited and Viscount Eudes of Porhoët claimed the duchy, leading to civil war.

SA42a.	Eudes II		1148–56	1179	expelled
SA42b.	Hoël (V)		1148–56	1179	expelled
SA43.	Conan IV	1138	1156–71	1171	

From 1166, Brittany passed under the control of Henry II of England.

SA44.	Constance	c1160	1171–87	1201	Styled duchess of Brittany; married Geoffrey Plantagenet, Henry II's son
SA45.	Geoffrey II Plantagenet	1158	1181–6	1186	killed in a tournament
SA46.	Arthur	1187	1187–1203	1203	murdered

When John lost Brittany to France the duchy passed to Arthur's half-sister Alice, the daughter of Constance's third marriage. She was married to Pierre of Dreux, whose descendants remained dukes of Brittany subject to France.

SB. AQUITAINE

Aquitaine had formed one of the early kingdoms of the Franks and, with the death of Theoderic IV in 741, the lordship of Aquitaine passed to his descendants, Guillaume of Toulouse (752–828), and Gerard of Auvergne. Gerard's son, Rainulf, who was also the grandson of Louis I of France, was invested as count of Poitou and duke of Aquitaine by Charles the Bald in 841.

Ref.	Ruler	Born	Reign	Died	Notes
SB1.	Rainulf (I)		841–67	867	
SB2.	Rainulf II	855	867–90	890	styled king of Aquitaine
SB3.	Ebles *Mancer*		890–3		deposed
SB4.	William (I)		893–918	918	count of Auvergne

Ref.	Ruler	Born	Reign	Died	Notes
SB5.	William II		918–26	926	count of Auvergne
(SB3)	Ebles (*restored*)		926–35	935	also became count of Auvergne
SB6.	William III		935–63	963	his daughter Adelais married Hugh Capet, king of France
SB7.	William IV	c937	963–95	995	
SB8.	William V the Great	c969	995–1030	1030	
SB9.	William VI		1030–8		
SB10.	Eudes or Odo		1038–9		
SB11.	William VII Pierre		1039–58	1058	
SB12.	William VIII Guy or Geoffrey	c1024	1058–86	1086	
SB13.	William IX	1071	1086–1127	1127	
SB14.	William X	1099	1127–37	1137	his daughter, Eleanor, married firstly (1137) Louis VII of France and secondly (1152) Henry II of England
SB15.	Eleanor	c1122	1137–1204	1204	duchess of Aquitaine
SB16.	Louis (VII of France)	1121	1137–52	1180	duke by right of marriage to Eleanor; divorced
SB17.	Henry (II of England)	1133	1152–72	1189	duke by right of marriage to Eleanor; invested title in his son Richard
SB18.	Richard (I of England)	1157	1172–99	1199	

After the death of Eleanor in 1204, John lost most of his lands in France to Philip Augustus. Both John and Henry III strove to regain the lands, but after 1224 all that remained in English hands was Gascony, the southern half of Aquitaine, between the Dordogne and Pyrenees. The English king retained the title duke of Aquitaine.

Ref.	Ruler	Born	Reign	Died	Notes
SB19.	Henry II (III of England)	1207	1216–54	1272	Henry invested the title duke of Gascony in his son Edward
SB20.	Edward (I of England)	1239	1254–1306	1307	duke of Gascony; invested the title duke of Aquitaine in his son Edward II
SB21.	Edward (II of England)	1284	1306–25	1327	title invested in his son, Edward III
SB22.	Edward (III of England)	1312	1325–62	1377	invested title of prince of Aquitaine on his son Edward
SB23.	Edward IV the Black Prince	1330	1362–75	1376	prince of Aquitaine; abdicated

Title remained dormant, as part of the crown possessions of the king (Richard II) until resurrected by Edward's brother, John of Gaunt.

Ref.	Ruler	Born	Reign	Died	Notes
SB24.	John	1340	1390–9	1399	
SB25.	Henry III (V of England)	1387	1399–1422	1422	created both prince and duke of Aquitaine
SB26.	Henry IV (VI of England)	1421	1422–53	1471	

The duchy was lost to the French in 1453.

SC. ANJOU

Anjou was established as a separate feudal fiefdom during the reign of Charles III of
France.

Ref.	Ruler	Born	Reign	Died	Notes
SC1.	Ingelger, viscount of Orleans		c870–98	898	
SC2.	Fulk (I) the Red	c865	898–941	941	
SC3.	Fulk II the Good	c900	941–58	958	
SC4.	Geoffrey I Grisgonelle (Greygown)	c940	958–87	987	killed in battle
SC5.	Fulk III the Black	c970	987–1040	1040	
SC6.	Geoffrey II Martel (the Hammer)	1006	1040–60	1060	
SC7.	Geoffrey III the Bearded	1040	1060–67	1098	grandson of Fulk III; deposed and imprisoned
SC8.	Fulk IV Rechin (the Bad Tempered)	1043	1067–1109	1109	brother of Geoffrey III
SC9.	Geoffrey IV	1073	1098–1106	1106	ruled jointly with father; died in battle
SC10.	Fulk V the Young	1092	1106–29	1143	abdicated to undertake a Crusade; was proclaimed king of Jerusalem, 1131
SC11.	Geoffrey V Plantagenet	1113	1129–51	1151	see also SD11; father of Henry II of England
SC12.	Henry	1133	1151–89	1189	Henry II of England

Henry's son, Henry "the Young King" was also styled count of Anjou from 1170–83.

Ref.	Ruler	Born	Reign	Died	Notes
SC13.	Richard	1157	1189–99	1199	Richard I of England
SC14.	John	1166	1199–1204	1216	John of England

*Neither Richard I nor John were formally styled count of Anjou. John lost the territory
in his war with France and the countship was later invested in Charles, son of Louis
VIII of France, in 1246.*

SD. NORMANDY

Normandy was a duchy established by Hrólfur, son of Ragnald I of Orkney, who
was granted land by treaty by Charles the Simple of France. The Normans acquired
the English throne by conquest in 1066 under Duke William II, and Normandy was
united with England until lost by John in 1204.

Ref.	Ruler	Born	Reign	Died	Notes
SD1.	Hrólfur or Rolf (also Rollo)	c860	911–27	927	
SD2.	William (I) Longsword	c900	927–43	943	

Ref.	Ruler	Born	Reign	Died	Notes
SD3.	Richard (I) the Fearless	c933	943–96	996	
SD4.	Richard II the Good	c958	996–1027	1027	
SD5.	Richard III	c1001	1027–8	1028	
SD6.	Robert I the Devil	c1008	1028–35	1035	
SD7.	William II the Bastard	c1027	1035–87	1087	William I of England
SD8.	Robert II Curthose or Shortshanks	c1052	1087–1106	1134	deposed by his brother Henry
SD9.	Henry I Beauclerc	1068	1106–35	1135	also Henry I of England
SD10.	William (III)	1103	Jun-Nov 1120	1120	invested as duke but drowned soon after

Although Stephen claimed the Duchy of Normandy after Henry's death he was never officially duke.

Ref.	Ruler	Born	Reign	Died	Notes
SD11.	Geoffrey of Anjou	1113	1144–51	1151	by right of conquest; see also SC11
SD12.	Henry II	1133	1151–89	1189	also Henry II of England
SD13.	Richard IV Lionheart	1157	1189–99	1199	Richard I of England
SD14.	John	1167	1199–1204	1216	

John lost the Duchy to Philippe II of France.

T. HIGH-KINGS OF IRELAND

There were more kings in Ireland than in the rest of the British Isles, and to do them justice requires a separate book. Their culture is rich in genealogies which purport to trace the kingships back many centuries BC, with the first high king of Ireland recorded as Slainge the Firbolg. Most recorded histories begin with Niall Noígiallach as the first to claim precedence over Ireland, but there is sufficient historicity to trace the high kings back several earlier generations. The rank of high king was not necessarily a position of overall sovereignty but a recognition of status. There were provincial kingdoms in Cashel and Munster, Ulster (Ulaid), Leinster (Laigin), Connaught, Meath and Ailech as well as many sub-kingdoms. It was from the provincial kingdoms, especially Ailech in Donegal, that the high king of Ireland was chosen and elected, ruling from the royal power base at Tara. The Irish rulers of Dál Riata, in Ulster, established themselves in Kintyre in Scotland around AD 500 and became the forebears of the Scots, while Irish settlers also ruled territory in Southern Wales (Demetia) in the fifth century. The Vikings conquered parts of eastern Ireland in the ninth century and established a kingdom based at Dublin, and these rulers are listed separately. The following lists the known high kings of Ireland from 1 BC, starting with Nuada, the 107th high king from Slainge. The dates for many of the reigns, especially pre-sixth century, are subject to dispute. My thanks to Peter Berresford Ellis for his help in compiling this list.

Ref.	Ruler	Born	Reign	Died	Notes
T107.	Nuada *Necht* (the White)		1 BC–AD 1		
T108.	Conaire *Mór*		1–65		
T109.	Lugaide *Riab nDerg* (of the Red Stripes)		65–73		
T110.	Conchobar *Abrat Ruadh* (of the Red Brows)		73–4	74	
T111.	Crimthann *Nia Nair* (the Modest Warrior)		74–90		
T112.	Carbery *Cinncat* (Cathead)		90–5		
T113.	Feradach Finn *Fachtnach*		95–117		
T114.	Fiatach Finn		117–19		
T115.	Fiacha Finnola		119–26		
T116.	Tuathal *Teachtmhair* (the Legitimate)		130–60		
T117.	Mal mac Rochride		160–4		
T118.	Fedlimid *Rechtmar* (the Law-Giver)		164–74	174	
T119.	Cathaeir *Mor*		174–7	177	killed in battle
T120.	Conn *of the Hundred Battles*		177–212	212	murdered
T121.	Conaire *Moglama*		212–20		
T122.	Art *Aenfer* (the Solitary)		220–50	250	killed in battle
T123.	Lugaid mac Conn		250–3		murdered
T124.	Fergus *Dubhdeadach* (of the Black Teeth)		253–4	218	killed in battle
T125.	Cormac mac Art		254–77	283	abdicated
T126.	Eochaid *Gunnat*		277–9		
T127.	Cairbre *Liffeachair* (of the Liffey)		279–97	297	killed in battle
T128.	Fiacha *Sraibtine*		297–327		
T129.	Colla *Huas*		327–31		
T130.	Muirdach *Tirech*		331–57		
T131.	Caelbad		357–8		
T132.	Eochaid *Mugmedon* (Slave-Lord)		358–66		
T133.	Crimthan *Mór*		366–79		
T134.	Niall *Noígiallach* (of the Nine Hostages)		379–405	405	killed in battle
T135.	Dathi or Nath I		405–28		
T136.	Lóeguire		429–63	463	
T137.	Ailill *Molt* mac Nath I		463–83	483	killed in battle
T138.	Lugaid mac Loeguiri		483–507		
T139.	Murtagh mac Erc		512–34	534	murdered by his wife
T140.	Tuathal *Máelgarb* mac Coirpri		534–44		

Ref.	Ruler	Born	Reign	Died	Notes
T141.	Diarmait mac Cerbaill		544–65	565	
T142.	Domnall *Ilchelgach* (*the Deceitful*)		565–6	566	ruled jointly with brother; died of the plague
T143.	Fergus mac Murtagh		565–6	566	ruled jointly with brother; died of the plague
T144.	Ainmere mac Sétnai		566–9	569	slain
T145.	Báetán mac Murtagh		569–72	572	ruled jointly with nephew; killed in battle
T146.	Eochaid mac Domnall		569–72	572	ruled jointly with uncle; killed in battle
T147.	Báetán mac Cairill		572–81	581	
T148.	Báetán mac Ninnedo		581–6	586	killed in battle
T149.	Aed mac Aenmere		586–98	598	may have ruled jointly with Colmán *Bec* mac Diarmid; slain in a skirmish
T150.	Aed Sláine mac Diarmid		598–604	604	rival claimant
T151.	Colmán *Rímid* (*the Celebrated*)		598–604	604	rival claimant; killed in battle
T152.	Aed *Uairidhnach* (*of the Ague*)		604–12	612	
T153.	Máel Cobo mac Aed		612–15	615	killed in battle
T154.	Suibne *Menn* (*the Little*)		615–28	628	killed in battle
T155.	Domnall [Donald] mac Aed		628–42	642	
T156	Conall Cóel mac Máel		642–54	654	ruled jointly with brother
T157.	Cellach mac Máel		642–56	656	ruled jointly with brother
T158.	Diarmit mac Aed		656–65	665	ruled jointly with brother
T159.	Blathmac mac Aed		656–65	665	ruled jointly with brother
T160.	Sechnussach mac Blathmac		665–71	671	
T161.	Cenn Fáelad mac Blathmac		671–5	675	
T162.	Fínnechtae *Fledach* (*the Festive*)		675–95	695	assassinated
T163.	Loingsech mac Angus		695–704	704	killed in battle
T164.	Congal Cinn Magair mac Fergus		704–10	710	
T165.	Fergal mac Máeldúin		710–22	722	
T166.	Fogartach mac Néill		722–4	724	
T167.	Cináed [Kenneth] mac Irgalaig		724–8	728	
T168.	Flaithbertach mac Loingsech		728–34	765	deposed
T169.	Aed *Alainn* (*the Handsome*)		734–43	743	killed in battle

T170.	Domnall Midi mac Murchado	743–63	763	
T171.	Niall *Frassach* (*of the Showers*)	763–70	778	abdicated
T172.	Dunnchad *Midi* mac Domnall	770–97	797	
T173.	Aed *Oirnide* (*the Dignified*)	797–819	819	
T174.	Conchobar mac Donnchad	819–33	833	
T175.	Niall *Caille* mac Aed	833–46	846	drowned
T176.	Máel Sechnaill (I)	846–62	862	
T177.	Aed *Findliath* (*White-Hair*)	862–79	879	
T178.	Flann *Sionna* (*the Fox*)	879–916	916	
T179.	Niall *Glúndubh* (*Black Knee*)	916–19	919	killed in battle
T180.	Dunnchad Donn mac Flainn	919–44	944	
T181.	Congalach Cnoba mac Máel Mithig	944–56	956	rival claimant
T182.	Ruaidrí [Rory] ua Canannáin	944–50	950	rival claimant
T183.	Domnall ua Néill	956–80	980	
T184.	Máel Sechnaill (II)	980–1002	1022	abdicated; later restored
T185.	Brian Bóru	1002–14	1014	killed in battle

After Brian's defeat at Clontarf the Irish high kingship suffered a severe setback. There were many rival claimants to the title, listed below, but it was not until the return of Turlogh O'Brien that the status of the high king was restored, though almost always "with opposition".

(T184)	Máel Sechnaill (II) (*restored*)	1014–22	1022	
T186.	Donnchad mac Brian	1022–63	1064	king of Munster; deposed and died in Rome on pilgrimage
T187.	Diarmait mac Máel	1042–72	1072	king of Leinster
T188.	Toirdelbach (Turlogh) O'Brien	1072–86	1086	king of Munster from 1063
T189.	Muirchertach (Murchadh) O'Brien	1086–1119	1119	king of Munster
T190.	Domnall Mac Lochlainn	1090–1121	1121	king of Ailech; rival claimant; killed in battle
T191.	Turlogh 1088 ua Conchobair	1121–50	1156	king of Connacht from 1106; deposed 1135–41; deposed again 1150
T192.	Muirchertach (Murtagh) mac Lochlainn	1150–66	1166	king of Ailech from 1136
T193.	Ruaidrí 1116 (Rory O'Connor)	1166–83	1198	king of Connacht from 1156; deposed

Rory O'Connor was the last recognized high king of Ireland. He acknowledged Henry II of England as his liege lord under the Treaty of Windsor in 1175. He was deposed by his *son, Conchobar, in 1183. Conchobar ruled as king of Connacht until his assassination in 1189. His brother Cathal was deposed in 1200. Thereafter King John of England claimed to be lord of Ireland. The provincial kingships continued for another three centuries, and occasional rulers had pretensions to the high kingship, but only two were recognized as having any official status by a majority vote.*

Ref.	Ruler	Born	Reign	Died	Notes
T194.	Brian *Catha an Duin*		1258–60	1260	killed in battle
T195.	Edward Bruce		1316–18	1318	brother of Robert the Bruce; killed in battle

U. VIKING RULERS OF DUBLIN

In the middle of the ninth century Danish and Norse adventurers captured territory on the eastern coast of Ireland which they were able to use as bases for their raids on Scotland, Wales and England. The territory was not a continuous kingdom but had its primary base at Dublin, with a secondary base at Waterford. For a brief period the rulers also established a kingdom at York (see Section NC on page xx).

Ref.	Ruler	Born	Reign	Died	Notes
U1.	Turgeis		840–5		first to style himself king of Dublin
U2.	Olaf (I)		853–71	872	probably killed in battle
U3.	Ivarr (I) Ragnarson, the Boneless		871–3	873	also king of Jorvik [NC1]
U4.	Eystein Olafson		873–5	875	killed in battle
U5.	Halfdan		875–7	877	king of Jorvik [NC2]; killed in battle
U6.	Bard		877–81		
U7.	Sigfrid Ivarson		881–8	888	
U8.	Sitric (I) Ivarson		888–96	896	deposed 893 but restored 894
U9.	Ivarr II		896–902	904	deposed
	Danish expelled from Dublin until 917.				
U10.	Sitric II *Caech* (the Squinty)		917–21	927	relinquished Dublin to become king of Jorvik [NC10]
U11.	Gothfrith		921–34	934	
U12.	Olaf II Gothfrithson	c919	934–41	941	also became king of Jorvik [NC12]
U13.	Blacar Gothfrithson		941–5	948	deposed
U14.	Olaf III Sitricson *Cuaran*	c920	945–8		left to regain kingdom of Jorvik [NC13]
	regained Dublin		952–80	981	retired to a monastery
U15.	Gothfrith Sitricson		948–52		
U16.	Gluniaran Olafson		980–9		
U17.	Sitric III Olafson, *Silkenbeard*		989–94		deposed
U18.	Ivar III Ivarson		994–5	1000	
(U17)	Sitric *Silkenbeard* (restored)		995–1035	1042	deposed again

| U19. Margad Ragnallson | 1035–38 | | deposed |
| U20. Ivar IV Haraldson | 1038–46 | 1054 | |

Kingdom regained by kings of Leinster.

| (U19) Margad Ragnallson (*restored*) | 1046–52 | 1064 | deposed again; became king of Man and Galloway [NA17] |
| U21. Godred Sitricson | 1072–4 | 1075 | deposed |

Kingship given to Toirrdelbach of Munster but soon regained by Leinster. From 1091–4 was ruled by Godred Crovan of Man (see NB20).

| U22. Thorfinn Thorkellson | 1118–24 | | |

Ruled again by Leinster.

U23. Ragnald Thorkellson	1136–46		
U24. Ottar Ottarson	1142–8		
U25. Brodar Thorkellson	1148–60		
U26. Astell Ragnaldson	1160–70	1171	deposed 1162–6

Kingdom conquered by Diarmait mac Donnchada, king of Leinster.

V. SCANDINAVIA

Early in its history Scandinavia was composed of many small kingdoms, often at war with each other. Over the years, as with the kingdoms in Britain, these were united into the kingdoms we know today. The main rivalry was between Norway and Denmark. Kings of one often ruled the other and, thanks to their seapower, also ruled lands overseas including almost half of Britain at one time.

VA. DENMARK

Denmark traces its monarchy back to the semi-legendary Skjold who ruled in the mid third century.

Ref.	Ruler	Born	Reign	Died	Notes
VA1.	Skjold		*fl* 250s		king of the Danes
VA2.	Fridleif		*fl* 280s		
VA3.	Frodi		*fl* 300s		
VA4.	Fridleif (II)		*fl* 320s		
VA5.	Havar		*fl* 340s		
VA6.	Frodi (II)		*fl* 360s		
VA7.	Vermund		*fl* 380s		
VA8.	Olaf		*fl* 400s		
VA9.	Dan		*fl* 430s		
VA10.	Frodi (III)		*fl* 450s		
VA11.	Fridleif (III)		*fl* 480s		
VA12.	Frodi (IV)		*fl* 500s		
VA13.	Halfdan		*fl* 530s		
VA14.	Hroar		*fl* 550s		king of Roeskilde
VA15.	Valdar		*fl* 570s		king of Roeskilde
VA16.	Harald (I)		*fl* 590s		king of Roeskilde
VA17.	Halfdan		*fl* 610s		king of Roeskilde and Sweden
VA18.	Ivar		*fl* 640s		king of Roeskilde, Lethra and Sweden

Ref.	Ruler	Born	Reign	Died	Notes

The next few generations are uncertain.

VA19.	Randver		*fl* 750s	*c*770	son of a ruler of Russia
VA20.	Sigurd (I)		*c*770–812	?812	

Several petty kings ruled after Sigurd including the short-lived Gothfrith and Hemming (both fl 810s) and Harthacanute, who ruled in the 830s and possibly 840s. The next few kings are uncertain, though it is possible Ragnar Lodbrok ruled earlier in the 840s and 850s.

VA21.	Eric (I)		850–4		
VA22.	Eric (II)		854– ?		
VA23.	Ragnar *Lodbrok* (*Hairy-Britches*)		860s	865	killed during a raid on York
VA24.	Sigurd *Snogoje*		865–73	873	
VA25.	Canute or Harthacanute		873–84	884	king of Sjaelland
VA26.	Frodo		884–5	885	king of Sjaelland
VA27.	Harald II *Parcus*		885–99	899	king of Sjaelland
VA28.	Gorm *the Old*		*c*900–*c*50	*c*950	King of Denmark
VA29.	Harald III *Bluetooth*	*c*911	*c*950– 86	986	
VA30.	Swein (I) *Forkbeard*	*c*960	986–1014	1014	see also M33
VA31.	Harald IV	*c*994	1014–18	1018	
VA32.	Canute (II) *the Great*	*c*995	1018–35	1035	see also M35 and VB16 note
VA33.	Canute III or Harthacanute	1018	1035–42	1042	see also M37
VA34.	Magnus *the Good* (of Norway)	1024	1042–7	1047	see also VB17
VA35.	Swein II *Interregnum*	1020	1047–74	1074	
VA36.	Harald III *the Simple*		1076–80	1080	
VA37.	Canute IV	1043	1080–6	1086	murdered
VA38.	Olaf IV *the Hungry*		1086–95		
VA39.	Erik (I) *the Good Interregnum*	1056	1095–1103	1103	
VA40.	Niels or Nicholas	1063	1105–35	1135	killed
VA41.	Erik II *the Memorable*		1135–7		
VA42.	Erik III *the Lamb*		1137–47		retired to a monastery
VA43.	Swein III		1147–57	1157	ruled jointly; beheaded
VA44.	Canute V		1147–57		ruled jointly; deposed
VA45.	Valdemar (I) *the Great*	1131	1157–82	1182	
VA46.	Canute VI *the Pious*	1163	1182–1202		

VA47.	Valdemar II *the Victorious*	1170	1202–41		
VA48.	Erik IV	1216	1241–50	1250	assassinated
VA49.	Abel	c1218	1250–2	1252	killed in battle
VA50.	Christopher (I)	1219	1252–9	1259	poisoned
VA51.	Erik V	1249	1259–86	1286	murdered
VA52.	Erik VI	1274	1286–1319	1319	
VA53.	Christopher II *Interregnum*	1216	1320–6	1333	deposed; restored 1330–2
VA54.	Valdemar III *Interregnum*	1320	1340–75	1375	
VA55.	Olaf V	1370	1375–87	1387	
VA56.	Margaret of Norway	1352	1387–1412	1412	also queen of Norway and Sweden
VA57.	Erik VII	1381	1397–1438	1459	also king of Norway and Sweden, initially jointly with Margaret; deposed
	Interregnum				
VA58.	Christopher III (of Sweden)	1418	1440–8		

Oldenburg Dynasty

VA59.	Christian I	1426	1448–81	1481	king of Norway (from 1450) and Sweden (from 1457); his daughter Margaret married (1469) James III of Scotland
VA60.	Hans	1455	1481–1513	1513	also king of Sweden (1497– 1501)
VA61.	Christian II *the Cruel*	1481	1513–23	1559	king of Sweden (1520–1); deposed; died in prison
VA62.	Frederik I	1471	1523–33	1533	
VA63.	Christian III	1503	1533–59	1559	
VA64.	Frederik II	1534	1559–88	1588	his daughter Anne married (1589) James VI of Scotland
VA65.	Christian IV	1577	1588–1648	1648	
VA66.	Frederik III	1609	1648–70	1670	his son George married (1683) the future Queen Anne of Great Britain
VA67.	Christian V	1646	1670–99	1699	died in a hunting accident
VA68.	Frederik IV	1671	1699–1730	1730	
VA69.	Christian VI	1699	1730–46	1746	
VA70.	Frederik V	1723	1746–66	1766	married (1743) Louisa, daughter of George II
VA71.	Christian VII	1749	1766–84	1808	grandson of George II; married (1766) Caroline, sister of George III; declared insane in 1784 and his son Frederik acted as regent
VA72.	Frederik VI	1768	1808–39	1839	regent from 1784; he was the great grandson of George II of Great Britain.

Ref.	Ruler	Born	Reign	Died	Notes
VA73.	Christian VIII	1786	1839–48	1848	
VA74.	Frederik VII	1808	1848–63	1863	
VA75.	Christian IX	1818	1863–1906	1906	his daughter Alexandra married (1863) the future Edward VII of Great Britain; he is therefore the great-great grandfather of Elizabeth II
VA76.	Frederik VIII	1843	1906–12	1912	
VA77.	Christian X	1870	1912–47	1947	
VA78.	Frederik IX	1899	1947–72	1972	
VA79.	Margaret II	1940	1972–		

VB. NORWAY

The kingdom of Norway had its roots in the Swedish colony of Vermeland, settled in about the year 680 by Olaf Tratelia who had been expelled from Sweden. He overthrew the petty local rulers and established the core of what became the Viking kingdom of Norway.

Ref.	Ruler	Born	Reign	Died	Notes
VB1.	Olaf *Tratelia* or *Tree-hewer*		680–710	710	king of Vestfold; slain
VB2.	Halfdan (I)		710–50	750	king of Vestfold
VB3.	Eystein (I)		750–80	780	king of Vestfold
VB4.	Halfdan II *Whitelegs*		780–800	800	king of Vestfold and of the Uplanders
VB5.	Gudrod *the Magnificent*	738	800–10	810	king of Vestfold, Vermaland, Vingulmark and Roumarike
VB6.	Olaf *Geirstade*	c770	810–40	840	King of Norway
VB7.	Halfdan III		840–63	863	drowned

Civil war erupted after the death of Halfdan, from which Harald Finehair emerged victorious as the first king of a united Norway.

VB8.	Harald *Härfager (Finehair)*	c860	885–933	934	retired
VB9.	Erik *Bloodaxe*	c885	933–c4	954	expelled; became ruler of Orkney (NB8) and Jorvik (NC11); slain
VB10.	Haakon *the Good*	c919	c934–63	963	killed in battle
VB11.	Harald II *Graafeld (Greycloak)*	c935	963–77	977	ruled with his brothers but sole ruler of southern Norway; kingship challenged by rivals Sigurd and Tryggve Olafson, both of whom ruled briefly; murdered

Kingdom subject to Denmark, 977–95.

VB12.	Haakon (Jarl of Lade)		977–95	995	vassal ruler under Danish sovereignty; deposed and later slain

VB13.	Olaf Tryggvason	c964	995–1000	1000	regained kingdom; killed in battle

Kingdom again subject to Denmark, 1000–16.

VB14.	Erik (Jarl of Lade)		1000–15		vassal ruler under Danish sovereignty
VB15.	Olaf II Haraldson	c995	1015–28	1030	regained kingdom 1016; expelled again and killed in battle trying to regain throne; later canonized; became Norway's patron saint

Kingdom again subject to Denmark, 1028–35, under overall rule of Canute.

VB16.	Swein	c1015	1030–35	c1036	appointed king by his father Canute; expelled

Regent: Elfgiva (c996–c1044), his mother; she was also expelled in 1035 after the death of Canute.

VB17.	Magnus (I) the Good	1024	1035–47	1047	also king of Denmark (VA34)
VB18.	Harald III Hardraade	1015	1047–66	1066	killed at Stamford Bridge during his attempted invasion of England
VB19.	Magnus II	c1048	1066–9	1069	ruled jointly with brother
VB20.	Olaf III *Kyrre* (the Quiet)	c1050	1066–93	1093	
VB21.	Magnus III Barefoot	c1073	1093–1103	1103	killed in battle in Ireland
VB22.	Sigurd (I) the Crusader	1090	1103–30	1130	also king of Orkney and Man (NA22;NB23)
VB23.	Olaf IV Magnusson	c1090	1103–15	1115	ruled jointly with brothers
VB24.	Eystein (II)	1089	1103–23	1123	ruled jointly with brothers
VB25.	Magnus IV the Blinded	c1115	1130–5	1139	deposed and blinded by Harald IV
VB26.	Harald IV Gillechrist	1103	1130–6	1136	ruled jointly with Magnus IV whom he then deposed; murdered

With Harald's murder civil war broke out; there were many contenders for the throne, some of whom listed below ruled jointly or in competition.

VB27.	Sigurd Slembediakn (the Mock Deacon)		1136–39		murdered Harald IV; released Magnus IV, ruling as the latter's "regent"
VB28.	Inge (I) Crookback	1135	1136–61	1161	ruled jointly with brothers
VB29.	Sigurd II *Mund*	1134	1136–55	1155	ruled jointly with brothers
VB30.	Eystein (III)	1125	1142–57	1157	ruled jointly with brothers
VB31.	Haakon II the Broadshouldered	1147	1161–2	1162	son of Sigurd II
VB32.	Magnus V	1156	1162–84	1184	drowned
VB33.	Sverre or Swerro	1152	1177–80		expelled
			1184–1202	1202	killed Magnus and regains throne
VB34.	Haakon III	c1177	1202–4	1204	poisoned ?

Ref.	Ruler	Born	Reign	Died	Notes
VB35.	Guthrum		Jan-Aug 1204	1204	
VB36.	Inge II Baardson	1195	1204–17	1217	
VB37.	Haakon IV *the Old*	1204	1217–63	1263	died during an unsuccessful campaign in Scotland and the Hebrides
VB38.	Magnus VI	1238	1263–80	1280	
VB39.	Erik II	1268	1280–99	1299	he married (1281) Margaret, daughter of Alexander III of Scotland; his daughter Margaret became queen of Scotland
VB40.	Haakon V	1270	1299–1319	1319	
VB41.	Magnus VII	1316	1319–55	1374	
VB42.	Haakon VI	1339	1355–80	1380	

Haakon was the last of his dynasty. After his death, Norway was ruled by the kings of Sweden and subsequently those of Denmark, until all three countries were united as Sweden from 1397–1523. Thereafter Norway remained united with Denmark until 1814 and then with Sweden. It did not regain independence until 1905.

Ref.	Ruler	Born	Reign	Died	Notes
VB43.	Haakon VII	1872	1905–57	1957	son of Frederik VIII of Denmark; married (1896) Maud, daughter of Edward VII
VB44.	Olaf V	1903	1957–91	1991	
VB45.	Harald V	1937	1991–		

W. HANOVER

An electorate in north-western Germany – an electorate was a state which had a vote in the election of the Holy Roman emperor. The state grew out of the former duchy of Brunswick and subsequently became a kingdom, until annexed by Prussia in 1866. From 1714 to 1837 the rulers of Hanover were also the kings of Great Britain.

Ref.	Ruler	Born	Reign	Died	Notes
W1.	Ernest-Augustus	1629	1679–98	1698	elevated to Elector in 1692
W2.	George I	1660	1698–1727	1727	also king of Great Britain from 1714
W3.	George II	1683	1727–60	1760	also George II of Great Britain
W4.	George III	1738	1760–1820	1820	also George III of Great Britain; status elevated to king of Hanover from 1814
W5.	George IV	1762	1820–30	1830	also George IV of Great Britain
W6.	William	1765	1830–7	1837	William IV of Great Britain
W7.	Ernest	1771	1837–51	1851	son of George III; Salic Law did not allow a woman to rule Hanover
W8.	George V	1819	1851–66	1878	deposed by Prussians

George was deposed when the Prussians conquered Hanover in 1866. His son, Ernest Augustus (1845–1923), was restored with the once hereditary title of duke of

Brunswick-Lüneberg in 1884, and this passed to his son, also Ernest Augustus (1887–1953), in 1923.

X. QUEEN AND KING CONSORTS

In pre-Norman times the wife of a monarch was seldom recognized as holding any authority, and they were seldom crowned or anointed as queen. Indeed, the West Saxons outlawed the crowning of the king's wife because of the wickedness of Beorhtric's wife Eadburh. Nevertheless some of the earlier queens were highly influential, especially in the rise of Christianity amongst the Saxons, starting with Bertha, the wife of Athelbert. The connection between the queen and the church gradually gave them a special status, which developed in the tenth century. By the time of some of the queens of the Middle Ages the king's wife had come to be regarded as a lady of power and authority. The queen ceases to be the queen when the king dies. If they are the mother of the successor they become the "Queen Mother"; otherwise they are known as the "Queen Dowager". The following lists all of the known Saxon queens, plus the later Queens of England and Scotland. By the nature of the role, few of the titles, especially in the early years, are continuous.

Ref.	Ruler	Born	Reign	Died	Notes

XA. Queens of Kent

Ref.	Ruler	Born	Reign	Died	Notes
XA1.	Bertha	post 561	c580–c601	c601	wife of Athelbert (I)

The name of Athelbert's second wife, who subsequently married Eadbald, is not known.

Ref.	Ruler	Born	Reign	Died	Notes
XA2.	Emma	c603	c618–40		post 640 wife of Eadbald
XA3.	Seaxburh		c640–64	c700	wife of Eorcenbert

Nothing is known of the later queens of Kent, except for the three wives of Wihtred, and it is not recorded whether they were consecrated as queens.

XB. Queens of Mercia

Ref.	Ruler	Born	Reign	Died	Notes
XB1.	Cynewise		fl630–55		wife of Penda

Cynewise appears to be Penda's only wife, and a sufficiently strong woman that she was left in charge of the kingdom when Penda undertook campaigns away.

Ref.	Ruler	Born	Reign	Died	Notes
XB2.	Eormenhild		c660–75	c700	wife of Wulfhere
XB3.	Osthryth		675–97	697	wife of Athelred; murdered

Identities of the next few queens are not known.

Ref.	Ruler	Born	Reign	Died	Notes
XB4.	Cynethryth		c769–96		wife of Offa; may be regarded as the first queen of the English
XB5.	Aelthryth		c796–821		wife of Cenwulf

Identities of the next few queens are not known.

Ref.	Ruler	Born	Reign	Died	Notes
XB6.	Saethryth		c840–52		wife of Beohrtwulf
XB7.	Athelswith		853–74	888	wife of Burgred, and daughter of Athelwulf of Wessex

XC. Queens of Northumbria

Ref.	Ruler	Born	Reign	Died	Notes
XC1.	Bebba		c595–c603	c603?	first wife of Athelfrith
XC2.	Acha	c586	c604–?	?	second wife of Athelfrith; it is not certain whether she pre-deceased him

Ref.	Ruler	Born	Reign	Died	Notes
XC3.	Athelburh	c595	625–33	647	wife of Edwin, and daughter of Athelbert (I) of Kent

Eanfrith had married a Pictish princess whose name is not recorded

XC4.	Cyneburh		c640–2	?	wife of Oswald, and daughter of Cynegils of Wessex
XC5.	Enfleda or Eanfled	c626	642–70	c704	wife of Oswy
XC6.	Etheldreda	c630	664–74	679	first wife of Egfrith; retired to monastery
XC7.	Eormenburh		679–85 after	685	second wife of Egfrith
XC8.	Cuthburh	c670	c695–c700	c725	wife of Aldfrith; retired to a monastery

Nothing is recorded of the subsequent wives of the Northumbrian kings or their status as queen.

XD. Queens of Wessex

The West Saxons or Gewisse did not usually recognize the king's wife as having any status until the reign of Ine.

XD1.	Athelburh		?688–?726		wife of Ine
XD2.	Frithugyth		?726–?40		wife of Athelheard

Subsequent wives are not recorded until the reign of Beorhtric.

XD3.	Eadburh		789–802	after 814	

Due to Eadburh's reputation, the title of queen was banned by the West Saxons.

XD4.	Judith	c843	856–8	after 870	second wife of Athelwolf and briefly wife of Athelbald

The title of queen again lapsed until the reign of Edgar. Even Alfred the Great's wife, Ealhswith, was never apparently consecrated queen. Their details however are provided here for completeness.

XD5.	Ealhswith		871–99	902	wife of Alfred
XD6.	Elfleda		c901–20	920	second wife of Edward the Elder
XD7.	Edgiva		c920–4	968	third wife of Edward the Elder
XD8.	Elgiva or Elfgiva		c940–c5	c945	wife of Edmund (I)
XD9.	Elgiva or Elfgiva		c957–8	959	wife of Edwy; marriage annulled; died in suspicious circumstances
XD10.	Athelfleda		c961–c4	c964?	first wife of Edgar

The Queens of England

XD11.	Elfrida	c945	c964–75	c1002	second wife of Edgar

Elfrida was the first woman to be crowned queen of England, on 11 May 973 at Bath.

XD12.	Elfgiva or Elgiva	c963	c985–1002	1002	first wife of Athelred II
XD13.	Emma (changed named to Elfgiva)	c985	1002–16	1052	second wife of Athelred II; subsequently married Canute (*see below*)
XD14.	Edith or Eadgyth		Apr-Nov 1016		wife of Edmund II
XD13.	Emma	c985	1017–1035	1052	wife of Canute and widow of Athelred II (*see above*)

XD15.	Edith	*c*1020	1045–1066	1075	wife of Edward the Confessor
XD16.	Edith	*c*1042	Jan-Oct 1066		wife of Harold II

Following the Norman Conquest the wife of the king was usually formally crowned as Queen Consort and these are the dates listed below. Where the marriage date is different it is included in the final column.

XD17.	Matilda	*c*1031	1068–83	1083	wife of William I, married 1053
XD18.	Edith (changed name to Matilda)	*c*1080	1100–18	1118	first wife of Henry I
XD19.	Adeliza (or Adela or Alice)	*c*1105	1121–35	1151	second wife of Henry I
XD20.	Matilda	*c*1103	1136–52	1152	wife of Stephen, married *c*1125
XD21.	Eleanor of Aquitaine	*c*1122	1154–89	1204	wife of Henry II, married 1152
XD22.	Berengaria of Navarre	*c*1163	1191–9	*c*1231	wife of Richard I
XD23.	Isabella of Angoulême	*c*1187	1200–16	1246	second wife of John
XD24.	Eleanor of Provence	*c*1223	1236–72	1291	wife of Henry III
XD25.	Eleanor of Castile	1241	1274–90	1290	first wife of Edward I, married 1254

Edward I's second wife, Margaret of France (1279–1318), whom he married in 1299, was never crowned queen.

XD26.	Isabella of France	*c*1292	1308–27	1358	wife of Edward II
XD27.	Philippa of Hainault	1311	1328–69	1369	wife of Edward III
XD28.	Anne of Bohemia	1366	1382–94	1394	first wife of Richard II
XD29.	Isabella of France	1389	1397–9	1409	second wife of Richard II
XD30.	Joan of Navarre	*c*1370	1403–13	1437	second wife of Henry IV
XD31.	Katherine of France	1401	1420–2	1437	wife of Henry V
XD32.	Margaret of Anjou	1429	1445–61	1482	wife of Henry VI, who was deposed in 1461 and briefly restored in 1471
XD33.	Elizabeth Wydville	*c*1437	1465–83	1492	wife of Edward IV
XD34.	Anne Nevill	1456	1483–5	1485	wife of Richard III, married 1472
XD35.	Elizabeth of York	1466	1487–1503	1503	wife of Henry VII
XD36.	Katherine of Aragon	1485	1509–33	1536	first wife of Henry VIII; divorced
XD37.	Anne Boleyn	*c*1500	1533–6	1536	second wife of Henry VIII; marriage annulled; executed

None of Henry VIII's remaining wives were crowned, although plans were in hand for Jane's coronation before she died. They are all listed below, however, for completeness.

XD38.	Jane Seymour	*c*1506	1536–7	1537	third wife of Henry VIII; not crowned; died after childbirth

Ref.	Ruler	Born	Reign	Died	Notes
XD39.	Anne of Cleves	1515	Jan-Jul 1540	1557	fourth wife of Henry VIII; divorced
XD40.	Katherine Howard	c1520	1540–2	1542	fifth wife of Henry VIII; executed
XD41.	Katherine Parr	c1512	1543–7	1548	sixth wife of Henry VIII
XD42.	Philip of Spain	1527	1554–8	1598	husband of Mary I; the only king consort of England; also king of Spain from 1556

XE. The Queens of Scotland

Records of the wives of the early Scottish rulers are virtually non-existent, and this includes the wives of the Pictish kings through whom inheritance passed. No queen consort was officially crowned until the reign of David II, but earlier queens are listed here, where known, for completeness.

Ref.	Ruler	Born	Reign	Died	Notes
XE1.	Sybilla		1034–?	?	wife of Duncan I; it is not known whether she predeceased him
XE2.	Gruoch	c1015	1040–?	?	wife of Macbeth; it is not known whether she predeceased him
XE3.	Ingibiorg		c1060–c9	c1069	first wife of Malcolm III
XE4.	Margaret	1046	1069–93	1093	second wife of Malcolm III
XE5.	Ethelreda		1094–?	?	wife of Duncan II; it is not known whether she predeceased him
XE6.	Sybilla	c1092	1107–22	1122	wife of Alexander I
XE7.	Matilda	c1072	1124–c30	c1130	wife of David I
XE8.	Ermengarde		1186–1214	1234	wife of William the Lyon
XE9.	Joan	1210	1221–38	1238	first wife of Alexander II
XE10.	Marie de Coucy		1239–49	?	second wife of Alexander II
XE11.	Margaret	1240	1251–75	1275	first wife of Alexander III
XE12.	Yolande of Dreux		1285–6	1323	second wife of Alexander III
XE13.	Isabella de Warrenne	1253	1292–6	?	wife of John Balliol, married 1281
XE14.	Elizabeth de Burgh		1306–27	1329	second wife of Robert I
XE15.	Joanna	1321	1329–62	1362	first wife of David II

Joanna was the first queen consort of Scotland to be anointed and crowned, on 24 November 1331.

Ref.	Ruler	Born	Reign	Died	Notes
XE16.	Margaret Drummond		1364–70	1375	second wife of David II; divorced
XE17.	Euphemia Ross	c1330	1371–87	1387	second wife of Robert II, married 1355; crowned 1372
XE18.	Annabella Drummond	c1350	1390–1401	1401	wife of Robert III, married 1366

XE19.	Joan Beaufort		1424–37	1445	wife of James I
XE20.	Mary of Gueldres	1433	1449–60	1463	wife of James II
XE21.	Margaret of Denmark	1456	1469–86	1486	wife of James III
XE22.	Margaret Tudor	1489	1503–13	1541	wife of James IV
XE23.	Madeleine of France	1520	Jan-Jul 1537	1537	first wife of James V; not crowned
XE24.	Mary of Guise	1515	1538–42	1560	second wife of James V; crowned 1540
XE25.	Henry Stuart (Lord Darnley)	1545	1565–7	1567	Mary's second husband, the only king consort to be proclaimed king of Scotland

XF. Queens of England and Scotland (Great Britain from 1701)

XF1.	Anne of Denmark	1574	1590–1619	1619	wife of James VI (I); crowned queen consort of England in 1603
XF2.	Henrietta Maria	1609	1625–49	1669	wife of Charles I; not crowned
XF3.	Katherine of Braganza	1638	1662–85	1705	wife of Charles II; not crowned
XF4.	Mary of Modena	1658	1685–8	1718	wife of James II
XF5.	George of Denmark	1653	1702–8	1708	husband of Anne; not officially created prince consort
XF6.	Caroline of Ansbach	1683	1727–37	1737	wife of George II, married 1705
XF7.	Charlotte	1744	1761–1818	1818	wife of George III
XF8.	Caroline of Brunswick	1768	1820–1	1821	wife of George IV; not crowned
XF9.	Adelaide	1792	1830–7	1849	wife of William IV, married 1818; crowned 1831
XF10.	Albert	1819	1840–61	1861	husband of Victoria; created Prince Consort 26 June 1857
XF11.	Alexandra	1844	1901–10	1925	wife of Edward VII; married 1863, crowned 1902
XF12.	Mary of Teck	1867	1910–36	1953	wife of George V; married 1893, crowned 1911; also crowned empress of India
XF13.	Elizabeth Bowes-Lyon	1900	1936–52		wife of George VI; married 1923, crowned 1937; also crowned empress of India, relinquished 1947
XF14.	Philip Mountbatten	1921	1952–		husband of Elizabeth II; married 1947; created Prince Philip 1957

Y. THE ENGLISH PRINCES OF WALES

Edward I bestowed the title prince of Wales on his eldest son, the future Edward II, and thereafter the title was always bestowed upon the heir apparent, usually the monarch's eldest son. Originally, the title brought with it not only the income from the principality but the allegiance of the Welsh lords, thus giving the prince of Wales authority, second to the king, over Wales. This authority waned over the years, usually because of the age of the holders and because the title was seldom held consecutively. The long gap in formal holders during the sixteenth century further weakened the role and it became a purely honorary title when it was revived in 1610. The title is not held separately by a ruling monarch.

Ref.	Ruler	Born	Reign	Died	Notes
Y1.	Edward	1284	1301–7	1327	future Edward II
Y2.	Edward, the Black Prince	1330	1343–76	1376	son of Edward III
Y3.	Richard	1367	1376–7	1400	future Richard II
Y4.	Henry	1387	1399–1413	1422	future Henry V
Y5.	Edward	1453	1454–71	1471	son of Henry VI
Y6.	Edward	1470	1471–83	1483	future Edward V
Y7.	Edward	1476	1483–4	1484	son of Richard III
Y8.	Arthur	1486	1489–1502	1502	son of Henry VII
Y9.	Henry	1491	1504–9	1547	future Henry VIII

Henry's son (the future Edward VI) was styled prince of Wales but never formally created

Ref.	Ruler	Born	Reign	Died	Notes
Y10.	Henry	1594	1610–2	1612	son of James I
Y11.	Charles	1600	1616–25	1649	future Charles I
Y12.	Charles	1630	1638–49	1685	future Charles II
Y13.	James	1688	Jul-Dec 1688	1766	"The Old Pretender"; unofficially retained title until 1701; his son, Charles, was also unofficially styled prince of Wales from his birth in 1720
Y14.	George	1683	1714–27	1760	future George II
Y15.	Frederick	1707	1729–51	1751	son of George II
Y16.	George	1738	1751–60	1820	future George III
Y17.	George	1762	1762–1820	1830	future George IV
Y18.	Albert Edward	1841	1841–1901	1910	future Edward VII
Y19.	George	1865	1901–10	1936	future George V
Y20.	Edward Albert David	1894	1910–1936	1972	future Edward VIII
Y21.	Charles	1948	1958–		son of Elizabeth I

THE GAZETTEER

This section covers those sites in Great Britain with a strong royal connection. In most cases these are where royalty were born, lived, married, died or were buried, but also covered are places of significant battles or other royal events. The gazetteer concentrates primarily on British locations but a few outside Britain are included where relevant.

Abbeycwmhir (*Powys*) *see* Cwm Hir Abbey

Aber (*Caernarfonshire and Merionethshire*) Known in full as Abergwyngregyn or Aber of the White Shells. One of the royal residences of the princes of Gwynedd, especially LLYWELYN THE GREAT who built a motte-and-bailey castle. Both his wife Joan (1237) and his son DAFYDD (1246) died here. It was here that LLYWELYN THE LAST rejected EDWARD I's sovereignty (1282) leading to Edward's subjugation of Wales.

Aberconwy *see* Conwy

Aberdeen (*Aberdeenshire*) Pictish village since 4th C. Settlement grew around church of St Machar (6th C). Bishopric established by DAVID I (1125) who made Old Aberdeen a royal burgh (1154); granted charter by WILLIAM THE LYON (1179); King's College founded by JAMES IV (1495; built 1500–6); General Assembly convened by JAMES VI (1616); William, duke of Cumberland (son of GEORGE II), stayed at Provost Skene's House prior to Culloden (1746).

Abererch (*Caernarfonshire and Merionethshire*) Small village on Lleyn Peninsula near Pwllheli. Legend states that RHYDDERCH HEN was buried here (612 or later).

Aberffraw *see* Anglesey

Aberhonddu *see* Brecon

Abernethy (*Fife*) Capital of the Southern Picts until 9th C; church dedicated to St Brigid by NECHTAN II (*c*620); MALCOLM III submitted to WILLIAM THE CONQUEROR (1072).

Acleah *see* Ockley

Adam's Grave (*Wiltshire*) Neolithic long-barrow in Vale of Pewsey, near Milk Hill, midway between Devizes and Marlborough. It was here that CEAWLIN of Wessex was defeated and expelled (588) and where CEOLRED of Mercia fought INE of Wessex (715).

Addinston (*Scottish Borders*) *see* Dawston

Agincourt (*France*) Small village 50km SE of Boulogne (now called Azincourt) renowned in English history because of HENRY V's victory over the French on 25 October 1415. The French outnumbered the English by six to one, but it is claimed that Henry lost only about 1,600 men compared to the French 10,000 (more likely 6,000). Henry owes his victory to the skill of the Welsh longbowmen.

Alclud *see* Dumbarton *and* Strathclyde

Aldborough (*North Yorkshire*) The ancient capital of the Brigantes and long a religious centre, as indicated by the Devil's Arrows, three prehistoric standing stones at nearby Boroughbridge. The Romans established a camp here called Isurium Brigantum, after the Celtic name for the town, Iseur. This was almost certainly the chief town of CARTIMANDUA. It also became a popular location for the royal villas of the later kings of Northumbria.

Alnwick (*Northumberland*) Saxon Ealnwic. Border town with frequent conflict between the Scots and English. MALCOLM III and his son Edward were killed during siege (1093); DAVID I captured town (1136); WILLIAM THE LYON captured during siege (1174); burned by JOHN (1215). William the Lyon's daughter, Isabella, married Roger Bigod, earl of Norfolk (1225). Original castle built by Normans in 1096 and extended by the de Vesci family in 12th and 13th Cs. The last De Vesci, William (illegitimate great-grandson of William the Lyon), sold castle to Henry Percy, and it became the stronghold of the earls of Northumberland (*see* Man, Isle of).

Althorp House (*Northants*) 6 miles NW of Northampton, this has been the home of the Spencer family since 1508. The original house has been much altered, particularly in 1660 and 1787. CHARLES I was playing bowls here when he was escorted to his final imprisonment (1647); Anne of Denmark stayed here whilst travelling to join her husband JAMES VI when he became James I of England (1603). It is best known today as the family home and last resting place of Lady Diana Spencer, princess of Wales, who was buried on an island in the lake in Althorp Park (1997).

Amesbury (*Wiltshire*). Town near Stonehenge and close to site of Woodhenge, a ceremonial hall and probably the stronghold of forgotten kings of around 2000BC. It is possible Amesbury was one of the forts of AMBROSIUS AURELIANUS, from whom it perhaps derives its name. According to legend, Guinevere retired to Amesbury after the death of ARTHUR. Another legend states that Elfrida, the widow of EDGAR, founded Amesbury in 980 in atonement for the murder of her stepson, EDWARD THE MARTYR, though this was more likely Wherwell Abbey. A medieval abbey was founded 1177. It was here that Eleanor of Brittany (granddaughter of HENRY II) was eventually laid to rest (after 1241) after thirty-nine years in prison. It was also where Eleanor of Provence (wife of HENRY III) retired as a nun in 1284. She died at Amesbury and was buried in the convent church. Many daughters and granddaughters of later monarchs became nuns at Amesbury including Isabella, great-granddaughter of Henry III and granddaughter of Edward of Lancaster, who was prioress (1344–47).

Anderida *see* Pevensey

Anglesey (*formerly part of Gwynedd*) Island also known as Ynys Môn, for centuries linked with the Isle of Man as one of the Menapian Islands, and long the stronghold of Druid power. Tradition links Anglesey with CARAUSIUS (287). Probably formed kingdom with rulers of Man and Rheged in 5th C, but was subject to intensive raids by Irish and Vikings. Captured by CADWALLON in early 6th C and became the heartland of Gwynedd for over six centuries with capital at Aberffraw, though was captured by Normans (1098). No relics of the early rulers of Gwynedd remain at Aberffraw, but nearby at Llangadwaladr church (named after CADWALADR, 634) is a stone inscribed to CADFAN – "wisest and most renowned of all kings". Inland on the NW of the island is Llanbabo claimed to be named after the Celtic chief PABO, who sought refuge here. RHODRI AB OWAIN was buried at Holyhead on Holy Island (1195); Joan, the wife of LLYWELYN THE GREAT, is buried at Llanfaes. EDWARD I built the castle at Beaumaris (1295–8), moving the inhabitants of that locality to Rhosyr, which he renamed Newborough (1303). Castle captured by OWAIN GLYN DWR (1403) but retaken (1405). Held for Royalists in Civil War but fell (1646) and abandoned (1705).

Anjou French province, originally a feudal county whose rulers became the Plantagenet dynasty of England. Three children of Fulk V, count of Anjou, married descendants of WILLIAM THE CONQUEROR: Alice (later called Matilda) married (1119) William, eldest son of HENRY I; Sybilla married (1123) William Clito, son of Robert, duke of Normandy; and Geoffrey (later Geoffrey V of Anjou) married (1128) MATILDA, daughter of Henry I. Matilda's son, HENRY II, inherited the county of Anjou in 1151 and his sons, RICHARD (I) and JOHN were also counts of Anjou. John lost the territory to Philip of France (1205); HENRY III renounced rights (1259); reconquered by EDWARD III but relinquished (1360). *See also* Le Mans.

Annan (*Dumfries*) Lordship of Annandale conferred by DAVID I (c1124) on Robert de Brus, son of Robert de Brus, one of William the

Conqueror's barons who came from Bruis, near Cherbourg. His son, Robert, married Isabella, illegitimate daughter of WILLIAM THE LYON. His grandson, Robert le Brus married another Isabella, niece of William the Lyon, and through him the Bruce's laid claim to the Scottish throne, ruled eventually by ROBERT I, 1306 (sixth in descent from the first lord of Annandale). EDWARD BALLIOL was defeated at battle of Annan (1332).

Appleton House *see* Sandringham

Aquitaine A Roman province that stretched from the River Loire south to the Pyrenees. It became an independent duchy under the Merovingian kings of Francia. At its greatest extent it incorporated Poitou and Gascony and was known for a while as Guyenne. It came to the English crown with the marriage of HENRY II to Eleanor of Aquitaine in 1152, and the title duke of Aquitaine was retained by the English king or one of his eldest sons. RICHARD (I) was especially possessive of his lands in Aquitaine. EDWARD III converted the duchy into a principality for his eldest son, Edward, the Black Prince (1362–75) and, though it reverted to France thereafter, the title duke of Aquitaine was regained by John of Gaunt in 1390, passing to his grandson, the future HENRY V in 1399. Aquitaine was lost to France by HENRY VI in 1452. *See also* Bordeaux.

Arbroath (*Angus*) Abbey founded by WILLIAM THE LYON (1178), who was buried here (1214). Scene of ROBERT I's declaration of independence (1320). Created royal burgh by JAMES VI (1599).

Arderydd *see* Arthuret

Ardtornish Castle (*Argyll*) On the Sound of Mull by Lochaline, facing the Isle of Mull, this was the main stronghold of the lords of the Isles from the 13th C. Treaty of Westminster-Ardtornish was signed here (1462) making JOHN OF THE ISLES a vassal of EDWARD IV of England.

Arfderydd *see* Arthuret

Armorica *see* Brittany

Arreton (*Isle of Wight*) An ancient manor house, the first building (9th C) being a royal manor of ALFRED THE GREAT's, possibly inherited from his mother whose family came from Wight. Remained in ownership of Saxon kings until Norman conquest when it was passed to the abbey of Quarr. Returned to royal ownership under HENRY VIII during dissolution of the monasteries (1536) until disposed of by CHARLES I to pay his debts. The current house dates from 1595–1612.

Arthuret (*Liddesdale, Dumfries*) The site associated with the battle of Arfderydd in 573, in which PEREDUR of York defeated GWENDDOLAU of Galloway. RHYDDERCH of Strathclyde may also have been involved in the battle on the side of PEREDUR, whilst some records also link AEDAN MAC GABHRAN and his son Artiur (*see* ARTHUR) in the conflict. Gwnedollau's counsellor was Merlin who, after the battle, fled to the court of Aedán after a period of remorse and madness in the Caledonian Forest.

Arundel Castle (*West Sussex*) Started in the reign of EDWARD THE CONFESSOR but completed by Robert de Montgomery (1086), first earl of Arundel, who was granted the lands by WILLIAM THE CONQUEROR. It was captured in 1102 by HENRY I, who granted the castle to William d'Albini, whose descendants, the dukes of Norfolk, still hold the castle. Albini gave refuge to the Empress MATILDA (1139) when it was besieged again by STEPHEN. Matilda's son, HENRY II, further extended the castle. HENRY IV married Mary de Bohun here (1380). It was severely damaged during the Civil War (1643) but was extensively restored in the 18th and 19th C, with additional furnishing for the visit of VICTORIA and Albert (1846).

Ashdown (*Oxford / Berkshire*) Territory long disputed between Wessex and Mercia, bequeathed by CUTHRED to CENWEALH (648). Site of victory by West Saxons (under ATHELRED I and ALFRED) over the Danes (under HALFDAN) in 871. Battle was probably on the Berkshire Downs, just north of Compton.

Ashingdon (*Essex*) Site of battle of Assandun (1016), five miles north of Southend, where CANUTE defeated EDMUND II leading to division of England between the Danes and the English.

Athelney (*Somerset*) Village on Somerset levels where ALFRED THE GREAT sought refuge from the Danes (878). The name means "island of the princes" suggesting that the whole royal family held fast here.

Atrebates A Belgic tribe whose territory was mostly in Hampshire and parts of Wiltshire and Sussex. Their chief fort was at Silchester. Although subjugated by the Romans their tribe no doubt survived within a *civitas* into the post-Roman period, and there were doubtless chieftains of the Atrebates who fought against AELLE and CERDIC in the 5th and 6th C.

Audley End House (*Essex*) A Jacobean manor house, 1 mile to W of Saffron Walden. Built (1603–16) on the site of Walden Abbey by Thomas Howard, earl of Suffolk, it was bought in 1669 by CHARLES II for £50,000. A huge house, rivalling Hampton Court, its upkeep became too expensive. Although the occasional residence of JAMES II and WILLIAM and MARY, it was returned to the 5th earl of Suffolk in 1701 in lieu of the balance of unpaid debt. It was much reduced in size after 1721.

Aylesford (*Kent*) A small medieval village to the north of Maidstone on the river Medway. The site of two important battles. CARATACUS was defeated here by the Romans (43AD); and VORTIMER fought the Angles under HENGIST (455). Victory is attributed to the Angles, although Hengist's brother Horsa was killed. Tradition states he was buried to the north of Aylesford at Horsted, though the name simply means a place where horses were kept.

Badon The site of a decisive battle where ARTHUR defeated the Saxons so convincingly that the Saxon onslaught was curbed for a generation or more. The date for the battle is reckoned variously between 490 and 516. Suggested sites for the battle include Badbury, south of Swindon, in Wiltshire; Badbury, near Wimborne in Dorset; Bath, in Somerset; or Badon Hill in Antrim, Northern Ireland. It is likely that there was more than one battle of Badon. That in the south of England saw the defeat of AELLE of the South Saxons and OISC of Kent and possibly, though less likely, CERDIC of the Gewisse. A later battle of Badon (665) was between MORGAN THE GENEROUS of Gwent and CENWEALH of Wessex.

Balmerino Abbey (*Fife*) On Firth of Tay opposite Dundee. Founded by ALEXANDER II (1227) at request of his mother, Ermengarde, widow of WILLIAM THE LYON; she was buried (1234) beneath the high altar.

Balmoral Castle (*Aberdeenshire*) Royal estate between Braemar and Ballater on the river Dee in the Grampians. An estate belonging to the earl of Huntly had existed here since the 15th C, but all remaining buildings were demolished and the new castle built in the neo-Gothic Scottish baronial style under instructions from Prince Albert after he and VICTORIA acquired the estate in 1852 at a price of £31,500. It was a private purchase with money from a legacy and thus was not crown property. It became a popular summer retreat for Victoria, though less so after Albert's death. It was not favoured so much by EDWARD VII and Alexandra, but has been a regular summer or autumn home for all succeeding monarchs and is a particular favourite of Prince Charles.

Bamburgh (*Northumberland*) Although the existing castle was mostly rebuilt in 1903 there has been a fortification on this site since pre-Roman times. Its original name was Din Guairi (the fort of the Guairi) and would have been occupied by a leading tribe of the Votadini known as the Brynaich, from whom the name Bernicia was derived. It was probably the fort of GERMANIANUS and possibly BRAN HEN and almost certainly MORCANT BULC. Its old name, sometimes rendered as Dinguayrdi, is not dissimilar to the name of Sir Lancelot's castle, Joyeuse Garde. Legend attributes the foundation of Din Guairi to Ebrauc, the founder of York. IDA captured the fortress in 557 and established the kingdom of Bernicia. His grandson ATHELFRITH married a Celtic princess, Bebbe, after whom Bamburgh (originally Bebbanburh), was named. Bamburgh was a formidable stronghold. It was unsuccessfully besieged by URIEN in the 580s and twice by PENDA around 650, and was eventually captured by the Danes under RAGNALL of York in 914. Even WILLIAM II could only take it by subterfuge (1095). It was not until the Wars of the Roses (1461) that Bamburgh found its thick walls could not withstand the power of cannon, when the castle was captured by Margaret of Anjou (wife of HENRY VI). Thereafter the castle fell into disrepair and was not restored until the 18th C. The castle was held for many years by the Percies of Northumberland, and during the border wars DAVID II of Scotland was held prisoner here (1346).

Bangor (*Caernarfonshire and Merionethshire*) Derives its name from the Celtic for enclosure, signifying the original monastery established by St Deiniol, a descendent of COEL HEN, in c525. It is likely to be this monastery to which MAELGWYN HIR retired briefly (520s). It is probable that several of the later kings of Gwynedd were buried at Bangor, certainly from the 9th C on, but the only ones known for sure are GRUFFYDD AP CYNAN (1137) and OWAIN GWYNEDD (1170).

Bangor-is-y-Coed or **Bangor-on-Dee** (*Wrexham*) An ancient monastic foundation is said to have existed here from the 2nd C. Its entire community of some 1200 monks were slaughtered by ATHELFRITH of Northumbria (615) for praying against him. The site is now a racecourse.

Bannockburn (*Stirling*) Small town SE of Stirling where ROBERT BRUCE soundly defeated EDWARD II on 24 June 1314, thereby re-establishing Scotland's independence. Much of the battlefield is now covered by buildings, but there is a statue of Robert on horseback overlooking the site, unveiled in 1964.

Bardney (*Lincolnshire*) Monastery in Lindsey founded, probably in the 680s, by ATHELRED of Mercia. His wife, Osthryth, who was murdered, was buried here (697). Athelred retired here as the abbot (704) and was also buried here (714). Osthryth had removed the relics of her uncle, the sainted OSWALD of Northumbria, here at the time of its foundation, though these were later translated to Gloucester. The monastery was destroyed by the Vikings (870) but refounded in 1087, and remained a Benedictine abbey until the reformation.

Barking (*Essex*) A monastery was founded here (c675) by Eorcenwald, bishop of London, almost certainly a member of the Kentish royal family,

for his sister, Athelburh, the first abbess. Queen Cuthburh, wife of ALDFRITH of Northumbria, retired here as a nun (c700), before founding the monastery at Wimborne. Later abbesses included Matilda, the illegitimate daughter of HENRY II (c1200), and Matilda, the illegitimate daughter of JOHN (c1210). The abbey was dissolved in 1539 and demolished. Only the Curfew Tower remains.

Barnard Castle (*Durham*) Founded by Guy de Bailleul from Normandy shortly after the Conquest but extensively developed by his nephew, Bernard, after 1150. His descendant was John de Balliol, regent of Scotland (1255), who founded Balliol College, Oxford (1263). His son was JOHN BALLIOL. The Castle passed from the Balliol family with the death of EDWARD BALLIOL (1364) to the earls of Warwick through which it came into the hands of RICHARD III (1472) from his wife Anne, daughter of the earl of Warwick. The castle fell into disrepair in the 16th C.

Barnet (*North London*) An obelisk erected in 1740 between Kitts' End and Hadley marks the site of the battle of Barnet (1471), when EDWARD IV defeated and killed the earl of Warwick.

Baschurch (*Shropshire*) Supposed burial place of CYNDDYLAN (655).

Basing (*Hampshire*) Old Basing, to the east of Basingstoke, was the site of a Saxon fortress. It was here that the Danes defeated ATHELRED and ALFRED in 871 just two weeks after the battle of Ashdown. A Norman castle was built on the same site and within its ruins a Tudor manor house, Basing House, was built in 1530 by William Paulet, marquess of Winchester, who served under all the Tudor monarchs. ELIZABETH I stayed here and was so extravagant that Paulet had to demolish part of the house to meet the costs. The house remained a frequent hot-spot for royal entertainment, particularly by Queen Henrietta Maria, wife of CHARLES I. It withstood sieges by the Parliamentarians over two years until captured and destroyed by Cromwell (1645).

Bath (*Somerset*) Geoffrey of Monmouth attributed the founding of Bath to BLAEDUD in around 650BC, but Bath is a Roman town (Aqua Sulis) which fell into much disrepair during the onslaught from the Saxons. It is one of the supposed sites for Badon. It was ruled by FARINMAIL when it was captured by CEAWLIN of Wessex in 577. The land passed in ownership between Wessex and Mercia. In 625 OSRIC of the Hwicce established a monastery here, and it was under the control of OFFA of Mercia when another monastery was founded (780). The abbey was chosen by Dunstan as the site for the first major coronation in 973 when EDGAR was crowned King of the English with his queen Elfrida. Captured by SWEIN (1013). Bath re-emerged as a spa in the 18th C when much of the centre was rebuilt and received much patronage from GEORGE III and his queen, Charlotte, who stayed in Sydney Place, and then from GEORGE IV.

Battle (*East Sussex*) The site of the battle of Hastings, fought on Senlac Hill on 14 October 1066 between HAROLD II of England and WILLIAM of Normandy. William vowed to build a church on the spot if he were victorious, and the high altar was placed on the spot where Harold fell, now the site of Harold's Stone (erected 1903). Little of the church and the abbey survive, although part of the abbey buildings were converted into a private school.

Bawtry (*Nottinghamshire / South Yorkshire*) The generally accepted site of the battle of the River Idle in 616, when the army of REDWALD of East Anglia, supporting the dispossessed EDWIN, defeated ATHELFRITH of Northumbria. As a result Edwin not only became king of Northumbria but introduced Christianity to the northern Angles.

Baynard's Castle *see* London

Beandun *see* Bindon

Bearsted (*Kent*) Small village now almost subsumed by Maidstone. It was here in 691 that WIHTRED called a council to issue his law code.

Beaumaris *see* Anglesey

Beauvale Priory (*Nottinghamshire*) One of the suggested locations for the burial of EDWARD BALLIOL (*c*1364), though it is possible he was buried at the original home of the Balliols at Bailleul in Normandy.

Bedricsworth *see* Bury St Edmunds

Benington (*Hertfordshire*) A royal villa of the kings of Mercia, near present-day Stevenage. BEOHRTWULF held a council-of-war here (850) to plan his campaign against the Danes.

Bensington *see* Benson.

Benson (*Oxfordshire*) The Saxon village of Bensington on the north side of the Thames, in land disputed between Mercia and Wessex. OFFA's defeat of CYNEWULF at Bensington (779) established Mercian supremacy for the next forty years.

Benton (*Devon*) *see* Bindon.

Berkeley Castle (*Gloucestershire*) Midway between Bristol and Gloucester this existing castle, overlooking the Severn estuary, was completed in 1153 by Lord Berkeley and has remained in the family's possession ever since, with few changes since the 14th C. The original site was granted to Roger de Berkeley by WILLIAM *the conqueror* in 1086. HENRY I stayed here in 1121. EDWARD II was murdered here (1327). The murder room remains as it was.

Berkhamstead Castle (*Hertfordshire*) The site of EDGAR ATHELING's submission to WILLIAM THE CONQUEROR towards the end of 1066. Situated in the foothills of the Chilterns, this castle was presented by William to his half-brother Robert, count of Mortain (1067), and it remained an important residence for the next six centuries. It was the home of Thomas Becket when he was Chancellor (1155–65). It was besieged by Louis, son of Philippe II of France (1216). The castle passed to the earls of Cornwall, starting with Richard, younger brother of HENRY III and briefly Holy Roman Emperor, who died here (1272), as had his second wife Sanchia, sister of Eleanor of Provence (1261). Richard's son, Edmund, who was "Guardian of the Realm" (1286–89) during EDWARD I's French campaigns, was born here (1249). It was the home of EDWARD II's favourite, Piers Gaveston, when he was made earl of Cornwall (1307–1312). Edward, the Black Prince, spent his final days here (1376), though he died at Westminster. The young HENRY VI spent some of his childhood here (1428). Cecilia Neville, the mother of EDWARD IV and RICHARD III died here (1495).

Bernicia (*Northumberland*) The name of a kingdom founded by the Angle IDA in 557. Later tradition ascribed the origin of the name to Bearnoch, Ida's wife, but the name was an anglicisation of the original Celtic name Bryneich or Beornice, which probably meant "the land of mountain passes". Its centre was at Bamburgh and at times it incorporated Lothian, stretching as far north as Edinburgh. Although Bernicia combined with Deira to form Northumbria under ATHELFRITH in 604, the two territories retained their individuality and occasionally had their own kings. When the Danes conquered York in 867, they installed separate kings in Bernicia and an earldom was established at Bamburgh which remained until 1041.

Berwick-on-Tweed (*Northumberland*) The northernmost town in England and one constantly in dispute with the Scots, having changed hands thirteen times since it was founded in 870 before it passed to England in 1482, though it enjoyed autonomous status from 1551 until the union of Scotland and England (1603). It was developed as a burgh by DAVID I in 1120s and formed part of the ransom paid to the English by WILLIAM THE LYON in 1174 to effect his release. William bought it back from RICHARD I who needed money to finance his Crusade (1189). It was sacked by JOHN in 1216. Here EDWARD I determined the heir to the Scottish throne (1292), and it was sacked by Edward during the subsequent wars with JOHN BALLIOL. DAVID II married EDWARD II's daughter Joan at Berwick (1328). HENRY VI granted Berwick to Scotland as part of the arrangement for his own protection (1461). The Treaty of Berwick (1357) allowed the release of David II; the second Treaty of Berwick (1560) declared ELIZABETH I's support of the Scots against the French, though this was never ratified by MARY Queen of Scots. Elizabeth decided on her own fortification of Berwick in 1558, resulting in the Elizabethan Wall, completed in 1565. *See also* Halidon Hill.

Bindon (*Devon*) Near Axminster on Devon-Somerset border. A possible site for the battle of Beandun (614) in which CYNEGILS defeated the British, killing over 2000 Britons. Benton, in North Devon, is another possible location.

Birdoswald (*Cumbria*) see Camlann

Birsay (*Orkneys*) The site of the original principal palace of the earls of Orkney. It is most closely associated with THORFINN THE MIGHTY, who established the first Christian church at Birsay (1048) and was buried here (*c*1060).

Bisham Abbey (*Berkshire*) An Augustinian priory built in the 14th C by William MONTACUTE on the site of a former Knights Templar preceptory, near Marlow. Several earls of Salisbury were buried here, as was Richard Neville, earl of Warwick (1471), called the King-Maker. The abbey was dismantled in 1557 but its remains can still be seen.

Bishop's Waltham (*Hampshire*) The site of the palace of the bishops of Winchester, near Southampton. Built in 12th C by Henry de Blois, brother of STEPHEN, it was at its height in the 15th C. The town was rich and strongly supported the Crusades. RICHARD I stayed here soon after his coronation (1189), during his brief stay in England. The castle was besieged and ruined during the Civil War (1644).

Blackheath (*Kent*) A village and open land south of Greenwich. It has long been a gathering place, both for rebellion and celebration. Wat Tyler assembled his supporters here in the Peasant's Revolt (1381), as did Jack Cade (1450). HENRY VII defeated Michael Joseph and the Cornish rebels (1497). HENRY V was welcomed here after his victory at Agincourt (1415); HENRY VIII first met Anne of Cleves (1540) and CHARLES II was welcomed back to England (1660). It was at Montague House, Blackheath, that Caroline of Brunswick established her orphanage (1797) that led to the subsequent scandal known as the "delicate investigation".

Blackmore (*Essex*) The former manor house of Jericho was the birthplace of HENRY VIII's illegitimate son Henry Fitzroy (1519) by Elizabeth Blount.

Blair Atholl (*Perth and Kinross*) A castle first built in 1269 by John Comyn, lord of Badenoch and a descendant of DONALD III, and subsequently the home of the dukes of Atholl. It was occupied by Bonnie Prince Charlie (1745/6) and besieged by government forces, probably the last castle siege in Britain.

Blickling (*Norfolk*) Village 14 miles N of Norwich. The original manor house was bought by Geoffrey Boleyn in 1452. His great grand-daughter Anne Boleyn was born here in about 1501, though she spent her childhood at Hever Castle. Blickling Hall was built on this site between 1616 and 1628.

Bodmin Moor (*Cornwall*) King Doniert's Stone on the southern edge of the Moor commemorates one of the last native kings of Kernow, who drowned nearby in the river Fowey (875).

Bognor Regis (*West Sussex*) A popular seaside resort favoured by Queen VICTORIA. Earned the title Regis when GEORGE V convalesced at the nearby Craigweil House (1929), which has since been demolished.

Bolingbroke Castle (*Lincolnshire*) 4 miles W of Spilsby, the castle was built by Ranulf, earl of Chester, in the 1220s. It came into the possession of John of Gaunt, son of Edward III, when he married Blanche, the daughter of the duke of Lancaster, in 1359. She died at Bolingbroke (1369). John's son, Henry (the future HENRY IV) was born here (1367). The castle was destroyed by the Parliamentarians in 1643 but has recently been partly restored.

Bolton Castle see Castle Bolton

Bordeaux (*France*) Bordeaux was part of HENRY II's Angevin Empire and was annexed when he married Eleanor of Aquitaine at Bordeaux Cathedral (1152). This was also where JOHN married Isabella of Angoulême (1200). The place was central to EDWARD III's French campaign and saw much tragedy. Edward's daughter Joan died here of the Black Death (1348). Edward's son, Edward the Black Prince, held his court here as Prince of Aquitaine (1362–73). The Black Prince's younger son, RICHARD II, was born here (1367), whilst his elder son, Edward, died here (1371). The city surrendered to Charles VII of France (1453) and was restored to French sovereignty, amidst much regret by its citizens whose prosperity declined.

Boroughbridge (*North Yorkshire*) A mile west of Aldborough, it superseded the older village when the Normans built a bridge here over the Ure (12th C). Here EDWARD II's forces defeated Thomas of Lancaster (1322) (*see under* Pontefract).

Boscobel House (*Shropshire*) 9 miles NW of Wolverhampton. Built around the year 1600 by John Giffard, this hunting lodge was designed as a retreat with many secret hiding places. It was here that CHARLES II fled after the battle of Worcester (1651) and hid in an oak tree in the grounds to evade the Parliamentarians. The present Royal Oak was purportedly grown from an acorn of the original tree. It led to the celebration of Oak-Apple Day. The house was subsequently significantly altered but has more recently been restored and refurbished.

Bosham (*West Sussex*) A Saxon village near Chichester, recorded as Bosanham as early as 731. A manor here was the home of Harold Godwinson (the future HAROLD II) and it was from here that he embarked on his ill-fated trip to Normandy (1064). The village claims to be the place where CANUTE ordered back the waves (*c*1027) though other chroniclers locate the site in the Thames estuary. Canute was also supposed to have had a daughter, whose name is not known but who apparently died at Bosham and was buried in the local church (*c*1027), but recent research has put this into doubt.

Bosworth Field (*Leicestershire*) Just south of Market Bosworth, the site of the battle of Bosworth fought on Monday, 22 August 1485 between RICHARD III and Henry Tudor (the future HENRY VII). Though not the last battle of the Wars of the Roses it was the decider, with Henry victorious and Richard killed. Legend may have taken over from fact, but the tradition is that Richard was killed during a rash attempt to fight Henry directly in the midst of the battle. His crown, which he had worn over his helmet, was found in the branches of a hawthorn bush by a soldier and placed on Henry's head by Thomas STANLEY, whose lack of support during the battle had been Richard's undoing. Richard's body was dumped over the back of a packhorse and removed to Leicester for burial. The battlefield is today part of a country park with displays and other facilities.

Boulogne (*France*) It has long had a close association with Britain. CARAUSIUS, who established himself as emperor in Britain (286), had his base at Bolougne. Mary, daughter of Malcolm III of Scotland, married Eustace III, count of Boulogne (*c*1101) and their daughter, Matilda, married STEPHEN (1125). Their son, EUSTACE, became count of Boulogne (1147–53) and was succeeded by his brother William (1153–59), and then his sister Mary in 1159. She was forcibly married to Matthew, count of Flanders, who assumed the countship of Boulogne, and it passed to their descendants. EDWARD II married Isabella of France at Boulogne Cathedral (1308). Boulogne was captured by HENRY VIII (1544) during his French wars but restored to the French in 1550.

Boyne (*Ireland*) The battle of the Boyne took place 3 miles W of Drogheda, near the estuary of the river Boyne, on 1 July 1690 and the Protestant forces led by William of Orange (WILLIAM III) defeated the Catholics under the deposed JAMES II.

Bradford-on-Avon (*Wiltshire*) The location of a battle (652) between CENWEALH of the West Saxons and the British, though it is possible that other Saxon factions (and even Angles of Mercia) were involved. Bradford was on the border of struggles between the West Saxons, Mercians and Celts. The oldest part of the surviving church of St Laurence may survive from a generation or two later, at the time of Aldhelm (late 7th C), who established a monastery at Bradford in the reign of INE.

Bradgate Manor (*Leicestershire*) 6 miles NW of Leicester, this was the home of Thomas Grey, earl of Huntingdon and 1st marquess of Dorset, who started it in 1490. It was here that Lady JANE Grey was born (1537) and spent the happiest years of her short life. The house is now a ruin but the surrounding parkland is open to the public.

Braemore (*Highland*) 7 miles W of Dunbeath. Above the town on Eagle Rock is a monument to George, duke of Kent, son of GEORGE V, who was killed here in a plane crash whilst on active service during the War (1942).

Brechin (*Angus*) It is recorded that in *c*990 KENNETH II "gave Brechin to the Lord", which may simply mean he took control of the territory, but also suggests that he founded a church or religious settlement. The existing Round Tower at Brechin probably dates from this period, though the subsequent cathedral and bishopric were not founded until around 1150. It was to the north of Brechin, in Strathcarro churchyard, that JOHN BALLIOL abdicated (1296). Brechin's name is purportedly derived from Brychan the son of BRYCHAN, who moved to this area from southern Wales (*see* Brecon). *See also* Fettercairn.

Brecon (*Powys*) The town, which gave its name to the old county of Brecknockshire, derives its name from BRYCHAN, the Celtic chieftain whose descendants ruled the kingdom of Brycheiniog. Brychan's grave is purportedly in the churchyard at Llanspyddid, 2 miles to the W of Brecon. RHYS AP TEWDWR was killed at Brecon (1093) and the Normans established a castle (1090s), which was rebuilt during the reign of EDWARD I and was besieged by LLYWELYN THE LAST (1282). It passed to Henry Bolingbroke (HENRY IV) with his marriage to Mary de Bohun (*c*1380) and was unsuccessfully besieged by OWAIN GLYN DWR (1404). The castle is now in ruins.

Brigantes One of the largest of the Celtic tribes of Britain which stretched across the Pennines of what is now Yorkshire and parts of Lancashire. Their main town was at Aldborough. Most of their rulers are not known by name, though the most notorious was CARTIMANDUA.

Brighton (*East Sussex*) Originally a small south-coast fishing village which erupted in popularity in the 1760s with the growing fashion for bathing and received royal patronage with the visits of George, prince of Wales (later GEORGE IV), which started in 1783. George leased a farmhouse at the mouth of the Steyne Valley in 1786, which was rebuilt as a Palladian mansion and renamed the Marine Pavilion. It became the favourite residence of the Prince; his (unofficial) wife, Maria Fitzherbert, had a villa nearby. In 1797 the Prince bought the Pavilion for £22,000 and over the next twenty years it was elaborately redesigned by the architect John Nash into the exotic oriental Pavilion that is such a tourist attraction today. George IV last visited it in 1827. WILLIAM IV often stayed here but VICTORIA found it vulgar and it was sold to Brighton Corporation in 1850 for £50,000.

Bristol Although an important Saxon town, with its own mint, and later England's second port, it has surprisingly few royal connections. Legend attributes its foundation to BRENNIUS in *c*380 BC. The Empress MATILDA held court here with her brother Robert (1139), and it was here that STEPHEN was held prisoner for nine months (1141). Eleanor of Brittany, the granddaughter of HENRY II, was confined by King JOHN in 1203 at various castles and remained captive for thirty-nine years till her death at Bristol Castle in 1241. She was buried at St James's Priory Church, Bristol, but later removed to Amesbury. St Augustine's Abbey (founded in 1148) was intended as the burial place of EDWARD II, who had been murdered at Berkeley Castle (1327), but the abbot refused the body, which was taken to Gloucester. The Abbey was dissolved in 1538 but was restored as a cathedral (1542). ELIZABETH I visited Bristol in 1574 and remarked that the Church of St Mary's was the "fairest and goodliest" church in the land.

Brittany Formerly Armorica, it was settled by the Celts of Britain driven out by the Saxon invasions in the mid fifth century. The first recorded king was CYNAN MERIADOC (*see also* DIONATUS *and* RIOTHAMUS). Brittany occasionally shared rulers with Dumnonia in south-west Britain during the fifth and sixth centuries and it is likely that both AMBROSIUS AURELIANUS and CERDIC spent some time in Brittany before their invasions of Britain. The last native Celtic king was Saloman (874) before it passed to the French. It came under the control of HENRY II (1166) but was lost by JOHN (1203), though it remained a separate duchy and was not formally incorporated into France until 1532.

Brixham (*Devon*) A fishing port on Tor Bay. Here William of Orange (WILLIAM III) first landed in England, declaring: "Mine goot people, I mean you goot, I am here for your goot, for all your goots."

Bruce's Cave *see* Kirkpatrick Fleming *and* Rathlin Island.

Brunanburh Although the exact site of the battle (937) is not known, its most likely location is somewhere near Nottingham (perhaps at Bourne in Lincolnshire). Other suggestions are as far south as Axminster in Devon, as far north as Burnswork in Scotland, or at Bromborough in the Wirral. It was one of the most decisive battles of the Saxon period, where the English army under ATHELSTAN defeated the Scots under CONSTANTINE II and the Vikings under OLAF GOTHFRITHSON and established the superiority of the Saxons over Britain.

Brycheiniog (*South Wales*) Kingdom established in the sixth century by Brychan and ruled by his descendants for four hundred years. It covered much of the region still called Brecknock in southern Powys. The chief royal residence was probably at Talgarth, though the centre of the region became Brecon.

Bryneich *see* Bernicia

Buckden (*Cambridgeshire; formerly Huntingdonshire*) Here stood the fortified palace of the bishops of Lincoln. Built in 1494, the palace was used to confine (virtually imprison) Katherine of Aragon from July 1533 to April 1534 while HENRY VIII awaited the Pope's verdict on the divorce. The palace was damp and unhealthy and contributed to Katherine's weakening constitution

Buckingham Palace *see* London

Builth Wells (*Powys*) Part of the old Welsh kingdom of Gwerthrynion, Builth, or more properly Llanfair-ym-Muallt, was probably the centre of PASCENT's kingdom in the fifth century. The Normans built a castle here in 1091 which was besieged by LLYWELYN THE LAST in 1260. A new castle was constructed by EDWARD I around 1280. The garrison refused Llywelyn shelter in 1282 as he fled from Edward, and as a result he was ambushed nearby and killed. The castle was destroyed in the 16th C and nothing now remains.

Burgh-by-Sands (*Cumbria*) EDWARD I died on his way to Scotland to strike at Robert the Bruce, and he lay in state at the church of St Michael's (1307) before the long procession back to Westminster. A monument to Edward stands just outside the village.

Burghead (*Moray*) *see* Elgin *and* Forres

Burnfoot (*Dumfries and Galloway*) *see* Dundrennan Abbey

Bury St Edmunds (*Suffolk*) Originally called Bedricsworth, a monastery was established here in 636. In 915 EDMUND, king of the East Angles who had been killed by the Danes in 870, was reburied here and a shrine established to his memory. A cult rapidly developed and the town's name became superseded by St Edmunds Bury. CANUTE granted the monastery abbey status and jurisdiction directly under the crown in 1032, and EDWARD THE CONFESSOR extended this authority over most of West Suffolk, making the abbey one of the richest in Saxon England. Stephen's son EUSTACE died here (1153) and Thomas, earl of Norfolk and son of Edward I, was buried at the Abbey (1338). A council of barons met here in secret in 1214 and drew up the terms of what became the Magna Carta (*see* JOHN). HENRY VI summoned a Parliament here in February 1447 because it was too risky in London. Humphrey, duke of Gloucester and son of Henry IV, was arrested for treason upon his arrival and imprisoned. He died a week later, some believed by poisoning. Henry VIII's sister, Mary Tudor, who had eloped and married Charles Brandon, duke of Suffolk, was buried at the Church of St Mary (1533).

Buxton (*Derbyshire*) A famous spa town. MARY, Queen of Scots, was allowed to visit the town in 1573 in the hope that the waters would improve her health.

Cadbury Castle (*Somerset*) The site of an ancient Celtic fort associated by many with Camelot. Whether or not this was the site of ARTHUR's castle, it was almost certainly the fortification of an important Celtic war-chief.

Cader Idris (*Caernarfonshire and Merionethshire*) The name means Chair of Idris and is associated with IDRIS, ruler of Meirionydd, who was killed in battle against the Saxons in 632. Idris was apparently something of a poet and there is a legend that anyone who can spend a night at the summit of Idris will find themselves either a poet or a lunatic.

Caerleon (*Monmouth, formerly Gwent*) The Romans established a fort here in AD 75 following their subjugation of the Silures. They called it Isca Silurum, after the river Usk, but it subsequently became known as the City of the Legions, or Caer-Leon. In later years it became associated with the capital of King ARTHUR.

Caernarvon (*Caernarfonshire and Merionethshire*) The site of the old Roman fort of Segontium (AD 77), the location was almost certainly of importance to the Ordovices and again to the subsequent kings of Gwynedd. It was attacked by CLYDNO and CINMARC (*c*560). Legend describes Segontium as the birthplace of CONSTANTINE THE GREAT (272), albeit apocryphally, and it was also claimed that his father, CONSTANTIUS was buried here (306). What was claimed as Constantius's body was found in 1283 during the construction of Caernarvon Castle and reburied here at EDWARD I's request. Edward's son, the future EDWARD II, was born here (1284) and invested as prince of Wales (1301). The castle took nearly forty years to build and was never properly finished. When RICHARD II sought refuge here on his return from Ireland (1399), he could only find a bed of straw. OWAIN GLYN DWR unsuccessfully besieged the castle (1403) and it managed to survive three sieges during the Civil War. It was partly dismantled in 1660 but the walls remain in a remarkable state of preservation. The future EDWARD VIII was invested here as prince of Wales in 1911, a ceremony which he found absurd; and Prince Charles was also invested here as prince of Wales in 1969.

Caistor (*Norfolk*) The capital of the Iceni, and the site of the Roman fort Venta Icenorum. This was the home of PRASUTAGUS and BOUDICCA.

Caithness (*Highlands*). The original Pictish division of Cat which almost certainly had its local rulers in pre-historic times. It was subject to Norse raids and under THORFINN (II) the Norse earls of Orkney also became earls of Caithness. HLODVIR of Orkney was buried at Hofn in Caithness (987). LIOT of Orkney was killed at Skidmoor (*c*984), which is also where SIGURD II defeated FINDLAECH of Moray (995). Although the earls remained subject to Scotland for the territory in Caithness they were virtually independent until ALEXANDER II regained Caithness in 1222. *See separate entries for* Duncansby, Thurso *and* Wick.

Calais (*France*) The last part of French soil to remain in English hands. It was captured by EDWARD III after a year's siege (1347). When the burghers came to surrender the town, Edward's wife Philippa successfully pleaded for their lives, a scene often reproduced in paintings and sculpture. RICHARD II married Isabella of France at St Nicholas's Church, in 1396. Present at the wedding was his uncle, Thomas, duke of Gloucester, who opposed the match and disliked the king. Thomas was later arrested at Pleshey in Essex and escorted back to Calais where he was imprisoned and found smothered the next day (1397). Calais remained in English hands, though it needed constant protection from the French. HENRY VIII landed here for his campaign of 1513 and it was near Calais that Henry had his summit meeting with François I of France at the Field of the Cloth of Gold (1520). It was finally taken by the French in 1558 and its loss was a sad blow to the last days of MARY I who claimed that when she was dead, "Calais will be found written on my heart."

Callington (*Cornwall*) The *ASC* records that in 838 EGBERT defeated a combined army of Danes and British at Hingston Down, just over the Tamar into Cornwall. Egbert was then into his sixties and probably did not take part in the battle, but it still demonstrated his abilities as a warrior king.

Cambridge (*Cambridgeshire*) Despite its antiquity and importance, Cambridge has surprisingly few royal connections other than in relation to the university. A centre for learning was developed by SIGEBERT (*c*630) through his monastic foundations but the Danish invasions destroyed much and it was not until the 12th C that it began to revive. King's Hall was founded by EDWARD II (1317) and enlarged by EDWARD III (1336). It formed the basis for the later Trinity College, established by HENRY VIII (1546), and attended by the future GEORGE VI (1919–20). King's College was founded by HENRY VI (1441), and Queen's College by his wife, Margaret of Anjou (1448).

Cambuskenneth Abbey (*Stirling*) An Augustinian abbey was founded here by DAVID I (*c*1140) and it was here that WILLIAM WALLACE defeated the English (1297). The abbey was the burial place of both JAMES III (1488) and his wife, Margaret of Denmark (1486). The abbey is just to the east of Stirling and is only a few miles north of the battlefields of Bannockburn and Sauchieburn.

Camelford (*Cornwall*) *see* Camlann

Camelon (*Falkirk*) *see* Camlann

Camelot The name of King ARTHUR's court. The name was first used by the French romancer Chrétien de Troyes at the start of *Lancelot* completed about 1177, and since he refers to Caerleon separately, a place often cited as Arthur's capital, it must be different. The name is probably a corruption of a renowned name at the time, the most likely candidate being Colchester, which was known to the Romans as Camulodunum. That might be the origin of the name but not necessarily the location of the place. Thomas Malory equates it with Winchester whilst other suggested sites are Cadbury Castle, Carlisle, or Stirling.

Camlann. The name of ARTHUR's last battle (*c*537 or later) in which he was mortally wounded while fighting his enemy, his incestuous son Mordred. The name derives from Camboglanna which, in Celtic, means "crooked branch", like an elbow in a river. There are many contenders for the site of Camlann associated with significant battles, and some also with the historical Arthurs. These include Maes Camlan, a field by a stream between Dinas Mawddwy and Aberangell in Merioneth,

where ARTHWYR of Dyfed probably fought; Camelon, west of Falkirk, where Artiur of Dalriada is supposed to have fought, as well as Camlanna or Comboglanna (a battle linked with that at Degsastan *c*603), along Hadrian's Wall (identified with the fort now called Birdoswald); Camelford in Cornwall (though this may be associated with a battle near Slaughterbridge, where EGBERT subdued the British in 825); or even Cambridge.

Canterbury (*Kent*) The capital of the Celtic tribe of the Cantii, where Julius Caesar defeated the British (55BC). It was called Durovernum by the Romans, and became the Saxon capital of Kent under ATHELBERT, whose palace and mint were both here. It was here that Augustine brought Roman Christianity to the Saxons in 597. His first church was that of St Martin's, already established by Athelbert's wife, Bertha. Augustine's Abbey and Church was dedicated in 602. Many of the Kentish kings were buried at Augustine's Abbey, and doubtless their wives, though records are not complete. Known burials include Athelbert (616) (*though see* Reculver), EADBALD (640), EORCENBERT (664), EGBERT I (673), WIHTRED (725), as well as Edgiva the third wife of Edward the Elder (968). The first pennies were minted in England at Canterbury (*c*770). The cathedral was sacked by the Danes in 1011 and destroyed by fire in 1067 and was completely rebuilt. It is usually the Archbishop of Canterbury who officiates at coronations, though historically most of these have happened at Kingston or Westminster Abbey. HARTHACANUTE was allegedly crowned here (1040), and STEPHEN held his second coronation here upon his restoration (1141). A few royal marriages have been conducted here, including HENRY III's marriage to Eleanor of Provence (1236) and EDWARD I's to Margaret of France (1299). Royalty buried here include Isabella, the first wife of JOHN (1217); Edward the Black Prince (1376) in a magnificent tomb in Trinity Chapel; HENRY IV (1413), the only post-Saxon king buried at Canterbury (*though see also* Faversham), and his queen, Joan of Navarre (1437). The last royal marriage at Canterbury was that of CHARLES I to Henrietta Maria in St Augustine's Church (1625). Canterbury is perhaps most famous (or notorious) for the murder of Thomas Becket (1170) on the inadvertent order of HENRY II. To atone for this Henry walked through the streets of Canterbury in sackcloth and was lashed by the monks. Becket's shrine, which was established in 1220, was destroyed by order of HENRY VIII in 1538, who declared Becket a traitor.

Cardiff (*Glamorgan*) Although now the capital of the principality of Wales (1955), Cardiff has only risen to prominence since the early nineteenth century. Prior to that it was a fishing village and small port though with evidence of occupation from Roman times, including a Viking settlement. The Normans built a castle here in 1091 on the site of the Roman fort. HENRY I imprisoned his brother Robert, duke of Normandy, at the castle from 1106–34. The castle was stormed by Ifor Bach, lord of Senghenydd (1158); it was again captured by OWAIN GLYN DWR (1404); and taken over by Jasper Tudor, uncle to the future HENRY VII (1488). Cardiff was granted city status by EDWARD VII when he visited in 1905. Since 1922 Cardiff has incorporated Llandaff within its suburbs, though this cathedral has had a more significant history as the central church of Gwent and Morgannwg since the 6th C.

Cardigan (*Cardiganshire; formerly Dyfed*), Welsh Aberteifi, on the borders between Ceredigion and Dyfed. A fortification has stood here since Celtic times, no doubt a frequent battlefield between the British and Irish. A stone castle was built here by the Normans (*c*1093). It was captured by RHYS AP GRUFFYDD (1170), who made it one of his residences and inaugurated the first official *eisteddfod* (1176). It was retaken by the earl of Pembroke who rebuilt it (1240). It fell to Parliamentarian forces in 1645.

Cardross Castle (*Argyll and Bute*) 8 miles W of Dumbarton. ROBERT THE BRUCE died here (1329).

Carew Castle (*Pembrokeshire; formerly Dyfed*) A castle was built here about 1100 by the Anglo-Norman Gerald de Windsor, whose wife Nest was the daughter of RHYS AP TEWDWR and mistress of HENRY I. Their son adopted the surname Carew. A stone castle was completed around the year 1320 and this was extended to include the Great Hall after 1480 when it was acquired by Sir Rhys ap Thomas. Henry Tudor (future HENRY VII) stayed here in 1485 after landing at Milford Haven on his way to the battle of Bosworth. In 1558 the castle was granted to Sir John Perrot, reputedly an illegitimate son of HENRY VIII, who further remodelled the castle. Perrot was subsequently tried for treason against his putative half-sister ELIZABETH and died in the Tower of London (1592).

Carham-on-Tweed (*Northumberland*) MALCOLM II and OWEN of Strathclyde defeated Eadulf of Bernicia (1018). The victory was such that Malcolm was able to re-annex Lothian to Scotland.

Carisbrooke Castle (*Isle of Wight*) A fort has stood on this site since Roman and Saxon times, and the first Norman castle was built in the 1070s and successively strengthened over the next century or two. CHARLES I was imprisoned here (1647–48) and his children Henry and Elizabeth remained prisoners even after his execution. Elizabeth died here, some say of a broken heart,

aged only 14 (1650), and was buried at St Thomas's Church, Newport.

Carlisle (*Cumbria*) A Celtic settlement since prehistoric times. The Romans established a fort here called Luguvallum (AD 80) and it subsequently formed the western end of Hadrian's Wall (130). It was the major frontier fort and became a significant legionary town. It was sacked by the Picts in 181 and 367 and subsequently became the centre of the post-Roman kingdom of Rheged. It may have been the central fortress of COEL HEN for a period, but it certainly was the capital of URIEN. It is also recognized in tradition as one of ARTHUR's courts. It was sacked by the Danes (875). It was conquered by EDMUND I in 945 and handed to MALCOLM I to control. It formed part of the sub-kingdom of Strathclyde, but occasional heirs were also made princes of Cumbria (*see* MALCOLM II). It was reclaimed by England after the Norman conquest and WILLIAM II restored the castle in 1092 and STEPHEN gave it to the Scots in 1138. DAVID I died here (1153). When MARY QUEEN OF SCOTS left Scotland, Carlisle Castle was her first place of imprisonment (May-July 1568). Royalist Carlisle fell to the Scots in 1645, and it was taken again by Bonnie Prince Charlie in 1745. *See also* Burgh-by-Sands.

Carreg Cennen Castle (*Carmarthenshire*) An imposing castle south-east of Llandeilo, set high on a limestone crag, most of its history is lost in legend. It was once claimed as a fortress of Arthur's knight URIEN. It is not known which of the Welsh rulers built the surviving stone castle but it dates to early in the 13th C. It was captured by the English in 1277. At various stages it was owned by John of Gaunt and Henry Bolingbroke (see HENRY IV). It was dismantled in 1462.

Castell Y Bere (*Caernarfonshire and Merionethshire*) The last stronghold of the Welsh in their fight against EDWARD I. A remote and atmospheric castle near Abergynolwyn, south of Dolgellau, now in ruins, it was built by the Welsh in the 1220s. After the death of Llywelyn the Last, his brother, DAFYDD AP GRUFFYDD made his last stand here. He was defeated (1283) and the castle taken. Dafydd was executed. Although the Welsh regained the castle in 1285, it was already too late as Welsh independence had been lost. The English re-captured the castle in 1294 and it was left to fall into ruin.

Castle Bolton (*North Yorkshire*) Built by Lord SCROPE in 1378, it passed briefly to the PERCY family when Scrope fell from favour. MARY QUEEN OF SCOTS stayed here (Jul-Dec 1568). An imposing shell of the castle remains.

Castle Dore (*Cornwall*) An Iron Age hill fort just north of Fowey, which is said to be the castle of MARK CUNOMOROS, uncle of TRISTAN.

The so-called Tristan Stone is now on the roadside north of Fowey.

Castle Rising (*Norfolk*) 4 miles NE of King's Lynn, the castle was built about 1150 by William d'Albini, earl of Sussex, who married the widow of HENRY I and who also owned Arundel Castle. From 1330 to 1358 it was the home and to all intents prison of Isabella of France, who was confined here by EDWARD III for the murder of his father (her husband) EDWARD II.

Catraeth (*North Yorkshire*) The Old British name for Catterick, and a name applicable to the British kingdom of York, which existed from the mid 5th C till the death of PEREDUR in *c*580. Any remnant of British control was destroyed by ATHELFRITH of Bernicia, the Angles' kingdom to the north, at the battle of Catraeth in 595, when OWAIN of Rheged was also killed.

Catuvellauni. A powerful Celtic tribe which established itself in the territory north of the Thames, including London and Hertfordshire. Its capital was at Wheathampstead and later moved to what is now St Albans. Its best known rulers were CASSIVELLAUNOS, TASCIOVANUS and CUNOBELINOS.

Cerdicesborg (*Hampshire*) *see* Stoke-in-Hurtsbourne.

Cerdicesford (*Hampshire*) The name given by the ASC to the landing place of CERDIC in 495, a date more likely to be 513 or later. The traditional landing site is at the head of the Solent although no archeological evidence exists to substantiate it.

Channel Islands These are the last remnants of the duchy of Normandy still in British hands, though the Islands retain a distinction shared with the Isle of Man in not being part of the United Kingdom, though the islanders may regard themselves as citizens of the United Kingdom, Islands and Colonies. From the islanders' perspective the Islands were never part of Britain but Britain has been part of the islands. Over the years they have shown intense loyalty to the English kings. The islands became part of the duchy of Normandy in 933 under William *Longsword* and thus became part of the Norman Empire when WILLIAM THE CONQUEROR claimed England in 1066. Although JOHN lost the duchy in 1204 he succeeded in retaining a special link with the Islands, which remained English and were governed through a Warden. John visited the Islands soon after 1204 to confirm these arrangements and many subsequent English kings have maintained this special attachment. HENRY III visited the Islands in 1230. The French captured and held Guernsey, Alderney and Sark between 1338 and 1345, when Guernsey was reclaimed but it was recaptured by the French briefly in 1356. After the Treaty of Calais the

French abandoned all claim to the Islands. This did not stop the French storming Jersey in 1461 but it was recaptured by EDWARD IV in 1468. The closest royal connections are with CHARLES II. During the Civil War the young Prince Charles sought refuge on Jersey, where George Carteret had been sent by Charles I to protect the royalists (1646). He stayed at Trinity Manor House. Prince Charles is rumoured to have had an illegitimate child by George's daughter, Margaret. The Islanders remained loyal to Charles, declaring him their king on the execution of his father (1649). The islands fell to the Parliamentarian forces in 1651, but upon the Restoration, they again promptly recognized CHARLES II as their king. Apart from the German occupation between 1940 and 1945, the Islands have remained Crown dependencies.

Chartley Castle (*Staffordshire*) Six miles N of Stafford, this was a moated manor house and the last place where MARY QUEEN OF SCOTS was held (December 1585–September 1586) before being taken to Fotheringhay for her trial and execution. It was at Chartley that her letters were intercepted and decoded and the evidence gained to determine her complicity in the Babington Plot.

Chatsworth Castle (*Derbyshire*) The magnificent home of the dukes of Devonshire near Bakewell in the Peak District, the present house was constructed between 1687 and 1707. The original mansion house was started in 1549 by Sir William Cavendish at the urging of his wife Bess of Hardwick. She outlived him and married the earl of Shrewsbury in 1568. Shrewsbury was made the custodian of MARY QUEEN OF SCOTS who was brought to Chatsworth in 1569 where she was detained in what is now called Queen Mary's Bower. She remained under his guardianship until 1585, spending most of those years at Sheffield Castle.

Chelsea *see* London

Chertsey (*Surrey*) A monastery was founded here in 666 by EGBERT I of Kent in the name of his kinsman Eorcenwald. The abbey was considerably extended a few years later by FRITHUWOLD of Surrey (*c*672). The abbey was refounded in 964 by EDGAR. After HENRY VI was murdered, his body was secretly borne down the Thames and buried at Chertsey Abbey (1471), though it was later reburied at Windsor.

Chester (*Cheshire*) The Romans founded a fortress here called Deva (AD 76) which became the base for the XXth Legion. The Roman town almost certainly formed the initial base for CUNEDDA (450s) for his incursion into Wales. ATHELFRITH of Northumbria defeated the Welsh at Chester (615). It was probably in Chester that ATHELBALD was married to his stepmother Judith (860). The town was well fortified against the

Danes by Athelflæd of Mercia (905), and it was here that the relics of St Werburh (the daughter of WULFHERE) were translated for safety from Hanbury. The town was of sufficient importance to the Saxons to serve as a mint and this mint also produced the coins for HYWEL DDA (940s). EDGAR held a royal convention here (973), where all the other kings of Britain recognized him as their overlord and where he was ceremonially rowed along the Dee. HAROLD II's wife Edith sought refuge in Chester after the Norman conquest and gave birth to Harold's posthumous sons, the twins Harold and Ulf (1066). Chester was the last major town in England to fall to the Normans (1071), and WILLIAM I granted it to Hugh d'Avranches, known as Hugh the Wolf. He held GRUFFYDD AP CYNAN prisoner at Chester for twelve years (1082–94). HENRY II met MALCOLM IV here (1157) when Malcolm was compelled to surrender Northumberland and Cumbria. The last Norman earl of Chester died in 1237 and the title reverted to the crown. Thereafter the eldest son of the monarch is granted the title of earl of Chester, the first being Prince Edward (later EDWARD I) in 1254. Thomas STANLEY, the chief justiciar of Chester was also king of Man and his family later inherited Stanley Palace (built 1591). CHARLES I sought refuge in the city during the Civil War at the home of Sir Francis Gamul (1645) and from the city walls saw his troops defeated at the battle of Rowton.

Chesters-on-the-Wall (*Northumberland*) A Roman cavalry base, Cilurnum, on Hadrian's Wall. The kings of Northumbria had a royal villa here and it was where king ELFWALD I was murdered in 788. The place became venerated as a light was seen shining over the spot where he was murdered and the church of St Cuthbert and St Oswald was founded here.

Chichester (*West Sussex*) The former capital of the Atrebates and later the Regnii, so named because they were the tribe of the king Cogidumnus, who had a palace at nearby Fishbourne. Chichester's name is attributed to CISSA, the son of AELLE, though the time of their arrival (late 5th C) is too early for the Saxon settlements in this area and it is likely to have been either a later Cissa, or named in his memory. Chichester Cathedral now houses a series of 16th C paintings by Lambert Barnard of all of the kings of England since WILLIAM I.

Chingford (*Essex*) *see* Waltham Forest

Chippenham (*Wiltshire*) A royal villa existed here in the 9th C. BURGRED of Mercia married Athelswith here (*c*854). ALFRED *THE GREAT* escaped from the Danes here (878) though the Danes wintered at the villa.

Cirencester (*Gloucestershire*) The capital of the Dobunni, it became established as an important Roman centre called Corinium Dobunorum (AD 43). By 305, when it became the administrative centre of the south-west (Britannia Prima), it was the second most important city in Britain, after London. It went into decline after the Roman era. CONDIDAN, the British king of Cirencester, was defeated by the Saxons (577); PENDA fought CYNEGILS here (628); the Danes under Guthrum raided Cirencester and wintered here (879–880); Canute held council here on his return to England (1020). Cirencester supported Henry Bolingbroke in his rise to the kingship and foiled an attempt by the earls of Salisbury and Kent to overthrow him (1399). In gratitude Henry bestowed a gift for the construction of the Perpendicular tower of the Church of St John the Baptist. Inside the church is a silver cup once owned by Anne Boleyn. Cirencester was captured by Prince Rupert of the Rhine during the English Civil War (1642).

Claremont House (*Surrey*) South of Esher, this house was originally built for Clive of India in 1772. In 1816 it became the home of Princess Charlotte, only daughter of the Prince Regent (the future GEORGE IV), where she tragically died in child-birth (1817). There is a statue to Charlotte in the nearby St George's Church, Esher. Claremont subsequently passed to the Saxe-Coburg family and thereby came into the possession of Prince Albert in 1840. It was used occasionally as a holiday home by VICTORIA, but the exiled French royal family took up residence in 1848 and Louis Philippe died here (1850).

Clithero (*Lancashire*) Here HENRY VI was captured by EDWARD IV's forces (1465).

Colchester (*Essex*) The capital of the Trinovantes under CUNOBELIN and the first Roman town founded in Britain, called Camulodunum, the name which is believed to be the origin of Camelot. It was sacked and destroyed by Boudica (60AD). Tradition links Colchester with King COEL, though this is all fabrication, as is its connection with Coel's supposed daughter St Helen, the mother of the Emperor CONSTANTINE. It was established by SWITHRED as the capital of the East Saxons (*c*750). In 1215 the castle was occupied by French troops supporting the civil war against JOHN but was successfully regained by John after a prolonged siege in 1216.

Combe Manor (*Berkshire*). Between Newbury and Andover, the manor at Combe is traditionally associated with CHARLES II and Nell Gwynn.

Compton Wynyates (*Warwickshire*) 10 miles W of Banbury, this was one of the first great Tudor manor houses. It was built in the 1480s on the site of an earlier Norman house built around 1204. The house was in the possession of the Compton family, who later became the earls of

Northampton, and who served the royal family. William Compton was courtier to HENRY VIII, who often stayed here with Katherine of Aragon. ELIZABETH I stayed here at great expense to Sir Henry Compton (1572). It was also visited by JAMES I and CHARLES I and fell to Parliamentary forces in 1644.

Conwy (*Aberconwy and Clwyd*) Cistercian abbey founded at Aberconwy under DAFYDD AB OWAIN (1172, completed 1187). LLYWELYN THE GREAT granted charter (1198), retired here as monk, (1238), died and was buried here (1240), as was DAFYDD AP LLYWELYN (1246). The abbey was dismantled by EDWARD I (1283) in order to build Conwy Castle (1283–87). Edward retreated here during uprising by Madog ap Llywelyn (1294) and was isolated for several days by the flooding river; RICHARD II stayed here in disguise (1399) and was betrayed to Henry Bolingbroke. The castle was captured by OWAIN GLYN DWR (1401); it fell into decay but was rebuilt and held by Royalist forces during Civil War, captured (1646), dismantled (1665). *See also* Deganwy.

Corbridge (*Northumberland*) Near the site of the old Roman supply fort, Corstopitum, Corbridge was the site of an Anglo-Saxon monastery. Here the Norse of York gained two victories over CONSTANTINE II of the Scots in 914 and 918.

Corfe Castle (*Dorset*) The atmospheric and rather sombre ruins are a reminder of the tragedies that have occurred at Corfe. Most notoriously it was the site of the murder of EDWARD THE MARTYR (978). The existing castle had been built by HENRY I in the 1130s and continued to be enlarged and strengthened by successive monarchs to EDWARD I, all of whom spent time here. It was the favourite residence of King JOHN when administering his royal estates at Purbeck. John despatched 22 French knights to Corfe in 1202, where they starved to death. The castle was destroyed by the Parliamentarians in 1646.

Corwen (*Denbighshire*) The town where OWAIN GLYN DWR established his headquarters prior to the battle of Shrewsbury (1403).

Cowes (*Isle of Wight*) A town popular with Queen VICTORIA who first stayed here at Norris Castle in 1831 and again in 1833. In later years Victoria and Albert acquired the estate at Osborne, near East Cowes, for £28,000 (1843). Osborne House was completed by 1846. It remained the Queen's favourite home, even after Albert's death, and she died here in 1901. EDWARD VII opened part of the house as a convalescent home for officers, and the house was opened to the public in 1954.

Craigmiller Castle *see* Edinburgh

Crail (*Fife*) Once a small fishing village. Near here in 877 CONSTANTINE MAC KENNETH was killed fighting the Norse. Constantine's Cave is the traditional spot. A castle, established here in the 12th C, was an occasional residence of DAVID I. His son, Henry of Huntingdon, granted the castle to his wife, Ada de Warenne, and it may be that at the castle the future kings MALCOLM IV and WILLIAM THE LYON were conceived, though whether they were born here or at her estates in Huntingdon is not known.

Crayford (*Kent*) A village on the outskirts of Greater London on the River Cray. The *ASC* records that in 457 HENGIST won a major victory over the British here, killing 4,000 men. The British fled to London, leaving Hengist in control of Kent.

Croydon (*Surrey*) The archbishops of Canterbury had a manor house here since 1070. This was developed over the years into Croydon Palace, now a girls' school. Many monarchs visited the Palace, including HENRY III, EDWARD I, HENRY IV, HENRY V, HENRY VII, HENRY VIII, MARY I and ELIZABETH I, while JAMES I of Scotland was held prisoner here (1412) during his captivity in England. Perhaps the strangest relic in Croydon are the bones of EDWARD THE MARTYR. These had been excavated at Shaftesbury Abbey in 1931. There were plans to reinter them at Brookwood Cemetery in 1984 but, following a dispute, they were exhumed and deposited at the Midland Bank in Croydon until a final resting place is resolved.

Cullen (*Moray*) ROBERT THE BRUCE established the Old Church here (1320s) and his wife, Elizabeth, died at Cullen Castle (1327). *See also* Findochty.

Culloden (*Highland*) The site of the last battle fought in Britain between the duke of Cumberland, son of GEORGE II, and Bonnie Prince Charlie on 16 April 1746. It was a disaster for CHARLES, "the Young Pretender", and resulted in the violent "pacification" of the Highlands.

Cumbria For many years Cumbria was part of the kingdom of Rheged from 450–595. It may have existed longer, though by then it was almost certainly a vassal kingdom to Northumbria. Cumbria became a retreat for Danes and Vikings during the 9th and 10th C until conquered by EDMUND I (945). It was granted to Scotland and formed part of the sub-kingdom of Strathclyde until it was reclaimed by WILLIAM II (1092). It remained in dispute with Scotland for over a century but was eventually annexed to England in 1237.

Cumnor Place (*Oxfordshire*) Just south of Oxford, Cumnor Place is notorious for the death of Amy Robsart, wife of Robert Dudley, a favourite of Queen Elizabeth. One night in 1560, she was found dead at the bottom of the stairs, and the cause of her fall was never resolved. Suspicion fell on Dudley because he was known to want Amy out of the way so that he could pursue his suit for the queen. However after Amy's death the queen was forced to distance herself from Dudley so as not to be associated with the incident. Although Cumnor Place is long demolished, memorabilia of Amy Robsart, including a statue of Elizabeth I, will be found in the local church.

Cupar Castle (*Fife*) Margaret, daughter of HENRY III of England and wife of ALEXANDER III of Scotland, died here of "decline" in 1275, aged only 34.

Cwm Hir Abbey (*Powys*) Founded in 1143 by Cistercian monks from Whitland, it was twice destroyed: in 1231 by HENRY III and in 1401 by OWAIN GLYN DWR. LLYWELYN THE LAST's body (less his head which had been sent to London) was buried here (1282).

Dalkeith (*Midlothian*) Dalkeith Palace was a 12th C castle which came into the ownership of the Scotts of Buccleuch in 1651. His daughter Anne married James, duke of Monmouth (1663), the illegitimate son of CHARLES II. After Monmouth was executed in 1685 Anne married Baron Cornwallis and lived until 1732, dying at Dalkeith Palace. Amongst her many descendants may be counted Lady Diana Spencer and Sarah Ferguson, duchess of York. Nearby is Newbattle Abbey, founded by DAVID I in 1140. Here was buried Marie de Coucy (1257) the second wife of ALEXANDER II.

Dartmouth (*Devon*) A village with a natural large harbour that made it a major port during the Middle Ages. It was from here that the fleet of the Second Crusade left in 1147, and from here that RICHARD I led the Third Crusade in 1190. It was here that EDWARD IV's invasion fleet landed (1470), and from here nine ships sailed to join Drake's fleet against the Armada. The present Naval College was built in 1905, though the future GEORGE V served as a naval cadet at Dartmouth in 1877, and the young Princess Elizabeth first met her future husband, Philip, at the naval college in 1939.

Dawston (*Scottish Borders*) The site of a vicious battle in 603, then called Degsaston, where ATHELFRITH of Northumbria destroyed the army of AEDAN of Dál Riata. The site is probably that of Dawston-in-Liddesdale, south of Hawick, though more recently it has been suggested the battle took place at Addinston, near Lauder, at least twenty miles further north. Addinston is a corruption of Aedan's stone. Some authorities suggest that this battle was a continuation of

Camlann and that it was here that the real ARTHUR – Artiur, son of Aedán, – was killed.

Deganwy (*Aberconwy and Clwyd*) Original settlement at estuary of Conwy (Dinas Conwy), centre of the Celtic Decangi; it became the primary court of MAELGWYN the Great (530s); overrun by BEORNWULF of Mercia (823); Normans built a succession of castles which were destroyed by the Welsh, the third built in 1211, captured by LLYWELYN THE GREAT (1213); HENRY III was besieged here during his Welsh campaign (1257); captured and destroyed by LLYWELYN THE LAST (1263). *See also* Conwy.

Degsaston (*Scotish Borders*) *see* Dawston

Deira A kingdom founded by AELLE in 569 and subsequently combined with Bernicia under ATHELFRITH to form Northumbria. Despite this forced union Deira strove to retain its independence, and there was frequent civil war between the Deirans and the Bernicians. When the Danes invaded York in 867, they re-established Deira as their own separate kingdom of Jorvik.

Demetia A separate kingdom in south-west Wales settled by the Irish under EOCHAID in the late fourth century. It subsequently formed the kingdom of Dyfed.

Dettingen (*Bavaria*) A battle in the War of the Austrian Succession on 16 June 1743 between the combined forces of the British, Hanoverian and Hessian armies and the French. It was the last occasion when a British sovereign, GEORGE II, led his troops into battle. The confederate forces were victorious.

Dinas Emrys (*Caernarfonshire and Merionethshire*) A hillfort above Lake Dinas near Beddgelert. This was the traditional stronghold of VORTIGERN where he retreated from the opposition of HENGIST and later AMBROSIUS AURELIANUS. This was the site of the legend concerning Vortigern's Tower and the prophecy of Merlin about Vortigern's fate.

Dinefwr or **Dynevor** (*Carmarthenshire*) Just south of Llandeilo, this was the ancient capital of Deheubarth and traditionally the last resting place of Merlin. Llandeilo itself takes its name from St Teilo, who founded a monastery here in the mid 6th C on land granted by AIRCOL of Demetia. A castle was built here by RHODRI MAWR (876), while a stone castle was established by RHYS AP GRUFFYDD (1196). Although LLYWELYN THE LAST defeated the English here in 1257, the castle eventually fell to EDWARD I in 1283. The castle fell into ruins but it now forms part of the Dinefwr estate under the management of the National Trust.

Dolwyddelan (*Aberconwy and Clwyd*) The castle of LLYWELYN THE GREAT, who was probably born here (*c*1173) soon after his father, Iorweth, completed the castle (*c*1170). LLYWELYN THE LAST also stayed here (1281), but the castle was captured by EDWARD I (1283).

Dorchester (*Oxfordshire*) The missionary Birinus baptized CYNEGILS of Wessex here and founded the first bishopric of Wessex (634). This was transferred to Winchester in 660.

Dover (*Kent*) Julius Caesar landed near here (BC 55). When WILLIAM of Normandy invaded England (1066), he hastened to Dover after the battle of Hastings and, though he sacked the town, he began fortification of the castle established by HAROLD II. King STEPHEN died here (1154). The existing castle was built by HENRY II (1180s). JOHN fortified the castle but it suffered under siege from the French (1216). In later years Dover Castle was noted for its royal meetings and romances. EDWARD II brought his new bride Isabella to Dover when she came to England (1308); RICHARD II met his young bride, Anne of Bohemia, here (1381); HENRY VIII stayed here with Katherine of Aragon on their way to the Field of the Cloth of Gold (1520); CHARLES I received Henrietta Maria of France here (1625) and JAMES II married Mary of Modena here (1673).

Driffield (*Humberside*) The site of one of the royal villas of the kings of Northumbria. ALDFRITH died here (704).

Duffus Castle (*Moray*) *see* Elgin

Dumbarton (*Strathclyde*) An ancient fortress on the estuary of the Clyde, it was for over four centuries a stronghold of the British – the name *Dun Breatann* means "fortress of the Britons". It was the capital of CERETIC in the fifth century and of the kings of Strathclyde until 1058. It had remained invulnerable for three hundred years but was captured by the Pictish king ANGUS and Eadbert of Northumbria in 756, and stormed by the Vikings in 871 when ARTGAL was betrayed.

Dumfries (*Dumfries*) Although these days more closely associated with the memories of Robert Burns and J.M. Barrie, in royal terms it saw the rebirth of the Scottish nation when, in 1306, Robert Bruce murdered John Comyn in the chapel of Grey Friars (which had been founded by John Balliol's mother Devorguilla) and went on to claim the throne of Scotland and cast off the English yoke.

Dunadd (*Argyll and Bute*) A rocky hill-fort, north of Lochgilphead, that was the capital of the kingdom of Dál Riata from at least 500–843. An Irish settlement was already here when FERGUS landed (*c*498). It was here that Columba performed the first Christian anointing of a king when he consecrated AEDAN MAC GABHRAN (574).

A formidable fortress it has withstood many sieges, including one by BRUDE (III) in 683, but was captured by ANGUS (I) in 736. The Stone of Destiny, upon which all later Scottish kings were anointed, was believed to have been brought to Dunadd from Ireland by Fergus, and it was taken from here to Scone (via Dunstaffnage Castle) by KENNETH MACALPIN in 843.

Dunaverty Castle (*Argyll and Bute*) A stronghold of the MacDonalds and one of the fortresses of the Lords of the Isles. It came into the possession of EDWARD I sometime before 1306 and the switch made by ANGUS OG to supporting ROBERT BRUCE that year and reclaiming the castle for Scotland was a major shift in Robert's fortunes. It remained staunchly Scottish despite attempts by later kings to anglicise Scotland. Sir John of Islay stormed the castle in 1494 and hanged the governor before the very eyes of JAMES IV. The castle was besieged by Covenanters in 1647 and, when the occupants surrendered, they were all slaughtered.

Dunbar (*East Lothian*) An ancient fortress which, for many years, was the key to control of Lothian. It is near to the site of the old capital of the Votadini at Traprain Law, which is three miles to the south-west, and it is likely that these two sites were the centre of the Gododdin, certainly under LEUDONUS (the Lot of Arthurian legend), who gave his name to Lothian (*c*470). The Gododdin abandoned Traprain at about this time and settled at Dun Eitin (Edinburgh). EGFRITH established his own sub-kingdom at Dunbar under BEORNHETH (670) which continued until the early 8th C. EDWARD I's forces defeated the Scots at Dunbar (1296), and it was from here that EDWARD II fled from Scotland after his defeat at Bannockburn (1314). The castle was heroically defended by Black Agnes, the daughter of the earl of Moray, against the forces of EDWARD III (1338). Joan, the wife of JAMES I, died here (1445). MARY Queen of Scots lived here with Bothwell (1567) and after she was deposed the castle was destroyed (1568). Cromwell devastated the Scots at Dunbar (1650). Just north of Dunbar is the impressively sited Tantallon Castle, near Auldhame, a fortress of the Douglases which remained impregnable from the time it was built (c.1375) until taken by Cromwell's forces (1651), defying sieges by JAMES IV (1491) and JAMES V (1528). It was here that ALEXANDER II of the Isles was imprisoned by JAMES I from 1433–35.

Dunblane (*Stirling*) Bishopric established here by DAVID I (*c*1150). Margaret Drummond, the mistress (or, as some claim, the secret wife) of JAMES IV, is buried in the cathedral. She and her two sisters were poisoned in 1502 because of her relationship with the king. North of Dunblane is Strathallan, where GIRIC defeated and killed AED (878).

Duncansby (*Highlands*) The north-easternmost tip of Scotland in the former shire of Caithness. Its name almost certainly derives from Duncan, the mórmaer of Caithness in the 10th C, who had a close relationship with the Norse earls of Orkney and whose daughter married THORFINN SKULLSPLITTER. MALCOLM II's grandson, THORFINN THE MIGHTY, was made earl of Caithness and lived his early years at Duncansby Castle before assuming his inheritance on Orkney.

Dundee (*Angus*) Although made a royal burgh by WILLIAM THE LYON about 1190, Dundee has surprisingly few royal connections. Most significantly, WILLIAM WALLACE attended the grammar school here (1280s) and apparently had a rebellious attitude even then, as tradition states that an argument about his dagger resulted in him fatally wounding a fellow student. The town suffered further under royal hands. It was attacked by ROBERT I (1313), burned by John of Gaunt (1385), plundered by HENRY VIII's forces (1547), looted by the marquess of Montrose (1645), and many of its citizens massacred by General Monck when it refused to surrender to Cromwell (1651).

Dundonald Castle (*South Ayrshire*) The family home of the Fitzallans, who were the hereditary High Stewards of Scotland. In 1315 Marjorie, daughter of Robert Bruce, married Walter, the 6th High Steward, and their son came to the throne as ROBERT II, the first of the Stewart kings of Scotland. Dundonald remained their family home and both Robert II and ROBERT III died here (1390 and 1406). Thereafter, however, the castle gradually fell into disuse and ruin.

Dundrennan Abbey (*Dumfries and Galloway*) The monastery was founded in 1142 by DAVID I, but is historically important because it was where Mary Queen of Scots purportedly spent her last night in Scotland before fleeing to England from Port Mary, then called Burnfoot (1568).

Dun Eitin *see* Edinburgh

Dunfermline (*Fife*) One of the most important royal centres in Scotland. Originally the site of a fort (the name means "fort of the crooked linn"), it was here that MALCOLM III rescued Margaret, sister of EDGAR ATHELING, who was fleeing from the Normans (1067). They were married here and established both a palace and a priory (1072). The palace became a favourite residence of the kings. Amongst the many royal children born here were DAVID II (1324), JAMES I (1394), Elizabeth, daughter of JAMES VI (1596) and CHARLES I (1600). EDWARD I held court here (1303) and set fire to the palace when he left (1304); it was rebuilt in 1315. The priory (raised to abbey status by DAVID I, 1128) became the main burial place of kings, starting with Malcolm III and his wife

Margaret (1093) and including DUNCAN II (1094) and his wife Ethelreda (c1100), EDGAR (1107), ALEXANDER I (1124), David I (1153), MALCOLM IV (1165), ALEXANDER III (1286) and his wife Margaret (1275), ROBERT I (1329) and his wife Elizabeth (1327), and Annabella, wife of ROBERT III (1401), besides many royal children. The town suffered heavily in the great fire of 1624. CHARLES II stayed here (1650) when trying to raise support against Cromwell.

Dunkeld (*Perth and Kinross*) The name means "fort of the Celts" (originally *Dun Chailleann*, "fort of the Caledonians"), and it was clearly a centre of considerable importance to the kingdom of the Southern Picts, Fortriu. A community of Celtic monks, driven from Iona, established themselves here in 729. The monastery was extended by CONSTANTINE MAC FERGUS around 800. KENNETH MACALPIN made this the ecclesiastical capital of his combined kingdom of the Scots and Picts in 849. The bishopric was revived by ALEXANDER I in 1107. Dunkeld has been the scene of many fierce battles. It was raided by Vikings (903) and again by MALCOLM of Moray (1027). It was the site of the battle where MACBETH defeated Crinan and MALDRED (1045). In 1689 Captain Munro massacred an army of Highland supporters of JAMES VII here. DONALD III was originally buried here (1099), before his remains were removed to Iona. The Cathedral marks the burial sites of Alexander, Wolf of Badenoch, the son of ROBERT II (1406), and of Charles Edward Stuart, Count Roehenstart, who died here as the result of a carriage accident in 1854. He was the grandson of Bonnie Prince Charlie.

Dunnichen (*Angus*) *see* Forfar

Dunollie Castle (*Argyll and Bute*) *see* Oban

Dunnottar Castle (*Aberdeenshire*) *see* Stonehaven

Dunsinane (*Perth and Kinross*) A few miles to the NE of Perth, this is the supposed location of MACBETH's castle and the site of his defeat by MALCOLM III (1057). However these events probably took place at Lumphanan, to the north. Dunsinane was the site where Macbeth was defeated by the forces of Siward of Northumbria a few years earlier (1054).

Dunstaffnage Castle (*Argyll and Bute*) *see* Oban

Dunvegan Castle (*Skye, Highlands*) On the NW side of Skye this Castle is the ancestral home of the MacLeods. They claim descent from Leod, nephew of MAGNUS, the last Norse king of Man (1265). They continued to support the claims of the later kings of the Isles, especially Torquil MacLeod, lord of Lewis, who supported Donald the Black (1501) in his attempts to regain the kingship.

Dupplin (*Perth and Kinross*) A few miles SW of Perth this was the site of a battle where EDWARD BALLIOL overthrew DAVID II's forces under the regent, the earl of Mar (1322).

Durham (*Durham*) Durham was established in 995 by monks from Lindisfarne, who eventually settled here seeking refuge from the Danes. They brought with them the relics of St Cuthbert and later the remains of Bede were also reburied here. MALCOLM II was defeated here by Uhtred of Northumbria (1006), and DUNCAN I besieged the town with many losses (1040). The castle become the home of the prince-bishops of Durham from 1072. Amongst the bishops was Antony Bek (1283), who was EDWARD I's principal advisor in the selection of JOHN BALLIOL as king of Scotland (1292). Bek subsequently received the sovereignty of the Isle of Man (1307). In the western suburbs of Durham is Neville's Cross, where DAVID II was defeated and captured by the English (1346).

Dyfed (*SW Wales*) A kingdom formerly named Demetia, which in the mid 8th C was divided into Rheinwg and Seisyllwg and which was later merged with parts of Ceredigion by HYWEL DDA to form Deheubarth.

Dynevor Castle *see* Dinefwr

Dyrham (*Gloucestershire*) The site of a major battle recorded by the *ASC* as happening in 577. CEAWLIN and CUTHWINE of Wessex defeated and killed three British kings, COINMAL, CONDIDAN and FARINMAIL, and thereby drove a land rift between the British of Wales and the Britons of the south-west peninsula.

Eamont Bridge (*Cumbria*) *see* Penrith

Eastwell (*Kent*) A tomb in the grounds of the ruined church of Eastwell Manor marks the burial place of Richard Plantagenet, believed to be the illegitimate son of RICHARD III who had fled Bosworth Field and kept his identity secret. He became a bricklayer, ending his days working on the Eastwell estate. He died in 1550.

Ebbsfleet (*Kent*) On the south side of the Isle of Thanet, opposite Richborough, where HENGIST and Horsa reputedly landed in 449. Ebbsfleet is the traditional landing place of Augustine's mission in 597 where he was received by ATHELBERT.

Edgehill (*Warwickshire*) Between Kineton and Radway, NW of Banbury, this was the site of the first major battle of the Civil War on 23 October 1642. The Royalist army was under the effective authority of Prince Rupert of the Rhine, nephew of CHARLES I, whilst the Parliamentarians were led by Robert Devereux, earl of Essex. It was a messy and indecisive battle with both sides retreating but it allowed King Charles the opportunity to move on to Oxford where he established his headquarters.

Edinburgh (*Lothian*) The capital of Scotland and a city with rich royal connections. A Celtic fort had existed here since pre-Roman times known as Dun Eitin or Dun Eadain ("the fort on the slope"). The Goddodin almost certainly moved their base here when they deserted Traprain Law in the fifth century because of onslaught by the Germanic invaders, perhaps as part of the plans of CUNEDDA. The surname of CLYDNO EITIN identified him with Dun Eitin, which was probably also ruled by his father CINBELIN (570s). MYNYDDOG was probably the last native Briton to rule the territory before it was overrun by ATHELFRITH of Northumbria (after 595). His successor EDWIN rebuilt the fortress (626), after which tradition conveniently states that it became known as Edwin's burgh, though the name is simply a derivation of Din Eitin. The Picts regained a foothold under GARTNAIT and BRUIDE, the sons of Gwid, but in 638 Eitin was again besieged, probably by OSWALD of Northumbria. Lothian remained in the possession of the kings of Northumbria for the next three centuries. ATHELSTAN stamped his authority over the Scots by invading Edinburgh and further north (934), but INDULF was able to regain Lothian from Northumbria during the 950s. Although Edinburgh did not become the capital of Scotland until 1498, it was the favoured residence of both MALCOLM III and EDGAR in the 11th C during whose reigns the town developed around the castle. It was raided and burned by RICHARD II (1385), by HENRY IV (1401), and by Edward Seymour marquess of Hertford (later duke of Somerset) (1544). There were riots in the city in 1596 and JAMES VI was attacked. After James left Scotland to become James I of England it was rare for a monarch to return. CHARLES I visited in 1633 (when he founded the Bishopric of Edinburgh) and 1641 and GEORGE IV in 1822, but starting with VICTORIA in 1842 royal visits became more regular. The main royal centres of interest are listed below.

Collegiate Church of the Holy Trinity Founded in 1462 by Mary of Gueldres, widow of JAMES II. She was buried here in 1463. When the church was demolished in 1848, what were believed to be her remains were transferred to the royal vault at Holyrood Palace. The church was situated next to what is now Waverley Station.

Craigmiller Castle Built about 1374, it belonged to the Preston family. JAMES III imprisoned his brothers here (1477), including John, earl of Mar, who died here (1480). The Castle was a favourite of MARY QUEEN OF SCOTS, who moved here in 1566 following the murder of Rizzio. It was here that the Craigmiller Conference of Scottish nobles met to plan the murder of Lord Darnley, Mary's husband.

Edinburgh Castle Legend dubbed the site *Castrum Puellarum*, the Castle of the Maidens, which probably means this was a home for the cherished Pictish princesses through whom the royal descent was conferred. The modern castle owes its origins to MALCOLM III and his wife Margaret who built a stone chapel in 1076. Margaret died here in 1093 as did King EDGAR (1107), DAVID II (1371), and Mary of Guise (1560). The only future king to be born in the castle was JAMES VI (1566), though there was a rumour that the infant died and the baby was a changeling. The castle fell to the troops of HENRY II (1174), EDWARD I (1296), and EDWARD III (1356). The earl of Morton captured it, with English help, from supporters of MARY QUEEN OF SCOTS (1573). ALEXANDER II held a parliament here (1215). The castle served as a prison on several occasions. JAMES III was held captive here in 1466 and again in 1482; JAMES V was imprisoned from 1526–28, and Donald the Black of the Isles from 1505–43.

Holyrood Abbey and Palace DAVID I established the Augustinian abbey of Holyrood in 1128 and an adjoining guest-house became the basis for the royal palace, Holyroodhouse, which was significantly enlarged in 1498. The abbey was the site of several royal events. DAVID II was buried here (1371); JAMES II, who was born at Holyrood (1430) was crowned (1437), married Mary of Gueldres (1449) and buried in the abbey (1460); JAMES III married Margaret of Denmark (1469) and JAMES IV married Margaret Tudor (1503), who were also crowned queens consort (as Mary of Gueldres had been); Mary of Guise (wife of JAMES V) was crowned (1540) as was Anne of Denmark (wife of JAMES VI) in 1590. CHARLES I was crowned separately here as king of Scotland (1633). Madeleine, the young French bride of JAMES V, died and was buried at Holyrood (1537). The last royal burial was that of Mary of Gueldres, widow of JAMES II, whose remains were moved here from the Church of the Holy Trinity in 1848. MARY QUEEN OF SCOTS married Lord Darnley at Holyrood Palace (1565) and then James Bothwell, two years later (1567). It was also at Holyrood that Darnley and his conspirators murdered Mary Queen of Scots's secretary, David Rizzio (1566). JAMES VI was resident at Holyrood when he learned that ELIZABETH I had died and he was now king of England. The castle has since rarely been used by royalty. Bonnie Prince Charlie took over Holyrood and established his court here in 1745, celebrating his recent victories. The exiled Louis XVIII of France and his brother (the future Charles X) found refuge here from 1795–9; GEORGE IV held festivities here in 1822. VICTORIA used it annually en route to Balmoral, and the future EDWARD VII stayed here in 1859 while studying at the university. The Picture Gallery contains portraits of all 111 Scottish kings, from the legendary FERGUS MAC FERADACH to CHARLES II. This is a unique set (no such series of portraits exists anywhere for any nation's rulers – even if half of them are legendary). They were produced by the Dutch painter Jacob de Wet between 1684 and 1686.

Kirk o' the Field The Collegiate Church of St Mary in the Fields was founded in 1510, but was damaged during the invasion of Edward Seymour by order of HENRY VIII in 1544. It was here that MARY QUEEN OF SCOTS brought her husband Lord Darnley to recuperate and where he was murdered after escaping from a massive explosion (1567). The site was later given to the Old University (1789).

Edington (*Wiltshire*) The generally accepted location for the battle of Ethandun (878), the decisive victory of ALFRED THE GREAT against the Danes under GUTHRUM. Following their defeat, the Danes retreated and surrendered two weeks later. Wessex, which only a few weeks earlier had been almost dominated by the Danes, was saved. The exact location of the battle is not known but it is likely to have been on the hill slopes by the famous Westbury White Horse.

Egilsay (*Orkneys*) One of the smaller islands of Orkney, where MAGNUS, earl of Orkney, was murdered (1116). He was later venerated as a saint, and the 12th C Church of St Magnus is almost certainly built on the site of the murder.

Eildon Hills (*Scottish Borders*) An Iron Age fort at the summit of Eildon Hills North, just south of Melrose, was the chief settlement of the Selgovae at the time of the Roman conquest. The Romans captured the fort (AD 79) and built a signal station. It is one of the locations in Arthurian legend where ARTHUR and his knights are said to sleep, awaiting to be recalled to save Britain. Here ATHELWOLD MOLL fought a bloody battle in 761 against the heirs of EADBERT.

Eilean Donan Castle (*Highlands*) On an islet in Loch Alsh this castle was built on the site of an earlier fort (1230) by ALEXANDER II to protect against raiders, notably the lords of the Isles. By a twist of fate it became the court of DONALD II, lord of the Isles (1387). It has for centuries been the home of the MacRaes. Although it was destroyed during the Jacobite rebellion, it was restored in 1932.

Elgin (*Moray*) Although first mentioned in 1190, Elgin is of considerable antiquity and no doubt was much associated with the men of Moray during the royal wars of the 10th and 11th C (*see* Cullen *and* Forres). It was near Elgin, either at Burghead or Pitgaveny, that DUNCAN I was killed by MACBETH. DAVID I stayed at Duffus Castle, north of Elgin, while selecting the site for Kinloss Abbey (*see* Forres). The town was partly destroyed by Alexander, the Wolf of Badenoch

(1390); restored, it became a favourite residence of JAMES II (1450s). Bonnie Prince Charlie stayed at Thunderton House in the fortnight before Culloden (1746). North of Elgin is Gordonstoun School (founded 1934), attended by both the duke of Edinburgh (1934) and Prince Charles (1962)

Eliseg's Pillar *see* Llangollen

Ellandun (*Wiltshire*) *see* Wroughton

Elmet (*Yorkshire*) A small British enclave survived into the early seventh century in the area around Leeds in the southern Pennines. It was probably established by Samwl in the mid 6th C. Its last king was CEREDIG, expelled by EDWIN of Northumbria no later than 625.

Eltham Palace (*Kent*) The original manor house was presented to Bishop Odo by WILLIAM I, after whom it passed through several families until Antony Bek, bishop of Durham, presented it to the prince of Wales (the future EDWARD II). Edward gave it to his queen, Isabella, who often stayed here. Their son John, later earl of Cornwall, was born here (1316); he became "Guardian of the Realm" in 1329 and 1331 during the king's absence. EDWARD III also often stayed here and received Jean II of France as captive. Further improvements were made by RICHARD II, HENRY IV and HENRY VI. HENRY VIII stayed here frequently in his youth and used the palace as one of the locations of his travelling court. He spent Christmas 1517 here with Katherine of Aragon watching a special Christmas play. Henry stayed here in November 1532 with his new mistress Anne Boleyn, and it is just possible ELIZABETH (I) was conceived here that December. Elizabeth spent some of her infancy at Eltham Palace but in later years seldom visited it, and it fell into disrepair. It was demolished in the early 1650s.

Ely (*Cambridgeshire*) A monastery was founded here on an island in the fens by Etheldreda, wife of Egfrith, the future king of Northumbria (673). She became abbess and died and was buried here (679). She later became venerated as a saint, her name evolved to Audrey, and the name St Audrey became corrupted to "tawdry" because of the cheap necklaces sold in her memory. It was to the Fenlands around Ely that ATHELBALD (the future king of Mercia) was banished around 709. In 870 the Danes sacked Ely and burned the church, but it was later restored and a Benedictine monastery established (879). A monastic school was founded (the basis for the later King's School) by EDGAR in 970, and it was here that EDWARD THE CONFESSOR was educated. Edward's younger brother Alfred, who had been in exile in Normandy, returned to England in 1036 to visit his mother at Winchester, but he was captured by Earl Godwin and taken to Ely where he was killed (probably on

the orders of HAROLD I) and buried (1036/7). Hereward the Wake maintained the last resistance against WILLIAM THE CONQUEROR at Ely (1071). HENRY I raised Ely to a bishopric in 1109. It was here that the disaffected barons rose up anew against HENRY III in 1267.

Epping Forest (*Essex, North London*) *see* Waltham Forest

Esher (*Surrey*) *see* Claremont House

Essie (*Aberdeenshire*) *see* Huntly

Ethandun (*Wiltshire*) *see* Edington

Eton College (*Berkshire*) Founded for "poor" scholars in 1440 by HENRY VI.

Evesham (*Worcestershire*) The site of the battle of Evesham (1265), where Prince Edward (the future EDWARD I) defeated and killed Simon de Montfort and rescued his father, HENRY III.

Exeter (*Devon*) On the southern border between the Britons of Dumnonia and the rest of Britain, Exeter was for centuries a frontier town, first with the Romans, who founded the city as Isca Damnoniorum, around AD 50, and then with the West Saxons, who gradually drove the Dumnonian borders back across Devon. CENWEALH was probably the first Saxon king to occupy Exeter. The British under GERAINT were further driven back by INE in 710. It was subject to many Danish attacks in the 9th C, and ATHELSTAN fortified the town in 926. Exeter was the focus of West Country resistance after the Norman conquest, where HAROLD II's mother fled. WILLIAM I rapidly negotiated peace and established a castle here in 1068. The castle surrendered to STEPHEN (1136), and EDWARD I held Parliament here (1286). It was besieged by Perkin WARBECK in 1497, and again by CHARLES I's troops in 1643. Charles's queen, Henrietta Maria, sought refuge in Exeter in May 1644 and here their daughter, Princess Henrietta, was born at Bedford House (16 June 1644). Exeter was the first city to welcome William of Orange (*see* WILLIAM III) in 1688, after his landing at Brixham.

Falkirk (*Falkirk*) The site of several battles. Camelon to the west of Falkirk has been suggested as a possible site for ARTHUR's last battle at Camlann (*c*537). Just north of Falkirk at Strathcarron OWEN MAP BILI of Strathclyde defeated and killed DOMNALL BRECC (642). In 1298 EDWARD I defeated WILLIAM WALLACE at Callendar Wood; and in 1746 Bonnie Prince Charlie rebuffed the advancing English forces at Bantaskyne.

Falkland (*Fife*) A castle has stood here since at least the 12th C belonging to the earls of Fife. It passed to ROBERT STEWART, later duke of Albany and governor of Scotland, in 1371 and it was here that ROBERT III's son DAVID STEWART died in prison (1401). The castle came into the possession of JAMES I of Scotland in 1425. In 1502 JAMES IV renovated the great hall, initiating conversion of the castle into Falkland Palace. JAMES V made significant additions to the palace, including the Royal Tennis Court (1539), and he often found the palace a place of solace and refuge. It was here that he pined away in the Golden Bed of Brahan (1542). His daughter, MARY Queen of Scots, spent much of her childhood here and visited it annually from 1561–5. JAMES VI frequently stayed here, but he was the last monarch to use it regularly. CHARLES I visited in 1633 and CHARLES II in 1650 but no monarch has stayed here since. Rob Roy occupied the Palace in 1715. It is still occupied by a Stewart descendent, the marquess of Bute, who is the hereditary keeper.

Farndon-on-Dee (*Cheshire*) EDWARD THE ELDER died here (924) while campaigning against the men of Chester, who were aiding the Welsh against the Saxons.

Farnham (*Surrey*) One of the sites associated with the final defeat of ALLECTUS by ASCLEPIODOTUS in 296, though the actual location is uncertain and may have been further west. Farnham Castle was constructed in the 1130s by Henry of Blois, brother of STEPHEN, as the seat of the bishops of Winchester. In 1155 HENRY II demolished everything that Henry of Blois had constructed and then rebuilt the castle which has remained in constant use ever since.

Faversham Abbey (*Kent*) Faversham has rich records of its occupation from prehistory through Roman and Saxon times. It seems likely that Faversham was originally the primary royal court of the kings of Kent in the 6th C under EORMENRIC, before it was superseded by Canterbury in the following century. The Roman and Saxon towns were just to the south of the present town, by Judd's Hill, near Ospringe. STEPHEN founded an abbey at Faversham (1147) and it was here that, in rapid succession, his wife Matilda (1152), his son Eustace (1153), and Stephen himself (1154) were buried. It is possible that somewhere in the creeks near Faversham lies the body of HENRY IV. He had requested a burial at Canterbury but en route by boat a storm erupted and legend has it that the crew cast the body overboard and later substituted another. It was to Faversham that JAMES II was brought and held captive at the Queen's Arms inn when he tried to leave the country (1688).

Fethanlea (*Oxfordshire*) *see* Stoke Lyne

Fettercairn (*Aberdeenshire*) A village north of Brechin, approached through a wooded valley along which MACBETH is believed to have retreated after his defeat at Dunsinane. This was once the site of Kincardine Castle, the royal palace from which JOHN BALLIOL penned his abdication to EDWARD I before declaring it from the nearby churchyard at Strathcarro (1296). Kincardine Castle has a history going back at least to the 10th C as it is associated with the murder of KENNETH II in 995 by Finella, the daughter of the lord of Angus, whose castle was on the hills outside Kincardine, her name remembered in Strath Finella. Kenneth was on a pilgrimage to the nearby shrine of St Palladius at Fordoun. VICTORIA and Albert visited Fettercairn in 1861 and a turreted arch commemorates the occasion as you enter the village.

Fetteresso (*Aberdeenshire*) *see* Stonehaven

Findochty (*Moray*) A few miles west of Cullen, it was here that INDULF was killed in battle against the Danes.

Fishbourne (*West Sussex*) The site of the palace of COGIDUMNUS, the client king of the Regnii, whose capital was at Chichester, a mile to the north. It was a splendid palace covering over ten acres and was built around AD 70, by the Romans in respect for Cogidumnus's loyalty.

Flint (*Flintshire*) Alongside the Dee, Flint has the earliest castle built in Wales by EDWARD I, started in 1277. It was here that EDWARD II met his court favourite, Piers Gaveston, who had returned from exile in Flanders (1312); and where RICHARD II surrendered to Henry Bolingbroke (1399).

Flodden Field (*Northumberland*) A few miles south of Coldstream in the disputed border territory between Scotland and England, this was the site of the battle where the English army, under the command of Thomas Howard, earl of Surrey, defeated the Scots. It was a bitter blow for the Scots, for they not only lost their king, JAMES IV, but twelve earls, fourteen lords and over ten thousand soldiers.

Fontevrault (*France*) A village in Anjou, near Chinon, where HENRY II (1189), RICHARD I (1199) and Henry's queen, Eleanor of Aquitaine (1204), are all buried.

Fordoun (*Aberdeenshire*) *see* Fettercairn

Forfar (*Angus*) The supposed site of the last major battle between the Picts and the Scots (845) before KENNETH MACALPIN united the kingdoms. The area around Forfar is rich in history. Dunnichen Moss, between Forfar and Letham, was once the site of Nechtansmere where the Picts under BRUDE MAC BILI slaughtered the Northumbrian army under EGFRITH (685) and thus freed the Picts of the English yoke for many years. One of the ancient stones at Aberlemno, north of Forfar, may depict the battle. NECHTAN (III) founded a priory at Restenneth for St Boniface (710); this was re-established by MALCOLM IV (1153). When DONALD III was deposed he was imprisoned at Rescobie Castle, where he died (1099). *See also* Glamis Castle.

Forres (*Moray*) An ancient site, traditionally associated with MACBETH, the royal castle has a bloody history, related to the rivalry between the men of Moray and the kings of the Scots. It was here that DONALD II was killed (900), and DUFF met his death at the hands of the governor of the castle (966). Forres was also the main residence of MALCOLM I in Moray and it is possible that he met his death at Blervie Castle just south of Forres (954), *but see also* Stonehaven. DUNCAN I held his court at Forres and was killed in battle with Macbeth between Forres and Elgin, possibly at Burghead or Pitgaveny. Hardmuir, near Brodie, just east of Forres, is where Macbeth is supposed to have met the three witches. Kinloss Abbey, 3 miles N of Forres, was founded in 1151 by DAVID I. Tradition states that David was led to the site by a white dove when he got lost in the forest. Forres suffered at the hands of Alexander, Wolf of Badenoch, in 1390, and thereafter the town declined.

Forteviot (*Perth and Kinross*) Just south of Dupplin near Perth this was the site of the ancient capital of the Pictish kingdom of Fortriu or Fortrenn. CONSTANTINE MAC FERGUS established his capital here in the early 800s, but it was destroyed by the Vikings in 839 and rebuilt around 850 by KENNETH MACALPIN, who moved the capital of the Scots from Dunadd. Kenneth died here (858) and soon after it was again plundered by Vikings (866).

Fotheringhay Castle (*Northants*) Between Oundle and Peterborough, this castle has two notorious associations. It was the birthplace of the future RICHARD III (1452) and the scene of the execution of MARY Queen of Scots (1587), both events happening in the same great hall. The castle had been the home of the dukes of York and Richard III's father, Richard, duke of York, was reinterred at the local collegiate church in 1476. Katherine of Aragon was almost removed to Fotheringhay in 1533 but she refused so defiantly, by locking herself in her room, that she was kept at Buckden. Mary Queen of Scots was brought here in September 1586, tried a few months later, and beheaded on 8 February 1587. Her body remained at Fotheringhay for six months until a state funeral was arranged at Peterborough. When her son, JAMES VI, became king of England he arranged his mother's re-burial at Westminster and had Fotheringhay Castle dismantled.

Fowey (*Cornwall*) *see* Bodmin Moor *and* Castle Dore

Framlingham Castle (*Suffolk*) The original castle was built about 1100. It was the home of the Bigod family, whose descendants became earls of Norfolk. The Bigods were sufficiently powerful to take on the king. Hugh Bigod challenged HENRY II in 1173 and was forced to surrender his castle. It was dismantled but rebuilt by his son Roger Bigod (1190), who entertained JOHN at Framlingham in 1213 but who fell from favour, was imprisoned, and subsequently supported the barons against John. The castle passed into royal possession. Mary Tudor moved to Framlingham for better protection after she learned that her brother EDWARD VI had died and that JANE was to be crowned queen (1553). The show of support given to Mary convinced her to claim the throne and she departed from Framlingham for London. The castle subsequently fell into disuse and was bequeathed to Pembroke College, Cambridge, for it to build a poor house on the site.

Frogmore House, Windsor *see* Windsor

Frome (*Somerset*) There was a Saxon villa here, where EADRED of Wessex died (955).

Gainsborough (*Lincolnshire*) A town with a diversity of royal interest. ALFRED THE GREAT was reputed to have courted his wife Ealhswith here (868). She was the daughter of Athelred, earl of the Gainas. SWEYN established his camp here at Thonock Park in 1013, where he died the following year. The Old Hall was built in 1484 by Lord de Burgh, who entertained RICHARD III upon its completion. HENRY VIII visited it in 1509. In 1526 Lord de Burgh's son married Katherine Parr. Seventeen years later she would become Henry VIII's last wife.

Galloway (*Scotland*) The south-westernmost part of Scotland, though not formally incorporated into the kingdom until 1034. As its name implies, it was originally the homeland of the Gaels or strangers, a word that might have referred to either the Irish or the Norse who settled here between the sixth and ninth centuries. It was for a while ruled as part of Strathclyde and also as part of the kingdom of Man. In earliest times it had its own ruler – St Ninian converted TUTAGUAL to Christianity in the early 5th C – and it remained fiercely independent even after it was incorporated into the kingdom of Scotland. In the 1150s the rebel lord Fergus of Galloway operated autonomously, styling himself king of Galloway until suppressed by MALCOLM IV in 1160. His son Gilbert and grandson Roland retained a high degree of independence until the time of Alan the last native lord of Galloway. He was an ancestor of John Balliol. Carrick was once part of Galloway and was thus the homeland of ROBERT I, who made his brother Edward lord of Galloway in about 1309.

Geddington (*Northants*) Here stands one of the three surviving crosses erected in memory of Eleanor of Castile, 1290 (*see under* Harby).

Gilling (*North Yorkshire*) OSWINE, king of Deira, was murdered at Gilling by order of OSWY of Northumbria (651). In expiation for the deed a monastery was built at the site and Oswine's relics were removed here.

Glamis Castle (*Angus*) There had been a royal hunting lodge on this site, near Forfar, since at least the 11th Century, and almost certainly earlier. MALCOLM II died here in his eightieth year (1034). Jean, the daughter of ROBERT II, married John Lyon in 1376, and he was granted the barony of Glamis. A descendant, Sir Patrick Lyon was made Lord Glamis in 1445 and his descendants became earls of Strathmore and Kinghorne. The castle was confiscated in 1537 when Lady Glamis, wife of the 6th Lord Glamis, was found guilty of witchcraft and plotting against JAMES V and was burned at the stake. She was later declared innocent and the castle was restored to the family. The descendants still live here. The present castle was built in the 17th C. JAMES STUART, the Old Pretender, stayed here in 1715. Lady Elizabeth Bowes-Lyon, wife of GEORGE VI, was born here in 1900, as was her daughter, Princess Margaret (1930).

Glasgow (*Glasgow*) Despite being Scotland's biggest city, Glasgow has remarkably few historical royal connections. WILLIAM WALLACE defeated the English here at Bell o' the Brae (1300) but was captured here in 1305; JAMES IV is believed to have stayed here in 1488; MARY QUEEN OF SCOTS stayed at the Provand's House in 1567 when visiting her sick husband, Lord Darnley; a year later she was defeated at Langside, in south Glasgow across the Clyde, where Queen's Park now stands.

Glastonbury (*Somerset*) A mystical site with strong Arthurian associations. The monks of Glastonbury Abbey claimed to have found the bodies of ARTHUR and Guinevere in 1191. The site of Glastonbury is ancient and legend claims that ARVIRAGUS granted Joseph of Arimathea twelve hides of land when he came to Britain in AD 63. A church was supposedly built here in the reign of LUCIUS in CAD 79. A monastery was established sometime in the early 7th C, as CENTWINE was a noted benefactor and probably retired here (685). The monastery was further embellished by INE (688). Dunstan, who was born near Glastonbury (*c*909) was made abbot by EDMUND I in 943. Edmund was buried here (946), as were EDGAR (975) and EDMUND II (1016). The abbey was damaged by fire in 1184 and it was during the construction of the new abbey that the relics of King Arthur were purportedly discovered, which did wonders for the abbey's revenues.

Glenfinnan (*Highland*) On 25 July 1745 Bonnie Prince Charlie landed at Loch nan Uamh (Loch of the Caves) and stayed at Kinlochmoidart until able to rendezvous with his supporters (who numbered about 1500) on 19 August at Glenfinnan, where he raised the Jacobite Standard in the name of his father, JAMES VIII. A monument commemorates the event.

Gloucester (*Gloucestershire*) In the heart of the territory of the Dobunni the Romans built their city of Glevum, though the founding is often attributed to ARVIRAGUS (CAD 47). Despite the Roman presence it seems to have remained strongly British. Tradition gives Gloucester as the burial place of TOGODUMNUS (AD 43), ARVIRAGUS (*c*67) and LUCIUS (*c*180). With the demise of Roman control, Gloucester became the heart of an emerging post-Roman kingdom under the control of VORTIGERN – possibly the same as Vitalinus, whose palace was found at Gloucester (430s). Gloucester might also have been the centre of operations of AMBROSIUS AURELIANUS (470s) and his descendants may have included AURELIANUS CANINUS (*c*500) and COINMAIL who was defeated by the Saxons at Dyrham (577). Along with Worcester it formed the boundary of the kingdom of the Hwicce which was merged into Mercia (7th C). OSRIC of Hwicce founded the monastery of St Peter here (681). It remained a key centre for Mercia. Both ATHELRED II and ATHELFLÆD of Mercia had their palace here where they were buried (911 and 918); ATHELSTAN spent his childhood here and died here (939), as did EDWY (959). After his long imprisonment by his brother HENRY (I), Robert of Normandy was laid to rest at Gloucester Cathedral (1134). It also holds the tomb of EDWARD II, cruelly murdered at Berkeley Castle (1327). The young HENRY III was hastily crowned at Gloucester (1216), where his mother had sought refuge during JOHN's war with the barons. Henry chose Gloucester as the site where the Welsh prince DAFYDD AP LLYWELYN paid him homage (1240).

Goodmanham (*Humberside*) see Market Weighton

Grafton Regis (*Northants*) Small village south of Northampton, near Stony Stratford, whose manor was the family home of the Wydvilles. It was here, on 1 May 1464, that EDWARD IV secretly married Elizabeth Wydville at a chapel called The Hermitage in the woods.

Greens Norton (*Northants*) West of Towcester, the manor here was the home of Sir Thomas Green, the grandfather of Katherine Parr, future wife of HENRY VIII. Katherine's father, Thomas Parr, died when she was only five, and the young Katherine was raised by her mother and frequently spent days at Greens Norton.

Greenwich (*Kent*) On the south side of the Thames, opposite the Isle of Dogs (apparently so called because the royal kennels were here), which in medieval times was known as the Stepney

Marshes. Greenwich Manor had always been a popular royal residence since Saxon times. It is known that both EDWARD I (1300) and HENRY IV (1408) stayed here. Henry's son, Humphrey, duke of Gloucester, built Greenwich Palace here in 1426. HENRY VI and Margaret of Anjou spent their honeymoon here (1445) and, after Humphrey's death in 1447, it passed into the king's ownership, who presented it to Queen Margaret. In turn EDWARD IV granted it to his wife, Elizabeth Wydville. HENRY VII threw Elizabeth out of Greenwich in 1490 and made it his own palace. His son, HENRY VIII was born here (1491), as were Henry's daughters MARY (1516) and ELIZABETH (1533). Henry VIII was married twice at Greenwich – to Katherine of Aragon in 1509 and to Anne of Cleves in 1540; his sister, Mary Tudor, officially married the duke of Suffolk here in 1515, having already eloped with him and married in secret. Henry once arranged a mock battle at Greenwich (1510), combining military training with entertainment; he also held the first masquerade in England here (1516). EDWARD VI was sent here to recuperate but died (1553). MARY I seldom used the palace, and one of the few times she did a cannon ball, fired in salute, struck the wall of her apartment. ELIZABETH used it as her main summer residence. It was here that she first met Walter Ralegh, when he allegedly placed his cloak over a puddle for her to walk over (1581), and where she knighted Francis Drake (1581). It was also where she signed MARY QUEEN OF SCOTS' death warrant (1587). JAMES I gave Greenwich Palace to his queen, Anne of Denmark (1605). Construction of a new house was started in the grounds of Greenwich Park (1616), but was not finished till the time of James's son, CHARLES I in 1640, whose wife Henrietta Maria so adored the place that it became known as the Queen's House. Although it was taken over by Parliamentary troops in 1642, it was restored to Henrietta in 1660, and was also the residence of the subsequent queens, Katherine of Braganza and Mary of Modena. Thereafter both the house and the palace fell out of royal favour (the palace was demolished in 1694) and, though the house was used occasionally over the next century (such as upon the first landing of GEORGE I in England in September 1714), both sites eventually came to form part of the National Maritime Museum and Royal Naval College. Greenwich Park is also the site of the Royal Observatory commissioned by CHARLES II in 1675.

Guernsey see Channel Islands

Guoloph (*Hampshire*) see Wallop

Haddington (*East Lothian*) The birthplace of ALEXANDER II (1198).

Haethfelth see Hatfield Chase

Hailes Abbey (*Gloucestershire*) A Cistercian abbey founded in 1246 by Richard, earl of Cornwall, brother of HENRY III. Henry and his queen, Eleanor of Provence, attended the dedication in 1251. Richard's wife, Sanchia, sister of Eleanor of Provence, was buried here in 1261, as were Richard (1272) and their son Edmund (1300). *See also* Winchcombe.

Halesowen (*West Midlands*) Now lost in the suburbs of Birmingham and Stourbridge, this was once the manor of Hales which was bestowed upon the Welsh prince DAFYDD AB OWAIN in 1177. He died here in 1203 and the manor passed to his son, Owain, from whom the name of Halesowen was derived. Although Owain had died by 1214, the name by then had become fixed. The manor formed the basis for the abbey built in 1218 and that in turn now forms part of Manor Farm.

Halidon Hill (*Scottish Borders*) Three miles north-west of Berwick is the site where EDWARD III's forces defeated the Scots under Sir Archibald Douglas, "Guardian of the Realm" during DAVID II's minority. Douglas was killed and the victory enabled Edward to take Berwick.

Hampton Court (*Greater London, formerly Middlesex*) The former manor of Hampton existed since Saxon times, and from 1236–1514 was used by the Knights of St John until acquired by Thomas Wolsey, who built himself a new palace on the old site. The palace was taken over by HENRY VIII in 1526, who moved into full possession in 1529. The palace was further extended and embellished, especially the grounds, which included what is now Bushey Park extending to over 1000 acres. All of Henry's wives lived here at some time except for Katherine of Aragon. It was most closely associated with Jane Seymour, who in 1537 gave Henry his long awaited son, the future EDWARD VI. Jane died a few days later and Henry, much grieved, fled to Windsor as he could not bear to be in the same residence as Jane's body. Jane was given a resplendent lying-in-state and a funeral procession to Windsor. Henry married Katherine Parr (1543) at Hampton Court. EDWARD VI lived at Hampton Court for most of his short life. Both MARY I and ELIZABETH regularly stayed here. Elizabeth took particular pride in the gardens, growing many of the exotic plants that her captains brought back from foreign lands, including the potato and tobacco plant. The great hall became renowned as an Elizabethan theatre, a tradition continued by JAMES I, and Shakespeare performed here in 1603. James I held a conference here in 1604, seeking to resolve issues between the English church and the Puritans. One of the outcomes was a new translation of the Bible. Hampton Court Palace remained the primary residence and court of the Stewart monarchs. James I's wife, Anne of Denmark, died here in 1619. CHARLES I (who spent his honeymoon here in 1625) later used it more as a refuge than a residence and, ironically, was held prisoner here during the Civil War (1646). CHARLES II (who also spent his honeymoon here in 1662) lived here after the restoration (1660) but his brother, JAMES II did not. WILLIAM and MARY loved the palace but had great plans for its modernisation, only part of which was done. Both ANNE and GEORGE I used the palace more as a private retreat than a court whilst GEORGE II, the last monarch to live here, used it more for festivities and hunting. Later monarchs, particularly GEORGE IV, took a special interest in the Royal Stud which had been started by Anne, but they shifted their primary London residence to Buckingham Palace. VICTORIA opened Hampton Court to the public in 1838.

Hanover (*Germany*) Once part of the Duchy of Brunswick, it became a separate electorate in 1692. Its first elector, Ernest Augustus, son of the duke of Brunswick, married Sophia, the daughter of Frederick V of Bohemia and Elizabeth, the daughter of JAMES I. Their eldest son GEORGE (I) became the eldest surviving Protestant heir to the throne of England when ANNE died in 1714. His mother had died just six weeks earlier, otherwise England would have been ruled by an eighty-four-year-old Queen Sophia. George had succeeded his father as duke and elector of Hanover in 1698, and the successive kings of England were also electors and, from October 1814, kings of Hanover. Since the Salic law denied succession by a woman, when Victoria became queen of England, her uncle Ernest Augustus became king of Hanover. The succession passed to his son, George Frederick in 1851, who was styled George V of Hanover. He was forced to abdicate on 20 September 1866 when Hanover was overrun by Prussia. The palace of the kings of Hanover was the Schloss Herrenhausen, built in 1665. It was here that the English king GEORGE II was born (1683) and that he married Caroline of Brandenburg (1705). George I died near Osnabrück in Hanover, where he had been born, and was buried at the Leinschloss in Hanover. His remains were transferred to the vaults of the Schloss Herrenhausen after the Second World War.

Harby (*Nottinghamshire*) Eleanor of Castile was following her husband, EDWARD I, north when she died of a fever at the manor house of Weston in Harby (1290). Edward was so griefstricken that he ordered the erection of a cross at each place where her body rested overnight on the journey back to Westminster. There were once twelve such Eleanor Crosses, of which only those at Geddington, Hardingstone and Waltham Cross survive. The others were at Lincoln, Grantham, Stamford, Stony Stratford, Woburn, Dunstable, St Albans, West Cheap and at Charing Cross, where a replica exists.

Hardingstone (*Northants*) *see* Northampton.

Hardmuir (*Highlands*) *see* Forres

Harewood House (*West Yorkshire*). This magnificent mansion, mid-way between Leeds and Harrogate, was built in the 1760s for the first Earl of Harewood. In 1922 Viscount Lascelles, who became the sixth earl in 1929, married Mary, the eldest daughter of George V. She became the countess of Harewood in 1929 and "Princess Royal" in 1932. She lived at Harewood from 1929 until her death on 28 March 1965. Her husband had died in 1947. She was buried alongside him in the family vault at Harewood church.

Hastings (*East Sussex*) Originally fortified by ALFRED THE GREAT in the 880s to protect against Danish attacks, Hastings is now intimately associated with WILLIAM of Normandy's invasion of 1066, although the famous Battle of Hastings actually took place six miles to the north (*see* Battle). William, who had landed at Pevensey, used Hastings as his base to prepare for the battle and invasion campaign. William subsequently established a castle at Hastings which was rebuilt in stone a century later.

Hatfield Chase (*South Yorkshire*) The generally accepted site of the battle of Haethfelth in 632/33, where EDWIN of Northumbria was killed by the confederate army of CADWALLON of Gwynedd and PENDA of Mercia.

Hatfield House and **Palace** (*Hertfordshire*) The original Hatfield Palace was built in the 1480s for Cardinal Morton, bishop of Ely and later archbishop of Canterbury. It was acquired in 1533 by HENRY VIII for his children. MARY was already seventeen by then and became something of a nurse to her young half-sister ELIZABETH who was only three months old. Elizabeth spent many of her childhood years at Hatfield, as did her brother EDWARD (VI), who was born four years later. Hatfield later served her as a retreat, almost a place of confinement, after she was released from the Tower of London in 1554. Tradition states that Elizabeth was sitting under an oak tree in the grounds at Hatfield when she received news of Mary's death and of her accession to the throne (1558). She sank to her knees and quoting from the Psalms, said: "This is the doing of the Lord; and it is marvellous in our eyes." She promptly held her first Council of State in the great hall. When JAMES I inherited Hatfield, he preferred the nearby Theobald's Place, owned by Robert Cecil, the earl of Salisbury and James's secretary of state and treasurer. The two exchanged houses in 1607. Salisbury demolished much of the Old Palace in 1611 in constructing the present Hatfield House, still the home of the Cecil family. Amongst the historical items on show at Hatfield are Elizabeth's silk stockings, believed to be the first such stockings in England.

Havering-atte-Bower (*Essex*) A village, north of Romford, which was once the site of an ancient royal palace in existence certainly as far back as EDWARD THE CONFESSOR (1040s). It was visited by most of the Plantagenet and Tudor monarchs – EDWARD III invested his grandson Richard here as prince of Wales (1376), for example. However, it was best remembered as a residence of English queens, who used that part of the palace known as The Bower. Joan, wife of ALEXANDER II of Scotland, died here while visiting her brother, HENRY III (1238). It was the favourite residence of Joan of Navarre, widow of HENRY IV. She was arrested here on a charge of witchcraft and held prisoner at Pevensey Castle from 1419 until 1422. She retired to Havering where she died in 1437. It was the official residence of Katherine of Aragon and Anne Boleyn, though by the time of Anne and Jane Seymour, the greater part of their time was spent at Hampton Court Palace. Havering fell into disuse after 1620 and was subsequently demolished, many of the stones being reused in the Bower House, built down the hill in 1729.

Heavenfield (*Northumberland*) *see* Hexham

Hedingham Castle (*Essex*) Queen Matilda, wife of STEPHEN, died here.

Hellesdon (*Norfolk*) Just outside Norwich, this was where EDMUND of East Anglia was killed in battle against the Vikings (869).

Hereford (*Herefordshire*) In the frontier zone between Mercia and Wales, Hereford was constantly the scene of fighting and it was significant that ATHELSTAN chose Hereford as the place to pronounce the boundary between Wales and England and to exact homage from the Welsh princes (926). Hereford was the centre of the kingdom of the Magonsæte and in 679 Theodore, archbishop of Canterbury, established a bishopric at Hereford for the sub-kingdom then ruled by MEREWALH. ATHELBERT of East Anglia was murdered by order of OFFA's wife near Hereford, at the royal villa of Sutton Walls, and cast into the river (794). His body was recovered and moved to Hereford Cathedral, which was dedicated in his name. Hereford was sacked by the Danes in 1050 and Athelbert's shrine destroyed. The town was sacked and burned by the Welsh under GRUFFYDD AP LLYWELYN in 1055 and again by the Welsh and Mercians in 1067, this time in retaliation against the Norman conquerors. CHARLES II's best known mistress, Nell Gwynne, was born in Hereford in 1650.

Hertford Castle (*Hertfordshire*). The castle was originally built by EDWARD THE ELDER (905) as a defence against the Danes – the frontier between Wessex and the Danelaw was the river Lea. It was rebuilt around 1100 but was damaged during the war between JOHN and his barons. EDWARD III had a close connection with the castle. When his mother died at Castle Rising, her body was kept at Hertford for three months (1358) before her tomb was ready in London. Edward had kept DAVID II of Scotland (his brother-in-law) captive at the castle for most of the previous ten years from 1346. David's wife, Joan, died while on a visit to her brother Edward III at Hertford Castle (1362). Jean II, king of France, was held prisoner here after the battle of Poitiers (1356). It was here that Henry Bolingbroke plotted the downfall of RICHARD II (1399). The infant king HENRY VI spent many of his childhood years here (1420s), as did the young Princess ELIZABETH when not at Hatfield (1540). The castle was eventually sold by JAMES I's son Charles, before he became king.

Hever Castle (*Kent*) A 13th C fortified farmhouse which was converted into a manor house when acquired by Geoffrey Boleyn, Lord Mayor of London, in 1462. The Boleyn family did not move here until after 1505. Anne Boleyn, who had been born at Blickling Manor, was raised and lived much of her life here until she married HENRY VIII in 1533. After Anne's execution the castle became forfeit and when her father died in 1538 it reverted to the Crown. Henry VIII granted it to Anne of Cleves upon their divorce in 1540. She only occasionally resided here. After her death the house fell into disrepair and was only restored to its former glory at the start of the 20th C by the American millionaire William Waldorf Astor.

Hexham (*Northumberland*) Just north of Hexham near Chollerford, by Hadrian's Wall, was Heavenfield, where OSWALD of Northumbria surprised and defeated CADWALLON in 634. The name received an added significance as Oswald reported having a vision of St Columba on the eve of the battle which bode well for his fortune. A monastery was founded at Hexham in 672 under the patronage of Queen Etheldreda, wife of EGFRITH of Northumbria, before she returned to her homeland and founded Ely. It was largely destroyed by the Danes in 810. ELFWALD I of Northumbria was buried here in 788. Hexham was also the site of a battle during the wars of the Roses when EDWARD IV's forces defeated HENRY VI (1464).

Highgrove House (*Gloucestershire*) A mile south of Tetbury, at Doughton, is the Georgian mansion and estate of Highgrove, the home of Prince Charles and Princess Diana after their marriage in 1981, acquired at a cost of £750,000 the previous year. Charles had a special passion for Highgrove, particularly in his delight for farming and horticulture, where he was able to explore some of his more radical innovations.

Holyrood Abbey and **Palace** *see* Edinburgh

Horsted *see* Aylesford

Huntly Castle (*Aberdeenshire*) Macbeth's son, LULACH, was killed near Huntly at Essie in Strathbogie. Huntly Castle was originally called Strathbogie Castle and was the stronghold of the earl of Fife. ROBERT BRUCE convalesced here (1307), but the lord of the castle turned against Bruce, with the result that Fife lost his lands and the castle passed to the Gordon family, whose descendants became earls of Huntly (1449). The Gordons came from Huntly in Berwickshire and they brought their home name with them. JAMES IV was a regular visitor and here was celebrated the marriage between Perkin WARBECK and James's cousin, Lady Catherine Gordon (1496). The modern castle was rebuilt after 1552, though it suffered twice when the Gordons rebelled against MARY QUEEN OF SCOTS (1562) and JAMES VI (1594), when much of the castle was destroyed. The castle was rebuilt but the 2nd marquess of Huntly chose the wrong side when he supported CHARLES I from 1639, and he was arrested and executed (1649).

Hwicce *see* Gloucester, Winchcombe *and* Worcester

Iceni *see* Caistor

Idle, River *see* Bawtry

Inchmahome Priory (*Stirling*) A small priory, on an island in the Lake of Menteith near Aberfoyle, founded in c1238. Here DAVID II married his second wife, Margaret Drummond (1364). It was also here that MARY QUEEN OF SCOTS was sent as a child for safety (1547) after the Scots defeat at the Battle of Pinkie.

Invergowrie (*Perth and Kinross*) On the western outskirts of Dundee this once small village was the favourite residence of ALEXANDER I (1110s).

Inverness (*Highland*) The fortress of Craig Phadrig on the west side of Inverness is believed to be the original capital of the Northern Picts. It was here that Columba visited BRUDE (I) in 565 to bring the Christian message and to seek Brude's blessing for his work throughout Pictland. There was constant strife between the Northern and Southern Picts, and the power base shifted from Inverness to Forteviot in the time of KENNETH MACALPIN (850). The northern vacuum was filled by the men of Moray, who believed they had equal claim to the kingship of the Scots. FINDLAECH of Moray's castle was at Inverness and he held in check the Norsemen to the north under SIGURD and the Scots to the south under MALCOLM I (1000). The deaths of Malcolm, DUFF, GILLECOMGAIN and DUNCAN I were all part of this

rivalry, which was only partly settled with the emergence of MACBETH, who inherited Findlaech's castle (1032). This castle was destroyed by MALCOLM III (1057) and a new castle founded by DAVID I (1140s). Inverness remained a centre of much hostility over the next six hundred years, particularly in the conflict between the Highlanders and the Scottish kings. JAMES I in 1428 summoned a council at Inverness, where he arrested and killed many of the Highland lords. It became the focus of the lords of the Isles and was captured by ANGUS (1480) and besieged by Angus and ALEXANDER of the Isles (1490–92). George Gordon, earl of Huntly, refused MARY QUEEN OF SCOTS admission to Inverness in 1562, for which he was subsequently hanged. Inverness Castle was occupied by the Jacobites in 1715 and 1745, when Bonnie Prince Charlie destroyed it.

Iona (*Highland*) The holy island of Columba, who was granted permission to establish a monastery here by CONALL of Dál Riata in 563. It was respected not only by the Scots but also by the Picts and the Angles. OSWALD and OSWY of Northumbria sought refuge here (617) and ALDFRITH spent some time in exile (684). It fell victim to the clash between the Celtic and Roman churches and in 717 NECHTAN III expelled the Celtic adherents from the monastery. It was plundered mercilessly by the Vikings several times between 795 and 825 so that by the time of KENNETH MACALPIN many of the relics, including those of Columba, were moved either to Kells (after 814) or to Dunkeld (after 849) for safe keeping. Even the Vikings recognized the faith in the end. OLAF SITRICSON retired to Iona and died here (981). Iona was long the burial place of the Pictish and Scottish kings, doubtless including many that were not recorded. The total number is recorded as 48 Scottish kings, 8 Norse, 4 Irish, though it is impossible today to account for all of these or even of the one or two French kings once alleged to be buried here. Of the Scottish it is known that here were buried BRUDE III (693), KENNETH I (858), DONALD I (862), CONSTANTINE I (877), AED (878), GIRIC (889), DONALD II (900), MALCOLM I (954), INDULF (962), DUFF (966), KENNETH II (995), CONSTANTINE III (997), GIRIC II (1005), MALCOLM II (1034), DUNCAN I (1040), MACBETH (1057), LULACH (1058) and DONALD III (about 1100). Thereafter burials were at Dunfermline, but the island continued to be the burial place for most West Highland chiefs. The monastery on Iona was restored by MALCOLM III's wife Margaret in the 1070s, and a Benedictine monastery was founded here by RAGNALD of the Isles in 1203. The later kings and lords of the Isles were also buried on Iona, as were two kings of Man who are numbered amongst the Norse burials. Perhaps the most surprising burial recorded on Iona is that of EGFRITH of Northumbria (685), the enemy of the Picts.

Islip (*Oxfordshire*) On Otmoor, above Oxford, an important royal palace was established here by the Saxon kings, probably in the time of ATHELSTAN early 10th C. It was the birthplace of EDWARD THE CONFESSOR in *c*1004.

Jedburgh (*Scottish Borders*) The castle and priory were founded by DAVID I in about 1138, with the priory raised to Abbey status in 1147. MALCOLM IV died at the Castle in 1165. It was also here that ALEXANDER III entered into his second and rather hasty marriage with Yolande of Dreux in 1285. A ghost appeared at the wedding feast in the castle which boded ill luck, and Alexander died less than five months later. MARY QUEEN OF SCOTS stayed at Jedburgh in 1566 and fell seriously ill. The house still remains.

Jersey *see* Channel Islands

Jorvik *see* York

Kelso (*Scottish Borders*) This town, and the former neighbouring town of Roxburgh, have often shifted between Scottish and English hands, and was subject to major English onslaughts in 1522, 1544 and 1545. The abbey was founded by DAVID I in 1128. Here lies buried Henry of Huntingdon (1152), son of David I and father of MALCOLM IV and WILLIAM THE LYON. While still in Scottish hands Roxburgh Castle, which was a favourite royal residence during the 12th and 13th C, saw the marriage of ALEXANDER II and Marie de Coucy in 1239 and the birth of their only son, the future ALEXANDER III (1241). It was at Roxburgh that EDWARD BALLIOL acknowledged English sovereignty (1332) and Roxburgh remained in English hands for the next 130 years. JAMES II was killed when a cannon exploded while the Scots were besieging Roxburgh Castle (1460). His wife, Mary of Gueldres, hastily came to the scene and successfully led the completion of the siege. The castle and town were totally destroyed. Their son was then crowned JAMES III of Scotland at Kelso Abbey (1460).

Kendal (*Cumbria*) Once part of the kingdom of Rheged and a stronghold of the Vikings (*see under* Carlisle *and* Cumbria). A Norman castle was built here in the 12th C and this came into possession of the Parr family. Thomas Parr was lord of the castle and his daughter, Katherine, the last wife of HENRY VIII, was born here around 1512.

Kenilworth Castle (*Warwickshire*) The first castle was built in the 1120s by Geoffrey de Clinton, treasurer and chamberlain to HENRY I, and it was expanded over succeeding generations with funds provided by HENRY II and JOHN. When the Crown realised how formidable a fortress it had become, it took possession of Kenilworth and exchanged land in Buckinghamshire for the Clintons. HENRY III continued to develop the castle until it was one of the most impregnable in England. Then, in a typical moment of weak judgment, Henry gave it to his sister Eleanor, and through her it passed to her husband, Simon de Montfort, on the occasion of their marriage in 1238. Shortly after De Montfort was made earl of Leicester, with Kenilworth as one of the possessions of that earldom. It was this same Simon who led the rebellion against Henry III twenty years later resulting in an English civil war. Henry's son, Prince Edward (the future EDWARD I), was captured at the battle of Lewes and held captive at Kenilworth (1264). He escaped the following year and defeated De Montfort at Evesham (1265). After the battle it was still necessary for Edward and his father to capture Kenilworth from De Montfort's supporters. Due to the sheer impregnability of the castle, the siege dragged on for nearly nine months before the occupants were forced to surrender through starvation. With De Montfort's death the castle passed with other titles and honours to Edward's brother Edmund (1267), though the command of the castle was given to Edward's close ally Roger de Mortimer, who staged a major tournament at Kenilworth based on the Arthurian concept of the Round Table (1279). Kenilworth remained a royal possession. It passed to Edmund's sons Thomas (1298) and Henry (1324). The mild-mannered Henry became the gaoler of the deposed EDWARD II (1326–27) before he was removed to Berkeley Castle. After the death of Henry's son, another Henry, the castle passed to his second cousin, John of Gaunt (1361) who undertook major rebuilding and extensions to the castle making it a sumptuous palace. It then passed to his son, HENRY IV (1399), whose son, Thomas, duke of Clarence, had been born at Kenilworth (1388). It remained a royal castle for the next 160 years. It was not just a residence, but also a prison. In 1441 Eleanor de Cobham, the wife of Henry VI's uncle, Humphrey of Gloucester, was arrested on a charge of witchcraft and for treasonable acts against the king. She was condemned to perpetual imprisonment and spent some years at Kenilworth in reasonable comfort, with twelve attendants. It seems that Kenilworth was a pleasure to everyone. In 1563 ELIZABETH I made a gift of it to her favourite Robert Dudley, creating him earl of Leicester. Further conversions were made, and no expense spared on entertainments for the queen. Quite possibly the most expensive series of banquets ever held were organized by Dudley for Elizabeth in 1575, spending £100,000 in advance on preparation and refurbishment, plus £1000 per day for each of the nineteen days she was here on entertainment and festivities. One of the guests later remarked that they had seen "none anywhere so memorable." This was Kenilworth's golden age. Thereafter it fell into decline and it was partially dismantled during the Civil War.

Kerrera, Isle of (*Argyll and Bute*) *see* Oban

Kew (*Surrey*) There were several houses at Kew attached to the original pleasure gardens of Sir Henry Capel. In 1728 Queen Caroline, the wife of GEORGE II, leased the Dutch House at Kew from Sir Henry. Three years later their son, Frederick, prince of Wales, rented the neighbouring White House. In 1736 he married Princess Augusta, who had an interest in gardening. Initially they created their own pleasure garden in the grounds but, after Prince Frederick's death in 1751, Augusta developed this as a formal botanic garden stretching as far as the grounds of her mother-in-law's at Richmond Lodge to the west. In the south-west corner of the Gardens stands Queen's Cottage, built in 1771 as a summerhouse for Queen Charlotte. After Augusta's death in 1772, the grounds and the two houses were combined and used frequently by GEORGE III and Queen Charlotte. The White House (which by then was known as Kew House) was demolished in 1802 and work commenced on a more ostentatious palace (which became known as the Castellated Palace) but this was not completed as the Prince Regent lost interest in it with his father's growing mental illness. Meanwhile the Dutch House (now known as the Old Palace) was the scene of a double wedding in 1818, when on 13 July the future WILLIAM IV married Princess Adelaide and his brother Edward, duke of Kent (and father of Queen Victoria) married Princess Victoria. There was sadness later that same year when in November, their mother, Queen Charlotte, died at the Dutch House. The Old Palace was then closed and the Prince Regent ordered that the half-finished Castellated Palace be demolished, which happened finally in 1828. The botanic gardens were handed over to the nation in 1840. Other royal mementoes in the Gardens include the Orangery, built for Princess Augusta in 1761; the Queen's Garden behind Kew Palace, named after ELIZABETH II who opened it to the public in 1969, and the Princess of Wales Conservatory, the largest of Kew's glasshouses, opened in 1987.

Kimbolton Castle (*Cambridgeshire; formerly Huntingdonshire*) This was the last residence of Katherine of Aragon. HENRY VIII had ordered her removal here in April 1534 and it served almost as a prison. She died here in January 1536. The house, which most recently has served as a school, was extensively redesigned in 1620 and again after 1707 when part of the building collapsed.

Kincardine Castle (*Aberdeenshire*) *see* Fettercairn

King's Langley (*Hertfordshire*) RICHARD II was buried at the Church of the Dominican Friars, King's Langley, after he died at Pontefract Castle (1400), but in 1413 his body was removed for a more ceremonial burial at Westminster Abbey.

There is still a richly decorated tomb at King's Langley which was probably Richard's.

Kinghorn (*Fife*) This was where ALEXANDER III met his death in 1286. He was riding back one night from court to the royal mansion at Pettycur when his horse stumbled on the track and Alexander fell down the cliff. A monument now marks the spot.

Kingston (*Surrey*) Although the capital of Wessex was at Winchester, the coronation of each new king took place at Kingston. The "King's stone" is still here, though it has been moved from its original site to a corner outside the Guild Hall. Simple though it sounds, the name Kingston does not derive from the "king's stone", but means the "king's manor", and it must have taken on added significance when EGBERT became recognized as overlord of all the English after 829. It is not recorded when the first coronation happened at Kingston, but it was most probably that of ATHELWOLF's in 839. Egbert had called a council at Kingston in 838 to ensure that the English Church at Canterbury recognized Athelfwolf as his successor and as protector of the monasteries. What must previously have been a standard ceremony of investment of authority now took on a more religious significance along the line that Offa had pursued with his son Egfrith in 787. All of the Saxon kings of England were crowned at Kingston from Athelwolf in 839 to ATHELRED II in 979. There is some uncertainty about ALFRED THE GREAT, because his accession came in the midst of the war with the Danes, but it is hard to imagine that any king would be accepted without some ceremonial inauguration, no matter how hurried. Also, whilst EDGAR must have had a standard coronation, he also had a special ceremony at Bath in 973 to celebrate his imperial authority over all of the kings of Britain. After Athelred, coronations took place at St Paul's Cathedral in London and then at Winchester before becoming customary at Westminster Abbey.

Kinlochmoidart (*Highland*) *see* Glenfinnan

Kinloss Abbey (*Moray*) *see* Forres

Kirkpatrick Fleming (*Dumfries and Galloway*) Just north of Gretna Green is a small village that boasts the cave in which ROBERT BRUCE hid and witnessed the spider spinning its web. Bruce's Cave is also claimed by Rathlin Island, but whichever is correct it is almost certain that Bruce was hidden here for three months by the owner of the local house (1306).

Kirkwall (*Orkney*) Now the capital of the Orkneys. It is first mentioned in the *Orkneyinga Saga* in the year 1046, when RAGNALD II settled here, just before he was killed by THORFINN II. At that stage it was just a collection of houses. The main earl's palace was at Birsay. After Ragnald's death it began to take on more significance, especially after 1137 when RAGNALD III founded the Cathedral of St Magnus, translating the former earl's relics here. Ragnald is also buried here (1158), making the cathedral purportedly the only one in Britain to have the bones of both its founder and its patron saint. The original Bishop's Palace was completed at about the same time. It was here that King Haakon of Norway died (1263) after his disaster at the battle of Largs. James, earl of Bothwell, husband of MARY QUEEN OF SCOTS tried to find support and refuge in Kirkwall in 1567, but was refused admittance to the castle and was forced to flee to Denmark.

Langside *see* Glasgow

Largs (*North Ayrshire*) The site of the battle of Largs on 2 October 1263, when ALEXANDER III defeated King Haakon of Norway. The result of this victory is that the Hebrides and Man, which had hitherto been under Norse sovereignty, were ceded to Scotland. The battle began at sea but a storm drove the Norse ships ashore. The Norse tried to unload their ships to make them easier to handle in the storm and sought to do this without attracting attention. However tradition cites that one of the Norsemen shouted when he trod on a thistle thus alerting the Scots. Thereafter the thistle became the emblem of Scotland.

Leeds (*West Yorkshire*) *see* Elmet, Harewood House *and* Temple Newsam.

Leeds Castle (*Kent*) Set on a lake in the river Len, in the small village of Leeds, east of Maidstone, this Castle, recognized as one of the most beautiful in England, has no connection with Leeds in Yorkshire. The derivation of the name has been attributed to Ledian, the chief advisor of ATHELBERT of the West Saxons who reputedly built a fort here in about 857, although the name has earlier origins relating to the name of the river Len at this point, *Hlyde*, "the noisy one". A Norman castle was started here about 1116, when it belonged to the de Crevecoeur family, but they forfeited it in 1265 because of their support for Simon de Montfort. The castle passed to the crown and it was under EDWARD I, whose queen, Eleanor of Castile, acquired the castle in 1278, that the main building works were undertaken. In 1321, during the rebellion against EDWARD II, his queen, Isabella, was refused admission to the castle. Edward laid siege successfully to the castle and hanged the castellan, Walter Culpeper, from the battlements. The deposed RICHARD II was held briefly at Leeds Castle for a few days in 1399, before being taken to less salubrious surroundings in Yorkshire. It remained a dower palace of the queens of England up to the time of Katherine of France, HENRY V's widow. Although by the time of HENRY VIII there were more sumptuous palaces at Greenwich and Hampton Court, the king was frequently entertained at Leeds by the castles constable, Sir Henry Guildford. He stayed here, for instance, in 1520 en route to the meeting in France known as the Field of the Cloth of Gold. The castle passed from royal hands in 1548, when it was granted to Sir Anthony St Leger.

Leicester (*Leicestershire*) The original capital of the Coritani; tradition states it was named after King LEAR, who was reputedly buried here. It was the site of a siege by EDMUND I in 939 when he defeated the Vikings. Leicester Castle was one of the seats of the earls of Leicester. John of Gaunt died here (1399). His son, the future HENRY IV, lived here before he became king, and his first wife, Mary de Bohun, was buried at St Mary's Church (1394). RICHARD III's body was brought after the battle of Bosworth (1485) to Greyfriars Church at Leicester, where he was buried. However his tomb was later despoiled during the Reformation and his bones thrown into the river Soar. It has never been certain whether they were recovered and reburied at Bow Bridge or were lost forever. There is a memorial to him in the cathedral.

Le Mans (*France*) Once capital of Maine, it was an important cathedral city of the Angevin Empire. The Empress Matilda married Geoffrey of Anjou here in 1128, and it was where her son, the future HENRY II, was born (1133). His son, HENRY THE YOUNG KING, was buried here (1183), as had been Geoffrey of Anjou (1151). RICHARD I's wife, Berengaria, founded the Abbey of L'Epau here (1230), where she died and was buried. Her remains were removed to Le Mans Cathedral in 1821.

Letham (*Angus*) *see* Dunnichen

Lewes (*Sussex*) The site of a battle in 1264 between the forces of Simon de Montfort and those of HENRY III. Thanks to the over-zealousness of the young Prince Edward, the royal army was defeated and both the king and Edward were captured (*see* Kenilworth). The house named after Anne of Cleves was one of her manors but is unlikely she ever lived here.

Lichfield (*Staffordshire*) This was one of the principal centres of the kingdom of Mercia. A bishopric was established here at the request of PEADA in 655. CEOLRED was buried here (716). The see was elevated to archiepiscopal status in 786 through the demands of OFFA. As part of the ceremonies Offa had his son EGFRITH crowned as king of Mercia in 787. It reverted to a bishopric in 803 under CENWULF. The cathedral was rebuilt in 1148, and again after it was severely damaged during the Commonwealth. Amongst its many statues at the front are 24 kings of England.

Lincoln (*Lincolnshire*) An important Roman city, which became the capital of the Roman province of Flavia Caesariensis (305), it was also the principal city of the Danish Five Boroughs (940s). Lincoln Castle was founded by WILLIAM THE CONQUEROR in 1068 and the cathedral was started in 1072. It was at Lincoln that the forces of the Empress MATILDA defeated and captured STEPHEN (1141). After Stephen regained power, he chose Lincoln for his third coronation (1146). At the end of JOHN's reign the barons invited Louis, the French heir, to be king of England and it was at Lincoln that his status was acknowledged (1216), but he was driven out of England the following year after the battle known as the Fair of Lincoln (1217). There are many royal memorabilia held in the Guildhall, including three presentation swords, of RICHARD II (1387), HENRY VII (1487) and CHARLES I (1642).

Lindisfarne (*Northumbria*) A monastery was established here by Aedán at the request of OSWALD of Northumbria (635). After Oswald's death in battle (*see* Oswestry), his head was buried at the monastery. CEOLWULF of Northumbria retired to the monastery (737) but did not die there till 764, during which period EADBERT violated its sanctuary. The Vikings plundered Lindisfarne in 793, and again over successive decades until the monks departed in 875.

Lindores Abbey (*Fife*) Founded in 1191 by David, earl of Huntingdon and brother of WILLIAM THE LYON, after he returned from the Holy Land. DAVID STEWART, duke of Rothesay, was buried here in 1402 after he had died in prison, and miracles were reported to happen at his tomb.

Linlithgow Palace (*West Lothian*) On the south side of the Forth west of Edinburgh, Linlithgow was made a royal burgh by DAVID I in 1138 and probably at about this time the original palace was developed, although no trace of that now remains. EDWARD I encamped here on three separate occasions, the first in 1298 before his battle against WILLIAM WALLACE at Falkirk. In 1302 Edward built a tower, which was destroyed by ROBERT THE BRUCE, rebuilt by DAVID II and then destroyed by fire in 1424. The next year JAMES I set about planning and designing a much grander palace. It became one of the principal residences of the Stewart kings, and it also served as the refuge for HENRY VI and Margaret of Anjou when in exile from England (1461). The young JAMES III was kidnapped from here (1466) while hearing the accounts. JAMES IV gave the palace to his wife, Margaret Tudor (1503). The future JAMES V was born here (1512); a year later it was where Queen Margaret heard news of the death of James IV at Flodden. MARY QUEEN OF SCOTS was born here (1542) and her son, JAMES VI,

regarded it as his favourite residence and undertook further embellishments. It became abandoned after James became James I of England, although his son, CHARLES I, who stayed here in 1633, had designs to make Linlithgow the capital of Scotland. It began to fall into ruin and was destroyed by fire in 1746, inadvertently caused by the army of the duke of Cumberland which stayed here after the battle of Falkirk.

Llanbabo *see* Anglesey

Llandaff *see* Cardiff

Llandeilo *see* Dinefwr

Llangadwaladr *see* Anglesey

Llangollen (*Powys*) The home of the International Music Eisteddfod every summer, Llangollen has one particular claim to historical fame – Eliseg's Pillar, erected in the valley in the early 9th C by CYNGEN AP CADELL to commemorate the achievements of his great-grandfather ELISEDD of Powys. The Pillar is just to the north of Valle Crucis Abbey, founded in 1201 by MADOG AP GRUFFYDD and where he lies buried (1236).

Llanspyddid *see* Brecon

Lochleven Castle (*Stirling*) A 14th C castle, best known today as the place where MARY QUEEN OF SCOTS was imprisoned (1567–8) and where she signed her deed of abdication. She was kept in the Round Tower and was not well treated, suffering a miscarriage. However she eventually won the hearts of at least two of her gaolers, who allowed her escape on 2 May 1568. She was defeated two weeks later at Langside and fled to England.

Lochmaben (*Dumfries*) Here stood the castle of the lords of Annandale, which claims (along with Writtle in Essex and Turnberry Castle) to have been the birthplace of ROBERT BRUCE (1274). It was also a favourite residence of JAMES IV and was visited by MARY QUEEN OF SCOTS with Lord Darnley (1565).

LONDON

Despite Geoffrey of Monmouth's claim that London was founded as New Troy by BRUTUS a few generations after the siege of Troy, there is no evidence to suggest there was any significant settlement in London prior to the Roman conquest of AD 43. The territory formed part of that of the Trinovantes, though the region was ruled over by CARATACUS of the Catuvellauni, with his capital near St Albans. London is supposed to take its name from LUD, the brother of CASSIVELAUNOS, four generations earlier than Caratacus, around 60 BC, who was reputedly buried at Ludgate. Legend also states that when Caratacus's father, BRAN, was killed his head was brought to London and buried at the White

Mount (the site of the Tower of London) facing France, to guard Britain against invasion. The Roman base was destroyed in BOUDICA's uprising in AD 60 but was soon re-established. HADRIAN visited London in 122. When SEPTIMIUS SEVERUS visited Britain (208), he split the island into two provinces and London became the capital of Britannia Superior. Its walls followed the line of what is still known as the City of London. The governor's palace was built on the site of what is now Cannon Street Station. When CARAUSIUS usurped power in 287, he used London as his base and established a mint. Britain was further subdivided after this revolt and London became the capital of Maxima Caesariensis (305). London was used as a fortress in 457 when the Britons fled to London from the army of HENGIST. There is some evidence that the British were drawn back into London in the late fifth century. It is quite possible that AMBROSIUS AURELIANUS used it as a base during his campaigns. Also a Celtic church dedicated to St Brigid (or St Bride) was established by a well alongside the Fleet around 550. Otherwise no mention is made of it until 604 when ATHELBERT of Kent established the first St Paul's cathedral under Bishop Mellitus. London later came under the jurisdiction of East Saxons. Under SAELRED its commercial significance as a port grew. This attracted the interest of ATHELBALD of Mercia, who gained authority over London (740s). It was plundered several times by the Vikings and Danes and was captured by SWEIN in 1013. The former West Saxon capital had been at Winchester, but London had increasingly become its commercial centre. ATHELRED II used it as his base and died here (1016) and EDWARD THE CONFESSOR constructed Westminster Abbey here (1066). WILLIAM THE CONQUEROR made it his capital after 1066, after which date the majority of the royal landmarks emerged and are covered separately below.

Battersea Park (*Battersea*) Formerly the common fields of Battersea, it has long been open land. It is possible that this was where Julius Caesar crossed the Thames to do battle with CASSIVELLAUNOS. It was also here that Thomas Blood hid during his assassination attempt on CHARLES II (1671).

Baynard's Castle (*City*) Situated on the north side of the Thames, just south of St Paul's Cathedral and west of Blackfriars. Built during the reign of WILLIAM THE CONQUEROR for Ralph Baynard, it passed to HENRY I. It later came into the possession of Robert Fitzwalter, leader of the barons against King JOHN. John is supposed to have ordered the dismantling of the castle because Fitzwalter opposed John's interest in his daughter Matilda who, following Fitzwalter's rebellion (1212), was arrested and died in the Tower of London. Although the castle was rebuilt, the land was later given to the church (1275) and Blackfriars was built on the site. A new castle was constructed to the east (1278) and

this was later acquired by Humphrey, duke of Gloucester (son of HENRY IV), who rebuilt it after a fire (1428). It reverted to the Crown on his death in 1447 and was granted to Richard, duke of York (1457). His widow, Cecilia, lived here after his death (1460) and it was at Baynard's Castle that her son, EDWARD (IV), was entreated to take the throne of England (1461). Richard of Gloucester (Cecilia's younger son) was also resident when he accepted the throne as RICHARD III. HENRY VII rebuilt it in 1487. In 1509 HENRY VIII gave it to Katherine of Aragon as her main residence in London, and it was also the subsequent home of Anne Boleyn and Anne of Cleves. Lady JANE Grey was proclaimed queen at Baynard's Castle (1553), and it was frequently used by later monarchs until destroyed in the Great Fire of London (1666). There are no remains, though the site was excavated in 1972, and Baynard Street retains the name.

Belgrave Square (*Belgravia, SW1*) Built in 1826 on land owned by Earl Grosvenor (later marquess of Westminster). Once the haunt of highwaymen and robbers, the new development rapidly became an area of exclusive residence. In 1840 VICTORIA took a lease on Ingestre House (Number 36) for her mother, the duchess of Kent, who lived there for five months before moving to Clarence House.

Bermondsey (*Southwark*) A Benedictine priory dedicated to St Saviour was founded in 1082 by Aylwyn Child, whose name is remembered in the Aylwyn Estate, and was later raised to status of abbey in 1399. MARY, the sister of Matilda (wife of Henry I) and daughter of Malcolm III, died and was buried here (1115). In 1140 STEPHEN granted the abbey the right to hold a court of law and in 1154 an early form of parliament met here by order of HENRY II. Henry's son, HENRY, THE YOUNG KING, was born here (1155); Katherine, widow of HENRY V, was banished to the abbey and died here (1437) as did Elizabeth Wydville, widow of EDWARD IV (1492). The abbey was dissolved in 1538 and demolished in 1541.

Blackfriars A Dominican community which existed on the site of what is now Blackfriars Station (and formerly Baynard's Castle) from 1278 to 1538. It became rich and powerful. At least two parliaments were called here (in 1311 and 1450) and HENRY VI's privy council often met here. The court was held here which judged the divorce case against Katherine of Aragon (1529).

Brandenburgh House (*Fulham*) Built in the early 17th C, and the headquarters of General Fairfax after the Civil War, it was bought just before his death by Prince Rupert of the Rhine, the cousin of CHARLES II, for his mistress Margaret Hughes and their child Ruperta. By 1792 it had come into the possession of the margrave of Brandenburg-Ansbach, which is how it acquired its name. Caroline of Brunswick, the estranged wife of GEORGE IV, stayed here while trying to establish her rights as queen and died here a few months later (1821). The house was demolished soon after.

Bridewell Originally a palace built alongside the River Fleet across from Blackfriars by the side of a well dedicated to St Bride (St Brigid). It was built between 1515 and 1520 for HENRY VIII. For a while after 1525 Henry's illegitimate son, Henry Fitzroy lived here. Katherine of Aragon stayed here while the papal legate judged her divorce case at Blackfriars (1528/9). She saw her husband for the last time here in November 1529 when they argued after dinner. In 1531 the palace was leased to the French ambassador. In 1553 EDWARD VI gave the palace to the City of London for the care of vagrants and minor offenders but it rapidly turned into a prison. The old building was destroyed in the Great Fire (1666).

Bruton Street (*W1*) A street running from Berkeley Square to New Bond Street; many of the houses were built in the 1740s. Number 17 was the town house of the earl of Strathmore, whose daughter, Elizabeth, was married to the future GEORGE VI. It was here in April 1926 that the future Queen ELIZABETH II was born. The house is now demolished.

Buckingham Palace (*Pimlico, SW1*) The original Buckingham House was built in 1702–5 by William Winde for John Sheffield, the 1st duke of Buckingham and Normanby. His wife, Katherine Darnley, was the illegitimate daughter of JAMES II. After the duke's death in 1721 she tried to sell it to the future GEORGE II – despite his initial interest, nothing came of it. GEORGE III bought it in 1762 for £28,000. The first royal child to be born here was Prince William, the future WILLIAM IV, on 21 August 1765. Ten more of George and Charlotte's children were born here, including Edward, the father of VICTORIA (1767), and Ernest Augustus, the future king of Hanover (1771). The first wedding to be conducted here was that of George's second son, Frederick, duke of York, who married Princess Frederica of Prussia on 23 November 1791. Here also was sealed the marriage of George's daughter Mary to his cousin, William, duke of Gloucester (1816).

When GEORGE IV came to the throne (1820), he decided that Buckingham House was not grand enough and requested an extensive rebuilding programme. His original plans were estimated to cost £500,000; Parliament approved £200,000; the final cost was in excess of £700,000. The rebuilding, most of which was designed by John Nash, took over twelve years. Neither George IV nor William IV lived here and work was still incomplete when VICTORIA took up residence in July 1837. Nash designed a magnificent Marble Arch in front of the palace, which was erected in 1827, but this was removed to its current site at Cumberland Gate, Hyde Park in 1851. Victoria soon came to like the palace and thereafter it remained the London residence of

the sovereign. All but one of her children were born here, starting with Princess Victoria (21 November 1840) and ending with Princess Beatrice (14 April 1857). This included Prince Edward (1841), the future EDWARD VII, who was the only monarch to die at Buckingham Palace (6 May 1910). Curiously there were no other royal births there until Prince Charles (1948), followed by Prince Andrew (1960) and Prince Edward (1964). Two of Edward VII's daughters were married at the Palace: Princess Louise to the marquess of MacDuff (1889) and Princess Maud to Prince Christian of Denmark – later King Haakon VII of Norway (1896). The most recent royal marriage at the palace, in the Private Chapel, was that of George V's son Henry, duke of Gloucester, to Alice Montagu-Douglas-Scott, daughter of the duke of Queensberry (1935). The chapel was destroyed during the Second World War, when the palace was struck by a series of bombs on 13 September 1940. It was restored and opened in 1961 as an art gallery exhibiting royal treasures.

Apart from being a tourist attraction, Buckingham Palace is a centre for displays of national celebration or mourning. Crowds gathered there to celebrate the end of World War II (1945) and more recently to join in the nation's grief at the death of Princess Diana (1997). The state apartments were opened to the public on an occasional basis in 1993. It is here that the changing of the guard happens daily at 11.30a.m. Security at the palace needs to be tight. There was a sensation in 1982 when Michael Fagan broke into Queen ELIZABETH II's bedroom and she needed to keep him calm until help arrived. This was not the first attempt at gaining entrance – it had happened as far back as 1840, when the 17–year-old Edmund Jones broke through security on three separate occasions.

The Palace Gardens extend for 45 acres and are noted for the royal garden parties in the summer. These grounds were originally owned by JAMES I and became known as the Mulberry Gardens, because he planted thousands of such trees in 1609 to encourage the silk industry. One of these mulberry trees still survives.

Carlton House (*Pall Mall*) The house was built in 1709 and was acquired by Frederick, prince of Wales, in 1732. His widow, Augusta, continued to live here when not at Kew. She died at Carlton House of cancer in 1772. In 1783 GEORGE III granted the house to his son, the prince of Wales (the future GEORGE IV), who converted it into the most ostentatious residence in London, at a cost of £225,000. The rising cost resulted in a parliamentary enquiry, and the king and government agreed to meet the prince's debts only if he entered into a formal marriage, which he did with extreme bad grace in 1795. His only child, Princess Charlotte, was born here in 1796, and she was also married at the house to Prince

Leopold of Saxe-Coburg in 1816. Carlton House saw many celebrations, all of sumptuous extravagance, including a huge fete to celebrate the prince's Regency in June 1811, and another as tribute to the duke of Wellington in 1814. When the Prince Regent ascended to the throne in 1820, he did not feel Carlton House was grand enough for his new status and set in train the renovation of Buckingham House into Buckingham Palace. Carlton House was demolished in 1829, though some of its furnishings and fittings were moved to Buckingham Palace or Windsor Castle. On its site John Nash built Carlton House Terrace.

Chapel Royal see London, St James's Palace

Charing Cross Here stood the last and most imposing of the twelve crosses erected by EDWARD I in memory of Eleanor of Castile, 1290 (see under Harby). It was pulled down in 1647. On its site now stands a statue of Charles I. A replica of the original Charing Cross was erected in 1863 outside Charing Cross Station.

Chelsea (SW3, SW10) A residential area which was once an exclusive riverside village, favoured by so many eminent people that by the sixteenth century it had become known as the "village of palaces". It was chosen by OFFA as the site for his synod (787) when Lichfield was granted archiepiscopal status. The locality grew in status after 1520 when Sir Thomas More built a country house here. HENRY VIII rebuilt the old manor house (1536) in what is now Cheyne Walk and gave it to Katherine Parr (1543). She retired to it (1547) and for a brief period the young ELIZABETH stayed here. Anne of Cleves spent her last years here (1555–6). The Manor House was demolished in 1755. Chelsea was often frequented by CHARLES II (1660s), who was responsible for founding the Royal Hospital (1682). King's Road, Chelsea, was so named because it was once a private road used by Charles II from St James's Palace to Hampton Court.

Clarence House (St James's) Built in 1828 for the future WILLIAM IV, who remained here when he became king because Buckingham Palace was still being renovated. It has always remained a family house. After his death in 1837 his sister Augusta moved in and after her death in 1840 it became the home of her sister-in-law, Victoria, the queen mother who stayed here until her death in 1861. It passed to her grandson, Prince Alfred, duke of Edinburgh, whose official residence it was from 1866 to his death in 1900. It passed to his brother, Arthur, duke of Connaught, who lived here till 1942 when he died, aged ninety-one. After the war the young Princess ELIZABETH lived here for three years (1947–50), and Princess Anne was born here (1950). It has been the official London residence of Queen Elizabeth, the queen mother, since 1953.

Cleveland House (St James's) Built in the 1620s this house once stood in Cleveland Row near St James's Palace. In 1666 it was briefly the home of Edward Hyde, earl of Clarendon, and father of JAMES II's wife, Anne. In 1668 it was acquired by CHARLES II for his mistress, Barbara Villiers, whom he created duchess of Cleveland in 1670, which is how the house acquired its name. She sold it after Charles's death to the earl of Bridgewater. The house was subsequently rebuilt (1790s) and then demolished (1841), and Bridgewater House was built on the site.

Drury Lane (WC2) A once fashionable residential area in the 17th C; residents included Oliver Cromwell (1646), Elizabeth, the former queen of Bohemia and daughter of JAMES I (1660–62), and CHARLES II's famous mistress, Nell Gwynne (1667). She was closely associated with the Drury Lane Theatre which had been built in 1663, but which burned down in 1672. It was rebuilt by Wren two years later. It was greatly patronised by CHARLES II and by many succeeding monarchs; and it was here that the future WILLIAM IV first saw Mrs Jordan (1790), who became his mistress and bore him ten children. It was also here that an assassination attempt was made on the future GEORGE II (1716) and again on GEORGE III (1800). The theatre burned down in 1809. The present theatre was built and opened in 1812.

Durham House (The Strand) A 13th C house built as the London residence of the bishops of Durham. When they were not in residence it was used by a variety of royal personages. Simon de Montfort stayed here in 1258 at the time of his growing opposition to his brother-in-law, HENRY III. Here the young Katherine of Aragon stayed before her marriage to Prince Arthur (1502), and Anne Boleyn stayed as she superseded Katherine of Aragon in HENRY VIII's eyes (1529). It was briefly the home of John Dudley, duke of Northumberland, and was thus the site of the marriage between his son Guilford Dudley and Lady Jane Grey (1553). Thereafter it became the residence of several court favourites, most notably Sir Walter Ralegh who lived here from 1583–1603, until ousted by JAMES I. The house was demolished in 1660 but Durham House Street, behind the Strand, betrays its former location.

Ely Place (Holborn) The London home of the bishops of Ely from 1290. Although the house was demolished in 1772, the neighbouring St Etheldreda's Church remains. It was an occasional residence of royalty, most notably EDWARD III's son John of Gaunt, who lived here from 1381–99. His mother, Philippa of Hainault, had stayed here in the weeks before her marriage to Edward III (1327/8).

Greyfriars Church and **Friary** (Newgate) This Franciscan friary was built in 1225 on land north of St Paul's by the city wall, south of St Bartholomew's Hospital. It received royal patronage and a significant gesture was made in 1291 when the heart of Eleanor of Provence, widow of HENRY III, was buried here. Margaret of France, the second wife of EDWARD I, sponsored the rebuilding of the church, which was of spectacular grandeur, second only to St Paul's. She was buried here in 1318 before the work was complete. Also buried here were Isabella, widow of EDWARD II (1358), and her daughter Joan, wife of DAVID II of Scotland (1362). The monastery was dissolved in 1538 and the church, by then renamed Christ Church, was destroyed in the Great Fire (1666). It was rebuilt by Wren but was destroyed again in the Blitz. The Royal Mail Postal Museum is now on the site.

Hampton Court Palace see Hampton Court

Kensington Palace (*Kensington*) Built in 1605, it acquired the name Nottingham House when later purchased by the earl of Nottingham. WILLIAM III and MARY II acquired it in 1689, preferring it to Hampton Court, and undertook several renovations. Both Mary (1694) and William (1702) died here. ANNE did little to the house but embellished the grounds, including the addition of an Orangery (1704). Her husband, George of Denmark, died here (1708), followed by Anne herself (1714). GEORGE I loved the house because it reminded him of his palace in Hanover, and he undertook many improvements. GEORGE II and Queen Caroline also used it as their main residence. They spent more money on the garden than the house. George died rather ignominiously of a heart attack on the toilet. GEORGE III preferred Buckingham House and Kensington Palace, as it had now become known, became delapidated until occupied in 1798 by Victoria's father Edward, duke of Kent, when extensive refurbishments were carried out, allowing for conversion into apartments for various members of the royal family. Edward soon moved out however and his brother, Augustus, duke of Sussex, took over (1806) and remained here till his death (1843). In the meantime the duke of Kent returned in 1819 and the young Princess VICTORIA was born at Kensington Palace on 24 May 1819. Victoria spent most of her childhood at Kensington Palace, and it was here that she learned of her accession to the throne in 1837. She moved out to Buckingham Palace and the duke and duchess of Teck moved in. Their daughter, Mary, the future wife of GEORGE V, was born here (1867). From 1880 it also became the residence of Princess Louise, later duchess of Argyll, who was a gifted artist and sculptor. Her apartments became a centre for artists and her own sculpture of the seated figure of Queen Victoria is outside the Palace. She died here in 1939, aged 91. More recently the palace was the home of several members of the royal family, none more memorable than Diana, princess of Wales, upon whose death (1997) the palace became a scene of national mourning.

Lambeth The archbishop of Canterbury's official London residence is Lambeth Palace. The original manor house was acquired by the see of Canterbury in 1190. Before that it had been owned by the Convent of St Andrew, Rochester, and it may have been in their ownership when HARTHACANUTE died here of convulsions at a wedding feast in 1042. The palace was overrun during the Peasants' Revolt in 1381. It is also likely that Katherine Howard, HENRY VIII's fifth wife, was born in Lambeth at the London residence of Lord Edmund Howard c1525.

Leicester House (*Leicester Square*) Built in the 1630s by the earl of Leicester. In 1662 Elizabeth, the former queen of Bohemia, died here of bronchitis, having moved in but five days earlier. In 1717 it became the home of the future GEORGE II, who had been thrown out of St James's Palace. Here Prince George and his wife Caroline established an alternative court for all those who disagreed with George I's actions. It became known as the Leicester House Set. In 1742 George II's son Frederick, prince of Wales, rented Leicester House. His last five children were born here between 1743 and 1751 and the future GEORGE III spent his childhood here. Frederick died here (1751) of a ruptured aneurysm, believed to have been caused by a blow from a cricket ball some months earlier. The last member of the royal family to live here was George III's younger brother Henry, duke of Cumberland, who moved out in 1767. The house was sold in 1792 and demolished. The Prince Charles Theatre and Lisle Street are on the site.

Marlborough House (*Pall Mall*) Built in 1711 for the duchess of Marlborough, who died here in 1744. The house stayed in the Marlborough family until 1817. It was then lived in by Leopold of Saxe-Coburg, the widowed husband of Princess Charlotte, who remained here until he became the king of the Belgians in 1831. From 1837 to 1849 it was the London home of the queen dowager Adelaide, widow of WILLIAM IV, though she spent many months each year away from the house because of her ill health. When Victoria's son, Edward, prince of Wales, married in 1863, he and Princess Alexandra moved into Marlborough House, and it remained their London residence until he succeeded to the throne as EDWARD VII in 1901. Their son, the future GEORGE V, was born here in 1865, and he lived here as prince of Wales from 1903–10. The widowed Queen Alexandra returned here after Edward's death in 1910 and she stayed here occasionally until her death in 1925, though she spent most of her time at Sandringham. On the death of GEORGE V (1936), his widow, Queen Mary, moved to Marlborough House and died here in 1953. The house is now the location of the Commonwealth Centre and Foundation.

Norfolk House (*St James's Square*) First built in the 1670s, it acquired its name when purchased by the duke of Norfolk in 1722, in whose family it remained until 1938. It was rented by Frederick, prince of Wales, in 1737, after he had been thrown out of St James's Palace. The future GEORGE III, was born here the next year. The house was demolished in 1748 and another built on the site.

St Clement Danes (*Strand*) At least one ancient source suggests that HAROLD I was buried here (*c*1043) or possibly at St Olave's Church in Southwark.

St James's Palace Built on the site of the former 11th C St James's Hospital for HENRY VIII (1531). MARY I died here (1558), a sad and embittered lady. Both ELIZABETH I and JAMES I held court here and James's son Henry, the heir to the throne, died here, probably of typhoid (1612), forbidden to see his family for fear of contagion. His brother, CHARLES I, lived here and also spent his last night here before his execution (1649). Both CHARLES II and JAMES II were born here (1630 and 1633). The young Prince James, duke of York, was held captive here after the Civil War (1646–8). Charles II made it his principal London residence after the Restoration (1660). James's first wife, Anne Hyde, died here (1671). Most of his children were born here, including the future queens MARY II (1662) and ANNE (1665) and his last child, JAMES "The Old Pretender" (1688). There was much suspicion at the time that he was a changeling smuggled into the bed chamber in a warming pan. Mary married the future WILLIAM III here (1677) and Anne married her consort, Prince George of Denmark (1683). The palace must have been the scene of many stormy arguments between the fathers and sons of the Hanoverian regime since none of them seemed compatible. In 1717 the future GEORGE II was thrown out of the palace by his father because of an argument over the choice of godparents for the son's new-born baby. They went to live in Leicester House. Ten years later George returned to St James's as the new king and, ironically, ten years further on, in 1737, he expelled his son, Frederick, prince of Wales. Frederick's son, GEORGE III, married Charlotte of Mecklenburg here (1761) and his first two children were born here, the future GEORGE IV (1762) and Frederick, duke of York (1763). Soon after George III and Queen Charlotte moved into Buckingham House and the palace was less frequently used. George IV was married here (1795), much against his wishes, and apparently spent his wedding night drunk in the fireplace. The palace was badly damaged by fire in 1809 and, after it was restored (1814), it was used more for official functions and visiting dignitaries rather than as a royal residence. VICTORIA and Albert were married here (1840), as were their daughter Victoria and Frederick of Prussia (1858) and the future GEORGE V and Mary of Teck (1893). The palace is still used by the Lord Chamberlain's department and continues to serve as the official location of the Court of St James, the official name of the royal court of Britain, which became established in the 18th C.

St Martin-in-the-Fields (*Trafalgar Square*) One of the better known London churches established in the 12th C, rebuilt in the 1540s and 1720s. It became noted for its royal associations in the 16th and 17th C. MARY I occasionally worshipped here; CHARLES II was christened here (1630) and Nell Gwynne was buried here (1687).

St Mary Overie (*Southwark*) The parish church of St Saviour, Southwark and originally the church of Southwark Cathedral, it was first built in the 7th C and rebuilt twice before the current church (1220). The name means "St Mary over the water". Here JAMES I of Scotland married Joan Beaufort (1424).

St Mary's Hospital (*Paddington*) Construction began in 1845 when Prince Albert laid the foundation stone. It was here, in 1928, that Alexander Fleming discovered penicillin. Its main royal connection is with the births of Prince William (1982) and Prince Henry (1984), children of Prince Charles and Princess Diana.

St Paul's Cathedral Founded in 604 by ATHELBERT of Kent, it subsequently came under the jurisdiction of the kings of Essex. Both SAEBERT and SEBBI were buried here (616 and 673). It suffered much from fire and the Danes, but in the 11th C superseded Kingston as the place of anointment and coronation of the new monarch. EDMUND II (1016) and CANUTE (1017) were each crowned here. Amongst the royal burials are Edward Atheling, the son of Edmund II (1057), Blanche of Lancaster, mother of HENRY IV (1369), and John of Gaunt (1399). The body of RICHARD II lay in state here (1400). HENRY VI chose it for the spectacle of his second coronation when he was briefly restored to the throne in 1470; within a few months his body was displayed at St Paul's, so that all would know he was dead (1471). Prince Arthur, son of HENRY VII, married Katherine of Aragon here (1501). In 1666 Old St Paul's, which had been built after the previous one was destroyed by fire in 1087, was itself destroyed in the Great Fire. The new Cathedral was started in 1675 and not finished until 1710. There were no further royal coronations or burials in the Cathedral, though here were occasional ceremonies, most notably the marriage of Prince Charles and Lady Diana Spencer (1981), the first royal wedding in the Cathedral for 480 years.

St Peter upon Cornhill (*Cornhill*) The church traditionally founded by LUCIUS in 179.

Smithfield (*Holborn*) The name now so closely associated with the meat market was once "Smoothfield", a flat open space beyond the city walls that was often used for tournaments and gatherings and became a famous horse market. A grand tournament was held here in 1357 in the presence of both EDWARD III of England and Jean II of France; another one was held here in 1384 in

honour of Edward's mistress, Alice Perrers.
Perhaps the most notorious event associated with
Smithfield was the climax of the Peasants' Revolt
(1381) where Wat Tyler met RICHARD II. It was
also the site of public hanging until 1388 when
this was shifted to Tyburn, though executions by
burning or roasting continued at Smithfield until
the 17th C, with many persecutions during the
reign of MARY I.

Somerset House (*Strand*) Known for many years
as the central deposit for certificates of
registration of births, deaths and marriages, and
more recently of wills, it was originally a palace,
built in 1550 for the Lord Protector, Edward
Seymour, brother of Jane Seymour. After his
execution in 1552, the house passed into royal
possession and was for a while used by Princess
ELIZABETH. It was here that Elizabeth was arrested
and detained at the Tower of London (1554) on
grounds of involvement in anti-Catholic
rebellion against her sister. On her accession,
Elizabeth occasionally stayed here, but it next
became an official royal residence in 1603 when it
was granted to JAMES I's wife, Anne of Denmark,
and it became renamed Denmark House. After
her death it was next given to Henrietta Maria,
wife of CHARLES I (1625–45; and again 1660–65),
and then CHARLES II's wife Katherine of Braganza
(1665–93). Thereafter no other members of
royalty lived here and it later became the home of
the Royal Academy (1771) and the Royal Society
(1780).

Tower of London Built on the site of the White
Mount by WILLIAM I soon after 1066, with a more
substantial keep following in 1078 which is still
known as the White Tower, a point reinforced
when it was whitewashed in 1240. Originally a
fortress, it was soon used as both a prison and a
royal residence. STEPHEN was the first king to live
here (1140). Further building works were carried
out during the reigns of HENRY II and JOHN to
form much of the castle as we know it today. John
used it as his main stronghold. He besieged it in
1191 in order to overthrow William Longchamp,
whom RICHARD I had installed as chancellor of
England, and John was himself besieged here in
1215 after he refused to accept the terms of the
Magna Carta. HENRY III added further buildings
including the first menagerie (1235). Henry
became virtually his own prisoner in the Tower
during the civil war of 1265. JOHN BALLIOL of
Scotland was imprisoned here (1296–9). JOAN,
daughter of EDWARD II and wife of DAVID II, was
born here (1321). David became a prisoner in the
Tower in 1346, but was soon moved out to make
way for the many French prisoners being shipped
back during EDWARD III's French wars. Although
it remained a royal residence, it was during these
years that its reputation as a prison grew.
RICHARD II was held here (1399), as were JAMES I
of Scotland (1406–8) and HENRY VI (1465–70);
the latter was murdered here (1471). Edward IV's

brother, George, duke of Clarence, died
mysteriously in the Tower (1478), allegedly
drowning in a butt of malmsey wine. The most
famous mystery associated with the Tower is the
disappearance (1483) of the Princes, EDWARD V
and his brother Richard, duke of York, believed
murdered by order of RICHARD III. Thereafter the
Garden Tower, in which they had been held,
became known as the Bloody Tower. Upon his
succession HENRY VII was so nervous about his
vulnerability that he was quick to imprison any
rivals in the Tower. Edward, earl of Warwick, was
held here (1485–99) as was Perkin WARBECK
(1497–99). Henry's wife Elizabeth of York died in
the Tower soon after giving birth to her eighth
child (1503). The 16th C was perhaps the Tower's
most notorious century. It saw the executions of
Anne Boleyn (1536), Katherine Howard (1542),
Lady JANE Grey and her husband Guilford
Dudley (1554), all of whom were buried in the
Chapel of St Peter ad Vincula within the Tower
precincts. It also saw the execution of many non-
royals, most notably Thomas More (1535), John
Fisher (1535), Thomas Cromwell (1540) and
Edward Seymour (1552). Princess Elizabeth was
imprisoned here from March to May 1554,
doubtless in fear of her life. JAMES I was the last
monarch to live at the Tower, though the
tradition of the coronation procession leaving
from the Tower to Westminster, which had
started with HENRY III in 1236, concluded with
that of CHARLES II (1661). At that time a new
collection of crown jewels was made, which
remain on display at the Tower, despite an early
attempt, by Thomas Blood, to steal them (1671).
James, duke of Monmouth, was executed on
Tower Hill (1685). The last man to be executed
here was Lord Lovat (1747), a Jacobite supporter,
although eleven spies were shot outside the
Martin Tower during the First World War.

Tyburn (*Marylebone*) The principal place of
hanging in London until 1783. The gallows stood
near the site of the present Marble Arch where
Tyburn Way runs. Roger Mortimer, who had
been responsible for the death of EDWARD II, was
the first to be executed here (1330) and others
with royal associations included the pretender
Perkin WARBECK (1499) and Elizabeth Barton
(1534), "the Maid of Kent", who denounced
HENRY VIII's marriage to Anne Boleyn. After the
Restoration (1660), several bodies were exhumed
and gibbeted at Tyburn before being buried at the
foot of the gallows, including that of Oliver
Cromwell.

Westminster Abbey A church was first
purportedly built on Thorney Island in the
Thames by SAEBERT of the East Saxons in the
early 7th C and later a Benedictine monastery was
established here, before EDWARD THE CONFESSOR
constructed his abbey (as well as the Palace of
Westminster) on this site. It was consecrated on
28 December 1065, just eight days before the

death of Edward, who became the first monarch to be buried here – his widow Edith followed in 1075. On the same day as Edward's funeral, HAROLD II became the first monarch to be crowned here. Thereafter all coronations of reigning monarchs have taken place at the abbey and, with few exceptions, also of their consorts. A full list is given on p. xxx, together with notable incidents. The coronation chair was made for EDWARD I to incorporate the Stone of Scone, which was brought to the Abbey in 1297. The first royal wedding at the abbey was that of HENRY I and Matilda (1100); Matilda was buried at the abbey in 1118. Much of the abbey was rebuilt during the reign of HENRY III (1245), who also added the Lady Chapel (1220). Henry III's Great Council met in the chapter house in 1257, which was later used for the meetings of the Commons until 1547. Henry III was the first monarch since the Conquest to be buried at the abbey (1272) and, though it became the principal site for the burial of the monarch, consort and children for the next five hundred years, this was not always straightforward. The kings and queens buried here are EDWARD I (1307) and his wife Eleanor of Castile (1290); EDWARD III (1377) and Philippa of Hainault (1369); RICHARD II, whose remains were brought here in 1413 to lie beside his wife Anne (1394); (HENRY IV died in the abbey after a fit while praying (1413), but he was buried at Canterbury); HENRY V (1422) and his widow Katherine (1437); the alleged remains of EDWARD V, who had been born within the sanctuary of Westminster Abbey in 1470, and of his brother Richard, which had been removed from the Tower of London (1674); Anne, wife of RICHARD III (1485). HENRY VII (1509) and Elizabeth of York (1507) were buried in the new chapel created by the king (1503), which became the place for all future royal burials – EDWARD VI (1553); Anne of Cleves (1557); MARY I (1558); ELIZABETH I (1603); MARY QUEEN OF SCOTS whose remains were brought here (1612); JAMES I (1625) and Anne of Denmark (1619); James II's wife Anne Hyde (1671); CHARLES II (1685); MARY II (1694) and WILLIAM III (1702); ANNE (1714) and George of Denmark (1708); GEORGE II (1760) and Caroline (1737). Apart from Henry I, the only reigning monarchs to be married in the abbey were Richard III with Anne Neville (1472), and Henry VII and Elizabeth of York (1486). However the future ELIZABETH II married Philip Mountbatten (1947) at the abbey, and it also saw the weddings of Princess Margaret and Lord Snowdon (1960), Princess Anne and Mark Phillips (1973) and Prince Andrew and Sarah Ferguson (1986).

Westminster, Palace of The original palace was built for EDWARD THE CONFESSOR and only just completed at the time of his death (1066). The palace was taken over by WILLIAM THE CONQUEROR and became the principal royal residence till the time of HENRY VIII. It was also

the centre of the court of England where the king's council met and where EDWARD I summoned his "Model" Parliament in 1295. Edward I was the only king to be born in the Palace (1239), though HENRY VI's heir, Edward, prince of Wales, was (1453) as was HENRY VIII's sister Margaret Tudor (1489), who became the wife of JAMES IV of Scotland. HENRY III died here (1272), as did Edward, the Black Prince (1376), EDWARD IV (1483) and Richard III's wife Anne Neville (1485). The only reigning monarch to be married within the palace was RICHARD II, who married Anne of Bohemia in St Stephen's Chapel (1382); however several wedding banquets were held in the adjoining Westminster Hall. St Stephen's Chapel became, after 1547, the meeting place for the House of Commons. Both Prince Arthur and his brother, the future Henry VIII, were invested at Westminster as prince of Wales (1490 and 1504). Although Henry attended Parliament at Westminster and frequently used the palace for celebrations and pageants, he did not use it as his primary residence, preferring Richmond, Greenwich and later Hampton Court. The royal apartments were damaged by a fire in 1512 and the palace was thereafter given over fully to Parliament. It was here in 1605 that the Gunpowder Plot to kill JAMES I was uncovered. It was also here in 1642 that CHARLES I entered St Stephen's Chapel to search for his enemies. He and his successors have been banned thenceforth from entering the chamber of the House of Commons. The trial of Charles I took place at Westminster Hall (1649). The Old Palace was destroyed by fire in 1834 and a new Palace of Westminster was completed by 1851, although the Victoria Tower, containing Big Ben, was not finished until 1860.

Whitehall Originally called York Place, because it had been the London residence of the archbishop of York since 1245, it was taken over by HENRY VIII after the fall from grace of Thomas Wolsey in 1530. Henry had extensive rebuilding works undertaken, making it, at 23 acres, the largest royal palace in Europe. It was renamed Whitehall. Henry secretly married Anne Boleyn here (1533) and more openly married Jane Seymour (1536). It was at Whitehall that Princesses Elizabeth and Mary were reunited under their caring stepmother Katherine Parr. Henry VIII died here (1547). It was the home of EDWARD VI but rather less of a home to MARY I or ELIZABETH I. JAMES I had grand plans for extending Whitehall, but only the Banqueting House was completed (1622). CHARLES I established a huge art collection at Whitehall. It was also here, outside the Banqueting House, that he was executed (1649). After the Commonwealth, during which Cromwell lived at Whitehall, CHARLES II instilled some gaiety, living openly with two of his mistresses at Whitehall. JAMES II was the last monarch to live here. After his flight from

England (1688), the crown was offered to
WILLIAM III, who preferred to live at Kensington
Palace where the air was purer for his asthma.
The old palace was damaged by fire in 1691 and
destroyed by fire in 1698.

Loudon Hill (*East Ayrshire*) 12 m E of
Kilmarnock, this was a rocky promontary where
ROBERT THE BRUCE defeated the earl of Pembroke
(1307), his first major victory.

Ludlow (*Shropshire*) Long a Saxon stronghold, a
Norman castle at Ludlow was built around 1085
for the earl of Shrewsbury. The castle supported
MATILDA during the civil war and it was besieged
by STEPHEN in 1139. Richard of York held Ludlow
at the outbreak of the Wars of the Roses (1457)
and it became the residence of his son, the future
EDWARD IV. His son, EDWARD V, lived at Ludlow
as prince of Wales, and was there when he learned
of his father's death and that he was now king
(1483). It was on his journey to London that he
was intercepted by his uncle, Richard of
Gloucester. The castle was later granted by Henry
VII to his son Arthur, prince of Wales, on his
wedding to Katherine of Aragon (1501), but
Arthur died here a few months later. MARY I spent
some of her youth here (1525–7), when she was
in her father's favour.

Lumphanan (*Aberdeenshire*) *see* Dunsinane

Lydford (*Devon*) An important Saxon town, well
fortified against the Danes and on the frontier of
the newly conquered kingdom of Dumnonia. It
even had its own mint. The earldorman of Devon
had his headquarters here and his daughter,
Elfrida, became the second wife of King EDGAR
(964), and the first women to be crowned queen
of the English (973) at Bath.

Lyme Regis (*Dorset*) The small but busy village
and port was granted the title *Regis* by EDWARD I
in 1285. Yet it was not an especially royal town. In
1644 it was held for Parliament and withstood a
two-month Royalist siege. In 1685 it welcomed
James, duke of Monmouth when his invasion
force landed here.

Machynlleth (*Powys*) The present Owen
Glendower Centre is believed to be on the site of
the fortress where OWAIN GLYN DWR held his first
Parliament in 1404.

Maes Camlan *see* Camlann

Maiden Stone *see* Pitcaple

Malmesbury (*Wiltshire*) The present Church of
St Mary is all that remains of the former
Malmesbury Abbey, established in 676 during the
reign of CAEDWALLA. Here ATHELSTAN was buried
(939) and a 15th C tomb to him remains. It was
also where EDMUND II married Edith (1015).

Man, Isle of The island has, over the centuries,
been under the possession of the British rulers of
Rheged, the Irish, the Scots, and the English. It is
closely linked with the early deity who may have
also been a real person, MANANNAN. At some
stage in the fifth century Man came under the
control of Rheged. Legend ascribes its rulership
to the descendents of LLYWARCH HEN. Whether
these were all rulers of Man, or represented a
mainland dynasty, is not clear. Man was
conquered by Báetán mac Cairill of Ireland in
577. The Irish were conquered in turn by AEDAN
MAC GABHRAN of Dál Riada in 582, and it may
have remained under Scottish domination until
conquered by EDWIN of Northumbria in 620. The
last independent ruler was GWRIAD, whose son,
MERFYN FRYCH, became king of Gwynedd and
Man in 825. Merfyn and his son RHODRI probably
ruled Man as part of the kingdom of Gwynedd,
but how long it remained in their possession is
not known. By the 850s the Western Isles became
subject to attacks by Vikings and a kingdom was
carved out by KETIL FLATNOSE. Thereafter Man
and the Western Isles was disputed between the
Norwegian kings of Dublin and the Danish kings
of York, until RAGNALL established his authority
across the North. SIGURD THE STOUT of Orkney
imposed his authority on the Western Isles from
989–1014, but it was regained by the kings of
Dublin under SITRIC OLAFSON from 1014–35.
THORFINN THE MIGHTY of Orkney in partnership
with RAGNALD II, reconquered the Isles around
1038 and demanded tribute from Man. Man
continued to be subject to Orkney until soon
after 1065, and a separate kingdom emerged
under GODRED CROVAN in 1079. In 1156
SOMERLED established the separate lordship of the
Isles, and he ruled the full kingdom of Man and
the Isles from 1158–64. Thereafter Man included
the Outer Hebrides under its jurisdiction until
1266, when the islands were granted to Scotland
under ALEXANDER III. In 1290 EDWARD I took
possession of the island for England placing it
under the governorship of Richard de Burgh, earl
of Ulster. JOHN BALLIOL reclaimed the island for
Scotland from 1293–6, otherwise it remained
under English control. During this period the
most stable period of governorship was under
Antony Bek, bishop of Durham, from 1298 to
1311. In 1313, ROBERT BRUCE again claimed Man
for Scotland. In 1316 the Irish ravaged the island
and it remained a battlefield plundered and
claimed by Ireland, Scotland and England until
the powerful reign of Edward III. In 1333 Edward
granted the island to William de MONTACUTE in
full possession. The kingship passed from the
Montacutes to Scrope to Percy, and then in 1405
settled on the powerful STANLEY family who ruled
Man until 1736, though they resigned the title of
king in 1504 and became lords of Man. It passed
finally to the MURRAY family and reverted to the
British crown in 1765.

Mancetter (*Warwickshire*) East of Tamworth near Atherstone, this is generally agreed to be the location where BOUDICA was defeated by the Romans under Suetonius (AD 61).

Mans, Le *see* Le Mans

Market Bosworth *see* Bosworth

Market Weighton (*Humberside*) The site of a royal villa, probably at nearby Goodmanham. It was here that EDWIN of Northumbria was born (*c*585); following Edwin's conversion to Christianity, the pagan temple was destroyed (627); and where OSWULF of Northumbria was murdered by his family (759).

Marlborough (*Wiltshire*) A Norman castle was established by the 12th C and HENRY I held his court here in 1110. JOHN married Isabella of Gloucester (1189); and Margaret of France, EDWARD I's second wife, died here in 1318. The present Marlborough College stands on the site of the castle.

Marston Moor (*North Yorkshire*) West of York, this marked the turning point in the Civil War with the victory of Cromwell's forces over those of CHARLES I (2 July 1644).

Martin (*Hampshire, formerly Wiltshire*) The likeliest but unconfirmed location of the Saxon royal villa of Meredune. It was here in 786 that CYNEWULF died in a revenge killing while visiting his mistress. It is likely to be the same place where the Danes defeated ATHELRED I and Prince ALFRED in 871, as a consequence of which Athelred died of his wounds and Alfred became king.

Maserfield (*Shropshire*) *see* Oswestry

Mathern (*Monmouthshire*) The traditional burial site of TEWDRIG (584).

Meifod (*Powys*) Now a small village north-west of Welshpool but once the ecclesiastical centre of Powys. It had almost certainly been a significant religious site from pre-Roman times, but in the early 7th C Tysilio, the son of BROCHFAEL OF THE TUSKS established a major church here which became the equivalent of the cathedral city of Powys and the burial place of its kings. It is not clear whether Brochfael himself was buried here but it is likely that all subsequent kings of Powys were, at least to the time of CYNGEN when Powys was overrun by Gwynedd (855). When Powys re-emerged as a separate kingdom, several of its later kings were also buried here including MADOG AP MAREDUDD (1160) and GRUFFYDD MAELOR (1191).

Melrose (*Scottish Borders*) The abbey was established in 1136 by DAVID I on the site of a former monastery founded by St Aedán (*c*640) when Melrose was in the English kingdom of Bernicia. ALEXANDER II was buried here (1249), but the site became symbolic of the Scottish nation when ROBERT BRUCE, who had restored the abbey in 1326, bequeathed his heart to it. When Robert died (1329) before he was able to embark on a Crusade, his heart was taken to Spain by William ST. CLAIR and Sir James Douglas, who threw Bruce's heart into the thick of the battle and charged after it. Douglas was killed but Bruce's heart was returned to Scotland and buried at Melrose by Sir William Keith (1331). Melrose was sacked by RICHARD II (1385) and was rebuilt, but when sacked again by Edward Seymour (1547), it sank into ruin.

Meredune, Meretune or Merton *see* Martin

Methven (*Perth and Kinross*) ROBERT I was defeated here (1306) by the earl of Pembroke. He forfeited the lands and later conferred them on his High Steward, Walter, whose son became ROBERT II. Methven Castle subsequently became a dower house for the Scottish queens Mary of Gueldres and Margaret of Denmark. In 1528 Margaret Tudor, sister of HENRY VIII and widow of JAMES IV, married Henry Stewart who was created Lord Methven. She died at Methven Castle (1541).

Middleham Castle (*North Yorkshire*) A 12th C castle which was acquired by the Neville family in the next century. In 1449 it passed to Richard Neville, earl of Warwick, possibly the richest noble in England at the time, who would become known as "the King-Maker". He embellished Middleham until it became known as the Windsor of the North. When EDWARD IV became king (1461), he sent his nine-year old brother Richard, duke of Gloucester (later RICHARD III), to Middleham to be educated. Later when Edward's fortunes waned, he was captured by Warwick and held prisoner at Middleham (1470), but his fortunes revived and he was restored to the throne after Warwick's death at Barnet (1471). Richard of Gloucester married Warwick's daughter, Anne (1472) and received Middleham Castle, from which he ruled the North on his brother's behalf. His son Edward, prince of Wales, was born (1473) and died here (1484). The castle was dismantled in 1646 but the ruins are still impressive.

Milltown (*Stirling*) *see* Sauchieburn

Minstead (*Hampshire*) *see* New Forest

Minster-in-Sheppey (*Kent*) The monastery was founded around 660 by Seaxburh, the daughter of ANNA of the East Angles and wife of EORCENBERT of Kent. She retired here as abbess in 664 but by all accounts remained a powerful force in Kent during a period of turbulence, providing sanctuary to the future kings EADRIC and WIHTRED who lived here as children. Seaxburh was succeeded as abbess in 679 by her daughter, Eormenhild, widow of WULFHERE of Mercia.

Minster-in-Thanet (*Kent*) A nunnery was founded here *c*670 by EGBERT I of Kent in reparation for the murder of his young cousins, whose sister Eafa, wife of MEREWALH, became the first abbess (673) and was succeeded by her daughter Mildrith and then by Eadburh (732–51), who established Minster as a major seat of learning. It is likely some of the royal princes were educated here.

Moncreiffe Hill (*Perth and Kinross*) The site of a Pictish fortress, probably of royal significance, as it was here that NECHTAN III defeated ALPIN.

Mondynes (*Aberdeenshire*) A village between Laurencekirk and Stonehaven which is believed to be the site of the battle of Monthecin in 1094, when DUNCAN II was killed by DONALD III.

Monmouth (*Monmouthshire*) Although Monmouth was a Roman town (Blestium), it was not an important town in the Welsh kingdom of Gwent. It came into its own with the building of the castle (1086), from where Gwent was subdued by the Normans. Geoffrey of Monmouth was probably a monk at the Benedictine priory in his youth (early 12th C) from where he may have gained some information for his later creation of the story of ARTHUR. But Monmouth's most famous royal son was HENRY V, who was born at the castle (1387).

Montacute Abbey (*Somerset*) An abbey existed near the site of the present Montacute House since before the Conquest. It was here that EDMUND, king of southern Scotland, was exiled as a monk (1097) and where he probably died and was buried.

Monthecin *see* Mondynes

Monzievaird (*Perth and Kinross*) Near the present site of Monzie Castle was where MALCOLM II defeated and killed KENNETH III and GIRIC II (1005).

Morven (*Highland*) *see* Braemore

Mugdock (*Stirling*) North of Glasgow, this was the site of the battle of Mygedawg (750) when TEUDEBUR of Strathclyde re-established his kingdom's importance when he defeated Talorgen, brother of ANGUS I of the Picts.

Mygedawg *see* Mugdock

Mynydd Carn (*Ceredigion; formerly Dyfed*) Here a decisive battle was fought in 1081, when GRUFFYDD AP CYNAN and RHYS AP TEWDWR killed CARADOG AP GRUFFYDD and TRAHERN AP CARADOG, allowing Gruffydd to reclaim the kingdom of Gwynedd and Rhys the kingdom of Deheubarth.

Nant Carno (*Powys*) The site of a battle (950) between the heirs of Gwynedd under IAGO AB IDWAL and IEUAF AB IDWAL and the heirs of Deheubarth under OWAIN AP HYWEL, in which the sons of Idwal were victors and restored the freedom of Gwynedd.

Naseby (*Northants*) Between Rugby and Kettering, this was the site of the decisive battle of the Civil War (14 June 1645) where Fairfax's New Model Army soundly defeated the Royalists under Prince Rupert of the Rhine. The victory soon led to CHARLES I's surrender.

Nechtansmere (*Angus*) *see* Dunnichen

Nefyn (*Caernarfonshire and Merionethshire*) The site of one of the former courts of Gwynedd where, in 1284, EDWARD I held his own Arthurian Round Table court in order to demonstrate his sovereignty over Wales. The court was so well attended that the floor fell through.

Neville's Cross *see* Durham

Newark (*Nottinghamshire*) A Saxon town, once owned by Lady Godiva (or Godgifu, wife of earl Leofric of Mercia), a Norman castle was built here around 1125 for the bishops of Lincoln because of their loyalty to STEPHEN. The castle was popular with King JOHN, who frequently stayed here and who died here (1216), some say of poison. JAMES VI of Scotland stopped here on his journey to London (1603) and was so shocked at the state of the prisoners that he released them all. The town remained intensely loyal to CHARLES I during the Civil War. The castle was impregnable and it was only at the command of King Charles that it surrendered, and was destroyed soon after.

Newborough *see* Anglesey

Newbattle Abbey *see* Dalkeith

New Forest (*Hampshire*) The ancient forest which was tamed and cultivated by WILLIAM THE CONQUEROR as a private royal forest for hunting. Bizarrely two of his sons were killed here. Richard, duke of Bernay, was gored to death by a stag (1081), whilst WILLIAM II was killed by accident or design while hunting near the present village of Minstead (1100).

Newmarket (*Suffolk*) A market town famous as the centre of horse-racing and the home of the turf: the first recorded race was in 1619. JAMES I came here to hunt and established a hunting-seat known as the King's House. CHARLES II was held prisoner here (1647). After the Restoration CHARLES II officially founded the race-course (1667). Charles even performed as a jockey at Newmarket in 1675. A fire at the race-course (1683) caused the early departure of Charles, which foiled the planned assassination known as the Rye-House Plot. Nearby is the Devil's Dyke, an earthwork which was probably thrown up as a defence by the East Angles under TYTILA against the Saxons.

Normandy *see* Channel Islands *and* Rouen

Northallerton (*North Yorkshire*) The battle of the Standard was fought at Standard Hill just north of Northallerton in 1138. Here DAVID I was defeated by STEPHEN's army under Archbishop Thurston of York, which curbed a planned Scottish invasion of England but did not stop David plundering northern towns.

Northampton (*Northants*) May have been the birthplace of HAROLD I (*c*1016). Just south of Northampton, at Hardingstone stands one of the three surviving crosses erected in memory of Eleanor of Castile by EDWARD I in 1290 (*see under* Harby). Northampton was the site for the ratification of the Treaty of Northampton (1328), whereby England recognized the independence of Scotland. At the battle of Northampton (1460) the Yorkists captured HENRY VI, thereby clearing the way for EDWARD IV to seize the throne. *See also* Althorp.

Nottingham (*Nottinghamshire*) Occupied by the Danes in 867, Nottingham was right in the thick of the wars between the Danes and the Saxons. EDWARD THE ELDER built further fortifications here in 920. WILLIAM I established his castle here (1068). It was twice destroyed during the civil war under STEPHEN, rebuilt by HENRY II (1154) and presented to JOHN (1174). John was left in command at Nottingham when RICHARD I left for the Crusade; thus the close association between John and Robin Hood. It was at Nottingham castle that Queen Isabella (widow of EDWARD II) and Roger Mortimer established their stronghold and where Mortimer was seized by EDWARD III (1330). JAMES I of Scotland was held prisoner here for a while during his long stay in England (1408). EDWARD IV was trapped here by the rebel army (1469). CHARLES I raised his standard here (1642), signalling the start of the English Civil War.

Oatlands Palace *see* Weybridge

Oban (*Argyll and Bute*) Although the modern town only emerged in the 19th century, the location has considerable history. It was here that Loarn, the brother of FERGUS settled in *c*498 and established a fort at Dunollie which remained the ancestral home of the Lorne family for generations. It was from here that AINBCELLACH and SELBACH made their bids for the kingship of Dál Riata (697). The family feud continued for many years, Selbach defeating Ainbcellach on his attempted resurgence at Findglen near Loch Avich, in the wild hills south of Oban (719). The castle was captured by the Pictish king ANGUS in 734 but remains in the hands of the MacDougalls,

the descendents of SOMERLED who became the lords of Lorne, to this day. Oban is protected from the sea by the Isle of Kerrera, where ALEXANDER II died (1249) while mounting an expedition against EWEN MacDougal of the Isles. Just to the north of Oban is Dunstaffnage Castle which was also a royal stronghold of the rulers of Dál Riata and where tradition states that the Stone of Destiny was held safe during a period of Norse and Pictish onslaught in the 9th C, by being built into the castle walls, before its removal to Scone. Flora Macdonald was held prisoner at Dunstaffnage (1746) for helping Bonnie Prince Charlie escape.

Ockley (*Surrey*) Believed to be the site where, in 851, ATHELWOLF had a resounding victory over the Danes.

Offa's Dyke The name given to a formidable earthwork which runs for 170 miles along the Welsh border from the Dee in the north to Tidenham in the south. It is named after OFFA, the king of Mercia who doubtless decreed its construction, though it was an extension of an earlier such ditch called Watt's Dyke. It was constructed in the 780s.

Olney (*Buckinghamshire*) This is where the treaty was signed between EDMUND II and CANUTE which divided England between them (1016).

Orkneys These islands would once have been part of the Pictish domain, though little is known about their early inhabitants despite the richness of their ancient remains. They were probably a sea-roving people because AEDAN MAC GABHRAN of Dál Riata fought against them in 580, presumably in response to raids on his own territory. The Pictish king BRUDE (III) also waged war against them (683). The islands were conquered by the Vikings under RAGNALD (*c*874) and became a separate earldom, subject to the kings of Norway but virtually autonomous. They remained under Norwegian sovereignty until 1469, although the earls of Orkney had been Scottish since 1379. *See also* Birsay, Egilsay *and* Kirkwall.

Osborne House (*Isle of Wight*) *see* Cowes

Oswestry (*Shropshire*) The name traditionally derives from "Oswald's tree", referring to OSWALD of Northumbria who was defeated here by PENDA of Mercia at the battle of Maserfield (642) and was crucified on a tree in the pagan manner. It was a year before his family could retrieve the remains. On the border between Wales and England, Oswestry was constantly subject to raids by either side. It was claimed by MADOG AP MAREDDUD of Powys in the 1140s; it was burned down by King JOHN (1215) and again by LLYWELYN THE GREAT (1233) and was ravaged by DAFYDD AP GRUFFYDD (1282). OWAIN GLYN DWR virtually destroyed the town (1400).

Otford (*Kent*) The site of a significant battle (776) where EGBERT II of Kent defeated the Mercians and re-established Kent's independence.

Oxford (*Oxfordshire*) The area around Oxford was briefly a sub-kingdom of Mercia ruled by DIDA (670), but the town really owes its origins to the fortifications by ALFRED THE GREAT against the Danes (879). The town remained part of Mercia and was only ceded to Wessex in 911. A royal villa existed here where ELFWEARD, the son of EDWARD THE ELDER, died (924). It suffered at the hands of the Danes and has often served as an alternative administrative centre to London. CANUTE was elected king here (1016) and summoned a national council (1018); HAROLD I was crowned here (1037) and died here (1040). WILLIAM I seized it as a key centre to his conquest (1068). The Empress MATILDA used it for the centre of her operations (1141–2) during the civil war. HENRY I favoured Oxford. He often stayed here at Beaumont Palace, which is where both RICHARD I and JOHN were born (1157 and 1167). He also maintained his mistress, Rosamund Clifford, here and she lies buried at Godstow Abbey (1176). HENRY III held his "Mad Parliament" here (1258). It was also the Royalist headquarters of CHARLES I during the Civil War (1642–6). The University has fewer royal connections than one might expect, though the future EDWARD VII attended Christ Church (1859–60) and the future EDWARD VIII, Magdalen (1912–14). The original University College was founded in 1249 by authority of HENRY III. Balliol College was founded (1263) by one of the forebears of JOHN BALLIOL; Oriel College was endowed by EDWARD II (1326); Queen's College was founded in 1340 and named in honour of Queen Philippa, wife of EDWARD III; All Souls College was founded (1438) to commemorate HENRY V's victory at Agincourt; Christ Church was founded by Thomas Wolsey (1525) as Cardinal College and re-formed by HENRY VIII (1546); Jesus College was founded by ELIZABETH I (1571) for Welsh scholars. Duke Humphrey, younger brother of HENRY V, donated his library of manuscripts to Oxford and, though most of these were lost during the Reformation, the gift was the basis of the later Bodleian Library.

Paisley (*Renfrewshire*) A monastery was founded here in the 7th C by St Mirren, but the later abbey was established in 1163 by Walter Fitzalan, the forerunner of the Stewarts. It was destroyed by the English in 1307 and not rebuilt until 1450. Walter and his descendants became the High Stewards of Scotland and each was buried at the Abbey. ROBERT BRUCE's daughter Marjorie married Walter, the 6th High Steward. She died

at Paisley after a fall from a horse that brought on the premature birth of her child, the future ROBERT II. Both Robert II's wives are buried here: Elizabeth Mure (1354) and Euphemia Ross (1387), as was his son ROBERT III (1406). JOHN II, the last lord of the Isles, retired to Paisley Abbey where he died (1498).

Paris (*France*) Paris has too many royal connections to catalogue here. Of immediate relevance are the following: HENRY VI was crowned king of France at the Cathedral of Notre Dame (1431), the same cathedral where MARY QUEEN OF SCOTS married the future François II (1558). Henrietta Maria, the wife of CHARLES I was buried at the abbey of St Denis (1669), as was her daughter Henrietta (1670). EDWARD (VIII), the Duke of Windsor, and his wife Wallis lived their latter years in the Bois de Boulogne, where he (1972) and she (1986) died.

Pembroke Castle (*Pembrokeshire*) Founded c1095 it was rebuilt several times before it passed to the first earl of Pembroke, Gilbert de Clare, in 1138. HENRY II stayed here (1172) while travelling to Ireland to assert his authority over Earl Richard (Strongbow). Jasper Tudor was created earl in 1453 and his nephew, Henry Tudor (the future HENRY VII) was born here (1457). The castle stood for the Parliamentarians during the Civil War but, at the last moment, changed to the Royalists and was sacked by Cromwell (1648) and thereafter dismantled.

Pengwern *see* Shrewsbury

Penrith (*Cumbria*) The capital of Cumbria in the 9th and 10th C, ATHELSTAN called a council here at Eamont Bridge (927) for the kings of Scotland and Strathclyde to pay him homage. One of those kings, OWEN CAESARIUS, is believed to be buried in Penrith churchyard in what is popularly known as the Giant's Grave (937). The Castle later came into the possession of the earl of Warwick, Richard Neville the Kingmaker, and, via his daughter, to Richard of Gloucester (later RICHARD III). The building of the present Gloucester Arms hotel (1477) is also believed to have been a residence of the duke. There are some rare stained glass windows in the parish church, apparently depicting the Neville family.

Penzance (*Cornwall*) At Penlee House is the cross of the 9th C king RICATUS.

Pershore Abbey (*Worcestershire*) Founded in 689 by OSWALD of Hwicce. The Abbey Church is dedicated to St Eadburh, the daughter of EDWARD THE ELDER, who died in 960 and whose remains were translated to Pershore upon her canonisation in 972.

Perth (*Perth and Kinross*) A settlement has been here since Roman times, and probably earlier, and it grew in importance during the 9th C after

KENNETH MACALPIN established his capital at Scone. The old town was destroyed in a flood in 1210 and the new town was created a royal burgh by WILLIAM THE LYON that year. It was regarded as the capital of Scotland during most of the 15th C and quite possibly earlier. The Treaty of Perth was signed here in 1266 by ALEXANDER III, whereby Hebrides and Man were ceded to Scotland. The town changed hands between the English and Scots several times between 1291 and 1339. John, earl of Cornwall, died here (1336), purportedly killed by his brother EDWARD III at the altar of the Church of St John. JAMES I was assassinated at Blackfriars (1437) and was buried at the nearby Charterhouse, as was his widow, Joan Beaufort (1445) and JAMES IV's widow, Margaret Tudor (1541), sister of HENRY VIII. In 1582 the young JAMES VI was detained at Ruthven Castle (now called Huntingtower, to the west of Perth) by the earl of Gowrie who made certain demands upon the King. 18 years later the next earl of Gowrie attempted to kidnap the king at Gowrie House, in what has become known as the Gowrie Conspiracy (1600). Perth was known for a while as St Johnstoune after its church. CHARLES I attended service here in 1633, as did CHARLES II (1650) and Bonnie Prince Charlie in 1745.

Peterborough (*Cambridgeshire*) A monastery was founded here, at what was then called Medeshamstede, by PEADA of the Middle Angles (655). Its name was changed in 689 during the reign of ATHELRED of Mercia when the monastery was dedicated to St Peter. It was destroyed by the Danes (870) and not restored until the reign of EDGAR (966). The monastery was destroyed twice more, once by Hereward the Wake (1070) and once by fire (1116). The new church was not completed until 1238. Katherine of Aragon was buried here (1536), though her tomb was destroyed in 1643. MARY QUEEN OF SCOTS was buried here (1587), though she was subsequently reburied at Westminster Abbey (1612). Mary de Bohun, the first wife of HENRY IV, died at Peterborough Castle (1394) in childbirth. Her daughter Philippa survived and went on to become the queen consort of Sweden (1406).

Peterhead (*Aberdeenshire*) This was where James, the Old Pretender, first landed in Scotland (1715).

Pevensey (*East Sussex*) The site of the old Roman fort of Anderida. AELLE purportedly landed here and defeated the British (491), establishing it as his base until 516. It was also where WILLIAM THE CONQUEROR landed (1066). Joan of Navarre, the stepmother of HENRY V, was imprisoned at Pevensey Castle for witchcraft in 1419–22.

Pitcaple (*Aberdeenshire*) West of Inverurie, here stands a 15th C castle owned by the Leslie family. When MARY QUEEN OF SCOTS visited (1562), she

danced under a large tree in the front grounds, and CHARLES II purportedly danced under the same tree in 1650. Just over a mile to the south is the Maiden Stone, near Chapel of Garioch, a very fine Pictish and Christian carved stone. It was believed that King AED WHITEFOOT was buried by this stone (878).

Pontefract (*West Yorkshire*) The castle became the property of the earls of Lancaster. Thomas, the cousin of EDWARD II, was executed and buried here (1322). It was also where RICHARD II was imprisoned and apparently starved to death (1400). Charles, duke of Orleans, was held here for several years after he had been captured at Agincourt (1415). It was a key castle during the Wars of the Roses, when it was in the possession of Richard, duke of York, father of EDWARD IV and RICHARD III, who was raised and buried here (1460). His body was later moved to Fotheringhay. It remained a Royalist stronghold during the Civil War but surrendered in 1648 and was dismantled.

Portchester (*Hampshire*) Set on the coastline within Portsmouth Harbour, this has been the site of fortifications since Roman times. Early in the 12th C HENRY I built a stone keep and an Augustinian priory was established just outside the castle (1133). RICHARD II developed the castle into a palace in the 1390s and it became a popular residence of monarchs visiting Portsmouth. EDWARD III sailed from here for his French campaign (1346) and it was from here that HENRY V left for Agincourt (1415). Both HENRY VII and HENRY VIII stayed here while reviewing the development of the docks at Portsmouth and the establishment of a Royal Navy. It remained a royal palace until 1632. See also Portsmouth.

Port Mary (*Dumfries*) see Dundrennan Abbey

Portskewett (*Gwent*) HAROLD II established a hunting lodge here (1063) in the name of EDWARD (THE CONFESSOR). It was raided in 1065 by CARADOG AP GRUFFYDD.

Portsmouth (*Hampshire*) The *ASC* records that Port landed at Portsmouth in 501 with his two sons and killed a young British nobleman. The Saxon's name is probably an invention derived by working back from Portsmouth, the landing was probably at Portchester, the British nobleman may have been GERAINT of Dumnonia, and the year was more likely 539, but despite these considerations we may safely assume that in the early 6th C a group of Saxons invaded Britain at this point. Robert of Normandy also landed here (1101), when he unsuccessfully campaigned against his brother HENRY I. RICHARD I established the first docks here (1194), and it was plundered and burned by the French (1369). HENRY VII developed the dockyard (1496), from which Portsmouth's growth began. CHARLES II married

Katherine of Braganza at the garrison church of St Thomas Becket (1662).

Powis Castle *see* Welshpool

Pucklechurch (*Gloucestershire*) Near Bristol, this was the site of a Saxon villa, where in 946 EDMUND I was killed while trying to arrest an outlaw.

Queenborough (*Kent*) Originally a small fishing village called Bynnee on the western side of the Isle of Sheppey, it was renamed Queenborough in 1377 after Philippa of Hainault, the queen of EDWARD III, who had built here a new castle – the only new royal castle built in the late Middle Ages. Edward III often stayed here in his later years and his son, John of Gaunt, was constable here. Although the castle was strengthened by HENRY VIII in 1539, it was totally destroyed by the Parliamentary forces in the Civil War and now not one stone remains above ground.

Rathlin Island (*Antrim*) One of the islands between Ireland and Kintyre, it served as a refuge for ROBERT BRUCE (1306). It has been suggested that it was here that Robert saw the spider rebuilding its web and caused Robert to consider "If at first you don't succeed, try, try again." Bruce also took refuge on the island of Sanda, while another Bruce's Cave is at Kirkpatrick Fleming.

Reading (*Berkshire*) An important Saxon site, its royal villa was attacked by the Danes in 870 and used as their winter camp. It was attacked again by Danes in 1006. HENRY I established an abbey here (1121) and he was buried here (1136), though the abbey was not consecrated until 1164 by Thomas Becket in the presence of HENRY II. John of Gaunt married Blanche of Lancaster at the Abbey in 1359. Reading was a regular stop on each king's royal progress. HENRY VIII took a liking to the place and, after the abbey was dissolved in 1539, he built a royal palace which remained in use for less than a hundred years.

Reculver (*Kent*) The site of a Roman fort, still visible, though the forlorn towers of the ruined Norman church are the main landmark. ATHELBERT I moved his palace here around 602, and it is possible, though not probable, he was buried here. A Saxon monastery was built here by grant of EGBERT I (669) on the site of Athelbert's palace. EADBERT I was buried here (762).

Rendlesham (*Suffolk*) North of Woodbridge, this was a royal villa in the 7th C and possibly the court of REDWALD. It was certainly the court of ATHELWOLD of the East Angles, for it was here under his sponsorship that SWITHHELM of the East Saxons was baptized by Cedd (*c*654). The nearby burial site of Sutton Hoo suggests a connection though it is uncertain whether the relics found here relate to Redwald or ANNA.

Renfrew (*Renfrewshire*) Now absorbed into the environs of Glasgow, this was once an ancient Celtic site. It was much patronised by DAVID I who established a small castle here (1130s). It was this that was the subject of attack by SOMERLED in 1164 when he died mysteriously before the battle.

Repton (*Derbyshire*) An important Mercian centre which later became the kingdom's capital. A monastery was founded here under PEADA in about 654 and it was the burial place of MEREWALH of the Magonsæte. Here also were buried the Mercian kings ATHELBALD (757), WIGLAF (839), WIGMUND (840) and WIGSTAN (850). The Vikings captured the site in 874, expelling BURGRED.

Rescobie (*Angus*) *see* Forfar

Restenneth Priory (*Angus*) *see* Forfar

Rhuddlan Castle (*Flintshire*) A motte-and-bailey castle had been established here since the 10th C and it became the principal court of GRUFFYDD AP LLYWELYN in the 1050s. A Norman castle was built in 1073 which was later captured by the Welsh under DAFYDD AB OWAIN (1177). EDWARD I captured Rhuddlan and began work on his castle in 1277. It was from here in 1284 that he issued his Statute of Rhuddlan, bringing Wales under English sovereignty.

Richmond Palace (*Surrey*) This site was originally called Shene, a name that still survives in the neighbouring Sheen. A royal manor house was established about 1125 for HENRY I, though it was used more by members of the court than royalty until EDWARD III developed it into a palace towards the end of his life. He died here (1377). RICHARD II loved the palace and frequently entertained here with his wife Anne of Bohemia. He was so griefstricken when she died of the plague that he could not bear to return to Shene and ordered that the palace be dismantled (1394). HENRY V sought to restore it and HENRY VI frequently held court here. EDWARD IV further embellished the palace and raised his children here, often holding tournaments on the Green. HENRY VII regarded Shene as his favourite palace. All his children were raised here (including the young princes Arthur and Henry – later HENRY VIII) and his daughter Mary, the future queen of France, was born here (1496). The Old Palace was destroyed by fire in 1499 but was rebuilt over the next few years and renamed Richmond Palace, after Henry's earldom in Yorkshire. Henry VII died here (1509). Katherine of Aragon had returned here from Ludlow after Arthur's death and it became her principal home after her marriage to HENRY VIII (1509). It was here she had her first four confinements (1510, 1511, 1513 and 1514). Only one of these children survived for more than a few hours, Prince Henry, who died at Richmond Palace seven weeks later of a chill arising from his christening (1511). In future years Henry visited Richmond less often, preferring Hampton Court and Windsor. Curiously JAMES IV's body was rumoured to have been "stored" at Richmond after it had been recovered from Flodden Field (1513) and he was purportedly buried at Shene Abbey. Henry gave Anne of Cleves Richmond Palace after their divorce (1540). The palace was still used by Henry's growing children. EDWARD VI often entertained here and MARY I spent part of her honeymoon here with Philip of Spain (1554). In the last half of her reign ELIZABETH I spent most summers here, and died here (1603). The Stuart kings were less interested in the palace. JAMES I gave it to his son Henry (1610) and after his death to Charles (1612), the future CHARLES I. Charles gave it to Henrietta Maria on their marriage (1625), but they seldom stayed here. After Charles's execution (1649), the palace was dismantled.

Richmond Park (*Surrey*) Originally the park surrounding Richmond Palace, it was enclosed by CHARLES I in 1637 as private hunting land. GEORGE II had a Palladian villa built in the park in 1729, which became known as the White Lodge. It was a favourite residence of Queen Caroline and her daughter Princess Amelia and was later the home of the duke and duchess of Teck. Their grandson, the future EDWARD VIII, was born here (1894). The future GEORGE VI also lived here for a while after his marriage to Elizabeth Bowes-Lyon (1923). The residential branch of the Royal Ballet School was established here in 1955.

Rochester (*Kent*) An important Roman and Saxon town at the first bridging point on the river Medway. The cathedral was established here in 604 by ATHELBERT of Kent. The town and cathedral were ransacked by ATHELRED of Mercia (676). The Norman castle was built in 1087, of which the stone keep, the highest in England, survives. It was successfully besieged by JOHN during his war with the barons (1215). CHARLES II stayed overnight in Rochester on his way back to London at the restoration of the monarchy (1660) and JAMES II was detained here for a week when he tried to flee the country in 1688.

Rockingham Castle (*Northants*) A royal residence from the time of WILLIAM THE CONQUEROR, popular because of the hunting in the nearby Rockingham Forest. WILLIAM II held council here in 1095 when he banished Archbishop Anselm and was in turn threatened with excommunication. JOHN hunted in the forest frequently. It remained a royal residence until ELIZABETH I granted it to the Watson family, whose descendants still live here.

Romsey Abbey (*Hampshire*) A church was founded here by EDWARD THE ELDER (907); his daughter Ethelfleda later became abbess. King EDGAR had close associations with the abbey since his step-daughter, also called Ethelfleda, was abbess here (*c*990) and his young son, Edmund, was buried here (*c*972). The abbey was rebuilt around 1120, perhaps in memory of HENRY I's wife Edith (Matilda). JOHN sent his daughter Joan (the future wife of ALEXANDER II) here to be educated (*c*1214) and he himself stayed in the area, building a hunting lodge nearby.

Rothesay (*Argyll and Bute*) A castle was built in the 12th C; it was stormed by USPAK, king of the Isles, who died of his wounds (1230). The castle fell again to the Norwegians under Haakon IV (1263) though it was a short-lived victory. The castle passed into royal ownership with ROBERT II (1371) and both he and ROBERT III stayed here often. Some of Robert III's children may well have been born here. His eldest son, DAVID STEWART, was created duke of Rothesay (1398), the first of the Scottish dukedoms and reserved always for the firstborn son of the monarch – the title is still held by Prince Charles. JAMES IV and JAMES V also stayed here regularly, using the castle as a base for their campaigns against the lords of the Isles. They built the great gatehouse tower (*c*1500). The castle suffered during the Civil War and was later burned, but was partly restored during the 19th C.

Rouen (*France*) The capital of the former duchy of Normandy. It was here at the Priory of St Gervais that WILLIAM I died (1087); HENRY I died near Rouen of food poisoning (1135); the heart of RICHARD I was buried here (1199) at the same time that the remains of his older brother, HENRY THE YOUNG KING, were removed here from Le Mans. JOHN lost Normandy in 1204, but it was retaken by HENRY V by 1419. Joan of Arc was burned here (1431). Richard Plantagenet, duke of York, was governor of Normandy in 1436–7 and again from 1440–5. Several of his children were born here, including the future EDWARD IV (1442). Rouen and Normandy were regained by France in 1449.

Roxburgh *see* Kelso

Runnymede (*Surrey / Berkshire*) The famous meadow where JOHN was forced by the barons to sign the Magna Carta on an island in the Thames on 15 June 1215.

Ruthven Castle or **Huntingtower Castle** *see* Perth

Saddell (*Argyll and Bute*) A Cistercian monastery was founded here by RAGNALD of the Isles (1207), who brought here the body of his father, SOMERLED. Ragnald was also buried here (1210).

St Albans (*Hertfordshire*) The Roman town of Verulamium was one of the most important in Britain. It had been built near to the primary fort of the Catuvellauni at Wheathamstead from where CARATACUS and his predecessors ruled (up to AD 51). It has been speculated that Caratacus's brother AMMINIUS was buried here. The Roman town was sacked by BOUDICA (61) but was soon re-established. Although the cult of St Alban grew in the 4th C and OFFA is presumed to be one of the benefactors of the church in the 8th C, the town was not known by its current name until the Norman abbey was founded in the 11th C – it was previously called *Wæclingcaster*, from which Watling Street derived its name. St Albans was the site of two battles in the Wars of the Roses. In the first (1455) HENRY VI was captured, but in the second (1461) his forces were victorious.

St Andrews (*Fife*) The first church was apparently founded here around 825, sponsored by ANGUS II. This had become a bishopric by the next century when CONSTANTINE II retired here as a monk (943) and was subsequently buried here (952). He was soon followed by INDULF (962). DAVID I made the town a royal burgh in 1140 and the cathedral was founded in 1160, though not formally consecrated until 1318, with ROBERT BRUCE in attendance. Robert held a parliament here (1309). The castle was built about 1200. JAMES III was born here (1452). JAMES V married Mary of Guise at the Cathedral in 1538, which was plundered by a mob in 1559. MARY QUEEN OF SCOTS visited St Andrews in 1563 and 1564; JAMES VI sought a retreat here in 1583 and thereafter was a regular visitor. CHARLES II was also a visitor in 1650.

St David's (*Pembrokeshire*) St David founded his church amongst the Irish of Demetia in the middle of the 6th C, not long after the reign of VORTEPOR. Although he became Wales's patron saint and many Welsh kings and princes undertook pilgrimages to his shrine, very few were buried here, at least so far as records go. It was not until the present cathedral was started around 1180 that it became the burial place of princes, and then only RHYS AP GRUFFYDD (1197) and RHYS GRYG (1234). It was also the last resting place of Edmund Tudor, whose remains were brought here in 1536.

Sanda (*Argyll and Bute*) A small island south of Kintyre where St Ninian had a chapel. ROBERT BRUCE sought refuge here in 1306.

Sandringham (*Norfolk*) Sandringham House, near King's Lynn, was acquired in 1862 for EDWARD VII, when he was prince of Wales, and it was significantly enlarged over the next twenty years. It is a private residence and has over the years become a traditional Christmas or New Year retreat for the royal family. Edward's youngest son, Alexander, was born here (1871) but unfortunately died the following day. Edward's eldest son Albert, duke of Clarence,

died here (1892). It was the favourite residence of GEORGE V. All of his children, except the eldest, were born here, including the future GEORGE VI (1895) at York Cottage, and Mary, Princess Royal (1897). Their youngest son John was also born here (1905), but as an epileptic remained out of the public eye and died young. He was buried at Sandringham Church (1919), which has many royal mementos. Queen Alexandra died at Sandringham (1925), as did George V (1936) and George VI (1952). Lady Diana Spencer was born at Park House on the Sandringham estate (1961).

Sauchieburn (*Stirling*) About a mile south-west of Bannockburn, where JAMES III was defeated by the rebel army headed by his son (the future JAMES IV) (1488). James III fell from his horse but his foot was caught in the stirrup. His unconscious body was dragged to a nearby mill (now called Milltown), where he was murdered.

Sawtry (*Cambridgeshire*) A small village between Huntingdon and Peterborough where a Cistercian abbey was founded in 1147, though little of it remains. David, earl of Huntingdon, brother of MALCOLM IV and WILLIAM THE LYON, who had died at Yardley in Northamptonshire, was buried here (1219).

Scone (*Perth and Kinross*) KENNETH MACALPIN made this the capital of his kingdom of Alba in around 843 when he united the kingdoms of the Picts and Scots. Scone, and nearby Forteviot, had long been a royal site for the southern Picts. Kenneth brought to the site the Stone of Destiny, which had been brought to Scotland by Fergus of Dál Riata and was purportedly the stone upon which Jacob had slept at Bethel and had his vision of angels descending from heaven. This stone had travelled to Egypt and from there to Spain from when the Milesians brought it to Ireland. It was thus the very heart of Celtic, and certainly Scottish, sovereignty. Although there are no records of their coronations, all of the Scottish kings since Kenneth I would have been inaugurated at Scone on the Stone (the ceremony taking place in Scone Abbey after it was re-founded by ALEXANDER I in 1120) through to JOHN BALLIOL (1292). EDWARD I of England seized the Stone in 1296 and brought it to Westminster. Coronations continued at Scone Abbey with ROBERT BRUCE (1306) through to JAMES I (1424). A parliament was held at Scone to determine whether the Stewart line should be the successor to that of Bruce (1371). The later Stewart kings were crowned at Holyrood with the exceptions of JAMES IV (1488) and CHARLES II (1651) who were crowned at Scone. The only Scottish king to be buried at Scone was ROBERT II (1390), though Matilda, the wife of DAVID I, was (c1130) and JOHN II, the last lord of the Isles (1498). The abbey and Bishop's Palace were destroyed during the Scottish reformation (1559) but a new palace was built (1581) and further enlarged (1808). James, the Old Pretender, established his court here (1716) and Bonnie Prince Charlie slept here (1745). Since 1606 the palace has been the family home of the earls of Mansfield.

Seckington (*Warwickshire, formerly Leicestershire*) Near Tamworth, this was the site of a royal villa of the kings of Mercia where ATHELBALD was murdered by his own bodyguard (757).

Selby (*North Yorkshire*) 13 miles S of York, this was where the future HENRY I was born (1068). WILLIAM THE CONQUEROR granted Benedict of Auxerre the land to establish a monastery and a small church was built in 1069, followed by the abbey which took over two hundred years to build.

Selkirk (*Scottish Borders*) EDWARD I defeated JOHN BALLIOL here (1296) and began his conquest of Scotland; a year later William WALLACE was proclaimed "Guardian of Scotland" at Selkirk in the Church of St Mary.

Senlac Hill (*Sussex*) *see* Battle

Shaftesbury (*Dorset*) The founding of Shaftesbury Abbey has long been associated with ALFRED THE GREAT in around 880 though recent evidence suggests the Abbey was founded later, perhaps into the 890s, if his daughter Athelgifu is to be recognized as the first abbess, or by his grandson EDMUND I, whose wife Elgifu (a variant of Athelgifu) may be the real first abbess (*c*944). Edmund's second wife also came to Shaftesbury some time after his death in 946 and was buried here some time after 975. The remains of EDWARD THE MARTYR, who had been buried at Wareham Abbey in 978, were brought to Shaftesbury with much ceremony in 981. CANUTE died at Shaftesbury in 1035.

Sheen Palace *see* Richmond Palace

Sheffield The long vanished Sheffield Castle, which was on the site of the Castle Market and former shopping centre, was the primary prison of MARY QUEEN OF SCOTS, throughout the 1570s.

Sherborne (*Dorset*) A bishopric was created here by INE of Wessex (706), and the West Saxon kings ATHELBALD (860) and ATHELBERT (866) were buried here. It was suggested by Alfred's biographer Asser, who was himself bishop of Sherborne in his final years, that Alfred was educated at Sherborne. Though this is very likely, it cannot be assumed without question since the authenticity of Asser's biography of Alfred has been cast into doubt.

Shrewsbury (*Shropshire*) The existing town of Shrewsbury came into existence in the 5th C when the former Celtic inhabitants of the Roman town of Wroxeter (or Viroconium) moved to a more easily defensible place. Then the town was called Pengwern and was the capital of the Welsh kingdom of South Powys under CYNGEN (550s) and BROCHFAEL YSGYTHROG (570s). It was conquered by the Mercians in the 8th C but remained a frontier town for centuries until GWENWYNWYN submitted there to JOHN (1208). Shrewsbury was also where HENRY IV's defeated the rebellious PERCYS of Northumberland (1403) – the site is called Battlefield, just north of the town.

Silchester (*Hampshire*) The Roman town of Calleva Atrebatum was built on the site of the chief fort of the Atrebates, from where COMMIUS and his son TINCOMMIUS ruled. Unlike other Roman towns, this one faded away after the Romans left and was not re-inhabited.

Skidmoore *see* Caithness

Stainmore (*Durham*) A remote stretch of moorland and forest between Barnard Castle and Brough, where ERIK BLOODAXE and his supporters were ambushed and killed after their retreat from York (954).

Stamford (*Lincolnshire*) Joan of Kent, the mother of RICHARD II, wife of Edward the Black Prince, and bigamous wife of William de MONTACUTE, was buried at Greyfriars Church (1385). Stamford was frequented by EDWARD IV during the Wars of the Roses and it was here that he ordered the execution of Lord Welles (1470) before defeating Welles's rebel son at Empingham.

Stamford Bridge (*Humberside*) 5 miles E of York, this was where HAROLD II defeated the army of Harald Hardraada of Norway on 25 September 1066 just three weeks before the Battle of Hastings.

Stanmore (*Greater London, formerly Middlesex*) Stanmore has many traditional links with early Britain. Brockley Hill is one of the traditional sites where Julius Caesar fought CASSIVELAUNOS of the Catuvellauni (54 BC). It was here that the Romans established their settlement of Sulloniace. The same site is also where BOUDICA was defeated by the Romans (AD 61) and the locals even claim that she is buried on Stanmore Common. In more recent times Stanmore Hill was the location for a meeting between the then Prince Regent (later GEORGE IV) and Louis XVIII of France (1814). In 1848 Queen Adelaide, the widow of WILLIAM IV, rented Bentley Priory, where she died (1849).

Stanwick (*North Yorkshire*) North of Richmond, this is the site of a fortification built by the Brigantes and where, in AD 74, VENUTIUS was defeated by the Romans in what was the last significant battle against the invaders.

Steyning (*West Sussex*) Here was a royal villa in the 9th C, where ATHELWOLF retired, died (858) and was buried on the site of the forerunner of the present St Andrew's Church.

Stirling (*Stirling*) The early history of Stirling is lost amongst the struggle of the Picts against the British of Strathclyde and the Votadini, the Irish of Dál Riata and the Angles of Bernicia. There was a fortification at Stirling for centuries before the existing castle was built for ALEXANDER I around 1120; he died here (1124), as did WILLIAM THE LYON (1214). It was taken by the English in 1296 but regained by William WALLACE after the battle of Stirling Bridge (1297). It was then the last castle in Scotland to fall to EDWARD I in 1304 and it remained in English hands until regained in 1314 after the Scots victory at Bannockburn. Thereafter it was a favourite residence of the Scottish kings, particularly the Stewarts. JAMES V (1513), MARY QUEEN OF SCOTS (1543) and JAMES VI (1567) were all crowned here as infants, the first two in the Chapel Royal at the castle and James VI at the Church of the Holy Rood. The Stewarts often found it a haven and retreat. It was here that JAMES II killed William Douglas (1452) and James V sought refuge from Alexander Douglas (1528). It was also from where the eccentric John Damian attempted to fly, encouraged by JAMES IV (1513). The castle was successfully besieged by Cromwell in 1651 and unsuccessfully by Bonnie Prince Charlie in 1746. *See also* Cambuskenneth Abbey *and* Sauchieburn.

Stoke-in-Hurtsbourne (*Hampshire*) The probable site of Cerdicesbeorg where CERDIC was buried (*c*554).

Stoke Lyne (*Oxfordshire*) Small village north of Bicester which is the likely site of the battle of Fethanlea, or Battle Wood, in 584 between CEAWLIN of the West Saxons and the British. The fact that there was a strong British enclave this far into England shows that the Saxons still did not control much of central Britain in the years before the growth of Mercia. Fethanlea was not an outright victory. Ceawlin's partner, CUTHA, was killed, and it seems that Ceawlin looted the territory more in anger than in victory.

Stonehaven (*Aberdeenshire*) To the west of Stonehaven MALCOLM I was killed in battle with the men of Moray in 954 at Fetteresso. Just south of Stonehaven is the impressive Dunnottar Castle, held by the English during the Wars of Independence and unsuccessfully besieged by William WALLACE in 1297. It was to Dunnottar that the Scottish crown jewels were brought during the Commonwealth (1649) and from where, when the castle was under siege in 1652, they were smuggled out by the local minister's wife and her serving woman.

Stony Stratford (*Buckinghamshire; formerly Northants*) EDWARD IV stayed here on 30 April 1464 on the pretext of hunting prior to his secret visit to Grafton Regis to marry Elizabeth Wydville. It was also here, nineteen years later to the day (30 April 1483), that Richard duke of Gloucester (the future RICHARD III) brought the young king EDWARD V under his "protection", and thereby paved his own way to the crown. The young king had stayed that night at the Rose and Crown Inn in the High Street, which still stands.

Strata Florida Abbey (*Ceredigion*) A Cistercian monastery, founded on the site of an earlier abbey in 1164 by Robert Fitzstephen. Before the abbey was completed the land was overrun by RHYS AP GRUFFYDD, who sponsored the completion of the abbey (1184). Deheubarth's resistance leader, CADELL AP GRUFFYDD, was buried here while the abbey was being built (1175), and Rhys's two sons, GRUFFYDD AP RHYS (1201) and MAELGWYN AP RHYS (1230) were also both buried here. In 1238 LLYWELYN THE GREAT summoned an assembly here for the Welsh princes to swear allegiance to his son DAFYDD. The name means Vale of Flowers.

Strata Marcella (*Powys*) A Cistercian monastery founded in 1170 by OWAIN CYFEILIOG. He retired here in 1195 and was buried here in 1197.

Strathallan *see* Dunblane

Strathbogie (*Aberdeenshire*) *see* Huntly Castle

Strathcarron *see* Falkirk

Strathclyde *see* Dumbarton

Sudeley Castle (*Gloucestershire*) *see* Winchcombe

Sutton Hoo *see* Rendlesham

Suttons Walls *see* Hereford

Syon House (*Greater London, formerly Middlesex*). Originally the site of a monastery where Katherine Howard was held before her execution (1542) and where HENRY VIII's coffin rested and burst open, allowing dogs to get at the remains (1547). Lord Protector Edward Seymour began construction of a house here soon after, and this passed to John Dudley, duke of Northumberland (1552), whose son Guilford married Lady JANE Grey. It was at Syon House that Jane was offered the crown of England (1553). After the executions of all three the house reverted to the Crown but was rarely used by either MARY or ELIZABETH and in 1594 Elizabeth granted it to Henry Percy, earl of Northumberland, in whose family the house remains.

Talgarth (*Powys*) *see* Brycheiniog

Tamworth (*Staffordshire*) An important town for the later kings of Mercia. OFFA established a royal villa here around 757 and it remained a favourite residence until the start of the tenth century. By then the Danish threat had caused the Mercian nobility to move south. ATHELFLÆD fortified Tamworth in 913 and died here in 918. A few years later ATHELSTAN chose Tamworth as the appropriate border town to meet with SITRIC of York for the marriage of his sister Eadgyth (926). It was devastated by the Vikings under OLAF GOTHFRITHSON in 939/940.

Tantallon Castle *see* Dunbar

Taunton (*Somerset*) A town whose association with royalty has appeared rather one-sided over the years. A castle was established here by INE in about 710 but within a few years Ine and his wife were besieging the town, which was protecting a rebel leader (722). STEPHEN favoured the town with special privileges to secure its support in his war against MATILDA (1140). The town supported Perkin WARBECK and declared him king as Richard IV (1497); it sided with the Parliamentarians during the Civil War (1644) and supported the Duke of Monmouth during his rebellion (1685). As a consequence of that, it had to face the Bloody Assizes of Judge Jeffries later that year.

Temple Newsam (*West Yorkshire*) Now in the suburbs of Leeds, this Tudor manor house was built by Lord Darcy around 1520. It passed to the crown after Darcy's execution in 1537 and was subsequently granted to the earl of Lennox by right of his wife, Margaret, who was Henry VIII's niece. Their son, Lord Darnley, the future husband of MARY QUEEN OF SCOTS, was born here in 1545.

Tewkesbury (*Gloucestershire*) The abbey was founded in 1092 and consecrated in 1121. Here lies buried Edward, prince of Wales and son of HENRY VI, who was killed in the bloody battle of Tewkesbury (1471), which signalled the end of the Wars of the Roses and the final victory of EDWARD IV. Also buried here is Edward's brother George, duke of Clarence (1478), who had died in the Tower of London, purportedly drowning in a vat of wine.

Thanet (*Kent*) *see* Ebbsfleet *and* Minster-in-Thanet

Theobald's Park *see* Waltham

Thetford (*Norfolk*) One of the principal towns of the later kings of East Anglia, it was plundered by the Danes in 869 when they killed king EDMUND. A castle was built here in the 12th C and dismantled by HENRY II (1174) during the rebellion of his sons, particularly HENRY THE YOUNG KING. It was also at Thetford that Henry Fitzroy, the illegitimate son of Henry VIII, was buried (1536). The King's House was once a hunting lodge used by JAMES I.

Thurso (*Caithness*) Early in its history this town had as much to do with Norway as Scotland, since it was the closest harbour in Britain to the Norse earls of Orkney. It was captured by ERLEND in 1155 and it was here that JOHN I of Orkney was killed (1231). *See also* Caithness.

Tilbury (*Essex*) A fort was established here in 1539 by HENRY VIII as part of his coastal defences. It was strengthened during ELIZABETH I's reign with the threat of the Spanish Armada, and it was here that Elizabeth made her rousing speech to her troops (1588).

Tintagel (*Cornwall*) The magnificent ruins of the castle have long been associated with the legend of King ARTHUR, although there is no basis for this. There was once a monastery on the site and it almost certainly had connections with the former kings of Kernow. The castle was built around 1140 by Reginald, earl of Cornwall, the illegitimate son of HENRY I.

Tintern (*Monmouthshire*) Famous for the ruins of its 12th C Cistercian Abbey Tintern was earlier the scene of a major battle between the Welsh under MEURIG and TEWDRIG and the Saxons, probably under CEAWLIN (584). *See also* Fethanlea.

Titchfield Abbey (*Hampshire*) Here the young RICHARD II nearly drowned in the fish-pond; HENRY VI in person married Margaret of Anjou (1445); and CHARLES I spent his last night of freedom (1646).

Towton (*North Yorkshire*) A vicious battle was fought here in a snowstorm on 29 March 1461. EDWARD IV drove home his earlier triumphs and defeated HENRY VI, thereby confirming his right to the throne. It was estimated that around 20,000 Lancastrians were killed, and 8,000 Yorkists.

Traprain Law *see* Dunbar

Turnberry (*South Ayrshire*) Here once stood a castle which belonged to the earls of Carrick and which has the most likely claim (challenged by Writtle in Essex and Lochmaben) to have been the birthplace of ROBERT BRUCE (1274). Certainly it was a stronghold of support for Bruce and was the castle from which he re-launched his campaign for the Scottish throne (1307).

Tutbury Castle (*Staffordshire*) Although now in ruins this castle, which owed much of its construction to John of Gaunt, is famous as one of the principal prisons of MARY QUEEN OF SCOTS. She was kept here for various long periods between 1569 and 1585.

Tynemouth (*Tyne and Wear*) A priory was established here in the 7th C and OSWINE of Deira was buried here after his murder (651), though his remains were later removed to Gilling. OSRED

II of Northumbria was also buried here in 790, and MALCOLM III of Scotland after his death in battle at Alnwick in 1093. His body was later transferred to Dunfermline.

Valle Crucis Abbey *see* Llangollen

Wakefield (*West Yorkshire*) A battle in the Wars of the Roses was fought at Sandal Castle, just south of Wakefield (1460). The victory went to the forces of Margaret of Anjou, wife of HENRY VI, who defeated and killed Richard, duke of York.

Walbottle (*Tyne and Wear*) The likely site of *Ad Murum*, referred to by Bede as where Finan, the bishop of Northumbria, baptized both PEADA of Mercia and SIGEBERT *SANCTUS* of the East Saxons into the Christian faith (653).

Wallingford (*Oxfordshire; formerly Berkshire*) Once a fortified Saxon town on the borders between Wessex and Mercia, it was sacked mercilessly by the Danes in 1006. Under the Treaty of Wallingford (1153), STEPHEN recognized HENRY II as his successor, and Henry II held a parliament here (1154). The castle was built in 1071. It was here that Joan, the widow of Edward the Black Prince and mother of RICHARD II, died (1385).

Wallop (*Hampshire*) The three villages of Nether Wallop, Middle Wallop and Over Wallop are the likely site of Guoloph, where in 437 VORTIGERN had a victory over AMBROSIUS THE ELDER which assured him of continuity in the high kingship.

Waltham Despite the administrative divide between Hertfordshire, Essex and Greater London, Waltham was originally all one community. The name means the village in the forest, referring to what was once called Waltham Forest but which residue is now better known as Epping Forest. The three centres are dealt with below.
Waltham Abbey (*Essex*) The abbey was founded in 1030 and rebuilt by Harold Godwinson (later HAROLD II) in 1060. His body was brought here for burial after the battle of Hastings (1066), along with his brothers Gyrth and Leofwine. Kings often stayed overnight at Waltham Abbey when hunting in the Forest. It was the last monastery in England to be dissolved (1540).
Waltham Cross (*Hertfordshire*) Here stands one of the three surviving crosses erected in memory of Eleanor of Castile, 1290 (*see under* Harby). Here also once stood Theobalds Palace, originally the home of Robert Cecil, earl of Salisbury. In 1607 JAMES I exchanged Hatfield House for Theobalds, which was his preferred residence, and he died here in 1625. It became a ruined shell during the Civil War and was sold by CHARLES II. Nothing now remains of the palace, though the park is open to the public.
Waltham Forest (*Essex, North London*) A London

borough created in 1965, comprising the former boroughs of Chingford, Leyton and Walthamstow, and which was the original name for what is now known as Epping Forest. This ancient forest which once stretched from the Thames to the Wash contains several Iron Age and ancient British fortifications. Ambersbury Banks, in the north of the forest, is alleged to be where BOUDICA fought her last battle against the Romans and where, witnessing defeat, committed suicide (however, *see also* Mancetter). The forest was regarded as a royal hunting forest, though in 1226 HENRY II allowed the citizens of London to hunt in the forest on Easter Monday (a privilege which remained until 1882). HENRY VIII had a hunting lodge built (Ranger's Road, Chingford) in order to watch the hunt (1543) and this was restored by ELIZABETH (1589), after whom it is still named. Copt Hall or Copped Hall, to the north of the Forest, is where Princess Mary (later MARY I) retreated during her brother's reign (1550). WILLIAM III also sought refuge at Copt Hall after almost being kidnapped in 1698.

Wantage (*Oxfordshire*) The town usually considered as the birthplace of ALFRED THE GREAT (*c*847), though at the time it was in Mercia, not Wessex, and the authenticity of Alfred's biographer Asser has been brought seriously into doubt. Nevertheless there is a superb statue to Alfred in the market square, designed by Count Gleichen and erected in 1877. Alfred did live at Wantage in his later years and bequeathed his estate here to his wife, Ealhswith (899). In 997 ATHELRED II issued his law code at Wantage.

Wareham (*Dorset*) An important Saxon town. A church was built here in the 7th or 8th C and both BEORHTRIC (802) and EDWARD THE MARTYR (978) were buried here. It was a site of fierce fighting during ALFRED THE GREAT's war with the Danes, and Alfred established a camp here in 876.

Welshpool (*Powys*) The territory around here was a scene of regular battles between the Welsh and first the Saxons and later the Normans. GRUFFYDD AP LLYWELYN defeated the Mercians here (1039). The original Powis Castle was the site for the treacherous murders of both BLEDDYN AP CYNFYN (1075) and his son CADWGAN AP BLEDDYN (1111). This castle was destroyed by LLYWELYN THE GREAT in 1233. A new castle was built by GRUFFYDD AP GWENWYNWYN after 1277 when he had become a vassal prince to EDWARD I. The castle subsequently passed into the ownership of the Herbert family (1586), who transformed it into a stately home.

Westhorpe Hall (*Suffolk*) This was the home of Mary Tudor, the sister of Henry VIII who had eloped with the duke of Suffolk in 1515. She died here in 1533 and was buried at Bury St Edmunds.

Westminster Abbey and Palace *see* London, Westminster

Weybridge (*Surrey*) Here once stood Oatlands Palace, acquired by HENRY VIII in 1537 and significantly developed over the next three years. Here he brought Katherine Howard to be married in secret (1540). It was also where Henry fled to wallow in his grief when he heard of Katherine's adultery. ELIZABETH liked Oatlands, calling it a "cheerful hunting box", and used to end her royal progress there and enjoy the thrill of the hunt. She was still hunting here as late as 1600. The Stewart kings used the house less, although CHARLES I's youngest son, Henry, was born here (1640). The palace fell into ruin during the Commonwealth and it was soon demolished. The name is now remembered in a local housing estate that covers the site.

Wherwell Abbey (*Hampshire*) The Abbey was founded in 986 by Elfrida, the widow of EDGAR, in atonement for the murder of her stepson, EDWARD THE MARTYR. She died and was buried at the Abbey (*c*1002). In 1043 EDWARD THE CONFESSOR banished his mother Emma to Wherwell (where his sister was abbess), because she had shown support for the claim of Magnus of Norway to the throne. She was also charged with complicity in the death of Edward's younger brother Alfred and even with attempting to poison Edward. Tradition states she had to face a trial by ordeal which involved walking over red-hot ploughshares. She survived unscathed and Edward begged forgiveness. A few years later (1051), when Edward's relationship soured with Earl Godwin, he banished his wife Edith (Godwin's daughter) to Wherwell on the grounds of infidelity, but he soon recanted and she was welcomed back.

Whitby (*North Yorkshire*) The abbey was founded in 657 by OSWY of Northumbria in thanks for his victory over PENDA at Winwæd. Its first abbess, Hild, was a great-granddaughter of AELLE of Deira. The Synod of Whitby, which was held here in 664, determined that the English church follow the Roman rites rather than the Celtic. Oswy's wife, Enfleda, became abbess of Whitby after Hild's death in 680 and translated to the abbey the remains of her father, EDWIN. Her daughter, Elfflæd, was abbess with her until her mother's death in 704 and then alone until 713. The abbey was destroyed by Danes in 867 and was not refounded until 1078. It is the ruins of this abbey which form such an impressive backdrop to the town.

Whithorn (*Dumfries and Galloway*) The name derives from the "white house" or chapel of St Ninian that was established here about the year 397 when Ninian helped cure the local king, TUTAGUAL, of blindness. It was a place of regular pilgrimage by many kings, especially ROBERT BRUCE and the Stewarts.

Whitland (*Carmarthenshire*) A monastery where HYWEL DDA convened an assembly in *c*945 in order to codify all the existing laws of Wales into one acceptable law code. The original name for the place Ty Gwyn means "White House", just like St Ninian's chapel in Galloway.

White Lodge, Richmond (*Surrey*) *see* Richmond Park

Wick (*Caithness*) The name comes from the Norse for "bay" and was closely associated with the Viking earls of Orkney. Here in 1198 HARALD II of Orkney defeated his rival HARALD THE YOUNGER.

Wight, Isle of Although the *ASC* links the Saxon conquest of Wight with CERDIC and later with WIHTGAR (530 and 534) the island had much stronger Jutish connections and was probably settled at much the same time as Kent under HENGIST and his mercenaries. Wight seems to have retained a separate kingship for about 150 years until the last ruler ARWALD was killed (687). *See also* Arreton, Carisbrooke *and* Cowes.

Wilton (*Wiltshire*) Here was a royal manor of the West Saxon kings, next to which a religious foundation was established at the end of the 8th C where EGBERT's half-sister, Ealburt, retired around 800, converting it into a nunnery. She died here (*c*810). The Danes attacked the royal estate in 871, forcing ALFRED into retreat. By the next century, however, the Danish threat was temporarily gone. Several of the daughters of EDWARD THE ELDER were buried at Wilton, as was the estranged wife of EDGAR, Athelfleda (*c*965). Although the importance of Wilton decreased after the Norman Conquest, it was still of strategic significance. STEPHEN fortified the defences here in his war against MATILDA but in 1142 suffered a humiliating defeat at Wilton. The abbey at Wilton was dissolved in 1544 and Wilton House built on the site.

Wimborne (*Dorset*) The site of a royal manor where a nunnery was founded by Cuthburh, sister of INE and widow of ALDFRITH, in *c*705. ATHELRED I was buried here (871), having died nearby at Witchampton of wounds received at Martin. The manor was evidently of singular importance for, after ALFRED's death, ATHELWOLD seized it in his bid for the kingship (899). Wimborne was later destroyed by the Danes, but EDWARD THE CONFESSOR established a religious college here which survived until the Reformation (1547).

Winchcombe (*Gloucestershire*) In the 9th C Winchcombe was the centre of its own administrative unit, a sub-kingdom which had survived from the earlier kingdom of Hwicce. It was the power base of CENWULF of Mercia (796). In 798 he captured and blinded EADBERT II of Kent and held him captive at Winchcombe Manor for many years, eventually releasing him into the care of Winchcombe Abbey, Cenwulf had founded the abbey around 805 with his daughter, Cwenthryth, as abbess. Cwenthryth has passed down through legend as a scheming woman responsible for the death of her brother Cynehelm, who was buried at Winchcombe (812) alongside his father (821). Cynehelm became venerated in later years and his shrine is still in the vaults of the existing Church of St Peter. South of Winchcombe is the former manor house of Sudeley, which was developed into a castle by RICHARD III in 1484. The house had a particular significance for Richard because its previous occupant had been Lady Eleanor Butler, the widow of Sir Thomas Butler, who had been granted Sudeley by his father (1450). There was a rumour that, after Butler's death (1461), his widow entered a secret marriage contract with EDWARD IV. Richard used this to annul Edward's later marriage with Elizabeth Wydville and thereby make EDWARD V illegitimate and free Richard's path to the throne. Sudeley remained a royal possession but was granted to Thomas Seymour, when he was created Lord Sudeley in 1547 upon his marriage to Katherine Parr, widow of HENRY VIII. She went to live at Sudeley but died there in childbirth in September 1548. Much of the castle, including Katherine's original tomb, was destroyed during the Civil War.

Winchester (*Hampshire*) An ancient town of importance to the Romans and Saxons. It eventually became the capital of Wessex and subsequently of England, but not until the 9th C. Its growth can be dated to the founding of a separate bishopric here in 660 by CENWEALH of Wessex about twelve years after he established the church. The bishopric grew and by the dawn of the 9th C Winchester had become the ecclesiastical and administrative centre of Wessex, with a royal palace established next to the minster. Many of the later Saxon kings are buried here. Most are in the cathedral itself, including EGBERT (839), ATHELWOLF (his body removed here from Steyning, EDWARD THE ELDER (924), ELFWEARD (924), EADRED (955), and EDWY (959). ALFRED THE GREAT was originally buried in the grounds of the nunnery he founded called New Minster, next to the Old Minster (899). EDGAR subsequently transferred the nunnery to Hyde Abbey and Alfred's remains were likewise transferred. After the abbey was dissolved, the site became St Bartholomew's Church off Hyde Street, where a slab by the east wall in the churchyard marks his last resting place. It was under Alfred that Winchester emerged as the capital of England. He and his wife Ealhswith were married here (868) and her remains now rest in the cathedral. Later

kings buried here are CANUTE (1035), HARTHACANUTE (1042) and WILLIAM II (1100) – the only Norman king buried here. Other royal burials include Emma, the queen of both ATHELRED II and CANUTE (who was reburied in the cathedral in 1190), Richard, the second son of WILLIAM I (1081), and Edmund, earl of Kent, the son of EDWARD I, who was executed at Winchester for supporting his brother, the deposed EDWARD II, and buried at the Church of the Dominican Friars (1330). The continued importance of Winchester can be seen in the number of coronations and royal marriages held here. EDWARD THE CONFESSOR, who was crowned here in 1043, married here in 1045; Matilda, the wife of William I, was crowned queen consort (1068); HENRY THE YOUNG KING was crowned here with his wife Margaret (1172); RICHARD I chose to have a second coronation here (1194); HENRY IV married Joan of Navarre (1403) and MARY I married Philip of Spain (1554). HENRY VII used Winchester Castle frequently as a royal residence and his son Arthur, the heir to the throne, was born here (1486). Other rulers born here include the future Empress MATILDA (1102) and HENRY III (1207). Those Welsh princes who had accepted first Saxon and later Norman authority often became friends of the monarchs and occasionally stayed at Winchester. Most noticeable were the regular visits in the 920s of HYWEL DDA, who learned much about court administration; MADOG AP MAREDDUD was also a friend of King HENRY II and he died at Winchester (1160). The Castle Hall contains King Arthur's Round Table made during the reign of either Henry III or more likely EDWARD I. Winchester was frequently subject to attack – first by the Danes in the 9th and 11th C; it was besieged during Stephen and Matilda's civil war (1141) – Winchester was the first to proclaim Matilda as queen and gave her possession of the treasury, castle and crown, but a few months later she found herself under siege from Stephen's brother Henry, who set fire to the castle and surrounding buildings that August – and then again in the Cromwellian Civil War, when the castle was dismantled (1645). CHARLES II thought of building a new palace here and work was started (1683) but was curtailed by his death.

Windsor Castle (*Berkshire*) The principal home of the royal family outside Buckingham Palace. It was originally a motte-and-bailey castle built by WILLIAM THE CONQUEROR as a defence along the Thames Valley soon after the Conquest. It was enlarged by HENRY I but it was HENRY II who established the first stone structures including the Round Tower. HENRY III conducted further building work, but it was EDWARD III who did the most to convert it into the centre of his kingdom and what would become one of the biggest castles in the world. He founded here the Order of the Knights of the Garter (1348). Almost every monarch has had a hand in extending and refurbishing the castle. EDWARD IV added St George's Chapel (1477) for the Order of the Garter and it subsequently became the burial place of kings. GEORGE IV's characteristically expensive works created the final scale and shape we recognize today. The castle was severely damaged by fire in 1992 and the cost of the refurbishment (since the royal palaces are not insured) was met from opening Buckingham Palace to the public at certain times.

The earliest royal event at the castle was the marriage of Henry I to Adeliza in 1121. The high king of Ireland, Rory O'Connor, here recognized Henry II as his overlord (1175). Since then there have been surprisingly few royal marriages or births. Edward the Black Prince married Joan of Kent (1361); and EDWARD VII married Alexandra in St George's Chapel (1863). Two kings were born here: EDWARD III (1312) and HENRY VI (1421); plus several queens: Matilda (1156), the daughter of Henry II who married Henry the Lion, Duke of Saxony and Bavaria; Margaret (1240) the daughter of Henry III and wife of ALEXANDER III; and Eleanor (1269), daughter of EDWARD I and wife of Alfonso III of Aragon. Unlike the Tower of London, the castle has not been used as a prison. JAMES I of Scotland was detained here for several years during the 1410s at the court of HENRY IV; also GEORGE III spent his last years of mental decline until his death in 1820 mostly in one room and adjacent corridors. Apart from the sumptuousness of the castle apartments, along with the many art and other treasures and the remarkable feeling of heritage and continuity over the centuries, perhaps the main feature of Windsor is St George's Chapel as the burial place of many kings and queens. The first king to be buried here was Edward IV (1483), though his elder sister Anne had been buried here a few years earlier (possibly as early as 1476). The remains of Henry VI, who had been buried at Chertsey in 1471, were removed to Windsor in 1484 by RICHARD III and found to be remarkably incorrupt. Other monarchs or their consorts buried in St George's Chapel are Edward IV's widow Elizabeth Wydville (1492), Jane Seymour (1537), HENRY VIII (1547), CHARLES I (1649), George III (1820) and his wife Charlotte (1818), George IV (1830), WILLIAM IV (1837) and his widow Adelaide (1849), EDWARD VII (1910) and Alexandra (1925), GEORGE V (1936) and Mary (1953) and GEORGE VI (1952). The parents of Queen VICTORIA were also originally buried here – Edward (1820) and Victoria (1861) – as was Victoria's husband Prince Albert (1861), but they were soon removed to a special mausoleum at Frogmore House (1862), where Victoria was also later buried (1901). EDWARD VIII (1972) and his widow Wallis (1986) are also buried at Frogmore. *Frogmore House* is about a mile south of Windsor Castle and was built in 1680 for CHARLES II's

architect Thomas May. It was occupied by several different families over the years until acquired by George III's wife, Charlotte (1792). It was subsequently lived in by George III's daughter Augusta and, from 1841 to 1861, Queen Victoria's mother. Both George V and George VI (when he was Duke of York) lived here for a while, though the Duke and his new bride, Elizabeth Bowes-Lyon lived at Windsor Royal Lodge from 1923 to 1936. Frogmore House fell into disrepair and was not renovated until the 1980s.

Wingfield Castle (*Suffolk*) Originally the home of the earls (later dukes) of Suffolk, established in 1384 by Michael de la Pole, a court favourite of RICHARD II. EDWARD IV's sister Elizabeth married John, the 2nd duke of Suffolk (1461), and lived at Wingfield until her death (1503) when she was buried in St Andrew's Church. Her son, Edmund de la Pole, believed he had greater right to the throne than Henry VII and sought the support of the Emperor Maximilian I (1501). He was eventually captured, imprisoned in the Tower and executed (1513). His brother Richard was recognized as king of England by Louis XII (1512) and, in conjunction with the French and Scots, he prepared to invade England, but he was killed at the battle of Pavia (1525), fighting for the French.

Winwæd At the battle of Winwæd (655) OSWY of Northumbria defeated and killed PENDA of Mercia. This gave Northumbria the ascendancy amongst the Saxon heptarchy for the next thirty years. The location of the battle is not known. It has been suggested that the Winwæd may be a tributary of the Don known as the Went and that the battle was fought somewhere near Leeds in the Aire marshes.

Witchampton *see* Wimborne

Wolf Hall (*Wiltshire*) *see* Wulfhall

Woodstock (*Oxfordshire*) A royal manor stood at Woodstock since Saxon times; certainly from the time of ATHELRED II (he held a Council here in 995) and probably earlier, as it is recorded as one of ALFRED's residences (888). It had become known as Woodstock Palace by the 12th C. HENRY I regularly stayed here, using it as a base for hunting in the neighbourhood. He also established a zoo in the grounds (1120). HENRY II held court here on a number of occasions. Most significant was his Council of 1163, where both the Welsh and Scottish rulers paid homage to him and where he first strongly disagreed with Thomas Becket. It was near here that Henry kept his mistress Rosamond Clifford (1174). The Scottish king WILLIAM THE LYON was married here (1186). EDWARD I's youngest son Edmund was born here (1301), as was EDWARD III's son Edward the Black Prince (1330). Princess Elizabeth was detained here for nearly a year

(1554/5). The palace was destroyed during the Civil War and it was in its grounds that Blenheim Palace was built (1705–22) for John Churchill, duke of Marlborough.

Worcester (*Worcestershire*) Originally part of the kingdom of Hwicce, a bishopric was established here by ATHELRED of Mercia (679). ATHELRED THE UNREADY held a Council here (992) to consider the Danish threat. Worcester suffered under HARTHACANUTE, who suppressed a rebellion here (1041). The cathedral, which was rebuilt in 1084, contains two royal tombs: King JOHN (1216), who was buried here by his own express wish, and Arthur (1502), elder brother of Henry VIII. Eleanor of Aquitaine, wife of Henry II, was crowned here in 1158, having been too far into her pregnancy to be crowned alongside her husband. It was here that LLYWELYN THE LAST married Eleanor de Montfort (1278), the niece of Henry III. Worcester remained staunchly royalist during the Civil War and was the last to surrender (1646). Five years later CHARLES II was defeated at Worcester (1651) and had to seek refuge.

Writtle (*Essex*) A small village near Chelmsford where King JOHN had a palace (*c*1200) and where it is alleged that ROBERT BRUCE was born (1274), though this is probably based on a misreading about Robert's father, also called Robert the Bruce. *See also* Lochmaben and Turnberry Castle.

Wroughton (*Wiltshire*) Generally agreed as the site of the battle of Ellandun (825), where EGBERT of Wessex defeated BEORNWULF of Mercia and shifted the balance in the control of England.

Wulfhall or **Wolf Hall** (*Wiltshire*) A manor in Savernake Forest, near Burbage, in the ownership of the Seymour family. Jane Seymour was born (*c*1508) and raised here and it is likely that Henry VIII's interest in her was roused when he stayed at Wulfhall in September 1535. They were married eight months later.

Yardley (*Northants*) *see* Sawtry

Yeavering (*Northumberland*) High in the Cheviot Hills west of Wooler and south of Kirknewton is the old Celtic fort of Yeavering Bell, probably a secondary fort to the Votadini of Traprain Law (*see* Dunbar) but also the main fortress of Bryneich (*see* Bernicia). When the Angles

subdued the British they established a royal palace at Yeavering. It was where EDWIN married Athelburh (625), the daughter of Athelbert of Kent, and where Paulinus baptized hundreds of Angles (627).

York (*North Yorkshire*) The site of a former Brigantian stronghold, the Romans established a fort here called Eboracum (AD 71), a name which Geoffrey of Monmouth maintains is derived from Ebrauc, the sixth king of Britain after Brutus (940 BC). Septimius SEVERUS died here (211), as did CONSTANTIUS (306). CONSTANTINE THE GREAT was proclaimed emperor here (306). In the post-Roman period the British chieftains returned of whom ELEUTHER and PEREDUR were renowned at York (6th C). The Angles established a kingdom under AELLE (*c*580), and York became the capital of Deira under EDWIN (625). He also established the archbishopric under Paulinus (627). Edwin was the first king to be buried at York Minster (633). York was subject to many invasions. It was burned by ATHELBALD of Mercia (740), besieged by the Danes (866) and captured by them (867); it was subsequently invaded by the Norse kings of Dublin, reclaimed by ATHELSTAN (297), retaken by OLAF GOTHFRITHSON (937 and 939), regained by EDMUND I of Wessex (945), besieged by EADRED (947), invaded by MALCOLM I of Scotland (948), conquered by WILLIAM of Normandy (1068) who established a new castle, captured by EDGAR ATHELING (1069) and consequently sacked by William I (1069). Throughout all of this turbulence it is not surprising that many records were lost and it is no longer certain where many of the later Northumbrian kings were buried. Two Scottish kings married at York: ALEXANDER II married Joan, the sister of HENRY III (1221), and ALEXANDER III married Margaret, Henry III's daughter (1251). It was also the scene of the wedding between EDWARD III and Philippa of Hainault (1328). Their fourth child, Prince William, died at Hatfield aged only two or three and was buried in the Minster (1337). The title of duke of York was created for Edward III's son Edmund in 1385 and is one of the royal dukedoms. Dukes of York who became monarchs were HENRY VIII, CHARLES I, GEORGE V and GEORGE VI. Royal marriages since Edward III's are rare. The most recent was that of Edward, duke of Kent, grandson of George V, on 8 June 1961.

BIBLIOGRAPHY AND ACKNOWLEDGEMENTS

In the thirty years or more that I have been fascinated with British and European monarchy, particularly the period before 1066, I have read and taken notes from more books about the subject than I can remember, and certainly many more than I have collected and consulted in compiling this present volume. The following is nevertheless as representative a list as I can produce of books that I have consulted in whole or in part in researching this book, in addition to the many specialist magazines and papers as well as countless visits to castles and royal homes over the years. I would also like to acknowledge the special help of Peter Berresford Ellis on Celtic matters, Martin Marix Evans for his experience and guidance on the format and structure of the book and Julian Lock for his invaluable historical knowledge and perception.

Adam, Frank, *The Clans, Septs, and Regiments of the Scottish Highlands*, Edinburgh: Johnston & Bacon, 1960 (6th edition, revised by Sir Thomas Innes).

Anderson, Marjorie O., *Kings & Kingship in Early Scotland*, Edinburgh: Scottish Academic Press, 1973.

Ashbee, Paul, *The Ancient British: A Social-Archaeological Narrative*, Norwich: University of East Anglia, 1978.

Ashdown, Dulcie M., *Queen Victoria's Family*, London: Robert Hale, 1975.

Ashdown, Dulcie M., *Royal Children*, London: Robert Hale, 1979.

Ashe, Geoffrey, *Kings and Queens of Early Britain*, London: Methuen, 1982.

Ashley, Maurice, *King John*, London: Weidenfeld and Nicolson, 1972.

Barber, Richard, *Henry Plantagenet*, Woodbridge: Boydell Press, 1972.

Barlow, Frank, *Edward the Confessor*, London: Eyre Methuen, 1970; revised New Haven: Yale University Press, 1997.

Barlow, Frank, *William Rufus*, London: Methuen, 1983.

Barnwell, P.S., *Emperor, Prefects and Kings: The Roman West, 395–565*, London: Duckworth, 1992.

Barnwell, P.S., *Kings, Courtiers & Imperium: The Barbarian West, 565–725*, London: Duckworth, 1997.

Barrow, G. W. S., *Kingship and Unity: Scotland 1000–1306*, London: Edward Arnold, 1981; revised, Edinburgh University Press, 1989.

Barrow, G.W.S., *Robert Bruce and the Community of the Realm of Scotland*, London: Eyre and Spottiswoode, 1965.

Bassett, Steven (ed), *The Origins of Anglo-Saxon Kingdoms*, Leicester University Press, 1989.

Bellenden, John (translator), *The History and Chronicles of Scotland* by Hector Boece, Edinburgh, 1821.

Bingham, Caroline, *The Crowned Lions: The Early Plantagenet Kings*, Newton Abbot: David & Charles, 1978.

Bingham, Caroline, *Edward II*, London: Weidenfeld and Nicolson, 1973.

Bingham, Caroline, *James V, King of Scots*, London: William Collins, 1971.

Bingham, Caroline, *The Kings and Queens of Scotland*, London: Weidenfeld & Nicolson, 1976.

Birley, Anthony, *The People of Roman Britain*, London: B.T. Batsford, 1979.

Blackett, A.T. and Wilson, Alan, *Arthur and the Charters of the Kings*, Cardiff: M.T. Byrd, 1981.

Blackett, A.T. and Wilson, Alan, *King Arthur: King of Glamorgan and Gwent*, Cardiff: M.T. Byrd, 1981.

Blakeley, Brian L. and Collins, Jacquelin, *Documents in English History*, London and New York: John Wiley, 1975.

Bradbury, Jim, *Stephen and Matilda: The Civil War of 1139–53*, Stroud: Alan Sutton, 1996.

Branigan, Keith, *Prehistoric Britain, An Illustrated Survey*, Bourne End, Buckinghamshire: Spurbooks, 1976.

Breeze, David J., *The Northern Frontiers of*

Roman Britain, London: B.T. Batsford, 1982.

Breeze, David J. and Dobson, Brian, Hadrian's Wall, London: Allen Lane, 1976.

Brooke, Christopher, The Saxon and Norman Kings, London: B.T. Batsford, 1963.

Brown, P. Hume, History of Scotland, Cambridge University Press, 1912 (3 volumes).

Bushell, T.A., Barracuda Guide to County History, Volume I – Kent, Chesham: Barracuda Books, 1976.

Casey, P.J., Carausius and Allectus: The British Usurpers, London: B.T. Batsford, 1994.

Chadwick, Nora K. (editor). Celt and Saxon: Studies in the Early British Border, Cambridge University Press, 1963.

Chadwick, Nora K. The Celts, London: Pelican Books, 1971.

Chapman, Hester W., Lady Jane Grey, London: Jonathan Cape, 1962.

Clarke, John, The Life and Times of George III, London: Weidenfeld & Nicolson, 1972.

Cleary, A.S. Esmonde, The Ending of Roman Britain, London: B.T. Batsford, 1989.

Clive, Mary, This Sun of York, London: Macmillan, 1973.

Collingwood, W.G., Scandinavian Britain, 1908; reprinted by Llanerch Publishers, 1993.

Crawford, Barbara E., Scandinavian Scotland, Leicester University Press, 1987.

Dark, K.R., Civitas to Kingdom, British Political Continuity 300–800, Leicester University Press, 1994.

Davies, John, A History of Wales, London: Allen Lane, 1993.

Davies, R.R., Conquest, Coexistence, and Change: Wales 1063–1415 (History of Wales, Volume II), University of Wales Press in association with Clarendon Press, Oxford: 1987.

Davies, R.R., The Revolt of Owain Glyn Dwr, Oxford University Press, 1995.

Davies, Wendy, Wales in the Early Middle Ages, Leicester University Press, 1982.

Donaldson, Frances, Edward VIII, London: Weidenfeld & Nicolson, 1974.

Donaldson, Gordon, Scottish Kings, London: B.T. Batsford, 1967.

Donaldson, Gordon & Morpeth, Robert S.,

A Dictionary of Scottish History, Edinburgh: John Donald, 1977.

Douglas, D.C., William the Conqueror, London: Eyre and Spottiswoode, 1964.

Dudley, Donald R. & Webster, Graham, The Rebellion of Boudicca, London: Routledge & Kegan Paul, 1962.

Duncan, Archibald A.M., Scotland: The Making of the Kingdom, Edinburgh: Oliver & Boyd, 1975.

Earle, Peter, Henry V, London: Weidenfeld & Nicolson, 1972.

Edwards, Nancy and Lane, Alan, The Early Church in Wales and the West, Oxford: Oxbow Books, 1992.

Ellis, Peter Berresford, Celt and Saxon: The Struggle for Britain, London: Constable, 1993.

Ellis, Peter Berresford, The Celtic Empire: The First Millenium of Celtic History, London: Constable, 1990.

Ellis, Peter Berresford, Macbeth, High King of Scotland 1040–57, London: Frederick Muller, 1980.

Falkus, Christopher, Charles II, London: Weidenfeld & Nicolson, 1972.

Falkus, Malcolm and Gillingham, John (eds), Historical Atlas of Britain, Book Club Associates by arrangement with Grisewood & Dempsey, 1981.

Farmer, David Hugh, The Oxford Dictionary of Saints, Oxford: University Press, 1992 (third edition).

Finberg, H.P.R., The Formation of England 550–1042, London: Hart-Davis, MacGibbon, 1974.

Fletcher, Richard, Who's Who in Roman Britain and Anglo-Saxon England, London: Shepheard-Walwyn, 1989.

Foster, Sally M., Picts, Gaels and Scots, London: Batsford, 1996.

Fraser, Antonia (editor), The Lives of the Kings & Queens of England, London: Weidenfeld & Nicolson, 1975.

Fraser, Antonia, King Charles II, London: Weidenfeld & Nicolson, 1979.

Fraser, Antonia, The Life and Times of King James, London: Weidenfeld & Nicolson, 1973.

Fraser, Antonia, Mary, Queen of Scots, London: Weidenfeld & Nicolson, 1969.

Fraser, Flora, The Unruly Queen, London: Macmillan, 1996.

Galliou, Patrick and Jones, Michael, The Bretons, Oxford: Basil Blackwell, 1991.

Gardner, Laurence, *Bloodline of the Holy Grail*, Shaftesbury: Element, 1996.

Garmonsway, G.N. (translator and editor), *The Anglo-Saxon Chronicle*, London: J.M. Dent, 1953.

Gelling, Margaret, *The West Midlands in the Early Middle Ages*, Leicester University Press, 1992.

Gillingham, John, *Richard I*, London: Weidenfeld & Nicolson, 1973.

Grimble, Ian, *Scottish Islands*, London: BBC, 1985.

Grinnell-Milne, Duncan, *The Killing of William Rufus*, Newton Abbot: David & Charles, 1968.

Hadfield, John, *The New Shell Guide to England*, London: Michael Joseph in association with Rainbird Publishing, 1981.

Hartley, Brian and Fitts, Leon, *The Brigantes*, Gloucester: Alan Sutton, 1988.

Hatton, Ragnald, *George I, Elector and King*, London: Thames and Hudson, 1978.

Haywood, John, *The Penguin Historical Atlas of the Vikings*, London: Penguin Books, 1995.

Head, Victor, *Hereward*, Stroud: Alan Sutton, 1995.

Hibbert, Christopher, *Edward VII*, London: Allen Lane, 1976.

Hibbert, Christopher, *George IV, Prince of Wales*, London: Longmans, 1972.

Hibbert, Christopher, *George IV, Regent and King*, London: Longmans, 1973.

Higham, Nicholas, *Rome, Britain and the Anglo-Saxons*, London: Seaby, 1992.

Higham, Nicholas, *The Northern Counties to AD 1000*, London, Longman, 1986.

Higham, Nicholas, *The Kingdom of Northumbria*, AD350–1100, Stroud: Alan Sutton, 1993.

Hill, David, *An Atlas of Anglo-Saxon England*, Oxford: Basil Blackwell, 1981.

Hood, A.B.E., *St. Patrick, His Writings and Muirchu's Life*, London and Chichester: Phillimore, 1978.

Hooke, Della, *The Anglo-Saxon Landscape: The Kingdom of the Hwicce*, Manchester University Press, 1985.

Howarth, Patrick, *George VI*, London: Hutchinson, 1987.

Ireland, S., *Roman Britain, A Sourcebook*, New York: St. Martin's Press, 1986.

Keynes, Simon and Lapidge, Michael, *Alfred the Great: Asser's Life of King Alfred and Other Contemporary Sources*, London: Penguin Classics, 1983.

Kightly, Charles, *Folk Heroes of Britain*, London: Thames and Hudson, 1982.

Kinvig, R.H., *The Isle of Man* (3rd ed., revised), Liverpool University Press, 1975.

Kirby, D.P., *The Earliest English Kings*, London: Unwin Hyman, 1991.

Kirby, J.L., *Henry IV of England*, London: Constable, 1970.

Lacey, Robert, *The Life and Times of Henry VIII*, London: Weidenfeld & Nicolson, 1972.

Lacey, Robert, *Majesty*, London: Hutchinson, 1977.

Laing, Lloyd, *The Archaeology of Late Celtic Britain and Ireland c.400–1200 AD*, London: Methuen, 1975.

Lambert, David and Gray, Randal, *Kings and Queens*, Glasgow: HarperCollins, 1991.

Lapidge, Michael and Dumville, David (eds), *Gildas: New Approaches*, Woodbridge: The Boydell Press, 1984.

Lawson, M.K., *Cnut: the Danes in England in the Early Eleventh Century*, London: Longman, 1993.

Lloyd, Sir John Edward, *A History of Wales*, London: Longmans, Green, 1939 (2 vols; third edition).

Lloyd, Sir John Edward and Jenkins, R.T. (eds), *The Dictionary of Welsh Biography, down to 1940*, Oxford: Basil Blackwell, 1959.

Lofts, Norah, *Queens of Britain*, London: Hodder & Stoughton, 1977.

Longford, Elizabeth, *Elizabeth R*, London: Weidenfeld & Nicolson, 1983.

Longford, Elizabeth, *Victoria R.I.*, London: Weidenfeld & Nicolson, 1964.

McClure, Judith and Collins, Roger (eds), Bede's *The Ecclesiastical History of the English People*, Oxford University Press, 1969.

Macdonald, Donald, *Lewis: A History of the Island*, Edinburgh: Gordon Wright, 1978.

McDonald, R. Andrew, *The Kingdom of the Isles*, East Linton: Tuckwell Press, 1997.

MacManus, Seamus, *The Story of the Irish Race*, 1921.

Mac Niocaill, Gearóid, *Ireland before the Vikings*, Dublin: Gill and Macmillan, 1972.

Maier, Bernhard, *Dictionary of Celtic Reli-*

gion and Culture, Woodbridge: Boydell Press, 1997.

Marsden, John, *Alba of the Ravens*, London: Constable, 1997.

Marsden, John, *The Fury of the Northmen*, London: Kyle Cathie, 1996.

Marsden, John, *Northanhymbre Saga: The History of the Anglo-Saxon Kings of Northumbria*, London: Kyle Cathie, 1992.

Marsden, John, *Sea-Road of the Saints*, Edinburgh, Floris Books, 1995.

Marsden, John, *The Tombs of the Kings: An Iona Book of the Dead*, Felinfach: Llanerch Publishers, 1994.

Middlemas, Keith, *The Life and Times of Edward VII*, London: Weidenfeld & Nicolson, 1972.

Mitchell, Stephen and Reeds, Brian, *Coins of England and the United Kingdom* (30th Edition), London: Seaby, 1995.

Mongan, Norman, *The Menapia Quest*, Dublin: The Herodotus Press, 1995.

Montgomery-Massingberd, Hugh (Editorial Director), *Burke's Guide to the Royal Family*, London: Burke's Peerage, 1973.

Moody, T.W., Martin, F.X., Byrne, F.J. (eds), *A New History of Ireland, Vol. IX: Maps, Genealogies, Lists*, Oxford University Press, 1984.

Morris, John, *The Age of Arthur*, 3 volumes, London & Chichester: Phillimore, 1977.

Morris, John, *Arthurian Sources Volume 2: Annals and Charters*, Chichester: Phillimore, 1995.

Morris, John, *Arthurian Sources Volume 3: Persons*, Chichester: Phillimore, 1995.

Morris, John, *Arthurian Sources Volume 4: Places & Peoples, & Saxon Archaeology*, Chichester: Phillimore, 1995.

Morris, John, *Arthurian Sources Volume 5: Genealogies and Texts*, Chichester: Phillimore, 1995.

Morris, John, *Arthurian Sources Volume 6: Studies in Dark-Age History*, Chichester: Phillimore, 1995.

Morris, John, *Nennius: British History and the Welsh Annals*, Chichester: Phillimore, 1980.

Myres, J.N.L., *The English Settlements*, Oxford University Press, 1986.

Nicolson, Harold, *George V: His Life and Reign*, London: Constable, 1952.

O Corráin, Donncha, *Ireland Before the Normans*, Dublin: Gill and Macmillan, 1972.

O Cróinín, Dáibhí, *Early Medieval Ireland 400–1200*, Harlow: Longman, 1995.

Oakley, Stewart, *The Story of Denmark*, London: Faber & Faber, 1972.

Packe, M., *King Edward III*, London: Routledge and Kegan Paul, 1983.

Palmer, Alan, *The Life and Times of George IV*, London: Weidenfeld & Nicolson, 1972.

Pálsson, Hermann and Edwards, Paul. *Orkneyinga Saga, The History of the Earls of Orkney*, London: Hogarth Press, 1978.

Pearce, Susan M., *The Kingdom of Dumnonia*, Padstow, Cornwall: Lodenek Press, 1978.

Powicke, Sir F. Maurice and Fryde, E.B., *Handbook of British Chronology*, London: Royal Historical Society, 1961 (3rd edition, 1986).

Richardson, Joanna, *Victoria and Albert*, London: J.M. Dent, 1977.

Ridley, Jasper, *Elizabeth I*, London: Constable, 1987.

Ridley, Jasper, *Henry VIII*, London: Constable, 1984.

Ridley, Jasper, *Mary Tudor*, Loondon: Weidenfeld & Nicolson, 1973.

Roberts, John L., *Lost Kingdoms*, Edinburgh: University Press, 1997.

Rollinson, William, *A History of Cumberland and Westmorland*, Chichester: Phillimore, 1978.

Ross, Charles, *Edward IV*, London: Eyre Methuen, 1974.

Ross, Stewart, *Monarchs of Scotland*, Moffat: Lochar Publishing, 1990.

Salway, Peter, *Roman Britain*, Oxford University Press, 1981.

Saul, Nigel (ed), *Historical Atlas of Britain: Prehistoric and Medieval*, Stroud: Alan Sutton for the National Trust, 1994.

Sawyer, P.H., *Kings and Vikings*, London: Methuen, 1982.

Scarre, Chris, *Chronicle of the Roman Emperors*, London: Thames and Hudson, 1995.

Simons, Eric N., *Henry VII: The First Tudor King*, London: Muller, 1968.

Sinclair, Andrew, *The Sword and the Grail*, London: Random House, 1993.

Smurthwaite, David. *Complete Guide to the Battlefields of Britain*, Exeter: Webb & Bower, 1984.

Smyth, Alfred P., *King Alfred the Great*, Oxford University Press, 1995.

Smyth, Alfred P., *Warlords and Holy Men*, London: Edward Arnold, 1984.

Somerset, Anne, *Elizabeth I*, London: Weidenfeld & Nicolson, 1991.

Stafford, Pauline, *The East Midlands in the Early Middle Ages*, Leicester University Press, 1985.

Stenton, Sir Frank, *Anglo-Saxon England*, Oxford University Press, 3rd edition, 1971.

Swanton, Michael (translator and editor). *The Anglo-Saxon Chronicle*, London: J.M. Dent, 1996.

Tapsell, R.F., *Monarchs, Rulers, Dynasties and Kingdoms of the World*, London: Thames and Hudson, 1983.

Taylor, Alexander Burt (trans). *The Orkneyinga Saga*, London and Edinburgh: Oliver and Boyd, 1938.

Thomas, Charles, *Christianity in Roman Britain to AD500*, London: B.T. Batsford, 1981.

Thorpe, Lewis (translator and editor), *The History of the Kings of Britain* by Geoffrey of Monmouth, Harmondsworth: Penguin Books, 1966.

Todd, Malcolm, *The Coritani*, Stroud: Alan Sutton, 1991 (revised).

Treharne, R.F. and Fullard, Harold (eds), *Muir's Historical Atlas, Ancient and Classical*, London: George Phillip, 1963 (sixth edition).

Vince, Alan, *Pre-Viking Lindsey*, Lincoln: City of Lincoln Archeological Unit, 1993.

Walker, Ian W., *Harold, the Last Anglo-Saxon King*, Stroud: Sutton Publishing, 1997.

Watson, D.R., *The Life and Times of Charles I*, London: Weidenfeld & Nicolson, 1972.

Webster, Graham, *Boudica*, London: B.T. Batsford, 1978, revised 1993.

Weir, Alison, *Britain's Royal Families: The Complete Genealogy*, London: The Bodley Head, 1989; revised edition, London: Pimlico, 1996.

Weir, Alison, *Children of England*, London: Jonathan Cape, 1996.

Weir, Alison, *Lancaster and York*, London: Jonathan Cape, 1995.

Weir, Alison, *The Princes in the Tower*, London: The Bodley Head, 1992.

Weir, Alison, *The Six Wives of Henry VIII*, London: The Bodley Head, 1991.

Whitelock, Dorothy, *English Historical Documents, Volume 1: c500–1042*, London: Eyre Methuen, 1979.

Whitlock, Ralph, *The Warrior Kings of Saxon England*, London: Moonraker Press, 1977.

Williams, Ann, Smyth, Alfred P., Kirby, D.P., *A Biographical Dictionary of Dark Age Britain*, London: Seaby, 1991.

Williams, Neville, *The Life and Times of Elizabeth I*, London: Weidenfeld & Nicolson, 1972.

Williamson, David, *Brewer's British Royalty*, London: Cassell, 1996.

Williamson, David, *Kings & Queens of Britain*, London: Webb & Bower, 1991.

Winterbottom, Michael (translator and editor), *Gildas: The Ruin of Britain and other documents*, London and Chichester: Phillimore, 1978.

Witney, K.P., *The Kingdom of Kent*, London and Chichester: Phillimore, 1982.

Woodruff, Douglas, *The Life and Times of Alfred the Great*, London: Weidenfeld & Nicolson, 1984.

Wroughton, John. *The Longman Companion to the Stuart Age, 1603–1714*, Harlow, Essex: Longman, 1997.

Yorke, Barbara, *Kings and Kingdoms of Early Anglo-Saxon England*, London: Seaby, 1990.

Yorke, Barbara, *Wessex in the Early Middle Ages*, London: Cassell on behalf of Leicester University Press, 1995.

Young, A.J., *The Swords of the Britons: A Military Review*, London: Regency Press, 1984.

INDEX TO PEOPLE

This index provides page references for all of the kings and queens as well as the majority of other individuals whose lives intermeshed with royalty. Where a ruler has a specific entry that entry reference is shown in brackets against their name, followed by the territory they ruled, e.g. Alfred the Great [M23] of Wessex. The page(s) for their primary entry are in bold print. All other individuals are listed with their birth-death dates in brackets (if known) and a brief description of their identity, e.g. Becket, Thomas (c1118–70), archbishop of Canterbury.

All entries are in alphabetical order. Where individuals share a common name the entries are in chronological order. However, for convenience, rulers of a common name within a kingdom are grouped together. Nicknames and patronymics (e.g. ab, ap, mac, map) form part of the alphabetical sequence, but ab and ap are not sorted separately. All queens are listed by their first name (e.g. Anne Boleyn, not Boleyn, Anne). All dukes and earls are listed by their family name and only exceptionally by their title.